BASIC AND CLINICAL SCIENCE COURSE

Ophthalmic Pathology and Intraocular Tumors

Section 4

2010–2011

(Last major revision 2007–2008)

LEO

LIFELONG
EDUCATION for the
OPHTHALMOLOGIST®

AMERICAN ACADEMY
OF OPHTHALMOLOGY
The Eye M.D. Association

The Basic and Clinical Science Course is one component of the Lifelong Education for the Ophthalmologist (LEO) framework, which assists members in planning their continuing medical education. LEO includes an array of clinical education products that members may select to form individualized, self-directed learning plans for updating their clinical knowledge. Active members or fellows who use LEO components may accumulate sufficient CME credits to earn the LEO Award. Contact the Academy's Clinical Education Division for further information on LEO.

The Academy provides this material for educational purposes only. It is not intended to represent the only or best method or procedure in every case, nor to replace a physician's own judgment or give specific advice for case management. Including all indications, contraindications, side effects, and alternative agents for each drug or treatment is beyond the scope of this material. All information and recommendations should be verified, prior to use, with current information included in the manufacturers' package inserts or other independent sources, and considered in light of the patient's condition and history. Reference to certain drugs, instruments, and other products in this course is made for illustrative purposes only and is not intended to constitute an endorsement of such. Some material may include information on applications that are not considered community standard, that reflect indications not included in approved FDA labeling, or that are approved for use only in restricted research settings. **The FDA has stated that it is the responsibility of the physician to determine the FDA status of each drug or device he or she wishes to use, and to use them with appropriate, informed patient consent in compliance with applicable law.** The Academy specifically disclaims any and all liability for injury or other damages of any kind, from negligence or otherwise, for any and all claims that may arise from the use of any recommendations or other information contained herein.

Cover image courtesy of Robert H. Rosa, Jr, MD.

General Introduction

The Basic and Clinical Science Course (BCSC) is designed to meet the needs of residents and practitioners for a comprehensive yet concise curriculum of the field of ophthalmology. The BCSC has developed from its original brief outline format, which relied heavily on outside readings, to a more convenient and educationally useful self-contained text. The Academy updates and revises the course annually, with the goals of integrating the basic science and clinical practice of ophthalmology and of keeping ophthalmologists current with new developments in the various subspecialties.

The BCSC incorporates the effort and expertise of more than 80 ophthalmologists, organized into 13 Section faculties, working with Academy editorial staff. In addition, the course continues to benefit from many lasting contributions made by the faculties of previous editions. Members of the Academy's Practicing Ophthalmologists Advisory Committee for Education serve on each faculty and, as a group, review every volume before and after major revisions.

Organization of the Course

The Basic and Clinical Science Course comprises 13 volumes, incorporating fundamental ophthalmic knowledge, subspecialty areas, and special topics:

1   Update on General Medicine
2   Fundamentals and Principles of Ophthalmology
3   Clinical Optics
4   Ophthalmic Pathology and Intraocular Tumors
5   Neuro-Ophthalmology
6   Pediatric Ophthalmology and Strabismus
7   Orbit, Eyelids, and Lacrimal System
8   External Disease and Cornea
9   Intraocular Inflammation and Uveitis
10 Glaucoma
11 Lens and Cataract
12 Retina and Vitreous
13 Refractive Surgery

In addition, a comprehensive Master Index allows the reader to easily locate subjects throughout the entire series.

References

Readers who wish to explore specific topics in greater detail may consult the references cited within each chapter and listed in the Basic Texts section at the back of the book.

These references are intended to be selective rather than exhaustive, chosen by the BCSC faculty as being important, current, and readily available to residents and practitioners.

Related Academy educational materials are also listed in the appropriate sections. They include books, online and audiovisual materials, self-assessment programs, clinical modules, and interactive programs.

Study Questions and CME Credit

Each volume of the BCSC is designed as an independent study activity for ophthalmology residents and practitioners. The learning objectives for this volume are given on page 1. The text, illustrations, and references provide the information necessary to achieve the objectives; the study questions allow readers to test their understanding of the material and their mastery of the objectives. Physicians who wish to claim CME credit for this educational activity may do so by mail, by fax, or online. The necessary forms and instructions are given at the end of the book.

Conclusion

The Basic and Clinical Science Course has expanded greatly over the years, with the addition of much new text and numerous illustrations. Recent editions have sought to place a greater emphasis on clinical applicability while maintaining a solid foundation in basic science. As with any educational program, it reflects the experience of its authors. As its faculties change and as medicine progresses, new viewpoints are always emerging on controversial subjects and techniques. Not all alternate approaches can be included in this series; as with any educational endeavor, the learner should seek additional sources, including such carefully balanced opinions as the Academy's Preferred Practice Patterns.

The BCSC faculty and staff are continuously striving to improve the educational usefulness of the course; you, the reader, can contribute to this ongoing process. If you have any suggestions or questions about the series, please do not hesitate to contact the faculty or the editors.

The authors, editors, and reviewers hope that your study of the BCSC will be of lasting value and that each Section will serve as a practical resource for quality patient care.

Objectives

Upon completion of BCSC Section 4, *Ophthalmic Pathology and Intraocular Tumors*, the reader should be able to

- describe a structured approach to understanding major ocular conditions based on a hierarchical framework of topography, disease process, general diagnosis, and differential diagnosis

- summarize the steps in handling ocular specimens for pathologic study, including obtaining, dissecting, processing, and staining tissues

- explain the basic principles of special procedures used in ophthalmic pathology, including immunohistochemistry, flow cytometry, molecular pathology, and diagnostic electron microscopy

- communicate effectively with the pathologist regarding types of specimens, processing, and techniques appropriate to the clinical situation

- summarize the histopathology of common ocular conditions

- correlate clinical and pathological findings

- list the steps in wound healing in ocular tissues

- summarize current information about the most common primary tumors of the eye

- identify those ophthalmic lesions that indicate systemic disease and/or are potentially life-threatening

- provide useful genetic information to families affected by retinoblastoma

- assess current and new treatment modalities for ocular tumors in terms of patient prognosis and ocular functioning

Introduction

This volume of the Basic and Clinical Science Course (BCSC), Section 4, *Ophthalmic Pathology and Intraocular Tumors*, is divided into 2 parts: Part I, Ophthalmic Pathology; and Part II, Intraocular Tumors: Clinical Aspects. Although these are 2 distinct disciplines, there is overlap, and it is critically important for the sight and life of the patient that the physician understand both the clinical and pathologic aspects of ocular neoplasia. The importance of correlating the clinical findings of other ophthalmic disciplines, such as cornea and retina, with the corresponding pathologic findings should not be neglected.

Part I, Ophthalmic Pathology, uses a hierarchy that moves from general to specific to help derive a differential diagnosis for a specific tissue. This concept was introduced by Curtis E. Margo, MD, and Hans E. Grossniklaus, MD, in the book *Ocular Histopathology: A Guide to Differential Diagnosis*, and it may be used as an organizational framework for the study of ophthalmic pathology.

Part II, Intraocular Tumors: Clinical Aspects, is a compilation of selected clinical aspects of importance to the general ophthalmologist. Because intraocular tumors may be both vision- and life-threatening, ophthalmologists must be aware of the basic principles of their diagnosis and treatment.

The tables that follow Part II outline the American Joint Committee on Cancer 2002 definitions and staging for the ocular and adnexal tumors discussed elsewhere in the book. These tables are referenced where appropriate throughout the main text.

The History of Ophthalmic Pathology

The establishment of ocular pathology as an independent science depended, obviously, on the development of our knowledge of the normal anatomy of the eye. Although animal eyes had been dissected for thousands of years, both Aristotle and Hippocrates held rather vague ideas about ocular anatomy. Only much later did the Greek school of Alexandria establish a formal structure of ocular anatomy. The first reports are by Rufus of Ephesus. He lived at the end of the first and the beginning of the second century AD and worked at least for a time in Egypt. His observations were astute, and, while he still believed that the crystalline lens was the seat of all vision, he wrote excellent descriptions of the anatomy of the eye and the orbit.

His counterpart in Rome was Aulus Cornelius Celsus, who lived from 25 BC to AD 50 and was the first to give us a systematic treatise on ophthalmology. However, he did not contribute anything original on the anatomy of the eye but rather followed the Greek authors in a slavish way.

The high point of anatomical work during the classical time was reached by the Greek physician Claudius Galenus (Galen). Galenus was born in AD 131 in Pergamon (Asia Minor) and died in Rome in AD 201. He was by far the most prominent of the physicians of Rome, and his anatomical descriptions remained in use until Zinn created the modern study of anatomy when he published his book in Gottingen in 1755.

Johann Gottfried Zinn was born in 1727 in Germany and was only 24 years old when he was appointed professor of medicine in Göttingen. At the same time, he became the director of the botanical gardens, and his important contributions to botany led Linnaeus to name a large family of flowers the zinnias. He died before he was 32. For a short time, Zinn was a pupil of the famous Swiss naturalist and physiologist Albrecht von Haller, who first described the cribriform plate and the ophthalmic artery with its branches. Zinn's book has remained the foundation of modern anatomy for the eye. The exact and detailed descriptions have made this work famous. The superb text by Zinn was later complemented by the beautiful atlas published by Samuel Thomas Soemmerring (1755–1830), which appeared in Frankfurt in 1801.

The next advance in normal anatomy study was a book by Julius Arnold that appeared in Leipzig in 1832, when the author was only 29 years old. He already used the microscope but not yet thin tissue sections.

The anatomical studies in the 19th century culminated in the book by Ernst von Brücke, who was born in Berlin and became a professor of physiology and anatomy in Vienna. In 1847 he wrote his anatomical description of the human eye. Von Brücke was the first to use thin sections to investigate the anatomical structures, and he found the longitudinal fibers of the ciliary muscle.

The first book on histology of the eye, written by Samuel Moritz Pappenheim (1811–1882), appeared in Breslau in 1842. The next step forward in this field was made by William Bowman in his book *Lectures on the Parts Concerned in the Operations on the Eye,* which appeared in 1849.

The first indications of a pathologic anatomy concerning vision appeared in the book *Sepulchretum,* published by Theophile Bonet. Bonet, who was born in 1620 in Geneva, died from rabies in his hometown in 1689. The book appeared in 1700 in Lyons. Among the cases described are an optic atrophy due to a brain tumor, a case of syphilis of the frontal bone, a large retinoblastoma, and a chiasmal cyst with optic atrophy.

A more systematic and extensive discussion of ocular pathology was written by Giambattista Morgagni, who first was an assistant to Valsalva (the pupil of Malpighi) in Bologna and then became professor of anatomy in Padua. He published his classic work *De Sedibus et Causis Morborum* . . . in 1761, when he was nearly 80 years old. His 13th letter gives an extensive description of pathologic changes of the visual organ. It contains excellent discussions of the pathologic anatomy of the cataract, vitreous opacities, and traumatic exophthalmos.

The first anatomical examination of diseased eyes occurred in the 18th century. The peculiar structure of the eye required special examination techniques, and these techniques developed slowly. It is therefore not surprising that the first real textbook on general pathologic anatomy, published by Mattias Baillie in London in 1793, does not discuss the visual organ at all.

The first book devoted entirely to ophthalmic pathology was written by James Wardrop (1782–1869), one of the foremost ophthalmologists of his time in the United Kingdom. He was born in Scotland but soon moved to London, where he became a member of the Royal College of Surgeons. After he had successfully treated the eye of a horse that belonged to the Prince Regent, he became the monarch's surgeon, and in 1828 he became surgeon to King George IV. His essays on the morbid anatomy of the human eye appeared in 1808, and a second volume was added in 1818. In his book Wardrop summarized numerous quotations from the world literature, adding valuable and important personal observations.

Although Wardrop was recognized for his scientific contributions, his personal life soon brought him into conflict with the establishment. As a convinced liberal, he was an ardent supporter of the Reform Movement, and his abrasive personality made him many enemies, especially at court. He withdrew from public life at an early age, hardly ever attended medical meetings, and was practically forgotten.

Albrecht von Graefe tells of being at a banquet in London in 1850. Seated next to him was James Wardrop. After they had introduced themselves, von Graefe asked Wardrop whether the author of the book on retinoblastoma, which had appeared in 1809, was his father or grandfather; Wardrop smiled and explained that he himself was the grandfather. Julius Hirschberg, a well-known ophthalmologist and historian, regarded Wardrop's books on pathology as a rich source of new and important facts destined to be of continuing value.

The second textbook on ocular pathologic anatomy was published by Dr. Matthias Johannes Albrecht Schoen in Hamburg in 1828. Schoen was born and practiced in that city. The book is complete in its contents and extremely well organized.

The third textbook was published by Friedrich August von Ammon. He was born in Göttingen in 1799 and became professor of pathology and pharmacology in Dresden in 1828. He later became surgeon to the court of Saxony. Many feel that von Ammon's contribution inaugurated the modern era of the study of pathologic anatomy of the eye.

Von Ammon's book was followed by a few important monographs, including one by John Dalrymple in English (1849–1852), one by Alan Williams Sichel in French (1852–1859), and one by George Theodor Ruete in German (1854–1860).

Heinrich Müller (1820–1864), a professor in Würzburg, is considered the founder of pathologic histology of the eye. He described the microscopic anatomy of the eye and its pathologic alterations. Müller made a number of important anatomical discoveries: the glial cells in the retina, the annular part of the ciliary muscle, and the smooth eyelid muscles are all named after him. At the same time, R. Albert Kolliker, one of the foremost histologists of his time, and Rudolf Virchow, the creator of modern pathology, worked at the University of Würzburg. It is not surprising that this university became the focal point of modern pathologic anatomy.

Müller attracted numerous pupils, but with his death and with Virchow's move to Berlin, Vienna became the center of ocular pathology. Here Karl Freiherr von Rokitansky pioneered in modern pathology. One of his pupils, the pathologist Carl Wedl, dedicated 10 years of his life to the study of ocular pathology. He published his famous atlas in 1861 in collaboration with the ophthalmologist Stellwag von Carion. Wedl greatly influenced the clinicians of that time, especially Carl Ferdinand Ritter von Arlt, the teacher of Ernst Fuchs (1851–1930), whose numerous contributions to ophthalmic pathology are well known.

A second center developed in Paris. Poncet de Cluny (died 1899) was one of the most prominent pupils of Louis Antoine Ranvier. The first French textbook on pathologic anatomy was published by Panas and André Rochon-Duvigneaud (1898).

The first histologic eye examinations in London were reported by J. W. Hulke (1859). This compilation was soon followed by the works of Edward Nettleship, the excellent textbook by J. Herbert Parsons, and the monograph by E. Treacher Collins and H. Stephen Mayou.

In Italy the science was taken up first by C. de Cincentiis (1872) and later by C. Circincione. Later German textbooks were by Adolf Alt of Toronto (1880), Wedl and Bock of Vienna (1886), and Otto Haab of Zurich (1890).

Ophthalmic pathology developed into a specialty in the 20th century. Jonas Stein Friedenwald (1897–1955) at Johns Hopkins combined scientific investigative skills and eye pathology to become a role model for experimental eye pathologists. Frederick Verhoeff (1874–1968) can be considered the father of American ophthalmic pathology. Verhoeff was the first ophthalmologist to graduate from the Johns Hopkins medical school, and he became the pathologist at the Massachusetts Eye and Ear Infirmary. He studied under Fuchs and Parsons and was their American counterpart. By midcentury, Norman Ashton (1913–2001), a general pathologist, had become the director of the Department of Pathology at Moorfields Hospital in London. Ashton used his general pathology training in diagnostic and experimental eye pathology. Ashton's American counterpart was Lorenz E. Zimmerman (1920–), a general pathologist who became director of the Department of Ophthalmic Pathology at the Armed Forces Institute of Pathology. Zimmerman has directly or indirectly trained many of the ophthalmic pathologists currently practicing in the United States and worldwide. Other prominent American eye pathologists who worked during the middle of the 20th century included Frederick C. Blodi (1917–1994), Michael Hogan (1907–1975), and Georgiana Dvorak-Theobald (1884–1971). The rich heritage of ophthalmic pathology has served as a basis for the clinical practice of ophthalmology and as a liaison between experimental and clinical ophthalmology.

PART I

Ophthalmic Pathology

CHAPTER 1

Introduction to Part I

The purpose of BCSC Section 4, *Ophthalmic Pathology and Intraocular Tumors,* is to provide a general overview of the fields of ophthalmic pathology and ocular oncology. Although there is some overlap between the 2 fields, it is useful to approach specific disease processes from the standpoint of 2 separate disciplines. This book contains numerous illustrations of entities commonly encountered in an ophthalmic pathology laboratory and in the practice of ocular oncology. In addition, important, but less common, entities are included for teaching purposes. For more comprehensive reviews of ophthalmic pathology and ocular oncology, the reader is referred to the excellent textbooks listed in Basic Texts at the end of this volume.

Part I of this text provides a framework for the study of ophthalmic pathology, with the following hierarchical organizational paradigm (explained in detail in the next section): topography, disease process, general diagnosis, differential diagnosis. Chapter 2 briefly covers basic principles and specific aspects of wound repair as it applies to ophthalmic tissues, which exhibit distinct responses to trauma, including end-stage processes such as phthisis bulbi. Chapter 3 discusses specimen handling, including orientation and dissection, and emphasizes the critical communication between the ophthalmologist and the pathologist. Although most ophthalmic pathology specimens are routinely processed and slides are stained with hematoxylin and eosin (H&E), special procedures are used in selected cases. Chapter 4 details several of these procedures, including immunohistochemical staining, flow cytometry, polymerase chain reaction (PCR), and electron microscopy. Also discussed are indications in some instances for special techniques in obtaining the specimen, such as fine-needle aspiration biopsy, and special ways of preparing slides for examination, such as frozen sections. Chapters 5 through 15 apply the organizational paradigm to specific anatomical locations.

Organization

Chapters 5 through 15 are each devoted to a particular ocular structure. Within the chapter, the text is organized from general to specific, according to the following hierarchical framework:

- topography
- disease process

- general diagnosis
- differential diagnosis

Topography

The microscopic evaluation of a specimen, whether on a glass slide or depicted in a photograph, should begin with a description of any normal tissue. For instance, the topography of the cornea is characterized by nonkeratinized stratified squamous epithelium, Bowman's layer, stroma, Descemet's membrane, and endothelium. By recognizing a particular structure, such as Bowman's layer or Descemet's membrane, in a biopsy specimen, an examiner might be able to identify the topography in question as cornea. It may not be possible, however, to identify the specific tissue source from the topography present on a glass slide or in a photograph. For example, a specimen showing the topographic features of keratinized stratified squamous epithelium overlying dermis with dermal appendages may be classified as skin; however, unless specific eyelid structures such as a tarsal plate are identified, that skin is not necessarily from the eyelid. See BCSC Section 2, *Fundamentals and Principles of Ophthalmology,* for a review of ophthalmic anatomy.

Disease Process

After identifying a tissue source, the pathologist should attempt to categorize the general disease process. These processes include

- congenital anomaly
- inflammation
- degeneration and dystrophy
- neoplasia

Congenital anomaly

Congenital anomalies usually involve abnormalities in size, location, organization, or amount of tissue. An example of congenitally enlarged tissue is congenital hypertrophy of the retinal pigment epithelium (CHRPE) (see Figs 11-5 and 17-10). Many congenital abnormalities may be classified as choristomas or hamartomas.

A *choristoma* consists of normal, mature tissue at an abnormal location. It occurs when 1 or 2 embryonic germ layers form mature tissue that is abnormal for a given topographic location. An example of a choristoma is a *dermoid:* skin that is otherwise normal and mature present at the abnormal location of the limbus. A tumor made up of tissue derived from all 3 embryonic germ layers is called a *teratoma* (Fig 1-1).

In contrast, the term *hamartoma* describes an exaggerated hypertrophy and hyperplasia (abnormal amount) of mature tissue at a normal location. An example of a hamartoma is a *cavernous hemangioma,* an encapsulated mass of mature venous channels in the orbit.

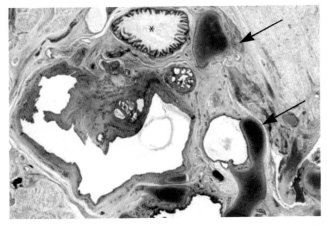

Figure 1-1 Orbital teratoma with tissue from 3 germ layers. Note gastrointestinal mucosa *(asterisk)* and cartilage *(arrows)* in the tumor. *(Courtesy of Hans E. Grossniklaus, MD.)*

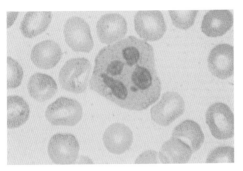

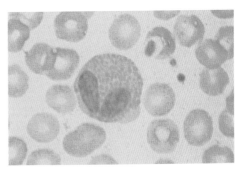

Figure 1-2 Polymorphonuclear leukocyte with multilobulated nucleus. *(Courtesy of Hans E. Grossniklaus, MD.)*

Figure 1-3 Eosinophil with bilobed nucleus and intracytoplasmic eosinophilic granules. *(Courtesy of Hans E. Grossniklaus, MD.)*

Inflammation

The next disease process in the schema, inflammation, is classified in several ways. It may be acute or chronic in onset and focal or diffuse in location. Chronic inflammation is subdivided further as either granulomatous or nongranulomatous. For example, a bacterial corneal ulcer is generally an acute, focal, nongranulomatous inflammation, whereas sympathetic ophthalmia is a chronic, diffuse, granulomatous inflammation.

Polymorphonuclear leukocytes (PMNs), eosinophils, and basophils all circulate in the blood and may be present in tissue in early phases of the inflammatory process (Figs 1-2, 1-3, 1-4). The types of leukocytes present at the site of inflammation vary according to the inflammatory response. PMNs, also known as *neutrophils,* typify acute inflammatory cells and can be recognized by a multisegmented nucleus and intracytoplasmic granules. They may be present in a variety of acute inflammatory processes; for example, they are associated with bacterial infection and found in the walls of blood vessels in some forms of vasculitis. *Eosinophils* have bilobed nuclei and prominent intracytoplasmic eosinophilic granules. They are commonly found in allergic reactions, although they may also be present in chronic inflammatory processes such as sympathetic ophthalmia. *Basophils* contain basophilic intracytoplasmic granules. *Mast cells* are the tissue-bound equivalent of the bloodborne basophils.

Inflammatory cells that are relatively characteristic of chronic inflammatory processes include monocytes (Fig 1-5) and lymphocytes (Fig 1-6). *Monocytes* may migrate from the intravascular space into tissue, in which case they are classified as *histiocytes*, or *macrophages*. Histiocytes have eccentric nuclei and abundant eosinophilic cytoplasm. In some instances, histiocytes may take on the appearance of epithelial cells, with abundant eosinophilic cytoplasm and sharp cell borders, becoming known in the process as *epithelioid histiocytes*. Epithelioid histiocytes may form a ball-like aggregate known as a *granuloma*, the sine qua non for granulomatous inflammation. These granulomas may contain only histologically intact cells ("hard" tubercles, Fig 1-7), or they may exhibit necrotic centers ("caseating" granulomas, Fig 1-8). Epithelioid histiocytes may merge to form a syncytium

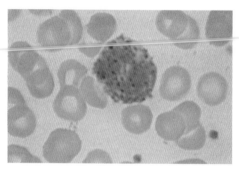

Figure 1-4 Basophil with intracytoplasmic basophilic granules. *(Courtesy of Hans E. Grossniklaus, MD.)*

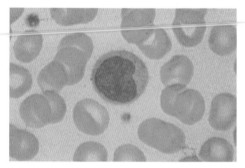

Figure 1-5 Monocyte with indented nucleus. *(Courtesy of Hans E. Grossniklaus, MD.)*

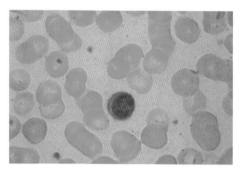

Figure 1-6 Lymphocyte with small, hyperchromatic nucleus and scant cytoplasm. *(Courtesy of Hans E. Grossniklaus, MD.)*

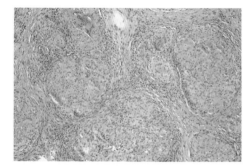

Figure 1-7 Noncaseating granulomas, or "hard" tubercles, are formed by aggregates of epithelioid histiocytes. *(Courtesy of Hans E. Grossniklaus, MD.)*

with multiple nuclei known as a *multinucleated giant cell.* Giant cells formed from histiocytes come in several varieties, including

- Langhans cells, characterized by a horseshoe arrangement of the nuclei (Fig 1-9)
- Touton giant cells, which have an annulus of nuclei surrounded by a lipid-filled clear zone (Fig 1-10)
- foreign body giant cells, with haphazardly arranged nuclei (Fig 1-11)

Lymphocytes are small cells with round, hyperchromatic nuclei and scant cytoplasm. Circulating lymphocytes infiltrate tissue in all types of chronic inflammatory processes. These cells terminally differentiate in the thymus *(T cells)* or bursa equivalent *(B cells),* although it is not possible to distinguish between B and T lymphocytes with routine histologic stains. B cells may produce immunoglobulin and differentiate into *plasma cells,* with eccentric "cartwheel," or "clockface," nuclei and a perinuclear halo corresponding to the Golgi apparatus. These cells may become completely distended with immunoglobulin and

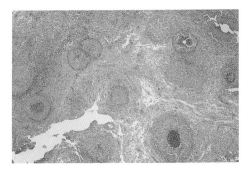

Figure 1-8 Granulomas with necrotic centers are classified as caseating granulomas. *(Courtesy of Hans E. Grossniklaus, MD.)*

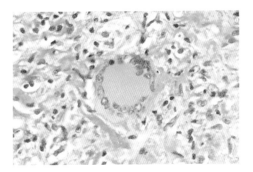

Figure 1-9 Langhans giant cell.

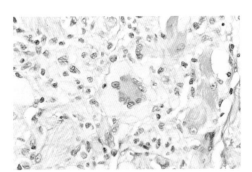

Figure 1-10 Touton giant cell.

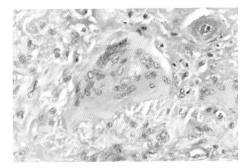

Figure 1-11 Foreign body giant cell.

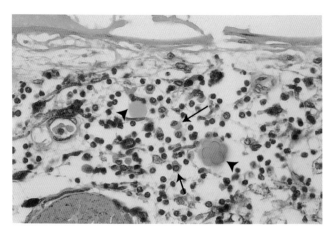

Figure 1-12 This aggregate of plasma cells *(arrows)* is associated with Russell bodies *(arrowheads)*. *(Courtesy of Hans E. Grossniklaus, MD.)*

form *Russell bodies,* which may be extracellular (Fig 1-12). BCSC Section 9, *Intraocular Inflammation and Uveitis,* discusses the cells involved in the inflammatory process in depth in Part I, Immunology.

Degeneration and dystrophy

The term *degeneration* refers to a wide variety of deleterious tissue changes that occur over time. Degenerative processes are not usually associated with a proliferation of cells; rather, there is often an accumulation of acellular material or a loss of tissue mass. Extracellular deposits may result from cellular overproduction of normal material or metabolically abnormal material. These processes, which have a variety of pathologic appearances, may occur in response to an injury or an inflammatory process. As used in this book, "degeneration" is an artificial category used to encompass a wide variety of disease processes. Various categories of diseases, such as those due to vascular causes, normal aging or involutional causes, and trauma, could be considered separately. However, in order to efficiently convey the hierarchical scheme used in this book, these causes are lumped under the rubric of "degeneration." *Dystrophies* are defined as bilateral, symmetric, inherited conditions that appear to have little or no relationship to environmental or systemic factors.

Degeneration of tissue may be seen in conjunction with other general disease processes. Examples include calcification of the lens (degeneration) in association with a congenital cataract (congenital anomaly); corneal amyloid (degeneration) in association with trachoma (inflammation); and orbital amyloid (degeneration) in association with a lymphoma (neoplasm). The ophthalmic manifestations of diabetes mellitus can be classified as degenerative changes associated with a metabolic disease.

Neoplasia

A *neoplasm* is a stereotypic, monotonous new growth of a particular tissue phenotype. Neoplasms can occur in either benign or malignant forms. Examples found in particular tissues include

- adenoma (benign) versus adenocarcinoma (malignant) in glandular epithelium

- topography + *oma* (benign) versus topography + *sarcoma* (malignant) in soft tissue
- hyperplasia/infiltrate (benign) versus leukemia/lymphoma (malignant) in hematopoietic tissue

Some neoplastic proliferations are called *borderline,* in that they are difficult to classify histologically as benign or malignant. Although most of the neoplasms illustrated and discussed in this text are classified as benign or malignant, the reader should be aware that tissue evaluation in a particular disease can give only a static portrait of a dynamic process. Thus, it may be impossible to determine whether the process will ultimately be benign or malignant, and in some instances "indeterminate" or "borderline" is a legitimate interpretation. Table 1-1 summarizes the origin, general classification of benign versus malignant, and growth pattern of neoplasms originating in various tissues.

The growth patterns described in Table 1-1 are shown in Figure 1-13. General histologic signs of malignancy include cellular pleomorphism, necrosis, hemorrhage, and mitotic activity.

Table 1-1 Classification of Neoplasia

Tissue Origin	Benign	Malignant	Growth Pattern
Epithelium	Hyperplasia/adenoma	Carcinoma Adenocarcinoma	Cords Tubules
Soft tissue	Topography + *oma*	Topography + *sarcoma*	Coherent sheets
Hematopoietic tissue	Hyperplasia/infiltrate	Leukemia Lymphoma	Loosely arranged

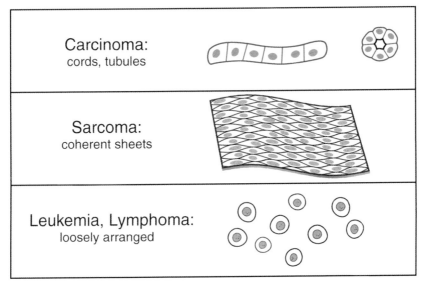

Figure 1-13 General classification and growth patterns of malignant tumors. *(Illustration by Christine Gralapp.)*

General Diagnosis

After considering the topography and disease process, the examiner formulates the general diagnosis. Recognizing a tissue *index feature* is a critical step in arriving at the general diagnosis. Index features are morphologic identifiers that help to define the disease process more specifically. Examples include the presence of pigment in a pigmented neoplasm, necrosis in a necrotizing granulomatous inflammation, and accumulation of smudgy extracellular material in a smudgy eosinophilic corneal degeneration. The index feature should differentiate the particular specimen from others demonstrating the same general disease process. For instance, retinoblastoma and melanoma are both intraocular malignant neoplasms; the former is a retinal malignancy, and the latter is a uveal tract malignancy. Other index features for distinguishing between these lesions could be "small, round, blue cell tumor" for the retinoblastoma and "melanocytic proliferation" for the melanoma. Although the most basic index features can be recognized without great difficulty, it takes experience and practice to identify subtle index features.

Differential Diagnosis

After the examiner has distinguished a key index feature and formulated a general diagnosis, developing a differential diagnosis is the next step. The differential diagnosis is a

---

Table 1-2 Organizational Paradigm for Ophthalmic Pathology

Topography
Conjunctiva
Cornea
Anterior chamber/trabecular meshwork
Sclera
Lens
Vitreous
Retina
Uveal tract
Eyelids
Orbit
Optic nerve

Disease Process
Congenital anomaly
  Choristoma versus hamartoma
Inflammation
  Acute versus chronic
  Focal versus diffuse
  Granulomatous versus nongranulomatous
Degeneration (includes dystrophy)
Neoplasia
  Benign versus malignant
  Epithelial versus soft tissue versus hematopoietic

General Diagnosis
Index feature

Differential Diagnosis
Limited list

limited list of specific conditions resulting from pathologic processes that were identified in the general diagnosis. For instance, the differential diagnosis based on the features of noncaseating granulomatous inflammation of the conjunctiva includes sarcoidosis, foreign body, fungus, and mycobacterium. The differential diagnosis of melanocytic proliferation of the conjunctiva includes nevus, primary acquired melanosis, and melanoma.

Readers are encouraged to practice working through the hierarchical framework by verbalizing each step in sequence while examining a pathologic specimen. Chapters 5 through 15 of this book provide tissue-specific examples of the differential diagnoses for each of the 4 disease process categories. The expanded organizational paradigm is shown in Table 1-2.

CHAPTER 2

Wound Repair

General Aspects of Wound Repair

Wound healing, though a common physiologic process, requires a complicated sequence of tissue events. The purpose of wound healing is to restore the anatomical and functional integrity of an organ or tissue as quickly and perfectly as possible. Repair may take a year, and the result of wound healing is a scar with variable consequences (Fig 2-1). A series of reactions follows a wound, including an acute inflammatory phase, regeneration/repair, and contraction:

- The *acute inflammatory phase* may last from minutes to hours. Blood clots quickly in adjacent vessels in response to tissue activators. Neutrophils and fluid enter the extracellular space. Macrophages remove debris from the damaged tissues, new vessels form, and fibroblasts begin to produce collagen.
- *Regeneration* is the replacement of lost cells; this process occurs only in tissues composed of labile cells (eg, epithelium), which undergo mitosis throughout life. *Repair* is the restructuring of tissues by granulation tissue that matures into a fibrous scar.
- Finally, *contraction* causes the reparative tissues to shrink so that the scar is smaller than the surrounding uninjured tissues.

Healing in Specific Ocular Tissues

The processes summarized in the following sections are also discussed in other volumes of the BCSC series: Section 7, *Orbit, Eyelids, and Lacrimal System;* Section 8, *External Disease and Cornea;* Section 9, *Intraocular Inflammation and Uveitis;* Section 11, *Lens and Cataract;* and Section 12, *Retina and Vitreous.* See also the appropriate chapters in this volume for a specific topography.

Cornea

A corneal *abrasion,* a painful but rapidly healing defect, is limited to the surface corneal epithelium, although Bowman's layer and superficial stroma may also be involved. Within an hour of injury the parabasilar epithelial cells begin to slide and migrate across the denuded area until they touch other migrating cells; then *contact inhibition* stops further migration. Simultaneously, the surrounding basal cells undergo mitosis to supply additional cells to

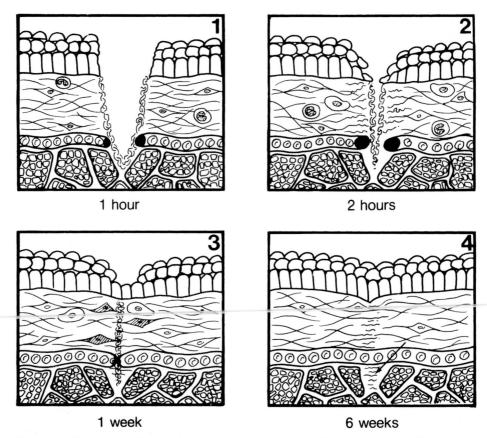

Figure 2-1 Sequence of general wound healing with an epithelial surface. **1,** The wound is created. Blood clots in the vessels; neutrophils migrate to the wound; the wounded edges begin to disintegrate. **2,** The wound edges are reapposed with the various tissue planes in good alignment. The epithelium is lost over the wound but starts to migrate. The subcutaneous fibroblasts enlarge and become activated. Fibronectin is deposited at the wound edges. The blood vessels begin to produce buds. **3,** The epithelium seals the surface. Fibroblasts and blood vessels enter the wound and lay down new collagen. Much of the debris is removed by macrophages. **4,** As the scar matures, the fibroblasts subside. Newly formed blood vessels recanalize. New collagen strengthens the wound, which contracts. Note that the striated muscle cells (permanent cells) at bottom are replaced by scar *(arrow).*

cover the defect. Although a large corneal abrasion is usually sealed within 24 hours, complete healing, which includes restoration of the full thickness of epithelium (4–6 layers) and re-formation of the anchoring fibrils, takes 4–6 weeks. The epithelial cells are labile; that is, some are continuously active mitotically and thus are able to completely replace the lost cells. If a thin layer of anterior cornea is lost with the abrasion, the shallow crater will be filled by epithelium, forming a facet.

Corneal stromal healing is avascular. Unlike with other tissues, healing in the corneal stroma occurs by means of fibrosis rather than by fibrovascular proliferation. This avascular aspect of corneal wound healing is critical to the success of penetrating keratoplasty as well as photorefractive keratectomy (PRK), laser in situ keratomileusis (LASIK), laser epithelial keratomileusis (LASEK), and other corneal refractive surgical procedures.

Following a central corneal wound, neutrophils are carried to the site by the tears (Fig 2-2), and the edges of the wound swell. Healing factors derived from vessels are not present. The matrix glycosaminoglycans, which in the cornea are keratan sulfate and chondroitin sulfate, disintegrate at the edge of the wound. The fibroblasts of the stroma become activated, eventually migrating across the wound, laying down collagen and fibronectin. The direction of the fibroblasts and collagen is not parallel to stromal lamellae. Hence, cells are directed anteriorly and posteriorly across a wound that is always visible microscopically as an irregularity in the stroma and clinically as an opacity. If the wound edges are separated, the gap is not completely filled by proliferating fibroblasts, and a partially filled crater results.

Both the epithelium and the endothelium are critical to good central wound healing. If the epithelium does not cover the wound within days, the subjacent stromal healing is limited and the wound is weak. Growth factors from the epithelium stimulate and sustain

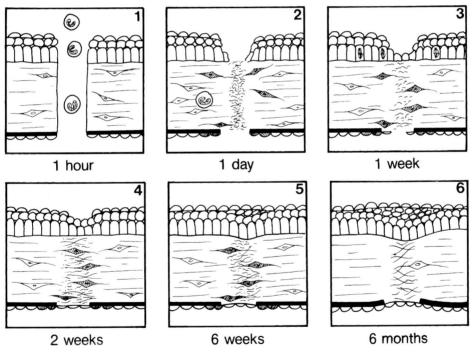

Figure 2-2 Clear corneal wound. **1,** The tear film carries neutrophils with lysozymes to the wound within an hour. **2,** With closure of the incision, the wound edge shows early disintegration and edema. The glycosaminoglycans at the edge are degraded. The nearby fibroblasts are activated. **3,** At 1 week, migrating epithelium and endothelium partially seal the wound; fibroblasts begin to migrate and supply collagen. **4,** Fibroblast activity and collagen and matrix deposition continue. The endothelium, sealing the inner wound, lays down new Descemet's membrane. **5,** Epithelial regeneration is complete. Fibroblasts fill the wound with type I collagen and repair slows. **6,** The final wound contracts. The collagen fibers are not parallel with the surrounding lamellae. The number of fibroblasts decreases.

healing. The endothelial cells adjacent to the wound slide across the posterior cornea; a few cells are replaced through mitotic activity. Endothelium lays down a new thin layer of Descemet's membrane. If the internal margin of the wound is not covered by Descemet's membrane, stromal fibroblasts may continue to proliferate into the anterior chamber as fibrous ingrowth, or the posterior wound may remain permanently open. The initial fibrillar collagen is replaced by stronger collagen in the late months of healing. Bowman's layer does not regenerate when incised or destroyed. In an ulcer, the surface is covered by epithelium, but little of the lost stroma is replaced by fibrous tissue. Modification of the healing process by use of topical antimetabolites, such as 5-fluorouracil and mitomycin C, may be desirable in certain clinical situations (see BCSC Section 10, *Glaucoma*, Chapter 8).

Sclera

The sclera differs from the cornea in that the collagen fibers are randomly distributed rather than laid down in orderly lamellae, and the glycosaminoglycan is dermatan sulfate. Sclera is relatively avascular and hypocellular. When stimulated by wounding, the episclera migrates down the scleral wound, supplying vessels, fibroblasts, and activated macrophages. The final wound contracts, creating a pinched-in appearance. If the adjacent uvea is damaged, uveal fibrovascular tissue may enter the scleral wound, resulting in a scar with a dense adhesion between uvea and sclera. Indolent episcleral fibrosis produces a dense coat around an extrascleral foreign body such as a scleral buckle.

Limbus

The limbus is a complex region of corneal, scleral, and episcleral tissues. Wounds of the limbus cause swelling in the cornea and shrinking of the sclera (Fig 2-3). Healing involves episcleral ingrowth and clear corneal fibroblastic migration. Collector channels in the sclera do not contribute to the healing. Alterations in surgical technique between clear corneal and limbal incisions may produce different healing responses. Differences include

- the potential for vascular ingrowth from episcleral vessels into a limbal wound and the absence of vascularity of a clear corneal wound
- surface remodeling of epithelium over a clear corneal wound that does not occur over a limbal wound

Uvea

Under ordinary circumstances, wounds of the iris do not stimulate a healing response in either the stroma or the epithelium. Though richly endowed with blood vessels and fibroblasts, the iridic stroma does not produce granulation tissue to close a defect. The pigmented epithelium may be stimulated to migrate in some circumstances, such as excessive inflammation, but its migration is usually limited to the subjacent surface of the lens capsule, where subsequent adhesion of epithelial cells occurs. When fibrovascular tissue forms, it usually does so on the anterior surface of the iris as an exuberant and aberrant membrane (eg, rubeosis iridis) that may cross iridectomy or pupillary openings. The fibrovascular tissue may arise from the iris, the chamber angle, or the cornea.

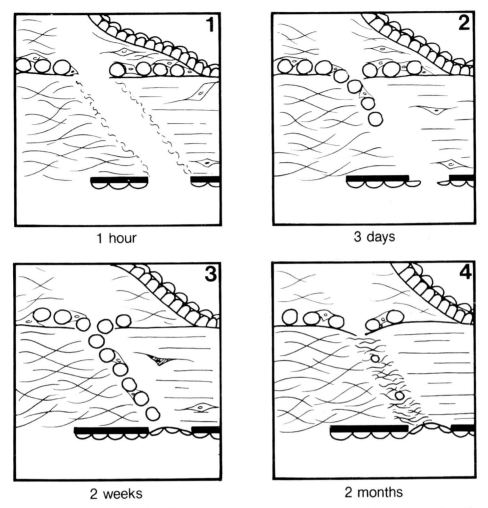

Figure 2-3 Limbal wound. **1,** The limbal wound with a conjunctival flap passes through episclera externally and enters the globe through Descemet's membrane and endothelium. Sclera is on the left and cornea on the right. The wound edge shows early disintegration. Neutrophils and macrophages are omitted in this diagram. **2,** Episcleral vessels and fibroblasts migrate down the wound. Some activity is present in the corneal fibroblasts. **3,** Episcleral fibrovascular migration in the wound is stopped at the endothelium crossing the internal margin of the incision. **4,** The number of vessels decreases in the late stage of healing. Irregular collagen fibers and matrix fill the contracting wound.

Stroma and melanocytes of the iris, ciliary body, and choroid do not regenerate after injury. Debris is removed, and a thin fibrous scar develops that appears white and atrophic clinically.

Dunn SP. Iris repair: putting the pieces back together. *Focal Points: Clinical Modules for Ophthalmologists.* San Francisco: American Academy of Ophthalmology; 2002, module 11.

Lens

Small rents in the lens capsule are sealed by nearby lenticular epithelial cells. When posterior synechiae make the lenticular epithelium anoxic or hypoxic, a metaplastic response occurs, producing fibrous plaques intermixed with basement membrane.

Retina

The retina is made of permanent cells that do not regenerate when fatally injured. Instead, a glial plug pulls the retina together after closure. Surgical techniques to close openings in the peripheral retina are successful when the neurosensory retina and retinal pigment epithelium (RPE) are destroyed (eg, cryotherapy, photocoagulation) and the surrounding tissues form an adhesive, atrophic scar.

Retinal scars are produced by glia rather than fibroblasts. After inflammatory cells have cleared away the debris, the tissues most damaged by the therapeutic modality remain as a thin, atrophic area in the center of the scar. Increasing numbers of residual viable cells ring the zone of greatest destruction. Adhesion between the residual neurosensory retina and Bruch's membrane develops according to the size of the original wound and the type of injury. The internal limiting membrane and Bruch's membrane provide the architectural planes for glial scarring. Adhesions from the internal limiting membrane to Bruch's membrane may incorporate a rare residual glial cell, and variable numbers of retinal cells and RPE may be present between the membranes. If the wound has damaged Bruch's membrane, choroidal fibroblasts and vessels may participate in the formation of the final scar. The end result is a metaplastic collagenous plaque in the sub–neurosensory retina and sub-RPE areas. The RPE usually proliferates rather exuberantly in such scars, giving rise to the dense black clumps seen clinically in scars of the fundus.

Vitreous

The vitreous has few cells and no blood vessels. Nonetheless, in conditions that cause vitreal inflammation, mediators stimulate the formation of membranes composed of new vessels and the proliferation of glial and fibrous tissue. With contraction of these membranes, the retina becomes distorted and detached.

Eyelid, Orbit, and Lacrimal Tissues

The rich blood supply of the skin of the eyelids supports rapid and complete healing. On about the third day after injury to the skin, myofibroblasts derived from vascular pericytes migrate around the wound and actively contract, resulting in a volumetric decrease in the size of the wound. Early invasion of ocular wounds by myofibroblasts does not occur, and the resultant early contraction does not happen. The eyelid and orbit are compartmentalized by intertwining fascial membranes enclosing muscular, tendinous, fatty, lacrimal, and ocular tissues that are distorted by scarring. Exuberant contracting distorts muscle action, producing dysfunctional scars. The striated muscles of the orbicularis oculi and extraocular muscles are made of permanent cells that do not regenerate, but the viable cells may hypertrophy. Contraction of tissue may occur after injury, hence the shrunken appearance of eyelids and globe following a crushing injury to the orbit.

Histologic Sequelae of Ocular Trauma

The anterior chamber angle structures, especially the trabecular beams, are vulnerable to distortion of the anterior globe. *Cyclodialysis* results from disinsertion of the longitudinal muscle of the ciliary muscle from the scleral spur (Fig 2-4). This condition can lead to hypotony because the aqueous of the anterior chamber now has free access to the suprachoroidal space, and, because the blood supply to the ciliary body is diminished, the production of aqueous is decreased.

Traumatic recession of the anterior chamber angle is a rupture of the face of the ciliary body (Fig 2-5). A plane of relative weakness starts at the ciliary body face and extends posteriorly between the longitudinal muscles of the ciliary body and the more centrally located oblique and circular muscle fibers. Concurrent damage to the trabecular meshwork may lead to glaucoma. The oblique and circular muscle fibers will usually atrophy, changing the overall shape of the cross-sectional appearance of the ciliary body from triangular to fusiform. The ciliary process will appear posteriorly and externally displaced as defined by a line drawn through the scleral spur parallel to the visual axis. In normal eyes, this line intersects the first ciliary process. These changes are also shown in Figure 7-10 in Chapter 7.

The uveal tract is attached to the sclera at 3 points: the scleral spur, the internal ostia of the vortex veins, and the peripapillary tissue. This anatomical arrangement is the basis of the evisceration technique and explains the vulnerability of the eye to expulsive choroidal hemorrhage. The borders of the dome-shaped choroidal hemorrhage are defined by the position of the vortex veins and the scleral spur (Fig 2-6).

An *iridodialysis* is a rupture of the iris at the thinnest portion of the diaphragm, the iris base, where it inserts into the supportive tissue of the ciliary body (Fig 2-7; see also Fig 7-11). Only a small amount of supporting tissue surrounds the iris sphincter. If the sphincter muscle is ruptured, contraction of the remaining muscle will create a notch at the pupillary border. The iris diaphragm may be lost completely through a relatively small limbal rupture associated with 360° iridodialysis.

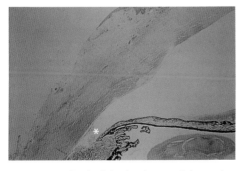

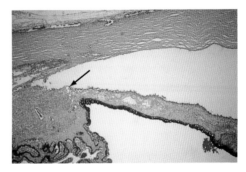

Figure 2-4 Cyclodialysis shows disinsertion of ciliary body muscle from the scleral spur *(asterisk). (Courtesy of Hans E. Grossniklaus, MD.)*

Figure 2-5 Angle recession shows a torn ciliary body muscle *(arrow). (Courtesy of Hans E. Grossniklaus, MD.)*

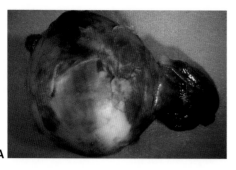 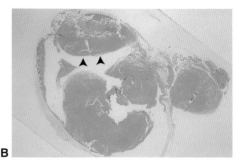

A **B**

Figure 2-6 **A,** This eye developed an expulsive hemorrhage after a corneal perforation. **B,** The intraocular choroidal hemorrhage is dome shaped *(arrowheads)*, delineated by the insertion of the choroid at the scleral spur. *(Courtesy of Hans E. Grossniklaus, MD.)*

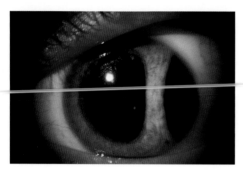 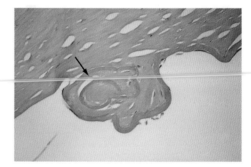

Figure 2-7 Iridodialysis shows a tear in the base of the iris. *(Courtesy of Hans E. Grossniklaus, MD.)*

Figure 2-8 A break in Descemet's membrane in keratoconus shows anterior curling of Descemet's membrane toward the corneal stroma *(arrow)*. *(Courtesy of Hans E. Grossniklaus, MD.)*

A *Vossius ring* appears when compression and rupture of iris pigment epithelial cells against the anterior surface of the lens occurs, depositing a ring of melanin pigment concentric to the pupil.

A *cataract* may form immediately if the lens capsule is ruptured. The lens capsule is thinnest at the posterior pole, a point farthest away from the lens epithelial cells. The epithelium of the lens may be stimulated by trauma to form an anterior lenticular fibrous plaque. The lens zonular fibers are points of relative weakness; if they are ruptured, displacement of the lens can be partial (subluxation) or complete (luxation). Focal areas of zonular rupture may allow formed vitreous to enter the anterior chamber.

Rupture of Descemet's membrane may occur after minor trauma (eg, in keratoconus, Fig 2-8) or major trauma (eg, after forceps injury, Fig 2-9). *Rupture of Bruch's membrane* can occur after compressive injuries (choroidal rupture); the rupture is often concentric to the optic disc. Ruptures of Bruch's membrane itself are not as functionally significant as the accompanying rupture of the overlying retina, which is usually undetectable clinically. A rupture of Bruch's membrane may also permit choroidal neovascularization by allowing the choroidal vasculature access to the sub–neurosensory retina space.

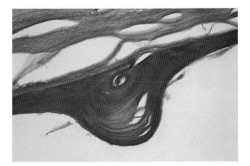

Figure 2-9 A break in Descemet's membrane as a result of forceps injury shows anterior curling of the original membrane and production of a secondary thickened membrane. *(Courtesy of Hans E. Grossniklaus, MD.)*

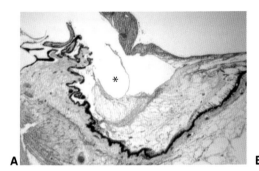

A

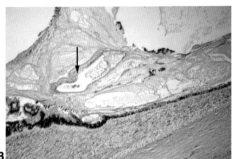

B

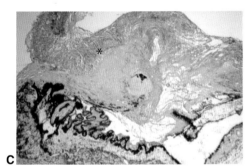

C

Figure 2-10 Anterior proliferative vitreoretinopathy (PVR). **A,** Traction of the vitreous base on the peripheral retina and ciliary body epithelium *(asterisk)*. **B,** Incorporation of peripheral retinal and ciliary body tissue into the vitreous base *(arrow)*. **C,** Proliferation of incorporated tissue in the vitreous base *(asterisk)*. *(Courtesy of Hans E. Grossniklaus, MD.)*

Retinal dialysis is most likely to develop in the inferotemporal or superonasal quadrant. The retina is anchored anteriorly to the nonpigmented epithelium of the pars plana. This union is reinforced by the attachment of the vitreous, which straddles the ora serrata. Deformation of the eye can result in a circumferential tear of the retina at the point of attachment of the ora or immediately posterior to the point of attachment of the vitreous base (Fig 2-10). Vitreoretinal traction may cause tears in a retina weakened by necrosis.

Intraocular *fibrocellular proliferation* may occur after a penetrating injury. Such proliferation may lead to vitreous/subretinal/choroidal hemorrhage; traction retinal detachment; proliferative vitreoretinopathy (PVR), including anterior PVR; hypotony; and ultimately phthisis bulbi. Formation of proliferative intraocular membranes may

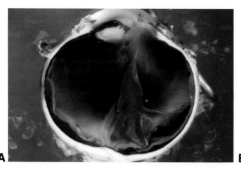 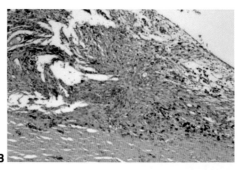

A   B

Figure 2-11 Focal posttraumatic choroidal granulomatous inflammation. **A,** Enucleated eye with a projectile causing a perforating limbal injury that extends to the posterior choroid. **B,** Microscopic examination shows a focus of choroidal granulomatous inflammation. *(Courtesy of Hans E. Grossniklaus, MD.)*

affect the timing of vitreoretinal surgery. The timing of the drainage of a ciliochoroidal hemorrhage is based on lysis of the blood clot (10–14 days). Hemosiderin forms at approximately 72 hours after hemorrhage. Sequelae of intraocular hemorrhage include siderosis bulbi, cholesterosis, and hemoglobin spherulosis.

Choroidal rupture may occur after direct or indirect injury to the globe. This results in granulation tissue proliferation and scar formation. Choroidal neovascularization may occur in an area of a choroidal rupture. A subset of direct choroidal ruptures, those usually occurring after a projectile injury, may result in *focal posttraumatic choroidal granulomatous inflammation* (Fig 2-11). This may be related to foreign material introduced into the choroid. A chorioretinal rupture and necrosis is known as *sclopetaria*.

Wilson MW, Grossniklaus HE, Heathcote JG. Focal posttraumatic choroidal granulomatous inflammation. *Am J Ophthalmol.* 1996;121:397–404.

Commotio retinae (Berlin edema) often complicates blunt trauma to the eye. Most prominent in the macula, commotio retinae can affect any portion of the retina. Originally, the retinal opacification seen clinically was thought to result from retinal edema (extracellular accumulation of fluid), but experimental evidence shows that a disruption in the architecture of the photoreceptor elements causes the loss of retinal transparency.

Phthisis bulbi is defined as atrophy, shrinkage, and disorganization of the eye and intraocular contents. Not all eyes rendered sightless by trauma become phthisical. If the nutritional status of the eye and near-normal intraocular pressure (IOP) are maintained during the repair process, the globe will remain clinically stable. However, blind eyes are at high risk of repeated trauma with cumulative destructive effects. Slow, progressive functional decompensation may also prevail. Many blind eyes pass through several stages of atrophy and disorganization into the end stage of phthisis bulbi:

- *Atrophia bulbi without shrinkage* (Fig 2-12). Initially, the size and shape of the eye are maintained. The atrophic eye often has elevated IOP. The following structures are most sensitive to loss of nutrition: the lens, which becomes cataractous; the retina, which atrophies and becomes separated from the RPE by serous fluid accumulation; and the aqueous outflow tract, where anterior and posterior synechiae develop.

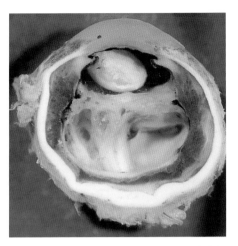

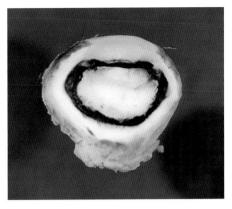

Figure 2-13 Phthisis bulbi. The size of the globe is markedly reduced, the sclera is thickened, and the contents of the eye are totally disorganized.

Figure 2-12 Atrophia bulbi without shrinkage. Note the dense cyclitic membrane and the corresponding detachment of the ciliary body.

- *Atrophia bulbi with shrinkage.* The eye becomes soft because of ciliary body dysfunction and progressive diminution of IOP. The globe becomes smaller and assumes a squared-off configuration as a result of the influence of the 4 rectus muscles. The anterior chamber collapses. Associated corneal endothelial cell damage results initially in corneal edema followed by opacification from degenerative pannus, stromal scarring, and vascularization. Most of the remaining internal structures of the eye will be atrophic but recognizable histologically.
- *Atrophia bulbi with disorganization (phthisis bulbi)* (Fig 2-13). The size of the globe shrinks from a normal average diameter of 24–26 mm to an average diameter of 16–19 mm. Most of the ocular contents become disorganized. In areas of preserved uvea, the RPE proliferates and drusen may be seen. Extensive calcification of Bowman's layer, lens, retina, and drusen usually occurs. Osseous metaplasia of the RPE may be a prominent feature. The sclera becomes massively thickened, particularly posteriorly.

CHAPTER 3

Specimen Handling

Communication

Communication with the pathologist before, during, and after surgical procedures is an essential aspect of quality patient care. The final histologic diagnosis reflects successful collaborative work between clinician and pathologist. The ophthalmologist should provide a relevant and reasonably detailed clinical history when the specimen is submitted to the laboratory. This history facilitates clinicopathologic correlation and enables the pathologist to provide the most accurate interpretation of the specimen. The clinical history portion of the pathology request form, therefore, should not be neglected, even in "routine" cases.

Where there is an ongoing relationship between a pathologist and an ophthalmologist, communication usually can be accomplished through the pathology request form and the pathology report. However, if a malignancy is suspected or if the biopsy will be used to establish a critical diagnosis, direct and personal communication between the ophthalmic surgeon and the pathologist can be essential. This preoperative consultation allows the surgeon and pathologist to discuss the best way to submit a specimen. For example, the pathologist may wish to have fresh tissue for immunohistochemical stains and molecular diagnostic studies, glutaraldehyde-fixed tissue for electron microscopy, and formalin-fixed tissue for routine paraffin embedding. If the tissue is simply submitted in formalin, the opportunity for a definitive diagnosis may be lost. Communication between clinician and pathologist is especially important in ophthalmic pathology, where specimens are often very small and require very careful handling. Biopsies may be incisional, in which only a portion of the tumor is sampled, or excisional, in which the entire lesion is removed. (See BCSC Section 7, *Orbit, Eyelids, and Lacrimal System,* Chapter 11, for further discussion.)

Any time a previous biopsy has been performed at the site of the present pathology, the sections of the previous biopsy should be requested and reviewed with the pathologist who will interpret the second biopsy. The surgical plan may be altered substantially if the initial biopsy was thought to represent, for example, a basal cell carcinoma when in fact the disease was a sebaceous carcinoma. In addition, the pathologist will be able to interpret intraoperative frozen sections more accurately when the case has been reviewed in advance.

If substantial disagreement arises between the clinical diagnosis and the histopathologic diagnosis, the ophthalmologist should contact the pathologist directly and promptly to resolve the discrepancy. Mislabeling of pathology specimens or reports through a simple typing error, for example, can have serious consequences. Merely correcting the patient age on the pathology request form may change the interpretation of melanotic lesions of the conjunctiva. Benign pigmental melanotic lesions in children may have a similar histologic appearance to malignant melanotic lesions in adults. Whether the patient is age 4 or age 44 makes a tremendous difference in interpretation.

Finally, the ophthalmologist who makes an effort to consult with the pathologist prior to surgery sends a clear signal both of special interest in the case and of respect for the contribution of the pathologist. This collaborative approach will ultimately benefit the patient by rendering the correct diagnosis in the most efficient manner.

Orientation

Globes may be oriented according to the location of the extraocular muscles and of the long posterior ciliary artery and nerve, which are located in the horizontal meridian. The medial, inferior, lateral, and superior rectus muscles insert progressively farther from the limbus. Locating the insertion of the inferior oblique muscle is very helpful in distinguishing between a right and a left eye (Fig 3-1). The inferior oblique inserts temporally over the macula, with its fibers running inferiorly. Once the laterality of the eye is determined, the globe may be transilluminated and dissected.

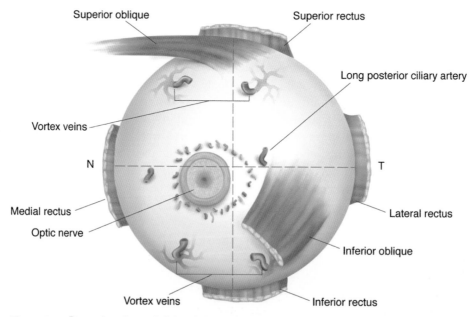

Figure 3-1 Posterior view of right globe. *(Modified by Cyndie Wooley from illustration by Thomas A. Weingeist, PhD, MD.)*

Transillumination

Eyes are transilluminated with bright light prior to gross dissection. This helps to identify intraocular lesions such as a tumor that blocks the transilluminated light and casts a shadow (Fig 3-2A). The shadow can be outlined with a marking pencil on the sclera (Fig 3-2B). This outline can then be used to guide the gross dissection of the globe so that the center of the section will include the maximum extent of the area of interest (Figs 3-2C to 3-2E).

Gross Dissection

A globe is opened so as to display as much of the pathologic change as possible on a single slide. The majority of eyes are cut so that the pupil and optic nerve are present in the same section, the *PO section.* The meridian, or clock-hour, of the section is determined by the

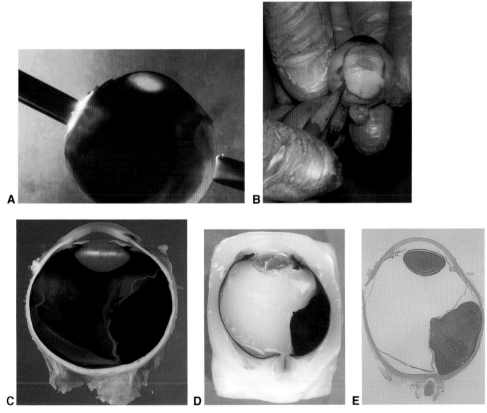

Figure 3-2 Preparation of an intraocular tumor specimen. **A,** Transillumination shows blockage to light secondary to an intraocular tumor. **B,** The area of blockage to light is marked with a marking pencil. **C,** The opened eye shows the intraocular tumor that was demonstrated by transillumination. **D,** The paraffin-embedded eye shows the intraocular tumor. **E,** The H&E-stained section shows that the maximum extent of the tumor demonstrated by transillumination is in the center of the section, which includes the pupil and optic nerve. *(Courtesy of Hans E. Grossniklaus, MD.)*

unique features of the case, such as the presence of an intraocular tumor or a history of previous surgery or trauma. In routine cases, with no prior surgery or intraocular neoplasm, most eyes are opened in the horizontal meridian, which includes the macula in the same section as the pupil and optic nerve (Fig 3-3). Globes with a surgical or nonsurgical wound should be opened so the wound will be perpendicular to, and included in, the PO section, which often means opening the globe vertically. Globes with intraocular tumors are opened in a way (horizontal, vertical, or oblique) that places the center of the tumor as outlined by transillumination in the PO section.

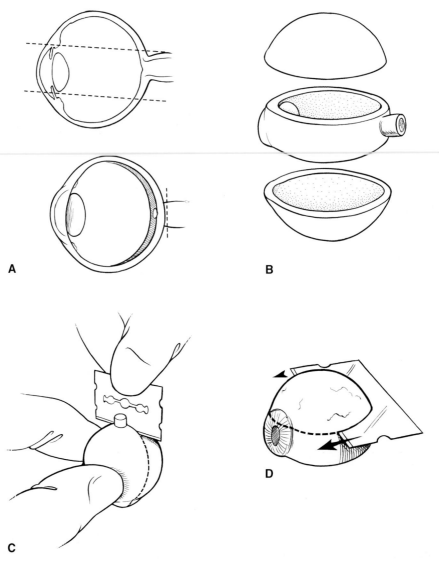

Figure 3-3 **A,** The goal of sectioning is to obtain a pupil–optic nerve (PO) section that contains the maximum area of interest. **B,** Two caps, or *calottes*, are removed to obtain a PO section. **C,** The first cut is generally performed from posterior to anterior. **D,** The second cut will yield the PO section. *(Illustration by Christine Gralapp.)*

The globe can also be opened coronally with separation of the anterior and posterior compartments. The tumor can be visualized directly with this technique, and a section including the maximum extent of the tumor may then be obtained.

Processing and Staining

Fixatives

The most commonly used fixative is 10% neutral buffered formalin. Formalin is a 40% solution of formaldehyde in water that stabilizes protein, lipid, and carbohydrates and prevents postmortem enzymatic destruction of the tissue (autolysis). In specific instances, other fixatives may be preferred, such as glutaraldehyde for electron microscopy and ethyl alcohol for cytologic preparations. Table 3-1 lists examples of some commonly used fixatives.

Formalin diffuses rather quickly through tissue. Because most of the functional tissue of the eye is within 2–3 mm of the surface, it is not necessary or desirable to open the eye. Opening the eye prior to fixation may damage or distort sites of pathology, making histologic interpretation difficult or impossible. The adult eye measures approximately 24 mm in diameter, and formalin diffuses at a rate of approximately 1 mm/hr; therefore, globes should be fixed at least 12 hours prior to processing. It is generally desirable to suspend an eye in formalin in a volume of approximately 10:1 for at least 24 hours prior to processing to ensure adequate fixation. Different institutions may use different protocols, and preoperative consultation is critical.

Tissue Processing

The infiltration and embedding process removes most of the water from the tissue and replaces the water with paraffin. Organic solvents used in this process will dissolve lipid and may dissolve some synthetic materials. Routine processing usually dissolves intraocular lenses made of polymethylmethacrylate (PMMA), polypropylene, and silicone, although the PMMA may fall out during sectioning. Silk, nylon, and other synthetic sutures do not dissolve during routine processing. Specimens are routinely processed through increasing concentrations of alcohol followed by xylene or another clearing agent prior to infiltration with paraffin. Alcohol dehydrates water and xylene replaces alcohol prior to paraffin infiltration. The paraffin mechanically stabilizes the tissue, making possible the cutting of sections.

Table 3-1 Common Fixatives Used in Ophthalmic Pathology

Fixative	Color	Examples of Use
Formalin	Clear	Routine fixation of all tissues
Bouin solution	Yellow	Small biopsies
B5	Clear	Lymphoproliferative tissue (eg, lymph node)
Glutaraldehyde	Clear	Electron microscopy
Ethanol/methanol	Clear	Crystals (eg, urate crystals of gout)
Michel fixative	Light pink	Immunofluorescence
Zenker acetic fixative	Orange	Muscle differentiation

The processing of even a "routine" specimen usually takes a day. Thus, it is unreasonable for a surgeon to expect an interpretation of a specimen sent for permanent sections to be available on the same day as the biopsy. Techniques for the rapid processing of special surgical pathology material are generally reserved for biopsy specimens that require emergent handling. Because the quality of histologic preparation after rapid processing is usually inferior to that of standard processed tissue, it should not be requested routinely. Surgeons should communicate directly with their pathologists about the availability and shortcomings of these techniques.

Tissue Staining

Tissue sections are usually cut at 4–6 µm. A tissue adhesive is sometimes used to secure the thin paraffin section to a glass slide. The cut section is colorless except for areas of indigenous pigmentation, and various tissue dyes—principally hematoxylin and eosin (H&E) and periodic acid–Schiff (PAS)—are used to color the tissue for identification (Fig 3-4). Other histochemical stains used in ophthalmic pathology are alcian blue or colloidal iron for acid mucopolysaccharides, Congo red for amyloid, Gram stain for bacteria, Masson trichrome for collagen, Gomori methenamine silver stain for fungi, and oil red O for lipid. A small amount of resin is placed over the stained section and covered with a thin glass coverslip to protect and preserve it. Table 3-2 lists some common stains and gives examples of their use in ophthalmic pathology.

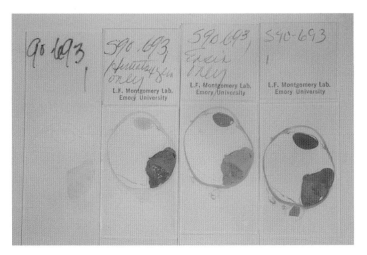

Figure 3-4 The section of paraffin-embedded tissue at the far left is colorless except for mild indigenous pigmentation in the tissue. Moving to the right are shown slides stained with hematoxylin only, eosin only, and both hematoxylin and eosin. *(Courtesy of Hans E. Grossniklaus, MD.)*

Table 3-2 Common Stains Used in Ophthalmic Pathology

Stain	Material Stained: Color	Example
Hematoxylin and eosin (H&E)	Nucleus: blue Cytoplasm: red	General tissue stain (Fig 3-2E)
Periodic acid–Schiff (PAS)	Neutral mucopolysaccharide: magenta	Fungi (Fig 6-6)
Alcian blue	Acid mucopolysaccharide: blue	Cavernous optic atrophy (Fig 15-8)
Alizarin red	Calcium: red	Band keratopathy
Colloidal iron	Acid mucopolysaccharide: blue	Macular dystrophy (Fig 6-14)
Congo red	Amyloid: orange, red-green dichroism	Lattice dystrophy (Fig 6-16)
Ziehl-Neelsen	Acid-fast organisms: red	Atypical mycobacterium
Gomori methenamine silver	Fungal elements: black	*Candida, Aspergillus*
Crystal violet	Amyloid: purple, violet	Lattice dystrophy

Gram stain (tissue Brown &
Brenn [B&B] or Brown &
Hopps [B&H] stain)
	Bacteria
	  Positive: blue
	  Negative: red
		Bacterial infection
		(Fig 5-6C)

Masson trichrome	Collagen: blue	Granular dystrophy (Fig 6-15)
	Muscle: red	Red deposits
Perls Prussian blue	Iron: blue	Hemosiderosis bulbi (Fig 6-19B)
Thioflavin T (ThT)	Amyloid: fluorescent yellow	Lattice dystrophy
Verhoeff–van Gieson	Elastic fibers: black	Temporal artery elastic layer
von Kossa	Calcium phosphate salts: black	Band keratopathy (Fig 6-8)

CHAPTER 4

Special Procedures

New technologies have contributed to improvements in the diagnosis of infectious agents and tumors as well as to the classification of tumors, especially the non–Hodgkin lymphomas (NHLs), childhood tumors, and sarcomas. Use of a more extensive test menu of paraffin-active monoclonal antibodies for immunohistochemistry; molecular cytogenetic studies, including standard cytogenetics; multicolor fluorescence in situ hybridization (FISH); polymerase chain reaction (PCR); and locus-specific FISH; as well as developments in high-resolution techniques, including microarray gene expression profiling and array comparative genomic hybridization (CGH), allow a more accurate diagnosis and more precise definition of biomarkers of value in risk stratification and prognosis. The ophthalmic surgeon is responsible for appropriately obtaining and submitting tissue for evaluation and consulting with the ophthalmic pathologist. See Table 4-1 for a checklist of important considerations when submitting tissue for pathologic consultation.

Immunohistochemistry

Pathologists making a diagnosis take advantage of the property that a given cell can express specific antigens. The immunohistochemical stains commonly used in ophthalmic pathology work because a primary antibody binds to a specific antigen in or on a cell, and because that antibody is linked to a chromogen, usually through a secondary antibody (Fig 4-1). The color product of the chromogens generally used in ophthalmic pathology is brown or red in tissue sections, depending on the chromogen selected for use (Fig 4-2). Red chromogen is especially helpful in working with ocular pigmented tissues and melanomas because it differs from the brown melanin (see Fig 4-7).

The precise cell or cells that display the specific antigen can be identified using these methods. Many antibodies are used routinely for diagnosis, treatment, and prognosis:

- cytokeratins for lesions composed of epithelial cells (adenoma, carcinoma)
- desmin, myoglobin, or actin for lesions with smooth muscle or skeletal muscle features (leiomyoma, rhabdomyoma)
- S-100 protein for lesions of neuroectodermal origin (schwannoma, neurofibroma, melanoma)
- HMB-45 and Melan A for melanocytic lesions (nevus, melanoma)

Table 4-1 Checklist for Requesting an Ophthalmic Pathologic Consultation

Routine Specimens (Cornea, pterygium, eyelid lesions, and so on)
1. Fill out requisition form
   a. Sex and age of patient
   b. Location of lesion (laterality and exact location)
   c. Previous biopsies of the site and diagnosis
   d. Pertinent clinical history
   e. Clinical differential diagnosis
   f. Ophthalmologist phone and fax numbers
2. Specimen submitted in adequately sealed container with
   a. ample amount of 10% formalin (at least 5 times the size of the biopsy)
   b. label with patient's name and location of biopsy
3. Drawing/map of site of biopsy for orientation of margins (eyelid lesions for margins, en bloc resections of conjunctiva, scleral, and ciliary body/iris tumors)

Frozen Sections
1. If possible, previous communication with ophthalmic pathologist
2. Fill out specific frozen section requisition form, specifying the reason for submitting tissue, such as
   a. Margins
   b. Diagnosis
   c. Adequacy of sampling
   d. Obtaining tissue for molecular diagnosis (retinoblastoma, rhabdomyosarcoma, metastatic neuroblastoma, etc) or flow cytometry
3. Map/diagram of lesion indicating margins and orientation
4. Labeling of tissue (ink, sutures) to orient according to the diagram (for margins)

FNAB and Cytology
1. Previous communication with ophthalmic pathologist to discuss
   a. Logistics of the biopsy
      i. Possible adequacy check during the biopsy (intraocular tumors)
      ii. Fixative to be used
      iii. Fresh tissue for possible molecular diagnosis
   b. Fill out specific cytology form

Molecular Techniques and Electron Microscopy
1. Previous communication with ophthalmic pathologist to discuss
   a. Differential diagnosis
   b. Fixative (fresh vs alcohol vs glutaraldehyde vs other)
   c. Logistics of the biopsy
      i. Time and date (availability of specialized personnel)

- chromogranin and synaptophysin for neuroendocrine lesions (metastatic carcinoid [see Fig 4-2], small cell carcinoma)
- leukocyte common antigen for lesions of hematopoietic origin (leukemia, lymphoma)
- Her2Neu and c-Kit for prognosis and treatment (metastatic breast carcinoma, mastocytosis)

These antibodies vary in their specificity and sensitivity. Specificities and sensitivities of new antibodies are continually being evaluated (for examples, see the online immunohistology query system at www.immunoquery.com). Automated equipment and antigen retrieval techniques are currently used to increase sensitivity and decrease turnaround

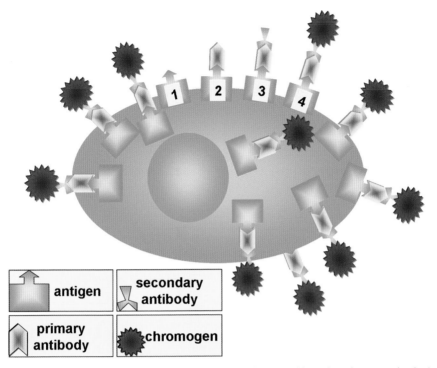

Figure 4-1 Schematic representation of the general immunohistochemistry method. *1,* The cellular antigen is recognized by the specific primary antibody, *2.* A secondary antibody, *3,* directed against the primary antibody reacts with the enzymatic complex to create the chromogen, *4.* The final product allows the visualization of the cell containing the antigen. *(Courtesy of Patricia Chévez-Barrios, MD.)*

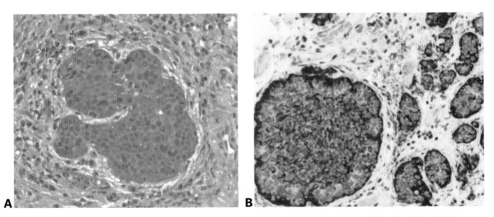

Figure 4-2 A metastatic carcinoid to the orbit seen by H&E **(A)** shows bland epithelial characteristics. **B,** Chromogranin antibody highlights the neuroendocrine nature of the cells. *(Courtesy of Patricia Chévez-Barrios, MD.)*

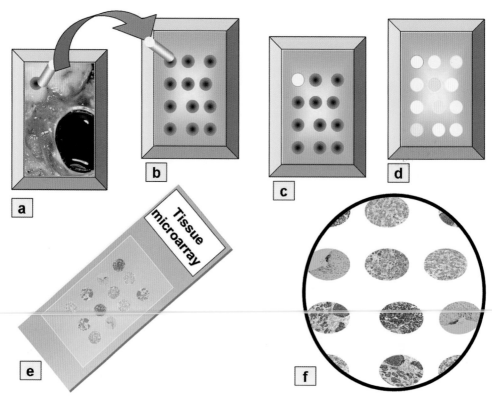

Figure 4-3 Tissue microarrays are constructed with small core biopsies of different tumors/tissues. A core is obtained from the donor paraffin block of the tumor *(a)*. A recipient paraffin block is prepared, creating empty cores *(b)*. The cores are incorporated into the slots *(c)* until all are occupied *(d)*. Glass slides are prepared and stained with a selected antibody *(e)*. Microscopic examination reveals the different staining patterns of each core *(f)*. *(Courtesy of Patricia Chévez-Barrios, MD.)*

time. Protein expression is presently evaluated, for research purposes mainly, in large series of tumors and tissues included in tissue microarrays (TMAs). Tissue microarrays are paraffin blocks constructed with multiple cores of different tumors/tissues, including positive controls. Microscopic slides are prepared from these blocks and immunohistochemistry performed on a single slide for the entire group of samples (Fig 4-3).

Flow Cytometry, Molecular Pathology, and Diagnostic Electron Microscopy

Flow Cytometry

Flow cytometry is used to analyze the physical and chemical properties of particles or cells moving in single file in a fluid stream (Fig 4-4, *a*). An example of flow cytometry is immunophenotyping of leukocytes. The cells need to be fresh (unfixed). Fluorochrome-labeled specific antibodies bind to the surface of lymphoid cells, and a suspension of labeled

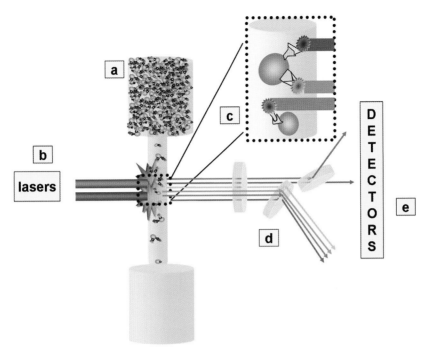

Figure 4-4 Flow cytometry analyzes particles or cells moving in single file in a fluid stream *(a)*. Fluorochrome-labeled specific antibodies bind to the surface of cells, and a suspension of labeled cells is sequentially illuminated by a laser *(b)*. As the excited fluorochrome returns to its resting energy level, a specific wavelength of light is emitted *(c)* that is sorted by wavelength *(d)* and received by a photodetector *(e)*. This signal is then converted to electronic impulses, which are in turn analyzed by computer software. *(Courtesy of Patricia Chévez-Barrios, MD.)*

cells is sequentially illuminated by a light source (usually argon laser) for approximately 10^{-6} second (Fig 4-4, *b*). As the excited fluorochrome returns to its resting energy level, a specific wavelength of light is emitted (Fig 4-4, *c*) that is sorted by wavelength stream (Fig 4-4, *d*) and received by a photodetector (Fig 4-4, *e*). This signal is then converted to electronic impulses, which are in turn analyzed by computer software. The results may be imaged by a multicolored dot-plot histogram (Fig 4-5). The most common use of flow cytometry in clinical practice is for immunophenotyping hematopoietic proliferations. This procedure may be performed on vitreous, aqueous, or ocular adnexal tissue.

In addition, multiple antibodies and cellular size can be analyzed, and the relative percentages of cells may be displayed. For example, CD4 (helper T cells), CD8 (suppressor T cells), both CD4+ and CD8+, or either CD4+ or CD8+ may be displayed for a given lymphocytic infiltrate. The advantage of this method is that it actually shows the percentages of particular cells in a specimen. Disadvantages are the failure to show the location and distribution of these cells in tissue and the possibility of sampling errors. Depending on the number of cells in the sample and on clinical information, the flow cytometrist chooses the panel of antibodies to be tested. Flow cytometric data should therefore be used as an adjunct to morphologic H&E and sometimes immunohistochemistry interpretation. Flow cytometric analysis is particularly useful for the evaluation of lymphoid proliferations.

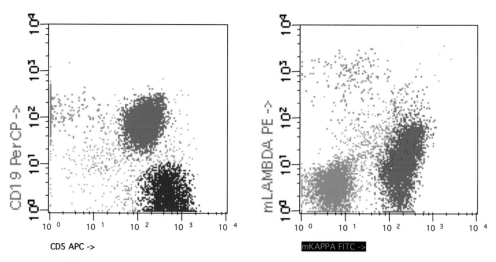

Figure 4-5 Flow cytometry scatter graphs showing a clonal population of CD19⁺ kappa restricted lymphocytes. Note that most of the CD19⁺ cells fail to express lambda light chains. *(Courtesy of Patricia Chévez-Barrios, MD.)*

Molecular Pathology

Molecular pathology techniques are used increasingly in diagnostic ophthalmic pathology and extensively in experimental pathology. A common molecular biological technique is the *polymerase chain reaction (PCR),* which amplifies a single strand of nucleic acid thousands of times, enabling recognition (Fig 4-6). Techniques used in diagnostic pathology are presented in brief in Table 4-2. Molecular pathology is used to identify tumor-promoting or tumor-inhibiting genes (CGH, PCR, array CGH), such as the retinoblastoma gene; and viral DNA or RNA strands, such as those seen in herpesviruses and Epstein-Barr virus (PCR, in situ hybridization [ISH]). The clinical relevance of detecting a PCR product depends on numerous variables, including the primers selected, the laboratory controls, and the demographic considerations. Therefore, PCR should be used to derive supplementary information for making a clinicopathologic diagnosis. For further information about the PCR technique, see Part III, Genetics, in BCSC Section 2, *Fundamentals and Principles of Ophthalmology.*

Leukemias, lymphomas, and soft tissue tumors represent a heterogeneous group of lesions whose classification continues to evolve as a result of advances in cytogenetic and molecular techniques. In the last decade, traditional diagnostic approaches were supplemented by the successful application of these newer techniques (see Table 4-2) to formalin-fixed, paraffin-embedded tissue, making it possible to subject a broader range of clinical material to molecular analysis. Thus, molecular genetics has already become an integral part of the workup in tumors, such as pediatric orbital tumors (rhabdomyosarcomas, neuroblastoma, peripheral neuroectodermal tumors [PNET]), that demonstrate characteristic translocations. Based on the results, treatment can be directed and prognostic features associated with certain mutations and translocations.

The evolution of molecular pathology techniques has made it possible not only to recognize the presence or absence of a strand of nucleic acid but also to demonstrate the localization in the specific cells (FISH, ISH).

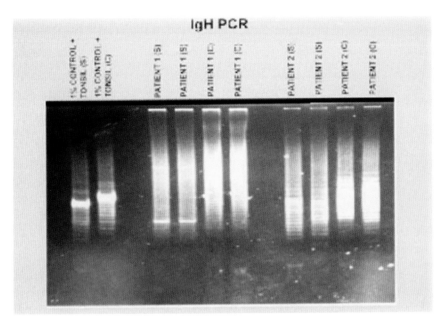

Figure 4-6 A patient's conjunctival lymphoid infiltrate was evaluated by PCR for clonality. PCR of the patient's infiltrate demonstrated a clonal band of IgH gene rearrangement in the lanes labeled "Patient 1 (S)." *(Courtesy of Hans E. Grossniklaus, MD.)*

Hicks J, Mierau GW. The spectrum of pediatric tumors in infancy, childhood, and adolescence: a comprehensive review with emphasis on special techniques in diagnosis. *Ultrastruct Pathol.* 2005;29:175–202.

Oostlander AE, Meijer GA, Ylstra B. Microarray-based comparative genomic hybridization and its applications in human genetics. *Clin Genet.* 2004;66:488–495.

Diagnostic Electron Microscopy

Diagnostic electron microscopy is used primarily to indicate the cell of origin of a tumor of questionable differentiation rather than to distinguish between benign and malignant processes. Although immunopathologic studies are less expensive and performed more rapidly than diagnostic electron microscopy, in some cases, diagnostic electron microscopy complements immunopathologic studies. Once again, the surgeon should consult with the pathologist before surgery to determine whether diagnostic electron microscopy might play a role in the study of a particular tissue specimen.

Special Techniques

Fine-Needle Aspiration Biopsy

Fine-needle aspiration biopsy (FNAB) has been used instead of excisional biopsy by non-ophthalmic surgeons and pathologists. It is especially useful if the physician performing the biopsy can grasp the lesion (usually between the thumb and forefinger) and make several passes with the needle to obtain representative areas. In the practice of general

Table 4-2 Summary of Molecular Techniques Used in Diagnostic Pathology

Technique	Year	Method	Advantages	Disadvantages
Karyotyping	1950s	Chromosomes treated to spread apart and arrange into pairs	Identification of specific chromosomal abnormalities	1. Need for dividing cells 2. Resolution limitations; cannot detect small aberrations
Chromosomal banding	1960s	Metaphase chromosomes stained, producing patterns of dark and light bands along the length of each chromosome	Gross chromosomal abnormalities, both numerical and structural, studied more easily	1. Need for dividing cells 2. Resolution limitations; cannot detect small aberrations
Fluorescence in situ hybridization (FISH)	1980s	Chromosome region-specific, fluorescent-labeled DNA probes (cloned pieces genomic DNA) able to detect their complementary DNA sequences	1. Localization in the lesion of positive cells 2. Fluorescent signal easily detected in fresh or fixed tissue	1. Known type and location of expected aberrations 2. Limited number of chromosomal loci at one time
Polymerase chain reaction (PCR)	1980s	Amplification of a single strand of nucleic acid thousands of times, enabling recognition	Quality snap-frozen tissue (optimal) and archival paraffin-embedded tissue	1. Variable success rate of DNA extraction 2. Contamination with other nucleic acid material
Reverse transcriptase-polymerase chain reaction (RT-PCR)	1990s	Detection of specific chimeric RNA transcripts	Quality snap-frozen tissue (optimal) and archival paraffin-embedded tissue	1. Variable success rate of RNA extraction 2. Contamination with other nucleic acid material
"Real time" quantitative RT-PCR	1999	Measurement of PCR-product accumulation during the exponential phase of the PCR reaction using a dual-labeled fluorogenic probe	Direct detection of PCR-product formation by measuring the increase in fluorescent emission continuously during the PCR reaction	Variable success rate of RNA extraction
Comparative genomic hybridization (CGH)	1990s	Genomic DNAs of test (patient) and reference (normal) samples, labeled green and red, respectively.	1. Detects and maps alterations in copy number of DNA sequences	Inability to detect mosaicism, balanced chromosomal translocations, inversions, and whole-genome ploidy changes

(Continued)

Table 4-2 *(continued)*

Technique	Year	Method	Advantages	Disadvantages
		Normal chromosomes = yellow (red + green) with ratio of 1. Deleted regions = red with ratio <1. Amplified regions = green with ratio >1.	2. Analyzes all chromosomes in a single experiment and no dividing cells required	
Microarray-based CGH (array CGH)	2000s	Differentially labeled test and reference DNAs, hybridized to cloned fragments, genomic DNA or cDNA, which are spotted on a glass slide (the array). The DNA copy number aberrations measured by detecting intensity differences in the hybridization patterns	High resolution	1. Inability to detect aberrations not resulting in copy number changes 2. Limited in its ability to detect mosaicism

surgical pathology, FNAB is very useful in assessing enlarged lymph nodes, thyroid nodules, salivary gland masses, and breast masses.

Intraocular FNAB may be useful in distinguishing between primary uveal tumors and metastases. The procedure is performed under direct visualization through a dilated pupil. Iris tumors may be accessible for FNAB during slit-lamp biomicroscopy. However, FNAB alone cannot reliably predict the prognosis of a uveal melanoma because the sample with intraocular FNAB is limited. Intraocular FNAB may also enable tumor cells to escape the eye; this possibility is an area of some controversy. In general, properly performed, FNAB does not pose a risk for seeding a tumor, but retinoblastoma is a notable exception. FNAB of a possible retinoblastoma lesion, if indicated, should be performed by an *ophthalmic oncologist* with ample experience in making the diagnosis and performing the procedure.

The cells obtained through FNAB can be processed through cytospin, liquid base cytology, or cell block (Fig 4-7). Cell block allows the pathologist to employ special stains, immunohistochemistry, and in situ hybridization, if necessary.

Some orbital surgeons have used FNAB in the diagnosis of orbital lesions, especially presumed metastases to the orbit and optic nerve tumors. However, because it is difficult to make several passes at different angles through an intraorbital tumor, FNAB of orbital masses may not adequately sample representative areas of the tumor. Specific indications

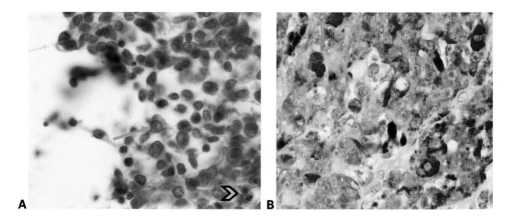

Figure 4-7 Fine-needle aspiration biopsy (FNAB) of choroidal tumor. **A,** Cytologic liquid-based preparation displays prominent nucleoli *(arrow)* and some brown pigment *(arrowhead)* suggestive of melanoma. **B,** Cell block of the aspirated cells, stained with HMB-45 using a red chromogen, is positive, confirming the diagnosis of melanoma. Notice the difference between the red chromogen and the brown melanin. *(Courtesy of Patricia Chévez-Barrios, MD.)*

for when and when not to perform intraocular or intraorbital FNAB are beyond the scope of this discussion, but some of these indications are discussed in Part II of this book, Intraocular Tumors: Clinical Aspects. Ophthalmic FNAB should be performed only when an ophthalmic pathologist or cytologist experienced in the preparation and interpretation of these specimens is available. The surgeon should be prepared to treat the patient appropriately when the FNAB results become known.

> Cohen VM, Dinakaran S, Parsons MA, Rennie IG. Transvitreal fine needle aspiration biopsy: the influence of intraocular lesion size on diagnostic biopsy result. *Eye.* 2001;15(Pt 2):143–147.
> Shields JA, Shields CL, Ehya H, Eagle RC Jr, De Potter P. Fine-needle aspiration biopsy of suspected intraocular tumors. The 1992 Urwick Lecture. *Ophthalmology.* 1993;100:1677–1684.

Frozen Section

Permanent sections (tissue that is processed after fixation through alcohols and xylenes, embedded in paraffin, and sectioned) are always preferred in ophthalmic pathology because of the inherent small size of samples. If the lesion is too small, it could be lost during frozen sectioning. A frozen section (tissue that is snap-frozen and immediately sectioned in a cryostat) is indicated when the results of the study will affect management of the patient in the operating room. For example, the most frequent indication for a frozen section is to determine whether the resection margins are free of tumor, especially in eyelid carcinomas. Appropriate orientation of the specimen (through drawings of the excision site, labeled margins, or margins of the excised tissue that are tagged with sutures or other markers) is crucial when submitting tissue for margin evaluation.

Two techniques are used for accessing the margins in eyelid carcinomas (basal cell carcinoma, squamous cell carcinoma, and sebaceous carcinoma): regular frozen sections and Mohs micrographic surgery. Mohs surgery preserves tissue while obtaining free margins. Eyelid lesions, especially those located in the canthal areas, require tissue conservation to maintain adequate cosmetic results and function. Other frequent indications for frozen sections are to determine whether the surgeon has biopsied representative material for diagnosis (metastasis) and to submit fresh tissue for flow cytometry and molecular genetics (sarcomas, lymphomas, and so on). Frozen sections are not indicated merely to satisfy the curiosity of the surgeon or the patient's family; the utilization of frozen sections is carefully monitored by most hospital quality assurance committees. Surgeons must keep in mind that the use of frozen sections is a time-intensive and costly process.

It is considered inappropriate to order frozen sections and then to proceed with a case before receiving the results from the pathologist. To ensure adequate understanding of the case and facilitate the best possible results for the patient, the surgeon should communicate with the pathologist ahead of time if a frozen section is anticipated.

Chévez-Barrios P. Frozen section diagnosis and indications in ophthalmic pathology. *Arch Pathol Lab Med.* 2005;129:1626–1634.

CHAPTER **5**

Conjunctiva

Topography

The conjunctiva is a mucous membrane lining the posterior surface of the eyelids and the anterior surface of the globe as far as the limbus. It can be subdivided into *palpebral, forniceal,* and *bulbar* sections. The conjunctiva consists of stratified, nonkeratinizing squamous epithelium that is flat and regular without goblet cells in the epibulbar area and, at the limbus, may be slightly pigmented (Fig 5-1A). In the palpebral area, the epithelium is thickened and covers nests of lymphocytes, vessels, and some lymphoid follicle in children and young adults (Fig 5-1B). The squamous epithelium is interspersed with mucus-containing goblet cells, which are most numerous in the fornices and plica semilunaris (Fig 5-1C, 5-1D). The epithelial layer covers a substantia propria that is thickest in the fornices and thinnest covering the tarsus. Constituents of this stromal layer include loosely arranged collagen fibers; vessels; nerves; and resident lymphocytes, plasma cells, and mast cells. In the medial canthal area, the conjunctiva forms a vertical fold, the *plica semilunaris,* and medial to this is the *caruncle.* The caruncle is covered by nonkeratinizing stratified squamous epithelium, and within the stroma are sebaceous glands, hair follicles, and accessory lacrimal glands. BCSC Section 8, *External Disease and Cornea,* also discusses the conjunctiva in depth.

Congenital Anomalies

Choristomas

Choristomas are congenital proliferations of histologically mature tissue elements not normally present at the site of occurrence. Examples include

- limbal dermoid
- dermolipoma
- ectopic lacrimal gland
- episcleral osseous choristoma

Dermoids are firm, dome-shaped, white-yellow papules at or straddling the limbus in the inferotemporal quadrant. Size varies from a few millimeters to more than 1 cm. They may occur in isolation or, particularly when bilateral, as a manifestation of a congenital

53

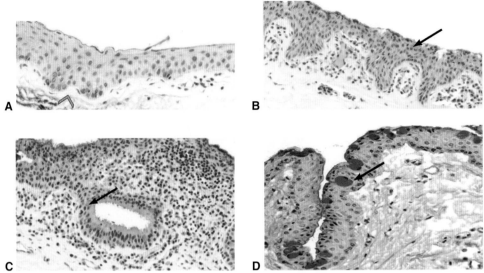

Figure 5-1 **A,** Epibulbar conjunctiva with regular, nonkeratinizing squamous epithelium with areas of light basal pigmentation at the limbus *(arrowhead)*. **B,** Palpebral conjunctiva with thickened epithelium covering vessels and inflammatory cells and containing some goblet cells *(arrow)*. **C,** Conjunctiva at the fornix may contain pseudoglands of Henle, infoldings of conjunctiva with abundant goblet cells *(arrow)*. **D,** Periodic acid–Schiff (PAS) stain highlights the mucinous origin of the goblet cells *(arrow)*. *(Courtesy of Patricia Chévez-Barrios, MD.)*

complex such as Goldenhar syndrome or linear nevus sebaceous syndrome. A dermoid recapitulates the tissues of the skin; that is, it contains epidermis and dermis, including dermal adnexal structures. The surface epithelium may or may not be keratinized. Figure 6-3, in Chapter 6, shows an example of a corneal dermoid.

Dermolipomas occur more frequently in the superotemporal quadrant toward the fornix and may extend posteriorly into the orbit. A dermolipoma is softer and yellower than a limbal dermoid as a result of the adipose tissue component present in the deeper layers of the choristoma (Fig 5-2). Histopathologically, it also differs from a dermoid in that the dermal adnexal structures are often absent. Dermolipomas may also be associated with Goldenhar syndrome or linear nevus sebaceous syndrome.

Complex choristomas, in addition to having the features of a dermoid or dermolipoma, include other tissues such as cartilage, bone, and lacrimal gland. Clinically, they usually are indistinguishable from dermoids or dermolipomas.

Spencer WH, ed. *Ophthalmic Pathology: An Atlas and Textbook.* Vol 1. 4th ed. Philadelphia: Saunders; 1996:chap 2.

Hamartomas

Hamartomas, in contrast to choristomas, are overgrowths of mature tissue normally present at that site. In the conjunctiva, the most common variety of hamartoma is *hemangioma,* although a hemangioma can also be considered to be a true neoplasm. Although it may involve only the conjunctiva, typically the hemangioma is also present in the eyelid, face,

Figure 5-2 A dermolipoma differs from a dermoid in that adnexal structures are often absent and significant amounts of mature adipose tissue are present in the deeper aspect of the choristoma. *(Courtesy of Harry H. Brown, MD.)*

and orbit. Congenital hemangiomas are detected at or shortly after birth as elevated, soft, red-purple nodules that may continue to grow in the first year of life before stabilizing. The majority of cases then begin a slow process of involution, resulting in complete regression. Intervention is necessary only when vision or ocular integrity is compromised. The histopathologic appearance varies depending on the stage at which the tissue is excised. Early, actively growing hemangiomas show a cellular proliferation of plump endothelial cells forming solid nests and cords within the connective tissue stroma. Mitotic figures are often present. In fully developed hemangiomas, the endothelial cells flatten, forming easily recognizable capillary lumina. In the involutional phase, the lobules of capillary proliferation are replaced by fibrous tissue.

Inflammations

Because the conjunctiva is an exposed surface, a variety of organisms, toxic agents, and allergens can initiate an inflammatory response known as *conjunctivitis*. Clinically, the response can be subdivided into acute or chronic conjunctivitis, according to the time frame of signs and symptoms. *Acute conjunctivitis* has a rapid onset of redness and irritation. Mucus production is particularly prominent in the acute phase and, in concert with the sloughing of necrotic epithelium and outpouring of acute inflammatory cells and fibrin, a surface membrane may form. A true membrane is formed when the underlying epithelium is ulcerated and granulation tissue forms beneath the fibrinopurulent exudate; attempts to remove a true membrane will result in petechial hemorrhages. However, if the underlying epithelium remains intact, removal does not cause bleeding and the surface material is known as a *pseudomembrane*.

The signs and symptoms of *chronic conjunctivitis* develop more insidiously. The inflammatory response is composed predominantly of lymphocytes and plasma cells, often causing localized nodules with infoldings of surface epithelium *(pseudoglands of Henle).*

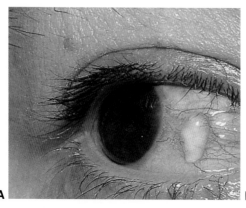 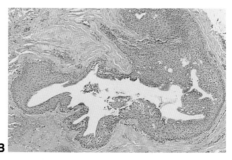

A   **B**

Figure 5-3 **A,** Epithelial inclusion cysts may follow conjunctival trauma. **B,** The cyst is lined by nonkeratinizing, stratified squamous epithelium, consistent with conjunctiva.

Although more commonly a sequela of trauma, epithelial inclusion cysts and calcification of inspissated secretions may also occur in the postinflammatory period (Fig 5-3).

Papillary versus Follicular Conjunctivitis

Conjunctivitis may be further subdivided into papillary and follicular types, according to the macroscopic and microscopic appearance of the conjunctiva (Fig 5-4). Neither is pathognomonic for a particular disease entity. *Papillary conjunctivitis* shows a cobblestone arrangement of flattened nodules with a central vascular core (Fig 5-5). It is most commonly associated with an allergic immune response, as in vernal and atopic keratoconjunctivitis, or is a response to a foreign body such as a contact lens or ocular prosthesis. Papillae coat the tarsal surface of the upper eyelid and may reach large size *(giant papillary conjunctivitis)*. Limbal papillae may occur in vernal keratoconjunctivitis *(Horner-Trantas dots)*. The histopathologic appearance is identical, regardless of the cause: closely packed, mesa-like nodules lined by conjunctival epithelium, with numerous eosinophils, lymphocytes, and plasma cells in the stroma surrounding a central vascular channel. Mast cells may also be conspicuous.

Follicular conjunctivitis is seen in a variety of conditions, including those caused by pathogens such as viruses; bacteria; chlamydiae; and toxins, including ocular topical medications (antiglaucomatous, over-the-counter ophthalmic decongestants, and so on; Fig 5-6). In contrast to papillae, follicles are small, dome-shaped nodules without a prominent central vessel. Histopathologically, they are composed of aggregates of lymphocytes and plasma cells in the superficial stroma between the tarsus and the fornix or within the palpebral and bulbar conjunctiva. Lymphocytes may form germinal centers within the follicles, complete with tingible body macrophages (histiocytes containing ingested intracytoplasmic nuclear debris).

Blondeau P, Rousseau JA. Allergic reactions to brimonidine in patients treated for glaucoma. *Can J Ophthalmol.* 2002;37:21–26.

Soparkar CN, Wilhelmus KR, Koch DD, Wallace GW, Jones DB. Acute and chronic conjunctivitis due to over-the-counter ophthalmic decongestants. *Arch Ophthalmol.* 1997;115:34–38.

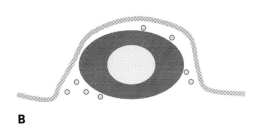

A   B

Figure 5-4 Schematic representation of papillary and follicular conjunctivitis. **A,** In papillary conjunctivitis, the conjunctival epithelium *(pale blue)* covers fibrovascular cores with blood vessels *(red)*, and the stroma contains eosinophils *(pink)* and lymphocytes and plasma cells *(dark blue)*. **B,** In follicular conjunctivitis, the conjunctival epithelium covers lymphocytes, forming follicles with paler follicular centers *(dark blue with central pale blue)*, and the surrounding stroma contains lymphocytes and plasma cells *(dark blue)*. *(Courtesy of Patricia Chévez-Barrios, MD.)*

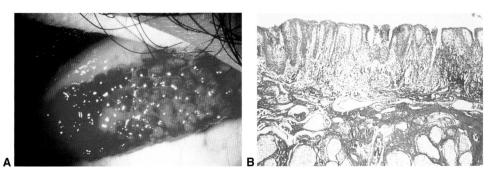

A   B

Figure 5-5 **A,** Papillae efface the normal palpebral conjunctival surface and form a confluent cobblestone pattern. **B,** Low-power photomicrograph highlights the closely packed, flat-topped papillae with central fibrovascular cores (trichrome stain). *(Courtesy of Harry H. Brown, MD.)*

Infectious Conjunctivitis

A wide variety of pathogens may infect the conjunctiva, including viruses, bacteria, fungi, and chlamydiae. The most common offending agents in children are bacterial *(Haemophilus influenzae)* and, in adults, viral; the usual culprits are adenovirus and the herpesviruses (simplex and zoster). Viral infections, in addition to inciting a follicular conjunctivitis, often affect the cornea, resulting in ulcers in herpetic disease and subepithelial infiltrates in adenoviral disease.

Bacterial infections cause about 50% of the cases of conjunctivitis in children and 5% of the cases in adults. See BCSC Section 8, *External Disease and Cornea,* for additional information on current pathogens.

When the conjunctiva alone is infected, fungi are rarely the inciting pathogen. *Rhinosporidium seeberi,* which may cause an isolated conjunctivitis, is seen most often in areas such as India and Southeast Asia.

Chlamydiae are obligate intracellular pathogens, among which *Chlamydia trachomatis* is a major cause of ocular infection, particularly in the Middle East. Serotypes A, B,

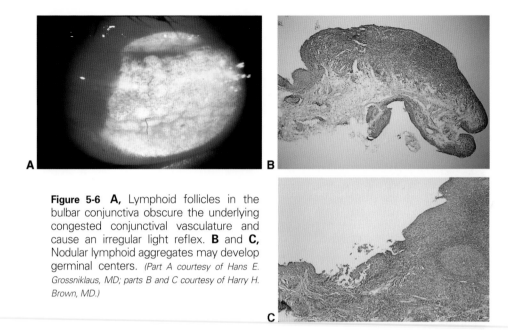

Figure 5-6 A, Lymphoid follicles in the bulbar conjunctiva obscure the underlying congested conjunctival vasculature and cause an irregular light reflex. **B** and **C,** Nodular lymphoid aggregates may develop germinal centers. *(Part A courtesy of Hans E. Grossniklaus, MD; parts B and C courtesy of Harry H. Brown, MD.)*

and C are associated with trachoma; serotypes D through K cause neonatal and adult inclusion conjunctivitis. *Microsporida* is another group of obligate intracellular parasites that may cause conjunctivitis, keratitis, or keratoconjunctivitis, particularly in patients with acquired immunodeficiency syndrome (AIDS). Exfoliative cytology of conjunctival or corneal epithelium (Giemsa stain) may be useful in demonstrating these intracellular organisms (Fig 5-7).

Kane KY, Meadows S, Ellis MR. Clinical inquiries. When should acute nonvenereal conjunctivitis be treated with topical antibiotics? *J Fam Pract.* 2002;51:312.

Wald ER. Conjunctivitis in infants and children. *Pediatr Infect Dis J.* 1997;16:S17–20.

Noninfectious Conjunctivitis

Sarcoidosis may involve any ocular tissues, including the conjunctiva. It manifests as small, tan nodules, primarily within the forniceal conjunctiva. Conjunctival biopsy can be a simple, expedient way of providing pathologic correlation in this systemic disease. Histopathologically, granulomas (aggregates of epithelioid histiocytes) are present within the conjunctival stroma with a variable, but usually minimal, cuff of lymphocytes and plasma cells. Multinucleated giant cells may or may not be present within the granuloma. Central necrosis is not characteristic and, if present, should suggest other causes of granulomatous inflammation, such as infection with mycobacteria, fungi, spirochetes, or parasites. Bacteria such as *Francisella tularensis* (tularemia) and *Bartonella henselae* (cat-scratch disease) are other considerations; these usually are accompanied by microabscesses. The diagnosis of sarcoidosis is tenable only when supported by clinical findings and after other causes of granulomatous inflammation have been excluded by histochemical stains and/or, most

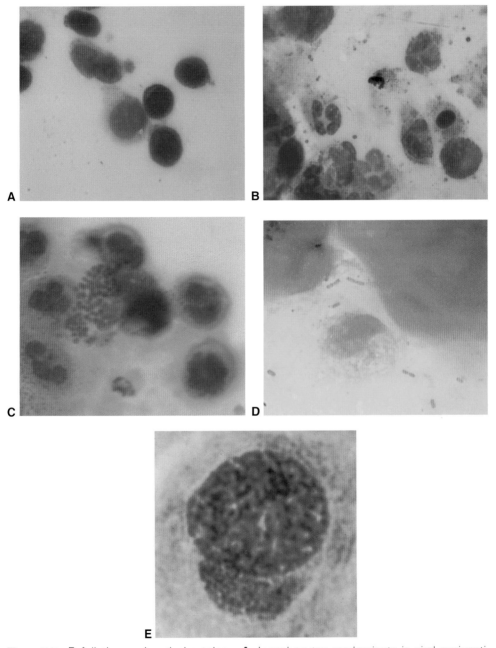

Figure 5-7 Exfoliative conjunctival cytology. **A,** Lymphocytes predominate in viral conjunctivitis. **B,** A mixture of polymorphonuclear leukocytes and eosinophils is typical of vernal conjunctivitis. **C,** Gram stain reveals the polymorphonuclear leukocyte response to gonococcal conjunctivitis. Note the intracellular, gram-negative diplococci. **D,** A case of *Moraxella lacunata* angular conjunctivitis demonstrating the bacilli, which often are found in pairs. **E,** *Chlamydia,* conjunctival scraping, Giemsa stain. The inclusion body, composed of multiple chlamydial organisms, can be seen capping the nucleus. A distinct space separates the inclusion body from the nuclear chromatin. Occasionally, crushing the cells during specimen preparation may cause chromatin to stream through a defect in the nuclear membrane, resulting in an appearance similar to that of a chlamydial inclusion body.

importantly, by culture. BCSC Section 9, *Intraocular Inflammation and Uveitis*, discusses sarcoidosis in greater detail. See also Chapter 12 in this volume.

Granulomatous conjunctivitis in association with preauricular lymphadenopathy is known as *Parinaud oculoglandular syndrome*. This condition is discussed in BCSC Section 6, *Pediatric Ophthalmology and Strabismus*, and Section 8, *External Disease and Cornea*.

As an exposed surface, the conjunctiva is vulnerable to contact with foreign bodies. Some may be transient and/or inert, whereas others may become embedded and incite a foreign-body reaction, identifiable as a granuloma surrounding the foreign object. Multinucleated giant cells are common. Viewing the slide under polarized light may be helpful in identifying the type of offending foreign material.

Degenerations

Pinguecula and Pterygium

A *pinguecula* is a small, yellowish gray nodule, often bilateral, situated at the nasal or temporal limbus (Fig 5-8). It is seen in individuals with prolonged exposure to sunlight and is therefore more common with advancing years. The overlying epithelium is often thinned but may be acanthotic (thickened) or dysplastic. The stromal collagen shows fragmentation and basophilic degeneration called *elastotic degeneration* because the degenerated collagen will stain positively with a histochemical stain for elastic fibers such as the Verhoeff–van Gieson stain (see Fig 5-8). However, pretreatment of the slide with elastase does not diminish the staining.

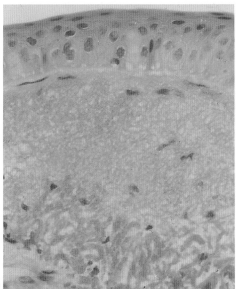
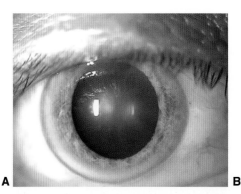

A   B

Figure 5-8 **A,** Pinguecula forms a dome-shaped yellow nodule adjacent to the limbus. **B,** Pinguecula showing the basophilic hue of elastotic degeneration, a type of collagen degeneration caused by ultraviolet light. A pterygium specimen would be similar except that a portion of Bowman's layer could be represented in the section. *(Part B courtesy of Hans E. Grossniklaus, MD.)*

A *pterygium* has similar etiology, location, and histologic features, but it encroaches onto the cornea in a winglike fashion (similar to an insect wing; Fig 5-9). Because they can interfere with vision, pterygia are excised when they threaten the visual axis. The destruction of Bowman's layer by the advancing fibrovascular tissue results in a corneal scar. So-called *recurrent pterygia* may completely lack the histopathologic feature of elastotic degeneration and are more accurately classified as an exuberant fibrous tissue response. Some studies have demonstrated that there is mutated p53 expression and loss of heterozygosity and microsatellite instability, especially in recurrent pterygia harboring dysplastic and cancerous epithelium.

Detorakis ET, Sourvinos G, Tsamparlakis J, Spandidos DA. Evaluation of loss of heterozygosity and microsatellite instability in human pterygium: clinical correlations. *Br J Ophthalmol.* 1998;82:1324–1328.

Dushku N, Hatcher SL, Albert DM, Reid TW. p53 expression and relation to human papillomavirus infection in pingueculae, pterygia, and limbal tumors. *Arch Ophthalmol.* 1999;117:1593–1599.

Gans LA. Surgical treatment of pterygium. *Focal Points: Clinical Modules for Ophthalmologists.* San Francisco: American Academy of Ophthalmology; 1996, module 12.

Amyloid Deposits

Amyloid deposition in the conjunctiva is most commonly a primary localized process seen in healthy young and middle-aged adults. Less often, it occurs secondary to preexisting, long-standing inflammation, such as with trachoma, or as an ocular manifestation of a systemic disease such as multiple myeloma. Deposits within the stroma cause a nodular or diffuse waxy, rubbery thickening of any portion of the conjunctiva (Fig 5-10). Amyloid is an eosinophilic, extracellular, hyaline-appearing substance within the stroma, often in a perivascular distribution. Congo red stain tints amyloid an orange-red, but amyloid deposits viewed with polarized light and a rotating analyzer polarization filter also exhibit dichroism (see Fig 5-10); that is, they change from orange-red to green-yellow as the analyzer is rotated. Other useful staining methods include crystal violet and thioflavin T. When describing amyloid deposits involving the eyelid, the physician should specify the location of the

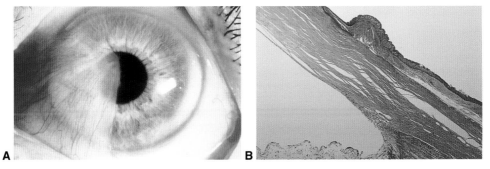

A   B

Figure 5-9 **A,** Pterygium is so named because of its winglike configuration across the corneal surface. **B,** Histologically, a pterygium differs from a pinguecula only in the encroachment onto the cornea and the destruction of Bowman's layer. *(Courtesy of Hans E. Grossniklaus, MD.)*

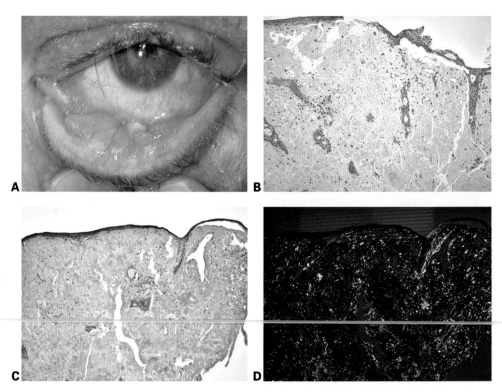

Figure 5-10 **A,** A 70-year-old man presented with a lower eyelid subconjunctival mass that was found to be an amyloid deposit. **B,** Amyloidosis characterized by extracellular amorphous eosinophilic material in the substantia propria of the conjunctiva *(asterisk).* **C,** Congo red stain shows the amyloid staining orange-red *(asterisk).* **D,** Under polarization, amyloid displays dichroism with the characteristic apple green color *(asterisk). (Part A courtesy of John B. Holds, MD; parts B, C, D courtesy of Nasreen A. Syed, MD.)*

deposit: amyloid deposits affecting the skin of the eyelid usually reflect a systemic condition, whereas amyloid deposits affecting the palpebral conjunctiva usually indicate localized pathology.

Neoplasia

Epithelial Lesions

Squamous papillomas are exophytic, pink-red, strawberry-like papillary growths with a biphasic age distribution, growth pattern, and site of involvement (Fig 5-11). In children they are most commonly multiple and pedunculated, involving the fornix, caruncle, or eyelid margin. In adults they are usually single and sessile, occurring at the limbus. Limbal papillomas cannot be clinically distinguished from precancerous dysplasia or invasive squamous cell carcinoma; they require excision for histopathologic diagnosis (Fig 5-12).

Human papillomavirus (HPV) has been detected in both pediatric and adult papillomas: HPV subtype 6 in the former and subtype 16 in the latter. The histopathologic examination of papillomas demonstrates papillary fibrovascular fronds covered by acanthotic squamous

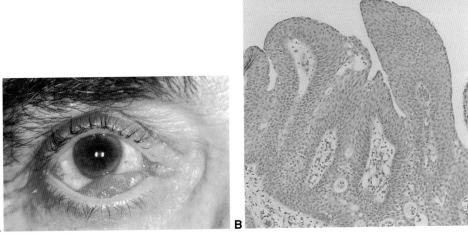

Figure 5-11 Squamous papilloma. **A,** Lower eyelid conjunctival papilloma. **B,** The epithelium is acanthotic and draped over fibrovascular cores. *(Part A courtesy of John B. Holds, MD.)*

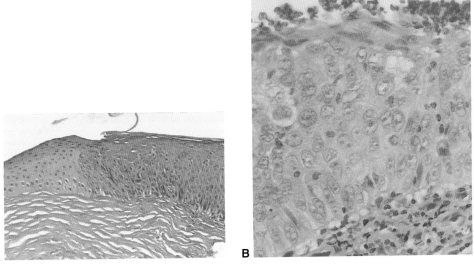

Figure 5-12 Conjunctival dysplasia. **A,** Note the sharp demarcation between normal and abnormal epithelium. The abnormal epithelial cells are confined to the lower half of the conjunctival epithelial thickness. **B,** This is carcinoma in situ, showing full-thickness abnormalities. Because of the difficulties in distinguishing between partial- and full-thickness abnormalities, the term *conjunctival intraepithelial neoplasia (CIN)* is used to describe the spectrum of abnormalities in these conditions.

epithelium. Pediatric papillomas often have an admixture of goblet cells and neutrophils within the epithelium. A chronic inflammatory infiltrate may occupy the stroma. Adult papillomas may exhibit various degrees of epithelial dysplasia, characterized by nuclear enlargement, increased nuclear-to-cytoplasmic ratio, loss of architectural maturation toward the epithelial surface, and mitotic figures above the basal epithelial layer.

Hereditary benign intraepithelial dyskeratosis (HBID) is a rare autosomal dominant disorder with incomplete penetrance. It is characterized by bilateral limbal conjunctival plaques combined with similar changes in the oral mucosa. The clinical and histologic findings are characteristic of HBID. The lesions are characterized histologically by dyskeratosis, acanthosis, parakeratosis, and a variable amount of subepithelial inflammation. Symptoms usually start in early childhood and show a waxing and waning course. HBID was first seen among Haliwa-Saponi Native Americans in North Carolina. It has now been found in other parts of the United States as well as in Europe. Malignant changes of the conjunctival or oral lesions have not been reported.

Haisley-Royster CA, Allingham RR, Klintworth GK, Prose NS. Hereditary benign intraepithelial dyskeratosis: report of two cases with prominent oral lesions. *J Am Acad Dermatol.* 2001;45:634–636.

Dysplasia of the conjunctival epithelium occurs in other clinical settings. *Dysplasias* are generally classified as focal and well circumscribed or diffuse and poorly demarcated (see Fig 5-12). As mentioned previously, dysplasia may arise in the epithelium covering areas of solar elastosis, similar to actinic keratoses of the skin. The dysplasia is focal and well delineated in this situation, often showing a white, flaky appearance (leukoplakia) caused by surface keratinization. When diffuse dysplasias occur in regions of the conjunctiva not exposed to the sun, the clinical appearance is more gelatinous and less well defined. Human papillomavirus subtype 16 has been demonstrated within some cases of dysplasia as well.

Dysplasia is graded as mild, moderate, or severe, according to the degree of involvement of the epithelium. Mild dysplasia, or *conjunctival intraepithelial neoplasia (CIN)* grade I, is defined as dysplasia confined to the lower third of the conjunctival epithelial thickness. Moderate dysplasia (CIN II) extends into the middle third, and severe dysplasia (CIN III) the upper third (Fig 5-13). The risk of invasive carcinoma developing from conjunctival dysplasia appears to be lower than in its counterpart in the uterine cervix, although it expresses mutated p53 in most of the dysplastic cells. Excision of affected epithelium with cryotherapy of the margins is the standard treatment. Topical mitomycin has shown efficacy as an adjunctive therapy in cases with multifocal or extensive surface involvement.

Auw-Haedrich C, Sundmacher R, Freudenberg N, et al. Expression of p63 in conjunctival intraepithelial neoplasia and squamous cell carcinoma. *Graefes Arch Clin Exp Ophthalmol.* 2006;244:96–103.

Kemp EG, Harnett AN, Chatterjee S. Preoperative and intraoperative local mitomycin C adjuvant therapy in the management of ocular surface neoplasias. *Br J Ophthalmol.* 2002;86:31–34.

Invasive *squamous cell carcinoma* of the conjunctiva is an uncommon sequela to preexisting dysplasia (Figs 5-14, 5-15). It occurs in older individuals, usually beginning at the limbus, then superficially invading the conjunctival stroma and spreading onto

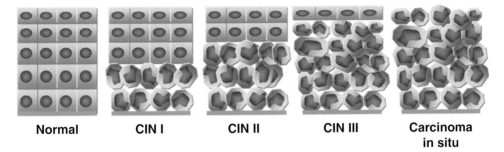

| Normal | CIN I | CIN II | CIN III | Carcinoma in situ |

Figure 5-13 Schematic representation of the progression of conjunctival dysplasia. The first panel represents normal epithelium with basement membrane *(pink)*. CIN I is the replacement of the deeper third of the epithelium by dysplastic, pleomorphic (irregular) cells. CIN II replaces half or more of the thickness of the epithelium with dysplastic cells. CIN III replaces almost the full thickness of the epithelium with dysplastic cells, leaving only 1 layer of nondysplastic epithelium. Carcinoma in situ is the complete replacement of epithelium by dysplastic cells, with the basement membrane still intact. *(Courtesy of Patricia Chévez-Barrios, MD.)*

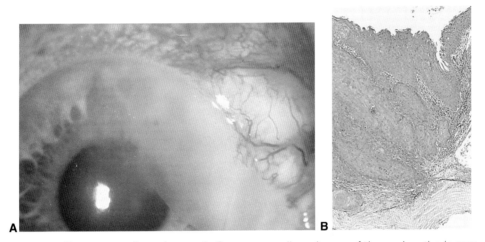

A B

Figure 5-14 Squamous cell carcinoma. **A,** Squamous cell carcinoma of the conjunctiva is commonly centered about the limbus and may spread to involve the corneal epithelium. **B,** The tumor has massively replaced the conjunctival substantia propria. The lamellar eosinophilic fibers at the bottom right of the photograph are sclera. It is unusual for squamous cell carcinoma of the conjunctiva to penetrate the sclera into the eye.

Invasive carcinoma

Figure 5-15 Schematic representation of invasive squamous cell carcinoma. Note the full thickness replacement of the epithelium by malignant cells plus the invasion of subepithelial stroma with infiltration through the basement membrane *(pink line)*. *(Courtesy of Patricia Chévez-Barrios, MD.)*

the corneal surface. Deep invasion of the cornea or sclera and intraocular spread are uncommon complications. Histopathologic examination demonstrates infiltrating nests that have penetrated the epithelial basement membrane and spread into the conjunctival stroma. Tumor cells may be well differentiated and easily recognizable as squamous, moderately differentiated, or poorly differentiated and difficult to distinguish from other malignancies, such as sebaceous carcinoma. Although regional lymph node metastasis is not common, dissemination and death are possible.

Mucoepidermoid carcinoma and *spindle cell carcinoma* are rare variants of squamous cell carcinoma. Both entities are more aggressive neoplasms with higher rates of recurrence and intraocular spread.

For the American Joint Committee on Cancer (AJCC) definitions and staging of carcinoma of the conjunctiva, see Table A-1 in the appendix.

Subepithelial Lesions

Clinically, both benign and malignant lymphoid lesions of the conjunctiva usually show a salmon pink appearance, are relatively flat with a smooth surface, and have a soft consistency (Fig 5-16). Most (approximately two thirds) of conjunctival lymphoid lesions are localized and *not* associated with systemic disease; however, nearly two thirds of lymphomas arising in the preseptal skin eventually show evidence of systemic involvement. Prediction of biological behavior based on clinical, histopathologic, and even immunophenotypic features is not always clear-cut in pathologic diagnosis of lymphoproliferative disorders of the conjunctiva. See also Chapter 14 on lymphoid lesions of the orbit and BCSC Section 7, *Orbit, Eyelids, and Lacrimal System.*

Histopathologic features favoring a diagnosis of *reactive lymphoid hyperplasia* include the presence of lymphoid follicles with germinal centers and an admixture of plasma cells and mature, small lymphocytes in the surrounding stroma (Fig 5-17). *Russell bodies,* eosinophilic spherules representing inspissated immunoglobulin, may be present

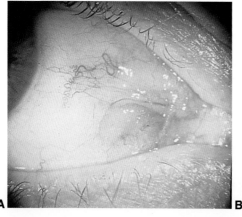

Figure 5-16 Benign reactive lymphoid hyperplasia of the conjunctiva. **A,** Clinical photograph (note the salmon patch). **B,** Note the irregularly shaped germinal centers in the conjunctival substantia propria.

either within plasma cell cytoplasm or extruded into the extracellular milieu. A diffuse sheet of monotonous, small, round or cleaved lymphocytes is more characteristic of a *low-grade malignant lymphoma* (Fig 5-18). *High-grade lymphomas* are readily recognized as malignant by virtue of their nuclear features and their high mitotic rate.

As expected, a histopathologically indeterminate zone exists between reactive hyperplasia and low-grade lymphoma, and ancillary studies may be helpful in classifying proliferations as benign or malignant. Immunophenotypic analysis, either by flow cytometry of fresh, unfixed tissue or by immunoperoxidase staining, may demonstrate B-cell monoclonality by revealing either κ or λ light chain predominance (Fig 5-19). More sophisticated molecular techniques may show monoclonality by revealing immunoglobulin gene rearrangements within tumor cells. However, although these advanced techniques are helpful, they are not definitive: not all lesions demonstrating monoclonality will behave in a malignant fashion that results in systemic disease. Other factors, such as host immune response, are important in determining clinical behavior of the lesion.

Albert DM, Jakobiec FA, eds. *Principles and Practice of Ophthalmology.* 2nd ed. Philadelphia: Saunders; 2000.

Shields CL, Shields JA, Carvalho C, Rundle P, Smith AF. Conjunctival lymphoid tumors: clinical analysis of 117 cases and relationship to systemic lymphoma. *Ophthalmology.* 2001;108:979–984.

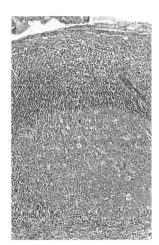

Figure 5-17 Note the large germinal center in this case of benign reactive lymphoid hyperplasia of the conjunctiva.

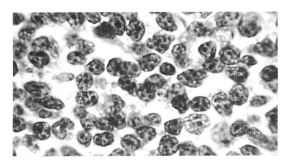

Figure 5-18 Lymphoma composed of sheets of atypical lymphocytes.

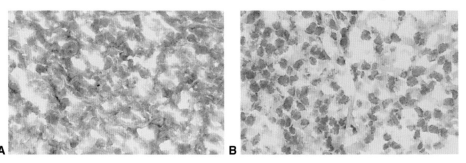

Figure 5-19 Conjunctival lymphoma. **A,** This is an immunoperoxidase stain for λ light chains. Note the diffuse brown staining. **B,** This is an immunoperoxidase stain for κ light chains. The stain is negative. The fact that only λ light stains were demonstrated in this tumor indicates that this is a monoclonal proliferation, consistent with the histologic impression of malignant lymphoma.

Melanocytic Lesions

As with hemangiomas, melanocytic nevi are classified by some authors as hamartomas and by others as neoplasms (Table 5-1). *Conjunctival melanocytic nevi* usually appear on the bulbar conjunctiva in childhood. Analogous to cutaneous melanocytic nevi, conjunctival nevi undergo evolutionary changes. In the initial junctional phase, nevus cells are confined to nests *(theques)* at the interface between the epithelium and the substantia propria. As the nevus evolves, the nests "drop off" into the substantia propria, eventually losing connection with the epithelium and existing solely in the substantia propria. Nevi with both junctional and subepithelial components are designated as *compound nevi;* those without junctional activity are termed *subepithelial* or *stromal nevi.* Subcategories of nevi (eg, Spitz nevus, halo nevus) and other types of nevi (eg, blue nevus) also exist. Epithelial cysts may be encountered within compound and subepithelial nevi (Fig 5-20). Nevi occur only rarely in the palpebral conjunctiva; pigmented lesions in this area are more likely to be primary acquired melanosis or melanoma.

Primary acquired melanosis (PAM) appears as a unilateral flat patch, or patches, of golden brown pigmentation with an irregular margin (Fig 5-21). It is most common in middle-aged persons. The lesions may wax and wane or grow slowly without remission over a period of 10 or more years. It is not possible to predict in which patient PAM is likely to progress to malignant melanoma on clinical grounds alone. However, histologic criteria have been developed to identify patients at high risk for malignancy. *PAM without atypia* denotes hyperplasia of melanocytes without atypical cytologic or architectural features (Fig 5-22A). PAM without atypia does not progress to melanoma. *PAM with atypia* will progress to invasive melanoma in approximately 46% of patients (Fig 5-22B).

Atypia in PAM is defined according to both cytomorphologic and architectural features. Atypical melanocytes show nuclear enlargement as compared with adjacent basal epithelial cells and may be spindled, polygonal, or epithelioid. Architectural features of atypia include lentiginous hyperplasia, intraepidermal migration of individual cells or nests *(pagetoid spread),* or complete replacement of the epithelium, mimicking carcinoma

Table 5-1   Clinical Comparison of Conjunctival Pigmentary Lesions

Lesion	Onset	Area	Location	Malignant Potential
Freckle	Youth	Small	Conjunctiva	No
Benign acquired melanosis	Adulthood	Patchy or diffuse	Conjunctiva	No
Conjunctival nevus	Youth	Small	Conjunctiva	Low (conjunctival melanoma)
Ocular and oculodermal melanocytosis	Congenital	Patchy or diffuse	Under conjunctiva	Yes (uveal melanoma)
Primary acquired melanosis	Middle age	Diffuse	Conjunctiva	Yes (conjunctival melanoma)

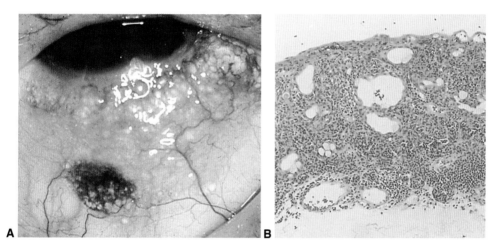

Figure 5-20   A, Compound nevus of the conjunctiva. Note the characteristic cysts. **B,** Histology of a compound conjunctival nevus. Note the cystic epithelial inclusions within the lesion, corresponding with the clinically observed cysts.

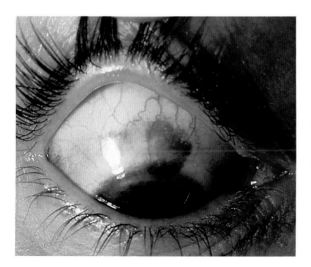

Figure 5-21   Primary acquired melanosis (PAM). Note the flat, patchy pigmentation of the conjunctiva. When examining this patient clinically, the physician should evert the eyelids to exclude involvement of the palpebral conjunctiva.

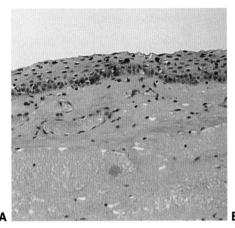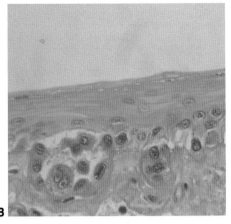

Figure 5-22 **A,** PAM without atypia. The basilar layer of the conjunctival epithelium is pigmented. There is no histologic evidence of melanocytic atypia. Note that in the term *PAM without atypia,* the word *atypia* refers to histologic findings, not to the clinical presentation. **B,** PAM with atypia. Highly atypical epithelioid melanocytes are present within the epithelium. The patient is at high risk for progression to melanoma.

in situ. Pagetoid spread by epithelioid melanocytes and full-thickness replacement of the epithelium are the most important of these features as predictors of subsequent invasive melanoma (75%–90% of cases). PAM with atypia should be treated by excision if the area is small or by cryotherapy for more extensive areas. Mitomycin C has been shown to cause regression in PAM with atypia and may be considered as an alternative therapy, particularly in extensive or multifocal cases; the efficacy of this treatment remains to be proven in a larger series.

> Demirci H, McCormick SA, Finger PT. Topical mitomycin chemotherapy for conjunctival malignant melanoma and primary acquired melanosis with atypia: clinical experience with histopathologic observations. *Arch Ophthalmol.* 2000;118:885–891.
>
> Helm CJ. Melanoma and other pigmented lesions of the ocular surface. *Focal Points: Clinical Modules for Ophthalmologists.* San Francisco: American Academy of Ophthalmology; 1996, module 11.

Approximately two thirds of cases of *conjunctival melanoma* arise from PAM with atypia (Fig 5-23A); the remainder develop either from a preexisting nevus or de novo. Tumors are usually nodular growths that may involve any portion of the conjunctiva; those not on the bulbar surface appear to behave more aggressively. Histopathologically, melanomas have diverse cellular morphology from pleomorphic, large, bizarre cells with prominent nucleoli to small, polygonal cells with mild anaplasia to spindle cells without identifiable melanin pigment. Immunohistochemical stains for S-100 protein and HMB-45 may help to identify problematic cases as melanocytic (Fig 5-23B). Conjunctival melanomas are more akin to cutaneous melanoma than to uveal melanoma in behavior.

The overall mortality rate from conjunctival melanoma is 25%. Typically, metastases first develop in parotid or submandibular lymph nodes. Unfavorable prognostic factors,

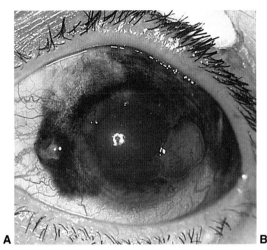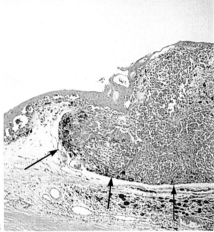

A **B**

Figure 5-23 **A,** Melanoma with PAM. Note the melanoma nodule at the 2 o'clock position at the limbus that has appeared on a background of PAM (diffuse, flat, brown pigmentation). **B,** Melanoma with PAM, histologic appearance. Intraepithelial atypical melanocytes (PAM) are present just to the left of the nodule of invasive melanoma *(arrows)*.

in addition to the conjunctival site, as just mentioned, include

- nonepibulbar location, orbital or scleral invasion
- histopathologic identification of pagetoid or full-thickness intraepithelial spread
- involvement of the eyelid skin margin

Tumor thickness can be measured objectively using a calibrated microscope; tumors thicker than 1.8 mm carry a greater risk for dissemination and death than thinner ones. However, even lesions less than 0.8 mm thick have resulted in patient mortality. The treatment for conjunctival melanoma is complete surgical removal. Detailed surgical planning with wide microsurgical excisional biopsy with minimal or no manipulation of the tumor ("no touch" technique) and supplemental alcohol corneal epitheliectomy, followed by conjunctival cryotherapy or brachytherapy, is the currently recommended treatment of choice. Melanomas can spread to regional lymph nodes of the preauricular or parotid and cervical nodes. Sentinel lymph node evaluation at the time of surgery has recently gained favor, as better techniques have evolved that decrease the chances of facial nerve paralysis. Metastases occur to the lungs, liver, skin, and brain.

Melanocytic lesions are discussed and illustrated extensively in Chapter 17. For AJCC definitions and staging of conjunctival melanoma, see Table A-2 in the appendix.

Albert DM, Jakobiec FA, eds. *Principles and Practice of Ophthalmology.* 2nd ed. Philadelphia: Saunders; 2000.

Missotten GS, Keijser S, De Keizer RJ, De Wolff-Rouendaal D. Conjunctival melanoma in the Netherlands: a nationwide study. *Invest Ophthalmol Vis Sci.* 2005;46:75–82.

Shields CL, Shields JA, Gunduz K, et al. Conjunctival melanoma: risk factors for recurrence, exenteration, metastasis, and death in 150 consecutive patients. *Arch Ophthalmol.* 2000;118:1497–1507.

CHAPTER **6**

Cornea

Topography

The normal cornea is composed of 5 layers: epithelium, Bowman's layer, stroma, Descemet's membrane, and endothelium (Fig 6-1). The average adult cornea has a horizontal diameter of 11–12 mm, a vertical diameter of 9–11 mm, and a thickness ranging between 0.52 mm centrally and 0.65 mm peripherally. The cornea is embryologically derived from surface ectoderm and neural crest. BCSC Section 8, *External Disease and Cornea,* discusses the structures and disorders of the cornea in depth.

The normal external surface of the cornea is composed of a stratified, squamous, non-keratinizing *epithelium* ranging between 5 and 7 cell layers in thickness. The 1–2 most superficial layers consist of flattened cells that are continually exfoliated and replaced by the underlying cells. The deepest epithelial layer is composed of basal cells, where mitotic activity is greatest. The basal cells are attached to the underlying basement membrane by hemidesmosomes and filaments that may be visualized with transmission electron microscopy. The epithelial basement membrane is thin and is best seen with the use of periodic acid–Schiff (PAS) stain.

Bowman's layer is present subjacent to the epithelial basement membrane. This layer is composed of acellular collagen and measures 8–14 nm in thickness. The posterior aspect of Bowman's layer blends imperceptibly with the underlying corneal stroma.

The corneal *stroma* makes up 90% of the total corneal thickness. The elongated collagenous lamellae are arranged in a precise orientation to allow for the orderly passage of light through the cornea. The ground substance, consisting of mucoprotein and glycoprotein, coats each collagen fibril and is responsible for the exact spacing required for corneal clarity.

The next layer, *Descemet's membrane,* is the basement membrane elaborated by the corneal endothelium. The production of Descemet's membrane begins during fetal development and continues throughout adulthood; therefore, the thickness of Descemet's membrane continually increases with age. Descemet's membrane is a true basement membrane, composed primarily of type IV collagen, and is strongly PAS-positive.

The corneal *endothelium* is a single layer derived from the neural crest. The primary function of the endothelium is to maintain corneal clarity by pumping water from the corneal stroma. The number of endothelial cells gradually decreases over time. As the endothelial cell number declines, the remaining cells flatten and elongate to provide coverage of the posterior corneal surface.

73

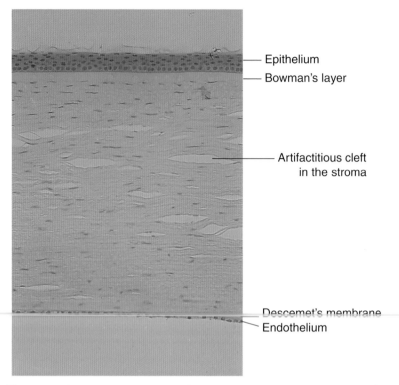

— Epithelium
— Bowman's layer

— Artifactitious cleft
  in the stroma

Descemet's membrane
Endothelium

Figure 6-1 The cornea is composed primarily of collagen. Because of dehydration of the tissue during processing for paraffin embedding, multiple areas of separation of the stromal lamellae are evident. If the lamellar separations are absent, corneal edema is suspected. This is an example of a meaningful artifact.

Congenital Anomalies

Congenital Hereditary Endothelial Dystrophy

The 2 forms of congenital hereditary endothelial dystrophy (CHED) causing bilateral congenital corneal edema are the autosomal recessive form and the autosomal dominant form. The more common autosomal recessive form is present at birth, remains stable, and is accompanied by nystagmus. Clinically, the cornea appears bluish white, is 2–3 times the normal thickness, and has a ground-glass appearance. The autosomal dominant form of CHED becomes apparent in the first or second year of life and exhibits slowly increasing edema of the corneal stroma. In these patients, the cornea has the same diffuse, blue-white appearance as in the autosomal recessive form, and patients may experience pain and photophobia (Fig 6-2A). Nystagmus, however, does not develop. The genetic loci for the AD and AR forms of CHED have been mapped to chromosomes 20p11.2-q11.2 and 20p13, respectively.

Despite the distinct clinical differences between autosomal recessive and autosomal dominant CHED, the 2 forms appear similar histologically. The corneal stroma is diffusely edematous, accounting for the marked increase in thickness observed clinically.

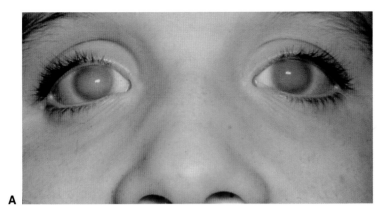

A

B

Figure 6-2 Congenital hereditary endothelial dystrophy. **A,** Clinical appearance. **B,** Note diffuse edema of the corneal epithelium and stroma. Descemet's membrane is diffusely thickened. *(Courtesy of Hans E. Grossniklaus, MD.)*

Descemet's membrane appears thickened, but guttae are not present (Fig 6-2B). The endothelium appears atrophic or may be focally absent. The primary abnormality is thought to be a degeneration of endothelial cells during or after the fifth month of gestation. CHED may be considered part of the spectrum of anterior segment dysgenesis abnormalities caused by abnormal differentiation of the neural crest ectoderm that forms the corneal endothelium. No systemic abnormalities are consistently associated with CHED.

Judisch GF, Maumenee IH. Clinical differentiation of recessive congenital hereditary endothelial dystrophy and dominant hereditary endothelial dystrophy. *Am J Ophthalmol.* 1978;85: 606–612.

Klintworth GK. The molecular genetics of the corneal dystrophies—current status. *Front Biosci.* 2003;8:d687–713.

Dermoid

Dermoid, a type of choristoma that may involve the cornea, is discussed in Chapter 5, Conjunctiva, and depicted in Figure 6-3.

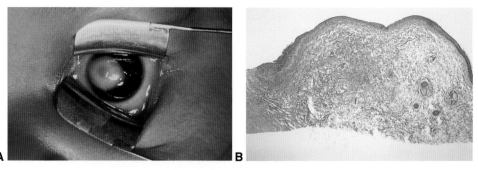

Figure 6-3 Corneal dermoid. **A,** Clinical photograph shows elevated, smooth, tan lesion on corneal surface. **B,** Histopathology shows keratinizing stratified epithelium overlying fibrous stroma containing scattered adnexal structures. *(Courtesy of Hans E. Grossniklaus, MD.)*

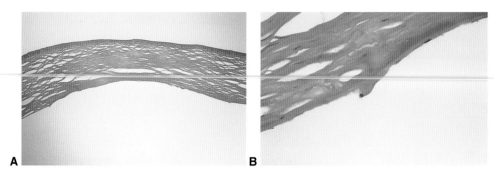

Figure 6-4 Posterior keratoconus. **A,** Anterior bowing of the posterior corneal surface accompanies corneal thinning. **B,** Descemet's membrane is thickened at the edge of the posterior concavity. *(Courtesy of Hans E. Grossniklaus, MD.)*

Posterior Keratoconus

A localized central or paracentral indentation of the posterior cornea without protrusion of the anterior surface is referred to as *posterior keratoconus,* also known as *internal ulcer of von Hippel.* The stroma may be thinned significantly, approaching one third normal corneal thickness, and often appears hazy. Descemet's membrane and endothelium are usually preserved in the area of the defect (Fig 6-4). Most cases occur in females and are unilateral, nonprogressive, and sporadic. Astigmatism and amblyopia may occur.

Haney WP, Falls HF. The occurrence of congenital keratoconus posticus circumscriptus in two siblings presenting a previously unrecognized syndrome. *Am J Ophthalmol.* 1961;52:53–57.

Sclerocornea

Sclerocornea, a nonprogressive, noninflammatory scleralization of the cornea, may be limited to the corneal periphery or may involve the entire cornea. The limbus is usually poorly defined, and superficial vessels that are extensions of normal scleral, episcleral, and conjunctival vessels extend across the cornea. Both sexes are affected equally, and 90%

of cases are bilateral. Half of the cases are sporadic; the remainder are either autosomal dominant or recessive, the latter form being more severe. The most common ocular association is cornea plana, found in 80% of cases.

Histologically, the stromal lamellae of the cornea are irregularly thickened, without differentiation between sclera and cornea. The small- to medium-sized vessels observed clinically are present in the superficial stroma. No evidence of inflammation is present.

Goldstein JE, Cogan DG. Sclerocornea and associated congenital anomalies. *Arch Ophthalmol.* 1962;67:761–768.

Congenital Corneal Staphyloma

Congenital corneal staphyloma is characterized by varying degrees of ectasia of the central, peripheral, or entire cornea. The posterior surface of the ectatic cornea is covered by remnants of anteriorly displaced iris. These findings may represent a severe expression of Peters anomaly or posterior keratoconus and may result from intrauterine trauma, maternal alcohol ingestion, or inflammation causing perforation.

Histologically, the scarred corneal and limbal tissues are thinned. Vascularization of the posterior aspect of the scar is often present in the area of the iris remnants. The anterior chamber is occluded by iris adhesions, and scattered collections of chronic inflammatory cells may be present.

Inflammations

Infectious

The cornea may be affected by infectious processes caused by a number of different microbial agents. Acute corneal inflammation is commonly characterized by edema and infiltration by inflammatory cells. Limbal hyperemia and iritis may be present. Severe inflammation can lead to corneal necrosis, ulceration, and perforation.

Bacterial infections

Corneal infections caused by bacterial agents often follow a disruption in the corneal epithelial integrity resulting from

- contact lens wear
- trauma
- contaminated ocular medications
- alteration in immunologic defenses (eg, use of topical or systemic immunosuppressives)
- antecedent corneal disease (eg, dry eye, corneal abrasion, bullous keratopathy, and so on)
- malposition of the eyelids

Some common bacterial organisms involved in corneal infections include *Staphylococcus aureus, Streptococcus pneumoniae, Pseudomonas aeruginosa,* and Enterobacteriaceae.

Scrapings obtained from infected corneas demonstrate collections of neutrophils admixed with necrotic debris. The presence of organisms may be demonstrated using tissue Gram stains such as Brown and Hopps (B&H) and Brown and Brenn (B&B). Growing the organism in culture remains the only method of obtaining accurate identification of specific organisms.

Herpes simplex virus keratitis

Usually a self-limited corneal epithelial disease, herpes simplex virus keratitis is characterized by a linear arborizing pattern of opacification and swelling of epithelial cells called a *dendrite*. Corneal scrapings obtained from a dendrite and prepared using the Giemsa stain reveal the presence of intranuclear viral inclusions. Infected epithelial cells may coalesce to form multinucleated giant cells. Chronic stromal keratitis may accompany or follow epithelial infection, leading to ulceration and scarring. With full-thickness stromal involvement, a granulomatous reaction can be seen, most often at the level of Descemet's membrane (Fig 6-5).

Fungal keratitis

Mycotic keratitis is often a complication of trauma or of corticosteroid use. Unlike most bacteria, fungi are able to penetrate the cornea and extend through Descemet's membrane into the anterior chamber. The most common organisms include *Aspergillus, Candida,* and *Fusarium.* Many fungi can be seen in tissue sections using special stains such as Grocott-Gomori methenamine–silver nitrate (GMS), PAS, or Giemsa (Fig 6-6). Other fungal organ-

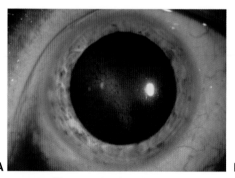
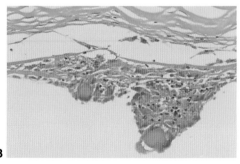

A **B**

Figure 6-5 Herpes simplex virus keratitis. **A,** Clinical photograph depicting corneal dendrites. **B,** Note the granulomatous response to Descemet's membrane. Herpesvirus antigen has been detected in this area. *(Part A courtesy of Sander Dubovy, MD.)*

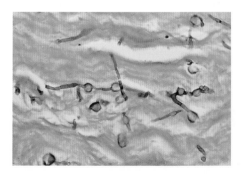

Figure 6-6 *Fusarium* keratitis. Grocott-Gomori methenamine–silver nitrate stain.

isms, including *Candida* and organisms causing mucormycosis, are visible with routine hematoxylin and eosin (H&E) preparations.

Acanthamoeba *keratitis*

Acanthamoeba protozoa most commonly cause infection in soft contact lens wearers who do not take appropriate precautions in cleaning and sterilizing their lenses. The most frequently involved species are *A castellani* and *A polyphagia*. Patients presenting with *Acanthamoeba* keratitis usually have severe eye pain. Clinically, a ring infiltrate and radial keratoneuritis may be present. (See Section 8, *External Disease and Cornea*, Fig 7-29.)

Biopsy specimens or scrapings from infected areas may demonstrate cysts and trophozoites that may be visualized in H&E sections (Fig 6-7). Other techniques, such as the use of monoclonal antibodies, may enhance the recognition of cysts and trophozoites in tissue sections. Special culture techniques and media, including nonnutrient blood agar layered with *E coli,* are required to grow *Acanthamoeba.* The pathologic findings in corneal buttons removed because of this infection are quite variable, ranging from no inflammation to a marked granulomatous reaction.

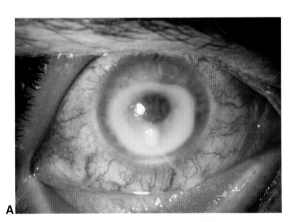
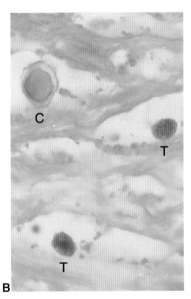

Figure 6-7 *Acanthamoeba* keratitis. **A,** Clinical photograph depicting ring infiltrate. **B,** Note the cyst *(C)* and trophozoite *(T)* forms. *(Part A courtesy of Sander Dubovy, MD.)*

Congenital syphilis

Transplacental infection of the fetus by *Treponema pallidum* may cause a nonsuppurative inflammation of the corneal stroma with relative sparing of the corneal epithelium and endothelium. Clinically, corneal stromal scarring at varying depths as well as deep stromal vascularization may be present. These changes are thought to result from an immunologic response to infectious microorganisms or their antigens in the corneal stroma. These clinical and histopathologic findings are frequently termed *interstitial keratitis*. Although congenital syphilis represents the classic cause of interstitial keratitis, other causative organisms include *Mycobacterium tuberculosis, M leprae, Borrelia burgdorferi,* and Epstein-Barr virus. (See also BCSC Section 8, *External Disease and Cornea*.)

Noninfectious

Corneal inflammation can also be caused by noninfectious agents. For example, foreign bodies may be retained in the cornea as a result of accidental or surgical trauma. Often, a localized granulomatous reaction may be present surrounding the foreign material. Foreign bodies are often birefringent and can be demonstrated on examination of tissue sections with polarized light.

Degenerations and Dystrophies

Degenerations

Corneal degenerations are secondary changes that occur in previously normal tissue. They are often associated with aging, are not inherited, and are not necessarily bilateral.

Salzmann nodular degeneration

Salzmann nodular degeneration is a noninflammatory corneal degeneration that may occur secondary to long-standing keratitis or may be idiopathic. It may be bilateral and is more commonly present in middle-aged and older women. Gray-white or blue-white raised lesions may be present, often in the central and paracentral cornea. Histopathologic examination discloses an absence of Bowman's layer and nodules composed of basement membrane–like material, hyaline material, cellular debris, and fibrocytes.

Vannas A, Hogan MJ, Wood I. Salzmann's nodular degeneration of the cornea. *Am J Ophthalmol.* 1975;79:211–219.

Band keratopathy

Seen clinically as calcific plaques in the interpalpebral zone, band keratopathy is characterized by the deposition of calcium in the epithelial basement membrane, Bowman's layer, and anterior stroma (Fig 6-8). The calcium deposits appear as basophilic granules in H&E sections; the presence of calcium can be further confirmed by use of special stains such as alizarin red or the von Kossa stain. Band keratopathy may develop in any chronic local corneal disease, in association with systemic hypercalcemic states, and in eyes with prolonged chronic inflammation.

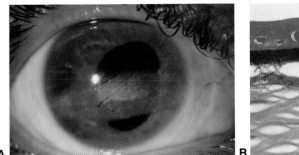
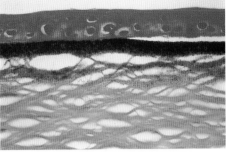

Figure 6-8 Band keratopathy. **A,** Clinical appearance shows white calcium deposition in the interpalpebral region of cornea. **B,** Calcium deposition in Bowman's layer appears black when stained with von Kossa stain. *(Part A courtesy of Sander Dubovy, MD; part B courtesy of Hans E. Grossniklaus, MD.)*

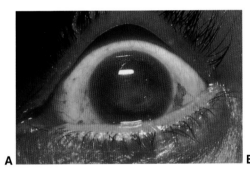

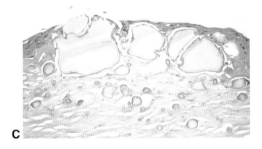

Figure 6-9 Actinic keratopathy (spheroidal degeneration). **A,** Clinical appearance shows golden-brown spheroidal deposits in the cornea. **B,** Gross appearance of corneal button. The air bubbles are artifacts. **C,** Histopathology shows lightly staining basophilic globules in the epithelium and superficial stroma. *(Courtesy of Hans E. Grossniklaus, MD.)*

Actinic keratopathy

Also known as *spheroidal degeneration* or *Labrador keratopathy,* actinic keratopathy involves damage to corneal collagen similar to that seen in pingueculae, pterygia, and solar elastosis of the skin. The actinic damage usually occurs within the palpebral fissure, similar to the pattern seen in band keratopathy. Clinical examination discloses translucent, golden-brown spheroidal deposits present in the superficial cornea. H&E-stained sections show basophilic globules in the superficial stroma, immediately subjacent to the epithelium. No associated inflammatory changes are present (Fig 6-9).

Pannus

Corneal pannus is the growth of tissue between the epithelium and Bowman's layer. This subepithelial fibrous tissue may have a significant vascular component, in which case the term *subepithelial fibrovascular pannus* is used. Bowman's layer may be disrupted (Fig 6-10). Pannus is frequently seen in cases of chronic corneal edema or prolonged corneal inflammation.

Bullous keratopathy

The end result of persistent stromal edema, bullous keratopathy is most frequently caused by the failure of the corneal endothelial cell layer to perform its normal pump function (Fig 6-11). The pump failure may occur either because the cells do not function normally or because there is a decrease in the number of endothelial cells below a critical level necessary to maintain corneal clarity. Although bullous keratopathy continues to be seen after

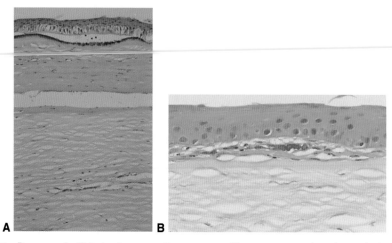

A   **B**

Figure 6-10 Pannus. **A,** This is degenerative pannus: fibrous connective tissue is interposed between the epithelium and Bowman's layer (note the basophilic stippling superficially in degenerative pannus, indicative of calcification). **B,** This is fibrovascular pannus, which may be accompanied by inflammatory cells and destruction of Bowman's layer (a condition sometimes called *inflammatory pannus*).

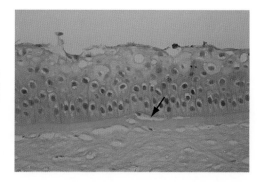

Figure 6-11 Bullous keratopathy. Note the swelling of the corneal epithelial cells (hydropic degeneration) and the subepithelial bulla *(arrow).*

cataract surgery, its incidence has decreased since the advent of intraoperative viscoelastic agents that protect the corneal endothelium and the decreased use of iris plane and anterior chamber intraocular lenses.

In corneal buttons, varying degrees of diffuse corneal edema are present. The epithelium is separated from the underlying Bowman's layer, creating microcysts or coalescing to form bullae. The epithelial basement membrane may be thickened and redundant, and intraepithelial basement membrane material similar to that seen in map-dot-fingerprint dystrophy is often observed. There is a paucity of endothelial cells, and those cells remaining are flattened and attenuated. Descemet's membrane is preserved intact.

Keratoconus

Keratoconus, a noninflammatory condition, is characterized by a bilateral central ectasia of the cornea with anterior protrusion of the cornea. Although the condition is bilateral, 1 eye may be more severely affected. The alteration in the normal corneal contour produces myopia and irregular astigmatism. Keratoconus can occur as an isolated finding, or it may be associated with other ocular disorders or with systemic conditions, including atopy, Down syndrome, and Marfan syndrome.

The earliest histologic changes are focal discontinuities of the epithelial basement membrane and Bowman's layer. Central stromal thinning and anterior stromal scarring are usually present. Iron deposition in the basal epithelial layers (Fleischer ring) can often be demonstrated using the Prussian blue stain or Perls test. Spontaneous breaks in Descemet's membrane can lead to acute stromal edema, or hydrops (Fig 6-12). Other causes of spontaneous breaks in Descemet's membrane include obstetric forceps injury, congenital glaucoma (Haab striae), Terrien marginal degeneration, and pellucid marginal degeneration.

Drug-related alterations

Amiodarone, an oral anti-arrhythmic agent, may produce a whorl-like keratopathy similar to that observed in Fabry disease. This distinctive pattern is a result of lysosomal deposits within the basal layer of the corneal epithelium. Other drugs that may produce a whorl-like keratopathy include chloroquine, chlorpromazine, and indomethacin. These corneal changes usually do not produce symptoms, although patients may complain of halos or blurry vision.

Dystrophies

Dystrophies of the cornea are primary, inherited, bilateral disorders, categorized by the layer of the cornea most involved. Keratoconus (previously discussed) is often considered a dystrophy. Only the most common corneal dystrophies are discussed in the following sections.

Epithelial dystrophy

Also called map-dot-fingerprint, Cogan microcystic, or anterior basement membrane dystrophy, epithelial dystrophy may be the most common of the corneal dystrophies seen by the comprehensive ophthalmologist (Fig 6-13). In this condition, the basement membrane is thickened and may extend into the epithelium. In addition, abnormal epithelial cells with microcysts are present. A deposition of fibrillar material forms between the basement membrane and Bowman's layer. Patients with epithelial dystrophy often present with symptoms of recurrent erosion syndrome.

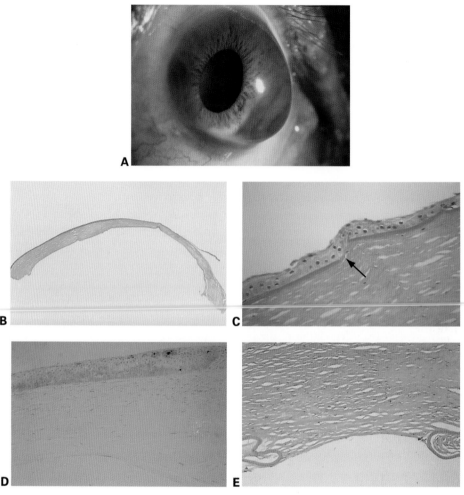

Figure 6-12 Keratoconus. **A,** Clinical appearance. **B,** Low-magnification view shows corneal stromal thinning. **C,** Masson trichrome stain demonstrates focal disruption of Bowman's layer *(arrow).* **D,** Intraepithelial iron deposition (Fleischer ring). **E,** Rupture of Descemet's membrane, with rolled edges of Descemet's membrane at the edge of the rupture site. *(Part A courtesy of Sander Dubovy, MD; part C courtesy of Hans E. Grossniklaus, MD.)*

Macular dystrophy

Macular dystrophy, an autosomal recessive stromal dystrophy, involves the entire cornea to the limbus. Clinically, it is characterized by poorly defined stromal lesions with hazy intervening stroma. Mucopolysaccharide material is deposited both intracellularly and extracellularly in the corneal stroma. The material stains blue with the alcian blue and colloidal iron stains (Fig 6-14). Corneal thinning may occur as well. Two types of macular dystrophy have been described; these depend on the specific abnormality in the keratan sulfate and dermatan sulfate–proteoglycan metabolism. The genes for macular dystrophy have been identified on chromosome 16q.

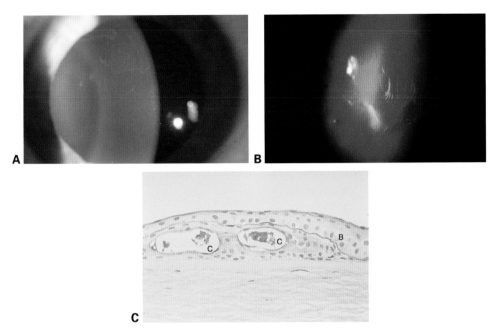

Figure 6-13 Epithelial dystrophy (map-dot-fingerprint dystrophy). **A,** Clinical appearance depicting fine, lacy opacities. **B,** Clinical appearance of cornea using retroillumination to demonstrate numerous wavy lines and dotlike lesions. **C,** The changes in primary map-dot-fingerprint dystrophy are almost identical to those seen in cases of chronic corneal epithelial edema. Note the intraepithelial basement membrane *(B)* and the degenerating intraepithelial cells trapped within cystic spaces *(C)*. *(Part A courtesy of Sander Dubovy, MD.)*

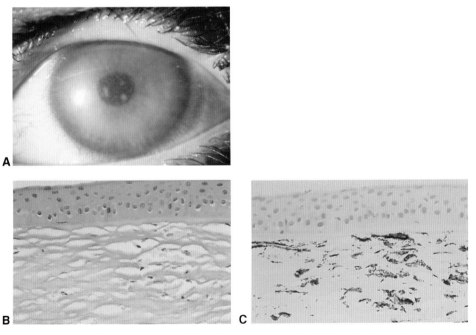

Figure 6-14 Macular dystrophy. **A,** Clinical appearance. **B,** H&E stain. Note the clear spaces surrounding the keratocytes and in the stroma. **C,** Colloidal iron stain for mucopolysaccharides. *(Part A courtesy of Sander Dubovy, MD.)*

Granular dystrophy

Granular dystrophy is an autosomal dominant stromal dystrophy that involves the central cornea and has sharply defined lesions with clear intervening stroma (Fig 6-15). Histologically, irregularly shaped, well-circumscribed depositions of hyaline material are visible in the stroma. This material stains bright red with the Masson trichrome stain.

Lattice dystrophy

Lattice dystrophy is an autosomal dominant condition that involves the central cornea and is characterized by refractile lines with hazy intervening stroma (Fig 6-16). The disorder is a primary localized corneal amyloidosis, in which the amyloid deposits may result from epithelial cells and keratocytes. Histologically, the amyloid deposits are concentrated most heavily in the anterior stroma, but they may also occur in the subepithelial area. The amyloid material stains positive with the Congo red stain and demonstrates metachromasia with crystal violet stain. The amyloid material is birefringent, appearing

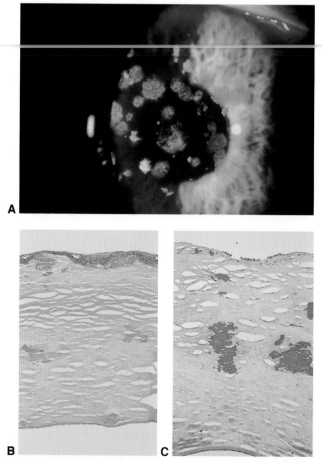

Figure 6-15 Granular dystrophy. **A,** Clinical appearance; note the clear intervening stroma. **B,** H&E stain. Note the chunky stromal deposits at all levels of the cornea. **C,** Masson trichrome stain. The corneal stroma stains blue, and the granular deposits stain brilliant red.

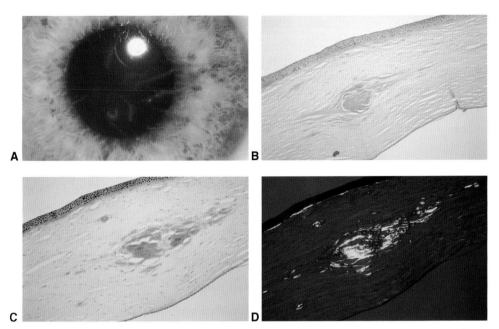

Figure 6-16 Lattice dystrophy. **A,** Clinical appearance. **B,** H&E stain shows scattered fusiform, eosinophilic material deposited at all levels of the stroma. **C,** Congo red stain demonstrates that the fusiform deposits are amyloid. **D,** Examination of Congo red stain with polarized light shows birefringence of amyloid deposits. *(Parts B, C, D, courtesy of Hans E. Grossniklaus, MD.)*

Table 6-1 Histopathologic Differentiation of Macular, Granular, and Lattice Dystrophies

Dystrophy	Masson	Alcian Blue	PAS	Congo Red	Birefringence
Macular	−	+	−	−	−
Granular	+	−	−	−	−
Lattice	+	−	+	+	+

apple green under polarized light. Recurrence of amyloid deposits in the corneal graft following penetrating keratoplasty occurs more frequently in lattice dystrophy than in granular or macular dystrophy.

See Table 6-1 for a histopathologic comparison of the macular, granular, and lattice dystrophies.

Avellino dystrophy

Features of both granular and lattice dystrophy appear in Avellino dystrophy, first described in patients tracing their ancestry to Avellino, Italy. Histologically, both hyaline deposits (typical of granular dystrophy) and amyloid deposits (characteristic of lattice dystrophy) are present within the corneal stroma. This dystrophy, like granular and lattice dystrophy, has been mapped to chromosome 5q.

Fuchs dystrophy

Fuchs dystrophy has a variable inheritance pattern and occurs more commonly in women. It is one of the leading causes of bullous keratopathy. This condition can be recognized clinically before corneal decompensation occurs by the appearance of guttae in Descemet's membrane. In corneal buttons, Descemet's membrane appears diffusely thickened. Focal, anvil-shaped excrescences of basement membrane material are seen protruding into the anterior chamber or buried within the thickened Descemet's membrane. The endothelial cells are usually sparse to absent. As in bullous keratopathy from other causes, there are varying degrees of secondary epithelial basement membrane changes and subepithelial fibrosis (Fig 6-17).

Pigment Deposits

Krukenberg spindle occurs in the pigment dispersion syndrome. The melanin pigment is primarily located within the endothelial cells but is also free on the posterior corneal surface (Fig 6-18).

Blood staining of the cornea may complicate hyphema when the intraocular pressure (IOP) is very high; however, if the endothelium is compromised, blood staining can occur

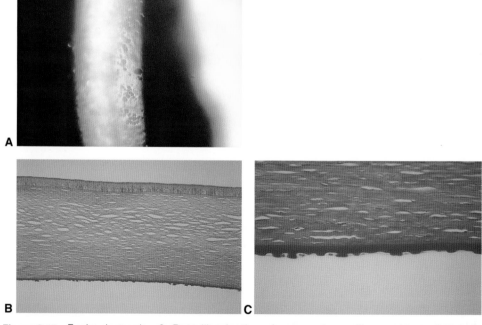

Figure 6-17 Fuchs dystrophy. **A,** Retroillumination of cornea shows "beaten bronze" appearance. **B,** Histology shows diffuse edema of corneal epithelium and stroma. **C,** Higher magnification of Descemet's membrane and posterior corneal stroma using PAS stain shows numerous focal areas of thickening of Descemet's membrane (guttae). *(Part A reproduced from* External Disease and Cornea: A Multimedia Collection. *San Francisco: American Academy of Ophthalmology; 2000. Parts B and C courtesy of Hans E. Grossniklaus, MD.)*

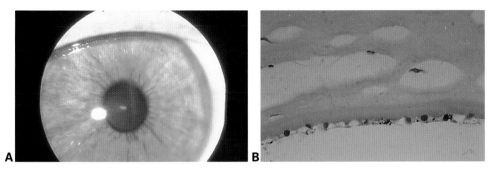

Figure 6-18 Pigment dispersion syndrome. **A,** Krukenberg spindle. **B,** Melanin is found within the endothelial cells. (See also Figure 7-13.) *(Part A courtesy of L.J. Katz, MD; part B courtesy of Debra J. Shetlar, MD.)*

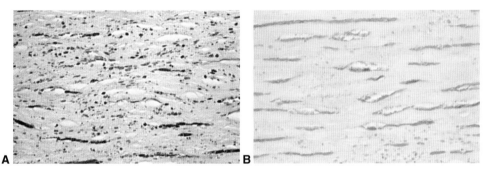

Figure 6-19 **A,** Corneal blood staining, H&E stain. The orange particles represent hemoglobin in the corneal stroma. **B,** An iron stain demonstrates iron confined to the stromal keratocytes. *(Courtesy of Hans E. Grossniklaus, MD.)*

even at normal or low IOP. In acute blood staining, hemoglobin is demonstrated in the corneal stroma. Later, iron may be demonstrated in the keratocytes (Fig 6-19).

Iron lines result from pooling of tears in areas where the corneal surface is irregular. Histologically, iron is found within the basal epithelial cells and can be demonstrated using the Prussian blue stain or Perls test. Some of the named iron lines include the following:

- Hudson-Stähli (junction of upper two thirds and lower one third of aging cornea)
- Fleischer (in keratoconus)
- Stocker (at the advancing edge of a pterygium)
- Ferry (anterior to a filtering bleb)

The *Kayser-Fleischer ring* is a brown ring seen in the periphery of the cornea in Wilson disease. It corresponds to copper deposition in Descemet's membrane.

Neoplasia

Primary conjunctival intraepithelial neoplasia may extend from the limbus and involve the corneal epithelium. *Dysplasia* of the corneal epithelium refers to abnormal maturation

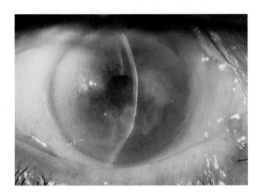

Figure 6-20 Clinical appearance of corneal epithelial dysplasia. Note the multiple, poorly demarcated superficial opacities. *(Courtesy of Sander Dubovy, MD.)*

of the epithelium as it differentiates from the basal layer to the superficial layers (Fig 6-20). This condition has been described further in Chapter 5, Conjunctiva. Rarely, primary intraepithelial neoplasia may arise in the clear cornea.

Carcinoma in situ describes full-thickness dysplastic involvement of the epithelium. Bowman's layer normally acts as a natural barrier against invasion by neoplasia; therefore, invasive squamous cell carcinoma involving the corneal stroma is seen only if the disease is very advanced or if Bowman's layer is compromised.

CHAPTER 7

Anterior Chamber and Trabecular Meshwork

Topography

The anterior chamber is bounded anteriorly by the corneal endothelium, posteriorly by the anterior surface of the iris–ciliary body and pupillary portion of the lens, and peripherally by the trabecular meshwork (Fig 7-1). The depth of the anterior chamber is about 3.4–3.7 mm. The trabecular meshwork is derived from the neural crest.

Trabecular Beams and Endothelium

The outermost corneoscleral meshwork is composed of multiple layers of collagenous sheets that are lined by very thin endothelium. This endothelium forms bridges between the sheets. The uveal meshwork, the innermost portion of the trabecular meshwork, is composed of 2 to 3 layers of intersecting trabecular beams that course meridionally from the ciliary body and iris root to the zone between the corneoscleral and trabecular endothelium. These beams, or cords, are covered by a slightly thicker layer of endothelium. Trabecular beams are thicker in individuals with primary infantile glaucoma than in normal individuals. Schlemm's canal encircles the trabecular meshwork and is joined to the corneoscleral meshwork by the internal collector channel. External collector veins channel aqueous back into the vascular system (Fig 7-2).

Congenital Anomalies

Schwalbe's line varies in prominence depending on the number and thickness of inserted cords at the zone of transition between the corneal and trabecular endothelium. Thickening of Schwalbe's line is known as *posterior embryotoxon* (Fig 7-3) and has been associated with open-angle glaucoma, sclerocornea, and other ocular and systemic anomalies related to maldevelopment of neural crest cells.

Axenfeld-Rieger syndrome represents a group of congenital anterior segment defects previously called *mesodermal dysgenesis* and a variety of eponyms. The single most important clinical feature of these phenotypes is that they confer at least a 50% risk of developing glaucoma. The syndrome is often hereditary with an autosomal dominant inheritance

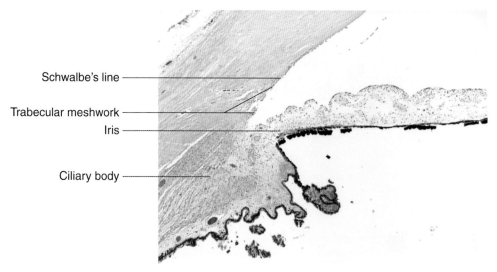

Schwalbe's line

Trabecular meshwork

Iris

Ciliary body

Figure 7-1 The normal anterior chamber angle, the site of drainage for the major portion of the aqueous humor flow, is defined by the anterior border of the iris, the face of the ciliary body, the internal surface of the trabecular meshwork, and the posterior surface of the cornea. *(Courtesy of Nasreen A. Syed, MD.)*

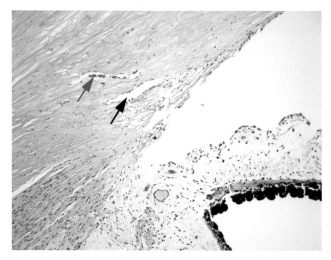

Figure 7-2 Light micrograph of the anterior chamber angle demonstrates Schlemm's canal *(black arrow)* external to the trabecular meshwork in the sclera. One of the external collector vessels can be seen adjacent to Schlemm's canal *(red arrow)*. *(Courtesy of Nasreen A. Syed, MD.)*

pattern. Mutations in the homeodomain transcription factor gene *PITX2* (chromosome 4q25) have been found in some patients with this syndrome. Other chromosomal loci, namely 6p25 and 13q14, have been linked to the related phenotypes. The following conditions are included under the name *Axenfeld-Rieger syndrome.*

Axenfeld anomaly is a congenital anomaly in which Schwalbe's line is anteriorly displaced and iris bands extend to the cornea (Fig 7-4). If the development of the meshwork is defective and glaucoma is present, the condition is called *Axenfeld syndrome.*

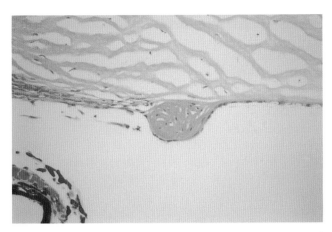

Figure 7-3 Posterior embryotoxon. Light micrograph shows a nodular prominence at the termination of Descemet's membrane. *(Courtesy of Hans E. Grossniklaus, MD.)*

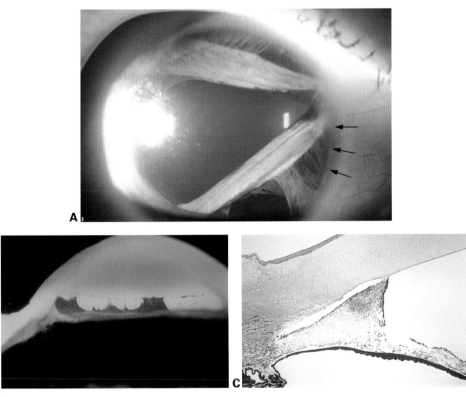

Figure 7-4 **A,** Clinical photograph of the anterior segment in a patient with Axenfeld-Rieger syndrome. Iris atrophy, polycoria, and iris strands in the periphery are present. Posterior embryotoxon can be seen laterally *(arrows).* **B,** Gross photograph shows a prominent Schwalbe's line and the anterior insertion of iris strands (Axenfeld anomaly). **C,** Light micrograph shows iris strands that insert anteriorly on Schwalbe's line. *(Part A courtesy of Wallace L.M. Alward, MD. Copyright University of Iowa; part B courtesy of Robert Y. Foos, MD; part C reproduced from Yanoff M, Fine BS. Ocular Pathology: A Color Atlas. New York: Gower; 1988.)*

Rieger anomaly is the term used to describe iris and pupillary abnormalities in combination with the findings of Axenfeld anomaly. Rieger anomaly is associated with the later onset of glaucoma. If Rieger anomaly is associated with dental and skeletal abnormalities, the condition is called *Rieger syndrome*.

Alward WL. Axenfeld-Rieger syndrome in the age of molecular genetics. *Am J Ophthalmol.* 2000;130:107–115.

Espinoza HM, Cox CJ, Semina EV, Amendt BA. A molecular basis for differential developmental anomalies in Axenfeld-Rieger syndrome. *Hum Mol Genet.* 2002;11:743–753.

Maclean K, Smith J, St. Heaps L, et al. Axenfeld-Rieger malformation and distinctive facial features: clues to a recognizable 6p25 microdeletion syndrome. *Am J Med Genet.* 2005;132:381–385.

Degenerations

Iridocorneal Endothelial Syndrome

The iridocorneal endothelial (ICE) syndrome refers to a spectrum of acquired abnormalities affecting the cornea, anterior chamber angle, and iris. Abnormal proliferation of corneal endothelium is a constant feature of all forms of the ICE syndrome. When these cells cover the angle, secondary angle-closure glaucoma develops. Over time, peripheral anterior synechiae may form, closing the angle (Fig 7-5). Three different clinical presentations are known:

- iris nevus (Cogan-Reese) syndrome
- Chandler syndrome
- essential iris atrophy

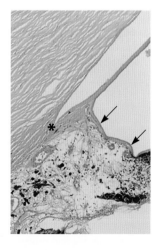

Figure 7-5 ICE syndrome. Descemet's membrane lines the anterior surface of the iris *(arrows)*. The iris is apposed to the cornea (peripheral anterior synechiae, *asterisk*).

The first letter for each type forms the mnemonic *ICE*. Most patients are young to middle-aged adults who are affected unilaterally. See also BCSC Section 10, *Glaucoma,* which discusses secondary angle-closure glaucoma and covers in depth the issues discussed throughout this chapter.

Albert DM, Miller JW, eds. *Albert & Jakobiec's Principles and Practice of Ophthalmology.* 3rd ed. Vol 1. Philadelphia: Elsevier; 2008:529–531.

Secondary Glaucoma With Material in the Trabecular Meshwork

Exfoliation syndrome

Sometimes known as *pseudoexfoliation,* exfoliation syndrome is a systemic condition, usually identified in people over 50 years of age and characterized by deposits of PAS-positive fibrils on the lens capsule, zonular fibers, iris, ciliary body, trabecular meshwork, cornea, conjunctiva, and orbital soft tissues. These deposits distinguish exfoliation syndrome from the rare *true exfoliation,* which is the splitting of the lens capsule induced by infrared radiation. Ocular involvement in exfoliation syndrome may be asymmetric. The deposits take the form of distinct fibrils that contain elements of elastic fibers such as fibrillin and α-elastin, as well as noncollagenous basement membrane material such as laminin. The fibrils are coated with the glycosaminoglycan hyaluronic acid (Figs 7-6, 7-7).

The trabecular meshwork in exfoliation syndrome also contains an excessive amount of pigment, but its distribution is more uneven than in pigmentary glaucoma (see "Pigment dispersion associations" later in the chapter). Transillumination defects and circumferential ridges are prominent in the posterior iris. About 10%–23% of patients with exfoliation syndrome have glaucoma: exfoliative glaucoma is the most common identifiable type of glaucoma. Exfoliation syndrome has been associated with systemic hypertension, cerebrovascular events, and myocardial infarction. There is increased risk of zonular dehiscence and capsular rupture during cataract extraction in patients with exfoliation syndrome.

Ritch R, Schlötzer-Schrehardt U. Exfoliation syndrome. *Surv Ophthalmol.* 2001;45:265–315.

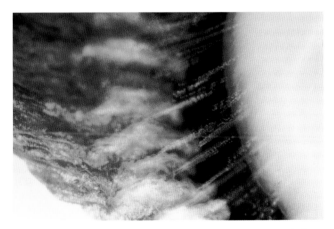

Figure 7-6 Gross photograph shows fibrillar deposits on the lens zonule in pseudoexfoliation. *(Courtesy of Hans E. Grossniklaus, MD.)*

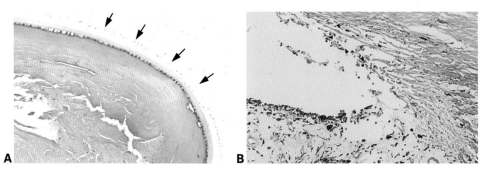

Figure 7-7 **A,** Abnormal material that resembles iron filings on the edge of a magnet *(arrows)* appears on the lens capsule. **B,** Note the intense pigmentation in the angle. *(Part A courtesy of Nasreen A. Syed, MD.)*

Phacolytic glaucoma

The condition known as *phacolytic glaucoma* occurs when denatured lens protein leaks from a hypermature cataract and occludes the trabecular meshwork. Although some controversy persists regarding the pathogenesis of phacolytic glaucoma, evidence suggests that the abnormal lens protein leaking into the anterior chamber may be directly responsible for the increased resistance to outflow. Macrophages, containing numerous vacuoles, may be present (Fig 7-8). BCSC Section 9, *Intraocular Inflammation and Uveitis,* discusses lens-induced uveitis in more detail.

Trauma

Following an intraocular hemorrhage, blood breakdown products may accumulate in the trabecular meshwork. Hemolyzed erythrocytes may obstruct aqueous outflow and lead to a secondary open-angle glaucoma known as *ghost cell glaucoma.* These ghost erythrocytes are tan in color, spherical in shape, and rigid. Their rigidity makes it difficult for the cells to escape through the trabecular meshwork (Fig 7-9).

In some cases of secondary open-angle glaucoma associated with chronic intraocular hemorrhage, histologic examination has revealed hemosiderin within endothelial cells of the trabecular meshwork and within macrophages. The effect of hemosiderin on the trabecular meshwork and on the pathogenesis of glaucoma is not known. The iron stored in the cells may be an enzyme toxin that damages trabecular function in hemosiderosis oculi. Alternatively, the hemosiderin may be a sign of damage that has occurred during oxidation of hemoglobin. Iron deposition in hemosiderosis oculi can be demonstrated within many ocular epithelial structures by means of the Prussian blue reaction.

In other cases of hemorrhage-associated glaucoma, macrophages in the anterior chamber are noted to contain phagocytosed erythrocytes. In *hemolytic glaucoma,* hemoglobin-laden macrophages block the trabecular outflow channels. It is possible that macrophages are a sign of trabecular obstruction rather than the actual cause.

Blunt injury to the globe may be associated with traumatic hyphema and with recession of the angle, the most common manifestation of this type of trauma. The probability that glaucoma will develop as a late sequela of hyphema depends, in part, on the amount

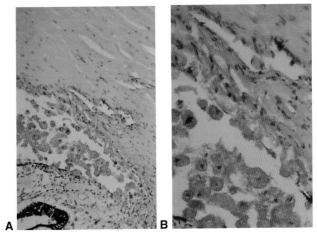

A   **B**

Figure 7-8 Phacolytic glaucoma. **A,** Low magnification of macrophages filled with degenerated lens cortical material in the angle. **B,** Higher magnification.

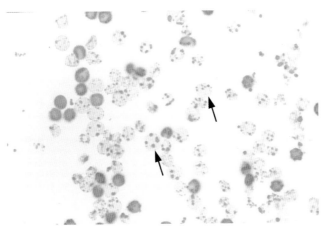

Figure 7-9 Aqueous aspirate demonstrating numerous ghost red blood cells. The degenerating hemoglobin is present as small globules known as Heinz bodies *(arrows)*. *(Courtesy of Nasreen A. Syed, MD.)*

of angle recession. Between 5% and 10% of patients having greater than 180° of angle recession eventually develop chronic glaucoma.

Histologically, angle recession represents a tear in the ciliary body between the longitudinal and circular muscles (Fig 7-10). If the longitudinal muscle is detached from the scleral spur, the tear is referred to as a *cyclodialysis.* Tears in the root of the iris *(iridodialysis)* may also occur with blunt trauma (Fig 7-11; see also Fig 2-7).

Although recession of the angle provides evidence of past blunt trauma, it does not necessarily mean that the trauma is the direct cause of glaucoma. Because glaucoma usually takes years to develop following angle recession, progressive degenerative changes in the remaining trabecular meshwork may be an important factor in the pathogenesis of postcontusion glaucoma.

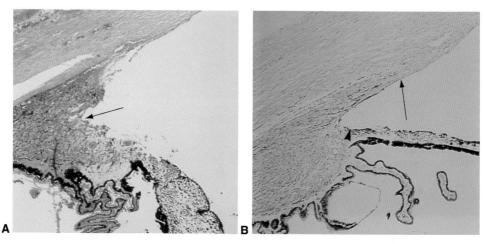

Figure 7-10 **A,** Contusion injury to the ciliary body. There is a rupture in the face of the ciliary body in the plane between the external longitudinal muscle fibers of the ciliary body and the internal circular and oblique fibers *(arrow)*. Concurrent injury to the trabecular meshwork often occurs. **B,** Contusion angle deformity. The iris root *(arrowhead)* is displaced posteriorly in relation to the longitudinal muscle bundle and its insertion into the scleral spur *(arrow)*. In the region of the injury, the anterior chamber may be deep. Although clinically and histologically unapparent, injury to the drainage structures can be significant.

Figure 7-11 Blunt trauma to the eye may cause rupture of the iris at its base *(arrows),* a point of relative weakness, resulting in iridodialysis.

Pigment dispersion associations

Pigment dispersion may be associated with a variety of other conditions in which pigment epithelium or uveal melanocytes are injured, such as uveitis (uveitic glaucoma) or uveal melanoma. These conditions are characterized by pigment within the trabecular meshwork and in macrophages littering the angle (Fig 7-12).

Secondary open-angle glaucoma can occur as a result of the *pigment dispersion syndrome* (Fig 7-13). This type of glaucoma is characterized by radially oriented defects in the midperipheral iris and pigment in the trabecular meshwork, the corneal endothelium

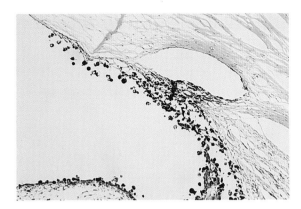

Figure 7-12 Secondary open-angle glaucoma. The trabecular meshwork is obstructed by macrophages that have ingested pigment from a necrotic intraocular melanoma *(melanomalytic glaucoma)*.

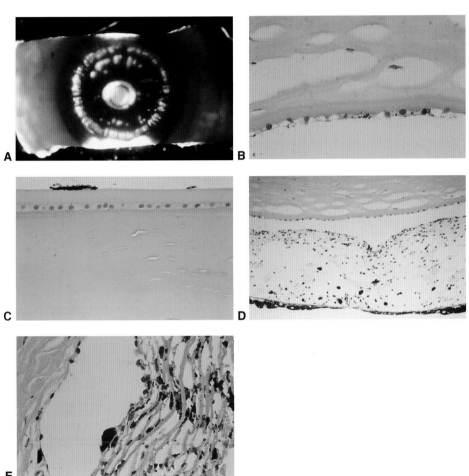

Figure 7-13 Pigment dispersion syndrome. **A,** Gross photograph demonstrating radially oriented transillumination defects in the iris. **B,** Krukenberg spindle. Melanin is present within the corneal endothelial cells. **C,** Scheie stripe. Melanin is present on the anterior surface of the lens. **D,** Note the focal loss of iris pigment epithelium. Chafing of the zonules against the epithelium may release the pigment that is dispersed in this condition. **E,** Note the accumulation of pigment in the trabecular meshwork.

(Krukenberg spindle), and other anterior segment structures such as the lens capsule. See Figure 6-18 for a clinical photograph of a Krukenberg spindle. The dispersed pigment is presumed to be iris pigment epithelium mechanically rubbed off by contact with lens zonular fibers. Histologic studies of eyes with pigmentary glaucoma show large accumulations of pigment granules and cellular debris in the trabecular meshwork and phagocytosed pigment in and on endothelial cells of the cornea. Pigment is present both intracellularly and extracellularly in the trabecular meshwork.

Neoplasia

Melanocytic nevi and melanomas that arise in the iris or extend to the iris from the ciliary body may obstruct the trabecular meshwork (Fig 7-14). See also Chapter 17, Melanocytic Tumors. In addition, pigment elaborated from the melanomas may be shed into the trabecular meshwork and produce secondary glaucoma.

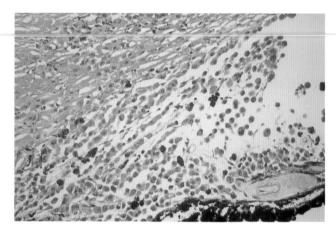

Figure 7-14 Photomicrograph shows malignant melanoma cells filling the anterior chamber angle and obstructing the trabecular meshwork. *(Courtesy of Hans E. Grossniklaus, MD.)*

CHAPTER 8

Sclera

Topography

The sclera is the white, nearly opaque portion of the outer wall of the eye, covering from four fifths to five sixths of the eye's circumference. It is continuous anteriorly at the limbus with the corneal stroma. Posteriorly, the outer two thirds of the sclera merges with the dura of the optic nerve sheath; the inner one third continues as the lamina cribrosa, through which pass the axonal fibers of the optic nerve. The diameter of the scleral shell averages 22.0 mm, and its thickness varies from 1.0 mm posteriorly to 0.3 mm just posterior to the insertions of the 4 rectus muscles. Histologically, the sclera is divided into 3 layers (from outermost inward): episclera, stroma, and lamina fusca (Fig 8-1). The sclera is derived from the neural crest.

Episclera

The episclera is a thin fibrovascular layer that covers the outer surface of the scleral stroma. It is thickest anterior to the rectus muscle insertions and immediately surrounding the optic nerve and thinnest at the limbus and posterior to the rectus muscle insertions at the equator of the eye. The episclera is composed of loosely arranged collagen fibers and a vascular plexus.

Stroma

The bulk of the sclera is made up of sparsely vascularized, dense, type I collagen fibers whose diameters range from 28 nm to more than 300 nm; the thicker fibers are more radially arranged. In general, collagen fibers in the stroma course parallel to the external surface of the scleral shell, but individual fibers are randomly arranged and may branch and curl. In comparison to the corneal stroma, scleral collagen fibers are thicker and more variable in thickness and orientation. Transmural emissarial channels provide outlets within the stroma as follows (Fig 8-2):

- in the posterior region, for posterior ciliary arteries and nerves
- in the equatorial region, for vortex veins
- in the anterior regions, for anterior ciliary arteries, veins, and nerves

Ciliary nerves may have pigmented melanocytes along their nerve sheaths that appear as pigmentation on the epibulbar surface (eg, Axenfeld nerve loop).

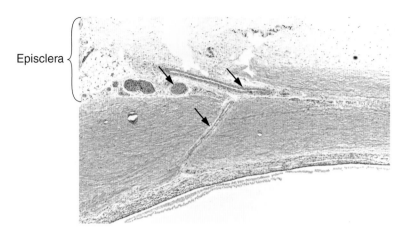

Episclera

Figure 8-1 Normal sclera demonstrating emissary structures, including ciliary arteries and nerves entering and traversing the sclera *(arrows)*. *(Courtesy of Nasreen A. Syed, MD.)*

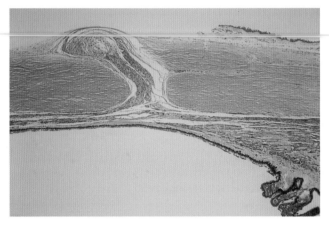

Figure 8-2 An emissarial channel through the sclera for the Axenfeld nerve loop is present overlying the pars plana (trichrome stain). *(Courtesy of Harry H. Brown, MD.)*

Lamina Fusca

The lamina fusca is a thin network of bridging collagen fibers that loosely binds the uvea to the sclera. Sclerouveal attachments are strongest along major emissarial canals and the anterior base of the ciliary body. The lamina fusca contains variable numbers of melanocytes.

Congenital Anomalies

Choristoma

Limbal dermoids are discussed in Chapter 5, Conjunctiva, and an example is shown in Figure 6-3.

Episcleral osseous choristomas are found most commonly in the superotemporal quadrant of the epibulbar surface, 0.5–1.0 cm posterior to the limbus. The clinical appearance is that of a single stationary hard white plaque, round to oval in shape, and measuring up to 1.0 cm in diameter, beneath the conjunctiva. No other congenital anomalies are associated. The histopathologic appearance demonstrates mature lamellar bony trabeculae; rarely, hematopoietic elements occupy the marrow space.

Nanophthalmos

An eye that is uniformly reduced in size except for the lens, which is normal or slightly enlarged, results in severe hyperopia. Nanophthalmos is usually bilateral. The sclera is abnormally thick, which is thought to predispose to uveal effusion because of reduced protein permeability and impaired venous outflow through the vortex veins. Glaucoma, which is common in nanophthalmic eyes, may be caused by a variety of mechanisms, including angle closure, pupillary block, and open angle with elevated episcleral venous pressure.

Inflammations

Episcleritis

Simple episcleritis most commonly presents as a slightly tender, movable, sectorial red area involving the anterior episclera. It affects males and females equally, most commonly in the third to fifth decades, and usually has no association with antecedent injury or systemic illness. Histopathologic examination shows vascular congestion and stromal edema associated with a chronic inflammatory infiltrate, composed primarily of lymphocytes, in a perivascular distribution. Granulomatous inflammation and necrosis are not present. The diagnosis is made on clinical findings, and complete resolution is the rule, with or without topical corticosteroid therapy. The condition may be recurrent, however, and can ultimately cause fibrosis and scar formation.

In contrast to simple episcleritis, *nodular episcleritis* more often affects females and those with rheumatoid arthritis. It is characterized by tender, elevated, rounded, pink-red nodules on the anterior episclera. Histopathologically, the nodules are composed of necrobiotic granulomatous inflammation, a palisading arrangement of epithelioid histiocytes around a central core of necrotic collagen. This light microscopic pattern is the same as that seen in rheumatoid nodules in subcutaneous tissue. Spontaneous resolution is the expected outcome, and topical corticosteroids or nonsteroidal anti-inflammatory drugs (NSAIDs) may reduce symptoms. See BCSC Section 8, *External Disease and Cornea,* for further discussion of this condition and of those covered in the following sections.

Scleritis

Scleritis is a painful, often progressive ocular disease with potentially serious sequelae. There is a high association with systemic autoimmune vasculitic connective tissue diseases.

Such diseases include

- rheumatoid arthritis
- systemic lupus erythematosus
- polyarteritis nodosa
- Wegener granulomatosis
- relapsing polychondritis
- Reiter syndrome

The inflammation may be localized to the anterior or the posterior sclera, or it may affect other ocular tissues, particularly the cornea and uvea. *Anterior scleritis* is usually a severely painful sectoral inflammation of episclera and sclera with intense photophobia (Fig 8-3). The disease is bilateral in approximately 50% of cases. *Posterior scleritis* is marked by a different constellation of signs and symptoms: patients present with unilateral proptosis, retrobulbar pain, gaze restriction, and visual field loss. Contiguous spread of inflammation may result in optic neuritis or retinal and choroidal detachments; thickening of the inflamed sclera may even give the mistaken impression of an intraocular neoplasm.

Histopathologic examination of scleritis reveals 2 main categories: necrotizing and nonnecrotizing inflammation. Either type may occur anteriorly or posteriorly. *Necrotizing inflammation* may be nodular or diffuse (so-called *brawny scleritis,* Fig 8-4). Both patterns demonstrate a palisading arrangement of epithelioid histiocytes and multinucleated giant cells surrounding sequestered areas of necrosis (Fig 8-5). Peripheral to the histiocytes is a rim of lymphocytes and plasma cells. Multiple foci may show different stages of evolution. In the course of healing, the necrotic stroma is resorbed, leaving in its wake a thinned scleral remnant prone to staphyloma formation (Fig 8-6). Severe ectasia of the scleral shell

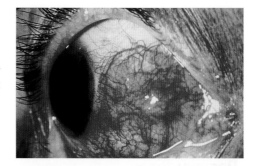

Figure 8-3 This patient has a sectoral nodular anterior scleritis that causes severe ocular pain and photophobia. *(Courtesy of Harry H. Brown, MD.)*

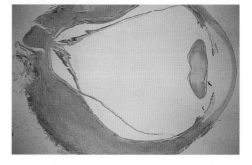

Figure 8-4 Diffuse posterior scleritis (brawny scleritis) demonstrates marked thickening of the posterior sclera. *(Courtesy of Harry H. Brown, MD.)*

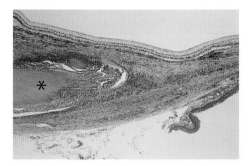

Figure 8-5 An area of necrosis *(asterisk)* is sequestered by a zonal inflammatory reaction of histiocytes, lymphocytes, and plasma cells in this necrotizing granulomatous scleritis. *(Courtesy of Harry H. Brown, MD.)*

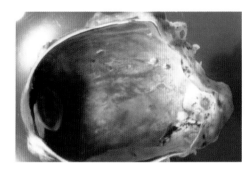

Figure 8-6 A posterior staphyloma is present in this eye as a sequela of scleritis. *(Courtesy of Hans E. Grossniklaus, MD.)*

predisposes to herniation of uveal tissue through the defect, a condition known as *scleromalacia perforans.*

Nonnecrotizing inflammation is characterized by a perivascular lymphocytic and plasma cell infiltrate without a granulomatous inflammatory component. Vasculitis may be present in the form of fibrinoid necrosis of vessel walls. Treatment with NSAIDs usually leads to resolution without significant weakening of the scleral shell.

> Dubord PJ, Chambers A. Scleritis and episcleritis: diagnosis and management. *Focal Points: Clinical Modules for Ophthalmologists.* San Francisco: American Academy of Ophthalmology; 1995, module 9.

Degenerations

Senile calcific plaques occur commonly in elderly persons as flat, firm, gray rectangular to oval patches that appear bilaterally and measure less than 1.0 cm in greatest dimension. They are located anterior to the insertions of the medial and lateral rectus muscles (Fig 8-7). On histologic sections, the calcium appears within the midportion of the scleral stroma. It initially occurs as a finely granular deposition but may progress to involve both superficial and deep layers as a confluent plaque. Senile calcific plaques may be highlighted by special stains such as the von Kossa stain. The etiology is unknown; dehydration and actinic damage have been proposed but not proven.

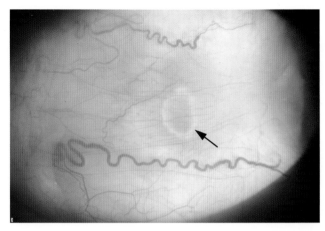

Figure 8-7 A calcific plaque of the sclera *(arrow)*. Such plaques are typically located just anterior to the insertion of the medial or lateral rectus muscles. *(Courtesy of Vinay A. Shah, MBBS.)*

Corneal staphylomas are discussed in Chapter 6, Cornea. *Scleral staphylomas* are ectasias lined by uveal tissue that may occur at points of weakness in the scleral shell, either in inherently thin areas (such as posterior to the rectus muscle insertions) or in areas weakened by tissue destruction (as in scleritis associated with rheumatoid arthritis; see Fig 8-6). In children, staphylomas may occur as a result of long-standing increased IOP or axial myopia, owing to the relative distensibility of the sclera in younger, as compared with older, individuals. Age at onset and location, therefore, vary according to the underlying etiology. Staphylomas appear as variably sized and shaped patches of blue-purple discoloration of the sclera caused by increased visibility of the underlying uveal pigment and vasculature. Histopathologic examination invariably reveals thinned sclera, with or without fibrosis and scarring, again depending on the cause.

Neoplasia

Neoplasms of the sclera are exceedingly rare. Tumors most likely originate in the episclera or Tenon's capsule rather than in the sclera proper. Reported examples include fibrous histiocytoma and melanocytoma. Nodular fasciitis is included in this discussion, although it is a reactive proliferative process.

Fibrous histiocytoma is a benign neoplasm formed by a proliferation of spindle cells, characteristically in a matlike *(storiform)* pattern. Although more common in the orbit, it may occasionally involve the sclera. For more information on this neoplasm, see Chapter 14, Orbit.

Nodular fasciitis is a reactive process that may, rarely, cause a tumor in the episclera. Antecedent trauma has been implicated as an etiologic factor for the development of nodular fasciitis in other body sites, but no such association has been identified in the sclera. The disease usually affects young adults as a rapidly growing, round to oval, firm white-gray nodule measuring 0.5–1.5 cm and appearing at the limbus or anterior to a rectus muscle insertion. Although self-limited, it is usually excised because of its rapid growth. Histopathologic examination reveals a circumscribed spindle cell proliferation in which individual cells are likened to the appearance of fibroblasts growing in tissue culture. These spindle cells aggregate in whorling fascicles, admixed with a chronic inflammatory infiltrate and lipid-laden histiocytes, in a myxoid background. Older lesions may show foci of dense collagen deposition. Although mitotic figures may be present, atypical (eg, tripolar) mitotic figures are absent. The cellular nature of these proliferations and the presence of mitotic figures may lead to the histologic misinterpretation as sarcoma (soft tissue malignancy), a pitfall to avoid.

CHAPTER 9

Lens

Topography

The crystalline lens is a soft, elastic, avascular, biconvex structure that in the adult measures 9–10 mm in diameter and 3.5 mm in anteroposterior thickness (Fig 9-1). The lens is derived from surface ectoderm. BCSC Section 11, *Lens and Cataract,* discusses in depth the structure, embryology, and pathology of the lens.

Capsule

The lens capsule is composed of a thick basement membrane that surrounds the entire lens and is elaborated by the lens epithelial cells. It is thickest anteriorly (12–21 μm) and peripherally near the equator and thinnest posteriorly (2–9 μm). The capsule provides insertions for the zonular fibers and plays an important part in molding the lens shape in accommodation.

Epithelium

The lens epithelium is derived from the cells of the original lens vesicle that did not differentiate into primary fibers. Although epithelial cells located centrally do not usually undergo mitosis, those located peripherally in the equatorial zone actively divide. The anterior or axial cells form a single layer of cuboidal cells with their basilar surface toward the anterior lens capsule, whereas the cells nearer the equator appear more elongated as they differentiate into lens fibers.

Cortex and Nucleus

New lens fibers are continuously laid down from the outside as the lens epithelial cells differentiate. The oldest fibers, the embryonic and fetal lens nucleus, were produced in embryonic life, have lost their nuclei, and persist in the center of the lens. The outermost fibers, which are the most recently formed, make up the cortex of the lens and are composed of fibers derived from the differentiated lens epithelial cells.

Zonular Fibers

The lens is supported by the zonular fibers that attach to the anterior and posterior lens capsule in the midperiphery (Fig 9-2). These fibers hold the lens in place through their attachments to the ciliary body processes.

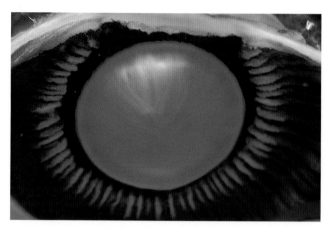

Figure 9-1 Posterior aspect of the crystalline lens, depicting its relationship to the peripheral iris and ciliary body. *(Courtesy of Hans E. Grossniklaus, MD.)*

Figure 9-2 Zonular fibers attached to the anterior and posterior aspect of the lens capsule. *(Reproduced with permission from Wilson DJ, Jaeger MJ, Green WR. Effects of extracapsular cataract extraction on the lens zonules. Ophthalmology. 1987;94:467–470.)*

Congenital Anomalies

Ectopia Lentis

With ectopia lentis, the lens may be partially dislocated *(subluxation)* or totally dislocated *(luxation)* (Fig 9-3). Congenital ectopia lentis may occur as an isolated phenomenon *(simple ectopia lentis)* or as part of an inherited syndrome that has systemic manifestations.

Marfan syndrome is a disorder of connective tissue with ocular, musculoskeletal, and cardiovascular manifestations. The lens is usually displaced upward or in a superotemporal

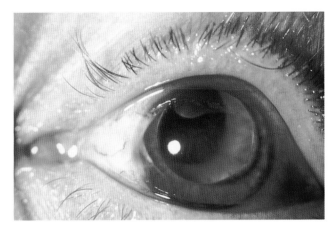

Figure 9-3 Anterior dislocation of the lens. The entire lens is present in the anterior chamber. *(Courtesy of Debra J. Shetlar, MD.)*

Table 9-1 Conditions Associated With Ectopia Lentis

With systemic abnormalities
Marfan syndrome: lens dislocated up
Homocystinuria: lens dislocated down
Weill-Marchesani syndrome: superotemporal or temporal displacement of spherophakic lens
Others: hyperlysinemia, Ehlers-Danlos syndrome, Crouzon disease, and oxycephaly

With other congenital ocular abnormalities
Aniridia
Uveal coloboma
Buphthalmos
Megalocornea
High myopia
Corectopia
Peters anomaly

direction, and axial myopia is often present. Marfan syndrome is caused by mutations in the fibrillin gene on chromosome 15.

In patients with *homocystinuria,* the lens is displaced inferonasally, or it may luxate into the anterior chamber or posterior segment. This autosomal recessive trait is caused by a defect in cystathionine β–synthase. Other conditions associated with ectopia lentis are listed in Table 9-1.

Congenital Cataract

Lens opacities present at birth or developing during the first year of life are called *congenital cataracts.* The term *infantile cataracts* is also used for those not seen at birth. Congenital cataracts may be unilateral or bilateral. In general, about one third of these cataracts are associated with other disease syndromes, one third occur as an inherited trait, and one third result from undetermined causes. See also BCSC Section 6, *Pediatric Ophthalmology and Strabismus.*

Posterior polar cataracts are congenital opacities that may range from the small white spot of a Mittendorf dot to a larger, plaque-shaped opacity that is due to persistence of the retrolental vascular tissue (persistent fetal vasculature [PFV]). The posterior capsule may rupture and lead to lens-induced inflammation and/or extension of vessels and fibroblasts into the lens. Removing these cataracts is difficult, as the lens capsule may be thinned or absent, leading to a high rate of posterior capsule rupture.

Rubella cataract

Rubella cataract occurs in the fetus if the mother is exposed to the rubella virus during the first or second trimester of pregnancy. The lens opacity is only one of several birth anomalies associated with in utero rubella exposure. Histologically, the lens is microsphrophakic, and retained lens fiber nuclei are present. Rubella virus may be cultured from surgically removed lenses.

Inflammations

Phacoantigenic Endophthalmitis

Also known as *lens-induced granulomatous endophthalmitis or phacoanaphylactic endophthalmitis,* this type of lens-induced intraocular inflammation is mediated by IgG immunoglobulins directed against lens protein. The inflammation may follow accidental or surgical trauma to the lens. Histologically, lens-induced granulomatous endophthalmitis consists of a central nidus of degenerating lens material surrounded by concentric layers of inflammatory cells (zonal granuloma). Multinucleated giant cells and neutrophils are present within the inner layer adjacent to the degenerating lens material. Lymphocytes and histiocytes make up the intermediate mantle of cells. These cells may be surrounded by fibrous connective tissue and collagen, depending on the duration of the inflammatory response (Figs 9-4, 9-5). See also BCSC Section 9, *Intraocular Inflammation and Uveitis.*

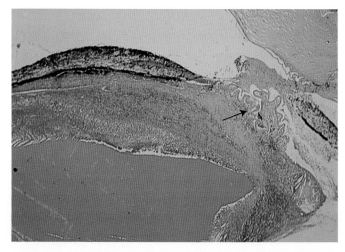

Figure 9-4 Phacoantigenic endophthalmitis, in which inflammatory reaction surrounds the lens *(lower left).* The torn capsule can be observed in the pupillary region *(arrow).* Also note corneal scar *(upper right),* representing the site of ocular penetration.

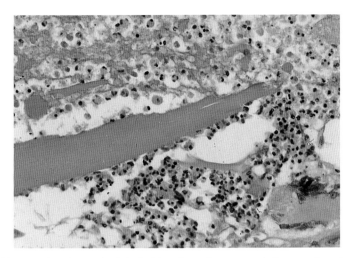

Figure 9-5 Phacoantigenic endophthalmitis. Granulomatous inflammation, including giant cells *(lower right)*, surrounds inciting lens fibers.

Phacolytic Glaucoma

In a hypermature cataract, the liquefied cortical material may leak through the capsule and gain access to the anterior chamber. This material incites a marked nongranuloma-tous inflammatory response in which numerous macrophages phagocytize the lens pro-tein material. Collections of these protein-laden macrophages, as well as extracellular lens protein, may obstruct the trabecular meshwork and thereby cause a type of secondary glaucoma known as *phacolytic glaucoma,* which was also discussed in Chapter 7. Cytologic examination of aqueous humor from patients with phacolytic glaucoma reveals collec-tions of macrophages containing eosinophilic lens protein and extracellular proteinaceous material (see Fig 7-8). The treatment for phacolytic glaucoma is surgical removal of the lens and irrigation of the anterior chamber.

Propionibacterium acnes Endophthalmitis

Chronic postoperative endophthalmitis secondary to *P acnes* may develop following cata-ract surgery, usually 2 months to 2 years later. It may be characterized by granulomatous keratic precipitates, a small hypopyon, vitritis, and a white plaque containing *P acnes* and residual lens material sequestered within the capsular bag (Figs 9-6, 9-7). Onset of the inflammation may follow Nd:YAG laser capsulotomy that allows release of the seques-tered organisms.

Degenerations

Cataract and Other Abnormalities

Capsule

Mild thickening of the lens capsule can be associated with pathologic proliferation of lens epithelium or with chronic inflammation of the anterior segment. Focal, internally directed

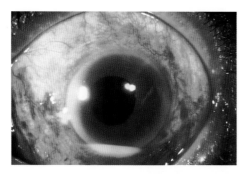

Figure 9-6 Clinical photograph of eye with *P acnes* endophthalmitis. Note injection of the conjunctiva and small hypopyon. *(Courtesy of William C. Lloyd III, MD, and Ralph C. Eagle, Jr, MD.)*

Figure 9-7 Histopathology of a lens capsule from a case of *P acnes* endophthalmitis. *(Courtesy of William C. Lloyd III, MD, and Ralph C. Eagle Jr, MD.)*

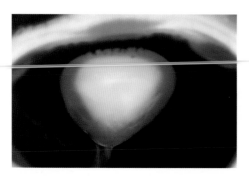

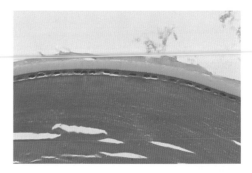

Figure 9-8 Posterior lenticonus. *(Courtesy of Hans E. Grossniklaus, MD.)*

Figure 9-9 Exfoliation syndrome (pseudoexfoliation). Abnormal material appears on the anterior lens capsule like iron filings on the edge of a magnet.

excrescences of the lens capsule are seen in several conditions, including aniridia and Lowe syndrome.

Coronary, or *cerulean, cataracts* consist of wartlike excrescences on the capsule. With time, these excrescences are replaced by clumps of epithelium, resulting in granular debris in the peripheral cortex.

In *posterior lenticonus,* the lens capsule is abnormally thin, and the lens bulges into the anterior aspect of the vitreous (Fig 9-8). The outermost layers of the adult nucleus and cortex in the region of the bulge become opacified. *Anterior lenticonus* is much rarer and shows more extensive cytoarchitectural abnormalities.

Exfoliation syndrome, also known as *pseudoexfoliation,* is not an abnormality of the lens capsule per se but is the result of the deposition of a fibrillary proteinlike material on the anterior lens capsule. The material is also deposited on other intraocular structures. Histologically, the eosinophilic deposits appear sprinkled on the surface of the capsule like iron filings standing upright on the surface of a magnet (Fig 9-9). See also Chapter 7, Anterior Chamber and Trabecular Meshwork.

Epithelium

A severe elevation of IOP causes injury to the lens epithelial cells, leading to degeneration of the cells. Clinically, patches of white flecks *(glaukomflecken)* are seen beneath the lens capsule. Histology shows focal areas of necrotic lens epithelial cells beneath the anterior lens capsule. Associated degenerated subepithelial cortical material is also present. See also BCSC Section 10, *Glaucoma.*

Chronic iritis may cause degeneration and necrosis, as well as proliferation of anterior lens epithelium. Epithelial hyperplasia may be associated with the formation of subcapsular fibrous plaques (Fig 9-10). In this situation, the epithelial cells have undergone metaplastic transformation into cells capable of producing collagen. These functionally transformed epithelial cells arise in response to a variety of stimuli, including chronic inflammation or trauma. Following resolution of the inciting stimulus, the lens epithelium may produce another capsule, thereby totally surrounding the fibrous plaque and producing a duplication cataract.

Retention of iron-containing metallic foreign bodies in the lens may lead to lens epithelial degeneration and necrosis secondary to *siderosis.* The presence of iron within the epithelial cells can be nicely demonstrated by the use of the Prussian blue stain or Perls test.

Posterior subcapsular cataract may be the most common abnormality involving the lens epithelium. This condition is often associated with cortical degeneration and nuclear sclerosis. The process begins with epithelial disarray at the equator, followed by posterior migration of the lens epithelium. As the cells migrate posteriorly, they enlarge and swell to 5–6 times their normal size. These swollen cells, referred to as *bladder cells* or *Wedl cells,* can cause significant visual impairment if they involve the axial portion of the lens (Fig 9-11). Conditions often associated with posterior subcapsular cataracts include chronic vitreal inflammation, ionizing radiation, and prolonged use of corticosteroids.

Disruption of the lens capsule often results in proliferation of the lens epithelial cells. Following extracapsular cataract extraction, for example, remaining epithelial cells can

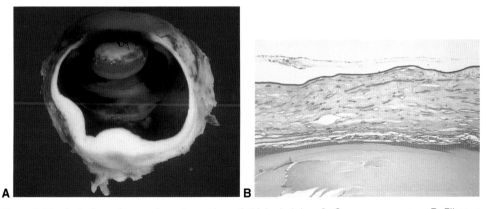

A   **B**

Figure 9-10 Anterior subcapsular cataract in a phthisical globe. **A,** Gross appearance. **B,** Fibrous plaque is present anterior to the original anterior capsule. *(Courtesy of Hans E. Grossniklaus, MD.)*

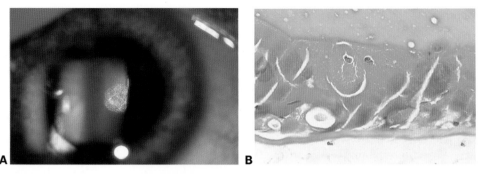

Figure 9-11 Posterior subcapsular cataract. **A,** Viewed at the slit lamp. **B,** With bladder cells (Wedl cells). *(Part A courtesy of CIBA Pharmaceutical Co., division of CIBA-GEIGY Corp. Reproduced with permission from* Clinical Symposia. *Illustration by John A. Craig; part B courtesy of Debra J. Shetlar, MD.)*

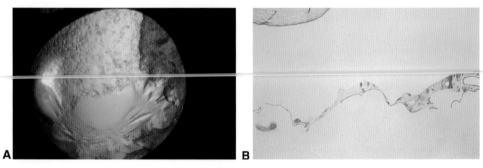

Figure 9-12 Elschnig pearls. **A,** Clinical appearance using retroillumination to demonstrate posterior capsule opacities. **B,** Histology depicting proliferating lens epithelium on posterior capsule. *(Part A courtesy of Sander Dubovy, MD; part B courtesy of Debra J. Shetlar, MD.)*

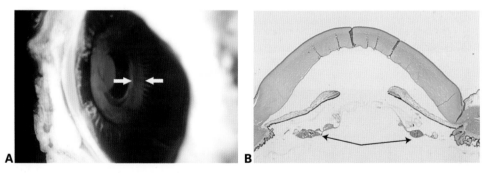

Figure 9-13 Soemmerring ring cataract. **A,** A ring cataract found adjacent to a posterior chamber intraocular lens *(arrows).* **B,** Ring cataract, photomicrograph *(arrows). (Part A courtesy of Sander Dubovy, MD.)*

proliferate and cover the inner surface of the posterior capsule. These collections of proliferating epithelial cells may form partially transparent globular masses called *Elschnig pearls* (Fig 9-12). Sequestration of proliferating lens fibers in the equatorial region, often as a result of incomplete cortical removal during cataract surgery, may create a doughnut-shaped configuration referred to as a *Soemmerring ring* (Fig 9-13).

Cortex

Opacities of the cortical lens fibers are most often associated with nuclear sclerosis or posterior subcapsular cataracts. Clinically, cortical degenerative changes fall into 2 broad categories:

1. generalized discolorations with loss of transparency
2. focal opacifications

Generalized loss of transparency cannot be diagnosed histologically with reliability, as histologic stains that are used to colorize the lens after it is processed prevent the assessment of lens clarity. The earliest sign of focal cortical degeneration is hydropic swelling of the lens fibers with decreased intensity of the eosinophilic staining. Focal cortical opacities become more apparent when fiber degeneration is advanced enough to cause liquefactive change. Light microscopy shows the accumulation of eosinophilic globules *(morgagnian globules)* in slitlike spaces between the lens fibers, which is a reliable histologic sign of cortical degeneration (Fig 9-14). As focal cortical lesions progress, the slitlike spaces become confluent, forming globular collections of lens protein. Ultimately, the entire cortex can become liquefied, allowing the nucleus to sink downward and the capsule to wrinkle *(morgagnian cataract)* (Fig 9-15).

Denatured lens protein can escape through an intact capsule and provoke an anterior chamber inflammatory reaction composed predominantly of macrophages. This condition, sometimes known as *phacolytic glaucoma,* was discussed earlier in this chapter and in Chapter 7.

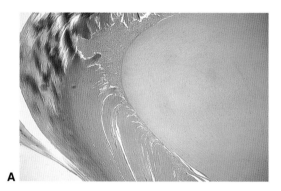

A

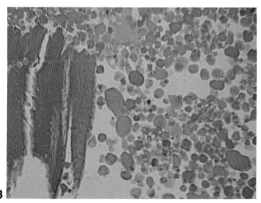

B

Figure 9-14 Cataract. **A,** Extensive cortical changes are present. **B,** Cortical degeneration. Lens cells (fibers) have swollen and fragmented to form morgagnian globules. The lenticular fragments are opaque and will increase osmotic pressure within the capsule. *(Courtesy of Hans E. Grossniklaus, MD.)*

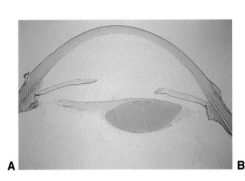

Figure 9-15 Morgagnian cataract. **A,** The lens cortex is liquefied, leaving the lens nucleus floating free within the capsular bag. **B,** Note the artifactitious (sharply angulated) clefts in this nuclear sclerotic cataract. A zone of morgagnian globules *(M)* is identified. *(Part A courtesy of Debra J. Shetlar, MD.)*

Nucleus

The continued production of lens fibers subjects the nucleus in the adult lens to the lifelong stress of mechanical compression. This compression causes hardening of the lens nucleus. Aging is also associated with alterations in the chemical composition of the nuclear fibers that may cause them to accumulate urochrome pigment. These changes in the nucleus increase the index of refraction, inducing a myopic shift of the refractive error.

The pathogenesis of nuclear discoloration is poorly understood and probably involves more than 1 mechanism. Clinically, the lens nucleus may appear yellow, brunescent, or deep brown. The histologic appearance, however, will not necessarily correlate to the clinical appearance because of the absorption of eosin dye (Fig 9-16).

Nuclear cataracts are difficult to assess histologically because they take on a subtle homogeneous eosinophilic appearance. The loss of cellular laminations probably correlates better with nucleus firmness than it does with optical opacification clinically. The more homogeneous the nucleus becomes, the less likely it is to artifactitiously fracture during sectioning.

Occasionally, crystalline deposits identified as calcium oxalate crystals may be identified within a nuclear cataract. The examiner can identify these crystals by viewing sections under polarized light.

Neoplasia and Associations With Systemic Disorders

There are no reported examples of neoplasms arising in the human lens. Premature opacification of the lens has been noted in many clinical situations, including the following:

- diabetes mellitus
- galactosemia

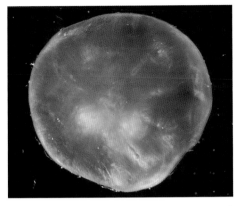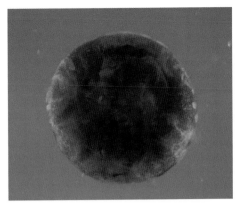

Figure 9-16 Surgically extracted lens nuclei showing varying degrees of brunescence and opacification. *(Courtesy of Hans E. Grossniklaus, MD.)*

- hypercupremia
- Fabry disease
- Down syndrome
- corticosteroid use

Exogenous agents, such as electric shock and radiation, may also play causative roles in the formation of cataracts. Retained intralenticular foreign bodies, especially those containing iron, may lead to cataract formation.

Pathology of Intraocular Lenses

Placement of an intraocular lens (IOL) following the removal of a cataract has become standard in most cases of cataract surgery. The selection of the type of IOL and the location of placement depends on a host of factors and may lead to a number of pathologic situations.

Decentration

Lens malpositions are almost certain to occur with asymmetric fixation of haptics. Placement of both haptics within the capsular bag is most likely to present with a well-centered optic (Fig 9-17). In the early 1980s, when posterior chamber IOLs were first introduced, the most likely etiology of decentration was surgical inexperience, with the haptics extending out of the capsular bag through tears in the anterior lens capsule after can-opener capsulotomy. With improvement of surgical techniques and the use of continuous curvilinear capsulorrhexis, the anterior capsule was made more stable and able to support a permanent in-the-bag fixation. Currently, the majority of IOLs are placed in the posterior chamber. However, IOLs may occasionally be placed in the anterior chamber, particularly if there is insufficient zonule support of the lens capsule (Fig 9-18).

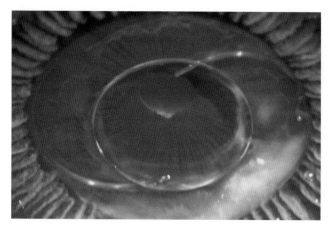

Figure 9-17 Posterior view of posterior chamber intraocular lens that is positioned within the capsular bag. *(Courtesy of Hans E. Grossniklaus, MD.)*

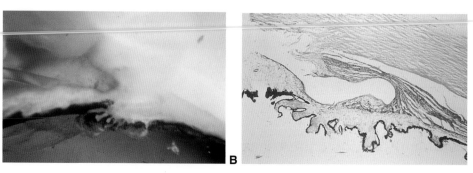

A   **B**

Figure 9-18 Anterior chamber IOL. **A,** Gross appearance of iris root and ciliary body with lens haptic. **B,** Microscopic appearance of anterior chamber. The IOL has been removed during tissue processing; the site where the haptic has partially eroded through the iris root can be seen. *(Reproduced with permission from Champion R, McDonnell PJ, Green WR. Intraocular lenses: histopathologic characteristics of a large series of autopsy eyes. Surv Ophthalmol. 1985;30:1–32. Photographs courtesy of W. Richard Green, MD.)*

Inflammation

Noninfectious causes

Inflammation following the implantation of an IOL may be caused by the lens itself through contact and chafing of the lens against the surrounding ciliary epithelium. This may lead to anterior segment inflammation and/or uveitis-glaucoma-hyphema (UGH) syndrome.

Infectious causes

Infectious generalized endophthalmitis may occur secondary to any intraocular procedure, including cataract extraction with IOL placement. Localized endophthalmitis may occur secondary to a focal sequestered infection that is present within the lens capsule and cataractous lens remnants (eg, *P acnes,* described earlier).

Corneal Complications

Corneal decompensation, including pseudophakic corneal edema and pseudophakic bullous keratopathy, may occur secondary to endothelial cell damage.

Retinal Complications

Cystoid macular edema may occur after cataract surgery, with fluid collecting within the inner and outer plexiform layers of the neural retina. See BCSC Section 12, *Retina and Vitreous*. Retinal detachment occurs in 2%–3% of eyes following intracapsular cataract extraction and in 0.5%–2.0% of eyes following extracapsular cataract extraction. The incidence following phacoemulsification is felt to be smaller. See BCSC Section 11, *Lens and Cataract*.

Apple DJ, Raab MF. *Ocular Pathology Clinical Applications and Self-Assessment*. 5th ed. St. Louis: Mosby-Year Book; 1998:161–179.

CHAPTER 10

Vitreous

Topography

The vitreous humor makes up most of the volume of the globe and is important in many diseases that affect the eye. BCSC Section 12, *Retina and Vitreous,* discusses the vitreous in detail.

The average volume of the adult vitreous is 4 cc. The vitreous is composed of 99% water and several macromolecules, including

- types II and IX collagen
- glycosaminoglycans
- soluble proteins
- glycoproteins

The outer portion of the vitreous has a greater number of collagen fibrils and is termed the *vitreous cortex.* The outer surface of the cortex is known as the *hyaloid face.*

The vitreous is bordered anteriorly by the lens, where its attachment to the lens capsule is called the *hyaloideocapsular ligament.* This attachment is firm in young patients and becomes increasingly tenuous with age. The vitreous is attached to the internal limiting membrane (ILM) of the retina by the insertion of the cortical collagen into the basement membrane structure that comprises the basal lamina of the ciliary epithelium and the ILM.

The vitreous attaches most firmly to the vitreous base, a 360° band that straddles the ora serrata and varies in width from 2 to 6 mm. The vitreous base extends more posteriorly with advancing age. Other relatively firm attachments of the vitreous are

- at the margins of the optic nerve head
- along the course of major retinal vessels
- in a circular area around the fovea
- at the edges of areas of vitreoretinal degeneration such as lattice degeneration

The strength of the vitreoretinal attachment is important in the pathogenesis of retinal tears and detachment, macular hole formation, and vitreous hemorrhage from neovascularization.

The embryologic development of the vitreous is generally divided into 3 stages:

1. primary vitreous
2. secondary vitreous
3. tertiary vitreous

The *primary vitreous* consists of fibrillar material; mesenchymal cells; and vascular components: the hyaloid artery, vasa hyaloidea propria, and tunica vasculosa lentis. The *secondary vitreous* begins to form at approximately the ninth week of gestation and is destined to become the main portion of the vitreous in the postnatal and adult eye. The primary vitreous atrophies with formation of the secondary vitreous, leaving only Cloquet's canal and, occasionally, the Bergmeister papilla and Mittendorf dot as vestigial remnants. The secondary vitreous is relatively acellular and completely avascular. The cells present in the secondary vitreous are called *hyalocytes,* and they exhibit features distinguishing them from macrophages and glial cells. The zonular fibers represent the *tertiary vitreous.*

Congenital Anomalies

Persistent Fetal Vasculature

Persistent fetal vasculature (PFV; also known as *persistent hyperplastic primary vitreous,* or *PHPV*) is characterized by the persistence of variable components of the primary vitreous and is most often unilateral. In most cases of clinically significant PFV, a fibrovascular plaque in the retrolental space extends laterally to involve the ciliary processes, which may be pulled centripetally by traction from the fibrovascular tissue. The clinical and gross appearance of elongated ciliary processes results. The anterior fibrovascular plaque is generally contiguous posteriorly with a remnant of the hyaloid artery that may attach to the optic nerve head (Fig 10-1). Involvement of the posterior structures may be more extensive, with tractional detachment of the peripapillary retina resulting from traction from preretinal membranes. The lens is often cataractous, and nonocular tissues such as adipose tissue and cartilage may be present in the retrolental mass. Eyes affected by PFV are often microphthalmic.

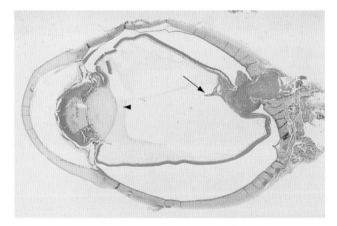

Figure 10-1 PFV. Note the prominent anterior fibrovascular plaque *(arrowhead)*. The posterior remnant of the persistent hyaloid is evident at the optic nerve head *(arrow)*. *(Courtesy of Hans E. Grossniklaus, MD.)*

Bergmeister Papilla

Persistence of a small part of the posterior portion of the hyaloid artery is referred to as a *Bergmeister papilla.* This anomaly generally takes the form of a veil-like structure overlying the optic nerve head or a finger-like projection extending from the surface of the optic nerve head.

Mittendorf Dot

The hyaloid artery attaches to the tunica vasculosa lentis just inferior and nasal to the center of the lens. With regression of these vascular structures, it is not uncommon to see a focal lens opacity at this site, which is referred to as a *Mittendorf dot* (see Fig 2-47 in BCSC Section 2, *Fundamentals and Principles of Ophthalmology*).

Peripapillary Vascular Loops

Retinal vessels may grow into a Bergmeister papilla and then return to the optic nerve head, creating the appearance of a vascular loop. These loops should not be mistaken for neovascularization of the optic nerve head.

Vitreous Cysts

Vitreous cysts generally occur in eyes with no other pathologic findings, but they have been seen in eyes with retinitis pigmentosa, with uveitis, and with remnants of the hyaloid system. Histologic studies have suggested the presence of hyaloid remnants in the vitreous cysts. The exact origin of the cysts is not known.

Inflammations

As a relatively acellular and completely avascular structure, the vitreous is not an active participant in inflammatory disorders. It does become involved secondarily in inflammatory conditions of adjacent tissues, however. The most notable involvement of the vitreous is in infectious endophthalmitis secondary to bacterial or fungal agents. The vitreous may also become involved secondarily with the inflammatory response associated with the following:

- toxocariasis
- toxoplasmosis
- acute retinal necrosis (ARN)
- cytomegalovirus (CMV) retinitis
- sarcoidosis
- pars planitis
- other forms of noninfectious retinitis

See also BCSC Section 9, *Intraocular Inflammation and Uveitis.*

Inflammatory conditions cause predictable changes in the vitreous. Marked neutrophilic infiltration of the vitreous occurs in acute inflammatory conditions such as bacterial endophthalmitis (Fig 10-2). This infiltration leads to liquefaction of the vitreous, with

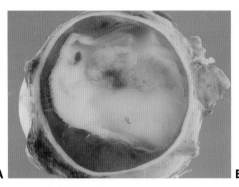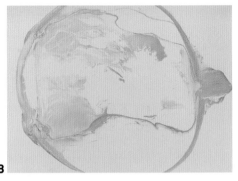

A   B

Figure 10-2 **A,** Gross photograph of opacification and infiltration of the vitreous as a result of bacterial endophthalmitis. **B,** Section shows cellular infiltration of vitreous in endophthalmitis (retinal detachment is artifactitious). *(Courtesy of Hans E. Grossniklaus, MD.)*

subsequent detachment of the posterior vitreous. Severe cases may be accompanied by formation of fibrocellular membranes, which typically form in the retrolental space and may exert traction on the peripheral retina. Chronic inflammatory conditions such as pars planitis (intermediate uveitis) and sarcoidosis may lead to infiltration of the vitreous with chronic inflammatory cells as well as to neovascularization of the anterior or posterior vitreous.

Degenerations

Syneresis and Aging

Syneresis of the vitreous is defined as liquefaction of the gel. Syneresis of the central vitreous is an almost universal consequence of aging. It also occurs as a consequence of vitreous inflammation and hemorrhage and in the setting of pathologic myopia. The prominent lamellae and strands that develop in aging and following inflammation or hemorrhage are the result of abnormally aggregated vitreous fibers around syneretic areas (Fig 10-3). Syneresis is one of the contributing factors leading to vitreous detachment.

Hemorrhage

A constellation of histopathologic findings may develop in the vitreous following vitreous hemorrhage. After 3–10 days, red blood cell clots undergo fibrinolysis and red blood cells may diffuse throughout the vitreous cavity. At this time, breakdown of the red blood cells also occurs. Loss of hemoglobin from the red blood cells produces ghost cells (Fig 10-4) and hemoglobin spherules (Fig 10-5). Obstruction of the trabecular meshwork by these cells may lead to *ghost cell glaucoma.* (See Fig 7-9 and BCSC Section 10, *Glaucoma.*)

The process of red blood cell dissolution attracts macrophages, which phagocytose the effete red blood cells. The hemoglobin is broken down to hemosiderin, then removed from the eye. In massive hemorrhages, cholesterol crystals caused by the breakdown of red blood cell membranes may be present, often surrounded by a foreign body giant cell reaction. Cholesterol

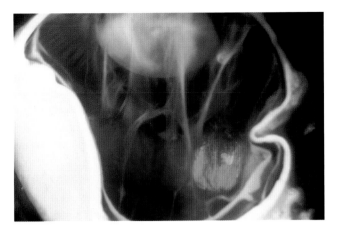

Figure 10-3 Gross photograph of vitreous condensations outlining syneretic cavities. *(Courtesy of Hans E. Grossniklaus, MD.)*

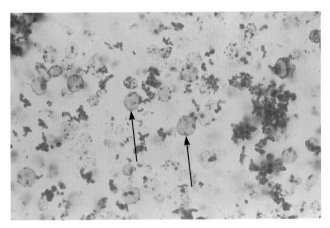

Figure 10-4 Ghost cells *(arrows)* represent red blood cells that have lost much of their intracellular hemoglobin. *(Courtesy of Hans E. Grossniklaus, MD.)*

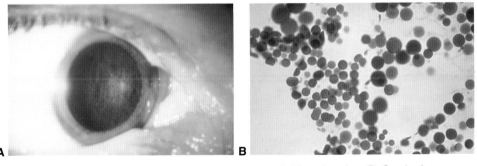

A   **B**

Figure 10-5 **A,** Clinical photograph of retrolental hemoglobin spherules. **B,** Cytologic preparation of hemoglobin spherules removed from the vitreous cavity. *(Reproduced with permission from Spraul CW, Grossniklaus HE. Vitreous hemorrhage. Surv Ophthalmol. 1997;42:3–39.)*

appears clinically as refractile intravitreal crystals. As mentioned previously, syneresis of the vitreous and posterior vitreous detachment are common after vitreous hemorrhage.

Asteroid Hyalosis

Asteroid hyalosis is a condition with a spectacular clinical appearance (see Fig 12-6, BCSC Section 12, *Retina and Vitreous*) but little clinical significance. Asteroid bodies are rounded structures measuring 10–100 nm that stain positively with alcian blue and positively with stains for neutral fats, phospholipids, and calcium (Fig 10-6). The bodies stain metachromatically and exhibit birefringence. Occasionally, asteroid bodies will be surrounded by a foreign body giant cell, but the condition is not generally associated with an inflammatory reaction.

The exact mechanism of formation of asteroid bodies is not known; however, element mapping by electron spectroscopic imaging has revealed a homogeneous distribution of calcium, phosphorus, and oxygen. The electron energy loss spectra of these elements show details similar to those found for hydroxyapatite. In addition, high contrast and sensitivity against a calcium-specific chelator highlights the crystalline, apatite-like nature of asteroid bodies. Immunofluorescence microscopy has revealed the presence of chondroitin-6-sulfate at the periphery of asteroid bodies; and carbohydrates specific for hyaluronic acid were observed by lectin-gold labeling to be part of the inner matrix of asteroid bodies. Thus, asteroid bodies exhibit structural and elemental similarity to hydroxyapatite, and proteoglycans and their glycosaminoglycan side chains appear to play a role in regulating the biomineralization process.

Winkler J, Lunsdorf H. Ultrastructure and composition of asteroid bodies. *Invest Ophthalmol Vis Sci.* 2001;42:902–907.

Vitreous Amyloidosis

The term *amyloidosis* refers to a group of diseases that lead to extracellular deposition of amyloid. Amyloid is composed of various proteins that have a characteristic ultrastructural appearance of nonbranching fibrils with variable length and a diameter of 75–100 Å (Fig 10-7). The proteins forming amyloid also have in common the ability to form a tertiary structure characterized as a β-pleated sheet, which then enables the proteins to bind Congo red stain and show birefringence in polarized light (Fig 10-8).

Amyloid may be derived from various types of protein, and the protein of origin is characteristic for different forms of amyloidosis. Amyloid deposits occur in the vitreous when

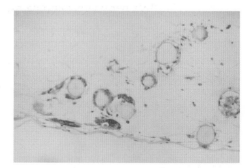

Figure 10-6 Asteroid bodies surrounded by a foreign-body reaction. *(Courtesy of Hans E. Grossniklaus, MD.)*

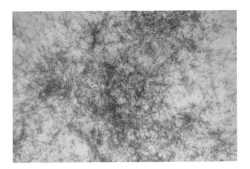

Figure 10-7 Electron photomicrograph shows characteristic amyloid fibrils. *(Courtesy of David J. Wilson, MD.)*

Figure 10-8 Polarized light photomicrograph of the Congo red–stained vitreous from a patient with familial amyloid polyneuropathy. *(Courtesy of David J. Wilson, MD.)*

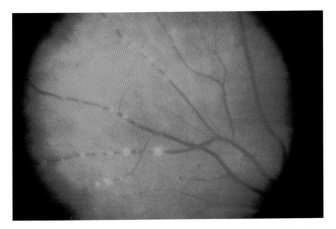

Figure 10-9 Perivascular sheathing associated with vitreous amyloidosis. *(Courtesy of Hans E. Grossniklaus, MD.)*

the protein forming the amyloid is *transthyretin,* previously known as *prealbumin.* Multiple genetic mutations have been described that result in various amino acid substitutions in the transthyretin protein. The most common mutations were originally described based on their clinical findings as *familial amyloid polyneuropathy (FAP)* types I and II. Systemic manifestations in patients with this type of amyloidosis include vitreous opacities and perivascular infiltrates (Fig 10-9), peripheral neuropathy, cardiomyopathy, and carpal tunnel syndrome.

The mechanism by which the vitreous becomes involved is not known with certainty. Because amyloid deposits are found within the walls of retinal vessels and in the retinal pigment epithelium (RPE), amyloid may gain access to the vitreous through these tissues. In addition, because transthyretin is a blood protein, it may gain access to the vitreous by crossing the blood–aqueous barrier at the ciliary body.

Posterior Vitreous Detachment

Posterior vitreous detachment (PVD) occurs when a dehiscence in the vitreous cortex allows fluid from a syneretic cavity to gain access to the potential subhyaloid space, causing the remaining cortex to be stripped from the ILM (Fig 10-10). As fluid drains out of the syneretic cavities under the newly formed posterior hyaloid, the vitreous body collapses anteriorly. Vitreous detachment generally occurs rapidly, so that over the course of a few hours to days the vitreous collapses anteriorly and remains attached only at its base.

A weakening of the adherence of the cortical vitreous to the ILM with age also plays a role in PVDs. The reported incidence of PVD varies between 31% and 65% at age 65 and is increased by intraocular inflammation, aphakia or pseudophakia, trauma, and vitreoretinal disease. PVD is important in the pathogenesis of many conditions, including retinal tears and detachment, vitreous hemorrhage, and macular hole formation.

Rhegmatogenous Retinal Detachment and Proliferative Vitreoretinopathy

Retinal tears form from vitreous traction on the retina during or after PVD or secondary to ocular trauma. Tears are most likely to occur at sites of greatest vitreoretinal adhesion, such as the vitreous base or the margin of lattice degeneration (Fig 10-11). The histopathology of retinal tears reveals that the vitreous is adherent to the retina along the flap of the tear. In the area of retina separated from the underlying RPE, there is loss of photoreceptors.

Retinal detachment occurs when vitreous traction and fluid currents resulting from eye movements combine to overcome the forces maintaining retinal adhesion to the RPE. The principal histopathologic findings in retinal detachment consist of the following:

- degeneration of the outer segments of the photoreceptors
- eventual loss of photoreceptor cells as a result of apoptosis, or programmed cell death
- migration of Müller cells
- proliferation and migration of RPE cells

Small cystic spaces develop in the detached retina, and in chronic detachment, these cysts may coalesce into large macrocysts (Fig 10-12).

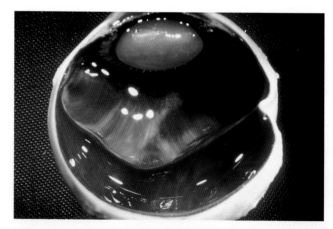

Figure 10-10 Gross photograph of posterior vitreous detachment. *(Courtesy of Hans E. Grossniklaus, MD.)*

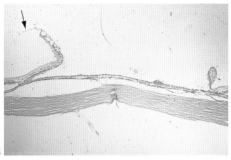

Figure 10-11   A, Gross photograph of retinal tears at vitreous base. **B,** Photomicrograph shows condensed vitreous *(arrow)* attached to anterior flap of retinal tear. *(Courtesy of W. Richard Green, MD.)*

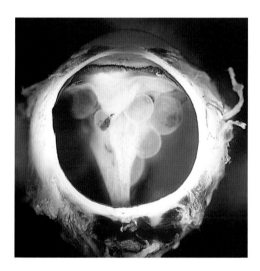

Figure 10-12 Long-standing total retinal detachment with macrocystic degeneration of the retina.

With rhegmatogenous retinal detachment, cellular membranes may form on either surface (anterior or posterior) of the retina (Fig 10-13). Clinically, this process is referred to as *proliferative vitreoretinopathy (PVR).* Membranes form as a result of proliferation of RPE cells and contain other cellular elements, including glial cells (Müller cells, fibrous astrocytes), macrophages, fibroblasts, myofibroblasts, and possibly hyalocytes. The cell biology of membrane formation in the vitreous is complex and involves the interaction of various growth factors, integrins, and cellular proliferation. Recent studies have shown a significant association between clinical grades of PVR and the expression levels of specific cytokines and/or growth factors in the vitreous fluid.

Harada C, Mitamura Y, Harada T. The role of cytokines and trophic factors in epiretinal membranes: involvement of signal transduction in glial cells. *Prog Retin Eye Res.* 2005;25:149–164; Dec 27 [Epub].

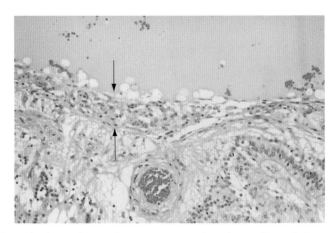

Figure 10-13 Preretinal membrane *(between arrows)* on the surface of the retina, secondary to proliferative vitreoretinopathy. *(Courtesy of David J. Wilson, MD.)*

Macular Holes

Idiopathic macular holes most likely form as the result of degenerative changes in the vitreous. Current imaging studies such as optical coherence tomography (OCT) have greatly advanced our understanding of the anatomical features of full-thickness macular holes and early macular hole formation. These studies are most consistent with a focal anteroposterior traction mechanism, but some inconsistencies in clinical cases suggest a role for degeneration of the inner retinal layers. Localized perifoveal vitreous detachment (an early stage of age-related PVD) appears to be the primary pathogenetic event in idiopathic macular hole formation (Fig 10-14). Detachment of the posterior hyaloid from the pericentral retina exerts anterior traction on the foveola and localizes the dynamic vitreous traction associated with ocular rotations into the perifoveolar region.

OCT has clarified the pathoanatomy of early macular hole stages, beginning with a foveal pseudocyst (stage 1a), typically followed by disruption of the outer retina (stage 1b), before progressing to a full-thickness dehiscence (stage 2). Histologically, full-thickness macular holes are similar to holes in other locations. A full-thickness retinal defect with rounded tissue margins (stage 3) is accompanied by loss of the photoreceptor outer segments in adjacent retina that is separated from the RPE by subretinal fluid (Fig 10-14D). An epiretinal membrane composed of Müller cells, fibrous astrocytes, and fibroblasts with myoblastic differentiation is often present on the surface of the retina adjacent to the macular hole. Cystoid macular edema in the parafoveal retina adjacent to the full-thickness macular hole is relatively common. Following surgical repair of macular holes, closer apposition of the remaining photoreceptors and variable glial scarring close the macular defect.

Gass JD. Reappraisal of biomicroscopic classification of stages of development of a macular hole. *Am J Ophthalmol.* 1995;119:752–759.

Johnson MW. Improvements in the understanding and treatment of macular hole. *Curr Opin Ophthalmol.* 2002;13:152–160.

Smiddy WE, Flynn HW Jr . Pathogenesis of macular holes and therapeutic implications. *Am J Ophthalmol.* 2004;137:525–537.

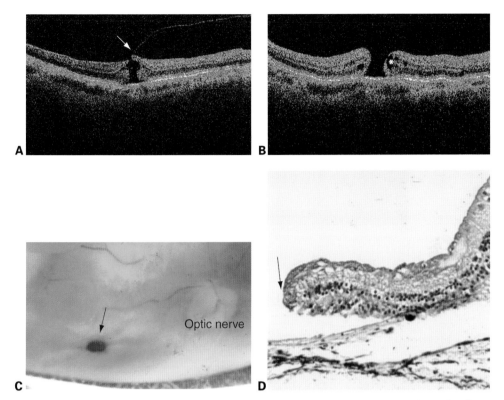

Figure 10-14 Macular holes. **A,** OCT of early stage 2 macular hole with vitreoretinal adhesion to lamellar flap *(arrow)*. **B,** OCT of stage 3 macular hole with full-thickness retinal defect, rounded margins, and CME *(asterisk)*. **C,** Gross photograph of full-thickness macular hole *(arrow)*. **D,** Histopathology of full-thickness macular hole showing rounded gliotic margin *(arrow)* with positive staining for glial fibrillary acidic protein (GFAP), highlighting the Müller cells and fibrous astrocytes. *(Parts A and B courtesy of Robert H. Rosa, Jr, MD, and Terry Hanke, CRA; parts C and D courtesy of Patricia Chévez-Barrios, MD.)*

Neoplasia

Intraocular Lymphoma

Primary neoplastic involvement of the vitreous is uncommon because of the relatively acellular nature of the vitreous. However, the vitreous can be the site of primary involvement in cases of B-cell lymphoma. This type of lymphoma has been referred to as *primary intraocular/central nervous system lymphoma, large cell lymphoma,* and *reticulum cell sarcoma.* Immunohistochemical and molecular genetic studies have confirmed that this entity is a B-cell lymphoma. In rare cases, vitreous involvement may occur in T-cell lymphomas.

The most common presentation of *primary intraocular lymphoma (PIOL)* is as a posterior uveitis. Some patients have sub-RPE infiltrates (Fig 10-15) with a very characteristic speckled pigmentation overlying tumor detachments of the RPE. The sub-RPE infiltrates are present in a minority of patients with intraocular lymphoma. Approximately 50% of

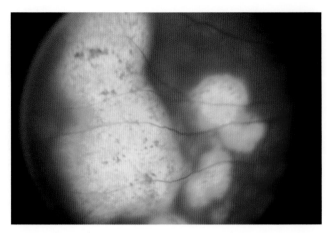

Figure 10-15 Sub-RPE infiltrates in a patient with primary intraocular lymphoma. Note the characteristic speckled pigmentation over the tumor detachments of the RPE. *(Courtesy of Robert H. Rosa, Jr, MD.)*

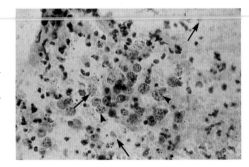

Figure 10-16 Cytologic preparation of vitreous lymphoma. Note the atypical cells *(arrowheads)* with large nuclei and multiple nucleoli. Cell ghosts *(arrows)* are also present. *(Courtesy of David J. Wilson, MD.)*

patients presenting with ocular findings have concomitant involvement of the central nervous system.

The diagnosis of intraocular lymphoma is made by cytologic analysis of vitrectomy specimens. Immunohistochemical study of cell markers, flow cytometry, or gene amplification studies can be performed on vitreous specimens, although the standard method of diagnosis is cytology.

Cytologically, the vitreous infiltrate in intraocular lymphoma is heterogeneous. The atypical cells are large lymphoid cells, frequently with a convoluted nuclear membrane and multiple, conspicuous nucleoli. An accompanying infiltrate of small lymphocytes almost always appears, and the normal cells may obscure the neoplastic cell population. These small round lymphocytes are largely reactive T cells. Numerous cell ghosts are usually present, and this feature is very suggestive of a diagnosis of intraocular lymphoma (Fig 10-16). Immunohistochemically, the viable tumor cells can be labeled as a monoclonal population of B cells. Demonstration of a monoclonal population is helped by the use of flow cytometry. Other laboratory tests that may be useful in the diagnosis and follow-up of patients with intraocular lymphoma are determination of the interleukin-10 to

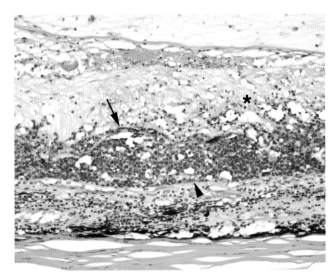

Figure 10-17 Primary intraocular lymphoma. Note the detachment of the RPE by tumor *(arrow)* overlying retinal gliosis *(asterisk)*, and intact Bruch's membrane *(arrowhead)*. Secondary chronic inflammation is present in the choroid. *(Courtesy of Robert H. Rosa, Jr, MD.)*

interleukin-6 ratio and the use of microdissection and polymerase chain reaction (PCR) for the detection of immunoglobulin gene rearrangement and translocation.

The subretinal/sub-RPE infiltrates are composed of atypical lymphoid cells (Fig 10-17). With or without treatment, the subretinal infiltrates tend to resolve, leaving a focal area of RPE atrophy. Optic nerve and retinal infiltration may also be present. Infiltrates in these locations tend to be perivascular and may lead to ischemic retinal or optic nerve damage. The choroid is most often free of atypical cells; however, secondary chronic inflammation may be present in the choroid. In the setting of systemic lymphoma with ocular involvement, the choroid (rather than the vitreous, retina, or subretinal space) is the primary site of involvement.

Coupland SE, Hummel M, Muller HH, Stein H. Molecular analysis of immunoglobulin genes in primary intraocular lymphoma. *Invest Ophthalmol Vis Sci.* 2005;46:3507–3514.

Levy-Clarke GA, Chan CC, Nussenblatt RB. Diagnosis and management of primary intraocular lymphoma. *Hematol Oncol Clin North Am.* 2005;19:739–749.

Read RW, Zamir E, Rao NA. Neoplastic masquerade syndromes. *Surv Ophthalmol.* 2002;47: 81–124.

CHAPTER 11

Retina and Retinal Pigment Epithelium

Topography

The retina and the retinal pigment epithelium (RPE) make up 2 distinct layers that together line the inner two thirds of the globe:

1. The RPE is a pigmented layer derived from the outer layer of the optic cup.
2. The neurosensory retina is a delicate, transparent layer derived from the inner layer of the optic cup.

Anteriorly, the RPE becomes continuous with the pigmented epithelium of the ciliary body, and the retina becomes continuous with the nonpigmented ciliary body epithelium. Posteriorly, the RPE terminates at the optic nerve, just prior to the termination of Bruch's membrane. The nuclear, photoreceptor, and synaptic layers of the retina gradually taper at the optic nerve head, and only the nerve fiber layer (NFL) continues on to form the optic nerve. BCSC Section 12, *Retina and Vitreous,* discusses in depth the anatomy of the retina, as well as other topics covered in this chapter.

Retina

The topographic variation in the structures of the retina is striking, with regional variation in the neural structures as well as the retinal vasculature. The neurosensory retina has 9 layers (Fig 11-1). Beginning on the vitreous side and progressing to the choroidal side, they are

1. internal limiting membrane (ILM; a true basement membrane synthesized by Müller cells)
2. nerve fiber layer
3. ganglion cell layer
4. inner plexiform layer
5. inner nuclear layer
6. outer plexiform layer

137

7. outer nuclear layer (nuclei of the photoreceptors)
8. external limiting membrane (ELM; not a true membrane but rather an apparent membrane formed by a series of desmosomes between Müller cells and photo-receptors)
9. photoreceptors (inner and outer segments) of the rods and cones

The arrangement of the retina (in tissue sections oriented perpendicular to the retinal surface) is vertical from outer to inner layers, except for the NFL, where the axons run horizontally toward the optic nerve head. Consequently, deposits and hemorrhages in the deep retinal layers have a round appearance clinically when viewed on edge, whereas those in the NFL have a feathery appearance.

The blood supply of the retina comes from 2 sources, with a watershed zone inside the inner nuclear layer. The *retinal blood vessels* supply the NFL, ganglion cell layer, inner plexiform layer, and inner two thirds of the inner nuclear layer. The *choroidal vasculature* supplies the outer one third of the inner nuclear layer, outer plexiform layer, outer nuclear layer, photoreceptors, and RPE. Because of this division of the blood supply to the retina, ischemic choroidal vascular lesions and ischemic lesions attributed to the retinal vasculature produce different histologic pictures. Ischemic retinal injury produces inner ischemic atrophy of the retina, and choroidal ischemia produces outer ischemic retinal atrophy.

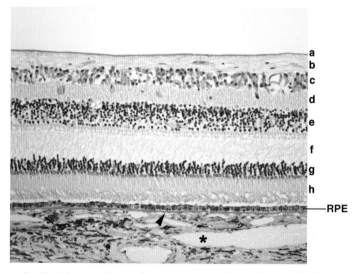

Figure 11-1 Normal retinal layers. From vitreous to choroid: **a,** internal limiting membrane; **b,** nerve fiber layer; **c,** ganglion cell layer; **d,** inner plexiform layer; **e,** inner nuclear layer; **f,** outer plexiform layer; **g,** outer nuclear layer; **h,** photoreceptors (inner/outer segments) for rods and cones. RPE = retinal pigment epithelium. Bruch's membrane, *arrowhead;* choroid, *asterisk.* The external limiting membrane (ELM) is not shown in this figure. *(Courtesy of Robert H. Rosa, Jr, MD.)*

Retinal Pigment Epithelium

The RPE consists of a monolayer of hexagonal cells with apical microvilli and a basement membrane at the base of the cells. This monolayer has the following specialized functions:

- vitamin A metabolism
- maintenance of the outer blood–retina barrier
- phagocytosis of the photoreceptor outer segments
- absorption of light
- heat exchange
- formation of the basal lamina of the inner portion of Bruch's membrane
- production of the mucopolysaccharide matrix that surrounds the photoreceptor outer segments
- active transport of materials into and out of the subretinal space

Compared with that of the retina, the topographic variation of the RPE is subtle. In the macula, the RPE is taller, narrower, and more heavily pigmented, and it forms a regular hexagonal array. In the equatorial and midperipheral area, the RPE cells are larger in diameter and thinner. Variability in the diameter of the RPE cells increases in the peripheral retina. The amount of cytoplasmic pigment, primarily lipofuscin, increases with age, particularly within the RPE in the macular region.

Macula

Histologically, the term *macula* refers to that area of the retina where the ganglion cell layer is thicker than a single cell (Fig 11-2). Clinically, this area corresponds approximately with the area of the retina bound by the inferior and superior vascular arcades. The macula is subdivided into the *foveola,* the *fovea,* the *parafovea,* and the *perifovea.* Only photoreceptor cells appear in the central foveola; the ganglion cells, other nucleated cells (including Müller cells), and blood vessels are not present. The concentration of cones is greater in the macula than in the peripheral retina, and only cones are present in the fovea.

Nerve fibers in the outer plexiform layer (nerve fiber layer of Henle) of the macula run obliquely (see Fig 11-2). This morphologic feature results in the flower-petal appearance of cystoid macular edema (CME) seen on fluorescein angiography and the star-shaped configuration of hard exudates seen ophthalmoscopically in conditions that cause macular edema. Xanthophyll pigment gives the macula its yellow appearance clinically and grossly (macula lutea), but the xanthophyll dissolves during tissue processing and is not present in histologic sections.

Congenital Anomalies

Albinism

Albinism is a general term that refers to a congenital dilution of the pigment of the skin, the eyes and the skin, or just the eyes. True albinism has been subdivided into *oculocutaneous*

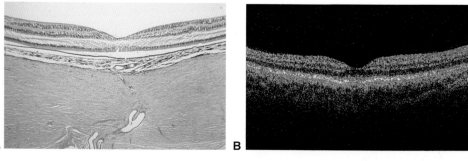

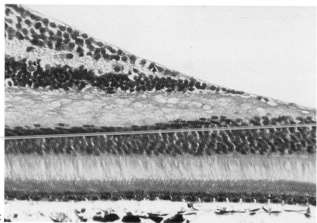

Figure 11-2 **A,** The normal macula is identified histologically by a multicellular, thick ganglion cell layer and an area of focal thinning, the foveola. Clinically, the macula lies between the inferior and superior vascular arcades. **B,** Optical coherence tomography (OCT) of the macula showing in vivo histologic assessment with tremendous details of the lamellar architecture of the retina. **C,** In the region of the foveola, the inner cellular layers are absent, with an increased density of pigment in the RPE. The incident light falls directly on the photoreceptor outer segments, reducing the potential for distortion of light by overlying tissue elements. *(Part B courtesy of Robert H. Rosa, Jr, MD, and Terry Hanke, CRA.)*

and *ocular albinism.* This distinction is somewhat helpful clinically, but in reality all cases of ocular albinism have some degree of mild cutaneous involvement. There is a pathophysiologic difference between the 2 types of albinism: in oculocutaneous albinism the amount of melanin in each melanosome is reduced, whereas in ocular albinism the number of melanosomes is reduced.

Many different types of oculocutaneous and ocular albinism have been described, but the ocular involvement always conforms to 1 of 2 clinical patterns:

1. congenitally subnormal visual acuity and nystagmus
2. normal or minimally reduced visual acuity and no nystagmus, a clinical pattern termed *albinoidism* because the visual consequences are much milder

Albinism and albinoidism share clinical features such as photophobia, iris transillumination, and hypopigmented fundi (Fig 11-3) as a result of the reduction in melanin content of the RPE and choroid. These 2 patterns also differ: albinism is accompanied by foveal hypoplasia, whereas albinoidism shows normal or nearly normal foveal architecture.

Two types of ocular albinism have important systemic associations:

1. *Hermansky-Pudlak syndrome:* albinism associated with a hemorrhagic disorder characterized by easy bruising
2. *Chédiak-Higashi syndrome:* an abnormality of neutrophils resulting in an increased susceptibility for infection

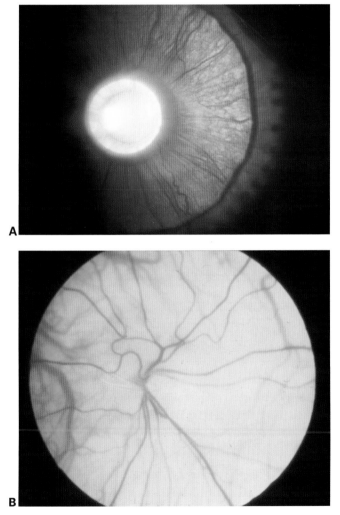

Figure 11-3 Albinisim. **A,** Iris transillumination. **B,** Fundus hypopigmentation. *(Courtesy of Robert H. Rosa, Jr., MD.)*

BCSC Section 6, *Pediatric Ophthalmology and Strabismus,* discusses albinism in greater detail.

Myelinated (Medullated) Nerve Fibers

Generally, myelination of the optic pathways terminates at the lamina cribrosa. However, myelination of the nerve fibers in the NFL can occur and produce a striking clinical appearance (see Fig 25-3, BCSC Section 6, *Pediatric Ophthalmology and Strabismus*). Areas of myelination are usually contiguous with the optic nerve head, but myelination may occur in isolation from the optic nerve head as well. The area of myelination is typically small, but large areas can produce a clinically significant scotoma. The myelin is produced by oligodendroglial cells within the NFL. Myelinated nerve fibers have been associated with myopia, amblyopia, strabismus, and nystagmus.

Vascular Anomalies

The numerous congenital anomalies of the retinal vasculature include

- capillary hemangioma (hemangioblastoma) and cavernous hemangioma
- proliferative retinopathy associated with anencephaly
- parafoveal telangiectasia
- Leber miliary aneurysm
- Coats disease
- familial exudative retinopathy
- racemose angioma (Wyburn-Mason syndrome)
- vascular loop

One histopathologic study of parafoveal telangiectasia revealed focal endothelial degeneration, accumulation of lipid within the walls of vessels, and extensive degeneration of pericytes. These findings were more pronounced in the area of clinically abnormal vessels but were also present diffusely in the retinal vasculature. In that study, no dilated or telangiectatic vessels were present.

Leber miliary aneurysm shows varying degrees of retinal capillary nonperfusion and aneurysmal dilation of retinal vessels. The changes in Leber miliary aneurysm are similar to those present to a greater degree in Coats disease. In Coats disease, exudative retinal detachment occurs as a result of leakage from abnormalities in the peripheral retina, including telangiectatic vessels, microaneurysms, and saccular dilations of retinal vessels (Fig 11-4). These changes are most often unilateral but may be bilateral. Histologically, retinal detachments secondary to Coats disease are characterized by the presence of "foamy" macrophages in the subretinal space.

Congenital Hypertrophy of the RPE

Congenital hypertrophy of the RPE (CHRPE), a relatively common congenital lesion, is characterized clinically by a flat, dark black lesion varying in size from a few to 10 mm in diameter (see Fig 17-10 in Chapter 17). Frequently, central lacunae and a peripheral zone of less dense pigmentation appear within the lesion. This lesion is histopathologically characterized by enlarged RPE cells with densely packed and larger-than-normal, spherical melanin granules (Fig 11-5). This benign congenital condition can generally be distinguished from choroidal nevi and malignant melanoma on the basis of ophthalmoscopic features. Adenocarcinoma of the RPE may develop, rarely, in an area of CHRPE.

In addition, CHRPE may be present in Gardner syndrome, or familial adenomatous polyposis. In this syndrome, bilateral or multiple (greater than 4) areas of RPE hypertrophy are a marker for the presence of the phenotype in members of pedigrees affected with the syndrome and indicate a significant risk for colorectal carcinoma. Four different types of RPE hypertrophy have been described in Gardner syndrome, and 1 of these types is similar to that present in CHRPE. Histopathologic study of the RPE changes in Gardner syndrome is more consistent with hyperplasia of the RPE than with hypertrophy. The RPE changes in Gardner syndrome are probably more appropriately termed *hamartomas*,

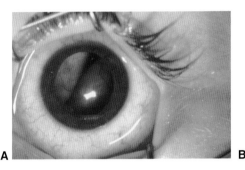

A

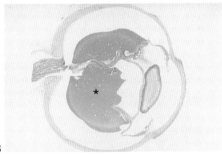

B

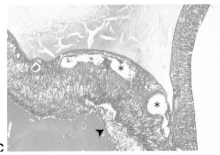

C

Figure 11-4 A, Leukocoria as a result of Coats disease. **B,** Total exudative retinal detachment in Coats disease. Note the dense subretinal proteinaceous fluid *(asterisk)*. **C,** Telangiectatic vessels *(asterisks)* and "foamy" macrophages *(arrowhead)* typical of Coats disease. *(Courtesy of Hans E. Grossniklaus, MD.)*

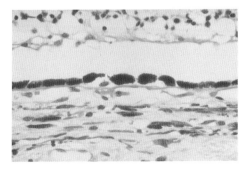

Figure 11-5 In CHRPE, the RPE cells are larger than normal and contain more densely packed melanin granules. For clinical images of CHRPE, see Figure 17-11 in Chapter 17. *(Courtesy of Hans E. Grossniklaus, MD.)*

consistent with the loss of regulatory control of cell growth that gives rise to the other soft-tissue changes in this syndrome.

Kasner L, Traboulsi EI, Delacruz Z, Green WR. A histopathologic study of the pigmented fundus lesions in familial adenomatous polyposis. *Retina*. 1992;12:35–42.

Inflammations

Infectious

Viral

Multiple viruses may cause retinal infections, including rubella, measles, human immunodeficiency virus (HIV), herpes simplex, herpes zoster, and cytomegalovirus (CMV). Two of the clinically most important entities are discussed here: acute retinal necrosis (ARN) and CMV infection.

Acute retinal necrosis is a clinically descriptive term that has been applied to the findings in patients with acute retinal infection caused by herpes simplex virus types 1 and 2 and herpes zoster. In at least 1 case, CMV has also been reported as a causative agent. The histopathologic findings are diffuse uveitis, vitritis, retinal vasculitis, and necrotizing retinitis (Fig 11-6). Electron microscopy has demonstrated viral inclusions in retinal cells. The involvement of the viruses just named in ARN has been demonstrated by culture, polymerase chain reaction (PCR), and immunohistochemistry.

CMV infection of the retina occurs as an opportunistic infection in approximately 37% of patients with AIDS and less commonly in patients immunosuppressed for other reasons (Fig 11-7). This infection is histopathologically characterized by retinal necrosis, which leads to a thin fibroglial scar with healing. Acute lesions show large neurons (20–30 μm) that contain large eosinophilic intranuclear or intracytoplasmic inclusion bodies. At the cellular level, CMV may infect vascular endothelial cells, retinal neurons, and macrophages.

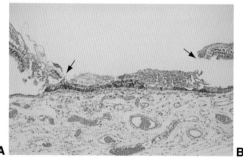 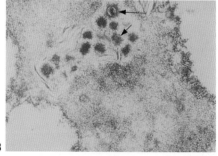

Figure 11-6 A, Acute retinal necrosis (ARN) is characterized by full-thickness necrosis of the retina *(between arrows)*. **B,** Electron microscopy demonstrates viral particles *(arrows)* within retinal cells. *(Courtesy of Hans E. Grossniklaus, MD.)*

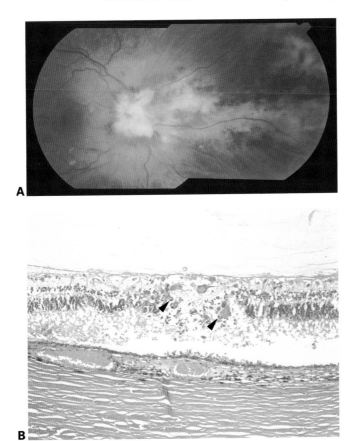

Figure 11-7 **A,** CMV retinitis/papillitis. Intraretinal hemorrhages and areas of opaque retina are present nasal to the optic disc. Note the marked optic disc and peripapillary retinal swelling and cotton-wool spots temporal to the optic disc. **B,** Histopathologically, full-thickness retinal necrosis, cytomegalo cells, and intranuclear *(arrowheads)* and/or intracytoplasmic inclusions are present. *(Part A courtesy of R. Doug Davis, MD; part B courtesy of Robert H. Rosa, Jr, MD.)*

Bacterial

See the discussion of endophthalmitis in Chapter 10. See also BCSC Section 9, *Intraocular Inflammation and Uveitis.*

Fungal

Fungal infections of the retina are uncommon, occurring almost exclusively in immunosuppressed patients as a result of fungemia. These infections usually begin as single or multiple foci of choroidal and retinal infection (Fig 11-8). The most common causative fungi are *Candida* species. Less common agents include *Aspergillus* species and *Cryptococcus neoformans.*

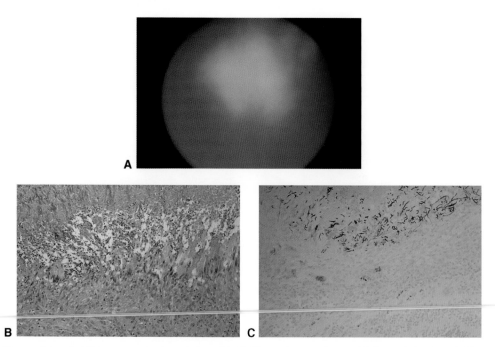

Figure 11-8 A, Vitreous, retinal, and choroidal infiltrate in a patient with fungal chorioretinitis. **B,** Granulomatous infiltration surrounding central area of necrosis. **C,** Gomori methenamine–silver nitrate stain of section parallel to **B** shows numerous fungal hyphae. *(Courtesy of David J. Wilson, MD.)*

Histopathologically, fungal infections are typified by necrotizing granulomatous inflammation. A central zone of necrosis is typically surrounded by granulomatous inflammation, and a surrounding infiltrate of lymphocytes is common. With treatment, the lesions heal with a fibrous scar. The causative agent can usually be identified by culture or by the specific features of the fungal hyphae in histopathologic material.

Toxoplasmosis

Most cases of toxoplasmosis represent reactivation of a transplacentally acquired retinal infection. Less commonly, toxoplasmic retinitis occurs as an acquired retinal infection in immunosuppressed patients. Microscopic examination of active toxoplasmic retinitis reveals necrosis of the retina, a prominent infiltrate of neutrophils and lymphocytes, and *Toxoplasma* organisms in the form of cysts and tachyzoites (Fig 11-9). There is generally a prominent lymphocytic infiltrate of the vitreous and the anterior segment. Healing brings resolution of the inflammatory cell infiltrate with encystment of the organisms in the retina adjacent to the chorioretinal scar.

Noninfectious

Noninfectious inflammatory retinal conditions include birdshot retinochoroidopathy, pars planitis, Eales disease, and cancer-associated retinopathy (CAR). See BCSC Section 9,

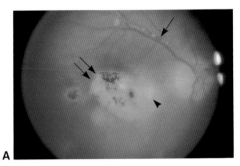 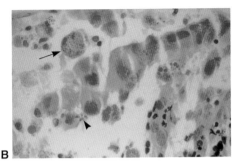

Figure 11-9 A, Chorioretinal scars with pigmentation *(double arrow)* typical of prior infection with toxoplasmosis. Active retinitis *(arrowhead)* and perivascular sheathing *(arrow)* are present. **B,** Cysts *(arrow)* and released organisms (bradyzoites, *arrowhead*) in active toxoplasmosis. *(Courtesy of Hans E. Grossniklaus, MD.)*

Intraocular Inflammation and Uveitis, and Section 12, *Retina and Vitreous,* for discussion of these conditions.

Sarcoidosis

Sarcoidosis, a systemic inflammatory process, is characterized by granulomatous inflammation without a demonstrable infectious cause (see Fig 12-8). Sarcoidosis can affect virtually any tissue within the eye, including the retina. Retinal involvement is characterized histopathologically by the presence of noncaseating granulomas. These are generally small, but when they are large, exudative retinal detachment may be present. Associated retinal findings include retinal periphlebitis, which corresponds to the clinical *taches de bougie,* or candlewax drippings; cystoid macular edema; retinal vascular occlusive disease; and retinal and optic nerve head neovascularization.

Degenerations

Typical and Reticular Peripheral Cystoid Degeneration

Typical peripheral cystoid degeneration (TPCD) is a universal finding in the eyes of people over the age of 20. In TPCD, cystic spaces develop in the outer plexiform layer. *Reticular peripheral cystoid degeneration (RPCD)* is less common. In RPCD, the cystic spaces are present in the NFL. When present, RPCD occurs posterior to areas of TPCD (Fig 11-10).

Typical and Reticular Degenerative Retinoschisis

Coalescence of the cystic spaces of TPCD forms typical degenerative retinoschisis. *Retinoschisis* is said to be present when the fluid-filled space in the outer plexiform layer is 1.5 mm or greater in diameter. *Typical degenerative retinoschisis* is present in approximately 1% of adults and is usually inferotemporal in location. *Reticular degenerative retinoschisis* is present in 1.6% of adults. In reticular degenerative retinoschisis, the splitting of retinal layers occurs in the NFL, so the inner layer of the schisis cavity is thinner than in typical

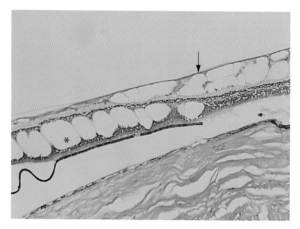

Figure 11-10 Retinal degeneration. Typical peripheral cystoid degeneration consists of cystoid spaces in the outer plexiform layer *(asterisk)* on the lower left (anterior retina). In the upper right (posterior retina), reticular peripheral cystoid degeneration *(arrow)* is present.

degenerative retinoschisis. Reticular degenerative retinoschisis tends to be more bullous than typical degenerative retinoschisis and is more likely to be associated with outer layer breaks and a more posterior location.

Lattice Degeneration

Lattice degeneration may be a familial condition (Fig 11-11). It is found in 8%–10% of the general population, but only a small number of affected persons develop retinal detachment. In contrast, lattice degeneration is seen in 20%–40% of all rhegmatogenous detachments. The most important histopathologic features of lattice degeneration include

- discontinuity of the internal limiting membrane of the retina
- an overlying pocket of liquefied vitreous
- sclerosis of the retinal vessels, which remain physiologically patent
- condensation and adherence of vitreous at the margins of the lesion
- variable degrees of atrophy of the inner layers of the retina

Although atrophic holes often develop in the center of the lattice lesion, they are rarely the cause of retinal detachment because the vitreous is liquefied over the surface of the lattice, and thus no vitreous traction occurs. Retinal detachment associated with lattice degeneration is generally the result of vitreous adhesion at the margin of lattice degeneration, leading to retinal tears in this location with vitreous detachment.

Radial perivascular lattice degeneration is a special type that has the same histopathologic features as typical lattice degeneration but occurs posteriorly along the course of retinal vessels. Radial perivascular lattice degeneration is more common in hereditary vitreoretinal degenerations such as Stickler syndrome and can be associated with severe forms of retinal detachment.

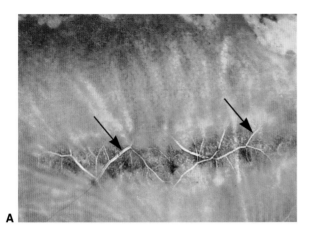

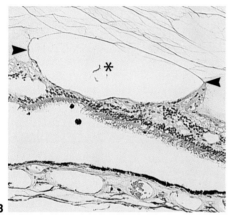

Figure 11-11 Retinal lattice degeneration. **A,** Lattice degeneration may present as prominent sclerotic vessels *(arrows)* in a wicker or lattice pattern. The clinical presentation has many variations. **B,** The vitreous directly over lattice degeneration is liquefied *(asterisk),* but formed vitreous remains adherent at the margins *(arrowheads)* of the degenerated area. The internal limiting membrane is discontinuous, and the inner retinal layers are atrophic.

Paving-Stone Degeneration

In contrast to retinal vascular occlusion, which leads to inner retinal ischemia, occlusion of the choriocapillaris can lead to loss of the outer retinal layers and RPE. This type of atrophy, called *cobblestone,* or *paving-stone, degeneration,* is very common in the retinal periphery. The well-demarcated, flat, pale lesions seen clinically correspond to circumscribed areas of retinal and RPE atrophy in which the inner nuclear layer is adherent to Bruch's membrane (Fig 11-12).

Ischemia

There are many causes of retinal ischemia, including

- diabetes
- retinal artery and vein occlusion
- radiation retinopathy
- retinopathy of prematurity
- sickle cell retinopathy
- vasculitis
- carotid occlusive disease

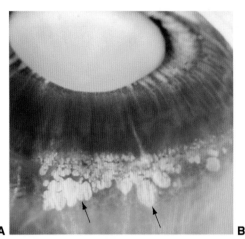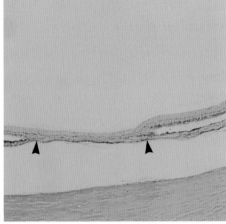

A **B**

Figure 11-12 **A,** Paving-stone degeneration appears as areas of depigmentation *(arrows)* in the periphery of the retina near the ora serrata. **B,** Histopathologically, paving-stone degeneration consists of atrophy of the outer retinal elements and chorioretinal adhesion to the remaining inner retinal elements. A sharp boundary *(arrowheads)* exists between normal and atrophic retina, corresponding to the clinical appearance of paving-stone degeneration.

Figure 11-13 Inner retinal ischemia. The photoreceptor nuclei (outer nuclear layer, *ON*) and the outer portion of the inner nuclear layer *(IN)* are identifiable. The inner portion of the inner nuclear layer is absent. There are no ganglion cells, and the NFL is absent. This pattern of ischemia corresponds to the supply of the retinal arteriolar circulation and may be observed in arterial and venular occlusions.

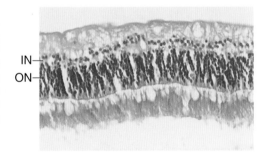

The specific aspects of some of these diseases are discussed later in the chapter. However, certain histopathologic findings are common to all the disorders that result in retinal ischemia. The retinal changes that occur with ischemia can be grouped into cellular responses and vascular responses.

Cellular responses

The neurons in the retina are highly active metabolically, requiring, on a per gram of tissue basis, large amounts of oxygen for production of adenosine triphosphate (ATP) (see also BCSC Section 2, *Fundamentals and Principles of Ophthalmology,* Part IV, Biochemistry and Metabolism). This makes them highly sensitive to interruption of their blood supply. With prolonged oxygen deprivation (greater than 90 minutes in experimental studies), the neuronal cells become pyknotic, and they are subsequently phagocytosed and disappear. The extent and location of the area of atrophic retina resulting from ischemia depends on the size of the occluded vessel and on whether it is a retinal or a choroidal blood vessel. As described earlier, the retinal circulation supplies the inner retina, and the choroidal circulation supplies the outer retina and RPE. Infarctions of the retinal circulation lead to *inner ischemic retinal atrophy* (Fig 11-13), and infarctions of the choroidal circulation lead to *outer ischemic retinal atrophy* (Fig 11-14).

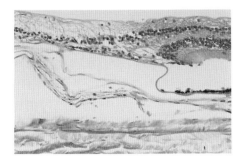

Figure 11-14 Begin at the right edge of the photograph and trace the ganglion cell and the inner nuclear layer toward the left. In this case, there is loss of the nuclei of the photoreceptor layer (outer nuclear layer), the photoreceptor inner and outer segments, and the RPE. This is the pattern of outer retinal atrophy, secondary to interruption in the choroidal vascular blood supply. Compare with Figure 11-13.

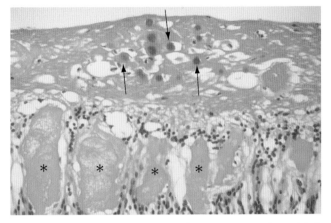

Figure 11-15 Cytoid bodies *(arrows)* within the NFL. Cystoid spaces *(asterisks)* are filled with proteinaceous fluid. *(Courtesy of W. Richard Green, MD.)*

The neuronal cells of the retina have no capacity for regeneration after ischemic damage. Following ischemic damage to the nerve fibers of the ganglion cells, *cytoid bodies* (swollen axons) become apparent histopathologically (Fig 11-15). These are localized accumulations of axoplasmic material that are present in ischemic infarcts of the NFL. *Cotton-wool spots* are the clinical correlate of ischemic infarcts of the NFL that resolve over 4–12 weeks, leaving an area of inner ischemic atrophy.

Glial cells, like axons, degenerate in areas of infarction. Proliferation of the glial cells may occur adjacent to local areas of infarction or in areas of ischemia without infarction, resulting in a glial scar.

Microglial cells are actually tissue macrophages rather than true glial cells. These cells are involved with the phagocytosis of necrotic cells as well as of extracellular material, such as lipid and blood, that accumulates in areas of ischemia. Microglial cells are fairly resistant to ischemia.

Vascular responses

Many of the vascular changes in retinal ischemia are mediated by vascular endothelial growth factor (VEGF). This growth factor is a potent mediator of vascular permeability and angiogenesis. It has been shown to play a role in numerous ocular conditions associated with vascularization.

In addition to the vascular changes secondary to ischemia itself, vascular changes may also be caused by the specific disease process responsible for the ischemia. Edema and hemorrhages are common with acute retinal ischemia. Retinal capillary closure, microaneurysms, lipid exudates, and neovascularization may develop with chronic retinal ischemia.

Edema, one of the earliest manifestations of retinal ischemia, is a result of transudation across the inner blood–retina barrier (Fig 11-16). Fluid and serum components accumulate in the extracellular space, and the fluid pockets are delimited by the surrounding neurons and glial cells. Exudate accumulating in the outer plexiform layer of the macula (Henle's layer) produces a star figure because of the orientation of the nerve fibers in this layer (Fig 11-17). In cases of chronic edema, the extracellular deposits will become richer in protein and lipids, as the water component of the exudate is more efficiently removed, resulting in so-called *hard exudates.* Histologically, retinal exudates appear as eosinophilic, sharply circumscribed spaces within the retina (Fig 11-18). Chronic edema may result in intraretinal lipid deposits that are contained within the microglial cells.

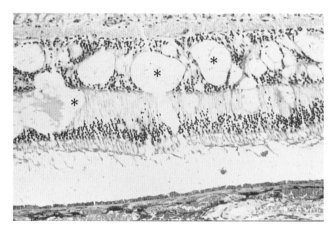

Figure 11-16 Cystoid spaces in inner nuclear and outer plexiform layers *(asterisks). (Courtesy of W. Richard Green, MD.)*

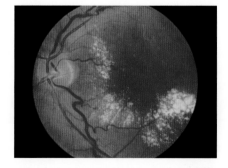

Figure 11-17 Intraretinal lipid deposits, or hard exudates. *(Courtesy of David J. Wilson, MD.)*

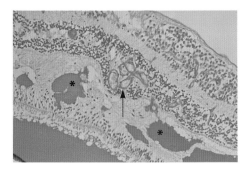

Figure 11-18 Intraretinal exudates *(asterisks)* surrounding intraretinal microvascular abnormalities *(arrow)*. *(Courtesy of W. Richard Green, MD.)*

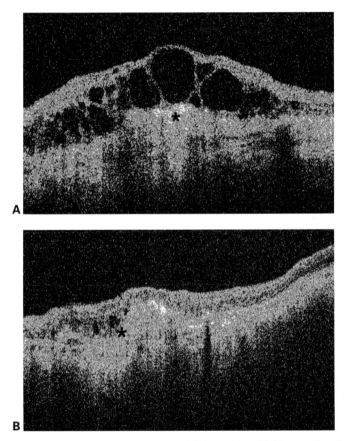

Figure 11-19 Cystoid macular edema and IVTA. OCT showing CME associated with choroidal neovascularization *(asterisk)* in exudative AMD before **(A)** and after **(B)** IVTA. *(Courtesy Robert H. Rosa, Jr, MD, and Terry Hanke, CRA.)*

Intravitreal triamcinolone acetonide (IVTA) has been employed in the treatment of various macular diseases associated with macular edema and choroidal neovascularization. Gain in visual acuity, which is mostly secondary to a decrease in macular edema, has been achieved with IVTA in such conditions as diffuse diabetic macular edema, central and branch retinal vein occlusions, pseudophakic cystoid macular edema, posterior uveitis, and choroidal neovascularization (Fig 11-19). Some studies have suggested that

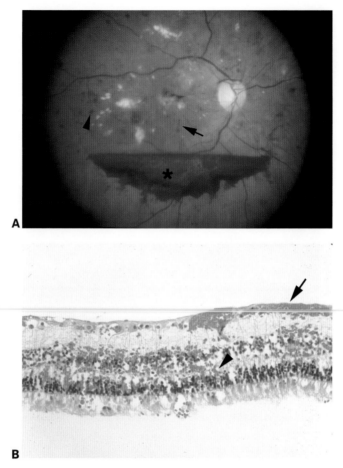

Figure 11-20 Intraretinal hemorrhage. **A,** Fundus photograph showing dot-and-blot *(arrowhead),* flame-shaped *(arrow),* and boat-shaped *(asterisk)* hemorrhages in diabetic retinopathy. **B,** Histopathologically, the dot-and-blot hemorrhage corresponds to blood in the middle layers (inner nuclear and outer plexiform layers) of the retina *(arrowhead).* The flame-shaped hemorrhage corresponds to blood in the NFL *(arrow),* and the boat-shaped hemorrhage corresponds to subhyaloid blood. *(Courtesy of Robert H. Rosa, Jr, MD.)*

IVTA may be useful as angiostatic therapy in eyes with iris neovascularization, proliferative ischemic retinopathies, and choroidal neovascularization. Hypotheses regarding the mechanism of action of IVTA include an anti-inflammatory effect, inhibition of VEGF, improvement in diffusion, and reestablishment of the blood–retina barrier through a reduction in permeability.

> Jonas JB. Intravitreal triamcinolone acetonide for treatment of intraocular oedematous and neovascular diseases. *Acta Ophthalmol Scand.* 2005;83:645–663.

Retinal hemorrhages also develop as a result of ischemic damage to the inner blood–retina barrier. As with edema and exudates, the shape of the hemorrhage conforms to the surrounding retinal tissue. Consequently, hemorrhages in the nerve fiber are

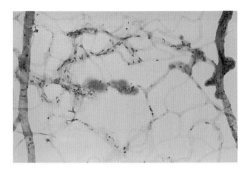

Figure 11-21 Trypsin digest preparation, illustrating acellular capillaries adjacent to dilated irregular vascular channels (IRMA). *(Courtesy of W. Richard Green, MD.)*

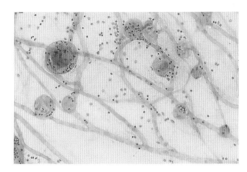

Figure 11-22 Retinal trypsin digest preparation, showing diabetic microaneurysms.

flame-shaped, whereas those in the nuclear or inner plexiform layer are circular, or "dot and blot" (Fig 11-20). Subhyaloid and sub-ILM hemorrhages have a boat-shaped configuration. White-centered hemorrhages *(Roth spots)* may be present in a number of conditions. The white centers of the hemorrhages can have a number of causes, including aggregates of white blood cells, platelets, and fibrin; or they may be due to retinal light reflexes. Hemorrhages clear over a period of time ranging from days to months.

Chronic retinal ischemia leads to architectural changes in the retinal vessels. The capillary bed becomes acellular in an area of vascular occlusion. Adjacent to acellular areas, dilated irregular vascular channels known as *intraretinal microvascular abnormalities (IRMA)* and microaneurysms often appear (Figs 11-21, 11-22). *Microaneurysms* are fusiform or saccular outpouchings of the retinal capillaries best seen clinically with fluorescein angiography and histologically with PAS-stained trypsin digest preparations. The density of the endothelial cells lining the microaneurysms and IRMA is frequently variable. Microaneurysms evolve from thin-walled hypercellular microaneurysms to hyalinized, hypocellular microaneurysms.

In some cases of retinal ischemia, neovascularization of the retina and the vitreous may occur, most commonly in diabetes and branch retinal vein occlusion. Retinal neovascularization generally consists of the growth of new vessels on the vitreous side of the ILM (Fig 11-23); only rarely does neovascularization occur within the retina itself. Hemorrhage may develop from retinal neovascularization as the associated vitreous exerts traction on the fragile new vessels. Retinal neovascularization should be distinguished from

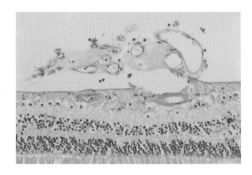

Figure 11-23 Retinal neovascularization. The new blood vessels have broken through the internal limiting membrane.

retinal collaterals and arteriovenous shunts, which represent dilation and increased flow in existing retinal vessels.

> Adamis AP, Miller JW, Bernal MT, et al. Increased vascular endothelial growth factor levels in the vitreous of eyes with proliferative diabetic retinopathy. *Am J Ophthalmol.* 1994;118:445–450.

Specific Ischemic Retinal Disorders

Central and branch retinal artery and vein occlusions

Central retinal artery occlusions (CRAO) result from

- localized arteriosclerotic changes
- an embolic event
- rarely, vasculitis (as in temporal arteritis)

As the retina becomes ischemic, it swells and loses its transparency. This swelling is best appreciated clinically and histopathologically in the posterior pole, where the NFL and the ganglion cell layer are the thickest (Fig 11-24). Because the ganglion cell layer and the NFL are thickest in the macula but absent in the fovea, the normal color of the choroid shows through in the fovea and produces a cherry-red spot, ophthalmoscopically suggesting CRAO. The retinal swelling eventually clears and leaves the classic histologic picture of inner ischemic atrophy (see Fig 11-13). Scarring and neovascularization are rare.

Branch retinal artery occlusion (BRAO) is usually the result of emboli that most frequently lodge at the bifurcation of a retinal arteriole. *Hollenhorst plaques,* which are cholesterol emboli within retinal arterioles, seldom occlude the vessel. Emboli may be the first or most important clue to a significant systemic disorder such as carotid vascular disease (Hollenhorst plaques), cardiac valvular disease (calcific emboli), or thromboembolism (platelet-fibrin emboli).

The histology of the acute phase of BRAO is characterized by swelling of the inner retinal layers with the death of all nuclei. As the edema resolves, a classic picture emerges of inner ischemic atrophy in the distribution of the retina supplied by the occluded arteriole. The NFL, the ganglion cell layer, the inner plexiform layer, and the inner nuclear layer are affected (see Fig 11-13). Arteriolar occlusions result in infarcts with complete postnecrotic atrophy of the affected layers.

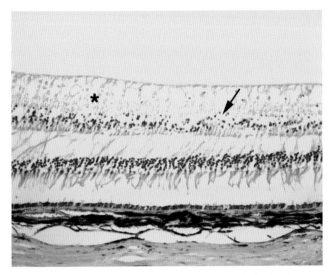

Figure 11-24 Acute central retinal artery occlusion. Histopathologically, necrosis occurs in the inner retina *(asterisk)* corresponding to the retinal whitening observed by ophthalmoscopic examination. Note the pyknotic nuclei *(arrow)* in the inner aspect of the inner nuclear layer. *(Courtesy of Robert H. Rosa, Jr, MD.)*

Central retinal vein occlusion (CRVO) occurs at the level of the lamina cribrosa. The pathophysiology of CRVO is the same as that of hemiretinal vein occlusion but different from that of branch retinal vein occlusion (see the following discussion). What has previously been called *papillophlebitis* represents a CRVO in a patient with good collateral circulation. Central retinal vein occlusions develop as a result of structural changes in the central retinal artery and the lamina cribrosa that lead to compression of the central retinal vein. This compression creates turbulent flow in the vein and predisposes to thrombosis. These structural changes occur in arteriosclerosis, hypertension, diabetes, and glaucoma.

CRVO is recognized clinically by the presence of retinal hemorrhages in all 4 quadrants. Usually, prominent edema of the optic nerve head occurs, along with dilation of the retinal veins and variable numbers of cotton-wool spots and amounts of macular edema. CRVO occurs in 2 forms: a milder perfused type and a more severe nonperfused type.

Nonperfused CRVO was defined in the CRVO study as a CRVO in which greater than 10 disc areas showed nonperfusion on fluorescein angiography. Nonperfused CRVOs typically have extensive retinal edema and hemorrhage. Marked venular dilation and a variable number of cotton-wool spots are found.

Baseline and early natural history report. The Central Vein Occlusion Study. *Arch Ophthalmol.* 1993;111:1087–1095.

Acute ischemic CRVO is characterized histologically by the following:

- marked retinal edema
- focal retinal necrosis
- subretinal, intraretinal, and preretinal hemorrhage

Vein occlusions can produce ischemia, allowing glial cells to survive and respond to the insult by replication and intracellular deposition of filaments *(gliosis)*. The hemorrhage, hemosiderosis, disorganization of the retinal architecture, and gliosis seen in vein occlusions distinguish the final histologic picture from that seen in CRAO (Fig 11-25). Numerous microaneurysms are present in the retinal capillaries following CRVO, and acellular capillary beds are present to a variable degree. With time, dilated collateral vessels develop at the optic nerve head. Neovascularization of the iris is common following CRVO.

A

B

Figure 11-25 **A,** Diffuse retinal hemorrhage following CRVO. The damaged retina will be replaced by gliosis. **B,** Histopathology of longstanding CRVO shows loss of the normal lamellar architecture of the retina, marked edema with cystic spaces *(asterisk)* containing blood and proteinaceous exudate, vitreous hemorrhage, and nodular hyperplasia of the RPE *(arrow)*. *(Part B courtesy of Robert H. Rosa, Jr, MD.)*

Branch retinal vein occlusion (BRVO) is occlusion of a tributary retinal vein. These occlusions occur almost universally at the site of an arteriovenous crossing. At the crossing of a branch retinal artery and vein, the 2 vessels share a common adventitial sheath. With arteriosclerotic changes in the arteriole, the retinal venule may become compressed, leading to turbulent flow, which predisposes to thrombosis. This condition is more common in patients with arteriosclerosis and hypertension.

BRVO occurs most commonly in the superotemporal quadrant (63% of cases). The occlusion leads to retinal hemorrhages and cotton-wool spots. Because BRVO does not always result in total inner retinal ischemia and death of all tissue, neovascularization of the optic nerve and retina may develop. Overall, 50%–60% of patients with BRVO maintain a visual acuity of 20/40 or better after 1 year. Findings in eyes with permanent visual loss from BRVO include

- CME
- retinal nonperfusion
- pigmentary macular disturbance
- macular edema with hard lipid exudates
- subretinal fibrosis
- epiretinal membrane formation

Photocoagulation therapy is considered for chronic macular edema and neovascularization.

The histologic picture of BRVO resembles that seen in CRVO but is localized to the area of the retina in the distribution of the occluded vein. Inner ischemic retinal atrophy is a characteristic late histologic finding in both retinal arterial and venous occlusions (see Fig 11-13). Numerous microaneurysms and dilated collateral vessels may be present. Acellular retinal capillaries are present to a variable degree, correlating with retinal capillary nonperfusion on fluorescein angiography.

Diabetic Retinopathy

Diabetic retinopathy is 1 of the 4 most frequent causes of new blindness in the United States and the leading cause among 20- to 64-year-olds. Early in the course of diabetic retinopathy, certain physiologic abnormalities occur:

- impaired autoregulation of the retinal vasculature
- alterations in retinal blood flow
- breakdown of the blood–retina barrier

Histologically, the primary changes occur in the retinal microcirculation. These changes include

- thickening of the retinal capillary basement membrane
- selective loss of pericytes compared with retinal capillary endothelial cells
- microaneurysm formation (see Fig 11-22)
- retinal capillary closure (see Fig 11-21) (histologically recognized as acellular capillary beds)

Dilated intraretinal telangiectatic vessels, or intraretinal microvascular abnormalities (IRMA), may develop, as shown in Figure 11-21, and neovascularization may follow (see Fig 11-23). Intraretinal edema, hemorrhages, exudates, and microinfarcts of the inner retina may develop secondary to the primary retinal vascular changes. Acutely, microinfarcts of the inner retina are characterized clinically as cotton-wool spots (see Fig 11-15). Subsequently, focal inner ischemic atrophy appears (see Fig 11-13).

Other histologic changes in diabetes

In diabetes, the corneal epithelial basement membrane is thickened. This change is associated with inadequate adherence of the epithelium to the underlying Bowman's layer, predisposing diabetic patients to corneal abrasions and poor corneal epithelial healing. Lacy vacuolation of the iris pigment epithelium occurs in association with hyperglycemia; histologically, the intraepithelial vacuoles contain glycogen (PAS-positive and diastase-sensitive). Histopathologically, thickening of the ciliary epithelial basement membrane is almost universally present in diabetic eyes. The incidence of cataract formation is increased.

Laser photocoagulation is often used in eyes with diabetic retinopathy. Argon laser photocoagulation, the type most frequently employed, results in variable destruction of the outer retina, destruction of the RPE, and occlusion of the choriocapillaris (Fig 11-26). These lesions heal by proliferation of the adjacent RPE and glial scarring.

Retinopathy of Prematurity

Retinal ischemia also plays a role in retinopathy of prematurity (ROP). This ischemia develops not because of the occlusion of existing vessels but rather because of the absence of retinal vessels in the incompletely developed retinal periphery. A decrease in retinal blood flow from oxygen-induced vasoconstriction may also be a contributing factor.

The clinical and histologic features of ROP are somewhat different from those present in other retinal ischemic states. Retinal edema and exudates do not develop. Retinal hemorrhages and retinal vascular dilation develop only in the most severe cases (*plus* or

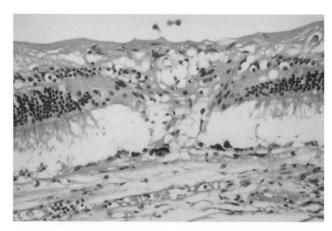

Figure 11-26 Laser photocoagulation scar characterized by absence of the RPE centrally with peripheral RPE hyperplasia and loss of the photoreceptors, the outer nuclear layer, and a portion of the inner nuclear layer. *(Courtesy of David J. Wilson, MD.)*

rush disease). Neovascularization of the retina and vitreous may develop as a result of proliferation of new vessels at the border between the vascularized and avascular peripheral retina. Fibrovascular proliferation into the vitreous at this site may lead to tractional retinal detachment, macular heterotopia, and high myopia.

Age-Related Macular Degeneration

Age-related macular degeneration (AMD) is the leading cause of new blindness in the United States. The precise pathogenesis of this disorder is not known, but genetic predisposition plays an important role. Environmental factors such as smoking and dietary intake of antioxidants may play a role in the pathogenesis of AMD. The retina seems particularly susceptible to oxidative stress because of its high concentration of oxygen, polyunsaturated fatty acids, and photosensitizers in combination with intense exposure to light. Randomized clinical trials have demonstrated a significant reduction in the risk of progression of AMD in elderly persons with a high dietary intake of antioxidants, including beta carotene, vitamins C and E, and zinc. In addition, laboratory studies have demonstrated the effects of different types of oxidative stress on the photoreceptors and RPE and suggested that the use of multiple antioxidants may be helpful in reducing oxidative damage to the photoreceptors/RPE. It is likely that AMD represents a general phenotype resulting from a variety of genetic mutations.

Age-Related Eye Disease Study Research Group. A randomized, placebo-controlled, clinical trial of high-dose supplementation with vitamins C and E, beta carotene, and zinc for age-related macular degeneration and vision loss: AREDS report no. 8. *Arch Ophthalmol.* 2001;119:1417–1436.

Lu L, Hackett SF, Mincey A, Lai H, Campochiaro PA. Effects of different types of oxidative stress in RPE cells. *J Cell Physiol.* 2006;206:119–125.

van Leeuwen R, Boekhoorn S, Vingerling JR, et al. Dietary intake of antioxidants and risk of age-related macular degeneration. *JAMA.* 2005;294:3101–3107.

Several characteristic changes in the retina, RPE, Bruch's membrane, and choroid occur in AMD. Perhaps the first detectable pathologic change is the appearance of deposits between the basement membrane of the RPE and the elastic portion of Bruch's membrane (basal linear deposits) and similar deposits between the plasma membrane of the RPE and the basement membrane of the RPE (basal laminar deposits). These deposits are not clinically visible and may require electron microscopy to be distinguished. In advanced cases, these deposits may become confluent and can be seen at the light microscopic level (Fig 11-27). This appearance has been described as *diffuse drusen,* for which there is no exact clinical correlate.

The first clinically detectable feature of AMD is the appearance of drusen. The clinical term *drusen* has been correlated pathologically to large PAS-positive deposits between the RPE and Bruch's membrane. Many eyes with clinically apparent drusen (especially soft drusen) are found to have basal laminar and/or basal linear deposits and diffuse drusen on histopathologic analysis. Drusen, which may be transient, have been classified clinically as follows:

- *hard (hyaline) drusen:* the typical discrete, yellowish lesions that are PAS-positive nodules composed of hyaline material between the RPE and Bruch's membrane (Fig 11-28)

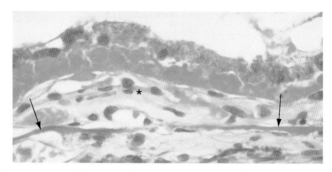

Figure 11-27 Diffuse drusen. There is diffuse deposition of eosinophilic material beneath the RPE. CNV *(asterisk)* is present between the diffuse drusen and the elastic portion of Bruch's membrane *(arrows)*. *(Courtesy of Hans E. Grossniklaus, MD.)*

Figure 11-28 Hard drusen *(arrow)*. Note the periodic acid–Schiff staining of the dome-shaped, nodular, hard druse. *(Reproduced with permission from Spraul CW, Grossniklaus HE. Characteristics of drusen and Bruch's membrane changes in postmortem eyes with age-related macular degeneration. Arch Ophthalmol. 1997;115:267–273. © 1997, American Medical Association.)*

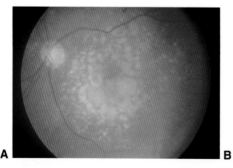

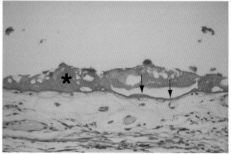

A **B**

Figure 11-29 A, Clinical photograph of multiple confluent drusen. **B,** Thick eosinophilic deposits *(asterisk)* between the RPE and the elastic portion *(arrows)* of Bruch's membrane. *(Reproduced with permission from Spraul CW, Grossniklaus HE. Characteristics of drusen and Bruch's membrane changes in postmortem eyes with age-related macular degeneration. Arch Ophthalmol. 1997;115:267–273. © 1997, American Medical Association.)*

- *soft drusen:* drusen with amorphous, poorly demarcated boundaries, usually >63 μm in size; histologically, they represent cleavage of the RPE and basal laminar or linear deposits from Bruch's membrane (Fig 11-29)
- *small drusen:* <63 μm
- *intermediate drusen:* 63–125 μm
- *large drusen:* >125 μm

- *basal laminar or cuticular drusen:* diffuse, small, regular, and nodular deposits of drusenlike material in the macula
- *calcific drusen:* sharply demarcated, glistening, refractile lesions usually associated with RPE atrophy

Photoreceptor atrophy occurs to a variable degree in macular degeneration. It is not clear whether this atrophy is a primary abnormality of the photoreceptors or is secondary to the underlying changes in the RPE and Bruch's membrane. In addition to photoreceptor atrophy, large zones of atrophy may appear in the RPE (Fig 11-30). When this occurs centrally, it is termed *central areolar atrophy of the RPE.* Drusen, photoreceptor atrophy, and RPE atrophy may all be present to varying degrees in *dry,* or *nonexudative, AMD.*

Eyes with choroidal neovascularization *(wet,* or *exudative, AMD)* have fibrovascular tissue present between the inner and outer layers of Bruch's membrane, beneath the

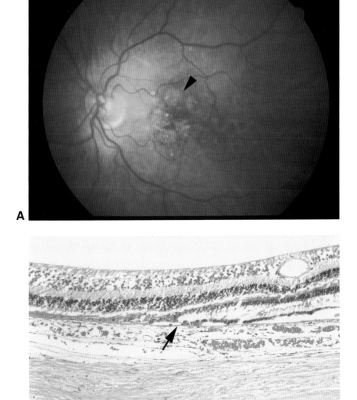

Figure 11-30 Geographic atrophy of the RPE. **A,** Fundus photograph shows focal geographic atrophy of the RPE *(arrowhead)* and drusen in nonexudative AMD. **B,** Histopathologically, there is loss of the photoreceptor cell layer, RPE, and choriocapillaris *(left of arrow)* with an abrupt transition zone *(arrow)* to a more normal-appearing retina/RPE *(right of arrow)*. Note the thickened ganglion cell layer identifying the macular region. *(Courtesy of Robert H. Rosa, Jr, MD.)*

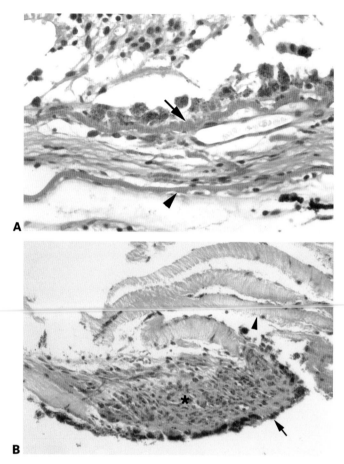

Figure 11-31 **A,** CNV located between the inner *(arrow)* and outer *(arrowhead)* layers of Bruch's membrane (sub-RPE, type 1 CNV). Note loss of the overlying photoreceptor inner and outer segments, RPE hyperplasia, and the PAS-positive basal laminar deposit *(arrow)*. **B,** Surgically excised CNV (subretinal, type 2 CNV) composed of fibrovascular tissue *(asterisk)* lined externally by RPE *(arrow)* with adherent photoreceptor outer segments *(arrowhead)*. *(Courtesy of Robert H. Rosa, Jr, MD.)*

RPE, or in the subretinal space (Fig 11-31), which leads to the exudative consequences of wet AMD. Choroidal neovascularization is associated with the presence of basal laminar deposits and diffuse drusen. The new blood vessels leak fluid, producing serous retinal detachments, and they rupture easily, leading to subretinal and intraretinal hemorrhages.

Subretinal neovascular membranes have been classified as type 1 or type 2, based on their pathologic and clinical features. *Type 1 neovascularization* (Fig 11-31A) is characterized by neovascularization within Bruch's membrane in the sub-RPE space. In this type of neovascularization, the RPE is often abnormally oriented or absent across a broad expanse of the inner portion of Bruch's membrane. *Type 2 neovascularization* (Fig 11-31B) occurs in the subretinal space and generally features only a small defect in which the RPE is abnormally oriented or absent. Type 1 neovascularization is more characteristic of AMD, whereas type 2 is more characteristic of ocular histoplasmosis. Type 2 membranes are more amenable to surgical removal than type 1 membranes because native RPE would be excised with a type 1 membrane, leaving an atrophic lesion (without RPE) in the area of membrane excision.

Grossniklaus HE, Gass JD. Clinicopathologic correlations of surgically excised type 1 and type 2 submacular choroidal neovascular membranes. *Am J Ophthalmol.* 1998;126:59–69.

Surgically excised choroidal neovascular membranes (see Fig 11-31) are composed of vascular channels, RPE, and various other components of the RPE–Bruch's membrane complex. These latter may include photoreceptor outer segments, basal laminar and linear deposits, hyperplastic RPE, and inflammatory cells.

Grossniklaus HE, Miskala PH, Green WR, et al. Histopathologic and ultrastructural features of surgically excised subfoveal choroidal neovascular lesions: submacular surgery trials report no. 7. *Arch Ophthalmol.* 2005;123:914–921.

Polypoidal Choroidal Vasculopathy

Polypoidal choroidal vasculopathy (PCV), previously described as *posterior uveal bleeding syndrome* and *multiple recurrent serosanguineous RPE detachments,* is a disorder in which dilated, thin-walled vascular channels (Fig 11-32), apparently arising from the short posterior ciliary arteries, penetrate into Bruch's membrane. Associated choroidal neovascularization is often present in these lesions, as observed in several histologic specimens. Ophthalmoscopically, the polypoidal lesions appear as elevated orange-red polyplike and

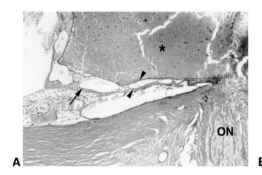

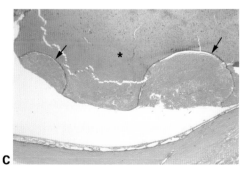

Figure 11-32 Polypoidal choroidal vasculopathy (PCV). **A,** Peripapillary dilated vascular channels *(arrow)* between the RPE and outer aspect of Bruch's membrane *(arrowheads).* Note the dense subretinal hemorrhage *(asterisk).* Optic nerve, *ON.* **B,** Higher-power view of thin-walled vascular channels *(asterisks)* interposed between the RPE and Bruch's membrane *(arrowhead).* **C,** Hemorrhagic RPE detachments *(arrows)* and serosanguineous subretinal fluid *(asterisk). (Courtesy of Robert H. Rosa, Jr, MD.)*

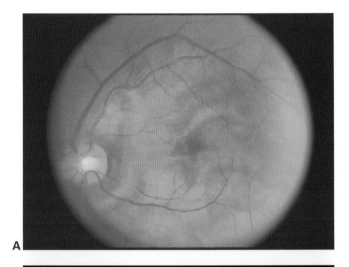

A

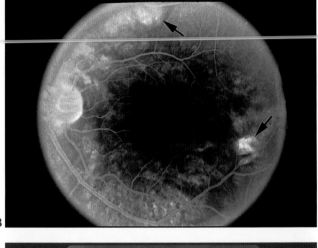

Figure 11-33 Polypoidal choroidal vasculopathy (PCV). **A,** Elevated, red-orange, nodular and tubular lesions in the peripapillary and macular regions. **B,** Late fluorescein angiogram (860 seconds) shows hyperfluorescent polypoidal lesions *(arrows)* without apparent leakage. **C,** Dense subretinal hemorrhage in same patient as in **A** and **B.** Note the persistent red-orange lesions nasal and superior to the optic disc. *(Courtesy of Robert H. Rosa, Jr, MD.)*

B

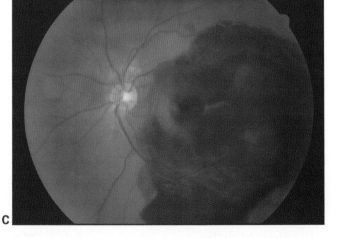

C

tubular subretinal lesions (Fig 11-33); they are often associated with serosanguineous detachments of the retina and RPE. The lesions may simulate hemorrhage from CNV associated with AMD. In Japanese and Chinese patients, the condition primarily affects men (~80%) and is generally unilateral (~85%); in Europe and the Americas, it preferentially affects darker pigmented patients (79%), with a female preponderance (96%), is more often bilateral (68%), and may be associated with hypertension (43%). More recently, polypoidal lesions have been identified in Caucasian patients, most of whom also have exudative AMD.

Rosa RH Jr, Davis JL, Eifrig CW. Clinicopathologic reports, case reports, and small case series: clinicopathologic correlation of idiopathic polypoidal choroidal vasculopathy. *Arch Ophthalmol.* 2002;120:502–508.

Macular Dystrophies

Fundus flavimaculatus and Stargardt disease

Fundus flavimaculatus and Stargardt disease are thought to represent 2 ends of the spectrum of a disease process characterized by yellowish flecks at the level of the RPE (Fig 11-34A; see also Fig 9-7, BCSC Section 12, *Retina and Vitreous*), a generalized vermillion color to the fundus on clinical examination, a dark choroid on fluorescein angiography (Fig 11-34B; see also Fig 9-8, BCSC Section 12, *Retina and Vitreous*), and gradually decreasing visual acuity. The inheritance pattern is generally autosomal recessive, but autosomal dominant forms have been reported as well. Several genetic mutations have been observed in patients with a Stargardt-like phenotype, including the *ABCA4, STGD4, ELOV4,* and *RDS/peripherin* genes. ABCA4 gene mutations are responsible for the majority of cases of Stargardt disease. The *ABCA4* gene encodes a protein called RIM protein, which is a member of the adenosine triphosphate (ATP)-binding cassette transporter family. It is expressed in the rims of rod and cone photoreceptor disc membranes and is involved in the transport of vitamin A derivatives to the RPE. The most striking feature on light and electron microscopy is the marked engorgement of RPE cells (Fig 11-34C and D; see also Fig 9-9, BCSC Section 12, *Retina and Vitreous*) with lipofuscin-like, PAS-positive material, with apical displacement of the normal RPE melanin granules.

Best disease

Best disease, or Best vitelliform macular dystrophy, is a dominantly inherited, early-onset macular degenerative disease that exhibits some histopathologic similarities to AMD. The diagnosis of Best disease is based on the presence of a vitelliform lesion (see Fig 9-10, BCSC Section 12, *Retina and Vitreous*) or pigmentary changes in the central macula and a reduced ratio of the light peak to dark trough in the electro-oculogram. Recently, mutations in the *VMD2* gene on chromosome 11q13 encoding the bestrophin protein were identified in Best disease. The gene product, bestrophin, localizes to the basolateral plasma membrane of the RPE and represents a newly identified family of chloride ion channels. Investigators have reported that bestrophins are volume-sensitive and may play a role in cell volume regulation in the RPE cells.

Fischmeister R, Hartzell HC. Volume sensitivity of the bestrophin family of chloride channels. *J Physiol.* 2005;562:477–491.

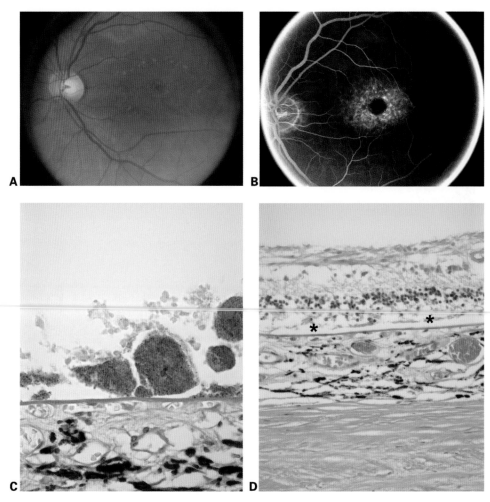

Figure 11-34 Stargardt disease. **A,** Fundus photograph shows characteristic retinal flecks and pigment mottling in the macular region. **B,** Fluorescein angiogram (midphase) shows late hyperfluorescence in a "bull's-eye" pattern in the central macula. Note the dark choroid (eg, absence of normal background choroidal blush), which is characteristic of Stargardt disease. **C,** Histopathology with periodic acid–Schiff (PAS) stain discloses hypertrophic RPE cells with numerous PAS-positive cytoplasmic granules containing lipofuscin. This histopathologic finding corresponds to the retinal flecks seen clinically. **D,** In advanced stages of Stargardt disease, geographic RPE atrophy with loss of the photoreceptor cell layer *(asterisks)* may be observed. *(Courtesy of Sander Dubovy, MD.)*

Marmorstein AD, Marmorstein LY, Rayborn M, Wang X, Hollyfield JG, Petrukhin K. Bestrophin, the product of the Best vitelliform macular dystrophy gene (VMD2), localizes to the basolateral plasma membrane of the retinal pigment epithelium. *Proc Natl Acad Sci USA.* 2000;97:12758–12763.

Pattern dystrophy

Pattern dystrophy is a heterogeneous group of retinal dystrophies that includes butterfly-shaped pattern dystrophy (BPD) and adult-onset foveomacular vitelliform dystrophy (AFMVD). BPD is characterized by a butterfly-shaped, irregular, depigmented lesion at the level of the RPE. AFMVD is characterized by the presence of slightly elevated, symmetric, solitary, round to oval, yellow lesions at the level of the RPE (Fig 11-35; see also

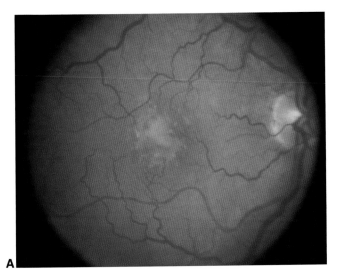

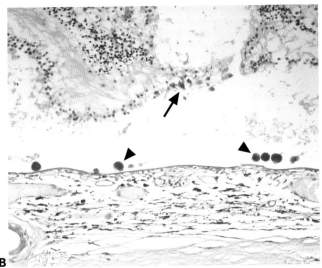

Figure 11-35 Adult-onset foveomacular vitelliform dystrophy. **A,** Yellowish, egg yoke–like lesion in the central macula. **B,** Histopathologic findings include pigment-containing cells in the subretinal space *(arrowheads)* and outer neurosensory retina *(arrow)*. **C,** Electron microscopy shows pigment-containing cells filled with lipofuscin *(arrowheads)*. *(Courtesy of Sander Dubovy, MD.)*

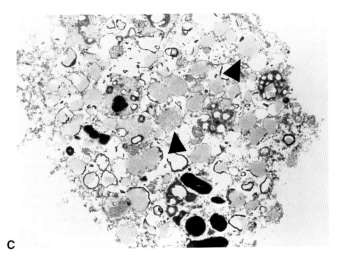

Fig 9-11, BCSC Section 12, *Retina and Vitreous*). Optical coherence tomography (OCT) has demonstrated elevation of the photoreceptor layer, with localization of the dystrophic material between the photoreceptors and RPE. The most common genetic mutation associated with the pattern dystrophies is in the *RDS/peripherin* gene. Histopathologic studies reveal central loss of the RPE and photoreceptor cell layer, with a moderate number of pigment-containing macrophages in the subretinal space and outer retina (see Fig 11-35). To either side, the RPE is distended with lipofuscin. Basal laminar and linear deposits are present throughout the macular region. The pathologic finding of pigmented cells with lipofuscin in the subretinal space correlates clinically with the vitelliform appearance.

Dubovy SR, Hairston RJ, Schatz H, et al. Adult-onset foveomacular pigment epithelial dystrophy: clinicopathologic correlation of three cases. *Retina*. 2000;20:638–649.

See BCSC Section 12, *Retina and Vitreous,* for further discussion and illustrations of macular dystrophies.

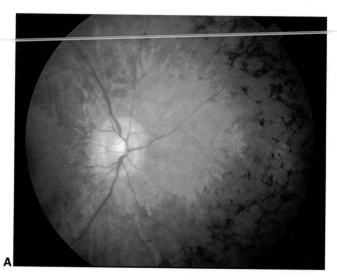

Figure 11-36 Retinitis pigmentosa. **A,** Fundus photograph shows mild optic atrophy, marked retinal arteriolar narrowing and bone spicule pigmentation in the fundus. **B,** Histopathologically, note the marked loss of photoreceptor cells and RPE pigment migration into the retina in a perivascular distribution, corresponding to the bone spicule–like pattern seen clinically. The retina is artifactitiously detached. *(Part A courtesy of Robert H. Rosa, Jr, MD.)*

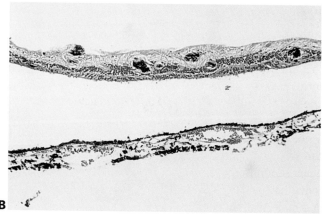

Generalized Chorioretinal Degeneration

The term *retinitis pigmentosa* is a misnomer, because clear evidence of inflammation is lacking. Retinitis pigmentosa (RP) is a group of inherited progressive retinal diseases affecting about 1 in 3500 people worldwide. The genetics of RP are complex. It can be sporadic, autosomal dominant, autosomal recessive, or X-linked. A large number of mutations can cause RP: deletions, insertions, or substitutions—all of which can cause missense, mutations, or truncations. The *RHO, RP1,* and *RPGR* genes contribute the greatest number of known mutations associated with RP. Mutations in the rhodopsin gene *(RHO)* are the most common cause of autosomal dominant RP. The disease is characterized primarily by the loss of rod photoreceptor cells by apoptosis. Cones are seldom directly affected by the identified mutations; however, they degenerate secondarily to rods.

Ophthalmoscopic findings include pigment arranged in a bone spicule–like configuration around the retinal arterioles, arteriolar narrowing, and optic disc atrophy (Fig 11-36). Microscopically, photoreceptor cell loss occurs, as well as RPE hyperplasia with migration into the retina around retinal vessels. The arterioles, although narrowed clinically, show no histologic abnormality initially. Later, thickening and hyalinization of the vessel walls appear. The optic nerve may show diffuse or sectoral atrophy, with gliosis as a late change.

Ben-Arie-Weintrob Y, Berson EL, Dryja TP. Histopathologic-genotypic correlations in retinitis pigmentosa and allied diseases. *Ophthalmic Genet.* 2005;26:91–100.

Neoplasia

Retinoblastoma

Retinoblastoma is the most common primary intraocular malignancy in childhood, occurring in 1 in 14,000–20,000 live births; the incidence varies slightly from country to country. Chapter 19 in this volume discusses retinoblastoma at length, from a more clinical point of view. Several other volumes of the BCSC cover various aspects of this topic as well; consult the *Master Index.* For American Joint Committee on Cancer (AJCC) definitions and staging of retinoblastoma, see Table A-3 in the appendix.

Pathogenesis

Although retinoblastoma was once considered to be of glial origin (lesions clinically simulating retinoblastoma were formerly called *pseudogliomas*), the neuroblastic origin of this tumor from the nucleated layers of the retina has now been established. Immunohistochemical studies have demonstrated that tumor cells stain positive for neuron-specific enolase, rod–outer segment photoreceptor–specific S antigen, and rhodopsin. Tumor cells also secrete an extracellular substance known as *interphotoreceptor retinoid-binding protein,* a product of normal photoreceptors. Recently, retinoblastoma tumor cells grown in culture have been shown to express a red and a green photopigment gene, as well as cone cell alpha subunits of transducin. These findings further support the concept that retinoblastoma may be a neoplasm of cone cell lineage. However, continuing immunohistochemical and molecular studies are adding data that complicate the hypothesis that a single cell type is the progenitor of retinoblastoma. The presence of small amounts of glial tissue within retinoblastoma suggests that tumor cells may possess the ability to differentiate into astroglia or that the resident glial cells proliferate in response to primary neoplastic cells.

The so-called *retinoblastoma gene*, localized to the long arm of chromosome 13, is deceptively named, as it does not actively cause retinoblastoma. The normal gene *suppresses* the development of retinoblastoma (and possibly other tumors, such as osteosarcoma). Retinoblastoma develops when both homologous loci of the suppressor gene become nonfunctional either by a deletion error or by mutation. Although 1 normal gene is sufficient to suppress the development of retinoblastoma, the presence of 1 normal gene and 1 abnormal gene is apparently an unstable situation that may lead to mutation in the normal gene and the loss of tumor suppression, thus allowing retinoblastoma to develop.

Dryja TP, Cavenee W, White R, et al. Homozygosity of chromosome 13 in retinoblastoma. *N Engl J Med.* 1984;310:550–553.

Histologic features

Histologically, retinoblastoma consists of cells with round, oval, or spindle-shaped nuclei that are approximately twice the size of a lymphocyte (Fig 11-37). Nuclei are hyperchromatic and surrounded by an almost imperceptible amount of cytoplasm. Mitotic activity is usually high, although pyknotic nuclei may make this difficult to assess. As tumors expand into the vitreous or subretinal space, they frequently outgrow their blood supply, creating a characteristic pattern of necrosis; calcification is a common finding in areas of necrosis (Fig 11-38). Cuffs of viable cells course along blood vessels with regions of ischemic necrosis beginning 90–120 μm from nutrient vessels. DNA released from necrotic cells may be detected within tumor vessels and within blood vessels in tissues remote from the tumor, such as the iris. Neovascularization of the iris can complicate retinoblastoma (Fig 11-39).

Cells shed from retinoblastoma tumors remain viable in the vitreous and subretinal space, and they may eventually give rise to implants throughout the eye. It may be difficult to determine histologically whether multiple intraocular foci of the tumor represent multiple

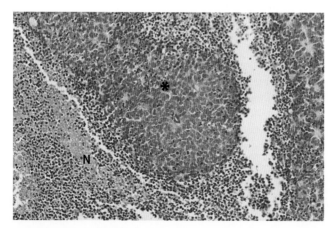

Figure 11-37 Retinoblastoma. Note the viable tumor *(asterisk)* aggregated around a blood vessel, and the alternating zones of necrosis *(N)*.

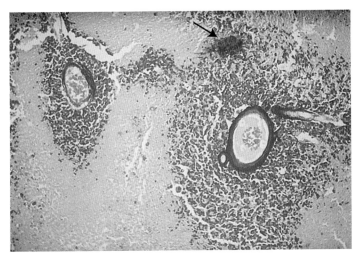

Figure 11-38 Retinoblastoma. Zones of viable tumor (usually surrounding blood vessels) alternate with zones of tumor necrosis. Calcium *(arrow)* is present in the necrotic area. The basophilic material surrounding the blood vessels is DNA, presumably liberated from the necrotic tumor.

Figure 11-39 Retinoblastoma. Note the thick iris neovascular membrane *(arrow)* and the free-floating tumor cells *(arrowhead)* in the anterior chamber.

primary tumors, implying a systemic distribution of the abnormal gene, or tumor seeds (see Fig 19-6 in Chapter 19).

The formation of highly organized *Flexner-Wintersteiner rosettes* is a characteristic feature of retinoblastoma that does not occur in other neuroblastic tumors, with the rare exception of some pinealoblastomas and ectopic intracranial retinoblastomas. Flexner-Wintersteiner rosettes are expressions of retinal differentiation. The cells of these rosettes surround a central lumen lined by a refractile structure. The refractile lining corresponds to the external limiting membrane of the retina that represents sites of attachments between photoreceptors and Müller cells. The rosette is characterized by a single row of columnar cells with eosinophilic cytoplasm and peripherally situated nuclei (Fig 11-40A). The chromatin of cell nuclei in rosettes is usually looser than that of nuclei from undifferentiated cells in adjacent tumor.

A less commonly encountered rosette, without features of retinal differentiation, known as the *Homer Wright rosette,* can be found in other neuroblastic tumors, such as neuroblastoma and medulloblastoma of the cerebellum, as well as in retinoblastoma. The

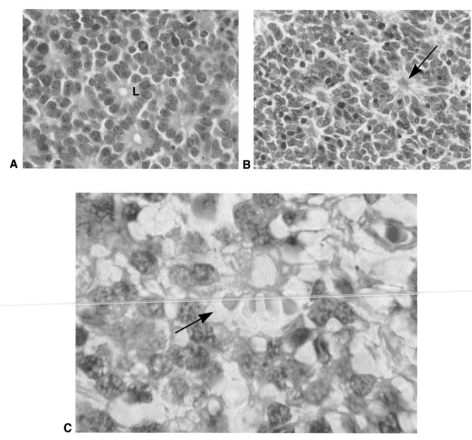

Figure 11-40 Retinoblastoma rosettes. **A,** Flexner-Wintersteiner rosettes: note the central lumen *(L)*. **B,** Homer Wright rosettes: note the neurofibrillary tangle *(arrow)* in the center of these structures. **C,** The fleurette *(arrow)* demonstrates bulbous cellular extension of retinoblastoma cells that represent differentiation along the lines of photoreceptor inner segments.

lumen of a Homer Wright rosette is filled with a tangle of eosinophilic cytoplasmic processes (Fig 11-40B).

Evidence of photoreceptor differentiation has also been documented for another flowerlike structure known as a *fleurette*. Fleurettes are curvilinear clusters of cells composed of rod and cone inner segments that are often attached to abortive outer segments (Fig 11-40C). The fleurette expresses a greater degree of retinal differentiation than does the Flexner-Wintersteiner rosette. In a typical retinoblastoma, the undifferentiated tumor cells greatly outnumber the fleurettes and Flexner-Wintersteiner rosettes, and differentiation is not an important prognostic indicator.

Progression

The most common route for retinoblastoma tumor to escape from the eye is by way of the optic nerve. Direct infiltration of the optic nerve can lead to extension into the brain. Cells that spread into the leptomeninges can gain access to the subarachnoid space, with the

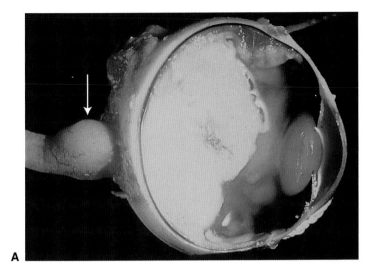

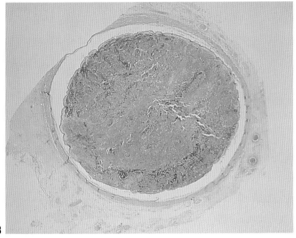

Figure 11-41 Retinoblastoma. **A,** Massive invasion of the globe posteriorly by retinoblastoma with bulbous enlargement of the optic nerve *(arrow)* caused by direct extension. **B,** A cross section of the optic nerve taken at the surgical margin of transection. Tumor is present in the nerve at this point, and the prognosis is poor.

potential for seeding throughout the central nervous system (Fig 11-41). Invasion of the optic nerve is a poor prognostic sign (Fig 11-42). See Chapter 19 for a discussion of prognosis.

Massive uveal invasion, in contrast, theoretically increases the risk of hematogenous dissemination. Spread to regional lymph nodes may be seen when a tumor involving the anterior segment grows into the conjunctival substantia propria, especially when the filtration angle is involved.

Spontaneous regression of retinoblastoma

Spontaneous regression of retinoblastoma is discussed in Chapter 19.

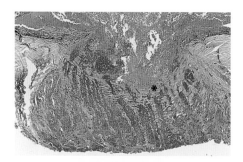

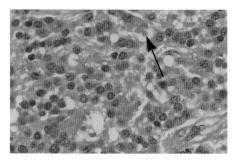

Figure 11-42 Retinoblastoma has invaded the optic nerve and extended to the margin of resection posterior to the lamina cribrosa *(asterisk).* This is an extremely poor prognostic sign.

Figure 11-43 Retinocytoma. Note the exquisite degree of photoreceptor differentiation with apparent stubby inner segments *(arrow).*

Retinocytoma

Retinocytoma is characterized histologically by numerous fleurettes admixed with individual cells that demonstrate varying degrees of photoreceptor differentiation (Fig 11-43). Retinocytoma should be distinguished from the spontaneous regression of retinoblastoma that is the end result of coagulative necrosis. See the discussion in Chapter 19.

Also referred to as *retinoma,* retinocytoma differs from retinoblastoma in the following ways:

- Retinocytoma cells have more cytoplasm and more evenly dispersed nuclear chromatin than do retinoblastoma cells. Mitoses are not observed in retinocytoma.
- Although calcification may be identified in retinocytoma, necrosis is usually absent.

Trilateral retinoblastoma

Trilateral retinoblastoma is discussed in Chapter 19.

Secondary malignancies

Patients with the genetic form of retinoblastoma have an increased risk for the development of secondary malignancies. The most common secondary malignancy is osteosarcoma. External-beam radiation therapy increases the risk of secondary malignancy. See Chapter 19 for more complete discussion of both genetic counseling for and management of retinoblastoma.

Medulloepithelioma

Also known as *diktyoma,* medulloepithelioma is a congenital neuroepithelial tumor arising from primitive medullary epithelium. This tumor usually occurs in the ciliary body but has also been documented in the retina and optic nerve. Clinically, medulloepithelioma may appear as a lightly pigmented or amelanotic, cystic mass in the ciliary body, with erosion into the anterior chamber and iris root (see Fig 23-1 in Part II, Intraocular Tumors). Although the tumor develops before the medullary epithelium shows substantial signs of differentiation, cells are organized into ribbonlike structures that have a distinct cellular

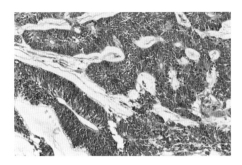

Figure 11-44 Medulloepithelioma. Histopathology shows ribbons and cords of tumor cells that seem to recapitulate the morphology of the ciliary epithelium.

polarity (Fig 11-44). These ribbonlike structures are composed of undifferentiated round to oval cells possessing little cytoplasm. Cell nuclei are stratified in 3 to 5 layers, and the entire structure is lined on one side by a thin basement membrane. One surface secretes a mucinous substance, rich in hyaluronic acid, that resembles primitive vitreous. Stratified sheets of cells are capable of forming mucinous cysts that are clinically characteristic. Homer Wright rosettes can also be seen.

Medulloepitheliomas that contain solid masses of neuroblastic cells indistinguishable from retinoblastoma are more difficult to classify. Medulloepitheliomas that have substantial numbers of undifferentiated cells with high mitotic rates and that demonstrate tissue invasion are considered malignant, although patients treated with enucleation have high survival rates, and "malignant" medulloepithelioma typically follows a relatively benign course if the tumor remains confined to the eye.

Heteroplastic tissue, such as cartilage or smooth muscle, may be found in medulloepitheliomas. Tumors composed of cells from 2 different embryonic germ layers are referred to as *teratoid medulloepitheliomas*. Malignant teratoid medulloepitheliomas demonstrate either solid areas of undifferentiated neuroblastic cells or sarcomatous transformation of heteroplastic elements.

Fuchs Adenoma

Fuchs adenoma, an acquired tumor of the nonpigmented epithelium of the ciliary body, may be associated with sectoral cataract and may simulate other iris or ciliary body neoplasms. Fuchs adenomas consist of hyperplastic, nonpigmented ciliary epithelium arranged in sheets and tubules with alternating areas of PAS-positive basement membrane material.

Combined Hamartoma of the Retina and RPE

A combined hamartoma of the retina and RPE is characterized clinically by the presence of a slightly elevated, variably pigmented mass involving the RPE, peripapillary retina, optic nerve, and overlying vitreous (see Fig 17-15). Frequently, a preretinal membrane is present that distorts the tumor's inner retinal surface. The lesion is often diagnosed in childhood, supporting a probable hamartomatous origin, but it is possible that the vascular changes are primary, with secondary changes in the adjacent RPE.

The tumor is characterized by thickening of the optic nerve head and peripapillary retina, with an increased number of vessels. The RPE is hyperplastic and frequently migrates into a perivascular location. Vitreous condensation and fibroglial proliferation may be present on the surface of the tumor.

Other Retinal Tumors

Other tumors of the retina are very rare. Massive gliosis of the retina may occur secondary to chronic retinal detachment or chronic inflammation. Various retinal tumors occur in association with some phakomatoses, including astrocytic hamartomas in tuberous sclerosis and hemangioblastomas in von Hippel–Lindau disease. The phakomatoses are discussed in BCSC Section 5, *Neuro-Ophthalmology,* and Section 6, *Pediatric Ophthalmology and Strabismus.*

Adenomas and Adenocarcinomas of the RPE

Neoplasia of the RPE is uncommon and is distinguished from hyperplasia of the RPE principally by the absence of a history or pathologic features suggesting prior trauma or eye disease. *Adenomas* of the RPE typically retain characteristics of RPE cells, including basement membranes, cell junctions, and microvilli. *Adenocarcinomas* are distinguished from adenomas by greater anaplasia, mitotic activity, and invasion of the choroid or retina. No metastases have ever been documented to occur in patients with RPE adenocarcinomas.

Spencer WH, ed. *Ophthalmic Pathology: An Atlas and Textbook.* 4th ed. Philadelphia: Saunders; 1997:1291–1313.

CHAPTER 12

Uveal Tract

Topography

The *iris, ciliary body,* and *choroid* constitute the uveal tract (Fig 12-1). The uveal tract is embryologically derived from mesoderm and neural crest. Firm attachments between the uveal tract and the sclera exist at only 3 sites:

1. scleral spur
2. exit points of the vortex veins
3. optic nerve

Iris

The iris is located in front of the crystalline lens. It separates the anterior segment of the eye into 2 compartments, the anterior chamber and the posterior chamber, and forms a circular aperture (pupil) that controls the amount of light transmitted into the eye. The iris is composed of 5 layers:

1. anterior border layer
2. stroma
3. muscular layer
4. anterior pigment epithelium
5. posterior pigment epithelium

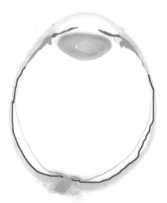

Figure 12-1 Uveal topography. The uveal tract consists of the iris *(red)*, the ciliary body *(green)*, and the choroid *(blue)*. *(Courtesy of Nasreen A. Syed, MD.)*

The anterior border layer represents a condensation of iris stroma and melanocytes and is coarsely ribbed with numerous crypts (Fig 12-2). The stroma contains blood vessels, nerves, melanocytes, fibrocytes, and clump cells. The clump cells are both macrophages containing phagocytosed pigment (type I, or clump cells of Koganei) and variants of smooth muscle cells (type II clump cells). The vessels within the stroma appear thick-walled because of a thick collar of collagen fibrils. The dilator and sphincter muscle make up the muscular layer. The posterior portion of the iris is lined by the anterior and posterior pigment epithelium, which is composed of a double layer of pigment epithelium arranged in an apex-to-apex configuration. The cell body of the anterior pigment epithelium gives rise to the dilator muscle. The color of the iris is determined by the number and size of the melanin pigment granules in the anterior stromal melanocytes.

Ciliary Body

The ciliary body, which is approximately 6.0–6.5 mm wide, extends from the base of the iris and becomes continuous with the choroid at the ora serrata. The ciliary body is composed of 2 areas:

1. the *pars plicata*, which contains the ciliary processes
2. the *pars plana*

The inner portion of the ciliary body is lined by a double layer of epithelial cells, the inner nonpigmented layer and the outer pigmented layer (Fig 12-3). The zonular fibers of the lens attach to the ciliary body processes. The ciliary muscle has 3 types of fibers:

1. longitudinal fibers (Brücke's muscle)
2. radial fibers
3. the innermost circular fibers (Müller's muscle)

These fiber groups function as a group during accommodation.

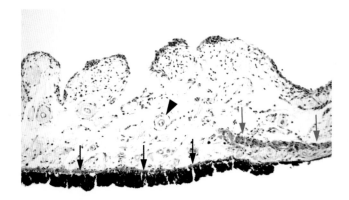

Figure 12-2 Histologic appearance of the iris: the anterior border layer is thrown into numerous crypts and folds. The sphincter muscle *(red arrows)* is present at the papillary border, whereas the dilator muscle *(black arrows)* lies just anterior to the posterior pigment epithelium. Normal iris vessels demonstrate a thick collagen cuff *(arrowhead). (Courtesy of Nasreen A. Syed, MD.)*

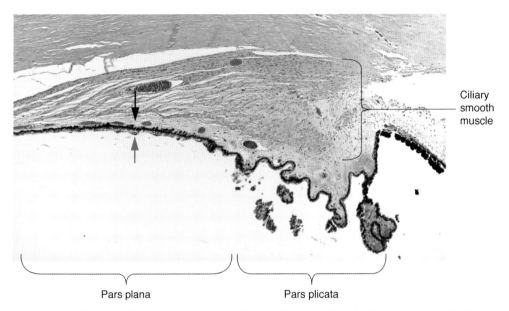

Ciliary smooth muscle

Pars plana

Pars plicata

Figure 12-3 Normal ciliary body. The ciliary body is lined with a double layer of epithelium. The inner layer is nonpigmented *(red arrow)* and the outer layer is pigmented *(black arrow)*. *(Courtesy of Nasreen A. Syed, MD.)*

Choroid

The choroid is the pigmented vascular tissue that forms the middle coat of the posterior part of the eye. It extends from the ora serrata anteriorly to the optic nerve posteriorly and consists of 3 principal layers:

1. lamina fusca (suprachoroid layer)
2. stroma
3. choriocapillaris

The choriocapillaris provides nutrients for the retinal pigment epithelium (RPE) and the outer retinal layers (Fig 12-4).

Congenital Anomalies

The entities described in the following sections are discussed in detail in BCSC Section 2, *Fundamentals and Principles of Ophthalmology,* and Section 6, *Pediatric Ophthalmology and Strabismus.*

Aniridia

True aniridia, or complete absence of the iris, is rare. Most cases of aniridia are incomplete, and a narrow rim of rudimentary iris tissue is present peripherally. Aniridia is usually bilateral, although it may be asymmetric. Histologically, the rudimentary iris consists

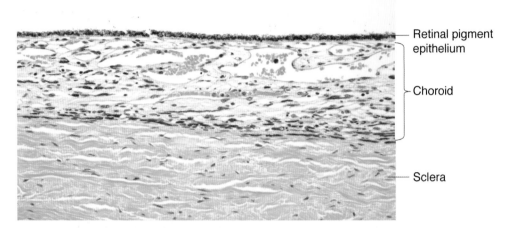

Figure 12-4 The choroid is a vascular, pigmented structure present between the retina and the sclera. The layer closest to the pigment epithelium is composed of capillaries and is known as the *choriocapillaris*. *(Courtesy of Nasreen A. Syed, MD.)*

of underdeveloped ectodermal–mesodermal neural crest elements. The anterior chamber angle is often incompletely developed, and peripheral anterior synechiae with an overgrowth of corneal endothelium are often present. These changes are most likely responsible for the high incidence of glaucoma associated with aniridia. Other ocular findings in aniridia include cataract, corneal pannus, and foveal hypoplasia.

Both autosomal dominant and recessive inheritance patterns for aniridia have been described. An association between sporadic aniridia and an increased incidence of Wilms tumor has been linked to 11p13 deletions and to mutations in the *PAX6* gene located in the same region. Microcephaly, mental retardation, and genitourinary abnormalities have also been described in association with aniridia.

> Hanson IM, Seawright A, Hardman K, et al. PAX6 mutations in aniridia. *Hum Mol Genet.* 1993;2:915–920.

Coloboma

A coloboma—the absence of part or all of an ocular tissue—may affect the iris, ciliary body, choroid, or all 3 structures. Colobomas may occur as isolated defects or as portions of more complex malformations. Typical colobomas occur as a result of faulty closure of the fetal fissure (optic groove) anywhere from the optic disc to the pupil in the inferonasal meridian. Atypical colobomas occur in locations outside the region of the fetal fissure. More than half of typical colobomas are bilateral, although they may be asymmetric.

Inflammations

BCSC Section 9, *Intraocular Inflammation and Uveitis,* discusses the conditions described in the following sections and also explains in depth the immunologic processes involved.

Infectious

The uveal tract may be involved in infectious processes that either seem restricted to a single intraocular structure or that may be part of a generalized inflammation affecting several or all coats of the eye. If the source of the infectious agent is introduced from outside the body, as with posttraumatic bacterial infection, the infection is termed *exogenous*. If, however, the infection originates elsewhere in the body, such as with a ruptured diverticulum, and subsequently spreads hematogenously to involve the uveal tract, the infection is referred to as *endogenous*. A wide variety of organisms have been shown to cause infections of the uveal tract, including bacteria, fungi, viruses, and protozoa. Obtaining a careful clinical history usually helps guide the physician in the consideration of causative agents.

Histopathology often shows a mixed acute and chronic inflammatory infiltrate within the choroid, ciliary body, or iris stroma. In cases of viral, fungal, or protozoal (eg, toxoplasmosis) agents, a granulomatous pattern of inflammation may be observed. Special tissue stains for microorganisms (tissue Gram, Gomori methenamine silver nitrate, PAS, Ziehl-Neelsen) are often helpful in identifying organisms admixed within the inflammatory reaction.

Noninfectious

Sympathetic ophthalmia

Sympathetic ophthalmia is a rare bilateral granulomatous panuveitis that occurs after accidental or surgical injury to 1 eye (the *exciting*, or *inciting, eye*) followed by a latent period and development of uveitis in the uninjured globe (the *sympathizing eye*). The inflammation in the sympathizing eye may occur as early as 9 days or as late as 50 years following the suspected triggering incident, but 4–8 weeks is the typical period of latency.

Histologically, a diffuse granulomatous inflammatory reaction appears within the uveal tract composed of lymphocytes and epithelioid histiocytes containing phagocytosed melanin pigment (Figs 12-5, 12-6). Typically, the choriocapillaris is spared. Varying degrees of

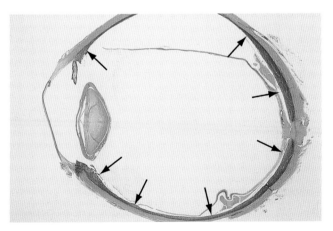

Figure 12-5 Sympathetic ophthalmia. Diffuse thickening of the uveal tract *(arrows)*. *(Courtesy of Hans E. Grossniklaus, MD.)*

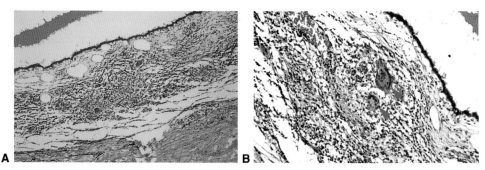

Figure 12-6 Sympathetic ophthalmia. **A,** Diffuse granulomatous inflammation within the choroid. **B,** Higher magnification shows the presence of multinucleated giant cells *(red arrows).* *(Courtesy of Hans E. Grossniklaus, MD.)*

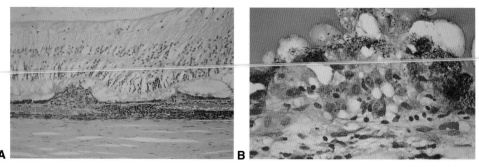

Figure 12-7 Dalen-Fuchs nodules in sympathetic ophthalmia. **A,** Focal collections of inflammatory cells are located between the RPE and Bruch's membrane. **B,** Higher magnification demonstrates the presence of epithelioid histiocytes within the nodules. *(Courtesy of Hans E. Grossniklaus, MD.)*

inflammation may be present in the anterior chamber, as evidenced by collections of histiocytes deposited on the corneal endothelium *(mutton-fat keratic precipitates). Dalen-Fuchs nodules,* which are collections of epithelioid histiocytes and lymphocytes between the RPE and Bruch's membrane, may be seen in some cases (Fig 12-7). However, Dalen-Fuchs nodules may be present in other diseases, such as Vogt-Koyanagi-Harada syndrome, and thus are not pathognomonic of sympathetic ophthalmia.

Although the etiology of sympathetic ophthalmia is not known, the pathogenesis may involve a hypersensitivity to melanin pigment, retinal S-antigen, or other retinal or uveal proteins. Experimental animal studies suggest that the penetrating ocular injury allows antigens to gain access to the lymphatic system, where they are processed and subsequently incite an immune response.

Vogt-Koyanagi-Harada syndrome

Vogt-Koyanagi-Harada (VKH) syndrome is a rare cause of posterior or diffuse uveitis that may have both ocular and systemic manifestations. The syndrome occurs more commonly in patients with Asian or Native American ancestry and usually affects individuals between 30 and 50 years of age. Ocular symptoms include bilateral decreased visual acuity, pain, redness, and photophobia. Systemic manifestations include alopecia, poliosis (loss of pigmentation of eyebrows and eyelashes), vitiligo, dysacusis, headaches, and seizures.

A chronic, diffuse granulomatous uveitis resembles that seen in sympathetic ophthalmia. In classic cases, the entire choroid is involved by the inflammatory reaction, however, without sparing of the choriocapillaris. The granulomatous inflammation may extend to involve the retina. Because the disease is one of exacerbation and remission, chorioretinal scarring and RPE hyperplasia may also be observed. Choroidal neovascularization has been described in some cases, and exudative retinal detachments may occur. The etiology of VKH syndrome is unknown. A proposed mechanism involves an immune reaction to uveal melanin-associated protein, melanocytes, or pigment epithelium. There is a strong association between HLA-DR4 and VKH syndrome.

Sarcoidosis

Sarcoidosis is a multisystem granulomatous disease characterized by inflammatory nodules, which can occur in various organs and tissues. These nodules are composed of collections of noncaseating epithelioid histiocytes admixed with lymphocytes (Fig 12-8). The uveal tract is the most common site of ocular involvement by sarcoidosis. Anteriorly, inflammatory nodules of the iris may be seen, either at the pupillary margin *(Koeppe nodules)* or elsewhere on the iris *(Busacca nodules)*. In the posterior segment, chorioretinitis, periphlebitis, and chorioretinal nodules may be seen. Periphlebitis may appear clinically as inflammatory lesions described as *candlewax drippings*. The optic nerve may be edematous due to inflammatory infiltration. Histologically, the involved tissues show infiltration by noncaseating granulomatous inflammation. Multinucleated giant cells are often present, and *asteroid bodies* (star-shaped, acidophilic bodies) and *Schaumann bodies* (spherical, basophilic, often calcified bodies) may be seen within the giant cells. Neither asteroid nor Schaumann bodies are pathognomonic for sarcoidosis, however.

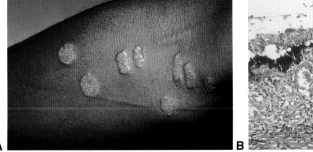
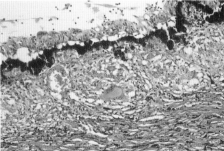

Figure 12-8 Sarcoidosis. **A,** Gross appearance of multiple discrete nodules on the skin of the upper extremity. **B,** Histopathology of sarcoid nodule showing epithelioid histiocytes and multinucleated giant cells. *(Part A courtesy of Curtis E. Margo, MD; part B courtesy of Hans E. Grossniklaus, MD.)*

Degenerations

Rubeosis Iridis

Rubeosis iridis, or neovascularization of the iris, is a common finding in surgically enucleated blind eyes. It may be associated with a wide variety of conditions (Table 12-1). Histopathologically, new vessels grow on the anterior surface of the iris and may extend to involve the angle, causing *neovascular glaucoma,* a secondary type of glaucoma. Initially, the vessels lack supporting tissue and do not possess the encircling thick fibrous cuff seen in normal iris vessels. The anterior surface of the iris leaflets often becomes flattened.

Less commonly, vessels may arise from the posterior surface of the iris. Fibrous tissue develops around the new vessels, creating fibrovascular membranes that line the anterior surface of the iris and cover the chamber angle. Myofibroblasts in the fibrovascular tissue may contract and lead to *ectropion uveae,* a displacement or dragging of the posterior iris pigment epithelium anterior to the level of the sphincter muscle. In the chamber angle, these fibrovascular membranes contribute to the formation of peripheral anterior synechiae. In advanced cases, atrophy of the dilator muscle, attenuation of the pigment epithelium, and stromal fibrosis occur.

A nonprogressive form of rubeosis iridis, consisting of small iris neovascular tufts at the pupillary margin, has also been described. The neovascular tissue may be isolated to 1 sector of the pupillary margin, or it may involve the entire margin. This condition has been described in patients with adult-onset diabetes mellitus and with myotonic dystrophy.

Table 12-1 Conditions Associated With Rubeosis Iridis

Vascular Disorders
Central retinal vein occlusion
Central retinal artery occlusion
Branch retinal vein occlusion
Carotid occlusive disease

Ocular Diseases
Intraocular inflammation
  Infectious (eg, severe corneal ulcer)
  Noninfectious (eg, uveitis)
Retinal detachment
Coats disease
Secondary glaucoma

Surgery and Radiation Therapy
Retinal detachment surgery
Radiation

Systemic Diseases
Diabetes mellitus
Sickle cell disease

Neoplastic Disease
Retinoblastoma
Melanoma of the choroid/iris
Metastatic carcinoma

Trauma

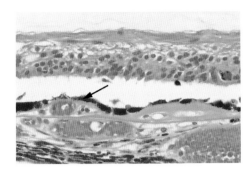

Figure 12-9 Sub-RPE neovascularization. A new blood vessel *(arrow)* lies between the RPE and Bruch's membrane.

Hyalinization of the Ciliary Body

Over time, the ciliary body processes become hyalinized and fibrosed. The thin, delicate processes become blunted and attenuated, and the stroma becomes more eosinophilic. This process is a normal aging change of the ciliary body and is not considered pathologic, although it does contribute functionally to the development of presbyopia.

Choroidal Neovascularization

New blood vessels may grow between the RPE and Bruch's membrane, a condition called *choroidal neovascularization.* Any condition that produces a disruption or break in Bruch's membrane, including age-related macular degeneration (AMD), angioid streaks, ocular histoplasmosis, and trauma, may predispose the eye to choroidal neovascularization. Complications of choroidal neovascularization include serous or hemorrhagic detachment of the RPE or retina, leading to fibrous tissue proliferation and disciform scarring (Fig 12-9). Choroidal neovascularization is discussed at length in BCSC Section 12, *Retina and Vitreous.*

Neoplasia

Iris

Nevus

An *iris nevus* represents a localized proliferation of melanocytic cells that generally appears as a darkly pigmented lesion of the iris stroma with minimal distortion of the iris architecture (see Fig 17-1). In some cases, the nevus may cause a distortion of the pupil or, less commonly, a sectoral cataract. Patients with neurofibromatosis have an increased incidence of iris nevi. There are conflicting data as to whether iris nevi occur more commonly in eyes containing posterior choroidal melanomas.

Iris nevi appear histologically as accumulations of branching dendritic cells or collections of bland-appearing spindle cells. A variety of growth patterns and cytologic appearances is possible, but cellular atypia and significant mitotic activity are not present. If the nevus is located near the pupillary margin, it may cause anterior displacement of the associated posterior pigment epithelium (ectropion uveae).

No treatment is indicated for iris nevi. They should be observed carefully over time, either through the use of photographs or with detailed drawings, to ascertain growth. See Chapter 17 for further discussion.

Melanoma

Melanomas arising in the iris tend to follow a nonaggressive clinical course compared to posterior melanomas arising in the ciliary body and choroid. The majority of iris melanomas occur in the inferior sectors of the iris (see Fig 17-3). The lesions can be quite vascularized and may occasionally cause spontaneous hyphema. Iris melanomas are uncommon, accounting for between 3.3% and 16.6% of all uveal melanomas. The average age of presentation of patients with iris melanomas is 10–20 years younger than that of patients with posterior melanomas, which ranges between 40 and 50 years. Iris melanomas may occur in the pediatric age group, however.

The modified Callender classification for posterior melanomas (see the discussion later in the chapter) may not be applicable to iris melanomas in terms of prognostic significance, because even iris melanomas containing epithelioid melanoma cell types have a relatively benign course compared with their posterior melanoma counterparts.

Although iris melanomas may grow in a localized aggressive fashion, they rarely metastasize. One exception occurs when melanomas grow to diffusely involve the entire iris stroma (Fig 12-10). In such cases, the melanoma may extend posteriorly into the chamber angle and involve the ciliary body, giving rise to the so-called *ring melanoma*. Cataract and secondary glaucoma may develop as complications of the tumor growth.

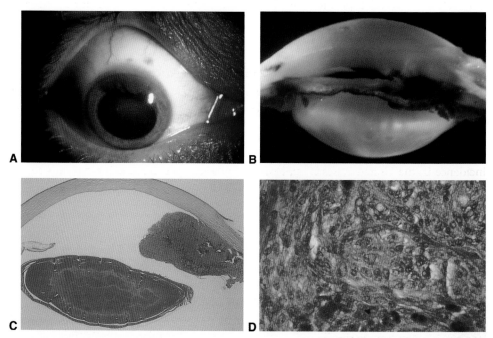

Figure 12-10   A, Clinical appearance of iris melanoma. The pigmented tumor is seen occupying the iris superiorly. **B,** Gross appearance of pigmented iris mass. **C,** Low magnification shows the iris melanoma completely replacing the normal iris stroma, extending into the anterior chamber, and touching the posterior cornea. **D,** Histopathology of iris melanoma shows numerous plump epithelioid melanoma cells containing prominent nucleoli. *(Courtesy of Hans E. Grossniklaus, MD.)*

Choroid and Ciliary Body

Nevus

Most nevi of the uveal tract occur in the choroid (see Fig 17-2). One review of 100 nevi showed that fewer than 6% involved the ciliary body; the remainder were present in the choroid. Four types of nevus cells have been described:

1. plump polyhedral
2. slender spindle (Fig 12-11)
3. plump fusiform dendritic
4. balloon cells

Depending on the size and location of the nevus, it may exert nonspecific effects on adjacent ocular tissues. The associated choriocapillaris may become compressed or obliterated, and drusen may be seen overlying the nevus. Less commonly, localized serous detachments of the overlying RPE or neurosensory retina develop.

The majority of choroidal nevi remain stationary over long periods of observation. However, the presence of nevus cells associated with some melanomas supplies evidence that melanomas may arise from previous choroidal nevi.

Melanocytoma

The melanocytoma is a specific type of uveal tract nevus (magnocellular nevus) that warrants separate consideration. These jet black lesions may occur anywhere in the uveal tract, but they most commonly appear in the peripapillary region (see Fig 17-12).

Histologically, a melanocytoma is composed of plump polyhedral cells with small nuclei and abundant cytoplasm. Because the nevus cells are so heavily pigmented, it is usually necessary to obtain bleached sections to accurately study the cytologic features. Areas of cystic degeneration or necrosis may be observed.

Melanoma

Choroidal melanoma is the most common primary intraocular malignancy in adults. The incidence in the United States is approximately 6 cases per million. The tumor is rare in children and primarily affects patients between 50 and 70 years old. Melanomas occur most commonly in whites or other lightly pigmented individuals. Ocular melanocytic conditions

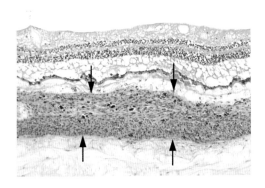

Figure 12-11 Spindle cell nevi *(between arrows)* are composed of slender, spindle-shaped cells with thin, homogeneous nuclei. *(Courtesy of Nasreen A. Syed, MD.)*

such as ocular and oculodermal melanocytosis (nevus of Ota) have been shown to be risk factors for the development of choroidal melanoma.

Ciliary body melanomas may be asymptomatic in their early stages, as they can remain hidden behind the iris. As they enlarge, they may cause displacement of the lens and sectoral cataracts. Ciliary body tumors may erode through the iris root and present as a peripheral iris mass. Other ciliary body melanomas can extend directly through the sclera, creating an epibulbar mass. Dilated episcleral vessels, *sentinel vessels,* may be visible directly over the tumor (see Fig 17-6). In rare cases, the tumor may grow circumferentially to involve the entire ciliary body. This growth pattern is referred to as a *ring melanoma.*

The location and size of posterior choroidal melanomas determine the patient's presenting symptoms. A peripheral lesion may go undetected for a protracted period, whereas a posterior pole tumor affecting the macula and, therefore, vision, may present quite early.

Choroidal melanomas are typically brown, elevated, dome-shaped subretinal masses. The degree of pigmentation is variable, ranging from dark brown to completely amelanotic. Over time, the tumor may break through the overlying Bruch's membrane, producing a collar-button or mushroom-shaped configuration. Prominent clumps of orange pigment (lipofuscin) at the level of the RPE may be present overlying the melanomas, and localized serous detachment of the sensory retina is frequently present.

Several factors have been significantly correlated with survival in patients with choroidal and ciliary body melanomas. The 2 most important variables associated with survival are

1. the size of the largest tumor dimension in contact with the sclera
2. the cell type making up the tumor

The modified Callender classification is used for the cytologic classification of uveal melanomas:

- spindle cell nevus
- spindle cell melanoma
- epithelioid melanoma
- mixed-cell type (mixture of spindle and epithelioid cells)

Occasionally, a melanoma undergoes extensive necrosis, which precludes classification.

Spindle cell melanoma has the best prognosis and epithelioid melanoma the worst. Melanomas of mixed-cell type have an intermediate prognosis. Some authors have suggested that survival following enucleation decreases with increasing proportions of epithelioid cells in mixed-cell melanomas. Totally necrotic melanomas assume the same prognosis as mixed-cell melanomas.

The modified Callender classification has some disadvantages. First, there is continuing controversy about the minimum number of epithelioid cells needed for a melanoma to be classified as mixed-cell type. Second, the scheme is difficult to reproduce, even among experienced ophthalmic pathologists. This difficulty arises because the cytologic features of the melanoma cells reflect a continuous spectrum (Figs 12-12 through 12-14).

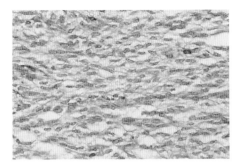

Figure 12-12 Spindle-A cells are characterized by low nuclear-to-cytoplasmic ratios. Neither nucleoli nor mitoses are observed, and a central stripe may be noted down the long axis of the nucleus. Tumors composed exclusively of spindle-A cells are considered to be nevi.

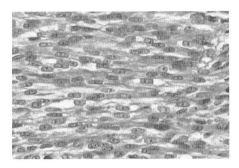

Figure 12-13 Spindle-B cells demonstrate a higher nuclear-to-cytoplasmic ratio; more coarsely granular chromatin; and plumper, large nuclei. Mitotic figures and nucleoli are present, although not in large numbers. Tumors composed of mixtures of spindle-A and spindle-B cells are designated spindle cell melanomas.

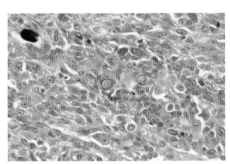

Figure 12-14 Epithelioid melanoma cells. Patients with this type of melanoma have the poorest prognosis. Cells resemble epithelium because of abundant eosinophilic cytoplasm and enlarged oval to polygonal nuclei. Epithelioid melanoma cells often lack cohesiveness and demonstrate marked pleomorphism, including the formation of multinucleated tumor giant cells. Nuclei have a conspicuous nuclear membrane, very coarse chromatin, and large nucleoli.

Cytomorphometric measurements of melanoma cells have been studied. One such measurement is the *mean of the 10 largest melanoma cell nuclei (MLN)*. This parameter has been shown to correlate well with mortality after enucleation. The correlation of morphometry is enhanced further when combined with the largest dimension of scleral contact by tumor.

Intrinsic tumor microvascular patterns have also been studied and shown to have prognostic significance. Tumors containing more complex microvascular patterns such as vascular closed loops or vascular networks (3 vascular loops located back-to-back) are associated with an increased incidence of the development of subsequent metastases (Fig 12-15).

As mentioned earlier, melanomas may break through the overlying Bruch's membrane and assume a mushroom-shaped configuration (Fig 12-16). Tumors may also contribute to serous detachments of the overlying and adjacent retina, with subsequent degenerative

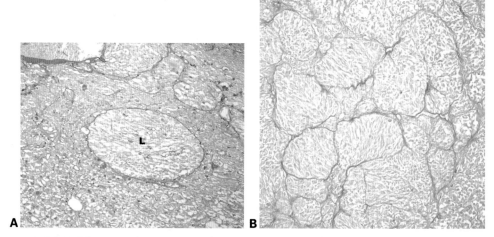

Figure 12-15 Microvascular patterns in uveal melanoma. **A,** Microvascular closed loop *(L)*. **B,** Microvascular network: 3 or more back-to-back loops. *(Courtesy of Nasreen A. Syed, MD.)*

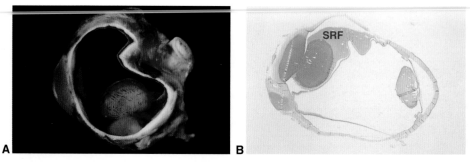

Figure 12-16 Choroidal melanoma with rupture through Bruch's membrane. **A,** Gross appearance. **B,** Microscopic appearance. Note the subretinal fluid *(SRF)* adjacent to the tumor.

changes in the outer segments of the photoreceptors. Melanomas may extend through scleral emissary channels to gain access to the episcleral surface and the orbit (Fig 12-17). Less commonly, aggressive melanomas may directly invade the underlying sclera or overlying retina (Fig 12-18).

Tumor necrosis can incite variable degrees of intraocular inflammation. Direct invasion of the anterior chamber may lead to secondary glaucoma. In addition, tumor necrosis may lead to the liberation of melanin pigment, which can then gain access to the anterior chamber and angle, causing a type of secondary glaucoma called *melanomalytic glaucoma*.

Lymphatic spread of ciliary body and choroidal melanomas is rare. Metastases almost invariably result from the hematogenous spread of melanoma to the liver. The reason for the propensity of melanomas to spread to the liver is unknown, although more than 95% of tumor-related deaths have liver involvement. In as many as one third of tumor-related deaths, the liver is the sole site of metastasis.

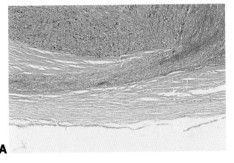

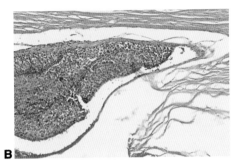

A

B

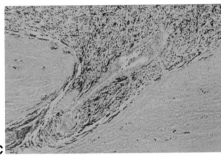

C

Figure 12-17 **A,** Note the melanoma cells tracking along scleral emissary canals. **B,** Melanoma is found within the vortex vein. **C,** Some melanomas track along the outer sheaths of vortex veins and nerves.

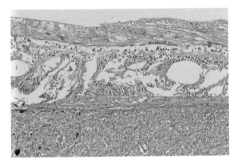

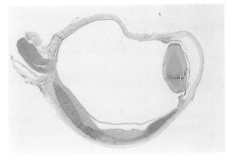

Figure 12-18 Note the retinal degeneration overlying this choroidal melanoma and the retinal invasion by tumor.

Figure 12-19 Some melanomas form diffuse, placoid growths.

Some types of uveal melanomas show biologic behavior that cannot be predicted according to the criteria just discussed. Survival rates of patients with diffuse ciliary body melanomas (ring melanoma) are particularly poor. These relatively flat tumors are almost always of mixed-cell type, and they may grow circumferentially without becoming significantly elevated. Diffuse choroidal melanomas similarly have a poor prognosis (Figs 12-19, 12-20).

For further discussion, see Chapter 17. For American Joint Committee on Cancer (AJCC) definitions and staging of uveal melanomas, see Table A-4 in the appendix.

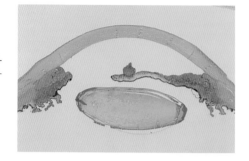

Figure 12-20 By definition, a ring melanoma follows the major arterial circle of the iris circumferentially around the eye.

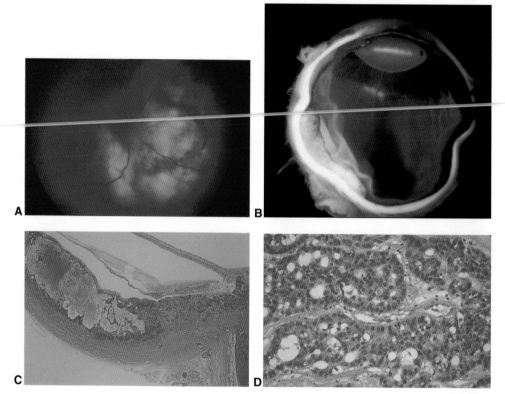

Figure 12-21 **A,** Clinical appearance of a metastatic lesion from a primary lung tumor. **B,** Gross appearance of lesion. **C,** Choroidal metastasis from lung adenocarcinoma; histopathology shows adenocarcinoma with mucin production. **D,** Higher magnification depicts a well-differentiated adenocarcinoma with distinct glandular appearance. *(Courtesy of Hans E. Grossniklaus, MD.)*

Metastatic Tumors

Metastatic lesions are the most common intraocular tumors in adults. These lesions most often involve the choroid, but any ocular structure can be affected. Unlike primary uveal melanoma, metastatic lesions are often multiple and may be bilateral. Although these lesions typically assume a flattened growth pattern, rare cases of collar-button or mushroom-shaped lesions have been reported. The most common primary tumors metastasizing to the eye are breast carcinoma in women and lung carcinoma in men (Fig 12-21).

Other primary tumors with reported metastases to the uveal tract include cutaneous melanoma, prostate adenocarcinoma, renal cell carcinoma, and carcinoid tumors. Histologically, metastatic tumors may recapitulate the appearance of the primary lesion, or they may appear less differentiated. Special histochemical and immunohistochemical stains can be helpful in diagnosing the metastatic lesion and determining its origin. The importance of a careful clinical history cannot be overemphasized. See Chapter 20 for further discussion and multiple photographs.

Other Uveal Tumors

Hemangioma

Hemangiomas of the choroid occur in 2 specific forms. The *localized* choroidal hemangioma typically occurs in patients without systemic disorders. It generally appears as a red or orange tumor located in the postequatorial zone of the fundus. Such tumors commonly produce a secondary retinal detachment. If the detachment extends into the foveal region, blurred vision, metamorphopsia, and micropsia may occur. These benign vascular tumors characteristically affect the overlying RPE and cause cystoid degeneration of the outer retinal layers.

The *diffuse* choroidal hemangioma is generally seen in patients with Sturge-Weber syndrome (encephalofacial angiomatosis). This choroidal tumor produces diffuse reddish orange thickening of the entire fundus, resulting in an ophthalmoscopic pattern commonly referred to as the *tomato catsup fundus.* Retinal detachment and glaucoma often occur in eyes with this lesion. (See also BCSC Section 5, *Neuro-Ophthalmology;* Section 6, *Pediatric Ophthalmology and Strabismus;* and Section 12, *Retina and Vitreous.*)

Histopathologically, both the diffuse and localized hemangiomas show collections of variably sized vessels within the choroid (Fig 12-22). The lesions may appear

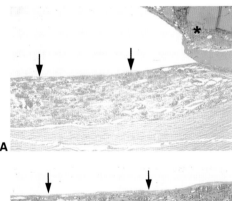

Figure 12-22 Choroidal hemangioma with a large number of thin-walled, variably sized vessels within the choroid. **A,** Low-magnification view illustrating exudative retinal detachment overlying the lesion *(asterisk). Arrows* designate Bruch's membrane. **B,** Higher magnification; *arrows* designate Bruch's membrane. *(Courtesy of Nasreen A. Syed, MD.)*

as predominantly capillary hemangiomas, cavernous hemangiomas, or a mixed pattern of both. The adjacent and overlying choroid may show compressed melanocytes, hyperplastic RPE, and fibrous tissue proliferation.

When choroidal hemangiomas are asymptomatic, generally no treatment is indicated. The most common complication is serous detachment of the retina involving the fovea, with resultant visual loss. If this complication occurs, the surface of the tumor can be treated lightly with argon laser photocoagulation. The treatment goal is not to destroy the tumor but rather to create a chorioretinal adhesion that prevents further accumulation of fluid. If the retinal detachment is extensive, photocoagulation is usually unsuccessful. Recurrent detachments are common, and the long-term visual prognosis in patients with macular detachment or edema is guarded. See also Chapter 18 and Figures 18-1 and 18-2.

Choroidal osteoma

Choroidal osteomas are benign bony tumors that typically arise from the juxtapapillary choroid and are seen in adolescent to young adult patients, more commonly women than men. The characteristic lesion appears yellow to orange and has well-defined margins (see Fig 17-14). Histopathologically, the tumor is composed of unremarkable-appearing compact bone located in the peripapillary choroid. The intratrabecular spaces are filled with a loose connective tissue containing large and small blood vessels, vacuolated mesenchymal cells, and scattered mast cells. The bony trabeculae contain osteocytes, cement lines, and occasional osteoclasts.

Choroidal osteomas typically enlarge slowly over many years. If the tumor involves the macula, vision is generally impaired. Subretinal neovascularization is a common complication of macular choroidal osteoma. Both choroidal osteoma and hemangioma may mimic a choroidal melanoma clinically and should, therefore, be included in the differential diagnosis of choroidal melanoma.

Neural sheath tumors

Schwannomas (neurilemomas) and neurofibromas are rare tumors of the uveal tract. Multiple neurofibromas may occur in the ciliary body, iris, and choroid in patients with neurofibromatosis. The histopathologic features of neurofibromas are discussed in Chapter 14, Orbit.

Leiomyoma

Neoplasms arising from the smooth muscle of the ciliary body have been reported only rarely. By light and transmission electron microscopy, these tumors may exhibit both myogenic and neurogenic features. In such cases, the term *mesectodermal leiomyoma* is employed.

Lymphoid proliferation

The choroid may be the site of lymphoid proliferation, either as a primary ocular process or in association with systemic lymphoproliferative disease.

Uveal lymphoid infiltration (formerly *reactive lymphoid hyperplasia*) of the uveal tract is similar to the spectrum of low-grade lymphoid lesions that occur in the orbit (see Chapter 14, Orbit) and conjunctiva. There may be diffuse involvement of the uveal

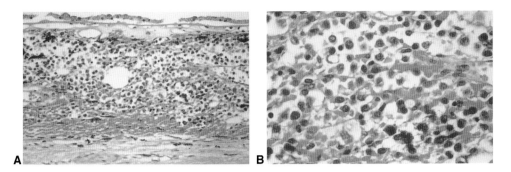

Figure 12-23 **A,** Diffuse expansion of choroid by lymphoma. **B,** Higher magnification depicts atypical lymphocytes. *(Courtesy of Hans E. Grossniklaus, MD.)*

tract by a mixture of lymphocytes and plasma cells, and lymphoid follicles may be present. Lymphocyte typing reveals a polymorphic population without clonal restriction; this finding distinguishes inflammatory pseudotumor from lymphoma.

> Grossniklaus HE, Martin DF, Avery R, et al. Uveal lymphoid infiltration: report of four cases and clinicopathologic review. *Ophthalmology.* 1998;105:1265–1273.

Lymphoma of the uveal tract occurs almost exclusively in association with systemic lymphoma (Fig 12-23). The classification of lymphomas is discussed in Chapter 14.

Trauma

The uveal tract is frequently involved in cases of ocular trauma. *Prolapse* of uveal tissue through a perforating ocular injury is a common association. *Rupture* of the choroid may occur as the result of a blunt or penetrating injury. The pattern of the rupture most frequently appears as semicircular lines circumscribing the peripapillary region. If the macula is involved, the prognosis for vision recovery is guarded. Subretinal neovascularization can occur as a late complication. More severe injury may cause rupture of both the choroid and retina, a condition termed *chorioretinitis sclopetaria.*

Choroidal detachment, either localized or diffuse, may occur after accidental or surgical trauma. Serous or hemorrhagic fluid accumulates in the suprachoroidal space between the choroid and the sclera. Depending on the etiology, the fluid may spontaneously resorb, allowing for reattachment of the choroid. In other cases, surgical drainage of the fluid may be required.

CHAPTER **13**

Eyelids

Topography

The eyelids extend from the eyebrow superiorly to the cheek inferiorly and can be subdivided into orbital and tarsal components. At the level of the tarsus, the eyelid consists of 4 main histologic layers, from anterior to posterior:

- skin
- orbicularis oculi muscle
- tarsus
- palpebral conjunctiva

A surgical plane of dissection through an incision along the gray line of the eyelid margin is possible between the orbicularis and the tarsus, functionally dividing the eyelid into anterior and posterior lamellae (Fig 13-1). BCSC Section 7, *Orbit, Eyelids, and Lacrimal System,* covers the anatomy of the eyelids as well as the conditions discussed later in this chapter in detail.

The skin of the eyelids is thinner than that of most other body sites. It consists of an epidermis of keratinizing stratified squamous epithelium, which also contains melanocytes and antigen-presenting Langerhans cells; and a dermis of loose collagenous connective tissue, which contains the following:

- cilia and associated sebaceous glands (of Zeis)
- apocrine sweat glands (of Moll)
- eccrine sweat glands
- pilosebaceous units

Lid retraction is effected by the *levator palpebrae superioris,* which in the eyelid is an aponeurosis, and the *Müller muscle* (smooth muscle connecting the upper border of the tarsus with the levator). Forceful eyelid closure is accomplished by the *orbicularis oculi* (striated skeletal muscle). The *tarsal plate,* a thick plaque of dense, fibrous connective tissue, contains the sebaceous meibomian glands. Also present near the upper border of the superior tarsal plate (and less so along the lower border of the inferior tarsal plate) are the accessory lacrimal glands of Wolfring; the accessory lacrimal glands of Krause are located in the conjunctival fornices. The *palpebral conjunctiva* is tightly adherent to the posterior

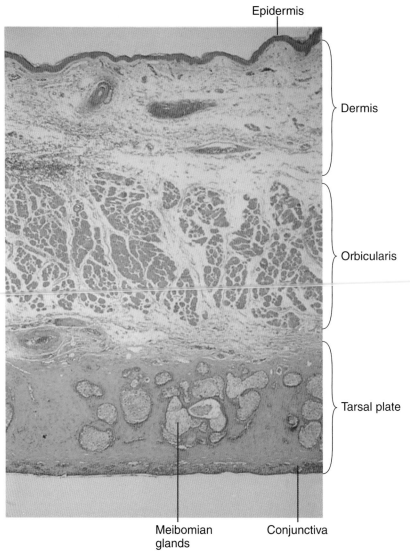

Figure 13-1 Cross section of a normal eyelid. Proceeding from top to bottom, note the epidermis, the dermis resting on the orbicularis, the tarsus surrounding the meibomian glands, and the palpebral (tarsal) conjunctiva.

Table 13-1 Glands of the Eyelid: Function and Pathology

Secretory Element	Normal Function	Pathology
Conjunctival goblet cells	Mucin secretion to enhance corneal wetting	Numbers diminished in some dry-eye states Present in mucoepidermoid carcinoma
Accessory lacrimal glands of Krause and Wolfring	Basal tear secretion of the aqueous layer	Sjögren syndrome Graft-vs-host disease Rare tumors (benign mixed tumor)
Meibomian glands	Secretion of lipid layer of tears to retard evaporation	Chalazion Sebaceous carcinoma
Sebaceous glands of Zeis	Lubrication of the cilia	External hordeolum Sebaceous carcinoma
Glands of Moll	Lubrication of the cilia	Ductal cyst (sudoriferous cyst, apocrine hidrocystoma) Apocrine carcinoma
Eccrine glands	Secretions for temperature control, electrolyte balance	Ductal cyst (sudoriferous cyst, eccrine hidrocystoma) Syringoma Sweat gland carcinoma

surface of the tarsus. Table 13-1 lists the normal functions of the eyelid glands and some of the pathologic conditions related to them.

Following are several terms used commonly in dermatopathology:

- *acanthosis:* increased thickness (hyperplasia) of the stratum malpighii (consisting of the strata basale, spinosum, and granulosum) of the epidermis
- *hyperkeratosis:* increased thickness of the stratum corneum of the epidermis
- *parakeratosis:* retention of nuclei within the stratum corneum with corresponding absence of the stratum granulosum
- *papillomatosis:* formation of fingerlike upward projections of epidermis lining fibrovascular cores
- *dyskeratosis:* premature individual cell keratinization within the stratum malpighii
- *acantholysis:* loss of cohesion (dissolution of intercellular bridges) between adjacent epithelial cells
- *spongiosis:* widening of intercellular spaces between cells in the stratum malpighii due to edema

Congenital Anomalies

BCSC Section 7, *Orbit, Eyelids, and Lacrimal System,* also discusses congenital anomalies, including those not mentioned here (eg, congenital ptosis).

Distichiasis

Distichiasis is the aberrant formation within the tarsus of cilia that exit the eyelid margin through the orifices of the meibomian glands. Although these lashes may rub against the eye, they are relatively well tolerated initially and may not cause symptoms of irritation until early childhood. Distichiasis is inherited in an autosomal dominant fashion and is usually the only congenital anomaly present. It may, however, be associated with other anomalies such as mandibulofacial dysostosis and trisomy 18. The pathogenesis of distichiasis is thought to be an anomalous formation within the tarsus of a complete pilosebaceous unit rather than the normal sebaceous (meibomian) gland.

Phakomatous Choristoma

A rare congenital tumor, phakomatous choristoma (Zimmerman tumor) is formed from the aberrant location of lens epithelium within the inferonasal portion of the lower eyelid. These cells may undergo cytoplasmic enlargement, identical to the "bladder" cell in a cataractous lens. PAS-positive basement membrane material is produced, recapitulating the lens capsule. The nodule formed is usually present at birth and enlarges slowly. Complete excision is the usual treatment.

Dermoid Cyst

Dermoid cysts may occur in the eyelid, but they are more common in the orbit and are discussed in Chapter 14.

Inflammations

Infectious

Depending on the causative agent, infections of the eyelids may produce disease that is localized (eg, hordeolum), multicentric (eg, papillomas), or diffuse (cellulitis). Routes of infection may be primary inoculation through a bite or wound, direct spread from a contiguous site such as a paranasal sinus infection, or hematogenous dissemination from a remote site. Infectious agents may be

- bacterial, such as *Staphylococcus aureus* in hordeolum and infectious blepharitis
- viral, as in papillomas caused by human papillomavirus (HPV)
- fungal, such as blastomycosis, coccidioidomycosis, or aspergillosis

Hordeolum

Also known as a *stye,* hordeolum is a primary, acute, self-limited inflammatory process typically involving the glands of Zeis and, less often, the meibomian glands of the upper eyelid. A small abscess, or focal collection of polymorphonuclear leukocytes and necrotic debris, forms at the site of infection. Healing occurs without visible scarring in most cases.

Cellulitis

The diffuse spread of acute inflammatory cells through tissue planes is known as *cellulitis.* The pathologic change is often accompanied by vascular congestion and edema (Fig 13-2).

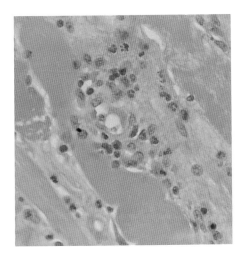

Figure 13-2 Polymorphonuclear leukocytes dissect between the skeletal muscle fibers of the orbicularis in this biopsy of a preseptal cellulitis of the eyelid.

Preseptal cellulitis involves the tissues of the eyelid anterior to the orbital septum, the fibrous membrane connecting the borders of the tarsal plates to the bony orbital rim. The condition most commonly affects the pediatric population and is most often secondary to upper respiratory tract infections caused by bacteria such as *Streptococcus pneumoniae*.

Viral infections

Examples of 2 types of viral infections involving the eyelids are viral papillomas and molluscum contagiosum. Virally induced *papillomas* of the eyelid are seen in young patients and are caused by HPV subtypes 6 and 11, those also associated with verruca. The papillomas are pedunculated growths along the eyelid margin composed of acanthotic and hyperkeratotic epidermis lining papillary fibrovascular cores. Koilocytotic cytoplasmic clearing of infected epithelial cells may be present. The growths may spontaneously regress over months to years if not surgically excised or ablated by cryotherapy. Lesions with a papillomatous appearance seen in middle-aged or elderly persons include seborrheic keratosis, actinic keratosis, intradermal nevus, and acrochordon (fibroepithelial polyp).

Molluscum contagiosum is caused by a member of the poxvirus family and also typically affects young or immunocompromised persons. Dome-shaped, waxy epidermal nodules with central umbilication form and, if present on the eyelid margin, may cause a secondary follicular conjunctivitis (Fig 13-3). Histopathologically, the lesions are distinctive, with a nodular proliferation of infected epithelium producing a central focus of necrotic cells that are extruded to the skin surface (Fig 13-4). As the replicating virus fills the cytoplasm, the nucleus is displaced peripherally and finally disappears as the cells are shed. Incision and curettage are usually curative.

Noninfectious

Chalazion

A chalazion is a chronic, often painless nodule of the eyelid that occurs when the lipid secretions of the meibomian glands or, less often, the glands of Zeis are discharged into the surrounding tissues, inciting a lipogranulomatous reaction (Fig 13-5). Because the lipid is dissolved by solvents during routine tissue processing, histologic sections show

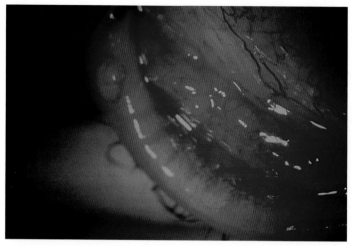

Figure 13-3 Molluscum contagiosum involving the eyelid margin. Note the associated follicular conjunctivitis.

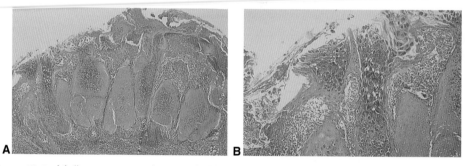

A   B

Figure 13-4 Molluscum contagiosum. **A,** Note the cup-shaped, thickened epidermis with a central crater. **B,** Note the eosinophilic inclusion bodies becoming basophilic as they migrate to the surface.

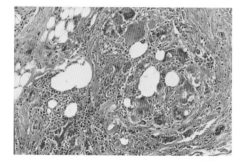

Figure 13-5 Chalazion. Granulomatous inflammation surrounds clear spaces formerly occupied by lipid (lipogranuloma).

histiocytes and multinucleated giant cells enveloping optically clear spaces. Lymphocytes, plasma cells, and neutrophils may also be present.

Degenerations

Xanthelasma

Xanthelasmas are single or multiple soft yellow plaques occurring in the nasal aspect of the upper and lower eyelids in middle-aged to elderly individuals, predominantly females. Associated hyperlipoproteinemic states, particularly hyperlipoproteinemia types II and III, are present in 30%–40% of patients with xanthelasma. These eyelid xanthomas consist of collections of histiocytes with microvesicular foamy cytoplasm clustered around vessels and adnexal structures within the dermis (Fig 13-6). Associated inflammation is minimal to nonexistent. Treatment is either by surgical excision or by carbon dioxide laser ablation.

Amyloid

The term *amyloid* refers to a heterogeneous group of extracellular proteins that exhibit bire-fringence and dichroism under polarized light when stained with Congo red (see Fig 10-8). These features result from the 3-dimensional configuration of the proteins into a β-pleated sheet. Examples of proteins that may form amyloid deposits include

- immunoglobulin light chain fragments (AL amyloid) in plasma cell dyscrasias
- transthyretin mutations in familial amyloid polyneuropathy (FAP) types I and II (see Chapter 10, Vitreous)
- gelsolin mutations in FAP type IV (Meretoja syndrome [lattice corneal dystrophy type II])

Amyloid within the skin of the eyelid is highly indicative of a systemic disease process, either primary or secondary, whereas deposits elsewhere in the ocular adnexa but not in the eyelid are more likely a localized disease process. Other systemic diseases with eyelid manifestations are listed in Table 13-2.

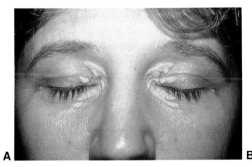 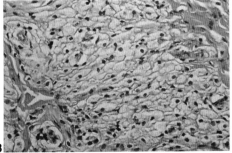

Figure 13-6 A, Patient with prominent xanthelasma. Note the yellow papules on the medial aspect of the upper and lower eyelids. **B,** Note the foam cells (filled with lipid) surrounding a venule at the left margin of this photograph. *(Part A from External Disease and Cornea: A Multimedia Collection. San Francisco: American Academy of Ophthalmology; 1994:slide 10.)*

Table 13-2 Eyelid Manifestations of Systemic Diseases

Systemic Condition	Eyelid Manifestation
Erdheim-Chester disease	Xanthelasma, xanthogranuloma
Hyperlipoproteinemia	Xanthelasma
Amyloidosis	Waxy papules, ptosis, pupura
Sarcoidosis	Papules
Wegener granulomatosis	Edema, ptosis, lower eyelid retraction
Scleroderma	Reduced mobility, taut skin
Polyarteritis nodosa	Focal infarct
Systemic lupus erythematosus	Telangiectasias, edema
Dermatomyositis	Edema, erythema
Relapsing polychondritis	Papules
Carney complex	Myxoma
Fraser syndrome	Cryptophthalmos
Treacher Collins syndrome	Lower eyelid coloboma

Modified from Wiggs JL, Jakobiec FA. Eyelid manifestations of systemic disease. In: Albert DM, Jakobiec FA, eds. *Principles and Practice of Ophthalmology.* Philadelphia: Saunders; 1994:1859.

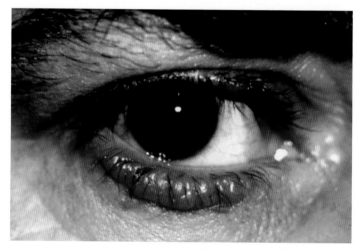

Figure 13-7 Cutaneous amyloid in a patient with multiple myeloma. Note the waxy elevation and the associated purpura. *(Courtesy of John B. Holds, MD.)*

Amyloid deposits in the skin are usually multiple, bilateral, symmetric, waxy yellow-white nodules. The deposition of amyloid within blood vessel walls in the skin causes increased vascular fragility and often results in intradermal hemorrhages, accounting for the purpura seen clinically (Fig 13-7). On routine histologic sections, amyloid appears as an amorphous to fibrillogranular, eosinophilic extracellular deposit, usually within vessel walls but also in connective tissue and around peripheral nerves and sweat glands. Other stains useful in demonstrating amyloid deposits include crystal violet and thioflavin T. Electron microscopy reveals the deposits to be composed of randomly oriented extracellular fibrils measuring 7.5–10.0 nm in diameter.

Albert DM, Jakobiec FA, eds. *Principles and Practice of Ophthalmology.* 2nd ed. Philadelphia: Saunders; 2000.

Garner A, Klintworth GK, eds. *Pathobiology of Ocular Disease: A Dynamic Approach.* 2nd ed. New York: Dekker; 1994:993–1007.

Neoplasia

Epidermal Neoplasms

Seborrheic keratosis

Seborrheic keratosis, a common benign epithelial proliferation, occurs in middle age. Clinically, 1 or more well-circumscribed, oval, dome-shaped to verrucoid "stuck-on" papules appear, principally on the trunk and face, varying from millimeters to centimeters in greatest dimension and from pink to brown in color. Histopathologically, several architectural patterns are possible, although all demonstrate hyperkeratosis, acanthosis, and some degree of papillomatosis. The acanthosis is a result of the proliferation of either polygonal or basaloid squamous cells without dysplasia.

A characteristic finding in most types of seborrheic keratoses is the formation of pseudohorn cysts, which are concentrically laminated collections of surface keratin within the acanthotic epithelium (Fig 13-8). Irritated seborrheic keratosis, also termed *inverted follicular keratosis* by some authors, shows nonkeratinizing squamous epithelial whorling, or squamous "eddies," instead of pseudohorn cysts (Fig 13-9). Heavy melanin phagocytosis by keratinocytes may impart a dark brown color to an otherwise typical seborrheic keratosis, which may then be confused clinically with malignant melanoma.

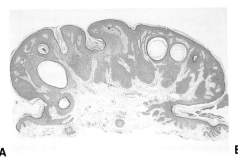
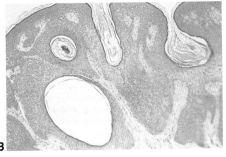

A　　　　　　　　　　　　　　　　　　　**B**

Figure 13-8 Seborrheic keratosis. **A,** The epidermis is acanthotic, and an excessive amount of keratin appears on the surface and within invaginations (hyperkeratosis). **B,** When serial histologic sections are studied, pseudohorn cysts within the epidermis are seen to represent crevices or infoldings of epidermis. *(Courtesy of Hans E. Grossniklaus, MD.)*

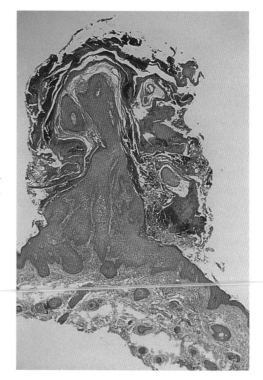

Figure 13-9 Inverted follicular keratosis. Clinically, this lesion appeared to be a cutaneous horn.

Table 13-3 Eyelid Neoplasms in Association With Systemic Malignancies

Syndrome	Eyelid Manifestation
Muir-Torre syndrome (visceral carcinoma, usually colon)	Keratoacanthoma, sebaceous neoplasm (adenoma, carcinoma)
Cowden disease (breast carcinoma; fibrous hamartomas of breast, thyroid, GI tract)	Multiple trichilemmomas
Basal cell nevus syndrome (medulloblastoma, fibrosarcoma)	Multiple basal cell carcinomas

Modified from Wiggs JL, Jakobiec FA. Eyelid manifestations of systemic disease. In: Albert DM, Jakobiec FA, eds. *Principles and Practice of Ophthalmology*. Philadelphia: Saunders; 1994:1859.

Sudden onset of multiple seborrheic keratoses is known as the *Leser-Trélat sign* and is associated with a malignancy, usually a gastrointestinal adenocarcinoma; these keratoses may in fact represent evolving acanthosis nigricans. Table 13-3 lists other systemic malignancies with cutaneous manifestations.

Keratoacanthoma

Keratoacanthoma is a rapidly growing epithelial proliferation with a potential for spontaneous involution that may be difficult to distinguish from squamous cell carcinoma both clinically and histopathologically. Recent evidence suggests that keratoacanthomas are a variant of a well-differentiated squamous cell carcinoma that has a tendency to regress. These studies are based on expression of proliferation markers (cyclins and cyclin-dependent kinases) and oncoproteins (mutated p53) that are expressed similarly by both entities. Dome-shaped nodules with a keratin-filled central crater may attain a considerable size, up to 2.5 cm in diameter, within a matter of 1–2 months (Fig 13-10). The natural history is typically spontaneous involution over several months, resulting in a slightly depressed scar. Histopathologically, keratoacanthomas show a cup-shaped invagination of well-differentiated squamous cells forming irregularly configured nests and strands and inciting a lymphoplasmacytic host response. The proliferating epithelial cells undermine the adjacent normal epidermis so that the edges of the lesion resemble the flying buttresses of a Gothic cathedral. At the deep aspect of the proliferating nodules, mitotic activity and nuclear atypia may occur, making the distinction between keratoacanthoma and invasive squamous cell carcinoma problematic. If unequivocal invasion is present, the lesion should be considered a well-differentiated squamous cell carcinoma. Many dermatopathologists and ophthalmic pathologists have ceased to use the term *keratoacanthoma* altogether and prefer to call it *well-differentiated keratinizing squamous cell carcinoma* because of the possible negative outcome of perineural invasion and metastasis. When the clinical differential diagnosis is keratoacanthoma versus squamous cell carcinoma, the lesion should be completely excised to permit optimal histopathologic examination of the lateral and deep margins of the tumor–host interface.

Hurt MA. Keratoacanthoma vs. squamous cell carcinoma in contrast with keratoacanthoma is squamous cell carcinoma. *J Cutan Pathol.* 2004;31:291–292.

Kerschmann RL, McCalmont TH, LeBoit PE. p53 oncoprotein expression and proliferation index in keratoacanthoma and squamous cell carcinoma. *Arch Dermatol.* 1994;130:181–186.

Tran TA, Ross JS, Boehm JR, Carlson JA. Comparison of mitotic cyclins and cyclin-dependent kinase expression in keratoacanthoma and squamous cell carcinoma. *J Cutan Pathol.* 1999;26:391–397.

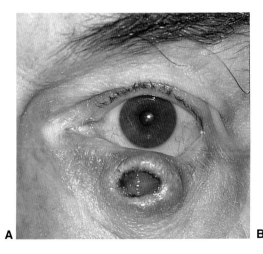
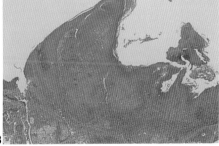

A **B**

Figure 13-10 **A,** Patient with keratoacanthoma. Note the cuplike configuration. In this case, the central crater was originally filled with keratin. **B,** Histologic photograph.

Actinic keratosis

More specifically known as *solar keratosis,* actinic keratosis appears as erythematous, scaly macules or papules developing in middle age on sun-exposed skin, particularly the face and the dorsal surfaces of the hands. Actinic keratoses range from millimeters up to 1 cm in greatest dimension. Hyperkeratotic types may form a cutaneous horn, and hyperpigmented types may clinically simulate lentigo maligna. Squamous cell carcinoma may develop from preexisting actinic keratosis; thus, biopsy of suspicious lesions and long-term follow-up are necessary in patients with this condition. However, when squamous cell carcinoma arises in actinic keratosis, the risk of subsequent metastatic dissemination is very low (0.5%–3.0%).

Histopathologically, there are 5 subtypes, ranging from hypertrophic to atrophic; the sine qua non for diagnosis in all types is the presence of

- nuclear dysplasia
- nuclear enlargement
- nuclear hyperchromasia
- nuclear membrane irregularity
- increased nuclear-to-cytoplasmic ratio

Nuclear changes in actinic keratosis range from mild (involving only the basal epithelial layers) to frank carcinoma in situ, or full-thickness involvement of the epidermis.

Dyskeratosis (premature individual cell keratinization) and mitotic figures above the basal epithelial layer are often present (Fig 13-11). The underlying dermis shows solar elastosis (fragmentation, clumping, and loss of eosinophils; Fig 13-12) of dermal collagen and a lichenoid chronic inflammatory infiltrate of varying intensity. The base of the lesion must be examined histopathologically to determine whether invasive squamous cell carcinoma has supervened; as with keratoacanthoma, superficial shave biopsies not including the base of the lesion are contraindicated.

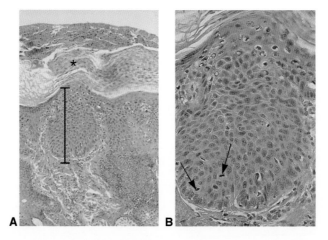

Figure 13-11 Actinic keratosis. **A,** Note the epidermal thickening (acanthosis *[I]*, disorganization within the epidermis (dysplasia), parakeratosis *(asterisk),* and inflammation within the dermis. Solar elastosis is also noted in the dermis. **B,** Note the epidermal disorganization and mitotic figures *(arrows).*

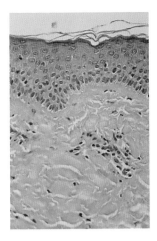

Figure 13-12 Solar elastosis. The collagen of the dermis appears blue in this H&E stain, instead of pink. This is a histopathologic marker of ultraviolet light–induced damage.

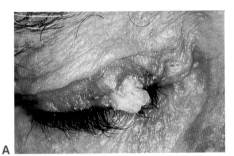

A

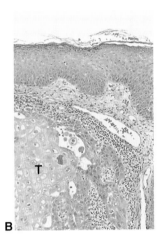

T

B

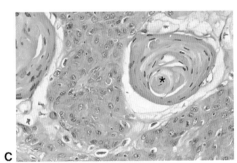

C

Figure 13-13 Squamous cell carcinoma. **A,** Clinical appearance. **B,** Note the tumor cells *(T)* invading the dermis. **C,** Keratin *(asterisk)* is produced in this well-differentiated squamous cell carcinoma.

Carcinoma

Although *squamous cell carcinoma* may occur in the eyelids, it is at least 10 and perhaps up to 40 times less common than basal cell carcinoma. Because the majority of squamous cell carcinomas arise in solar-damaged skin (actinic keratoses), the lower eyelid is more frequently involved than the upper. The clinical appearance is diverse, ranging from ulcers to plaques to fungating or nodular growths. Accordingly, the clinical differential diagnosis is a long list, and pathologic examination of excised tissue is necessary for accurate diagnosis. Histopathologic examination shows atypical squamous cells forming nests and strands, extending beyond the epidermal basement membrane, infiltrating the dermis, and inciting a desmoplastic fibrous tissue reaction (Fig 13-13).

Tumor cells may be

- well differentiated, forming keratin and easily recognizable as squamous
- moderately differentiated
- poorly differentiated, requiring ancillary studies to confirm the nature of the neoplasm

The presence of intercellular bridges between tumor cells should be sought when the diagnosis is in question. Perineural and lymphatic space invasion may be present and should be reported when identified microscopically. The use of frozen section (conventional or Mohs microsurgery) or permanent section margin control is indicated to treat this tumor adequately. Regional lymph node metastasis is reported to occur in 1%–21% of patients with squamous cell carcinoma of the eyelid.

Basal cell carcinoma is by far the most common malignant neoplasm of the eyelids, accounting for more than 90% of all eyelid malignancies. As with squamous cell carcinoma, exposure to sunlight is a risk factor. Lesions typically occur on the face, and the lower eyelid is more commonly involved than the upper. Tumors in the medial canthal area are more likely to be deeply invasive and to involve the orbit. The classic description is that of a "rodent" ulcer (*ulcus rodens,* or ulcer reminiscent of an object that has been chewed up by a rodent)— that is, a slowly enlarging ulcer with pearly, raised, rolled edges (Fig 13-14). The morpheaform, or fibrosing, basal cell carcinoma, however, is a flat or slightly depressed pale yellow indurated plaque; this type is often infiltrative, and its extent is difficult to determine clinically (Fig 13-15). Other growth patterns include nodular (most common) and multicentric.

As the name implies, basal cell carcinomas originate from the stratum basale, or stratum germinativum, of the epidermis. Tumor cells are characterized by relatively bland, monomorphous nuclei and a high nuclear-to-cytoplasmic ratio; anaplastic features and abnormal mitotic figures are uncommon. Basal cell carcinoma forms cohesive nests with nuclear palisading of the peripheral cell layer. A helpful diagnostic feature, albeit a presumed artifact of tissue processing, is the characteristic cleftlike separation of the tumor from its surround-

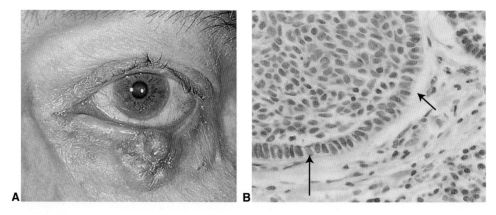

Figure 13-14 Basal cell carcinoma. **A,** Clinical appearance of a nodular "rodent" ulcer. **B,** Note the characteristic palisading of the cells around the outer edge of the tumor *(long arrow)* and the artifactitious separation between the nest of tumor cells and the dermis (cracking artifact, *short arrow).*

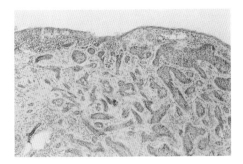

Figure 13-15 Basal cell carcinoma, morphea-form (sclerosing) type. Thin strands and cords of tumor cells are seen in a fibrotic (desmoplastic) dermis.

ing stroma (see Fig 13-14). Basal cell carcinomas may exhibit a variety of cytologic and architectural patterns, including squamous (metatypical), sebaceous, adenoid, and cystic differentiation. Fibrosing basal cell carcinomas are almost always undifferentiated.

Complete excision is the treatment of choice and margin control is required. Multicentric and infiltrating fibrosing basal cell carcinomas require frozen section examination of surgical margins or Mohs micrographic surgical technique for adequate excision. Morbidity in basal cell carcinomas is almost always the result of local spread; metastatic spread is extremely unusual.

Chévez-Barrios P. Frozen section diagnosis and indications in ophthalmic pathology. *Arch Pathol Lab Med.* 2005;129:1626–1634.

Dermal Neoplasms

Capillary hemangiomas are common in the eyelids of children. They usually appear at or shortly after birth as a red-purple nodule that may exhibit slow but worrisome growth over weeks to months. Spontaneous involution, however, is the rule, and lesions usually disappear by school age. Intervention is reserved for those lesions that diminish vision because of proptosis or astigmatism, promoting amblyopia. The histopathologic appearance depends on the stage of evolution of the hemangioma. Early lesions may be very cellular, with solid nests of plump endothelial cells and correspondingly little vascular luminal formation. Established lesions typically show well-developed, flattened, endothelium-lined capillary channels in a lobular configuration. Involuting lesions demonstrate increased fibrosis and hyalinization of capillary walls with luminal occlusion.

Appendage Neoplasms

A *sebaceous carcinoma* most commonly involves the upper eyelid of elderly persons. It may originate in the meibomian glands of the tarsus, the glands of Zeis in the skin of the eyelid, or the sebaceous glands of the caruncle. Clinical diagnosis is often missed or delayed because of this lesion's propensity to mimic a chalazion or chronic blepharoconjunctivitis (Fig 13-16). Histopathologically, well-differentiated sebaceous carcinomas are readily identified through the microvesicular foamy nature of the tumor cell cytoplasm (Fig 13-17). Moderately differentiated tumors may exhibit some degree of sebaceous differentiation. Poorly differentiated tumors, however, may be difficult to distinguish from the other, more common epithelial malignancies. The demonstration of lipid within the cytoplasm of tumor cells by special stains, such as oil red O or Sudan black, is diagnostic, but it must be performed on tissue prior to processing and paraffin embedding. Alternatively, osmium staining of tissue processed for electron microscopy will highlight intracytoplasmic lipid.

When sebaceous carcinoma is suspected clinically, the pathologist should be alerted so that frozen section slides can be generated for lipid stains. Another feature, characteristic of but not pathognomonic for sebaceous cell carcinoma, is the dissemination of individual tumor cells and clusters of tumor cells within the epidermis or conjunctival epithelium, known as *pagetoid spread* (see Fig 13-16). Another pattern in the conjunctiva is that of complete replacement of conjunctival epithelium by tumor cells. A rare variant of sebaceous carcinoma involves only the epidermis and conjunctiva without demonstrable invasive tumor.

Treatment recommendations include wide local excision of nodular lesions. Large or deeply invasive tumors may require exenteration. Suboptimal cytologic preservation and difficulty in distinguishing goblet cells from pagetoid spread of tumor cells may reduce

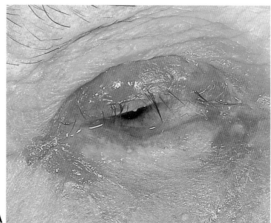

A

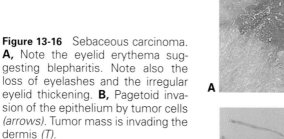

Figure 13-16 Sebaceous carcinoma. **A,** Note the eyelid erythema suggesting blepharitis. Note also the loss of eyelashes and the irregular eyelid thickening. **B,** Pagetoid invasion of the epithelium by tumor cells *(arrows)*. Tumor mass is invading the dermis *(T)*.

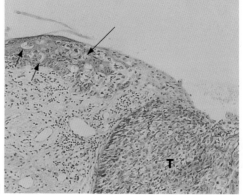

B

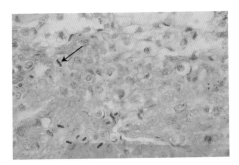

Figure 13-17 Sebaceous carcinoma. Note the mitotic figures *(arrow)* and tumor cells with foamy cytoplasm.

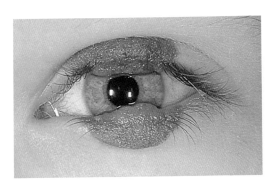

Figure 13-18 Congenital split, or "kissing," nevus of the eyelid.

the accuracy of intraoperative frozen section diagnosis of margins. Preoperative mapping by routine processing of multiple biopsies may afford a more accurate assessment of the extent of spread of the carcinoma. Survival rates for sebaceous carcinoma are worse than those for squamous cell carcinoma but have improved in recent years as a result of increased awareness, earlier detection, more accurate diagnosis, and appropriate treatment. Metastases first involve regional lymph nodes.

For American Joint Committee on Cancer definitions and staging of malignant neoplasms of the eyelid, see Table A-5 in the appendix.

Albert DM, Jakobiec FA, eds. *Principles and Practice of Ophthalmology.* 2nd ed. Philadelphia: Saunders; 2000.

Melanocytic Neoplasms

Nevocellular nevi occur commonly on the eyelids and may be visible at birth (congenital nevi) or become apparent in adolescence or adulthood. Congenital nevi are often larger than those appearing in later years, sometimes reaching substantial size. Nevi greater than 20 cm in diameter are referred to as *giant congenital melanocytic nevi.* The risk for development of melanoma in congenital nevi is proportional to the size of the nevus; close follow-up and/or excision of congenital nevi is warranted. Congenital melanocytic nevi in the eyelid may develop in utero prior to the separation of the upper and lower eyelids and result in the clinical appearance of "kissing" nevi (Fig 13-18). Features associated with congenital nevi include the presence of nevus cells within and around adnexal structures, vessel walls, and the perineurium; extension into the deep reticular dermis or subcutaneous tissue; and a single- or double-file arrangement of nevus cells.

Melanocytic nevi appearing after childhood typically begin as small (less than 0.5 cm), round brown macules, gradually attaining increased thickness to become papules that may or may not be pigmented. This growth pattern corresponds to the histopathologic classification of melanocytic nevi. Macular (flat) nevi histopathologically show nests of melanocytes along the dermal–epidermal junction and are consequently termed *junctional nevi* (Fig 13-19). A junctional nevus is clinically indistinguishable from an ephelis, or freckle. Histopathologically, however, an ephelis is a result of increased melanization of basal keratinocytes without proliferation or aggregation of melanocytes. As the junctional nests, or theques, of the nevus begin to migrate into the superficial dermis, the nevus becomes a dome-shaped, or papillomatous, papule. When both junctional and intradermal components are present, the histopathologic classification becomes *compound nevus* (Fig 13-20). Finally, the junctional component disappears, leaving only nevus cells within the dermis, and the classification accordingly becomes *intradermal nevus* (Fig 13-21).

An evolution in the cytomorphology of the nevus cells also takes place: those in the superficial portion of the nevus are polygonal, or epithelioid, in shape (type A nevus cells). Within the midportion of the nevus, the cells become smaller, have less cytoplasm, and resemble lymphocytes (type B nevus cells). At the deepest levels, the nevus cells become spindled and appear similar to Schwann cells of peripheral nerves (type C nevus cells). Recognition of this "maturation" is useful in classifying melanocytic neoplasms as benign. Other histopathologic criteria favoring a benign melanocytic process include the following:

- absence of intraepidermal migration of nevus cells
- absence of mitotic activity in the dermal component of the mass
- absence of nuclear enlargement or prominent nucleoli
- cytoplasmic melanin pigment content greatest in superficial layers and absent in deeper layers

Multinucleated giant melanocytes and interspersed adipose tissue are common in older nevi.

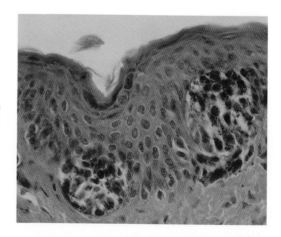

Figure 13-19 Junctional nevus. Nests of nevus cells are seen at the junction between epidermis and dermis.

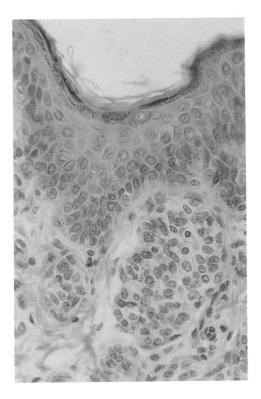

Figure 13-20 Compound nevus. Nests of nevus cells are present in the dermis as well as at the junction of epidermis and dermis.

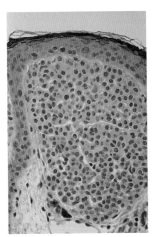

Figure 13-21 Intradermal nevus. The nests of nevus cells are confined to the dermis.

Nevi that show some clinical or pathologic atypicality include the Spitz nevus and the dysplastic nevus. *Spitz nevi* develop in late childhood or in adolescence and are uncommon after the second decade. In contrast to the clinical picture of the usual nevus, they may be larger (up to 1.0 cm) and have a pink-red color. Histopathologically, they are usually compound and exhibit nuclear and cytoplasmic enlargement and pleomorphism. Other features suggesting malignancy, however, such as atypical mitotic figures, intraepidermal migration, and lack of maturation, are generally lacking.

Clinical features suggesting a *dysplastic nevus* may include size greater than 0.5 cm, irregular margins, and irregular pigmentation. Nevi are considered dysplastic when they demonstrate certain architectural or cytomorphologic characteristics on histopathologic examination. Architectural features include lentiginous (single-cell) melanocytic hyperplasia, bridging of melanocytes across the bases of adjacent rete pegs, and lamellar fibrosis of the papillary dermis. Cytologic atypia is characterized by nuclear enlargement, hyperchromasia, and prominent nucleoli. Clinically suspicious lesions should be completely excised. Persons with multiple dysplastic nevi are at increased risk for development of melanoma and may represent a genetic susceptibility, suggesting that family members should also be examined and followed closely.

Cutaneous malignant melanoma is a rare occurrence on the eyelids. It may be associated with a preexisting nevus or it may develop de novo. Clinical features suggesting malignancy are the same as those just mentioned for dysplastic nevi; in addition, invasive melanoma is heralded by a vertical (perpendicular to the skin surface) growth phase that results in an elevated or indurated mass. There are 4 main histopathologic subtypes of malignant melanoma:

1. superficial spreading
2. lentigo maligna
3. nodular
4. acral-lentiginous

Superficial spreading is the most common type of cutaneous melanoma and demonstrates a radial (intraepidermal) growth pattern extending beyond the invasive component, distinguishing it from nodular melanoma. Lentigo maligna melanoma occurs on the face of elderly individuals, with a long preinvasive phase. Acral-lentiginous melanoma, as the name implies, involves the extremities and is not seen in the eyelid.

Histopathologic features characteristic of melanoma include pagetoid intraepidermal spread of atypical melanocytic nests and single cells, nuclear abnormalities as listed earlier, lack of maturation in the deeper portions of the mass, and atypical mitotic figures. A bandlike lymphocytic host response along the base of the mass is more common in melanoma than in benign proliferations, with the exception of a halo nevus. Prognosis is correlated with depth of invasion in stage I (localized) disease. Metastases, when they occur, typically involve regional lymph nodes first.

Font RL. Eyelids and lacrimal drainage system. In: Spencer WH, ed. *Ophthalmic Pathology: An Atlas and Textbook.* 4th ed. Philadelphia: Saunders; 1996:2263–2277.

McLean IW, Burnier MN, Zimmerman LE, Jakobiec FA. *Tumors of the Eye and Ocular Adnexa.* Washington: Armed Forces Institute of Pathology; 1995.

CHAPTER **14**

Orbit

Topography

Bony Orbit and Soft Tissues

Seven bones form the boundaries of the orbit (Fig 14-1). These 7 bones are the

- frontal
- zygoma
- palatine
- lacrimal
- sphenoid
- ethmoid
- maxilla

The orbital cavity is pear-shaped and has a volume of 30 cc. Other structures and tissues occupying the cavity are the

- globe
- lacrimal gland
- muscles
- tendons
- fat
- fascia
- vessels
- nerves
- sympathetic ganglia
- cartilaginous trochlea

Inflammatory and neoplastic processes that increase the volume of the orbital contents lead to *proptosis* (protrusion) of the globe and/or *displacement* (deviation) from the horizontal or vertical position. The degree and direction of ocular displacement help to localize the position of the mass.

The *lacrimal gland* is situated anteriorly in the superotemporal quadrant of the orbit. The gland is divided into orbital and palpebral lobes by the aponeurosis of the levator palpebrae superioris muscle. The acini of the glands are composed of low cuboidal epithelium. The ducts, which lie within the fibrovascular stroma, are lined by low cuboidal epithelium with a second outer layer of low, flat myoepithelial cells.

219

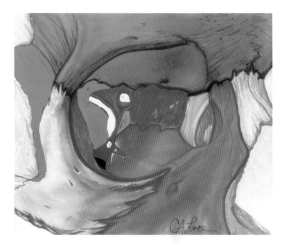

Figure 14-1 Bony components of the right orbit identified by color: maxilla *(orange)*; zygoma *(beige)*; sphenoid bone, greater wing *(light blue)*, lesser wing *(dark blue)*; palatine bone *(light green)*; ethmoid bone *(purple)*; lacrimal bone *(pink)*; frontal bone *(green)*. *(Reproduced with permission from Zide BM, Jelks GW, eds. Surgical Anatomy of the Orbit. New York: Raven; 1985:3.)*

BCSC Section 2, *Fundamentals and Principles of Ophthalmology,* covers orbital anatomy in Part I, Anatomy. BCSC Section 7, *Orbit, Eyelids, and Lacrimal System,* also discusses orbital anatomy, as well as the conditions covered in the following pages, in detail.

Congenital Anomalies

Dermoid and Other Epithelial Cysts

Dermoid cysts are believed to arise as embryonic epithelial nests that became entrapped during embryogenesis. They may protrude through the frontozygomatic suture to take a dumbbell shape. Most manifest in childhood as a mass in the superotemporal quadrants of the orbit. Rupture of cyst contents may produce a marked granulomatous reaction. Histologically, dermoid cysts are encapsulated, lined by keratinized stratified squamous epithelium. The cysts contain keratin and hair, and the walls of the cysts are lined with adnexal structures, including sebaceous glands, hair roots, sweat glands, and may include glandular tissue (Fig 14-2). If the wall does not bear adnexal structures, the term *epidermal cyst* is applied. Intraorbital cysts may also be lined by respiratory epithelium or conjunctival epithelium.

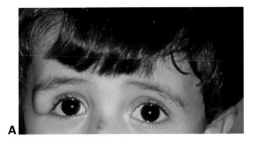

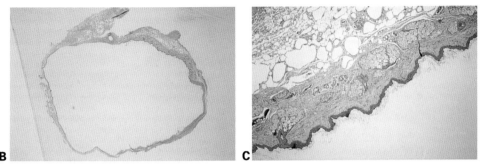

Figure 14-2 **A,** Clinical appearance of dermoid cyst of the orbit. Note the typical superotemporal location. **B,** Low-power photomicrograph discloses a cyst lined by stratified squamous epithelium. **C,** The wall of the cyst contains sebaceous glands and adnexal structures. *(Part A courtesy of Sander Dubovy, MD; parts B and C courtesy of Hans E. Grossniklaus, MD.)*

Inflammations

Infectious

Bacterial infections

The causes of bacterial infections of the orbit include bacteremia, trauma, retained surgical hardware, and adjacent sinus infection. Infection may involve a variety of organisms, including *Haemophilus influenzae, Streptococcus, Staphylococcus aureus, Clostridium, Bacteroides, Klebsiella,* and *Proteus.* Histologically, acute inflammation, necrosis, and abscess formation may be present. Tuberculosis, which rarely involves the orbit, produces a necrotizing granulomatous reaction.

Fungal and parasitic infections

A common fungal infection of the orbit is caused by sinus infection from mucormycosis (zygomycosis). Poorly controlled diabetes can make patients particularly prone to mucormycosis, although any immunocompromised condition may increase susceptibility. Histologically, acute and chronic inflammation appear in a background of necrosis, often with histiocytes. Broad, nonseptated hyphae may be identified in periodic acid–Schiff (PAS) and Gomori methenamine silver (GMS) stains. Diagnosis is achieved by biopsy of necrotic-appearing tissues in the nasopharynx. These fungi can invade blood vessel walls and produce a thrombosing vasculitis.

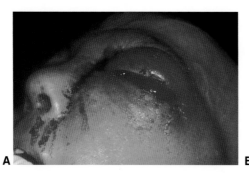
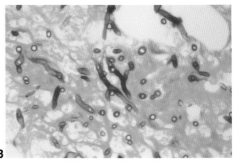

A   **B**

Figure 14-3 *Aspergillus* infections of the orbit generally produce severe, insidious orbital inflammation. **A,** Clinical appearance. **B,** Microscopic section demonstrates the branching hyphal structure on silver stains. *(Courtesy of Hans E. Grossniklaus, MD.)*

Aspergillus infection of the orbit may occur in immunocompromised or otherwise healthy individuals. Often, the symptoms are slowly progressive and insidious, producing a sclerosing granulomatous disease. *Aspergillus* has often been difficult to culture but may be observed in tissue as septated hyphae with 45° angle branching (Fig 14-3). Despite aggressive surgical therapy and adjunctive therapy with amphotericin B, orbital infections with either *Aspergillus* or mucormycosis may be fatal if extension into the brain occurs. Allergic fungal sinusitis has also been noted to extend into the orbit in some instances.

Parasitic infections of the orbit are rare and may be produced by *Echinococcus*, *Taenia solium* (cysticercosis), *Onchocerca volvulus* (onchocerciasis), and *Loa loa* (loiasis). These infections are mostly seen in patients who come from, or have traveled to, areas where the infections are endemic.

Noninfectious

Thyroid-associated orbitopathy

Also known as *Graves disease* and *thyroid ophthalmopathy,* thyroid-associated orbitopathy is related to thyroid dysfunction and is the most common cause of unilateral or bilateral proptosis (exophthalmos) in adults. A cellular infiltrate of mononuclear cells, lymphocytes, plasma cells, mast cells, and fibroblasts involves the interstitial tissues of the extraocular muscles, most commonly the inferior and medial rectus muscles (Fig 14-4). The muscles appear firm and white, and the tendons are usually not involved. The fibroblasts produce mucopolysaccharide, leading to increased water content in the tissues. As a result of the increased bulk, the optic nerve may be compromised at the orbital apex and papilledema may result. Progressive fibrosis results in restriction of ocular movement, and exposure keratitis is also a complication. BCSC Section 1, *Update on General Medicine,* and Section 7, *Orbit, Eyelids, and Lacrimal System,* discuss thyroid disease in greater detail.

Albert DM, Jakobiec FA, eds. *Principles and Practice of Ophthalmology.* 2nd ed. Philadelphia: Saunders; 2000.

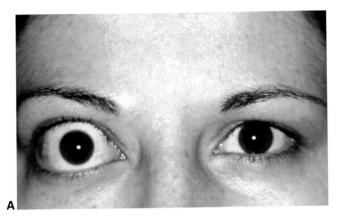

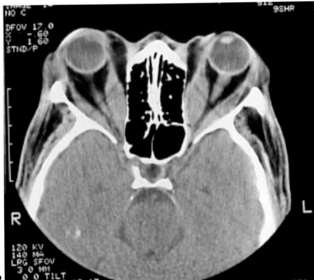

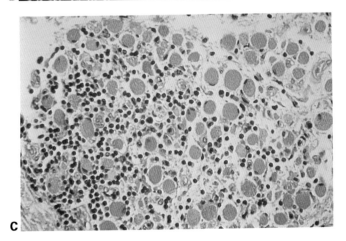

Figure 14-4 Thyroid-associated orbitopathy (Graves disease or thyroid ophthalmopathy). **A,** Clinical appearance demonstrating asymmetric proptosis and eyelid retraction. **B,** CT scan (axial view) showing fusiform enlargement of the extraocular muscles. **C,** The muscle bundles of the extraocular muscle are separated by fluid, accompanied by an infiltrate of mononuclear inflammatory cells. The inflammatory process expands the volume of the muscles, potentially causing proptosis and, in extreme cases, corneal exposure. *(Parts A and B courtesy of Sander Dubovy, MD.)*

Idiopathic orbital inflammation

Idiopathic orbital inflammation, or *orbital inflammatory syndrome (sclerosing orbititis),* refers to a space-occupying inflammatory disorder that simulates a neoplasm (thus, it is sometimes known as *orbital pseudotumor*) but has no recognizable cause, such as Graves disease or a ruptured epidermal inclusion cyst. This disorder accounts for about 5% of orbital lesions. Clinically, patients have an abrupt course and usually complain of pain. The condition may affect children as well as adults. The inflammatory response may be diffuse or compartmentalized. When localized to an extraocular muscle, the condition is called *orbital myositis* (Fig 14-5); when localized to the lacrimal gland, it is frequently called *sclerosing dacryoadenitis.*

In the early stages, inflammation predominates, with a polymorphous inflammatory response (eosinophils, neutrophils, plasma cells, lymphocytes, and macrophages) that is often perivascular and that frequently infiltrates muscle, producing fat necrosis. In later stages, fibrosis is the predominant feature, often with interspersed lymphoid follicles bearing germinal centers. The fibrosis may inexorably replace orbital fat and encase extraocular muscles and the optic nerve (Fig 14-6). The majority of patients with early idiopathic orbital inflammation respond promptly to corticosteroids; patients with the advanced stages of fibrosis may be unresponsive. See BCSC Section 7, *Orbit, Eyelids, and Lacrimal System,* for further discussion.

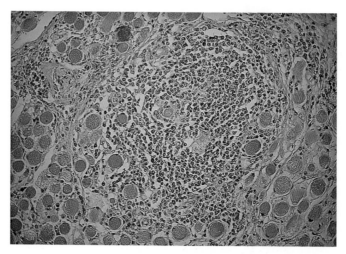

Figure 14-5 Idiopathic orbital inflammation (orbital inflammatory syndrome). In this case, an inflammatory infiltrate involves extraocular muscle. Unlike Graves disease, in which the tendons of the muscles typically are spared, this condition can affect any orbital structure, including the muscle tendons.

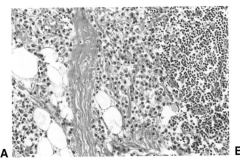
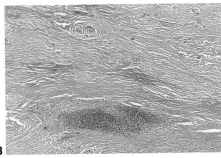

A   **B**

Figure 14-6   Idiopathic orbital inflammation. **A,** Note the mixture of inflammatory cells in the bundle of collagen running through the orbital fat. **B,** Diffuse fibrosis dominates the histologic picture of this fibrosing orbititis, considered by some authorities to represent a later stage of the condition illustrated in part **A**.

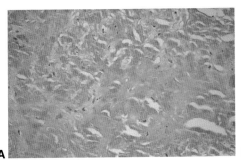
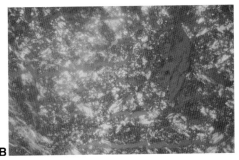

A   **B**

Figure 14-7   Orbital amyloidosis. **A,** Tissue infiltration by pink amorphous material. **B,** Polarized light of a Congo red–stained section demonstrates red-green dichroism. *(Courtesy of Hans E. Grossniklaus, MD.)*

Degenerations

Amyloid

Amyloid deposition in the orbit occurs in primary systemic amyloidosis; when it involves the extraocular muscles and nerves, it can produce ophthalmoplegia and ptosis. Amyloid-osis may also be localized within the orbit and have no systemic manifestations. Histologic sections stained with Congo red dye show deposits of a hyalinized amorphous material that exhibits green-red dichroism with polarized light (Fig 14-7). Electron microscopy demonstrates characteristic fibrils. Amyloid deposition may be associated with a plasma cell dyscrasia or atypical lymphomatous proliferation. BCSC Section 8, *External Disease and Cornea,* discusses both systemic and localized amyloidosis in greater detail.

Neoplasia

Neoplasms of the orbit may be primary, secondary from adjacent structures, or metastatic. The incidence of primary neoplasms is low, with hemangioma and lymphoma being the most common. Secondary tumors from adjacent sinuses are slightly more common than primary tumors.

In children, approximately 90% of orbital tumors are benign. Most benign lesions are cystic (dermoid or epidermoid cysts), and most malignant tumors are rhabdomyosarcomas. The orbit may be involved secondarily by retinoblastoma, neuroblastoma, or leukemia/lymphoma.

The various tumors discussed in the following sections are covered at greater length in BCSC Section 7, *Orbit, Eyelids, and Lacrimal System.*

Lacrimal Gland Neoplasia

Pleomorphic adenoma

Pleomorphic adenoma (benign mixed tumor) describes the most common epithelial tumor of the lacrimal gland. Initially, the tumor is encapsulated; it grows slowly by expansion. This progressive expansive growth may indent the bone of the lacrimal fossa, producing excavation of the area. Tumor growth stimulates the periosteum to deposit a thin layer of new bone (cortication). The adjacent orbital bone is not eroded. Typically, the patient experiences no pain. This tumor is more common in men than in women, and the median age at presentation is approximately 35 years.

The histologic appearance of pleomorphic adenoma is a mixture of epithelial and stromal elements. The epithelial component may form nests or tubules lined by 2 layers of cells, the outermost layer blending imperceptibly with the stroma (Fig 14-8). The stroma may appear myxoid and may contain heterologous elements, including cartilage and bone. Although the tumor may appear to be encapsulated, microscopic lobules can prolapse through the capsule, which is formed by the compression of adjacent normal orbital tissue and is not an anatomical barrier cleanly separating the tumor from the adjacent orbit.

Although pleomorphic adenoma is a benign neoplasm, tumor left behind in the orbit after incomplete surgical removal may produce clinically significant recurrences that are difficult to extirpate surgically. The possibility of orbital recurrence leads to 2 important surgical principles. The surgeon should

1. try to excise the tumor with a rim of normal orbital tissue and not merely shell it out
2. avoid incisional biopsies into this tumor to prevent seeding of the orbit

Transformation into a malignant mixed tumor may take place in a long-standing pleomorphic adenoma with relatively rapid growth after a period of relative quiescence. Carcinomas, including adenocarcinoma and adenoid cystic carcinoma, may also arise in recurrent pleomorphic adenomas.

Spencer WH, ed. *Ophthalmic Pathology: An Atlas and Textbook.* 4th ed. Philadelphia: Saunders; 1996:2484–2494.

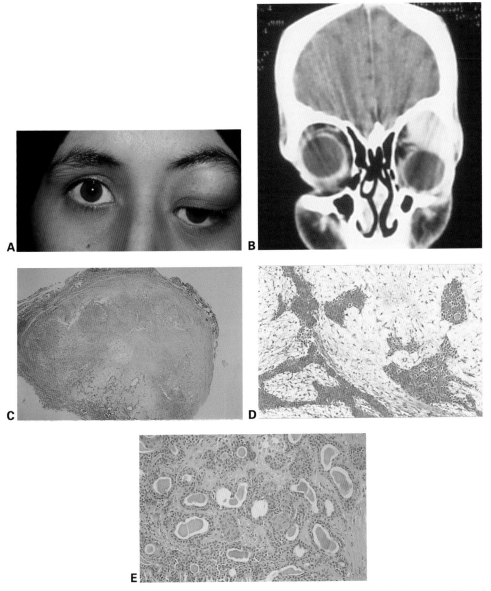

Figure 14-8 Pleomorphic adenoma (benign mixed tumor) of the lacrimal gland. **A,** Clinical appearance. A superotemporal orbital mass is present, causing proptosis and downward displacement of the left globe. **B,** CT scan (coronal view) demonstrating left orbit tumor. **C,** Low power shows the circumscribed nature of this pleomorphic adenoma. **D,** Note both the epithelial and the mesenchymal elements. **E,** Well-differentiated glandular structures (epithelial component). *(Parts A and B courtesy of Sander Dubovy, MD; parts C–E courtesy of Hans E. Grossniklaus, MD.)*

Adenoid cystic carcinoma

As mentioned in the previous section, adenoid cystic carcinoma can arise in a pleomorphic adenoma or de novo in the lacrimal gland. The tumor is slightly more common in women than in men, and the median age of presentation is about 40. Unlike pleomorphic adenoma, adenoid cystic carcinoma is not encapsulated; it tends to erode the adjacent bone and invade orbital nerves, accounting for the pain that is a frequent presenting complaint. Grossly, the appearance is grayish white, firm, and nodular. Histologically, a variety of patterns may appear, including the Swiss cheese (cribriform) pattern (Fig 14-9). Other histologic patterns include basaloid (solid), comedo, sclerosing, and tubular. Presence of the basaloid pattern has been associated with a worse prognosis (5-year survival of 21%) than those tumors without a basaloid component (5-year survival of 71%). Because of the diffuse infiltration of this tumor, exenteration may be recommended, often with removal of adjacent bone. Despite aggressive surgical intervention, the long-term prognosis is poor.

For American Joint Committee on Cancer (AJCC) definitions and staging of lacrimal gland carcinomas, see Table A-6 in the appendix.

Font RL, Smith SL, Bryan RG. Malignant epithelial tumors of the lacrimal gland: a clinico-pathologic study of 21 cases. *Arch Ophthalmol.* 1998;116:613–616.

Lymphoproliferative Lesions

Most classifications of lymphoid lesions have been based on lymph node architecture, and such nodal classifications have been difficult to apply to so-called extranodal lymphoid lesions. Because there are no lymph nodes in the orbit, it is problematic to classify these lesions according to the criteria used for lymph nodes. The development of classification schemes for lymphomas is, thus, an ongoing and controversial process. The most recent classification schemes, which incorporate data from morphology, immunophenotyping, and gene rearrangement studies, have attempted to include orbital lymphomas. Data that reveal the prognosis of patients with orbital lymphomas using these classifications are just beginning to emerge. Many lymphoid masses in the orbit that were previously classified as reactive would now be considered neoplastic.

Malignant lymphoma

Malignant lymphomas of the orbit may be a presenting manifestation of systemic lymphomas, or they may arise primarily from the orbit. The incidence of orbital involvement in systemic lymphomas is 1.3%. Hodgkin disease is exceedingly rare in the orbit, and the majority of primary malignant orbital lymphomas are non–Hodgkin lymphomas of diffuse architecture that mark immunophenotypically as B cells (Fig 14-10). The classification of non–Hodgkin lymphomas is controversial and continues to evolve. The current Revised European-American Lymphoma (REAL) classification includes extranodal lymphomas.

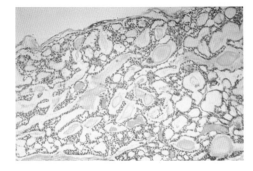

Figure 14-9 Adenoid cystic carcinoma of the lacrimal gland. Note the characteristic Swiss cheese (cribriform) pattern of tumor cells. *(Courtesy of Ben J. Glasgow, MD.)*

Harris NL, Jaffe ES, Stein H, et al. A revised European-American classification of lymphoid neoplasms: a proposal from the International Lymphoma Study Group. *Blood.* 1994;84:1361–1392.

The most commonly encountered low-grade orbital lymphoma in the REAL classification is an extranodal marginal zone, or mucosa-associated lymphoid tissue (MALT), lymphoma. The MALT lymphoma often shows poorly formed follicles with heterogeneous cellular composition, including small atypical cells with cleaved nuclei, monocytoid cells, small lymphocytes, and plasma cells. The neoplastic monocytoid B-cell population may expand the marginal zone and infiltrate follicles (follicular colonization). MALT lymphomas are characterized by a B-cell immunophenotype that is generally CD5- and CD10-negative (Fig 14-11).

The lymphomas of the chronic lymphocytic leukemia (CLL) type are also low grade and are composed of homogeneous sheets of small, mature-appearing lymphocytes.

In some studies, follicular center lymphoma is the most common secondary type of lymphoma to involve the orbit. In this low-grade B-cell lymphoma, follicles are well formed and dominated by cleaved cells (centrocytes), with fewer noncleaved cells (centroblasts).

High-grade lymphomas of the orbit in the REAL classification include large cell lymphoma, lymphoblastic lymphoma, and Burkitt lymphoma. With the exception of Burkitt

Figure 14-10 B-cell lymphoma of the orbit. Orbital soft tissues are diffusely replaced by sheets of cytologically malignant lymphocytes.

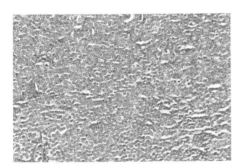
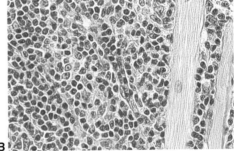

A **B**

Figure 14-11 MALT. **A,** Low power shows a hint of follicular architecture in a dense lymphoid infiltrate with infiltration of muscle. **B,** Higher magnification demonstrates a heterogeneous infiltrate that includes small lymphocytes, plasma cells, and cleaved and noncleaved cells, as well as atypical lymphocytes with cytoplasmic clearing (monocytoid B cells). *(Courtesy of Ben J. Glasgow, MD.)*

lymphoma, orbital lymphoma is not likely to occur in children, although leukemic infil-trates and so-called granulocytic sarcomas are encountered in children.

Neither immunophenotypic nor gene rearrangement studies to identify clonal lym-phocyte populations have thus far proven helpful in predicting the development of sys-temic disease. Location is 1 factor that may have a bearing on prognosis; conjunctival lesions have a better prognosis than orbital lesions, for example. Eyelid lesions may have the highest association with systemic involvement (67%).

It is important for the ophthalmologist to distinguish orbital lymphoproliferative lesions from orbital inflammatory syndrome. Unlike patients with orbital inflammatory syndrome, those with orbital lymphoproliferative lesions present with a gradual, painless progression of proptosis. Every patient with an orbital lymphoproliferative lesion must be investigated for evidence of systemic lymphoma, including examination for lymphade-nopathy, a complete blood count (CBC) and differential, and imaging of the thoracic and abdominal viscera. In general, biopsy of an accessible lymph node is preferred over an orbital biopsy because nodal architecture is helpful in diagnosis and the procedure may be safer. A bone marrow biopsy is preferred to an aspirate because it includes bone spicules; the presence of a paratrabecular lymphoid infiltrate may indicate systemic lymphoma. In contrast to most cases of idiopathic orbital inflammation, which are treated with cortico-steroids, lymphoproliferative lesions confined to the orbit are treated with radiation.

The ophthalmologist taking a biopsy of an orbital or conjunctival lymphoproliferative lesion should consult with the pathologist to determine the optimal method for handling the tissue. Fresh (unfixed) tissue is preferred for touch preparations, immunohistochemis-try, flow cytometry, and gene rearrangement studies. The type of fixative used for perma-nent sections varies from one laboratory to another. Exposure of the biopsy specimen to air for long periods of time should be avoided. Tissue samples may be wrapped in saline-moistened gauze and transported on ice. It is very important that the tissue be handled gently; crush artifact can prevent the pathologist from rendering a diagnosis.

Albert DM, Jakobiec FA, eds. *Principles and Practice of Ophthalmology.* 2nd ed. Philadelphia: Saunders; 2000.

Vascular Tumors

Lymphangiomas occur in children and are characterized by fluctuation in proptosis. Lymphangiomas of the orbit are unencapsulated, diffusely infiltrating tumors that feature lymphatic vascular spaces and well-formed lymphoid aggregates in a fibrotic interstitium (Fig 14-12).

Hemangioma in the adult is encapsulated and consists of cavernous spaces *(cavern-ous hemangioma)* with thick, fibrosed walls (Fig 14-13). Vessels may show thrombosis and calcification. Hemangioma in the child is unencapsulated, more cellular, and composed of capillary-sized vessels *(capillary hemangioma)* (Fig 14-14).

Hemangiopericytoma occurs mainly in adults (median age is 42 years) and manifests with proptosis, pain, diplopia, and decreased visual acuity. Histologically, a staghorn vas-cular pattern is displayed with densely packed oval to spindle-shaped cells. The reticulin stain is useful in demonstrating tumor cells that are individually wrapped in a network of collagenous material (Fig 14-15). Hemangiopericytomas include a spectrum of benign,

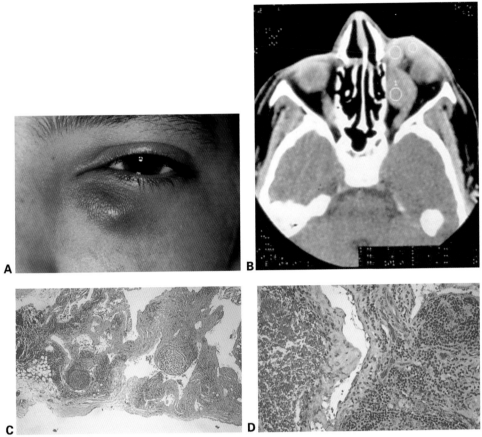

Figure 14-12 Lymphangioma. **A,** Clinical appearance. A young boy with an inferior orbital lesion extending anteriorly to the right lower lid. **B,** CT scan (axial view) showing a multilobulated mass within the left orbit. **C,** Photomicrograph shows numerous vascular channels with a fibrotic interstitium. **D,** Higher magnification demonstrates the lymphocytes and plasma cells within the fibrous walls. *(Parts A and B courtesy of Sander Dubovy, MD; parts C and D courtesy of Ben J. Glasgow, MD.)*

intermediate, and malignant lesions. Features of malignancy include an infiltrating border, anaplasia, mitotic figures, and necrosis. However, these features may be absent in tumors that eventually metastasize.

Tumors With Muscle Differentiation

Rhabdomyosarcoma

Rhabdomyosarcoma is the most common primary malignant orbital tumor of childhood (average age of onset is 7–8 years). Proptosis is often sudden and rapidly progressive, and it requires emergency treatment. Reddish discoloration of the eyelids is *not* accompanied by local heat or systemic fever, as it is in cellulitis. Orbital rhabdomyosarcomas are classified slightly differently and have a better prognosis (overall 5-year survival of 92%) than do their extraorbital counterparts.

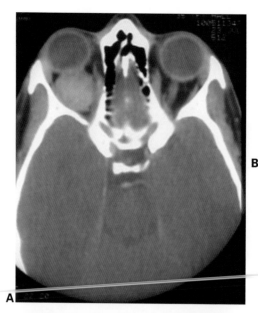

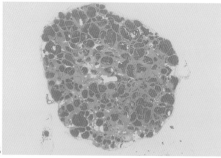

Figure 14-13 Cavernous hemangioma. **A,** CT scan (axial view) showing a well-circumscribed retrobulbar mass. **B,** Large spaces of blood are separated by thick septa. *(Part A courtesy of Sander Dubovy, MD; part B courtesy of Hans E. Grossniklaus, MD.)*

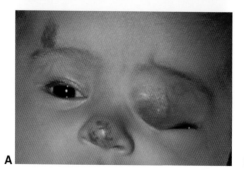

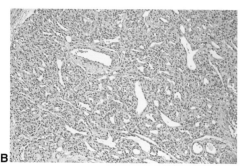

Figure 14-14 Capillary hemangioma. **A,** Infant with multiple capillary hemangiomas. **B,** Note the small capillary-sized vessels and the proliferation of benign endothelial cells. *(Part A courtesy of Sander Dubovy, MD.)*

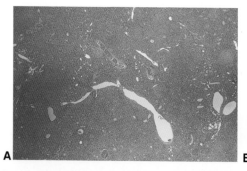

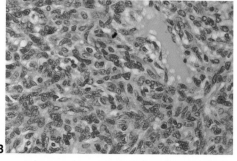

Figure 14-15 Hemangiopericytoma. **A,** Photomicrograph demonstrates a dense spindle-cell tumor with a characteristic branching vascular pattern. **B,** Higher magnification demonstrates closely packed, round to oval cells with vesicular nuclei. *(Courtesy of Ben J. Glasgow, MD.)*

Three histologic types of orbital rhabdomyosarcoma are recognized (Fig 14-16):

1. embryonal (the most common)
2. alveolar
3. differentiated (pleomorphic)

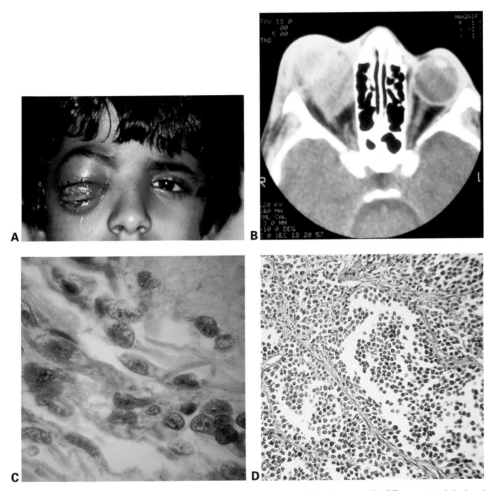

Figure 14-16 Rhabdomyosarcoma. **A,** Child with a large orbital mass. **B,** CT scan (axial view) showing a large, poorly circumscribed orbital tumor. **C,** The neoplastic cells tend to differentiate toward muscle cells. In this moderately differentiated embryonal example, cross-striations representing Z-bands of actin–myosin complexes within the cytoplasm can be easily identified. It is common for these cells to be more primitive, with a featureless abundant cytoplasm. In the less-differentiated cases, electron microscopy and immunohistochemistry may be necessary to correctly identify this neoplasm. **D,** Poorly cohesive rhabdomyoblasts separated by fibrous septa into "alveoli" are low-magnification histologic features of the alveolar variant of rhabdomyosarcoma. This variant may have a less favorable natural history than the more common embryonal type. *(Parts A and B courtesy of Sander Dubovy, MD.)*

Embryonal rhabdomyosarcoma may develop in the conjunctiva and may present as grape-like submucosal clusters *(botryoid variant)*. Histologically, spindle cells are arranged in a loose syncytium with occasional cells bearing cross-striations, which are found in about 60% of embryonal rhabdomyosarcomas. Well-differentiated rhabdomyosarcomas feature numerous cells with striking cross-striations. Immunohistochemical reactivity for desmin and muscle-specific actin may be identified. Electron microscopy is often helpful, especially in the less well-differentiated cases of embryonal rhabdomyosarcoma, to demonstrate the typical sarcomeric banding pattern.

Leiomyomas and leiomyosarcomas

Tumors with smooth-muscle differentiation are rare. *Leiomyomas* are benign tumors that typically manifest with slowly progressive proptosis in patients in the fourth and fifth decades. Histologically, these spindle-cell tumors show blunt-ended, cigar-shaped nuclei and trichrome-positive filamentous cytoplasm. *Leiomyosarcomas* are malignant lesions that typically occur in patients in the seventh decade. Histologically, more cellularity, necrosis, pleomorphism, and mitotic figures appear in leiomyosarcomas than in leiomyomas.

Tumors With Fibrous Differentiation

Fibrous histiocytoma (fibroxanthoma) is one of the most common mesenchymal tumors of the orbit in adults. The median age at presentation is 43 years (with a range of 6 months to 85 years), and the upper nasal orbit is the most common site. Most fibrous histiocytomas are benign. The tumor is composed of an admixture of histiocytes and fibroblasts, some of which form a storiform (matlike) pattern (Fig 14-17). Although most are benign, intermediate and malignant varieties do exist. Malignant tumors are identified by a high rate of mitotic activity (more than 1 mitotic figure per high-power field), pleomorphism, and necrosis. Other primary tumors of fibrous connective tissue include nodular fasciitis, fibroma, solitary fibrous tumor, and fibrosarcoma.

Bony Lesions of the Orbit

Fibrous dysplasia of bone may be monostotic or polyostotic. When the orbit is affected, the condition is usually monostotic, and the patient often presents during the first 3 decades of life. The tumor may cross suture lines to involve multiple orbital bones. Narrowing of the optic canal and lacrimal drainage system can occur. Plain radiographic studies show a ground-glass appearance with lytic foci. Cysts containing fluid also appear. As a result of

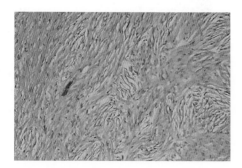

Figure 14-17 Fibrous histiocytoma. This photomicrograph illustrates the storiform (matlike) pattern.

arrest in the maturation of bone, trabeculae are composed of woven bone with a fibrous stroma that is highly vascularized rather than lamellar bone. The bony trabeculae often have a C-shaped appearance.

Katz BJ, Nerad JA. Ophthalmic manifestations of fibrous dysplasia: a disease of children and adults. *Ophthalmology.* 1998;105:2207–2215.

Juvenile ossifying fibroma, a variant of fibrous dysplasia, is characterized histologically by spicules of bone rimmed by osteoblasts. At low magnification, ossifying fibroma may be confused with a psammomatous meningioma. The inexperienced histologist can find the correct identification difficult.

Osseous and cartilaginous tumors are rare; of these, *osteoma* is the most common. It is slow growing, well circumscribed, and composed of mature bone. Most commonly, an osteoma arises from the frontal sinus. Other primary tumors in this group include

- osteoblastoma
- giant cell tumor
- chondroma
- Ewing sarcoma
- osteogenic sarcoma
- chondrosarcoma

For AJCC definitions and staging of orbital sarcomas, see Table A-7 in the appendix.

Nerve Sheath Tumors

Neurofibromas are the most common nerve sheath tumor. This slow-growing tumor includes an admixture of endoneural fibroblasts, Schwann cells, and axons. Neurofibromas may be circumscribed but are not encapsulated. The consistency is firm and rubbery. Microscopically, the spindle-shaped cells are arranged in ribbons and cords in a matrix of myxoid tissue and collagen that contains axons.

Isolated neurofibromas do not necessarily indicate systemic involvement, but the plexiform type of neurofibroma is associated with neurofibromatosis type 1, also called von Recklinghausen disease (Fig 14-18).

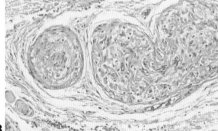

Figure 14-18 Plexiform neurofibroma. **A,** Clinical photograph depicting a typical S-shaped deformity of the upper eyelid. **B,** The trunk of the nerve is enlarged by proliferation of endoneural fibroblasts and Schwann cells. Axons may be demonstrated within the lesion. *(Part A courtesy of Sander Dubovy, MD.)*

The *neurilemoma* (also called *schwannoma*) arises from Schwann cells. Slow growing and encapsulated, this yellowish tumor may show cysts and areas of hemorrhagic necrosis. It may be solitary or associated with neurofibromatosis. Two histologic patterns appear microscopically: Antoni A spindle cells are arranged in interlacing cords, whorls, or palisades that may form Verocay bodies, or collections of fibrils resembling sensory corpuscles. Antoni B tissue is made up of stellate cells with a mucoid stroma. Vessels are usually prominent and thick-walled, and no axons are present (Fig 14-19).

Adipose Tumors

Lipomas are rare in the orbit. Pathologic characteristics include encapsulation and a distinctive lobular appearance. Because lipomas are histologically difficult to distinguish from normal or prolapsed fat, their incidence might have been previously overestimated.

Liposarcomas are malignant tumors that are extremely rare in the orbit. Histologic criteria depend on the type of liposarcoma, but the unifying diagnostic feature is the presence of lipoblasts. These tumors tend to recur before they metastasize.

Metastatic Tumors

Secondary tumors are those that invade the orbit by direct extension from adjacent structures such as sinus, bone, or eye. *Metastatic* tumors are those that spread from a primary site such as the breast in women and the prostate in men. In children, neuroblastoma is the most common primary origin.

McLean IW, Burnier MN, Zimmerman LE, Jakobiec FA. *Tumors of the Eye and Ocular Adnexa.* Washington: Armed Forces Institute of Pathology; 1995:215–298.

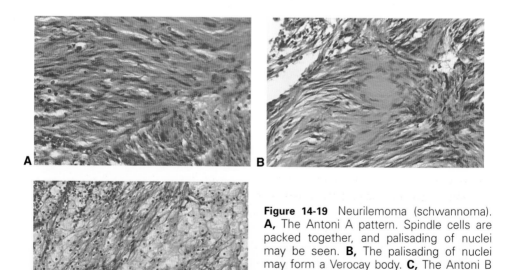

Figure 14-19 Neurilemoma (schwannoma). **A,** The Antoni A pattern. Spindle cells are packed together, and palisading of nuclei may be seen. **B,** The palisading of nuclei may form a Verocay body. **C,** The Antoni B pattern represents degeneration within the tumor. The histologic structures are loosely teased apart.

CHAPTER 15

Optic Nerve

Topography

The optic nerve, embryologically derived from the optic stalk, is a continuation of the optic tract; thus, the pathology of the optic nerve reflects that of the central nervous system (CNS). The optic nerve is 35–55 mm in length and extends from the eye to the optic chiasm (Fig 15-1). Its axons originate from the retinal ganglion cell layer and have a myelin coat posterior to the lamina cribrosa. The intraocular portion is 0.7–1.0 mm in length, the intraorbital portion 25–30 mm, and the intracanalicular portion 4–10 mm. The length of the intracranial portion varies according to the position of the chiasm but averages 10 mm. The diameter is 3.0–3.5 mm, tapering to 1.5 mm in the scleral canal.

Oligodendrocytes, astrocytes, and microglial cells are glial cells (*glia* = glue). Oligodendrocytes produce and maintain the myelin that sheaths the optic nerve. Myelination stops at the lamina cribrosa (Fig 15-2). Occasionally, aberrant patches of myelin are seen in the nerve fiber layer of the retina as discrete, flat, feathery white patches. Astrocytes are involved with support and nutrition. Microglial cells (CNS histiocytes) have a phagocytic function.

The coat of meninges includes the dura mater (which merges with the sclera), the cellular arachnoid layer, and the vascular pia. Arachnoid cells may lie in nests that can contain corpora arenacea; these nests are most obvious in young patients. The pial vessels extend into the optic nerve and subdivide the nerve fibers into fascicles. The subarachnoid space, which contains cerebrospinal fluid (CSF), ends blindly at the termination of the meninges (Fig 15-3).

Blood supply to different portions of the optic nerve comes from a variety of sources. The ophthalmic artery comes through the pia and supplies the intraorbital and intraocular portion. In general, the periaxial fibers are supplied by the pial vessels, and the axial fibers by the central retinal artery, which passes directly through the subarachnoid space to the nerve. The vein, however, is oblique and has a variable course.

BCSC Section 2, *Fundamentals and Principles of Ophthalmology,* discusses and illustrates the anatomy of the optic nerve. Section 5, *Neuro-Ophthalmology,* also covers the physiology and pathology of the optic disc and optic nerve.

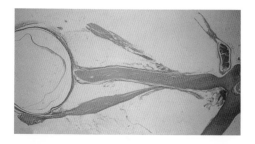

Figure 15-1 Low-power photomicrograph shows the relationship of the optic nerve to the eye and extraocular muscle. *(Courtesy of Hans E. Grossniklaus, MD.)*

Figure 15-2 Photomicrograph shows the termination of myelinated axons at the lamina cribrosa *(arrows)*.

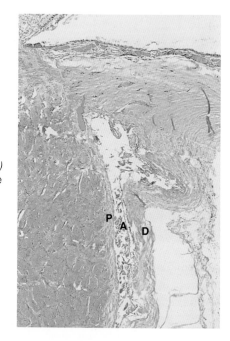

Figure 15-3 Normal optic nerve. The dura mater *(D)* is continuous with the sclera anteriorly. Note the arachnoid *(A)* and the pia *(P)*.

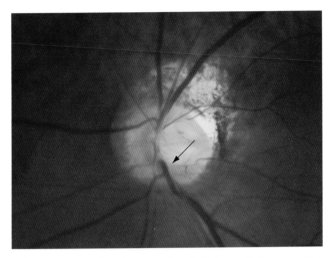

Figure 15-4 Clinical appearance of optic nerve head pit *(arrow). (Courtesy of Debra J. Shetlar, MD.)*

Congenital Anomalies

Pits

Optic nerve head pits presumably arise as defects in closure of the fetal fissure. Pits usually appear temporally and are associated with visual field defects, serous retinal detachments, and occasionally colobomas in the fellow eye. Loss of retinal ganglion cells and nerve fibers occurs in the region of the pit, and meningeal cysts have been described in association with closed pits (Fig 15-4).

Colobomas

Colobomas of the optic nerve head result from failure of closure of the fetal fissure. Optic nerve head colobomas are located inferior to the nerve head and are associated with colobomas of the retina, choroid, ciliary body, and iris. Cystic outpouchings in the sclera may produce a cyst lined by degenerated choroid and gliotic retina (microphthalmos with cyst). (See BCSC Section 6, *Pediatric Ophthalmology and Strabismus*, Chapter 25, Fig 25-2.)

Inflammations

Infectious

Infections of the optic nerve may be secondary to bacterial and mycotic infections of adjacent anatomical structures, such as the eye, brain, or sinus, or they may occur as part of a systemic infection, particularly in the immunosuppressed patient. Fungal infections include mucormycosis, cryptococcosis, and coccidioidomycosis. Mucormycosis generally results from contiguous sinus infection. Cryptococcosis results from direct extension of the infection from the CNS and often produces multiple foci of necrosis with little inflammatory reaction. Coccidioidomycosis produces necrotizing granulomas.

Viral infections of the optic nerve are usually associated with other CNS lesions. Multiple sclerosis and acute disseminated myelitis produce loss of myelin early, but initially the axons are undamaged, and visual function may return. The damaged myelin is removed by macrophages (Fig 15-5). Astrocytic proliferation then occurs to produce a glial scar, which is known as a *plaque*.

Noninfectious

Noninfectious inflammatory disorders of the optic nerve include giant cell arteritis and sarcoidosis. *Giant cell arteritis* may produce granulomatous mural inflammation and occlusion of posterior ciliary vessels with liquefactive necrosis of the optic nerve.

Sarcoidosis of the optic nerve is often associated with retinal, vitreal, and uveitic lesions (Fig 15-6; see also Fig 12-8). Unlike the characteristic noncaseating granulomas in the eye, optic nerve lesions may feature necrosis.

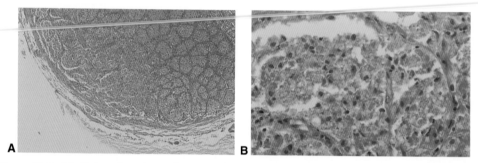

Figure 15-5 Multiple sclerosis, optic nerve. **A,** Luxol-fast blue stain, counterstained with H&E. The blue-staining area indicates normal myelin. Note the absence of myelin in the lower left corner of the optic nerve, corresponding to a focal lesion. **B,** Higher magnification. The blue material (myelin) is engulfed by macrophages.

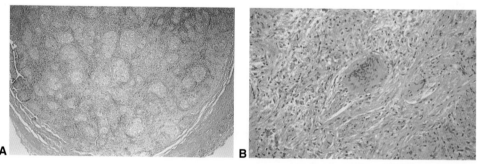

Figure 15-6 Sarcoidosis. **A,** Low-magnification photomicrograph of the optic nerve with discrete noncaseating granuloma. **B,** Higher magnification shows multinucleated giant cells in the granulomas. *(Courtesy of Hans E. Grossniklaus, MD.)*

Degenerations

Optic Atrophy

Loss of retinal ganglion cells because of glaucoma or infarction results in degeneration of their axons and is known as *ascending atrophy.* (See BCSC Section 5, *Neuro-Ophthalmology,* Chapter 3, Fig 3-2.) Pathologic processes within the cranial cavity or orbit result in *descending atrophy.* Axonal degeneration is accompanied by loss of myelin and oligodendrocytes. The optic nerve shrinks despite the proliferation of astrocytes, and thickened pial strands result from proliferation of connective tissue (Fig 15-7).

The portion of the optic nerve nearer the lateral geniculate body is described as *central,* and the portion nearer the retina is described as *peripheral.* Injury to the retina or to any peripheral portion of the optic nerve results in rapid ascending atrophy of the central portion. Initially, the axons at the peripheral portion swell. Retrograde degeneration of the axons then occurs with loss of retinal ganglion cells.

Cavernous optic atrophy of Schnabel is characterized microscopically by large cystic spaces containing mucopolysaccharide material, which stains with alcian blue, posterior to the lamina cribrosa (Fig 15-8). The intracystic material that penetrates into the parenchyma

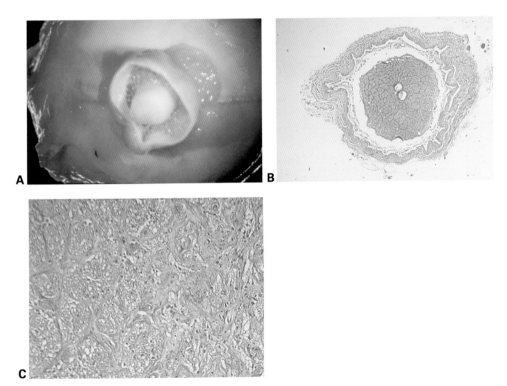

Figure 15-7 Atrophic optic nerve. **A,** Gross appearance of atrophic optic nerve. **B,** Low magnification. Note the widened subdural space. **C,** Higher magnification shows changes in the dura mater, arachnoid, and pia. *(Part A courtesy of Debra J. Shetlar, MD.)*

through the internal limiting membrane of the optic nerve head is thought to be vitreous. These changes occur most commonly in patients with glaucoma after acute IOP elevation, but they have also been seen in nonglaucomatous elderly patients with generalized arteriosclerotic disease.

Albert DM, Jakobiec FA, eds. *Principles and Practice of Ophthalmology.* 2nd ed. Philadelphia: Saunders; 2000:3875–3877.

Drusen

Drusen of the optic disc consist of hyaline-like calcified material within the nerve substance (Fig 15-9). They are usually bilateral and may be complicated by neovascularization and hemorrhage. They are thought to result from intracellular mitochondrial calcification within the axons. Optic disc drusen may produce field defects, and their presence can cause enlargement of the papilla that may be mistaken for papilledema (pseudopapilledema).

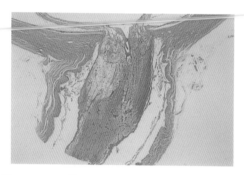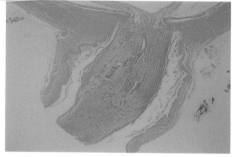

Figure 15-8 Cavernous optic atrophy of Schnabel. Photomicrographs show cystic atrophy within the optic nerve. The cystic space is filled with alcian blue–staining material. *(Courtesy of Hans E. Grossniklaus, MD.)*

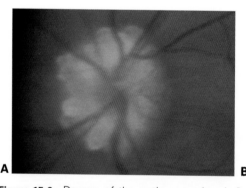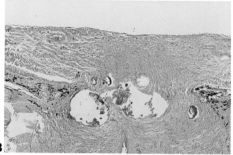

A   B

Figure 15-9 Drusen of the optic nerve head. **A,** Clinical appearance of optic disc drusen. **B,** Note the local zones of calcification just anterior to the lamina cribrosa. *(Part A courtesy of Debra J. Shetlar, MD.)*

Giant drusen are associated with the phakomatoses such as tuberous sclerosis and neurofibromatosis, which are considered to be hamartomatous proliferations of astrocytes with secondary calcification. (See BCSC Section 6, *Pediatric Ophthalmology and Strabismus,* for further discussion of the phakomatoses.) Giant drusen lie anterior to the lamina cribrosa.

Optic disc drusen may be associated with acquired disease such as angioid streaks, papillitis, optic atrophy, chronic glaucoma, and vascular occlusions. They may occur in otherwise normal eyes and are occasionally dominantly inherited. They can be diagnosed using B-scan echography, ultrasound, or fundus photography with a fluorescein filter in place (autofluorescence).

Spencer WH, ed. *Ophthalmic Pathology: An Atlas and Textbook.* 4th ed. Philadelphia: Saunders; 1996:537–541.

Neoplasia

Tumors may affect the optic nerve head (eg, melanocytoma, peripapillary choroidal melanoma, pigment epithelium proliferation, and hemangioma) or the retrobulbar portion of the optic nerve (eg, glioma and meningioma).

Melanocytoma

A melanocytoma is a benign, deeply pigmented melanocytic tumor situated eccentrically on the disc, projecting less than 2 mm into the vitreous and extending into the lower temporal retina and posteriorly beyond the lamina (Fig 15-10). Slow growth may occur. A bleached section shows closely apposed plump cells of uniform character with abundant cytoplasm and small nuclei with little chromatin. Nucleoli are small and regular. See also Chapter 17.

Glioma

A glioma may arise in any part of the visual pathway, including the optic disc and optic nerve. The most common cell of origin is the spindle-shaped or hairlike (pilocytic) astrocyte (juvenile pilocytic astrocytoma) (Fig 15-11A and B). Optic nerve gliomas are frequently associated with neurofibromatosis (NF1), an autosomal dominant disorder, with

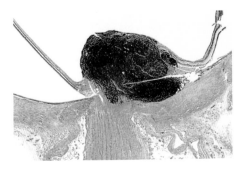

Figure 15-10 Melanocytoma of the optic nerve. The choroid adjacent to the optic nerve is also involved by this tumor. The cells of the tumor are so densely packed with melanin that the cytologic detail is not visible without higher magnification and melanin bleaching.

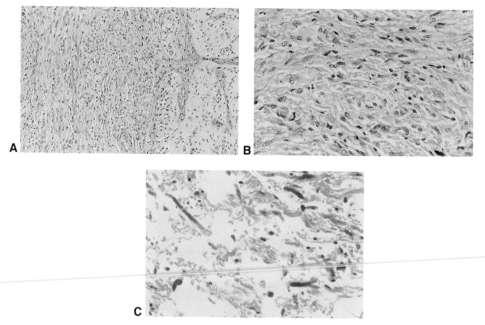

Figure 15-11 Astrocytoma of the optic nerve. **A,** The right side of this photograph demonstrates normal optic nerve, and the left side shows a pilocytic astrocytoma. **B,** The neoplastic glial cells are elongated to resemble hairs (hence the term *pilocytic*). **C,** Degenerating eosinophilic filaments, known as *Rosenthal fibers,* are not unique to astrocytoma of the optic nerve.

the gene, a tumor suppressor, located on the long arm of chromosome 17q11. The tumors most commonly present in the first decade and are of low grade.

Enlarged, deeply eosinophilic filaments, representing degenerating cell processes known as *Rosenthal fibers,* may be found in these low-grade tumors (Fig 15-11C). Foci of microcystic degeneration and calcification may occur, and the pial septa are thickened. The meninges show a reactive hyperplasia with proliferation of spindle-shaped meningeal cells and infiltration with astrocytes. The dura mater remains intact, so the nerve appears tubular or sausage-shaped. Some evidence indicates that these tumors may undergo slow, progressive growth.

High-grade tumors (grade 4 astrocytomas, glioblastoma multiforme) rarely involve the optic nerve. When this does occur, the optic nerve is usually involved secondarily from a brain tumor.

Meningioma

Primary optic nerve sheath meningiomas occur much less frequently than secondary orbital meningiomas. Optic nerve meningiomas arise within the arachnoid of the optic nerve, whereas secondary orbital meningiomas extend from an intracranial primary site (Fig 15-12A and B). Extradural tumors that arise from ectopic meningothelial cells, within the muscle cone or at the roof or orbital floor, are rare.

The mean age at presentation of primary meningioma is lower than that of the secondary type (20% of patients are less than 10 years of age). Tumor growth is slow. Primary

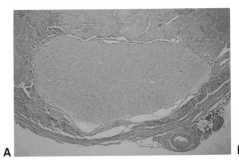

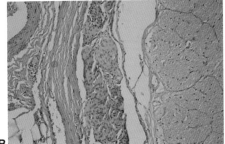

A

B

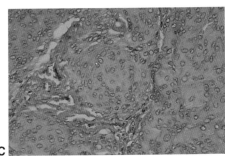

C

Figure 15-12 Optic nerve meningioma. **A,** This meningioma has grown circumferentially around the optic nerve and has compressed the nerve. **B,** Meningioma of the optic nerve originates from the arachnoid. **C,** Note the whorls of tumor cells, characteristic of the meningothelial type of meningioma, the most common histologic variant arising from the optic nerve.

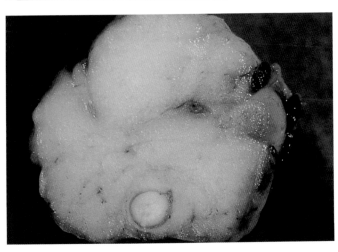

Figure 15-13 Optic nerve meningioma. The shaggy border of this gross specimen emphasizes the tendency of the perioptic meningioma to invade surrounding orbital tissues.

optic nerve meningiomas may invade the nerve and the eye and may extend through the dura mater to invade muscle (Fig 15-13).

Microscopically, the tumor (primary or secondary) is usually of the meningotheliomatous type, with plump cells arranged in whorls (Fig 15-12C). Psammoma bodies tend to be sparse. Patient survival is longer (up to 19 years) with primary orbital meningiomas than with those of secondary type (up to 15 years). Although meningioma may rarely be associated with neurofibromatosis in the younger age group, it is a less frequent hallmark of NF1 than is optic nerve glioma.

Albert DM, Jakobiec FA, eds. *Principles and Practice of Ophthalmology.* 2nd ed. Philadelphia: Saunders; 2000:3881–3883.

PART **II**

Intraocular Tumors:
Clinical Aspects

CHAPTER **16**

Introduction to Part II

Intraocular tumors comprise a broad spectrum of benign and malignant lesions that can lead to loss of vision and loss of life. Effective management of these lesions depends on accurate diagnosis. In most cases, experienced ophthalmologists diagnose intraocular neoplasms by clinical examination and ancillary diagnostic tests, and investigators in the Collaborative Ocular Melanoma Study (COMS) reported a misdiagnosis rate of less than 0.2%. One diagnostic aid that may be used to evaluate intraocular tumors is fine-needle aspiration biopsy (FNAB), although the indications for this technique are limited. FNAB may help to confirm the presence of choroidal metastases or provide tumor for cytogenetic studies in patients with choroidal melanoma, but FNAB of tumors suspected to be retinoblastoma is strongly discouraged, as it may result in extraocular dissemination of the disease. (FNAB is discussed in greater detail in Chapter 4.)

Important information concerning the most common primary intraocular malignancy in adults, choroidal melanoma, was gathered in the COMS. The COMS, which was funded in 1985, incorporated both randomized clinical trials for patients with medium and large choroidal melanomas and an observational study for patients with small choroidal melanomas. The COMS reported outcomes for enucleation versus brachytherapy for the treatment of medium tumors and for enucleation alone versus pre-enucleation external-beam radiotherapy for large melanomas. Survival data from the large, medium, and small treatment arms of the COMS are available. In addition to the study's primary objectives, the COMS has provided data regarding local tumor failure rates after iodine 125 brachytherapy as well as visual acuity outcomes following this globe-conserving treatment. These findings have shifted the primary treatment of choroidal melanoma from enucleation toward globe-conserving brachytherapy. (See Chapter 17.)

The predisposing gene for retinoblastoma has been isolated, cloned, and sequenced. As with choroidal melanoma, retinoblastoma therapy is also undergoing a transition toward globe-conserving therapy, with a renewed interest in combined-modality therapy focused particularly on systemic chemotherapy coupled with focal therapy. This trend toward chemotherapy has been fueled by our growing understanding of the potential risks of primary external-beam radiotherapy for increasing the incidence of secondary (radiation-induced) malignancies in children with a germline mutation of the retinoblastoma gene. Advances in our understanding of the molecular genetics of retinoblastoma continue to enhance our ability to screen and treat this pediatric ocular malignancy. (See Chapter 19.)

CHAPTER 17

Melanocytic Tumors

Iris Nevus

An iris nevus generally appears as a darkly pigmented lesion of the iris stroma with minimal distortion of the iris architecture (Fig 17-1). The true incidence of iris nevi remains uncertain because many of these lesions produce no symptoms and are recognized incidentally during routine ophthalmic examination. Iris nevi may present in 2 forms:

1. *circumscribed iris nevus:* typically nodular, involving a discrete portion of the iris
2. *diffuse iris nevus:* may involve an entire sector or, rarely, the entire iris

In some cases, the lesion causes slight ectropion iridis and sectoral cataract. The incidence of iris nevi may be higher in the eyes of patients with neurofibromatosis.

Iris nevi are best evaluated by slit-lamp biomicroscopy coupled with gonioscopic evaluation of the angle structures. Specific attention should be given to lesions involving the angle structures to rule out a previously unrecognized ciliary body tumor. The most important possibility in the differential diagnosis of iris nevi is iris melanoma. When iris melanoma is included within the differential diagnosis, close observation with scheduled serial reevaluation is indicated. Clinical evaluation of suspicious iris nevi should include slit-lamp photography and high-frequency ultrasound biomicroscopy. Iris nevi usually require no treatment once they are diagnosed, but, when suspected, they should be followed closely and photographed to evaluate for growth.

Nevus of the Ciliary Body or Choroid

Nevi of the ciliary body are occasionally incidental findings in histopathologic examination of globes that are enucleated for other reasons. Choroidal nevi may occur in up to 7% of the population. In most cases, they have no clinical symptoms and are recognized on routine ophthalmic examination. The typical choroidal nevus appears ophthalmoscopically as a flat or minimally elevated pigmented (gray-brown) choroidal lesion with indistinct margins (Fig 17-2). Some nevi are amelanotic and may be less apparent. Choroidal nevi may be associated with overlying RPE disturbance, serous detachment, drusen, choroidal neovascular membranes, and orange pigment; and they may produce visual field defects. On fluorescein angiography, choroidal nevi may either hypofluoresce or hyperfluoresce, depending on the associated findings. Ocular and oculodermal

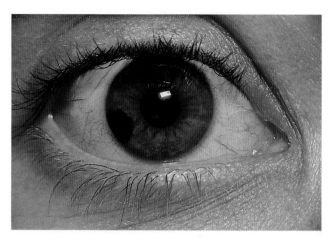

Figure 17-1 Iris nevus, clinical appearance. The lesion is only slightly raised from the iris surface, and lesion color is homogeneous brown.

melanocytosis may predispose to uveal malignancy, with an estimated lifetime risk of 1 in 400 in the white population. Choroidal nevi are distinguished from choroidal melanomas by clinical evaluation and ancillary testing. No single clinical factor is pathognomonic for benign versus malignant choroidal melanocytic lesions. The differential diagnosis for pigmented lesions in the ocular fundus most commonly includes the following:

- choroidal nevus
- malignant melanoma
- atypical disciform scar associated with age-related macular degeneration (AMD)
- suprachoroidal hemorrhage
- RPE hyperplasia
- congenital hypertrophy of the retinal pigment epithelium (CHRPE)
- choroidal hemangioma with RPE hyperpigmentation
- melanocytoma
- metastatic carcinoma with RPE hyperpigmentation
- choroidal osteoma

Virtually all choroidal melanocytic tumors thicker than 3 mm are melanomas, and virtually all choroidal melanocytic lesions thinner than 1 mm are nevi. Many lesions 1–2 mm in thickness (apical height) may be benign, although the risk of malignancy increases with height. It is difficult to classify with certainty tumors that are 1–2 mm in thickness. Flat lesions with a basal diameter of 10 mm or less are almost always benign. The risk of malignancy increases for lesions that are larger than 10 mm in basal diameter.

Clinical risk factors for enlargement of choroidal melanocytic lesions have been well characterized and include

- subjective clinical symptoms such as metamorphopsia, photopsia, visual field loss
- presence of orange pigmentation
- associated subretinal fluid

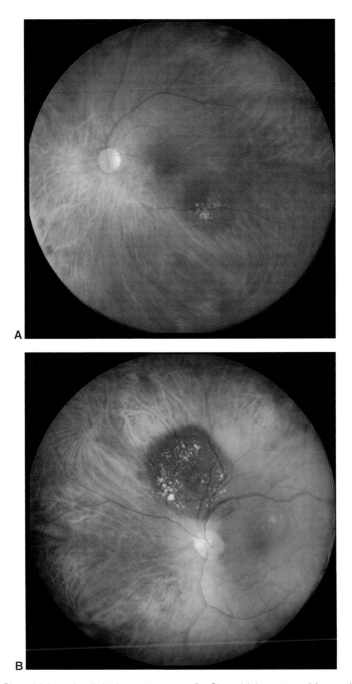

Figure 17-2 Choroidal nevi, clinical appearance. **A,** Choroidal nevus with overlying drusen, under the lower temporal retinovascular arcade. **B,** Medium-sized choroidal nevus with overlying drusen, superior to the optic nerve head. *(Courtesy of Jacob Pe'er, MD.)*

- larger size at presentation
- juxtapapillary location
- absence of drusen or RPE changes
- hot spots on fluorescein photography
- homogeneity on ultrasonography

If definite enlargement is documented, malignant change should be suspected.

The recommended management of choroidal nevi is photographic documentation for lesions less than 1 mm in thickness and photographic and ultrasonographic documentation for lesions greater than 1 mm in thickness, coupled with regular, periodic reassessment for signs of growth.

Melanocytoma of the Iris, Ciliary Body, or Choroid

Melanocytomas are rare tumors with a characteristic large, polyhedral shape; small nuclei; and cytoplasm filled with melanin granules (see Fig 15-10). Cells from iris melanocytomas may seed to the anterior chamber angle, causing glaucoma. Melanocytomas of the ciliary body are usually not seen clinically due to their peripheral location. In some cases, extrascleral extension of the tumor along an emissary canal appears as a darkly pigmented, fixed subconjunctival mass. Melanocytomas of the choroid appear as elevated, pigmented tumors, simulating a nevus or melanoma. Melanocytomas have been reported to undergo malignant change in some instances. When a melanocytoma is suspected, photographic and echographic studies are appropriate. If growth is documented, the lesion should be treated as a malignancy.

Iris Melanoma

Iris melanomas account for 3%–10% of all uveal melanomas. Small malignant melanomas of the iris may be impossible to differentiate clinically from benign iris nevi and other simulating lesions. The following conditions may be included in a differential diagnosis of iris melanoma:

- iris nevus
- primary iris cyst (pigment epithelial and stromal)
- iridocorneal endothelial syndrome
- iris foreign body
- peripheral anterior synechiae
- metastatic carcinoma to iris
- aphakic iris cyst
- iris atrophy, miscellaneous
- pigment epithelial hyperplasia or migration

- juvenile xanthogranuloma
- medulloepithelioma
- retained lens material simulating iris nodule

Signs suggesting malignancy include extensive ectropion iridis, prominent vascularity, sectoral cataract, secondary glaucoma, seeding of the peripheral angle structures, extrascleral extension, lesion size, and documented progressive growth. Iris melanomas range in appearance from amelanotic to dark brown lesions, and three quarters of them involve the inferior iris (Fig 17-3). In rare instances, they assume a diffuse growth pattern, producing a syndrome of unilateral acquired hyperchromic heterochromia and secondary glaucoma. Clinical evaluation is identical to that for iris nevi. The differential diagnosis of iris nodules is listed in Table 17-1; Figure 17-4 illustrates the various iris nodules. See also Figure 12-10 in Chapter 12.

Recent advances in high-frequency ultrasonography allow for excellent characterization of tumor size and anatomical relationship to normal ocular structures (Fig 17-5). Fluorescein angiography may document intrinsic vascularity, although this finding is of limited value in establishing a differential diagnosis. In rare instances, biopsy may be considered when the management of the lesion is in question. In most cases, when growth or severe glaucoma occurs, diagnostic and therapeutic excisional treatment is indicated. Brachytherapy using custom-designed plaques may be used in selected cases. Specifically designed proton-beam radiotherapy has also been reported for iris melanoma. The prognosis for most patients with iris melanomas is excellent, with a lower mortality rate (1%–4%) than that for ciliary body and choroidal melanomas, possibly because the biological behavior of most of these iris tumors appears distinctly different from that of ciliary or choroidal melanoma.

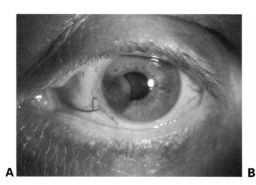

A

B

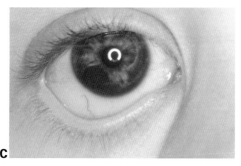

C

Figure 17-3 Iris melanoma, clinical appearance. **A,** Mildly pigmented iris melanoma on the nasal side, involving also the anterior chamber angle. A sentinel vessel is growing toward the area of the melanoma. **B,** Melanoma in the lower part of the iris. **C,** Melanoma in the lower temporal area, spreading to other parts of the iris. *(Photographs courtesy of Jacob Pe'er, MD.)*

Table 17-1 Differential Diagnostic Features of Iris Nodules (alphabetical list)

Lesion	Features
Brushfield spots (Down syndrome) (Fig 17-4A)	Elevated white to light yellow spots in periphery of iris, 10–20 per eye. Incidence in Down syndrome is 85%; otherwise, 24%. Histopathologically, the spots are areas of relatively normal iris stroma surrounded by a ring of mild iris hypoplasia. Anterior border layer slightly increased in density.
Epithelial invasion, serous cyst, solid or pearl cyst, implantation membrane	Each follows surgery or injury. Appears as serous or solid cysts in continuity with the wound or as implantation cysts or membranes on the anterior iris surface.
Foreign body, retained	Usually becomes secondarily pigmented and may be associated with chronic iridocyclitis and peripheral anterior synechiae.
Fungal endophthalmitis	Irregular yellow-white mass on iris. May be accompanied by hypopyon or only mild inflammatory signs.
Iridocyclitis	The iris nodules of classic granulomatous anterior uveitis occur either superficially or deeply within the iris. Koeppe nodules occur at the pupillary border, and Busacca nodules lie on the anterior iris surface. Microscopically, they are composed of large and small mononuclear cells.
Iris freckle (Fig 17-4B)	Stationary, lightly to darkly pigmented flat areas on anterior iris surface composed of anterior border layer melanocytes containing increased pigmentation without increase in number of melanocytes.
Iris nevus (Fig 17-1)	Discrete mass(es) or nodule(s) on anterior iris surface and in the iris stroma. Variable pigmentation. Composed of benign nevus cells. Increased incidence of iris nevi in patients with neurofibromatosis.
Iris nevus syndrome (Cogan-Reese)	Acquired diffuse nevus of iris associated with unilateral glaucoma, heterochromia, peripheral anterior synechiae, and extension of endothelium and Descemet's membrane over trabecular meshwork. Obliteration of normal iris architecture. (See ICE syndrome, Chapter 7.)
Iris pigment epithelial cysts (Fig 17-4C)	Cysts encompassing both layers of neuroepithelium. Produce a localized elevation of stroma and may be pigmented. May transilluminate. May be better seen after dilation. B-scan ultrasonography of value in diagnosis.
Iris pigment epithelial proliferation	Congenital or acquired (trauma or surgery) plaques of pigment epithelium displaying a black, velvety appearance.
Juvenile xanthogranuloma	Yellowish to gray, poorly demarcated iris lesions associated with raised orange skin lesion(s) (single or multiple) appearing in the first year of life. May be associated with spontaneous hyphema and secondary glaucoma. Histopathologically, there is a diffuse granulomatous infiltrate with lipid-containing histiocytes and Touton giant cells. The lesions regress spontaneously. May also be found in ciliary body, anterior choroid, episclera, cornea, eyelids, and orbit.
Leiomyoma	May be well localized and even pedunculated, often diffuse and flat, and usually lightly pigmented. Electron microscopy required for clear differentiation between leiomyoma and amelanotic spindle cell melanoma.
Leukemia (Fig 17-4D)	Very rare nodular or diffuse milky lesions with intense hyperemia. Often, the iris loses its architecture, becomes thickened, and develops heterochromia. Pseudohypopyon is common.

(Continued)

Table 17-1 *(continued)*

Lesion	Features
Lisch nodules (neurofibromatosis) (Fig 17-4E)	One of the diagnostic criteria for neurofibromatosis. Multiple lesions varying from tan to dark brown and about the size of a pinhead. May be flat or project from the surface. Histopathologically, they are composed of collections of nevus cells.
Malignant melanoma (Fig 17-3)	Occurs as nodular or flat growths, usually in the periphery, especially inferiorly or inferotemporally. Variably pigmented, often with satellite pigmentation and pigmentation in the anterior chamber angle and nutrient vessels. Pupil may dilate irregularly, and elevated IOP may be present.
Melanocytosis, congenital ocular and oculodermal	Generally unilateral with diffuse uveal nevus causing heterochromia iridis associated with blue or slate gray patches of sclera and episclera. In oculodermal melanocytosis, eyelid and brow are also involved. Malignant potential exists.
Metastatic carcinoma	Gelatinous to white vascularized nodules on the iris surface and in the anterior chamber angle. May be associated with anterior uveitis, hyphema, rubeosis, and glaucoma.
Retinoblastoma	White foci on the anterior iris surface or in the anterior chamber angle, or a pseudohypopyon.
Tapioca melanoma	Tapioca-like nodules lying over a portion or all of the iris. May be translucent to lightly pigmented in color. Often associated with unilateral glaucoma.

Butler P, Char DH, Zarbin M, Kroll S. Natural history of indeterminate pigmented choroidal tumors. *Ophthalmology.* 1994;101:710–716.

Demirci H, Shields CL, Shields JA, Eagle RC Jr, Honavar SG. Diffuse iris melanoma: a report of 25 cases. *Ophthalmology.* 2002;109:1553–1560.

Girkin CA, Goldberg I, Mansberger SL, Shields JA, Shields CL. Management of iris melanoma with secondary glaucoma. *J Glaucoma.* 2002;11:71–74.

Jakobiec FA, Silbert G. Are most iris "melanomas" really nevi? A clinicopathologic study of 189 lesions. *Arch Ophthalmol.* 1981;99:2117–2132.

Marigo FA, Finger PT, McCormick SA, et al. Iris and ciliary body melanomas: ultrasound biomicroscopy with histopathologic correlation. *Arch Ophthalmol.* 2000;118:1515–1521.

Shields CL, Shields JA, Kiratli H, De Potter P, Cater JR. Risk factors for growth and metastasis of small choroidal melanocytic lesions. *Ophthalmology.* 1995;102:1351–1361.

Singh AD, De Potter P, Fijal BA, Shields CL, Shields JA, Elston RC. Lifetime prevalence of uveal melanoma in white patients with oculo(dermal) melanocytosis. *Ophthalmology.* 1998;105:195–198.

Singh AD, Kalyani P, Topham A. Estimating the risk of malignant transformation of a choroidal nevus. *Ophthalmology.* 2005;112:1784–1789.

Sumich P, Mitchell P, Wang JJ. Choroidal nevi in a white population: the Blue Mountains Eye Study. *Arch Ophthalmol.* 1998;116:645–650.

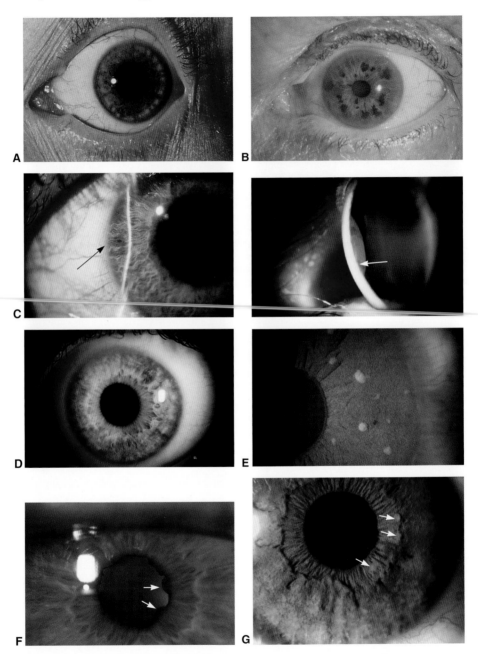

Figure 17-4 **A–G,** Iris nodules. **A,** Brushfields spots in Down syndrome. **B,** Iris freckles. **C,** Pigment epithelial cyst. Prior to dilation *(left),* the iris stroma is bowed forward *(arrow)* in the area of the cyst, which is invisible posteriorly. After dilation *(right),* the cyst of the posterior iris epithelium can be seen *(arrow)* with eye adduction. **D,** Leukemic infiltration of the iris. Note heterochromia, prominent vascularity, and stromal thickening. **E,** Multiple Lisch nodules in neurofibromatosis. **F,** Koeppe nodules at pupil margin *(arrows)* in sarcoidosis. **G,** Busacca nodules in mid-iris *(arrows)* in sarcoidosis. *(Part A courtesy of W.R. Green, MD; parts B and E courtesy of Timothy G. Murray, MD; parts F and G courtesy of R. Christopher Walton, MD.)*

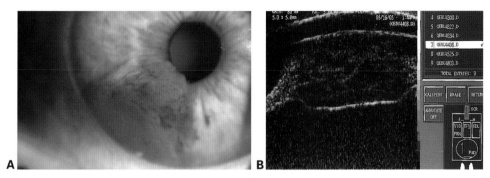

Figure 17-5 **A,** Iris melanoma, clinical appearance. **B,** High-resolution ultrasound, showing replacement of the normal iris stroma by a melanoma. *(Courtesy of Matthew W. Wilson, MD.)*

Melanoma of the Ciliary Body or Choroid

Ciliary body and choroidal melanomas are the most common primary intraocular malignancies in adults. The incidence in the United States is approximately 6–7 cases per million. The tumor, extremely rare in children, primarily affects patients in their 50s and early 60s; it has a predilection for lightly pigmented individuals. Risk factors have not been conclusively identified but may include

- light-colored complexion (white skin, blue eyes, blond hair)
- ocular melanocytic conditions such as melanosis oculi and oculodermal melanocytosis
- genetic predisposition (dysplastic nevus syndrome)
- cigarette smoking

Ciliary body melanomas can be asymptomatic in the early stages. Because of their location behind the iris, ciliary body melanomas may be rather large by the time they are detected. Patients who have symptoms most commonly note visual loss, photopsias, or visual field alterations. Ciliary body melanomas are not usually visible unless the pupil is widely dilated (Fig 17-6A). Some erode through the iris root into the anterior chamber and eventually become visible on external examination or with gonioscopy. Rarely, tumors extend directly through the sclera in the ciliary region, producing a dark epibulbar mass. The initial sign of a ciliary body melanoma may be dilated episcleral sentinel vessels in the quadrant of the tumor (Fig 17-6B). The tumor may eventually become quite large, producing a sectoral or diffuse cataract, subluxated lens (Fig 17-6C), secondary glaucoma, retinal detachment, and even iris neovascularization. Rarely, a ciliary body melanoma assumes a diffuse growth pattern that extends 180°–360° around the ciliary body. This type of melanoma is called a *ring melanoma* (see Fig 12-20 in Chapter 12).

The typical *choroidal melanoma* is a pigmented, elevated, dome-shaped subretinal mass (Fig 17-7A, B). The degree of pigmentation ranges from totally amelanotic to dark brown. With time, many tumors erupt through Bruch's membrane to assume a mushroom-like shape (Fig 17-7C, D). Prominent clumps of orange pigment at the RPE level may appear over the surface of the tumor, and serous detachment of the neurosensory

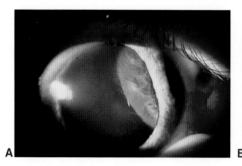
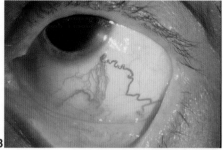

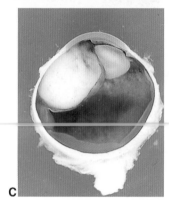

Figure 17-6 **A,** Ciliary body melanoma, clinical appearance. Such tumors may not be evident unless the pupil is widely dilated. **B,** Sentinel vessels. **C,** Ciliary body melanoma, gross pathology. Note mostly amelanotic appearance of this tumor, which is subluxing the lens and causing secondary angle closure. *(Part B courtesy of Timothy G. Murray, MD.)*

retina is common. If an extensive retinal detachment develops, anterior displacement of the lens–iris diaphragm and secondary angle-closure glaucoma occasionally occur. Neovascularization of the iris may also appear in such eyes, and there may be spontaneous hemorrhage into the subretinal space. Vitreous hemorrhage is usually seen only in cases when the melanoma has erupted through Bruch's membrane.

Accuracy of diagnosis of choroidal melanomas in the Collaborative Ocular Melanoma Study. COMS report no. 1. *Arch Ophthalmol.* 1990;108:1268–1273.

Gallagher RP, Elwood JM, Rootman J, et al. Risk factors for ocular melanoma: Western Canada Melanoma Study. *J Natl Cancer Inst.* 1985;74:775–778.

Hu DN, Yu GP, McCormick SA, Schneider S, Finger PT. Population-based incidence of uveal melanoma in various races and ethnic groups. *Am J Ophthalmol.* 2005;140:612–617.

Seddon JM, Gragoudas ES, Glynn RJ, Egan KM, Albert DM, Blitzer PH. Host factors, UV radiation, and risk of uveal melanoma: a case-control study. *Arch Ophthalmol.* 1990;108:1274–1280.

Diagnostic Evaluation

Clinical evaluation of all suspected posterior uveal melanomas of the ciliary body and the choroid should include a history, ophthalmoscopic evaluation, and ancillary testing to definitively establish the diagnosis. When used appropriately, the tests described here enable accurate diagnosis of melanocytic tumors in almost all cases. Atypical lesions may be characterized by several other testing modalities, such as FNAB; or, when appropriate,

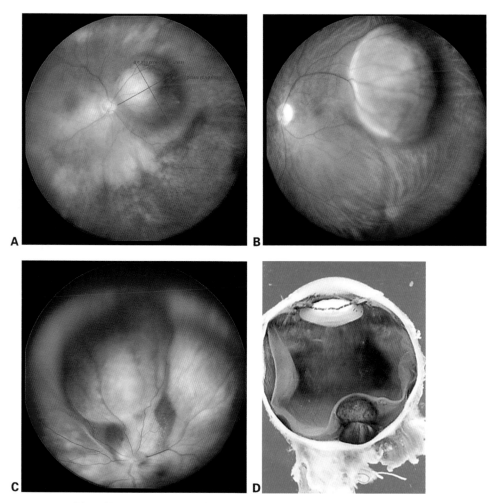

Figure 17-7 Choroidal melanoma. **A,** Small choroidal melanoma touching the nasal border of the optic nerve head, with digital measurement of the tumor diameter. **B,** Medium-sized choroidal melanoma temporal to the macula. **C,** A large choroidal melanoma surrounding the optic nerve head and extending upward to the ora serrata. Note the retinal detachment in the lower half of the retina. **D,** Gross pathology. Note the mushroom-shaped cross section of this darkly pigmented tumor and the associated retinal detachment. *(Parts A–C courtesy of Jacob Pe'er, MD.)*

lesions may be observed for characteristic changes in clinical behavior that will establish a correct diagnosis.

Indirect ophthalmoscopic viewing of the tumor remains the gold standard. It is the single most important diagnostic technique for evaluating patients with intraocular tumors, as it provides stereopsis and a wide field of view and facilitates visualization of the peripheral fundus, particularly when performed with scleral depression. Indirect ophthalmoscopy allows for clinical assessment of tumor basal dimension and apical height. However, it is not useful in eyes with opaque media, which require other diagnostic methods, such as ultrasonography, computed tomography (CT), and/or magnetic resonance imaging (MRI).

Slit-lamp biomicroscopy used in combination with *gonioscopy* offers the best method for establishing the presence and extent of anterior involvement of ciliary body tumors. The use of high-frequency ultrasonography (biomicroscopy) enables excellent visualization of anterior ocular structures and is a significant adjunct to slit-lamp photography for the evaluation and documentation of anterior segment pathology.

In addition, the presence of sectoral cataract, secondary angle involvement, or sentinel vessel formation may be a clue to the diagnosis of ciliary body tumor. Hruby, Goldmann, and other wide-field fundus lenses can be used with the slit lamp to evaluate lesions of the posterior fundus under high magnification. High-magnification fundus evaluation can delineate neurosensory retinal detachment, orange pigmentation, rupture of Bruch's membrane, intraretinal tumor invasion, and vitreous involvement. Fundus biomicroscopy with the 3-mirror contact lens is useful in assessing lesions of the peripheral fundus.

Ultrasonography is the most important ancillary study for evaluating ciliary body and choroidal melanomas (Fig 17-8). It also remains the ancillary test of choice for detection of orbital extension associated with intraocular malignancy. Standardized A-scan ultrasonography provides an accurate assessment of a lesion's internal reflectivity, vascularity, and measurement. Serial examination with A-scan ultrasonography can be used to document growth or regression of an intraocular tumor.

A-scan ultrasonography usually demonstrates a solid tumor pattern with high-amplitude initial echoes and low-amplitude internal reflections (low internal reflectivity). Spontaneous vascular pulsations can also be demonstrated in most cases. B-scan examination provides information about the relative size (height and basal diameters), general shape, and position of intraocular tumors. Occasionally, cross-sectional tumor shape and

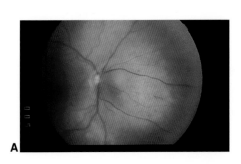

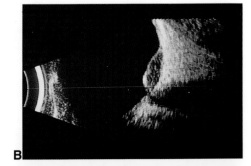

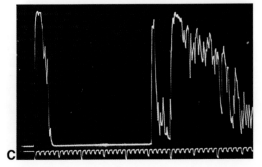

Figure 17-8 **A,** Peripapillary choroidal melanoma. **B,** The peripapillary tumor is seen nasal to the optic nerve. B-scan ultrasonography is used primarily to show the tumor location and its topography. **C,** The A-scan ultrasonogram shows characteristic low internal reflectivity. The pattern of the A scan is used to differentiate tumor types more reliably than does the B-scan pattern.

associated retinal detachment can be detected more easily by ultrasonography than by ophthalmoscopy. B-scan ultrasonography usually shows a dome- or mushroom-shaped choroidal mass with a highly reflective anterior border, acoustic hollowness, choroidal excavation, and occasional orbital shadowing. B-scan ultrasonography can be used to detect intraocular tumors in eyes with either clear or opaque media.

Ultrasonography for ciliary body melanomas is more difficult to interpret because the peripheral location of these tumors makes the test technically more demanding to perform. High-frequency ultrasonography is not limited by the technical difficulties associated with standard B-scan testing and enables excellent imaging of the anterior segment and ciliary body.

Although ultrasonography is generally considered highly reliable in the differential diagnosis of posterior uveal malignant melanoma, it may be difficult or impossible to differentiate a necrotic melanoma from a small subretinal hematoma or a metastatic carcinoma. Advances in 3-dimensional ultrasound imaging may allow for better evaluation of tumor volume, and advances in high-resolution imaging may be able to determine tumor microvasculature patterns predictive of tumor biology (see Chapter 12).

Transillumination may be helpful in evaluating suspected ciliary body or anterior choroidal melanomas. It is valuable in assessing the degree of pigmentation within a lesion and in determining basal diameters of anterior tumors. The shadow of a tumor is visible with a transilluminating light source, preferably a high-intensity fiberoptic device, placed either on the surface of the topically anesthetized eye in a quadrant opposite the lesion or directly on the cornea with a smooth, dark, specially designed corneal cap (Fig 17-9). Fiberoptic transillumination is used during surgery for radioactive applicator insertion to locate the uveal melanoma and delineate its borders.

Fundus photography is valuable for documenting the ophthalmoscopic appearance of choroidal melanoma and for identifying interval changes in the basal size of a lesion in follow-up examinations. Wide-angle fundus photographs (60°–180°) of intraocular tumors can reveal the full extent of most lesions and can document the relationship between lesions and other intraocular structures. The relative positions of retinal blood vessels can be helpful markers of changes in the size of a lesion. New wide-angle fundus cameras enable accurate measurement of the basal diameter of a choroidal melanoma as well as changes in its size, using intrinsic scales. No patterns of *fluorescein angiography* are pathognomonic for choroidal melanoma.

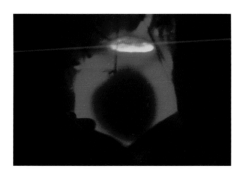

Figure 17-9 Choroidal melanoma, transillumination shadow.

Although *CT* and *MRI* are not widely used in the assessment of uncomplicated intra-ocular melanocytic tumors, these modalities are useful in identifying tumors in eyes with opaque media and in determining extrascleral extension and involvement of other organs. MRI may be helpful in differentiating atypical vascular lesions from melanocytic tumors.

Differential Diagnosis

The most common lesions that should be considered in the differential diagnosis of pos-terior uveal malignant melanoma include suspicious choroidal nevus, disciform macular and extramacular lesions, congenital hypertrophy of the RPE (CHRPE), choroidal heman-gioma (see Chapter 18), melanocytoma, hemorrhagic detachment of the choroid or RPE, metastatic carcinoma (see Chapter 20 and later in this chapter), and choroidal osteoma. Table 17-2 offers a more complete list to be considered in cases with *amelanotic* choroidal masses.

Choroidal nevus has been discussed previously, but it should be reemphasized that no single clinical characteristic is pathognomonic of choroidal melanoma. Diagnostic accuracy is associated with clinical experience and outstanding ancillary testing facili-ties. Evaluation and management of these complex cases within regional ocular oncology referral centers appears to enhance patient outcome.

Age-related macular degeneration (AMD) may present with extramacular or macular subretinal neovascularization and fibrosis accompanied by varying degrees and patterns of pigmentation. Hemorrhage, a common finding associated with disciform lesions, is not commonly seen with melanomas unless the tumor extends through Bruch's mem-brane. Clinical evaluation of the fellow eye is important in documenting the presence of degenerative changes in AMD. Fluorescein angiography results are virtually patho-gnomonic, revealing early hypofluorescence secondary to blockage from the hemorrhage, often followed by late hyperfluorescence in the distribution of the choroidal neovascular

---

Table 17-2 DIfferential Diagnosis of Amelanotic Choroidal Mass

Amelanotic melanoma
Choroidal metastasis
Choroidal hemangioma
Choroidal osteoma
Age-related macular or extramacular degeneration
Choroidal detachment
Uveal effusion syndrome
Posterior scleritis
Chorioretinal granuloma
Toxoplasmic retinochoroiditis
Rhegmatogenous retinal detachment
Degenerative retinoschisis
Presumed acquired retinal hemangioma
Neurilemoma
Leiomyoma
Retinal cavernous hemangioma
Combined hamartoma of the retinal pigment epithelium

Modified from Shields JA, Shields CL. Differential diagnosis of posterior uveal melanoma. In: Shields JA, Shields CL. *Intraocular Tumors: A Text and Atlas*. Philadelphia: Saunders; 1992:137–153.

membrane. Ultrasound testing may reveal increased heterogeneity and a lack of intrinsic vascularity on standardized A scan. Serial observation will document involutional alterations of the evolving disciform lesion.

Congenital hypertrophy of the RPE (CHRPE) is a well-defined, flat, darkly pigmented lesion ranging in size from 1 mm to greater than 10 mm in diameter. Patients are asymptomatic, and the lesion is noted during ophthalmic examination, typically in patients in their teens or twenties. In younger patients, CHRPE often appears homogeneously black; in older individuals, foci of depigmentation (lacunae) often develop (Fig 17-10).

Histologically, CHRPE consists of tall, melanin-containing pigment epithelial cells with large spherical pigment granules. The histology is identical to a condition known as *grouped pigmentation of the retina,* or *bear tracks* (Fig 17-11). The presence of multiple patches of congenital hypertrophy in family members of patients with Gardner syndrome, a familial polyposis, appears to be a marker for the development of colon carcinoma. Fundus findings enable the ophthalmologist to help the gastroenterologist determine the recommended frequency of colon carcinoma screening in family members (see Chapter 11).

Melanocytoma (magnocellular nevus) of the optic disc typically appears as a dark brown to black epipapillary lesion, often with fibrillar margins as a result of extension into the nerve fiber layer (Fig 17-12; see also Fig 15-10 in Chapter 15). It is usually located

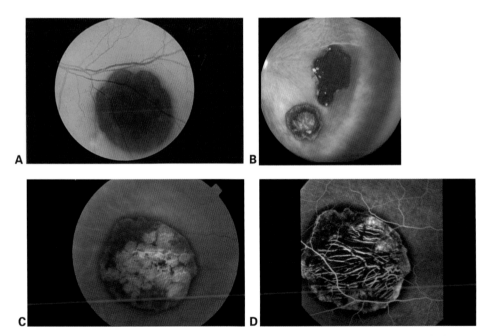

Figure 17-10 Congenital hypertrophy of the RPE (CHRPE). Examples of varying clinical appearances. **A,** CHRPE. Note the homogeneous black color and well-defined margins of the nummular lesion. **B,** Two lesions of CHRPE in the nasal periphery of the fundus. **C, D,** Color fundus photograph and corresponding fluorescein angiogram of a large CHRPE. Note loss of RPE architecture and highlighted choroidal vasculature. *(Part B courtesy of Jacob Pe'er, MD; parts C and D courtesy of Timothy G. Murray, MD.)*

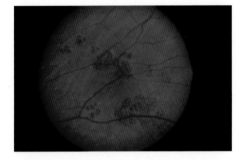

Figure 17-11 Bear tracks. Grouped pigmentation of the retina/RPE represents a form fruste of CHRPE. Note the distinct bear track configuration and heavy pigmentation.

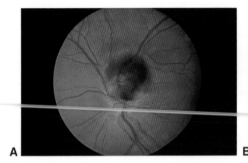
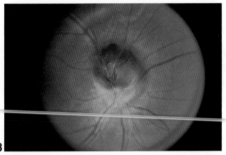

A   B

Figure 17-12 Melanocytoma of the optic disc. Note varying clinical appearance in these 2 examples based on degree of choroidal pigmentation: lesion in **(A)** darkly pigmented fundus and **(B)** lightly pigmented fundus. *(Part B courtesy of Timothy G. Murray, MD.)*

eccentrically over the optic disc and may be elevated. It is important to differentiate this lesion from melanoma, because a melanocytoma has minimal malignant potential.

Recent studies have shown that about one third of optic disc melanocytomas have a peripapillary nevus component and that 10% of cases will show minimal but definite growth over a 5-year period. In addition, these lesions can produce an afferent pupillary defect and a variety of visual field abnormalities, ranging from an enlarged blind spot to extensive nerve fiber layer defects.

Suprachoroidal detachments present in 2 forms: *hemorrhagic* and *serous*. These lesions are often associated with hypotony and may present in the immediate period after ophthalmic surgery. Clinically, hemorrhagic detachments are often dome-shaped, involve multiple quadrants, and are associated with breakthrough vitreous bleeding. A- and B-scan ultrasonography readings may closely resemble melanoma but show an absence of intrinsic vascularity and an evolution of the hemorrhage over time. Observational management is indicated in the majority of cases. MRI with gadolinium enhancement may be of benefit in selected cases to document characteristic alterations.

Choroidal osteomas are benign bony tumors that typically arise from the juxtapapillary choroid in adolescent to young adult patients (more commonly in women than men) and are bilateral in 20%–25% of cases. The characteristic lesion appears yellow to orange, and it has well-defined pseudopod margins (Fig 17-13). Ultrasonography reveals a high-amplitude echo corresponding to the plate of bone and loss of the normal orbital echoes

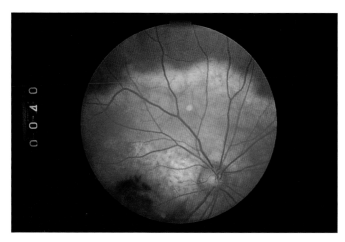

Figure 17-13 Choroidal osteoma, clinical appearance. Note the yellow-orange color, well-defined pseudopod-like margins, and characteristic spotted pigmentation on the surface of this circumpapillary tumor.

behind the lesion. These tumors can also be seen on CT; their hallmark is calcification. Choroidal osteomas typically enlarge slowly over many years. If these lesions involve the macula, vision is generally impaired. Subretinal neovascularization is a common complication of macular choroidal osteomas. The etiology of these lesions is unknown, but chronic low-grade choroidal inflammation has been suspected in some cases (see Chapter 12).

Accuracy of diagnosis of choroidal melanomas in the Collaborative Ocular Melanoma Study. COMS report no. 1. *Arch Ophthalmol.* 1990;108:1268–1273.

Byrne SF, Marsh MJ, Boldt HC, Green RL, Johnson RN, Wilson DJ. Consistency of observations from echograms made centrally in the Collaborative Ocular Melanoma Study. COMS report no. 13. *Ophthalmic Epidemiol.* 2002;9:11–27.

Mukai S, Reinke MH, Gragoudas ES. Diagnosis of choroidal melanoma. In: Albert DM, Jakobiec FA, eds. *Principles and Practice of Ophthalmology.* 2nd ed. Philadelphia: Saunders; 2000:5017–5027.

Scott IU, Murray TG, Hughes JR. Evaluation of imaging techniques for detection of extraocular extension of choroidal melanoma. *Arch Ophthalmol.* 1998;116:897–899.

Shields CL, Shields JA, Augsburger JJ. Choroidal osteoma. *Surv Ophthalmol.* 1988;33:17–27.

Classification

Melanomas of the ciliary body and choroid have been categorized by size in a number of different ways. Although a size classification based on tumor volume is logical, no simple and reliable method for assessing tumor volume is currently available. The common practice of estimating tumor volume by multiplying maximal basal diameter, minimal basal diameter, and thickness yields only a crude assessment of actual tumor size. Most commonly, posterior uveal melanomas are classified as small, medium, or large based on maximal thickness and basal diameter (Table 17-3). See also Table A-4 in the appendix for the American Joint Committee on Cancer definitions and staging.

Table 17-3 Classification of Posterior Uveal Melanoma by Tumor Dimension

	Basal Diameter (mm)	Thickness (mm)
Nevus	<5	<2
Small	5–10	2–3
Medium	10–15	3–5
Large	15–20	5–10
Extra large	>20	>10

Modified from Shields JA, Shields CL. *Intraocular Tumors: A Text and Atlas.* Philadelphia: Saunders; 1992.

Metastatic Evaluation

In a study by Kujala and colleagues, the incidence of metastatic uveal melanoma was observed to be as high as 50% at 25 years after treatment for choroidal melanoma. The Collaborative Ocular Melanoma Study (COMS) reported an incidence of metastatic disease of 25% at 5 years after initial treatment and 34% at 10 years. Nevertheless, clinically evident metastatic disease at the time of initial presentation can be detected in less than 2% of patients. Currently, it is hypothesized that many patients have undetectable micrometastatic disease at the time of their primary treatment. Despite achieving great accuracy in correctly diagnosing uveal melanoma, mortality owing to this tumor has not changed significantly for many years. In general, survival with metastatic uveal melanoma is poor, with a median survival of less than 6 months, although early detection and prompt treatment of liver metastases can increase survival time significantly.

The liver is the predominant organ involved in metastatic uveal melanoma. Liver involvement also tends to be the first manifestation of metastatic disease. In the presence of liver involvement, lung, bone, and skin are other sites that may be affected. An assessment of metastatic disease patterns in COMS revealed liver involvement in 89% of patients, lung involvement in 24%, bone involvement in 17%, and skin and subcutaneous tissue involvement in 12%. In cases that were autopsied, liver involvement was found in 100% and lung involvement in 50% of the patients with metastatic disease.

All patients require metastatic evaluation prior to definitive treatment of the intraocular melanoma (Table 17-4). The purpose of this evaluation is twofold:

1. To determine whether the patient has any other medical conditions that contraindicate surgical treatment or need to be ameliorated before surgery. For example, in one small series, 15% of the patients had a second malignancy at the time of presentation or during the course of a 10-year follow-up; the COMS found preexisting independent primary cancers in about 10% of patients. If there is any question whether the lesion in the eye is a metastatic tumor, this possibility must be ruled out with a thorough medical evaluation directed at determining the site of primary malignancy.

Table 17-4 **Clinical Evaluation of Metastatic Uveal Melanoma**

- Liver imaging—ultrasound in routine evaluation
- Liver function test
- Chest x-ray

If any of the above are abnormal:
- Triphasic liver CT
- CT-PET of the abdomen/chest
- MRI of the abdomen/chest

2. To rule out the possibility of detectable metastatic melanoma from the eye. Only rarely is metastatic disease from uveal melanoma detectable at the time of initial presentation. If metastatic disease is clinically present during the pretreatment evaluation of the eye tumor, enucleation is inappropriate unless the eye is painful.

In order to detect metastatic disease of uveal melanoma at an early stage, metastatic evaluation should be performed on all patients on a yearly follow-up basis, and some centers will do so every 6 months. Metastatic evaluation should include a comprehensive physical examination and liver function tests. Chest x-ray is also usually performed, although its yield was found to be low. Recently, research has been performed in several centers investigating possible blood markers for early detection of metastatic uveal melanoma.

Liver imaging studies are included in the metastatic evaluation at some centers. Ultrasound of the abdomen is usually sufficient, but when a suspicion of metastatic disease is raised, triphasic CT or PET-CT is usually recommended in order to evaluate the extent of the disease. A liver or other organ site biopsy may be confirmatory of metastatic disease and is appropriate prior to institution of any treatment for metastatic disease.

The interval between the diagnosis of primary uveal melanoma and its metastasis depends on various clinical, histopathologic, cytogenetic, and molecular genetic factors. It varies from 1–2 years to over 15–20 years. When metastatic disease is diagnosed early enough, before developing miliary spread, the options for treatment of the metastasis, mainly liver metastasis, include surgical resection; chemotherapy, including intra-arterial hepatic chemotherapy and chemoembolization; and immunotherapy.

Development of metastatic disease after enrollment in the COMS trials for treatment of choroidal melanoma: Collaborative Ocular Melanoma Study Group report no. 26. *Arch Ophthalmol.* 2005;123:1639–1643.

Eskelin S, Pyrhonen S, Summanen P, Prause JU, Kivela T. Screening for metastatic malignant melanoma of the uvea revisited. *Cancer.* 1999;85:1151–1159.

Kaiserman I, Amer R, and Pe'er J. Liver function tests in metastatic uveal melanoma. *Am J Ophthalmol.* 2004;137:236–243.

Kujala E, Makitie T, Kivela T. Very long term prognosis of patients with malignant uveal melanoma. *Invest Ophthalmol Vis Sci.* 2003;44:4651–4659.

Singh AD, Topham A. Survival rate with uveal melanoma in the United States: 1973–1997. *Ophthalmology.* 2003;110:962–965.

Treatment

Management of posterior uveal melanomas has long been the subject of considerable controversy. Two factors lie at the heart of this controversy:

1. the limited amount of data on the natural history of untreated patients with posterior uveal malignant melanoma
2. the lack of groups of patients matched for known and for unknown risk factors and managed by different therapeutic techniques to assess the comparative effectiveness of those treatments

In 1882, Fuchs wrote that all intraocular melanomas were treated by enucleation and the only untreated cases were in the "older literature." Presently, both surgical and radiotherapeutic management are used for intraocular melanoma. The COMS has reported randomized, prospectively administered treatment outcomes for patients with medium and large choroidal melanomas. The methods of patient management currently in use depend on several factors:

- size, location, and extent of the tumor
- visual status of the affected eye and of the fellow eye
- age and general health of the patient

Observation

In certain instances, serial observation without treatment of an intraocular tumor is indicated. Most types of benign retinal and choroidal tumors, such as choroidal nevi, choroidal osteoma, or hyperplasia of the RPE, can be managed with observation. Growth of small melanocytic lesions of the posterior uvea that are less than 1.0 mm in thickness can be documented periodically by fundus photography and ultrasonography. Significant controversy persists regarding the management of small choroidal melanomas. Lesions greater than 1.0 mm in thickness, with documented growth, should be evaluated for indications for definitive treatment. Observation of active larger tumors may be appropriate in very elderly and systemically ill patients who are not candidates for any sort of therapeutic intervention.

Enucleation

Historically, enucleation has been the gold standard in the treatment of malignant intraocular tumors. Although some authors in the past hypothesized that surgical manipulation of eyes containing malignant melanoma leads to tumor dissemination and increased mortality, this hypothesis is no longer accepted, and enucleation remains appropriate for some medium-sized, many large, and all extra-large choroidal melanomas. The COMS compared the application of pre-enucleation external-beam radiation therapy followed by enucleation with enucleation alone for patients with large choroidal melanomas and found no statistically significant survival difference in 5-year mortality rates. Enucleation remains one of the most common primary treatments for choroidal melanoma.

Radioactive plaque (brachytherapy)

The application of a radioactive plaque to the sclera overlying an intraocular tumor is probably the most common method of treating uveal melanoma. It allows the delivery of a high dose of radiation to the tumor and a relatively low dose to the surrounding normal structures of the eye. The technique has been available for 50 years. Although various isotopes have been used, the most common today are iodine 125 and ruthenium 106. Cobalt 60 plaques, which were the main source for brachytherapy in the past, are rarely used today. Other isotopes that have been used are strontium 90, iridium 192, and palladium 103. In the United States, iodine 125 is the isotope most frequently used in the treatment of ciliary body and choroidal melanomas. Advances in intraoperative localization, especially the use of ultrasound, have increased local tumor control rates to as high as 96%. In most patients, the tumor decreases in size (Fig 17-14); in others, the result is total flattening of the tumor with scar formation or no change in tumor size, although clinical and ultrasound changes can be seen. Regrowth is diagnosed in only 4%–5% of the treated tumors. Late radiation complications, especially optic neuropathy and retinopathy, are visually limiting in as many as 50% of patients undergoing treatment. Radiation complications appear dose-dependent, and they increase for tumors involving, or adjacent to, the macula or optic nerve.

Charged-particle radiation

High-linear-energy transfer radiation with charged particles (protons and helium ions) has been used effectively in managing ciliary body and choroidal melanomas. The technique requires surgical attachment of tantalum clips to the sclera to mark the basal margins of the tumor prior to the first radiation fraction. The charged-particle beams deliver a more

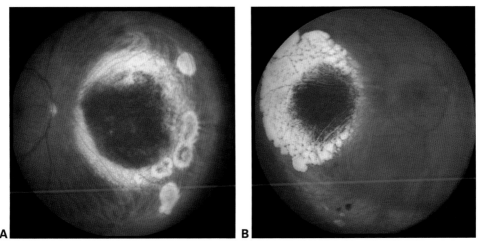

Figure 17-14 Choroidal melanoma treated by radioactive brachytherapy. **A,** Mildly elevated remnants of melanoma surrounded by atrophic chorioretinal scarring, nasal to the optic nerve head. **B,** Flat remnants of melanoma pigmentation surrounded by chorioretinal scarring located temporal to the macula. *(Parts A and B courtesy of Jacob Pe'er, MD.)*

homogeneous dose of radiation energy to a tumor than does a radioactive plaque, and the lateral spread of radiation energy from such beams is less extensive (Bragg peak effect). Local tumor control rates of up to 98% have been reported. The response is similar to that seen after brachytherapy.

Unfortunately, charged-particle radiation often delivers a higher dose to anterior segment structures. Radiation complications, most commonly anterior, lead to uncontrolled neovascular glaucoma in 10% of treated eyes and vision loss in approximately 50%.

External-beam radiation

Conventional external-beam radiation therapy is ineffective as a single-modality treatment for malignant melanoma. Pre-enucleation external-beam radiotherapy combined with enucleation appears to limit orbital recurrence in large melanomas and showed a non–statistically significant reduction in 5-year mortality in the COMS large-tumor trial. In recent years, several centers have used fractionated stereotactic radiotherapy and gamma knife radiosurgery, reporting good results.

Cataract may develop following all types of radiotherapy. Surgical removal of radiation-induced cataract is indicated if the intraocular tumor is nonviable and the patient appears to have visual limitations attributable to the cataract. No increase in mortality after cataract extraction has been documented.

Alternative treatments

Photoablation and hyperthermia Photocoagulation has played a limited role in the treatment of melanocytic tumors. Reports of focal/grid treatment to eradicate active subretinal fluid in choroidal melanoma have documented a propensity for accelerated tumor growth with rupture of Bruch's membrane. Recently, advances in the delivery of hyperthermia (heat) using transpupillary thermotherapy (TTT) have been reported. Direct diode laser treatment using long duration, large spot size, and relatively low-energy laser have been associated with a reduction in tumor volume. Some reports have suggested that TTT is associated with an increased rate of local tumor recurrence compared with brachytherapy.

Cryotherapy Although cryotherapy using a triple freeze-thaw technique has been tried in the treatment of small choroidal melanomas, it is not considered standard therapy and is not currently undergoing further evaluation for efficacy.

Transscleral diathermy Diathermy is *contraindicated* in the treatment of malignant intraocular tumors because the induced scleral damage may provide a route for extrascleral extension of tumor cells.

Surgical excision of tumor Surgical excision has been performed successfully in many eyes with malignant and benign intraocular tumors. Concerns regarding surgical excision include the inability to evaluate tumor margins for residual disease and the high incidence of pathologically recognized scleral, retinal, and vitreous involvement in medium and large choroidal melanomas. When this treatment is used, the surgical techniques are generally quite difficult, requiring an experienced surgeon. In some instances, local excision of uveal melanoma has been coupled with globe-conserving radiotherapy, such as brachytherapy.

Chemotherapy Currently, chemotherapy is not effective in the treatment of primary or metastatic uveal melanoma. Various regimens have been used, however, for palliative treatment of patients with metastatic disease.

Immunotherapy Presently, immunotherapy is under investigation in the treatment of gross and microscopic metastatic disease. Immunotherapy uses systemic cytokines, immuno-modulatory agents, or local vaccine therapy to try to activate a tumor-directed T-cell immune response.

Exenteration Exenteration, traditionally advocated for patients with extrascleral extension of a posterior uveal melanoma, is rarely employed today. The current trend is toward more conservative treatment for these patients, with enucleation plus a limited tenonectomy. The addition of local radiotherapy appears to achieve survival outcomes similar to those of exenteration.

Bergman L, Nilsson B, Lundell G, Lundell M, Seregard S. Ruthenium brachytherapy for uveal melanoma, 1979–2003: survival and functional outcomes in the Swedish population. *Ophthalmology.* 2005;112:834–840.

The Collaborative Ocular Melanoma Study (COMS) randomized trial of pre-enucleation radiation of large choroidal melanoma, II: initial mortality findings. COMS report no. 10. *Am J Ophthalmol.* 1998;125:779–796.

Damato B, Jones AG. Uveal melanoma: resection techniques. *Ophthalmol Clin North Am.* 2005;18:119–128.

Diener-West M, Earle JD, Fine SL, et al. The COMS randomized trial of iodine 125 brachytherapy for choroidal melanoma, III: initial mortality findings. COMS report no. 18. *Arch Ophthalmol.* 2001;119:969–982.

Gragoudas ES, Marie Lane A. Uveal melanoma: proton beam irradiation. *Ophthalmol Clin North Am.* 2005;18:111–118.

Harbour JW, Murray TG, Byrne SF, et al. Intraoperative echographic localization of iodine 125 episcleral radioactive plaques for posterior uveal melanoma. *Retina.* 1996;16:129–134.

Shields JA, Shields CL. Current management of posterior uveal melanoma. *Mayo Clin Proc.* 1993;68:1196–1200.

Prognosis and Prognostic Factors

A meta-analysis from the published literature of tumor mortality after treatment documented a 5-year mortality rate of 50% for large choroidal melanoma and 30% for medium-sized choroidal melanoma; 5-year melanoma-related mortality in treated patients with small choroidal melanoma has been reported to be as high as 12%. Retrospective analysis among patients with melanoma suggests that clinical risk factors for mortality are

- larger tumor size at time of treatment
- tumor growth
- anterior tumor location
- extraocular extension
- older age
- tumor regrowth after globe-conserving therapy
- rapid decrease in tumor size after globe-conserving therapy
- juxtapapillary tumors

Histopathologic features associated with a higher rate of metastases include

- epithelioid cells
- high mitotic index and high cell proliferation indices
- complex microvascular patterns (loops, networks of loops, and parallel with cross-linking)
- mean of 10 largest nuclei
- tumor-infiltrating lymphocytes
- monosomy 3
- trisomy 8

A more in-depth discussion is provided in Chapter 12.

Coleman DJ, Rondeau MJ, Silverman RH, et al. Correlation of microcirculation architecture with ultrasound backscatter parameters of uveal melanoma. *Eur J Ophthalmol.* 1995;5:96–106.

Folberg R, Pe'er J, Gruman LM, et al. The morphologic characteristics of tumor blood vessels as a marker of tumor progression in primary human uveal melanoma: a matched case-control study. *Hum Pathol.* 1992;23:1298–1305.

Mueller AJ, Freeman WR, Folberg R, et al. Evaluation of microvascular pattern visibility in human choroidal melanomas: comparison of confocal fluorescein with indocyanine green angiography. *Graefes Arch Clin Exp Ophthalmol.* 1999;237:448–456.

Sisley K, Rennie IG, Parsons MA, et al. Abnormalities of chromosomes 3 and 8 in posterior uveal melanoma correlate with prognosis. *Genes Chromosomes Cancer.* 1997;19:22–28.

Collaborative Ocular Melanoma Study (COMS)

Survival data from the COMS have now been reported for the randomized clinical trials of large and medium choroidal melanoma and for the observational study of small choroidal melanoma. These results provide the framework for patient discussions concerning treatment-related long-term survival, rates of globe conservation with iodine 125 brachytherapy, and predictors of small-tumor growth.

- COMS Large Choroidal Melanoma Trial

  - evaluated 1003 patients with choroidal melanomas >16 mm in basal diameter and/or >10 mm in apical height
  - compared enucleation alone with enucleation preceded by external-beam radiotherapy
  - reported a 5-year survival rate of 57% and 62%, respectively, between cohorts
  - concluded that adjunctive radiotherapy did not improve overall survival
  - established the appropriateness of primary enucleation alone in managing large choroidal melanomas that are not amenable to globe-conserving therapy

- COMS Medium Choroidal Melanoma Trial

  - evaluated 1317 patients with choroidal melanomas ranging in size from 6 mm to 16 mm in basal diameter and/or 2.5 mm to 10 mm in apical height
  - compared standardized enucleation and iodine 125 brachytherapy
  - all-cause mortality at 5 years: 18% and 19%, respectively
  - histologically confirmed metastases at 5 years found in 9% of patients treated with brachytherapy as opposed to 11% in patients who underwent enucleation

- secondary finding in enucleated eyes:
    - —only 2/660 (0.3%) enucleated eyes misdiagnosed as having a choroidal melanoma
- secondary findings in patients undergoing brachytherapy:
    - —10.3% local tumor recurrence at 5 years
    - —12.5% risk of enucleation after brachytherapy at 5 years
    - —local tumor recurrence weakly associated with a reduced survival, with an adjusted risk ratio of 1.5
    - —decline in visual acuity to 20/200 in 43% of patients at 3 years
    - —quadrupling of the visual angle (6 lines of visual loss) in 49% of patients at 3 years

- COMS Small Choroidal Tumor Trial

    - observational study of 204 patients with tumors measuring 4.0–8.0 mm in basal diameter and/or 1.0–2.4 mm in apical height
    - melanoma-specific mortality 1% at 5 years
    - clinical growth factors included
        - —greater initial thickness and basal diameter
        - —presence of orange pigmentation
        - —absence of drusen and/or retinal pigment epithelial changes
        - —presence of tumor pinpoint hyperfluorescence on angiography

Detailed findings of the COMS can be found at www.jhu.edu/wctb/coms.

Pigmented Epithelial Tumors of the Uvea and Retina

Adenoma and Adenocarcinoma

Benign adenomas of the nonpigmented and pigmented ciliary epithelium may appear indistinguishable clinically from melanomas arising in the ciliary body. Benign adenomas of the RPE are very rare. These lesions occur as oval, deeply melanotic tumors arising abruptly from the RPE. Adenomas rarely enlarge and seldom undergo malignant change. Adenocarcinomas of the RPE are also very rare; only a few cases have ever been reported in the literature. Although these lesions have malignant features histologically, their metastatic potential appears to be minimal.

Rare benign asymptomatic cysts of the ciliary epithelium may occur. Opacified ciliary epithelial cysts are formed in myeloma and macroglobulinemia.

Fuchs adenoma (pseudoadenomatous hyperplasia) is usually an incidental finding at autopsy and rarely becomes apparent clinically. It appears as a glistening, white, irregular tumor arising from a ciliary crest. Histologically, it consists of benign proliferation of the nonpigmented ciliary epithelium with accumulation of basement membrane–like material.

Green WR. Retina. In: Spencer WH, ed. *Ophthalmic Pathology: An Atlas and Textbook.* 4th ed. Philadelphia: Saunders; 1996:1291–1313.

Acquired Hyperplasia

Hyperplasia of the pigmented ciliary epithelium or the retinal pigment epithelium usually occurs in response to trauma, inflammation, or other ocular insults. Ciliary body lesions, because of their location, often do not become evident clinically. Occasionally, however, they may reach a large size and simulate a ciliary body melanoma. Posteriorly located lesions may be more commonly recognized and can lead to diagnostic uncertainty. In the early management of these atypical lesions, observation is often appropriate to document stability of the lesion. Adenomatous hyperplasia, which has been reported only rarely, may clinically mimic a choroidal melanoma.

Combined Hamartoma

Combined hamartoma of the RPE and retina is a rare disorder that occurs most frequently at the disc margin. Typically, it appears as a darkly pigmented, minimally elevated lesion with retinal traction and tortuous retinal vessels (Fig 17-15). Histologically, it consists of a proliferation of RPE cells, glial cells, and retinal blood vessels. The glial cells may contract, producing the traction lines seen clinically in the retina. This lesion has been mistaken for malignant melanoma because of its dark pigmentation and slight elevation. In rare cases, a combined hamartoma may be situated in the peripheral fundus.

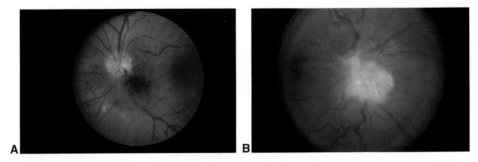

Figure 17-15 **A,** Peripapillary combined hamartoma of the retina and RPE. Note the radiating traction lines through the fovea. **B,** Example of medium-sized combined hamartoma. *(Part B courtesy of Timothy G. Murray, MD.)*

CHAPTER 18

Angiomatous Tumors

Hemangiomas

Choroidal Hemangiomas

Hemangiomas of the choroid occur in 2 specific forms: circumscribed and diffuse. The *circumscribed choroidal hemangioma* typically occurs in patients with no other systemic disorders. It generally appears as a red or orange tumor located in the postequatorial zone of the fundus, often in the macular area (Fig 18-1). Such tumors commonly produce a secondary retinal detachment that extends into the foveal region, resulting in visual blurring, metamorphopsia, and micropsia. These benign vascular tumors characteristically affect the overlying RPE and cause cystoid degeneration of the outer retinal layers.

The principal entities in the differential diagnosis of circumscribed choroidal hemangioma include

- amelanotic choroidal melanoma
- choroidal osteoma
- metastatic carcinoma to the choroid
- granuloma of the choroid

The *diffuse choroidal hemangioma* is generally seen in patients with Sturge-Weber syndrome (encephalofacial angiomatosis). This choroidal tumor produces diffuse reddish orange thickening of the entire fundus, resulting in an ophthalmoscopic pattern commonly referred to as *tomato catsup fundus* (Fig 18-2). Retinal detachment and glaucoma often occur in eyes with this lesion. See BCSC Section 12, *Retina and Vitreous,* for a discussion of choroidal hemangioma, and BCSC Section 6, *Pediatric Ophthalmology and Strabismus,* for a discussion of intraocular vascular tumors and Sturge-Weber syndrome.

Ancillary diagnostic studies may be of considerable help in evaluating choroidal hemangiomas. Fluorescein angiography reveals the large choroidal vessels in the prearterial or arterial phases with late staining of the tumor and the overlying cystoid retina. This pattern is not pathognomonic of choroidal hemangiomas. Ultrasonography has been helpful in differentiating choroidal hemangiomas from amelanotic melanomas and other simulating lesions. A-scan ultrasonography generally shows a high-amplitude initial echo and high-amplitude broad internal echoes ("high internal reflectivity"; see Fig 18-1B). B-scan ultrasonography demonstrates localized or diffuse choroidal thickening with prominent internal reflections (acoustic heterogeneity) without choroidal excavation or orbital shadowing (see

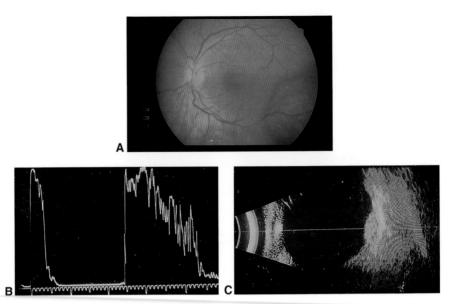

Figure 18-1 A, Circumscribed choroidal hemangioma. **B,** A-scan ultrasound study shows characteristic high internal reflectivity. **C,** B-scan ultrasound study shows a highly reflective tumor.

Fig 18-1C). Radiographic studies, particularly CT scanning, can be helpful in differentiating a choroidal hemangioma from a choroidal osteoma.

Asymptomatic choroidal hemangiomas require no treatment. The most common complication is serous detachment of the retina involving the fovea, with resultant visual loss. Traditionally, this has been managed by laser photocoagulation. The surface of the tumor is treated lightly with laser photocoagulation in an effort not to destroy the tumor but rather to create a chorioretinal adhesion that prevents further accumulation of fluid. Often, repeated treatments are necessary to eliminate active exudation of subretinal fluid. If the retinal detachment is extensive, this type of photocoagulation is usually unsuccessful. Recurrent detachments are common, and the long-term visual prognosis in patients with macular detachment or edema is guarded.

Photodynamic therapy (PDT) has recently been used to treat patients with circumscribed choroidal hemangioma and associated decreased visual function. PDT applied over the entire surface of the lesion appears to be effective in the resolution of subretinal fluid and in the involution of the vascular tumor. Further clinical experience is needed to better define the therapeutic indications and parameters for this evolving laser therapy.

Radiation, in the forms of brachytherapy, charged-particle, and external-beam, has been used to treat choroidal hemangiomas. Brachytherapy and charged-particle therapy have been used to treat patients with circumscribed choroidal hemangiomas, and external-beam radiotherapy (low dose, fractionated) has been used to treat patients with diffuse choroidal hemangioma. Each modality has been reported to cause involution of the hemangiomas, with subsequent resolution of the associated serous retinal detachment. Complications from the radiation and the serous retinal detachment may limit vision in patients who are irradiated.

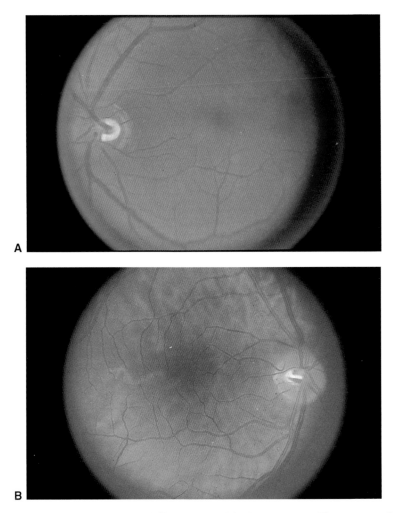

Figure 18-2 Choroidal hemangioma, diffuse type, clinical appearance. The saturated red color of the affected fundus **(A)** contrasts markedly with the color of the unaffected fundus **(B)** of the same patient.

New horizons in the treatment of choroidal hemangiomas may involve the periocular or intraocular use of antiangiogenic agents.

See Chapter 12 for further discussion of choroidal hemangiomas.

Augsburger JJ, Freire J, Brady LW. Radiation therapy for choroidal and retinal hemangiomas. *Front Radiat Ther Oncol.* 1997;30:265–280.

Chao AN, Shields CL, Shields JA, Krema H. Plaque radiotherapy for choroidal hemangioma with total retinal detachment and iris neovascularization. *Retina.* 2001;21:682–684.

Lee V, Hungerford JL. Proton beam therapy for posterior pole circumscribed choroidal haemangioma. *Eye.* 1998;12:925–928.

Madreperla SA, Hungerford JL, Plowman PN, Laganowski HC, Gregory PT. Choroidal hemangiomas: visual and anatomic results of treatment by photocoagulation or radiation therapy. *Ophthalmology.* 1997;104:1773–1778.

Meyer K, Augsburger JJ. Independent diagnostic value of fluorescein angiography in the evaluation of intraocular tumors. *Graefes Arch Clin Exp Ophthalmol.* 1999;237:489–494.

Porrini G, Giovannini A, Amato G, Ioni A, Pantanetti M. Photodynamic therapy of circumscribed choroidal hemangioma. *Ophthalmology.* 2003;110:674–680.

Schilling H, Bornfeld N. Long-term results after low-dose ocular irradiation for choroidal hemangiomas. *Curr Opin Ophthalmol.* 1998;9:51–55.

Singh AD, Kaiser PK, Sears JE, Gupta M, Rundle PA, Rennie IG. Photodynamic therapy of circumscribed choroidal haemangioma. *Br J Ophthalmol.* 2004;88:1414–1418.

Retinal Angiomas

Capillary hemangioma

Retinal capillary hemangioma (angiomatosis retinae) is a rare autosomal dominant condition with a reported incidence of 1 in 40,000. Typically, patients are diagnosed in the second to third decades of life, although retinal lesions may be present at birth. The retinal capillary hemangioma *(hemangioblastoma)* appears as a red to orange tumor arising within the retina with large-caliber, tortuous afferent and efferent retinal blood vessels (Fig 18-3). Associated yellow-white retinal and subretinal exudates that seem to have a predilection for foveal involvement may appear. Exudative detachments often occur in eyes with hemangioblastomas. Atypical variations include hemangiomas arising from the optic disc, which may appear as encapsulated lesions with or without pseudopapilledema, and in the retinal periphery, where vitreous traction may elevate the tumor from the surface of the retina, giving the appearance of a free-floating vitreous mass.

When a capillary hemangioma of the retina occurs as a solitary finding, the condition is generally known as *von Hippel disease.* This condition is familial in about 20% of cases and bilateral in about 50%. The lesions may be multiple in 1 or both eyes. If retinal capillary hemangiomatosis is associated with a cerebellar hemangioblastoma, the term *von Hippel–Lindau syndrome* is applied. The gene for von Hippel–Lindau syndrome has been isolated on chromosome 3. A number of other tumors and cysts may occur in patients with von Hippel–Lindau syndrome. The most important of these lesions are cerebellar hemangioblastomas, renal cell carcinomas, and pheochromocytomas. Genetic screening now allows for subtyping of patients with von Hippel–Lindau to determine risk for systemic

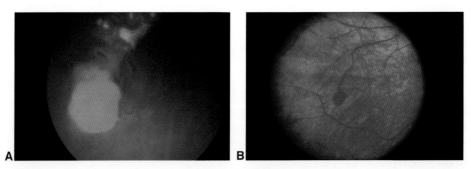

A B

Figure 18-3 Retinal capillary hemangioma (hemangioblastoma). **A,** Note dilated, tortuous retinal vessels supplying this vascular tumor. **B,** Retinal capillary hemangiomas may be small and difficult to observe clinically. *(Part A courtesy of Timothy G. Murray, MD.)*

manifestations of the disease. When this diagnosis is suspected, appropriate consultation and screening are critical for long-term follow-up of ocular manifestations and the associated systemic complications.

Fluorescein angiography of retinal capillary hemangiomas demonstrates a rapid arteriovenous transit, with immediate filling of the feeding arteriole, subsequent filling of the numerous fine blood vessels that constitute the tumor, and drainage by the dilated venule. Massive leakage of dye into the tumor and vitreous can occur.

Treatment of retinal capillary hemangiomas includes photocoagulation for smaller lesions, cryotherapy for larger and more peripheral lesions, and scleral buckling with cryotherapy or penetrating diathermy for extremely large lesions with extensive retinal detachment. Cryotherapy, and to a lesser extent laser photocoagulation, however, may be associated with vascular decompensation leading to massive exudative retinal detachment. Eye-wall resection as well as external-beam and charged-particle radiotherapy have also been used. Recent case reports have suggested the utility of targeted antiangiogenic therapy in the management of retinal capillary hemangiomas that are unresponsive to standard treatment. The efficacy of antiangiogenic agents in the treatment of these vascular lesions is of compelling interest to von Hippel–Lindau patients, who have a lifelong risk of developing retinal angiomas. Visual prognosis remains guarded for patients with large retinal lesions. Aggressive screening and early treatment may reduce the late complications of total exudative retinal detachment. Screening for systemic vascular anomalies (eg, cerebellar hemangioblastomas) and malignancies (eg, renal cell carcinoma) may reduce mortality.

> Aiello LP, George DJ, Cahill MT, et al. Rapid and durable recovery of visual function in a patient with von Hippel–Lindau syndrome after systemic therapy with vascular endothelial growth factor receptor inhibitor su5416. *Ophthalmology*. 2002;109:1745–1751.

Cavernous hemangioma

Cavernous hemangioma of the retina is an uncommon lesion that resembles a cluster of grapes (Fig 18-4). In contrast to the lesions in Coats disease and retinal capillary hemangiomatosis, cavernous hemangiomas are generally not associated with exudates. However, small hemorrhages as well as areas of gliosis and fibrosis may appear on the surface of the lesion. Within the vascular spaces of the cavernous hemangioma, a plasma–erythrocyte separation may appear that can best be demonstrated on fluorescein angiography. Cavernous hemangiomas may occur on the optic disc, where their appearance resembles that in the extrapapillary retina. Cavernous hemangiomas of the retina are sometimes associated with similar skin and CNS lesions, and patients with intracranial lesions may have seizures.

Fluorescein angiography is virtually diagnostic of cavernous hemangiomas of the retina. In contrast to a retinal capillary hemangioma, a retinal cavernous hemangioma fills very slowly, and the fluorescein often pools in the upper part of the vascular space, while the cellular elements (erythrocytes) pool in the lower part. The fluorescein remains in the vascular spaces for an extended period of time. Unlike tumors in Coats disease and retinal capillary hemangiomatosis, cavernous hemangiomas generally show no leakage of fluorescein into the vitreous.

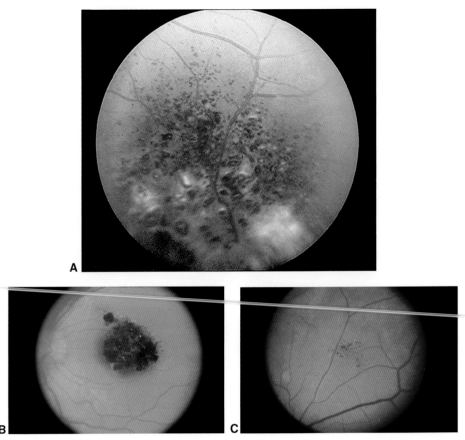

Figure 18-4 Retinal cavernous hemangioma. **A,** Note multiple tiny vascular saccules and associated white fibrovascular tissue. **B,** Note clumped vascular saccules (grape cluster configuration). **C,** When lesions are small, findings may be subtle. *(Part B courtesy of Timothy G. Murray, MD.)*

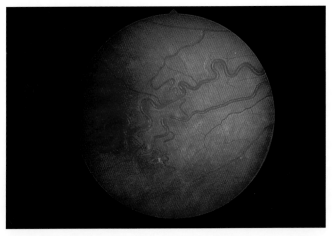

Figure 18-5 Retinal arteriovenous malformation, clinical appearance. Note the absence of capillary bed between the afferent and efferent arms of this retinal arteriovenous communication.

Histologically, a cavernous retinal hemangioma consists of dilated, thin-walled vascular channels that are interconnected by small orifices. The dilated vessels may protrude upward beneath the internal limiting membrane, and associated gliosis and hemorrhage may be seen. Treatment is rarely required.

Arteriovenous Malformation

Congenital retinal arteriovenous malformation (racemose hemangioma) is an anomalous artery-to-vein anastomosis ranging from a small, localized vascular communication near the disc or in the periphery to a prominent tangle of large, tortuous blood vessels throughout most of the fundus (Fig 18-5). When associated with an arteriovenous malformation of the midbrain region, this condition is generally referred to as *Wyburn- Mason syndrome* (see also discussions of phakomatoses in BCSC Section 5, *Neuro-Ophthalmology,* and Section 6, *Pediatric Ophthalmology and Strabismus*). Associated similar arteriovenous malformations may appear in the orbit and mandible.

CHAPTER 19

Retinoblastoma

Retinoblastoma is the most common primary intraocular malignancy of childhood, second only to uveal malignant melanoma as the most common primary intraocular malignancy in all age groups (Table 19-1). The frequency of retinoblastoma ranges from 1 in 14,000 to 1 in 20,000 live births, depending on the country. It is estimated that approximately 250–300 new cases occur in the United States each year. In Mexico, 6.8 cases per million population have been reported compared to 4 cases per million in the United States. In Central America, there has been an increased incidence in recent years. There is no sexual predilection, and the tumor occurs bilaterally in 30%–40% of cases. The mean age at diagnosis depends on family history and the laterality of the disease:

- patients with a known family history of retinoblastoma: 4 months
- patients with bilateral disease: 14 months
- patients with unilateral disease: 24 months

About 90% of cases are diagnosed in patients under 3 years old.

Augsburger JJ, Oehlschlager U, Manzitti JE. Multinational clinical and pathologic registry of retinoblastoma. Retinoblastoma International Collaborative Study report 2. *Graefes Arch Clin Exp Ophthalmol.* 1995;233:469–475.

Rubenfeld M, Abramson DH, Ellsworth RM, Kitchin FD. Unilateral vs. bilateral retinoblastoma: correlations between age at diagnosis and stage of ocular disease. *Ophthalmology.* 1986;93:1016–1019.

Sanders BM, Draper GJ, Kingston JE. Retinoblastoma in Great Britain 1969–1980: incidence, treatment, and survival. *Br J Ophthalmol.* 1988;72:576–583.

Tamboli A, Podgor MJ, Horm JW. The incidence of retinoblastoma in the United States: 1974 through 1985. *Arch Ophthalmol.* 1990;108:128–132.

Genetic Counseling

Retinoblastoma is caused by a mutation in the *RB1* gene located on the long arm of chromosome 13 at locus 14 (13q14). Both copies of the *RB1* gene must be mutated in order for a tumor to form. If a patient has bilateral retinoblastoma, there is approximately a 98%

Table 19-1 Epidemiology of Retinoblastoma

Most common intraocular cancer of childhood
Third most common intraocular cancer overall after melanoma and metastasis
Incidence is 1/14,000–1/20,000 live births
90% of cases present before 3 years of age
Occurs equally in males and females
Occurs equally in right and left eyes
No racial predilection
60%–70% unilateral (mean age at diagnosis, 24 months)
30%–40% bilateral (mean age at diagnosis, 14 months)

chance that it represents a germline mutation. Only 6% of retinoblastoma patients have a family history of retinoblastoma. The children of a retinoblastoma survivor who has the hereditary form of retinoblastoma have a 45% chance of being affected (50% chance of inheriting and 90% chance of penetrance). In these cases, the child inherits an abnormal gene from the affected parent. This abnormal gene coupled with somatic mutations in the remaining normal RB1 allele leads to the development of multiple tumors in 1 or both eyes.

Sporadic cases constitute about 94% of all retinoblastomas. Of these, 60% of patients have unilateral disease with no germline mutations. The remaining patients have new germline mutations and will develop multiple tumors. It should be noted that approximately 15% of the sporadic unilateral patients are carriers of a germline RB1 mutation. Unless there are multiple tumors in the affected eye, these patients cannot be distinguished from children without a germline mutation. Children with unilateral retinoblastoma and a germline mutation, much like their counterparts with bilateral retinoblastoma, are more likely to present at an earlier age. Commercial laboratories are now available to test the blood of all retinoblastoma patients for germline mutations. There is approximately a 95% chance of finding a new mutation if one exists.

Genetic counseling for retinoblastoma can be very complex (Fig 19-1). A bilateral retinoblastoma survivor has a 45% chance of having an affected child, whereas a unilateral survivor has a 7% chance of having an affected child. Normal parents of a child with bilateral involvement have less than a 5% risk of having another child with retinoblastoma. If 2 or more siblings are affected, the chance that another child will be affected increases to 45%. See Chapter 11 for further discussion of the genetic origins of the retinoblastoma tumor as well as descriptions of histologic features. BCSC Section 6, *Pediatric Ophthalmology and Strabismus,* also discusses retinoblastoma in its chapter on ocular tumors in childhood.

Abramson DH, Mendelsohn ME, Servodidio CA, Tretter T, Gombos DS. Familial retinoblastoma: where and when? *Acta Ophthalmol Scand.* 1998;76:334–338.

Gallie BL, Dunn JM, Chan HS, Hamel PA, Phillips RA. The genetics of retinoblastoma: relevance to the patient. *Pediatr Clin North Am.* 1991;38:299–315.

Murphree, AL. Molecular genetics of retinoblastoma. *Ophthalmol Clin North Am.* 1995;8:155–166.

Scott IU, O'Brien JM, Murray TG. Retinoblastoma: a review emphasizing genetics and management strategies. *Semin Ophthalmol.* 1997;12:59–71.

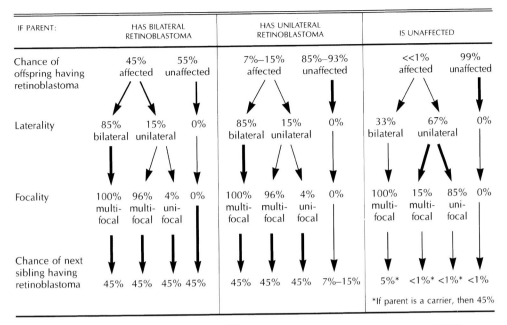

IF PARENT:	HAS BILATERAL RETINOBLASTOMA			HAS UNILATERAL RETINOBLASTOMA			IS UNAFFECTED		
Chance of offspring having retinoblastoma	45% affected	55% unaffected		7%–15% affected	85%–93% unaffected		<<1% affected	99% unaffected	
Laterality	85% bilateral	15% unilateral	0%	85% bilateral	15% unilateral	0%	33% bilateral	67% unilateral	0%
Focality	100% multi-focal	96% multi-focal	4% uni-focal	0%	100% multi-focal	96% multi-focal	4% uni-focal	0%	100% multi-focal	15% multi-focal	85% uni-focal	0%
Chance of next sibling having retinoblastoma	45%	45%	45% 45%	45%	45%	45%	7%–15%	5%*	<1%* <1%* <1%

*If parent is a carrier, then 45%

Figure 19-1 Genetic counseling for retinoblastoma. *(Chart created by David H. Abramson, MD.)*

Smith BJ, O'Brien JM. The genetics of retinoblastoma and current diagnostic testing. *J Pediatr Ophthalmol Strabismus.* 1996;33:120–123.

Diagnostic Evaluation

The presenting signs and symptoms of retinoblastoma are determined by the extent and location of tumor at the time of diagnosis. In the United States, the most common presenting signs of retinoblastoma are leukocoria (white pupillary reflex), strabismus, and ocular inflammation (Table 19-2; Fig 19-2). Other presenting features, such as heterochromia, spontaneous hyphema, and "cellulitis" are uncommon. In rare instances, a small lesion may be found on routine examination. Visual complaints are infrequent because most patients are preschool-age children.

The diagnosis of retinoblastoma can generally be suspected on the basis of a complete ocular examination in the office. The initial examination should include an assessment of visual function, slit-lamp biomicroscopy of the anterior segment and vitreous, and indirect ophthalmoscopy with scleral depression. Ultrasound may confirm the presence of intraocular calcifications.

Retinoblastoma begins as a translucent, gray to white intraretinal tumor, fed and drained by dilated, tortuous retinal vessels (Fig 19-3). As the tumor grows, foci of calcification develop, giving the characteristic chalky white appearance. Exophytic tumors grow beneath the retina and may have an associated serous retinal detachment (Fig 19-4). As the tumor grows, the retinal detachment may become extensive, obscuring visualization of the tumor (Fig 19-5). Endophytic tumors grow on the retinal surface into the vitreous

Table 19-2 **Presenting Signs of Retinoblastoma**

Among Patients <5 Years of Age	Among Patients ≥5 Years of Age
Leukocoria (54%–62%)	Leukocoria (35%)
Strabismus (18%–22%)	Decreased vision (35%)
Inflammation (2%–10%)	Strabismus (15%)
Hypopyon	Floaters (4%)
Hyphema	Pain (4%)
Heterochromia	
Spontaneous globe perforation	
Proptosis	
Cataract	
Glaucoma	
Nystagmus	
Tearing	
Anisocoria	

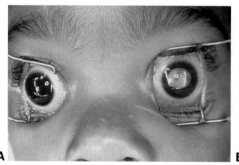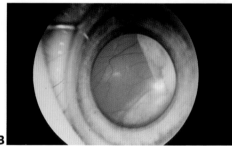

A **B**

Figure 19-2 Retinoblastoma. **A,** Clinical appearance shows leukocoria and strabismus associated with advanced intraocular tumor. **B,** High magnification. Note large retrolental tumor and secondary total exudative retinal detachment. *(Courtesy of Timothy G. Murray, MD.)*

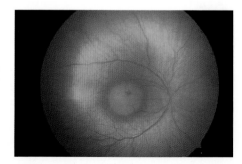

Figure 19-3 Retinoblastoma, clinical appearance. Small, discrete white tumor supplied by dilated retinal blood vessels. *(Courtesy of Timothy G. Murray, MD.)*

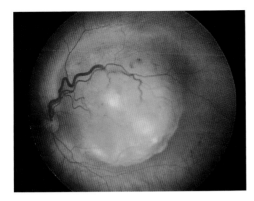

Figure 19-4 Retinoblastoma. Note the dilated retinal blood vessels, foci of calcification, cuff of subretinal fluid, and overlying luteal pigment. *(Courtesy of Matthew W. Wilson, MD.)*

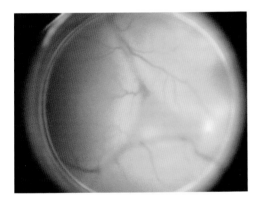

Figure 19-5 Retinoblastoma. Complete exudative detachment obscures tumor visualization. Note normal-appearing retinal vessels as opposed to those found in Coats disease. *(Courtesy of Matthew W. Wilson, MD.)*

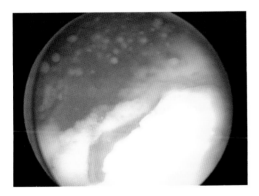

Figure 19-6 Retinoblastoma. Large endophytic tumor with extensive vitreous seeding. *(Courtesy of Matthew W. Wilson, MD.)*

cavity. Blood vessels may be difficult to discern in this tumor. Endophytic tumors are more apt to give rise to vitreous seeds (Fig 19-6). Cells shed from retinoblastoma remain viable in the vitreous and subretinal space and may eventually give rise to tumor implants throughout the eye. Vitreous seeds may also enter the anterior chamber, where they can aggregate on the iris to form nodules or settle inferiorly to form a pseudohypopyon (Fig 19-7). Secondary glaucoma and rubeosis iridis occur in about 50% of such cases. A rare variant of retinoblastoma is the *diffuse infiltrating retinoblastoma,* which is detected at a later age and is typically unilateral. Diffuse infiltrating retinoblastoma presents a diagnostic dilemma, as the retina may be difficult to see through the dense vitreous cells. It is often mistaken for an intermediate uveitis of unknown etiology.

Retinoblastoma cells most commonly escape the eye by invading the optic nerve and extending into the subarachnoid space. Figure 11-41 in Chapter 11 illustrates bulbous enlargement of the optic nerve following invasion by a retinoblastoma tumor. Tumor cells may also traverse emissary canals or erode through the sclera to enter the orbit. Extraocular extension may result in proptosis as the tumor grows in the orbit (Fig 19-8). In the anterior chamber, tumor cells may invade the trabecular meshwork, gaining access to the conjunctival lymphatics. The patient may subsequently develop palpable preauricular and cervical nodes. In the United States, patients rarely present with systemic metastasis and intracranial extension at the time of diagnosis. The most frequently identified sites of metastatic involvement in children with retinoblastoma include skull bones, distal bones, brain, spinal cord, lymph nodes, and abdominal viscera.

Abramson DH, Frank CM, Susman M, Whalen MR, Dunkel IJ, Boyd NW 3rd. Presenting signs of retinoblastoma. *J Pediatr.* 1998;132:505–508.

Albert DM. Historic review of retinoblastoma [review of 86 references]. *Ophthalmology.* 1987;94:654–662.

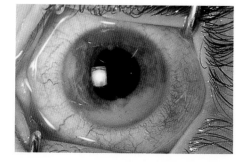

Figure 19-7 Retinoblastoma, clinical appearance. Pseudohypopyon resulting from migration of tumor cells into the anterior chamber (masquerade syndrome).

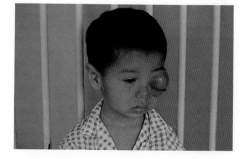

Figure 19-8 Retinoblastoma, clinical appearance. Proptosis caused by retinoblastoma with orbital invasion.

Clinical Examination

Children with retinoblastoma should have a complete history and physical examination by a pediatric oncologist. An examination under anesthesia (EUA) is needed in all patients to permit a complete assessment of the extent of ocular disease prior to treatment (Fig 19-9). The location of multiple tumors should be clearly documented. Intraocular pressure and corneal diameters should be measured intraoperatively. Ultrasonography can be helpful in the diagnosis of retinoblastoma by demonstrating characteristic calcifications within the tumor. Although these calcifications can also be seen on CT scan, MRI has become the preferred diagnostic modality for evaluating the optic nerve, orbits, and brain. Not only does MRI offer better soft tissue resolution, but it also avoids potentially harmful radiation exposure. Recent studies have suggested that systemic metastatic evaluation, typically bone marrow and lumbar puncture, is not indicated in children without neurologic abnormalities or evidence of extraocular extension. If optic extension is suspected, lumbar puncture may be performed. Parents and siblings should be examined for evidence of untreated retinoblastoma or retinoma, as this would provide evidence for a hereditary predisposition to the disease.

Differential Diagnosis

A number of lesions simulate retinoblastoma. Lesions that resemble small to medium-sized retinoblastomas include retinal astrocytic hamartomas commonly seen in tuberous sclerosis; exudative deposits, such as those that occur with Coats disease and retinal capillary hemangiomatosis; and peripheral or posterior pole granulomas, such as those associated with nematode endophthalmitis. The differential diagnoses for the patients with leukocoria and a retinal detachment include Coats disease, persistent fetal vasculature, ocular toxocariasis, and retinopathy of prematurity (Table 19-3). Most of these conditions can be differentiated from retinoblastoma on the basis of a comprehensive history, clinical examination, and appropriate ancillary diagnostic testing.

Coats disease

Coats disease is clinically evident within the first decade of life and is more common in boys. The lesion is typically characterized by unilateral retinal telangiectasia associated

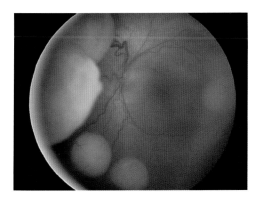

Figure 19-9 Retinoblastoma. Multiple tumor foci in an eye of a patient with a germline RB1 mutation. *(Courtesy of Matthew W. Wilson, MD.)*

Table 19-3 Differential Diagnosis of Retinoblastoma

Clinical Diagnosis in Pseudoretinoblastoma	265 Cases*	Percent	76 Cases†	Percent
Persistent fetal vasculature	51	19.0	15	20.0
Retinopathy of prematurity	36	13.5	3	4.0
Posterior cataract	36	13.5	5	7.0
Coloboma of choroid or optic disc	30	11.5	7	9.0
Uveitis	27	10.0	2	3.0
Larval granulomatosis	18	6.5	20	26.0
Congenital retinal fold	13	5.0		
Coats disease	10	4.0	12	16.0
Organizing vitreous hemorrhage	9	3.5	3	4.0
Retinal dysplasia	7	2.5		
Assorted other disorders	28	10.5	9	12.0

*From Howard GM, Ellsworth RM. Dfferential diagnosis of retinoblastoma. *Am J Ophthalmol.* 1965; 60: 610–618.

†From Shields JA, Stephens RT, Sarin LK. The differential diagnosis of retinoblastoma. In: Harley RD, ed. *Pediatric Ophthalmology.* 2nd ed. Philadelphia: Saunders; 1983.114.

with intraretinal yellow exudation without a distinct mass (Fig 19-10). The progressive leakage of fluid may lead to an extensive retinal detachment. Ultrasound documents the absence of a retinal tumor and shows the convection of cholesterol in the subretinal fluid. Fluorescein angiography shows classic telangiectatic vessels. Laser photocoagulation or cryoablation of the vascular anomalies eliminates the exudative component of the disease and may restore visual function. Subretinal fluid may be drained to facilitate these procedures. Serial evaluation and follow-up is critical for these patients.

Persistent fetal vasculature

Persistent fetal vasculature (PFV), previously known as persistent hyperplastic primary vitreous (PHPV), is typically recognized within days or weeks of birth. The condition is unilateral in two thirds of cases and is associated with microphthalmos, a shallow or flat anterior chamber, a hypoplastic iris with prominent vessels, and a retrolenticular fibrovascular mass that draws the ciliary body processes inward. On indirect ophthalmoscopy, a vascular stalk may be seen arising from the optic nerve head and attaching to the posterior lens capsule. Ultrasound confirms the diagnosis by showing persistent hyaloid remnants arising from the optic nerve head, usually in association with a closed funnel retinal detachment. No retinal tumor is seen, and the axial length of the eye is shortened. Calcification may be present. PFV may be managed with combined lensectomy and vitrectomy approaches in selected cases. See Chapter 10 in this volume and BCSC Section 6, *Pediatric Ophthalmology and Strabismus.*

Ocular toxocariasis

Ocular toxocariasis typically occurs in older children with a history of soil ingestion or exposure to puppies. Toxocara presents with posterior and peripheral granulomas, with an associated uveitis. Organized vitreoretinal traction and cataracts may be present. Ultrasound shows the vitritis, granulomas, retinal traction, and the absence of calcium. See BCSC Section 9, *Intraocular Inflammation and Uveitis.*

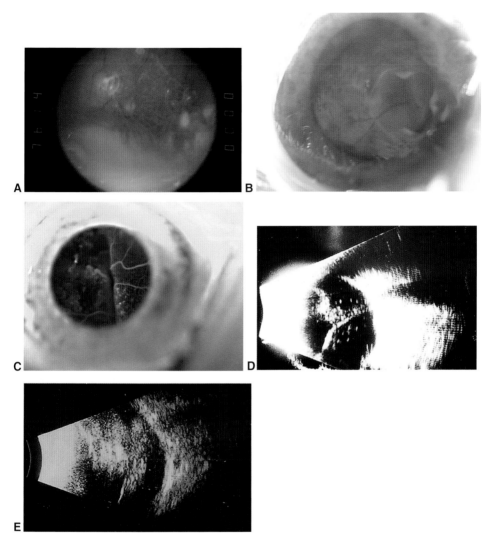

Figure 19-10 Coats disease. **A,** Clinical appearance of characteristic lightbulb aneurysms seen in a patient with Coats disease. There is an inferior exudative retinal detachment. **B,** In advanced cases, there can be a complete exudative retinal detachment. In this case, the retina is visible behind the lens. **C,** Fluorescein angiogram showing classic telangiectatic vessels. **D,** Patient with Coats disease shows an exudative retinal detachment on ultrasound. **E,** In contrast, this ultrasound scan of a patient with retinoblastoma shows a total retinal detachment, but in this case a large tumor mass is also present. *(Parts B and C courtesy of Matthew W. Wilson, MD.)*

Astrocytoma

Retinal astrocytoma, or astrocytic hamartoma, generally appears as a small, smooth, white, glistening tumor located in the nerve fiber layer of the retina (Fig 19-11). It may be single or multiple, unilateral or bilateral. In some cases, it may become larger and calcified, typically having a mulberry appearance. Astrocytomas occasionally arise from the optic disc; such tumors are often referred to as *giant drusen*. Astrocytomas of the retina

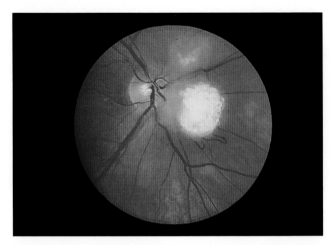

Figure 19-11 Retinal astrocytic hamartomas, clinical appearance. Note the more subtle opalescent lesion superonasal from the optic disc and the larger mulberry lesion inferonasal from the disc.

commonly occur in patients with tuberous sclerosis but may also be seen in patients with neurofibromatosis. Most retinal astrocytomas are not associated with a phakomatosis.

Shields JA, Parsons HM, Shields CL, Shah P. Lesions simulating retinoblastoma. *J Pediatr Ophthalmol Strabismus.* 1991;28:338–340.

Shields JA, Shields CL. *Intraocular Tumors: A Text and Atlas.* Philadelphia: Saunders; 1992: 341–362.

Ulbright TM, Fulling KH, Helveston EM. Astrocytic tumors of the retina. Differentiation of sporadic tumors from phakomatosis-associated tumors. *Arch Pathol Lab Med.* 1984;108: 160–163.

Classification

The Reese-Ellsworth clinical classification is the most commonly used method of categorizing intraocular retinoblastoma (Table 19-4); it does not classify extraocular retinoblastoma. The classification takes into account the number, size, and location of tumors and the presence or absence of vitreous seeds. According to this classification, eye tumors are grouped from very favorable (group I) to very unfavorable (group V) by probability of eye preservation when treated with external-beam radiation alone. The Reese-Ellsworth classification does not provide prognostic information about patient survival or vision. The use of external-beam radiotherapy has given way to the use of primary systemic chemotherapy for the treatment of bilateral retinoblastoma. As a result, the Children's Oncology Group (COG) is currently evaluating a new International Classification System, which will be used in a series of upcoming clinical trials. The hope is to develop a schema that better predicts an eye's response to chemotherapy (Table 19-5). For American Joint Com-

Table 19-4   Reese-Ellsworth Classification of Retinoblastoma

Group	A	B
Group I (very favorable)	Solitary tumor 4 disc diameters (DD) at or behind equator	Multiple tumors 4 DD at or behind equator
Group II (favorable)	Solitary tumor 4–10 DD or behind equator	Multiple tumors 4–10 DD at or behind equator
Group III (doubtful)	Any lesion anterior to equator	Solitary tumor 10 DD posterior to equator
Group IV (unfavorable)	Multiple tumors, some larger than 10 DD	Any lesion anterior to ora serrata
Group V (very unfavorable)	Massive tumor occupying half or more of retina	Vitreous seeding

Table 19-5   International Classification System

Group A	Small tumors (≤3 mm) confined to the retina; >3 mm from the fovea; >1.5 mm from the optic disc
Group B	Tumors (>3 mm) confined to the retina in any location, with clear subretinal fluid ≤6 mm from the tumor margin
Group C	Localized vitreous and/or subretinal seeding (<6 mm in total from tumor margin). If there is more than 1 site of subretinal/vitreous seeding, then the total of these sites must be <6 mm.
Group D	Diffuse vitreous and/or subretinal seeding (≥6 mm in total from tumor margin). If there is more than 1 site of subretinal/vitreous seeding, then the total of these sites must be ≥6 mm. Subretinal fluid >6 mm from tumor margin.
Group E	• No visual potential; *or* • Presence of any 1 or more of the following: 　▪ tumor in the anterior segment 　▪ tumor in or on the ciliary body 　▪ neovascular glaucoma 　▪ vitreous hemorrhage obscuring the tumor of significant hyphema 　▪ phthisical or pre-phthisical eye 　▪ orbital cellulitis–like presentation

mittee on Cancer (AJCC) definitions and staging of retinoblastoma, see Table A-3 in the appendix.

Gallie BL, Truong T, Heon E, et al. Retinoblastoma ABC classification survey. 11th International Retinoblastoma Symposium, Paris, France; 2003.

Reese AB. *Tumors of the Eye.* 3rd ed. Hagerstown, MD: Harper & Row; 1976:90–132.

Shields CL, Mashaykekhi A, Demirci H, Meadows AT, Shields JA. Practical approach to the management of retinoblastoma. *Arch Ophthalmol.* 2004;122:729–735.

Associated Conditions

Retinocytoma

Retinocytoma is clinically indistinguishable from retinoblastoma. Chapter 11 describes the histologic characteristics that distinguish retinocytoma from retinoblastoma (see Fig 11-43). The developmental biology of retinocytoma is subject to controversy. Some authorities consider retinocytoma to be retinoblastoma that has undergone differentiation, analogous to ganglioneuroma, the differentiated form of neuroblastoma. Many other authorities contend that retinocytoma is a benign counterpart of retinoblastoma.

Although histologically benign, retinocytoma carries the same genetic implications as retinoblastoma. A child harboring a retinoblastoma in 1 eye and a retinocytoma in the other should be considered capable of transmitting a faulty tumor suppressor gene to offspring.

Trilateral Retinoblastoma

The term *trilateral retinoblastoma* is reserved for cases of bilateral retinoblastoma associated with ectopic intracranial retinoblastoma. The ectopic focus is usually located in the pineal gland or the parasellar region and historically has been termed a *pinealoblastoma*. This tumor affects 2%–5% of children with a germline RB1 mutation. Rarely, a child may present with ectopic intracranial retinoblastoma prior to ocular involvement. More commonly, this independent malignancy presents months to years after treatment of the intraocular retinoblastoma.

Several different observations support the concept of primary intracranial retinoblastoma. CT helped to establish that intracranial tumors in some patients dying from retinoblastoma are anatomically separate from the primary tumors in the orbit. These intracranial tumors are not associated with metastatic disease elsewhere in the body, and, unlike metastatic retinoblastoma, they often demonstrate features of differentiation such as Flexner-Wintersteiner rosettes (see Fig 11-40 in Chapter 11). Embryologic, immunologic, and phylogenic evidence of photoreceptor differentiation in the pineal gland offers further support for the concept of trilateral retinoblastoma.

All patients with retinoblastoma should undergo baseline neuroimaging studies to exclude intracranial involvement. Patients with germline RB1 gene mutations (ie, bilateral retinoblastoma, unilateral multifocal retinoblastoma, or unilateral retinoblastoma with a positive family history) should undergo serial imaging of the CNS. Studies suggest that serial MRI with and without contrast is most sensitive for CNS involvement and does not expose the child to radiation. Median survival of patients with retinoblastoma with CNS involvement is approximately 8 months. Recent studies report a decrease in the incidence of trilateral retinoblastoma in patients treated with systemic chemotherapy, suggesting a possible prophylactic effect.

Holladay DA, Holladay A, Montebello JF, Redmond KP. Clinical presentation, treatment, and outcome of trilateral retinoblastoma. *Cancer.* 1991;67:710–715.

Jubran RF, Erdreich-Epstein A, Butturini A, Murphree AL, Villablanca JG. Approaches to treatment for extraocular retinoblastoma: Children's Hospital Los Angeles experience. *J Pediatr Hematol Oncol*. 2004;26:31–34.

Shields CL, Meadows AT, Shields JA, Carvalho C, Smith AF. Chemoreduction for retinoblastoma may prevent intracranial neuroblastic malignancy (trilateral retinoblastoma). *Arch Ophthalmol*. 2001;119:1269–1272.

Treatment

When treating retinoblastoma, it is first and foremost important to understand that it is a malignancy. When the disease is contained within the eye, survival rates exceed 95% in the Western world. However, with extraocular spread, survival rates decrease to under 50%. Therefore, in deciding on a treatment strategy, the first goal must be preservation of life, then preservation of the eye, and, finally, preservation of vision. The modern management of intraocular retinoblastoma currently incorporates a combination of different treatment modalities, including enucleation, chemotherapy, photocoagulation, cryotherapy, external-beam radiation therapy, and plaque radiotherapy. Metastatic disease is managed using intensive chemotherapy, radiation, and bone marrow transplantation. The treatment of children of children with retinoblastoma requires a team approach, including an ocular oncologist, pediatric ophthalmologist, pediatric oncologist, and radiation oncologist.

Abramson DH, Schefler AC. Update on retinoblastoma. *Retina*. 2004;24:828–848.

Shields CL, Meadows AT, Leahey AM, Shields JA. Continuing challenges in the management of retinoblastoma with chemotherapy. *Retina*. 2004;24:849–862.

Enucleation

Enucleation remains the definitive treatment for retinoblastoma, providing, in most cases, a complete surgical resection of the disease. Typically, enucleation is considered an appropriate intervention when

- the tumor involves more than 50% of the globe
- orbital or optic nerve involvement is suspected
- anterior segment involvement, with or without neovascular glaucoma, is noted

Enucleation techniques are aimed at minimizing the potential for inadvertent globe penetration while obtaining the greatest length of resected optic nerve that is feasible, typically longer than 10 mm. Porous integrated implants, such as hydroxyapatite or porous polyethylene, are currently used by most surgeons.

Attempts at globe-conserving therapy should be undertaken only by ophthalmologists well versed in the management of this rare childhood tumor and in conjunction with similarly experienced pediatric oncologists. Failed attempts at eye salvage may place a child at inadvertent risk of metastatic disease.

Chemotherapy

A significant advance in the management of bilateral intraocular retinoblastoma in the past decade has been the use of primary systemic chemotherapy. Systemic administration of chemotherapy reduces tumor volume, allowing for subsequent application of consolidative focal therapy with laser, cryotherapy, or radiotherapy (Fig 19-12). These changes have come about as a result of improvements in the treatment of both brain tumors and metastatic retinoblastoma. Current regimens incorporate varying combinations of carboplatin, vincristine, etoposide, and cyclosporine. Children receive drugs intravenously every 3–4 weeks for 4–9 cycles of chemotherapy. Meanwhile, serial EUAs are performed, during which tumor response is observed and focal therapies are administered. Drug regimens, routes of administration, and dose schedules should be determined by a pediatric oncologist experienced in the treatment of children with retinoblastoma. Newer transgenic mouse models of retinoblastoma may now facilitate the screening of newer chemotherapeutic agents (see the following section).

Bechrakis NE, Bornfeld N, Schueler A, Coupland SE, Henze G, Foerster MH. Clinicopathologic features of retinoblastoma after primary chemoreduction. *Arch Ophthalmol.* 1998;116:887–893.

Doz F, Khelfaoui F, Mosseri V, et al. The role of chemotherapy in orbital involvement of retinoblastoma: the experience of a single institution with 33 patients. *Cancer.* 1994;74:722–732.

Dyer MA, Rodriguez-Galindo C, Wilson MW. Use of preclinical models to improve treatment of retinoblastoma. *PloS Med.* 2005;2:e332.

Finger PT, Czechonska G, Demirci H, Rausen A. Chemotherapy for retinoblastoma: a current topic [review of 111 references]. *Drugs.* 1999;58:983–996.

Gallie BL, Budning A, DeBoer G, et al. Chemotherapy with focal therapy can cure intraocular retinoblastoma without radiotherapy. *Arch Ophthalmol.* 1996;114:1321–1328. [Erratum: *Arch Ophthalmol.* 1997;115:525.]

Murphree AL, Villablanca JG, Deegan WF III, et al. Chemotherapy plus local treatment in the management of intraocular retinoblastoma. *Arch Ophthalmol.* 1996;114:1348–1356.

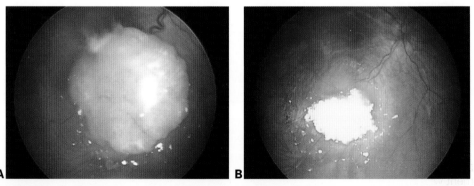

Figure 19-12 Retinoblastoma. **A,** Before chemotherapy. **B,** Reduced tumor volume after 2 cycles of chemotherapy alone.

Shields CL, De Potter P, Himelstein BP, Shields JA, Meadows AT, Maris JM. Chemoreduction in the initial management of intraocular retinoblastoma. *Arch Ophthalmol.* 1996;114: 1330–1338.

Wilson MW, Haik BG, Liu T, Merchant TE, Rodriguez-Galindo C. Effect on ocular survival of adding early intensive focal treatments to a two-drug chemotherapy regimen in patients with retinoblastoma. *Am J Ophthalmol.* 2005;140:397–406.

Periocular chemotherapy

Periocular chemotherapy is being included in upcoming COG trials based on recent data using subconjunctival carboplatin as treatment for retinoblastoma. In phase 1 and 2 clinical trials, both vitreous seeds and retinal tumors were found to be repsonsive to this treatment. Minor local toxicity in the form of orbit myositis has been seen after administration and responds to oral corticosteroids, and more severe reactions, including optic atrophy, have been reported.

Abramson DH, Frank CM, Dunkel IJ. A phase I/II study of subconjunctival carboplatin for intraocular retinoblastoma. *Ophthalmology.* 1999;106:1947–1950.

Harbour JW, Murray TG, Hamasaki D, et al. Local carboplatin therapy in transgenic murine retinoblastoma. *Invest Ophthalmol Vis Sci.* 1996;37:1892–1898.

Photocoagulation and Hyperthermia

Xenon arc and argon laser (532 nm) have traditionally been used to treat retinoblastomas smaller than 3 mm in apical height with basal dimensions less than 10 mm. Two to 3 rows of encircling retinal photocoagulation destroy the tumor's blood supply, with ensuing regression. Newer lasers now allow for direct confluent treatment of the tumor surface. The diode laser (810 nm) is used to provide hyperthermia. Direct application to the surface increases the tumor's temperature to the 45°–60° Celsius range and has a direct cytotoxic effect, which can be augmented by both chemotherapy and radiation (Fig 19-13).

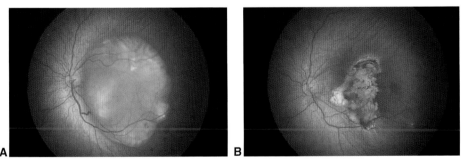

Figure 19-13 Retinoblastoma. **A,** Before treatment. **B,** Same eye 6 months later, after treatment with chemoreduction and laser therapy. *(Courtesy of Timothy G. Murray, MD.)*

Cryotherapy

Also effective for tumors in the size range of less than 10 mm in basal dimension and 3 mm in apical thickness, cryotherapy is applied under direct visualization with a triple freeze-thaw technique. Typically, laser photoablation is chosen for posteriorly located tumors and cryoablation for more anteriorly located tumors. Repetitive tumor treatments are often required for both techniques, along with close follow-up for tumor growth or treatment complications.

External-Beam Radiation Therapy

Retinoblastoma tumors are responsive to radiation. Current techniques use focused megavoltage radiation treatments, often employing lens-sparing techniques, to deliver 4000–4500 cGy over a 4–6 week treatment interval. Typically, those treated are children with bilateral disease not amenable to laser or cryotherapy. Globe salvage rates are excellent, with up to 85% of eyes being retained. Visual function is often excellent and limited only by tumor location or secondary complications.

Two major concerns have limited the application of external-beam radiotherapy using standard techniques:

1. the association of germline mutations of the *RB1* gene with a lifelong increase in the risk of second, independent primary malignancies (eg, osteosarcoma) that is exacerbated by exposure to external-beam radiotherapy
2. the potential for radiation-related sequelae, including midface hypoplasia, radiation-induced cataract, and radiation optic neuropathy and vasculopathy

Evidence suggests that combined-modality therapy that uses lower-dose external-beam radiotherapy coupled with chemotherapy may allow for increased globe conservation with decreased radiation morbidity. In addition, the use of systemic chemotherapy may delay the need for external-beam radiotherapy, allowing for greater orbital development and significantly decreasing the risk of second malignancies once the child is older than 1 year.

Abramson DH, Frank CM. Second nonocular tumors in survivors of bilateral retinoblastoma: a possible age effect on radiation-related risk. *Ophthalmology.* 1998;105:573–574.

Hungerford JL, Toma NM, Plowman PN, Doughty D, Kingston JE. Whole-eye versus lens-sparing megavoltage therapy for retinoblastoma. *Front Radiat Ther Oncol.* 1997;30:81–87.

Murray T. Cancer incidence after retinoblastoma: radiation dose and sarcoma risk. *Surv Ophthalmol.* 1998;43:288–289.

Tucker MA, D'Angio GJ, Boice JD Jr, et al. Bone sarcomas linked to radiotherapy and chemotherapy in children. *N Engl J Med.* 1987;317:588–593.

Plaque Radiotherapy (Brachytherapy)

Radioactive plaque therapy may be used both as salvage therapy for eyes in which globe-conserving therapies have failed to destroy all viable tumor and as a primary treatment for some children with relatively small to medium-sized tumors. This technique is generally applicable for tumors less than 16 mm in basal diameter and 8 mm in apical thickness. The most commonly used isotopes are iodine 125 and ruthenium 106. Intraoperative localization with ultrasound enhances local tumor control for plaque brachytherapy. A greater likelihood of radiation optic neuropathy or vasculopathy may be associated with this radiotherapy modality compared with external-beam radiotherapy. Limiting the radiation dose to periocular structures may lower the incidence of radiation-induced second malignancies.

> Freire JE, De Potter P, Brady LW, Longton WA. Brachytherapy in primary ocular tumors. *Semin Surg Oncol.* 1997;13:167–176.
>
> Shields CL, Shields JA, De Potter P, et al. Plaque radiotherapy in the management of retinoblastoma: use as a primary and secondary treatment. *Ophthalmology.* 1993;100:216–224.

Targeted Therapy

New frontiers in the treatment of retinoblastoma include the use of gene therapy for treating vitreous seeds. Adenoviral-mediated transfection of tumor cells with thymidine kinase renders the tumor susceptible to systemically administered ganciclovir. Phase 1 clinical trials have been completed, documenting both safety and efficacy. Although currently reserved as salvage therapy for remaining eyes failing all conventional modalities of treatment, there is hope that this new targeted therapy may become a mainstream treatment.

> Chévez-Barrios P, Chintagumpala M, Mieler W, et al. Response of retinoblastoma with vitreous tumor seeding to adenovirus-mediated delivery of thymidine kinase followed by ganciclovir. *J Clin Oncol.* 2005;23:7927–7935.

Spontaneous Regression

Retinoblastoma is one of the more common malignant tumors to undergo complete and spontaneous necrosis (although this is rarely recognized with active disease). Spontaneous regression is recognized clinically after involutional changes such as phthisis have occurred. The incidence of spontaneous regression is unknown, as no child with active retinoblastoma is observed in the hopes of spontaneous involution. Although the mechanism by which spontaneous regression occurs is not understood, its histologic appearance is diagnostic. The vitreous cavities of these phthisical eyes are filled with islands of calcified cells embedded in a mass of fibroconnective tissue. Close inspection of the peripheral portion of these calcified islands reveals the ghosted contours of fossilized tumor cells. The process is often accompanied by exuberant proliferation of retinal pigment and ciliary epithelia.

Prognosis

Children with intraocular retinoblastoma who have access to modern medical care have a very good prognosis for survival, with overall survival rates of over 95% for children in developed countries. The most important risk factor associated with death is extraocular extension of tumor, either directly through the sclera or, more commonly, by invasion of the optic nerve, especially to the surgically resected margin (see Fig 11-42 in Chapter 11). The importance of choroidal invasion is unclear. Although a multivariate analysis of a large case series has shown that choroidal invasion is not predictive of metastases, the significance of this pathologic finding remains the subject of debate. A current multicenter study by the COG is investigating this further. Some evidence suggests, however, that bilateral tumors may increase the risk of death because of their association with primary intracranial tumors (see the discussion of trilateral retinoblastoma earlier in the chapter).

Children who survive bilateral retinoblastoma have an increased incidence of non-ocular malignancies later in life. The mean latency for second tumor development is approximately 9 years from management of the primary retinoblastoma. The RB1 mutation is associated with a 26.5% incidence of second tumor development within 50 years in patients treated without exposure to radiation therapy. External-beam radiation therapy decreases the latency period, in turn increasing the incidence of second tumors in the first 30 years of life, as well as increasing the proportion of tumors in the head and neck. The most common type of second cancer in these patients appears to be osteogenic sarcoma. Other relatively common second malignancies include pinealomas, brain tumors, cutaneous melanomas, soft-tissue sarcomas, and primitive unclassifiable tumors (Table 19-6). Estimates suggest that as many as 10%–20% of patients who have bilateral retinoblastoma will develop an apparently unrelated neoplasm within 20 years and that 20%–40% will develop a third malignancy within 30 years. The prognosis for survival in retinoblastoma patients who later develop sarcomas is less than 50%.

Table 19-6 Nonretinoblastoma Malignancies in Retinoblastoma Survivors

Pathologic Type	Tumors Arising in the Field of Radiation of the Eye No. Cases	Percent
Osteosarcoma	25	40.3
Fibrosarcoma	6	9.7
Soft-tissue sarcoma	5	8.1
Anaplastic and unclassifiable	5	8.1
Squamous cell carcinoma	3	4.8
Rhabdomyosarcoma	3	4.8
Assorted other	15	24.2
	Total 62	

Pathologic Type	Tumors Arising Outside the Field of Radiation No. Cases	Percent
Osteosarcoma	12	36.4
Malignant melanoma	4	12.1
Pinealoma	3	9.1
Ewing sarcoma	2	6.1
Papillary thyroid carcinoma	2	6.1
Assorted other	10	30.3
	Total 33	

From Abramson DH, Ellswoth RM, Kitchin FD, el al. Second nonocular tumors in retinoblastoma survivors. Are they radiation-induced? *Ophthalmology.* 1984;91:1351–1355.

Eng C, Li FP, Abramson DH, et al. Mortality from second tumors among long-term survivors of retinoblastoma. *J Natl Cancer Inst.* 1993;85:1121–1128.

Kopelman JE, McLean IW, Rosenberg SH. Multivariate analysis of risk factors for metastasis in retinoblastoma treated by enucleation. *Ophthalmology.* 1987;94:371–377.

Roarty JD, McLean IW, Zimmerman LE. Incidence of second neoplasms in patients with bilateral retinoblastoma. *Ophthalmology.* 1988;95:1583–1587.

Shields CL, Shields JA, Baez K, Cater JR, De Potter P. Optic nerve invasion of retinoblastoma: metastatic potential and clinical risk factors. *Cancer.* 1994;73:692–698.

CHAPTER 20

Secondary Tumors of the Eye

Metastatic Carcinoma

Since the first description in 1872 of a metastatic tumor in the eye of a patient with carcinoma, a large body of literature has indicated that the most common type of intraocular or orbital tumor in adults is metastatic. There are several comprehensive studies of ocular metastatic tumor: some have reported the incidence of tumor metastases in a consecutive series in autopsies, some have dealt with tumor incidence in patients with generalized malignancy, and others have used a clinicopathologic approach. As long-term survival from systemic primary malignancy continues to increase, the ophthalmologist will be confronted with a growing incidence of intraocular and orbital metastatic disease requiring prompt recognition and appropriate diagnostic and therapeutic management.

Metastases to the eye are being diagnosed with increasing frequency for various reasons:

- increasing incidence of certain tumor types that metastasize to the eye (eg, lung, breast)
- prolonged survival of patients with certain cancer types (eg, breast cancer)
- increasing awareness among medical oncologists and ophthalmologists of the pattern of metastatic disease

Bloch RS, Gartner S. The incidence of ocular metastatic carcinoma. *Arch Ophthalmol.* 1971;85: 673–675.

Ferry AP, Font RL. Carcinoma metastatic to the eye and orbit. I. A clinicopathologic study of 227 cases. *Arch Ophthalmol.* 1974;92:276–286.

Grossniklaus HE, Green WR. Uveal tumors. In: Garner A, Klintworth GK, eds. *Pathobiology of Ocular Disease: A Dynamic Approach.* 2nd ed. New York: Marcel Dekker; 1994:1455–1459.

Shields CL, Shields JA, Gross NE, Schwartz GP, Lally SE. Survey of 520 eyes with uveal metastases. *Ophthalmology.* 1997:104:1265–1276.

Volpe NJ, Albert DM. Metastases to the uvea. In: Albert DM, Jakobiec FA, eds. *Principles and Practice of Ophthalmology.* 2nd ed. Philadelphia: Saunders; 2000:5073–5084.

Primary Tumor Sites

The vast majority of metastatic solid tumors to the eye are carcinomas from various organs. Cutaneous melanoma rarely metastasizes to the eye. Table 20-1 shows the most common primary tumors that metastasize to the choroid.

Table 20-1 Primary Sites of Choroidal Metastasis

Males (N = 137)	Females (N = 287)
Lung (40%)	Breast (68%)
Unknown (29%)	Lung (12%)
Gastrointestinal (9%)	Unknown (12%)
Kidney (6%)	Others (4%)
Prostate (6%)	Gastrointestinal (2%)
Skin (4%)	Skin (1%)
Others (4%)	Kidney (<1%)
Breast (1%)	

Modified from Shields CL, Shields JA, Gross NE, et al. Survey of 520 eyes with uveal metastases. *Ophthalmology*. 1997;104:1265–1276.

Mechanisms of Metastasis to the Eye

The mechanism of intraocular metastasis depends on hematogenous dissemination of tumor cells. The anatomy of the arterial supply to the eye dictates the predilection of tumor cell deposits within the eye. The posterior choroid, with its rich vascular supply, is the most favored site of intraocular metastases, and it is affected 10–20 times more frequently than is the iris or ciliary body. The retina and optic disc, supplied by the single central retinal artery, are rarely the sole site of involvement. Bilateral ocular involvement has been reported in 20%–25% of cases, and multifocal deposits are frequently seen within the involved eye. Many patients with ocular metastases also have concurrent CNS metastases.

Clinical Evaluation

The clinical features of intraocular metastases depend on the site of involvement. Metastases to the iris and ciliary body usually appear as white or gray-white gelatinous nodules (Figs 20-1, 20-2, 20-3). The clinical features of anterior uveal metastases may include

- iridocyclitis
- secondary glaucoma
- rubeosis iridis
- hyphema
- irregular pupil

Anterior segment tumors are best evaluated with slit-lamp biomicroscopy coupled with gonioscopy. High-resolution ultrasound imaging may quantify tumor size and anatomical relationships.

Patients with tumor in the posterior pole commonly complain of loss of vision. Pain and photopsia may be concurrent symptoms. Indirect binocular ophthalmoscopy may reveal a nonrhegmatogenous retinal detachment associated with a placoid amelanotic tumor mass (Figs 20-4, 20-5, 20-6). Multiple or bilateral lesions may be present in approximately 25% of cases, highlighting the importance of close evaluation of the fellow eye. These lesions are usually relatively flat and ill defined, often gray-yellow or yellow-white, with secondary alterations at the level of the RPE presenting as clumps of brown pigment ("leopard spotting"; Fig 20-7).

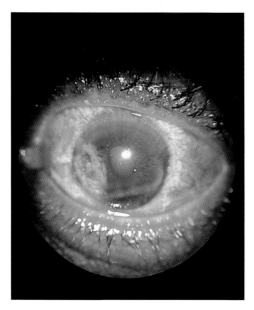

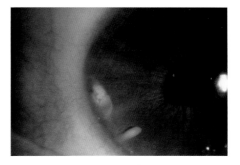

Figure 20-1 Metastasis to the iris associated with hyphema.

Figure 20-2 Metastasis from breast carcinoma to the iris. *(Courtesy of Timothy G. Murray, MD.)*

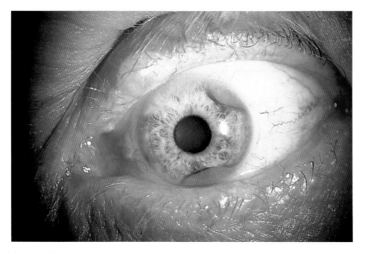

Figure 20-3 Metastatic cutaneous melanoma to the iris. Note both lesions at periphery.

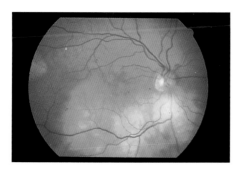

Figure 20-4 Multiple metastatic lesions to the choroid. Note the pale yellow color and relative flatness.

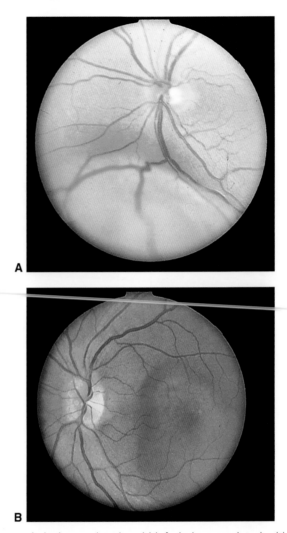

Figure 20-5 **A,** Metastatic lesion to the choroid inferiorly, associated with bullous retinal detachment. **B,** Subtle metastatic lesion to the choroid, near the fovea, associated with serous effusion.

The mushroom configuration frequently seen in primary choroidal melanoma from breakthrough of Bruch's membrane is rarely present in uveal metastases. The retina overlying the metastasis may appear opaque and become detached. Rapid tumor growth with necrosis and uveitis are occasionally seen. Dilated epibulbar vessels may be seen in the quadrant overlying the metastasis. For a differential diagnosis of choroidal metastasis, see Table 20-2.

Ancillary Tests

Although *fluorescein angiography* may be helpful in defining the margins of a metastatic tumor, it is typically less useful in differentiating a metastasis from a primary intraocular neoplasm. The double circulation pattern and prominent early choroidal filling often seen in choroidal melanomas are rarely found in metastatic tumors.

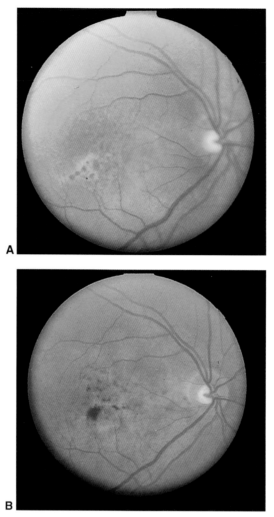

Figure 20-6 A, Metastatic carcinoma to the choroid. Vision was reduced to finger counting because of macular involvement. Note irregular pigmentation on surface. **B,** Same eye, 1 month after radiation therapy. Visual acuity has improved to 20/20. Note increased pigmentation, characteristic of irradiation effects.

Ultrasonography is diagnostically valuable in patients with metastatic tumor. B scan shows an echogenic choroidal mass with an ill-defined, sometimes lobulated, outline. Overlying secondary retinal detachment is commonly detected in these cases. A scan demonstrates moderate to high internal reflectivity.

Fine-needle aspiration biopsy may be helpful in rare cases when the diagnosis cannot be established by noninvasive procedures. Although metastatic tumors may recapitulate the histology of the primary tumor, they are often less differentiated. Special histochemical and immunohistochemical stains assist in the diagnosis of metastatic tumors, but they are usually not useful in determining the precise origin.

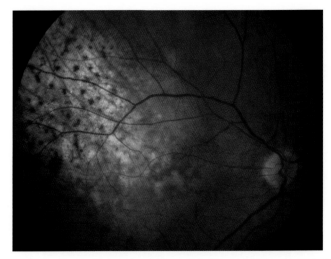

Figure 20-7 Breast metastases, clinical appearance. Note the amelanotic infiltrative choroidal mass with secondary overlying retinal pigment epithelial changes accounting for the characteristic "leopard spots." *(Courtesy of Matthew W. Wilson, MD.)*

Table 20-2 Differential Diagnosis of Choroidal Metastasis

Amelanotic nevus	VKH syndrome
Amelanotic melanoma	Central serous retinopathy
Choroidal hemangioma	Infectious lesions
Choroidal osteoma	Organized subretinal hemorrhage
Posterior uveal effusion syndrome	Extensive neovascular membranes
Posterior scleritis	Rhegmatogenous retinal detachment

Metastases to the optic nerve may produce disc edema, decreased visual acuity, and visual field defects. Because the metastases may involve the parenchyma or the optic nerve sheath, MRI as well as ultrasonography may be valuable in detecting the presence and location of the lesion(s).

Metastases to the retina, which are very rare, appear as white, noncohesive lesions, often distributed in a perivascular location suggestive of cotton-wool spots (Fig 20-8). Because of secondary vitreous seeding of tumor cells, these metastases sometimes resemble retinitis more than they do a true tumor. Vitreous aspirates for cytologic studies may confirm the diagnosis.

Other Diagnostic Factors

One of the most important diagnostic factors in the evaluation of suspected metastatic tumors is a history of systemic malignancy. More than 90% of patients with uveal metastasis from carcinoma of the breast, for example, have a history of treatment prior to the development of ocular involvement. In the remaining 10% of patients, the primary tumor can usually be diagnosed by breast examination at the time the suspicious ocular lesion is detected. For other patients, however, there is no prior history of malignancy.

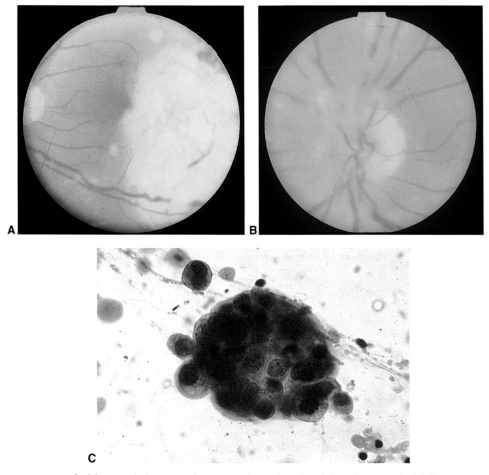

Figure 20-8 **A,** Metastatic lung carcinoma to the retina, involving the macula. Vision was reduced to finger counting. **B,** Same eye, showing characteristic perivascular distribution of metastases. **C,** Vitreous aspirate from same eye, showing a morula of cells, characteristic of adenocarcinoma of the lung.

This is especially true of patients with ocular metastasis from the lung. A complete review of systems, a family history, and a history of smoking may alert the ophthalmologist to the suspected site of an occult primary tumor. Any patient with an amelanotic fundus mass suspected of being a metastatic focus should have a thorough systemic evaluation, including imaging of the breast, chest, abdomen, and pelvis. CT-PET scanning may help direct a more targeted evaluation.

Prognosis

The diagnosis of tumor metastatic to the uvea implies a poor prognosis, because widespread dissemination of the primary tumor has usually occurred. In one report, the survival time following diagnosis of metastasis to the uvea ranged from 1 to 67 months, depending on the primary cancer type. Metastatic carcinoid is associated with long survival times. Patients with breast carcinoma metastatic to the uvea survive an average of 9–13 months after the metastasis is recognized, but cases with long-term survival have now been reported. Shorter survival time is typically seen in patients with lung carcinoma and carcinomas arising from the gastrointestinal or genitourinary tracts, in which metastases herald the presence of the primary tumor.

The goal in ophthalmic management of ocular metastases is preservation or restoration of vision and palliation of pain. Radical surgical procedures and treatments with risks greater than the desired benefits should be avoided.

Treatment

Indications for treatment include decreased vision, pain, diplopia, and severe proptosis. The patient's age and health status and the condition of the fellow eye are also critical in the decision-making process. The treatment modality in patients with metastatic ocular disease should be individually tailored. When ocular metastases are concurrent with widespread metastatic disease, systemic chemotherapy alone or in combination with local therapy is reasonable. In patients manifesting metastases in the eye alone, local therapy modalities may be safe, allowing conservation of visual functions with minimal systemic morbidity.

Chemotherapy or hormonal therapy for sensitive tumors (eg, breast cancer) may induce a prompt response. In such patients, no additional ocular treatment may be indicated. However, when vision is endangered by choroidal metastases in spite of chemotherapy, additional modalities of local therapy such as external irradiation, brachytherapy, and laser photocoagulation or transpupillary thermotherapy may be necessary. Radiotherapy is frequently associated with rapid improvement of the patient's symptoms, along with rapid resolution of exudative retinal detachment and, often, direct reduction in tumor size. Rarely, enucleation is performed because of severe, unrelenting pain.

Amer R, Pe'er J, Chowers I, Anteby I. Treatment options in the management of choroidal metastases. *Ophthalmologica*. 2004;218:372–377.

Shields JA, Shields CL, Brotman HK, Carvalho C, Perez N, Eagle RC Jr. Cancer metastatic to the orbit: the 2000 Robert M. Curts Lecture. *Ophthal Plast Reconstr Surg*. 2001;17:346–354.

Direct Intraocular Extension

Direct extension of extraocular tumors into the eye is rare. Intraocular extension occurs most commonly with conjunctival squamous cell carcinoma and less frequently with conjunctival melanoma and basal cell carcinoma of the eyelid. The sclera is usually an effective barrier against intraocular invasion. Only a small minority of carcinomas of the conjunctiva ever successfully penetrate the globe, but those that do are often variants of squamous cell carcinoma: mucoepidermoid carcinoma or spindle cell variant. These more aggressive neoplasms usually recur several times after local excision before they invade the eye.

CHAPTER **21**

Lymphomatous Tumors

Intraocular Lymphoma

Intraocular lymphoma is almost always non-Hodgkin large cell lymphoma of the B-cell type. T-cell lymphoma involves the eye only rarely. Historically, the terminology for intraocular lymphoma was *histiocytic lymphoma* or *reticulum cell sarcoma,* but these terms are not used in the recent literature. Intraocular lymphoma can infiltrate any part of the eye, including the vitreous, retina, sub-RPE space, subretinal space, and uveal tract.

Two types of lymphoma may involve intraocular structures. The much more common one is *primary central nervous system lymphoma (PCNSL),* in which approximately one quarter of the patients have intraocular involvement. In these cases, the vitreous and retina are involved. More rarely, the eye can be involved in *systemic/visceral/nodal lymphoma.* In these cases, the uveal tract is more commonly involved, usually in a pattern of metastatic disease. In advanced cases, the intraocular findings of the 2 types may overlap. In recent decades, the incidence of PCNSL has been increasing significantly in both immunocompetent and immunocompromised persons; thus, the incidence of intraocular lymphoma is more frequent than in the past.

Clinical Evaluation

Ocular signs and symptoms may occur before systemic or CNS findings. In such cases, the disease may manifest as a masquerade syndrome, simulating nonspecific uveitis. The onset of bilateral posterior uveitis in patients over the age of 50 years should be considered suggestive of large cell lymphoma, as should "chronic" uveitis in patients in their fifth to seventh decades. Although 30% of patients present with unilateral involvement, delayed involvement of the second eye occurs in approximately 85% of patients.

Diffuse vitreous cells may be associated with deep subretinal yellow-white infiltrates. Often, fine details of the retina are obscured by the density of the vitritis ("headlight in the fog"). Retinal vasculitis and/or vascular occlusion may be noted. The RPE may reveal characteristic clumping overlying the subretinal infiltrates (see Fig 10-15 in Chapter 10). Anterior chamber reaction may be minimal.

Photographic and fluorescein angiographic studies document baseline clinical findings but are rarely helpful in defining a differential diagnosis. Ultrasound examination may reveal discrete nodular or placoid infiltration of the subretinal space, associated retinal detachment, and vitreous syneresis with increased reflectivity. Clinical history and neurologic evaluation may reveal neurologic deficits in up to 10% of patients, and 60% of patients show concomitant CNS involvement at the time of presentation. If the diagnosis is suspected, neurologic consultation coupled with CT or MRI studies and lumbar puncture should be coordinated with diagnostic vitrectomy.

Pathologic Studies

Diagnostic confirmation of ocular involvement requires sampling of the vitreous and, when appropriate, the subretinal space. Coordinated planning with the surgical pathologist prior to surgery regarding sample handling is important. The surgical pathologist should be skilled in the handling of small-volume intraocular specimens and experienced in the evaluation of vitreous samples.

The best approach to pathologic evaluation of the specimen remains controversial. Complete diagnostic 3-port pars plana vitrectomy is indicated to obtain an undiluted vitreous specimen. If a subretinal nodule is accessible in a region of the retina unlikely to compromise visual function, subretinal aspiration of the lesion can be performed. A single-vitrectomy biopsy may not be adequate, and a repeat biopsy may be required. Evaluation of the vitreous and subretinal specimen may be performed using cytopathology (see Fig 10-16), including immunohistochemical studies for subclassification of the cells, flow cytometry, and PCR analysis for gene rearrangements (see Chapters 3, 4, and 10).

Preferably, a pathologist familiar with the diagnosis of intraocular large cell lymphoma should evaluate the specimen. If an adequate specimen is obtained, multiple pathologic approaches may be employed. Cytologic evaluation is essential in establishing the diagnosis, with flow cytometry and PCR serving as ancillary studies. Specimens that reveal malignant lymphocytic cells establish the diagnosis (Fig 21-1), and evaluation of cell surface markers may allow for subclassification of the tumor.

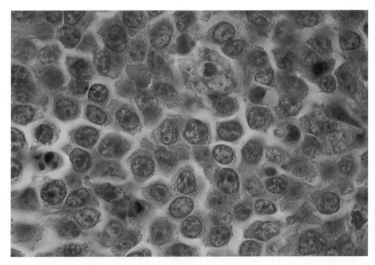

Figure 21-1 Large cell lymphoma, cytology. Note the unusual nuclei and prominent nucleoli of these neoplastic lymphoid cells obtained by fine-needle aspiration biopsy.

Treatment

Because the blood–ocular barriers may limit penetration of chemotherapeutic agents into the eye, irradiation of the affected eye using fractionated external-beam radiation has remained popular in many centers for treatment of intraocular lymphoma. However, although radiotherapy may induce an ocular remission, the tumor invariably recurs, and further irradiation places the patient at high risk for irreversible visual loss caused by radiation retinopathy. Concern regarding the disadvantages of ocular irradiation has led several groups to use intraocular chemotherapy, injecting high-dose methotrexate into the vitreous, with very good response and low recurrence rate. Parallel to the treatment of the intraocular disease is the treatment of the CNS and systemic lymphoma by a medical oncologist.

Prognosis

The prognosis for patients with large cell lymphoma is poor, although advances in early diagnosis have produced a cohort of long-term survivors. Serial follow-up with consultative management by an experienced medical oncologist is critical in the management of this disease. Patients with primary CNS lymphoma should be followed carefully by an ophthalmologist for possible ocular involvement, even after remission of the CNS disease.

Uveal Lymphoid Infiltration

Uveal lymphoid infiltration, formerly known as *reactive lymphoid hyperplasia,* typically presents in patients in the sixth decade; it can occur at any uveal site. Similar lymphoid proliferation can occur in the conjunctiva and orbit (see also Chapter 5 for conjunctival involvement, Chapter 12 for uveal involvement, and Chapter 14 for orbital involvement).

Clinical Evaluation

Patients typically notice painless, progressive visual loss. Ophthalmoscopically, a diffuse or, rarely, nodular amelanotic thickening of the choroid is noted. Exudative retinal detachment and secondary glaucoma may be present in up to 85% of eyes. Frequently, delay between the onset of symptoms and diagnostic intervention is significant.

This rare disorder is characterized pathologically by localized or diffuse infiltration of the uveal tract by lymphoid cells. The etiology is unknown. Clinically, this condition can simulate posterior uveal melanoma, metastatic carcinoma to the uvea, sympathetic ophthalmia, Vogt-Koyanagi-Harada syndrome, and posterior scleritis. Proptosis of the affected eye occurs in approximately 10%–15% of patients who develop simultaneous orbital infiltration with benign lymphoid cells. Ultrasound testing reveals a diffuse, homogeneous choroidal infiltrate with associated secondary retinal detachment. Extraocular extension or orbital involvement may be best demonstrated with echography.

Pathologic Studies

Biopsy confirmation should be targeted to the most accessible tissue. If extraocular involvement is present, biopsy of the involved conjunctiva or orbit may be considered.

FNAB or pars plana vitrectomy with biopsy may be indicated for isolated uveal involvement. Coordination with the surgical pathologist is crucial to achieve the greatest likelihood of appropriate confirmation and cell marker studies.

Treatment

Historically, eyes with this type of lymphoid infiltration were generally managed by enucleation because of presumed malignancy. Current management emphasizes globe-conserving therapy aimed at visual preservation. High-dose oral steroids may induce tumor regression and decrease exudative retinal detachment. Early intervention with low-dose ocular and orbital fractionated external-beam radiotherapy may definitively manage the disease.

Prognosis

The prognosis for survival is excellent for patients with uveal lymphoid infiltration, with the rare exception of patients with systemic lymphoma. Preservation of visual function appears related to primary tumor location and secondary sequelae, including exudative retinal detachment or glaucoma. Early intervention appears to enhance the likelihood for visual preservation.

Chan CC, Wallace DJ. Intraocular lymphoma: update on diagnosis and management. *Cancer Control.* 2004;11:285–295.

Coupland SE, Hummel M, Muller HH, Stein H. Molecular analysis of immunoglobulin genes in primary intraocular lymphoma. *Invest Ophthalmol Vis Sci.* 2005;46:3507–3514.

Grossniklaus HE, Martin DF, Avery R, et al. Uveal lymphoid infiltration: report of four cases and clinicopathologic review. *Ophthalmology.* 1998;105:1265–1273.

Read RW, Zamir E, Rao NA. Neoplastic masquerade syndromes. *Surv Ophthalmol.* 2002;47:81–124.

Smith JR, Rosenbaum JT, Wilson DJ, et al. Role of intravitreal methotrexate in the management of primary central nervous system lymphoma with ocular involvement. *Ophthalmology.* 2002;109:1709–1716.

Specht CS, Laver NM. Benign and malignant lymphoid tumors, leukemia, and histiocytic lesions. In: Albert DM, Jakobiec FA, eds. *Principles and Practice of Ophthalmology.* 2nd ed. Philadelphia: Saunders; 2000:5146–5168.

CHAPTER 22

Ocular Manifestations of Leukemia

Ocular involvement with leukemia is common, occurring in as many as 80% of the eyes of patients examined at autopsy. Clinical studies have documented ophthalmic findings in as many as 40% of patients at diagnosis. Although retinal lesions are the most frequently observed clinical finding, histologic studies have shown that the choroid is affected more often. Furthermore, the uveal tract may serve as a "sanctuary site," predisposing the eye to be the first clinical manifestation of recurrent disease (Fig 22-1). Choroidal infiltrates may be difficult to detect with indirect ophthalmoscopy; they may be better detected on ultrasound as a thickening of the choroids. Serous retinal detachments may overlie these infiltrates. Leukemic involvement of the iris is also manifested as a diffuse thickening, and in some cases small nodules may be seen at the margin of the pupil (see Fig 17-4D). Tumor cells in the anterior chamber may layer to form a pseudohypopyon. Infiltration of the angle by these cells can give rise to a secondary glaucoma.

Retinal findings such as hard exudates, cotton-wool spots, and white-centered retinal hemorrhages (pseudo–Roth spots) are usually the result of associated anemia or thrombocytopenia. However, leukemic infiltrates can be seen as yellow deposits in the retina and the subretinal space. Gray-white nodules of various sizes have been seen in a case of chronic myelogenous leukemia. Occasionally, perivascular leukemic infiltrates can produce gray-white streaks in the retina.

Vitreous involvement by leukemias is rare; however, opacities may develop. If necessary, a diagnostic vitrectomy can be performed to establish a diagnosis. Leukemic infiltration of the optic nerve may present with severe visual loss and optic nerve edema. One or both eyes may be affected. This is an ophthalmic emergency and requires immediate treatment to preserve as much vision as possible. Systemic and intrathecal chemotherapy will be needed with or without radiation.

Leukemic infiltrates may also involve the orbital soft tissue, with resultant proptosis. These tumors, which are more common with myelogenous leukemias, are referred to as *granulocytic sarcomas* or *chloromas*. They have a predilection for the lateral and medial walls of the orbit.

Patients with leukemia and allied disorders may be immunocompromised and thus susceptible to opportunistic infections. Endogenous infections must be considered in the differential diagnosis of leukemic infiltration.

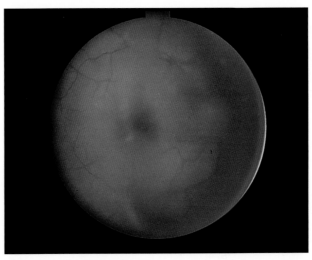

Figure 22-1 Leukemic infiltration of the vitreous, clinical appearance. View of the fundus is hazy because of dispersed tumor cells in the vitreous.

Treatment of leukemic involvement of the eye generally consists of low-dose radiation therapy to the eye and systemic chemotherapy. The prognosis for vision depends on the type of leukemia and the extent of ocular involvement.

Guyer DR, Schachat AP, Vitale S, et al. Leukemic retinopathy: relationship between fundus lesions and hematologic parameters at diagnosis. *Ophthalmology.* 1989;96:860–864.

Reddy SC, Jackson N. Retinopathy in acute leukaemia at initial diagnosis: correlation of fundus lesions and haematological parameters. *Acta Ophthalmol Scand.* 2004;82:81–85.

Schachat AP, Jabs DA, Graham ML, Ambinder RF, Green WR, Saral R. Leukemic iris infiltration. *J Pediatr Ophthalmol Strabismus.* 1988;25:135–138.

Schachat AP, Markowitz JA, Guyer DR, Burke PJ, Karp JE, Graham ML. Ophthalmic manifestations of leukemia. *Arch Ophthalmol.* 1989;107:697–700.

Sharma T, Grewal J, Gupta S, Murray PI. Ophthalmic manifestations of acute leukaemias: the ophthalmologist's role. *Eye.* 2004;18:663–672.

CHAPTER 23

Rare Tumors

Medulloepithelioma

Medulloepithelioma, or diktyoma, is a tumor of the nonpigmented ciliary epithelium that occurs in both benign and malignant forms (see Fig 11-44). Medulloepitheliomas are congenital neuroepithelial tumors arising from primitive medullary epithelium. This type of tumor typically becomes clinically evident in children 4–12 years old, but it may also occur in adults. It usually appears as a variably pigmented mass arising from the ciliary body but has also been documented in the retina and optic nerve. The tumor may erode into the anterior chamber and become visible at the iris root. Large cysts may be seen on the surface of the tumor or within the lesion on diagnostic imaging (Fig 23-1). Chapter 11 discusses the histologic features of medulloepithelioma.

Management usually consists of enucleation or observation. Surgical resection is specifically avoided for the majority of these tumors because of late complications and documented metastases associated with this treatment. Fortunately, metastasis is rare with appropriate management, even if the tumor appears frankly malignant on histologic examination. Small lesions have been successfully treated with iodine 125 plaque brachytherapy.

Davidorf FH, Craig E, Birnhaum L, Wakely P. Management of medulloepithelioma of the ciliary body with brachytherapy. *Am J Ophthalmol.* 2002;133:841–843.

Garner A, Klintworth GK, eds. *Pathology of Ocular Disease: A Dynamic Approach.* 2nd ed. New York: Marcel Dekker; 1994:1405–1413.

Lumbroso L, Desjardins L, Coue O, Ducourneau Y, Pechereau A. Presumed bilateral medulloepithelioma. *Arch Ophthalmol.* 2001;119:449–450.

Leiomyomas, Neurilemomas, and Neurofibromas

Leiomyomas, neurilemomas, and neurofibromas of the uveal tract are extremely rare tumors that are usually misdiagnosed clinically as amelanotic primary uveal melanomas. The role of ancillary diagnostic tests for such lesions is uncertain.

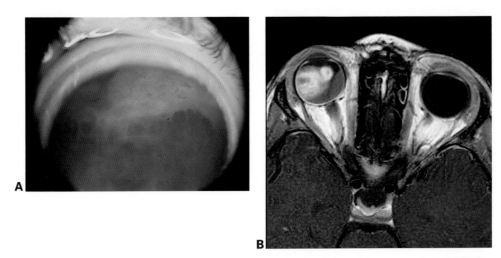

Figure 23-1 Medulloepithelioma. **A,** Pigmented lesion arising in ciliary body with amelanotic apex. **B,** T1-weighted MRI with gadolinium, showing diffuse enhancement and multiple cystic spaces. *(Courtesy of Matthew W. Wilson, MD.)*

American Joint Committee on Cancer (AJCC) Definitions and Staging of Ocular Tumors, 2002

Table A-1 Carcinoma of the Conjunctiva

The following definitions apply to both clinical and pathologic staging

Primary Tumor (T)

TX	Primary tumor cannot be assessed
T0	No evidence of primary tumor
Tis	Carcinoma in situ
T1	Tumor ≤5 mm in greatest dimension
T2	Tumor >5 mm in greatest dimension, without invasion of adjacent structures
T3	Tumor invades adjacent structures, excluding the orbit
T4	Tumor invades the orbit with or without further extension
	T4a Tumor invades orbital soft tissues without bone invasion
	T4b Tumor invades bone
	T4c Tumor invades adjacent paranasal sinuses
	T4d Tumor invades brain

Regional Lymph Nodes (N)

NX	Regional lymph nodes cannot be assessed
N0	No regional lymph node metastasis
N1	Regional lymph node metastasis

Distant Metastasis (M)

MX	Distant metastasis cannot be assessed
M0	No distant metastasis
M1	Distant metastasis

Stage Grouping	No stage grouping is presently recommended

Histologic Grade (G)

GX	Grade cannot be assessed
G1	Well differentiated
G2	Moderately differentiated
G3	Poorly differentiated
G4	Undifferentiated

Residual Tumor (R)

RX	Presence of residual tumor cannot be assessed
R0	No residual tumor
R1	Microscopic residual tumor
R2	Macroscopic residual tumor

Table A-2 Malignant Melanoma of the Conjunctiva

Clinical Definitions (cTNM)

Primary Tumor (T)

TX	Primary tumor cannot be assessed
T0	No evidence of primary tumor
T1	Tumor of the bulbar conjunctiva
T2	Tumor of the bulbar conjunctiva with corneal extension
T3	Tumor extending into the conjunctival fornix, palpebral conjunctiva, or caruncle
T4	Tumor invades the eyelid, globe, orbit, sinuses, or central nervous system

Pathologic Definitions (pTNM)

Primary Tumor (T)

pTX	Primary tumor cannot be assessed
pT0	No evidence of primary tumor
pT1	Tumor of the bulbar conjunctiva confined to the epithelium
pT2	Tumor of the bulbar conjunctiva ≤0.8 mm in thickness with invasion of the substantia propria
pT3	Tumor of the bulbar conjunctiva >0.8 mm in thickness with invasion of the substantia propria or tumors involving palpebral or caruncular conjunctiva
pT4	Tumor invades the eyelid, globe, orbit, sinuses, or central nervous system

Regional Lymph Nodes (N)

pNX	Regional lymph nodes cannot be assessed
pN0	No regional lymph node metastasis
pN1	Regional lymph node metastasis

Distant Metastasis (M)

pMX	Distant metastasis cannot be assessed
pM0	No distant metastasis
pM1	Distant metastasis

Stage Grouping   No stage grouping is presently recommended

Histologic Grade (G)

(Histopathologic grade represents the origin of the primary tumor)

GX	Origin cannot be assessed
G0	Primary acquired melanosis without cellular atypia
G1	Conjunctival nevus
G2	Primary acquired melanosis with cellular atypia (epithelial disease only)
G3	De novo malignant melanoma

Residual Tumor (R)

RX	Presence of residual tumor cannot be assessed
R0	No residual tumor
R1	Microscopic residual tumor
R2	Macroscopic residual tumor

Table A-3 **Retinoblastoma**

Clinical Definitions (cTNM)

Primary Tumor (T)

TX	Primary tumor cannot be assessed
T0	No evidence of primary tumor
T1	Tumor confined to the retina (no vitreous seeding or significant retinal detachment)

       T1a Any eye in which the largest tumor is ≤3 mm in height *and* no tumor is located closer than 1 DD (1.5 mm) to the optic nerve or fovea

       T1b All eyes in which the tumor(s) are confined to the retina regardless of location or size (up to half the volume of the eye). *No* vitreous seeding. *No* retinal detachment or subretinal fluid >5 mm from the base of the tumor.

T2	Tumor with contiguous spread to adjacent tissues or spaces (vitreous or subretinal space)

       T2a *Minimal tumor spread to vitreous and/or subretinal space.* Fine local or diffuse vitreous seeding and/or serous retinal detachment up to total detachment may be present, but *no* clumps, lumps, snowballs, or avascular masses are allowed in the vitreous or subretinal space. Calcium flecks in the vitreous or subretinal space are allowed. The tumor may fill up to 2/3 the volume of the eye.

       T2b *Massive tumor spread to the vitreous and/or subretinal space.* Vitreous seeding and/or subretinal implantation may consist of lumps, clumps, snowballs, or avascular tumor masses. Retinal detachment may be total. Tumor may fill up to 2/3 the volume of the eye.

       T2c Unsalvageable intraocular disease. Tumor fills more than 2/3 of the eye *or* there is no possibility of visual rehabilitation *or* one or more of the following are present: tumor-associated glaucoma, either neovascular or angle closure; anterior segment extension of tumor; ciliary body extension of tumor; hyphema (significant); massive vitreous hemorrhage; tumor in contact with lens; orbital cellulitis–like clinical presentation (massive tumor necrosis)

T3	Invasion of the optic nerve and/or optic coats
T4	Extraocular tumor

Regional Lymph Nodes (N)

NX	Regional lymph nodes cannot be assessed
N0	No regional lymph node involvement
N1	Regional lymph node involvement (preauricular, submandibular, or cervical)
N2	Distant lymph node involvement

Distant Metastasis (M)

MX	Distant metastasis cannot be assessed
M0	No distant metastasis
M1	Metastases to central nervous system and/or bone, bone marrow, or other sites

(Continued)

Table A-3 *(continued)*

Pathologic Definitions (pTNM)

Tumor (pT)

pTX	Primary tumor cannot be assessed
pT0	No evidence of primary tumor
pT1	Tumor confined to the retina, vitreous, or subretinal space. No optic nerve or choroidal invasion
pT2	Minimal invasion of optic nerve and/or optic coats
	pT2a Tumor invades optic nerve up to, but not through, the level of the lamina cribrosa
	pT2b Tumor invades choroid focally
	pT2c Tumor invades optic nerve up to but not through the level of the lamina cribrosa *and* invades the choroid focally
pT3	Significant invasion of the optic nerve and/or optic coats
	pT3a Tumor invades optic nerve through the level of the lamina cribrosa but not to the line of resection
	pT3b Tumor massively invades the choroid
	pT3c Tumor invades the optic nerve through the lamina cribrosa but not to the line of resection *and* massively invades the choroid
pT4	Extraocular extension, which includes:

- Tumor invades optic nerve to the line of resection
- Tumor invades the orbit through the sclera
- Tumor extends both anteriorly and posteriorly into orbit
- Extension into the brain
- Extension into the subarachnoid space of the optic nerve
- Extension to the apex of the orbit
- Extension to, but not through, the chiasm, or
- Extension into the brain beyond the chiasm

Regional Lymph Nodes (N)

pNX	Regional lymph nodes cannot be assessed
pN0	No regional lymph node metastasis
pN1	Regional lymph node metastasis

Distant Metastasis (M)

pMX	Distant metastasis cannot be assessed
pM0	No distant metastasis
pM1a	Bone marrow
pM1b	Other sites

Stage Grouping No applicable stage grouping for pathologic or clinical

Residual Tumor (R)

RX	Presence of residual tumor cannot be assessed
R0	No residual tumor
R1	Microscopic residual tumor
R2	Macroscopic residual tumor

Table A-4   Malignant Melanoma of the Uvea

The following definitions apply to both clinical and pathologic staging

All Uveal Melanomas (T)

TX   Primary tumor cannot be assessed

T0   No evidence of primary tumor

Iris (T)

T1   Tumor limited to the iris

        T1a Tumor limited to the iris (≤3 clock-hours in size)

        T1b Tumor limited to the iris (>3 clock-hours in size)

        T1c Tumor limited to the iris with melanomalytic glaucoma

T2   Tumor confluent with or extending into the ciliary body and/or choroid

        T2a Tumor confluent with or extending into the ciliary body and/or choroid with melanomalytic glaucoma

T3   Tumor confluent with or extending into the ciliary body and/or choroid with scleral extension

        T3a Tumor confluent with or extending into the ciliary body with scleral extension and melanomalytic glaucoma

T4   Tumor with extraocular extension

Ciliary Body and Choroid (T)

T1*   Tumor ≤10 mm in greatest diameter and ≤2.5 mm in greatest height (thickness)

        T1a Tumor ≤10 mm in greatest diameter and ≤2.5 mm in greatest height (thickness) without microscopic extraocular extension

        T1b Tumor ≤10 mm in greatest diameter and ≤2.5 mm in greatest height (thickness) with microscopic extraocular extension

        T1c Tumor ≤10 mm in greatest diameter and ≤2.5 mm in greatest height (thickness) with macroscopic extraocular extension

T2*   Tumor >10 mm but ≤16 mm in greatest basal diameter and between 2.5 and 10 mm in maximum height (thickness)

        T2a Tumor 10–16 mm in greatest basal diameter and between 2.5 and 10 mm in maximum height (thickness) without microscopic extraocular extension

        T2b Tumor 10–16 mm in greatest basal diameter and between 2.5 and 10 mm in maximum height (thickness) with microscopic extraocular extension

        T2c Tumor 10–16 mm in greatest basal diameter and between 2.5 and 10 mm in maximum height (thickness) with macroscopic extraocular extension

T3*   Tumor >16 mm in greatest diameter and/or >10 mm in maximum height (thickness) without extraocular extension

T4*   Tumor >16 mm in greatest diameter and/or >10 mm in maximum height (thickness) with extraocular extension

(Continued)

Table A-4 *(continued)*

The following definitions apply to both clinical and pathologic staging

Regional Lymph Nodes (N)

NX	Regional lymph nodes cannot be assessed
N0	No regional lymph node metastasis
N1	Regional lymph node metastasis

Distant Metastasis (M)

MX	Distant metastasis cannot be assessed
M0	No distant metastasis
M1	Distant metastasis

Stage Grouping

Stage	T	N	M
Stage I	T1	N0	M0
	T1a	N0	M0
	T1b	N0	M0
	T1c	N0	M0
Stage II	T2	N0	M0
	T2a	N0	M0
	T2b	N0	M0
	T2c	N0	M0
Stage III	T3	N0	M0
	T4	N0	M0
Stage IV	Any T	N1	M0
	Any T	Any N	M1

Histologic Grade (G)

GX	Grade cannot be assessed
G1	Spindle cell melanoma
G2	Mixed cell melanoma
G3	Epithelioid cell melanoma

Residual Tumor (R)

RX	Presence of residual tumor cannot be assessed
R0	No residual tumor
R1	Microscopic residual tumor
R2	Macroscopic residual tumor

Venous Invasion (V)

VX	Venous invasion cannot be assessed
V0	Veins do not contain tumor
V1	Microscopic venous invasion
V2	Macroscopic venous invasion

* Note: When basal dimension and apical height do not fit this classification, the largest tumor diameter should be used for classification. In clinical practice, the tumor base may be estimated in optic disc diameters (DD) (average: 1 DD = 1.5 mm). The height may be estimated in diopters (average: 3 diopters = 1 mm). Techniques such as ultrasonography, visualization, and photography are frequently used to provide more accurate measurements.

Table A-5 Carcinoma of the Eyelid

The following definitions apply to both clinical and pathologic staging

Primary Tumor (T)

TX	Primary tumor cannot be assessed
T0	No evidence of primary tumor
Tis	Carcinoma in situ
T1	Tumor of any size, not invading the tarsal plate, or, at the eyelid margin, ≤5 mm in greatest dimension
T2	Tumor invades tarsal plate or is at the eyelid margin, >5 mm but ≤10 mm in greatest dimension
T3	Tumor involves full eyelid thickness or is at the eyelid margin, >10 mm in greatest dimension
T4	Tumor invades adjacent structures, which include bulbar conjunctiva, sclera and globe, soft tissues of the orbit, perineural space, bone and periosteum of the orbit, nasal cavity and paranasal sinuses, and central nervous system

Regional Lymph Nodes (N)

NX	Regional lymph nodes cannot be assessed
N0	No regional lymph node metastasis
N1	Regional lymph node metastasis

Distant Metastasis (M)

MX	Distant metastasis cannot be assessed
M0	No distant metastasis
M1	Distant metastasis

Stage Grouping   No stage grouping is presently recommended

Histologic Grade (G)

GX	Grade cannot be assessed
G1	Well differentiated
G2	Moderately differentiated
G3	Poorly differentiated
G4	Undifferentiated or differentiation is not applicable

Residual Tumor (R)

RX	Presence of residual tumor cannot be assessed
R0	No residual tumor
R1	Microscopic residual tumor
R2	Macroscopic residual tumor

Table A-6 Carcinoma of the Lacrimal Gland

The following definitions apply to both clinical and pathologic staging

Primary Tumor (T)

TX	Primary tumor cannot be assessed
T0	No evidence of primary tumor
T1	Tumor ≤2.5 cm in greatest dimension, limited to the lacrimal gland
T2	Tumor >2.5 cm but ≤5 cm in greatest dimension limited to the lacrimal gland
T3	Tumor invades the periosteum
	T3a Tumor ≤5 cm invades the periosteum of the lacrimal gland fossa
	T3b Tumor >5 cm in greatest dimension with periosteal invasion
T4	Tumor invades the orbital soft tissues, optic nerve, or globe with or without bone invasion; tumor extends beyond the orbit to adjacent structures including the brain

Regional Lymph Nodes (N)

NX	Regional lymph nodes cannot be assessed
N0	No regional lymph node metastasis
N1	Regional lymph node metastasis

Distant Metastasis (M)

MX	Distant metastasis cannot be assessed
M0	No distant metastasis
M1	Distant metastasis

Stage Grouping   No stage grouping is presently recommended

Histologic Grade (G)

GX	Grade cannot be assessed
G1	Well differentiated
G2	Moderately differentiated; includes adenoid cystic carcinoma without basaloid (solid) pattern
G3	Poorly differentiated; includes adenoid cystic carcinoma with basaloid (solid) pattern
G4	Undifferentiated

Residual Tumor (R)

RX	Presence of residual tumor cannot be assessed
R0	No residual tumor
R1	Microscopic residual tumor
R2	Macroscopic residual tumor

Table A-7 **Sarcoma of the Orbit**

The following definitions apply to both clinical and pathologic staging

Primary Tumor (T)

TX	Primary tumor cannot be assessed
T0	No evidence of primary tumor
T1	Tumor ≤15 mm in greatest dimension
T2	Tumor >15 mm in greatest dimension without invasion of globe or bony wall
T3	Tumor of any size with invasion of orbital tissues and/or bony walls
T4	Tumor invasion of globe or periorbital structures, such as eyelids, temporal fossa, nasal cavity and paranasal sinuses, and/or central nervous system

Regional Lymph Nodes (N)

NX	Regional lymph nodes cannot be assessed
N0	No regional lymph node metastasis
N1	Regional lymph node metastasis

Distant Metastasis (M)

MX	Distant metastasis cannot be assessed
M0	No distant metastasis
M1	Distant metastasis

Stage Grouping   No stage grouping is presently recommended

Histologic Grade (G)

GX	Grade cannot be assessed
G1	Well differentiated
G2	Moderately differentiated
G3	Poorly differentiated
G4	Undifferentiated

Residual Tumor (R)

RX	Presence of residual tumor cannot be assessed
R0	No residual tumor
R1	Microscopic residual tumor
R2	Macroscopic residual tumor

Basic Texts

Ophthalmic Pathology and Intraocular Tumors

Albert DM, Jakobiec FA, eds. *Atlas of Clinical Ophthalmology.* Philadelphia: Saunders; 1996.

Albert DM, Jakobiec FA, eds. *Principles and Practice of Ophthalmology.* 6 vols. 2nd ed. Philadelphia: Saunders; 2000.

Apple DJ, Rabb MF. *Ocular Pathology: Clinical Applications and Self-Assessment.* 5th ed. St Louis: Mosby; 1998.

Bornfeld N, Gragoudas ES, Höpping W, et al, eds. *Tumors of the Eye.* New York: Kugler; 1991.

Char DH. *Clinical Ocular Oncology.* 2nd ed. Philadelphia: Lippincott Williams & Wilkins; 1998.

Cohen IK, Diegelmann RF, Lindblad WJ, eds. *Wound Healing: Biochemical and Clinical Aspects.* Philadelphia: Saunders; 1992.

Dutton JJ. *Atlas of Clinical and Surgical Orbital Anatomy.* Philadelphia: Saunders; 1994.

Garner A, Klintworth GK, eds. *Pathobiology of Ocular Disease: A Dynamic Approach.* 2nd ed. New York: Marcel Dekker; 1994.

Isenberg SJ, ed. *The Eye in Infancy.* 2nd ed. St Louis: Mosby; 1994.

Margo CE, Grossniklaus HE. *Ocular Histopathology: A Guide to Differential Diagnosis.* Philadelphia: Saunders; 1991.

McLean IW, Burnier MN, Zimmerman LE, Jakobiec FA. *Tumors of the Eye and Ocular Adnexa.* Washington: Armed Forces Institute of Pathology; 1994.

Nauman GOH, Apple DJ. *Pathology of the Eye.* New York: Springer-Verlag; 1986.

Rootman J, Stewart B, Goldberg RA. *Orbital Surgery. A Conceptual Approach.* Philadelphia: Lippincott; 1995.

Sanborn GE, Gonder JR, Shields JA. *Atlas of Intraocular Tumors.* Philadelphia: Saunders; 1994.

Sassani JW, ed. *Ophthalmic Pathology With Clinical Correlations.* Philadelphia: Lippincott Williams & Wilkins; 1997.

Shields JA, Shields CL. *Atlas of Eyelid and Conjunctival Tumors.* Philadelphia: Lippincott Williams & Wilkins; 1999.

Shields JA, Shields CL. *Atlas of Intraocular Tumors.* Philadelphia: Lippincott Williams & Wilkins; 1999.

Spencer WH, ed. *Ophthalmic Pathology: An Atlas and Textbook.* 4th ed. Philadelphia: Saunders; 1996.

Yanoff M, Fine BS. *Ocular Pathology.* 5th ed. St Louis: Mosby; 2002.

Related Academy Materials

Focal Points: Clinical Modules for Ophthalmologists

Galetta SL, Liu GT, Volpe NJ. Pseudotumor cerebri (Module 12, 2003).

Helm CJ. Melanoma and other pigmented lesions of the ocular surface (Module 11, 1996).

Lane Stevens JC. Retinoblastoma (Module 1, 1990).

Margo CE. Nonpigmented lesions of the ocular surface (Module 9, 1996).

Stefanyszyn MA. Orbital tumors in children (Module 9, 1990).

Publications

Berkow JW, Flower RW, Orth DH, Kelley JS. *Fluorescein and Indocyanine Green Angiography: Technique and Interpretation.* 2nd ed. (Ophthalmology Monograph 5, 1997).

Kline LB, ed. *Optic Nerve Disorders* (Ophthalmology Monograph 10, 1996).

Singh AD, Damato BE, Pe'er J, Murphree AL, Perry JD, eds. *Clinical Ophthalmic Oncology.* Philadelphia: Elsevier Saunders; 2007.

Stewart WB, ed. *Surgery of the Eyelid, Orbit, and Lacrimal System* (Ophthalmology Monograph 8. Vol 1, 1993; reviewed for currency 2001. Vol 2, 1994; reviewed for currency 2003. Vol 3, 1995; reviewed for currency 2000).

Wilson FM II, ed. *Practical Ophthalmology: A Manual for Beginning Residents.* 5th ed. (2005).

Wirtschafter JD, Berman EL, McDonald CS. *Magnetic Resonance Imaging and Computed Tomography: Clinical Neuro-Orbital Anatomy* (Ophthalmology Monograph 6, 1992).

To order any of these materials, please call the Academy's Customer Service number at (415) 561-8540, or order online at www.aao.org.

Credit Reporting Form

Basic and Clinical Science Course, 2010–2011
Section 4

The American Academy of Ophthalmology is accredited by the Accreditation Council for Continuing Medical Education to provide continuing medical education for physicians.

The American Academy of Ophthalmology designates this educational activity for a maximum of 10 *AMA PRA Category 1 Credits*™. Physicians should only claim credit commensurate with the extent of their participation in the activity.

If you wish to claim continuing medical education credit for your study of this Section, you may claim your credit online or fill in the required forms and mail or fax them to the Academy.

To use the forms:

1. Complete the study questions and mark your answers on the Section Completion Form.
2. Complete the Section Evaluation.
3. Fill in and sign the statement below.
4. Return this page and the required forms by mail or fax to the CME Registrar (see below).

To claim credit online:

1. Log on to the Academy website (www.aao.org/cme).
2. Select Review/Claim CME.
3. Follow the instructions.

Important: These completed forms or the online claim must be received at the Academy by June 2013.

I hereby certify that I have spent _____ (up to 10) hours of study on the curriculum of this Section and that I have completed the study questions.

Signature: _____
                                                                            Date

Name: _____

Address: _____

City and State: _____ Zip: _____

Telephone: (_____) _____ Academy Member ID# _____
                    area code

Please return completed forms to: **Or you may fax them to:** 415-561-8575
American Academy of Ophthalmology
P.O. Box 7424
San Francisco, CA 94120-7424
Attn: CME Registrar, Customer Service

2010–2011
Section Completion Form

Basic and Clinical Science Course

Answer Sheet for Section 4

Question	Answer	Question	Answer
1	a b c d	26	a b c d
2	a b c d	27	a b c d
3	a b c d	28	a b c d e
4	a b c d	29	a b c d
5	a b c d e	30	a b c d
6	a b c d e	31	a b c d
7	a b c d	32	a b c d
8	a b c d	33	a b c d
9	a b c d	34	a b c d e
10	a b c d	35	a b c d e
11	a b c d	36	a b c d
12	a b c d	37	a b c d
13	a b c d	38	a b c d
14	a b c d	39	a b c d e
15	a b c d e	40	a b c d
16	a b c d	41	a b c d e
17	a b c d	42	a b c d e
18	a b c d	43	a b c d
19	a b c d	44	a b c d
20	a b c d	45	a b c d e
21	a b c d	46	a b c d
22	a b c d	47	a b c d
23	a b c d	48	a b c d
24	a b c d	49	a b c d
25	a b c d		

Section Evaluation

Please complete this CME questionnaire.

1. To what degree will you use knowledge from BCSC Section 4 in your practice?

   ☐ Regularly

   ☐ Sometimes

   ☐ Rarely

2. Please review the stated objectives for BCSC Section 4. How effective was the material at meeting those objectives?

   ☐ All objectives were met.

   ☐ Most objectives were met.

   ☐ Some objectives were met.

   ☐ Few or no objectives were met.

3. To what degree is BCSC Section 4 likely to have a positive impact on health outcomes of your patients?

   ☐ Extremely likely

   ☐ Highly likely

   ☐ Somewhat likely

   ☐ Not at all likely

4. After you review the stated objectives for BCSC Section 4, please let us know of any additional knowledge, skills, or information useful to your practice that were acquired but were not included in the objectives.

5. Was BCSC Section 4 free of commercial bias?

   ☐ Yes

   ☐ No

6. If you selected "No" in the previous question, please comment.

7. Please tell us what might improve the applicability of BCSC to your practice.

Study Questions

Although a concerted effort has been made to avoid ambiguity and redundancy in these questions, the authors recognize that differences of opinion may occur regarding the "best" answer. The discussions are provided to demonstrate the rationale used to derive the answer. They may also be helpful in confirming that your approach to the problem was correct or, if necessary, in fixing the principle in your memory.

1. Which of the following choices best describes the sequence of specific processes that occur during wound healing in clear cornea?
   a. epithelial wound repair, wound edge digestion, fibroblast activation, wound contraction
   b. wound edge digestion, epithelial wound repair, fibroblast activation, wound contraction
   c. fibroblast activation, wound contraction, wound edge digestion, epithelial wound repair
   d. wound edge digestion, fibroblast activation, epithelial wound repair, wound contraction

2. Which of the following special techniques in diagnostic pathology is quantitative in its standard form?
   a. immunohistochemistry
   b. electron microscopy
   c. flow cytometry
   d. PCR-based gene rearrangement studies

3. Which of the following best describes the differences between macular dystrophy of the cornea and granular and lattice dystrophies?
   a. deposited material and visual disability
   b. genetic transmission, deposited material, and visual disability
   c. genetic transmission, tissue distribution, visual disability, and deposited material
   d. genetic transmission and tissue distribution

4. Which of the following would *not* be detected by Prussian blue staining?
   a. Fleischer line
   b. Stocker line
   c. Ferry line
   d. Krukenberg spindle

5. The most important and helpful imaging tool in the diagnosis of choroidal and ciliary body melanoma is
   a. fluorescein angiography
   b. ultrasonography
   c. computed tomography (CT)
   d. magnetic resonance imaging (MRI)
   e. PET-CT

6. Which of the following about iris melanoma compared to choroidal melanoma is *true*?

   a Iris melanoma is as common as choroidal melanoma.

   b. Iris melanoma metastasizes at a rate similar to that of choroidal melanoma.

   c. Histologically, iris melanoma may contain the same type of cells as choroidal melanoma.

   d. Like choroidal melanoma, iris melanoma is usually treated by brachytherapy.

   e. Iris melanoma is diagnosed, like choroidal melanoma, by both A-scan and B-scan modes of ultrasonography.

7. Two tumors commonly associated with so-called *masquerade syndromes* are

   a. conjunctival lymphoma, choroidal melanoma

   b. conjunctival lymphoma, intraocular lymphoma

   c. eyelid sebaceous carcinoma, intraocular lymphoma

   d. basal cell carcinoma, retinoblastoma

8. The most common secondary tumor in retinoblastoma patients is

   a. fibrosarcoma

   b. melanoma

   c. pinealoblastoma

   d. osteosarcoma

9. The primary treatment for a child with unilateral retinoblastoma filling more than 50% of the vitreous cavity with diffuse vitreous seeding is

   a. chemotherapy alone

   b. enucleation

   c. radiation alone

   d. chemotherapy and radiation

10. Which of the following statements about pleomorphic adenoma of the lacrimal gland is *false*?

   a. It can recur in a diffuse manner.

   b. It can transform to a malignant tumor if present long enough.

   c. Recurrences can transform to malignancy.

   d. It can resolve spontaneously.

11. Intraocular calcification in the eye of a child is most diagnostic of

   a. retinoblastoma

   b. toxocara

   c. persistent fetal vasculature

   d. Coats disease

12. Histopathologic characteristics of ciliochoroidal melanoma that correlate with patient prognosis include

    a. modified Callender classification, erosion through Bruch's membrane, intrinsic micro-vascular pattern

    b. tumor size, intrinsic microvascular patterns, immunohistochemical positivity for HMB-45

    c. modified Callender classification, tumor size, intrinsic microvascular patterns

    d. modified Callender classification, invasion of optic nerve, intrinsic microvascular patterns

13. Which of the following ocular histologic changes is not considered to be associated with diabetes mellitus?

    a. lacy vacuolization of the iris

    b. retinal hemorrhages

    c. iris hemorrhages

    d. thickened basement membranes

14. Histologic differentiation between primary and recurrent pterygia can be based on

    a. the degree of vascularity in the lesion

    b. the presence of more fibrous tissue in the recurrent lesion

    c. the absence of elastotic degeneration in recurrent pterygia

    d. the presence of Bowman's layer in recurrent but not primary pterygia

15. The most common primary sites and type of choroidal metastasis are

    a. lung carcinomas in males and females

    b. prostate carcinomas in males and breast carcinomas in females

    c. lung carcinomas in males and breast carcinomas in females

    d. gastrointestinal carcinomas in males and breast carcinomas in females

    e. carcinomas of unknown origin in males and breast carcinomas in females

16. Which of the following extraocular muscles inserts farthest from the limbus?

    a. superior rectus

    b. inferior rectus

    c. inferior oblique

    d. superior oblique

17. Which of the following antigens would allow identification of a spindle cell tumor as a melanoma?

    a. cytokeratin

    b. S-100

    c. HMB-45

    d. desmin

18. Histologically, the term *angle recession* refers to which of the following conditions?
    a. a tear between the ciliary body and the sclera
    b. a tear between the iris and the ciliary body
    c. a tear between the longitudinal and circular portions of the ciliary muscle
    d. posterior displacement of the iris root without alteration of the ciliary body

19. The following entity results in synechial angle-closure glaucoma:
    a. melanomalytic glaucoma
    b. iridocorneal endothelial (ICE) syndrome
    c. ghost cell glaucoma
    d. hemosiderosis bulbi

20. The sclera shows what variation in thickness and is composed primarily of what type of collagen?
    a. tenfold thickness variation; type I collagen
    b. threefold thickness variation; type IV collagen
    c. twofold thickness variation; type IV collagen
    d. threefold thickness variation; type I collagen

21. Anterior scleritis is likely to
    a. be bilateral in 50% of cases
    b. be associated with pain on eye movement
    c. cause exophthalmos
    d. be painless

22. Mutations in the fibrillin gene on chromosome 15 lead to lens displacement
    a. down
    b. inferonasally
    c. superotemporally
    d. anteriorly

23. Which of the following is the most common primary malignancy of the eyelid?
    a. basal cell carcinoma
    b. squamous cell carcinoma
    c. sebaceous carcinoma
    d. melanoma

24. When a parent has bilateral retinoblastoma, each child
    a. has an 85% chance of developing retinoblastoma
    b. who develops retinoblastoma will have bilateral disease
    c. will be affected only if male
    d. has a 45% chance of developing retinoblastoma

25. In the final scar of the average wound,
    a. myofibroblasts and fibroblasts contract
    b. most of the vessels persist
    c. the recently laid collagen parallels the uninjured surrounding collagen
    d. macrophages remain, producing enzymes

26. At the time of enucleation, most blind, painful eyes have either
    a. absolute glaucoma or expulsive hemorrhage
    b. phthisis bulbi or absolute glaucoma
    c. fibrous ingrowth or absolute glaucoma
    d. epithelial downgrowth or absolute glaucoma

27. Conjunctival and corneal epithelial cells
    a. never grow inside the eye
    b. can invade the eye by burrowing through intact cornea
    c. produce free-floating solid masses of cells in the eye
    d. may grow down a tract or wound edge to the inside of the eye

28. Cotton-wool spots
    a. are diagnostic of collagen vascular disease
    b. contain swollen glial cells
    c. never disappear once they are formed
    d. are transudates from the superficial capillary plexus
    e. represent coagulative necrosis of the nerve fiber layer

29. The most commonly used fixative in ophthalmic pathology is
    a. gluteraldehyde
    b. formalin
    c. B5
    d. RPMI

30. An appropriate use of surgical frozen sections is to
    a. provide a rapid diagnosis for anxious family members
    b. freeze all of the excised tissue
    c. determine if representative tissue has been sampled
    d. determine the margins of resection of primary acquired melanosis (PAM) with atypia

31. A giant cell with an annulus of nuclei surrounded by a lipid-filled zone is classified as a
    a. Langhans giant cell
    b. foreign body giant cell
    c. tumor giant cell
    d. Touton giant cell

32. Vitreous amyloidosis is associated with
    a. peripheral neuropathy
    b. cranial nerve paralysis
    c. lattice dystrophy
    d. peripheral vascular disease

33. Which of the following statements about Descemet's membrane is *false*?
    a. It is developmentally derived from the neural crest.
    b. It is elaborated by the corneal endothelial cells.
    c. It remains static throughout life.
    d. It is composed of type IV collagen.

34. Band keratopathy is characterized by
    a. randomly distributed deposits in the cornea
    b. calcium deposition within the deep corneal stroma
    c. occurrence only in patients with hypercalcemia
    d. involvement of the epithelial basement membrane and Bowman's layer
    e. association with other congenital malformations

35. All of the following may be associated with congenital cataracts *except*
    a. anterior lenticonus
    b. cerulean cataracts
    c. aniridia
    d. rubella
    e. siderosis

36. Which of the following sites for ocular adnexal lymphoid neoplasms has the strongest association with systemic lymphoma?
    a. eyelid
    b. palpebral conjunctiva
    c. bulbar conjunctiva
    d. orbit

37. The conjunctival melanocytic proliferation most commonly associated with subsequent development of conjunctival malignant melanoma is
    a. ephelis
    b. nevus
    c. ocular melanocytosis
    d. primary acquired melanosis (PAM)

38. Exfoliation syndrome (pseudoexfoliation) does not include
    a. systemic deposition of fibrillin
    b. a history of infrared exposure
    c. transillumination defects of the iris
    d. deposition of a flaky material on lens zonule fibers

39. Which method is not effective in treating posterior uveal melanoma?
    a. enucleation
    b. brachytherapy
    c. charged-particle radiation
    d. conventional external-beam radiation
    e. surgical excision

40. Which of the following statements about uveal melanoma is *true*?
    a. Uveal melanomas rarely metastasize.
    b. Melanomas of the ciliary body have the best prognosis.
    c. Metastases always occur within 2½ years of treatment.
    d. Survival is directly related to tumor volume.

41. Which of the following statements about persistent hyperplastic primary vitreous (PHPV) is *true*?
    a. Visual prognosis is excellent.
    b. Early angle-closure glaucoma is common.
    c. Retinal detachment is rare.
    d. The eye is usually normal in size.
    e. Cataract is uncommon.

42. Medulloepitheliomas
    a. are tumors arising from surface ectoderm-derived cells
    b. are congenital lesions often containing cartilage
    c. are usually malignant in nature
    d. can be caused by trauma to the ciliary body
    e. usually metastasize to the liver

43. Which of the following tumors develops in the absence of a normal tumor-suppressor gene?
    a. choroidal melanoma
    b. melanocytoma
    c. medulloepithelioma
    d. retinoblastoma

44. The average volume of the adult vitreous cavity is
    a. 3 cc
    b. 4 cc
    c. 5 cc
    d. 6 cc

45. Which of the following statements about corneal dystrophies is *true*?
    a. They may occur unilaterally.
    b. They are inherited disorders.
    c. Their development often follows surgical or accidental trauma to the eye.
    d. They rarely cause visual symptoms or impairment.
    e. They are never associated with stromal thinning.

46. von Hippel–Lindau syndrome is distinguished from von Hippel disease by the association of
    a. intracranial calcifications, ash leaf spots, retinal astrocytomas
    b. café-au-lait spots, Lisch nodules, optic pathway gliomas
    c. pheochromocytomas, cerebellar hemangioblastomas, renal cell carcinoma
    d. limbal dermoids, upper eyelid colobomas, ear tags

47. Which of the following statements regarding the sclera is *true*?
    a. It consists of type I collagen fibers.
    b. It appears white due to a regular, periodic arrangement of collagen fibers.
    c. The thickest areas are in the region of rectus muscle insertions.
    d. It derives nutrition from its own capillary bed.

48. In intraocular lymphoma associated with CNS lymphoma,
    a. T-cell lymphoma is common
    b. the vitreous and retina are usually involved
    c. the diagnosis is made using routine histopathologic preparations
    d. systemic and intrathecal chemotherapy usually result in a good response

49. Which of the following choices best matches the following description: a lymphoid infiltrate with a vaguely follicular pattern that includes the proliferation of monocytoid B lymphocytes and a heterogeneous mix of small lymphocytes and plasma cells?
    a. reactive lymphoid hyperplasia
    b. mucosa-associated lymphoid tissue (MALT)
    c. small B-cell lymphoma
    d. orbital inflammatory syndrome

Answers

1. **b.** Although many of the processes overlap, this is the overall sequence of events. If this sequence is disrupted, the wound healing process may be altered.

2. **c.** Although immunohistochemistry and PCR can be performed to yield quantitative results, only flow cytometric analysis is inherently quantitative.

3. **c.** Macular dystrophy is autosomal recessive, involves the entire cornea to the limbus, may cause earlier visual disability, and represents deposition of mucopolysaccharide.

4. **d.** Prussian blue detects iron. A Krukenberg spindle is composed of melanin pigment in the endothelium.

5. **b.** B-scan ultrasonography provides information about the size, shape, and position of the tumor; A-scan ultrasonography provides an accurate assessment of the lesion's internal reflectivity, vascularity, and height.

6. **c.** In iris melanoma, as in choroidal melanoma, spindle A, spindle B, and epithelioid cell types can be identified histologically.

7. **c.** Primary intraocular lymphoma and sebaceous cell carcinoma represent 2 of the most common and feared tumors; their presentation can simulate uveitis or other conditions. Although retinoblastoma can masquerade, basal cell carcinoma rarely does this.

8. **d.** Osteosarcoma represents 40% of secondary tumors within, and 36% outside, the field of radiation in patients previously treated for retinoblastoma.

9. **b.** Enucleation remains the recommended treatment for a child with unilateral retinoblastoma filling 50% of the vitreous cavity with diffuse vitreous seeding.

10. **d.** The first 3 behaviors are well accepted for this tumor; however, it does not characteristically resolve.

11. **a.** Intraocular calcification is most diagnostic of retinoblastoma.

12. **c.** The major risk factors found on histopathology that correlate with prognosis include cell type, as defined by the modified Callender classification; tumor size; tumor location (anterior to equator or adjacent to optic nerve); and intrinsic microvascular patterns. Erosion through Bruch's membrane is not correlated with prognosis and occurs frequently. Melanomas rarely invade the optic nerve, more often escaping the eye by eroding through the sclera. Most melanomas are HMB-45–positive, as an indication of their melanocytic origin.

13. **c.** Although iris neovascularization is a typical feature of diabetic ocular disease, iris hemorrhages are not.

14. **c.** Recurrent pterygia represent exuberant healing responses and do not show the elastotic degeneration typical of primary pterygia, which are of long-standing duration.

15. **c.** Breast carcinomas in women are by far the most common source of metastasis to the choroid. Lung carcinomas are the most common source of metastasis to the choroid in men.

16. **c.** The location of the oblique muscles is a key feature in orienting a globe. The inferior oblique inserts most posteriorly, in close proximity to the optic nerve and over the macula.

17. **c.** Although S-100 is expressed in melanomas, it is also expressed in other tumors and tissues of neuroectodermal origin. HMB-45 is more specific for melanocytic lesions and can differentiate a melanoma from other neuroectodermal tumors.

18. **c.** Choice *a* is a cyclodialysis, *b* is an iridodialysis. Angle recession involves separation of the longitudinal portion from the remainder of the ciliary muscle, with corresponding displacement of the iris and a change in angle configuration.

19. **b.** ICE syndrome involves the proliferation of corneal endothelium over the trabecular meshwork and iris, sealing the angle closed. Melanomalytic and ghost cell glaucoma are due to an accumulation of material in the trabecular meshwork, or secondary open-angle glaucoma. Hemosiderosis results in iron deposition and toxicity in the meshwork without other visible changes in the meshwork.

20. **d.** The sclera varies from 0.3 mm behind the rectus muscle insertions to 1 mm posteriorly and is composed mainly of type I collagen.

21. **a.** Anterior scleritis is typically painful and is bilateral in half the cases. Posterior scleritis is associated with exophthalmos and pain with eye movement.

22. **c.** Fibrillin gene mutations are seen in Marfan syndrome, in which the lens is typically displaced superotemporally.

23. **a.** Basal cell carcinoma is by far the most common primary malignancy of the eyelid. It is probably more common than squamous cell carcinoma, sebaceous carcinoma, and melanoma of the eyelid combined.

24. **d.** If a parent has bilateral disease, there is a 98% chance that he or she has a germinal mutation. If the parent has a germinal mutation, the risk for each child is 45%.

25. **a.** The final scar shrinks because of the contraction of myofibroblasts and fibroblasts. The vessels decrease markedly as the scar matures, but a few remain. Part of the distortion of any scar occurs because the collagen laid down in the healing process is not in synchrony with that in the surrounding tissues. Macrophages, which produce many factors in the active healing stage, subside and are absent from the final scar.

26. **b.** Blind eyes may become painful after many years and are enucleated to relieve the pain. Most eyes develop either high intraocular pressure and absolute glaucoma or cease to produce aqueous in adequate amounts to sustain the eye. In the latter case, the eye shrinks and becomes phthisical. The other choices are serious conditions, and each may lead to either glaucoma or phthisis.

27. **d.** The epithelial cells gain access to the globe by migrating along a preexisting tract or wound edge; they are unable to invade normal tissues. Once inside the eye, the epithelium may extend as a sheet over available surfaces, such as posterior cornea or iris, or may form epithelial cysts. Free-floating masses of solid epithelium do not form.

28. **e.** Cotton-wool spots are characteristic of, but not diagnostic of, collagen vascular diseases; they occur in a variety of ischemic retinopathies. They contain swollen nerve fibers, not glial cells. They usually disappear with time. They represent infarcts, with resultant coagulative necrosis of the nerve fiber layer. They are not typically associated with transudates.

29. **b.** Formalin is the most commonly used tissue fixative. Gluteraldehyde is used to fix tissue for electron microscopy. B5 is a mercury-based fixative used for preservation of cytologic detail, primarily in lymphoid tissue. RPMI may be used for flow cytometry specimens.

30. **c.** Frozen sections are not used to satisfy the curiosity of the surgeon or to relieve the anxiety of a patient's family. One should never freeze all excised tissue, because adequate fixation and avoidance of freezing artifact are needed to properly evaluate surgical specimens for diagnostic purposes. One should not try to evaluate the margins of melanocytic proliferations, including melanoma, with frozen sections. Adequate specimen preservation and processing are needed for such evaluation. An appropriate use of frozen sections is to determine if representative tissue is being sampled; if so, more tissue should be submitted in fixative for processing.

31. **d.** A Langhans giant cell has a horseshoe-shaped ring of nuclei around the periphery of the cytoplasm. Langhans giant cells may be encountered in tuberculosis and sarcoidosis, among other diseases. Foreign body giant cells have haphazardly arranged nuclei. Some malignant neoplasms, including melanoma, may contain multinucleated tumor giant cells. Touton giant cells have central nuclei and a peripheral lipid-filled area. Touton giant cells may be seen in association with chalazion, xanthogranuloma, and xanthelasma, among other diseases. Langhans, foreign body, and Touton giant cells are not diagnostic for any single disease process.

32. **a.** Vitreous amyloidosis and peripheral neuropathy are associated with a transthyretin abnormality.

33. **c.** The production of Descemet's membrane by the endothelial cells begins during fetal development and continues throughout adulthood. Therefore, the thickness of Descemet's membrane slowly increases with age.

34. **d.** Band keratopathy involves the interpalpebral region of the cornea and consists of calcium deposition in the epithelial basement membrane and Bowman's layer. Although band keratopathy may occur in patients with hypercalcemia, it also occurs in chronically inflamed eyes of patients with normal serum calcium levels. Band keratopathy is an acquired lesion and is, therefore, not associated with congenital malformations.

35. **e.** Siderosis is caused by the retention of iron-containing metallic foreign bodies in the lens, resulting in lens epithelial degeneration and necrosis. As such, it is an acquired condition rather than a congenital one.

36. **a.** Lymphomas manifesting in the eyelid are associated with systemic lymphoma in approximately 80% of cases; conjunctival and orbital lymphomas are more often localized than disseminated.

37. **d.** PAM with atypia is associated with approximately two thirds of cases of conjunctival melanoma; preexisting nevi are seen in fewer than one fourth. Ocular melanocytosis is

associated with an increased risk of melanoma. Ephelis, or freckle, is not associated with melanoma.

38. **b.** Unlike true exfoliation, exfoliation syndrome (pseudoexfoliation) is not associated with a history of infrared exposure.

39. **d.** Conventional external-beam radiation is not effective in treating uveal melanoma and is not used. Special methods of external-beam radiation such as fractionated stereotactic radiotherapy and gamma knife radiosurgery have been used with good results.

40. **d.** Smaller uveal tumors have the best prognosis overall. Melanomas often metastasize, and 30%–40% of patients die within 5 years of metastatic disease. Ciliary body melanomas in a relatively hidden area often become large before symptoms develop and have a poorer prognosis. The mean duration from treatment to the onset of metastases of uveal melanoma is 7 years.

41. **b.** Because the ciliary processes are often displaced centripetally by a central fibrovascular plaque, early angle-closure glaucoma is common. PHPV commonly occurs in microphthalmic eyes and is associated with cataract and retinal detachment. Visual prognosis is poor.

42. **b.** Medulloepitheliomas are derived from neuroectoderm. They are usually benign choristomas and, even if they are malignant, follow a benign course if the eye is removed with the tumor confined to it. There are developmental lesions—so-called adult medulloepitheliomas—that are actually reactive hyperplasias of the ciliary epithelium and usually related to ocular trauma.

43. **d.** Choroidal melanoma, melanocytoma, and medulloepithelioma are not associated with a tumor-suppressor gene.

44. **b.** The adult vitreous occupies four fifths of the eye, measures 4 cc, and weighs 4 g.

45. **b.** The corneal dystrophies are primary, inherited, bilateral disorders. Patients may have symptoms of recurrent erosion or loss of visual acuity. Some of the dystrophies, such as macular dystrophy, may be associated with stromal thinning.

46. **c.** von Hippel disease consists of a solitary retinal angioma, whereas von Hippel–Lindau includes the spectrum of pheochromocytomas, cerebellar hemangioblastomas, and renal cell carcinomas.

47. **a.** The sclera appears white due to the random arrangement and variable thickness of its collagen fibers compared with the collagen fibers of the cornea, which are parallel, relatively uniform, and regularly arranged. The sclera is thinnest in the region just posterior the rectus muscle insertions, a common location for traumatic scleral rupture. The scleral has blood vessels that pass through it—emissary vessels—but it does not have its own capillary bed. It derives its nutrition from the choroid and episcleral vessels.

48. **b.** Whereas in systemic/visceral/nodal lymphomas the uvea is the most common site of metastasis, in up to 25% of CNS lymphomas the vitreous and retina are the site of involvement.

49. **b.** The best diagnosis in this example is mucosa-associated lymphoid tissue (MALT), also known as extranodal marginal zone lymphoma (EMZL).

Index

(*f* = figure; *t* = table)

INTRODUCTION to

java™ and software Design

Nell Dale

University of Texas, Austin

Chip Weems

University of Massachusetts, Amherst

Mark Headington

University of Wisconsin–La Crosse

JONES AND BARTLETT PUBLISHERS

Sudbury, Massachusetts

BOSTON   TORONTO   LONDON   SINGAPORE

World Headquarters
Jones and Bartlett Publishers
40 Tall Pine Drive
Sudbury, MA 01776
978-443-5000
info@jbpub.com
www.jbpub.com

Jones and Bartlett Publishers
Canada
2406 Nikanna Road
Mississauga, ON L5C 2W6
CANADA

Jones and Bartlett Publishers
 International
Barb House, Barb Mews
London W6 7PA
UK

Library of Congress Cataloging-in-Publication Data
Dale, Nell B.
  Introduction to Java and software design / Nell Dale, Chip Weems, Mark Headington.
     p. cm.
   ISBN 0-7637-2030-5
     1. Java (Computer programming language) 2. Computer software Development.   I. Weems,
Chip. II. Headington, Mark R. III. Title.

QA76.73.J38 D34 2000
005.13'3 dc21   00-062547

Chief Executive Officer: Clayton Jones
Chief Operating Officer: Don W. Jones, Jr.
Executive Vice President and Publisher: Tom Manning
V.P., Managing Editor: Judith H. Hauck
V.P., College Editorial Director: Brian L. McKean
V.P., Design and Production: Anne Spencer
V.P., Sales and Marketing: Paul Shepardson
V.P., Manufacturing and Inventory Control: Therese Br uer
Senior Acquisitions Editor: Michael Stranz
Development and Product Manager: Amy Rose
Marketing Director: Jennifer Jacobson
Production Assistant: Tara McCormick
Editorial Assistant: Amanda Green
Cover Design: Kristen E. Ohlin
Project Coordination: Trillium Project Management
Composition: Northeast Compositors, Inc.
Text Design: Anne Spencer
Printing and Binding: Courier Westford
Cover printing: John Pow Company, Inc.

This book was typeset in QuarkXPress 4.1 on a Macintosh G4. The font families used were Rotis Sans Serif, Rotis Serif, and Prestige Elite. The first printing was printed on 45 lb. Utopia Book Matte.

Printed in the United States of America

04 03 02   10 9 8 7 6 5 4 3 2

To Al, my husband and best friend, and to our children and our children's children.

N.D.

To Lisa, Charlie, and Abby with love.

C.W.

To Professor John Dyer-Bennet, with great respect.

M.H.

To quote Mephistopheles, one of the chief devils, and tempter of Faust,

...My friend, I shall be pedagogic,
And say you ought to start with Logic...
...Days will be spent to let you know
That what you once did at one blow,
Like eating and drinking so easy and free,
Can only be done with One, Two, Three.
Yet the web of thought has no such creases
And is more like a weaver's masterpieces;
One step, a thousand threads arise,
Hither and thither shoots each shuttle,
The threads flow on, unseen and subtle,
Each blow effects a thousand ties.
The philosopher comes with analysis
And proves it had to be like this;
The first was so, the second so,
And hence the third and fourth was so,
And were not the first and second here,
Then the third and fourth could never appear.
That is what all the students believe,
But they have never learned to weave.

As you study this book, do not let the logic of algorithms bind your imagination, but rather make it your tool for weaving masterpieces of thought.

J. W. von Goeth, *Faust*, Walter Kaufman trans., New York, 1963, 199.

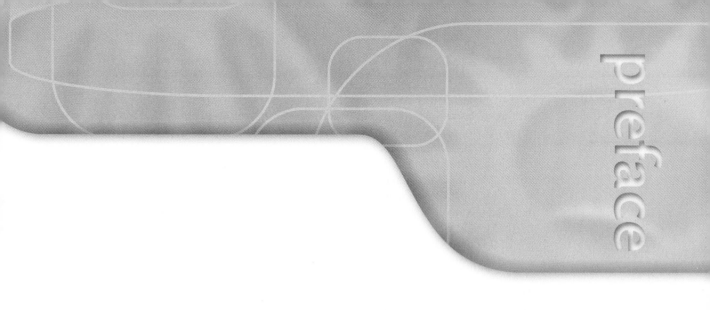

Introduction to Java and Software Design represents a significant transition in the development of the Dale series, with much that is new. This book has been developed from the ground up to be a Java text. It is not a "Java translation" of our previous texts. However, we have retained our familiar easy-to-read style and clear approach to introducing new topics. The chapters retain the same overall organization with each chapter containing a full problem-solving case study, testing and debugging hints, summary, and five types of end-of-chapter exercises. Also, some topics—such as problem solving—are independent of the programming language and thus contain familiar discussions.

The text uses real Java I/O classes rather than ones we supply. We have seen many introductory programming texts that introduce either C- or Pascal-like command-line I/O classes or simplified windowing classes that automatically handle events. However, our view is that event-driven I/O is the dominant model not only in Java but in the modern world of programming in general. Students come to our classes already familiar with event-driven interfaces and expect to learn how to write programs that have them.

Event handling is now a fundamental control structure and must be treated that way from the start. We therefore introduce event handling even before branching and looping. On the other hand, it is easy for students to be overwhelmed by the sheer number and complexity of Java I/O classes. We have taken great care to select a tiny but sufficient subset of the library to illustrate all of the fundamental concepts. The result is that when students are finished with the course, they can write real Java programs without being dependent on a text-supplied library. They also have developed the ability to extend their knowledge of I/O classes to include the many optional features that are available.

There is some confusion, which we would like to address, about what the term "Java 2" refers to. Java 2 refers to the second version of the Sun Java Software Development Kit (compilers, debuggers, and other tools). We do not cover these specific tools, as they are often hidden inside of an integrated development environment, and there are too many different environments to cover them all at a useful level of detail. It was in version 1.2 that the Java class library was heavily extended with new classes such as Swing. Other than Swing and the comparable interface, most of the new classes are well beyond the introductory computer science curriculum. The remaining classes that might be presented at this level are unnecessary for covering the curriculum. They are bells and whistles that may be interesting in their own right, but omitting them has no impact on learning the fundamentals of problem solving and software design. The Java language itself has not changed since version 1.1. Thus, the Java that students learn from this text is fully compatible with Java 2, as well as with version 1.3 of the language.

In this book we consciously chose the AWT library over Swing for pragmatic reasons. At this point, Swing is not available on all platforms, and our experience has been that some Swing implementations aren't stable or are inconsistent with others. These are the kinds of problems that greatly trouble beginners, so we've chosen to avoid them by using the older, more reliable AWT package in this first edition. In addition, at this level the programming differences between AWT and Swing are quite trivial. For those students and instructors who would like to experiment with Swing, Appendix H describes how to convert our AWT programs to Swing, and provides as an example a Swing version of the case study program from Chapter 6.

All of the programs In this book have been tested with Symantec Café® and Metrowerks CodeWarrior®. The program code is available for download from the Jones and Bartlett web site at www.jbpub.com/disks.

Chapter Coverage

Chapter 1 begins with basic definitions, computer concepts, problem-solving techniques, ethical issues, and a case study. We introduce objects from the very beginning, with their definition in this first chapter and the consistent use of object-oriented terminology.

In Chapter 2 we examine the String class and aspects of its interface. Through the next several chapters, we introduce new library classes and point out their design features. We also tread carefully through the process of declaring a reference variable, instantiating an object, assigning it to the variable, and using the object. These are difficult but essential concepts for beginners to grasp. Our goal is for students to gradually develop a complete and deep understanding of what an object is, how it works, and what makes its interface well-designed. Then, by Chapters 7 and 8, students are ready to build significant and realistic classes.

Chapter 2 further covers sequential control flow, and simple output to system.out. This gets students off to a quick start with a working program and past the mechanics of program entry and execution. Then, in Chapter 3 we switch to using the Frame class and a Label for output. Simple event handling is then introduced for a WindowClosing event. The WindowClosing event is conceptually simpler than others because it doesn't need to be registered. Its handler can be written with a simple syntactic template that uses Java's anonymous inner-class mechanism to avoid becoming bogged down in general class syntax at this early stage.

In Chapter 4, we turn to the numeric types and expression syntax. We cover type conversions, precedence rules, the use of numeric types, and additional methods that can be applied to String objects. We also reinforce the distinction between the reference and primitive types in this chapter. Students gain further experience with Frame output and event handling in this chapter.

With Chapter 5, we take the next step in event handling by introducing the essential elements of an input dialog. Students learn how to use a TextField for data input and a Button to signal when the field is ready. The Button class is the first event source they see that must be registered. The concepts of an event source, an action listener, and an event handler are covered in the simplest context possible. Together, these constructs enable the students to implement a program with an event loop for reading a series of inputs. One of the key pedagogical differences in moving to event-driven I/O is that the looping control structure isn't required, as it would be in a command-line I/O environment.

Along the way, students are introduced to the syntax for a specific user-defined class and method that conforms to the ActionListener interface. This experience with the syntax, though limited, simplifies its formal introduction in Chapter 7. We also examine the conversion of strings to numeric values. The chapter closes with a discussion of object-oriented design that introduces the CRC card (Classes, Responsibilities, and Collaborators) as a mechanism for organizing an object oriented design.

The primary goal of Chapter 6 is to introduce branching and the boolean type. But the motivation for its use, in the end, is for students to be able to handle events from multiple sources in a single event handler. Students then have learned all of the basic user interface elements necessary to write a wide range of interactive programs.

Chapters 7 and 8 are the heart of the text. In these chapters we bring together all of the informal discussion of classes and objects to formally introduce the mechanisms for defining new classes, methods, and derived classes. Students learn how to read the documentation for a class hierarchy and how to determine the inherited members of a class. They also see how the classes are related through Java's scope rules. Package syntax is introduced so that multifile programs can be written and user-defined classes can be created and imported to other code. The key object-oriented concepts of encapsulation, inheritance, and polymorphism are treated thoroughly, and their use is demonstrated in the case studies.

Users who are familiar with procedural languages may wonder, at this point, "What happened to looping?" The answer is that event driven I/O has permitted us to postpone it to Chapter 9, where it naturally fits with file I/O and prepares students for the upcoming chapters on arrays. As always, we cover the basic concepts of looping using only the *while* loop. Object-oriented languages haven't changed the basic fact that beginners have to make conceptual leaps to understand looping. Because there is more syntax to learn in an object-oriented language, it is tempting to relegate all those "old-fashioned" control structures to a single chapter and just breeze by them as if they are suddenly made easier in the presence of the additional complexity.

We find that students are still well-served by a careful study of the basic programming elements. We focus on how loops are used in algorithms while introducing only the minimum syntax necessary to illustrate the concepts. In that way, students don't develop the misperception that the different forms of control structures are bound to the different syntactic structures in a language. This approach also avoids the situation that we commonly see in which a student is focused on their confusion over choosing among different looping statements when they are really still unsure of the underlying algorithmic mechanism that they wish to express. For those instructors who feel strongly that they prefer to show students all of the control structure syntax at one time, Chapter 10 covers the additional branching and looping structures in a manner that enables appropriate sections to be covered as extensions to Chapters 6 and 9.

Chapter 10 is the "ice cream and cake" section of the book, covering the additional control structures that make the coding of certain algorithms easier. In addition to the *switch*, *do*, and *for* statements, Chapter 10 introduces the concept of exception handling. We show students how to use a *try-catch* statement to catch exceptions. Because we've already covered inheritance, it is a simple matter to define new exception classes that can be thrown between sections of user code. Students then are able to write code that is robust in the face of errors that cannot be handled directly with testing and branching.

Chapters 11, 12, and 13 are devoted to composite data structures. In Chapter 12, the basic concept of a composite structure is introduced and illustrated with the Java array. In Chapter 13, we show how an array can be used to implement a general-purpose list class. Our prior class designs have been in the context of specific applications, and this is the first taste of an object-oriented design that does not have a predefined client. Then, in Chapter 13, we extend the discussion of arrays to multiple dimensions, and through a case study we show how they can be used to represent mathematical matrices. Given this numerically motivated case study, it is also natural to review the limitations of floating-point numbers as they are represented in the computer.

Chapter 14 concludes the text with a quick tour of the concept of recursion and some example algorithms. As in our previous texts, this chapter is designed so that it can be assigned for reading along with earlier chapters. The first half of the chapter can be covered after Chapter 6, although the contrasting iterative examples won't be readable until after Chapter 9. The second half of the chapter can be read after Chapter 11, as it applies recursion to arrays.

Chapter Features

Goals   Each chapter begins with a list of learning objectives for the student. These goals are reinforced and tested in the end-of-chapter exercises.

Problem-Solving Case Studies   A full development of a problem from its statement to a working Java application is developed. In chapters beginning with 5, the CRC card design strategy is employed to develop object-oriented designs that are then translated into code. Test plans and sample test data are also presented for many of these case studies.

Testing and Debugging   These sections consider the implications of the chapter material with regard to testing of applications or classes. They conclude with a list of testing and debugging hints.

Quick Checks   These questions test the student's recall of major points associated with the chapter goals. Upon reading each question, the student immediately should know the answer, which he or she can verify by glancing at the answer at the end of the section. The page number on which the concept is discussed appears at the end of each question so that the student can review the material in the event of an incorrect response.

Exam Preparation Exercises   To help the student prepare for tests, these questions usually have objective answers and are designed to be answerable with a few minutes of work. Answers to selected questions are given in the back of the book, and the remaining questions are answered in the Instructor's Guide.

Programming Warm-Up Exercises   These questions provide the student with experience in writing Java code fragments. The student can practice the syntactic constructs in each chapter without the burden of writing a complete program.

Programming Problems   These exercises require the student to design solutions and write complete Java applications.

Case Study Follow-Up Exercises   Much of modern programming practice involves reading and modifying existing code. These exercises provide the student with an opportunity to strengthen this critical skill by answering questions about the case study code, or making changes to it.

Supplements

Instructor's ToolKit CD-ROM

Also available to adopters on request from the publisher is a powerful teaching tool entitled Instructor's ToolKit. This CD-ROM contains an electronic version of the Instructor's Guide, a computerized test bank, PowerPoint lecture presentations, and the complete programs from the text (see below).

Programs

The programs contain the source code for all of the complete Java applications and stand-alone classes that are found within the textbook. They are available on the Instructor's ToolKit CD-ROM and also as a free download for instructors' and students from the publisher's Web site: www.jbpub.com/disks. The programs from all of the case studies, plus several programs that appear in the chapter bodies are included. Fragments or snippets of code are not included nor are the solutions to the chapter-ending Programming Problems. These application files can be viewed or edited using any standard text editor, but in order to compile and run the applications, a Java compiler must be used.

Student Lecture Companion: A Note-Taking Guide

Designed from the PowerPoint™ presentation developed for this text, the Student Lecture Companion is an invaluable tool for learning. The notebook is designed to encourage students to focus their energies on listening to the lecture as they fill in additional details. The skeletal outline concept helps students organize their notes and readily recognize the important concepts in each chapter.

A Laboratory Course in Java

Written by Nell Dale, this lab manual follows the organization of the text. The lab manual is designed to allow the instructor maximum flexibility and may be used in both open and closed laboratory settings. Each chapter contains three types of activities: Prelab, Inlab, and Postlab. Each lesson is broken into exercises that thoroughly demonstrate the concept covered in the chapter. A disk that contains the applications, application shells (partial applications), and data files accompanies the lab manual.

Acknowledgments

We would like to thank the many individuals who have helped us in the preparation of this text. We are indebted to the members of the faculties of the Computer Science Departments at the University of Texas at Austin, The University of Massachusetts at Amherst, and the University of Wisconsin–La Crosse.

We extend special thanks to Jeff Brumfield for developing the syntax template metalanguage and allowing us to use it in this text.

For their many helpful suggestions, we thank the lecturers, teaching assistants, consultants, and student proctors who run the courses for which this book was written, and the students themselves.

We are grateful to the following people who took the time to review the manuscript at various stages in its development: John Connely, California Polytechnic State University; John Beidler, University of Scranton; Hang Lau, Concordia University; Thomas Mertz, Millersville University; Bina Ramamurthy, State University of New York College at Buffalo; James Roberts, Carnegie Mellon University; David Shultz, University of New Mexico; Kenneth Slonneger, University of Iowa; Sylvia Sorkin, Community College of Baltimore County.

We also thank Brooke Albright, Bobbie Lewis, and Mike and Sigrid Wile along with the many people at Jones and Bartlett who contributed so much, especially J. Michael Stranz, Jennifer Jacobson, Anne Spencer, and W. Scott Smith. Our very special thanks go to Amy Rose, our Project Manager, who taught us a lesson in professionalism while she was winning her gold stars.

Anyone who has ever written a book—or is related to someone who has—can appreciate the amount of time involved in such a project. To our families—all the Dale clan and the extended Dale family (too numerous to name); to Lisa, Charlie, and Abby; to Anne, Brady, and Kari—thanks for your tremendous support and indulgence.

N. D.
C. W.
M. H.

10 Additional Control Structures and Exceptions   451

11 One-Dimensional Arrays   495

Overview of Programming and Problem Solving

Goals

- To be able to define *computer program, algorithm,* and *high-level programming language.*
- To be able to list the basic stages involved in writing a computer program.
- To be able to distinguish between machine code and Bytecode.
- To be able to describe what compilers and interpreters are and what they do.
- To be able to describe the compilation, execution, and interpretation processes.
- To be able to list the major components of a computer and describe how they work together.
- To be able to distinguish between hardware and software.
- To be able to discuss some of the basic ethical issues confronting computing professionals.
- To be able to apply an appropriate problem-solving method for developing an algorithmic solution to a problem.

1.1   Overview of Programming

com·put·er \kəm-'pyüt-ər\ *n. often attrib* (1646): one that computes; *specif:* a programmable electronic device that can store, retrieve, and process data*

What a brief definition for something that has, in just a few decades, changed the way of life in industrialized societies! Computers touch all areas of our lives: paying bills, driving cars, using the telephone, shopping. In fact, it might be easier to list those areas of our lives in which we do *not* use computers. You are probably most familiar with computers through the use of games, word processors, Web browsers, and other programs. Be forewarned: This book is not just about using computers. This is a text to teach you how to program them.

What Is Programming?

Much of human behavior and thought is characterized by logical sequences of actions applied to objects. Since infancy, you have been learning how to act, how to do things; and you have learned to expect certain behavior from other people.

A lot of what you do every day you do automatically. Fortunately, it is not necessary for you to consciously think of every step involved in a process as simple as turning a page by hand:

1. Lift hand.
2. Move hand to right side of book.
3. Grasp top-right corner of page.
4. Move hand from right to left until page is positioned so that you can read what is on the other side.
5. Let go of page.

Think how many neurons must fire and how many muscles must respond, all in a certain order or sequence, to move your arm and hand. Yet you do it unconsciously.

Much of what you do unconsciously you once had to learn. Watch how a baby concentrates on putting one foot before the other while learning to walk. Then watch a group of three-year-olds playing tag.

On a broader scale, mathematics never could have been developed without logical sequences of steps for manipulating symbols to solve problems and prove theorems. Mass production never would have worked without operations taking place on component parts in a certain order. Our whole civilization is based on the order of things and actions.

---

*By permission. From *Merriam-Webster's Collegiate Dictionary*, Tenth Edition © 1994 by Merriam-Webster Inc.

We create order, both consciously and unconsciously, through a process called programming. This book is concerned with the programming of one tool in particular, the computer.

Notice that the key word in the definition of computer is data. Computers manipulate data. When you write a program (a plan) for a computer, you specify the properties of the data and the operations that can be applied to it. Those operations are then combined as necessary to solve a problem. Data is information in a form the computer can use—for example, numbers and letters. Information is any knowledge that can be communicated, including abstract ideas and concepts such as "the Earth is round."

Data comes in many different forms: letters, words, integer numbers, real numbers, dates, times, coordinates on a map, and so on. Virtually any kind of information can be represented as data, or as a combination of data and operations on it. Each kind of data in the computer is said to have a specific data type. For example, if we say that two data items are of type `int` (a name that Java uses for integer numbers), we know how they are represented in memory and that we can apply arithmetic operations to them.

> **Programming** Planning or scheduling the performance of a task or an event.
>
> **Electronic Computer** A programmable device that can store, retrieve, and process data.
>
> **Data** Information in a form a computer can use.
>
> **Information** Any knowledge that can be communicated.
>
> **Data type** The specification of how information is represented in the computer as data and the set of operations that can be applied to it.
>
> **Computer programming** The process of specifying the data types and the operations for a computer to apply to data in order to solve a problem.
>
> **Computer program** Data type specifications and instructions for carrying out operations that are used by a computer to solve a problem.

Just as a concert program lists the pieces to be performed and the order in which the players perform them, a computer program lists the types of data that are to be used and the sequence of steps the computer performs on them. From now on, when we use the words *programming* and *program*, we mean computer programming and computer program.

The computer allows us to do tasks more efficiently, quickly, and accurately than we could by hand—if we could do them by hand at all. In order for this powerful machine to be a useful tool, it must be programmed. That is, we must specify what we want done and how. We do this through programming.

How Do We Write a Program?

A computer is not intelligent. It cannot analyze a problem and come up with a solution. A human (the *programmer*) must analyze the problem, develop the instructions for solving the problem, and then have the computer carry out the instructions. What's the advantage of using a computer if it can't solve problems? Once we have written a solution for the computer, the computer can repeat the solution very quickly and consistently, again and again. The computer frees people from repetitive and boring tasks.

To write a program for a computer to follow, we must go through a two-phase process: *problem solving* and *implementation* (see Figure 1.1).

PROBLEM-SOLVING PHASE IMPLEMENTATION PHASE

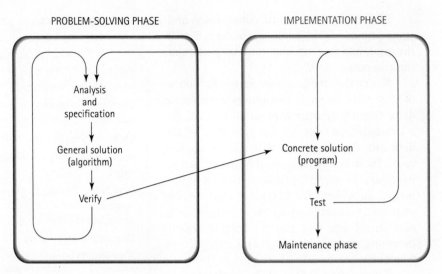

Figure 1.1 *Programming process*

Problem-Solving Phase

1. *Analysis and Specification.* Understand (define) the problem and what the solution must do.

2. *General Solution (Algorithm).* Specify the required data types and the logical sequences of steps that solve the problem.

3. *Verify.* Follow the steps exactly to see if the solution really does solve the problem.

Implementation Phase

1. *Concrete Solution (Program).* Translate the algorithm (the general solution) into a programming language.

2. *Test.* Have the computer follow the instructions. Then manually check the results. If you find errors, analyze the program and the algorithm to determine the source of the errors, and then make corrections.

Once a program has been written, it enters a third phase: *maintenance.*

Maintenance Phase

1. *Use.* Use the program.

2. *Maintain.* Modify the program to meet changing requirements or to correct any errors that show up in using it.

> **Algorithm** Instructions for solving a problem or sub-problem in a finite amount of time using a finite amount of data.

The programmer begins the programming process by analyzing the problem, breaking it into manageable pieces, and developing a general solution for each piece called an algorithm. The solutions to the pieces are collected together to form a program that solves the original problem. Understanding and analyzing a problem take up much more time than Figure 1.1 implies. They are the heart of the programming process.

If our definitions of a computer program and an algorithm look similar, it is because a program is simply an algorithm that has been written for a computer.

An algorithm is a verbal or written description of a logical sequence of actions applied to objects. We use algorithms every day. Recipes, instructions, and directions are all examples of algorithms that are not programs.

When you start your car, you follow a step-by-step procedure. The algorithm might look something like this:

1. Insert the key.
2. Make sure the transmission is in Park (or Neutral).
3. Depress the gas pedal.
4. Turn the key to the start position.
5. If the engine starts within six seconds, release the key to the ignition position.
6. If the engine doesn't start in six seconds, release the key and gas pedal, wait ten seconds, and repeat Steps 3 through 6, but not more than five times.
7. If the car doesn't start, call the garage.

Without the phrase "but not more than five times" in Step 6, you could be trying to start the car forever. Why? Because if something is wrong with the car, repeating Steps 3 through 6 over and over will not start it. This kind of never-ending situation is called an *infinite loop*. If we leave the phrase "but not more than five times" out of Step 6, the procedure doesn't fit our definition of an algorithm. An algorithm must terminate in a finite amount of time for all possible conditions.

Suppose a programmer needs an algorithm to determine an employee's weekly wages. The algorithm reflects what would be done by hand:

1. Look up the employee's pay rate.
2. Determine the hours worked during the week.
3. If the number of hours worked is less than or equal to 40, multiply the hours by the pay rate to calculate regular wages.
4. If the number of hours worked is greater than 40, multiply 40 by the pay rate to calculate regular wages, and then multiply the difference between the hours worked and 40 by 1½ times the pay rate to calculate overtime wages.
5. Add the regular wages to the overtime wages (if any) to determine total wages for the week.

The steps the computer follows are often the same steps you would use to do the calculations by hand.

After developing a general solution, the programmer tests the algorithm, "walking through" each step mentally or manually with paper and pencil. If the algorithm doesn't work, the programmer repeats the problem-solving process, analyzing the problem again and coming up with another algorithm. Often the second algorithm is just a variation of the first. When the programmer is satisfied with the algorithm, he or she translates it into a programming language. We use the Java programming language in this book.

Programming language A set of rules, symbols, and special words used to construct a computer program.

A programming language is a simplified form of English (with math symbols) that adheres to a strict set of grammatical rules. English is far too complicated and ambiguous for today's computers to follow. Programming languages, because they limit vocabulary and grammar, are much simpler.

Although a programming language is simple in form, it is not always easy to use. Try giving someone directions to the nearest airport using a limited vocabulary of no more than 25 words, and you begin to see the problem. Programming forces you to write very simple, exact instructions.

Translating an algorithm into a programming language is called *coding* the algorithm. The products of the translation—the code for all the algorithms in the problem—are tested by collecting them into a program and running (*executing*) the program on the computer. If the program fails to produce the desired results, the programmer must *debug* it—that is, determine what is wrong and then modify the program, or even one or more of the algorithms, to fix it. The combination of coding and testing the algorithms is called *implementation*.

Code Data type specifications and instructions for a computer that are written in a programming language.

Code is the product of translating an algorithm into a programming language. The term *code* can refer to a complete program or to any portion of a program.

There is no single way to implement an algorithm. For example, an algorithm can be translated into more than one programming language. Each translation produces a different implementation (see Figure 1.2a). Even when two people translate an algorithm into the same programming language, they are likely to come up with different implementations (see Figure 1.2b). Why? Because every programming language allows the programmer some flexibility in how an algorithm is translated. Given this flexibility, people adopt their own *styles* in writing programs, just as they do in writing short stories or essays. Once you have some programming experience, you develop a style of your own. Throughout this book, we offer tips on good programming style.

Some people try to speed up the programming process by going directly from the problem definition to coding the program (see Figure 1.3). A shortcut here is very tempting and at first seems to save a lot of time. However, for many reasons that become obvious to you as you read this book, this kind of shortcut actually takes *more* time and effort. Developing a general solution before you write a program helps you manage the problem, keep your thoughts straight, and avoid mistakes. If you don't take the time at the beginning to think out and polish your algorithm, you spend a lot of

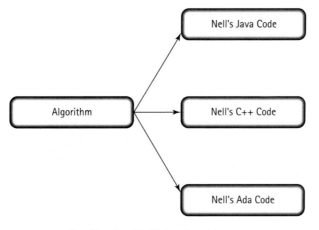

a. Algorithm translated into different languages

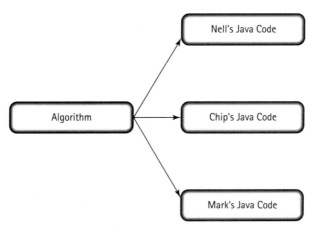

b. Algorithm translated by different people

Figure 1.2   *Differences in implementation*

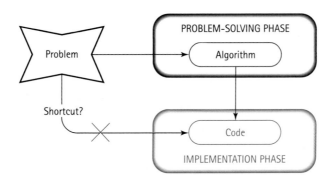

Figure 1.3   *Programming shortcut?*

extra time debugging and revising your program. *So think first and code later!* The sooner you start coding, the longer it takes to write a program that works.

Once a program has been put into use, it is often necessary to modify it. Modification may involve fixing an error that is discovered during the use of the program or changing the program in response to changes in the user's requirements. Each time the program is modified, it is necessary to repeat the problem-solving and implementation phases for those aspects of the program that change. This phase of the programming process is known as *maintenance* and actually accounts for the majority of the effort expended on most programs. For example, a program that is implemented in a few months may need to be maintained over a period of many years. Thus it is a cost-effective investment of time to carefully develop the initial problem solution and program implementation. Together, the problem-solving, implementation, and maintenance phases constitute the program's *life cycle*.

Documentation   The written text and comments that make a program easier for others to understand, use, and modify

In addition to solving the problem, implementing the algorithm, and maintaining the program, writing documentation is an important part of the programming process. Documentation includes written explanations of the problem being solved and the organization of the solution, comments embedded within the program itself, and user manuals that describe how to use the program. Many different people are likely to work on a program over a long period of time. Each of those people must be able to read and understand the code.

Theoretical Foundations

Binary Representation of Data

In a computer, data is represented electronically by pulses of electricity. Electric circuits, in their simplest form, are either on or off. Usually, a circuit that is on represents the number 1; a circuit that is off represents the number 0. Any kind of data can be represented by combinations of enough 1s and 0s. We simply have to choose which combination represents each piece of data we are using. For example, we could arbitrarily choose the pattern 1101000110 to represent the name *Java*.

Data represented by 1s and 0s is in *binary form*. The binary (base–2) number system uses only 1s and 0s to represent numbers. (The decimal [base–10] number system uses the digits 0 through 9.) The word *bit* (short for binary digit) often is used to refer to a single 1 or 0. So the pattern 1101000110 has 10 bits. A binary number with 10 bits can represent 2^{10} (1,024) different patterns. A *byte* is a group of eight bits; it can represent 2^{8} (256) patterns. Inside the computer, each character (such as the letter *A*, the letter *g*, or a question mark) is usually

continued ▼

Binary Representation of Data

represented by a byte.[1] Groups of 16, 32, and 64 bits are generally referred to as *words* (although the terms *short word* and *long word* are sometimes used to refer to 16-bit and 64-bit groups, respectively).

The process of assigning bit patterns to pieces of data is called *coding*—the same name we give to the process of translating an algorithm into a programming language. The names are the same because the only language that the first computers recognized was binary in form. Thus, in the early days of computers, programming meant translating both data and algorithms into patterns of 1s and 0s.

Binary coding schemes are still used inside the computer to represent both the instructions that it follows and the data that it uses. For example, 16 bits can represent the decimal integers from 0 to $2^{16}-1$ (65,535). More complicated coding schemes are necessary to represent negative numbers, real numbers, and numbers in scientific notation. Characters also can be represented by bit combinations. In one coding scheme, 01001101 represents *M* and 01101101 represents *m*.

The patterns of bits that represent data vary from one family of computers to another. Even on the same computer, different programming languages can use different binary representations for the same data. A single programming language may even use the same pattern of bits to represent different things in different contexts. (People do this too. The four letters that form the word *tack* have different meanings depending on whether you are talking about upholstery, sailing, sewing, paint, or horseback riding.) The point is that patterns of bits by themselves are meaningless. It is the way in which the patterns are used that gives them their meaning.

Fortunately, we no longer have to work with binary coding schemes. Today the process of coding is usually just a matter of writing down the data in letters, numbers, and symbols. The computer automatically converts these letters, numbers, and symbols into binary form. Still, as you work with computers, you continually run into numbers that are related to powers of 2—numbers like 256, 32,768, and 65,536—reminders that the binary number system is lurking somewhere nearby.

---

[1]Most programming languages use the American Standard Code for Information Interchange (ASCII) to represent the English alphabet and other symbols. ASCII characters are stored in a single byte. Java recognizes both ASCII and a newer standard called Unicode, which includes the alphabets of many other human languages. A single Unicode character takes up two bytes in the computer's memory.

1.2   How Is a Program Converted into a Form That a Computer Can Use?

In the computer, all data, whatever its form, is stored and used in binary codes, strings of 1s and 0s. Instructions and data are stored together in the computer's memory using these binary codes. If you were to look at the binary codes representing instructions and data in memory, you could not tell the difference between them; they are distinguished only by the manner in which the computer uses them. It is thus possible for the computer to process its own instructions as a form of data.

When computers were first developed, the only programming language available was the primitive instruction set built into each machine, the machine language, or *machine code.*

> **Machine language**   The language, made up of binary-coded instructions, that is used directly by the computer

Even though most computers perform the same kinds of operations, their designers choose different sets of binary codes for each instruction. So the machine code for one family of computers is not the same as for another.

When programmers used machine language for programming, they had to enter the binary codes for the various instructions, a tedious process that was prone to error. Moreover, their programs were difficult to read and modify. In time, assembly languages were developed to make the programmer's job easier.

> **Assembly language**   A low-level programming language in which a mnemonic is used to represent each of the machine language instructions for a particular computer

Instructions in an assembly language are in an easy-to-remember form called a *mnemonic* (pronounced "ni-ˈmän-ik"). Typical instructions for addition and subtraction might look like this:

Assembly Language	Machine Language
ADD	100101
SUB	010011

Although assembly language is easier for humans to work with, the computer cannot directly execute the instructions. Because a computer can process its own instructions as a form of data, it is possible to write a program to translate assembly language instructions into machine code. Such a program is called an assembler.

> **Assembler**   A program that translates an assembly language program into machine code
>
> **Compiler**   A program that translates a program written in a high-level language into machine code

Assembly language is a step in the right direction, but it still forces programmers to think in terms of individual machine instructions. Eventually, computer scientists developed high-level programming languages. These languages are easier to use than assembly languages or machine code because they are closer to English and other natural languages (see Figure 1.4).

A program called a compiler translates algorithms written in certain high-level languages (Java, C++, Pascal, and Ada, for example) into machine language. If you write a program in a high-level language, you can run it on any computer that has the appropriate compiler. This is possible because most high-level languages are *standardized,* which means that an official description of the language exists.

Figure 1.4   *Levels of abstraction*

The text of an algorithm written in a high-level language is called source code. To the compiler, source code is just input data. It translates the source code into a machine language form called object code (see Figure 1.5).

A benefit of standardized high-level languages is that they allow you to write

Source code   Data type specifications and instructions written in a high-level programming language

Object code   A machine language version of a source code

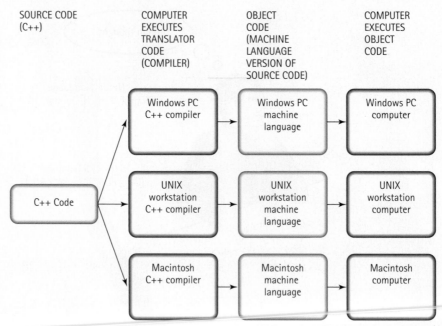

SOURCE CODE (C++)

COMPUTER EXECUTES TRANSLATOR CODE (COMPILER)

OBJECT CODE (MACHINE LANGUAGE VERSION OF SOURCE CODE)

COMPUTER EXECUTES OBJECT CODE

Figure 1.5   *High-level programming languages allow programs to be compiled on different systems.*

portable (or *machine-independent*) code. As Figure 1.5 emphasizes, a single C++ program can be run on different machines, whereas a program written in assembly language or machine language is not portable from one computer to another. Because each computer family has its own machine language, a machine language program written for computer A may not run on computer B.

Java takes a somewhat different approach than we have described in order to achieve greater portability. Java programs are translated into a standard machine language called Bytecode.

> **Bytecode**   A standard machine language into which Java source code is compiled

However, there are no computers that actually use Bytecode as their machine language. In order for a computer to run Bytecode programs, it must have another program called the Java Virtual Machine (JVM) that serves as a language interpreter for the program. Just as an interpreter of human languages listens to words spoken in one language and speaks a translation of them in a language that another person understands, the JVM reads the Bytecode machine language instructions and translates them into machine language operations that the particular computer executes. Interpretation is done as the program is running, one instruction at a time. It is not the same as compilation, which is a sepa-

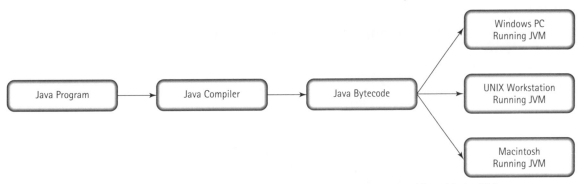

Figure 1.6 *Java compiler produces Bytecode that can be run on any machine with the JVM.*

rate step that translates all of the instructions in a program prior to execution. Figure 1.6 shows how the Java translation process achieves greater portability.

As Figure 1.6 illustrates, the compiled Java code can be run on any computer that has the JVM program to interpret for it, which means that the Java program does not have to be compiled for each different type of computer. This level of portability has grown in importance as computers across the globe are connected by the World Wide Web (sometimes simply called the Web). A programmer can write a Java program and make its Bytecode available to the public via the Web without having to compile it for all of the different types of computers that may be used to run it.

1.3 How Is Interpreting a Program Different from Executing It?

There is a significant distinction between direct execution and interpretation of a program. A computer can directly execute a program that is compiled into machine language. The JVM is one such machine language program that is directly executed. The computer cannot directly execute Bytecode. It must execute the JVM to interpret each Bytecode instruction in order to run the compiled Java program. The JVM does not produce machine code, like a compiler, but instead it reads each Bytecode instruction and gives the computer a corresponding series of operations to perform. Because each Bytecode instruction must first be interpreted, the computer cannot run Bytecode programs as quickly as it can execute machine language. Slower execution is the price we pay for increased portability.

> **Direct execution** The process by which a computer performs the actions specified in a machine language program
>
> **Interpretation** The translation, while a program is running, of non-machine language instructions (such as Bytecode) into executable operations

1.4 How Is Compilation Related to Interpretation and Execution?

It is important to understand that *compilation* and *execution* are two distinct processes. During compilation, the computer runs the compiler program. During execution, the object program is loaded into the computer's memory unit, replacing the compiler program. The computer then directly executes the object program, doing whatever the program instructs it to do (see Figure 1.7).

We can use the JVM as an example of the process shown in Figure 1.7. The JVM is written in a high-level programming language such as C++ and then compiled into machine language. The machine language is loaded into the computer's memory, and the JVM is executed. Its input is a Java program that has been compiled into Bytecode. Its results are the series of actions that would take place if the computer could directly execute Bytecode. Figure 1.8 illustrates this process.

In looking at Figure 1.8, it is important to understand that the output from the compilers can be saved for future use. Once the JVM and the Java program have been compiled, they can be used over and over without being compiled again. You never need to compile the JVM because that has already been done for you. We have shown

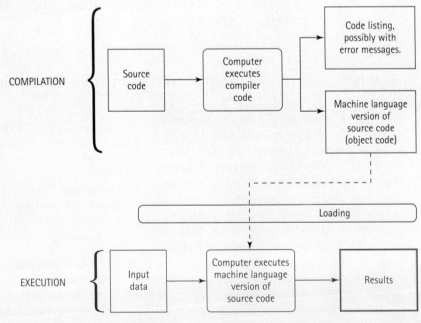

Figure 1.7 *Compilation/Execution*

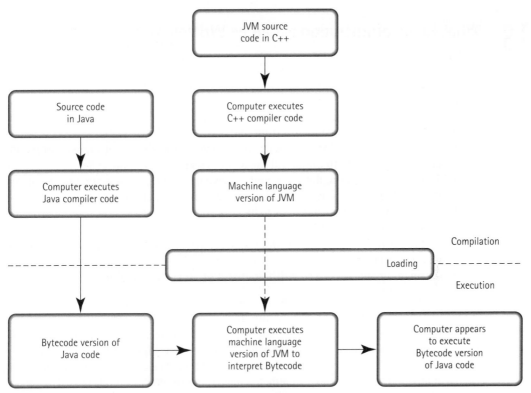

Figure 1.8   *Compilation and execution of JVM combined with compilation and interpretation of Bytecode*

its compilation in Figure 1.8 simply to illustrate the difference between the traditional compile-execute steps and the compile-interpret steps that are used with Java.

Viewed from a different perspective, the JVM makes the computer look like a different computer that has Bytecode as its machine language. The computer itself hasn't changed—it is still the same collection of electronic circuits—but the JVM makes it appear that it has become a different machine. When a program is used to make one computer act like another computer, we call it a virtual machine. For convenience we may refer to the computer as "executing a Java program," but keep in mind this is just short-hand for saying that "the computer is executing the JVM running a Java program."

Virtual machine   A program that makes one computer act like another

1.5 What Kinds of Instructions Can be Written in a Programming Language?

The instructions in a programming language reflect the operations a computer can perform:

- A computer can transfer data from one place to another.
- A computer can get data from an input device (a keyboard or mouse, for example) and write data to an output device (a screen, for example).
- A computer can store data into and retrieve data from its memory and secondary storage (parts of a computer that we discuss in the next section).
- A computer can compare data values for equality or inequality and make decisions based on the result.
- A computer can perform arithmetic operations (addition and subtraction, for example) very quickly.
- A computer can branch to a different section of the instructions.

Programming languages require that we use certain *control structures* to express algorithms as a source code. There are four basic ways of structuring statements (instructions) in most programming languages: by sequence, selection, loop, and with subprograms. Java adds a fifth way: asynchronously (see Figure 1.9). A *sequence* is a series of statements that are executed one after another. *Selection*, the conditional control structure, executes different statements depending on certain conditions. The repetitive control structure, the *loop*, repeats statements while certain conditions are met. The *subprogram* allows us to structure our code by breaking it into smaller units. *Asynchronous* control lets us write code that handles events that originate outside of our program, such as the user clicking a button on the screen with their mouse. Each of these ways of structuring statements controls the order in which the computer executes the statements, which is why they are called control structures.

Assume you're driving a car. Going down a straight stretch of road is like following a *sequence* of instructions. When you come to a fork in the road, you must decide which way to go and then take one or the other branch of the fork. This is what the computer does when it encounters a *selection* control structure (sometimes called a *branch* or *decision*) in a program. Sometimes you have to go around the block several times to find a place to park. The computer does the same sort of thing when it encounters a *loop* in a program.

A *subprogram* is a named sequence of instructions written separately from the main program. When the program executes an instruction that refers to the name of the subprogram, the code for the subprogram is executed. When the subprogram has finished executing, execution of the program resumes at the next instruction. Suppose, for example, that every day you go to work at an office. The directions for getting from home to work form a procedure called "Go to the office." It makes sense, then, for someone to give you directions to a meeting by saying, "Go to the office, then go four

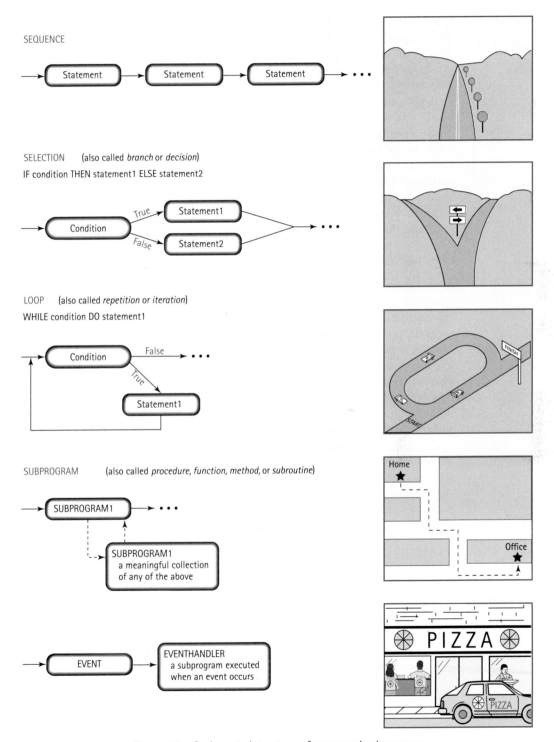

Figure 1.9   *Basic control structures of programming languages*

blocks west"—without listing all the steps you have to take to get to the office. Subprograms allow us to write parts of our programs separately and then assemble them into final form. They can greatly simplify the task of writing large programs.

Responding to asynchronous events is like working as a pizza delivery person. You wait around the dispatch station with all of the other delivery people. The dispatcher calls your name and gives you some pizzas and a delivery address. You go deliver the pizzas and return to the dispatch station. At the same time, other delivery people may be out driving.[2] The term asynchronous means "not at the same time." In this context it refers to the fact that the user can, for example, click the mouse on the screen at any time while the program is running. The mouse click does not have to happen at some particular time corresponding to certain instructions within the program. The event shown in Figure 1.9 is like the dispatcher. You do not have to write it as part of your program because it is included in Java. You simply write the event-handler subprograms that the event calls.

Object-Oriented Programming Languages

Early programming languages focused their attention on the operations and control structures of programming. These *procedural* languages paid little explicit attention to the relationships between the operations and the data. At that time, a typical computer program used only simple data types such as integer and real numbers, which have obvious sets of operations defined by mathematics. Those operations were built directly into early programming languages. As people gained experience with the programming process, they began to realize that in solving complex problems, it is helpful to define new types of data, such as dates and times; these aren't a standard part of a programming language. Each new type of data typically has an associated set of operations, such as determining the number of days between two dates.

Procedural languages thus evolved to include the feature of *extensibility*: the capability to define new data types. However, they still treated the data and operations as separate parts of the program. A programmer could define a data type to represent the time of day and then write a subprogram to compute the number of minutes between two times, but could not explicitly indicate that the two are related.

Modern programming languages such as Java allow us to collect a data type and its associated operations into a single entity called an object. They are thus called object-oriented programming languages. The advantage of an object is that it makes the relationships between the data type and operations explicit. The result is that an object is a complete, self-contained unit that can be reused again

> **Object**   A collection of data values and associated operations

---

[2]Java actually allows us to write more general asynchronous programs using a construct called a *thread*. Threaded programs are beyond the scope of this text. We restrict our use of asynchronous structures to handling events.

in other programs. Reusability enables us to write a significant portion of our programs using existing objects, thereby saving us a considerable amount of time and effort.

A class is a description of one or more like objects. Classes are usually collected into groups called packages. When we need an object in a program, we instantiate the class that describes the object. That is, we tell the Java compiler to provide us with one or more of the objects described by a specified class. One characteristic of an object-oriented programming language is having a large library of classes. In this text we present only a small subset of the classes that are available from the Java library. It is easy to be overwhelmed by the sheer size of Java's library, but many of those objects are highly specialized and unnecessary for learning the essential concepts of programming.

> **Class** A description of an object that specifies the types of data values that it can hold and the operations that it can perform
>
> **Instantiate** To create an object based on the description supplied by a class

In the next few chapters we consider how to write simple codes that instantiate just a few of the classes in Java's library. By Chapter 7 we develop enough of the basic concepts of programming to start designing our own classes. Leading up to that point, we learn how to write some specific classes using patterns of Java code that we provide.

1.6 What Is a Computer?

You can learn a programming language, how to write programs, and how to run (execute) these programs without knowing much about computers. But if you know something about the parts of a computer, you can better understand the effect of each instruction in a programming language.

Most computers have six basic components: the memory unit, the arithmetic/logic unit, the control unit, input devices, output devices, and auxiliary storage devices. Figure 1.10 is a stylized diagram of the basic components of a computer.

The **memory unit** is an ordered sequence of storage cells, each capable of holding a piece of data. Each memory cell has a distinct address to which we refer in order to store data into it or retrieve data from it. These storage cells are called *memory cells*, or *memory locations*.[3] The memory unit holds data (input data or the product of computation) and instructions (programs), as shown in Figure 1.11.

> **Memory unit** Internal data storage in a computer

---

[3]The memory unit is also referred to as RAM, an acronym for random-access memory (because we can access any location at random).

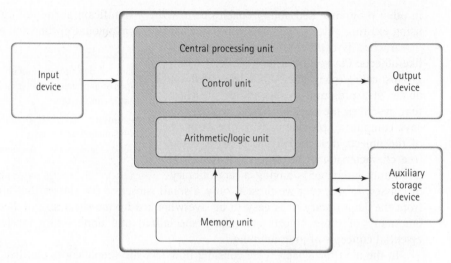

Figure 1.10   *Basic components of a computer*

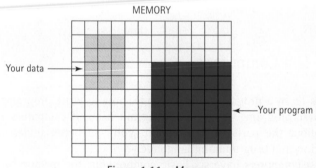

Figure 1.11   *Memory*

Central processing unit (CPU) The part of the computer that executes the instructions (program) stored in memory; made up of the arithmetic/logic unit and the control unit

Arithmetic/Logic unit (ALU) The component of the central processing unit that performs arithmetic and logical operations

Control unit The component of the central processing unit that controls the actions of the other components so that instructions (the program) are executed in the correct sequence

The part of the computer that follows instructions is called the central processing unit (CPU). The CPU usually has two components. The arithmetic/logic unit (ALU) performs arithmetic operations (addition, subtraction, multiplication, and division) and logical operations (comparing two values). The control unit controls the actions of the other components so that program instructions are executed in the correct order.

For us to use computers, we must have some way of getting data into and out of them. Input/Output (I/O) devices accept data to be processed (input) and present data that have been processed (output). A keyboard is a common input device. Another is a *mouse*, a "pointing" device. A video display is a common output device, as are printers and liquid crystal display (LCD) screens.

> **Input/Output (I/O) devices**   The parts of the computer that accept data to be processed (input) and present the results of that processing (output)

For the most part, computers simply move and combine data in memory. The many types of computers differ primarily in the size of their memories, the speed with which data can be recalled, the efficiency with which data can be moved or combined, and limitations on I/O devices.

When a program is executing, the computer proceeds through a series of steps, the *fetch-execute cycle*:

1. The control unit retrieves (*fetches*) the next coded instruction from memory.

2. The instruction is translated into control signals.

3. The control signals tell the appropriate unit (arithmetic/logic unit, memory, I/O device) to perform (*execute*) the instruction.

4. The sequence repeats from Step 1.

Computers can have a wide variety of peripheral devices. An auxiliary storage device, or *secondary storage device*, holds coded data for the computer until we actually want to use the data. Instead of inputting data every time, we can input it once and have the computer store it onto an auxiliary storage device. Whenever we need to use the data, we tell the computer to transfer the data from the auxiliary storage device to its memory. An auxiliary storage device therefore serves as both an input and an output device. Typical auxiliary storage devices are disk drives and magnetic tape drives. A *disk drive* is a cross between a compact disk player and a tape recorder. It uses a thin disk made out of magnetic material. A read/write head (similar to the record/playback head in a tape recorder) travels across the spinning disk, retrieving or recording data. A CD-ROM or a DVD-ROM drive uses a laser to read information stored optically on a plastic disk. The CD-R and DVD-RAM forms of the CD and DVD can be used to both read and write data. A *magnetic tape drive* is like a tape recorder and is most often used to back up (make a copy of) the data on a disk in case the disk is ever damaged.

> **Peripheral device**   An input, output, or auxiliary storage device attached to a computer
>
> **Auxiliary storage device**   A device that stores data in encoded form outside the computer's main memory

Together, all of these physical components are known as hardware. The programs that allow the hardware to operate are called software. Hardware usually is fixed in design;

> **Hardware**   The physical components of a computer
>
> **Software**   Computer programs; the set of all programs available on a computer

software is easily changed. In fact, the ease with which software can be manipulated is what makes the computer such a versatile, powerful tool.

In addition to the programs that we write or purchase, there are programs in the computer that are designed to simplify the user/computer interface, making it easier for us to use the machine. The interface between user and computer is a set of I/O devices—for example, the keyboard, mouse, and a screen—that allows the user to communicate with the computer. We work with the keyboard, mouse, and screen on our side of the interface boundary; wires attached to the keyboard and the screen carry the electronic pulses that the computer works with on its side of the interface boundary. At the boundary itself is a mechanism that translates information for the two sides.

Interface   A connecting link at a shared boundary that allows independent systems to meet and act on or communicate with each other

When we communicate directly with the computer through an interface, we are using an interactive system. Interactive systems allow direct entry of programs and data and provide immediate feedback to the user. In contrast, *batch systems* require that all data be entered before a program is run and provide feedback only after a program has been executed. In this text we focus on interactive systems, although in Chapter 9 we discuss file-oriented programs, which share certain similarities with batch systems.

Interactive system   A system that allows direct communication between user and computer

The set of programs that simplifies the user/computer interface and improves the efficiency of processing is called *system software*. It includes the JVM and the Java compiler as well as the operating system and the editor (see Figure 1.12). The operating system manages all of the computer's resources. It can input programs, call the compiler, execute object programs, and carry out any other system commands. The editor is an interactive program used to create and modify source programs or data.

Operating system   A set of programs that manages all of the computer's resources

Editor   An interactive program used to create and modify source programs or data

1.7 Ethics and Responsibilities in the Computing Profession

Every profession operates with a set of ethics that help to define the responsibilities of people who practice the profession. For example, medical professionals have an ethical responsibility to keep information about their patients confidential. Engineers have an ethical responsibility to their employers to protect proprietary information, but they also have a responsibility to protect the public and the environment from harm that may result from their work. Writers are ethically bound not to plagiarize the work of others, and so on.

For example, a car thief who gains access to the state motor vehicle registry could print out a "shopping list" of valuable car models together with their owners' addresses. An industrial spy might steal customer data from a company database and sell it to a competitor. Although these are obviously illegal acts, computer professionals face other situations that are not so obvious.

Suppose your job includes managing the company payroll database. In that database are the names and salaries of the employees in the company. You might be tempted to poke around in the database and see how your salary compares to your associates—this act is unethical and an invasion of your associates' right to privacy. This information is confidential. Any information about a person that is not clearly public should be considered confidential. An example of public information is a phone number listed in a telephone directory. Private information includes any data that has been provided with an understanding that it will be used only for a specific purpose (such as the data on a credit card application).

A computing professional has a responsibility to avoid taking advantage of special access that he or she may have to confidential data. The professional also has a responsibility to guard that data from unauthorized access. Guarding data can involve such simple things as shredding old printouts, keeping backup copies in a locked cabinet, not using passwords that are easy to guess (such as a name or word), and more complex measures such as *encryption* (keeping it stored in a secret coded form).

Use of Computer Resources

If you've ever bought a computer, you know that it costs money. A personal computer can be relatively inexpensive, but it is still a major purchase. Larger computers can cost millions of dollars. Operating a PC may cost a few dollars a month for electricity and an occasional outlay for paper, disks, and repairs. Larger computers can cost tens of thousands of dollars per month to operate. Regardless of the type of computer, whoever owns it has to pay these costs. They do so because the computer is a resource that justifies its expense.

The computer is an unusual resource because it is valuable only when a program is running. Thus, the computer's time is really the valuable resource. There is no significant physical difference between a computer that is working and one that is sitting idle. By contrast, a car is in motion when it is being used. Thus, unauthorized use of a computer is different from unauthorized use of a car. If one person uses another's car without permission, that individual must take possession of it physically—that is, steal it. If someone uses a computer without permission, the computer isn't physically stolen, but just as in the case of car theft, the owner is being deprived of a resource that he or she is paying for.

For some people, theft of computer resources is a game—like joyriding in a car. The thief really doesn't want the resources; it is just the challenge of breaking through a computer's security system and seeing how far he or she can get without being caught. Success gives a thrilling boost to this sort of person's ego. Many computer thieves think that their actions are acceptable if they don't do any harm, but whenever real work is displaced from the computer by such activities, then harm is clearly being done. If nothing else, the thief is trespassing in the computer owner's property. By analogy, consider that even though no physical harm may be done by someone who breaks into your bedroom and takes a nap while you are away, such an action is certainly disturbing to you because it poses a threat of potential physical harm. In this case, and in the case of breaking into a computer, mental harm can be done.

Other thieves can be malicious. Like a joyrider who purposely crashes a stolen car, these people destroy or corrupt data to cause harm. They may feel a sense of power from being able to hurt others with impunity. Sometimes these people leave behind programs that act as time bombs, to cause harm long after they have gone. Another kind of program that may be left is a virus—a program that replicates itself, often with the goal of spreading to other computers. Viruses can be benign, causing no other harm than to use up some resources. Others can be destructive and cause widespread damage to data. Incidents have occurred in which viruses have cost billions of dollars in lost computer time and data.

Virus　Code that replicates itself, often with the goal of spreading to other computers without authorization, and possibly with the intent of doing harm

Computing professionals have an ethical responsibility never to use computer resources without permission. This includes activities such as doing personal work on an employer's computer. We also have a responsibility to help guard resources to which we have access—by using unguessable passwords and keeping them secret, by watching for signs of unusual computer use, by writing programs that do not provide loopholes in a computer's security system, and so on.

Software Engineering

Humans have come to depend greatly on computers in many aspects of their lives. That reliance is fostered by the perception that computers function reliably; that is, they work correctly most of the time. However, the reliability of a computer depends on the care that is taken in writing its software.

Errors in a program can have serious consequences. Here are a few examples of real incidents involving software errors. An error in the control software of the F–18 jet fighter caused it to flip upside down the first time it flew across the equator. A rocket launch went out of control and had to be blown up because there was a comma typed in place of a period in its control software. A radiation therapy machine killed several patients because a software error caused the machine to operate at full power when the operator typed certain commands too quickly.

Even when the software is used in less critical situations, errors can have significant effects. Examples of such errors include

- an error in your word processor that causes your term paper to be lost just hours before it is due.
- an error in a statistical program that causes a scientist to draw a wrong conclusion and publish a paper that must later be retracted.
- an error in a tax preparation program that produces an incorrect return, leading to a fine.

Programmers thus have a responsibility to develop software that is free from errors. The process that is used to develop correct software is known as software engineering.

> **Software engineering**   The application of traditional engineering methodologies and techniques to the development of software

Software engineering has many aspects. The software life cycle described at the beginning of this chapter outlines the stages in the development of software. Different techniques are used at each of these stages. We address many of the techniques in this text. In Chapter 5 we introduce methodologies for developing correct algorithms. We discuss strategies for testing and validating programs in every chapter. We use a modern programming language that enables us to write readable, well-organized programs, and so on. Some aspects of software engineering, such as the development of a formal, mathematical specification for a program, are beyond the scope of this text.

1.8   Problem-Solving Techniques

You solve problems every day, often unaware of the process you are going through. In a learning environment, you usually are given most of the information you need: a clear statement of the problem, the necessary input, and the required output. In real life, the process is not always so simple. You often have to define the problem yourself and then decide what information you have to work with and what the results should be.

After you understand and analyze a problem, you must come up with a solution—an algorithm. Earlier we defined an algorithm as a step-by-step procedure for solving a problem in a finite amount of time with a finite amount of data. Although you work with algorithms all the time, most of your experience with them is in the context of *following* them. You follow a recipe, play a game, assemble a toy, or take medicine. In the problem-solving phase of computer programming, you will be *designing* algorithms, not following them. This means you must be conscious of the strategies you use to solve problems in order to apply them to programming problems.

Ask Questions

If you are given a task orally, you ask questions—When? Why? Where?—until you understand exactly what you have to do. If your instructions are written, you might put question marks in the margin, underline a word or a sentence, or in some other way indicate that the task is not clear. Your questions may be answered by a later paragraph, or you might have to discuss them with the person who gave you the task.

These are some of the questions you might ask in the context of programming:

- What do I have to work with—that is, what is my data?
- What do the data items look like?
- What are the operations to be performed on the data?
- How much data is there?

- How will I know when I have processed all the data?
- What should my output look like?
- How many times is the process going to be repeated?
- What special error conditions might come up?

Look for Things That Are Familiar

Never reinvent the wheel. If a solution exists, use it. If you've solved the same or a similar problem before, just repeat your solution. People are good at recognizing similar situations. We don't have to learn how to go to the store to buy milk, then to buy eggs, and then to buy candy. We know that going to the store is always the same; only what we buy is different.

In programming, certain problems occur again and again in different guises. A good programmer immediately recognizes a subtask he or she has solved before and plugs in the solution. For example, finding the daily high and low temperatures is really the same problem as finding the highest and lowest grades on a test. You want the largest and smallest values in a set of numbers (see Figure 1.13).

In Chapter 8, we see how this problem-solving strategy can be implemented in Java using a mechanism called *inheritance*, which allows us to define a new object that adds to the capabilities of an existing object.

Solve by Analogy

Often a problem reminds you of one you have seen before. You may find solving the problem at hand easier if you remember how you solved the other problem. In other

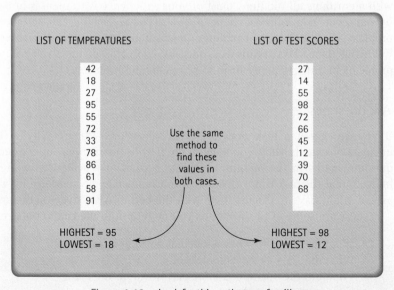

Figure 1.13   *Look for things that are familiar.*

A library catalog system can give insight into how to organize a parts inventory.

Figure 1.14 *Analogy*

words, draw an analogy between the two problems. For example, a solution to a perspective projection problem from an art class might help you figure out how to compute the distance to a landmark when you are on a cross-country hike. As you work your way through the new problem, you come across things that are different than they were in the old problem, but usually these are just details that you can deal with one at a time.

Analogy is really just a broader application of the strategy of looking for things that are familiar. When you are trying to find an algorithm for solving a problem, don't limit yourself to computer-oriented solutions. Step back and try to get a larger view of the problem. Don't worry if your analogy doesn't match perfectly—the only reason for starting with an analogy is that it gives you a place to start (see Figure 1.14). The best programmers are people who have broad experience solving all kinds of problems.

Means-Ends Analysis

Often the beginning state and the ending state are given; the problem is to define a set of actions that can be used to get from one to the other. Suppose you want to go from Boston, Massachusetts to Austin, Texas. You know the beginning state (you are in Boston) and the ending state (you want to be in Austin). The problem is how to get from one to the other.

In this example, you have lots of choices. You can fly, walk, hitchhike, ride a bike, or whatever. The method you choose depends on your circumstances. If you're in a hurry, you'll probably decide to fly.

Once you've narrowed down the set of actions, you have to work out the details. It may help to establish intermediate goals that are easier to meet than the overall goal. Let's say there is a really cheap, direct flight to Austin out of Newark, New Jersey. You might decide to divide the trip into legs: Boston to Newark and then Newark to Austin. Your intermediate goal is to get from Boston to Newark. Now you only have to examine the means of meeting that intermediate goal (see Figure 1.15).

The overall strategy of means-ends analysis is to define the ends and then to analyze your means of getting between them. The process translates easily to computer programming. You begin by writing down what the input is and what the output should be.

Start: Boston **Goal:** Austin	**Means:** *Fly*, walk, hitchhike, bike, drive, sail, bus
Start: Boston **Goal:** Austin	**Revised Means:** Fly to Chicago and then Austin; *fly to Newark and then Austin:* fly to Atlanta and then Austin
Start: Boston **Intermediate Goal:** Newark **Goal:** Austin	**Means to Intermediate Goal:** *Commuter flight*, walk, hitchhike, bike, drive, sail, bus
Solution: Take commuter flight to Newark and then catch cheap flight to Austin	

Figure 1.15   *Means-ends analysis*

Then you consider the actions a computer can perform and choose a sequence of actions that can transform the input into the results.

Divide and Conquer

We often break up large problems into smaller units that are easier to handle. Cleaning the whole house may seem overwhelming; cleaning the rooms one at a time seems much more manageable. The same principle applies to programming. We break up a large problem into smaller pieces that we can solve individually (see Figure 1.16). In fact, the object-oriented design and functional decomposition methodologies, which we describe in Chapter 5, are both based on the principle of divide and conquer.

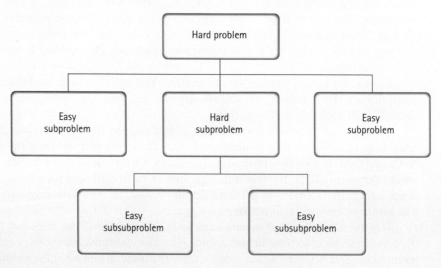

Figure 1.16   *Divide and conquer*

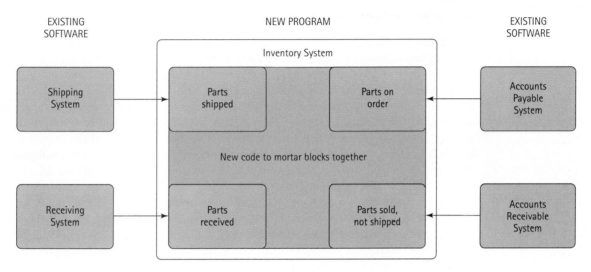

Figure 1.17 *Building-block approach*

The Building-Block Approach

Another way of attacking a large problem is to see if any solutions for smaller pieces of the problem exist. It may be possible to put some of these solutions together end to end to solve most of the big problem. This strategy is just a combination of the look-for-familiar-things and divide-and-conquer approaches. You look at the big problem and see that it can be divided into smaller problems for which solutions already exist. Solving the big problem is just a matter of putting the existing solutions together, like mortaring together blocks to form a wall (see Figure 1.17).

With an object-oriented programming language, we often solve a problem by first looking in the class library to see what solutions have been developed previously and then writing a small amount of additional code to put the pieces together. As we see later, this problem-solving technique is the basis for the methodology called *object-based design*.

Merging Solutions

Another way to combine existing solutions is to merge them on a step-by-step basis. For example, to compute the average of a list of values, we must both sum and count the values. If we already have separate solutions for summing values and for counting the number of values, we can combine them. But if we first do the summing and then do the counting, we have to read the list twice. We can save steps if we merge these two solutions: read a value and then add it to the running total and add 1 to our count before going on to the next value. Whenever the solutions to subproblems duplicate steps, think about merging them instead of joining them end to end.

Mental Blocks: The Fear of Starting

Writers are all too familiar with the experience of staring at a blank page, not knowing where to begin. Programmers have the same difficulty when they first tackle a big problem. They look at the problem and it seems overwhelming (see Figure 1.18).

Remember that you always have a place to begin solving any problem: Write it down on paper in your own words so that you understand it. Once you paraphrase the problem, you can focus on each of the subparts individually instead of trying to tackle the entire problem at once. This process gives you a clearer picture of the overall problem. It helps you see pieces of the problem that look familiar or that are analogous to other problems you have solved. And it pinpoints areas where something is unclear, where you need more information.

As you write down a problem, you tend to group things together into small, understandable chunks of data and operations, which may be natural places to split the problem up—to divide and conquer. Your description of the problem may collect all of the information about data and results into one place for easy reference. Then you can see the beginning and ending states necessary for means-ends analysis.

Most mental blocks are caused by not really understanding the problem. Rewriting the problem in your own words is a good way to focus on the subparts of the problem, one at a time, and to understand what is required for a solution.

Figure 1.18   *Mental block*

Algorithmic Problem Solving

Coming up with an algorithm for solving a particular problem is not always cut-and-dried. In fact, it is usually a trial-and-error process requiring several attempts and refinements. We test each attempt to see if it really solves the problem. If it does, fine. If it doesn't, we try again. We typically use a combination of the techniques we've described to solve any nontrivial problem.

Remember that the computer can only do certain things (see p. 16). Your primary concern, then, is how to make the computer transform, manipulate, calculate, or process the input data to produce the desired output. If you keep in mind the allowable instructions and data types in your programming language, you won't design an algorithm that is difficult or impossible to code.

In the case study that follows, we develop a program for calculating employees' weekly wages. It typifies the thought processes involved in writing an algorithm and coding it as a program, and it shows you what a complete Java program looks like.

Problem-Solving Case Study

A Company Payroll Program

Problem   A company needs an program to figure its weekly payroll. The input data, consisting of each employee's identification number, pay rate, and hours worked, is on the file datafile.dat in secondary storage. The program should input the data for each employee, calculate the weekly wages, save the input information for each employee along with the weekly wages on a file, and display the total wages for the week on the screen, so that the payroll clerk can transfer the appropriate amount into the payroll account.

Discussion   At first glance, this seems like a simple problem. But if you think about how you would do it by hand, you see that you need to ask questions about the specifics of the process: What is the employee data that we need and how is the data written on the file? How are wages computed? In what file should the results be stored? How does the program know that all of the employees have been processed? How should the total be displayed?

- The data for each employee includes an employee identification number, the employee's hourly pay rate, and the hours worked. Each data value is written on a separate line.
- Wages equal the employee's pay rate times the number of hours worked up to 40 hours. If an employee worked more than 40 hours, wages equal the employee's pay rate times 40 hours, plus 1½ times the employee's regular pay rate times the number of hours worked above 40.
- The results should be stored in a file called payfile.dat.
- The program knows to finish the processing when there is no more data on the input file.
- The total should be shown in a window on the screen that can be closed by the user.

We begin by *looking for things that are familiar.* An experienced Java programmer immediately recognizes that this problem contains many different objects that are represented as classes in the Java library. The input file and the output file are objects, as is the window in which the total payroll is displayed on the screen. Closing the window is an event represented by another class in the library. The employee identification number, pay rate, hours worked, wages earned, and total wages are objects in the problem that we must find a way to represent in our algorithm. Here's a list of the objects we've identified:

- Input file, datafile.dat, represented by one of the Java file classes
- Output file, payfile.dat, represented by another Java file class
- Display window, represented by a Java Frame class
- Window closing event, represented by a Java Event class
- Employee identification number
- Pay rate
- Hours worked
- Wages
- Total wages

Now that we know the objects we are working with, we need to fit them together with operations that enable them to exchange information. The operations coordinate the behavior of the objects in a way that solves the problem, like the choreography that coordinates ballet dancers to move around a stage, interacting with each other.

Let's apply the *divide-and-conquer* approach to identify the main operations in which our objects must participate. It's clear that there are two main steps to be accomplished. One is to process the input file, and the other is to display the total on the screen. Let's look at each of those steps separately, once again applying *divide-and-conquer.*

First we consider the processing of the data on the input file. Each data set represents one employee, and we process each employee's data in turn. There are three obvious steps in almost any problem of this type. For each person, we must

1. Get the data
2. Compute the results
3. Output the results

Our first step is to get the data. (By *get*, we mean *read* or *input* the data.) We need three pieces of data for each employee: employee identification number, hourly pay rate, and number of hours worked. Each data value is written on the input file. Therefore, to input the data, we take these steps:

Read the employee number.
Read the pay rate.
Read the number of hours worked.

The next step is to compute the wages. Let's expand this step with *means-ends analysis.* Our starting point is the set of data values that was input; our desired ending, the payroll for the week. The means at our disposal are the basic operations that the computer can perform, which include calculation and control structures. Let's begin by working backward from the end.

We know that there are two formulas for computing wages: one for regular hours and one for overtime. If there is no overtime, wages are simply the pay rate times the number of hours worked. If the number of hours worked is greater than 40, however, wages are 40 times the pay rate, plus the number of overtime hours times 1½ times the pay rate. The overtime hours are computed by subtracting 40 from the total number of hours worked. Here are the two formulas:

wages = hours worked × pay rate
wages = (40.0 × pay rate) + (hours worked − 40.0) × 1.5 × pay rate

We now have the means to compute wages for each person. Our intermediate goal is then to execute the correct formula given the input data. We must decide which formula to use and employ a branching control structure to make the computer execute the appropriate formula. The decision that controls the branching structure is simply whether more than 40 hours have been worked. We now have the means to get from our starting point to the desired end. To figure the wages, then, we take the following steps:

If hours worked is greater than 40.0, then
    wages = (40.0 × pay rate) + (hours worked − 40.0) × 1.5 × pay rate
otherwise
    wages = hours worked × pay rate

The last step, outputting the results, is simply a matter of directing the computer to write the employee number, the pay rate, the number of hours worked, and the wages onto `payfile.dat`:

Write the employee number, pay rate, hours worked, and wages onto `payfile.dat`

We now have an algorithm that processes the data for one employee. We need to extend this algorithm to handle all of the employees. Let's use the *building-block approach* to enclose our three main steps (getting the data, computing the wages, and outputting the results) within a looping structure that continues until each employee has been processed. Once we have computed the wages for one employee, we need to add them to a running total so that we can display it at the end of processing. Our algorithm now coordinates the behavior of the objects to accomplish the first of our two major steps.

The second major step is to display the total wages. We again used *divide-and-conquer* to break this into a series of steps:

Prepare an empty window
Write the total into the window
Show the window on the screen
Respond to the window-closing event by removing the window and stopping the program

Finally, we must take care of housekeeping chores. Before we start processing, we must prepare the input file for reading, prepare the output file to receive the results, and set the running total to zero.

What follows is the complete algorithm. Calculating the wages is written as a separate subalgorithm that is defined below the main algorithm. Notice that the algorithm is simply a very precise description of the same steps you would follow to do this process by hand.

Main Algorithm

Prepare to read a list of employee information (open file object datafile.dat)
Prepare to write a list of the employees' wages (open file object `payfile.dat`)
Set the total payroll to zero
while there is more data on file `dataFile`
    Read employee number
    Read the pay rate
    Read the number of hours worked
    Calculate pay
    Add the employee's wages to the total payroll
    Write the employee number, pay rate, hours worked, and wages onto the list (file
      `payFile`)
Prepare an empty window (a `Frame` class object)
Write the total into the window
Show the window on the screen
Respond to the window-closing event by removing the window and stopping the program

Subalgorithm for Calculating Pay

if number of hours worked is greater than 40.0, then

  wages = (40.0 × pay rate) + (hours worked − 40.0) × 1.5 × pay rate

else

  wages = hours worked × pay rate

Before we implement this algorithm, we should test it by hand, simulating the algorithm with specific data values. Case Study Follow-Up Exercise 2 asks you to carry out this test.

What follows is the Java program for this algorithm. It's here to give you an idea of what you'll be learning. If you've had no previous exposure to programming, you probably won't understand most of the program. Don't worry; you will soon. In fact, throughout this book as we introduce new constructs, we refer you back to the Payroll program. One more thing: The remarks following the symbols `//` are called comments. They are here to help you understand the program; the compiler ignores them. Words enclosed by the symbols `/*` and `*/` also are comments and are ignored by the compiler.

```java
import java.awt.*;
import java.awt.event.*;
import java.io.*;

public class Payroll
{
   private static Frame outputDisplay;          // Declare a Frame for total

   static double calcPay(double payRate,        // Employee's pay rate
                         double hours)           // Hours worked

   // CalcPay computes wages from the employee's pay rate
   // and the hours worked, taking overtime into account

   {
      final double MAX_HOURS = 40.0;            // Maximum normal work hours
      final double OVERTIME = 1.5;              // Overtime pay rate factor
      if (hours > MAX_HOURS)                    // Is there overtime?
         return (MAX_HOURS * payRate) +         // Yes
             (hours - MAX_HOURS) * payRate * OVERTIME;
```

```
      else
        return hours * payRate;                // No
    }


    public static void main(String args[])
                        throws IOException, NumberFormatException
    // Main is where execution starts. It opens dataFile and payFile, and
    //    processes the data file. After that, it shows the total in a Frame on
    //    the screen and exits when the user closes the window
    {
      String empNum;                           // Employee ID Number
      double payRate;                          // Employee's pay rate
      double hours;                            // Hours worked
      double wages;                            // Wages earned
      double total = 0.0;                      // Total company payroll
      BufferedReader dataFile;                 // Declare dataFile for input
      PrintWriter payFile;                     // Declare payFile for printing
      // Open company payroll files
      dataFile = new BufferedReader(new FileReader("datafile.dat"));
      payFile = new PrintWriter(new FileWriter("payfile.dat"));
      // Process the input on dataFile, outputting results on payFile
      empNum = dataFile.readLine();            // Read employee ID number
      while (empNum != null)
      {
        payRate = Double.valueOf(dataFile.readLine()).doubleValue();
                                               // Read payRate
        hours = Double.valueOf(dataFile.readLine()).doubleValue();
                                               // Read hours
        wages = CalcPay(payRate, hours);       // Compute wages
        total = total + wages;                 // Add wages to total
        // Put results into payFile
        payFile.println(empNum + " " + payRate + " " + hours + " " +
                    wages);
        empNum = dataFile.readLine();          // Get next ID number
      }


      dataFile.close();                        // Close input file
      payFile.close();                         // Close output file


      // Create a Frame and display it on the screen
      outputDisplay = new Frame();             // Instantiate a Frame object
      // Specify layout manager for frame
      outputDisplay.setLayout(new FlowLayout());
```

```
   outputDisplay.add(new Label("Total payroll for the week is $" + total));
   outputDisplay.add(new Label("Close window to exit program."));
   outputDisplay.pack();                          // Pack the frame
   outputDisplay.show();                          // Show the frame on the screen
   // Event handler for window closing
   outputDisplay.addWindowListener(new WindowAdapter()
   // Create a WindowAdapter
     {
       // Method to handle event
       public void windowClosing(WindowEvent event)
       {
         outputDisplay.dispose();                 // Remove frame from the screen
         System.exit(0);                          // Quit the program
       }
     });
 }
}
```

Given the following input on file `datafile.dat`:

```
534923445
6.54
45
103428439
12.82
38
131909545
8.20
52
739219803
10.00
40
```

The program outputs the following on file `payfile.dat`:

```
534923445 6.54 45.0 310.65000000000003
103428439 12.82 38.0 487.16
131909545 8.2 52.0 475.6
739219803 10.0 40.0 400.0
```

And then it displays the following window:

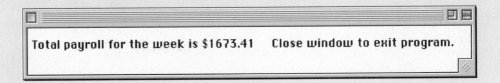

Total payroll for the week is $1673.41   Close window to exit program.

For such a simple task, the length of this program is rather daunting. Don't worry. A large part of this program involves preparation for inputting and outputting data. These steps become second nature to you very shortly, and you can use the same algorithmic steps again and again (the building-block approach).

Summary

We think nothing of turning on the television and sitting down to watch it. It's a communication tool we use to enhance our lives. Computers are becoming as common as televisions, just a normal part of our lives. And like televisions, computers are based on complex principles but are designed for easy use.

Computers are dumb; they must be told what to do. A true computer error is extremely rare (usually due to a component malfunction or an electrical fault). Because we tell the computer what to do, most errors in computer-generated output are really human errors.

Computer programming is the process of planning a sequence of steps for a computer to apply to data. It involves a problem-solving phase and an implementation phase. After analyzing a problem, we develop and test a general solution (algorithm). This general solution becomes a concrete solution—our program—when we write it in a high-level programming language. The sequence of instructions that makes up our program is then either compiled into machine code (the language the computer uses) or Bytecode (the language the Java Virtual Machine or JVM uses). After correcting any errors or "bugs" that show up during testing, our program is ready to use.

Once we begin to use the program, it enters the maintenance phase. Maintenance involves correcting any errors discovered while the program is being used and changing the program to reflect changes in the user's requirements.

Data and instructions are represented as binary numbers (numbers consisting of just 1s and 0s) in electronic computers. The process of converting data and instructions into a form usable by the computer is called coding.

A programming language reflects the range of operations a computer can perform. In this text, you will learn to write programs in the high-level programming language called Java. The basic control structures in the Java programming language—sequence, selection, loop, subprogram, and asynchronous—are based on the fundamental operations of the computer. Java provides the ability to collect data and operations into self-contained units called objects that can be reused in other programs.

Computers are composed of six basic parts: the memory unit, the arithmetic/logic unit, the control unit, input drivers, output devices, and auxiliary storage devices. The arithmetic/logic unit and control unit together are called the central processing unit. The physical parts of the computer are called hardware. The programs that are executed by the computer are called software.

System software is a set of programs designed to simplify the user/computer interface. It includes the compiler, the operating system, the JVM, and the editor.

Computing professionals are guided by a set of ethics, as are members of other professions. Among the responsibilities that we have are: copying software only with permission and including attribution to other programmers when we make use of their code, guarding the privacy of confidential data, using computer resources only with permission, and carefully engineering our programs so that they work correctly.

We've said that problem solving is an integral part of the programming process. Although you may have little experience programming computers, you have lots of experience solving problems. The key is to stop and think about the strategies that you use to solve problems, and then use those strategies to devise workable algorithms. Among those strategies are asking questions, looking for things that are familiar, solving by analogy, applying means-ends analysis, dividing the problem into subproblems, using existing solutions to small problems to solve a larger problem, merging solutions, and paraphrasing the problem in order to overcome a mental block.

The computer is widely used today in science, engineering, business, government, medicine, production of consumer goods, and the arts. Learning to program in Java can help you use this powerful tool effectively.

Quick Check

The Quick Check is intended to help you decide if you've met the goals set forth at the beginning of each chapter. If you understand the material in the chapter, the answer to each question should be fairly obvious. After reading a question, check your response against the answers listed at the end of the Quick Check. If you don't know an answer or don't understand the answer that's provided, turn to the page(s) listed at the end of the question to review the material.

1. What is a computer program? (p. 3)
2. What are the three phases in a program's life cycle? (p. 4)
3. Is an algorithm the same as a program? (p. 4–5)
4. What is a programming language? (p. 6)
5. What are the advantages of using a high-level programming language? (pp. 10–11)
6. What does a compiler do? (p. 10)
7. What is the difference between machine code and Bytecode? (pp. 12–13)
8. What part does the Java Virtual Machine play in the compilation and interpretation process? (pp. 12–13)
9. Name the five basic ways of structuring statements in Java. (pp. 16–18)

10. What are the six basic components of a computer? (pp. 19–21)
11. What is the difference between hardware and software? (pp. 21–22)
12. In what regard is theft of computer time like stealing a car? How are the two crimes different? (pp. 25–26)
13. What is the divide-and-conquer approach? (p. 30)

Answers

1. A computer program is a sequence of instructions performed by a computer. 2. The three phases of a program's life cycle are problem solving, implementation, and maintenance. 3. No. All programs are algorithms, but not all algorithms are programs. 4. A set of rules, symbols, and special words used to construct a program. 5. A high-level programming language is easier to use than an assembly language or a machine language, and programs written in a high-level language can be run on many different computers. 6. The compiler translates a program written in a high-level language into machine language or Bytecode. 7. Machine code is the native binary language that is directly executed by any particular computer. Bytecode is a standard portable machine language that is executed by the Java Virtual Machine, but it is not directly executed by the computer. 8. It translates the Bytecode instructions into operations that are executed by the computer. 9. Sequence, selection, loop, subprogram, and asynchronous. 10. The basic components of a computer are the memory unit, arithmetic/logic unit, control unit, input and output devices, and auxiliary storage devices. 11. Hardware is the physical components of the computer; software is the collection of programs that run on the computer. 12. Both crimes deprive the owner of access to a resource. A physical object is taken in a car theft, whereas time is the thing being stolen from the computer owner. 13. The divide-and-conquer approach is a problem-solving technique that breaks a large problem into smaller, simpler subproblems.

Exam Preparation Exercises

1. Explain why the following series of steps is not an algorithm, then rewrite the series so it is.

   Shampooing

   1. Rinse.
   2. Lather.
   3. Repeat.

2. Describe the input and output files used by a compiler.
3. In the following recipe for chocolate pound cake, identify the steps that are branches (selection) and loops, and the steps that are references to subalgorithms outside the algorithm.

Preheat the oven to 350 degrees
Line the bottom of a 9-inch tube pan with wax paper
Sift 2 ¾ c flour, ¾ t cream of tartar, ½ t baking soda, 1 ½ t salt, and 1 ¾ c sugar into a large bowl
Add 1 c shortening to the bowl
If using butter, margarine, or lard, then
    add 2/3 c milk to the bowl,
else
    (for other shortenings) add 1 c minus 2 T of milk to the bowl
Add 1 t vanilla to the mixture in the bowl
If mixing with a spoon, then
    see the instructions in the introduction to the chapter on cakes,
else
    (for electric mixers) beat the contents of the bowl for 2 minutes at medium speed, scraping the
        bowl and beaters as needed
Add 3 eggs plus 1 extra egg yolk to the bowl
Melt 3 squares of unsweetened chocolate and add to the mixture in the bowl
Beat the mixture for 1 minute at medium speed
Pour the batter into the tube pan
Put the pan into the oven and bake for 1 hour and 10 minutes
Perform the test for doneness described in the introduction to the chapter on cakes
Repeat the test once each minute until the cake is done
Remove the pan from the oven and allow the cake to cool for 2 hours
Follow the instructions for removing the cake from the pan, given in the introduction to the chapter
        on cakes
Sprinkle powdered sugar over the cracks on top of the cake just before serving

4. Put a check next to each item below that is a peripheral device.

    _____   a. Disk drive
    _____   b. Arithmetic/logic unit
    _____   c. Magnetic tape drive
    _____   d. Printer
    _____   e. CD-ROM drive
    _____   f. Memory
    _____   g. Auxiliary storage device
    _____   h. Control unit
    _____   i. LCD display
    _____   j. Mouse

5. Next to each item below, indicate whether it is hardware (H) or software (S).
   _____ a. Disk drive
   _____ b. Memory
   _____ c. Compiler
   _____ d. Arithmetic/logic unit
   _____ e. Editor
   _____ f. Operating system
   _____ g. Object program
   _____ h. Java Virtual Machine
   _____ i. Central processing unit
6. Means-ends analysis is a problem-solving strategy.
   a. What are three things you must know in order to apply means-ends analysis to a problem?
   b. What is one way of combining this technique with the divide-and-conquer strategy?
7. Show how you would use the divide-and-conquer approach to solve the problem of finding a job.
8. Distinguish between information and data.

Programming Warm-Up Exercises

1. Write an algorithm for driving from where you live to the nearest airport that has regularly scheduled flights. Restrict yourself to a vocabulary of 47 words plus numbers and place names. You must select the appropriate set of words for this task. An example of a vocabulary is given in Appendix A, the list of *reserved words* (words with special meaning) in the Java programming language. Notice that there are just 47 words in that list. The purpose of this exercise is to give you practice writing simple, exact instructions with an equally small vocabulary.
2. Write an algorithm for making a peanut butter and jelly sandwich, using a vocabulary of just 47 words (you choose the words). Assume that all ingredients are in the refrigerator and that the necessary tools are in a drawer under the kitchen counter. The instructions must be very simple and exact because the person making the sandwich has no knowledge of food preparation and takes every word literally.
3. In Exercise 1 above, identify the sequential, conditional, repetitive, and subprogram steps.

Case Study Follow-Up Exercises

1. Using Figure 1.16 as a guide, construct a divide-and-conquer diagram of the Problem-Solving Case Study, A Company `Payroll` Program.
2. Use the following data set to test the payroll algorithm presented on page 36. Follow each step of the algorithm just as it is written, as if you were a computer. Then check your results by hand to be sure that the algorithm is correct.

ID Number	Pay Rate	Hours Worked
327	8.30	48
201	6.60	40
29	12.50	40
166	9.25	51
254	7.00	32

3. In the Company Payroll case study, we used means-ends analysis to develop the subalgorithm for calculating pay. What are the *ends* in the analysis? That is, what information did we start with and what information did we want to end up with?

4. In the `Payroll` program, certain remarks are preceded by the symbols //. What are these remarks called, and what does the compiler do with them? What is their purpose?

Java Syntax and Semantics, and the Program Entry Process

- To be able to describe the composition of a Java program.

- To be able to read syntax templates in order to understand the formal rules governing Java programs.

- To be able to create and recognize legal Java identifiers.

- To be able to declare named constants and variables of type `char` and class `String`.

- To be able to distinguish reserved words in Java from user-defined identifiers.

- To be able to assign values to variables and objects.

- To be able to construct simple string expressions made up of constants, variables, and the concatenation operator.

- To be able to construct a code segment that displays a message on the screen.

- To be able to determine what is displayed by a given code segment.

- To be able to use comments to clarify your programs.

- To be able to construct simple Java application programs.

- To learn the steps involved in entering and running a program.

Programmers develop solutions to problems using a programming language. In this chapter, we start looking at the rules and symbols that make up the Java programming language. We also review the steps required to create a program and make it work on a computer.

2.1 Syntax and Symantics

A programming language is a set of rules, symbols, and special words used to construct a program. There are rules for both syntax (grammar) and semantics (meaning).

Syntax is a formal set of rules that defines exactly what combinations of letters, numbers, and symbols can be used in a programming language. There is no room for ambiguity in the syntax of a programming language because the computer can't think; it doesn't "know what we mean." To avoid ambiguity, syntax rules themselves must be written in a very simple, very precise, formal language called a metalanguage.

> **Syntax**   The formal rules governing how valid instructions are written in a programming language
>
> **Semantics**   The set of rules that determines the meaning of instructions written in a programming language
>
> **Metalanguage**   A language that is used to describe the syntax rules for another language

Learning to read a metalanguage is like learning to read the rules of a sport. Once you understand the notation, you can read the rule book. It's true that many people learn a sport simply by watching others play, but what they learn is usually just enough to allow them to take part in casual games. You could learn Java by following the examples in this book, but a serious programmer, like a serious athlete, must take the time to read and understand the rules.

Syntax rules are the blueprints we use to "build" instructions in a program. They allow us to take the elements of a programming language—the basic building blocks of the language—and assemble them into *constructs*, syntactically correct structures. If our program violates any of the rules of the language—by misspelling a crucial word or leaving out an important comma, for instance—the program is said to have *syntax errors* and cannot compile correctly until we fix them.

Theoretical Foundations

Metalanguages

Metalanguage is the word *language* with the prefix *meta*, which means "beyond" or "more comprehensive." A metalanguage is a language that goes beyond a normal language by allowing us to speak precisely about that language. It is a language for talking about languages. It is like an English grammar book describing the rules of English.

One of the oldest computer-oriented metalanguages is the *Backus-Naur Form (BNF)*, which is named for John Backus and Peter Naur, who developed it in 1960. BNF syntax definitions are written out using letters, numbers, and special symbols. For example, an *identifier* (a name for something) in Java must be at least one letter, underscore, or dollar sign, which may or may not be followed by additional letters, underscores, dollar signs, or digits. The BNF definition of an identifier in Java is

```
<identifier> ::= <letter> | <letter> <letter-digit-sequence>
<letter-digit-sequence > ::= <letter-or-digit> |
          <letter-or-digit> <letter-digit-sequence>
<letter-or-digit> ::= <letter> | <digit>
<letter> ::= _ | $
         | A | B | C | D | E | F | G | H | I | J | K | L
         | M | N | O | P | Q | R | S | T | U | V | W | X | Y | Z
         | a | b | c | d | e | f | g | h | i | j | k | l
         | m | n | o | p | q | r | s | t | u | v | w | x | y | z
<digit>   ::= 0 | 1 | 2 | 3 | 4 | 5 | 6 | 7 | 8 | 9
```

where the symbol ::= is read "is defined as," the symbol | means "or," the symbols < and > are used to enclose words called *nonterminal symbols* (symbols that still need to be defined), and everything else is called a *terminal symbol*.

The first line of the definition reads: "An identifier is defined as a letter or a letter followed by a letter-digit-sequence." This line contains nonterminal symbols that must be defined. In the second line, the nonterminal symbol `<letter-digit-sequence>` is defined as a `<letter-or-digit>` or as a `<letter-or-digit>` followed by another `<letter-digit-sequence>`. The self-reference in the definition is a roundabout way of saying that a `<letter-digit-sequence>` can be a series of one or more letters or digits. In the fourth line, a `<letter-or-digit>` is defined to be either a `<letter>` or a `<digit>`. In the fifth and last lines, we finally encounter terminal symbols that define `<letter>` to be an underscore, dollar sign, or any of the upper- or lowercase letters and `<digit>` as any one of the numeric characters 0 through 9.

continued ▼

Metalanguages

BNF is an extremely simple language, but that simplicity leads to syntax definitions that can be long and difficult to read. An alternative metalanguage, the *syntax diagram*, is easier to follow. It uses arrows to indicate how symbols can be combined. Here are the syntax diagrams that define an identifier in Java:

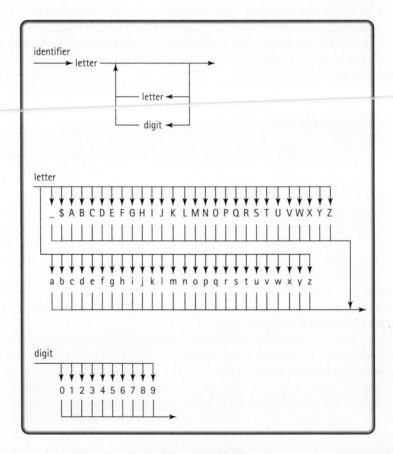

continued ▼

Metalanguages

To read the diagrams, start at the left and follow the arrows. When you come to a branch, take any one of the branch paths.

The first diagram shows that an identifier can consist of a letter and optionally any number of letters or digits. The remaining diagram defines the nonterminal symbols *letter* and *digit* to be any one of the alphabetic or numeric characters. Here, we have eliminated the BNF nonterminal symbols `⟨letter-digit-sequence⟩` and `⟨letter-or-digit⟩` by using arrows in the first syntax diagram to allow a sequence of consecutive letters or digits.

Syntax diagrams are easier to interpret than BNF definitions, but they still can be difficult to read. In this text, we introduce another metalanguage, called a *syntax template*. Syntax templates show at a glance the form a Java construct takes.

One final note: Metalanguages only show how to write instructions that the compiler can translate. They do not define what those instructions do (their semantics). Formal languages for defining the semantics of a programming language exist, but they are beyond the scope of this text. Throughout this book, we describe the semantics of Java in English.

Syntax Templates

In this book, we write the syntax rules for Java using a metalanguage called a *syntax template*. A syntax template is a generic example of the Java construct being defined. Graphic conventions show which portions are optional and which can be repeated. A colored word or symbol is written in the Java construct just as it is in the template. A noncolored word can be replaced by another template. A square bracket is used to indicate a set of items from which one can be chosen.

Let's look at an example. This template defines a Java identifier, which is Java's way of naming something in a program:

Identifier

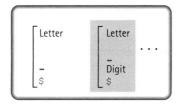

The shading indicates the part of the definition that is optional. The three dots (. . .) mean that the preceding symbol or shaded block can be repeated. So an identifier in

Java is a letter, an underscore, or dollar sign that may be optionally followed by one or more letters, digits, underscores, or dollar signs.

Remember that a word not in color can be replaced with another template. These are the templates for letter and digit:

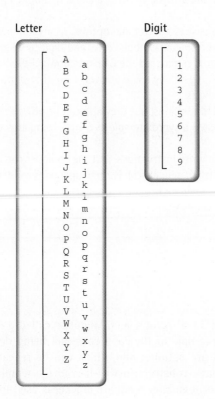

Letter

Digit

In this template, the brackets again indicate lists of items from which any one can be chosen. So a letter can be any one of the upper- or lowercase letters, and a digit can be any of the numeric characters 0 through 9.

Naming Program Elements: Identifiers

As we noted in our discussion of metalanguages, an identifier is used in Java to name something. For example, an identifier could be the name of a class, a subprogram (called a method, in Java), or a place in the computer's memory that holds data (called a field in Java). Identifiers are made up of an indefinite sequence of letters (A–Z, a–z), digits (0–9), the under-

Identifier   A name associated with a package, class, method, or field and used to refer to them

Method   A subprogram in Java

Field   A named place in memory that holds a data value or a reference to an object

score character (_), and the dollar sign ($), but must begin with a letter, underscore, or dollar sign.

Identifiers beginning with an underscore have special meaning in some Java systems, so it is best to begin an identifier with a letter. Similarly, the dollar sign has special meaning in some Java systems, and should not be used at all in identifiers that you write. We have included it in the syntax template so that you can recognize its use if you encounter it in a Java program that someone else has written.

Here are some examples of valid identifiers:

```
sum_of_squares  J9  box_22A  getData  Bin3D4  count    Count
```

Note that the last two of these identifiers (count and Count) are completely different names to the Java compiler. The uppercase and lowercase forms of a letter are two distinct characters to the computer. Here are some examples of invalid identifiers and the reasons why they are invalid:

Invalid Identifier	Explanation
40Hours	Identifiers cannot begin with a digit.
Get Data	Blanks are not allowed in identifiers.
box-22	The hyphen (-) is a math symbol (minus) in Java.
empty_?	Special symbols such as ? are not allowed.
int	The word int is predefined in the Java language.

The last identifier in the table, int, is an example of a reserved word. Reserved words are words that have specific uses in Java; you cannot use them as programmer-defined identifiers. Appendix A lists all of the reserved words in Java.

> **Reserved word**   A word that has special meaning in Java; it cannot be used as a programmer-defined identifier.

In the following table we have listed some of the programmer-defined identifiers used in the Payroll program in Chapter 1. Notice that we chose the names to convey how the identifiers are used. You can also see that there is a wide range of program elements that Java allows us to name.

Identifier	How It Is Used
MAX_HOURS	Maximum normal work hours
total	The sum of weekly wages for all employees (total company payroll)
payFile	The output file (where the employee's number, pay rate, hours, and wages are written)
outputDisplay	The name of an object representing a window on the screen
hours	A real number representing hours worked
wages	A variable that holds the result of calculating the wages for an employee
calcPay	A method for computing an employee's wages
empNum	A string of characters indicating the employee ID number

Matters of Style

Using Meaningful, Readable Identifiers

The names we use to refer to things in our programs are totally meaningless to the computer. The computer behaves in the same way whether we call the value 3.14159265 `pi` or `cake`, as long as we always call it the same thing. However, it is much easier for somebody to figure out how a program works if the names we choose for elements actually tell something about them. Whenever you have to make up a name for something in a program, try to pick one that is meaningful to a person reading the program.

Java is a *case-sensitive* language. Uppercase letters are different from lowercase letters. The identifiers

```
PRINTTOPPORTION pRiNtToPpOrTiOn printTopPortion PrintTopPortion
```

are four distinct names and are not interchangeable in any way. As you can see, the last two of these forms are easier to read. In this book, we use combinations of uppercase letters, lowercase letters, and underscores in identifiers. Many Java programmers use different capitalizations of identifiers as a way to indicate what they represent. Later in this chapter we show you the conventions that we, and many Java programmers, use.

Now that we've seen how to write identifiers, we look at some of the things that Java allows us to name.

2.2 Data Types

A computer program operates on data (stored internally in memory, stored externally on disk or tape, or input from a keyboard, mouse, scanner, or electrical sensor) and produces output. As we said in Chapter 1, in Java each piece of data must be of a specific data type. The data type determines how the data is represented in the computer and the kinds of processing the computer can perform on it.

Some types of data are used so frequently that Java provides them for us. Java defines several of these standard (or built-in) types. You are already familiar with three of them from everyday life: integer numbers, real numbers, and characters. By the end of Chapter 6 you'll be equally familiar with a fourth type, Boolean.

> **Standard (built-in) type** A data type that is automatically available for use in every Java program

Additionally, Java allows programmers to define their own data types—*programmer-defined* (or *user-defined*) *types*. In Java, each of these types is called a *class*. In this chapter, we focus on the `char` data type and the `String` class that enable us to work with character data. In Chapter 4, we examine the numeric types (such as `int`, `long`, `float`, and `double`) in detail.

Background Information

Data Storage

Where does a program get the data it needs to operate? Data is stored in the computer's memory. Remember that memory is divided into a large number of separate locations or cells, each of which can hold a piece of data. Each memory location has a unique address we refer to when we store or retrieve data. We can visualize memory as a set of post office boxes, with the box numbers as the addresses used to designate particular locations.

Of course the actual address of each location in memory is a binary number in a machine language code. In Java we use identifiers to name memory locations; then the compiler and JVM translate them into binary for us. This is one of the advantages of a high-level programming language: It frees us from having to keep track of the numeric addresses of the memory locations in which our data and instructions are stored.

The `char` *Data Type* The built-in type `char` describes data consisting of one alphanumeric character—a letter, a digit, or a special symbol. Java uses a particular *character set*, the set of alphanumeric characters it can represent. Java's character set is called Unicode, and includes characters for writing in many human languages. In this text we use a subset of Unicode that corresponds to an older character set called the American Standard Code for Information Interchange (ASCII). ASCII consists of the alphabet for the English language, plus numbers and symbols. Here are some example values of type `char`.

```
'A'    'a'    '8'    '2'    '+'    '-'    '$'    '?'    '*'    ' '
```

Notice that each character is enclosed in single quotes (apostrophes). The Java compiler needs the quotes to differentiate between the character data and other elements of Java. For example, the quotes around the characters `'A'` and `'+'` distinguish them from the identifier `A` and the addition sign. Notice also that the blank, `' '`, is a valid character.

How do we write the single quote itself as a character? If we write `''`, Java complains that this is a syntax error. The second quote indicates the end of the (empty) character value, and the third quote starts a new character value. Java provides a special case called an *escape sequence* that allows us to write a single quote as a character. The sequence of two characters `\'`, is treated by Java as a single character representing the quote. When we want to write the quote as a character in Java, we thus write

```
'\''
```

Notice that we use the backwards slash, or backslash (\), as the escape character rather than the regular slash (/). As we see in the next chapter, Java uses the regular slash as a division sign, so it is important to recognize that they are different from each other. A moment's thought reveals that this scheme introduces a new problem: How do we write the backslash as a character? The answer is that Java provides a second escape sequence, \\, that allows us to write a backslash. Thus, we write the `char` value of backslash in Java as follows.

```
'\\'
```

Java provides operations that allow us to compare data values of type `char`. The Unicode character set has a *collating sequence*, a predefined ordering of all the characters. In Unicode, `'A'` compares less than `'B'`, `'B'` less than `'C'`, and so forth. And `'1'` compares less than `'2'`, `'2'` less than `'3'`, and so on. None of the identifiers in the `Payroll` program is of type `char`.

2.3 Classes and Objects

In Chapter 1 we outlined two phases of programming: the problem-solving phase and the implementation phase. Often the same vocabulary is used in different ways in the two phases. In the problem-solving phase, an object is an entity or some *thing* that makes sense in the context of the problem being solved. A group of objects with similar properties and behaviors is described by an *object class*, or class for short. Object-oriented problem solving involves isolating the objects that make up the problem. Objects interact with one another by sending messages.

In the implementation phase, a `class` is a Java construct that allows the programmer to describe one or more objects. A `class` contains fields (data values) and methods (subprograms) that define the behavior of the object. Think of a class in the general sense as a pattern for what an object looks like and how it behaves and the Java `class` as the construct that allows you to simulate the object in code. If a class is a description of an

Class (general sense) A description of the behavior of a group of objects with similar properties and behaviors

`class` **(Java construct)** A pattern for an object

Object (general sense) An entity or thing that is relevant in the context of a problem

Object (Java) An instance of a class

Method A subprogram that defines one aspect of the behavior of a class

Instantiation Creating an object, an instance of a class

object, how do we get an object that fits the description? We use an operator called `new`, which takes the class name and returns an object of the class type. The object that is returned is an *instance* of the class. The act of creating an object from a class is called instantiation. These definitions provide new meanings for the terms *object* and *class* in addition to how we defined them in Chapter 1. Here is the syntax diagram for a class.

Class

```
ImportDeclaration; ...

Modifiers ... class Identifier

{

    ClassDeclaration ...

}
```

Modifiers

```
[ private
  ⋮
  public ]
```

A Java class may optionally begin with a series of import declarations. An object-oriented language such as Java provides a very large library of classes that are available for us to use in our programs. There are so many of these in Java's library, in fact, that they must be organized into smaller groups called packages. Import declarations are statements that tell the Java compiler which library packages we are using in our class. We do not use a Java package in this chapter, so we postpone looking at the syntax for an `import` statement until the next chapter.

Package A named collection of program building blocks or components in Java that can be imported by a class

The next line may optionally begin with a series of access modifiers, which are then followed by the word `class` and an identifier. This line is called the heading of the class. The heading gives the class a name (the identifier) and may optionally specify some general properties of the class (the modifiers). Modifiers are Java keywords. We have listed two of Java's modifiers in the syntax diagram that are relevant here: `public` and `private`. They are called access modifiers because they specify whether elements outside of the class can use the class. What's outside of the class? Any of the packages that we list in `import` declarations are outside the class. In addition, every program class actually resides within a package called `java` that is part of the JVM. Thus, if we declare an identifier to be `public`, we are allowing the JVM and all imported packages to make use of it. Because we want the JVM to be able to execute our program class, we specify that its name is `public`.

After the heading you see an open brace, a series of class declarations, and a closing brace. These three elements make up the *body* of the class. The braces indicate where the body begins and ends, and the class declarations contain all of the statements that tell the computer what to do. The simplest Java class we can write would look like this

```
class DoNothing
{
}
```

and as its name implies, it does absolutely nothing. It is a completely empty shell of a program. Our job as programmers is to add useful instructions to this empty shell.

The `String` Class　　Whereas a value of type `char` is limited to a single character, a *string* (in the general sense) is a sequence of characters, such as a word, name, or sentence, enclosed in double quotes. In Java, a string is an object, an instance of the `String` class. For example, the following are strings in Java:

```
"Introduction to "     "Java"     " and Software Design "     "."
```

A string must be typed entirely on one line. For example, the string

```
"This string is invalid because it
is typed on more than one line."
```

is not valid because it is split across two lines before the closing double quote. In this situation, the Java compiler issues an error message at the first line. The message may say something like QUOTE EXPECTED, depending on the particular compiler.

The quotes are not considered to be part of the string but are simply there to distinguish the string from other parts of a Java program. For example, `"amount"` (in double quotes) is the character string made up of the letters *a, m, o, u, n,* and *t* in that order. On the other hand, `amount` (without the quotes) is an identifier, perhaps the name of a place in memory. The symbols `"12345"` represent a string made up of the characters *1, 2, 3, 4,* and *5* in that order. If we write `12345` without the quotes, it is an integer quantity that can be used in calculations.

A string containing no characters is called the *empty string.* We write the empty string using two double quotes with nothing (not even spaces) between them.

```
""
```

The empty string is not equivalent to a string of spaces; it is a special string that contains no characters.

To write a double quote within a string, we use another escape sequence, \". Here is a string containing both quotation marks and the escape sequence for a backslash.

```
"She said, \"Don't forget that \\ is not the same as the / character.\""
```

The value of this string is

```
She said, "Don't forget that \ is not the same as the / character."
```

Notice that within a string we do not have to use the escape sequence \' to represent a single quote. Similarly, we can write the double quote as a value of type `char` (`'"'`) without using an escape sequence. But we have to use \\ to write a backslash as a `char` value or within a string.

Java provides operations for joining strings, comparing strings, copying portions of strings, changing the case of letters in strings, converting numbers to strings, and converting strings to numbers. We look at some of these operations later in this chapter and cover the remaining operations in subsequent chapters. In the `Payroll` program, the identifier `empNum` is of class `String`, and string values are used directly in several places.

2.4 Defining Terms: Declarations

How do we tell the computer what an identifier represents? We use a declaration, a statement that associates a name (an identifier) with a description of an element in a Java program (just as a dictionary definition associates a name with a description of the thing being named). In a declaration, we name an identifier and what it represents. For example, the `Payroll` program uses the declaration

> **Declaration** A statement that associates an identifier with a field, a method, a class, or a package so that the programmer can refer to that item by name

```
String empNum;
```

to announce that `empNum` is the name of a field whose contents are an instance of class `String`. When we declare a field, the compiler picks a location in memory to be associated with the identifier. We don't have to know the actual address of the memory location because the computer automatically keeps track of it for us.

Fields and the actual instructions in a program are stored in various memory locations. We use identifiers to refer to fields. We have also seen that a method can be given an identifier. In addition, a name can be associated with a programmer-defined class, which is a collection of fields and methods.

In Java you must declare every identifier before you use it. This allows the compiler to verify that the use of the identifier is consistent with what it was declared to be. If you declare an identifier to be a field that can hold a `char` value and later try to store a number into the field, the compiler detects this inconsistency and issues an error message.

A field can be either a constant or a variable. In other words, a field identifier can be the name of a memory location whose contents are not allowed to change or it can be the name of a memory location whose contents can change. There are different forms of declaration statements for constants, variables, methods, and classes in Java.

Variables   A program operates on data. Data is stored in memory. While a program is executing, different values may be stored in the same memory location at different times. This kind of memory location is called a variable, and its contents are the *variable value*. The symbolic name that we associate with a memory location is the *variable name* or *variable identifier*. In practice, we often refer to the variable name more briefly as the *variable*.

> **Variable**   A location in memory, referenced by an identifier, that contains a data value that can be changed

Declaring a variable means specifying both its name and its data type or class. This tells the compiler to associate a name with a memory location, and that the values to be stored in that location are of a specific type or class (for example, `char` or `String`). The following statement declares `myChar` to be a variable of type `char`:

```
char myChar;
```

Notice that the declaration does not specify what value is stored in `myChar`. It only specifies that the name `myChar` can hold a value of type `char`. At this point, `myChar` has been reserved as a place in memory but it contains no data. Shortly, we see how to actually put a value into a variable. (See Figure 2.1.)

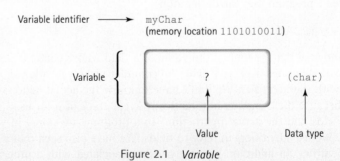

Figure 2.1   *Variable*

Java is a *strongly typed language.* This means that a variable can contain a value only of the type or class specified in its declaration. Because of the above declaration, the variable `myChar` can contain *only* a `char` value. If the Java compiler comes across an instruction that tries to store a value of the wrong type, it gives an error message, usually something like "Cannot assign String to char."

Here's the syntax template for a variable declaration:

VariableDeclaration

> Modifiers TypeName Identifier, Identifier • • • ;

TypeName is the name of a type or class such as `char` or `String`. Notice that a declaration always ends with a semicolon. Modifiers are Java reserved words. Different modifiers have different meanings, and we introduce each one and explain its use as the need arises throughout the next several chapters. Notice that the syntax template shows that they are optional. We can declare variables without using any of the modifiers.

From the syntax template, you can also see that it is possible to declare several variables in one statement:

```
char letter, middleInitial, ch;
```

Here, all three variables are declared to be `char` variables. Our preference, though, is to declare each variable with a separate statement:

```
char letter;
char middleInitial;
char ch;
```

Declaring each variable with a separate statement allows you to attach comments to the right of each declaration, for example:

```
String firstName;        // A person's first name
String lastName;         // A person's last name
String title;            // A person's title, for example Dr.
char middleInitial;      // A person's middle initial
char myChar;             // A place to store one letter
```

These declarations tell the compiler to reserve memory space for three `String` variables—`firstName`, `lastName`, and `title`—and two `char` variables, `middleInitial`, and `myChar`. The comments explain to someone reading the program what each variable represents.

In the syntax template for a class, we saw that it contains a set of class declarations, and some of those declarations are variables. For example, here is a class with two variable declarations, also showing how we might use a `private` modifier as part of a declaration.

```
public class Sample          // The start of a class called Sample
{
   private char myChar;      // A char type variable declared in class
                             //  Sample
   private String myString;  // A String variable declared in class Sample
}                            // The end of class Sample
```

Constants All single characters (enclosed in single quotes) and strings (enclosed in double quotes) are constants.

```
'A'    '@'    "Howdy boys"    "Please enter an employee number:"
```

Literal value Any constant value written in a program

Named constant (symbolic constant) A location in memory, referenced by an identifier, that contains a data value that cannot be changed

In Java, as in mathematics, a constant is something whose value never changes. When we use the actual value of a constant in a program, we are using a literal value (or *literal*).

An alternative to the literal constant is the named constant (or symbolic constant), which is introduced in a declaration statement. A named constant is just another way of representing a literal value. Instead of using the literal value in an instruction, we give the literal value a name in a declaration statement, then use that name in the instruction. For example, we can write an instruction that prints the title of this book using the literal string `"Introduction to Java and Software Design"`. Or we can declare a named constant called `BOOK_TITLE` that equals the same string and then use the constant name in the instruction. That is, we can use either

```
"Introduction to Java and Software Design"
```

or

```
BOOK_TITLE
```

in the instruction.

Using the literal value of a constant may seem easier than giving it a name and then referring to it by that name. But, in fact, named constants make a program easier to read because they make the meaning of literal constants clearer. And named constants also make it easier to change a program later on.

The syntax template for a constant declaration is similar to the template for a variable declaration:

ConstantDeclaration

```
Modifiers final TypeName Identifier = LiteralValue;
```

The only difference is that we must include the modifier `final`, a reserved word, and we follow the identifier with an equal sign (=) and the value to be stored in the constant. The `final` modifier tells the Java compiler that this value is the last and only value we want this field to have.

The following are examples of constant declarations:

```
final String STARS = "*********";
final char   BLANK = ' ';
final String BOOK_TITLE = "Introduction to Java and Software Design";
final String MESSAGE = "Error condition";
```

As we have done above, many Java programmers capitalize the entire identifier of a named constant and separate the English words with an underscore. The idea is to let the reader quickly distinguish between variable names and constant names when they appear in the middle of code.

It's a good idea to add comments to constant declarations as well as variable declarations. For example:

```
final String STARS = "*********"; // Row of stars to use as a separator
final char   BLANK = ' ';         // A single blank
```

Matters of Style

Capitalization of Identifiers

Programmers often use capitalization as a quick, visual clue to what an identifier represents. Different programmers adopt different conventions for using uppercase letters and lowercase letters. Some people use only lowercase letters, separating the English words in an identifier with the underscore character:

```
pay_rate   emp_num   pay_file
```

continued ▼

Capitalization of Identifiers

The convention used by many Java programmers and the one we use in this book is the following:

- Variables and methods begin with a lowercase letter and capitalize each successive English word.

  ```
  lengthInYards   middleInitial   hours
  ```

- Class names begin with an uppercase letter but are capitalized the same as variable names thereafter.

  ```
  PayRollFrame   Sample   MyDataType   String
  ```

  Capitalizing the first letter allows a person reading the program to tell at a glance that an identifier represents a class name rather than a variable or method. Java reserved words use all lowercase letters, so type `char` is lowercase. `String` is a class, so it begins with a capital letter.

- Identifiers representing named constants are all uppercase with underscores used to separate the English words.

  ```
  BOOK_TITLE   OVERTIME   MAX_LENGTH
  ```

These conventions are only that—conventions. Java does not require this particular style of capitalizing identifiers. You may wish to capitalize in a different fashion. But whatever you use, it is essential that you use a consistent style throughout your program. A person reading your program will be confused or misled if you use a random style of capitalization.

2.5 Taking Action: Executable Statements

Up to this point, we've looked at ways of declaring variables and constants in a program. Now we turn our attention to ways of acting, or performing operations, on data.

Assignment The value of a variable can be set or changed through an assignment statement. For example,

> **Assignment statement** A statement that stores the value of an expression into a variable

```
lastName = "Lincoln";
```

assigns the string value `"Lincoln"` to the variable `lastName` (that is, stores the sequence of characters `"Lincoln"` into the memory associated with the variable named `lastName`).

Here's the syntax template for an assignment statement:

AssignmentStatement

> Variable = Expression;

The assignment operator (=) means "is set equal to" or "gets"; the variable *is set equal to* the value of the expression. Any previous value in the variable is destroyed and replaced by the value of the expression.

Only one variable can be on the left-hand side of an assignment statement. An assignment statement is *not* like a math equation (*x* + *y* = *z* + 4); the expression (what is on the right-hand side of the assignment operator) is evaluated, and the resulting value is stored into the single variable on the left of the

> **Expression**   An arrangement of identifiers, literals, and operators that can be evaluated to compute a value of a given type
>
> **Evaluate**   To compute a new value by performing a specified set of operations on given values

assignment operator. A variable keeps its assigned value until another statement stores a new value into it.

Because you are accustomed to reading from left to right, the way that the assignment operator moves a value from right to left may at first seem awkward. Just remember to read the = as "is set equal to" or "gets" and it seems more natural.

The value assigned to a variable must be of the same type as the variable. Given the declarations

```
String firstName;
String middleName;
String lastName;
String title;
char middleInitial;
char myChar;
```

the following assignment statements are valid:

```
firstName = "Abraham";
middleName = firstName;
middleName = "";
lastName = "Lincoln";
title = "President";
middleInitial = ' ';
myChar = 'B';
```

However, these assignments are not valid:

Invalid Assignment Statement	Reason
`middleInitial = "A.";`	`middleInitial` is of type `char`; `"A."` is a string.
`letter = firstName;`	`letter` is of type `char`; `firstName` is of class `String`.
`letter = " ";`	`letter` is of type `char`, `" "` is only one character but it is a string because of the double quotes.
`firstName = Thomas;`	`Thomas` is an undeclared identifier.
`"Edison" = lastName;`	Only a variable can appear to the left of `=`.
`lastName = ;`	The expression to the right of `=` is missing.

Figure 2.2 shows variable `myChar` with the letter B stored in it.

String Expressions Although we can't perform arithmetic on strings, Java provides the `String` class with a special string operation, called *concatenation*, that uses the + operator. The result of concatenating (joining) two strings is a new string containing the characters from both strings. For example, given the statements

```
String bookTitle;
String phrase1;
String phrase2;

phrase1 = "Introduction to Java and ";
phrase2 = "Software Design";
```

we could write

```
bookTitle = phrase1 + phrase2;
```

which results in `bookTitle` being set equal to the character string

```
"Introduction to Java and Software Design"
```

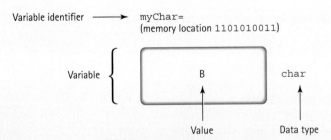

Figure 2.2 *Variable with value*

The order of the strings in the expression determines how they appear in the resulting string. If we instead write

```
bookTitle = phrase2 + phrase1;
```

then `bookTitle` is set equal to the string

```
"Software DesignIntroduction to Java and "
```

Concatenation works with named `String` constants and literal strings as well as `String` variables. For example, if we have declared the following constants:

```
final String WORD1 = "Introduction";
final String WORD3 = "Java";
final String WORD5 = "Design";
```

then we could write the following statement to assign the title of this book to the variable `bookTitle`:

```
bookTitle = WORD1 + " to " + WORD3 + " and Software " + WORD5;
```

As a result, `bookTitle` is assigned the string

```
"Introduction to Java and Software Design"
```

The preceding example demonstrates how we can combine identifiers and literal strings in a concatenation expression. Of course, if we simply want to assign the complete string to `bookTitle`, we can do so directly:

```
bookTitle = "Introduction to Java and Software Design";
```

But occasionally we need to assign a string literal that is too long to fit on one line and then a concatenation expression is necessary, as in the following statement.

```
longSentence = "The Red-Wing Blackbird hovered precariously in the gusty " +
               "breeze as he tried to display his brilliant red and yellow " +
               "epaulets to his rival suitor. ";
```

Sometimes we may also encounter a situation in which we want to add some characters to an existing string value. Suppose that `bookTitle` already contains `"Introduction to Java"` and that we wish to complete the title. We could use a statement of the form

```
bookTitle = bookTitle + " and Software Design";
```

Such a statement retrieves the value of `bookTitle` from memory, concatenates the string `" and Software Design"` to form a new string, and then assigns the new string back to `bookTitle`. The new string replaces the old value of `bookTitle` (which is destroyed).

Concatenation works only with values of type `String`. However, if we try to concatenate a value of one of Java's built-in types with a string, Java automatically converts the value into an equivalent string and performs the concatenation. For example, the code segment:

```
String result;
result = "The square of 12 is " + 144;
```

assigns the string `"The square of 12 is 144"` to the variable `result`. Java converts the integer literal `144` into the string `"144"` before performing the concatenation.

Fields   The similarity in appearance between variable and constant declarations in Java is not a coincidence. Java doesn't actually distinguish between the declaration of named constants and variables because they are just different kinds of fields. A named constant is merely a field that is given an initial value, together with the modifier `final`, which says that the value can never be changed. If we extend the template for a variable declaration to include the syntax necessary to give the variable an initial value, and add the keyword `final` to the list of modifiers, then we have a generic template for a field declaration in Java. Now that we have defined expressions, we generalize the initial value syntax to include expressions.

FieldDeclaration

```
Modifiers TypeName Identifier = Expression , Identifier = Expression ;
```

The following declarations are legal:

```
final String WORD1 = "Introduction";
final String WORD3 = "Java " + WORD1;
final String WORD5 = "Design " + WORD3;
```

and store `"Design Java Introduction"` as the value for constant `WORD5`.

Output   Have you ever asked someone, "Do you know what time it is?" only to have the person smile smugly, and say, "Yes, I do!"? This situation is like the one that currently exists between you and the computer. You now know enough Java syntax to tell the computer to assign values to variables and to concatenate strings, but the computer won't give you the results until you tell it to display them.

Early computers used printers to display their output. Older programming languages thus had output statements, such as *print* or *write* that would type the contents of a variable or a constant on the printer. As technology advanced, printers were replaced by display screens, but output was still shown on the screen as if it was being typed by a printer, line by line. In the 1970s, computer scientists at the Xerox Palo Alto Research Center developed a new approach to output in which a program could display separate panels on the screen and print or draw on each panel independently. The panels were called windows, and opened a new era in the design of user interfaces for computer programs.

Today, virtually every computer operating system supports a graphical user interface (GUI) based on windows. Such interfaces make it much easier for people to use programs; however, they require more work on the part of the programmer than did the old-fashioned printer style of output. Because Java was developed after the GUI became the standard mechanism for interactive input and output, it has built-in features to simplify the programming of a user interface, which we cover in the next chapter. Here we introduce a very simple way of writing messages on the screen.

Java provides an object that represents an output device, which is, by default, the screen. We can send messages to this object asking it to print something on the screen. The name of the object is `System.out` and the messages we can send (methods that we can apply) are `print` and `println`. For example,

```java
System.out.print("Susy" + "  " + "Sunshine");
```

prints

```
Susy  Sunshine
```

in a window on the screen. There are several things to notice about this statement. The method is invoked (message sent) by placing the method name next to the object with a dot in between. The "something" that is to be printed is called a *parameter* and is placed within the parentheses. What do you think the next code fragment prints?

```java
System.out.print("Susy");
System.out.print("  ");
System.out.print("Sunshine");
```

If you said that the two code fragments print the same thing, you would be correct. Successive messages sent via the `print` method print the strings next to each other on the same line. If you want to go to the next line after the string is printed, you use the `println` method. The code fragment,

```java
System.out.println("Susy");
System.out.println("  ");
System.out.println("Sunshine");
```

prints

Susy

Sunshine

Note that the `println` method does not go to the next line until *after* the string is printed. The second line contains two blanks, it is not the empty string. We can print variables as well as literals.

```
String myName = "Susy  Sunshine";
System.out.println(myName);
```

prints exactly the same thing on the screen as the statement

```
System.out.print("Susy  Sunshine");
```

There is a difference, however. If this example is followed by another message to `System.out`, the next string would begin on the same line. If the previous example is followed by another message to `System.out`, the next string would begin on the next line.

Beyond Minimalism: Adding Comments to a Program

All you need to create a working program is the correct combination of declarations and executable statements. The compiler ignores comments, but they are of enormous help to anyone who must read the program. Comments can appear anywhere in a program except in the middle of an identifier, a reserved word, or a literal constant.

Java comments come in two forms. The first is any sequence of characters enclosed by the `/*   */` pair. The compiler ignores anything within the pair no matter how many lines are enclosed. Here's an example:

```
String idNumber;    /* Identification number of the aircraft */
```

There is one special note about using this form of comment. When the first character of the comment is an asterisk, the comment has a special meaning that indicates it is to be used by an automatic documentation generation program called `javadoc`. For the time being, since we do not discuss `javadoc` in this text, we recommend that you avoid comments that start with `/**`.

The second, and more common, form begins with two slashes (`//`) and extends to the end of that line of the program:

```
String idNumber;    // Identification number of the aircraft
```

The compiler ignores anything after the two slashes to the end of the line.

Writing fully commented programs is good programming style. A comment should appear at the beginning of a program to explain what the program does:

```
// This program computes the weight and balance of a Beechcraft
// Starship-1 airplane, given the amount of fuel, number of
// passengers, and weight of luggage in fore and aft storage.
// It assumes that there are two pilots and a standard complement
// of equipment, and that passengers weigh 170 pounds each
```

Another good place for comments is in constant and variable declarations, where the comments explain how each identifier is used. In addition, comments should introduce each major step in a long program and should explain anything that is unusual or difficult to read (for example, a lengthy formula).

It is important to make your comments concise and to arrange them in the program so that they are easy to see and it is clear what they refer to. If comments are too long or crowd the statements in the program, they make the program more difficult to read—just the opposite of what you intended! In this text we use color to make the comments stand out from the rest of the Java code in our examples.

Program Construction

We have looked at the basic elements of Java codes: identifiers, declarations, variables, constants, expressions, assignment statements, method calls, and comments. Now let's see how to collect these elements into a program. A Java program, usually called an application, is a class containing class declarations: fields and methods. In order for the class to be a Java application, one of the methods must be named `main`. The `main` method is where execution of the Java program begins.

We have already shown the template for a field declaration; now let's look at how to declare a method. A method declaration consists of the method heading and its body, which is delimited by left and right braces. The following syntax template represents the declaration of a method.

MethodDeclaration

```
Modifiers void Identifier ( ParameterList )
{
      Statement · · ·
}
```

Here's an example of a program with just one method, the `main` method. Note that the name of the program, the class that includes `main`, is up to the programmer; we chose `PrintName`. Because a program is a class, we begin the name with an upper-case `P`.

```
//***************************************************************************
// PrintName program
// This program prints a name in two different formats
//***************************************************************************
public class PrintName
{

   public static void main(String[] args)
   {
      final String FIRST  = "Herman";     // Person's first name
      final String LAST   = "Herrmann";   // Person's last name
      final char   MIDDLE = 'G';          // Person's middle initial
      String firstLast;                   // Name in first-last format
      String lastFirst;                   // Name in last-first format

      firstLast = FIRST + " " + LAST;
      System.out.println("Name in first-last format is " + firstLast);
      lastFirst = LAST + ", " + FIRST + ", ";
      System.out.println("Name in last-first-initial format is " +
                         lastFirst + MIDDLE + ".");

   }
}
```

The program begins with a comment that explains what the program does. Next comes the class heading, which begins with the modifier public. In order to execute the class, it must be public so that the JVM can find it. If you look a little further down in the program, you see that the heading of the main method also begins with public. The JVM must also be able to find main in order to start execution there. In later chapters we see situations where we want to limit access to a field, method, or class. We do this by using the modifier private. If we used the private modifier with main, then the method would be invisible to the JVM and it wouldn't know where to start.

The class heading is followed by an open brace that begins the body of the class. The class contains the method declaration for the main method. The first line is the method heading. We are not going to explain the construction of main's heading at this point. For the time being, just memorize this heading, and use it in your programs. It is not until the end of Chapter 11 that we can explain it completely. The body of the method contains declarations of three String constants (FIRST, LAST, and MIDDLE) and two String variables (firstLast and lastFirst) and a list of executable statements. The compiler translates these executable statements into Bytecode instructions. During the execution phase of the program, these are the instructions that are executed.

Note that neither the public nor the private modifier precedes the variables declared within main. The reason is that fields declared inside the body of a method are said to be *local* to that method, which means that they are accessible only within the method. Thus, there is no need to explicitly specify that they are `private`, and they cannot be made `public`. In fact, the only modifier allowed in a local declaration is `final`.

Notice how we use spacing in the `PrintName` program to make it easy for someone to read. We use blank lines to separate statements into related groups, and we indent the entire body of the class and the `main` method. The compiler doesn't require us to format the program this way; we do so only to make it more readable. We have more to say in the next chapter about formatting a program.

Here is what the program displays on the screen when it executes:

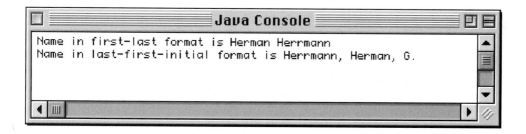

Blocks

The body of a method is an example of a *block*. This is the syntax template for a block:

Block

A block is just a sequence of zero or more statements enclosed (delimited) by a { } pair. Now we can redefine a method declaration as a heading followed by a block:

MethodDeclaration

In later chapters we define the syntax of Heading in greater detail. In the case of the `main` method, Heading is simply `public static void main(String[] args)`. Here is the syntax template for a statement, limited to the Java statements discussed in this chapter:

Statement

```
┌ NullStatement
│ LocalFieldDeclaration
│ AssignmentStatement
│ MethodCall
└ Block
```

A statement can be empty (the *null statement*). The null statement is just a semicolon (;) and looks like this:

```
;
```

It does absolutely nothing at execution time; execution just proceeds to the next statement. It is not used often.

As the syntax template shows, a statement also can be a local field declaration, an executable statement, or even a block. The latter means that you can use an entire block wherever a single statement is allowed. In later chapters where we introduce the syntax for branching and looping structures, this fact is very important.

We use blocks often, especially as parts of other statements. Leaving out a { } pair can dramatically change the meaning as well as the execution of a program. This is why we always indent the statements inside a block—the indentation makes a block easy to spot in a long, complicated program.

Notice in the syntax templates for the block and the statement that there is no mention of semicolons. Yet the `PrintName` program contains many semicolons. If you look back at the templates for class field declaration, local field declaration, assignment statement, and method call, you can see that a semicolon is required at the end of each kind of statement. However, the syntax template for the block shows no semicolon after the right brace. The rule for using semicolons in Java, then, is quite simple: Terminate each statement *except* a block with a semicolon.

One more thing about blocks and statements: According to the syntax template for a statement, a field declaration is officially considered to be a statement. A declaration, therefore, can appear wherever an executable statement can. In a block, we can mix local declarations and executable statements if we wish. However, a declaration must come before it is used.

```
{
    char ch;                        // Declaration
    ch = 'A';
    System.out.println(ch);
    String str;                     // Declaration
```

```
  str = "Hello";
  System.out.println(str);
}
```

In this book we group the declarations together because we think it is easier to read, and is therefore better style.

```
{
  // Declarations
  char    ch;
  String str;
  // Executable statements
  ch = 'A';
  System.out.println(ch);
  str = "Hello";
  System.out.println(str);
}
```

2.6 Program Entry, Correction, and Execution

Once you have a program on paper, you must enter it on the keyboard. In this section, we examine the program entry process in general. You should consult the manual for your specific computer to learn the details.

Entering a Program

The first step in entering a program is to get the computer's attention. With a personal computer, this usually means turning it on. Workstations connected to a network are usually left running all the time. You must *log on* to such a machine to get its attention. This means entering a user name and a password. The password system protects information that you've stored in the computer from being tampered with or destroyed by someone else.

Once the computer is ready to accept your commands, you tell it that you want to enter a program by running the editor. The editor is a program that allows you to create and modify programs by entering information into an area of the computer's secondary storage called a file.

> **File** A named area in secondary storage that is used to hold a collection of data; the collection of data itself

A file in a computer system is like a file folder in a filing cabinet. It is a collection of data that has a name associated with it. You usually choose the name for the file when you create it with the editor. From that point on, you refer to the file by the name you've given it.

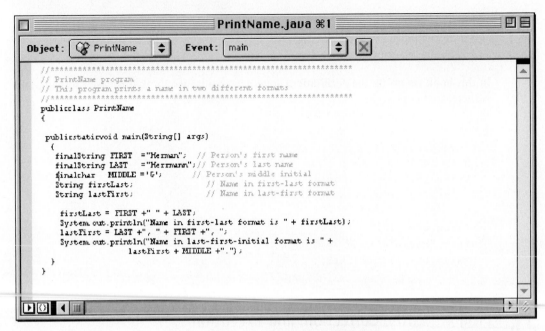

Figure 2.3 *Display screen for an editor*

There are so many different types of editors, each with different features, that we can't begin to describe them all here. But we can describe some of their general characteristics.

The basic unit of information in an editor is a display screen full of characters. The editor lets you change anything that you see on the screen.

When you create a new file, the editor clears the screen to show you that the file is empty. Then you enter your program, using the mouse and keyboard to go back and make corrections as necessary. Figure 2.3 shows an example of an editor's display screen.

Compiling and Running a Program

Once your program is stored in a file, you compile it by issuing a command to run the Java compiler. The compiler translates the program, then stores the Bytecode version into a file. The compiler may display a window with messages indicating errors in the program. Some systems let you click on an error message to automatically position the cursor in the editor window at the point where the error was detected.

If the compiler finds errors in your program (syntax errors), you have to determine their cause, go back to the editor and fix them, and then run the compiler again. Once your program compiles without errors, you can run (execute) it.

Some systems automatically run a program when it compiles successfully. On other systems, you have to issue a separate command to run the program. Whatever series of commands your system uses, the result is the same: Your program is loaded into memory and executed by the JVM.

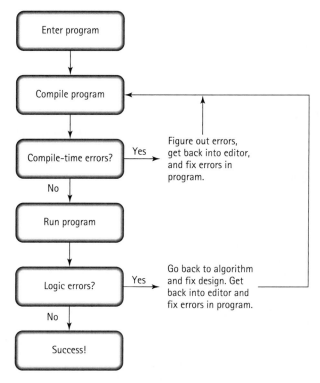

Figure 2.4   *Debugging process*

Even though a program runs, it still may have errors in its design. The computer does exactly what you tell it to do, even if that's not what you wanted it to do. If your program doesn't do what it should (a *logic error*), you have to go back to the algorithm and fix it, and then go to the editor and fix the program. Finally, you compile and run the program again. This *debugging* process is repeated until the program does what it is supposed to do (see Figure 2.4).

Finishing Up

On a workstation, once you finish working on your program, you have to *log off* by typing a command. This frees up the workstation so that someone else can use it. It also prevents someone from walking up after you leave and tampering with your files.

On a personal computer, when you're done working, you save your files and quit the editor. Turning off the power wipes out what's in the computer's memory, but your files are stored safely on disk. It is a wise precaution to periodically make a copy of your code files on a removable diskette. When a disk in a computer suffers a hardware failure, it often makes it impossible to retrieve your files. Having a backup copy on a diskette enables you to restore your files to the disk once it is repaired.

Be sure to read the manual for your particular system and editor before you enter your first program. Don't panic if you have trouble at first—almost everyone does. It becomes much easier with practice. That's why it's a good idea to first go through the process with a program such as `PrintName`, where mistakes don't matter—unlike a class programming assignment!

Problem-Solving Case Study

Display a Date in Multiple Formats

Problem   You are beginning to work on a program that needs to output dates in several formats. As a start, you decide to write a short Java application that takes a single date and displays it in the different formats, so you can be certain that all of your string expressions are correct.

Output   A window showing the date in four formats:

    Month day, year (August 18, 2001)
    day Month year (18 August 2001)
    mm/dd/yyyy (8/18/2001)
    dd/mm/yyyy (18/8/2001)

Discussion   You could easily just type the dates in the four formats as string literals in the program, but the purpose of this exercise is to develop and test the string expressions you need for the larger program.

   Because you plan to eventually use the same expressions in another program, you decide that this preliminary program should start with a set of named string constants containing the parts of a date. Then the program can use concatenation expressions to form string variables in the different date formats. In that way, all the date strings can be created before the output statements are executed.

   A date consists of three parts, the month, day, and year, but you need to write the month both by name and by number so there must be a total of four string constants. Here is the algorithmic solution:

....

Define Constants

```
MONTH_NAME = "August"
MONTH_NUMBER = "8"
DAY = "18"
YEAR = "2001"
```

Create First Format

Set first to MONTH_NAME + " " + DAY + ", " + YEAR

Create Second Format

Set second to DAY + " " + MONTH_NAME + " " + YEAR

Create Third Format

Set third to MONTH_NUMBER + "/" + DAY + "/" + YEAR

Create Fourth Format

Set fourth to DAY + "/" + MONTH_NUMBER + "/" + YEAR

Display the Dates

Print first
Print second
Print third
Print fourth

From the algorithm, we can create tables of constants and variables that help us write the declarations in the program.

Constants

Name	Value	Description
MONTH_NAME	"August"	The name of the month
MONTH_NUMBER	"8"	The number of the month
DAY	"18"	The day of the month
YEAR	"2001"	The four-digit year number

Variables

Name	Data Type	Description
first	String	Date in Month day, year format
second	String	Date in day Month year format
third	String	Date in mm/dd/yyyy format
fourth	String	Date in dd/mm/yyyy format

Now we're ready to write the program. Let's call it DateFormats. We can take the declarations from the tables and create the executable statements from the algorithm. We also include comments as necessary.

Here is the program:

```java
//*************************************************************************
// DateFormats program
// This program prints a date in four different formats by
// building strings up from the component parts of the date
// using string concatenation expressions
//*************************************************************************

public class DateFormats
{
  public static void main(String[] args)
  {
    final String MONTH_NAME = "August";    // The name of the month
    final String MONTH_NUMBER = "8";       // The number of the month
    final String DAY = "18";               // The day of the month
    final String YEAR = "2001";            // The four-digit year number
    String first;                          // Date in Month day, year format
    String second;                         // Date in day Month year format
    String third;                          // Date in mm/dd/yyyy format
    String fourth;                         // Date in dd/mm/yyyy format

    first = MONTH_NAME + " " + DAY + ", " + YEAR;     // Create Month day,
                                                      //  year format
    second = DAY + "  " + MONTH_NAME + " " + YEAR;    // Create day Month
                                                      //  year format
    third = MONTH_NUMBER + "/" + DAY + "/" + YEAR;    // Create mm/dd/yyyy
                                                      //  format
    fourth = DAY + "/" + MONTH_NUMBER + "/" + YEAR;   // Create dd/mm/yyyy
                                                      //  format

    // Print the dates on the screen
```

```
    System.out.println(first);
    System.out.println(second);
    System.out.println(third);
    System.out.println(fourth);
  }
}
```

The output from the program is

```
┌────────────────────────────────────────────────┐
│ □ ═══════════ Java Console ═══════════  🗗 🗒   │
├────────────────────────────────────────────────┤
│ August 18, 2001                             ▲  │
│ 18  August 2001                             ▒  │
│ 8/18/2001                                       │
│ 18/8/2001                                       │
│                                             ▼  │
├────────────────────────────────────────────────┤
│ ◄  ▦                                    ►      │
└────────────────────────────────────────────────┘
```

Testing and Debugging

1. Every identifier that isn't a Java reserved word must be declared. If you use a name that hasn't been declared, you get an error message.

2. If you try to declare an identifier that is the same as a reserved word in Java, you get an error message from the compiler. See Appendix A for a list of reserved words.

3. Java is a case-sensitive language. Two identifiers that are capitalized differently are treated as two different identifiers. The word `main` and all Java reserved words use only lowercase letters.

4. Check for mismatched quotes in `char` and string literals. Each `char` literal begins and ends with an apostrophe (single quote). Each string literal begins and ends with a double quote.

5. Be sure to use only the single quote (') to enclose `char` literals. There is also a reverse apostrophe (`) on most keyboards that is easily confused with the single quote. If you use the reverse apostrophe, the compiler issues an error message.

6. To use a double quote within a literal string, use the two symbols \" in a row. If you use just a double quote, it ends the string, and the compiler then sees the remainder of the string as an error. Similarly, to write a single quote in a `char` literal, use the two symbols \' without any space between them (that is, '\" is the `char` literal for a single quote).

7. In an assignment statement, be sure that the identifier to the left of = is a variable and not a named constant.

8. In assigning a value to a `String` variable, the expression to the right of = must be a `String` expression or a literal string.

9. In a concatenation expression, at least one of the two operands of + must be of class `String`.

10. Make sure your statements end in semicolons (except compound statements, which do not have a semicolon after the right brace).

11. On most Java systems, the filename that holds the program must be the same as the name of the class, but with the extension `.java`. Thus, program `DateFormats` is stored in a file called `DateFormats.java`. Using another name produces an error message from the compiler.

12. Be careful when using the `/*    */` pair to delimit comments. If you forget the `*/`, then everything that follows until the end of the next `/*    */` comment (or the end of your program) is treated as a comment. Also, remember to avoid starting comments of this form with two asterisks (`/**`) because comments of that form are used by the `javadoc` program.

13. Check that every open brace ({) in your program is matched by a close brace (}) in the right place. Braces determine the beginning and end of blocks in Java, and their placement affects the structure of the program. Similarly, it is always wise to check that parentheses are used in matched pairs in your program.

Summary of Classes

Programming with an object-oriented language depends heavily on the use of class types from the language's standard library. As we progress through this book we steadily introduce you to new classes in the Java library. In this section we summarize all of the classes and methods that a chapter has added to your repertoire. The summary is presented as a table, organized hierarchically. The major divisions of the table are the packages containing the classes (the name you need to include in an `import` declaration). Within a package we list the classes and what the class provides.

Package Name

Class Name	Comments
`java.lang`	Automatically imported to every Java program
`String`	
`System.out`	Instantiated automatically
Instance Methods: `print(String)`	
`println(String)`	

Summary

The syntax (grammar) of the Java language is defined by a metalanguage. In this text, we use a form of metalanguage called syntax templates. We describe the semantics (meaning) of Java statements in English.

Identifiers are used in Java to name things. Some identifiers, called reserved words, have predefined meanings in the language; others are created by the programmer. The identifiers you invent are restricted to those *not* reserved by the Java language. Reserved words are listed in Appendix A.

Identifiers are associated with memory locations by declarations. A declaration may give a name to a location whose value does not change (a constant) or to one whose value can change (a variable). Every constant and variable has an associated data type or class. Java provides many predefined data types and classes. In this chapter we have examined the type `char` and `String` class. A class contains fields and methods that describe the behavior of an object. An object is an instance of the class that describes it.

The assignment operator is used to change the value of a variable by assigning it the value of an expression. At execution time, the expression is evaluated and the result is stored in the variable. With the `String` class, the plus sign (+) is an operator that concatenates two strings. A string expression can concatenate any number of strings to form a new `String` value.

Simple output to the screen is accomplished by using the `System.out` object that is provided in Java. There are two methods defined on this object: `print` and `println`. `System.out.print("A string")` prints whatever is between the parentheses on the screen. `println` behaves exactly the same as `print`, except that `println` goes to the next line after it finishes the printing.

A Java application program is a class containing one or more class declarations, which are fields and methods. One of the methods *must* be named `main`. Execution of a program class always begins with the `main` method.

Quick Check

1. Every Java program consists of at least how many methods? (p. 72)
2. Use the following syntax template to decide whether your last name is a valid Java identifier. (p. 50)

Identifier

3. Write a Java constant declaration that gives the name ZED to the value 'Z'. (pp. 62–63)

4. Which of the following words are reserved words in Java? (*Hint*: Look in Appendix A.)

```
public static final  pi  float  integer  sqrt
```

(p. 53)

5. Declare a char variable named letter and a String variable named street. (pp. 60–61)

6. Assign the value "Elm" to the String variable street. (pp. 60–61)

7. Write an output statement that prints the title of this book (*Introduction to Java and Software Design*) on the screen. (pp. 68–69)

8. What does the following code segment output on the screen?

```
String str;
str = "Abraham";
System.out.println("The answer is " + str + "Lincoln");
```

(pp. 68–70)

9. The following program code is incorrect. Rewrite it, using correct syntax for the comment.

```
String address;   / Employee's street address,
                  / including apartment
```

(pp. 70–71)

10. Fill in the blanks in this program.

```
_____ class QuickCheck
{
  public static void _____(String args[])
  ____
    final _____ TITLE = "Mr";   // First part of title
    String guest1;              // First guest
    String guest2;              // Second guest
    guest1 ____ TITLE + ". " + "Jones";
    guest2 ____ TITLE + "s. " + "Smith";
    System._____.print("The guests in attendance were " _____;
    System.out._____(guest1 _____ " and " + guest2);
  ____
}
```

(pp. 71–72)

11. Show precisely the output produced by running the program in Question 10 above. (pp. 71-72)

Answers

1. A program must have at least one method—the `main` method.
2. Unless your last name is hyphenated, it probably is a valid Java identifier.
3. `private final char ZED = 'Z';`
4. `public`, `static`, `final`, `float`
5. `private char letter;`
   `private String street;`
6. `street = "Elm";`
7. `System.out.print("Introduction to Java and Software Design");`
8. The answer is AbrahamLincoln
9. `String address;   // Employee's street address,`
   `                   // including apartment`

   or

   `String address;   /* Employee's street address,`
   `                      including apartment         */`

10.

```
public class QuickCheck
{

  public static void main(String args[])

  {

     final String TITLE = "Mr";   // First part of title
     String guest1;               // First guest
     String guest2;               // Second guest

     guest1 = TITLE + ". " + "Jones";
     guest2 = TITLE + "s. " + "Smith";

     System.out.print("The guests in attendance were " );
     System.out.println(guest1 + " and " + guest2);
  }
}
```

11. The guests in attendance were Mr. Jones and Mrs. Smith

Exam Preparation Exercises

1. Mark the following identifiers either valid or invalid.

		Valid	Invalid
a.	item#1	_____	_____
b.	data	_____	_____
c.	y	_____	_____
d.	3Set	_____	_____
e.	PAY_DAY	_____	_____
f.	bin-2	_____	_____
g.	num5	_____	_____
h.	Sq Ft	_____	_____

2. Given these four syntax templates:

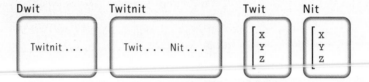

mark the following "Dwits" either valid or invalid.

		Valid	Invalid
a.	XYZ	_____	_____
b.	123	_____	_____
c.	X1	_____	_____
d.	23Y	_____	_____
e.	XY12	_____	_____
f.	Y2Y	_____	_____
g.	ZY2	_____	_____
h.	XY23X1	_____	_____

3. Match each of the following terms with the correct definition (1 through 15) given below. There is only one correct definition for each term.

_____ a. program   _____ g. variable
_____ b. algorithm   _____ h. constant
_____ c. compiler   _____ i. memory
_____ d. identifier   _____ j. syntax
_____ e. compilation phase _____ k. semantics
_____ f. execution phase   _____ l. block

(1) A symbolic name made up of letters, digits, underscores, and dollar signs but not beginning with a digit
(2) A place in memory where a data value that cannot be changed is stored
(3) A program that takes a program in a high-level language and translates it into machine code or Bytecode
(4) An input device
(5) The time spent planning a program
(6) Grammar rules

(7) A sequence of statements enclosed by braces

(8) Meaning

(9) A program that translates assembly language instructions into machine code

(10) When the compiled version of a program is being run

(11) A place in memory where a data value that can be changed is stored

(12) When a program in a high-level language is converted into machine code or Bytecode

(13) A part of the computer that can hold both program and data

(14) Instructions for solving a problem in a finite amount of time with a finite amount of data

(15) Data type specifications and instructions used by a computer to solve a problem

4. Which of the following are reserved words and which are programmer-defined identifiers?

	Reserved	*Programmer-Defined*
a. `char`	_____	_____
b. `sort`	_____	_____
c. `INT`	_____	_____
d. `new`	_____	_____
e. `Public`	_____	_____

5. Reserved words can be used as variable names. (True or False?)

6. In a Java program containing just one method, that method can be named either `main` or `Main`. (True or False?)

7. If `s1` and `s2` are `String` variables containing `"blue"` and `"bird"`, respectively, what does each of the following statements print?
   a. `System.out.println("s1 = " + s1 + "s2 = " + s2);`
   b. `System.out.println("Result:" + s1 + s2);`
   c. `System.out.println("Result:   " + s1 + s2);`
   d. `System.out.println("Result:   " + s1 + ' ' + s2);`

8. Show precisely what is output by the following statement.

```
System.out.println("A rolling" +
    "stone" +
    "gathers" +
    "no" +
    "moss");
```

9. How many characters can be stored into a variable of type `char`?

10. How many characters are in the empty string?

11. A variable of class `String` can be assigned to a variable of type `char`. (True or False?)

12. A literal string can be assigned to a variable of class `String`. (True or False?)

13. What is the difference between the literal string `"computer"` and the identifier `computer`?

14. What is output by the following code segment? (All variables are of class String.)

```
street = "Elm St.";
address = "1425B";
city = "Amaryllis";
state = "Iowa";
streetAddress = address + " " + street;
System.out.println(streetAddress);
System.out.println(city);
System.out.println(", " + state);
```

15. Correct the following program so that it displays "Martin Luther King Jr."

```
// This program is full of errors
class LotsOfErrors;
{
  void main (string[] args);
  {
    constant String FIRST : Martin";
    constant String MID : "Luther;
    constant String LAST : King

    String name;
    character initial;
    name = Martin + Luther + King;
    initial = MID;
    LAST = "King Jr.";
    System.out.println('Name = ' + name));
    System.out.println(mid
  }
```

Programming Warm-Up Exercises

1. Write the output statement that prints your name.
2. Write three consecutive output statements that print the following three lines.

```
The moon
is
blue.
```

3. Write declaration statements to declare three variables of class String and two variables of type char. The String variables should be named make, model, and color. The char variables should be named plateType and classification.

4. Write a series of output statements that display the values in the variables declared in Exercise 3. Each value should be preceded by an identifying message.

5. Change the `PrintName` program (page 72) so that it also prints the name in the format

```
First-name Middle-initial. Last-name
```

Make `MIDDLE` a `String` constant rather than a `char` constant. Define a new `String` variable to hold the name in the new format. Use the existing named constants, any literal strings that are needed for punctuation and spacing, and concatenation operations to create the new string. Print the string, labeled appropriately.

6. Print the following groups of text.

   a. `Four score`
      `and seven years ago`
   b. `Four score`
      `and seven`
      `years ago`
   c. `Four score`
      `and`
      `seven`
      `years ago`
   d. `Four`
      `score`
      `and`
      `seven`
      `years`
      `ago`

7. Enter and run the following program. Be sure to type it exactly as it appears here.

```
//*************************************************************
// HelloWorld program
// This program displays two simple messages
//*************************************************************
public class HelloWorld
{
  public static void main(String[] args)
  {
    final String MSG1 = "Hello world.";
    String msg2;
```

```
    System.out.println(MSG1);
    msg2 = MSG1 + " " + MSG1 + " " + MSG1;
    System.out.println(msg2);
  }
}
```

Programming Problems

1. Write a Java application that displays a series of Haiku poems. A Haiku poem is written in three phrases. The first phrase has five syllables, the second has seven syllables, and the last phrase again has five syllables. For example:

   Bright flash then silence
   My expensive computer
   Has gone to heaven

   Your application should define string constants with four phrases of five syllables and two phrases of seven syllables. Use string concatenation expressions to construct every possible 5–7–5 permutation of these phrases and display each one. Do not use the same phrase twice in any poem. See if you can create phrases that make sense together in every permutation. Be sure to include appropriate comments in your program, choose meaningful identifiers, and use indentation as we do in the programs in this chapter.

2. Write an application that simulates the child's game "My Grandmother's Trunk." In this game, the players sit in a circle, and the first player names something that goes in the trunk: "In my grandmother's trunk, I packed a pencil." The next player restates the sentence and adds something new to the trunk: "In my grandmother's trunk, I packed a pencil and a red ball." Each player in turn adds something to the trunk, attempting to keep track of all the items that are already there.

   Your application should simulate just five turns in the game. Starting with the empty string simulate each player's turn by concatenating a new word or phrase to the existing string, and print the result.

3. Write a program that prints its own grading form. The program should output the name and number of the class, the name and number of the programming assignment, your name and student number, and labeled spaces for scores reflecting correctness, quality of style, late deduction, and overall score. An example of such a form is the following:

   ```
   CS-101 Introduction to Programming and Problem Solving

   Programming Assignment 1

   Sally A. Student    ID Number 431023877

   Grade Summary:
   ```

```
Program Correctness:      Quality of Style:
Late Deduction:           Overall Score:
Comments:
```

Case Study Follow-Up Exercises

1. Change the `DateFormats` program so that the four formats are shown in the opposite order on the screen.
2. In the `DateFormats` program, explain what takes place in the statement that assigns a value to the string variable `third`.
3. Change the `DateFormats` program so that the third and fourth formats use hyphens (-) instead of slashes (/).
4. Change the `DateFormats` program so that your birth date is displayed in the four formats.

Event-Driven Output

■ To be able to construct a code segment that creates a window on the screen.

■ To be able to construct a code segment that displays a message in a window on the screen.

■ To be able to use a layout manager to organize messages in a window.

■ To be able to invoke a method.

■ To be able to use a constructor to instantiate an object.

■ To be able to determine what is displayed by a given code segment.

■ To be able to write an event listener for a window-closing event.

In the last chapter, we looked at the components that make up a program: classes, fields, and methods. We described the object that Java provides for writing simple information on the screen (`System.out`). In this chapter we look at two fundamental capabilities that Java provides. The first is the ability to create a window on the screen and display information in the window, and the second is the ability to recognize and handle an asynchronous event—the closing of a window.

3.1 Classes and Methods

In Chapter 1, we defined an interface as a connecting link at a shared boundary that allows independent systems to meet and act on or communicate with each other. In this chapter we use an interface: The independent systems are the computer and you the programmer. The shared boundary is the screen, and the link is the set of capabilities that Java provides for writing information on the screen.

Java supports many different classes of windows and interface components. In fact, entire books have been written just to explain all of the features that Java supports for output. In this text, we use a very simple subset of Java's capabilities. Once you thoroughly understand the basics, you can easily learn about Java's other interface features on your own.

Frames

The type of window that we use in this text is called a *frame*. It has all of the basic features that you are used to seeing in a window on a personal computer: the ability to change size, to be closed, to be turned into an icon (a small pictorial representation of the window), and so on. Our programs won't support all of these features. When you try to click on one of them, the window may simply do nothing in response. In later chapters, we show you how to handle more of a frame's features in your programs.

To use a frame for output in Java, your program must perform seven steps:

1. Import the package containing the `Frame` class from Java's library.
2. Declare a variable of class `Frame`.
3. Ask Java to create an instance of class `Frame` (an object) and assign it to the variable.
4. Specify a layout manager for the `Frame` object.
5. Add output to the `Frame` object.
6. Pack the `Frame` object (adjust its size to fit the output it contains).
7. Show the `Frame` object on the screen.

In the remainder of this section we examine each of these steps in turn. Along the way, we also review the syntax and semantics for calling a method in Java, and we show you how to use additional types that Java defines for output.

Packages In order to access the tools that you need to create and manipulate a window, you must import some classes available in a Java package. Here is the syntax diagram for a such declaration:

ImportDeclaration

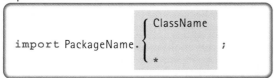

As the template shows, an import declaration begins with the keyword `import`, the name of a package and a dot (period). Following the period you can either write the name of a class in the package, or type an asterisk (*). The declaration ends with a semicolon. If you know that we want to use exactly one class in a particular package, then you can simply give its name (Class-name) in the import declaration. More often, however, you'll want to use more than one of the classes in a package, and the asterisk is a shorthand notation to the compiler that says, "Import whatever classes from this package that this program uses."

Why would you ever want to use the first form, when the asterisk has the same effect and is easier to type? The answer is that the first form documents the specific class that you intend to use, and it causes the compiler to warn you if you mistakenly attempt to use some additional class from the package. In this text the asterisk typically is used instead of the Class-name, but a comment is used to document the class(es) being imported.

For example, the `Frame` class is contained in the Java package called `awt` (which stands for abstract window toolkit). Many of Java's library packages are contained in the master package called `java`, which we mentioned previously. Java requires us to indicate that `awt` is part of the `java` package; we do this by writing the two names joined by a period in our import declaration:

```
import java.awt.*;   // Supplies Frame class for output display
```

Declaring and Instantiating a `Frame` Object Once you have imported the `Frame` class, you can declare a variable of type `Frame` the same way that you declare a `char` or `String` variable:

```
Frame outputDisplay;   // A variable of class Frame
```

Recall that an object is an instance of a class. This declaration says to set aside a place in memory called `outputDisplay` that is to contain an object of class `Frame`. Like any other variable, the variable called `outputDisplay` is empty until you assign it a value. What sort of value is assigned to a `Frame` field? The answer to this question is both trivial and deep: A `Frame` object is assigned. The answer is trivial because it seems so obvious, like the answer to the question "Who is buried in Grant's tomb?" In practice, it is really that simple. You can just write the following assignment statement using the new operator:

```
outputDisplay = new Frame();
```

Java then instantiates a new object of class `Frame` and assigns it to `outputDis-play`. The answer to our question is deep because the actual contents of a `Frame` object are quite complex. You could read a biography of President Grant as one way of knowing who is buried in his tomb. Likewise, you could read all of the source code in the `awt` package to learn how `Frame` objects work. Fortunately, Java makes it unnecessary for you to do this through the principle of abstraction: You don't have to understand what makes `Frame` objects work in order to use them.

The `Frame` that is referenced by `outputDisplay` is an empty window that is waiting to be filled and then shown on the screen. You fill it by adding display elements to it.

How does Java know where the elements should be placed within the window? You can either tell it manually or let Java handle their layout automatically. Manual placement of elements allows you to precisely control the appearance of output within the window, but it requires that you compute the location of each element and specify it in your program. We take the simpler approach of letting Java handle the layout automatically.

Because Java provides several different styles of automatic layout, you have to indicate which one to use. The style of layout is determined by specifying the name of a layout manager through a method associated with the `Frame` object assigned to `outputDis-play`. The method is called `setLayout`.

> **Layout manager**   A class that automatically manages the placement of display elements within a window on the screen

Method Invocation

Recall that methods are subprograms that are called upon to perform some predefined set of actions. You can use the `print` and `println` methods to print strings on the screen. Using object-oriented terminology, we say that we are sending messages to an object called `System.out`. Technically, we say that we are *calling* methods associated with the object.

A call to a method is another form of executable statement in Java. You can write the call statement simply by specifying the name of the method, followed by a list of parameters enclosed in parentheses. The parameters to `print` and `println` are the strings to be printed. We say that the parameters are *passed* to a method.

> **Call**   A statement that causes a method to be executed. In Java, a method is called by writing its name, followed by a list of parameters enclosed in parentheses.
>
> **Parameter**   An expression used for communicating values to a method

In a call, the method name may or may not have to be appended to an object name with a dot in between. (We explain these different forms of a call statement shortly.)

The effect of the call is to cause control of the computer to jump to the instructions in the method, which make use of the values given to it as parameters. Control of the computer returns to the statement following the call when the method has completed its task.

Here is the syntax template for a call statement.

Call

```
ObjectName . MethodName ( parameter , parameter . . .) ;
```

In Java, methods come in three flavors: instance methods, class methods, and helper methods. Instance methods are associated with individual objects. Class methods are associated with classes. Helper or auxiliary methods are subprograms within a class that help other methods in the class. Instance methods are covered here.

When you create an object of a given class, it has a set of instance methods associated with it. Because there can be more than one object of a given class, you must also identify the object when you call the method. In object-oriented terms, you must designate the object to which the message is being sent. The object name is appended in front of the method name with a dot in between. In the following call

```
System.out.println("Good morning.");
```

`System.out` is the name of the object with which the `println` method is associated.

As you examine the template, you should note that the parameters in a call are optional, but the parentheses are required. You sometimes write call statements of the form

```
myObject.methodName();
```

in which there are no parameters.

After a method's job is done, control passes to the next statement after the call. This form of method call is used as a separate statement in the code. Methods that are used in this way are called void methods. In the next chapter we examine a different form of method call that is written within an expression to compute a value as part of evaluating the expression.

> **Void method** A method that is called as a separate statement. The method does not return a value.

The `setLayout` method takes one parameter, a layout manager object. A layout manager is another of Java's classes that you instantiate with the use of `new`, just as you did to create a new `Frame` object. Let's use the simplest of Java's layout managers, called `FlowLayout`. Thus, a call to the `setLayout` method associated with the `Frame` object `outputDisplay` is written as follows

```
outputDisplay.setLayout(new FlowLayout());
```

The `FlowLayout` manager's responsibility is to automatically place elements that you add to a frame in the order that you add them. The first element goes in the upper-left corner of the window, and the next element goes to the right of it, on the same line. When there is no more room left on a line, the manager moves to the next line in the window and continues adding elements there.

Let's review the steps covered so far.

```
import java.awt.*;          // Supplies Frame class for output display
    ⋮
Frame outputDisplay;        // Declare a variable of class Frame
outputDisplay = new Frame(); // Assign the variable a new Frame object
// Call the setLayout method associated with outputDisplay
// An object of class FlowLayout is passed as a parameter
outputDisplay.setLayout(new FlowLayout());
```

It is important to note that we can instantiate an object within a parameter list. The parameter of `setLayout` is an object of type `FlowLayout` created by `new`.

Putting Elements in the Window We have now seen how to import the `Frame` class, declare a `Frame` variable, instantiate a `Frame` object, and specify the layout manager for the frame. A frame is called a container class because you can add elements into it. The remaining steps are to add elements to the frame, pack the frame, and show it on the screen. All of these steps involve additional instance method calls.

Container class A class into which you can add other elements

Initially, we just add elements called labels to our frames. A *label* is a block of text that is placed into the frame. We can add the label to the frame using the `add` instance method. Here is an example:

```
outputDisplay.add(new Label("This is the text in the label. "));
```

The `add` method places a new object into the frame.

We can also declare a variable to be of class `Label`, assign it a value, and pass the variable as a parameter to the `add` method, as shown below.

```
Label someLabel;
someLabel = new Label("This is the text in the label. ");
outputDisplay.add(someLabel);
```

The first way of adding a label to a frame is simpler. But when you need a label that can be added to a frame at multiple points in a program, it's easier to declare and instantiate it separately. Then, you can add it to the frame at any point in the program simply by writing:

```
outputDisplay.add(someLabel);
```

Constructors In the example in the last section, you used the `new` operation to create an object of class `Label` within the parameter list of the `add` method call:

```
outputDisplay.add(new Label("This is the text in the label. "));
```

Once again, because of Java's use of abstraction, you don't need to know the details of what a `Label` object contains. You can simply accept that it has been properly defined in the Java library and that the `add` method uses it appropriately.

You might notice that the portion of the parameter list following `new` looks very similar to a method call: It is an identifier followed by a value within parentheses. That is because it is really a call to a special method, known as a constructor, that is part of every class. The constructor for a given class is called whenever a new object of that class is created, and its purpose is to provide the instructions the computer follows in instantiating the object.

> **Constructor** A method that has the same name as the class containing it; this method is called whenever an object of that class is instantiated

Constructors are class methods with the special feature that they have the same name as the class.[1] In the case of the constructor for the `Label` class, there is one parameter, a string that specifies the text to appear in the label.

If you look back through this section, you should now recognize that we have used two other constructors: `Frame()` and `FlowLayout()`. Both of these constructors have empty parameter lists.

The capitalization of constructor names doesn't follow our usual rule of starting a method name with a lowercase letter. The reason is that the Java library uses the convention that class names begin with an uppercase letter, and the constructor name *must* be spelled exactly the same as the name of the class that contains it.

The call to the constructor method isn't preceded by an object name. The reason is that the constructor is a class method not an instance method; it is associated with the class itself, rather than with an object. This makes sense if you stop to consider that the constructor is used to create an object *before* it is assigned to a field. Thus, it can't be associated with a particular object name.

---

[1] A class method can have any name, but when its name is the same as the class containing it, then it is also a constructor.

Only two steps remain to cause our frame to be displayed on the screen. You must pack it by calling a method that adjusts its size to fit its contents. And you must call a method to show it on the screen. These two method calls are quite simple:

```
outputDisplay.pack();
outputDisplay.show();
```

As you can see by the way that the calls are written, they are both void methods. Now let's put all the pieces together to show their relationship to each other. Our list of seven steps is repeated here within the comments in the code.

```
import java.awt.*;     // Import the package containing the Frame class

public class FrameExample ...

private static Frame outputDisplay;  // Declare a field of class Frame

final String WORDS = "Java and Software Design";
...
// Create a new instance of class Frame and assign it to outputDisplay
outputDisplay = new Frame();

// Specify a layout manager for the frame object
outputDisplay.setLayout(new FlowLayout());

// Add output to the frame object
outputDisplay.add(new Label("The title of this book is "));
outputDisplay.add(new Label("Introduction to " + WORDS));

// Specify a layout manager for the frame object
outputDisplay.pack(); // Pack the frame (adjust its size to fit the output)
outputDisplay.show(); // Show the frame on the screen
...
```

The ellipses (…) in this code segment indicate pieces of the Java program that are yet to be filled in. Let's now put all these steps together into a program. Let's redo the program that prints Mr. Herrmann's name in two formats, but let's use a window that the program constructs rather than using System.out.

```
//***********************************************************************
// PrintName program
// This program prints a name in two different formats
//***********************************************************************
import java.awt.*;     // Contains Frame class
public class PrintName
{
  public static void main(String[] args)
```

```
{
    final String FIRST   = "Herman";     // Person's first name
    final String LAST    = "Herrmann";   // Person's last name
    final char   MIDDLE = 'G';           // Person's middle initial
    Frame outputDisplay;                 // Declare frame object

    String firstLast;                    // Name in first-last format
    String lastFirst;                    // Name in last-first format

    outputDisplay = new Frame();              // Create a Frame object
    outputDisplay.setLayout(new FlowLayout()) // Specify layout manager

    firstLast = FIRST + " " + LAST;
    outputDisplay.add (new Label("Name in first-last format is "
        + firstLast));

    lastFirst = LAST + ", " + FIRST + ", ";
    outputDisplay.add(new Label("Name in last-first-initial format is "
        + lastFirst + MIDDLE + "."));

    outputDisplay.pack();
    outputDisplay.show();
  }
}
```

The output screen from this program is shown on page 105.

 ## Background Information

The Origins of Java

If we were to chart the history of programming languages, we would find several distinct families of languages that have their origins in the early days of computing. When the idea of high-level languages first arose, it seemed that everybody had their own notion of the ideal form for a programming language. The result is known as the *Tower of Babel* period of programming languages. As more programs were written, the cost of rewriting them to use the features of a new language increased, and the computing world concentrated on a few languages. These included FORTRAN, Algol, COBOL, Basic, PL/1, Lisp, and BCPL.

As computers were used in more sophisticated ways, it was necessary to create more powerful languages. In many cases, these new languages were just expanded versions of older languages. Expanding a language allows older programs to be used unchanged, but enables

continued ▼

The Origins of Java

programmers to add to programs using the language's new features. This strategy is known as *upward compatibility*. A good example is the FORTRAN series that began with FORTRAN, then FORTRAN II, FORTRAN IV, FORTRAN 77, FORTRAN 90, and now High Performance FORTRAN.

Sometimes, however, different extensions to a language result in excess complexity. The solution is to redesign the language to eliminate conflicting features while preserving its desirable qualities. For example, Pascal replaced the Algol language series and was itself superseded by the Modula series of languages. Java is a redesign of languages derived from BCPL (Basic Combined Programming Language).

In the 1960s, BCPL had a small but loyal following, primarily in Europe. From BCPL, another language arose with its name abbreviated to B. In the early 1970s, Dennis Ritchie, working on a new language at AT&T Bell Labs, adopted features from the B language and decided that the successor to B naturally should be named C.

In 1985 Bjarne Stroustrup, also of Bell Labs, invented the C++ programming language. To the C language he added features for object-oriented programming. Instead of naming the language D, the Bell Labs group named it C++ in a humorous vein. As we see later, ++ signifies the *increment* operation in the C, C++, and Java languages. Given a variable *x*, the expression *x*++ means to increment (add 1 to) the current value of *x*. Therefore, the name C++ suggests it is the successor of the C language.

C includes many features that are close to the level of machine code, allowing programmers to write detailed instructions for the computer. C++ adds features that enable programmers to write instructions at a very powerful and abstract level that is far removed from machine language. If used with care, this combination of features enables programmers to "shift gears" between easily programming complex operations and writing instructions that are close to machine code. However, many people find it difficult to keep the features separate and view the combination as fraught with potential for introducing errors.

In the early 1990s, James Gosling, working at Sun Microsystems, needed a language for programming microprocessors being used in consumer electronics (for example, digital cameras). Like Stroustrop, he began with C but decided to eliminate features that would conflict with the structures that he was adding. The Algol family of languages, as well as several experimental programming languages inspired some of the new features. He called his language Oak, and spent several years experimenting with it and refining it. When the popularity of the Internet began to grow, Gosling worked with a team of designers at Sun to adapt Oak for writing programs that could operate over the network. The revised language was renamed Java and released to the public in May of 1996.

Java achieves many of the capabilities of C++ in a less complicated fashion. It supports programming for the Internet and writing programs with graphical user interfaces that are now the standard for interactive I/O. In addition, Java programs are highly portable. These features combined to cause the popularity of Java to skyrocket in the first year after it was released. It is very rare for a new programming language to appear and achieve popularity so quickly. Because Java is powerful yet simple, it has also become popular as a language for teaching programming.

3.2 Formatting Output

To format a program's output means to control how it appears visually on the screen or on a printer. In the last section we used the layout manager called `FlowLayout` to arrange our output on the screen. In this section, we introduce another layout manger, called `GridLayout`, and examine how to align text within labels.

Using `GridLayout` for Tabular Output

We introduced `FlowLayout` as the simplest of Java's layout managers. The advantage of `FlowLayout` is that it entirely manages the placement of labels as we add them to a frame. This simplicity is convenient, but it also prevents us from controlling the appearance of output on the screen. For example, in the Case Study at the end of this chapter we display a date in various formats. We do not have the option of telling `FlowLayout` to place each date on a separate line. If we use the `GridLayout` manager, however, we gain the ability to control the position of a label with respect to others in the frame.

GridLayout works much the same as `FlowLayout` in that we simply add labels to the frame, and the layout manager places them consecutively into the available space. The only difference is that `GridLayout` partitions the frame into a fixed number of rows and columns—a rectangular grid. Starting with the top row and the leftmost column, `GridLayout` fills successive columns, moving to the next row when it has filled every column on the row. Every column is the same size as every other column, and the rows are also equal in size. Figure 3.1 shows a frame with a 3 × 2 grid.

To specify `GridLayout` as the manager for the frame, you must provide the constructor with a pair of integer parameters that determine the number of rows and columns in the frame. If one of the parameters is zero, then that dimension isn't specified and the grid grows as needed in that direction to accommodate the contents of the frame. The first parameter is the number of rows and the second parameter is the number of columns.

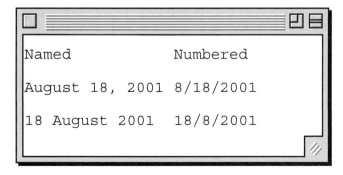

Figure 3.1   *A grid layout with three rows and two columns*

For example, if we are printing dates in two columns as shown in Figure 3.1, the layout is specified with a method call to setLayout as shown here.

```
dateWindow.setLayout(new GridLayout(3, 2));   // 3 rows and 2 columns
```

If you wanted the dateWindow frame to have two columns and an arbitrary number of rows, you would write the call with the first parameter to the GridLayout constructor being zero.

```
dateWindow.setLayout(new GridLayout(0, 2));   // Any # of rows of 2 columns
```

Using zero for the number of columns (the second parameter) would allow Grid-Layout to partition the frame into any number of columns. The number it chooses depends on the size of the largest label (since all columns are equal in size) and the number of these labels that can fit horizontally on the screen. Because this could lead to some rather strange column configurations, it is more common for the user to specify the number of columns. The most common use of GridLayout is to display a table of values, often with a text label at the top of each column (called a *column heading*) that explains what is contained in the column. Figure 3.1 uses the column headings "Named" and "Numbered."

Alignment of Text within Labels

By default, the text within a label begins at the left edge of the label. Sometimes, however, you'll want to center the text within the label or have it appear as far to the right as possible within the label. Java allows you to do this by providing a second parameter for use when calling the Label constructor. The parameter can be any of three predefined constants that are imported with the Label class. The constants are Label.LEFT, Label.CENTER, and Label.RIGHT. For example, if you want the column heading "Named" in Figure 3.1 to be centered, you would write:

```
dateWindow.add(new Label("Named", Label.CENTER));
```

If instead you write

```
dateWindow.add(new Label("Named", Label.RIGHT));
```

then the text would be positioned as far to the right as possible within the label. Because the usual position for text is toward the left, you rarely need to use Label.LEFT. Figure 3.2 shows the result of centering the headings from the example in Figure 3.1.

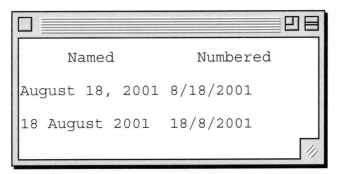

Figure 3.2   *A grid with centered headings in the first row*

3.3 Handling Events

If you enter the `PrintName` program on page 100 into the computer and run it, the result is a window like that shown here. Compare this window with the one from the version of `PrintName` in Chapter 2.

If you run this application yourself, you discover that the window just stays there. Nothing you do, short of using an operating system command to stop the program, makes it go away. The situation that now exists between you and the computer is analogous to asking someone what time it is, only to have them hold their watch in front of your face, refusing to take it away. We're able to get the computer to tell us its results, but it does so with rather poor manners.

Typically, a user would expect to make the window go away by closing it. On most systems, closing a window is a matter of clicking on some symbol at the top of the window. However, this has no effect on your frame because your program doesn't contain any instructions that tell the computer what to do when the user clicks with the mouse.

Recall from Chapter 1 that one of the control structures in a Java program is asynchronous control. A mouse click is an action that can trigger the program to perform a set of instructions at any time during its execution. That is why it is called asynchronous, which means not connected with a specific moment in time. The program can be busily working away performing some operation; you can choose that random moment to click the mouse. The program has to stop what it is doing and transfer control to the

> **Asynchronous**   Not occurring at the same moment in time as some specific operation of the computer. In other words, not synchronized with the program's actions.

instructions that take care of the mouse click. Once it has responded to your action, control returns to the program at the point at which it was interrupted. In Java, a user action of this form is called an event, and responding to it is called event handling Events are handled by special methods called event handlers.

The event-handling process sounds very much like calling a method, but there is a basic difference. A method call is a statement in our program that calls the method at a specific point in the program's execution. An event handler, on the other hand, can implicitly be called at any time, and there is no corresponding method call statement anywhere in the program. How then is the event handler called?

The answer is that there are objects called event listeners whose purpose is to watch for (i.e., listen for) events to occur and respond to them. An object that generates an event is called an event source. When an event source generates an event, we say that the source is firing the event. Every event source keeps a list of the listeners that want to be notified when that kind of event occurs. Letting an event source know that a listener wants to be notified is called registering the listener.

> **Event** An action, such as a mouse click, that takes place asynchronously with respect to the execution of the program
>
> **Event handling** The process of responding to events that can occur at any time during execution of the program
>
> **Event handler** A method that is part of an event listener and is invoked when the listener receives a corresponding event
>
> **Event listener** An object that is waiting for one or more events to occur
>
> **Event source** An object that generates an event
>
> **Firing an event** An event source generating an event
>
> **Registering the listener** Adding the listener to an event source object's list of interested listeners

Each listener has one or more methods that are designed to respond to (handle) events. These listeners are waiting in the background, watching diligently for events to occur. When an event occurs, the appropriate listeners are notified and the appropriate event handlers are invoked. When the event handler returns (method finishes executing), the program continues executing. Figure 3.3 illustrates the process. If there is no listener that is interested or the interested listener doesn't have an event handler for that particular type of event, the event is ignored and the program continues uninterrupted.

Because program `PrintName` doesn't have an event listener with an event-handling method for the window-closing event, it just ignores our attempt to close the window and continues to show us the frame. You need to add an event listener with a handler method to the program so that it behaves with better manners.

3.4 Register an Event Listener

As we've already said, an event handler is a method of the listener object. But how do you tell the event source that the listener wants to be notified when the event occurs? The answer is that you have to register the listener with the event source object. To put this in more familiar terms, let's look at an analogy.

Suppose you are traveling and have told a friend to call you, and you give her the phone number of your hotel. She calls the hotel and the hotel operator answers. Your friend asks for you and the operator connects the call to your room phone. In this analogy, your friend is an event source, the operator is the event listener, and your

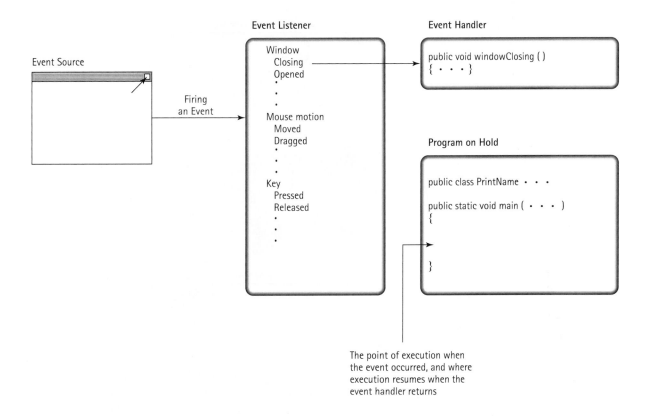

Figure 3.3   *Event handling*

room phone is the event handler. By giving the number to your friend, you registered the listener with the event source.

The hotel has multiple guests and takes many calls, with the operator directing each call to the proper room. In the same way, a single event listener can have multiple event-handler methods for different kinds of events. When the event listener is invoked, it is passed an object of one of Java's Event classes. The Event object includes a method that the event listener can call to determine the specific type of event that has occurred, and from that information the listener decides which of its event handlers to call. Figure 3.4 illustrates this analogy.

Registering an event listener is accomplished by calling a method associated with the event-source object. By convention, the method that registers a listener is add plus the listener name. The listener for window events is WindowListener, so the method to register the listener is addWindowListener. Registering the listener in program Print-Name would be done as follows.

```
outputDisplay.addWindowListener(myListener);
```

Figure 3.4 *An analogy representing the event-listener registration and calling process*

Notice that the parameter is an object of class `WindowListener` that is registered with the event. This class defines the methods that handle the various window events. Java recognizes seven different kinds of window events, so the `WindowListener` class contains a handler (method) corresponding to each of these events. Each of the seven methods has a specific name that the event source recognizes. Here you are just interested in the one that closes the window, called `windowClosing`. The `addWindow-Listener` method registers the `WindowListener` object with the `outputDisplay Frame` object. But you still must write the `windowClosing` event handler, which is a method in the `WindowListener` class.

3.5 Event-Handler Methods

On the surface, writing a method called `windowClosing` sounds quite simple. Just as you wrote a method named `main` that the JVM recognizes as the place to start execution, you can write a method with a special name that the event listener recognizes. The problem is that the method has to be part of a user-defined class, and we won't look at how to write our own nonapplication classes until Chapter 7. Also, the class must include methods for all seven types of window events. It's inconvenient to have to write seven methods when you just want to handle one specific event. Fortunately, Java provides a pair of shortcuts that solve these problems.

The first shortcut is a predefined class called `WindowAdapter`. An object of type `WindowAdapter` can be used in place of an object of type `WindowListener`. A

`WindowAdapter` object automatically supplies empty shells for all seven of the window event-handler methods. For example, you can write:

```
outputDisplay.addWindowListener(new WindowAdapter());
```

If you pass a `WindowAdapter` object as a parameter when you register the listener, the listener can call these seven empty methods. Calling an empty method has the same effect as having no event handler at all, so the use of `WindowAdapter` would be pointless if it wasn't for the second shortcut that Java provides.

When you use `new` to create an object of class `WindowAdapter`, Java allows you to follow the call to the constructor with a block containing declarations that are effectively added to the object.

```
outputDisplay.addWindowListener(new WindowAdapter()
  {declaration block});
```

If you write a method declaration in the block using the same name as one of the methods supplied by `WindowAdapter`, then your method replaces it. The other empty methods aren't replaced, so the effect is that `addWindowListener` is passed a `WindowAdapter` object that has all of the required methods. Six of those methods still do nothing (because you aren't explicitly handling those events), and the seventh contains our code for responding to closing of the window.

Look carefully at the following code segment that illustrates how you write an event handler. Notice that the declaration block is contained within the parameter list of the call to `addWindowListener`, immediately following the call to the constructor for `WindowAdapter`.

```
outputDisplay.addWindowListener(    // Within the parameter list
           new WindowAdapter()   // Create object of type WindowAdapter
  { // Start a block of declarations to add to the WindowAdapter

    // Here we write a method to replace WindowAdapter's
    //   empty windowClosing method
    public void windowClosing(WindowEvent event)
    {
      outputDisplay.dispose();  // Remove the window from the screen
      System.exit(0);           // Stop the program
    }                           // End of the method
  // End of the declaration block and end of addWindowListener parameters
  });
```

Figure 3.5 shows the relationship between the method written in the code, the `WindowAdapter` object, the `addWindowListener` method, the `WindowListener`, and the `WindowEvent` object. Once the modified `WindowAdapter` is received, the event listener is able to call the method whenever a window closing event occurs.

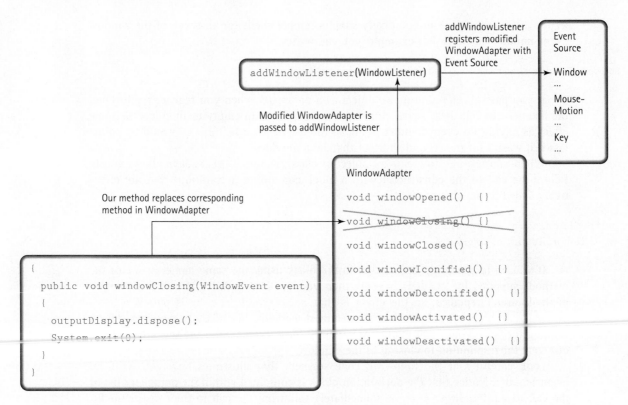

Figure 3.5   *An event handler is added to an event listener, and the event listener is registered with an event source.*

The heading of the windowClosing method shows that it has to accept a parameter of type WindowEvent that is passed to it by the event source. The value that the event source assigns to the parameter includes the name of the window associated with the event. Java makes it possible for programs to have multiple windows that are distinguished by different names, but because you are using just one window in the program, you can ignore the value in the parameter at this point.

Notice also that the heading begins with the modifier public. It is being declared within the WindowAdapter class, and so it must be public to be accessible outside of that class. In the body of the method you can find two method calls. The first, dispose, simply removes the window from the screen. The second, System.exit is a special Java method that tells the JVM that the program is finished. Zero is passed to System.exit to indicate to the JVM that no problems were encountered. If any other value is passed, the JVM displays a warning message that the program ended with an abnormal condition.

Let's see how the event handler fits into program PrintName. There is one other detail that we need to take care of first, however. The classes for handling events are contained in a separate package called java.awt.event. Thus, you must add a second import declaration to the start of the program. Otherwise, it is just a matter of inserting our event-handling code at the end of main.

```
//***********************************************************
// PrintName program
// This program prints a name in two different formats
//***********************************************************
import java.awt.*;                        // Import Frame type, etc.
import java.awt.event.*;                  // Import event handling types

public class PrintName
{
  private static Frame outputDisplay;     // Declare Frame variable
  public static void main(String[] args)
  {
    final String FIRST  = "Herman";       // Person's first name
    final String LAST   = "Herrmann";     // Person's last name
    final char   MIDDLE = 'G';            // Person's middle initial

    String firstLast;                     // Name in first-last format
    String lastFirst;                     // Name in last-first format

    outputDisplay = new Frame();          // Create new Frame object
    outputDisplay.setLayout(new FlowLayout()); // Specify layout manager

    firstLast = FIRST + " " + LAST;
    outputDisplay.add(new Label("Name in first-last format is " +
                          firstLast));

    lastFirst = LAST + ", " + FIRST + ", ";
    outputDisplay.add(new Label("Name in last-first-initial format is " +
                          lastFirst + MIDDLE + "."));
    outputDisplay.pack();                 // Pack the frame
    outputDisplay.show();                 // Show the frame on the
                                          //  screen
    // Event handler for window closing
    outputDisplay.addWindowListener(new WindowAdapter()
      {
        public void windowClosing(WindowEvent event)  // Replacement method
        {
          outputDisplay.dispose();                    // Remove the window
                                                      //  from the screen
          System.exit(0);                             // Stop the program
        }
      });
  }
}
```

The output from this version of `PrintName` looks identical to the earlier version. When we click on the icon for closing the window, however, it politely vanishes and the program halts its execution.

Notice that a method, `windowClosing`, has been declared as part of creating a new (nameless) object that is an instance of class `WindowAdapter`. The `windowClosing` method is being added to the `WindowAdapter` class just for this specific object instantiation. If you think of the class like the blueprint for building a house, and the `new` operator as being the actual construction of the house from the blueprint, then the declaration of `windowClosing` is like customizing a standard blueprint for the construction of a specific house.

Before we leave this example, there is one additional change that we made from the prior version that requires some explanation. The declaration of the `Frame` variable has been moved from within `main` to a point preceding `main`, and we've added the modifiers `private` and `static`. The reason for this move is that `windowClosing` cannot refer to variables declared within `main`, even though it appears inside of `main` itself. What really happens is that the Java compiler discovers that `windowClosing` is being added to the `WindowAdapter` class. Thus, `windowClosing` effectively becomes part of `WindowAdapter`, which is outside of `main`. If we declare the `Frame` variable within `main`, then it can be accessed only from within `main`. So we must declare it outside of `main` to enable `windowClosing` to use it.

When it is declared outside of `main`, the `Frame` variable becomes one of the class declarations, just like `main`. Also, as with `main`, we use the `static` modifier. Unlike `main`, however, there is no reason for the JVM to access the `Frame` variable, so we declare it `private` instead of `public`.

Problem–Solving Case Study

Display a Date in Multiple Formats

Problem You are beginning to work on a program that needs to output dates in several formats. As a start, you decide to write a short Java application that takes a single date and displays it in the different formats, so you can be certain that all of your string expressions are correct. *Does this sound familiar?* It should, this is the beginning of the Case Study for Chapter 2. However, there are added constraints: There should be labels showing how the date is written next to the example. The output should be in two columns, with the first column labeled "Format" and the second labeled "Example."

Output   A window showing the date in four formats:

Format	Example
Month day, year	August 18, 2001
day Month year	18 August 2001
mm/dd/yyyy	8/18/2001
dd/mm/yyyy	18/8/2001

Discussion   To organize the screen as this problem requires means that we must use a `Frame` object rather than `System.out` to create the output. The design we used in the original problem can be used to create the date strings, but we must write the labels for each date. In order to line them up in two columns, we should use `GridLayout` with five rows and two columns. The first row is the label for each column. We must add a `Frame` variable to the list of variables and instantiate the `Frame` object. Otherwise, the design remains the same until we reach the Display the Dates algorithm.

Set Up FrameObject

```
Frame outDisplay = new Frame();

outDisplay.setLayout(new GridLayout(5, 2)
```

Display the Labels

```
Add label "Format"
Add label "Example"
```

Display the Dates

```
Add label Month day, year
Add label first
Add label day Month year
Add label second
Add label mm/dd/yyyy
Add label third
Add label dd/mm/yyyy
Add label fourth
```

In the first version, we were not using a frame, so we didn't need to close the window. Here, however, we do. We can use the code for `addWindowListener` directly from this chapter.

```java
//**************************************************************************
// DateFormats program
// This program prints a date in four different formats by
//   building strings up from the component parts of the date
//   using string concatenation expressions
//**************************************************************************
import java.awt.*;
import java.awt.event.*;
public class DateFormats
{
  public static Frame outDisplay;            // Declare a frame variable
  public static void main(String[] args)
  {
    final String MONTH_NAME = "August";   // The name of the month
    final String MONTH_NUMBER = "8";      // The number of the month
    final String DAY = "18";              // The day of the month
    final String YEAR = "2001";           // The four-digit year number
    String first;                         // Date in Month day, year form
    String second;                        // Date in day Month year format
    String third;                         // Date in mm/dd/yyyy format
    String fourth;                        // Date in dd/mm/yyyy format

    outDisplay = new Frame();
    outDisplay.setLayout(new GridLayout(5, 2));
    // Set up headings
    outDisplay.add(new Label("Format"));
    outDisplay.add(new Label("Example"));

    // Add information to the screen
    outDisplay.add(new Label("Month day, year"));
    first = MONTH_NAME + " " + DAY + ", " + YEAR;
    outDisplay.add(new Label(first));

    outDisplay.add(new Label("day Month year"));
    second = DAY + "  " + MONTH_NAME + " " + YEAR;
    outDisplay.add(new Label (second));

    outDisplay.add(new Label("mm/dd/yyyy"));
    third = MONTH_NUMBER + "/" + DAY + "/" + YEAR;
    outDisplay.add(new Label(third));

    outDisplay.add(new Label("dd/mm/yyyy"));
    fourth = DAY + "/" + MONTH_NUMBER + "/" + YEAR;
```

```
outDisplay.add(new Label(fourth));
outDisplay.pack();
outDisplay.show();
outDisplay.addWindowListener(new WindowAdapter()
  // Create a WindowAdapter
  {
    public void windowClosing(WindowEvent event)
    // Method to replace the empty one
  {
    outDisplay.dispose();        // Remove the window from the screen
    System.exit(0);              // Stop the program
  }
 });
}
}
```

The output from the program is

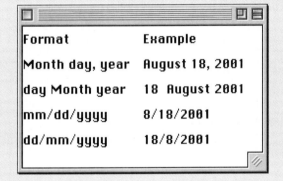

Format	Example
Month day, year	August 18, 2001
day Month year	18 August 2001
mm/dd/yyyy	8/18/2001
dd/mm/yyyy	18/8/2001

Testing and Debugging

1. Use new to instantiate an object of a class. Only objects can be assigned to class variables.

2. When instantiating an object in a parameter list, be sure to include the new operator before the class name.

3. Objects to which methods are being applied must have the method appended to the object name with a dot in between.

4. If clicking the window does not remove it from the screen, you have probably forgotten to register the WindowListener with the event handler.

5. If your window does not appear on the screen, be sure you have included the show method.

6. Don't forget the closing parenthesis at the end of the parameter list of `addWindowListener`. Because you are inserting a declaration block in the parameter list, the parenthesis that closes the list appears far removed from the start of the list.

7. Remember that Java is case-sensitive: `Gridlayout` is not the same as `GridLayout`.

8. Be sure to include the `awt` and `awt.event` packages when using the `Frame` class.

Summary of Classes

Package Name

Class Name		Comments
`java.lang`		
`System.exit(0)`		Proper exit from an application with a `Frame` object
`java.awt`		
`FlowLayout`		
Constructor:	`FlowLayout()`	
`GridLayout`		
Constructor:	`GridLayout(int, int)`	Used as a parameter to setLayout method of class Frame
`Frame`		
Constructor:	`Frame()`	
Instance Methods:	`add(Label)`	
	`addWindowListener(WindowListener)`	
	`dispose()`	
	`pack()`	
	`setLayout(FlowLayout)`	
	`setLayout(GridLayout)`	
	`show()`	
`Label`		
Constructor:	`Label(String)`	
`Java.awt.event`		
`WindowListener`		
Constructor:	`WindowListener()`	Listener for Window events
`WindowAdapter`		Can be substituted for WindowListener
Constructor:	`WindowAdapter()`	

Summary

Window output is accomplished by means of the `Frame` class, along with its `add` method. Each add operation adds a display element to the frame. When the `pack` and `show` methods are called, the frame is displayed on the screen containing whatever elements have been added to it.

In order to allow the user to close the window, we must provide an event handler that can be called by the event source. An event handler is a method in a listener class. Listeners are objects that are associated with events. When a listener is registered with an event, the event can invoke a handler from the listener class when the event fires. We modify the `WindowAdapter` class to include a method called `windowClosing` that replaces its empty method of the same name, and then register the listener using the `addWindowListener` method.

Quick Check

1. What type of window do we use in this text? (p. 94)
2. What is the Java reserved word that provides access to classes in a package? (p. 95)
3. Write a statement that instantiates a `Frame` object called `outDisplay`. (pp. 95–96)
4. What is an expression used for communicating values to a method? (pp. 96–97)
5. What is the responsibility of a layout manager? (p. 98)
6. How many columns and how many rows will be in the frame that is formatted according to the following statement? (p. 103)

   ```
   out.setLayout(new GridLayout(4, 3));
   ```

7. Give an example of a method call to `System.out`. (p. 97)
8. Write a statement that adds the label "This is my answer" to `outDisplay`. (pp. 98–99)
9. What object is waiting for an event to occur? (pp. 105–106)
10. What is an event handler? (p. 106)
11. What is the method name that is used to register a window listener? (p. 107)

Answers

1. A frame 2. `import` 3. `outDisplay = new Frame();` 4. A parameter 5. To automatically place elements that we add to a frame in the order that we add them
6. 4 rows of 3 columns 7. `System.out.print("Oh what a beautiful morning...");` or `System.out.println("Oh what a beautiful morning...");`
8. `outDisplay.add(new Label("This is my answer"));` 9. A listener object 10. An event handler is a method in a listener class. 11. `addWindowListener`

Exam Preparation Exercises

1. Name two operations that can be applied to a `Frame` object.
2. How do we gain access to the `Frame` class?
3. How do you instantiate an object of a `Frame` class?
4. Describe the contents of a package.
5. Name three kinds of methods.
6. How do you invoke an instance method?
7. Name two instance methods associated with the `System.out` object.
8. What does the expression "sending a message to" mean?
9. Describe the role of a parameter list.
10. What is a class called that can contain other components?
11. What is the function of the `add` method of class `Frame`?
12. What is a synonym for a void method?
13. We have used the convention that method names begin with a lowercase letter. Why does a constructor have to begin with an uppercase letter?
14. If your frame fails to appear on the screen, what might the error be?
15. a. What is the purpose of the `setLayout` method?
    b. Name two layout managers. What is the difference between them?
16. The `Label` class has a second constructor that can take two parameters rather than one. What is the second parameter?
17. What is the object whose role in life is to wait for an event to occur?
18. What is an event handler?
19. Where is an event handler defined?
20. What is an event source?
21. What does it mean to register an event listener?
22. What can be used in place of an object of class `WindowListener`?
23. Where is the code for the `windowClosing` method contained?
24. Why does the `Frame` variable have to be declared outside of `main` in the Case Study program?
25. What is output by the following code segment? (All variables are of type `String`. Assume that the frame variable `out` has been declared and given a value.)

```
street = "Elm St.";
address = "1425B";
city = "Amaryllis";
state = "Iowa";
streetAddress = address + " " + street;
out.add(new Label(streetAddress));
out.add(new Label(city));
out.add(new Label(", " + state));
out.pack();
out.show();
```

26. Correct the following program so that it displays "Martin Luther King Jr."

```
// This program is full of errors
import Java.awt
class LotsOfErrors;
{
  constant String FIRST : Martin";
  constant String MID : "Luther;
  constant String LAST : King
  private static Frame : out;

  void main (string[] args);
  {
    out = new Frame;
    out.FlowLayout(new setLayout());
    String name;
    character initial;

    name = Martin + Luther + King;
    initial = MID;
    LAST = "King Jr.";
    out.add(new Label('Name = ' + name));
    out.add(new Label(mid
    out.pack
    out.show();
  }
```

Programming Warm-Up Exercises

1. Write the output statement that displays your name in a frame called `display` (assume that `display` has already been set up properly and that `display.pack` and `display.show` are called after your statement is executed).

2. Write three consecutive output statements that display the following three lines of text as separate labels:

```
The moon
is
blue.
```

3. Write declaration statements to declare three variables of class `String` and two variables of type `char`. The `String` variables should be named `make`, `model`, and `color`. The `char` variables should be named `plateType` and `classification`.

4. Write a series of output statements that display the values in the variables declared in Exercise 3 in a frame called `auto`. Each value should be preceded by an identifying message.

5. Change the `PrintName` program (page 111) so that it also prints the name in the format

```
First-name Middle-initial. Last-name
```

Make `MIDDLE` a `String` constant rather than a `char` constant. Define a new `String` variable to hold the name in the new format and assign it the string using the existing named constants, any literal strings that are needed for punctuation and spacing, and concatenation operations. Display the string, labeled appropriately.

6. Write Java output statements that declare and properly set up a frame called `address`.

7. Display the following groups of text in the frame called `address` that was set up in Exercise 6, with each line of text in a separate label.

a. `Four score`
   `and seven years ago`
b. `Four score`
   `and seven`
   `years ago`
c. `Four score`
   `and`
   `seven`
   `years ago`
d. `Four`
   `score`
   `and`
   `seven`
   `years`
   `ago`

8. Enter and run the following program. Be sure to type it exactly as it appears here.

```java
//***********************************************************************
// HelloWorld program
// This program displays two simple messages
//***********************************************************************
import java.awt.*;
import java.awt.event.*;

public class HelloWorld
{
  private static final String MSG1 = "Hello world.";
  private static Frame out;
```

```
public static void main(String[] args)
{
  String msg2;
  out = new Frame();
  out.setLayout(new FlowLayout());
  out.add(new Label(MSG1));
  msg2 = MSG1 + " " + MSG1 + " " + MSG1;
  out.add(new Label(msg2));
  out.pack();
  out.show();
  out.addWindowListener(new WindowAdapter()
    {
      public void windowClosing(WindowEvent event)
      {
        out.dispose();
        System.exit(0);
      }
    });
}
}
```

a. Write a statement that assigns the `GridLayout` manager to `Frame` variable `outDisplay` with two rows and three columns.

b. Write a statement that assigns the `GridLayout` manager to `Frame` variable `outDisplay` with an unspecified number of rows and three columns.

c. Write a statement that adds a new label to `Frame` variable `outDisplay` that centers the text in the label.

d. The following output appeared on the screen:

```
The dollar amount is 23dollarsand52cents.
```

Write the correct output using `System.out`.

Programming Problems

1. Problem 1 in Chapter 2 asked you to write a Java application that displayed a series of Haiku poems. Recall that a Haiku poem is written in three phrases. The first phrase has five syllables, the second has seven syllables and the last phrase again has five syllables. For example:

```
Bright flash then silence
My expensive computer
Has gone to heaven
```

Your program was to define string constants with four phrases of five syllables and two phrases of seven syllables. Use string concatenation expressions to construct every possible 5-7-5 permutation of these phrases and display each one. Rewrite this application using a `Frame` object rather than `System.out`.

2. Rewrite the solution to Chapter 2, Problem 2 that simulates the child's game "My Grandmother's Trunk." In this game, the players sit in a circle, and the first player names something that goes in the trunk: "In my grandmother's trunk, I packed a pencil." The next player restates the sentence and adds something new to the trunk: "In my grandmother's trunk, I packed a pencil and a red ball." Each player in turn adds something to the trunk, attempting to keep track of all the items that are already there.

   Your program should simulate just five turns in the game. Starting with the null string, simulate each player's turn by concatenating a new word or phrase to the existing string, and add the result to a frame.

3. Write an application that uses the `GridLayout` manager to write your name left-justified on the first line, your address centered on the next line, and your phone number right-justified on the third line.

Case Study Follow-Up Exercises

1. Change the `DateFormats` program so that the four formats are shown in the opposite order on the screen.

2. In the `DateFormats` program, explain what takes place in the statement that assigns a value to the label that goes with string variable `third`.

3. Change the `DateFormats` program so that the third and fourth formats use hyphens (-) instead of slashes (/).

4. Change the `DateFormats` program so that your birth date is displayed in the four formats.

Numeric Types and Expressions

- To be able to declare named constants and variables of type `int` and `double`.

- To be able to construct simple arithmetic expressions.

- To be able to evaluate simple arithmetic expressions.

- To be able to construct and evaluate expressions that include multiple arithmetic operations.

- To understand implicit type conversion and explicit type casting.

- To be able to use Java math methods in expressions.

- To learn and be able to use additional operations associated with the `String` type.

- To be able to format the statements in a program in a clear and readable fashion.

In Chapters 2 and 3, we examined enough Java syntax to be able to construct simple programs using assignment and output. We focused on the `char` and `String` types and saw how to construct expressions using the concatenation operator. In this chapter we continue to write programs that use assignment and output, but we concentrate on additional built-in data types: `int`, `long`, `float`, and `double`. These numeric types include multiple operators that enable us to construct complex arithmetic expressions. We show how to make expressions even more powerful by using calls to Java's value-returning math methods.

4.1   Overview of Java Data Types

The Java built-in data types are organized into primitive types and reference types (see Figure 4.1).

You might have noticed that the `String` type isn't listed in Figure 4.1. In Chapter 2 we noted that `String` is an example of a class, which is one of the reference types. In fact, most of the types that we use in this text, other than the primitive types, are classes. In Chapter 3 we used classes such as `Frame`, `Label`, and `WindowAdapter`. Recall that our convention is to capitalize the first letter of all classes in this manner, to help you identify them in programs.

The division of Java's data types into *primitive* and *reference* types stems from the way that Java stores values of each of the types in memory. Recall from Chapter 2 that we said Java chooses an address in the computer's memory where it stores each value and keeps track of the address so that we don't have to remember it. Each primitive type takes up a fixed amount of space in memory, so Java stores each primitive value at the memory address it chooses for it. When you assign a value to a variable of a primitive type, Java copies the value into the address that has been chosen for the variable. This action is possible because each primitive type takes a specified amount of space.

The reference types are more complex. Because they can contain different numbers of fields, they take up different amounts of the computer's memory. Most are too large to fit into a single memory location, so Java can't just assign the new object by copying

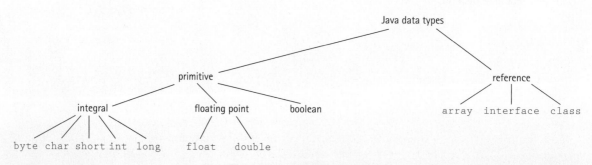

Figure 4.1   *Java data types*

one memory location to another. Instead of storing the object at the chosen location, Java stores the object in one or more additional locations in another part of memory. If Java doesn't put the object into the chosen location, then what does it put there? It stores the *address* of the memory location where the object can be found. That is, the chosen location contains a binary number that tells the computer where the object is stored. When Java assigns an object to a variable, it copies this address into the variable.

Let's look at a pair of examples that demonstrate the difference between primitive values and reference values.

```
char letter;
String title;
String bookName;
letter = 'J';
title = "Introduction to Java and Software Design";
bookName = title;
```

When you declare variables `letter`, `title`, and `bookName`, locations in memory are chosen for these variables. When you assign the value `'J'` to the `char` variable `letter`, Java stores the value `'J'` into it. When you assign the string `"Introduction to Java and Software Design"` to the `String` variable `title`, Java chooses locations into which to store the string, and stores the *address* of the first location into `title`. If you assign the value of `title` to the `String` variable called `bookName`, then Java just copies the value stored in `title` (the address) to the place it chose for `book-Name`. Figure 4.2 illustrates the difference between primitive and reference types.

Figure 4.2 also shows that a reference type has the advantage of saving memory space when copying values that take up multiple locations in memory. The lengthy value is stored just once, and the variables that are assigned the value each take up just one location. If Java stored reference types the same way it stores primitive types, it would have to store a copy of the whole value in each variable, which would take up more space.

The term "reference," by the way, comes from the fact that the contents of a reference variable *refer* to another place in memory. You can think of a reference type as being analogous to the call number of a library book. If you have the call number, you can go into the library and find the book. If a friend wants to find the same book, you give a copy of the call number to him or her, which is much easier than making a copy of the book.

Do not feel overwhelmed by the quantity of data types shown in Figure 4.1. Our purpose is simply to give you an overall picture of what is available in Java. Except for the `String` and output classes, this chapter works mainly with the primitive types. Details of the reference types come later in the book. First we look at the primitive integral types (those used primarily to represent integers), and then we consider the floating types (used to represent real numbers containing decimal points). We postpone talking about the remaining primitive type, `boolean`, until Chapter 6.

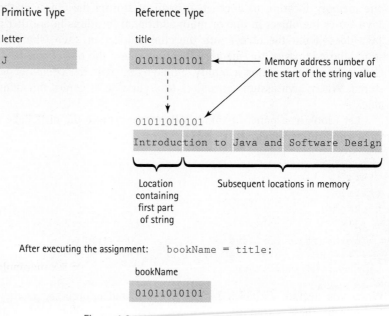

Figure 4.2 *Primitive types and reference types*

4.2 Numeric Data Types

You already are familiar with the basic concepts of integer and real numbers in mathematics. However, as used on a computer, the corresponding data types have certain limitations, which we now examine.

Integral Types

The data types `byte`, `short`, `int`, and `long` are known as integral types (or integer types) because they refer to integer values—whole numbers with no fractional part. In Java, the simplest form of integer value is a sequence of one or more digits:

```
22   16   1   498   0   4600
```

Commas are not allowed.

A minus sign preceding an integer value makes the integer negative:

```
-378   -912
```

The data types `byte`, `short`, `int`, and `long` are intended to represent different sizes of integers, from smaller (fewer bits) to larger (more bits), as shown in Figure 4.3.

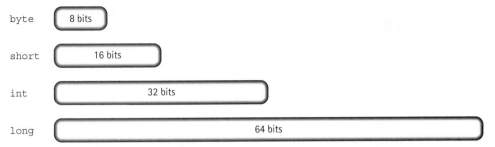

Figure 4.3   *The integral types in Java*

The Java language specifies the sizes of the integral types to be just as shown in the figure. The more bits there are in the type, the larger the integer value that can be stored.

The int type is by far the most common data type for manipulating integer data. byte and short types are used far less frequently. In Java you nearly always use int for manipulating integer values, but sometimes you may choose to use long if your program requires values larger than the maximum int value. The range of int values is from -2147483648 through +2147483647. As we noted in Chapter 1, numbers like these remind us that the binary number system is working in the background.

A variable of type int can hold any value with up to nine decimal digits, such as a social security number. But for values with more digits, such as a telephone number with country and area codes, it isn't large enough. Such numbers require the long type, which can hold any integer up to 18 digits in length.

When you write a literal integer value, it is automatically assumed by Java to be of type int. To write a literal of type long, you must follow the last digit of the number with the letter "L". You may also use the lowercase "l", but it looks so much like the digit "1" that it may be impossible for a person to recognize the literal as long when reading your program. We use only the uppercase "L" in this text. Here are some examples of literals of type int and long.

Literal	Type
0	int
0L	long
2001	int
18005551212L	long
18005551212	invalid (11 digits are too large for type int)

If your program tries to compute a value larger than a type's maximum value, the result is *integer overflow*. Some programming languages give you an error message when overflow occurs, but Java doesn't. If a computation in Java produces a value that is too large for the type to represent, you simply get an erroneous result.

One caution about integer literals in Java: A literal constant beginning with a zero is taken to be an octal (base–8) number instead of a decimal (base–10) number. If you write

```
015
```

the Java compiler takes this to mean the decimal number 13. If you aren't familiar with the octal number system, don't worry about why an octal 15 is the same as a decimal 13. The important thing to remember is not to start a decimal integer literal with a zero (unless you want the number 0, which is the same in both octal and decimal).

Floating-Point Types

Floating-point types (or floating types) are used to represent real numbers. Floating-point numbers have an integer part and a fractional part, with a decimal point in between. Either the integer part or the fractional part, but not both, may be missing. Here are some examples:

```
18.0      127.54      0.57      4.      193145.8523      .8
```

Starting `0.57` with a 0 does not make it an octal number. It is only with integer values that a leading 0 indicates an octal number.

Just as the integral types in Java come in different sizes (`byte`, `short`, `int`, and `long`), so do the floating-point types. In increasing order of size, the floating-point types are `float` and `double` (meaning double-precision). Type `double` gives us a wider range of values and more precision (the number of significant digits in the number) than type `float`, but at the expense of twice the memory space to hold the number. In Java, `int` and `float` values take up the same amount of memory space (32 bits), and both `long` and `double` take up 64 bits of memory space.

Floating-point values also can have an exponent, as in scientific notation. (In scientific notation, a number is written as a value multiplied by 10 to some power.) Instead of writing 3.504×10^{12}, in Java we write `3.504E12`. The E (you can also use e) means exponent of base 10. The number preceding the letter E doesn't need to include a decimal point. Here are some examples of floating-point numbers in scientific notation:

```
1.74536E-12      3.652442E4      7E20      -8.01994E-23      -6e12
```

A `float` value can represent seven-digit decimal numbers with an exponent in the range of −45 through 38. A `double` value can represent 15-digit decimal numbers with an exponent ranging from −324 to 308.

In Java, floating-point literals of the form we have shown are automatically assumed by the compiler to be of type `double`. To write a literal of type `float`, you must end the number with the letter F (or f). In the `Payroll` program, the identifiers

MAX_HOURS, OVERTIME, payRate, hours, wages, and total are all of type double. Here are some examples of floating-point literals.

Literal	Type
0.0	double
0.0f	float
2.001E3	double
2.001E3F	float
1.8E225F	invalid (exponent 225 too great for type float)

We talk more about floating-point numbers in Chapter 13. But there is one more thing you should know about them now. Computers cannot always represent floating-point numbers exactly. You learned in Chapter 1 that the computer stores all data in binary (base-2) form. Many decimal floating-point values can only be approximated in the binary number system. Don't be surprised if your program prints out the number 4.8 as 4.7999998. In most cases, slight inaccuracies in the rightmost fractional digits are to be expected and are not the result of programmer error.

4.3 Declarations for Numeric Types

Just as with the types char and String, we can declare named constants and variables of type int, long, float, and double. Such declarations use the same syntax as before, except that the literals and the names of the data types are different.

Named Constant Declarations

In the case of named constant declarations, the literal values in the declarations are numeric instead of being characters in single or double quotes. For example, here are some constant declarations that define values of type int and float. For comparison, declarations of char and String values are included.

```
final double  PI = 3.14159;
final float   E = 2.71828F;
final long    MAX_TEMP = 1000000000L;
final int     MIN_TEMP = -273;
final char    LETTER = 'W';
final String  NAME = "Elizabeth";
```

Although character and string literals are put in quotes, literal integers and floating-point numbers are not, because there is no chance of confusing them with identifiers. Why? Because identifiers must start with a letter or underscore, and numbers must start with a digit or sign.

Software Engineering Tip
Using Named Constants Instead of Literals

It's a good idea to use named constants instead of literals. In addition to making your program more readable, named constants can make your program easier to modify. Suppose you wrote an application last year to compute taxes. In several places you used the literal 0.05, which was the sales tax rate at the time. Now the rate has gone up to 0.06. To change your program, you must locate every literal 0.05 and change it to 0.06. And if 0.05 is used for some other reason—to compute deductions, for example—you need to look at each place where it is used, figure out what it is used for, and then decide whether to change it.

The process is much simpler if you use a named constant. Instead of using a literal constant, suppose you had declared a named constant, TAX_RATE, with a value of 0.05. To change your program, you would simply change the declaration, setting TAX_RATE equal to 0.06. This one modification changes all of the tax rate computations without affecting the other places where 0.05 is used.

Java allows us to declare constants with different names but the same value. If a value has different meanings in different parts of an application, it makes sense to declare and use a constant with an appropriate name for each meaning.

Named constants also are reliable; they protect us from mistakes. If you mistype the name PI as PO, the Java compiler tells you that the name PO has not been declared. On the other hand, even though we recognize that the number 3.14149 is a mistyped version of pi (3.14159), the number is perfectly acceptable to the compiler. It won't warn us that anything is wrong.

Variable Declarations

We declare numeric variables the same way in which we declare char and String variables, except that we use the names of numeric types. Here are some sample declarations.

```
int     studentCount;   // Number of students
int     sumOfScores;    // Sum of their scores
long    sumOfSquares;   // Sum of squared scores
double  average;        // Average of the scores
float   deviation;      // Standard deviation of scores
char    grade;          // Student's letter grade
String  stuName;        // Student's name
```

Given these declarations

```
int    num;
int    alpha;
double rate;
char   ch;
```

the following are appropriate assignment statements:

Variable	Expression
alpha =	2856;
rate =	0.36;
ch =	'B';
num =	alpha;

In each of these assignment statements, the data type of the expression matches the data type of the variable to which it is assigned. Later in the chapter we see what happens if the data types do not match.

4.4 Simple Arithmetic Expressions

Now that we have looked at declaration and assignment, we consider how to calculate with values of numeric types. Calculations are performed with expressions. We first look at simple expressions that involve at most one operator so that we may examine each operator in detail. Then, we move on to compound expressions that combine multiple operations.

Arithmetic Operators

Expressions are made up of constants, variables, and operators. The following are all valid expressions:

```
alpha + 2     rate - 6.0     4 - alpha     rate     alpha * num
```

The operators allowed in an expression depend on the data types of the constants and variables in the expression. The *arithmetic operators* are

+	Unary plus
-	Unary minus
+	Addition
-	Subtraction
*	Multiplication
/	{ Floating-point division (floating-point result) { Integer division (no fractional part)
%	Modulus (remainder from division)

The first two operators are unary operators—they take just one operand. The remaining five are binary operators, taking two operands. Unary plus and minus are used as follows:

```
-54    +259.65    -rate
```

> **Unary operator** An operator that has just one operand
>
> **Binary operator** An operator that has two operands

Programmers rarely use the unary plus. Without any sign, a numeric constant is assumed to be positive anyway.

You may not be familiar with integer division and modulus (%). Let's look at these operations more closely. Note that % can be used with both integers and floating-point numbers. When you divide one integer by another, you get an integer quotient and a remainder. Integer division gives only the integer quotient, and % gives only the remainder.

$$
\begin{array}{ll}
3 \leftarrow 6/2 & 3 \leftarrow 7/2 \\
2\overline{)6} & 2\overline{)7} \\
\underline{6} & \underline{6} \\
0 \leftarrow 6\%2 & 1 \leftarrow 7\%2
\end{array}
$$

In Java, the sign of the remainder is the same as the sign of the dividend. For example,

```
 3 %  2 =  1
 3 % -2 =  1
-3 %  2 = -1
-3 % -2 = -1
```

In contrast to integer division, floating-point division yields a floating-point result. The expression

```
7.2 / 2.0
```

yields the value 3.6.

The floating-point remainder operation returns the remainder after dividing the dividend by the divisor a whole number of times. For example,

```
7.2 % 2.1
```

yields the value 0.9 because 2.1 goes into 7.2 exactly 3 times (3 * 2.1 = 6.3), with 0.9 remaining.

Here are some expressions using arithmetic operators and their values:

Expression	Value
3 + 6	9
3.4 - 6.1	−2.7
2 * 3	6
8 / 2	4
8.0 / 2.0	4.0
8 / 8	1

Expression	Value
8 / 9	0
8 / 7	1
8 % 8	0
8 % 9	8
8 % 7	1
0 % 7	0
5.0 % 2.3	0.4

Be careful with division and modulus. The expressions `7 / 0` and `7 % 0` produce an error message. The computer cannot divide an integer by zero. With floating-point values, however, the expressions `7.0 / 0.0` and `7.0 % 0.0` do not result in an error message. The result of the expression `7.0 / 0.0` is a special value representing *infinity*. The result of `7.0 % 0.0` is another special value called *Not a Number* (NaN).

Calculations involving these special values produce unusual results. For example, the result of any arithmetic operation involving NaN is also NaN. If you encounter such results, it is an indication that you need to carefully reexamine the expressions in your program to be certain that the division operation and remainder do not have a zero divisor.

Because variables are allowed in expressions, the following are valid assignments:

```
alpha = num + 6;
alpha = num / 2;
num = alpha * 2;
num = 6 % alpha;
alpha = alpha + 1;
num = num + alpha;
```

As we saw with assignment statements involving `String` expressions, the same variable can appear on both sides of the assignment operator. In the case of

```
num = num + alpha;
```

the value in `num` and the value in `alpha` are added together, and then the sum of the two values is stored back into `num`, replacing the previous value stored there. This example shows the difference between mathematical equality and assignment. The mathematical equality

$$num = num + alpha$$

is true only when alpha equals zero. The assignment statement

```
num = num + alpha;
```

is valid for *any* value of `alpha`.

Here's a simple program that uses arithmetic expressions:

```
//*************************************************************************
// FreezeBoil program
// This program computes the midpoint between
// the freezing and boiling points of water
//*************************************************************************


import java.awt.*;                          // Import Frame type, etc.
import java.awt.event.*;                    // Import event handling types

public class FreezeBoil
{

  private static Frame out;                 // Declare a variable of type Frame
  public static void main(String[]  args)
  {
    final double FREEZE_PT = 32.0;          // Freezing point of water
    final double BOIL_PT = 212.0;           // Boiling point of water

    double avgTemp;                         // Holds the result of averaging
                                            //    FREEZE_PT and BOIL_PT
    out = new Frame();                      // Create new value of type Frame
    out.setLayout(new FlowLayout());        // Specify layout manager for frame
    out.add(new Label("Water freezes at " + FREEZE_PT));
    out.add(new Label("and boils at " + BOIL_PT + " degrees."));


    avgTemp = FREEZE_PT + BOIL_PT;
    avgTemp = avgTemp / 2.0;


    out.add(new Label("Halfway between is " + avgTemp + " degrees."));
    out.pack();                             // Pack the frame
    out.show();                             // Show the frame on the screen
    out.addWindowListener(new WindowAdapter()
    // Create a WindowClosing method to replace the empty one
      public void windowClosing(WindowEvent event)
      {
        out.dispose();                          // Remove the frame from the screen
```

```
      System.exit(0);                  // Stop the program
    }
  });
 }
}
```

The program begins with a comment that explains what the program does. In the class declaration section we declare the variable `out` of class `Frame`. The body of the `main` method includes a definition of constants `FREEZE_PT` and `BOIL_PT` and the declaration of the local variable `avgTemp` and then a sequence of executable statements. These statements display labels, add `FREEZE_PT` and `BOIL_PT`, divide the sum by 2, show the result, and finally set up handling of the window closing event. Here is the output from the application:

Water freezes at 32.0   and boils at 212.0 degrees.   Halfway between is 122.0 degrees.

Increment and Decrement Operators

In addition to the arithmetic operators, Java provides *increment* and *decrement operators*:

++   Increment
- -   Decrement

These are unary operators that take a single variable name as an operand. For integer and floating-point operands, the effect is to add 1 to (or subtract 1 from) the operand. If `num` currently contains the value 8, the statement

```
num++;
```

causes `num` to contain 9. You can achieve the same effect by writing the assignment statement

```
num = num + 1;
```

but Java programmers typically prefer using the increment operator.

The ++ and - - operators can be either *prefix operators*

```
++num;
```

or *postfix operators*

```
num++;
```

Both of these statements behave in exactly the same way; they add 1 to whatever is in num. The choice between these two is a matter of personal preference, although most Java programmers favor the latter form.

Java allows the use of ++ and - - in the middle of a larger expression:

```
alpha = num++ * 3;
```

In this case, note that the postfix form of ++ gives a different result from the prefix form. In Chapter 10, we explain the ++ and - - operators in more detail. In the meantime, you should use them only to increment or decrement a variable as a separate, standalone statement:

IncrementStatement

```
Variable ++  ;
++ Variable ;
```

DecrementStatement

```
Variable - -  ;
- - Variable ;
```

4.5 Compound Arithmetic Expressions

The expressions we've used so far have contained at most a single arithmetic operator. We also have been careful not to mix integer and floating-point values in the same expression. Now we look at more complicated expressions—ones that are composed of several operators and ones that contain mixed data types.

Precedence Rules

Arithmetic expressions can be made up of many constants, variables, operators, and parentheses. In what order are the operations performed? For example, in the assignment statement

```
avgTemp = FREEZE_PT + BOIL_PT / 2.0;
```

is `FREEZE_PT + BOIL_PT` calculated first or is `BOIL_PT / 2.0` calculated first?

The five basic Java arithmetic operators (+ for addition, – for subtraction, * for multiplication, / for division, and % for modulus) and parentheses are ordered the same way mathematical operators are, according to *precedence rules*:

Highest precedence:	( )	
	++ (postfix increment)	– – (postfix decrement)
	++ (prefix increment)	– – (prefix decrement)
	unary + unary -	
	* / %	
Lowest precedence:	+ -	

In the example above, we first divide `BOIL_PT` by `2.0` and then add `FREEZE_PT` to the result.

You can change the order of evaluation by using parentheses. In the statement

```
avgTemp = (FREEZE_PT + BOIL_PT) / 2.0;
```

`FREEZE_PT` and `BOIL_PT` are added first, and then their sum is divided by `2.0`. We evaluate subexpressions in parentheses first and then follow the precedence of the operators.

When there are multiple arithmetic operators with the same precedence, their *grouping order* (or *associativity*) is from left to right. The expression

```
int1 - int2 + int3
```

means (`int1` − `int2`) + `int3`, not `int1` − (`int2` + `int3`). As another example, we would use the expression

```
(double1 + double2) / double1 * 3.0
```

to evaluate the expression in parentheses first, then divide the sum by `double1`, and then multiply the result by 3.0. Following are some more examples.

Expression	Value
`10 / 2 * 3`	15
`10 % 3 - 4 / 2`	−1
`5.0 * 2.0 / 4.0 * 2.0`	5.0
`5.0 * 2.0 / (4.0 * 2.0)`	1.25
`5.0 + 2.0 / (4.0 * 2.0)`	5.25

Type Conversion and Type Casting

Integer values and floating-point values are stored differently inside a computer's memory. The pattern of bits that represents the constant 2 does not look at all like the pattern of bits representing the constant 2.0. (In Chapter 13, we examine why floating-point numbers need a special representation inside the computer.) What happens if we mix integer and floating-point values together in an assignment statement or an arithmetic expression? Let's look first at assignment statements.

Assignment Statements If you make the declarations

```
int     someInt;
double  someDouble;
```

then `someInt` can hold *only* integer values, and `someDouble` can hold *only* double-precision floating-point values. The assignment statement

```
someDouble = 12;
```

may seem to store the integer value 12 into `someDouble`, but this is not true. The computer refuses to store anything other than a `double` value into `someDouble`. The compiler inserts extra Bytecode instructions that first convert 12 into 12.0 and then store 12.0 into `someDouble`. This implicit (automatic) conversion of a value from one data type to another is known in Java as type conversion.

Type conversion The implicit (automatic) conversion of a value from one data type to another

The statement

```
someInt = 4.8;
```

also causes type conversion. When a floating-point value is assigned to an `int` variable, the fractional part is truncated (cut off). As a result, `someInt` is assigned the value 4.

With both of the assignment statements above, the program would be less confusing for someone to read if we avoided mixing data types:

```
someDouble = 12.0;
someInt = 4;
```

More often, it is not just constants but entire expressions that are involved in type conversion. Both of the assignments

```
someDouble = 3 * someInt + 2;
someInt = 5.2 / someDouble - anotherDouble;
```

lead to type conversion. Storing the result of an `int` expression into a `double` variable doesn't cause loss of information; a whole number such as 24 can be represented in floating-point form as 24.0. In the Java language, a type conversion that does not result in a loss of information is known as a widening conversion. Assigning `int` values to `long` variables or a `float` values to `double` variables are additional examples of widening conversions.

However, storing the result of a floating-point expression into an `int` variable can cause a loss of information because the fractional part is truncated. Java refers to such a conversion as a narrowing conversion. It is easy to overlook the assignment of a floating-point expression to an `int` variable, a `double` value to a `float` variable, or a `long` value to an `int` variable when we try to discover why our program is producing the wrong answers.

To make our programs as clear (and error-free) as possible, we should use explicit type casting. A Java *cast operation* consists of a data type name within parentheses, then the expression to be converted:

> **Widening conversion** A type conversion that does not result in a loss of information[1]
>
> **Narrowing conversion** A type conversion that may result in a loss of some information, as in converting a value of type `double` to type `float`
>
> **Type casting** The explicit conversion of a value from one data type to another; also called type conversion

```
someDouble = (double)(3 * someInt + 2);
someInt = (int)(5.2 / someDouble -
anotherDouble);
```

Both of the statements

```
someFloat = someInt + 8;
someFloat = (float)(someInt + 8);
```

produce identical results. The only difference is in clarity. With the cast operation, it is perfectly clear to the programmer and to others reading the program that the mixing of types is intentional, not an oversight. Countless errors have resulted from unintentional mixing of types.

Note that there is a nice way to round off rather than truncate a floating-point value before storing it into an `int` variable. Here is the way to do it:

```
someInt = (int)(someDouble + 0.5);
```

With pencil and paper, see for yourself what gets stored into `someInt` when `someDouble` contains 4.7. Now try it again, assuming `someDouble` contains 4.2.

---

[1]In non-Java terminology, implicit conversions are called coercions and explicit conversions are casts.

(This technique of rounding by adding 0.5 assumes that `someDouble` is a positive number.)

Arithmetic Expressions   So far we have been talking about mixing data types across the assignment operator (=). It's also possible to mix data types within an expression:

```
someInt * someDouble
4.8 + someInt - 3
```

Such expressions are called mixed type (or mixed mode) expressions.

> **Mixed type expression**   An expression that contains operands of different data types; also called a mixed mode expression

Whenever an integer value and a floating-point value are joined by an operator, implicit type conversion occurs as follows.

1. The integer value is temporarily converted to a floating-point value.
2. The operation is performed.
3. The result is a floating-point value.

Let's examine how the machine evaluates the expression `4.8 + someInt - 3`, where `someInt` contains the value 2. First, the operands of the + operator have mixed types, so the value of `someInt` is converted to 2.0. (This conversion is only temporary; it does not affect the value that is stored in `someInt`.) The addition takes place, yielding a value of 6.8. Next, the subtraction (-) operator joins a floating-point value (6.8) and an integer value (3). The value 3 is converted to 3.0, the subtraction takes place, and the result is the floating-point value 3.8.

Just as with assignment statements, you can use explicit type casts within expressions to lessen the risk of errors. Writing expressions like

```
(double)someInt * someDouble
4.8 + (double)(someInt - 3)
```

makes it clear what your intentions are.

Not only are explicit type casts valuable for program clarity, in some cases they are mandatory for correct programming. Given the declarations

```
int    sum;
int    count;
double average;
```

suppose that `sum` and `count` currently contain 60 and 80, respectively. If `sum` represents the sum of a group of integer values and `count` represents the number of values, let's find the average value:

```
average = sum / count;    // Gives the wrong answer
```

Unfortunately, this statement stores the value 0.0 into `average`. Here's why. The expression to the right of the assignment operator is not a mixed type expression. Both operands of the / operator are of type `int`, so integer division is performed. Dividing 60 by 80 yields the integer value 0. Next, the machine implicitly converts 0 to the value 0.0 before storing it into `average`. The way to find the average correctly, as well as clearly, is this:

```
average = (double)sum / (double)count;
```

This statement gives us floating-point division instead of integer division. As a result, the value 0.75 is stored into `average`.

As a final remark about type conversion and type casting, you may have noticed that we have concentrated only on the `int` and `double` types. It is also possible to stir `byte`, `long`, `short`, and `float` values into the pot. The results can be confusing and unexpected. You should avoid unnecessarily mixing values of these types within an expression. Whenever it is necessary to do so, you should use explicit type conversion to clarify your intentions.

String Conversion   Just as Java attempts to convert between numeric types when you mix them in expressions, it also tries to convert numeric values to strings when you mix them into expressions with the string concatenation operator. If you declare a `String` object called `answer`, you can write an assignment expression of the following form

```
answer = "The average is: " + average;
```

If `average` contains the value 27.65, then the outcome of this assignment is that `answer` contains the string

```
"The average is: 27.65"
```

When one of the operands of the + operator is a string and the other operand is a numeric type, the numeric type is converted to a string prior to concatenation. The + operator has the same precedence whether it is adding numeric values or concatenating strings. String conversion is a useful feature of Java for formatting output in which we mix numeric values with text that explains their meaning. For example, you might use the preceding expression in a label as follows:

```
out.add(new Label("The average is: " + average));
```

You can use a series of concatenation operators to create complex strings. For example,

```
answer = "The results are: " + 27 + 18 + " and " + 9;
```

produces the string

```
"The results are: 2718 and 9"
```

Notice, however that the values 27 and 18 were concatenated without any spaces between them. String conversion of numeric values doesn't add any space around the digits of the number. You must explicitly include any spaces that you need as part of the expression:

```
answer = "The results are: " + 27 + ", " + 18 + " and " + 9;
```

It is also important to note that the result of the original expression wasn't

```
"The results are: 45 and 9"
```

Why doesn't the subexpression 27 + 18 perform an integer addition? The answer is found in the precedence rules. Let's take a closer look at how this expression is evaluated. All of the operators in the expression have the same precedence and are thus evaluated left to right. The first operand is a string, so the first + is a concatenation. The second operand is converted to a string and concatenated, with a string

```
"The results are: 27"
```

as the result. This string becomes the first operand of the second + operator, so it too is a concatenation. The number 18 is thus converted to a string and concatenated with the result of the first operator to produce a new string

```
"The results are: 2718"
```

The third operator has two strings as its operands, so no conversion is necessary and it produces

```
"The results are: 2718 and "
```

The last operator then has a string as its first operand and an integer as its second operand. The integer is converted to a string and concatenated to form the final result, which is assigned to answer.

As you can see from the preceding discussion, when an expression mixes strings and numeric types, you must consider the entire expression in light of the precedence rules. Take a look at the following expression and see if you can determine what its result is.

```
answer = 27 + 18 + 9 + " are the results."
```

If you think it is

```
"27189 are the results."
```

then you are forgetting the impact of the left-to-right evaluation precedence rule. Its actual result is

```
"54 are the results."
```

The first two + operators are integer additions because neither of their operands are strings. Only the last + sign is a concatenation, and its left operand is the sum of the three numbers, which it converts into a string. If a chain of + operators begins with a concatenation, then the succeeding operators are also concatenations. The following is an invalid assignment:

```
answer = 27 + 18 + 9;              // Invalid; expression type is int
```

String conversion occurs only with the concatenation operator, not with assignment. The result of this expression is an `int` value, which can't be assigned to a string. However, there is a trick that you can use to turn this expression into a series of string concatenations. You can concatenate the values with the empty string.

```
answer = "" + 27 + 18 + 9;        // Valid; expression type is String
```

The value stored in `answer` is then `"27189"`. But what if you want `answer` to contain the string representing the sum of these integers? That is, how do you get Java to first compute the integer sum before applying string conversion? You can do it the same way that you change the order of evaluation of any expression: use parentheses.

```
answer = "" + (27 + 18 + 9);
```

Now the expression `27 + 18 + 9` is evaluated first, and because all of the operands are integers, the + operators perform addition. Once the sum is computed, it is converted to a string and concatenated with the null string. The assignment then stores `"54"` into `answer`.

To summarize, string conversion is a useful feature of Java for formatting numeric output. But keep in mind that it works only as part of string concatenation. And remember that you must be careful to consider the precedence rules whenever you write a complex expression in which you there are multiple numeric values.

May We Introduce...

Blaise Pascal

One of the great historical figures in the world of computing was the French mathematician and religious philosopher Blaise Pascal (1623–1662), the inventor of one of the earliest known mechanical calculators.

Pascal's father, Etienne, was a noble in the French court, a tax collector, and a mathematician. Pascal's mother died when Pascal was three years old. Five years later, the family moved to Paris and Etienne took over the education of the children. Pascal quickly showed a talent for mathematics. When he was only 17, he published a mathematical essay that earned the jealous envy of René Descartes, one of the founders of modern geometry. (Pascal's work actually had been completed before he was 16.) It was based on a theorem, which he called the *hexagrammum mysticum*, or mystic hexagram, that described the inscription of hexagons in conic sections (parabolas, hyperbolas, and ellipses). In addition to the theorem (now called Pascal's theorem), his essay included over 400 corollaries.

When Pascal was about 20, he constructed a mechanical calculator that performed addition and subtraction of eight-digit numbers. That calculator required the user to dial in the numbers to be added or subtracted; then the sum or difference appeared in a set of windows. It is believed that his motivation for building this machine was to aid his father in collecting taxes. The earliest version of the machine does indeed split the numbers into six decimal digits and two fractional digits, as would be used for calculating sums of money. The machine was hailed by his contemporaries as a great advance in mathematics, and Pascal built several more in different forms. It achieved such popularity that many fake, nonfunctional copies were built by others and displayed as novelties. Several of Pascal's calculators still exist in various museums.

Pascal's box, as it is called, was long believed to be the first mechanical calculator. However, in 1950, a letter from Wilhelm Shickard to Johannes Kepler written in 1624 was discovered. This letter described an even more sophisticated calculator built by Shickard 20 years prior to Pascal's box. Unfortunately, the machine was destroyed in a fire and never rebuilt.

During his twenties, Pascal solved several difficult problems related to the cycloid curve, indirectly contributing to the development of differential calculus. Working with Pierre de Fermat, he laid the foundation of the calculus of probabilities and combinatorial analysis. One of the results of this work came to be known as Pascal's triangle, which simplifies the calculation of the coefficients of the expansion of $(x + y)^n$, where n is a positive integer.

Pascal also published a treatise on air pressure and conducted experiments that showed that barometric pressure decreases with altitude, helping to confirm theories that had been proposed by Galileo and Torricelli. His work on fluid dynamics forms a significant part of the foundation of that field. Among the most famous of his contributions is Pascal's law, which states that pressure applied to a fluid in a closed vessel is transmitted uniformly throughout the fluid.

continued ▼

Blaise Pascal

When Pascal was 23, his father became ill, and the family was visited by two disciples of Jansenism, a reform movement in the Catholic Church that had begun six years earlier. The family converted, and five years later one of his sisters entered a convent. Initially, Pascal was not so taken with the new movement, but by the time he was 31, his sister had persuaded him to abandon the world and devote himself to religion.

His religious works are considered no less brilliant than his mathematical and scientific writings. Some consider *Provincial Letters*, his series of 18 essays on various aspects of religion, as the beginning of modern French prose.

Pascal returned briefly to mathematics when he was 35, but a year later his health, which had always been poor, took a turn for the worse. Unable to perform his usual work, he devoted himself to helping the less fortunate. Three years later, he died while staying with his sister, having given his own house to a poor family.

4.6   Additional Mathematical Methods

Certain computations, such as taking square roots or finding the absolute value of a number, are very common in programs. It would be an enormous waste of time if every programmer had to start from scratch and create methods to perform these tasks. To help make the programmer's life easier, the `Math` class provides a number useful methods. Note that the class name must precede each of these methods with a dot in between the two names.

Method	Parameter Type(s)	Result Type	Result
`Math.abs(x)`	`int`, `long`, `float`, or `double`	same as parameter	Absolute value of x
`Math.cos(x)`	`double`	`double`	Cosine of x (x is in radians)
`Math.sin(x)`	`double`	`double`	Sine of x (x is in radians)
`Math.log(x)`	`double`	`double`	Natural logarithm of x
`Math.pow(x, y)`	`double`	`double`	x raised to the power y (if $x = 0.0$, y must be positive; if $x \leq 0.0$, y must be a whole number)
`Math.min(x, y)`	`int`, `long`, `float`, or `double`	same as parameter	Smaller of x and y
`Math.max(x, y)`	`int`, `long`, `float` or `double`	same as parameter	Larger of x and y
`Math.sqrt(x)`	`double`	`double`	Square root of x ($x \geq 0.0$)

When you call a `Frame` class method like `add` as a separate statement, it simply does some work and returns control to the next statement. But the calls to the `Math` methods like those in this table are used in *expressions* within assignment statements or in the parameter lists of other method calls. A method that is called as part of an expression does some work for you, but it also returns a value that takes its place in the expression. The statement

```
rootX = Math.sqrt(x);
```

calls the `Math.sqrt` method, which returns the square root of `x` that is assigned to `rootX`. Methods such as `Math.sqrt`, which return a value, are called value-returning methods. The third column in the preceding table tells you the type of the value that is returned.

Value-returning method A method that is called from within an expression. The method returns a value that takes its place in the expression, allowing further operations to be performed on the value; also called a function.

Notice that these arithmetic value-returning methods (such as `Math.abs` and `Math.sqrt`) are called without having to specify the name of an object. Recall from Chapter 3 that methods can be instance methods or class methods. These methods are class methods because they are associated with the class itself, rather than with a particular object. The Math class belongs to the package `java.lang`, which is automatically imported into every program by the Java compiler.

Matters of Style

Program Formatting

As far as the compiler is concerned, Java statements are *free format*: They can appear anywhere on a line, more than one can appear on a single line, and one statement can span several lines. The compiler needs blanks (or comments or new lines) to separate important symbols, and it needs semicolons to terminate statements. However, it is extremely important that your programs be readable, both for your sake and for the sake of anyone else who has to examine them.

When you write an outline for an English paper, you follow certain rules of indentation to make it readable. These same kinds of rules can make your programs easier to read. It is much easier to spot a mistake in a neatly formatted program than in a messy one. Thus you should keep your program neatly formatted while you are working on it. If you've gotten lazy and let your program become messy while making a series of changes, take the time to straighten it up. Often the source of an error becomes obvious during the process of formatting the code.

continued ▼

Program Formatting

Take a look at the following program for computing the cost per square foot of a house. Although it compiles and runs correctly, it does not conform to any formatting standards.

```java
// HouseCost program
// This program computes the cost per square foot of
// living space for a house, given the dimensions of
// the house, the number of stories, the size of the
// nonliving space, and the total cost less land
import java.awt.*; import java.awt.event.*; import java.text.*;
public class UglyHouseCost {private static Frame out;// Declare a variable of
                                                     //  type Frame
public static void main(String[] args){
final double WIDTH = 30.0;
final double LENGTH = 40.0;// Length of the house
final double STORIES = 2.5;// Number of full stories
final double NON_LIVING_SPACE = 825.0;  // Garage, closets, etc.
final double PRICE = 150000.0;// Selling price less land
double grossFootage;// Total square footage
double livingFootage;// Living area
double costPerFoot;// Cost/foot of living area
out = new Frame(); out.setLayout(new FlowLayout());  // Specify layout manager
                                                     //   for frame
   grossFootage = LENGTH * WIDTH * STORIES;  // Compute gross footage
       livingFootage = grossFootage - NON_LIVING_SPACE;  // Compute net footage
   costPerFoot = PRICE / livingFootage;  // Compute cost per usable foot
   out.add(new Label("Cost per square foot is " + costPerFoot));
out.pack();   out.show();  // Show the frame on the screen
// Event handler for window closing
   out.addWindowListener(new WindowAdapter(){
   public void windowClosing(WindowEvent event){ out.dispose();
System.exit(0);}});}}
```

Now look at the same program with proper formatting:

```java
//*****************************************************************************
// HouseCost program
// This program computes the cost per square foot of
```

continued ▼

Program Formatting

```java
// living space for a house, given the dimensions of
// the house, the number of stories, the size of the
// nonliving space, and the total cost less land
//********************************************************************
import java.awt.*;                              // Import Frame type, etc.
import java.awt.event.*;                        // Import event handling
                                                //   types


public class HouseCost
{
  // Declare a variable of type Frame
  private static Frame out;

  public static void main(String[] args)
  {
    final double WIDTH = 30.0;                  // Width of the house
    final double LENGTH = 40.0;                 // Length of the house
    final double STORIES = 2.5;                 // Number of full stories
    final double NON_LIVING_SPACE = 825.0;      // Garage, closets, etc.
    final double PRICE = 150000.0;              // Selling price less land

    double grossFootage;                        // Total square footage
    double livingFootage;                       // Living area
    double costPerFoot;                         // Cost/foot of living area

    out = new Frame();                          // Instantiate Frame object
    out.setLayout(new FlowLayout());            // Specify layout manager
                                                //   for frame

    grossFootage = LENGTH * WIDTH * STORIES;    // Compute gross footage
    livingFootage = grossFootage - NON_LIVING_SPACE;  // Compute net footage
    costPerFoot = PRICE / livingFootage;        // Compute cost per
                                                //   usable foot

    out.add(new Label("Cost per square foot is " +   // Add result to frame
          costPerFoot));
```

continued ▼

Program Formatting

```
    out.pack();                                  // Pack the frame
    out.show();                                  // Show the frame on
                                                 //  the screen

    // Event handler for window closing
    out.addWindowListener(new WindowAdapter()    // Create a
                                                 //  WindowClosing method

      {
        public void windowClosing(WindowEvent event)  //  to replace the empty
                                                 //   one

        {
          out.dispose();                         // Remove the frame from
                                                 //  the screen

          System.exit(0);                        // Stop the program
        }
      });
    }
}
```

Need we say more?
   Appendix F talks about programming style. Use it as a guide when you are writing programs.

4.7 Additional String Operations

Now that we have introduced numeric types and method calls, we can take advantage of additional features of the String data type. Here we introduce three useful methods that operate on strings: length, indexOf, and substring. The methods are value-returning methods.

The length Method

The length method, when applied to a String object, returns an int value that equals the number of characters in the string. If myName is a String object, a call to the length method looks like this:

```
myName.length()
```

The `length` method requires no parameters to be passed to it, but you still must use parentheses to signify an empty parameter list. Because `length` is a value-returning method, the method call must appear within an expression:

```
String firstName;                    // Local declarations
String fullName;
int    len;

firstName = "Alexandra";
len = firstName.length();            // Assigns 9 to len
fullName = firstName + " Jones";
len = fullName.length();             // Assigns 15 to len
```

The `indexOf` Method

The `indexOf` method searches a string to find the first occurrence of a particular substring and returns an `int` value giving the result of the search. The substring, passed as a parameter to the method, can be a literal string or a `String` expression. If `str1` and `str2` are of type `String`, the following are valid method calls with each returning an integer:

```
str1.indexOf("the")     str1.indexOf(str2)     str1.indexOf(str2 + "abc")
```

In each case above, `str1` is searched to see if the specified substring can be found within it. If so, the method returns the position in `str1` where the match begins. (Positions are numbered starting at 0, so the first character in a string is in position 0, the second is in position 1, and so on.) For a successful search, the match must be exact, including identical capitalization. If the substring could not be found, the method returns the value −1.

Given the code segment

```
String phrase;
int position;
phrase = "The dog and the cat";
```

then the statement

```
position = phrase.indexOf("the");
```

assigns to `position` the value 12, whereas the statement

```
position = phrase.indexOf("rat");
```

assigns to `position` the value −1, because there was no match.

The parameter to the `indexOf` method can also be a `char` value. In this case, `indexOf` searches for the first occurrence of that character within the string and returns its position (or −1, if the character was not found). For example, the code segment

```
String theString;

theString = "Abracadabra";
position = theString.indexOf('a');
```

assigns the value 3 to `position`, which is the position of the first occurrence of a lowercase *a* in `theString`. (Remember the first position is 0.)

Below are some more examples of calls to the `indexOf` method, assuming the following code segment has been executed:

```
String str1;
String str2;

str1 = "Programming and Problem Solving";
str2 = "gram";
```

Method Call	Value Returned by Method
`str1.indexOf("and")`	12
`str1.indexOf("Programming")`	0
`str2.indexOf("and")`	−1
`str1.indexOf("Pro")`	0
`str1.indexOf("ro" + str2)`	1
`str1.indexOf("Pr" + str2)`	−1
`str1.indexOf(' ')`	11

Notice in the fourth example that there are two copies of the substring `"Pro"` in `str1`, but `indexOf` returns only the position of the first copy. Also notice that the copies can be either separate words or parts of words—`indexOf` merely tries to match the sequence of characters given in the parameter list. The final example demonstrates that the parameter can be as simple as a single character, even a single blank.

The `substring` Method

The `substring` method returns a particular substring of a string. Assuming `myString` is of type `String`, here is a sample method call:

```
myString.substring(5, 20)
```

The parameters are integers that specify positions within the string. The method returns the piece of the string that starts with the position specified by the first parameter and continues to the position given by the second parameter minus 1. Thus, the length of the substring returned by the example call is 20 − 5 = 15 characters. Note that `sub-string` doesn't change `myString`; it returns a new `String` value that is a copy of a portion of the string. Below are some examples, assuming the statement

```
myString = "Programming and Problem Solving";
```

has been executed.

Method Call	String Contained in Value Returned by Method
`myString.substring(0, 7)`	`"Program"`
`myString.substring(7, 15)`	`"ming and"`
`myString.substring(10, 10)`	`""`
`myString.substring(24, 31)`	`"Solving"`
`myString.substring(24, 25)`	`"S"`

In the third example in the preceding list, specifying the second parameter to be the same as the first produces the empty string as the result. The last example illustrates how to obtain a single character from a given position in the string. If either of the parameters specifies a position beyond the end of the string, or if the second parameter is smaller than the first, the call to `substring` results in an error message. One way to avoid such errors is to write the call to `substring` in the following form. Here, `start` is an `int` variable containing the starting position, and `len` is another `int` variable containing the length of the desired substring.

```
myString.substring(start, Math.min(start+len, myString.length()))
```

Recall from our discussion of Java's math methods that `Math.min` returns the smaller of its two parameters. If `start+len` is accidentally greater than the length of the string, `min` returns the length of `myString` instead. We have thus ensured that the second parameter in the call to `substring` can be no greater than the length of `myString`. We are assuming `start` is less than the length of the string, but we can use the same sort of formula as the first parameter if we aren't certain that this assumption is valid.

Because `substring` returns a value of type `String`, you can use it with the concatenation operator (+) to copy pieces of strings and join them together to form new strings. The `indexOf` and `length` methods can be useful in determining the location and end of a piece of a string to be passed to `substring` as parameters.

Here is a code segment that uses several of the `String` operations:

```
fullName = "Jonathan Alexander Peterson";
startPos = fullName.indexOf("Peterson");
name = "Mr. " + fullName.substring(startPos, fullName.length());
```

This code assigns "Mr. Peterson" to name when it is executed. First, it stores a string into the variable fullName, and then it uses indexOf to locate the start of the name Peterson within the string. Next, it builds a new string by concatenating the literal "Mr. " with the characters Peterson, which are copied from the original string. As we see in later chapters, string operations are an important aspect of many computer programs.

4.8 Formatting Numeric Types

By default, consecutive integer and string values are output with no spaces between them. If the variables i, j, and k contain the values 15, 2, and 6, respectively, the statement

```
out.add(new Label("Results: " + i + j + k));
```

displays a label containing

```
Results: 1526
```

Without spacing between the numbers, this output is difficult to interpret. To separate the output values, you could insert a single blank (as a char literal) between the numbers:

```
out.add(new Label("Results: " + i + ' ' + j + ' ' + k));
```

This statement produces the label contents

```
Results: 15 2 6
```

If you want even more spacing between items, you can use literal strings containing blanks:

```
out.add(new Label("Results: " + i + "    " + j + "    " + k));
```

Here, the resulting label contains

```
Results: 15    2    6
```

What do you suppose happens if we reverse the order of the parameters in our first example? That is, what does the following statement output?

```
out.add(new Label(i + j + k + " are the results."));
```

You might think it would display

```
1526 are the results
```

But you'd be wrong. It actually displays

```
23 are the results
```

Remember that a chain of + operators is evaluated left to right, and a + performs concatenation only if one of its operands is a string.

 Software Engineering Tip

Understanding Before Changing

When you are in the middle of getting a program to run and you come across an error, it's tempting to start changing parts of the program to try to make it work. *Don't!* You'll nearly always make things worse. It's essential that you understand what is causing the error and that you carefully think through the solution. The only thing you should try is running the program with different data to determine the pattern of the unexpected behavior.

There is no magic trick—inserting an extra semicolon or right brace, for example—that can automatically fix a program. If the compiler tells you that a semicolon or a right brace is missing, you need to examine the program in light of the syntax rules and determine precisely what the problem is. Perhaps you accidentally typed a colon instead of a semicolon. Or maybe there's an extra left brace.

If the source of a problem isn't immediately obvious, a good rule of thumb is to leave the computer and go somewhere where you can quietly look over a printed copy of the program. Studies show that people who do all of their debugging away from the computer actually get their programs to work in less time *and in the end produce better programs* than those who continue to work on the machine—more proof that there is still no mechanical substitute for human thought.[2]

[2]Basili, V. R., Selby, R. W., "Comparing the Effectiveness of Software Testing Strategies," *IEEE Transactions on Software Engineering*, Vol. SE–13, No. 12, pp. 1278–1296, Dec. 1987.

Problem-Solving Case Study

Map Measurements

Problem You're spending a day in the city. You plan to visit the natural history museum, a record store, a gallery, and a bookshop, and then go to a concert. You have a tourist map that shows where these places are located. You want to determine how far apart they are and how far you'll walk during the entire day. Then you can decide when it would be better to take a taxi. According to the map's legend, one inch on the map equals one quarter of a mile on the ground.

Output The distance between each of the places and the total distance, rounded to the nearest tenth of a mile. The values on which the calculations are based also should be displayed for verification purposes.

Discussion You can measure the distances between two points on the map with a ruler. The program must output miles, so you need to multiply the number of inches by 0.25. You then write down the figure, rounded to the nearest tenth of a mile. When you've done this for each pair of places, you add the distances to get the total mileage.

What are the objects in our by-hand solution? Distances. We can represent each distance as a floating-point number. The operations on the objects are the same as those that we did by hand.

The only tricky part is how to round a value to the nearest tenth of a mile. This is easy to do in our head; how do we calculate it in our program? In this chapter, we showed how to round a floating-point value to the nearest integer by adding 0.5 and using a type cast to truncate the result:

```
(int)((double)Value + 0.5))
```

To round to the nearest tenth, we first multiply the value by 10, round the result to the nearest integer, and then divide by 10 again. For example, if `doubleValue` contains 5.162, then

```
(double)((int)(doubleValue * 10.0 + 0.5)) / 10.0
```

gives 5.2.

Let's treat all of the quantities as named constants so that it is easier to change the program later. From measuring the map, you know that the distance from the museum to the record store is 1.5 inches, from the record store to the gallery is 2.3 inches, from the gallery to the bookshop is 5.9 inches, and from the bookshop to the concert is 4.0 inches. Our distance objects are represented by these constants.

Define Constants

DISTANCE1 = 1.5
DISTANCE2 = 2.3
DISTANCE3 = 5.9
DISTANCE4 = 4.0
SCALE = 0.25

Initialize the Total Miles

Set totMiles to 0.0

Initialize the Frame

Set the layout manager to GridLayout with one column and any number of rows

Compute Miles for Each Distance on the Map

Set miles to (double)((int)(DISTANCE1 * SCALE * 10.0 + 0.5)) / 10.0
Display DISTANCE1, miles to one decimal place
Add miles to totMiles
Set miles to (double)((int)(DISTANCE2 * SCALE * 10.0 + 0.5)) / 10.0
Display DISTANCE2, miles to one decimal place
Add miles to totMiles
Set miles to (double)((int)(DISTANCE3 * SCALE * 10.0 + 0.5)) / 10.0
Display DISTANCE3, miles to one decimal place
Add miles to totMiles
Set miles to (double)((int)(DISTANCE4 * SCALE * 10.0 + 0.5)) / 10.0
Display DISTANCE4, miles to one decimal place
Add miles to totMiles

Before we go on, let's examine the Compute Miles algorithm again. There are four statements that are alike except for the distance object being used in the calculation. Wouldn't it be nice if we could write that calculation equation only once but have it be applied four times to four different values? Well, this is an example of the third kind of method, a helper method.

9. Examine each method call to see that you have the correct number of parameters and that the data types of the parameters are correct.

10. If the cause of an error in a program is not obvious, leave the computer and study a printed listing. Change your program only after you understand the source of the error.

Summary of Classes

In this chapter we introduced value-returning methods, so we add this form of method to our table that summarizes the classes discussed in the chapter.

Package Name

Class Name	Comments
`java.lang`	Automatically imported to every Java program
`Math`	

Value-Returning Class Methods:

`abs(int)`	Returns `int`
`abs(long)`	Returns `long`
`abs(float)`	Returns `float`
`abs(double)`	Returns `double`
`cos(double)`	Returns `double`
`log(double)`	Returns `double`
`max(int, int)`	Returns `int`
`max(long, long)`	Returns `long`
`max(float, float)`	Returns `float`
`max(double, double)`	Returns `double`
`min(int, int)`	Returns `int`
`min(long, long)`	Returns `long`
`min(float, float)`	Returns `float`
`min(double, double)`	Returns `double`
`pow(double, double)`	Returns `double`
`sin(double)`	Returns `double`
`sqrt(double)`	Returns `double`

`String`

Value-Returning Instance Methods:

`length()`	Returns `int`
`indexOf(String)`	Returns `int`
`indexOf(char)`	Returns `int`
`substring(int, int)`	Returns `String`

Summary

Java provides several built-in numeric data types, of which the most commonly used are `int` and `double`. The integral types are based on the mathematical integers, but the computer limits the range of integer values that can be represented. The floating-point types are based on the mathematical notion of real numbers. As with integers, the computer limits the range of floating-point numbers that can be represented. In addition, it limits the number of digits of precision in floating-point values. We can write literals of type `double` in several forms, including scientific (E) notation. Java provides the standard mathematical operations to go with these data types: addition (+), subtraction (-), multiplcation (*), division (/), and remainder (%). Java also provides an increment operation (++) and a decrement operation (- -).

Mixing values of the integer and floating-point types in an expression results in automatic type conversion to achieve compatibility between the operands of all of the operators. If you aren't careful, these automatic conversions can have unanticipated results. It is best to explicitly use type cast operations whenever you need to mix types within expressions.

Much of the computation of a program is performed in arithmetic expressions. Expressions can contain more than one operator. The order in which the operations are performed is determined by precedence rules. In arithmetic expressions, the unary operators (such as negation) are performed first, then type casts, then multiplication, division, and modulus are performed, and lastly addition and subtraction. Multiple arithmetic operations of the same precedence are grouped from left to right. You can use parentheses to override the precedence rules.

Not only should the output produced by a program be easy to read, but the format of the program itself should be clear and readable. Java is a free-format language. A consistent style that uses indentation, blank lines, and spaces within lines helps you (and other programmers) understand and work with your programs.

Quick Check

1. Write a local Java constant declaration that gives the name PI to the value 3.14159. (p. 129)
2. Declare an `int` variable named `count` and a `double` variable named `sum`. (pp. 130–131)
3. You want to divide 9 by 5.
   a. How do you write the expression if you want the result to be the floating-point value 1.8? (pp. 138–139)
   b. How do you write it if you want only the integer quotient? (pp. 138–139)
4. What is the value of the following Java expression?

   `5 % 2`

   (pp. 131–133)

5. What is the result of evaluating the expression

```
(1 + 2 * 2) / 2 + 1
```

(p. 137)

6. How would you write the following formula as a Java expression that produces a floating-point value as a result? (pp. 138–139)

$$\frac{9}{5}c + 32$$

7. Add type casts to the following statements to make the type conversions clear and explicit. Your answers should produce the same results as the original statements. (pp. 138–139)

a. `someDouble = 5 + someInt;`

b. `someInt = 2.5 * someInt / someDouble;`

8. You want to compute the square roots and absolute values of some floating-point numbers. Which Java methods would you use? (pp. 145–146)

9. If the `String` variable `str` contains the string "Now is the time", what is the result of the following expression? (pp. 149–153)

```
str.length() + ' ' + str.substring(1, 3)
```

10. Reformat the following program to make it clear and readable. (pp. 146–149)

```
//*********************************************************************
                    // SumProd program
    // This program computes the sum and product of two integers
//*********************************************************************
import java.awt.*; public class SumProd {
private static Frame out;
public static void main(String[] args){
    final int INT2=8;
    out = new Frame();
    out.setLayout (new FlowLayout());
final int INT1=20; out.add(new Label(
"The sum of " + INT1 + " and "
+ INT2 + " is " + INT1+INT2)); out.add(new Label (
"Their product is " + (INT1*INT2))); out.pack(); out.show(); }
}
```

11. What should you do if a program fails to run correctly and the reason for the error is not immediately obvious? (p. 154)

Answers

1. `final double PI = 3.14159;`
2. `int    count;`
   `float sum;`
3. a. `9.0 / 5.0` *or* `(double) 9 / (double) 5`   b. `9 / 5`
4. The value is 1.
5. The result is 3.
6. `9.0 / 5.0 * c + 32.0`
7. a. `someDouble = (double)(5 + someInt);`
   b. `someInt = (int)(2.5 * (double)(someInt) / someDouble);`
8. `math.sqrt` **and** `math.abs`   9. `15 ow`
10.

```
//*****************************************************************
// SumProd program
// This program computes the sum and product of two integers
//*****************************************************************
import java.awt.*;

public class SumProd
{
  private static Frame out;
  public static void main(String[] args)
  {
    final int INT1 = 20;
    final int INT2 = 8;

    out = new Frame();
    out.setLayout(new FlowLayout());
    out.add(new Label("The sum of " + INT1 + " and "
    + INT2 + " is " + INT1+INT2));
    out.add(new Label ("Their product is " + (INT1*INT2)));
    out.pack();
    out.show();
  }
}
```

11. Print out the program, leave the computer, and study the program until you understand the cause of the problem. Then correct the algorithm and the program as necessary before you go back to the computer and make any changes in the program file.

Exam Preparation Exercises

1. Mark the following constructs either valid or invalid. Assume all variables are of type `int`.

	Valid	*Invalid*
a. `x * y = c;`	_____	_____
b. `y = con;`	_____	_____
c. `private static final int x : 10;`	_____	_____
d. `int x;`	_____	_____
e. `a = b % c;`	_____	_____

2. If `alpha` and `beta` are `int` variables with `alpha` = 4 and `beta` = 9, what value is stored into `alpha` in each of the following? Answer each part independently of the others.

   a. `alpha = 3 * beta;`
   b. `alpha = alpha + beta;`
   c. `alpha++;`
   d. `alpha = alpha / beta;`
   e. `alpha--;`
   f. `alpha = alpha + alpha;`
   g. `alpha = beta % 6;`

3. Compute the value of each legal expression. Indicate whether the value is an integer or a floating-point value. If the expression is not legal, explain why.

	Integer	*Floating Point*
a. `10.0 / 3.0 + 5 * 2`	_____	_____
b. `10 % 3 + 5 % 2`	_____	_____
c. `10 / 3 + 5 / 2`	_____	_____
d. `12.5 + (2.5 / (6.2 / 3.1))`	_____	_____
e. `-4 * (-5 + 6)`	_____	_____
f. `13 % 5 / 3`	_____	_____
g. `(10.0 / 3.0 % 2) / 3`	_____	_____

4. What value is stored into the `int` variable `result` in each of the following?

   a. `result = 15 % 4;`
   b. `result = 7 / 3 + 2;`
   c. `result = 2 + 7 * 5;`
   d. `result = 45 / 8 * 4 + 2;`
   e. `result = 17 + (21 % 6) * 2;`
   f. `result = (int)(4.5 + 2.6 * 0.5);`

5. If `a` and `b` are `int` variables with `a` = 5 and `b` = 2, what output does each of the following statements produce?

   a. `out.add(new Label("a = " + a + "b = " + b));`
   b. `out.add(new Label("Sum:" + a + b));`
   c. `out.add(new Label("Sum:   " + a + b));`
   d. `out.add(new Label(a / b + " feet"));`

6. What does the following program print?

```java
import java.awt.*
public class ExamPrep
{
  private static Frame out;
  public static void main(String[] args)
  {
    final int LBS = 10;
    int  price;
    int  cost;
    char ch;
    out = new Frame();
    out.setLayout(new GridLayout(0,1));
    price = 30;
    cost = price * LBS;
    ch = 'A';
    out.add(new Label("Cost is "));
    out.add(new Label(cost));
    out.add(new Label("Price is " + price + "Cost is " + cost));
    out.add(new Label("Grade " + ch + " costs "));
    out.add(new Label(cost));
    out.pack();
    out.show();
  }
}
```

7. Translate the following Java code into algebraic notation. (All variables are `double` variables.)

```java
y = -b + sqrt(b * b - 4.0 * a * c);
```

8. Given the following program fragment:

```java
int    i;
int    j;
double z;

i = 4;
j = 17;
z = 2.6;
```

determine the value of each expression below. If the result is a floating-point value, include a decimal point in your answer.

a. i / (double)j

b. 1.0 / i + 2

c. z * j

d. i + j % i
e. (1 / 2) * i
f. 2 * i + j - i
g. j / 2
h. 2 * 3 - 1 % 3
i. i % j / i
j. (int)(z + 0.5)

9. To use each of the following statements, a Java program must `import` which package(s)?
a. `out.add(new Label(x));`
b. `new WindowAdapter();`
c. `out.setLayout(new GridLayout(0, 2));`
d. `out.pack();`

10. Evaluate the following expressions. If the result is a floating-point number, include a decimal point in your answer.
a. `Math.abs(-9.1)`
b. `Math.sqrt(49.0)`
c. `3 * (int)7.8 + 3`
d. `Math.pow(4.0, 2.0)`
e. `Math.sqrt((double)(3 * 3 + 4 * 4))`
f. `Math.sqrt(abs(-4.0) + Math.sqrt(25.0))`

11. Given the statements

```
String heading;
String str;
heading = "Exam Preparation Exercises";
```

what is the output of each code segment below?
a. `out.add(new Label(heading.length()));`
b. `out.add(new Label(heading.substring(6, 16)));`
c. `out.add(new Label(heading.indexOf("Ex")));`
d. `str = heading.substring(2, 26);`
   `out.add(new Label(str.indexOf("Ex")));`
e. `str = heading.substring(heading.IndexOf("Ex") +`
   `                     2, heading.length());`
   `out.add(new Label(str.indexOf("Ex")));`

12. Formatting a program incorrectly causes an error. (True or False?)

Chapter 4: Numeric Types and Expressions

Programming Warm-Up Exercises

1. Change the program in Exam Preparation Exercise 6 so that it prints the cost for 15 pounds.

2. Write an assignment statement to calculate the sum of the numbers from 1 through n using Gauss's formula:

$$\text{Sum} = \frac{n(n+1)}{2}$$

Store the result into the int variable sum.

3. Given the declarations

```
int    i;
int    j;
double x;
double y;
```

write a valid Java expression for each of the following algebraic expressions.

a. $\dfrac{x}{y} - 3$ e. $\dfrac{i}{j}$ (the floating-point result)

b. $(x + y)(x - y)$ f. $\dfrac{i}{j}$ (the integer quotient)

c. $\dfrac{1}{x + y}$ g. $\dfrac{\dfrac{x+y}{3} - \dfrac{x-y}{5}}{4x}$

d. $\dfrac{1}{x} + y$

4. Given the declarations

```
int    i;
long   n;
double x;
double y;
```

write a valid Java expression for each of the following algebraic expressions. Use calls to math methods wherever they are useful.

a. $|i|$ (absolute value)

e. $\dfrac{x^3}{x+y}$

b. $|n|$

f. $\sqrt{x^6+y^5}$

c. $|x+y|$

g. $\left(x+\sqrt{y}\right)^7$

d. $|x| + |y|$

5. Write expressions to compute both solutions for the quadratic formula. The formula is

$$\frac{-b \pm \sqrt{b^2 - 4ac}}{2a}$$

The $\pm$ means "plus or minus" and indicates that there are two solutions to the equation, one in which the result of the square root is *added* to $-b$ and one in which the result is *subtracted* from $-b$. Assume all variables are `float` variables.

6. Enter the following program into your computer and run it. In the initial comments, replace the items within parentheses with your own information. (Omit the parentheses.)

```
//**********************************
// Programming Assignment One
// (your name)
// (date program was run)
// (description of the problem)
//**********************************
import java.awt.*;

class WarmUp
{
  public static void main(String[] args)
  {
    private static Frame out;        // Frame for output
    final double DEBT = 300.0;       // Original value owed
    final double PMT = 22.4;         // Payment
    final double INT_RATE = 0.02;    // Interest rate
```

```
    double charge;        // Interest times debt
    double reduc;         // Amount debt is reduced
    double remaining;     // Remaining balance

    out = new Frame();
    out.setLayout(new FlowLayout());
    charge = INT_RATE * DEBT;
    reduc = PMT - charge;
    remaining = DEBT - reduc;
    out.add(new Label("Payment: " + PMT + " Charge: " + charge
                        + " Balance owed: " + remaining));
    out.pack();
    out.show();
  }
}
```

7. Enter the following program into your computer and run it. Add comments, using the pattern shown in Exercise 6 above. (Notice how hard it is to tell what the program does without the comments.)

```
import java.awt.*;
class WarmUp2
{
  private static Frame out;
  public static void main(String[] args)
  {
    final int TOT_COST = 1376;
    final int POUNDS = 10;
    final int OUNCES = 12;

    int     totOz;
    double uCost;

    out = new Frame();
    out.setLayout(new FlowLayout());
    totOz = 16 * POUNDS;
    totOz = totOz + OUNCES;
    uCost = TOT_COST / totOz;
    out.add(new Label("Cost per unit: " + uCost));
    out.pack();
    out.show();
  }
}
```

8. Complete the following Java program. The program should find and output the perimeter and area of a rectangle, given the length and the width. Be sure to label the output, and don't forget to use comments.

```java
//***************************************************
// Rectangle program
// This program finds the perimeter and the area
// of a rectangle, given the length and width
//***************************************************
import java.awt.*;
class Rectangle
{
  private static Frame out;        // Frame for output
  public static void main(String[] args)
  {

    double length;              // Length of the rectangle
    double width;               // Width of the rectangle
    double perimeter;           // Perimeter of the rectangle
    double area;                // Area of the rectangle

    length = 10.7;
    width = 5.2;
```

9. Write an expression whose result is the position of the first occurrence of the characters "res" in a String variable named sentence. If the variable contains the first sentence of this question, then what is the result? (Look at the sentence carefully!)

10. Write a sequence of Java statements to output the positions of the second and third occurrences of the characters "res" in the String variable named sentence. You may assume that there are always at least three occurrences in the variable. (*Hint*: Use the substring method to create a new string whose contents are the portion of sentence following an occurrence of "res".)

Programming Problems

1. Java systems provide a set of classes that duplicate the names of primitive types except that the first letter of the type name is capitalized (for example, Double and Long instead of double and long). The two exceptions are that the class corresponding to int is called Integer and the class corresponding to char is called Character. Each of these types contains declarations of constants related to the corresponding primitive type. Two of these constants are Integer.MAX_VALUE and Integer.MIN_VALUE, the largest and smallest int

values that Java allows. Write an application to display the values of `Integer.MAX_VALUE` and `Integer.MIN_VALUE`. The output should identify which value is `Integer.MAX_VALUE` and which value is `Integer.MIN_VALUE`. Be sure to include appropriate comments in your program, and use indentation as we do in the programs in this chapter. Each of these types defines similar constants, so you may want to extend your program to display `Long.MIN_VALUE`, and so on, just to learn what the actual maximum and minimum numbers are for each of the primitive types.

2. Write an application that outputs three labels, displayed on separate lines as follows:

```
7 / 4 using integer division equals  <result>
7 / 4 using floating point division equals  <result>
7 modulo 4 equals  <result>
```

where <result> stands for the result computed by your program. Use named constants for 7 and 4 everywhere in your program (including the output statements) to make the program easy to modify. Be sure to include appropriate comments in your program, choose meaningful identifiers, and use indentation as we do in the programs in this chapter.

3. Write a Java application that converts a Celsius temperature to its Fahrenheit equivalent. The formula is

$$\text{Fahrenheit} = \frac{9}{5}\text{Celsius} + 32$$

Make the Celsius temperature a named constant so that its value can be changed easily. The program should print both the value of the Celsius temperature and its Fahrenheit equivalent, with appropriate identifying messages. Be sure to include appropriate comments in your program, choose meaningful identifiers, and use indentation as we do in the programs in this chapter.

4. Write an application to calculate the diameter, the circumference, and the area of a circle with a radius of 6.75. Assign the radius to a `float` variable, and then output the radius with an appropriate message. Declare a named constant `PI` with the value 3.14159. The program should output the diameter, the circumference, and the area, each on a separate line, with identifying labels. Be sure to include appropriate comments in your program, choose meaningful identifiers, and use indentation as we do in the programs in this chapter.

5. You have bought a car, taking out a loan with an annual interest rate of 9%. You expect to make 36 monthly payments of $165.25 each. You want to keep

track of the remaining balance you owe after each monthly payment. The formula for the remaining balance is

$$\text{Bal}_k = \text{pmt}\left(\frac{1 - (1 + i)^{k-n}}{i}\right)$$

where

Bal_k = balance remaining after the kth payment
  k = payment number (1, 2, 3, ...)
pmt = amount of the monthly payment
  i = interest rate per month (annual rate ÷ 12)
  n = total number of payments to be made

Write an application to calculate and display the balance remaining after the first, second, and third monthly car payments. Before showing these three results, the program should output the values on which the calculations are based (monthly payment, interest rate, and total number of payments). Display an identifying message with each numerical result. Be sure to include appropriate comments in your program, choose meaningful identifiers, and use indentation as we do in the programs in this chapter.

Case Study Follow-Up Exercises

1. What is the advantage of using named constants instead of literal constants in the Walk program?
2. Modify the Walk program to include a round-off factor so that the rounding of miles can be modified easily. Currently, the program uses a literal constant (10.0) in several places to round miles to the nearest tenth, requiring us to make multiple changes if we want a different round-off factor.
3. Should the round-off factor in Question 2 be a constant or a variable? Explain.
4. In the Walk program, a particular pattern of statements is repeated four times with small variations. Identify the repeating pattern. Next, circle those parts of the statements that vary with each repetition. Having done this, now modify the Walk program to work with a fifth distance measurement.

Event-Driven Input and Software Design Strategies

- To be able to construct statements to display a data entry field on the screen.

- To be able to display a button on the screen and register it as an event source.

- To be able to write statements to read values from a data entry field into a program when a button is pressed.

- To be able to write an event handler for a button event and register it as a listener.

- To know how to convert strings containing numbers into numeric types.

- To be able to write appropriate prompting labels for interactive programs.

- To be able to describe the basic principles of object-oriented design and functional decomposition.

- To be able to apply the object-oriented design strategy to solve a simple problem.

- To be able to apply the functional decomposition strategy to solve a simple problem.

- To be able to take a design for a software solution and code it in Java, using self-documenting code.

A program needs data on which to operate. We have been writing all of the data values in the program itself, in literal and named constants. If this were the only way we could enter data, we would have to rewrite a program each time we wanted to apply it to a different set of values. In this chapter, we look at ways of entering data into a program while it is running.

Once we know how to input data, process the data, and output the results, we can begin to think about designing more complicated programs. We have talked about general problem-solving strategies and writing simple programs. For a simple problem, it's easy to choose a strategy, write the algorithm, and code the program. But as problems become more complex, we have to use a more organized approach. In the second part of this chapter, we look at two general strategies for developing software: object-oriented design and functional decomposition.

5.1 Getting Data into Programs

One of the biggest advantages of computers is that a program can be used with many different sets of data. To do so, we must keep the data separate from the program until the program is executed. Then instructions in the program copy values from the data set into variables in the program. After storing these values into the variables, the program can perform calculations with them (see Figure 5.1).

The process of placing values from an outside data set into variables in a program is called *input*. In widely used terminology, the computer is said to *read* outside data into the variables. The data for the program can come from an input device (such as a keyboard or mouse) or from a file on an auxiliary storage device. We look at file input in Chapter 9; here we consider data entered from the keyboard.

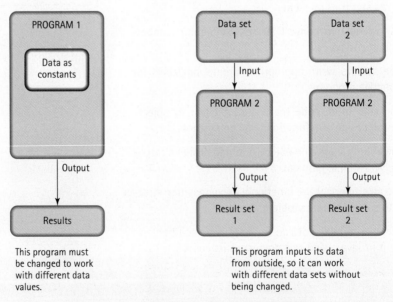

Figure 5.1   *Separating the data from the program*

5.2 Entering Data Using Fields in a Frame

If the `Payroll` program in Chapter 1 had used interactive input, the frame in Figure 5.2 would have been appropriate.

This frame contains three labels and a button (Done) in the left column of its grid. The right column has three data entry fields.

It's important to note that a data entry field and a Java field (a declaration in a class) are not the same. One is an area on the screen and the other is a name representing a constant or variable. This is a case where the Java designers use the same word to mean two different things. When discussing fields, we must clearly indicate which kind we are referring to. Syntactically, Java doesn't confuse them because a data entry field is a type of object and a class field is part of a class declaration.

> **Button**   A component of a frame that fires an event (called a *button event*) when the user clicks on it with the mouse
>
> **Field**   A component of a frame in which the user can type a value. The user must first place the cursor in the field by clicking inside the field.

The user clicks within a data entry field to position the cursor there and then types a value into the field using the keyboard. As shown in Figure 5.2, the program displays each field with an initial value that the user can delete before entering a value. Such an initial value is called a *default value*. A program can also be written to display a field without a default value. Including a default value is one way to show the user how to type data within the field.

The user can enter the data into the fields in any order and can go back to any field and correct a mistyped value. None of the user's actions are seen by the program until the button is clicked. Of course, the computer is responding to the user's keystrokes and mouse clicks, so some program must be handling these actions. What is it? The JVM, working together with the operating system, handles the individual keystrokes and mouse actions.

There is a separate variable in the program that corresponds to each field object in the frame. The operating system keeps a copy of each field's contents in objects assigned to these variables. Meanwhile, the program is doing nothing because it has turned control over to the JVM. You can picture a program covering its eyes while the user makes changes to its field variables via the operating system and JVM.

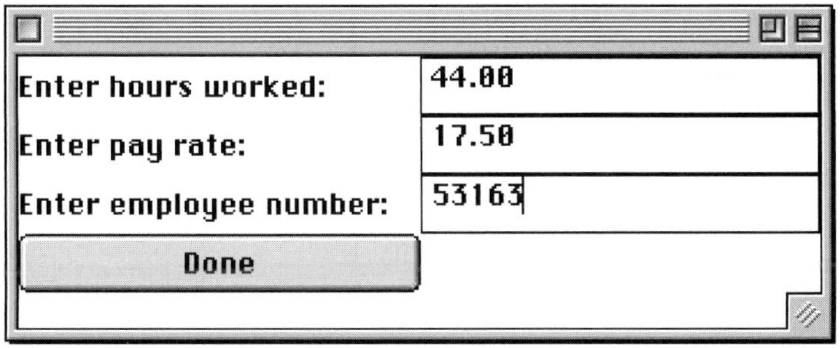

Figure 5.2   *Possible data entry frame for the* `Payroll` *program*

When the user clicks on the button, the button event is fired and the appropriate handler within the button listener is invoked. The event handler springs into action (the program uncovers its eyes) and processes the values that are currently stored in the variables associated with the fields. The event handler then restores the values in the fields to their default values and returns control to the JVM. Seeing the fields return to their default values is a signal to the user that he or she can enter another set of values. This process is shown in Figure 5.3.

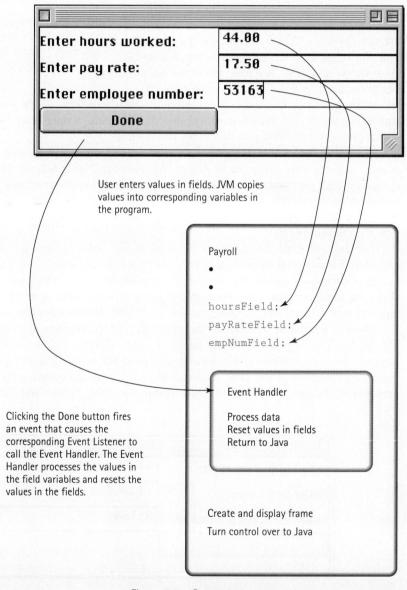

Figure 5.3 *Data entry process*

Entering data in the manner that we have just described is typical of modern programs, and is called a dialog. In a theatrical play, a dialog is an exchange between two characters. In the case of the computer, a dialog is an exchange between the user and a program. The program initiates the dialog by displaying a frame, the user replies by entering data into the fields of the frame and clicking a button, the program processes the data and responds by updating the frame.

> **Dialog** A style of user interface in which the user enters data and then performs a separate action (such as clicking a button) when the entered values are ready to be processed by the program
>
> **Event loop** The repetitive calling of an event handler to respond to a series of events, until some condition causes the program to exit the cycle.

If the program needs to have a series of values entered, it can again display the frame in its initial form and the user replies again. This data entry cycle is called an event loop. The event loop continues until the user indicates that there is no more data to enter, perhaps by entering a special data value or clicking another button.

Later we consider the finer points of designing a dialog so that it is easy to use. Such considerations are especially important when a dialog involves entering data into multiple fields in a frame. Until then, we focus our attention on a simple dialog using a frame that contains a single field, a label for the field, and a button.

5.3 Creating a Data Entry Field

Creating a data entry field in Java is very similar to creating a label. The essential steps are the same, with only minor differences. Those steps are:

1. Declare a variable of the appropriate field class
2. Instantiate an object of the class
3. Add the object to the frame using the add method

We saw in Chapter 3 that a label is simply an object of type Label. A data entry field is an object of type TextField. For example, you can declare a variable called inputField as follows:

```
TextField inputField;     // Declare a field for data entry
```

When you create a Label object with new, you pass a string to the Label constructor that tells it what text to display in the label. For example, here is a statement that creates and assigns a Label object containing the string "Enter data here:" to a Label variable called fieldLabel.

```
fieldLabel = new Label("Enter data here:");
```

When creating an object of type TextField, you provide the constructor with the size of the field. Here is an example of creating and assigning a TextField object to the variable inputField.

```
inputField = new TextField(6);
```

In this example, the object assigned to `inputField` is specified to have space for typing six characters within it. You can give the field a default value by including a string as the first parameter to the constructor. For example,

```
inputField = new TextField("Replace Me", 10);
```

would cause the `TextField` object to be created with space for 10 characters, and initially the words `"Replace Me"` would appear within the field.

The last step in creating a field is to add it to a frame. Just as with a label, you can use the frame's `add` method. If you have a frame called `dataEntryFrame`, then you would write:

```
dataEntryFrame.add(inputField);
```

When you call `dataEntryFrame.show()`, the frame appears on the screen with a field for entering data. As you can see, creating a field really is just as simple as creating a label. There is one very important difference between a `Label` field and a `TextField` field: The user cannot change the text written in a `Label` but can change the text in the `TextField`.

In some of our examples, we've instantiated labels directly within the parameter list of `add`. Java lets us do the same thing with a `TextField`, but we should never do so. The reason is that objects instantiated in this manner aren't assigned to a variable, so there is no name that we can use to access them. These are called *anonymous* objects. Sometimes we `add` a `Label` to a `Frame` and then never access it again; in that case it's OK for it to be anonymous. But the reason for adding a `TextField` is to later access its contents for input data. So a `TextField` object must be assigned to a variable to be useful.

Now let's look at how to get the data from the field in which it has been entered.

5.4 Extracting a Value from a Field

Just as a `Frame` object has methods such as `add`, `pack`, and `show` associated with it, a `TextField` object also comes with a set of methods. One of those methods, called `getText`, enables us to get the current value in the field as it appears on the screen. The `getText` method returns a value of type `String` that holds a copy of the contents of the field. For example, if you declare a `String` variable called `fieldContents`, you can write

```
fieldContents = inputField.getText();
```

to store the characters currently contained in `inputField` into `fieldContents`.

Note that we have not yet said anything about when or where to call the `getText` method. We have considered the steps of creating the field and taking data from it in isolation from the rest of the program. In the following sections, we examine how these steps are related to handling a button event that tells the program when the user is ready to have it look at the data. Before that, however, there is one more `TextField` method that we would like to introduce.

You saw in the last section how a field can be given a default value by its constructor. Once a field has been created and shown on the screen, it is often useful to be able to change its contents. For example, after the program has processed the contents of the field, it may replace them with the default value so that the user knows that he or she can enter a new value. The `setText` method replaces the current contents of a field with a string that is passed to it. Here is an example of calling `setText`:

```
inputField.setText("Replace Me");
```

Notice that `setText` is a `void` method. It does not return a value, and it is called as a separate statement. If you want to clear the field so that it appears empty, you simply call `setText` with an empty string:

```
inputField.setText("");
```

A call to `setText` immediately changes the contents of the field on the screen. You do *not* call the frame's `show` method again to update the field. Figure 5.4 shows a window with one `TextField` object.

You might notice another similarity between a `Label` object and a `TextField` object; a `Label` object also has a `setText` method that allows you to change its contents after it has been displayed on the screen. For example, you can write

```
fieldLabel.setText("Enter more data:");
```

which changes the text in `fieldLabel` to the string, `"Enter more data:"`.

Figure 5.4   *A* `Frame` *with one* `TextField`

Given all of their similarities, it is important to remember the major distinction between a `Label` object and a `TextField` object: The user cannot change what is displayed in a `Label`, but he or she can change the contents of a `TextField`.

5.5 Creating a Button

Before you can handle a button event, you have to put a button into the frame and register a listener with the button object. First, let's consider how to add a button to a frame. The process is very much like adding a label or a field.

1. Declare a variable of the appropriate button class
2. Instantiate an object of the class
3. Add the object to the frame using the `add` method

In the case of a button, the appropriate class is called `Button`. An example declaration is:

```
Button done;          // Declare a Button variable called done
```

The call to its constructor includes the string that should appear inside of the button. For example,

```
done = new Button("Done");          // Create a Button object
```

The call to the `add` method for a frame called `dataEntryField` is written:

```
dataEntryFrame.add(done);
```

When the `show` method for the frame is called, a button is included in the frame with the word `"Done"` appearing inside of it. Note that we are using our convention of starting a variable identifier with a lowercase letter, but the string that appears in the button is capitalized. Java may not use proper English capitalization, but our user interface should! The identifier `done` with a lowercase d is the name of a button object; `"Done"` with an uppercase D is the string that appears on the button on the screen. Now let's examine the button registration process.

Each event listener must be registered with the appropriate event source. When the event fires, the object that generated it calls the appropriate method within the listener to process the event. Each Java application has its own set of possible events and corresponding event listeners. Registration is a two-part process: giving a name to the event and registering a corresponding listener. In the case of closing the window, however, you didn't have to give a name to the event. Because Java predefines all of the events that a window can generate, it automatically names them when you create a frame.

Java doesn't know in advance what buttons are added to a frame or what they are called. There could be dozens of buttons on the screen at once and all of them could have the same listener. So each event must have a name that distinguishes it from the others. Giving the event a name is simply a matter of calling a method associated with its `Button` object. The method is called `setActionCommand` and it takes one parameter, a string that names the event. Here is an example:

```
done.setActionCommand("done");
```

The example call tells the `Button` object called `done` that when it generates an event it should supply the string `"done"` to any listener that responds to the event. Note that the string doesn't have to be the same as the name of the object. It can be any string of our choosing. However, it's easier to remember a single name for both, so that is the style we follow in this text. Keep in mind that there are two strings associated with a button, the one that is displayed on the screen and the one that names the event that the button generates.

If a user interface has multiple buttons, when the event handler is called, it doesn't automatically know which one was clicked. To tell them apart, it looks at the event name string associated with the event. Because we use frames with just one button in this chapter, we needn't be concerned with using the name in our event handler method. Even so, we still give the button event a name as a matter of good programming practice. In Chapter 6, we use the event name to handle events from multiple buttons.

Let's put together all of the elements we've seen in this chapter to show how to create the example frame.

```
Frame dataEntryFrame;                         // Declare a frame
Label fieldLabel;                             // Declare a label
TextField inputField;                         // Declare a field
Button done;                                  // Declare a button
:
dataEntryFrame = new Frame();                 // Give the frame a value
fieldLabel = new Label("Enter data here:");   // Give the label a value
inputField = new TextField("Replace me", 10); // Give the field a value
done = new Button("Done");                     // Give the button a value
done.setActionCommand("done");                // Name the button event

dataEntryFrame.setLayout(new FlowLayout());   // Set the layout manager
dataEntryFrame.add(fieldLabel);               // Add the label to frame
dataEntryFrame.add(inputField);               // Add the field to frame
dataEntryFrame.add(done);                     // Add the button to frame
dataEntryFrame.pack();                        // Pack the frame
dataEntryFrame.show();                        // Show the frame
```

The above code segments result in a frame with the following appearance.

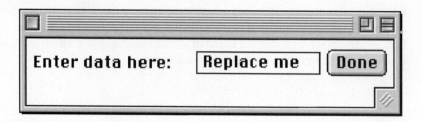

Of course, when the user clicks on the `Done` button, nothing appears to happen. In fact, something does happen: An event is fired, but we have not registered the listener with the button. Since the button doesn't know what to do, it simply ignores the event. Now let's look at how to create such a handler.

5.6 Creating and Registering a Button Event Listener

In Chapter 3 we were able to handle a `windowClosing` event by adding a method to a `WindowAdapter` as its constructor was creating it. For example, our `PrintName` program had the following code segment:

```
// Event handler for window closing
out.addWindowListener(new WindowAdapter()
// Create WindowClosing method
  {                                          //  to replace the empty one
    public void windowClosing(WindowEvent event)
    {
      out.dispose();                         // Remove frame from screen
      System.exit(0);                        // Stop the program
    }
  });
```

Recall that when we first discussed the `addWindowListener` method in Chapter 3, we said that it must be passed a parameter of type `WindowListener`. We then introduced the `WindowAdapter` type as a shortcut to save us from having to define the `WindowListener` type.

Button event listeners are registered with the event source through a similar method call. The corresponding method to register the event listener is called `addActionListener`, which takes as a parameter an object of the listener class. Thus far, registering a button listener is basically the same as registering a window event listener. Unfortunately, here is where the similarity breaks down: Java was able to provide the `WindowAdapter` shortcut for the window listener class because it predefines all of the window events that can happen. However, button events aren't predefined, so there is no `ActionAdapter` in Java. We have to define a new listener class that meets the specifications in `ActionListener` in order to handle button events.

Defining classes in Java is a straightforward process. However, there are many optional aspects to defining a new class that could easily divert our attention from the essential task at hand. Fortunately, in the case of a button listener class, Java gives us a precise model to follow. We don't have to consider any of the options until we get to Chapter 7. The model that Java provides for us is called an interface. Previously, we defined an interface in the general sense. In Java, however, an interface is part of the language; it is a way of specifying the fields and methods that must be present in a class that is an implementation of the interface. Likewise, we said in Chapter 1 that implementation is the stage in the software development life cycle in which an algorithm is translated into a programming language. But in Java, an implementation is a specific part of the language. The Java designers have used these general terms in a very specific way to define part of the language.

> **Interface**   (In Java) A model for a class that specifies the fields and methods that must be present in a class that implements the interface
>
> **Implementation**   (In Java) A class containing the definitions of the methods specified in an interface

The `ActionListener` interface specifies that you need to write a class that has one method called `actionPerformed`, which takes the event source object as a parameter. You've already seen how to write a class (each of our programs is a class), and you've seen how to write a method (that's what `main` is). The following example should thus look somewhat familiar to you.

```
private static class ButtonHandler implements ActionListener
{
  public void actionPerformed(ActionEvent event) // Event handler method
  {
    // Body of button event handler method goes here
  }
}                                                  // End of ButtonHandler
```

The only major differences are that:

1. The class that implements `ActionListener` is contained within our program class as a declaration.
2. Instead of having a `main` method, the new class has a method called `actionPerformed`.

There are some other minor differences that are summarized in the following table.

Type of Class	Program Class	Class Implementing `ActionListener`
Class modifiers	`public`	`private static`
Extra class clauses	none	`implements ActionListener`
Method heading	`public static void main`	`public void actionPerformed`
Method parameter	`(String[] args)`	`(ActionEvent event)`

As the table shows, the class that implements `ActionListener` is modified by `private` and `static` instead of `public`. These modifiers are consistent with the other declarations that are internal to our application. Class `ButtonHandler` is used only within the application to declare an object of that class, and is not used outside of the application. Thus, there is no need to make it `public`. Just as we get to choose the name of our application class, we also get to choose the name (`ButtonHandler`) of the class that implements `ActionListener`.

The name of the class is followed by the keyword `implements` and the name of the interface (`ActionListener`). The fact that our new class `implements` the `ActionListener` interface means that we can pass a `ButtonHandler` object to a method that expects a parameter of class `ActionListener` (such as `addActionListener`).

With respect to the methods `main` and `actionPerformed`, the table indicates that `main` is modified by `public` and `static`, while `actionPerformed` has only `public` as a modifier. There are deeper reasons for this difference that we consider in a later chapter, but for now we simply note that the designer of `ActionListener` chose to use only the `public` modifier, and we have to precisely match the interface in our implementation. Similarly, the interface specifies that `actionPerformed` takes one parameter of class `ActionEvent` (a predefined class that represents a source event). We can choose any name that we wish for the parameter, but here we simply call it `event`.

Let's look at how this class definition is written within a program. Here is a skeleton of a program that includes just the essential parts of the two classes.

```
public class ButtonDemo                        // Our program class
{
  // As part of the declarations for the program, we define another class
  //  called ButtonHandler that implements Java's ActionListener interface
  private static class ButtonHandler implements ActionListener
  {
    public void actionPerformed(ActionEvent event) // Event handler method
    {
      // Body of button event handler method goes here
    }
  }                                              // End of ButtonHandler class

  // More declarations for the program (ButtonDemo)

  public static void main(String[] args)         // main, just as usual
  {
    // Body of main goes here
  }
}
```

As you can see from this skeleton, it is an application just like previous ones, except that it contains another class with one method inside of it. It looks basically like a application within an application. The inner "application" however, defines a new class called `ButtonHandler`. Although we use the identifier `"ButtonHandler"` for the class, it is actually a listener class. Because the listener contains the method that handles the event, we use the linguistic shortcut of calling it a button handler rather than calling it "the listener that contains the method that handles the button event." All we have to do to complete the type definition is fill in the body of the `actionPerformed` method with statements to be executed when the button event fires. Those statements might be, for example,

```
fieldContents = inputField.getText();
inputField.setText("Replace me");
```

We return to the discussion of processing within a button event handler in the next section. Before we turn to that topic, there are three steps we need to take to register the listener with the event source.

1. Declare a variable of class `ButtonHandler`.
2. Instantiate an object of class `ButtonHandler`.
3. Call the `addActionListener` method associated with the button and pass it the object of class `ButtonHandler`.

When you define a new class, you specify a blueprint for Java to use in creating an object of that class. You still must declare a variable to hold such an object. The situation here is no different than for any other class in Java. For example, the existence of the `String` class doesn't create any `String` variables—you have to declare them. You now have a class called `ButtonHandler`, and you can use it to declare variables of that class. Here's an example:

```
ButtonHandler buttonEventHandler;
```

This statement declares a variable called `buttonEventHandler` to handle button events. Having declared such a variable, you can assign it an object that you create with `new`:

```
buttonEventHandler = new ButtonHandler();
```

and then pass it to `addActionListener` to register the listener with the event source:

```
done.addActionListener(buttonEventHandler);
```

Because `addActionListener` is an instance method associated with `done`, this particular event listener is registered with the event that is generated by the button.

You have seen how to create fields and buttons, how to name a button event and register its listener, and how to extract data from a field when the button is pressed. You now have all of the syntax that you need to program a user interface dialog that inputs data. There are still some algorithmic and style issues that must be considered in writing the body of our event handler, and we examine these in the next section.

5.7 Handling a Button Event

Once a button's event handler has been registered, the user can click on the button and the result is that the event transfers control to the first statement in the event handler. But what should the event handler do? In this case, the event is a signal from the user that some data has been typed into a field and is now ready for processing. Because we have just been exploring the mechanics of getting to this point in the program, rather than solving an actual problem, we don't know just yet what the data represents or what should be done with it.

Our discussion up to this point has put the cart before the horse. In solving a real problem, we begin by identifying the input data and what should be done with it. Then we design the user interface to enable the user to enter the data and generate the events that cause the program to process it.

Let's look at a trivial problem that we can use to illustrate the design process for building an event handler. Suppose we want the user to be able to enter a string and have it appear in a label in the same frame when he or she is done typing. Here is a formal definition of the problem.

Input: A string that the user enters.
Output: The input string, displayed in a label.
Processing: Copy the input string from the data entry field to the label.

When does the program copy the input string to the label? We need an event to signal when the user is done typing. Let's use a button called "Copy" to generate the event. What happens after the program copies the string? The problem statement doesn't answer this question. We could end the program, but then the frame disappears before the user has a chance to see the output. We need a second event to indicate when the user has finished looking at the output. Such an event could be generated by a second button, but we're not quite ready to handle events from multiple buttons. Instead, we can do what we've done in prior programs and let the user close the window to end the program. We thus have to write two event handlers.

The event handler for the button simply copies the data from the input field to the output label. For example,

```
fieldContents = inputField.getText();
outputLabel.setText(fieldContents);
```

We can even shorten these two lines to just one and eliminate the string variable `fieldContents` as follows:

```
outputLabel.setText(inputField.getText());
```

This single line of code carries out the main action that we want to perform on the data. The button event handler that contains it is written just as before, except that we insert this line into the body of the method.

```
private static class ButtonHandler implements ActionListener
{
   public void actionPerformed(ActionEvent event)   // Event handler method
   {
     outputLabel.setText(inputField.getText());
   }
}                                                    // End of ButtonHandler
```

After this method executes, it returns control to the JVM. If the user then closes the window, the window closing event calls the window-closing event handler. The code for this event handler is basically the same as in our other programs. Let's call the frame dataFrame.

```
// Event handler for window closing
out.addWindowListener(new WindowAdapter()
// Create WindowClosing method to replace the empty one
   {
     public void windowClosing(WindowEvent event)
     {
       dataFrame.dispose();                    // Remove frame from screen
       System.exit(0);                         // Stop the program
     }
   });
```

All that remains is to declare the appropriate variables, assign them objects, add them to the frame, and then show the frame on the screen. We saw in Chapter 3 that the Frame object had to be declared outside of the main method and needed the modifier static. Do any of the other declarations here need to be declared outside of main with a static modifier? Yes. Recall that we declared the Frame object outside of main because Java views the extension of the WindowAdapter class as also being declared outside of main, and its method refers to the Frame. Similarly, the method inside of class ButtonHandler refers directly to outputLabel and inputField, so they must also be declared outside of main. The other variables can remain local to main. Here is the complete program, which we call CopyString.

```
import java.awt.*;                              // User interface classes
import java.awt.event.*;                        // Event handling classes


public class CopyString
   // This program displays a frame with a data entry field and copies its
   //   contents to a label when the user clicks a button marked "Copy"
   {
   // Define a button listener
   private static class ButtonHandler implements ActionListener
   {
```

```
        public void actionPerformed(ActionEvent event) // Event handler method
        {
          outputLabel.setText(inputField.getText());
        }
    }                                                    // End of ButtonHandler

    // Declare pieces of the user interface shared by main and CopyString
    private static Frame dataFrame;               // User interface frame
    private static Label outputLabel;             // Label for output
    private static TextField inputField;          // Input field

    public static void main(String[] args)
    { // Declare pieces of the user interface accessed only by main
      Label entryLabel;                           // Label for input field
      Button copy;                                // Copy button
      ButtonHandler copyAction;                   // Action handler

      // Instantiate the pieces of the interface
      dataFrame = new Frame();
      entryLabel = new Label("Enter a string:");
      outputLabel = new Label("");
      inputField = new TextField("", 30);
      copy = new Button("Copy");
      copy.setActionCommand("copy");              // Give button event a name
      copyAction = new ButtonHandler();           // Instantiate listener
      copy.addActionListener(copyAction);         // Register listener

      // Make the frame and put interface parts in it
      dataFrame.setLayout(new GridLayout(2,2));
      dataFrame.add(entryLabel);
      dataFrame.add(inputField);
      dataFrame.add(copy);
      dataFrame.add(outputLabel);
      dataFrame.pack();
      dataFrame.show();

      // Register window closing event handler
      dataFrame.addWindowListener(new WindowAdapter()
        {
          public void windowClosing(WindowEvent event)
          {
            dataFrame.dispose();                  // Close the frame
            System.exit(0);                       // Quit the program
          }
        });
    }
}
```

The program initially displays a frame that looks like this:

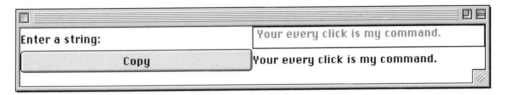

After the user enters a string and clicks the copy button, the frame appears as follows:

When the user closes the window, the program removes the frame from the screen and quits. But what happens if the user doesn't close the window? What if the user types some more data and clicks the button again? The button sends another event to the event manager, which dutifully calls the event handler again, and the output label is updated with the new input value. The user can keep entering new data values until he or she closes the window. In future programs we see that this pattern is useful as a way to enter a series of data values. For this problem, however, our intent was to allow the user to enter just one value.

How can we prevent the user from entering another value? We can have the event handler remove the button from the frame so that it can't be clicked a second time. Every `Frame` object supports a `remove` method that allows us to delete items that we've previously inserted with `add`. We can thus write a second line in our event handler that calls this method for `dataFrame`, passing it the button `copy`.

```
dataFrame.remove(copy);
```

Now, as soon as the user clicks on the Copy button, the button disappears. At the same time the input string appears in the output label. The only event that the user can then generate is closing the window.

5.8 Interactive Input/Output

In Chapter 1 we defined an interactive program as one in which the user communicates directly with the computer. Many of the programs that we write are interactive. There is a certain "etiquette" involved in writing interactive programs that has to do with instructions for the user to follow.

To get data into an interactive program, we begin with *input prompts*, labels that explain what the user should enter into an adjacent field. Without these messages, the user has no idea what data values to type. In many cases, a program also should display the data values typed in so that the user can verify that they were entered correctly. Displaying input values is called *echo printing*.

The amount of information you put into your prompts depends on who is going to be using a program. If you are writing a program for people who are not familiar with computers, the prompts should be more detailed. For example, "Type a four-digit part number, then click the button marked Enter." If the program is going to be used frequently by the same people, you might shorten the prompt to "Enter PN."

Whether a program echo prints its input or not also depends on how experienced the users are and on the task it is to perform. If the users are experienced and the prompts are clear, then echo printing is probably not required. If the users are novices or multiple values can be input at once, echo printing should be used. If the program inputs a large quantity of data and the users are experienced, rather than echo print the data, it may be stored in a separate file that can be checked after all of the data is input. We'll see how to store data into a file in a later chapter.

When data is not entered in the correct form, a message that indicates the problem should be displayed. For users who haven't worked much with computers, it's important that these messages be informative and friendly. The message

```
ILLEGAL DATA VALUES!!!!!!!
```

is likely to upset even an experienced user. Moreover, it doesn't offer any constructive information. A much better message would be

```
That is not a valid part number.
Part numbers must be no more than four digits long.
Please reenter the number in its proper form:
```

In Chapter 10, we introduce statements that allow us to catch and handle erroneous data.

5.9 Converting Strings to Numeric Values

Many of the problems solved with computers involve the entry of numerical data; values of the types int, long, float, and double. A TextField object enables you to enter a String. How then do you input a number? The answer is that you can't—at least not directly. Java provides only for the input of strings. You have to enter a number as a string and then convert the string into one of the numeric types using methods from Java's library.

As noted previously, Java's standard library includes a set of classes that correspond to the built-in numeric types. These classes provide methods and constants that are useful in working with the numeric types. The following table lists these predefined classes and the built-in type that each one corresponds to.

Class Name: Name	Superclass:	Subclassess:
Responsibilities	**Collaborations**	
Know first		
Know middle		
Know last		

Figure 5.8   *A CRC card with initial responsibilities*

With this particular question, we might pick up the User Interface card and say, "I have a responsibility to get the person's name from the user." That responsibility gets written down on the card. Once the name is input, the User Interface must collaborate with other objects to look up the name and get the corresponding address. What object should it collaborate with?

We've found a hole in our list of classes! The Entry objects should be organized into a Book object. We quickly write out a Book CRC card. The User Interface card-holder then says. "I'm going to collaborate with the book class to get the address." The collaboration is written in the right column of the card, and it remains in the air. The owner of the Book card holds it up, saying, "I have a responsibility to find an address in the list of Entry objects that I keep, given a name." That responsibility gets written on the Book card. Then the owner says, "I have to collaborate with each Entry to compare its name with the name sent to me by the User Interface." Figure 5.9 shows a team in the middle of a walk-through.

Now comes a decision. What are the responsibilities of Book and Entry for carrying out the comparison? Should Book get the name from Entry and do the comparison, or should it send the name to Entry and receive an answer that indicates whether they are equal? The team decides that Book should do the comparing, so the Entry card is held in the air, and its owner says, "I have a responsibility to provide the full name as a string. To do that I must collaborate with Name." The responsibility and collaboration are recorded and the Name card is raised.

Name says, "I have the responsibilities to know my first, middle, and last names. These are already on my card, so I'm done." And the Name card is lowered. Entry says, "I concatenate the three names into a string with spaces between them, and return the result to Book, so I'm done." The Entry card is lowered.

Book says, "I keep collaborating with Entry until I find the matching name. Then I must collaborate with Entry again to get the address." This collaboration is placed on its card and the Entry card is held up again, saying, "I have a responsibility to provide an address. I'm not going to collaborate with Address, but am just going to return the

Figure 5.9   *A scenario walk-through in progress*

object to Book." The Entry card has this responsibility added and then goes back on the table. Its CRC card is shown in Figure 5.10.

Now Book can say, "I have the Address, and I return it to User Interface, so I'm done." The Book card is lowered. Figure 5.11 shows its CRC card. Then the holder of User Interface (whose arm is getting very tired) says, "I need to collaborate with Address to get each line of the address as a string that I can place in a pair of labels." Address is raised, saying, "I have responsibilities to know my street, city, state, and zip code, and those are already on my list." User Interface says, "I can concatenate the last three to

Class Name: Entry	Superclass:	Subclassess:
Responsibilities	**Collaborations**	
Provide name as a string	Get first from Name	
	Get middle from Name	
	Get last from Name	
Provide Address	None	

Figure 5.10   *The CRC card for Entry*

Class Name: Book	Superclass:	Subclassess:
Responsibilities	**Collaborations**	
Find address, given a name	Get name string from Entry	
	Get address from Entry	

Figure 5.11   *The CRC card for Book*

form the second line, so that satisfies the collaboration." The collaboration is recorded, and User Interface says, "Now I display the labels and provide buttons to either quit or get another address, and I'm done." The last card is lowered and the scenario ends.

Reading about the scenario makes it seem longer and more complex than it really is. Once you get used to role playing, the scenarios move quickly and the walk-through becomes more like a game. However, to keep things moving, it is important to avoid becoming bogged-down with implementation details. Book should not be concerned with how the Entry objects are organized on the list. Address doesn't need to think about whether the zip code is stored as an int or a String. Explore each responsibility only as far as you need to decide whether a further collaboration is needed or whether it can be solved with the available information.

Subsequent Scenarios

We began the first scenario with a "What happens when..." question for the most obvious case. The next step is to brainstorm some additional questions that produce new scenarios. For example, here is list of some further scenarios.

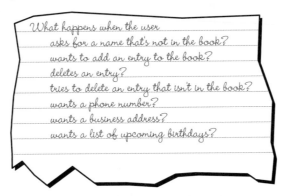

What happens when the user
asks for a name that's not in the book?
wants to add an entry to the book?
deletes an entry?
tries to delete an entry that isn't in the book?
wants a phone number?
wants a business address?
wants a list of upcoming birthdays?

We walk through each of the scenarios, adding responsibilities and collaborations to the CRC cards as necessary. After several scenarios have been tried, the number of additions decreases. When one or more scenarios take place without adding to any of the cards, then we brainstorm further to see if we can come up with new scenarios that may not be covered. When all of the scenarios that we can envision seem to be doable with the existing classes, responsibilities, and collaborations, then the design is done.

The next step is to implement the responsibilities for each class. The implementation may reveal details of a collaboration that weren't obvious in the walk-through. But knowing the collaborating classes makes it easy to change their corresponding responsibilities. The implementation phase should also include a search of available class libraries to see if any existing classes can be used. For example, the `java.util.Calendar` class represents a date that can be used directly to implement Birthday.

Inheritance

In walking through the scenario in which the user requests a business address, we should notice that the Work Address class is nearly identical with the Address class, except that it also provides a Business Name and a Second Address Line. Rather than copy all of the responsibilities and collaborations from the Address card to this one, we can list Address as the superclass of Work Address.

Because Work Address is a subclass of Address, it *inherits* all of the responsibilities that are in Address. A subclass is automatically able to use the responsibilities of its superclass and also add its own. In addition, a subclass can replace an inherited responsibility with a new definition of the responsibility. The new definition is a way of retaining the same form of interface but customizing its implementation to reflect the differences between the superclass and the subclass. In OOD this concept is called inheritance, and it allows you to adapt an existing class to satisfy additional responsibilities.

> **Inheritance** A mechanism that enables us to define a new class by adapting the definition of an existing class

We used inheritance to write our `windowClosing` event handler. Recall from Chapter 3 that the `WindowAdapter` class provides empty methods for all of the different events that a window can generate, and we supply a replacement for its `windowClosing` method. When we do this we are actually defining a new class that inherits all of the other empty methods from the `WindowAdapter` class. Java calls this an *anonymous inner class*—a fancy name that simply means we are using some syntax shortcuts to define the new class without giving it a name and as part of instantiating the object. In terms of our house building analogy, you can think of an anonymous inner class as giving the construction crew some last minute changes in the design without bothering to redraw the blueprints. Figure 5.12 illustrates the use of inheritance in defining a `windowClosing` event handler.

Enhancing CRC Cards with Additional Information

The CRC card design is informal. There are many ways that the card can be enhanced. For example, when a responsibility has obvious steps, we can write them below its name. Each step may have specific collaborations, and we write these beside the steps in the right column. We often recognize that certain data must be sent as part of the message that activates a responsibility, and we can record this in parentheses beside the calling collaboration and the responding responsibility. Figure 5.13 shows a CRC card

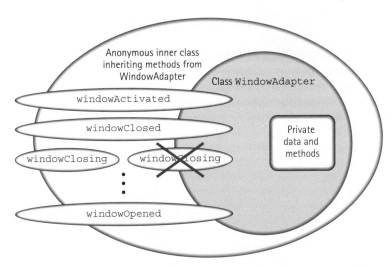

Figure 5.12 *A* windowClosing *event handler defines a new class that inherits all but one of the methods from Class* WindowAdapter

Class Name: *Entry*	Superclass:		Subclassess:
Responsibilities		**Collaborations**	
Provide name as a string			
Get first name		*Name*	
Get middle name		*Name*	
Get last name		*Name*	
Provide Address		*None*	
Change Name (name string)			
Break name into first, middle, last		*String*	
Update first name		*Name, changeFirst(first)*	
Update middle name		*Name, changeMiddle(middle)*	
Update last name		*Name, changeLast(last)*	

Figure 5.13 *A CRC card that is enhanced with additional information*

that includes design information in addition to the basic responsibilities and collaborations.

To summarize the CRC card process, first brainstorm the objects in a problem and then abstract them into classes. Then filter the list of classes to eliminate duplicates. For each class, create a CRC card and list any obvious responsibilities that it should support. Then walk through a common scenario, recording responsibilities and collaborations as they are discovered. After that, walk through additional scenarios, moving from common cases to special and exceptional cases. When it appears that all of the scenarios have been covered, brainstorm additional scenarios that may need more responsibilities and collaborations. When all ideas for scenarios are exhausted and all the scenarios are covered by the existing CRC cards, the design is done.

In this section, we have presented only an introduction to OOD. A more complete discussion requires knowledge of topics that we explore in Chapters 6 through 8: flow of control, programmer-written methods, class definitions, and interface design. Until then, our programs are relatively small, and we consider problems that can be solved with object-based programming. Keep in mind that a CRC card design doesn't have to lead to the design of new classes.

5.14 Functional Decomposition

The second design technique we use is functional decomposition (also called *structured design, top-down design, stepwise refinement*, and *modular programming*). It allows us to use the divide-and-conquer approach, which we talked about in Chapter 1.

When a responsibility clearly involves a series of major steps, you can break it down (decompose it) into pieces. In the process, you move to a lower level of abstraction—that is, some of the implementation details (but not too many) are now specified. Each of the major steps becomes an independent subproblem that you can work on separately. The process continues until each subproblem cannot be divided further or has an obvious solution.

By subdividing the problem, you create a hierarchical structure called a *tree structure*. Each level of the tree is a complete solution to the problem that is less abstract (more detailed) than the level above it. Figure 5.14 shows a generic solution tree for a problem. Steps that are shown in black type have enough implementation details to be translated directly into Java statements. These are concrete steps. Those in colored type are abstract steps; they reappear as subproblems in the next level down. Each box in the figure represents a module. Modules are the basic building blocks in a functional decomposition. The diagram in Figure 5.14 is also called a *module structure chart*.

Concrete step   A step for which the implementation details are fully specified

Abstract step   A step for which some implementation details remain unspecified

Module   A self-contained collection of steps that solves a problem or subproblem; can contain both concrete and abstract steps

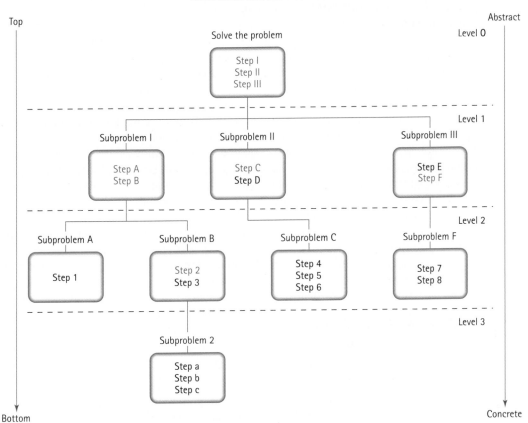

Figure 5.14 *Hierarchical solution tree*

Writing Modules

Here's one approach to writing modules:

1. Think about how you would solve the subproblem by hand.

2. Begin writing down the major steps.

3. If a step is simple enough so that you can see how to implement it directly in Java, it is at the concrete level; it doesn't need any further refinement.

4. If you have to think about implementing a step as a series of smaller steps or as several Java statements, it is still at an abstract level.

5. If you are trying to write a series of steps and start to feel overwhelmed by details, you probably are bypassing one or more levels of abstraction. Stand back and look for pieces that you can write as more abstract steps.

We could call this the "procrastinator's technique." If a step is cumbersome or difficult, put it off to a lower level; don't think about it today, think about it tomorrow. Of course, tomorrow does come, but the whole process can be applied again to the subproblem. A trouble spot often seems much simpler when you can focus on it. And eventually the whole problem is broken up into manageable units.

As you work your way down the solution tree, you make a series of design decisions. If a decision proves awkward or wrong (and many times it does!), you can backtrack (go back up the tree to a higher-level module) and try something else. You don't have to scrap your whole design—only the small part you are working on. There may be many intermediate steps and trial solutions before you reach a final design.

Before OOD was developed, functional decomposition was used to solve entire problems. However, by itself, it results in designs that lack flexibility. Applications developed entirely this way are hierarchical in nature, and often at the bottom of the hierarchy you are implementing multiple versions of the same responsibility. With OOD, you can define a superclass and a set of subclasses to organize these responsibilities and save yourself programming effort. But functional decomposition doesn't allow for this kind of organization.

Today, we typically use functional decomposition as a way to design the algorithm for a complex responsibility. For example, in a class that supports image processing, a morphing responsibility that distorts part of an image might have no need of any other collaboration. Yet there may be many mathematically sophisticated steps in the algorithm that transforms the image data. Functional decomposition provides a way to break such a problem down into simpler pieces that are easier to solve.

Pseudocode

You'll find it easier to implement a design if you write the steps in pseudocode. *Pseudocode* is a mixture of English statements and Java-like control structures that can be translated easily into Java. (We've already been using pseudocode in the algorithms in the Problem-Solving Case Studies.) When a concrete step is written in pseudocode, it should be possible to rewrite it directly as a Java statement in a program.

Remember that the problem-solving phase of the programming process takes time. If you spend the bulk of your time analyzing and designing a solution, coding (implementing) the program takes relatively little time.

 ## Software Engineering Tip

Documentation

As you create your functional decomposition or object-oriented design, you are developing documentation for your program. *Documentation* includes the written problem specifications, design, development history, and actual code of a program.

continued ▼

Documentation

Good documentation helps other programmers read and understand a program and is invaluable when software is being debugged and modified (maintained). If you haven't looked at your program for six months and need to change it, you'll be happy that you documented it well. Of course, if someone else has to use and modify your program, documentation is indispensable.

Documentation is both external and internal to the program. External documentation includes the specifications, the development history, and the design documents. Internal documentation includes the program format and **self-documenting code**— meaningful identifiers and comments. You can use the pseudocode from your design as comments in your programs.

> **Self-documenting code** Program code containing meaningful identifiers as well as judiciously used clarifying comments

This kind of documentation may be sufficient for someone reading or maintaining your programs. However, if a program is going to be used by people who are not programmers, you must provide a user's manual as well.

Be sure to keep documentation up-to-date. Indicate any changes you make in a program in all of the pertinent documentation. Use self-documenting code to make your programs more readable.

Now let's look at a case study that demonstrates the design process.

Problem-Solving Case Study

Averaging Rainfall Amounts

Problem   You are working for a scientific research project that is keeping track of the average rainfall in your area. Observers from different locations call you to report how much rain has fallen at the end of a storm. You need to enter the numbers as they come in and print the running average.

Brainstorming   Because this is such a small project, you are the "team." Therefore, you must do a solitary brainstorm. Grady Booch suggested that underlining nouns in a problem statement is a good way to begin.[2] So you begin your brainstorming by looking at the nouns in the problem statement: *you, project, average, rainfall, observers,* and *storm.* So, here is your first pass at the classes in the problem.

---

[2]Grady Booch, "What Is and Isn't Object-Oriented Design." *American Programmer*, Special Issue on Object Orientation, Vol. 2, no. 7–8, Summer 1989.

you
project
average
rainfall
observers
storm

Filtering   *Project* and *storm* are not really objects; they just give information about the context of the problem. *Average* and *rainfall* are numeric values, so we don't need classes for them. What are *observers*? They are the people who provide the rainfall values, so they are not a class in our problem solution. However, this reminds us that we must have a window object to input the rainfall values. What does *you* represent? It represents the processing that must be done. Since you cannot actually do the processing within the machine, *you* is represented as the application class. Let's call the application class `RainFall`. Here is the filtered list of classes.

RainFall
Window object

Scenarios   The main class (`RainFall`) is responsible for seeing that the values are input and the running average is calculated and printed. Some of the tasks should be done in the `main` method and some in the button handlers for the input. We can use the built-in classes `Frame`, `Button`, `Label`, `String`, and `TextField` to implement the window. Because the classes we need for the window are built in, we don't need to set up CRC cards for them, but we do for class `Rainfall`.

Class Name: RainFall	Superclass:	Subclassess:
Responsibilities	**Collaborations**	
Prepare the window for input	TextField, Label, String, Buttons	
Handle input events (using buttons)	Buttons	
Handle window closing	Frame	

Responsibility Algorithms   At this point, let's switch to a functional decomposition to write the algorithms for implementing the responsibilities. Preparing the window for input (more generally called *preparing the user interface*) requires us to declare each of the components of the interface, to instantiate each component, and to add each component to the frame. These are abstract steps because they each involve a series of actions. We defer a closer examination of them until later. After the frame has been built, we pack and show it. We also need to register its window-closing event handler. These steps can all be translated into individual Java statements, so they are concrete.

Prepare Window for Input   **Level 1**

> Declare the interface variables
> Instantiate each interface object
> Add each interface object to the frame
> Pack the frame
> Show the frame
> Handle window closing

Declaring the interface objects is essentially making a list of the components of our user interface. We need a frame to hold everything, two labels (one for input and one for output), a field for entering data, and a button for the user to click when a value is ready for input.

Declare the Interface Variables   **Level 2**

> Declare a Frame, inputFrame
> Declare a Label, entryLabel
> Declare a Label, outputLabel
> Declare a TextField, inputField
> Declare a Button, enter

Each declared object variable should also be assigned an instantiated object.

Instantiate Each Interface Object

> Set inputFrame to new Frame
> Set entryLabel to new Label, "Enter amount here:"
> Set outputLabel to new Label
> Set inputField to new TextField, empty with 10 spaces
> Set enter to new Button, "Enter"
> Register the event listener for the Enter button

We have added one more abstract step, which we can now expand. Registering an event listener for a button involves four steps. We declare a variable of the listener class that implements interface `ActionListener`, set the action command for the button, instantiate the object, and then add the object to the button. Let's call the listener `ActionHandler`. These four steps are all concrete, as shown in the following module.

Register the Event Listener for the Enter Button   Level 3

Declare action of class ActionHandler
setActionCommand for button enter to "enter"
Instantiate action
Add action as listener for button

Next, we must assemble the user interface components into a frame. We start by specifying a layout manager for the frame. Let's use a 2 by 2 grid for this interface to keep it compact. Now we simply add each of the components to the frame: the two labels, the input field, and the button.

Add Each Interface Object to the Frame   Level 2

Set layout manager for inputFrame to 2 $\times$ 2 grid
Add entryLabel to inputFrame
Add outputLabel to inputFrame
Add inputField to inputFrame
Add enter button to inputFrame

Handling the input events is where the real work of the program is accomplished. When the user clicks the Enter button, we need to get the value from the input field and convert it to a numerical value. Because we have input a new data value, we need to add 1 to the count of the entries. We also add the input value to the total rainfall. The updated total and count can then be used to compute the average, which we display for the user to see. Lastly, we should clear out the input field so that the user can enter a new value. Each of these steps is concrete, as shown in the following module.

Handle Input Events   Level 1

Get the entry string from the input field
Set rainfall to numerical value (double) of entry string
Add 1 to the number of entries
Add rainfall to total
Set average to total divided by number of entries
Display average
Clear input field

This module must be implemented as a method called `actionPerformed` in a class that implements `ActionListener`, the interface that all button handlers must implement. We have called the class `ActionHandler`.

The last responsibility is to handle the window closing. When the user closes the window, it is time to quit the program. What should we do if there is a value in the input field? Let's ignore it, on the assumption that it is only valid if the user clicks the Enter button. There are two housekeeping steps to be done in quitting the program. We should clear the frame from the screen and then exit the program. Each of these is a concrete step.

....

Handle Window Closing   **Level 1**

> Dispose of the frame
> Exit the program

We used OOD to determine the objects and their responsibilities. We then used functional decomposition to write the algorithms to implement the responsibilities. Each abstract step in each algorithm has been expanded into concrete steps that are functionally equivalent. All that remains is for us to gather together the concrete steps in the proper order to give a complete algorithm consisting of concrete steps. To perform the gathering process, we begin at the lowest level, substituting the concrete steps of each module for the corresponding abstract step in the level above it. That is, we replace each line of colored type with the corresponding lines of black type.

For example, the four lines in the Level 3 module would be substituted for the colored line at the end of the Level 2 module called "Instantiate Each Interface Object." That module then consists entirely of concrete steps that can replace the abstract step by the same name in the Level 1 module called "Prepare Window for Input."

Once all of the substitutions are complete, we have an algorithmic solution consisting entirely of concrete steps. Because each concrete step can be directly translated into a Java statement, writing the program is simply a matter of converting each line of the algorithm into a corresponding line of code. The resulting algorithm and program are known as a *flat* or *inline implementation* because our series of substitutions produces a solution with just a single level. We are flattening the two-dimensional, hierarchical structure of the solution by writing all of the steps as one long sequence. This kind of implementation is adequate when the implementation of a responsibility is short.

From our design we collect a list of all of the variables that our program uses, to help in writing their declarations. The variables referenced outside of `main` must be declared outside of `main` and have the modifier `static`. To remind us, we mark these variables with an asterisk.

Variables

Name	Data Type	Description
inputFrame*	Frame	A frame
entryLabel	Label	Label for input
outputLabel*	Label	Label for output
inputField*	TextField	Input field
enter	Button	Enter button
total*	double	Keeps running total
numberEntries*	double	Keeps count of entries
action	ActionHandler	Action handler
amount	double	Holds input value
average	double	Holds computed average

At this stage we should look over this list of variables and ask ourselves if there are any that we have forgotten to initialize. `total` keeps the running total of the rainfall so far, so it should be initialized to zero. `numberEntries` is a counter that tells how many values have been read, so it should also be set to zero. We must set these values in `main` where they are declared. We have marked the identifiers used outside of main; we need to make them `private static` class declarations.

Here is the complete program. We have used the steps in the design as the basis for its comments.

```java
import java.awt.*;                              // User interface classes
import java.awt.event.*;                        // Event handling classes
public class Rainfall
{
 // Define a button listener
  private static class ActionHandler implements ActionListener
  {
    public void actionPerformed(ActionEvent event)
    // Handles events from the Enter button in inputFrame
    {
      double amount;                            // Holds input value
      double average;                           // Holds computed average
      // Convert string in inputField to a double value
      amount = Double.valueOf(inputField.getText()).doubleValue();
      numberEntries++;                          // Increment entries
      total = total + amount;                   // Add value to sum
      average = total / numberEntries;          // Compute average
      outputLabel.setText("" + average);        // Display average
      inputField.setText("");                   // Clear input field
    }
  }
```

```
private static Frame inputFrame;                        // User interface frame
private static Label outputLabel;                       // Label for output
private static TextField inputField;                    // Input field
private static double total;                            // Keeps running total
private static double numberEntries;                    // Keeps count of entries

public static void main(String[] args)
{
  {  // Declare local variables
  Label entryLabel;                                     // Label for input field
  Button enter;                                         // Enter button
  ActionHandler action;                                 // Declare listener
  // Initialize/instantiate variables
  total = 0.0;
  numberEntries = 0.0;
  inputFrame = new Frame();
  entryLabel = new Label("Enter amount here:");
  outputLabel = new Label("0.0", Label.RIGHT);
  inputField = new TextField("", 10);
  enter = new Button("Enter");
  enter.setActionCommand("enter");                      // Name the button event
  action = new ActionHandler();                         // Instantiate listener
  enter.addActionListener(action);                      // Register the listener
  // Add components to frame
  inputFrame.setLayout(new GridLayout(2,2));
  inputFrame.add(entryLabel);
  inputFrame.add(inputField);
  inputFrame.add(enter);
  inputFrame.add(outputLabel);
  inputFrame.pack();                                    // Pack the frame
  inputFrame.show();                                    // Show the frame
  inputFrame.addWindowListener(new WindowAdapter()
  // Declare window closing event handler
    {
      public void windowClosing(WindowEvent event)
      {
        inputFrame.dispose();                           // Close the frame
        System.exit(0);                                 // Quit the program
      }
    });
  }
}
```

When the program executes, the frame shown below is displayed. The contents shown in the frame are the result of entering the following series of values, with the frame appearing as it does just before Enter is clicked to cause the last value to be processed.

1.300
0.800
1.200
2.000
0.950
1.410

```
┌─────────────────────────────────────────┐
│ □ ▓▓▓▓▓▓▓▓▓▓▓▓▓▓▓▓▓▓▓▓▓▓▓▓▓▓▓▓▓  ◱ ◲ │
├─────────────────────────────┬───────────┤
│ Enter amount here:          │ 1.41      │
├─────────────────────────────┴───────────┤
│           Enter                     1.25 │
├──────────────────────────────────────────┤
│                                        ◿ │
└──────────────────────────────────────────┘
```

Background Information

Programming at Many Scales

To help you put the topics in this book into context, we describe in broad terms the way programming in its many forms is done in "the real world." Obviously, we can't cover every possibility, but we'll try to give you a flavor of the state of the art.

Programming projects range in size from the small scale, in which a student or computer hobbyist writes a short program to try out something new, to large-scale multicompany programming projects involving hundreds of people. Between these two extremes are efforts of many other sizes. There are people who use programming in their professions, even though it isn't their primary job. For example, a scientist might write a special-purpose program to analyze data from a particular experiment.

Even among professional programmers there are many specialized programming areas. An individual might have a specialty in business data processing, in writing compilers or developing word processors (a specialty known as "tool making"), in research and development support, in graphical display development, in writing entertainment software, or in one of many other areas. However, one person can produce only fairly small programs (a few tens of thousands of lines of code at best). Work of this kind is called *programming in the small.*

A larger application, such as the development of a new operating system, might require hundreds of thousands or even millions of lines of code. Such large-scale projects require teams of programmers, many of them specialists, who must be organized in some manner or they waste valuable time just trying to communicate with one another.

Usually, a hierarchical organization is set up. One person, the *chief architect* or *project director*, determines the basic structure of the program and then delegates the responsibility of implementing the major components. The components may be implemented by teams or by individual programmers. This sort of organization is called *programming in the large.*

Programming languages and software tools can help a great deal in supporting programming in the large. For example, if a programming language lets programmers develop, compile,

continued ▼

Programming at Many Scales

and test parts of a program independently before they are put together, then it enables several people to work on the program simultaneously. Of course, it is hard to appreciate the complexity of programming in the large when you are writing a small program for a class assignment. However, the experience you gain in this course will be valuable as you begin to develop larger programs.

The following is a classic example of what happens when a large program is developed without careful organization and proper language support. In the 1960s, IBM developed a major new operating system called OS/360, which was one of the first true examples of programming in the large. After the operating system was written, more than 1,000 significant errors were found. Despite years of trying to fix these errors, the programmers never did get the number of errors below 1,000, and sometimes the "fixes" produced far more errors than they eliminated.

What led to this situation? Hindsight analysis showed that the code was badly organized and that different pieces were so interrelated that nobody could keep it all straight. A seemingly simple change in one part of the code caused several other parts of the system to fail. Eventually, at great expense, an entirely new system was created using better organization and tools.

In those early days of computing, everyone expected occasional errors to occur, and it was still possible to get useful work done with a faulty operating system. Today, however, computers are used more and more in critical applications such as medical equipment and aircraft control systems where errors can prove fatal. Many of these applications depend on large-scale programming. If you were stepping onto a modern jetliner right now, you might well pause and wonder, "Just what sort of language and tools did they use when they wrote the programs for this thing?" Fortunately, most large, life-critical, software development efforts today use a combination of good methodology, appropriate language, and extensive organizational tools—an approach known as *software engineering*.

Testing and Debugging

An important part of implementing a program is testing it (checking the results). By now you should realize that there is nothing magical about the computer. It is infallible only if the person writing the instructions and entering the data is infallible. Don't trust it to give you the correct answers until you've verified enough of them by hand to convince yourself that the program is working.

From here on, these Testing and Debugging sections offer tips on how to test your programs. We offer suggestions for what to do if a program doesn't work as expected. It's much easier to prevent bugs than to fix them.

With programs that input data from fields, the most common error is to try to assign the field contents directly to an `int` or `double` variable. Remember that Java only inputs `String` values and that you must convert the input to any other type. Another problem that often occurs is that the user enters a number that causes integer overflow. When you want a field to input an integer value, limit its size (through the constructor call) to nine characters. As we noted before, we are not yet ready to handle errors in which the user enters nonnumeric data into such a field. Your program will simply crash with an error message if this happens.

In testing programs that perform numeric calculations, be sure to test whether input values can result in overflow or division by zero. In Chapter 6 we see how to catch these errors before the calculation takes place. Until then you should document the limitations of your program with comments.

By giving you a framework that can help you organize and keep track of the details involved in designing and implementing a program, OOD and functional decomposition should help you avoid errors in the first place.

Testing and Debugging Hints

1. Remember to label each input field with a prompting message.

2. Be certain that every field, label, or button follows the three basic steps: declare it, instantiate it, and add it to the frame.

3. Remember to specify a layout manager for a frame.

4. The value in a field is a string. If you need to input a number, you must use `get-Text` to input the string, and then convert the string to a number, using methods such as `valueOf` and `doubleValue` or `valueOf` and `intValue`. Applying these methods to a nonnumeric value causes the program to halt with an error message such as Number Format Error.

5. Call `setActionCommand` for each button to name it.

6. A button event listener declaration must follow exactly the pattern of headings specified by the `ActionListener interface`. You can choose the name of the class, but the rest of the class and method headings must appear exactly as shown on page 185.

7. Once the button event listener class is declared, there are three steps that must be performed to register the event listener: declare an object of the same type as the class, instantiate the object, and call the button's `addActionListener` method with the object as its parameter.

8. Use the design methodologies presented in this chapter to carefully design a complete algorithmic solution to a problem before you start writing Java code. The design should be sufficiently detailed that converting it to Java is almost a mechanical process.

Summary of Classes

Package Name

Class Name	Comments
`java.lang`	Automatically imported to every Java program
`Double`	
Class Constants: `MAX_VALUE`	Highest `double` value
`MIN_VALUE`	Lowest `double` value
Constructor: `Double(double)`	
Value-Returning Class Method:	
`valueOf(String)`	Returns `Double`
Value-Returning Instance Method:	
`doubleValue()`	Returns `double`
`Float`	
Class Constants: `MAX_VALUE`	Highest `float` value
`MIN_VALUE`	Lowest `float` value
Constructor: `Float(float)`	
Value-Returning Class Method:	
`valueOf(String)`	Returns `Float`
Value-Returning Instance Method:	
`floatValue()`	Returns `float`
`Integer`	
Class Constants: `MAX_VALUE`	Highest `int` value
`MIN_VALUE`	Lowest `int` value
Constructor: `Integer(int)`	
Value-Returning Class Method:	
`valueOf(String)`	Returns `Integer`
Value-Returning Instance Method:	
`intValue()`	Returns `int`
`Long`	
Class Constants: `MAX_VALUE`	Highest `long` value
`MIN_VALUE`	Lowest `long` value
Constructor: `Long(long)`	
Value-Returning Class Method:	
`valueOf(String)`	Returns `Long`
Value-Returning Instance Method:	
`longValue()`	Returns `long`

Package Name

Class Name	Comments
`java.awt`	
`ActionEvent`	Passed to event handler
`ActionListener`	An `interface`
`Button`	
Constructor: `Button(String)`	
Void Instance Methods:	
`setActionCommand(String)`	
`addActionListener(`**implementation of** `ActionListener)`	
`Frame`	
Void Instance Methods:	
`add(Button)`	
`add(TextField)`	
`remove(Button)`	
`remove(Label)`	
`remove(TextField)`	
`TextField`	
Constructors: `TextField(int)`	
`TextField(String, int)`	
Value-Returning Instance Method:	
`getText()`	Returns `String`
Void Instance Method:	
`setText(String)`	

Summary

Programs operate on data. If data and programs are kept separate, the data is available to use with other programs, and the same program can be run with different sets of input data.

The `TextField` class enables us to input data from the keyboard, storing the data into the variable specified in a call to its `getText` method. The `getText` method inputs the contents of the field as a string. We must use additional methods such as `valueOf` and `doubleValue` to convert an input string to a numeric value. Reading of the text in a field is usually triggered by a user event such as closing a window or clicking a button.

We must register an event listener with its button to activate the button. The button is named with a call to `setActionCommand`, and the event listener is registered with a call to `addActionListener`. The event handler itself is a method in a class definition that follows the specification of the `ActionListener` interface.

Interactive programs prompt the user for each data entry and directly inform the user of results and errors. Designing an interactive dialogue is an exercise in the art of communication. Noninteractive input/output allows data to be prepared before a program is run and allows the program to run again with the same data in the event that a problem crops up during processing.

Object-oriented design (OOD) and functional decomposition are methods for tackling nontrivial programming problems. The two methodologies are often used in combination, and experienced programmers often switch between them in solving a problem. We use OOD to design the overall solution to a complex problem, and then apply functional decomposition to aid in writing the algorithm for the individual responsibilities of each object.

Object-oriented design produces a problem solution by focusing on objects and their associated operations. The first step is to brainstorm the major objects in the problem and create classes that are abstract descriptions of them. We filter the initial classes, eliminating duplicate and inappropriate classes. We then walk through a series of scenarios, working from common cases to exceptional cases to determine the responsibilities and collaborations of the classes. The use of CRC cards helps us to keep track of this information as we explore the scenarios. The result of the design process is a program consisting of self-contained objects that have responsibilities for managing their own data and collaborating with other objects by invoking each other's methods.

Functional decomposition begins with an abstract solution that then is divided into major steps. Each step becomes a subproblem that is analyzed and subdivided further. A concrete step is one that can be translated directly into Java; those steps that need more refining are abstract steps. A module is a collection of concrete and abstract steps that solves a subproblem.

Careful attention to program design, program formatting, and documentation produces highly structured and readable programs.

Quick Check

1. What is one of the biggest advantages of computers? (p. 176)
2. Where is an event sent when a user clicks on a button with a mouse? (p. 178)
3. What happens when a user clicks a button? (p. 178)
4. Who or what participates in a computer dialog? (p. 179)
5. Declare a `TextField` called `dataField`. (p. 179–180)
6. Assign a value to `dataField` with a fieldwidth of 10. (pp. 179–180)
7. Assign a default value "Replace me" to `dataField`. (p. 180)
8. Add `dataField` to Frame object `dataFrame`. (p. 180)
9. Write the statement that stores the values entered in field `dataField` into the `String` variable `dataValue`. (pp. 180–181)
10. Write the statement that converts the `dataValue` into `doubleValue` of type `double`. (pp. 192–194)

11. Write a statement that declares a `Button` variable `press`. (p. 182)
12. Write the statement that gives the name "Press" to `press`. (pp. 182–183)
13. Write a statement that declares an object of listener class `ButtonListener`. (pp. 184–187)
14. Write the statement to register the button listener. (p. 187)
15. Object-oriented design produces a collection of _____. (objects, tasks) (p. 200)
16. Functional design produces a hierarchy of _____. (objects, tasks) (p. 210)

Answers

1. A program can be run with many different data sets.   2. Event handler within an event listener.   3. The JVM recognizes the button event and calls the event handler within the appropriate event listener.   4. A computer dialog is an exchange between the program and a user.
5. `private static TextField dataField`
6. `dataField = new TextField(10);`
7. `dataField = new TextField("Replace me", 10);`
8. `dataFrame.add(dataField);`
9. `dataValue = dataField.getText();`
10. `someDouble = Double.valueOf(dataValue).doubleValue();`
11. `Button press;`
12. `press.setActionCommand("Press");`
13. `ButtonListener buttonHear;`
14. `press.addActionListener(ButtonHear);`
15. objects   16. tasks

Exam Preparation Exercises

1. Name three objects that can be contained in a `Frame` object.
2. What are the steps in adding a data entry field to a `Frame` object?
3. When instantiating a `Label` object, what is passed to the constructor?
4. When instantiating a `TextField` object, what is passed to the constructor?
5. What happens if you forget to include the statement `dataFrame.show()`?
6. What are the three steps needed to add a `Button` object to a frame?
7. What are the steps necessary in creating a `Button` object?
8. What are the steps necessary in creating a `Button` listener?
9. What happens when a user clicks a button but there is no listener registered for the event?
10. What is an interface in Java?
11. What is an interface implementation in Java?
12. How are application classes and classes that implement the `ActionListener` interface different?
13. `actionPerformed` takes one parameter of a predefined Java type. What is the name of the type?

14. What three steps are necessary to register an event listener?
15. Why do you not have to write an implementation of `WindowListener` to handle the window-closing event?
16. What determines the amount of information in a prompt?
17. Java provides input only for strings. How can we enter numeric values into our programs?
18. What are the object types that correspond with the built-in numeric types?
19. Distinguish between instance methods and class methods.
20. If it is natural to think of the solution to a problem in terms of a collection of component parts, which design technique is more appropriate?
21. If it is natural to think of the solution to a problem in terms of a series of steps, which design technique is more appropriate?
22. If a method is modified by `static`, is it a class method or an instance method?
23. Distinguish between an abstract step and a concrete step.
24. List the steps in performing an object-oriented design.
25. At which point in an object-oriented design is functional decomposition useful?

Programming Warm-Up Exercises

1. a. Write the statement that declares a `Label` field named `textLabel`.
   b. Write the statement that instantiates `textLabel` with the string `"Enter data"`.
   c. Write the statement that declares a `TextField` named `dataField`.
   d. Write the statement that stores the values entered in field `dataField` into `String` variable `dataValue`.
   e. Write the statement that converts `dataValue` to an integer value and stores it in `intValue`.
   f. Write a statement to replace the current contents of `dataField` with `"Next Value"`.
2. a. Declare a `Button` variable called `stop`.
   b. Instantiate the `Button` object, calling it `"Stop"`.
   c. Name the `Button` object `"stop"`.
   d. Declare and instantiate a `Button` listener object.
   e. Register the `Button` listener.
   f. Add the button to frame `dataFrame`.
3. a. Write the statements to create a frame (`exampleFrame`) with one label (`exampleLabel`), one field (`exampleField`), and one button (`example-Button`).
   b. Write the statements that define a class (`ExampleClass`) that is an implementation of `ActionListener`. When the `exampleButton` is clicked, the contents of `exampleField` are stored in `exampleValue` and removed from `exampleField`.
   c. Write the statements that declare and instantiate `example_EventHandler` of class `ExampleClass`.

    d. Write the statements that name `exampleButton` and register its associated event listener `exampleEventHandler`.

4. a. What is the type of the following expression `Integer.valueOf("1999")`?

    b. Is `valueOf` an instance method or a class method?

    c. If `Integer.valueOf("1999")` returns a value of type `Integer`, how can you convert it to type `int`?

5. Write the statements that store the number 2,000 into variable `data` of type `int`.

6. Write the statement that takes the string representing an integer number in `exampleField` and stores it into `data`.

7. You are to read the three coefficients of a quadratic polynomial and write the two floating-point solutions. Assume that the discriminant (the portion of the formula inside the square root) is nonnegative. You may use the standard method `Math.sqrt`. The quadratic formula is

$$\frac{-b \pm \sqrt{b^2 - 4ac}}{2a}$$

    a. Use object-oriented design to determine the objects in the problem. Discuss the problem in the following phases: brainstorming, filtering, scenarios, CRC cards, and responsibility algorithms.

    b. Use functional decomposition to write an algorithm for the problem.

    c. Compare your object-oriented design and your functional design.

Programming Problems

1. Design and code a Java application to read an invoice number, quantity ordered, and unit price (all integers) and compute the total price. The application should write out the invoice number, quantity, unit price, and total price on the screen with identifying phrases. Format your program with consistent indentation; use appropriate comments and meaningful identifiers. The data is prompted for and read from the screen. Use buttons where appropriate.

2. How tall is a rainbow? Because of the way in which light is refracted by water droplets, the angle between the level of your eye and the top of a rainbow is always the same (the so-called magic angle). If you know the distance to the rainbow, you can multiply it by the tangent of that angle to find the height of the rainbow. The magic angle is 42.3333333 degrees. The Java standard library works in radians, however, so you have to convert the angle to radians with this formula:

$$radians = degrees \times \frac{\pi}{180}$$

where π equals 3.14159265.

`Math.tan` is a value-returning method that takes a floating-point parameter and returns a floating-point result:

```
x = Math.tan(someAngle);
```

If you multiply the tangent by the distance to the rainbow, you get the height of the rainbow.

Design and code a Java application to read a single floating-point value—the distance to the rainbow—from the screen and compute the height of the rainbow. The program should print the distance to the rainbow and its height with phrases that identify which number is which. Format your program with consistent indentation, and use appropriate comments and meaningful identifiers.

3. Sometimes you can see a second, fainter rainbow outside a bright rainbow. This second rainbow has a magic angle of 52.25 degrees. Modify the program in Exercise 2 so that it prints the height of the main rainbow, the height of the secondary rainbow, and the distance to the main rainbow, with a phrase identifying each of the numbers.

Case Study Follow-Up Exercises

1. Does `RainFall` crash if the window is closed before the user enters any values? Explain.
2. Outline a testing strategy for application `RainFall`.
3. `Rainfall` stops when the user closes the window. What other ways could the program allow the user to quit? Explain.
4. What happens when a negative value is input?

Conditions, Logical Expressions, and Selection Control Structures

- ■ To be able to construct a simple logical (Boolean) expression to evaluate a given condition.

- ■ To be able to construct a complex Boolean expression to evaluate a given condition.

- ■ To be able to construct an *if-else* statement to perform a specific task.

- ■ To be able to construct an *if* statement to perform a specific task.

- ■ To be able to construct a set of nested *if* statements to perform a specific task.

- ■ To be able to describe an algorithm walk-through and tell how it is used.

- ■ To be able to explain the purpose of tracing the execution of Java code.

- ■ To be able to test and debug a Java program.

So far, the statements in our programs have been executed in the same order that we write them, except when an event occurs. The first statement is executed, then the second, and so on. The method call and the event handler, which execute a separate sequence of statements, provide variations of this ordering. But what if we want the computer to execute the statements in an order other than sequentially? Suppose we want to check the validity of input data and then perform a calculation *or* display an error message, not both. To do so, we must be able to ask a question and then, based on the answer, choose one or another course of action.

The *if* statement allows us to execute statements in an order that is different from their physical order. We can ask a question with it and do one thing if the answer is yes (true) or another if the answer is no (false). In the first part of this chapter, we deal with asking questions; in the second part, we deal with the *if* statement itself.

6.1 Flow of Control

The order in which statements are executed in a program is called the flow of control. In a sense, the computer is under the control of one statement at a time. When a statement has been executed, control is turned over to the next statement (like a baton being passed in a relay race).

Flow of control The order in which the computer executes statements in a program

Control structure A statement used to alter the normally sequential flow of control

Flow of control is normally sequential (see Figure 6.1). That is, when one statement is finished executing, control passes to the next statement in the program. If you want the flow of control to be nonsequential, you can use control structures, special statements that transfer control to a statement other than the one that physically comes next. You have already seen that method calls, especially event handlers, are control

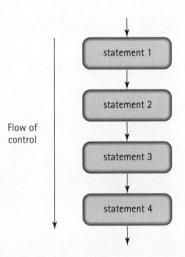

Flow of control

Figure 6.1   *Sequential control*

structures that alter the flow of control so that a separate sequence of statements can be executed.

Selection

You can use a selection (or branching) control structure when you want the computer to choose between alternative actions. You make an assertion, a claim that is either true or false. If the assertion is true, the computer executes one statement. If it is false, it executes another (see Figure 6.2). The computer's ability to solve practical problems is a product of its ability to make decisions and execute different sequences of instructions.

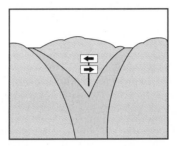

The `Payroll` program in Chapter 1 shows the selection process at work. The computer must decide whether or not a worker has earned overtime pay. It does this by testing the assertion that the person has worked more than 40 hours. If the assertion is true, the computer follows the instructions for computing overtime pay. If the assertion is false, the computer simply computes the regular pay. Before examining selection control structures in Java, let's look closely at how we get the computer to make decisions.

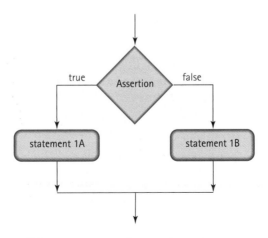

Figure 6.2   *Selection (branching) control structure*

6.2 Conditions and Logical Expressions

To ask a question in Java, we don't phrase it as a question; we state it as an assertion. If the assertion we make is true, the answer to the question is yes. If the statement is not true, the answer to the question is no. For example, if we want to ask, "Are we having spinach for dinner tonight?" we would say, "We are having spinach for dinner tonight." If the assertion is true, the answer to the question is yes. If not, the answer is no.

So, asking questions in Java means making an assertion that is either true or false. The computer *evaluates* the assertion, checking it against some internal condition (the values stored in certain variables, for instance) to see whether it is true or false.

The `boolean` Data Type

The `boolean` data type consists of just two values, the constants `true` and `false`. The reserved word `boolean` is pronounced bool-e-un.[1] Boolean data is used for testing conditions in a program so that the computer can make decisions (as in a selection control structure).

We declare variables of type `boolean` the same as we declare variables of other standard types, by writing the name of the data type and then an identifier:

```
boolean dataOK;     // True if the input data is valid
boolean done;       // True if the process is done
boolean taxable;    // True if the item has sales tax
```

Each variable of type `boolean` can contain one of two values: `true` or `false`. It's important to understand right from the beginning that `true` and `false` are not variable names and they are not strings. They are special constants in Java and, in fact, are reserved words.

Logical Expressions

In programming languages, assertions take the form of *logical expressions* (also called *Boolean expressions*). Just as an arithmetic expression is made up of numeric values and operations, a logical expression is made up of logical values and operations. Every logical expression has one of the two `boolean` values: `true` or `false`.

Here are some examples of logical expressions:

- A `boolean` variable or constant
- An arithmetic expression followed by a relational operator followed by an arithmetic expression
- A logical expression followed by a logical operator followed by a logical expression

---

[1]The name `boolean` is a tribute to George Boole, a nineteenth-century English mathematician who described a system of logic using variables with just two values, True and False. (See the Background Information box on page 242.)

Let's look at each of these in detail.

Boolean Variables and Constants As we have seen, a `boolean` variable is a variable declared to be of type `boolean`, and it can contain either the value `true` or the value `false`. For example, if `dataOK` is a `boolean` variable, then

```
dataOK = true;
```

is a valid assignment statement.

Relational Operators Another way of assigning a value to a `boolean` variable is to set it equal to the result of comparing two expressions with a *relational operator*. Relational operators test a relationship between two values.

Let's look at an example. In the following program fragment, `lessThan` is a `boolean` variable and `i` and `j` are `int` variables:

```
lessThan = (i < j);   // Compare i and j with the "less than" relational
                      //  operator, and assign the value to lessThan
```

By comparing two values, we assert that a relationship (such as "less than") exists between them. If the relationship does exist, the assertion is true; if not, it is false. These are the relationships we can test for in Java:

Operator	Relationship Tested
==	Equal to
!=	Not equal to
>	Greater than
<	Less than
>=	Greater than or equal to
<=	Less than or equal to

An expression followed by a relational operator followed by an expression is called a *relational expression.* The result of a relational expression is of type `boolean`. For example, if `x` is 5 and `y` is 10, the following expressions all have the value `true`:

```
x != y
y > x
x < y
y >= x
x <= y
```

If `x` is the character `'M'` and `y` is `'R'`, the values of the expressions are still `true` because the relational operator `<`, used with letters, means "comes before in the alphabet," or, more properly, "comes before in the collating sequence of the character set." For example, in the ASCII subset of the Unicode character set, all of the uppercase letters are in alphabetical order, as are the lowercase letters, but all of the uppercase letters come before the lowercase letters. So

`'M' < 'R'`

and

`'m' < 'r'`

have the value `true`, but

`'m' < 'R'`

has the value `false`.

Of course, we have to be careful about the data types of things we compare. The safest approach is always to compare identical types: `int` with `int`, `double` with `double`, `char` with `char`, and so on. If you mix data types in a comparison, implicit type conversion takes place just as in arithmetic expressions. If an `int` value and a `double` value are compared, the computer temporarily converts the `int` value to its `double` equivalent before making the comparison. As with arithmetic expressions, it's wise to use explicit type casting to make your intentions known:

`someDouble >= (double)someInt`

If you try to compare a `boolean` value with a numeric value (probably by mistake), the compiler gives you an error message. Values of type `boolean` cannot be converted to any type other than `String`. When a `boolean` variable is concatenated with a string, its value is automatically converted to either `"true"` or `"false"`. No type can be converted to `boolean`.

Be careful to compare `char` values only with other `char` values. For example, the comparisons

`'0' < '9'`

and

`0 < 9`

are appropriate, but comparing a digit in quotes (a character) and a digit such as

`'0' < 9`

generates an implicit type conversion and a result that probably isn't what you expect. The character for the digit `'0'` is converted to its Unicode `int` value, which is 79, and the comparison returns `false` because 79 is greater than 9.

You can use relational operators not only to compare variables or constants, but also to compare the values of arithmetic expressions. The following table shows the results of using the relational operators to compare expressions made up of adding 3 to x and multiplying y by 10 for different values of x and y:

Value of x	Value of y	Expression	Result
12	2	x + 3 <= y * 10	true
20	2	x + 3 <= y * 10	false
7	1	x + 3 != y * 10	false
17	2	x + 3 == y * 10	true
100	5	x + 3 > y * 10	true

Caution: It's easy to confuse the assignment operator (=) and the == relational operator. These two operators have very different effects in a program. Some people pronounce the relational operator as "equals-equals" to remind themselves of the difference.

Comparing Strings   You cannot compare strings using the relational operators. Syntactically, Java lets you write the comparisons for equality (==) and inequality (!=) between values of class String, but the comparison that this represents is not what you typically want. Recall from Chapter 3 that String is a reference type. That is, the content of a String variable is the memory address number for the beginning of the string. When you assign one string to another, Java just copies this address. Similarly, when you compare two strings, Java checks to see that they have the same address. It does not check to see if they contain the same sequence of characters.

Forgetting that Java applies comparison to strings in this manner, and mistakenly using == or != can produce some insidious errors. The comparison sometimes seems to work and sometimes it fails. The reason is that most Java compilers are quite clever about how they store String literals. If you type the same literal in two different places in your program, the compiler recognizes their equality and stores the character sequence just once, and then uses the same address in the Bytecode. Thus, comparing a String literal to a variable that has been assigned an identical literal elsewhere in the program is likely to work (if the Java compiler is well designed).

On the other hand, if you get a string from a TextField object and compare it to a String literal, the two will always compare as unequal, even when they contain the exact same sequence of characters. The string from the TextField object and the String literal are stored in different places in memory, which means that their addresses compare as unequal.

Rather than using the relational operators, we compare strings with a set of value-returning instance methods that Java supplies as part of the String class. Because they are instance methods, the method name is written following a String object, separated by a dot. The string that the method name is appended to is one of the strings in the comparison, and the string in the parameter list is the other. Because there are times we want to compare strings ignoring capitalization, the String class provides methods called toLowerCase and toUpperCase that convert all the characters of a string to lowercase or uppercase, respectively. The two most useful comparison methods are summarized in the following table, along with toLowerCase and toUpperCase.

Method Name	Parameter Type	Returns	Operation Performed
equals	String	boolean	Tests for equality of string contents.
compareTo	String	int	Returns 0 if equal, a positive integer if the string in the parameter comes before the string associated with the method, and a negative integer if the parameter comes after it.
toLowerCase		String	Returns a new identical string, except the characters are all lowercase.
toUpperCase		String	Returns a new identical string, except the characters are all lowercase.

For example, if `lastName` is a `String` variable, you can write

```
lastName.equals("Olson")   // Tests whether lastName equals "Olson"
```

Because every `String` literal is also a `String` object, Java lets you append the method call to a literal, if you so choose.

```
"Olson".equals(lastName)   // Tests whether lastName equals "Olson"
```

As another example, you might write

```
0 > lastName.compareTo("Olson")   // Tests if lastName comes before "Olson"
```

Comparison of strings follows the collating sequence of the Unicode character set. When the computer tests a relationship between two strings, it begins with the first character of each, compares them according to the collating sequence, and if they are the same, repeats the comparison with the next character in each string. The character-by-character test proceeds until a mismatch is found, the final characters have been compared and are equal, or one string runs out of characters. If all their characters are equal, then the two strings are equal. If a mismatch is found, then the string with the character that comes before the other is the "lesser" string. If their characters are equal throughout the shorter string, the shorter string comes before the longer string.

For example, given the statements

```
String word1;
String word2;

word1 = "Tremendous";
word2 = "Small";
```

the following relational expressions have the values shown.

Expression	Value	Reason
`word1.equals(word2)`	`false`	They are unequal in the first character.
`0 < word1.compareTo(word2)`	`true`	'T' comes after 'S' in the collating sequence.
`0 < word1.compareTo("small")`	`false`	'T' comes before 's' in the collating sequence.
`0 > word1.compareTo("Tremble")`	`false`	Fifth characters don't match, and 'b' comes before 'e'.
`word2.equals("Small")`	`true`	They are equal.
`0 == "cat".compareTo("dog")`	`false`	They are unequal.

In most cases, the ordering of strings corresponds to alphabetical ordering. But when strings have mixed case letters, you can get nonalphabetical results. For example, in a phone book we expect to see Macauley before MacPherson, but the Unicode collating sequence places all English uppercase letters before the lowercase letters, so the string "MacPherson" compares as less than "Macauley". To compare strings for strict alphabetical ordering, all the characters must be in the same case. Here we see examples in which `toLowerCase` and `toUpperCase` are used to perform the comparison correctly.

```
lowerCaseString = myString.toLowerCase();
upperCaseString = myString.toUpperCase();
```

You can use these methods directly in a comparison expression. For example, the following expressions convert `word1` and `word2` to the same case before comparing them. It doesn't matter whether the strings are both converted to uppercase or both are converted to lowercase, as long as they are the same.

```
0 > word1.toLowerCase().compareTo(word2.toLowerCase())
0 > word1.toUpperCase().compareTo(word2.toUpperCase())
```

If two strings with different lengths are compared and the comparison is equal up to the end of the shorter string, then the shorter string compares as less than the longer string. For example, if `word2` contains `"Small"`, the expression

```
0 > word2.compareTo("Smaller")
```

yields `true` because the strings are equal up to their fifth character position (the end of the string on the left) and the string on the right is longer.

Logical Operators In mathematics, the *logical* (or *Boolean*) *operators* AND, OR, and NOT take logical expressions as operands. Java uses special symbols for the logical operators: `&&` (for AND), `||` (for OR), and `!` (for NOT). By combining relational operators with logical operators, you can make more complex assertions. For example, suppose you want to determine whether a final score is greater than 90 *and* a midterm score is greater than 70. In Java, you would write the expression this way:

```
finalScore > 90 && midtermScore > 70
```

The AND operation (`&&`) requires both relationships to be true in order for the overall result to be true. If either or both of the relationships are `false`, the entire result is `false`.

The OR operation (`||`) takes two logical expressions and combines them. If *either* or *both* are true, the result is `true`. Both values must be `false` for the result to be `false`. Now you can determine whether the midterm grade is an A *or* the final grade is an A. If either the midterm grade or the final grade equals A, the assertion is `true`. In Java, you can write the expression like this:

```
midtermGrade == 'A' || finalGrade == 'A'
```

The `&&` and `||` operators always appear between two expressions; they are binary (two-operand) operators. The NOT operator (`!`) is a unary (one-operand) operator. It precedes a single logical expression and gives its opposite as the result. If (`grade == 'A'`) is false, then `!(grade == 'A')` is true. NOT gives a convenient way of reversing the meaning of an assertion. For example,

```
!(hours > 40)
```

is the equivalent of

```
hours <= 40
```

In some contexts, the first form is clearer; in others, the second makes more sense.

The following pairs of expressions are equivalent:

Expression	Equivalent Expression
`!(a == b)`	`a != b`
`!(a == b || a == c)`	`a != b && a != c`
`!(a == b && c > d)`	`a != b || c <= d`

Take a close look at these expressions to be sure you understand why they are equivalent. Try evaluating them with some values for `a`, `b`, `c`, and `d`. Notice the pattern: The expression on the left is just the one to its right with `!` added and the relational and logical operators reversed (for example, `==` instead of `!=` and `||` instead of `&&`). Remember this pattern. It allows you to rewrite expressions in the simplest form.[2]

---

[2]In Boolean algebra, the pattern is formalized by a theorem called *DeMorgan's law*.

Logical operators can be applied to the results of comparisons. They also can be applied directly to variables of type `boolean`. For example, instead of writing

```
isElector = (age >= 18 && district == 23);
```

to assign a value to the `boolean` variable `isElector`, you could use two intermediate `boolean` variables, `isVoter` and `isConstituent`:

```
isVoter = (age >= 18);
isConstituent = (district == 23);
isElector = isVoter && isConstituent;
```

The two tables below summarize the results of applying `&&` and `||` to a pair of logical expressions (represented here by `boolean` variables x and y).

Value of x	Value of y	Value of (x && y)
true	true	true
true	false	false
false	true	false
false	false	false

Value of x	Value of y	Value of (x || y)
true	true	true
true	false	true
false	true	true
false	false	false

The following table summarizes the results of applying the `!` operator to a logical expression (represented by Boolean variable x).

Value of x	Value of !x
true	false
false	true

Short-Circuit Evaluation   Consider the logical expression

```
i == 1 && j > 2
```

Some programming languages use *full evaluation* of logical expressions. With full evaluation, the computer first evaluates both subexpressions (both `i == 1` and `j > 2`) before applying the `&&` operator to produce the final result.

Short-circuit (conditional) evaluation   Evaluation of a logical expression in left-to-right order with evaluation stopping as soon as the final Boolean value can be determined

In contrast, Java uses short-circuit (or conditional) evaluation of logical expressions. Evaluation proceeds from left to right, and the computer stops evaluating subexpressions as soon as possible—that is, as soon as it knows the Boolean value of the entire expression. How can the computer know if a lengthy logical expression yields `true` or `false` if it doesn't examine all the subexpressions? Let's look first at the AND operation.

An AND operation yields the value `true` only if both of its operands are `true`. In the previous expression, suppose that the value of i happens to be 95. The first subexpression yields `false`, so it isn't necessary even to look at the second subexpression. The computer stops evaluation and produces the final result of `false`.

With the OR operation, the left-to-right evaluation stops as soon as a subexpression yielding `true` is found. Remember that an OR produces a result of `true` if either one or both of its operands are `true`. Given this expression:

```
c <= d || e == f
```

if the first subexpression is `true`, evaluation stops and the entire result is `true`. The computer doesn't waste time evaluating the second subexpression.

Java provides a second set of logical operators that result in full evaluation of Boolean expressions. The single & and | perform logical AND and OR operations, respectively, with full evaluation. We don't recommend their use at this stage in your experience with programming. In Java these operators have another meaning with variables or constants of types `byte`, `short`, `int`, and `long`, which can lead to errors that are hard to find.

 Background Information

George Boole

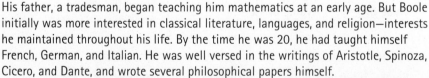

Boolean algebra is named for its inventor, English mathematician George Boole, born in 1815. His father, a tradesman, began teaching him mathematics at an early age. But Boole initially was more interested in classical literature, languages, and religion—interests he maintained throughout his life. By the time he was 20, he had taught himself French, German, and Italian. He was well versed in the writings of Aristotle, Spinoza, Cicero, and Dante, and wrote several philosophical papers himself.

At 16, to help support his family, he took a position as a teaching assistant in a private school. His work there and a second teaching job left him little time to study. A few years later, he opened a school and began to learn higher mathematics on his own. In spite of his lack of formal training, his first scholarly paper was published in the *Cambridge Mathematical Journal* when he was just 24. Boole went on to publish over 50 papers and several major works before he died in 1864, at the peak of his career.

continued ▼

George Boole

Boole's *The Mathematical Analysis of Logic* was published in 1847. It would eventually form the basis for the development of digital computers. In the book, Boole set forth the formal axioms of logic (much like the axioms of geometry) on which the field of symbolic logic is built.

Boole drew on the symbols and operations of algebra in creating his system of logic. He associated the value 1 with the universal set (the set representing everything in the universe) and the value 0 with the empty set, and restricted his system to these two quantities. He then defined operations that are analogous to subtraction, addition, and multiplication. Variables in the system have symbolic values. For example, if a Boolean variable *P* represents the set of all plants, then the expression $1 - P$ refers to the set of all things that are not plants. We can simplify the expression by using $-P$ to mean "*not* plants." ($0 - P$ is simply 0 because we can't remove elements from the empty set.) The subtraction operator in Boole's system corresponds to the ! (NOT) operator in Java. In a Java program, we might set the value of the Boolean variable `plant` to `true` when the name of a plant is entered, and `!plant` is `true` when the name of anything else is input.

The expression $0 + P$ is the same as *P*. However, $0 + P + F$, where *F* is the set of all foods, is the set of all things that are either plants or foods. So the addition operator in Boole's algebra is the same as the Java || (OR) operator.

The analogy can be carried to multiplication: $0 \times P$ is 0, and $1 \times P$ is *P*. But what is $P \times F$? It is the set of things that are both plants and foods. In Boole's system, the multiplication operator is the same as the && (AND) operator.

In 1854, Boole published *An Investigation of the Laws of Thought, on Which Are Founded the Mathematical Theories of Logic and Probabilities*. In the book, he described theorems built on his axioms of logic and extended the algebra to show how probabilities could be computed in a logical system. Five years later, Boole published *Treatise on Differential Equations*, then *Treatise on the Calculus of Finite Differences*. The latter is one of the cornerstones of numerical analysis, which deals with the accuracy of computations. (In Chapter 13, we examine the important role numerical analysis plays in computer programming.)

Boole received little recognition and few honors for his work. Given the importance of Boolean algebra in modern technology, it is hard to believe that his system of logic was not taken seriously until the early twentieth century. George Boole was truly one of the founders of computer science.

Precedence of Operators

In Chapter 4, we discussed the rules of precedence, the rules that govern the evaluation of complex arithmetic expressions. Java's rules of precedence also govern relational and logical operators. Here's a list showing the order of precedence for the arithmetic, relational, and logical operators (with the assignment operator thrown in as well):

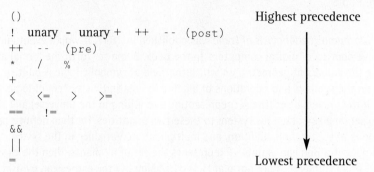

```
()                                           Highest precedence
!   unary -  unary +   ++   -- (post)
++   --   (pre)
*    /    %
+    -
<    <=    >    >=
==    !=
&&
||
=                                            Lowest precedence
```

Operators on the same line in the list have the same precedence. If an expression contains several operators with the same precedence, most of the operators group (or *associate*) from left to right. For example, the expression

```
a / b * c
```

means (a / b) * c, not a / (b * c). However, the ! operator groups from right to left. Although you'd never have occasion to use this expression:

```
!!badData
```

the meaning of it is !(!badData) rather than the meaningless (!!)badData. Appendix B, Operator Precedence, lists the order of precedence for all operators in Java. In skimming the appendix, you can see that a few of the operators associate from right to left (for the same reason we just described for the ! operator).

Parentheses are used to override the order of evaluation in an expression. If you're not sure whether parentheses are necessary, use them anyway. The compiler disregards unnecessary parentheses. So if they clarify an expression, use them. Some programmers like to include extra parentheses when assigning a relational expression to a boolean variable:

```
dataInvalid = (inputVal == 0);
```

The parentheses are not needed; the assignment operator has the lowest precedence of all the operators we've just listed. So we could write the statement as

```
dataInvalid = inputVal == 0;
```

but the parenthesized version is more readable.

One final comment about parentheses: Java, like other programming languages, requires that parentheses always be used in pairs. Whenever you write a complicated expression, take a minute to go through and pair up all of the opening parentheses with their closing counterparts.

PEANUTS reprinted by permission of United Features Syndicate, Inc.

Software Engineering Tip
Changing English Statements into Logical Expressions

In most cases, you can write a logical expression directly from an English statement or mathematical term in an algorithm. But you have to watch out for some tricky situations. Remember our sample logical expression:

```
midtermGrade == 'A' || finalGrade == 'A'
```

In English, you would be tempted to write this expression: "Midterm grade or final grade equals A." In Java, you can't write the expression as you would in English. That is,

```
midtermGrade || finalGrade == 'A'
```

won't work because the `||` operator is connecting a `char` value (`midtermGrade`) and a logical expression (`finalGrade == 'A'`). The two operands of `||` must be logical expressions. This example generates a syntax error message.

A variation of this mistake is to express the English assertion "*i* equals either 3 or 4" as

```
i == 3 || 4
```

But the syntax is incorrect. In the second subexpression, `4` is an `int` rather than a `boolean` value. The `||` operator (and the `&&` operator) can only connect two `boolean` expressions. Here's what we want:

```
i == 3 || i == 4
```

In math books, you might see a notation like this:

$12 < y < 24$

continued ▼

Changing English Statements into Logical Expressions

which means "y is between 12 and 24." This expression is illegal in Java. First, the relation $12 < y$ is evaluated, giving a `boolean` result. The computer then tries to compare it with the number 24. Because a `boolean` value cannot be converted to any type other than `String`, the expression is invalid. To write this expression correctly in Java, you must use the `&&` operator as follows:

```
12 < y && y < 24
```

Relational Operators with Floating-Point Types

So far, we've talked only about comparing `int`, `char`, and `String` values. Here we look at `float` and `double` values.

Do not compare floating-point numbers for equality. Because small errors in the rightmost decimal places are likely to arise when calculations are performed on floating-point numbers, two `float` or `double` values rarely are exactly equal. For example, consider the following code that uses two `double` variables named `oneThird` and `x`:

```
oneThird = 1.0 / 3.0;
x = oneThird + oneThird + oneThird;
```

We would expect `x` to contain the value 1.0, but it probably doesn't. The first assignment statement stores an *approximation* of 1/3 into `oneThird`, perhaps 0.333333. The second statement stores a value like 0.999999 into `x`. If we now ask the computer to compare `x` with 1.0, the comparison yields `false`.

Instead of testing floating-point numbers for equality, we test for *near* equality. To do so, we compute the difference between the two numbers and test to see if the result is less than some maximum allowable difference. For example, we often use comparisons like this:

```
Math.abs(r - s) < 0.00001
```

where `Math.abs` is the absolute value method from the Java library. The expression `Math.abs(r - s)` computes the absolute value of the difference between two variables `r` and `s`. If the difference is less than 0.00001, the two numbers are close enough to call them equal. We discuss this problem with floating-point accuracy in more detail in Chapter 13.

6.3 The if Statement

Now that we've seen how to write logical expressions, let's use them to alter the normal flow of control in a program. The *if statement* is the fundamental control structure that allows branches in the flow of control. With it, we can ask a question and choose a course of action: *if* a certain condition exists (the assertion is true), perform one action, *else* perform a different action.

The computer performs just one of the two actions under any given set of circumstances. Yet we must write *both* actions into the program. Why? Because, depending on the circumstances, the computer can choose to execute *either* of them. The *if* statement gives us a way of including both actions in a program and gives the computer a way of deciding which action to take.

The *if-else* Form

In Java, the *if* statement comes in two forms: the *if-else* form and the *if* form. Let's look first at the *if-else*. Here is its syntax template:

IfStatement (the if–else form)

```
if   ( Expression )
        Statement1A
else
        Statement1B
```

The expression in parentheses must produce a `boolean` result. At run time, the computer evaluates the expression. If the value is `true`, the computer executes Statement1A. If the value of the expression is `false`, Statement1B is executed. Statement1A often is often called the *then-clause*; Statement1B, the *else-clause*. Figure 6.3 illustrates the flow of control of the *if-else*. In the figure, Statement2 is the next statement in the program after the entire *if* statement.

Notice that a Java *if* statement uses the reserved words `if` and `else` but the *then-clause* does not include the word *then*. The code fragment below shows how to write an *if* statement in a program. Observe the indentation of the *then*-clause and the *else*-clause, which makes the statement easier to read. And notice the placement of the statement following the *if* statement.

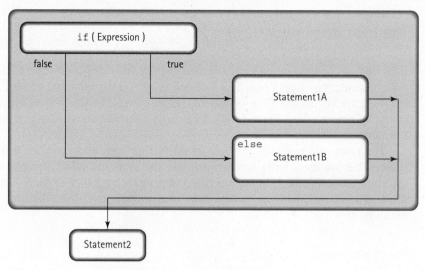

Figure 6.3   *if-else flow of control*

```
if (hours <= 40.0)
  pay = rate * hours;
else
  pay = rate * (40.0 + (hours - 40.0) * 1.5);
out.add(new Label("Pay is " + pay));
```

In terms of instructions to the computer, the above code fragment says, "If hours is less than or equal to 40.0, compute the regular pay and then go on to execute the output statement. But if hours is greater than 40, compute the regular pay and the overtime pay, and then go on to execute the output statement." Figure 6.4 shows the flow of control of this *if* statement.

If-else statements are often used to check the validity of input. For example, before we ask the computer to divide by a data value, we should be sure that the value is not zero. (Even computers can't divide something by zero. If you try it with int values, the computer halts the execution of your program. With floating-point types, you get the special infinity value.) If the divisor is zero, our program should thus display an error message. Here's an example that adds an error message label to a frame called out.

```
Label errorMsg;
errorMsg = new Label("Division by zero is not allowed. " +
          " Enter a new value for divisor and press Done button." );
if (divisor != 0)
  result = dividend / divisor;
else
  out.add(errorMsg);
```

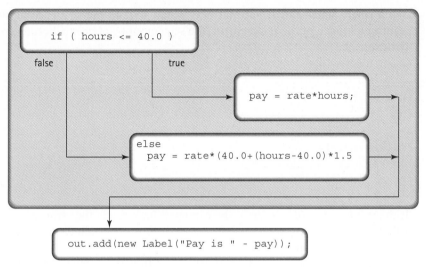

Figure 6.4   *Flow of control for calculating pay*

If this code fragment is within the handler for a button controlling screen input, the program waits until another event occurs, either the pressing of the button or the closing of the input window.

Before we look any further at *if* statements, take another look at the syntax template for the *if-else.* According to the template, there is no semicolon at the end of an *if* statement. In both of the program fragments above—the worker's pay and the division-by-zero examples—there seems to be a semicolon at the end of each *if* statement. However, the semicolons belong to the statements in the *then*-clause and the *else*-clause in those examples; assignment statements end in semicolons, as do method calls. The *if* statement doesn't have its own semicolon at the end.

Blocks (Compound Statements)

In our division-by-zero example, suppose that when the divisor is equal to zero we want to do *two* things: add the error message to the frame *and* set the variable named `result` equal to a special value like `Integer.MAX_VALUE`. We would need two statements in the same branch, but the syntax template seems to limit us to one.

What we really want to do is turn the else-clause into a *sequence* of statements. This is easy. Remember from Chapter 2 that the compiler treats the block (compound statement) like a single statement. If you put a { } pair around the sequence of statements you want in a branch of the *if* statement, the sequence of statements becomes a single block. For example:

```
if (divisor != 0)
  result = dividend / divisor;
else
{
  out.add(errorMsg);
  result = Integer.MAX_VALUE;
}
```

If the value of `divisor` is zero, the computer both prints the error message and sets the value of `result` to `Integer.MAX_VALUE` before continuing with whatever statement follows the *if* statement.

Blocks can be used in both branches of an *if-else* statement. For example:

```
private static Label errorMsg;
private static Label oKMsg;
errorMsg = new Label("Division by zero is not allowed.");
oKMsg = new Label("Division performed.");
if (divisor != 0)
{
  result = dividend / divisor;
  out.add(oKMsg);
}
else
{
  out.add(errorMsg);
  result = Integer.MAX_VALUE;
}
```

When you use blocks in an *if* statement, there's a rule of Java syntax to remember: *Never use a semicolon after the right brace of a block.* Semicolons are used only to terminate simple statements such as assignment statements and method calls. If you look at the examples above, you won't see a semicolon after the right brace that signals the end of each block.

Matters of Style

Braces and Blocks

Java programmers use different styles when it comes to locating the left brace of a block. The style we use puts the left and right braces directly below the words `if` and `else`, each brace on its own line:

```
if (n >= 2)
{
    alpha = 5;
    beta = 8;
}
else
{
    alpha = 23;
    beta = 12;
}
```

Another popular style is to place the statements following `if` and `else` on the same line as the left brace; the right braces still line up directly below the left braces.

```
if (n >= 2)
{ alpha = 5;
    beta = 8;
}
else
{ alpha = 23;
    beta = 12;
}
```

It makes no difference to the Java compiler which style you use (and there are other styles as well, such as placing the left braces at the ends of the lines containing `if` and `else`.). It's a matter of personal preference. Whichever style you use, though, you should always use the same style throughout a program. Inconsistency can confuse a person reading your program and give the impression of carelessness.

The *if* Form

Sometimes you run into a situation where you want to say, "*If* a certain condition exists, perform some action; otherwise, don't do anything." In other words, you want the computer to skip a sequence of instructions if a certain condition isn't met. You could do this by leaving the `else` branch empty, using only the null statement:

```
if (a <= b)
  c = 20;
else
  ;
```

Better yet, you could simply leave off the `else` part. The resulting statement is the *if* form of the *if* statement. This is its syntax template:

IfStatement (the if form)

```
if    ( Expression )
        Statement
```

Here's an example of an *if* form. Notice the indentation and the placement of the statement that follows the *if*.

```
if (age < 18)
  out.add(new Label("Not an eligible "));
out.add(new Label("voter."));
```

This statement means that if `age` is less than 18, first add the label `"Not an eligible "` to Frame `out` and then add the label `"voter."`. If `age` is not less than 18, skip the first statement and go directly to adding the label `"voter."`. Figure 6.5 shows the flow of control for an *if* form.

Like the two branches in an *if-else* form, the one branch in an *if* can be a block. For example, let's say you are writing a program to compute income taxes. One of the lines on the tax form says, "Subtract line 23 from line 17 and enter result on line 24; if result is less than zero, enter zero and check box 24A." You can use an *if* statement to do this in Java:

```
Label checkMsg;
checkMsg = new Label("Check box 24A");
result = line17 - line23;
if (result < 0.0)
```

To see how this *if-else-if* structure works, consider the branch that tests for `temperature` greater than 70. If it has been reached, you know that `temperature` must be less than or equal to 85 because that condition causes this particular *else* branch to be taken. Thus, you need to test only whether `temperature` is above the bottom of this range (> 70). If that test fails, then you enter the next *else*-clause knowing that `temperature` must be less than or equal to 70. Each successive branch checks the bottom of its range until you reach the final *else*, which takes care of all the remaining possibilities.

Note that if the ranges aren't consecutive, then you must test the data value against both the highest and lowest value of each range. You still use an *if-else-if* structure because that is best for selecting a single branch from multiple possibilities, and you can arrange the ranges in consecutive order to make them easier for a human reader to follow. But there is no way to reduce the number of comparisons when there are gaps between the ranges.

The Dangling else

When *if* statements are nested, you may find yourself confused about the *if-else* pairings. That is, to which *if* does an *else* belong? For example, suppose that if a student's average is below 60, you want to display "Failing"; if it is at least 60 but less than 70, you want to display "Passing but marginal"; and if it is 70 or greater, you don't want to display anything.

You can code this information with an *if-else* structure nested within an *if*:

```
Label failing;
Label passing;
failing = new Label("Failing");
passing = new Label("Passing but marginal");
if (average < 70.0)
  if (average < 60.0)
    out.add(failing);
  else
    out.add(passing);
```

How do you know to which *if* the *else* belongs? Here is the rule that the Java compiler follows: In the absence of braces, an *else* is always paired with the closest preceding *if* that doesn't already have an *else* paired with it. The code is indented to reflect this pairing.

Suppose you write the fragment like this (assuming the declarations of the labels are the same):

```
if (average >= 60.0)          // Incorrect version
  if (average < 70.0)
    out.add(passing);
else
  out.add(failing);
```

Here you want the *else* branch attached to the outer *if* statement, not the inner, so the code is indented as you see it. But indentation does not affect the execution of the code. Even though the *else* aligns with the first *if*, the compiler pairs it with the second *if*. An *else* that follows a nested *if* is called a *dangling else*. It doesn't logically belong with the nested *if* but is attached to it by the compiler.

To attach the *else* to the first *if*, not the second, you can turn the outer *then*-clause into a block:

```
if (average >= 60.0)                 // Correct version
{
  if (average < 70.0)
    out.add(passing);
}
else
  out.add(failing);
```

The { } pair indicates that the first *if* statement has a compound first clause that contains an *if* statement (with no *else* clause), so the *else* must belong to the outer *if*.

6.5 Handling Multiple Button Events

When we first discussed the handling of button events in a frame, we restricted our user interface to a single button. The reason for our restriction was that all button events for a frame can be sent to the same listener method (actionPerformed) and we had not yet seen the *if* statement, which is what we use to distinguish among events from multiple buttons. Now we have the ability to respond to each event differently. In this section we consider the handling of events from multiple buttons, which also nicely illustrates the use of branching.

Immediately after we instantiate a button with new, we call setActionCommand with a String parameter that identifies the button. (This is not the string that appears on the button, though they may be the same string.) If we do not call setActionCommand, the listener assumes that the name of the button is the same as the string used when instantiating the Button object. We then call addActionListener to tell the event, "Here's a button listener to be called when this button fires."

For example, suppose we provide a user interface with two buttons, Copy and Done, as follows: We create one ButtonHandler listener object, and we register it with both buttons as follows.

```
buttonAction = new ButtonHandler();
// Instantiate a ButtonHandler object, and assign it to the variable
//  buttonAction
copy = new Button("Copy");
// Instantiate a Button object that is displayed with the word "Copy"
//  assign it to the variable copy
copy.setActionCommand("copy");
// Give button a string to identify it
copy.addActionListener(buttonAction);
// Register button listener using the ButtonHandler assigned to
//  buttonAction
done = new Button("Done");
// Instantiate a second Button thatdisplays the word "Done" inside it
//  and assign it to the variable done
done.setActionCommand("done");
// Give button a string to identify it
done.addActionListener(buttonAction);
// Register button listener using the ButtonHandler stored in buttonAction
```

Figure 6.6 shows a frame with these buttons in it.

When either one of these buttons is pressed, `actionPerformed` is called by its source event, just as we saw in Chapter 5. How does `actionPerformed` decide which button was pressed? Recall that when we write the heading for the `actionPerformed` method, we include a parameter of type `ActionEvent`. The source event passes an object to the method through that parameter. That object has a field containing the name of the button, which is either the default string from the constructor or the string in the call to `setActionCommand`. We access the name string by calling the value returning method `getActionCommand` that is associated with the parameter object.

For example, if the heading for `actionPerformed` is written this way:

```
public void actionPerformed(ActionEvent buttonEvent)
```

Then we obtain the string that names the pressed button using the following statement.

```
command = buttonEvent.getActionCommand();
```

Figure 6.6 *Frame with two buttons*

Within our declaration of the method, we use string comparisons and branches to perform the necessary action for the particular button. For example, we might extend the event handler in our `CopyString` class from Chapter 5 as follows.

```
private static class ButtonHandler implements ActionListener
{
  public void actionPerformed(ActionEvent buttonEvent) // Event handler method
  {
    String command;                                    // String to hold button name
    command = buttonEvent.getActionCommand();          // Get the button's name
    if (command.equals("copy"))                        // When the name is "copy"
      outputLabel.setText(inputField.getText());       //  copy the field
    else if (command.equals("done"))                   // When the name is "done"
    {
      dataFrame.dispose();                             // close the frame and
      System.exit(0);                                  // quit the program
    }
    else                                               // Otherwise, it's an error
      outputLabel.setText("An unexpected event occurred.");
  }
}
```

When the event source calls `actionPerformed`, the method gets the button's name using `getActionCommand`. If `setActionCommand` has been called to name the button, its parameter string is returned. If not, the parameter string used in the button's instantiation is returned. Why do we bother to explicitly name the button? There may be times when a different internal name is more meaningful than the string used to label the button in the window. For example, if you are writing an application to be used in France, you might want the button to have a meaningful English name, but the label would be in French.

The eventhandler then uses an *if-else-if* structure to decide which button was pressed and execute the appropriate statements. Although `getActionCommand` should never return a name other than `"copy"` or `"done"`, you can provide a branch for other names just to be safe. Some time in the future the program could be changed to add another button. If you forget to add a corresponding branch to handle that event, the program displays an error message instead of crashing.

There is another way that you can handle multiple button events. For each button you can declare a separate listener class. For example, instead of one class called `ButtonHandler`, you could declare two classes called `CopyHandler` and `DoneHandler`, each of which has its own `actionPerformed` method. You would then write

```
copyAction = new CopyHandler();      // Instantiate copyAction
copy = new Button("Copy");           // Instantiate copy, labeled "Copy"
copy.setActionCommand("copy");       // Give copy button a string to
                                     //  identify it
```

```
copy.addActionListener(copyAction);   // Register the button listener using
                                      //   the CopyHandler assigned to
                                      //   copyAction
done = new Button("Done");            // Instantiate done, labeled "Done"
doneAction = new DoneHandler();       // Instantiate the handler
done.setActionCommand("done");        // Name the button
done.addActionListener(doneAction);   // Register the button listener using
                                      //   the DoneHandler assigned to
                                      //   doneAction
```

This code registers a different event listener for each button. The source event calls the `actionPerformed` method within the appropriate listener. With this approach you avoid writing a branch to decide which button has been pressed, but you must declare a new class for each button. Look back at Figure 6.6. The buttons generated from this code fragment are identical to those in Figure 6.6; how the buttons are handled when they are pressed, however, is different.

When a user interface contains buttons that perform simple or related tasks, it makes sense to combine the handling of their events into a single method. If pressing a button causes complex processing that is unrelated to other buttons, then it is more sensible to use a separate event handler. For example, when a button press results in a branch to a different part of the program where the user interface is replaced by a new set of fields and buttons, then the code belongs in a separate event listener.

The following code segment shows the declaration of the `CopyHandler` and `DoneHandler` classes, along with the subsequent declaration of variables of those types. The same names are used as in the preceding code segment.

```
private static class CopyHandler implements ActionListener
{
  public void actionPerformed(ActionEvent event)
  // Copy event handler method
  {
    outputLabel.setText(inputField.getText());   // Copy the field
  }
}

private static class DoneHandler implements ActionListener
{
  public void actionPerformed(ActionEvent event)
  // Done event handler method
  {
    dataFrame.dispose();                          // Close the frame
    System.exit(0);                               // Quit the program
  }
}

CopyHandler copyAction;                            // CopyHandler variable
DoneHandler doneAction;                            // DoneHandler variable
```

Problem-Solving Case Study

A Simple Calculator

Problem   It's useful to have a calculator that you can display on your computer screen when you look around and can't find your handheld one. Let's write a Java application that simulates a simple calculator. Once we have the basic design it is easy to extend it to provide other functions.

Brainstorming   You pick up your pocket calculator. After all, this problem is one of simulating the pocket calculator. What are the objects that you see? A register on the top that shows what you are entering and displays the answer, an ON button, buttons for each of the ten decimal digits, buttons for each of the four basic operations, a CLEAR button, and a button marked with an equal sign. There are buttons for percent and square root, but you do not use them often enough to add them to the simulation. So the first list of proposed classes is as follows:

```
register
on button
buttons for each digit
buttons for four operations
clear button
equal button
```

Filtering   We certainly need a register to show the output. Do we need an ON button? No, running the program is equivalent to the ON button. However, we do need some way of quitting the program. We could have a quit button or we could let the window closing end the program. We need an object to represent the calculator itself; that is, we need a window to hold all the other objects. What about the buttons for each digit? No, we can let the user input a number into a text field rather than pushing individual buttons. This means that we need a label for the text field. Do we need an enter button? No, we can let the button for the operation signal that the value is ready to be read. We do need buttons for each operation. We certainly need a CLEAR button to set the register value to zero. What about the equal button? On the calculator it signals that we want to see the results so far in the register. Instead of entering an equal button, let's just display the result of each operation in the register as we go along.

We know from our experience with the Case Study in Chapter 5 that we need a class that contains `main` to organize the window and a class that implements `ActionListener`. This class becomes the application. Let's call it `Calculator`. Here, then, is our second pass at the classes for our application:

a register
window
text field for number input
label for input text field
four buttons for the operations
clear button

Scenarios The register is simply a label that displays what is put into it, so it actually has no further responsibility. The window object is a container into which labels, text fields, and buttons are placed, so it collaborates with each of these. The text field for the input has no responsibilities; it just collaborates with the appropriate button handler. The label for the text field has only one responsibility: to display the input prompt. What happens when the operation buttons are pressed? The four operator buttons are event sources; they have no responsibility, but their handlers do. When one is pressed, the JVM calles the appropriate button handler, which collaborates with the text field to input a value, performs a calculation, and sends the value to the register. The clear button is different in function from the others but its only responsibility is to be an event source. However, its event handler must collaborate with the register to set it to zero. It makes sense to use one button handler for the four arithmetic buttons, but a separate one for the CLEAR button.

The application has responsibility for setting up the window, handling the button events through the inclusions of the two listener classes, and handling the window-closing event.

CRC cards All of the objects are instances of classes provided in the Java window and event-handling packages. So the only CRC card is for class `Calculator`.

Class Name: Calculator	Superclass:		Subclasses:
Responsibilities		**Collaborations**	
Prepare the window for input		TextField, Label, String, Buttons	
Handle numeric button events		Buttons, register (text field)	
Handle clear button event		Buttons, register (text field)	
Handle window closing		Frame	

Responsibility Algorithms   Do you remember in Chapter 1, after the long first program, that we said that much of the code dealt with input and output, which would soon become second nature to you? Well the first responsibility should sound comfortingly familiar. It is exactly the same as the first responsibility for Chapter 5's Case Study. Does this mean that we can just cut and paste the algorithms? No, the objects in the window are not the same, but the steps used to create them are the same, so we can reuse the top-level module.

Prepare Window for Input   Level 1

> Declare the interface variables
> Instantiate each interface object
> Add each interface object to the frame
> Pack the frame
> Show the frame

Declaring the interface variables requires us to make a list of the components in the window. We need a frame to hold everything, two labels (one for input and one for the register), a field for entering a data value, four buttons for the user to click to indicate the operation when a value is ready for input, and a button for the user to click to clear the register.

Before we go on, let's simplify the problem somewhat. Let's first create a calculator with only plus and minus functions. After we verify this simplified version of the program, we can come back and add division and multiplication. (See Case Study Follow-Up Question 1.)

Declare Interface Variables   Level 2

> Declare a Frame, calcFrame
> Declare a Label, resultLabel
> Declare a Label, register
> Declare a Label, entryLabel for prompting
> Declare a TextField, inputField for input
> Declare a Button, add
> Declare a Button, subtract
> Declare a Button, clear

Instantiate Each Interface Object

> Set calcFrame to new Frame, as a four-row, two-column grid
> Set resultLabel to new Label, "Result:"
> Set register to new Label, "0.0"
> Set entryLabel to new Label, "Enter #:"
> Set inputField to new TextField, empty with 10 spaces
> Set add to new Button, "+"
> Set subtract to new Button, "-"
> Set clear to new Button, "Clear"
> Register the event listener for the numeric buttons
> Register the event listener for the clear button

We have added two more abstract steps, which we can now expand. Registering an event listener for a button involves four steps that: declare a variable of the listener class, set the action command for the button, instantiate the listener class, and then add the listener object to the button. Let's call the listener for the numeric operations `NumericHandler`. These four steps are all concrete as shown in the following module.

....

Register the Event Listener for the Numeric Buttons   Level 3

> Declare a NumericHandler, operation
> setActionCommand for button add to "add"
> setActionCommand for button subtract to "subtract"
> Instantiate operation
> Add operation as listener for numeric button

Let's call the listener for the clear operation `ClearHandler`.

....

Register the Event Listener for the Clear Button

> Declare a ClearHandler, clearOperation
> setActionCommand for button clear to "Clear"
> Instantiate clearOperation
> Add clearOperation as listener for clear button

....

Add Each Interface Object to the Frame   Level 2

> Add resultLabel to calcFrame
> Add register to calcFrame
> Add entryLabel to calcFrame
> Add inputField to calcFrame
> Add add to calcFrame
> Add subtract to calcFrame
> Add clear to calcFrame

We have now completed the first responsibility for class `Calculator`. The second responsibility is to handle the numeric buttons; that is, write the listener for the numeric buttons. We have said that the listener class is called `NumericHandler`. What should the `actionPerformed` method do when an add or subtract button is pushed? First, it should get the value to be used in the calculation from the input field and convert it to a real number. If the user enters a string that does not represent a legitimate real number, a `NumberFormatException` may be thrown. In Chapter 10 we show you how to handle this exception; here we assume correct input.

The next step is to determine which operation is to be applied to the number, addition or subtraction. Wait a minute: Addition and subtraction are binary operations. We have one value; where is the other one? Actually, the value just input is the second operand. The first operand is the value in the register. Rather than extract it from the window each time, we

should keep a copy in numeric form. (We must be sure to set that value to zero originally.) Back to the question of determining which button was pushed: We can use the parameter to the `actionPerformed` method to tell us.

Handle Numeric Button Events   Level 1

> Get the entry string from the input field
> Set secondOperand to numerical value (double) of entry string
> Set whichButton to source event
> if whichButton is "add"
>   Set result to result + secondOperand
> else
>   Set result to result − secondOperand
> Display result in register
> Clear inputField

The third responsibility is even simpler; all we have to do is set the register and input field to zero as well as the variable that contains the same value. These actions are performed in the `actionPerformed` method of class `ClearHandler`.

Handle Clear Button Event   Level 1

> Set result to zero
> Display result in register
> Clear inputField

The fourth responsibility is one that you should see in all of your applications that use windows: Handle window closing.

Handle Window Closing   Level 1

> Dispose of the frame
> Exit the program

Objects and Variables

Name	Type	Description
In *main:*		
calcFrame*	Frame	Frame to display on screen
resultLabel	Label	Indicates output area
register*	Label	Label to show output
entryLabel	Label	Label indicating input field
inputField*	TextField	Field for user input
add	Button	Add button
subtract	Button	Subtract button
clear	Button	Clear button
result*	double	Keeps current value
operation	NumericHandler	Listener for numeric buttons
clearOperation	ClearHandler	Listener for clear button
In *NumericHandler.actionPerformed:*		
secondOperand	double	Holds input value
whichButton	String	Holds button's name

The coding of the program into Java is now easy—tedious but straightforward. Here is the result.

```java
import java.awt.*;                              // User interface classes
import java.awt.event.*;                        // Event handling classes


public class Calculator
{
  // Define action listener for numeric buttons
  private static  class NumericHandler implements ActionListener
  {
    public void actionPerformed(ActionEvent event)
    // Handles events from the numeric buttons in calcFrame
    {
      double secondOperand;                      // Holds input value
      String whichButton;                        // Holds the button's name
      // Get the operand
      secondOperand = Double.valueOf(inputField.getText()).doubleValue();
      whichButton = event.getActionCommand();    // Get the button's name

      if (whichButton.equals("add"))             // When the name is "add"
```

```
          result = result + secondOperand;          //  add the operand
      else                                           // Otherwise
        result = result - secondOperand;             //  subtract the operand

      register.setText("" + result);                 // Display result
      inputField.setText("");                        // Clear input
    }
  }

  private static class ClearHandler implements ActionListener
  {
    public void actionPerformed(ActionEvent event)
    // Handles events from the Clear button in calcFrame
    {
      result = 0.0;                                  // Set result back to zero
      register.setText("0.0");                       // Reset register
      inputField.setText("");                        // Clear input
    }
  }


  private static TextField inputField;               // Data field
  private static Label register;                     // Result shown on screen
  private static Frame calcFrame;                    // Declare a frame
  private static double result;                      // Keeps current value

  public static void main(String[] args)
  {
    // Declare numeric listener
    NumericHandler operation;
    ClearHandler clearOperation;                     // Declare clear listener
    Label resultLabel;                               // Indicates output area
    Label entryLabel;                                // Label for input field
    Button add;                                      // Add button
    Button subtract;                                 // Subtract button
    Button clear;                                    // Clear button

    operation = new NumericHandler();                // Instantiate operation
    // Instantiate clearOperation
    clearOperation = new ClearHandler();
    result = 0.0;                                    // Initialize result

    // Instantiate labels and initialize input field
    calcFrame = new Frame();                         // Give the frame a value
```

```
calcFrame.setLayout(new GridLayout(4,2));        // Set the layout manager
resultLabel = new Label("Result:");
register = new Label("0.0", Label.RIGHT);
entryLabel = new Label("Enter #:");
inputField = new TextField("", 10);

// Instantiate button objects
add = new Button("+");
subtract = new Button("-");
clear = new Button("Clear");

// Name the button events
add.setActionCommand("add");
subtract.setActionCommand("subtract");
clear.setActionCommand("clear");

// Register the button listeners
add.addActionListener(operation);
subtract.addActionListener(operation);
clear.addActionListener(clearOperation);

// Add interface elements to calcFrame
calcFrame.add(resultLabel);
calcFrame.add(register);
calcFrame.add(entryLabel);
calcFrame.add(inputField);
calcFrame.add(add);
calcFrame.add(subtract);
calcFrame.add(clear);
calcFrame.pack();                                        // Pack the frame
calcFrame.show();                                        // Show the frame
calcFrame.addWindowListener(new WindowAdapter()
// Define window-closing event handler
  {
    public void windowClosing(WindowEvent event)
    {
      calcFrame.dispose();                               // Close the frame
      System.exit(0);                                    // Quit the program
    }
  });
}
}
```

When we run the program, it displays a window like the one shown below.

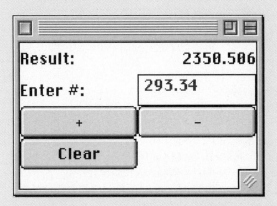

Testing and Debugging

In Chapter 1, we discussed the problem-solving and implementation phases of computer programming. Testing is an integral part of both phases. Testing in the problem-solving phase is done after the solution is developed but before it is implemented. In the implementation phase, we test after the algorithm is translated into a program, and again after the program has compiled successfully. The compilation itself constitutes another stage of testing that is performed automatically.

Testing Strategies

When an individual programmer is designing and implementing a program, he or she can find many software errors with pencil and paper. Desk checking the design solution is a very common method of manually verifying a design or program. The programmer writes down essential data (variables, input values, parameters of subprograms, and so on) and walks through the design, manually simulating the actions of the computer and recording changes in the data on the paper. Portions of the design or code that are complex or that are a source of concern should be double-checked.

Desk checking Tracing an execution of a design or program on paper

Deskchecking can be done by an individual, but most sizable computer programs are developed by *teams* of programmers. Two extensions of desk checking that are used effectively by programming teams are design or code walk-throughs and inspections. These are formal team activities, the intention of which is to move the responsibility for uncovering bugs from the individual programmer to the group. Because testing is time-consuming and errors cost more the later they are discovered, the goal is to identify errors before testing begins.

In a *walk-through* the team performs a manual simulation of the design or program with sample test inputs, keeping track of the program's data by hand. Unlike thorough program testing, the walk-through is not intended to simulate all possible test cases. Instead, its purpose is to stimulate discussion about the way the programmer chose to design or implement the program's requirements.

Walk-through   A verification method in which a *team* performs a manual simulation of the program or design

Inspection   A verification method in which one member of a team reads the program or design line by line and the others point out errors

At an *inspection*, a reader (not necessarily the program's author) goes through the design or code line by line. Inspection participants point out errors, which are recorded on an inspection report. Some errors are uncovered just by the process of reading aloud. Others may have been noted by team members during their preinspection preparation. As with the walk-through, the chief benefit of the team meeting is the discussion that takes place among team members. This interaction among programmers, testers, and other team members can uncover many program errors long before the testing stage begins.

At the high-level design stage, the design should be compared to the application requirements to make sure that all required responsibilities have been included and that this application or class correctly interfaces with other software in the system. At the low-level design stage, when the design has been filled out with more details, it should be reinspected before it is implemented.

After the code is written, you should go over it line by line to be sure that you've faithfully reproduced the algorithm—a process known as a *code walk-through*. In a team programming situation, you ask other team members to walk through the algorithm and code with you, to double-check the design and code.

You also should take some actual values and hand-calculate what the output should be by doing an execution trace (or *hand trace*). When the program is executed, you can use these same values as input and then check the results. The computer is a very literal device—it does exactly what we tell it to do, which may or may not be what we want it to do. We try to make sure that a program does what we want by tracing the execution of the statements.

Execution trace   The process of going through the program with actual values recording the state of the variables

When a program contains branches, it's a good idea to retrace its execution with different input data so that each branch is traced at least once. In the next section, we describe how to develop data sets that test each of a program's branches.

To test an application with methods, we need to execute each method. If a method contains branches, we need to execute each branch at least once and verify the results. For example, there are two `actionPerformed` methods, one of which contains an *if* statement. Therefore, we need at least three data sets to test the methods and the different branches. For example, the following combination of buttons and input values cause all of the methods and branches to be executed:

	Button	Value
Set 1	+	12.5
Set 2	-	2.5
Set 3	Clear	

Every branch in the program is executed at least once through this series of test runs. Eliminating any of the test data sets would leave at least one branch untested. This series of data sets provides what is called *minimum complete coverage* of the program's branching structure. Whenever you test a program with branches in it, you should design a series of tests that covers all of the branches. Because an action in one branch of a program often affects processing in a later branch, it is critical to test as many *combinations of branches*, or paths, through a program as possible. By doing so, you can be sure that there are no interdependencies that could cause problems. Should you try all possible paths? Yes, in theory you should. However, the number of paths in even a small program can be very large.

The approach to testing that we've used here is called *code coverage* because the test data is designed by looking at the code of the program. Code coverage is also called *white-box* (or *clear-box*) *testing* because you are allowed to see the program code while designing the tests. Another approach to testing, *data coverage*, attempts to test as many allowable data values as possible without regard to the program code. Because you need not see the code in this form of testing, it is also called *black-box testing*—the same set of tests would be used even if the code were hidden in a black box. Complete data coverage is as impractical as complete code coverage for many programs. For example, the `NumericHandler.actionPerformed` method reads one `double` value and thus has an immense number of possible input values.

Often, testing is a combination of these two strategies. Instead of trying every possible data value (data coverage), the idea is to examine the code (code coverage) and look for ranges of values for which processing is identical. Then test the values at the boundaries and, sometimes, a value in the middle of each range. For example, a simple condition such as

```
alpha < 0
```

divides the integers into two ranges:

1. `Integer.MIN_VALUE` through `-1`
2. `0` through `Integer.MAX_VALUE`

Thus, you should test the four values `Integer.MIN_VALUE`, -1, 0, and `Integer.MAX_VALUE`. A compound condition such as

```
alpha >= 0 && alpha <= 100
```

divides the integers into three ranges:

1. `Integer.MIN_VALUE` through `-1`
2. `0` through `100`
3. `101` through `Integer.MAX_VALUE`

Thus, you have six values to test. In addition, to verify that the relational operators are correct, you should test for values of 1 (> 0) and 99 (< 100).

Conditional branches are only one factor in developing a testing strategy. We consider more of these factors in later chapters.

The Test Plan

We've discussed strategies and techniques for testing programs, but how do you approach the testing of a specific program? You do it by designing and implementing a test plan—a document that specifies the test cases that should be tried, the reason for each test case, and the expected output. Test plan implementation involves running the program using the data specified by the test cases in the plan and checking and recording the results.

> **Test plan** A document that specifies how a program is to be tested
>
> **Test plan implementation** Using the test cases specified in a test plan to verify that a program outputs the predicted results

The test plan should be developed together with the design. The following table shows a partial test plan for the `Calculator` application. The first test case assumes that the calculator has an initial value of 0.0. Successive test cases use the preceding result as one of the two operands for a calculation. To be more thorough, we should check that the program properly handles closing of the window, and we should include some negative as well as positive values.

Implementing a test plan does not guarantee that a program is completely correct. It means only that a careful, systematic test of the program has not demonstrated any bugs. The situation shown in Figure 6.7 is analogous to trying to test a program without

Test Plan for the Calculator Application

Reason for Test Case	Input Values	Expected Output	Observed Output
Test add command	12.5, +	12.500	
Test subtract command	2.5, -	10.000	
Test clear command	none, Clear	0.000	
Test window closing	none	window disappears	

a plan—depending only on luck, you may completely miss the fact that a program contains numerous errors. Developing and implementing a written test plan, on the other hand, casts a wide net that is much more likely to find errors.

Tests Performed Automatically During Compilation and Execution

Once a program is coded and test data has been prepared, it is ready for compiling. The compiler has two responsibilities: to report any errors and (if there are no errors) to translate the program into object code or Bytecode.

Errors can be syntactic or semantic. The compiler finds syntactic errors. For example, the compiler warns you when reserved words are misspelled, identifiers are unde-

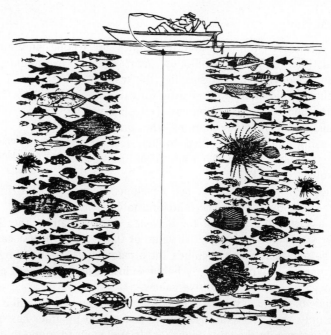

Figure 6.7   *When you test a program without a plan, you never know what you might be missing*

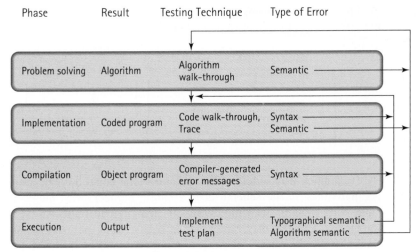

Phase	Result	Testing Technique	Type of Error
Problem solving	Algorithm	Algorithm walk-through	Semantic
Implementation	Coded program	Code walk-through, Trace	Syntax, Semantic
Compilation	Object program	Compiler-generated error messages	Syntax
Execution	Output	Implement test plan	Typographical semantic, Algorithm semantic

Figure 6.8 *Testing process*

clared, semicolons are missing, and operand types are mismatched. But it won't find all of your typing errors. If you type > instead of <, you won't get an error message; instead, you get erroneous results when you test the program. It's up to you to design a test plan and carefully check the code to detect errors of this type.

Semantic errors (also called *logic errors*) are mistakes that give you the wrong answer. They are more difficult to locate than syntactic errors and usually surface when a program is executing. Java detects only the most obvious semantic errors—those that result in an invalid operation (dividing by zero, for example). Although typing errors sometimes cause semantic errors, they are more often a product of a faulty algorithm design.

By walking through the algorithm and the code, tracing the execution of the program, and developing a thorough test strategy, you should be able to avoid, or at least quickly locate, semantic errors in your programs.

Figure 6.8 illustrates the testing process we've been discussing. The figure shows where syntax and semantic errors occur and in which phase they can be corrected.

Testing and Debugging Hints

1. Java has three pairs of operators that are similar in appearance but different in effect: == and =, && and &, and || and |. Double-check all of your logical expressions to be sure you're using the "equals-equals," "and-and," and "or-or" operators. Then check them again to make certain that you didn't double type the < or > operators.

2. If you use extra parentheses for clarity, be sure that the opening and closing parentheses match up. To verify that parentheses are properly paired, start with the

innermost pair and draw a line connecting them. Do the same for the others, working your way out to the outermost pair. For example,

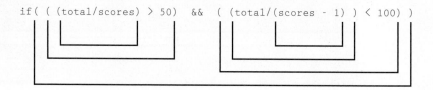

3. Here is a quick way to tell whether you have an equal number of opening and closing parentheses. The scheme uses a single number (the "magic number"), whose value initially is 0. Scan the expression from left to right. At each opening parenthesis, add 1 to the magic number; at each closing parenthesis, subtract 1. At the final closing parenthesis, the magic number should be 0. In the following example the digits indicate the total number so far, working from left to right.

```
if (((total/scores) > 50) && ((total/(scores - 1)) < 100))
 0   123         2     1    23     4        32      10
```

4. Don't use =< to mean "less than or equal to"; only the symbol <= works. Likewise, => is invalid for "greater than or equal to"; you must use >= for this operation.

5. Don't compare strings with the == operator. Use the associated instance methods such as equals and compareTo. When testing for alphabetical order, remember to convert the strings to the same case before comparison.

6. When comparing values of different types, use explicit casting to clarify how the values should be converted before comparison.

7. Don't compare floating-point types for exact equality. Check that the difference between the values is less than some small amount.

8. In an *if* statement, remember to use a { } pair if the first clause or the *else*-clause is a sequence of statements. And be sure not to put a semicolon after the right brace.

9. Test for bad data. If a data value must be positive, use an *if* statement to test the value. If the value is negative or 0, an error message should be displayed; otherwise, processing should continue.

10. Take some sample values and try them by hand. Develop a test plan before you start testing your program.

11. If your program produces an answer that does not agree with a value you've calculated by hand, try these suggestions:

   • Redo your arithmetic.
   • Recheck your input data.

- Carefully go over the section of code that does the calculation. If you're in doubt about the order in which the operations are performed, insert clarifying parentheses.

- Check for integer overflow. The value of an `int` variable may have exceeded `Integer.MAX_VALUE` in the middle of a calculation. Java doesn't give an error message when this happens.

- Check the conditions in branching statements to be sure that the correct branch is taken under all circumstances.

Summary of Classes

In this chapter we introduced additional instance methods for the `String` class that enable us to compare the values contained in strings. We also introduced methods to get the action command string from an event.

Package Name

Class Name	Comments
`java.lang`	Automatically imported to every Java program
`String`	
Value-Returning Instance Methods:	
`equals(String)`	True if string contents match parameter
`compareTo(String)`	0 if equal, positive int if parameter comes before string, negative int if parameter comes after string
`toUpperCase`	Returns an identical string, with all characters uppercase
`toLowerCase`	Returns an identical string, with all character lowercase
`java.awt.event`	
`ActionEvent`	
Value-Returning Instance Method:	
`getActionCommand()`	Returns String registered with button

Summary

Using logical expressions is a way of asking questions while a program is running. The program evaluates each logical expression, producing the value `true` if the expression is true or the value `false` if the expression is not true.

The *if* statement allows you to take different paths through a program based on the value of a logical expression. The *if-else* statement is used to choose between two courses of action; the *if* statement is used to choose whether or not to take a particular course of action. The branches of an *if* or *if-else* can be any statement, simple or compound. They can even be another *if* statement.

When a user interface includes multiple buttons, we can use the action command string associated with each button to determine which one was pressed. The event handler is passed an `ActionEvent` value as a parameter, and we call its associated value-returning instance method, `getActionCommand`, to retrieve the string given to the button.

The algorithm walk-through is a manual simulation of the algorithm at the design phase. By testing our design in the problem-solving phase, we can eliminate errors that can be more difficult to detect in the implementation phase.

An execution trace is a way of finding program errors once we've entered the implementation phase. It's a good idea to trace a program before you run it, so that you have some sample results against which to check the program's output. A written test plan is an essential part of any program development effort.

Quick Check

1. Write a Java expression that compares the variable `letter` to the constant `'Z'` and yields `true` if `letter` is less than `'Z'`. (pp. 237–238)
2. Write a Java expression that yields `true` if `letter` is between `'A'` and `'Z'` inclusive. (pp. 237–239)
3. What form of the *if* statement would you use to make a Java program print out "Is an uppercase letter" if the value in `letter` is between `'A'` and `'Z'` inclusive, and print out "Is not an uppercase letter" if the value in `letter` is outside that range? (pp. 247–249)
4. What form of the *if* statement would you use to make a Java program print out "Is a digit" only if the value in the variable `someChar` is between `'0'` and `'9'` inclusive? (pp. 252–253)
5. On a telephone, each of the digits 2 through 9 has a segment of the alphabet associated with it. What kind of control structure would you use to decide which segment a given letter falls into and to print out the corresponding digit? (pp. 254–257)
6. If operands of a relational expression are characters rather than numeric values, what do the relational operators measure?
7. What is the handler method to which all button events for a frame are sent? (pp. 258–261)

8. In what phase of the program development process should you carry out an execution trace? (pp. 270–272)
9. You've written an application that displays the corresponding digit on a phone, given a letter of the alphabet. Everything seems to work right except that you can't get the digit '5' to display; you keep getting the digit '6'. What steps would you take to find and fix this bug? (pp. 274–275)

Answers

1. `letter < 'Z'`   2. `letter >= 'A' && letter <= 'Z'`   3. The *if-else* form
4. The *if* form   5. A nested *if* statement   6. The relative position of the characters within the collating sequence of the character set   7. `actionPerformed`   8. The implementation phase
9. Carefully review the section of code that should print out '5'. Check the branching condition and the output statement there. Try some sample values by hand.

Exam Preparation Exercises

1. What is the purpose of a control structure?
2. What is a logical expression?
3. Given the following relational expressions, state in English what they say.

Expression	Meaning in English
`one == two`	
`one != two`	
`one > two`	
`one < two`	
`one >= two`	
`one <= two`	

4. Given these values for the Boolean variables x, y, and z:

   `x = true, y = false, z = true`

   evaluate the following logical expressions. In the blank next to each expression, write a T if the result is `true` or an F if the result is `false`.

   _____   a. `x && y || x && z`
   _____   b. `(x || !y) && (!x || z)`
   _____   c. `x || y && z`
   _____   d. `!(x || y) && z`

5. Given these values for variables i, j, p, and q:

   `i = 10, j = 19, p = true, q = false`

add parentheses (if necessary) to the expressions below so that they evaluate to true.

a. `i == j || p`

b. `i >= j || i <= j && p`

c. `!p || p`

d. `!q && q`

6. Given these values for the `int` variables `i`, `j`, `m`, and `n`:

   $i = 6$, $j = 7$, $m = 11$, $n = 11$

   what is the output of the following code?

```
out.add(new Label("Madam"));
if (i < j)
  if (m != n)
    out.add(new Label("How"));
  else
    out.add(new Label("Now"));
out.add(new Label("I'm"));
if (i >= m)
  out.add(new Label("Cow"));
else
  out.add(new Label("Adam"));
```

7. Given the `int` variables `x`, `y`, and `z`, where `x` contains 3, `y` contains 7, and `z` contains 6, what is the output from each of the following code fragments?

a.
```
if (x <= 3)
  out.add(new Label('x' + 'y'));
out.add('x' + 'y');
```

b.
```
if (x != -1)
  out.add(new Label("The value of x is " + x));
else
  out.add(new Label("The value of y is " + y));
```

c.
```
if (x != -1)
  {
  out.add(new Label("" + x));
  out.add(new Label("" + y));
  out.add(new Label("" + z));
  }
else
  out.add(new Label("y"));
  out.add(new Label("z"));
```

8. Given this code fragment:

```
if (height >= minHeight)
  if (weight >= minWeight)
    out.add(new Label("Eligible to serve."));
  else
    out.add(new Label("Too light to serve."));
else
  if (weight >= minWeight)
    out.add(new Label("Too short to serve."));
  else
    out.add(new Label("Too short and too light to serve."));
```

a. What is the output when `height` exceeds `minHeight` and `weight` exceeds `minWeight`?

b. What is the output when `height` is less than `minHeight` and `weight` is less than `minWeight`?

9. Match each logical expression in the left column with the logical expression in the right column that tests for the same condition.

_____   a. `x < y && y < z`   (1) `!(x != y) && y == z`

_____   b. `x > y && y >= z`   (2) `!(x <= y || y < z)`

_____   c. `x != y || y == z`   (3) `(y < z || y == z) || x == y`

_____   d. `x == y || y <= z`   (4) `!(x >= y) && !(y >= z)`

_____   e. `x == y && y == z`   (5) `!(x == y && y != z)`

10. The following expressions make sense but are invalid according to Java's rules of syntax. Rewrite them so that they are valid logical expressions. (All the variables are of type `int`.)

a. `x < y <= z`

b. `x`, `y`, and `z` are greater than 0

c. `x` is equal to neither `y` nor `z`

d. `x` is equal to `y` and `z`

11. Given these values for the Boolean variables x, y, and z,

```
x = true, y = true, z = false
```

indicate whether each expression is `true` (T) or `false` (F).

_____   a. `!(y || z) || x`

_____   b. `z && x && y`

_____   c. `!y || (z || !x)`

_____   d. `z || (x && (y || z))`

_____   e. `x || x && z`

12. For each of the following problems, decide which is more appropriate, an *if-else* or an *if-*(then). Explain your answers.

a. Students who are candidates for admission to a college submit their SAT scores. If a student's score is equal to or above a certain value, print a letter of acceptance for the student. Otherwise, print a rejection notice.

b. For employees who work more than 40 hours a week, calculate overtime pay and add it to their regular pay.

c. In solving a quadratic equation, whenever the value of the discriminant (the quantity under the square root sign) is negative, print out a message noting that the roots are complex (imaginary) numbers.

d. In a computer-controlled sawmill, if a cross section of a log is greater than certain dimensions, adjust the saw to cut four-inch by eight-inch beams; otherwise, adjust the saw to cut two-inch by four-inch studs.

13. What causes the error message "UNEXPECTED ELSE" when this code fragment is compiled?

```
if (mileage < 24.0)
{
  out.add(new Label("Gas "));
  out.add(new Label("guzzler."));
};
else
  out.add(new Label("Fuel efficient."));
```

14. The following code fragment is supposed to print "Type AB" when Boolean variables typeA and typeB are both true, and print "Type O" when both variables are false. Instead, it prints "Type O" whenever just one of the variables is false. Insert a { } pair to make the code segment work the way it should.

```
if (typeA || typeB)
  if (typeA && typeB)
    out.add(new Label("Type AB"));
else
  out.add(new Label("Type O"));
```

15. The nested *if* structure below has five possible branches depending on the values read into char variables ch1, ch2, and ch3. To test the structure, you need five sets of data, each set using a different branch. Create the five test data sets.

```
if (ch1 == ch2)
  if (ch2 == ch3)
    out.add(new Label("All initials are the same."));
  else
    out.add(new Label("First two are the same."));
else if (ch2 == ch3)
  out.add(new Label("Last two are the same."));
else if (ch1 == ch3)
  out.add(new Label("First and last are the same."));
else
  out.add(new Label("All initials are different."));
```

a. Test data set 1: ch1 = _____ ch2 = _____ ch3 = _____
b. Test data set 2: ch1 = _____ ch2 = _____ ch3 = _____
c. Test data set 3: ch1 = _____ ch2 = _____ ch3 = _____
d. Test data set 4: ch1 = _____ ch2 = _____ ch3 = _____
e. Test data set 5: ch1 = _____ ch2 = _____ ch3 = _____

16. If x and y are Boolean variables, do the following two expressions test the same condition?

```
x != y
(x || y) && !(x && y)
```

17. The following *if* condition is made up of three relational expressions:

```
if (i >= 10 && i <= 20 && i != 16)
    j = 4;
```

If i contains the value 25 when this *if* statement is executed, which relational expression(s) does the computer evaluate? (Remember that Java uses short-circuit evaluation.)

18. a. If strings cannot be compared using the relational operators in Java, how can you compare two strings?
    b. Fill in the following table that describes methods that can be applied to string objects.

Method Name	Parameter	Returns	English Description
equals			
compareTo			
toUpperCase			
toLowerCase			

19. How do you associate a string with a button event?
20. Why are there two strings associated with each button event? Explain.
21. What happens if you do not call the setActionCommand to name the button?
22. Describe the two ways that multiple buttons can be distinguished.

Programming Warm–Up Exercises

1. Declare eligible to be a Boolean variable, and assign it the value true.
2. Write a statement that sets the Boolean variable available to true if numberOrdered is less than or equal to numberOnHand minus numberReserved.
3. Write a statement containing a logical expression that assigns true to the Boolean variable isCandidate if satScore is greater than or equal to 1100, gpa is not less than 2.5, and age is greater than 15. Otherwise, isCandidate should be false.

4. Given the declarations

```
boolean leftPage;
int    pageNumber:
```

write a statement that sets `leftPage` to `true` if `pageNumber` is even. (*Hint:* Consider what the remainders are when you divide different integers by two.)

5. Write an *if* statement (or a series of *if* statements) that assigns to the variable `biggest` the greatest value contained in variables `i`, `j`, and `k`. Assume the three values are distinct.

6. Rewrite the following sequence of *if*-(then) as a single *if-else* statement.

```
if (year % 4 == 0)
  out.add(new Label(year + " is a leap year."));
if (year % 4 != 0)
{
  year = year + 4 - year % 4;
  out.add(new Label(year + " is the next leap year."));
}
```

7. Simplify the following program segment, taking out unnecessary comparisons. Assume that `age` is an `int` variable.

```
if (age > 64)
  out.add(new Label("Senior voter"));
if (age < 18)
  out.add(new Label("Under age"));
if (age >= 18 && age < 65)
  out.add(new Label("Regular voter"));
```

8. The following program fragment is supposed to print out the values 25, 60, and 8, in that order. Instead, it prints out 50, 60, and 4. Why?

```
length = 25;
width = 60;
if (length == 50)
  height = 4;
else
  height = 8;
out.add(new Label("" + length + ' ' + width + ' ' + height));
```

9. The following Java program segment is almost unreadable because of the inconsistent indentation and the random placement of left and right braces. Fix the indentation and align the braces properly.

```
// This is a nonsense program segment
if (a > 0)
if (a < 20)
      {
  out.add(new Label("A is in range."));
```

```
calcFrame.add(subtract);
calcFrame.add(clear);
calcFrame.pack();
calcFrame.show();
calcFrame.addWindowListener(new WindowAdapter()
  {
     public void windowClosing(WindowEvent event)
     {
       calcFrame.dispose();
       System.exit(0);
     }
  });
  }
}
```

2. List the statements that relate to the Clear button, describing in English what each one does.
3. Complete the original Calculator project by adding buttons for multiplication and division.
4. Write a test plan to test the final project and implement the test plan.

Classes and Methods

- ■ To be able to apply the concepts of abstraction and encapsulation in object-oriented design.

- ■ To be able to design the public interface for a class.

- ■ To be able to implement a class responsibility as a method.

- ■ To be able to design and implement a constructor for a class.

- ■ To be able to distinguish between immutable and mutable objects.

- ■ To be able to implement a new class.

- ■ To be able to determine the lifetime of an object or a class field.

- ■ To be able to recognize the conditions under which an object is garbage collected.

- ■ To be able to collect a set of classes together in a package.

- ■ To be able to test classes in a package.

Prior to this chapter we have written Java application classes in which we have occasionally nested other class definitions. These classes have followed specific patterns that enabled us to write them without learning all the rules and options that Java provides for implementing a class. As we have seen from our use of CRC cards, however, it is common to create new classes that don't follow an existing formula.

In this chapter we consider the principles that result in a well-designed class implementation. Primary among these is the concept of encapsulation. We'll also see how to bundle one or more classes into a package that can be imported by applications.

Up to this point we've also been writing just a few specific methods such as `main`. It's time to see how to write methods that can implement an arbitrary class responsibility.

7.1 Encapsulation

The dictionary provides several definitions of the word *capsule*. For example, it can be a sealed gelatin case that holds a dose of medication. Early spacecraft were called capsules because they were sealed containers that carried passengers through space. A capsule protects its contents from outside contaminants or harsh conditions. To encapsulate something is to place it into a capsule.

Encapsulation Designing a class so that its implementation is protected from the actions of external code except through the formal interface

Abstraction The separation of the logical properties of an object from its implementation

What does encapsulation have to do with classes and object-oriented programming? One goal in designing a class is to protect its contents from being damaged by the actions of external code. If the contents of a class can be changed only through a well-defined interface, then it is much easier to use the class and to debug errors in an application.

Why is it important to encapsulate a class? Encapsulation is the basis for abstraction in programming. Recall, for example, that it is abstraction that lets us use a `Frame` without having to know the details of its implementation.

We simplify the design of a large program through abstraction: We design classes that can be described in simple terms. There are implementation details of each class that are irrelevant to using it. Those details are hidden by encapsulation. The programmer who implements the class doesn't have to understand how the larger application uses it, and the programmer who uses the class doesn't have to think about how it is implemented.

Modifiability The property of an encapsulated class definition that allows the implementation to be changed without having an effect on code that uses it (except in terms of speed or memory space)

Reuse The ability to import a class into any program without additional modification to either the class or the program; the ability to extend the definition of a class

Even when you are the programmer in both cases, abstraction simplifies your job because it allows you to focus on different parts of the program in isolation from each other. What seems like a huge programming problem at first is much more manageable when you break it into little pieces that you can solve separately (the divide-and-conquer strategy from Chapter 1).

Separating a class into a logical description (an interface) and an encapsulated implementation has two additional benefits: modifiability and reuse.

Encapsulation enables us to modify the implementation of a class after its initial development. Perhaps we are rushing to meet a deadline, so we create a simple but inefficient implementation. Later, we can replace the implementation with one that is more efficient. The modification is undetectable by users of the class with the exception that their programs run faster and/or require less memory.

If we write a class in a manner that exposes implementation details, user code may try to exploit some of those details. If we later change the implementation, the user code would stop working. Figure 7.1 illustrates an encapsulated implementation versus one that is exposed to external code.

Encapsulation also allows us to use a class in other applications. An encapsulated class is self-sufficient so that it doesn't depend on declarations in the application. It can thus be imported into different applications without requiring changes to either the class or the application. Our event listener classes have directly accessed variables that are also directly accessed by main, and therefore are not encapsulated.

As we see in Chapter 8, reuse also means that an encapsulated class can be easily extended to form new related classes. For example, suppose you are working for a utility company developing software to manage their fleet of vehicles. As shown in Figure 7.2, an encapsulated class that describes a vehicle could be used in the applications that schedule its use and keep track of maintenance as well as the tax accounting application that computes its operating cost and depreciation. Each of those applications could add extensions to the vehicle class to suit its particular requirements.

Reuse is a way to save programming effort and also ensures that objects have the same behavior every place that they are used. Consistent behavior helps us to avoid and detect programming errors.

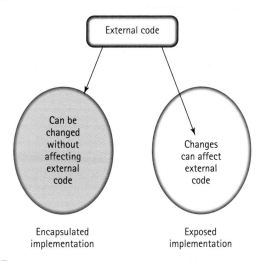

Figure 7.1 *Encapsulated versus exposed implementation*

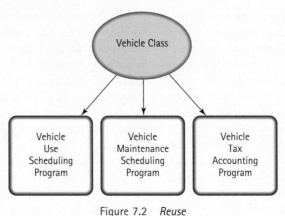

Figure 7.2 *Reuse*

It is important to understand that encapsulation isn't a Java language construct. We achieve encapsulation by carefully designing the class interface. Once that's done, we take advantage of Java features that simplify implementation of an encapsulated class.

Abstraction

How do we design a class with an encapsulated implementation? We begin with the abstraction for the object, as written on our CRC card. That way, we focus on the class interface independently of how we may implement it. Then the implementation is automatically separated from the interface.

We thus begin with a discussion of abstraction in programming, then turn to class interface design, and finally look at implementation. Along the way we'll take a short detour to look at method implementation in Java.

Data and Control Abstraction Creation of a new class begins when there is a need for a new object type. At the conclusion of the brainstorming and filtering steps in a design, if we find a CRC card that isn't in the Java library, we create a new class from the responsibilities on the card. Some responsibilities require us to supply data to the class (for example, constructors), while others provide data (such as Know First Name). Each responsibility has a control component (what it does) and a data component (the information it needs or returns). Encapsulation allows us to create an abstraction of either or both of these components.

> **Data abstraction** The separation of the logical representation of an object's range of values from their implementation

Data abstraction is the separation of the external representation of an object's values from their internal implementation. For example, the external representation of a date might be integer values for the day and year, and a string that specifies the name of the month. But we might implement the date within the class using a standard value that calendar makers call the Julian day, which is the number of days since January 1, 4713 B.C.

The advantage of using the Julian day is that it simplifies arithmetic on dates, such as computing the number of days between dates. All of the complexity of dealing with leap years and the different number of days in the months is captured in formulas that convert between the conventional representation of a date and the Julian day. From the user's perspective, however, the responsibilities of a `Date` object receive and return a date as two integers and a string.[1]

In many cases, the external representation and the implementation of the values are identical. However, we won't tell that to the user, in case we decide to change the implementation in the future.

Control abstraction is the separation of the logical properties of the actions of a responsibility from their implementation. For example, the documentation for the `Date` class says that it takes into account all of the special leap-year rules. In the implementa-

> **Control abstraction** The separation of the logical properties of the operations on an object from their implementation

tion, only the conversion formulas handle those rules, and the other responsibilities merely perform simple arithmetic on the Julian day number.

A user can simply imagine that every `Date` responsibility is separately computing leap years. But control abstraction lets us program a more efficient implementation and hide that complexity from the user.

Object State Any object that stores information is said to have state. The object's state is the current set of values that it contains. Some of those values may be represented in the data abstraction and some may be hidden.

> **State** The current values contained within an object

An object's state can also contribute to its control abstraction. For example, an object that simulates a traffic light may only return its current color, but internally it keeps track of the time so that it knows when to change color.

The state of an object, its data and control abstractions, and its collaborations combine to precisely determine its behavior.

An object is instantiated with an initial state. If any of its methods can subsequently change its state, then the object is said to be mutable. A `Frame` is an example of a mutable object; its `add` method changes its state. If an object doesn't have any methods that can change its state, it is immutable. A `String` is an immutable object; we can only retrieve its contents.

> **Mutable** An object whose state can be changed after it is created
>
> **Immutable** An object whose state cannot be changed once it is created

---

[1]The Java library includes a `Date` class, `java.util.Date`. However, the familiar properties of dates make them a natural example to use in explaining the concepts of class interface design. So we ignore the existence of the library class in the discussion that follows, as if we must design our own `Date` class. In writing real programs, however, you would probably use the `Calendar` library class that replaced `Date` in Java 1.1.

Theoretical Foundations

Categories of Instance Responsibilities

Class instance responsibilities generally fall into three categories: constructors, transformers, and observers.

A constructor is an operation that creates a new instance of a class. Operators that modify the state of an object are transformers. For example, an operation that changes the year of a Date object is a transformer. Observers are operations that allow us to observe the state of an object. The knowFirstName method of a Name class is an example of an observer.

Some operations are combinations of observers and constructors. An operation that takes a Date object and an integer value and returns a new Date object that is the original date plus that number of days is an example of an observer (of the original Date object) and a constructor (of the new Date object). This particular case is an example of a copy constructor.

In addition to the three basic categories of responsibility, there is a fourth category that is less common: iterators.

In later chapters we examine classes that are made up of multiple values all of the same type. An iterator allows us to observe each of these components one at a time. For example, given a class representing a list of names, an iterator would enable us to go through the list, observing or transforming each of the names one by one.

Constructor   An operation that creates a new instance of a class

Transformer   An operation that changes the internal state of an object

Observer   An operation that allows us to observe the state of an object without changing it

Copy constructor   An operation that creates a new instance of a class by copying an existing instance, possibly altering some or all of its state in the process

Iterator   An operation that allows us to process—one at a time—all the components in an object

For example, examine the following class shell that represents a traffic light.

```
public class TrafficLight
{
   // Instance variables
   String currentColor;
   int timeRemaining;
   // Constructor
   public TrafficLight()
   {
   }
   // Observer methods
   public String knowCurrentColor()
   {
   }
```

```
public int knowTimeRemaining()
{
}
// Transformers
public void changeColor()
{
}
public void decrementTimeRemaining()
{
}
}
```

The values stored in `currentColor` and `timeRemaining` are the state of the object. We know that any object of class `TrafficLight` is a mutable object because transformer methods are defined.

7.2 Class Interface Design

Let's begin our discussion of designing the class interface by looking at the CRC card for a new class, `Name`, with three fields, `First`, `Middle`, and `Last`.

Class Name: *Name*		Superclass:		Subclasses:
Responsibilities		**Collaborations**		
Create itself (First, Middle, Last)		*None*		
Know its first name		*None*		
return String				
Know its middle name		*None*		
return String				
Know its last name		*None*		
return String				
Name in firstMidLast form		*String*		
return String				
Name in lastFirstMid form		*String*		
return String				
Are two names equal?		*String*		
return boolean				
Compare two names		*String*		
return int				

As you can see, a `Name` has eight responsibilities. As we discussed in Chapter 5, we have extended the basic CRC card to include notes about the data that a responsibility needs and that it returns. This additional information arises naturally in the scenario discussions as we play out the collaborations, and we simply write it on the CRC card to remember it.

From the preceding discussion we can classify the eight responsibilities as follows:

Responsibility	Classification
Create itself	Constructor
Know its first name	Observer
Know its middle name	Observer
Know its last name	Observer
Name in firstMidLast form	Observer
Name in lastFirstMid form	Observer
Is this name equal to (anotherName)?	Observer
Compare this name to (anotherName)	Observer

We know that the first responsibility (Create itself) must be a constructor that uses `new` to instantiate itself. The remaining responsibilities all return information about a name, so they are observers. There are no transformers among the responsibilities. Thus an instance of this class is an immutable object; once it is created it doesn't change. None of the responsibilities are iterators. This information can be added to the CRC card for future reference.

Now let's look at how we turn this CRC card into a design for a class. Note that at this stage, we begin to convert the responsibilities from phrases or sentences to names that represent the responsibility.

Public Interface Design

There are two ways that the data abstraction of an object can be provided to the user, the fields that it makes publicly accessible and the parameters of its methods. We briefly consider `public` field values, and then look at methods and parameters.

Public Field Values One way to implement the `Name` class would be to keep each part of the name in a `String` declared as a field:

```
String first;
String middle;
String last;
```

The Know first, Know middle, and Know last responsibilities return these values, so we might consider simply declaring the corresponding fields `public` and letting the user access them directly. However, this defeats the encapsulation of the class by revealing its internal representation to the user.

We can achieve encapsulation by making each of these responsibilities a method. If we later change the internal representation, the methods can be rewritten to convert the new internal representation into the existing external form.

Would we ever want to declare a `public` field in a class? Yes. Sometimes it's useful to provide constants that a collaborator can pass to responsibilities. For example, the names of the primary colors for a `Spectrum` object could be represented by `public` constants.

The constant `RED` could be an `int` with a value of `1` or a `String` with a value of `"RED"`. The collaborator doesn't know how the class represents the constant. It merely passes the class-supplied constant as a parameter to a method, as in this example:

```
colorObject.mixWith(Spectrum.RED);
```

In Java, such constants are declared `static`; that is, they belong to the class rather than to an instance. We want every object of a given class to use the same set of constants, so they should be kept centrally located in the class.

The `Name` class doesn't have any such constants on its CRC card. Normally, they would be identified during the scenario phase, and it would be noted that responsibilities receive one value from among a small set. Here's part of the CRC card for `Spectrum` that illustrates the need for constants.

Class Name: Spectrum	Superclass:	Subclasses:
Responsibilities		**Collaborations**
mixWith (a color, one of red, orange, yellow, green, blue, indigo, or violet)		None
. . .		

Responsibilities as Methods   Each responsibility on the CRC card can be implemented by a method in the class. If we know the information that is needed and returned by each one, then the design is straightforward.

An observer naturally returns a value, so we implement it as a Java value-returning method. Constructors have a special syntax in Java that we review later in this chapter. A transformer is typically a void method. Iterators may be either value-returning or void, but we won't consider them until we work with arrays in Chapter 12.

If a responsibility implicitly refers to an object, then it should be implemented as an instance method. Constructors, observers, transformers, and iterators are always instance methods. They implicitly take their associated object as a parameter and have access to its fields. In addition they can receive values through the parameter list, as noted on the CRC card.

Class methods are used to implement responsibilities that are not associated with a particular object, such as the `Math.abs` method. Class methods may also affect all the instances of a class. For example, setting the maximum score for all `TestScore` objects so that they can be checked for errors. None of the responsibilities of the `Name` class are appropriate for a class method implementation.

Let's add this information to the CRC card for the class. We abbreviate value-returning as V-R on the card.

Class Name: *Name*	Superclass:		Subclasses:
Responsibilities		**Collaborations**	
Create itself (first, middle, last), Constructor		None	
Know its first name, Observer, V-R instance		None	
return String			
Know its middle name, Observer, V-R instance		None	
return String			
Know its last name, Observer, V-R instance		None	
return String			
Name in firstMidLast form, Observer, V-R instance		String	
return String			
Name in lastFirstMid form, Observer, V-R instance		String	
return String			
Are two names equal?, Observer, V-R instance		String	
return boolean			
Compare two names, Observer, V-R instance		String	
return int			

7.3 Internal Data Representation

The first implementation step for a class is to decide on the internal representation of data. Then we can use the means-ends analysis technique from Chapter 1 to design the algorithms for translating between the abstract and internal representations. These algorithms form the basis for the constructor and observer methods, and parts of some transformer and iterator methods.

As we saw with our example of a `Date` object, the internal representation (Julian day) and the abstract representation (month, day, year) can be quite different. In other cases, such as class `Name`, the internal representation may be exactly the same as the abstract form of the data. We choose the internal form to be useful for the programmer rather than the user.

Our goal in selecting an internal representation should be to simplify our task and to make the object efficient in terms of storage space and execution time. These goals are sometimes in conflict, and we must balance simplicity against efficiency.

Two problem-solving strategies that are valuable in designing the internal data representation are looking for things that are familiar and solving by analogy. In the case of the `Date` class, you can go to the library and research calendars. For the `Name` class, you already know how to write down a name.

It's rare that you have to invent an entirely new data representation. Most programs are written to solve problems that people have dealt with in the past. Consider who would normally use such data, and consult with those people or look in texts that they would use (Figure 7.3). For example, astronomers use dates in computing the positions of planets over many years. You can find the formulas for computing the Julian day in some astronomy texts.

As another example, a geography professor gave an assignment to draw a map showing nearby airports with their elevations and the lengths of their runways. Most students spent hours poring through almanacs and topographic maps to gather the data. Even so, their maps were inaccurate. One student, however, got a perfect grade because she stopped to consider who would use such data. She went to a pilot supply shop and bought a precise map of nearby airports.

While there, she noticed a book that lists information for airports using an especially efficient representation. If she ever had to develop a computerized version of the map, she would start with that representation.

From the preceding discussion it should be clear that we can't give you a set of rules that lead you to an internal data representation for a class. Each situation you encounter is different. Be prepared to give this part of your design some careful thought, to go to a library and do some research, to consult with other people, and to trade off issues of efficiency and complexity.

In some cases you may discover that there is no one representation that is always best. Or there may not be enough information to choose among several options. In those cases, you simply have to pick a representation and use it. In the end, it may not turn out to be the best choice. But remember that the beauty of encapsulation is that you can go back later and change to a better internal representation!

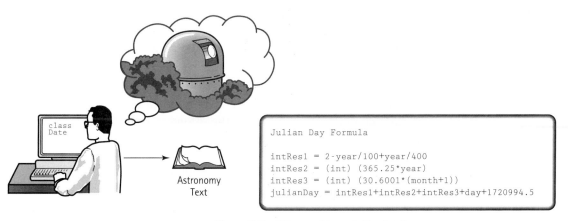

Figure 7.3 *Who would use similar data?*

Data Lifetime

There are three categories of data that we use in implementing a class, instance data, class data, and local data. We tend to focus more on the instance data because it is the internal representation of a given object. However, the other two categories are also important. Class data provides information common to all objects of a class. Local data is specific to a given call of a method.

> **Instance data**   Data that is associated with a specific object
>
> **Class data**   Data that is associated with a class and accessible by all objects of that class
>
> **Local data**   Data that is associated with a specific call to a method

Storage space for data in a Java application is automatically supplied by the JVM for as long as the data is needed. Depending on the category of the data, it is needed at different stages in the execution of the application. The period during which storage space is assigned to data is called its lifetime.

As you implement the internal representation for a class, you need to choose one of the categories for each variable, constant, or object, and that choice largely depends upon the desired lifetime of the data. Let's look at each of the three categories in turn.

Instance Data   Each class instance contains data that distinguishes it from other instances. For example, a `Name` object contains three strings that hold the first, middle, and last names.

> **Lifetime**   For a variable, constant, or object, the portion of an application's execution time during which it is assigned storage space in the computer's memory
>
> **Allocate**   To assign memory space at run time for use by an object
>
> **Free pool (heap)**   An area of memory, managed by the JVM, that is used to provide storage space for objects

We've said many times that the JVM instantiates an object when we use `new`. To instantiate an object, the JVM must provide memory space for it. The JVM manages an area of memory called the free pool or heap for storing objects.

When an object is instantiated we say that `new` allocates memory space from the free pool to the object. An object is destroyed when the JVM detects that no variable refers to it. If no variable contains the address of the object, there is no longer any way to access its contents.

For example, consider the following code segment.

```
labelVar = new Label("Instance data for one object.");
labelVar = new Label("Instance data for another object.");
```

In the first statement `new` instantiates a `Label`, allocating space for it. The assignment causes `labelVar` to refer to this object. The second statement also instantiates a `Label` and assigns it to `labelVar`. After the second statement, `labelVar` no longer refers to the first object, nor does any other variable. There is no way to refer to that first object, and we say that the object is unreachable.

> **Unreachable**   A condition of an object such that there is no way to refer to it

When an object is unreachable, the JVM marks it as garbage. Periodically, the JVM performs an operation known as garbage collection, in which it finds all of the unreachable objects and **deallocates** their storage space, making it once again available in the free pool for the creation of new objects.[2]

This approach, of creating and destroying objects at different points in the application by allocating and deallocating space in the free pool is called dynamic memory management. Without it, the computer would be much more likely to run out of storage space for data.

> **Garbage** The set of currently unreachable objects
>
> **Garbage collection** The process of finding all unreachable objects and destroying them by deallocating their storage space
>
> **Deallocate** To return the storage space for an object to the pool of free memory so that it can be reallocated to new objects
>
> **Dynamic memory management** The allocation and deallocation of storage space as needed while an application is executing

The point of the preceding discussion is to impress upon you that the lifetime of instance data is shorter than the execution time of the application and is the same as the lifetime of its object. It is thus a way of storing object-specific information between method calls.

Instance data thus records the object's state for as long as the object exists. We implement a field for an instance value by omitting the `static` modifier in its declaration. It is often helpful to gather together the instance variables into one section of the class declaration for easy reference—for example,

```
// Private instance variables
private String first;
private String middle;
private String last;
```

To identify the parts of the internal representation that are instance data, answer this question:

> Which parts of the internal representation does each object of this class need to store independently for its lifetime?

Class Data Fields declared as `static` belong to the class rather than to a specific instance. Space for class data is allocated at the start of the application and exists until it is finished. That is, its lifetime is the whole time that the application is running. It provides a way for us to record information about a class that survives across the creation and destruction of objects.

A common use for class data is to provide constants that are available to all instances of the class. For example, a `Measurement` class might declare constants for conversion between metric and English units.

---

[2]The term garbage collection dates back to programming languages of the 1960s. If the technique had been invented more recently, it would probably be called recyclable collection.

```
public class Measurement
{
   // Class constants
   static final double INCHES_TO_CENTIMETERS = 2.54;
   static final double METERS_TO_YARDS = 1.1;
      .
      .
      .
```

As you can see from these examples, class data has many uses. It is a way of storing information that is separate from any particular object. In implementing the class, ask yourself:

What information needs to be kept that is independent of any instance or that must remain throughout the execution of the application?

Local Data   Local data exists only within a method call. As we have seen with `main` and our event handler methods, we can declare local constants and variables within the body of a method that are accessible only to statements within the method.

```
public void actionPerformed(ActionEvent event)
{ // Local variable declarations
   double secondOperand;
   String whichButton;
   .
   .
   .
```

The JVM allocates space for this data when the method is called and deallocates it as soon as the method returns. Local data has the most limited lifetime of the three categories.

We use local data whenever we need to store information that is specific to a particular method. For example, computing the Julian day number requires intermediate values to be computed and then combined in a final formula. The method needs local variables in which to keep these values. The values aren't needed by any other methods, so they do not have to be kept in instance variables.

As you develop the algorithm for each method, keep a list of the values that are needed. Those that are not parameters, instance values, or class values are probably local. To be certain, for each value ask yourself:

Is this information needed anywhere outside of the method?

If the answer is no, then you know the value is local. The following table summarizes the lifetime of each category of data.

Category	Lifetime
Class	Execution of application program
Instance	From creation to destruction of its object
Local	From method call until return

Internal Representation Example

Our `Name` class needs to represent a first, middle, and last name for each of its instances. Clearly, these are instance variables because they are distinct values for each object. What other information does `Name` need to carry out its responsibilities?

The `lastFirstMid` responsibility must provide punctuation to separate the names. We could write this punctuation directly in the necessary string expression, or we could declare a named constant with the punctuation string. The constant could be associated— either with the instance or with the class. Because the same punctuation characters are used in every instance, let's make it a class constant.

Here is the Java code that declares the internal representation for `Name`.

```
static final String PUNCT = ", ";  // Class constant
// Instance variables
private String first;
private String middle;
private String last;
```

Notice that we use `static` to indicate that the constant belongs to the class, and omitting this modifier from the variable declarations associates them with instances of the class. When the following expression is executed:

```
new Name("Martha", "Bette", "Casey")
```

the JVM allocates space to the three string variables in the new `Name` object. For each additional `Name` object that we instantiate, the JVM allocates space for three more strings. But there is just one copy of `PUNCT`, and it exists for the lifetime of the application.

7.4 Class Syntax

The syntax for writing a new class is exactly like that of our application class. Here we show a syntax template for a class. It consists of a heading, followed by a block containing class declarations:

Class

```
ClassModifier  . . .  class  Identifier
{
    ClassDeclaration  . . .
}
```

The following template for a ClassDeclaration shows that it can be either a field declaration (such as a variable, constant, or object), or a method declaration:

ClassDeclaration

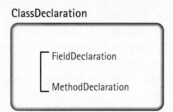

Here's an example class declaration.

```
public class Name
{
    static final String PUNCT = ", ";  // Class constant
    // Instance variables
    private String first;
    private String middle;
    private String last;
    // Declare methods that implement responsibilities of Name
}
```

We already know how to declare fields in a class from our experience with writing fields in the application class. However, we have not examined the process of declaring methods. The mechanics of writing a method are quite simple: We just write its heading and then follow it with the block of code that does the work. In the next section we see how to write a method declaration, and we focus extensively on its heading and especially its parameters.

7.5 Declaring Methods

Up to now, we've restricted our method declarations to a small set of precise recipes. We know how to declare main, windowClosing, and actionPerformed, all of which have their headings predefined for us. In this section we look at how to write headings for arbitrary methods. Here we repeat the syntax templates from Chapter 2 that show the form of a method declaration.

MethodDeclaration

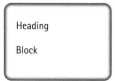

Heading

Block

Block

{

Statement . . .

}

In Chapter 2 we left *Heading* undefined. Now we can provide the syntax template that defines it.

Heading

Modifiers   ResultType   Identifier (TypeName   Identifier , TypeName   Identifier   . . .   )

From this template we see that a method heading can optionally begin with modifiers such as `public`, `private`, `final`, `abstract`, and `static`. Next in the heading is the result type (`void` if no value is returned, or the name of a type or class if the method returns a value). After the result type comes the name that we are giving to the method. Then, enclosed in parentheses is an optional list of the parameters accepted by the method, with commas separating them. Each parameter declaration consists of a type (or class) name and an identifier. Notice that the parentheses are required. Here are some examples of method headings.

```
void doNothing()                                    // The simplest heading
public void skipValue()                             // Example with a modifier
int trimax(int num1, int num2, int num3)            // Shows multiple parameters
private static int square(int number)               // One parameter, returns int
public static double cube(double number)            // A public class method
public abstract void readname(FileReader inFile)    // An abstract method
```

The first example is the simplest form of instance method heading, and illustrates that the parentheses are required even when there are no parameters. When we omit any access modifiers from the heading, it is said to have *package* accessibility. We explain package accessibility later in this chapter when we look at how to create packages. The second example shows a similar heading with the addition of the `public` access modifier. The third example shows a heading for a value-returning instance method that has three parameters, all of type `int`.

The fourth case shows a heading for a `private` value-returning class (`static`) method that takes one parameter of type `int`. A `private` class method can only be called from other methods within the class (either class or instance methods). The fifth example is a `public` value-returning class method that can be called by users of the class.

The last example shows the heading for an `abstract` method. We discuss `abstract` methods in Chapter 12. At this point there is no need for you to write `abstract` methods, so you should avoid using this modifier in method headings.

Parameter   An identifier declared between the parentheses in a method heading

Argument   An expression listed in the call to a method

The parameter list in the method heading provides one mechanism by which the method call and the method exchange information. Identifiers declared in the method heading are called parameters and expressions in the method call are arguments.

Arguments are matched to parameters by their relative position within the two lists. Here is an example that illustrates the matching between the lists in a method heading and a call.

```
public void someMethod (int param1, double param2, String param3)



          someMethod (argumentA*2, argumentB, argumentC)
```

Parameter passing   The transfer of data between the arguments and parameters in a method call

When the JVM executes a call to a method, it first copies the values of the arguments into their corresponding parameters. We refer to this step as parameter passing. Then it transfers control to the first statement in the method's block. As soon as the last statement in the block has been executed, the values in the parameters are destroyed and control returns to the point following the call.

The parameters are just like local variables declared within the method's block. The only difference is that they are automatically given initial values when the method is called, because the values of the arguments are copied into the parameters. If the method is called again with different arguments, then the method starts executing with these new values in its parameters.

Parameters

When a method is executed, it uses the values of the arguments passed to it in the call. But because of the distinction between simple and reference types, the effect of passing different types of arguments varies.

With simple types, such as `int`, `double`, and `boolean`, the parameter receives a copy of the value of the argument. The method can use and change the value in the parameter. Keep in mind that the argument can be any expression that computes a value of the appropriate type. Frequently, however, our arguments are just individual variables.

When we pass a variable as an argument to a parameter, it is easy to think that the two identifiers are connected in some way, as if the parameter becomes a synonym for the argument. But their only connection is at the moment when the value of the argument is copied to the parameter. Otherwise, they are independent of each other. That is, operations on the parameter do not affect the argument.

When the method returns, whatever value is in a parameter is discarded. It is not copied back into a variable in the argument. Thus, values of simple types may be passed into methods, but changes to those values aren't returned. Figure 7.4 illustrates the passing of simple types as parameters.

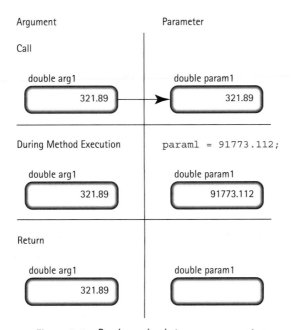

Figure 7.4 *Passing a simple type as a parameter*

With reference types such as `String` and other classes, a variable contains the address of where an object's fields are stored in memory. This address is the value copied from the argument to the parameter. There is only one copy of the object's fields, which is used by both the calling code and the method. If the method changes the values in those locations, then the calling code sees those changes when the method returns.

Therefore, you must be careful when using reference type parameters because changes made to their fields affect the value of the argument. Figure 7.5 illustrates the difference between passing simple and reference types to a method.

Each argument must have the same type or class as the parameter in the same position. You sometimes see Java code that seems to violate this rule, for example, in passing an `int` argument to a `float` parameter. But in this case, Java automatically inserts a widening conversion that forces the argument to have the same type as the parameter. Proper programming style would use an explicit conversion of the argument. There must also be the same number of arguments in a call as there are parameters in the method heading, or a compiler error message results.

When a method has several parameters of the same type, be careful that the arguments are in the correct order. For example, given the following heading for a method that computes the amount of water resulting from snow melting during one day at a specified temperature,

```
public double meltEstimate(int temperature, int snowDepth)
```

the following call is syntactically correct, but the arguments are clearly reversed and produce a meaningless result.

```
runOff = meltEstimate(237, -12);
```

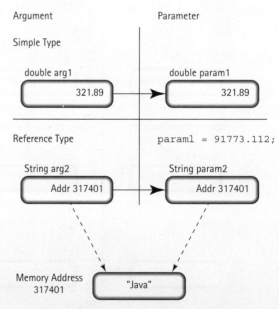

Figure 7.5 *Passing simple and reference types*

This example also demonstrates that we can pass a literal constant as an argument.

Changes to the parameter do not affect the literal constant argument when a simple type is being used. But what about literals of type String, which is a reference type? Wouldn't a change to the parameter change the argument? For many reference types the answer would be yes, but String is an immutable class.

There is no way to change a string object. We can only assign a new value to a String variable. Because each string value occupies a different place in memory, the effect of assigning a new value to a String variable is to store a different address in it. A parameter of type String is initially given a copy of the address of the string literal, and when we assign it a new value, the address is replaced by the address of the new value. The argument is left unchanged. Figure 7.6 illustrates what happens when we change the value of a parameter of type String.

In contrast to the simple types and immutable classes like String, there are classes that provide methods for directly changing instance fields. For example, Java allows us to write a method that takes a Frame as a parameter, and adds a label containing the

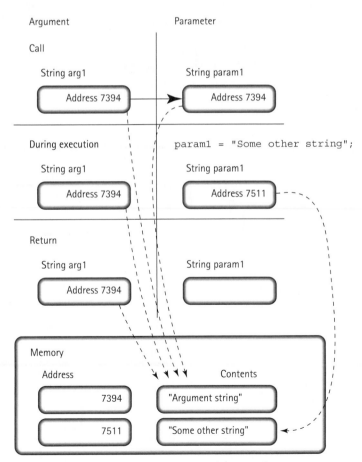

Figure 7.6   *The effect of assigning a new value to a reference type parameter*

string "Java" to the frame. The method's parameter receives the address where the Frame is stored. Calling add with the parameter directly changes the same Frame that the argument refers to.

Figure 7.7 shows this process, and you should carefully compare it to Figure 7.6 to be sure that you understand the difference. Assigning a new value (a different object) to a reference type parameter does not change the object to which the argument refers. But changes to the fields of the object referred to by the parameter are made to the argument object.

We recommend that you avoid modifying the contents of a reference parameter within a method. Our example of passing a Frame to a method that adds a label to it is poor programming practice. We used this example only to show that a reference parameter *could be* changed. However, reference parameters *should not be* changed. Although Java permits us to write a method that changes its parameter, when another programmer reads a call statement, his or her expectation is that the object referred to by the argument is unchanged.

Because it is poor practice to do so, Java programmers have adopted the convention that a reference value passed as an argument to a method should not be changed. In Java, arguments should be used only for sending data into a method. A method that changes its arguments is said to have a side effect. That is, it makes a change to values outside of itself, in a manner that isn't expected.

Side effect   Any change made by a method to values that are declared outside of its block that isn't explicit in its interface

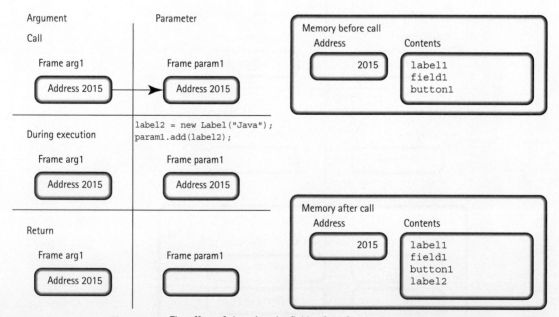

Figure 7.7   *The effect of changing the fields of a reference type parameter*

A Parameter-Passing Analogy

To help you remember the behavior of simple and reference parameters, we offer another analogy. Suppose you have in your hand a slip of paper and you are talking to someone who has another slip of paper. You are like the call and the other person is like the method. You read to her what's written on your paper and she writes it down. If your slip contains a simple type, such as a number representing the current temperature, she can use her copy of that number to perform some task. She could also replace the number with a different one. When she is done, she throws away her paper and your paper remains unchanged. (See Figure 7.8.)

Now suppose your slip of paper contains the address of a house (a reference type). The other person can use a copy of the address to go look at the house. If the person changes the address on the slip of paper (assigns a new value to the reference type parameter), then that person can go to a different house but she would no longer have the address of the first house. When done, the person throws away her paper. Your slip of paper still has the original address and so you can go and look at the house, and you find it unchanged.

Lastly, suppose that you again have an address on your slip of paper, but this time the person goes to the house and, instead of just looking at it, she goes inside and rearranges the furniture. When she is done, she throws away her paper, but your paper

Figure 7.8

still has the address of the house. When you go to the house, you find that its contents have changed.

Note that in every case, your slip of paper remained unchanged. In Java, the argument is never affected by a method call. But in the last situation, the method made changes to the object at the address it was given. So even though the address in the argument was untouched, the object it refers to has been altered. Whenever you are writing a method that changes a reference parameter, and you are unsure about how the operation is going to behave, stop and ask yourself, "Am I going inside the house, or am I going to a different address?"

Implementing a Responsibility as a Method

Once you have the design for the responsibilities listed on the CRC card, you need to turn each into Java code that implements it. Observers return information, transformers change information, and observers, constructors, and transformers may all receive information. We have already seen that parameters enable methods to receive information. How do we return information, and how do we change values? The mechanisms vary somewhat depending on whether the information is a simple type or a reference type. Figure 7.9 shows the mechanisms that we need and which ones we now know how to achieve.

As you might expect, one way of returning information from a method is to write it as a value-returning method. Recall that a value-returning method is called from within an expression and returns a value that takes its place in further computations. In our discussion of the syntax for method headings we saw that a value-returning method includes the type or class of its return value preceding the name of the method. For example, if we want to return a `String` from the `knowFirstName` instance method, we write the following heading (our CRC card indicates that it has no parameters).

```
public String knowFirstName()
```

The heading tells Java that the method returns a value. The class name allows Java to determine whether the value that it returns is compatible with the expression that contains the call. For example, we can't call `knowFirstName` in an expression that tries to assign its return value to a `boolean` variable. But how do we actually return a value? We use a `return` statement. Here is the syntax template for this new statement.

	Simple Type	Reference Type
Receives	Parameter	Parameter
Returns	???	???
Changes	???	???

Figure 7.9   *Method mechanisms for implementing a responsibility*

ReturnStatement

```
return expression ;
```

We write the `return` statement at the point in the method where we are ready to return control to the calling expression. The expression in the `return` statement computes the value that is returned. The result of the expression must be compatible with the class or type specified in the method's heading.

Note that a value-returning method enables us to return just one value. What if we need to return multiple values? Then we bind them together into an object that is returned. Our scenario discussions should reveal when a responsibility must return an object rather than a simple value, so this should never come as a surprise. Figure 7.10 shows the interface implementation mechanisms we have seen.

Now we consider mechanisms for changing values. Changing simple types can't be done directly in Java. We use a value-returning method and simply replace the value that was passed to it. For example,

```
value = Math.abs(value);
```

As we saw earlier, changing a reference type parameter within a method is poor practice. Instead of passing the object we wish to change as a parameter, we define an instance method that has direct access to the fields of the object. You might be tempted to think that the instance fields are like extra parameters to the method, but there is a big difference: They are not copied when the method is called. Remember that they are declared in the same block as the method.

Class methods also have access to fields, but as you might expect, they can access only the class fields. Note that when a method changes a class field, it is not changing a specific instance—it is changing a value accessible to all instances of that class.

Now we have seen the basic mechanisms that Java provides for implementing a method interface, and we can fill in the blanks from Figure 7.10 as shown in Figure 7.11.

	Simple Type	Reference Type
Receives	Parameter	Parameter
Returns	`return` statement	`return` statement
Changes	???	???

Figure 7.10 *Method mechanisms for implementing a responsibility*

	Simple Type	Reference Type
Receives	Parameter	Parameter Instance method accesses field of object without changing.
Returns	return statement	return statement
Changes	return with replacement assignment after method returns	Implement as instance method Implement as class method

Figure 7.11 *Method mechanisms for implementing a responsibility*

Here is the implementation of the `knowFirstName` observer, within the declaration of class `Name`. We examine the implementation of the remaining observer responsibilities of `Name` in the Case Study at the end of the chapter.

```
public class Name
{
   static final String PUNCT = ", ";   // Class constant
   // Instance variables
   String first;
   String middle;
   String last;
   // Declare methods that implement responsibilities of Name
   public String knowFirstName()
   {
      return first;
   }
}
```

There is one last bit of Java syntax that we need for implementing the responsibilities of `Name`. We must still see how to write a constructor.

Constructors

Now that we know how to write a method, writing a constructor is easy. Syntactically, a constructor heading looks just like other method headings except that its name is the same as the name of the class, and it has neither a `return` type nor the keyword `void`. Just as with a normal method, the heading is followed by a block.

ConstructorHeading

For example, we can write the constructor for a `Name` as follows.

```
public Name(String firstName, String middleName, String lastName)
{
   first = firstName;
   middle = middleName;
   last = lastName;
}
```

The constructor might be invoked with a statement such as

```
someName = new Name("Martha", "Bette", "Casey");
```

A constructor is a special kind of method that is called when `new` instantiates the object. Like an instance method, it has access to all of the instance fields of the object. But because the object has not yet been given a name, its call can't be written in the usual manner with an object name and a period preceding the method name. Because a constructor is like an instance method, we never use the `static` modifier in its heading.

You might think that constructor `Name` returns a value of class `Name`, but that's the job of the `new` operator. When you use `new`, it looks at the type of the constructor and creates an empty object of that type. It then calls the constructor, which has access to its fields, and thus can give them initial values. When the constructor returns, `new` returns the initialized object for use in the expression. One way to think of a constructor invocation is that `new` takes the place of the object name and period until the object value is given a name (by assigning it to an object identifier). In our example, the expression assigns the initialized object value to an identifier of class `Name` called `someName`.

Because a constructor is called when an object is instantiated, its primary function is to initialize fields within the object. Some of these values may be supplied through parameters while others may be constants (called default values). In some cases, a constructor may perform more complex work, such as calculating a value for a field from several parameters, accessing a file for its initial values, and so on. The majority of constructors that we write in this text, however, simply initialize fields from parameters and constants.

7.6 Packages

As we noted previously, Java lets us group related classes together into a unit called a *package*. Classes within a package can access each other's nonprivate members, saving us programming effort and making it more efficient to access their data. The other advantage of packages is that they can be compiled separately and imported into our programs.

Together with the access levels, packages provide the means for implementing encapsulation because they allow us to distribute our classes as Bytecode files. The unreadable nature of Bytecode prevents users from seeing the implementation details.

Package Syntax

The syntax for a package is extremely simple. We've been writing our applications as unnamed packages all along, so all we have to do is to specify the package name at the start of the application. The first line of a package is the keyword `package` followed by an identifier and a semicolon. By convention, Java programmers start a package identifier with a lowercase letter to distinguish package names from class names.

```
package someName;
```

After this we can write our `import` declarations and then one or more declarations of classes. Java calls this a compilation unit, and its syntax diagram is shown here.

Package

```
packageIdentifier;

ImportDeclaration      . . .

Class                  . . .
```

As you can see from the syntax diagram, we can write a series of `class` declarations following the `import` declarations. Those classes are members of the package. All of the package members (the classes) have access to each other's nonprivate members. Recall that we said that a field or method that doesn't have an access modifier has package access.

Classes that are imported into the package can be used by any of the classes declared in the package. From the perspective of the imported classes, the declared classes are user code and thus can only access their `public` members. Note that imported classes are not members of the package.

Although we can declare multiple classes in a compilation unit, only one of them can be declared `public`. The others must have the package level of access. If a compilation unit can hold at most one `public` class, how do we create packages with multiple `public` classes? We have to use multiple compilation units, as we describe next.

Packages with Multiple Compilation Units

Each Java compilation unit is stored in its own file. The Java system names the file using a combination of the package name and the name of the `public` class in the compilation unit. Java restricts us to having a single `public` class in a file so that it can use file names to locate all `public` classes. Thus, a package with multiple `public` classes must be implemented with multiple compilation units, each in a separate file.

Using multiple compilation units has the further advantage that it provides us with more flexibility in developing the classes of a package. Team programming projects would be very cumbersome if Java made multiple programmers share a single package file.

We split a package among multiple files simply by placing its members into separate compilation units with the same package name. For example, we can create one file containing the following code (the ... between the braces represents the code for each class):

```
package someName;
public class One{ ... }
class Two{ ... }
```

and a second file containing:

```
package someName;
class Three{ ... }
public class Four{ ... }
```

with the result that the package `someName` contains four classes, all of which have access to each other's nonprivate members. Two of the classes, `One` and `Four` are public, and so are available to be imported by user code.

Many programmers simply place every class in its own compilation unit. Others gather the nonpublic classes into one unit, separate from the public classes. How you organize your packages is up to you, but you should be consistent to make it easy to find the members of the package among all of its files.

How does the Java compiler manage to find these pieces and put them together? The answer is that it requires that all of the compilation unit files for a package be kept in a single directory or folder. For our preceding example, a Java system would store the source code in files called `One.java` and `Four.java` in a directory called `someName`.

Splitting a package among multiple files has one other benefit. Each compilation unit can have its own set of `import` declarations. Thus, if the classes in a package need to use different sets of imported classes, you can place them in separate compilation units, each with just the `import` declarations that are required.

Problem-Solving Case Study

Implementing the Name Class

Earlier in the chapter we showed the CRC card design for a class called Name. Here we complete its implementation. Here is the CRC card for the class.

Class Name: Name	Superclass:		Subclasses:
Responsibilities		**Collaborations**	
Create itself (First, Middle, Last)		None	
Know its first name		None	
return String			
Know its middle name		None	
return String			
Know its last name		None	
return String			
Name in firstMidLast form		String	
return String			
Name in lastFirstMid form		String	
return String			
Are two names equal?		String	
return boolean			
Compare two names		String	
return int			

We need to develop a method algorithm for each of the responsibilities. We've already done this for the first two responsibilities, but here we want to take a moment to revisit our choice of internal representation.

Internal Representation

Because we already have the interface design, we can skip ahead to specifying the internal representation for the class, after which we apply our algorithmic problem-solving techniques to each of the methods.

Our initial approach was to use three separate strings to represent the parts of the name. But we could conserve storage space by combining all of the parts of a name into one `String` variable. Then the JVM would have to store just one address instead of an address for the start of each string that holds a part of a name.

Along with the single string, we would use a set of `int` variables to record the character position where the middle and last parts of the name begin in the string. Retrieving a part of a name is then a matter of calling the `substring` method using the `int` variables as parameters. For example, if the start of the middle name is stored in the string at a position recorded by the `int` variable `midStart` and is followed by the last name at position `lastStart`, then we would retrieve the middle name with the following call:

```
middleName = wholeName.substring(midStart, lastStart);
```

This approach sounds attractive, but we've actually started down a dead-end path to illustrate a point. This representation has some merit, but it also has some disadvantages. Before you read the next paragraph, stop and think about what the disadvantages might be. Then read on and see if you've spotted them all.

The most obvious disadvantage is that we are making the computer perform extra operations to retrieve the parts of a name. We have traded processing speed for some saving in memory space. Secondly, the more complex the implementation, the more likely it is to have errors. And lastly, we may not really be saving any memory space. Let's consider this last point more closely.

Each part of the name (except the first name, which starts at zero) has a corresponding `int` variable, which in many systems takes up the same space as the address of a `String` object. So as Figure 7.12 shows, we still use the same amount of space! Have we gone to all this trouble for nothing? Not quite.

On some systems an address takes up more space than an `int`, so sometimes we do save space. And some systems allocate more memory for a string than is required to hold the exact number of characters. Combining all the strings into one saves that wasted space.

Thus, any reduction in space is dependent on the particular Java system. Yet for every system, we have increased the processing time and the likelihood of errors in the code. The amount of space we save may be significant if we are storing millions of names, but for a small number it is a tiny portion of the computer's memory.

The point we set out to make is that sometimes the simplest implementation is the best. While it is good to explore other possibilities, be sure to weigh the benefits against the costs, keeping in mind how the object may be used.

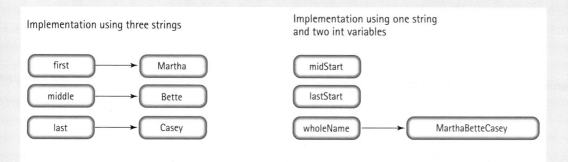

Figure 7.12 *Two possible implementations of a name object*

Responsibility Algorithms

We've chosen the simpler implementation of the Name class with a separate string for each part of the name. The strings are instance variables. With this representation the algorithm for the constructor is trivial. We just assign the parameters to the corresponding instance variables.

Here is the algorithm for the constructor (which we coded earlier).

public Name(String firstName, String middleName, String lastName)

```
Set first to firstName
Set middle to middleName
Set last to lastName
```

It might seem that this implementation violates the encapsulation. We are directly storing the address of a string supplied by the user. Shouldn't we make a copy of the string so that we have our own internal version of its contents? Recall that String is an immutable class.

If String objects were mutable, the answer would be yes because the user could directly change the contents of our object. That could lead to side-effect errors that would be difficult to locate. But the immutability of String objects makes them immune to such side effects. We need to make a copy only when a constructor is passed a mutable object.

The algorithms for the basic observers also are simple. They just return the corresponding instance variable. Here is the algorithm for the observer that returns the first name. The other basic observers are equally simple.

public String knowFirstName()

```
return first
```

public String knowMiddleName()

```
return middle
```

public String knowLastName()

```
return last
```

The preceding algorithms illustrate a particular aspect of object-oriented programming. Many classes contain large numbers of trivial methods whose purpose is simply to ensure encapsulation of instances. Once an interface has been designed, it is possible to code much of its implementation with a minimum of algorithmic problem solving. There may then be only a few methods left that require additional thought.

The next two responsibilities on the CRC card return the name in different formats. These algorithms merely have to concatenate the parts of the name in different orders. In the case of lastFirstMid, we use the class constant called PUNCT, which we defined earlier.

public String firstMidLast()

```
return first + " " + middle + " " + last
```

public String lastFirstMid()

```
return last + punct + first + " " + middle
```

The next responsibility on the CRC card is `equals`. Objects of type `String` have an `equals` method, so we can use this to compare all of the parts of a `Name` object to another name that's supplied as a parameter. Here's the algorithm for `equals`.

public boolean equals(Name otherName)

```
return
    first.equals(otherName.first) and
    middle.equals(otherName.middle) and
    last.equals(otherName.last)
```

The last responsibility of `Name` is `compareTo`. We can use the `compareTo` method of class `String` to compare last names. If the last names are equal, we compare first names. If the first names are equal, we compare middle names. Only if all three are equal can we say that the names are equal. Is that all we have to do? Not quite. As we've seen before, names should be converted to all upper or lower case before they are compared.

public boolean compareTo(Name otherName)

```
Set result to last.toUpperCase().compareTo(otherName.last.toUppercase())
if result is not zero
    return result
else
    Set result to
        first.toUpperCase().compareTo(otherName.first.toUpperCase())
    if result if not zero
        return result
    else
        return
            middle.toUpperCase().compareTo(otherName.middle.toUpperCase())
```

Notice that in the preceding two algorithms we directly access the fields of `otherName` rather than use its observer methods to retrieve their values. Because these are instances of the same class and they are declared with package level access, their methods are allowed to access each other's fields. The accesses are all occurring inside of the capsule, so there is no violation of the encapsulation.

Our design is now complete and can be coded in Java. Here is the complete code for the `name` package. (From this Case Study on we omit the list of variables in order to save space.)

Package

```
package name;

public class Name
// This class defines a name consisting of three parts
{
  // Class constant
  final String PUNCT = ", ";        // Punctuation for formatting
  // Instance variables
  String first;
  String middle;
  String last;

  // Constructors
  public Name(String firstName, String middleName,
              String lastName)
  // Initializes a Name object with first, middle and last name
  {
    first = firstName;
    middle = middleName;
    last = lastName;
  }

  // Basic observers that return the value of each field

  public String knowFirstName()
  {
    return first;
  }

  public String knowMiddleName()
  {
    return middle;
  }

  public String knowLastName()
  {
    return last;
  }

  // Additional observers

  public String firstMidLast()
  {
    return first + " " + middle + " " + last;
  }

  public String lastFirstMid()
  {
    return last + PUNCT + first + " " + middle;
  }
```

```java
public boolean equals(Name otherName)
{
  return
    first.equals(otherName.first) &&
    middle.equals(otherName.middle) &&
    last.equals(otherName.last);
}

public int compareTo(Name otherName)
  {
    int result;
    result = last.toUpperCase().compareTo(othername.first.toUpperCase());
    if (result != 0)
      return result;
    else
    {
      result = first.toUpperCase().compareTo(otherName.first.toUpperCase());
      if (result != 0)
        return result;
      else
        return
          middle.toUpperCase().compareTo(otherName.middle.toUpperCase());
    }
  }
}
```

Testing

The Name class contains eight methods. Each one should be tested. As you can see, designing a class and writing its code is just the beginning of the process. Testing can be as much work or more.

In order to test the methods of a class, we need to write an application that can call each method. We call such an application a driver.

The class we have just written is contained in the name package and so we can simply import it into the driver with a statement like the following:

> **Driver** A simple application class that is used to call methods being tested. The use of a driver permits direct control of the testing process.

```java
import name.*;
```

Once the package has been imported, our driver has access to all of the public interface components, and we simply need to write statements that call each of the methods with the necessary arguments to test that their responsibilities are met. In principle this sounds straightforward. But with eight methods, we must carefully write out a plan that lists every test to ensure that we don't miss any cases.

Because testing a package requires some new organizational concepts, we leave the development of the driver for the Name class to the Testing and Debugging section that follows.

Testing and Debugging

Now that our code is becoming more complex, we need to extend our formal test plan to help us organize the larger number of tests. In Chapter 6 we introduced the test plan as a table with four columns: Reason for Test Case, Input Values, Expected Output, and Observed Output. Our test plan was written for a single method in a class.

With the large number of methods in a typical package, it's more convenient to combine multiple tests into a single driver. Thus, to help us write this driver, we expand the test plan to include Class, Method, and Test Number columns. Together with the class and method names, the test number uniquely identifies what's being tested.

The simplest approach to developing a package test plan is to create an empty table with seven columns and as many rows as there are methods. Insert the class and method names in the order that they appear in the code. Then, for each method, determine the number of different tests that are needed and add the necessary rows to the table, filling them in before moving on to the next method.

For many methods, such as basic observers, there may be just a single test. Methods with branches have multiple tests. Once all of the tests for a method are listed, you can number them. As an example, here is a test plan for our `Name` class. We omit the empty Observed Output column here to save space.

Class	Method	Test #	Reason for Test	Input Values	Expected Output
Name	Name	1	Constructor	"John", "Kirk", "Herrel"	Name object with three fields
Name	knowFirstName	1	Observer	instance from constructor test	"John"
Name	knowMiddleName	1	Observer	instance from constructor test	"Kirk"
Name	knowLastName	1	Observer	instance from constructor test	"Herrel "
Name	firstMidLast	1	Observer	instance from constructor test	"John Kirk Herrel"
Name	lastFirstMid	1	Observer	instance from constructor test	"Herrel, John Kirk"
Name	equals	1	Equality test	instance, second object with same values	true
Name	equals	2	Inequality test	instance, second object with other values	false
Name	compareTo	1	Equality test	instance, second object with same value	0
Name	compareTo	2	Greater than test	instance, second object with lesser value	Positive int
Name	compareTo	3	Less than test	instance, second object with greater value	Negative int

Once we have a plan of all the tests, it is simply a matter of writing a driver to perform them. Below is the code for the driver to test the Name class in the name package.

```
import name.*;

public class PersonDriver
// This class is a test driver for the Name class in package name
{
  static Name testName;        // Name object for testing
  static Name otherName;       // Another Name object

  public static void main(String[] args)
  {
    // Output headings
    System.out.println("Test Results for Package name");
    System.out.println();
    System.out.println("Class      Method        Test#  " +
                " Expected Output     Observed Output");
    // Constructor test
    testName = new Name("John", "Kirk", "Herrel");
    if (testName.knowFirstName().equals("John") &&
        testName.knowMiddleName().equals("Kirk") &&
        testName.knowLastName().equals("Herrel"))
      System.out.println("Name       Name          1    " +
        "3-field Name       3-field Name");
    else
      System.out.println("Name       Name          1    " +
        "3-field Name       Fields don't match");

    // Basic observer tests
    System.out.println("Name       first         1    " +
      "John              " + testName.knowFirstName ());
    System.out.println("Name       middle        1    " +
      "Kirk              " + testName.knowMiddleName ());
    System.out.println("Name       last          1    " +
      "Herrel            " + testName.knowLastName ());
    // Additional observer tests
    otherName = new Name("John", "Kirk", "Herrel");
    System.out.println("Name       equals        1    " +
      "true              " +
      testName.equals(otherName));
    otherName = new Name("John", "Patrick", "Herrel");
    System.out.println("Name       equals        2    " +
      "false             " +
```

```
            testName.equals(otherName));
        otherName = new Name("John", "Kirk", "Herrel");
        System.out.println("Name          compareTo        1    " +
            "0                        " +
            testName.compareTo(otherName));
        otherName = new Name("John", "Kirk", "Altman");
        System.out.println("Name          compareTo        2    " +
            "Positive int             " +
            testName.compareTo(otherName));
        otherName = new Name("John", "Kirk", "Zigman");
        System.out.println("Name          compareTo        3    " +
            "Negative int             " +
            testName.compareTo(otherName));
    }
}
```

Here is the output from running `PersonDriver`.

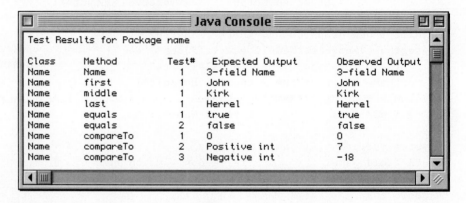

We have kept the driver as simple as possible to emphasize how the test plan is converted into a program. If you were writing a driver for your own use, you would probably want to add features such as displaying a summary of the testing at the end of the run.

You may also notice that the test for the constructor depends on the correct functioning of the basic observers. In fact, by the time we've tested the constructor, we've effectively tested every basic observer.

The encapsulation of an object makes us dependent on its user interface for the testing process. We can't check the effects of a constructor without using a basic observer, and we can't test a basic observer without first calling a constructor to create an object. However, we can at least see that an error has occurred in one or more tests, which tells us to reexamine our code.

Having separate tests for the basic observers helps us to determine whether an error detected in a constructor is really with the constructor or with one of the observers. If we see an unexpected result from both a constructor and a basic observer that was used to check the constructor, we can assume that the error is really in the observer.

Testing and Debugging Hints

1. Make sure your class designs are encapsulated to avoid the possibility of side-effect errors.

2. Use the CRC card process to design the user interface before you begin to think about the implementation.

3. Make classes immutable unless the abstraction truly requires its objects to change without being copied. Immutable objects are less prone to side effects.

4. When choosing an internal representation, carefully consider the tradeoff between saving space or improving speed and the complexity of the required code. One benefit of encapsulation is that you can start with a simple implementation and then go back and make improvements after you have the class working.

5. Consciously consider whether data should be associated with a class, an instance (object) of the class, or a particular method call.

6. When writing methods, be careful not to use parameter names, local names, or method names that duplicate class or instance identifiers. Parameters and local identifiers hide class and instance identifiers with the same name. (More on this in the next chapter.)

7. Don't write a semicolon at the end of a class heading or at the end of a method heading.

8. Be sure that the braces that begin and end a class are properly matched. It requires some effort to check that the braces match because they may be separated by many lines of code and multiple nested blocks. Being careful about consistently indenting your code makes this easier.

9. A method heading always has a pair of parentheses, even when there are no parameters.

10. Remember that arguments and parameters are matched by their position and the types of each argument must be compatible (in the sense of the assignment operator) with its corresponding parameter.

11. Assigning a new value to a parameter of a reference type causes it to refer to a new place in memory and leaves the arguments unchanged. Modifying the contents of the object at the location specified by the parameter modifies the same object that the argument refers to. Such side effects are considered poor programming practice.

12. Only one value (simple or reference type) can be returned with a *return* statement. Every value returning method must have at least one *return* statement.

13. A constructor must have the same name (including capitalization) as the class. Its heading does not include either a `return` type or the keyword `void`. Constructors typically take the `public` modifier.

14. Use the package level of access for each data field unless your design specifically calls for it to be `public`, `protected`, or `private`.

15. Be sure to store multifile packages in the same directory. Otherwise, you get an error message saying that the classes in the package can't be found.

16. Make a test plan and use it to write your driver(s).

Summary of Classes

Package Name

Class Name		Comments
name		
Name		
Constructors: `Name(first, middle, last)`		
Value-Returning Instance Methods:		
	`knowFirstName()`	All return `String` unless otherwise noted
	`knowMiddleName()`	
	`knowLastName()`	
	`firstMidLast()`	
	`lastFirstMid()`	
	`equals(otherName)`	**Returns** `boolean`
	`compareTo(otherName)`	**Returns** `int`

Summary

Encapsulation is the separation of the implementation of a class from external code except through a formal interface. Abstraction is the separation of the logical properties of an object from its implementation. Abstraction helps us to design a well-encapsulated class. Together they lead to classes that are immune to side-effects, that are easily modified and reused.

Abstraction can be divided into data abstraction (separating the internal and external representations of the data stored in a class) and control abstraction (separating the logical properties of operations from their implementations).

Class responsibilities can be divided into four categories: constructors, observers, transformers, and iterators. Constructors create objects, observers return the abstract contents of objects, and transformers directly change the contents of objects. When an object has multiple parts that can be accessed in some sequence, an iterator is used to step through the parts.

Objects can be mutable or immutable. Immutable objects do not have transformer operations.

Java allocates memory space for objects from a free pool in memory. When an object no longer has any identifiers that refer to it, the garbage collector returns its space to the free pool. Because instance data is associated with an object, its lifetime starts with allocation and ends when it becomes garbage (is unreachable). The lifetime of class data is for the entire execution of an application. Local data exists only for the lifetime of an individual method call.

Methods provide the means for implementing the responsibilities of a class. We design the method interface from the CRC card specification of a responsibility. The interface includes the parameters that receive the arguments that are passed to the method, the method's return value (if any), and access to class and instance fields of an object. We categorize the information that flows through the interface as receives, returns, and changes.

A method heading defines the parameters that receive the corresponding arguments from a call to the method. In Java a copy of the argument is given to the method. Simple type arguments that are passed to a method cannot be modified by it. Assigning a new value to a reference type parameter doesn't change the argument because the assignment causes the address stored in the parameter to refer to a different object. However, the object associated with a reference type argument can be changed by a method if it assigns new values to the fields of the object, but this is bad practice.

The return statement in combination with a value-returning method provides a mechanism to return a value from a method. If a method's responsibility is to change the values in an object, the method should be an instance method applied to the object and not a method that takes the object as a parameter. An instance method has the option to receive, return, or change any object field.

A constructor is a special type of method that is called with the `new` operator to initialize a newly created object. The constructor has access to all the fields of the new object. The heading for a constructor doesn't include a return type or the keyword `void`. The name of a constructor is the same as the name of its class including capitalization.

A package collects a set of related classes into a common structure that can be imported by other classes. The Java compiler allows just one `public` class per compilation unit, so a package consists of multiple files, all of which begin with identical `package` statements.

Test plans are especially important for verifying the correct operation of a new class or package. Because there may be many methods to test, we need to take an organized and methodical approach to testing each one with no case omitted. We can often combine multiple tests into a single driver to save work.

Quick Check

1. What are the benefits of a well-designed interface? (p. 294)
2. What is abstraction? (p. 294)
3. Which do you design first, the class interface or the implementation? (p. 294)
4. What the four categories of responsibility? (pp. 298–299)

5. (True or False?) Transformer operations may be defined on an immutable object. (p. 300)
6. What is the default modifier for a declaration? (p. 310)
7. What is the purpose of a constructor for a class? (pp. 318–319)
8. What is an iterator? (pp. 298–299)
9. Before this chapter, you have written three method declarations on numerous occasions. What are they? (p. 308)
10. What do we call the transfer of data between the arguments and parameters in a method call? (pp. 310–311)
11. Distinguish between simple and reference types. (pp. 311–314)
12. When a method is invoked, how does the system match up arguments and parameters? (p. 310)
13. What does "lifetime of a variable or constant" mean? (p. 304)
14. What is the Java syntactic construct that bundles related classes? (p. 320)

Answers

1. A well-designed interface makes a class easy to use and to debug.   2. The separation of the logical properties of an object from its implementation.   3. Abstraction dictates that the interface must be designed first.   4. Constructor, observer, transformer, iterator.   5. False   6. package   7. A constructor is a method that initializes the data fields of a new class instance.   8. An iterator is an operation that allows the user to view members in a collection one at a time.   9. `main`, `windowClosing`, and `actionPerformed`.   10. parameter passing   11. A variable of a simple type contains a value. A variable of a reference type contains the address of a value.   12. Arguments and parameters are matched by position: The first argument is copied into the first parameter, the second argument is copied into the second parameter, etc.   13. "Lifetime" refers to the portion of a program's execution during which a variable or constant is assigned storage space in memory.   14. package

Exam Preparation Exercises

1. What is the goal of designing a new class?
2. Why is it important to encapsulate a new class?
3. Name two benefits of encapsulating a class's implementation.
4. Explain the advantages of modifiability.
5. Explain the advantages of reuse.
6. How can exposing implementation details cause an error in a user program?
7. What are the five basic control structures?
8. Constructors have a strange syntax. Explain.
9. Can one object have another object as a part?
10. a. What is data abstraction?
    b. What is control abstraction.
    c. Differentiate between data abstraction and control abstraction within an object.
11. Distinguish between class and instance methods at the logical level.

12. Distinguish between class and instance methods at the syntactic level.
13. Distinguish between a parameter and an argument.
14. a. If a parameter is of a simple type, what does the parameter receive?
    b. Can the method change the value in the parameter?
    c. Is the argument changed?
15. a. If a parameter is not a simple type, what does the parameter receive?
    b. Can the method change the value in the parameter?
    c. Is the argument changed?
16. Why doesn't changing a parameter of type `String` change the argument?
17. What does a constructor do? Give an example.
18. a. What does a transformer do? Give an example.
    b. What does an observer do? Give an example.
19. a. What does an iterator do?
    b. Distinguish between a transformer iterator and an observer iterator.
20. Fill in the following table showing three categories of data, specifying the lifetime of each and what code can access each.

Types of Data	Lifetime of Data	From Where Data Is Accessible

21. How does the Java compiler distinguish between class data and instance data?
22. a. From where does the JVM get the space it needs to create an object?
    b. Define allocate.
    c. Define deallocate.
    d. Define dynamic memory management.
23. a. What does it mean when we say an object is unreachable?
    b. What is the term used for unreachable objects?
    c. What is the process of going through memory and reclaiming the memory assigned to unreachable objects?
24. a. What is a compilation unit?
    b. Can there be many public classes in one compilation unit?
    c. Where is each compilation unit stored?
    d. How is the file containing a compilation unit named?
    e. Can multiple public classes be put in the same package?
25. a. What are the two places in which the data abstraction is visible to the user?
    b. Should the public constants be initialized in their declarations or in assignment statements?
    c. Can variables be marked `public` in Java?

26. Distinguish between an immutable and a mutable object.

27. (True or False?) Transformer operations may be defined on a mutable object.

28. a. How can you change a value in an immutable object?

    b. How do you create a new object with the same values as another object?

Programming Warm-Up Exercises

1. Declare the following instance variables for a class called `AddressLabel`: `name`, `address`, `state`, `zipCode`, `city`, and `country`. `zipCode` is a `long`; the others are strings.

2. Write the heading for a copy constructor for class `AddressLabel` that changes the `address` field.

3. Write the heading for a constructor for class `AddressLabel` that has four `String` parameters, `name`, `address`, `city`, and `state`, and one long parameter, `zipCode`. The country is set by default to the United States.

4. Write the heading for a constructor for class `AddressLabel` that has four `String` parameters: `name`, `address`, `state`, and `country` and one `long` parameter, `zipCode`.

5. What basic observer operations should our `AddressLabel` class have?

6. Declare a package named `somePackage` with headings for `public` class `AddressLabel` and class `PrintLabel`.

7. Declare a package named `somePackage` with headings for `public` class `AddressLabel` and `public` class `PrintLabel`.

8. How does Java manage to put all the pieces of a package together?

9. Write the code for a class method call to class `Integer`, followed by an instance method call to the newly created object.

10. Write a Java statement that declares an integer-returning `public` method named `myExample`.

11. Write a Java statement that assigns 1066 as the return value of `myExample`.

12. Design and declare an integer method that inputs an integer value from a `TextField` and returns it.

13. Design and declare a `float` method that inputs a `float` value from a `TextField`.

Programming Problems

1. Design and implement an address book object that contains a person's name, home address and phone number, business address and phone number, and numbers for their fax machine, cellular phone, and pager. Write a test plan for the object and implement a driver that tests it.

2. Design, implement, and test a package of one or more classes to represent a catalog entry for a music library. The objects in the library are albums, which can be in the form of tapes, records, compact disks, DVDs, and electronic files. Each album has a title, name of the recording group, name of the record company, the

catalog number or URL used to order the recording, number of songs, total playing time, and an index used to identify the album in the library.

3. Design, implement, and test a package of one or more classes to represent a car. The information associated with a car object is its make, model, production year, color, vehicle identification number, registration number, and owner's name and address.

Case Study Follow–Up Exercises

1. Add an iterator method to the `Name` class that returns each of the parts of a name in the order that they are listed in the class. That is, the first time the iterator is called, it returns the `first` field. The second time it is called, it returns the `middle` field, etc. After it returns the `last` field, it should reset to the `first` field for the next call.

2. Modify the test plan and extend the driver program as necessary to test the iterator developed for Exercise 1.

Inheritance, Polymorphism, and Scope

- To be able to visualize the hierarchical nature of classes in object-oriented programming.

- To be able to demonstrate the concept of inheritance in a class hierarchy.

- To be able to distinguish between overriding and hiding in Java.

- To be able to define polymorphism.

- To be able to differentiate between deep and shallow copying of objects.

- To be able to use the access rules for Java classes.

- To be able to apply the assignment compatibility rules for objects.

- To be able to identify the interface components of a class in a hierarchy.

- To be able to design a derived class to extend an existing class hierarchy.

- To be able to implement a derived class using inheritance.

- To be able to use the keywords `super` and `this` to disambiguate references.

- To be able to explain the concept of overloading in Java.

In Chapter 7 you saw how to create a new class from a CRC card design by choosing an internal representation and implementing the responsibilities as methods. Using the CRC card technique naturally results in a design that is encapsulated. An encapsulated class has the advantage of being reusable in different programs. We also mentioned that another form of reuse is to create additional classes that are variations of the base class. In this chapter we look at how to design and implement such derived classes.

The relationship between derived classes (subclasses) and their superclass is defined by Java's rules of inheritance that tell us which parts of the superclass are automatically included in the derived classes. Another aspect of Java that is similar to the inheritance rules is called scope of access. Java provides a set of rules that determine the fields and methods of a class that can be accessed by derived classes, classes in the same package, user code, and so on. Understanding these rules helps us to preserve encapsulation as the relationships between classes become more sophisticated.

8.1 Inheritance

Let's look at an analogy between the work of an architect and the work of a programmer. The way that an architect handles the complexity of a large building design sheds some light on how we can organize our programming work. The analogy lets us consider the same concepts but without the distraction of Java syntax and semantics.

An Analogy

The architect begins by considering the overall requirements for a building: square footage, number of occupants, types of usage, size of the building lot, height limits, and so on. Once some initial decisions are made, the architect is faced with a basic aspect of any design: the building is composed of floors. In many buildings the floors all have common characteristics: the same size and shape, the same number and location for elevator shafts, stairways, and utility trunks, and so on. The architect could then begin by designing a basic empty floor with all of the common elements in place. Once she installs this plan in the library of the CAD (computer-aided design) program, she can use it repeatedly as the starting point for designing each floor of the building.

The architect may further decide that there are two main types of floors: office floors and mechanical equipment floors. The office floors might be of two types: executive office space and standard office space. Starting from the basic empty floor design, she adds components such as lavatories and hallways to make an empty office floor. She can then add offices and conference rooms to the empty space. Each of the four types of floors is thus derived from the basic empty floor plan and is added to the library (see Figure 8.1). Drawing the entire building is then simply a matter of creating an instance of one of these four floor plans for each story.

The architect uses the same process to design the components that make up the floors. She might design a basic type of office with a door, windows, lights, heating, wiring, and so forth and then derive several types of offices from that one design. From a given type of office, such as secretarial, she might further refine the design into subtypes such as general secretarial, secretary/receptionist, and executive secretary.

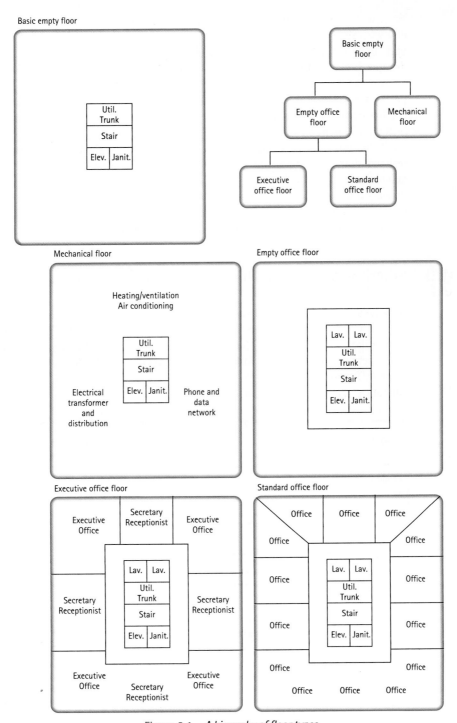

Figure 8.1   *A hierarchy of floor types*

Creating hierarchies of designs simplifies the architect's job. She begins each hierarchy with the most general form of a building component, such as the basic empty floor, and then derives new designs by adding details to the more general forms. The new designs *inherit* all of the characteristics of the general form, saving the architect from having to redraw those pieces they have in common. In some cases she replaces existing parts of a design, as when she substitutes a wider door for a reception area than is in the basic secretarial office. The replacement part *overrides* what was originally specified in the more general form.

In addition to the components of individual floors, the architect can specify characteristics that are common to all floors, such as a color scheme. Each floor inherits these general properties. Sometimes she *hides* or deletes portions of the general properties, as in customizing the color scheme for a particular floor that has been rented in advance by a company with its own corporate colors. We see later that inheritance, overriding, and hiding are formally defined mechanisms in Java.

8.2 Inheritance and the Object–Oriented Design Process

Now let's consider how a class hierarchy originates in the CRC card-design process. At the end of the filtering phase we sometimes discover that there are several classes that are similar. For example, in the Address Book example of Chapter 5, we noted the similarity between the Address and Work Address classes. Let's look at the CRC cards for some different address objects. There are no class members, so we don't bother to write "instance" by each member field.

Class Name: Work Address	Superclass:	Subclasses:
Responsibilities		**Collaborations**
Create itself (name, company, street, mail stop, city, state, zip code), Constructor		Name: Name
Know its name, Observer return String		Name: First Middle Last
Know its company, Observer return String		None
Know its street, Observer return String		None
Know its mail stop, Observer return String		None
Know its city, Observer return String		None
Know its state, Observer return String		None
Know its zip code, Observer return String		None

Class Name: HomeAddress	Superclass:	Subclasses:
Responsibilities	**Collaborations**	
Create itself (name, street, apartment, city, state, zip code), Constructor	Name: Name	
Know its name, Observer return String	Name: First Middle Last	
Know its street, Observer return String	None	
Know its apartment, Observer return String	None	
Know its city, Observer return String	None	
Know its state, Observer return String	None	
Know its zip code, Observer return String	None	

Class Name: BoxAddress	Superclass:	Subclassess:
Responsibilities	**Collaborations**	
Create itself (name, company, box, city, state, zip code), Constructor	Name: Name	
Know its name, Observer return String	Name: First Middle Last	
Know its company, Observer return String	None	
Know its box, Observer return String	None	
Know its city, Observer return String	None	
Know its state, Observer return String	None	
Know its zip code, Observer return String	None	

These CRC cards might originate in the brainstorming phase or they could result from a series of scenarios. No matter how they arise, it is quite obvious that they have several responsibilities in common: Know Its Name, Know Its City, Know Its State, and Know Its

Superclass A class that is extended by one or more derived classes (its subclasses)

Subclass A class that is derived from another class (its superclass)

Zip Code. We can save ourselves duplicate effort by defining a superclass, Address, that has the common responsibilities. In addition, two of the classes share the "Know its company" responsibility. We can thus define a subclass of Address called Company Address that becomes the superclass of these two. The third class directly extends Address with its specific responsibilities. Here are the revised CRC cards:

Class Name: *Address*	Superclass:	Subclasses: *Home Address, Company Address*
Responsibilities	**Collaborations**	
Create itself (name, city, state, zip code), Constructor	Name: Name	
Know its name, Observer return String	Name: First Middle Last	
Know its city, Observer return String	None	
Know its state, Observer return String	None	
Know its zip code, Observer return String	None	

Class Name: *Company Address*	Superclass: *Address*	Subclasses: *Work Address, Box Address*
Responsibilities	**Collaborations**	
Create itself (name, company, city, state, zip code)	Name: Name	
Know its company, Observer return String	None	

Class Name: *Work Address*	Superclass: **CompanyAddress**	Subclasses:
Responsibilities	**Collaborations**	
Create itself (name, company, street, mail stop, city, state, zip code)	Name: Name	
Know its street, Observer return String	None	
Know its mail stop, Observer return String	None	

Class Name: *Box Address*	Superclass: *Company Address*	Subclasses:
Responsibilities	**Collaborations**	
Create itself (name, company, box, city, state, zip code)	*Name: Name*	
Know its Box (Observer, instance) return String	*None*	

Class Name: *Home Address*	Superclass: *Address*	Subclassess:
Responsibilities	**Collaborations**	
Create itself (name, street, apartment, city, state, zip code)	*Name: Name*	
Know its street, Observer return String	*None*	
Know its apartment, Observer return String	*None*	

Figure 8.2 shows the relationships between these classes. Address is the most general form and is thus at the top of its hierarchy, just below Java's most general class, which is called Object.

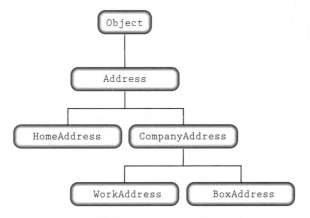

Figure 8.2   *Address class hierarchy*

> **Inheritance** A mechanism by which one class acquires the properties—the data fields and methods—of another class

The ability of a programming language to support the creation of superclasses and subclasses is known as inheritance. Each of the subclasses inherits the responsibilities that are defined by its superclass, including all of the responsibilities that it has inherited. In addition, subclasses are assignment compatible with the superclasses above them in the hierarchy. That is, we can assign a `WorkAddress` object to a `WorkAddress` variable, a `CompanyAddress` variable, an `Address` variable, or an `Object` variable.

Periodically in the CRC card design process it is useful to look for similarities among the cards and decide whether a superclass should be created. Another situation where inheritance is used can be seen when we start to create a new class and realize that is just a variation of an existing class. For example, a field for input of numeric values is just an extension of the familiar `TextField`. We simply have to add `getInt` and `getDouble` methods that read the field and convert it to a numeric value. The derived class could be called `NumericField`. There is no need to define an entirely new class when we can simply extend one that already exists. As you look for things that are familiar in solving a problem, keep in mind the existing classes.

In our Address example, we collected responsibilities from similar classes to form a superclass. In the `TextField` case, we recognize the existence of a class with the properties that make it suitable as a superclass. Whenever you encounter either of these situations, you should immediately consider how you can take advantage of it through inheritance.

8.3 How to Read a Class Hierarchy

In Java, all classes can eventually trace their roots back to the `Object` class, which is so general that it does almost nothing; objects of type `Object` are nearly useless by themselves. But `Object` does define several basic methods: comparison for equality, conversion to a string, and so on.

The Java library defines numerous classes that directly extend the `Object` class and thus inherit all of its methods. For example, there is a class called `Component` that extends `Object` with the basic operations needed to display something in a `Frame`. We can't instantiate objects of class `Component` directly, however, because they are incomplete. Java calls such classes abstract. Returning to our analogy, the architect would never include the basic empty floor in a building plan, but uses it instead as the basis for designing floors that are complete. Similarly, we would never instantiate an object of an `abstract` class in a program, but we use it as the superclass for defining new subclasses that are complete.

> **Abstract** A modifier of a class or field that indicates that it is incomplete and must be fully defined in a derived class
>
> **Derived class** A class that is created as an extension of another class in the hierarchy

The familiar `Button` and `Label` classes are subclasses of the `Component` abstract class. The `TextField` class is derived from a class called `TextComponent`, which is in turn derived from `Component`. As you can see, the hierarchy of classes can be multiple levels in depth, so it can become difficult to keep track of who's descended from whom.

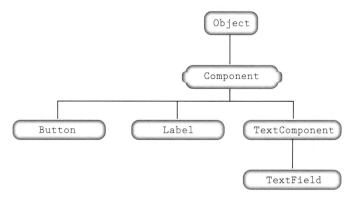

Figure 8.3   *Hierarchy of component classes*

Figure 8.3 shows how these classes are related. We use boxes with their corners cut out to represent the incomplete nature of the abstract class.

When the architect looks at a floor plan with her CAD program, she sees all of its parts including those that are derived from the basic empty floor. But when we look at the documentation for a Java class, we see only the fields that are added by that specific class, and the name of its superclass.

For example, let's look at the documentation for the TextField class. Java class documentation is typically written in a form similar to a class declaration section.

```
public class TextField extends TextComponent
{
  public TextField();
  public TextField(int cols);
  public TextField(String text);
  public TextField(String text, int cols);
  public void addNotify();
  public boolean echoCharIsSet();
  public int getColumns();
  public char getEchoChar();
  public Dimension minimumSize();
  public Dimension minimumSize(int cols);
  protected String paramString();
  public Dimension preferredSize();
  public Dimension preferredSize(int cols);
  public void setEchoCharacter(char c);
}
```

A first glance at the class is somewhat disappointing. Where are the getText and setText methods that we've been using? But wait! The class header says that TextField *extends* TextComponent. That one little bit of code tells us that this definition is just part of the story. We have to look at the documentation for `TextComponent` to determine what `TextField` inherits from it. `TextComponent` is defined as follows:

```
public class TextComponent extends Component
{
   public String getSelectedText();
   public int getSelectionEnd();
   public int getSelectionStart();
   public String getText();
   public boolean isEditable();
   protected String paramString();
   public void removeNotify();
   public void select(int selStart, int selEnd);
   public void selectAll();
   public void setEditable(boolean b);
   public void setText(String s);
}
```

Now we see where `getText` and `setText` are defined. We also see additional methods for dealing with selected text within the field. There is one feature of Java in this definition that we haven't examined yet. The modifier `protected` is used with method `paramString`. We'll take a closer look at this modifier later in this chapter when we discuss Java's rules for accessing fields in other classes.

The class heading for `TextComponent` indicates that there is still more, because it `extends` the class `Component`. If we look at the documentation for that class, we find that it defines 75 more methods. We'll just list a few of them here, together with the class heading.

```
public abstract class Component extends Object
{
   public void enable();
   public void disable();
   public void hide();
   public void show();
   public boolean isEnabled();
   public boolean isVisible();
   .
   .
   .
}
```

You should notice the use of the `abstract` modifier in the class heading. Whenever you see the keyword `abstract` in a class declaration, it tells you that the class being defined is incompletely specified and cannot be instantiated.

When a class is declared as `abstract`, its purpose is to provide a placeholder for a definition to be supplied in a derived class. Class `Component` doesn't have any constructors. It doesn't define the structure of a useful object that we can instantiate.

Instead, it defines a collection of methods that are common to various objects that can appear in a `Frame`. By deriving those objects from this common class, Java makes it easy to ensure that they all behave in a consistent manner.

As we can see from its definition, `Component` extends `Object`, which is the top of the entire hierarchy. We rarely use `Object`'s methods directly, and several of them are related to features of Java that are beyond the scope of this text. Here we list just the ones that are familiar.

```
public class Object
{
  public Object();                 // Constructor
  public boolean equals(Object obj);
  public String toString();
  .
  .
  .
}
```

Now that we have the specification for every class that is an ancestor of `TextField`, we can determine the methods that it has available. The following table illustrates how we do this.

TextField	TextComponent	Component	Object
TextField()	getSelectedText()	enable()	equals(Object obj)
TextField(int cols)	getSelectionEnd()	disable()	toString()
TextField(String text)	getSelectionStart()	hide()	.
TextField(String text, int cols)	getText()	show()	.
addNotify()	isEditable()	isEnabled()	.
echoCharIsSet()	removeNotify()	isVisible()	
getColumns()	select(int start, int end)	.	
getEchoChar()	selectAll()	.	
minimumSize()	setEditable(boolean b)	.	
minimumSize(int cols)	setText(String s)		
paramString()	paramString()		
preferredSize()			
preferredSize(int cols)			
setEchoCharacter(char c)			

We begin at the bottom of the hierarchy (`TextField`) and write down all of its members. In the next column we write the members of its superclass (excluding its constructors, because constructors technically aren't members and they aren't inherited). We repeat this process in the third column, adding the members of `Component`. Note that `Component` is written in italics to remind us that it is `abstract`. Lastly, we write the members of `Object` (excluding its constructors) in the fourth column.

Overriding

Notice that `TextComponent` defines a method called `paramString`. `TextField` then redefines (overrides) `paramString`, substituting its own version of `paramString`. Thus, we write the `TextComponent` member name in color to indicate that it is redefined by `TextField`.

> **Override** To provide an instance method in a derived class that has the same form of heading as an instance method in its superclass. The method in the derived class redefines (overrides) the method in its superclass. We cannot override class methods.

Together, the columns in the table tell us every member that is available in the class `TextField`. When we first looked at the documentation for `TextField`, it appeared that there were just 14 members in the class. Now, however, we can count 32 members in the table, and if we had bothered to list all of the members of `Component` and `Object`, we would see over 100 members. This example illustrates the power of using inheritance in a hierarchy of classes. Just as the architect saves effort by defining a hierarchy of building parts, we can save ourselves a lot of work by using inheritance.

Hiding

In our `TextField` example, we considered only inheritance of methods, but fields may also be inherited through the hierarchy. When a derived class defines a field with the same name as one in its superclass, the field in the derived class hides the one in the superclass. Java also distinguishes the case of overriding a `static` (class) method with another class method as a form of hiding. The term overriding technically applies only to instance methods.

> **Hide** To provide a field in a derived class that has the same name as a field in its superclass. To provide a class method that has the same form of heading as a class method in its superclass. The field or class method is said to hide the corresponding component of the superclass.

If you look at the `TextField` hierarchy carefully, you may notice that nothing is deleted as a result of inheritance (except constructors). In Java, there is no way to remove a member that is inherited. We can cover over a member with a replacement member, but we can't delete it. This is an aspect of the philosophy of object-oriented design: As we go deeper in the hierarchy, we add or change functionality, but we do not lose functionality. In object-oriented design, a derived class is always an extension of its superclass.

For example, we would say that a `TextField` *is a* `TextComponent`. In object-oriented design, a fundamental concept is the "is a" relationship between a derived class and its superclass. A derived class *is a* form of its superclass. The closest that we can get to deleting a member of a superclass in a derived class is to override it or hide it with a member of the same name that does nothing. However, this would be considered poor programming practice.

Polymorphism

Let's take a closer look at the mechanizm that allows `paramString` to have two different implementations, which is called polymorphism. Object oriented languages, such as Java, give us the ability to implement subclasses with methods that override superclass methods. Our definition of `paramString` in class `TextField` that overrides the method in superclass `TextComponent` is an example. Polymorphism further enables the compiler and JVM to decide which version of `paramString` is appropriate

> **Polymorphism** The ability of a language to have duplicate method names in an inheritance hierarchy and to apply the method that is appropriate for the object to which the method is applied

to call depending on the class of the object to which it is applied. For example, when `paramString` is applied to a `TextField` it has one implementation, but when applied to a `TextComponent`, it has another. In object-oriented terms, we say that `paramString` is polymorphic. That is, it has multiple forms. Java decides which form to use depending on the class of the object.

Together with inheritance and encapsulation, polymorphism gives us the ability to flexibly implement a hierarchy of objects. We use polymorphism to substitute different implementations of a responsibility as required by variations in the internal representation of classes at different levels of the hierarchy. For example, `Address` might represent the zip code as a single string, but then we might redefine its representation in the `CompanyAddress` class so that the four-digit extension is kept separately. Thus, the Know Zip Code responsibility would be implemented differently in `CompanyAddress` than in `Address`.

8.4 Derived Class Syntax

The declaration of a derived class looks very much like the declaration of any other class. Here is the syntax template for a class declaration.

Class

```
ClassModifier  . . .  class Identifier  extends ClassName
{
      ClassDeclaration  . . .
}
```

The only difference between this template and the one in Chapter 7 is that we've added the optional `extends` clause that allows us to indicate the superclass that our new class is derived from. Here's an example declaration.

```
public class NumericField extends TextField
{
   // Declare new methods that add numeric input to TextField
}
```

This new class inherits all of the fields and methods of `TextField` (including everything `TextField` has inherited) and then adds some of its own. Is that all there is to implementing a derived class? In terms of syntax, yes. But in terms of semantics, there is more we need to know.

In Chapter 7, we learned how to create individual classes that are fully encapsulated. With inheritance and polymorphism we are beginning to create related sets of classes. Java lets us group related classes in a package so that encapsulation protects the whole collection. But within the package, Java allows the related classes to communicate directly. Direct access is more efficient than converting back and forth between external and internal representations when classes share a common internal representation.

Also, when a derived class overrides or hides members of its superclass, it can no longer refer to them directly. Java provides additional syntax and semantics that enable a subclass to access such superclass members when the need arises.

In the next section we thus examine the Java semantics for accessing members from different places. Then we can return to the specifics of implementing a hierarchy of derived classes.

May We Introduce...

Ada Lovelace

On December 10, 1815 (the same year that George Boole was born), a daughter—Augusta Ada Byron—was born to Anna Isabella (Annabella) Byron and George Gordon, Lord Byron. In England at that time Byron's fame derived not only from his poetry but also from his wild and scandalous behavior. The marriage was strained from the beginning, and Annabella left Byron shortly after Ada's birth. By April of 1816, the two had signed separation papers. Byron left England, never to return. Throughout the rest of his life he regretted that he was unable to see his daughter. At one point he wrote of her,

I see thee not. I hear thee not.
But none can be so wrapt in thee.

Before he died in Greece, at age 36, he exclaimed,

Oh my poor dear child! My dear Ada!
My God, could I but have seen her!

Meanwhile, Annabella, who eventually was to become a baroness in her own right, and who was educated as both a mathematician and a poet, carried on with Ada's upbringing and education. Annabella gave Ada her first instruction in mathematics, but it soon became clear that Ada was gifted in the subject and should receive more extensive tutoring. Ada received further training from Augustus DeMorgan, today famous for one of the basic theorems of Boolean Algebra. By age eight, Ada had demonstrated an interest in mechanical devices and was building detailed model boats.

continued ▼

Ada Lovelace

When she was 18, Ada visited the Mechanics Institute to hear Dr. Dionysius Lardner's lectures on the "Difference Engine," a mechanical calculating machine being built by Charles Babbage. She became so interested in the device that she arranged to be introduced to Babbage. It was said that, upon seeing Babbage's machine, Ada was the only person in the room to understand immediately how it worked and to recognize its significance. Ada and Charles Babbage became lifelong friends. She worked with him, helping to document his designs, translating writings about his work, and developing programs for his machines. In fact, Ada today is recognized as the first computer programmer in history.

When Babbage designed his Analytical Engine, Ada foresaw that it could go beyond arithmetic computations and become a general manipulator of symbols, and thus would have far-reaching capabilities. She even suggested that such a device eventually could be programmed with rules of harmony and composition so that it could produce "scientific" music. In effect, Ada foresaw the field of artificial intelligence more than 150 years ago.

In 1842, Babbage gave a series of lectures in Turin, Italy, on his Analytical Engine. One of the attendees was Luigi Menabrea, who was so impressed that he wrote an account of Babbage's lectures. At age 27, Ada decided to translate the account into English, with the intent to add a few of her own notes about the machine. In the end, her notes were twice as long as the original material, and the document, "The Sketch of the Analytical Engine," became the definitive work on the subject.

It is obvious from Ada's letters that her "notes" were entirely her own and that Babbage was acting as a sometimes unappreciated editor. At one point, Ada wrote to him,

> I am much annoyed at your having altered my Note. You know I am always willing to make any required alterations myself, but that I cannot endure another person to meddle with my sentences.

Ada gained the title Countess of Lovelace when she married Lord William Lovelace. The couple had three children, whose upbringing was left to Ada's mother while Ada pursued her work in mathematics. Her husband was supportive of her work, but for a woman of that day, such behavior was considered almost as scandalous as some of her father's exploits.

Ada died in 1852, just one year before a working Difference Engine was built in Sweden from one of Babbage's designs. Like her father, Ada lived only to age 36, and even though they led very different lives, she undoubtedly had admired him and took inspiration from his unconventional and rebellious nature. In the end, Ada asked to be buried beside him at the family's estate.

8.5 Scope of Access

In writing a Java class we declare variables, constants, methods, and inner classes that are given identifiers. Java defines a set of rules that specify where those identifiers can then be used, both inside and outside of the class. We say that the rules determine the

> **Scope of access (scope)**   The region of program code where it is legal to reference (use) an identifier
>
> **Scope rules**   The rules that determine where in a program an identifier may be referenced, given the point where the identifier is declared and its specific access modifiers

scope of access of an identifier. The term is usually shortened to *scope*, and the rules are thus called the scope rules of the language.

The scope rules for access within a class are straightforward and do not depend on the access modifiers attached to an identifier. External access scope rules determine where an identifier can be used outside of a class and depend on both the access modifiers and where the access takes place. We look first at internal scope, then at external scope.

Internal Scope

Any identifier declared as a `static` or instance member of a class can be used anywhere within the class with two exceptions. You can't use one class variable to initialize another before the first one has been defined. And, within its block, a local identifier overrides a static or instance member of the same name. Let's take a closer look at each of these exceptions.

Order of Definition   Suppose you are defining a `Circle` class and you want to provide class variables that are initially set to `PI` and `PI` times two. The first of the following two declarations is illegal because its initialization expression uses the second identifier before it has been given a value.

```
public static double twoPI = PI * 2; //PI isn't defined yet
public static double PI = 3.14159265358979323846;
```

Reversing the order of the statements makes them both legal.

```
public static double PI = 3.14159265358979323846;
public static double twoPI = PI * 2; //PI already has a value
```

The scope rule that requires us to define a variable's value before it is used applies only to references in expressions that initialize other variables as part of their declaration.

It's otherwise legal to refer to variables before they are defined. For example, the following declarations are legal.

```
public static int circumference(Circle anyCircle)
{
    return anyCircle.radius * twoPI;
}
public static double PI = 3.14159265358979323846;
public static double twoPI = PI * 2;
```

The method is allowed to refer to the variable `twoPI` before it is defined. Why is this case different? The JVM performs all variable declaration initializations before it starts executing statements in `main`, and it does them in the order that they are written in the code. So an initialization expression can only use variables that have already been given values.

The method `circumference` isn't executed until it is called from some point in the program, which can happen only after all of the variable declaration initializations are complete. In terms of the order of execution, all initialization expressions are executed before any other use of a variable.

Note that regular assignment statements that initialize variables in methods are distinct from declaration initialization expressions. They are executed in the normal flow of control, which starts after all of the declaration initializations.

Constant declarations do not follow this rule because the compiler computes constant values at compile time. The compiler first searches through our code to find all the constant declarations before it computes their values. So it doesn't require us to define a constant before using it. The JVM isn't able to search through the Bytecode in the same way, so it requires us to initialize variables before their use.

To make life easier for human readers of your code, it's good form to define constants ahead of any references to them. Some programmers even make a point of writing all constant declarations preceding the variable declarations, just as a reminder that constants are given their values first.

Name Precedence The scope rule that says local identifiers hide members of the class with the same name is called name precedence.

In Java, the scope of a local identifier is the entire block in which it is declared. The block includes all of the statements between the { and } that contain the declaration. For example:

Name precedence   A scope rule specifying that a local identifier declaration hides the declaration of an identifier in the class with the same name (also called name hiding)

```
public class someClass
{
   public static int var;              // Class member var
   public static final int CONST = 5;  // Class member CONST
   public static Label label1;
   public static void someMethod(int param)
   {
      int var;
      final int CONST = 10;
      var = param * CONST;
      label1.setText("" + var);
   }
}
```

Scope of local variable `var` and local constant `CONST`, each of which overrides the same identifier declared as a class member

Notice in this example that the scope of the local declarations extends to the entire block. Thus, if we used CONST to initialize var, the initialization would refer to the local version of CONST. Of course, the compiler would report this as an error because we're using CONST before we've defined it.

Using this *to Overcome Name Precedence* Java provides a keyword, this, to refer to members that are hidden by local declarations. With regard to their scope, formal parameters are treated as local identifiers that are declared at the beginning of the method body. Their scope thus includes the entire body of the method.

Here's an example showing the use of this to access hidden class members.

```java
public class someClass
{
  public int var = -1;          // Member var
  public final int const = 5; // Member CONST
  public int param = 0;         // Member param

  public static int someMethod(int param)  // Local param
  {
    int var;                              // Local var
    // Set local CONST to class CONST * 2
    final int CONST = this.CONST*2;       // Local CONST
    // Compare local and member params
    if (param > this.param)
      var = param * CONST;                // Use local values
    else
      this.var = this.param * this.CONST; // Use member values
    return var;
  }
}
```

Understanding the internal scope rules helps to avoid or locate errors in implementing the internal representation of the class. For example, a scope-related error occurs when you declare a local identifier that overrides a class member but misspell the name in the local declaration. The compiler won't complain and merely directs all of the references to the local identifier to its correctly spelled class member equivalent, as shown here.

```java
public class SomeClass
{
  public static int var;            // Member var
  public static Label label1;       // Member label1

  public static void SomeMethod(int param);
  {
    int ver;                        // Misspelling of var
    var = param * param;            // Refers to member var
    label1.setText("" + var);       // Refers to members
  }
}
```

The program exhibits erroneous behavior in which a class member is changed and displayed as a side effect of calling a method. Knowing the scope rules leads us to look for references to the class member within the method and then to check the local declarations.

External Scope

The external access scope rules for members control their use by code that is outside of the class. There are three external places from which Java allows class members to be accessed: derived classes, members of the same package, and code external to the package.

A package contains a set of related classes, and sometimes we want to make members of those classes accessible to each other, even if they aren't `public`. For example, suppose that a `Date` class is part of a `calendar` package. There is another class, called `ShowWeek`, in the package that displays a week surrounding a given date. Both of the classes use the Julian day as their internal representation. It is thus more efficient for a `Date` object to make its Julian day member directly accessible to `ShowWeek` than to require conversion of the date to its external form and back to a Julian day in the other object. The user is unaware of this shortcut, so the encapsulation is preserved.

Classes naturally belong together in a package if they have common internal representations. In that case, they can bypass each other's encapsulations because the common details of their implementations are already known to anyone who's working with them.

Java defines four levels of access for class members, three of which enable direct access by other package members. The four levels of access are `public`, `protected`, default (package), and `private`. There are keywords that we use as access modifiers for each of these levels except package, which is the default level. If you omit an access modifier from the declaration of a class member, it is at the package level of access.

Public Access   A `public` member can be accessed from anywhere outside of the class. User code, derived classes, and other classes in the same package can all access a `public` member. The member may still be hidden by a declaration of the same name in another class, in which case references to it must be qualified with its class or instance name.

Here's an example of using qualified names. If class `ShowWeek` defines a `julianDay` member and `Date` also defines `julianDay` as a `static` member, then `ShowWeek` would need to refer to

```
Date.julianDay
```

to access the static field of `Date`. If `julianDay` is an instance member of `Date` and the particular object is called `instanceName`, then `ShowWeek` must refer to it as:

```
instanceName.julianDay
```

Protected Access   A `protected` member is accessible to classes in the same package and can be inherited by derived classes outside of the package. Code that is outside of the package can only inherit `protected` members of a class. It can't access them directly.

The following code segment shows the definition of two packages. The second package has a class (DerivedClass) that is derived from the class in the first package (SomeClass). DerivedClass inherits the protected field someInt from SomeClass. Notice that it doesn't include its own declaration of someInt.

DerivedClass defines a method that has one parameter of class SomeClass and another of its own class. It then tries to access the someInt field in both parameters.

```
package one;
public class SomeClass
{
  protected int someInt;
}


package two;
import one.*;
public class DerivedClass extends SomeClass
{
  void demoMethod (SomeClass param1, DerivedClass param2)
  {
    param1.someInt = 1;    // Generates compiler error
    // Can't access member of SomeClass in other package
    param2.someInt = 1;    // This access is legal
    // It refers to the inherited member in this package
  }
}
```

The compiler issues an error message for the first assignment statement because it is illegal to access the protected field of a superclass when the superclass is in a different package. The second assignment is valid because it refers to the inherited field within DerivedClass.

The protected modifier provides the least restrictive level of access that isn't public. We use protected to enable users to extend our class with a subclass. The subclass inherits its own copies of the protected members and cannot access the originals.

It is unusual to use protected in an application designed with CRC cards because all of the responsibilities and collaborations are known in advance. But if a package of classes is independent of an application (such as the java.util package), it is often desirable to enable the user to derive their own classes from the library classes.

Package Access When no access modifier is specified, then classes in the same package can access the member. No other external access is allowed. A member at the package level of access cannot be inherited by a derived class in another package. Up to this point, we've only given examples in which every member of a class is inherited by a subclass. With the introduction of the package level of access, we see that Java also lets us selectively restrict the members that are inherited.

A derived class in the same package still has access to the members of its superclass that are at the package level of access. All classes within the same package have access to each other's `public`, `protected`, and package members.

Here's the preceding example, but with both classes in the same package and `someInt` at the package level of access. In this case, both assignment statements are valid.

```
package one;
public class SomeClass
{
   int someInt;
}


package one;
public class DerivedClass extends SomeClass
{
   void demoMethod (SomeClass param1, DerivedClass param2)
   {
     param1.someInt = 1;  // Accesses someInt in param1 superclass object
     param2.someInt = 1;  // Accesses someInt inherited from superclass
   }
}
```

Private Access   Lastly, the `private` modifier cuts off all external access, even by classes in the same package. A `private` member of a class can be referred to only by other members of the class, and only the internal scope rules apply to it. It isn't even permissible for a derived class in the same package to access a `private` member of its superclass.

Instances of a class can refer to each other's `private` members. A member is `private` to its class, which includes all instances of the class. Thus, two objects, `someObj` and `otherObj` that have `private int` fields called `someInt` can refer to each other's fields. That is, `someObj` can refer to `otherObj.someInt` and `otherObj` can refer to `someObj.someInt`.

Note that within a method, all local identifiers are automatically `private` and Java doesn't allow us to declare them with access modifiers. The reason is that the lifetime of a local identifier is limited to a particular method call, so it simply doesn't exist when external code is running. The following table summarizes the external scope rules.

External access	public	protected	default (package)	private
Same package	yes	yes	yes	no
Derived class in another package	yes	yes (inheritance only)	no	no
User code	yes	no	no	no

Thus far we have primarily used the `public` and package levels of access, keeping data members at the package level and making most methods and classes `public`. This simple scheme provides encapsulation and a consistent user interface that is strictly a set of method calls. However, the scheme is inflexible and limits our ability to provide for either extension or the construction of related classes that are grouped into a package.

Now that we have a better understanding of the Java access rules, we must consider which access modifier is most appropriate for each member of a class. Once you have identified all of its members, take a second look at each one and ask the following question.

Do I want to access this member from other classes in the same package, from derived classes, or from user code?

Based on your answer to each part of this question, you can use the preceding table to decide which access modifier is most appropriate.

8.6 Implementing a Derived Class

Given the CRC card design for a subclass and its superclass, you can determine what it is that you must include in the subclass to implement its responsibilities. You may find that you simply need to change the operation of an inherited method, which means that you override or hide it with a new version. Because a derived class doesn't inherit any constructors, it probably needs one or more new constructors. We often implement new constructors by calling the old ones to do much of the work, and then adding a few statements to take care of initializing any fields that we've added. In some cases you may find it necessary to change the internal representation of the subclass.

After you have designed the subclass interface and its internal representation, you implement it by writing the necessary field and method declarations within a class declaration that `extends` the superclass. Here are the steps in the form of a checklist.

1. Study the interfaces of the superclass and the subclass, identifying the members that are inherited.
2. Determine whether the internal representation must change in the subclass.
3. Provide constructors as needed.
4. Add fields and methods to those that are inherited, as necessary.
5. Hide any inherited fields or class methods that you wish to replace.
6. Override any instance methods that you wish to replace.

We have already seen how to read an existing class hierarchy to determine what is inherited by a subclass. When we are creating a new hierarchy we start from a set of CRC cards. During the enactment of the scenarios, it may become clear that certain responsibilities are `public`, `private`, or package in their access requirements and this should be written on the cards. As we've noted, it is rare for a CRC card design to result in a `protected` responsibility.

As we design the internal representation for a class, we may also notice that certain fields need an access level other than package. For example, we might define some `public` class constants. Once we have this information, we can list the members that a subclass inherits.

Next we reconsider the choice of internal representation given the responsibilities of the subclass. Unless there is a good reason for making the representation different from the superclass, it should remain the same. Thus, we begin with the inherited representation and look for any omissions. We can easily add extra fields.

Sometimes an inherited field is inappropriate for the subclass. Perhaps the superclass uses an `int` field for part of its representation, and the purpose of the subclass is to extend its range by using `long`. Then we must hide the inherited field in the subclass.

Once we have the interface and internal representation, we can begin to implement the constructors. Java has some special rules regarding constructors in derived classes that we examine next.

Constructors in Derived Classes

What would happen if we forgot to include a constructor in the declaration of a derived class? Java automatically provides a default constructor that calls the superclass constructor with an empty parameter list. If the superclass doesn't have a constructor of that form, then the compiler issues an error message.

In fact, Java requires every constructor in a derived class to call a constructor in its superclass. That call must be the first statement in the constructor, even before any declarations. If it isn't the first statement, Java automatically inserts the same default call.

The reason that Java requires us to call a superclass constructor is that every derived class is a specialized form of its superclass. An object of the subclass can be assigned to a variable of both its own class and of its superclass (and by extension, any of the classes above it in the hierarchy). The superclass may perform initialization operations to create a valid object. Rather than requiring every derived class to duplicate those operations, Java simply enforces the rule that one of the superclass constructors must be called, either explicitly in our constructor or implicitly by default.

Of course, the superclass constructor must call a constructor for its superclass, and so on until the constructor for `Object` is called. Thus, the process of instantiating an object calls a chain of constructors that provides essential initialization all the way up to `Object`. Next we examine how Java identifies methods and the Java syntax for calling a constructor in the superclass.

Overloading and Method Signatures

If you were to examine the interface of class `TextField`, you would discover that it has not one but four constructors.

```
public TextField();
public TextField(String text);
public TextField(int columns);
public TextField(String text, int columns);
```

We've always been careful to avoid declaring duplicate identifiers in our programs, yet `TextField` has four constructors all with the same name. How is this possible? In the case of methods, Java uses more than just the name to identify them; it also uses the parameter list. A method's name, the number and type of parameters that are passed to it, and the arrangement of the different parameter types within the list, combine into what Java calls the signature of the method.

Signature The distinguishing features of a method heading. The combination of the method name with the number and type(s) of its parameters in their given order

Overloading The repeated use of a method name with a different signature

Java allows us to use the name of a method as many times as we wish, as long as each one has a different signature. When we use a method name more than once, we are overloading its identifier. The Java compiler needs to be able to look at a method call and determine which version of the method to invoke. The four constructors in class `TextField` all have different signatures: one takes no arguments, the second takes a `String`, the third takes an `int`, and the fourth takes both a `String` and an `int`. Java decides which version to call according to the arguments in the statement that invokes `TextField`.

The following method headings have different signatures and thus overload each other.

```
public static void someName(int param1, int param2, int param3)
public static void someName(int param1, double param2, int param3)
public static void someName(double param1, int param2, int param3)
public static void someName(int param1, int param2, String param3)
```

Even though the parameters all have the same names, the differences in their types enable Java to distinguish between them. For example, the statement

```
someName(1, 2.0, 3)
```

calls the second version because it has an `int` value, a `double` value, and another `int` value as its arguments. If we write the call as

```
someName(1.0, 2, 3)
```

then the `double`, `int`, `int` pattern of its arguments identifies the third version of the method as the target of the call.

The following method headings all have the same signature, and cannot be declared together in a class. Their signature is the method name (`aName`) and the presence of three parameters of types `int`, `double`, and `String` in that order.

```
public static void aName(int param1, double param2, String param3)
public static void aName(int large, double medium, String small)
public void aName(int red, double green, String blue)
static int aName(int thing1, double thing2, String hatCat)
```

Keep in mind that the types of the parameters determine the signature of a method. The names of the parameters, the return type, and the modifiers of a method are not part of its signature.

Overloading is related to but different from hiding and overriding. Hiding and overriding are mechanisms whereby a name is replaced when the same name is declared in a new context. For example, an instance method identifier overrides a method with the same name in its superclass if it has the same signature. The declaration in the derived class results in an identifier that duplicates the one in the superclass. But because they are in different classes, the duplication is acceptable. When we use the identifiers, we indicate which one we mean. An instance identifier is associated with a specific object of one or the other class type, and a class identifier is preceded with the name of the class and a period.

If we declare a method with the same name as an inherited superclass method, but their signatures are different, then the new method overloads the name of the superclass method. The two identifiers are the same, but the different signatures allow them to be distinguished. Different signatures also serve to distinguish overloaded methods within the same class. The Java compiler decides which version to call by comparing the types of the arguments with the types of the parameters in each signature.

To summarize, overloading allows us to add new versions of a name that can exist together in a single context, while hiding and overriding provide a way to replace a name with a new declaration in a different context.

Accessing Overridden and Hidden Methods and Fields

Suppose you need to extend the `Frame` class so that, when a window is closed, a confirmation is requested of the user. The interface of this derived class is the same as the superclass except that you are overriding the `dispose` instance method with a new version. Within your version of `dispose`, you present the message to the user, handle the event that signals the user has acknowledged the message, and then `dispose` of the `Frame` if the user has confirmed the closing.

There's just one problem with this approach. To actually `dispose` of the `Frame` you need to call the `dispose` method that's defined by the superclass. But you just overrode `dispose` with a local definition that has the same signature. If it was a class method, you could access the hidden form by writing the full name of the method: the superclass name, a period and the method name. That is, if `dispose` was a class method, you could write

```
Frame.dispose()
```

to access its hidden form. But `dispose` is an instance method, and there's no instance (object) of class `Frame` to refer to.

Java solves this problem by providing the keyword `super`, which refers to the superclass of a derived class. We write

```
super.dispose()
```

to refer to the `dispose` method in `Frame` from within a derived class that overrides `dispose`. We can also use `super` as an alternative to naming the superclass when referring to a hidden method or field.

The reference to `super.dispose()` invokes the method from the superclass just like any other instance method inherited by the derived class. Our example illustrates an important point regarding hiding and overriding: All the fields and methods from the inheritance interface of the superclass are inherited, but some of them are covered-up by new declarations in the derived class. In effect, they are still there, and `super` simply provides a way to uncover them for a particular reference.

Using `super` followed by a parameter list refers to the constructor in the superclass with the same signature.

For example, in a class derived from `TextField`, we can write

```
myField = super("Initial string", 25);
```

to call the version of the `TextField` constructor that has a `String` and an `int` as its two parameters. We would write

```
myField = super();
```

to explicitly call the default constructor for the superclass. Recall that the constructor is not inherited. Thus, even though it has not been overridden, we can't call it by name. The statement

```
myField = new TextField("Initial String", 25);  // Invalid reference
```

is invalid if written in a class derived from `TextField`.

Keep in mind that there are only two cases where you have to use `super` or the name of the superclass:

1. To access a method or field that has been overridden or hidden

2. To access a superclass constructor

Otherwise, the name has been inherited and you can refer to it directly.

There is one other situation in which hiding can occur. A local declaration that takes name precedence over a class declaration is said to hide the class declaration. As we have already seen, in this situation we use the keyword `this` to refer to the class declaration.

Before we move on to a Case Study, there is one more technique that we would like to introduce. In Chapter 7 we mentioned that it is sometimes useful to create constructors that take an existing instance and use its contents to build a new instance. These are called copy constructors and we use them to illustrate the difference between shallow and deep copying of objects.

8.7   Copy Constructors

One way to simplify the creation of a new instance of an immutable object from an old one is to provide a constructor that takes an existing object as a parameter. It may also have other parameters that take values to substitute in creating the new object. Here's an example of the heading and documentation for such a constructor.

```
public SavingsAccount(SavingsAccount oldAcct, String address)
// oldAcct must contain valid account information.
//  A SavingsAccount object is created with its
//  contents equal to those of the old account except that
//  the address is set equal to the address parameter
```

Here's an example of how it would be called, where `oldAccount` is an existing object of type `SavingAccount` and `address` is a string holding a new address value for the account.

```
account = new SavingsAccount(oldAccount, address)
```

The body of the constructor would copy every field from `oldAccount` to its own equivalent fields, substituting the value in its `address` parameter for the one in the `address` field of `oldAccount`. Note that if any of the fields in the object are themselves objects, it is necessary to use their observers to copy the actual values from the fields of the nested objects. Otherwise, the new object simply refers to the same places in memory as `oldAccount`.

This copy constructor is said to perform a deep copy of the object. A deep copy copies what a reference refers to, rather than the reference itself. A shallow copy ignores the presence of nested objects, treating them like fields of simple types. Figure 8.4 illustrates shallow copying and Figure 8.5 shows deep copying. In both figures, the colored arrows indicate that a field is a reference type with an address that specifies another place in memory. The black arrows indicate copying of values.

> **Deep copy**   An operation that copies one class instance to another, using observer methods as necessary to eliminate nested references and copy only the simple types that they refer to. The result is that the two instances do not contain any duplicate references.
>
> **Shallow copy**   An operation that copies a source class instance to a destination class instance, simply copying all references so that the destination instance contains duplicate references to values that are also referred to by the source

Now that we have seen the mechanics of implementing a derived class and discussed the method for designing a class interface, let's bring all the pieces together in a Case Study that illustrates the process.

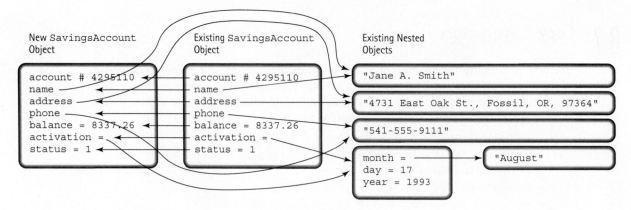

Figure 8.4   *Shallow copying*

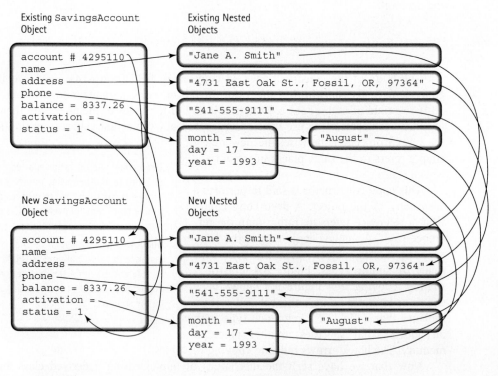

Figure 8.5   *Deep copying*

Problem–Solving Case Study

Extending `TextField` *for Numeric Input and Output*

Problem   Reading a numeric value from a field requires us to perform two type conversions. The expressions containing the conversions are tiresome to write and difficult to read. It would be much nicer to have a field object that specifically handles numeric input, automatically doing the conversion for us. The nearest superclass is type `TextField`. We can extend it with a set of methods, each of which reads the field and returns a value of a specific numeric type.

Brainstorming   The Java class library documentation tells us that `TextField` extends `TextComponent`, which extends `Component`, which extends `Object`. To study the interface of our superclass, we thus work our way upward through this hierarchy. We showed this process earlier in the chapter, so we won't repeat the analysis here. Recall that we found that `TextField` has access to over 100 methods.

Filtering   Of all the methods in the `TextField` hierarchy, there are three that we need to examine closely because they deal with input and output in the field: `getText`, `setText`, and `getSelectedText`. We have used `getText` and `setText` before; `getSelectedText` returns the part of the string that the user has highlighted within the text field. We should add equivalent methods that handle numeric values. The remaining methods in `TextComponent` are not related to our extension of the class.

For numeric input, we would like our derived class to have responsibilities similar to these three for each of the numeric types—for example, `getint`, `setint`, and `getSelectedint`. Rather than add responsibilities for every numeric type, here we simply add the ones for the `int` and `double` types. We leave it as an exercise to develop the responsibilities for Java's remaining numeric types. Thus, we have six responsibilities in our `NumericField` class. The responsibilities that get values are observers, and those that set the value in the field are transformers.

We also must provide constructors for our new class. The superclass has four constructors, two of which allow the user to display an initial string in the field. Because we want the field to contain only numbers, we should supply a constructor for creating the field with an initial value of the appropriate numeric types.

The constructors for the `TextField` class include a form that allows the user to specify an initial string without specifying the width of the field as a number of columns. An analogous constructor in our new class would enable us to specify an `int` or `double` value and have the field be automatically sized to fit. However, if we write the constructor heading

```
NumericField(int value)
```

we get a constructor with the same signature as

```
NumericField(int columns)
```

and such duplication isn't allowed. We can't eliminate the latter form of constructor because it enables us to initially display the field with nothing in it. So we instead choose to forego the ability to create a numeric field with the width set automatically to fit its initial contents.

Because we are extending an existing class in a specified manner, we don't need to walk through any scenarios. However, if we were creating this extension for a real application, then we would need to consider its use. We can identify its collaborations simply by noting that each of our responsibilities needs to use the corresponding methods in TextField. Here's a the CRC card for our new class:

Class Name: NumericField	Superclass: TextField	Subclasses:
Responsibilities	**Collaborations**	
Create itself, default	Textfield: Textfield	
Create itself (int columns)	Textfield: Textfield	
Create itself (int value, int columns)	Textfield: Textfield	
Create itself (double value, int columns)	Textfield: Textfield	
Get int, Observer return int	Textfield: Get Text	
Set int (int value), Transformer	Textfield: Set Text	
Get selected int, Observer return int	Textfield: GetSelected Text	
Get double, Observer return double	TextField: Get Text	
Set double (double value), Transformer	TextField: Set Text	
Get selected double, Observer return double	TextField: GetSelected Text	

Responsibility Algorithms Now that we've designed the method interfaces, let's design their algorithms. We begin with the constructors. The first form of constructor takes no parameters and relies on the default size established by TextField. We thus create it by calling the corresponding constructor for TextField, by using super with a parameter list that matches the signature, as shown below. Note that this satisfies Java's requirement that each constructor call a constructor for its superclass before doing anything else.

....

NumericField()

```
super()
```

Similarly, for the constructor that creates a field with a width of a specified number of columns, we can use the corresponding constructor from `TextField`.

NumericField(int columns)

```
super(columns)
```

The next constructor takes two integer values, the first to be printed and the second to set the number of columns. We can use `TextField`'s constructor that takes a string to be printed and the number of columns, but we must convert the numeric input into a string.

NumericField(int value, int columns)

```
super(" "+ value, columns)
```

The fourth constructor is identical to the third, except that its first parameter is a floating-point value.

NumericField(double value, int columns)

```
super(" " + value, columns)
```

The remaining methods use the corresponding methods from the superclass to get or set the text in the field, but with appropriate conversion to or from a numeric type.

getint

```
return super.getText() converted to int
```

setint(int value)

```
super.setText(" " + value)
```

getSelectedint

```
return super.getSelectedText() converted to int
```

getdouble

```
return super.getText() converted to double
```

---

setdouble(double value)

```
super.setText(" " + value)
```

---

getSelecteddouble

```
return super.getSelectedText() converted to double
```

Now we're ready to code the implementation of our class. In the comments, we note that if the user enters a string that's an invalid number, an error occurs. In Chapter 10, we show how you can handle this error.

```
package numericField;
public class NumericField extends TextField
// This class provides a set of methods for directly getting and setting
//   numeric values in a TextField derived object. It does not check for
//   number format exceptions. No TextField methods are overridden. Only
//   int and double are supported
{
  // Constructors
  public NumericField()
  {                                         // Default constructor
    super();
  }
  public NumericField(int columns)
  {                                         // Makes empty field, columns wide
    super(columns);
  }
  public NumericField(int value, int columns)
  {                                         // Field with int value, width
    super("" + value, columns);
  }
  public NumericField(double value, int columns)
  {                                         // Field with double value, width
    super("" + value, columns);
  }
  // Added methods
  public int getint()
  {                                         // Get an int from the field
    return Integer.valueOf(super.getText()).intValue();
  }
```

```
public void setint(int value)
{                                       // Change int value in field
  super.setText("" + value);
}
public int getSelectedint()
{                                       // Get int from user selection
  return Integer.valueOf(super.getSelectedText()).intValue();
}
public double getdouble()
{                                       // Get a double from the field
  return Double.valueOf(super.getText()).doubleValue();
}
public void setdouble(double value)
{                                       // Change double value in field
  super.setText("" + value);
}
public double getSelecteddouble()
{                                       // Get double from user
                                        //   selection
  return Double.valueOf(super.getSelectedText()).doubleValue();
}
}
```

To test this class, we must import it into a driver that can call its methods.

Testing and Debugging

As we noted in our discussion of the driver for class Name in Chapter 7, when we test a class we can usually test multiple methods with one driver to reduce the amount of user interface code that we have to write. For the NumericField class, there are four constructors and six methods to test. Because each of the methods is independent of the others, there are a total of 10 tests to be performed. When a class has methods that can affect each other's behavior, then we need to test the combinations of methods as well. For example, if one method stores a value in a field of the class that another method then uses, we have to test the combination of these two methods.

Each method is tested to verify that it satisfies its responsibilities if it is called with the proper inputs. We may also test a method to verify its operation when its inputs are erroneous. For example, we may check that a method throws an appropriate exception when it is given invalid data. When a method contains a branch, then we must apply the testing strategies for that control structure to the method just as we would apply them to an application.

The driver is responsible for setting up the proper conditions prior to each method call and reporting the conditions after it returns. It supplies arguments or initializes an object as necessary, and after the call it outputs the results from the method. In some cases, the output is simply a statement that the responsibilities were satisfied. In other cases it is more useful to display the actual return value or fields of the object. It is up to you to decide what to output, but in general the more information that you have, the easier it is to identify errors.

To test the `NumericField` class, we need a driver that first declares and initializes an object of that class. We must also provide a frame to display the field and some labels to provide instructions to the user and to show the results of the method calls. Each of the methods has a single line of code in its body, so there are no control structures to test. We simply call each one to either display a value in the field or to get a value from the field.

We can create a separate `NumericField` object for each test case or we can create a single object and use it in multiple cases. We choose the latter here because it simplifies the user interface to just have one data entry field in the frame. The `main` method declares the object, gives it an initial value and prepares the user interface. The actual testing must take place in the button listener because we can only get information from the field when the user signals through an event that its contents are ready.

We want to perform a series of tests that together cover all of the methods. Each test involves handling a user event. We use the same event (pressing a button) for all of the tests, so within the listener class `ActionHandler` we need a way to determine which test is being performed. We can declare an `int` field, `testNumber`, in the program class that keeps track of the test number between events. The `main` method initializes `testNumber` to 1, and at the end of each test we assign it the number for the next test. The `actionPerformed` method then contains an *if-then-else-if* control structure that branches to the appropriate test depending on `testNumber`.

```
public void actionPerformed(ActionEvent event)
{
  // Declarations
  if (testNumber == 1)
  {
    // Perform first test
  }
  else if (testNumber == 2)
  {
    // Perform second test
  }
  else if (testNumber == 3)
  {
    // Perform third test
  }
  // And so on...
}
```

We can combine testing of more than one method into a single branch in this control structure. For example, we can use `setInt` to place a number in the field in preparation for testing `getSelectedint`. We would thus combine testing of `getint` and `setint` in a single branch, followed by a separate test of `getSelectedint`.

The typical form of an individual test is getting a value from the field, displaying it in a label, setting `testNumber` to the next test, and packing and showing the revised frame. The different tests vary this pattern slightly but are all very similar. Testing `NumericField` is very straightforward because we have added methods that are very similar to each other, which is fairly common in extending a class.

Here is the complete driver for testing class `NumericField`.

```java
import java.awt.*;                          // User interface classes
import java.awt.event.*;                    // Event handling classes
import numericField.*;                      // Class being tested

public class NumericFieldDriver
{

// Define a button listener
private static class ActionHandler implements ActionListener
{
  public void actionPerformed(ActionEvent event)
  // Handles events from the Enter button in inputFrame
  {
    int intAmount;
    double doubleAmount;
    if (testNumber == 1)
    {
      // Convert string in testField to a double value and display
      doubleAmount = testField.getdouble();           // Test getdouble
      outputLabel.setText("You input: " + doubleAmount); // Show results
      testField.setdouble(doubleAmount);              // Test setdouble
      // Show instructions
      entryLabel.setText("Select part of the field " +
                         "and press enter");
      // Set up for test 2
      testNumber = 2;
      inputFrame.pack();
      inputFrame.show();
    }
    else if (testNumber == 2)
    {
      // Convert selected string in testField to a double value and display
      // Test getSelecteddouble
      doubleAmount = testField.getSelecteddouble();
      outputLabel.setText("You input: " + doubleAmount); // Show results
```

```
        testField.setText("");                              // Clear field
        // Show instructions
        entryLabel.setText("Type an integer " +
                           "and press enter");
        // Set up for test 3
        testNumber = 3;
        inputFrame.pack();
        inputFrame.show();
      }
      else if (testNumber == 3)
      {
        // Convert string in testField to an int value and display
        intAmount = testField.getint();                     // Test getint
        outputLabel.setText("You input: " + intAmount);     // Show results
        testField.setint(intAmount);                        // Test setint
        // Show instructions
        entryLabel.setText("Select part of the field " +
                           "and press enter");
        // Set up for test 4
        testNumber = 4;
        inputFrame.pack();
        inputFrame.show();
      }
      else if (testNumber == 4)
      {
        // Convert selected string in testField to an intvalue and display
        // Test getSelectedint
        intAmount = testField.getSelectedint();
        entryLabel.setText("You input: " + intAmount);      // Show results
        // Show instructions
        outputLabel.setText("End of test. " +
                           "Please close the window.");
        inputFrame.remove(enter);                           // Remove button
        inputFrame.remove(testField);                       // Remove field
        inputFrame.pack();
        inputFrame.show();
      }
    }
  }


  static Frame inputFrame;                    // Declare a frame
  static Label entryLabel;                    // Label for input
```

```
static Label outputLabel;                    // Label for output
static NumericField testField;               // Input field
static Button enter;                         // Enter button
static ActionHandler action;                 // Declare the action handler
static int testNumber;                       // Keeps track of which test


public static void main(String[] args)
{ // Prepare user interface components
  inputFrame = new Frame();
  entryLabel = new Label("Enter a real number here:");
  outputLabel = new Label("Press enter when input is ready.",
      Label.RIGHT);
  testField = new NumericField(10);
  enter = new Button("Enter");
  enter.setActionCommand("enter");
  action = new ActionHandler();
  enter.addActionListener(action);
  testNumber = 1;                            // Initialize test number
  // Add user interface components to the frame and display it
  inputFrame.setLayout(new GridLayout(2,2));
  inputFrame.add(entryLabel);
  inputFrame.add(testField);
  inputFrame.add(enter);
  inputFrame.add(outputLabel);
  inputFrame.pack();
  inputFrame.show();
  // Define window closing event handler
  inputFrame.addWindowListener(new WindowAdapter()
    {
      public void windowClosing(WindowEvent event)
      {
        inputFrame.dispose();
        System.exit(0);
      }
    });
}
}
```

Here is the series of dialogs that appears on the screen when the test is executed.

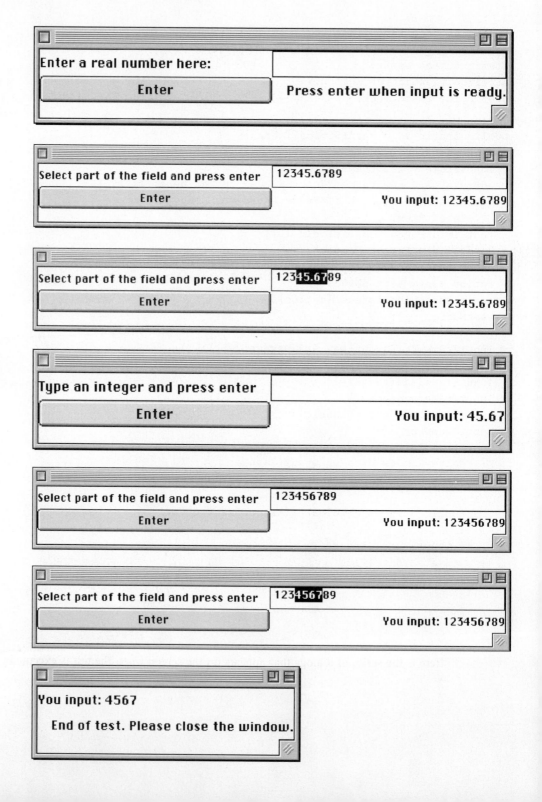

Note that we tested just one of the constructors in our driver program. You can test the other constructors by modifying the statement

```
testField = new NumericField(10);
```

in main to call a different constructor and recompile and run the program. Then repeat the process for each of the constructors. An alternative would be to create a separate driver that simply declares a frame with four fields, each created by a different constructor. Here's how the first part of the main method for such a driver could be written.

```
static Frame inputFrame;              // Declare a frame
static NumericField testField1;       // Field1
static NumericField testField2;       // Field2
static NumericField testField3;       // Field3
static NumericField testField4;       // Field4

public static void main(String[] args)
{
  inputFrame = new Frame();                    // Give the frame a value
  testField1 = new NumericField();             // Give field1 a value
  testField2 = new NumericField(10);           // Give field2 a value
  testField3 = new NumericField(1234, 10);     // Give field3 a value
  testField4 = new NumericField(12.34, 10);    // Give field4 a value

  inputFrame.setLayout(new GridLayout(2,2));   // Set the layout manager
  inputFrame.add(testField1);                  // Add field1 to frame
  inputFrame.add(testField2);                  // Add field2 to frame
  inputFrame.add(testField3);                  // Add field3 to frame
  inputFrame.add(testField4);                  // Add field4 to frame
  inputFrame.pack();                           // Pack the frame
  inputFrame.show();                           // Show the frame
  //
} . . .
```

Once a class has been thoroughly tested, it can be used in many different programming projects. One of the major goals of object-oriented design is to enable the reuse of code in multiple programs. But if a class has an error in it, then the error gets transferred to every program that uses it. You would be very upset if you built a program on top of a class that was written by someone else, only to discover that the class has bugs that make your program fail. Be sure to test your classes thoroughly so that you don't cause similar problems for other programmers!

Testing and Debugging Hints

1. Study the entire hierarchy for a class before you try to use or extend it. Watch out for cases of overriding and hiding that change the semantics of a class member.

2. An abstract class cannot be instantiated as an object; a derived class must be written to use it.

3. Overriding applies to instance methods, hiding applies to class methods. You cannot hide an instance method with a class method or override a class method with an

instance method. However, Java does allow static and instance fields to hide and override each other.

4. When you write a class that extends a superclass, be sure that the compilation unit (program or package) imports the superclass if it isn't one of the standard ones that is always imported.

5. The access modifiers for a method that overrides or hides a method in a superclass must grant the same level of access or greater. The most restrictive form of access is `private`, then `protected`, then `public`. You can override a `private` method with a `public` one, but you can't use `private` to override a `public` method.

6. Be sure that the first statement of every constructor is a call to one of the superclass constructors. If you omit the call, Java automatically inserts a call to `super()`.

7. Overloading a method requires that the two methods have a different signature. The signature is the name of the method plus the types of its parameters in their specific order. The return type and modifiers are not part of the signature.

8. Use `super` to access fields or methods of a superclass that have been hidden or overridden by a derived class.

9. Use `this` to access class fields that have been hidden by a local declaration.

10. Thoroughly document the interface of a class to facilitate its proper use, ensure its correct design, and to simplify testing.

Summary of Classes

Package Name

Class Name	Comments

```
numericField
   NumericField extends TextField
```

Constructors:

```
         NumericField()
         NumericField(int)
         NumericField(int, int)
         NumericField(double, int)
```

Value-Returning Instance Methods:

`getint()`	**Returns** `int`
`setint(int)`	
`getSelectedint()`	**Returns** `int`
`getdouble()`	**Returns** `double`
`setdouble(double)`	
`getSelecteddouble()`	**Returns** `double`

Summary

Object-oriented languages such as Java organize class data types into a hierarchy. At the top of Java's hierarchy is a class called `Object` that provides a few basic operations. Using inheritance, other classes extend `Object` and are said to be derived from it. Derived classes inherit all of the public and protected fields and methods of their superclass except for its constructors. We must explore the entire inheritance hierarchy for a class to determine its full interface.

Instance methods can override superclass instance methods, and class methods and fields can hide superclass class methods and fields. Overriding and hiding provide ways for us to change the meaning of a method or field when extending a superclass with a derived class. The derived class can thus retain the same form of interface, but operate in a different manner.

Constructors are not inherited by derived classes. The first statement in a constructor must be a call to a constructor for the superclass; otherwise, Java automatically inserts such a call to the default constructor for the superclass.

Java allows us to declare multiple methods with the same name as long as they have different signatures. The method name is then said to be overloaded. The signature is the combination of the method name and the types of its parameters in their given order. The return type and modifiers are not part of the signature. Java determines which version of an overloaded method to call by examining the types in the argument list and selecting the method with the matching parameter list.

Sometimes we need to access a method or field in a superclass that has been overridden or hidden. We can use the `super` keyword to refer to the superclass version of a field or method instead of the local version. Similarly, a method can define a local variable or parameter with the same name as a field in the class and we can use `this` to refer to the class version instead of the local version.

Scope rules determine the range of code that has access to an identifier. Internal scope rules specify where class members can be accessed within a class. In Java, members can be used anywhere within a class except that class variables must be defined before they are used to initialize other variables, and local variables can override class variables (name precedence).

External scope specifies where a member can be accessed outside of a class. Java provides four levels of external access. The default level is package, and extends access to all classes in the same package. With `protected` access, derived classes are also able to access a member. A member with `public` access can be used by any code that imports the class. The `private` access level restricts access to only the class containing the member.

In this chapter we have learned how to declare derived classes. The advantage of a derived class is that we have the interface from the superclass as the model for our design. We benefit from inheriting many fields and methods that give our derived class powerful capabilities with no extra work on our part. In some cases, however, a new object is sufficiently different from anything that exists in the standard hierarchy that we have to design it entirely from the ground up. Now that you know how to design and implement both derived classes and top-level classes, you are prepared to explore a wide range of useful and general abstractions that computer scientists have identified as fundamental to the development of more advanced algorithms. The remainder of this text primarily examines some of these abstractions and their implementation.

Quick Check

1. What is the most general class in Java? (p. 346)
2. What is the mechanism that allows one class to extend another class? (pp. 345–346)
3. What do you call a class that is an extension of another class in the hierarchy? (pp. 346–347)
4. Overriding refers to _____ methods; hiding refers to fields and _____ methods. (pp. 350–351)
5. What kinds of members are *not* accessible to a derived class? (p. 359)
6. What is an operation that has multiple meanings depending on the object to which it is applied? (p. 351)
7. Are constructors inherited? (p. 361)
8. An object of a _____ class can be assigned to an object of its _____ class. (p. 361)
9. Explain the meaning of the keyword `extends`. (pp. 346–348, 351)
10. What do we call the rules that determine where in a program that an identifier can be recognized? (pp. 353–355)
11. What keyword refers to a class's superclass? (pp. 363–364)
12. What keyword refers to hidden class members? (p. 364)

Answers

1. `Object` 2. Inheritance 3. Derived class 4. instance, class 5. `private` 6. a polymorphic operation 7. Class constructors are not inherited. 8. derived, super 9. `extends` tells the compiler the class from which this class is being derived. 10. scope rules 11. `super` 12. `this`

Exam Preparation Exercises

1. a. Name two kinds of scope.
   b. Do both internal and external scope depend on the access modifiers of an identifier?
   c. Define internal scope.
   d. What are these two exceptions noted in 1c?
   e. What is name precedence?
   f. Is it legal to define local variables with the same identifier in nested blocks?
2. Name the three external places from which Java allows class members to be accessed.
3. a. List the four levels of access for class members.
   b. Which of the four is the default access?
   c. From where can a `public` member be accessed?
   d. From where can a member with no access modifier be accessed?
   e. From where can a `private` member be accessed?
   f. From where can a `protected` member be accessed?

4. a. What nonpublic members should be part of the interface?
   b. How do you make them part of the interface?
5. What happens if we forget to include a constructor in our new class?

6. a. Distinguish between a deep copy and a shallow copy.
   b. Under what conditions are a deep copy and a shallow copy the same?
7. To what class can all Java objects trace themselves back?
8. What is the modifier of a class or field that indicates that it is incomplete?
9. What does the inheritance mechanism allow one class to acquire from another?
10. What do you call the class that is extended by a derived class?
11. When we examine a derived class, we have access to more than just the methods and fields defined in the class. Explain.
12. What happens if a derived class defines an instance method with the same form of heading as a method in its superclass?
13. What happens if a derived class defines a data field with the same name as a data field in the superclass?
14. Distinguish between overriding and hiding.
15. Is it possible to remove a member that is inherited?
16. Overloading, overriding, and hiding are similar, yet different. Fill in the following table showing whether the sentence describes overloading, overriding, or hiding.

Situation	Hiding	Overriding	Overloading
A class method has the same name and signature of a superclass method.			
An instance method has the same name and signature of a superclass instance method.			
A class has two methods with the same name but different signatures.			
A field in a derived class has the same name as a field in its superclass.			
An instance method has the same name but a different signature of a superclass instance method.			
A method declares a field with the same name as a field in the class.			
A method has a formal parameter with the same name as a field in the class.			

17. What parts of a superclass's interface cannot be inherited?

Programming Warm-Up Exercises

1. Declare three constructors for class `MyClass`.
2. Fill in the blanks in the documentation in the following code segment.

```
public class MyName extends YourName
{
    public static int myField;      // myField is a _____ field.

    public MyName(int myField)

    // _____ with a parameter that hides the _____ _____
    {
        // Assign the _____ to the _____ field.
        this.myField = myField;
    }
}
```

3. a. How does the syntax of a constructor differ from that of an ordinary method?
   b. How is a constructor invoked?
   c. How many constructors can a class have?
   d. What is the signature of a method?
   e. What happens if a class does not have a constructor?
   f. What must be the first statement in every constructor?
4. a. Declare a public class `SomeClass`.
   b. Write the heading for a public class method `someMethod`.
   c. Write the heading for an integer class method `someMethod` that should be accessible by the classes in the package but not to derived classes.
   d. Write the heading for an integer class method `someMethod` that should be accessible only to other methods in the class.
   e. Write the heading for a character class method `someMethod` that should be accessible by classes in the package and any derived classes.
5. a. Write the heading for a `public` method `someMethod`.
   b. Write the heading for an integer method `someMethod` that should be accessible by the classes in the package but not to derived classes.
   c. Write the heading for an integer method `someMethod` that should be accessible only to other methods in the class.
6. Is the following code segment correct? If so, to what does each reference to var refer?

```
public static class someClass
{
    public static int var;            // Class member var
    public static final int const;    // Class member const
    public static void someMethod(int param);
    {
        int var;
```

```
var = param * const;
final int const = 10;
{
    var = 5;
    label1.setText("" + this.var);
}
}
}
```

7. Examine the following constructor headings and list the signature for each.

```
public someClass()
public someClass(int)
public someClass(double)
public someClass(String, int, double)
```

8. Examine the following method headings and list the signature for each. Can this set of signatures be declared in the same class?

```
public int someMethod()
public void someMethod()
public double someMethod()
public double someMethod(int)
public double someMethod(String)
public double someMethod(int, int)
```

9. Are these code segments correct? If not, why not?
   a. `public double taxRate = 29.3;`
      `public double myRate = taxRate*1.1;`
   b. `public double myRate = taxRate*1.1;`
      `public double taxRate = 29.3;`

Programming Problems

1. Take the CRC cards used to design the Address hierarchy and complete the design and implementation of a package that contains the five classes. Design and implement a test plan for the package.
2. Design and implement an application that creates an electronic address book. Use the name class from Chapter 7 and the HomeAddress class from this chapter. The application prompts the user to enter a name and an address. When the name has been entered and verified by the user, it is written to a file. Design and implement a test plan for the application.
3. Design, implement, and test a class that represents a telephone number. There should be fields for the local number, the area code, and the country code.

Case Study Follow-Up Exercises

1. To extend class NumericField to handle values of type float, what new methods would you need to declare?
2. Would you need to add a constructor?
3. Write the interface for your new methods.
4. Implement and test your new methods.

File I/O and Looping

- ■ To be able to recognize when noninteractive input/output is appropriate and describe how it differs from interactive input/output.

- ■ To be able to write applications that use data files for input and output.

- ■ To be able to construct syntactically correct *while* loops.

- ■ To be able to construct count-controlled loops with a *while* statement.

- ■ To be able to construct event-controlled loops with a *while* statement.

- ■ To be able to use the end-of-file condition to control the input of data.

- ■ To be able to use sentinels to control the execution of a *while* statement.

- ■ To be able to construct counting loops with a *while* statement.

- ■ To be able to construct summing loops with a *while* statement.

- ■ To be able to choose the correct type of loop for a given problem.

- ■ To be able to construct nested *while* loops.

- ■ To be able to choose data sets that test a looping application comprehensively.

In Chapters 1 through 8, we have used interactive input. We have written our programs so that the user could enter more than one set of data values by continuing to push a button indicating input data is ready to be read; that is, we have used events to control data input. This strategy works well when the data sets are small. However, there are times when the data sets are too large to be entered in this fashion, so they are stored on a file. In this chapter we examine how to read data into our program that has been previously stored on a file.

Entering data from a file leads to the need for an additional control structure that allows us to explicitly repeat a process rather than relying on a user-initiated event to control the processing.

9.1 File Input and Output

In everything we've done so far, we've assumed that input is via the user interface on the screen. We have used both the `System.out` object and the user interface to send messages to the screen. We look now at input/output (I/O) with files.

Files

Earlier we defined a file as a named area in secondary storage that holds a collection of information (for example, the program code we have typed into the editor). The information in a file usually is stored on an auxiliary storage device, such as a disk (see Figure 9.1).

Figure 9.1 *Disks used for file storage*

Reading and writing data on files is a different process than input and output on the screen. A file contains a sequence of values and has a distinct beginning and end, that is, a first value and a last value. You may think of reading a file as analogous to reading a book in that it is read from the front to the back. Just as you might use a bookmark to keep track of where you are in a book, Java uses something called the *file pointer* to remember its place in a file. Each time some data is read from the file, the file pointer advances to the point where reading should next resume. Each read operation copies a value from the file into a variable in the program and advances the file pointer. A series of read operations eventually reads the last value in the file, and the pointer is said to be at end-of-file (EOF).

Writing data on a file is like writing in an empty notebook. At the beginning, the file is empty, and then data is written onto it from front to back. The file pointer always indicates the end of the last value written so that writing can resume after that point. In effect, the file pointer is always at EOF when a file is being written. The size of the file increases with each write operation. The only limit to the size of a file is the amount of disk space available to the program.

Why would we want a program to read data from a file instead of the user interface? If a program is going to read a large quantity of data, it is easier to enter the data into a file with an editor than to enter it while the program is running. With the editor, we can go back and correct mistakes. Also, we do not have to enter the data all at once; we can take a break and come back later. And if we want to rerun the program, having the data stored in a file allows us to do so without retyping the data.

Why would we want the output from a program to be written to a disk file? The contents of a file can be displayed on a screen or printed. This gives us the option of looking at the output over and over again without having to rerun the program. Also, the output stored in a file can be read into another program as input. For example, the Payroll program writes its output to a file named payFile. We can take payFile and read it into another program, perhaps one that prints out paychecks.

Using Files

If we want a program to use file I/O, we have to do five things:

1. Import the library package java.io.*.
2. Use declaration statements to declare the file variable identifiers we are going to use.
3. Instantiate a file object for each variable.
4. Use methods associated with the file objects to read or write data.
5. Call a method to close the files when we are through with them.

Import the Package java.io.* The first thing we must do any time we want to read from or write to a file is import the package containing the classes that define files.

```
import java.io.*;
```

Through the package `java.io.*`, Java defines many classes for different forms of I/O. In the case of our programs we use just four of these classes, `FileReader`, `FileWriter`, `BufferedReader`, and `PrintWriter`. The `FileReader` and `Buffered-Reader` classes represent streams of characters coming from an input file. `FileWriter` and `PrintWriter` represent streams of characters going to an output file. We first go through the five steps using the simpler `FileReader` and `FileWriter` classes and then look at the extra capabilities offered by `FileWriter` and `BufferedReader`.

Declare the File Identifiers   In a program, you declare file identifiers the same way that you declare any variable—you specify the class and then the name:

```
FileWriter outFile;
FileReader inFile;
```

Note that `FileReader` is for input files only, and `FileWriter` is for output files only. With these classes, you cannot read from and write to the same file. The classes `FileReader` and `FileWriter` allow us to read and write individual characters on files. They are useful when we need to control every aspect of input or output on a character by character basis.

The data in character stream files are organized into lines. A line is a string of characters that ends with a special character called an end-of-line (EOL) mark. When you examine such a file with an editor, each line in the file appears as a line of text on the screen. The editor doesn't display the EOL mark. The EOL mark simply tells the editor when to go to the next line as it places the characters on the screen.

Instantiate the File Objects   The third thing we have to do is to instantiate the file objects. Part of instantiating a file object involves telling the operating system the name of the file on the disk. Thus, we pass the file's name on the disk to the constructor for the object. That way, the JVM and operating system know which disk file to use when the program performs an operation on the file.

For example, we can write these statements:

```
outFile = new FileWriter("outfile.dat");
inFile = new FileReader("infile.dat");
```

Exactly what do these statements do? The constructors create file objects for use in your program and associate them with physical files on disk. The object is then assigned to a file variable that you can reference in other statements in your program. The first statement creates a connection between the file variable `outFile` and the disk file named `outfile.dat`. (Names of file variables must be Java identifiers. But many computer systems do not use Java syntax for file names on disk. For example, file names can include dots and slashes (/) but file variable identifiers cannot.) Similarly, the second statement associates the identifier `inFile` with the disk file `infile.dat`.

The constructor performs additional operations depending on whether the file is an input file or an output file. With an input file, the constructor places the file pointer at the first piece of data in the file. (Each input file has its own file pointer.)

With an output file, the constructor checks to see whether the file already exists. If the file doesn't exist, it creates a new, empty file for you. If the file does exist, it erases the old contents of the file. Then the file pointer is placed at the beginning of the empty file (see Figure 9.2). As output proceeds, each successive output operation advances the file pointer to add data to the end of the file.

Because calling the constructor creates a file object and prepares the file for reading or writing, you must call it before you can use any input or output methods that refer to the file. It's a good habit to call the constructor early in the program to be sure that the files are prepared before any attempts to perform file I/O.

```java
public static void main(String[] args)
{
  FileWriter outFile;
  FileReader inFile;
  // Instantiate the file objects
  outFile = new FileWriter("outfile.dat");
  inFile = new FileReader("infile.dat");
        .
        .
        .
}
```

Use Methods Associated with the File Object To Read or Write Data   Once a file has been declared and instantiated, we are ready to use it. The main operation that we can perform on a file of class `FileWriter` is to write a value onto it. The `write` method can

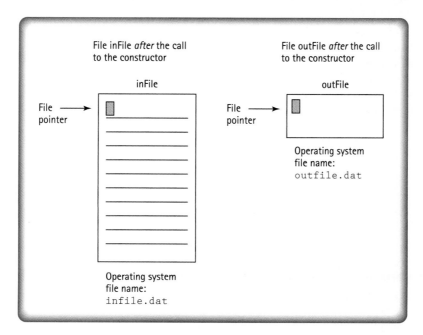

Figure 9.2   *The effect of calling a constructor for a character stream file object*

either be passed a value of type int or a String object. The int value is converted into the corresponding character code and written to the file as a character. If you use a value of type char in place of an int, Java automatically converts the char value to type int before calling write.

The conversion from char to int before the value is then output as a character seems rather convoluted, and you may wonder why write doesn't simply take a value of type char directly. The reason is that there are characters we can't type directly on the keyboard, but all characters have a numerical equivalent in the Unicode character set. Thus, if you want to output one of these characters, you can look up its corresponding number and pass that value to write (see Appendix D for a partial listing of the Unicode characters and their numerical values).

Here are some examples of calls to write. Recall from Chapter 2 that a literal of type char is enclosed in single quotes and contains just one character.

```
outFile.write('X');
outFile.write(88);                              // Code 88 = 'X'
outFile.write("This is a string value.");
```

These statements write

```
XXThis is a string value.
```

onto outFile. To separate the values from each other in the output we can explicitly insert blanks. For example, the statements

```
outFile.write('X');
outFile.write(' ');
outFile.write(88);                              // Code 88 = 'X'
outFile.write(' ');
outFile.write("This is a string value.");
```

produce the following output on the file:

```
X X This is a string value.
```

We can also separate the values by explicitly inserting the EOL, or new line mark (\n), as follows.

```
outFile.write('X');
outFile.write('\n');
outFile.write(88);                              // Code 88 = 'X'
outFile.write('\n');
outFile.write("This is a string value.");
```

Recall from Chapter 2 that we said to use the escape sequence \' to write a single quote as a `char` literal. Similarly, Java interprets the pair of characters \n as a single character corresponding to the EOL mark. The output from this code segment is:

```
X
X
This is a string value.
```

Some operating systems do not immediately write data to a file after each call to `write`. Instead, they keep the data in an area of main memory called a *buffer* and write the data to the disk only when the buffer is full. The reason that this is done is to make the program run faster. A disk access is about 100,000 times slower than copying data between locations in memory. The operating system might save the data from 1,000 write operations in main memory before transferring the data to the disk, making the program run nearly 1,000 times faster.

Occasionally, we need to force the operating system to write a partially filled buffer to the disk. The `FileWriter` class has a method called `flush` that does this for us. For example, if a user is entering data slowly, it could take an hour to fill the buffer, and a power failure would lead to the loss of all the data in the buffer. We could write our program so that every 10 minutes it calls `flush` to save the buffer's contents on the disk and thus reduce the potential for lost data. When we close the file, as discussed in the next section, the buffer is automatically flushed.

Now we turn our attention to file input. The `FileReader` class has just one method that we use for input. Reasonably enough, the name of the method is called `read`. Unlike `write`, however, `read` is a value-returning method. It is called with no parameters and returns an `int` value containing the code for a single Unicode character. If the file contains no more data when `read` is called (the file pointer is at EOF), then `read` returns the value −1, which is not a valid character code. As we will see later in this chapter, detecting when there is no more data to be read is an important aspect of working with files. Assuming that the variable `datum` is of type `int`, we can write a call to `read` from the `FileReader` object `inFile` as follows:

```
datum = inFile.read();
```

When this statement executes, a single character is read from the disk file associated with `inFile`, converted to the `int` value in the Unicode character set that represents it, and then stored in `datum`. In addition, the file pointer advances to the next character in the file. If the character `'M'` had been written on the file, `datum` would contain the integer 77, because 77 is the character code for the letter M. If the digit 8 had been written on the file, datum would contain 56, the character code for an 8. If the value in `datum` is −1, then the file pointer is at EOF. If the value in `datum` is not −1, then it can be converted to type `char` with an explicit type conversion. For example, if `letter` is of type `char`, we can write:

```
letter = (char)datum;
```

If `datum` contained 77, `letter` would contain `'M'`. If `datum` contained 56, `letter` would contain `'8'`.

A value that has been input with `read` can be output to another file with `write`. For example,

```
outFile.write(datum);
```

places the *character* associated with `datum` on the disk file associated with `outFile`. That is, the value in `datum` is automatically converted to the character that it represents before writing it on the file.

Reading data from a file does *not* destroy the data on the file. But because the file pointer moves in just one direction, we cannot go back and reread data that has been read from the disk file unless we return the pointer to the beginning of the file and start over. As we see in the next section, closing a file and reassigning it to a file object with `new` causes the file pointer to return to the start of the file.

Another method associated with objects of class `FileReader` is called `skip`. We pass a `long` value to `skip`, which causes the file pointer to skip over that many characters in the file. Recall that we write a literal value of type `long` with an L at the end. For example, the statement

```
inFile.skip(100L);
```

skips the next 100 characters in the file. Reading can then resume at the new position of the file pointer. If `skip` reaches EOF before it has skipped the specified number of characters, then the program halts with an error message.

Call a Method To Close the File After we have finished reading from or writing to a file, it must be closed. Closing a file tells the operating system that we no longer need the file, and makes it available for use by another program. Once a file is closed, it is no longer associated with the corresponding identifier in our program. Each of the file classes that we have discussed in this chapter has a void method called `close` associated with it. The `close` method does not take any parameters. The following code segment closes the files that we have been using in our discussions.

```
inFile.close();
outFile.close();
```

Although most Java systems automatically close every file when the program exits, it is good programming practice to explicitly close each file. Also, once a program has finished using a file, it should be closed immediately. You don't have to wait until the end of a program to close a file.

Once a file is closed, it can again be assigned a file object with a call to `new`. For example, if the file `infile.dat` is associated with the file object `inFile`, we can write:

```
inFile.close();
inFile = new FileReader("infile.dat");
```

The effect of these two statements is to temporarily break the association between the disk file (`infile.dat`) and the file identifier (`inFile`), and then restore their connection. A side effect of these operations is that the file pointer is reset to the start of the file as part of the constructor call. After the call to `close`, it would also be possible to assign a different disk file to `inFile`, or to assign `infile.dat` to a different file identifier. Here's an example that does both:

```
inFile.close();
inFile = new FileReader("somefile.dat");
differentFile = new FileReader("infile.dat");
```

Extending File I/O with `PrintWriter` and `BufferedReader`

Java provides two file classes, `PrintWriter` and `BufferedReader`, which add useful operations to those of `FileWriter` and `FileReader`. The `BufferedReader` and `PrintWriter` classes allow us to read or write an entire line at once. These are generally more convenient than single character I/O.

We follow the same five steps for using these two new classes. The first step, importing `java.io.*`, is exactly the same for all four file classes. We need not discuss it further, except to note that it has only to be done once in a program, regardless of which file classes we actually use. Now let's look at the second step.

Declare the File Identifier The declaration of identifiers for `PrintWriter` and `BufferedReader` is done in the same way as for `FileReader` and `FileWriter`, except that we use the corresponding class names. Here's an example:

```
PrintWriter payFile;
BufferedReader dataFile;
```

Instantiate the File Object The `BufferedReader` and `PrintWriter` file classes are also instantiated with `new`, but the values passed to their constructors are different. We pass file names to the constructors for `FileWriter` and `FileReader` objects. But `BufferedReader` and `PrintWriter` are derived from `FileWriter` and `FileReader` and simply add some extra methods so that we can read and write whole lines at once.

The extra methods work by repeatedly calling the methods associated with `FileReader` and `FileWriter` objects that input and output individual characters. Thus, when we instantiate a `BufferedReader` object, we pass a `FileReader` object to its constructor, and when we instantiate a `PrintWriter` object we pass a `FileWriter` object to its constructor. For example, given the following declarations and statements,

```
FileWriter outFile;
FileReader inFile;
PrintWriter payFile;
BufferedReader dataFile;
outFile = new FileWriter("outfile.dat");
inFile = new FileReader("infile.dat");
```

we can then write:

```
payFile = new PrintWriter(outFile);
dataFile = new BufferedReader(inFile);
```

Both `payFile` and `outFile` now refer to the disk file called `outfile.dat`. Similarly, `dataFile` and `inFile` are objects that represent the file that the operating system calls `infile.dat`. The objects `payFile` and `dataFile` merely have some extra methods associated with them. When we don't need those methods, there's no reason to use `PrintWriter` or `BufferedReader` to extend `FileWriter` and `FileReader`. Figure 9.3 illustrates the relationship between these types in the context of our example declarations and assignments.

Because the `PrintWriter` and `BufferedReader` classes include the same methods as the `FileWriter` and `FileReader` classes, we don't have to use the `outFile` and `inFile` objects once the `payFile` and `dataFile` objects have been created. In fact, when the only use for a `FileWriter` or `FileReader` is to give a value to a `Print-Writer` or `BufferedReader`, we don't even need to separately declare names for them.

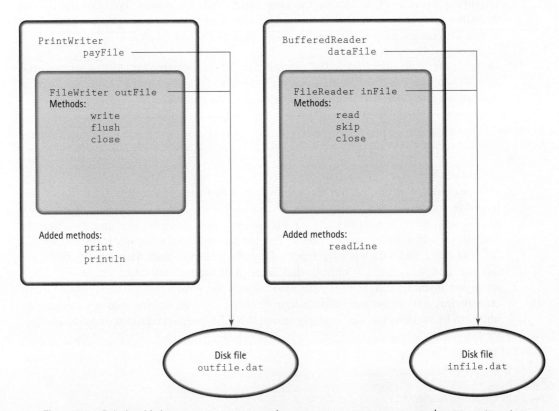

Figure 9.3 *Relationship beween* `FileWriter` *and* `Printwriter`, `FileReader` *and* `BufferedReader`

We can create anonymous (nameless) `FileWriter` and `FileReader` objects within the calls to the `PrintWriter` and `BufferedReader` constructors. That is, where we previously wrote

```
outFile = new FileWriter("outfile.dat");
payFile = new PrintWriter(outFile);
```

we can write:

```
payFile = new PrintWriter(new FileWriter("outfile.dat"));
```

And in place of writing

```
inFile = new FileReader("infile.dat");
dataFile = new BufferedReader(inFile);
```

we can just write:

```
dataFile = new BufferedReader(new FileReader("infile.dat"));
```

In most of our example applications we use `PrintWriter` and `BufferedReader`. But on occasion, when we don't need the ability to write and read whole lines at once, we declare and use objects of the `FileWriter` and `FileReader` classes.

Use Methods Associated with the File Object To Read or Write The `PrintWriter` class adds two more methods to those of the `FileWriter` classes: `print` and `println`. These methods are programming conveniences that avoid the need to convert values to `char` and `String`. In the case of `println`, we are also freed from having to write the EOL escape sequence. Both `print` and `println` can be passed values of any of the built-in Java data types. This is especially useful when you want to output a value of type `int`. With a `FileWriter`, an `int` value is converted to the corresponding Unicode character. But if we write

```
payFile.print(7419);
```

then the string `"7419"` is written out to the file.

When `print` and `println` write numbers on a file, they do not apply any formatting. All of the significant digits of a number are output so that it is possible for another program to read the values back into main memory without any loss of precision.

The only difference between `print` and `println` is that `println` automatically adds the EOL mark at the end of whatever it writes. For example, the following statements do exactly the same thing.

```
payFile.print("Rate = " + rate + "\n");
payFile.println("Rate = " + rate);
```

Using `println` merely saves a small amount of extra typing. This example also illustrates the typical usage of the string concatenation operator to combine several values in a single output statement. The value of the `double` variable `rate` is automatically converted to class `String` before the concatenations take place.

We can also call `println` with no parameters as follows.

```
payFile.println();
```

What do you suppose this call does? Even when there is nothing for `println` to output, it still writes an EOL mark on the file. This call is equivalent to writing,

```
payfile.print('\n');
```

In both cases, the result is that an EOL mark is written at the end of the file, indicating that any subsequent output starts on a new line. If you need to write multiple values on one output line, you can use a series of calls to `print`, followed by a call to `println`:

```
payFile.print("Rate = ");
payFile.print(rate);
payFile.println();
```

The preceding three statements are equivalent to the following single statement.

```
payFile.println("Rate = " + rate);
```

Why would we ever want to write three statements when we can use just one? Sometimes values are computed in different sections of a program, yet you want them to all appear together on one line. As each value is computed, you can write it to the file with a call to `print`, and after all of the values have been written, you can start a new line using a call to `println`.

A series of calls to `println` can be used to produce blank lines in the output. For example, if we run the following code segment,

```
payFile.println('X');
payFile.println();
payFile.println(88);
payFile.println();
payFile.println("This is a string value.");
```

the output is:

```
X

88


This is a string value.
```

We can rewrite these five statements as a single call to `println`,

```
payFile.println('X' + "\n\n" + 88 + "\n\nThis is a string value.");
```

but notice that this statement does not look much like the actual output. It is easier for a human reader to determine what is output by the longer version. Calling `println` five times in a row with simple values as parameters obviously writes five lines to the file. With the shorter version, you must count the number of `\n` escape sequences and add 1 for the EOL that `println` automatically inserts, to know how many lines are output. As you gain experience in reading programs written by other programmers, you grow to appreciate every effort that makes the code easier to understand.

If you write a floating-point value to a file (or a text field, for that matter) that has been calculated within the program, you have no control over the number of digits printed. For example, in the extended `Calculator` program, if you divide 1 by 3, you get .333333333. . . . You can use the `String` class `valueOf` method in conjunction with `String` methods `indexOf` and `substring` to print only as many decimal digits as you wish. The `valueOf` method is a class method that takes a value of a numeric type as a parameter and returns a string representation of the value. We ask you to explore this technique in the exercises.

Everything that we have said about writing to a file should sound somewhat familiar. Recall the `System.out` object we introduced in Chapter 2. This object behaves in much the same way as a `PrintWriter` object. However, `System.out` displays the output on the screen, is automatically instantiated, and we don't have to close it.

The `BufferedReader` class extends the `FileReader` type with a value-returning method called `readLine` that returns an object of class `String`. The returned string contains a line of input from the file, but without the EOL mark at the end of the line. The `readLine` method actually reads the EOL mark but then discards it instead of storing it in the string. The file pointer thus advances to the start of the next line. If we read a line from one file we can write it out to another file with `println`. For example, if `dataLine` is a `String` object, we can write

```
dataLine = dataFile.readLine();
payFile.println(dataLine);
```

When `println` outputs the string in `dataLine`, it appends an EOL mark that replaces the one discarded by `readLine`. The advantage of having `readLine` discard the EOL mark is that is it easier to work with the input string. For example, if we want to add some characters to the end of the string before we write it to `payFile`, we can simply use string concatenation:

```
dataLine = dataFile.readLine();
dataLine = dataLine + "***";
payFile.println(dataLine);
```

If `readLine` did *not* discard the EOL mark, then after the concatenation there would be an EOL mark between the last character from the input line and the appended stars. The call to `println` would then output two lines on `payFile`.

What happens when we call `readLine` and the file pointer is at EOF? The answer is similar to what happens with `read`. Recall that `read` returns an `int` value (-1) that isn't a valid character code. Because `readLine` returns a instance of class `String`, it can't return -1. There is no corresponding invalid value of class `String`; even the empty string (`""`) is a valid string. So Java defines a special value called `null` that signifies that a reference type variable contains an invalid value. When `readLine` discovers that the file pointer is already at EOF, it returns the value `null`. Note that `null` is not the same as the empty string. It is a unique value in Java that does not correspond to any valid data value.

If `readLine` returns a string, how do we get numbers into our program? We do it exactly the same way we did when using `TextField` variables. `getText` returns a string that we must convert to a numeric value; we must do the same with the string returned from `readLine`. Here is the example we used when getting a floating-point value from the frame.

```
number = Double.valueOf(inputField.getText()).doubleValue();
```

Using this as a model, we see that we can input a floating-point value from the file as follows.

```
double floatNumber;
floatNumber = Double.valueOf(dataFile.readLine()).doubleValue();
```

Likewise, an integer value can be read as

```
int intNumber;
intNumber = Integer.valueOf(dataFile.readLine()).intValue();
```

We return to the subject of reading data from files later in this chapter. Except for some trivial cases, we must combine reading operations with loops to read through all of the data on a file.

Call a Method To Close the File The last step is exactly the same for `PrintWriter` and `BufferedReader` as for `FileWriter` and `FileReader`. Here's an example:

```
dataFile.close();
payFile.close();
```

Exceptions with Input and Output

Recall in our discussion of the `FileReader` methods that we said there are situations when calling `skip` can cause the program to halt with an error message. If we try to assign a value to an input file object and the file doesn't exist on the disk, the program also halts with an error message. These kinds of errors are representative of an unusual situation that Java calls an exception.

When a method signals that one of these unusual errors has occurred, it is said to throw an exception. We shall see in Chapter 10 how a Java program can in turn catch an exception. If an exception isn't caught by the program, then it is subsequently caught by the JVM, which halts the program and displays an error message.

> **Exception**   An unusual situation that is detected while a program is running. An exception halts the normal execution of the method.
>
> **Throw**   The act of signaling that an exception has occurred. Throwing an exception is said to abnormally terminate execution of a method.
>
> **Catch**   The processing of a thrown exception by a section of code called an exception handler

Java recognizes two types of exceptions, *checked* and *unchecked*. A checked exception must be explicitly recognized by a program, whereas unchecked exceptions can be ignored. For example, there are several exceptions that can happen when we work with strings. Because Java defines the `String` class so that its exceptions are unchecked, we can simply write our string operations and allow the JVM to catch any exceptions that are thrown. The file object types, `FileReader` and `BufferedReader`, and `FileWriter` define several exceptions that are checked. We cannot simply ignore these exceptions. But Java does give us an option to avoid catching a checked exception: We can explicitly ignore it by forwarding it.

When you forward an exception, you are effectively saying, "OK, Java, I acknowledge that you want me to catch this exception, but I'm not going to do it here; I'm sending it on to a higher authority." You can think of forwarding as the computer equivalent of "passing the buck." If the exception is never

> **Forward**   When a method calls another method that throws an exception, it may pass the exception to its own caller rather than catch the exception.

caught within the program, it eventually ends up at the desk of the JVM, which effectively has a big sign saying "The Buck Stops Here!" The JVM is the ultimate higher authority for a Java program.

To forward an exception, you simply add a `throws` clause to a method heading. The clause specifies the name of the exception that is being forwarded. The `FileReader`, `BufferedReader`, and `FileWriter` classes all throw an exception called `IOException`. Thus, we need to add the clause `throws IOException` to the end of the heading for each of our methods that call any of their methods. Here is an example of the heading for `main` with the appropriate `throws` clause:

```
public static void main(String[] args) throws IOException
```

Note that we haven't mentioned `PrintWriter` in any of the preceding discussion. That is because `PrintWriter` methods do not throw any exceptions. However, even if your program uses only `PrintWriter` objects for file output, you still need to forward or catch an `IOException` because you have to create and pass a `FileWriter` object to the `PrintWriter` constructor, and that `FileWriter` can throw an exception.

An Example Program Using Files

Now let's put all of our discussion of file I/O together by writing a simple application. The application should read a single line from an input file and display it in a field on the screen so that the user can edit it. When the user closes the window, the contents of the field are then written to an output file. Our user interface needs a label to prompt the user, and a field to display the data, but there is no need for a button. Thus, the only event handler that is required is the one that handles closing of the window. However, that event handler is also where we write the contents of the field to the output file and then close the file.

We use `BufferedReader` and `PrintWriter` file objects to simplify the input and output of the line. They are given values that associate them with files called `infile.dat` and `outfile.dat`. We can call `readLine` directly within the call to the `Textfield`'s constructor because `readLine` returns a string and the constructor takes a string as a parameter that specifies its default contents. Once the line has been read, we close the input file.

When the window-closing event handler is called, it retrieves the contents of the field using `getText`. The string that is returned by `getText` is passed directly to `println`, which writes it on the file. After closing the output file, the event handler removes the frame from the screen and halts the program.

```
import java.awt.*;                                    // User interface classes
import java.awt.event.*;                              // Event handling classes
import java.io.*;                                     // File classes

public class EditLine
{
  private static Frame editFrame;                     // Declare a frame
  private static Label entryLabel;                    // Label for field
  private static TextField lineField;                 // Editing field
  private static PrintWriter outFile;                 // Output data file
  private static BufferedReader inFile;               // Input data file

  public static void main(String[] args) throws IOException
  {
    inFile = new BufferedReader(
          new FileReader("infile.dat"));              // Prepare input file
    outFile = new PrintWriter(
          new FileWriter("outfile.dat"));             // Prepare output file
    editFrame = new Frame();                          // Instantiate the frame
```

```
entryLabel = new Label("Edit then close window:"); // Give label a value
// Put input value in field
lineField = new TextField(inFile.readLine(), 40);
inFile.close();                                     // Done reading,
                                                    //  close file


editFrame.setLayout(new FlowLayout());              // Set the layout
                                                    //  manager
editFrame.add(entryLabel);                          // Add field label
                                                    //  to frame
editFrame.add(lineField);                           // Add edit field to
                                                    //  frame
editFrame.pack();                                   // Pack the frame
editFrame.show();                                   // Show the frame
editFrame.addWindowListener(new WindowAdapter()
  {                                                 //  event listener
    // Register window closing
    public void windowClosing(WindowEvent event)
    {
      // Put edited value on file
      outFile.println(lineField.getText());
      outFile.close();                              // Close output file
      editFrame.dispose();                          // Close the frame
      System.exit(0);                               // Quit the program
    }
  });
}
}
```

If `infile.dat` contains the string `"27.000"`, then here is how the frame initially appears on the screen.

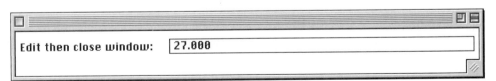

Here is the frame after being edited by the user.

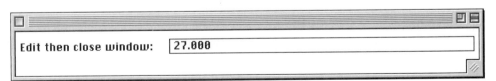

After the window is closed, examination of `outfile.dat` with a text editor reveals that it contains the single line,

```
This is a line of data to output to a file.
```

Before we move on, let's take a closer look at the statements that perform the file input and output operations in program `EditLine`. Both of them are examples of nested method calls, which you have seen before:

```
lineField = new TextField(inFile.readLine(), 40);
outFile.println(lineField.getText());
```

Because Java depends so heavily on the use of method calls, it is quite natural to see one call nested inside another in this manner. Nesting calls avoids having to declare a separate variable or object to hold the return value, and saves an assignment operation. They can be used whenever a return value has no other use than to be passed directly to another method. If the return value is needed at any other point in the program, then it should be assigned to an identifier, and that identifier can then be used in all of the places where the return value is needed. For example, if the input line is to be written both in its original and its edited form onto the output file, then we would instead declare a string variable, such as `lineData`, to hold the return value and write the input section of the program as follows:

```
lineData = inFile.readLine();
lineField = new TextField(lineData, 40);
outFile.println(lineData);
```

9.2 Looping

In Chapter 6, we said that the flow of control in a program can differ from the physical order of the statements. The *physical order* is the order in which the statements appear in a program; the order in which we want the statements to be executed is called the *logical order*.

The *if* statement is one way of making the logical order different from the physical order. Looping control structures are another. A loop executes the same statement (simple or compound) over and over, as long as a condition or set of conditions is satisfied.

> **Loop** A control structure that causes a statement or group of statements to be executed repeatedly.

LOOP   (also called *repetition* or *iteration*)
WHILE condition DO statement1

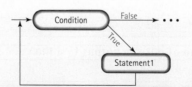

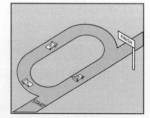

In this chapter, we discuss different kinds of loops and how they are constructed using the *while* statement. We also discuss *nested loops* (loops that contain other loops) and introduce a notation for comparing the amount of work done by different algorithms.

The *while* Statement

The *while* statement, like the *if* statement, tests a condition. Here is the syntax template for the *while* statement:

WhileStatement

```
while ( Expression )
    Statement
```

and this is an example of one:

```
count = 1;
while (count <= 25)
    count = count + 1;
```

The *while* statement is a looping control structure. The statement to be executed each time through the loop is called the *body* of the loop. In the example above, the body of the loop is a statement that adds 1 to the value of `count`. This *while* statement says to execute the body repeatedly as long as `count` is less than or equal to 25. The *while* statement is completed (hence, the loop stops) when `count` is greater than 25. The effect of this loop, then, is to count through the `int` values from 1 to 25.

Just like the condition in an *if* statement, the condition in a *while* statement must be an expression of type `boolean`. The *while* statement says, "If the value of the expression is `true`, execute the body and then go back and test the expression again. If the expression's value is `false`, skip the body." So the loop body is executed over and over as long as the expression is `true` when it is tested. When the expression is `false`, the program skips the body and execution continues at the statement immediately following the loop. Of course, if the expression is `false` to begin with, the body is not even executed. Figure 9.4 shows the flow of control of the *while* statement, where Statement1 is the body of the loop and Statement2 is the statement following the loop.

The body of a loop can be a block of statements, which allows us to execute any group of statements repeatedly. Most often we use *while* loops in the following form:

```
while (Expression)
{
    .
    .
    .
}
```

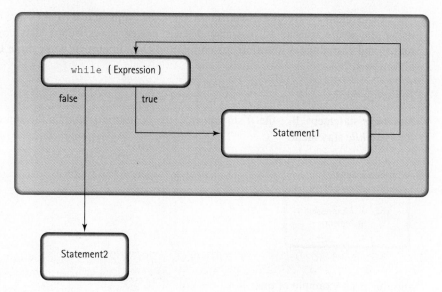

Figure 9.4   *while statement flow of control*

In this structure, if the expression is `true`, the entire sequence of statements in the block is executed, and then the expression is checked again. If it is still `true`, the statements are executed again. The cycle continues until the expression becomes `false`.

Although in some ways the *if* and *while* statements are alike, there are fundamental differences between them (see Figure 9.5). In the *if* structure, Statement1 is either skipped or executed exactly once. In the *while* structure, Statement1 can be skipped, executed once, or executed over and over. The *if* is used to *choose* a course of action; the *while* is used to *repeat* a course of action.

Phases of Loop Execution

The body of a loop is executed in several phases:

Loop entry   The point at which the flow of control reaches the first statement inside a loop

Iteration   An individual pass through, or repetition of, the body of a loop

- The moment that the flow of control reaches the first statement inside the loop body is the loop entry.
- Each time the body of a loop is executed, a pass is made through the loop. This pass is called an iteration.

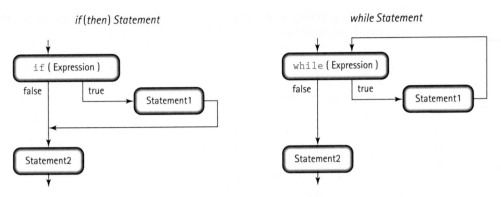

Figure 9.5 *A comparison of if and while*

- Before each iteration, control is transferred to the loop test at the beginning of the loop.
- When the last iteration is complete and the flow of control has passed to the first statement following the loop, the program has exited the loop. The condition that causes a loop to be exited is the termination condition. In the case of a *while* loop, the termination condition is that the *while* expression becomes false.

> **Loop test** The point at which the *while* expression is evaluated and the decision is made either to begin a new iteration or skip to the statement immediately following the loop
>
> **Loop exit** The point at which the repetition of the loop body ends and control passes to the first statement following the loop
>
> **Termination condition** The condition that causes a loop to be exited

Notice that the loop exit occurs only at one point: when the loop test is performed. Even though the termination condition may become satisfied midway through the execution of the loop, the current iteration is completed before the computer checks the *while* expression again.

The concept of looping is fundamental to programming. In this chapter, we spend some time looking at typical kinds of loops and ways of implementing them with the *while* statement. These looping situations come up again and again when you are analyzing problems and designing algorithms.

Loops Using the while Statement

In solving problems, you will come across two major types of loops: count-controlled loops, which repeat a specified number of times, and event-controlled loops, which repeat until something happens within the loop. In the context of a loop, we use the word *event* to mean a specific condition that

> **Count-controlled loop** A loop that executes a specified number of times
>
> **Event-controlled loop** A loop that terminates when something happens inside the loop body to signal that the loop should be exited

we expect to occur during some iteration of the loop and that can be tested by a `boolean` expression. Don't confuse looping events with those that are caused by asynchronous processes such as buttons. The latter cause an asynchronous transfer of control to an event handler, while looping events are merely Boolean conditions that are checked in the loop test.

If you are making an angel food cake and the recipe reads, "Beat the mixture 300 strokes," you are executing a count-controlled loop. If you are making a pie crust and the recipe reads, "Cut with a pastry blender until the mixture resembles coarse meal," you are executing an event-controlled loop; you don't know ahead of time the exact number of loop iterations.

Count-Controlled Loops

A count-controlled loop uses a variable we call the *loop control variable* in the loop test. Before we enter a count-controlled loop, we have to *initialize* (set the initial value of) the loop control variable and then test it. Then, as part of each iteration of the loop, we must *increment* (increase by 1) the loop control variable. Here's an example:

```
loopCount = 1;                    // Initialization
while (loopCount <= 10)           // Test
{
  .
  .                               // Repeated actions
  .
  loopCount = loopCount + 1;      // Incrementation
}
```

Here `loopCount` is the loop-control variable. It is set to 1 before loop entry. The *while* statement tests the expression

```
loopCount <= 10
```

and executes the loop body as long as the expression is `true`. The dots inside the compound statement represent a sequence of statements to be repeated. The last statement in the loop body increments `loopCount` by adding 1 to it.

Look at the statement in which we increment the loop control variable. Notice its form:

```
variable = variable + 1;
```

This statement adds 1 to the current value of the variable, and the result replaces the old value. Variables that are used this way are called *counters*. In our example, `loopCount` is incremented with each iteration of the loop—we use it to count the iterations. The loop control variable of a count-controlled loop is always a counter.

We've encountered another way of incrementing a variable in Java. The incrementation operator (++) increments the variable that is its operand. The statement

```
loopCount++;
```

has precisely the same effect as the assignment statement

```
loopCount = loopCount + 1;
```

From here on, we typically use the ++ operator, as do most Java programmers.

When designing loops, it is the programmer's responsibility to see that the condition to be tested is set correctly (initialized) before the *while* statement begins. The programmer also must make sure the condition changes within the loop so that it eventually becomes `false`; otherwise, the loop is never exited.

```
loopCount = 1;   ←   Variable loopCount must be initialized
while (loopCount <= 10)
{
    .
    .
    .
    loopCount++;   ←   loopCount must be incremented
}
```

A loop that never exits is called an *infinite loop* because, in theory, the loop executes forever. In the code above, omitting the incrementation of `loopCount` at the bottom of the loop leads to an infinite loop; the *while* expression is always `true` because the value of `loopCount` is forever 1. If your program goes on running for much longer than you expect it to, chances are that you've created an infinite loop. You may have to issue an operating system command to stop the program.

How many times does the loop in our example execute—9 or 10? To determine this, we have to look at the initial value of the loop control variable and then at the test to see what its final value is. Here we've initialized `loopCount` to 1, and the test indicates that the loop body is executed for each value of `loopCount` up through 10. If `loopCount` starts out at 1 and runs through 10, the loop body is executed 10 times. If we want the loop to execute 11 times, we have to either initialize `loopCount` to 0 or change the test to

```
loopCount <= 11
```

Event-Controlled Loops

There are several kinds of event-controlled loops: sentinel-controlled, end-of-file-controlled, and flag-controlled. In all of these loops, the termination condition depends on some event occurring while the loop body is executing.

Sentinel-Controlled Loops Loops often are used to read in and process long lists of data. Each time the loop body is executed, a new piece of data is read and processed.

Often a special data value, called a *sentinel* or *trailer value*, is used to signal the program that there is no more data to be processed. Looping continues as long as the data value read is *not* the sentinel; the loop stops when the program recognizes the sentinel. In other words, reading the sentinel value is the event that controls the looping process.

A sentinel value must be something that never shows up in the normal input to a program. For example, if a program reads calendar dates, we could use February 31 as a sentinel value:

```
// This code is incorrect:
while ( !date.equals("0231") )
{
  date = dataFile.readLine();          // Get a date
    .                                    // Process it
    .
    .
}
```

There is a problem in the loop in the example above. The value of `date` is not defined before the first pass through the loop. Somehow we have to initialize this string. We could assign it an arbitrary value, but then we would run the risk that the first value input is the sentinel value, which would then be processed as data. Also, it's inefficient to initialize a variable with a value that is never used.

We can solve the problem by reading the first data value *before* entering the loop. This is called a *priming read.* (The idea is similar to priming a pump by pouring a bucket of water into the mechanism before starting it.) Let's add the priming read to the loop:

```
// This is still incorrect:
date = dataFile.readLine();           // Get a date--priming read
while ( !date.equals("0231") )
{
  date = dataFile.readLine();          // Get a date
    .                                    // Process it
    .
    .
}
```

With the priming read, if the first value input is the sentinel value, then the loop correctly does not process it. We've solved one problem, but now there is a problem when the first value input is valid data. Notice that the first thing the program does inside the loop is to get a date, destroying the value obtained by the priming read. Thus, the first date in the data list is never processed. Given the priming read, the *first* thing that the loop body should do is process the data that's already been read. But then at what point do we read the next input value? We do this *last* in the loop. In this way, the *while* condition is applied to the next input before it gets processed. Here's how it looks:

```
// This version is correct:
date = dataFile.readLine();           // Get a date--priming read
while ( !date.equals("0231") )
```

```
{
   .
   .
   .                                     // Process it
   date = dataFile.readLine();           // Get a date
}
```

This segment works fine. The first value is read in; if it is not the sentinel, it gets processed. At the end of the loop, the next value is read in, and we go back to the beginning of the loop. If the new value is not the sentinel, it gets processed just like the first. When the sentinel value is read, the *while* expression becomes `false`, and the loop exits (*without* processing the sentinel).

Many times the problem dictates the value of the sentinel. For example, if the problem does not allow data values of 0, then the sentinel value should be 0. Sometimes a combination of values is invalid. The combination of February and 31 as a date is such a case. Sometimes a range of values (negative numbers, for example) is the sentinel. And when you process `char` data, one line of input at a time, the newline character (`'\n'`) often serves as the sentinel. Here's a code segment that reads and prints all of the characters on an input line (`inChar` is of type `char`):

```
inChar = (char)inFile.read();           // Get first character
while (inChar != '\n')
{
   outFile.write(inChar);               // Echo it
   inChar = (char)inFile.read();        // Get next character
}
```

(Notice that for this particular task we use the `read` method, not the `readLine` method, to input a single character.)

When you are choosing a value to use as a sentinel, what happens if there aren't any invalid data values? Then you may have to input an extra value in each iteration, a value whose only purpose is to signal the end of the data. For example, look at this code segment:

```
data = dataFile.readLine();             // Get first data line
sentinel = data.substring(0, 1);        // Extract sentinel character
while (sentinel.equals("Y"))
{
   // Extract data value from line and convert to double
   value = Double.valueOf(data.substring(1, data.length())).doubleValue();
      .
      .                                  // Process data value
      .
   data = dataFile.readLine();          // Get next data line
   sentinel = data.substring(0, 1);     // Extract sentinel character
}
```

The first value on each line of the following data set is used to indicate whether or not there are more lines of data. In this data set, when the sentinel value is anything other than "Y", there is no more data; when it is "Y", there is more data.

Sentinel Values	Data Values
Y	12.78
Y	-47.90
Y	5.33
Y	21.83
Y	-99.01
N	59.99

What happens if you forget to include the sentinel value? Once all the data has been read from the file, the loop body is executed again. However, there isn't any data left because the computer has reached the end of the file. In the next section, we describe a way to use the end-of-file situation as an alternative to using a sentinel.

End-of-File-Controlled Loops   After a program has read the last piece of data from an input file, the computer is at the end of the file (EOF, for short). The next time that we attempt to read from the file, there is nothing to read and thus there is nothing for the read or readLine method to return. What happens? Each method has its own sentinel value to return, which signals EOF. The read method normally returns a positive int value corresponding to the code for a single character, so it returns the sentinel value -1. The readLine method normally returns a String value that holds the contents of the line, and so it returns the null string as its sentinel.

Thus, to read and process lines from a file, we can write a sentinel-controlled loop like the following:

```
line = dataFile.readLine();            // Get a line--priming read
while ( line != null )
{
  .
  .                                     // Process it
  .
  line = dataFile.readLine();           // Get the next line
}
```

Notice that the test in this *while* statement uses the relational operator != instead of the equals method. The reason is that equals compares the contents of two strings, but the meaning of null is that the String variable doesn't even contain the address of a String object. Thus, a null String has no contents to compare with. Be sure that you understand the distinction between a null String and an empty string (""). If the empty string is assigned to a String variable, then the variable contains the address of a place in memory where a String object of length 0 is stored. When null is assigned to a `String` variable, it is given an invalid address value that refers to nowhere in memory. The comparison

```
line.equals(null)
```

always returns `false`, because the `null String` has no contents that can be compared to `line`. Even when

```
line == null
```

is `true`, the `equals` method in the preceding example returns `false` because it can't find any contents to compare.

Java provides a convenient way of avoiding the need to separately write the priming read and the read that gets the next value. When the input operation consists of a simple assignment statement, we can instead write the loop as follows.

```
while ((line = dataFile.readLine()) != null)   // Get a line
{
       .
       .                                        // Process it
       .
}
```

At first glance, the expression in the *while* statement looks rather strange. The reason for its strangeness is that there is an aspect of the assignment operator that we haven't discussed yet. We have been writing the assignment operator in assignment statements, such as

```
x = 2;
```

But the assignment operator can also appear in expressions, where it has a value and a side effect. The side effect is the action we normally associate with assignment statements: The result of the expression to the right of = is assigned to the variable to its left. The value that = returns is the same as the value that is assigned to the variable. An assignment statement is really just a special form of assignment expression where the side effect (the assignment) takes place and then the value returned by the expression is discarded. For example, in the following comparison,

```
(x = 2 + 2) == 5
```

the value 4 is assigned to the `int` variable x as a side effect, and the subexpression (x = 2 + 2) has the result 4, which is compared to the literal 5, giving a final result of `false`. When we use the result of an assignment expression in a comparison, we must enclose the assignment expression in parentheses because = has the lowest precedence of all the operators. Note that this is another example of why you must be careful not to confuse the = and == operators in writing a comparison!

In the *while* statement,

```
while ((line = dataFile.readLine()) != null)     // Get a line
{
   .
   .                                             // Process it
   .
}
```

`line` is thus assigned the value returned by `readLine`, and that same value (the result of the assignment expression) is compared to `null` by the `!=` operator.

Because the parentheses force the input operation to happen before the first comparison, the effect is the same as using a separate priming read. When control flow reaches the end of the loop, it returns to the test in the *while* statement where another input operation takes place before the comparison, with the same effect as using a separate input operation at the end of the loop body. Thus, the input operation in the assignment expression within the *while* statement's comparison takes the place of two separate input operations.

If we can write the *while* statement in this manner, why would we ever need the longer form with the two separate input operations? When the test in the *while* statement depends on something other than the value returned by the input operation, we need to use the longer form. For example, if an input line contains three numbers that must be converted to `int` values and their sum is then compared to zero to decide if the loop should exit, we can't use a simple assignment expression within the *while*. Whenever the condition in the *while* depends on performing multiple operations on the input value, it is best to code the input and the operations as separate priming and updating statements before and within the loop.

Looping Subtasks

We have been looking at ways to use loops to affect the flow of control in programs. But looping by itself does nothing. The loop body must perform a task in order for the loop to accomplish something. In this section, we look at two tasks—counting and summing—that often are used in loops.

Counting A common task in a loop is to keep track of the number of times the loop has been executed. For example, the following program fragment reads and counts input characters until it comes to a period. (`inChar` and `count` are of type `int`.) The loop in this example has a counter variable; but the loop is not a count-controlled loop because the variable is not being used as a loop control variable.

```
count = 0;                          // Initialize counter
inChar = inFile.read()              // Read a character
while ((char)inchar != '.')         // Test the character
{
  count++;                          // Increment counter
  inChar = inFile.read();           // Read a character
}
```

The loop continues until a period is read. After the loop is finished, `count` contains one less than the number of characters read. That is, it counts the number of characters up to, but not including, the sentinel value (the period). Notice that if a period is the first character, the loop body is not entered and `count` contains a zero, as it should. We use a priming read here because the loop is sentinel-controlled, and because we are storing the input character as an `int` but need to convert it to a `char` for the comparison.

The counter variable in this example is called an iteration counter because its value equals the number of iterations through the loop. According to our definition, the loop control variable of a count-controlled loop is an iteration counter. However, as you've just seen, not all iteration counters are loop control variables.

> **Iteration counter** A counter variable that is incremented with each iteration of a loop

What happens if our example loop encounters EOF before it reads a period? It runs forever (or at least until we terminate the program with an operating system command). The reason is that `read` returns -1 when the file pointer is at EOF. The `(char)` conversion translates this into a character code that doesn't correspond to any valid character. Thus, the result of comparing this invalid character for inequality with `'.'` is always `true`, and the loop continues executing forever. The test in the *while* statement is thus more properly written as follows:

```
while (inchar != -1 && (char)inchar != '.')          // Test the character
```

Summing Another common looping task is to sum a set of data values. Notice in the following example that the summing operation is written the same way, regardless of how the loop is controlled.

```
sum = 0;                                             // Initialize sum
count = 1;
while (count <= 10)
{
  number = Integer.valueOf(dataFile.readLine()).intValue(); // Input a value
  sum = sum + number;                                // Add value to sum
  count++;
}
```

We initialize `sum` to 0 before the loop starts so that the first time the loop body executes, the statement

```
sum = sum + number;
```

adds the current value of `sum` (0) to `number` to form the new value of `sum`. After the entire code fragment has executed, `sum` contains the total of the 10 values read, `count` contains 11, and `number` contains the last value read.

Here `count` is incremented in each iteration. For each new value of `count`, there is a new value for `number`. Does this mean we could decrement `count` by 1 and inspect the previous value of `number`? No. Once a new value has been read into `number`, the previous value is gone forever unless we've saved it in another variable.

Let's look at another example. This time, let's also check for EOF. We want to count and sum the first 10 odd numbers in a data set. We need to test each number to see if it is even or odd. (We can use the modulus operator to find out. If `number % 2` equals 1, `number` is odd; otherwise, it's even.) If the input value is even, we do nothing. If it is odd, we increment the counter and add the value to our sum. We use a flag to control the loop because this is not a normal count-controlled loop. In the following code segment, all variables are of type `int` except the `String line` and the Boolean flag, `notDone`.

```
count = 0;                                  // Initialize event counter
sum = 0;                                    // Initialize sum
notDone = true;                             // Initialize loop control flag
while (notDone)
{
  line = dataFile.readLine();               // Get a line
  if (line != null)                         // Got a line?
  {                                         // Try converting line to an int
    number = Integer.valueOf(line).intValue();
    if (number % 2 == 1)                    // Is the int value odd?
    {
      count++;                              // Yes--Increment counter
      sum = sum + number;                   // Add value to sum
      notDone = (count < 10);               // Update loop control flag
    }
  }
  else                                      // Hit EOF unexpectedly
  {
    errorFile.println("EOF reached before ten odd values read.");
    notDone = false;                        // Update loop control flag
  }
}
```

We control the loop with the flag `notDone`, because the loop exits when either of two events occur: reading and processing 10 odd values or reaching EOF. Because we use a Boolean flag to control the loop, this type of loop is often called a *flag-controlled loop*.

In this example, there is no relationship between the value of the counter variable and the number of times the loop is executed. Note that `count` is incremented only when an odd number is read; it is an event counter. We initialize an event counter to 0 and increment it only when a certain event occurs. The

Event counter A variable that is incremented each time a particular event occurs

counter in the previous example was an *iteration counter*; it was initialized to 1 and incremented during each iteration of the loop.

How to Design Loops

It's one thing to understand how a loop works when you look at it and something else again to design a loop that solves a given problem. In this section, we look at how to design loops. We can divide the design process into two tasks: designing the control flow and designing the processing that takes place in the loop. And we can break each task into three phases: the task itself, initialization, and update. It's also important to specify the state of the program when it exits the loop, because a loop that leaves variables and files in a mess is not well designed.

There are seven different points to consider in designing a loop:

1. What is the condition that ends the loop?
2. How should the condition be initialized?
3. How should the condition be updated?
4. What is the process being repeated?
5. How should the process be initialized?
6. How should the process be updated?
7. What is the state of the program on exiting the loop?

We use these questions as a checklist. The first three help us design the parts of the loop that control its execution. The next three help us design the processing within the loop. The last question reminds us to make sure that the loop exits in an appropriate manner.

Designing the Flow of Control

The most important step in loop design is deciding what should make the loop stop. If the termination condition isn't well thought out, there's the potential for infinite loops and other mistakes. So here is our first question:

- What is the condition that ends the loop?

This question usually can be answered through a close examination of the problem statement. For example:

Key Phrase in Problem Statement	Termination Condition
"Sum 365 temperatures"	The loop ends when a counter reaches 366 (count-controlled loop).
"Process all the data in the file"	The loop ends when EOF occurs (EOF-controlled loop).
"Process until 10 odd integers have been read"	The loop ends when 10 odd numbers have been input (event counter).
"The end of the data is indicated by a negative test score"	The loop ends when a negative input value is encountered (sentinel-controlled loop).

Now we need statements that make sure the loop gets started correctly and statements that allow the loop to reach the termination condition. So we have to ask the next two questions:

- How should the condition be initialized?
- How should the condition be updated?

The answers to these questions depend on the type of termination condition.

Count-Controlled Loops   If the loop is count controlled, we initialize the condition by giving the loop control variable an initial value. For count-controlled loops in which the loop control variable is also an iteration counter, the initial value is usually 1. If the process requires the counter to run through a specific range of values, the initial value should be the lowest value in that range.

The condition is updated by increasing the value of the counter by 1 for each iteration. (Occasionally, you may come across a problem that requires a counter to *count down* from some higher value to a lower value. In this case, the initial value is the greater value, and the counter is decremented by 1 for each iteration.) So, for count-controlled loops that use an iteration counter, these are the answers to the questions:

- Initialize the iteration counter to 1.
- Increment the iteration counter at the end of each iteration.

If the loop is controlled by a variable that is counting an event within the loop, the control variable usually is initialized to 0 and is incremented each time the event occurs. For count-controlled loops that use an event counter, these are the answers to the questions:

- Initialize the event counter to 0.
- Increment the event counter each time the event occurs.

Sentinel-Controlled Loops   In sentinel-controlled loops, a priming read may be the only initialization necessary. It also may be necessary to open the file in preparation for reading. To update the condition, a new value is read at the end of each iteration. So, for sentinel-controlled loops, we answer our questions this way:

- Open the file, if necessary, and input a value before entering the loop (priming read).
- Input a new value for processing at the end of each iteration.

EOF-Controlled Loops   EOF-controlled loops require the same initialization as sentinel-controlled loops. You must open the file, if necessary, and perform a priming read. Updating the loop condition happens implicitly; the input value reflects the success or failure of the operation. However, if the loop doesn't read any data, it never reaches EOF, so updating the loop condition means the loop must keep reading data.

Flag-Controlled Loops   In flag-controlled loops, the Boolean flag variable must be initialized to `true` or `false` and then updated when the condition changes.

- Initialize the flag variable to `true` or `false`, as appropriate.
- Update the flag variable as soon as the condition changes.

In a flag-controlled loop, the flag variable essentially remains unchanged until it is time for the loop to end. Then the code detects some condition within the process being repeated that changes the value of the flag (through an assignment statement). Because the update depends on what the process does, at times we have to design the process before we can decide how to update the condition.

Designing the Process within the Loop

Once we've determined the looping structure itself, we can fill in the details of the process. In designing the process, we first must decide what we want a single iteration to do. Assume for a moment that the process is going to execute only once. What tasks must the process perform?

- What is the process being repeated?

To answer this question, we have to take another look at the problem statement. The definition of the problem may require the process to sum up data values or to keep a count of data values that satisfy some test. For example:

> *Count the number of integers in the file* `howMany`*.*

This statement tells us that the process to be repeated is a counting operation.
Here's another example:

> *Read a stock price for each business day in a week and compute the average price.*

In this case, part of the process involves reading a data value. We have to conclude from our knowledge of how an average is computed that the process also involves summing the data values.

In addition to counting and summing, another common loop process is reading data, performing a calculation, and writing out the result. Many other operations can appear in looping processes. We've mentioned only the simplest here; we look at some other processes later on.

After we've determined the operations to be performed if the process is executed only once, we design the parts of the process that are necessary for it to be repeated correctly. We often have to add some steps to take into account the fact that the loop executes more than once. This part of the design typically involves initializing certain variables before the loop and then reinitializing or updating them before each subsequent iteration.

- How should the process be initialized?
- How should the process be updated?

For example, if the process within a loop requires that several different counts and sums be performed, each must have its own statements to initialize variables, increment counting variables, or add values to sums. Just deal with each counting or summing operation by itself—that is, first write the initialization statement, and then write the incrementing or summing statement. After you've done this for one operation, you go on to the next.

The Loop Exit

When the termination condition occurs and the flow of control passes to the statement following the loop, the variables used in the loop still contain values. And if an input file has been used, the reading marker has been left at some position in the file. Or maybe an output file has new contents. If these variables or files are used later in the program, the loop must leave them in an appropriate state. So, the final step in designing a loop is answering this question:

* What is the state of the program on exiting the loop?

Now we have to consider the consequences of our design and double-check its validity. For example, suppose we've used an event counter and later processing depends on the number of events. It's important to be sure (with an algorithm walk-through) that the value left in the counter is the exact number of events—that it is not off by 1.

Look at this code segment:

```
commaCount = 1;                        // This code is incorrect
while ((inChar = (char)inFile.read()) != '\n')
  if (inChar == ',')
    commaCount++;
outLabel.setText("" + commaCount);
```

This loop reads characters from an input line and counts the number of commas on the line. However, when the loop terminates, commaCount equals the actual number of commas plus 1 because the loop initializes the event counter to 1 before any events take place. By determining the state of commaCount at loop exit, we've detected a flaw in the initialization. commaCount should be initialized to zero. Note that this code segment is also an example of using an assignment expression within a loop test, and because there is just a single statement in the loop (the *if* statement) there is no need for the usual brackets to enclose a block of statements.

Designing correct loops depends as much on experience as it does on the application of design methodology. At this point, you may want to read through the Problem-Solving Case Study at the end of the chapter to see how the loop-design process is applied to a real problem.

Nested Loops

In Chapter 6, we described nested *if* statements. It's also possible to nest *while* statements. Both *while* and *if* statements contain statements and are themselves statements. So the body of a *while* statement or the branch of an *if* statement can contain other *while* and *if* statements. By nesting, we can create complex control structures.

Suppose we want to extend our code for counting commas on one line, repeating it for all the lines in a file. We put an EOF-controlled loop around it:

```
inChar = inFile.read();                 // Initialize outer loop
while (inChar != -1)                     // Outer-loop test for EOF
{
  commaCount = 0;                        // Initialize inner loop
  // Priming read is taken care of by outer loop's priming read
  while (inChar != -1 && (char)inChar != '\n' )  // Inner-loop test
  {
    if (inChar == ',')
      commaCount++;
    // Update inner-termination condition
    inChar = inFile.read();
  }
  outLabel.setText("" + commaCount);
  // Update outer-termination condition
  inChar = inFile.read();
}
```

In this code, notice that we have omitted the priming read for the inner loop. The priming read for the outer loop has already "primed the pump." It would be a mistake to include another priming read just before the inner loop; the character read by the outer priming read would be destroyed before we could test it. Our inner-loop test checks for both end of line (\n) and for EOF (-1), just in case the last line in the file doesn't end with the newline character.

General Pattern

Let's examine the general pattern of a simple nested loop. The dots represent places where the processing and update may take place in the outer loop.

Notice that each loop has its own initialization, test, and update. It's possible for an outer loop to do no processing other than to execute the inner loop repeatedly. On the other hand, the inner loop might be just a small part of the processing done by the outer loop; there could be many statements preceding or following the inner loop.

Let's look at another example. For nested count-controlled loops, the pattern looks like this (where outCount is the counter for the outer loop, inCount is the counter for the inner loop, and limit1 and limit2 are the number of times each loop should be executed):

```
outCount = 1;                               // Initialize outer-loop counter
while (outCount <= limit1)
{
  .
  .
  .
  inCount = 1;                              // Initialize inner-loop counter
  while (inCount <= limit2)
  {  .
     .
     .
    inCount++;                              // Increment inner-loop counter
  }
  .
  .
  .
  outCount++;                               // Increment outer-loop counter
}
```

Here, both the inner and outer loops are count-controlled loops, but the pattern can be used with any combination of loops. The following program fragment shows a count-controlled loop nested within an EOF-controlled loop. The outer loop inputs an integer value telling how many asterisks to print on each line of an output file. (We use the numbers to the right of the code to trace the execution of the program.)

```
line = dataFile.readLine();                            1
while (line != null)                                   2
{
  starCount = Integer.valueOf(line).intValue();        3
  loopCount = 1;                                       4
  while (loopCount <= starCount)                       5
  {
    outFile.print('*');                                6
    loopCount++;                                       7
  }
  outFile.println();                                   8
  line = dataFile.readLine();                          9
}
outFile.println("End");                                10
```

To see how this code works, let's trace its execution with these data values (<EOF> denotes end-of-file):

```
3
1
<EOF>
```

We'll keep track of the variables line, starCount, and loopCount, as well as the logical expressions. To do this, we've numbered each line (except those containing only a left or right brace). As we trace the program, we indicate the first execution of line 3 by 3.1, the second by 3.2, and so on. Each loop iteration is enclosed by a large brace, and true and false are abbreviated as T and F (see Table 9.1).

Table 9.1 Code trace

	Variables		Logical Expressions			
Statement	line	starCount	loopCount	line != null	loopCount <= starCount	Output
1.1	'3'	—	—	—	—	—
2.1	'3'	—	—	T	—	—
3.1	'3'	3	—	—	—	—
4.1	'3'	3	1	—	—	—
5.1	'3'	3	1	—	T	—
6.1	'3'	3	1	—	—	*
7.1	'3'	3	2	—	—	—
5.2	'3'	3	2	—	T	—
6.2	'3'	3	2	—	—	*
7.2	'3'	3	3	—	—	—
5.3	'3'	3	3	—	T	—
6.3	'3'	3	3	—	—	*
7.3	'3'	3	4	—	—	—
5.4	'3'	3	4	—	F	—
8.1	'3'	3	4	—	—	\n (newline)
9.1	'1'	3	4	—	—	—
2.2	'1'	3	4	T	—	—
3.2	'1'	1	4	—	—	—
4.2	'1'	1	1	—	—	—
5.5	'1'	1	1	—	T	—
6.4	'1'	1	1	—	—	*
7.4	'1'	1	2	—	—	—
5.6	'1'	1	2	—	F	—
8.2	'1'	1	2	—	—	\n (newline)
9.2	null	1	2	—	—	—
2.3	null	1	2	F	—	—
10.1	null	1	2	—	—	End

Here's the output on outFile from the program given the input used for our trace.

```
* * *
*
End
```

Because `starCount` and `loopCount` are variables, their values remain the same until they are explicitly changed, as indicated by the repeating values in Table 9.1. The values of the logical expressions `line != null` and `loopCount <= starCount` exist only when the test is made. We indicate this fact with dashes in those columns at all other times.

Designing Nested Loops

To design a nested loop, we begin with the outer loop. The process being repeated includes the nested loop as one of its steps. Because that step is more complex than a single statement, our functional decomposition methodology tells us to make it a separate module. We can come back to it later and design the nested loop just as we would any other loop.

For example, here's the design process for the outer loop for the preceding code segment:

1. *What is the condition that ends the loop?* EOF is reached in the input.
2. *How should the condition be initialized?* A priming read should be performed before the loop starts.
3. *How should the condition be updated?* An input statement should occur at the end of each iteration.
4. *What is the process being repeated?* Using the value of the current input integer `starCount`, the code should print that many asterisks across one output line.
5. *How should the process be initialized?* No initialization is necessary.
6. *How should the process be updated?* A sequence of asterisks is output and then a newline character is output. There are no counter variables or sums to update.
7. *What is the state of the program on exiting the loop?* File `dataFile` is at EOF, `starCount` contains the last integer read from the input stream, and the rows of asterisks have been printed along with a concluding message.

From the answers to these questions, we can write this much of the algorithm:

```
Read line from dataFile
while NOT EOF
     Set starCount to the integer equivalent to the string in line
     Set loopCount = 1
     while loopCount <= starCount
         Print '*' on outFile
         Increment loopCount
     Output newline on outFile
     Read line from dataFile
Print "End"
```

After designing the outer loop, it's obvious that the process in its body (printing a sequence of asterisks) is a complex step that requires us to design an inner loop. So we repeat the methodology for the corresponding lower-level module:

1. *What is the condition that ends the loop?* An iteration counter exceeds the value of starCount.
2. *How should the condition be initialized?* The iteration counter should be initialized to 1.
3. *How should the condition be updated?* The iteration counter is incremented at the output file.
4. *What is the process being repeated?* The code should print a single asterisk on the output file
5. *How should the process be initialized?* No initialization is needed.
6. *How should the process be updated?* No update is needed.
7. *What is the state of the program on exiting the loop?* A single row of asterisks has been printed, the writing marker is at the end of the current output line, and loopCount contains a value one greater than the current value of starCount.

Now we can write the algorithm:

```
Read line from dataFile
while NOT EOF
        Set starCount to the integer equivalent to the string in line
        Print starCount asterisks
        Output newline on outFile
        Read line from dataFile
Print "End"
```

Of course, nested loops themselves can contain nested loops (called *doubly-nested loops*), which can contain nested loops (*triply-nested loops*), and so on. You can use this design process for any number of levels of nesting. The trick is to defer details using the functional decomposition methodology—that is, focus on the outermost loop first, and treat each new level of nested loop as a module within the loop that contains it.

It's also possible for the process within a loop to include more than one loop. For example, here's an algorithm that reads people's names from a file and prints them on another file, omitting the middle name in the output:

```
Read and print first name (ends with a comma)
while NOT EOF
    Read and discard characters from middle name (ends with a comma)
    Read and print last name (ends at newline)
    Output newline
    Read and print first name (ends with a comma)
```

The steps for reading the first name, middle name, and last name require us to design three separate loops. All of these loops are sentinel-controlled.

This kind of complex control structure would be difficult to read if written out in full. There are simply too many variables, conditions, and steps to remember at one time. When a responsibility algorithm becomes this complex, it is an indication that we have missed some objects in the brainstorming and scenario phases. In this case, we should extend `FileReader` with new methods that get the first, middle, and last names. We could call the new class `NameFileReader`.

 Theoretical Foundations

Analysis of Algorithms

If you are given the choice of cleaning a room with a toothbrush or a broom, you probably would choose the broom. Using a broom sounds like less work than using a toothbrush. True, if the room is in a doll house, it may be easier to use the toothbrush, but in general a broom is the faster way to clean. If you are given the choice of adding numbers together with a pencil and paper or a calculator, you would probably choose the calculator because it is usually less work. If you are given the choice of walking or driving to a meeting, you would probably choose to drive; it sounds like less work.

What do these examples have in common? What do they have to do with computer science? In each of the settings mentioned, one of the choices seems to involve significantly less work. Precisely measuring the amount of work is difficult in each case, because there are unknowns. How large is the room? How many numbers are there? How far away is the meeting? In each case, the unknown information is related to the size of the problem. If the problem is especially small (for example, adding 2 plus 2), our original estimate of which approach

continued ▼

Analysis of Algorithms

to take (using the calculator) might be wrong. However, our intuition is usually correct, because most problems are reasonably large.

In computer science, we need a way of measuring the amount of work done by an algorithm relative to the size of a problem, because there is usually more than one algorithm that solves any given problem. We often must choose the most efficient algorithm—the algorithm that does the least work for a problem of a given size.

The amount of work involved in executing an algorithm relative to the size of the problem is called the complexity of the algorithm. We would like to be able to look at an algorithm and determine its complexity. Then we could take two algorithms that perform the same task and determine which completes the task faster (requires less work).

> **Complexity** A measure of the effort expended by the computer in performing a computation, relative to the size of the computation

How do we measure the amount of work required to execute an algorithm? We use the total number of *steps* executed as a measure of work. One statement, such as an assignment, may require only one step; another, such as a loop, may require many steps. We define a step as any operation roughly equivalent in complexity to a comparison, an I/O operation, or an assignment.

Given an algorithm with just a sequence of simple statements (no branches or loops), the number of steps performed is directly related to the number of statements. When we introduce branches, however, we make it possible to skip some statements in the algorithm. Branches allow us to subtract steps without physically removing them from the algorithm because only one branch is executed at a time. But because we usually want to express work in terms of the worst-case scenario, we use the number of steps in the longest branch.

Now consider the effect of a loop. If a loop repeats a sequence of 15 simple statements 10 times, it performs 150 steps. Loops allow us to multiply the work done in an algorithm without physically adding statements.

Now that we have a measure for the work done in an algorithm, we can compare algorithms. For example, if Algorithm A always executes 3,124 steps and Algorithm B always does the same task in 1,321 steps, then we can say that Algorithm B is more efficient—that is, it takes fewer steps to accomplish the same task.

If an algorithm, from run to run, always takes the same number of steps or fewer, we say that it executes in an amount of time bounded by a constant. Such algorithms are referred to as having *constant-time* complexity. Be careful: Constant time doesn't mean small; it means that the amount of work done does not exceed some amount from one run to another regardless of the size of the problem.

If a loop executes a fixed number of times, the work done is greater than the physical number of statements but still is constant. What happens if the number of loop iterations can change from one run to the next? Suppose a data file contains *N* data values to be processed in a loop. If the loop reads and processes one value during each iteration, then the loop executes *N* iterations. The amount of

continued ▼

Analysis of Algorithms

work done thus depends on a variable, the number of data values. The variable N determines the size of the problem in this example.

If we have a loop that executes N times, the number of steps to be executed is some factor times N. The factor is the number of steps performed within a single iteration of the loop. Specifically, the work done by an algorithm with a data-dependent loop is given by the expression

$$\overbrace{S_1 \times N}^{\substack{\text{Steps performed} \\ \text{by the loop}}} + \underbrace{S_0}_{\substack{\text{Steps performed} \\ \text{outside the loop}}}$$

where S_1 is the number of steps in the loop body (a constant for a given simple loop), N is the number of iterations (a variable representing the size of the problem), and S_0 is the number of steps outside the loop. Mathematicians call expressions of this form *linear*; hence, algorithms such as this are said to have *linear-time* complexity. Notice that if N grows very large, the term $S_1 \times N$ dominates the execution time. That is, S_0 becomes an insignificant part of the total execution time. For example, if S_0 and S_1 are each 20 steps, and N is 1,000,000, then the total number of steps is 20,000,020. The 20 steps contributed by S_0 are a tiny fraction of the total.

What about a data-dependent loop that contains a nested loop? The number of steps in the inner loop, S_2, and the number of iterations performed by the inner loop, L, must be multiplied by the number of iterations in the outer loop:

$$\overbrace{(S_2 \times L \times N)}^{\substack{\text{Steps performed} \\ \text{by the nested loop}}} + \overbrace{(S_1 \times N)}^{\substack{\text{Steps performed} \\ \text{by the outer loop}}} + \overbrace{S_0}^{\substack{\text{Steps performed outside} \\ \text{the outer loop}}}$$

By itself, the inner loop performs $(S_2 \times L)$ steps, but because it is repeated N times by the outer loop, it accounts for a total of $(S_2 \times L \times N)$ steps. If L is a constant, then the algorithm still executes in linear time.

Now, suppose that for each of the N outer loop iterations the inner loop performs N steps ($L = N$). Here the formula for the total steps is

$$(S_2 \times N \times N) + (S_1 \times N) + S_0$$

continued ▼

Analysis of Algorithms

or

$$\left(S_2 \times N^2\right) + \left(S_1 \times N\right) + S_0$$

Because N^2 grows much faster than N (for large values of N), the inner-loop term $(S_2 \times N^2)$ accounts for the majority of steps executed and the work done. So the corresponding execution time is essentially proportional to N^2 Mathematicians call this type of formula quadratic. If we have a doubly nested loop, where each loop depends on N, then the expression is

$$\left(S_3 \times N^3\right) + \left(S_2 \times N^2\right) + \left(S_1 \times N\right) + S_0$$

and the work and time are proportional to N^3 whenever N is reasonably large. Such a formula is called *cubic*.

The following table shows the number of steps required for each increase in the exponent of N, where N is a size factor for the problem, such as the number of input values.

N	N^0 (Constant)	N^1 (Linear)	N^2 (Quadratic)	N^3 (Cubic)
1	1	1	1	1
10	1	10	100	1,000
100	1	100	10,000	1,000,000
1,000	1	1,000	1,000,000	1,000,000,000
10,000	1	10,000	100,000,000	1,000,000,000,000
100,000	1	100,000	10,000,000,000	1,000,000,000,000,000

As you can see, each time the exponent increases by 1, the number of steps is multiplied by an additional order of magnitude (factor of 10). That is, if N is made 10 times greater, the work involved in an N^2 algorithm increases by a factor of 100, and the work involved in an N^3 algorithm increases by a factor of 1,000. To put this in more concrete terms, an algorithm with a doubly-nested loop, in which each loop depends on the number of data values, takes 1,000 steps for 10 input values and 1 quadrillion steps for 100,000 values. On a computer that executes 1 billion instructions per second, the latter case would take more than 10 days to run.

The table also shows that the steps outside of the innermost loop account for an insignificant portion of the total number of steps as N gets bigger. Because the innermost loop dominates the total time, we classify the complexity of an algorithm according to the highest order of N that appears in its complexity expression, called the *order of magnitude*, or simply the *order* of that expression. So we

continued ▼

Analysis of Algorithms

talk about algorithms having "order N-squared complexity" (or cubed or so on) or we describe them with what is called *Big-O notation*. We express the complexity by putting the highest order term in parentheses with a capital O in front. For example, O(1) is constant time; O(N) is linear time; O(N^2) is quadratic time; and O(N^3) is cubic time.

Determining the complexities of different algorithms allows us to compare the work they require without having to program and execute them. For example, if you had an O(N^2) algorithm and a linear algorithm that performed the same task, you probably would choose the linear algorithm. We say *probably* because an O(N^2) algorithm actually may execute fewer steps than an O(N) algorithm for small values of N. Remember that if the size factor N is small, the constants and lower-order terms in the complexity expression may be significant.

Let's look at an example. Suppose that algorithm A is O(N^2) and that algorithm B is O(N). For large values of N, we would normally choose algorithm B because it requires less work than A. But suppose that in algorithm B, S_0 = 1,000 and S_1 = 1,000. If N = 1, then algorithm B takes 2,000 steps to execute. Now suppose that for algorithm A, S_0 = 10, S_1 = 10, and S_2 = 10. If N = 1, then algorithm A takes only 30 steps. Here is a table that compares the number of steps taken by these two algorithms for different values of N.

N	Algorithm A	Algorithm B
1	30	2,000
2	70	3,000
3	130	4,000
10	1,110	11,000
20	4,210	21,000
30	9,310	31,000
50	25,510	51,000
100	101,010	101,000
1,000	10,010,010	1,001,000
10,000	1,000,100,010	10,001,000

From this table we can see that the O(N^2) algorithm A is actually faster than the O(N) algorithm B, up to the point that N equals 100. Beyond that point, algorithm B becomes more efficient. Thus, if we know that N is always less than 100 in a particular problem, we would choose algorithm A. For example, if the size factor N is the number of test scores on an exam and the class size is limited to 30 students, algorithm A would be more efficient. On the other hand, if N is the number of scores at a university with 25,000 students, we would choose algorithm B.

Constant, linear, quadratic, and cubic expressions are all examples of *polynomial* expressions. Algorithms whose complexity is characterized by such expressions are therefore said to execute in

continued ▼

Analysis of Algorithms

polynomial time and form a broad class of algorithms that encompasses everything we've discussed so far.

In addition to polynomial-time algorithms, we encounter a logarithmic-time algorithm in Chapter 12. There are also factorial ($O(N!)$), exponential ($O(N^N)$), and hyperexponential ($O(N^{N^N})$) class algorithms, which can require vast amounts of time to execute and are beyond the scope of this book. For now, the important point to remember is that different algorithms that solve the same problem can vary significantly in the amount of work they do.

Problem-Solving Case Study

Average Income by Gender

Problem   You've been hired by a law firm that is working on a sex discrimination case. Your firm has obtained a file of incomes, `gender.dat`, which contains the salaries for every employee in the company being sued. Each salary amount is preceded by `'F'` for female or `'M'` for male. As a first pass in the analysis of this data, you've been asked to compute the average income for females and the average income for males. The output should be saved on a file to be reviewed later.

Brainstorming   Most of the nouns in this problem statement relate to the reason for the problem, not the problem itself. There are two file objects, one for input and one for output. The result of the application is a pair of averages, one for males and one for females. These averages are `double` values, not classes. Therefore, we only have three classes.

Filtering   No filtering is necessary in a problem this simple.

Scenarios   What happens when we see an `'F'`? We add the corresponding salary to the female sum. Otherwise, we add the salary to the male sum. When all of the figures have been read and summed, we calculate the average female's salary and the average male's salary. Calculate the average—we mustn't forget to keep track of how many males and females there are. All the responsibility for this application lies in the application class; let's call it class `Incomes`. Because there is no event processing in this application and there is only one class, all the processing is done in class `Incomes`.

CRC card

Class Name: *Incomes*		Superclass: *Object*	Subclasses:
Responsibilities		**Collaborations**	
Prepare the file for input		*FileReader, BufferedReader*	
Prepare the file for output		*FileWriter, PrintWriter*	
Calculate the averages		*BufferedReader*	
Write results to file		*PrintWriter*	

Responsibility Algorithms

The algorithms for preparing the input and output files are very straightforward.

Prepare File for Input   Level 1

```
Declare BufferedReader, inFile
Instantiate inFile, "incomes.dat"
```

Prepare File for Output   Level 1

```
Declare PrintWriter, outFile
Instantiate outFile, "results.dat"
```

Calculating the averages is more difficult. We remember the basic algorithm from application `RainFall`. To calculate a single average we sum the values and divide by the number of values. In that problem the processing was done in the event handler for the input button. Here we must explicitly write the loop, which involves a loop with several subtasks, because we must calculate two averages instead of just one. We use our checklist of questions to develop these subtasks in detail.

1. *What is the condition that ends the loop?* The termination condition is EOF on the file `inFile`. It leads to the following loop test (in pseudocode).

```
while NOT EOF on inFile
```

2. *How should the condition be initialized?* A priming read must take place to enter a gender code and amount.

3. *How should the condition be updated?* We must input a new data line with a gender code and amount at the end of each iteration.

   We must input each data line as a string. Then we need to extract the gender code and amount from the string. Because the input of the line is a single operation, we can combine the priming read and the updating read using Java's assignment expression shortcut. Here's the resulting algorithm:

   > **while** Reading inLine from inFile does not return EOF
   >   Extract gender code and amount from inLine
   >   : (Process being repeated)

4. *What is the process being repeated?* From our knowledge of how to compute an average, we know that we have to count the number of amounts and divide this number into the sum of the amounts. Because we have to do this separately for females and males, the process consists of four parts: counting the females and summing their incomes, and then counting the males and summing their incomes. We develop each of these in turn.

5. *How should the process be initialized?* `femaleCount` and `femaleSum` should be set to zero. `maleCount` and `maleSum` should also be set to zero.

6. *How should the process be updated?* When a female income is input, `femaleCount` is incremented, and the income is added to `femaleSum`. Otherwise, an income is assumed to be for a male, so `maleCount` is incremented, and the amount is added to `maleSum`.

7. *What is the state of the program on exiting the loop?* The file `inFile` is at EOF; `femaleCount` contains the number of input values preceded by `'F'`; `femaleSum` contains the sum of the values preceded by `'F'`; `maleCount` contains the number of values not preceded by `'F'`; and `maleSum` holds the sum of those values.

   From the description of how the process is updated, we can see that the loop must contain an *if* structure, with one branch for female incomes and the other for male incomes. Each branch must increment the correct event counter and add the income amount to the correct total. After the loop has exited, we have enough information to compute the averages, dividing each total by the corresponding count.

Now we're ready to write the complete algorithm:

....

Calculate the Averages   Level 1

> Initialize variables
> **while** Reading inLine from inFile does not return EOF
>   Extract gender code and amount from inLine
>   Update process
> Compute average incomes

Initialize Variables   Level 2

Set femaleCount to 0
Set femaleSum to 0.0
Set maleCount to 0
Set maleSum to 0.0

Extract Gender Code and Amount from inLine

Set gender to char at position 0 of inLine
Set amountString to substring of inLine starting at position 2, through end of inLine
Set amount to amountString converted to double

We haven't discussed the operation of getting a single character from a string. The `String` class provides a value-returning instance method called `charAt` that takes an `int` value as its parameter. The `int` specifies the position of the character to be copied from the string and the method returns the character as a value of type `char`. We can thus implement the first line of this algorithm with the statement:

```
gender = inLine.charAt(0);
```

Update Process

if gender is 'F'
     Increment femaleCount
     Add amount to femaleSum
else
     Increment maleCount
     Add amount to maleSum

Compute Average Incomes

Set femaleAverage to femaleSum / (double)femaleCount
Set maleAverage to maleSum / (double)maleCount

Write Results to File   Level 1

Println "For " + femaleCount + " females, the average income is " + femaleAvg + "."
Println "For " + maleCount + " males, the average income is " + maleAvg + "."

All of these algorithms depend on the file being created in a certain way. These assumptions should be stated in a special section of the design.

Assumptions There is at least one male and one female among all the data sets. The data sets are all entered properly in the input file, with the gender code in the first character position on each line and a floating point number starting in the third character position. The only gender codes in the file are 'M' and 'F'—any other codes are counted as 'M'. (This last assumption invalidates the results if there are any illegal codes in the data. Case Study Follow-Up Exercise 1 asks you to change the program as necessary to address this problem.)

Before we write the program, we need to look back over the algorithm and see if there are repeating processes that should be encapsulated into helper methods. The summing and counting are the same for both males and females. There could be a summing and counting method, but it would need three parameters for a two statement method body. Let's just code it inline.

Here is the code for the application.

```java
import java.io.*;                           // File types

public class Incomes
// This program reads a file of income amounts classified by
//   gender and computes the average income for each gender
{
  public static void main(String[] args) throws IOException
  {
    int femaleCount;                        // Keeps count of females
    double femaleSum;                       // Keeps total of salaries
    double femaleAvg;                       // Holds average salary
    int maleCount;                          // Keeps count of males
    double maleSum;                         // Keeps total of salaries
    double maleAvg;                         // Holds average salary
    String inLine;                          // A line from the file
    char gender;                            // Indicates gender
    String amountString;                    // Amount part of input line
    double amount;                          // Salary amount
    BufferedReader inFile;                  // Input data file
    PrintWriter outFile;                    // Output data file

    // Prepare files for reading and writing
    inFile = new BufferedReader(new FileReader("gender.dat"));
    outFile = new PrintWriter(new FileWriter("results.dat"));

    // Calculate averages
    // Initialize process
    femaleCount = 0;
    femaleSum = 0.0;
    maleCount = 0;
```

```
            maleSum = 0.0;

            while ((inLine = inFile.readLine()) != null)
            {
              // Update process
              // Extract gender code and amount from input line
              gender = inLine.charAt(0);              // Gender is the first character
              //  Amount begins in the third position.
              amountString = inLine.substring(2, inLine.length());
              amount = Double.valueOf(amountString).doubleValue();

              // Process amount based on gender code
              if (gender == 'F')
              { // female
                femaleCount++;
                femaleSum = femaleSum + amount;
              }
              else
              { // male
                maleCount++;
                maleSum = maleSum + amount;
              }
            }

            // Compute average incomes
            femaleAvg = femaleSum / (double)femaleCount;
            maleAvg = maleSum / (double)maleCount;

            // Write results
            outFile.println ("For " + femaleCount + " females, the average income "
              "is " +  femaleAvg + ".")
            outFile.println ("For " + maleCount + " males, the average income is " +
              maleAvg + ".")
            inFile.close();
            outFile.close();
          }
        }
```

Testing   Given the following data on file `incomes.dat`:

```
F 24345.23
F 17812.99
F 59207.34
M 38119.29
```

```
M 29228.99
M 89101.73
F 47237.83
M 31820.04
F 32933.73
F 45910.86
```

program `Incomes` writes the following on file `results.dat`:

```
For 6 females, the average income is 37907.99666666667.
For 4 males, the average income is 47067.51250000004.
```

With an EOF-controlled loop, the obvious test cases are a file with data (as shown above) and an empty file. We should test input values of both `'F'` and `'M'` for the gender, and try some typical data (so we can compare the results with our hand-calculated values) and some atypical data (to see how the process behaves). The application assumed that the data file included at least one woman and one man, but in general, an atypical data set for testing a counting operation is an empty file, which should result in a count of zero. Any other result for the count indicates an error. For a summing operation, atypical data might include negative or zero values.

The `Incomes` program is not designed to handle empty files or negative income values; the assumption that the file was not empty and contained at least one male and one female was written in the design. An empty file causes both `femaleCount` and `maleCount` to equal zero at the end of the loop. Although this is correct, the statements that compute average income cause the program to produce invalid results (infinity) because they divide by zero. And a negative income would be treated like any other value, even though it is probably a mistake.

To correct these problems, we should insert *if* statements to test for the error conditions at the appropriate points in the program. When an error is detected, the program should either display an error message or write an error report to a file instead of carrying out the usual computation. This prevents a crash and allows the program to keep running. We call a program that can recover from erroneous input and keep running a *robust program*.

Testing and Debugging

Loop-Testing Strategy

Even if a loop has been properly designed, it is still important to test it rigorously, because the chance of an error creeping in during the implementation phase is always present. To test a loop thoroughly, we must check for the proper execution of both a single iteration and multiple iterations.

Remember that a loop has seven parts (corresponding to the seven questions in our checklist). A test strategy must test each part. Although all seven parts aren't implemented separately in every loop, the checklist reminds us that some loop operations serve multiple purposes, each of which should be tested. For example, the incrementing statement in a count-controlled loop may be updating both the process and the ending condition. So it's important to verify that it performs both actions properly with respect to the rest of the loop.

Consider what the acceptable ranges of variables are and what sorts of I/O operations you expect to see in the loop. Try to devise data sets that could cause the variables to go out of range or leave the files in unexpected states.

It's also good practice to test a loop for four special cases: (1) when the loop is skipped entirely, (2) when the loop body is executed just once, (3) when the loop executes some normal number of times, and (4) when the loop fails to exit.

Statements following a loop often depend on its processing. If a loop can be skipped, those statements may not execute correctly. If it's possible to execute a single iteration of a loop, the results can show whether the body performs correctly in the absence of the effects of previous iterations, which can be very helpful when you're trying to isolate the source of an error. Obviously, it's important to test a loop under normal conditions, with a wide variety of inputs. If possible, you should test the loop with real data in addition to mock data sets. Count-controlled loops should be tested to be sure they execute exactly the right number of times. And finally, if there is any chance that a loop might never exit, your test data should try to make that happen.

Testing a program can be as challenging as writing it. To test a program, you need to step back, take a fresh look at what you've written, and then attack it in every way possible to make it fail. This isn't always easy to do, but it's necessary if your programs are going to be reliable. (A *reliable program* is one that works consistently and without errors regardless of whether the input data is valid or invalid.)

Test Plans Involving Loops

In Chapter 6, we introduced formal test plans and discussed the testing of branches. Those guidelines still apply to programs with loops, but here we provide some additional guidelines that are specific to loops. In general, the goal of testing a loop is to verify that it behaves as expected.

Unfortunately, when a loop is embedded in a larger program, it sometimes is difficult to control and observe the conditions under which the loop executes using test data and output alone. In come cases we must use indirect tests. For example, if a loop reads floating-point values from a file and prints their average without echo-printing them, you cannot tell directly that the loop processes all the data. If the data values in the file are all the same, then the average appears correct as long as even one of them is processed. You must construct the input file so that the average is a unique value that can be arrived at only by processing all the data.

What we would like to do to simplify our testing of such loops is to observe the values of the variables involved in the loop at the start of each iteration. How can we observe the values of variables while a program is running? Two common techniques are the use of the system's *debugger* program and the use of extra output statements designed solely for debugging purposes. We discuss these techniques in the section Testing and Debugging Hints.

Now let's look at some test cases that are specific to the different types of loops that we've seen in this chapter.

Count-Controlled Loops When a loop is count-controlled, you should include a test case that specifies the output for all the iterations. It may help to add an extra column to the test plan that lists the iteration number. If the loop reads data and outputs a result, then each input value should produce a different output to make it easier to spot errors. For example, in a loop that is supposed to read and print 100 data values, it is easier to tell that the loop executes the correct number of iterations when the values are 1, 2, 3 ... 100 than if they are all the same.

If the program inputs the iteration count for the loop, you need to test the cases in which the count is invalid. For example, when a negative number is input, an error message should be output and the loop should be skipped. You should also test various valid cases. When a count of 0 is input, the loop should be skipped; when a count of 1 is input, the loop should execute once; and when some typical number of iterations is input, the loop should execute the specified number of times.

Event-Controlled Loops In an event-controlled loop, you should test the situation in which the event occurs before the loop, in the first iteration, and in a typical number of iterations. For example, if the event is that EOF occurs, then try an empty file, a file with one data set, and another with several data sets. If your testing involves reading from test files, you should attach printed copies of the files to the test plan and identify each in some way so that the plan can refer to them. It also helps to identify where each iteration begins in the Input and Expected Output columns of the test plan.

When the event is the input of a sentinel value, you need the following test cases: The sentinel is the only data set, the sentinel follows one data set, and the sentinel follows a typical number of data sets. Given that sentinel-controlled loops involve a priming read, it is especially important to verify that the first and last data sets are processed properly.

Testing and Debugging Hints

1. For each file that a program uses, check that all five of the required steps are performed: import the package `java.io.*`, declare an object of the given file class, instantiate the file object, use the methods associated with the file object to perform input or output operations, and close the file when you are done using it.

2. Remember that the constructor for a `FileReader` or a `FileWriter` can be passed the name of the disk file, but the constructor for a `BufferedReader` must be passed an object of type `FileReader` and the constructor for a `PrintWriter` must be passed a `FileWriter` object.

3. Keep in mind that if you pass an integer value to the `write` method of a `FileWriter` object, the number is converted into a Unicode character. In contrast, the `print` method of a `PrintWriter` object outputs the integer as a string of digit characters.

4. If you use file I/O, remember that `main` must have the `throws IOException` clause appended to its heading.

5. Plan your test data carefully to test all sections of a program.

6. Beware of infinite loops, where the expression in the *while* statement never becomes `false`. The symptom: the program doesn't stop.

 If you have created an infinite loop, check your logic and the syntax of your loops. Be sure there's no semicolon immediately after the right parenthesis of the *while* condition:

```
while (expression);              // Wrong
   statement;
```

 This semicolon causes an infinite loop in most cases; the compiler thinks the loop body is the null statement (the do-nothing statement composed only of a semicolon). In a count-controlled loop, make sure the loop control variable is incremented within the loop. In a flag-controlled loop, make sure the flag eventually changes.

7. Check the loop-termination condition carefully, and be sure that something in the loop causes it to be met. Watch closely for values that cause one iteration too many or too few (the "off-by–1" syndrome).

8. Write out the consistent, predictable part of a loop's behavior in each iteration. Look for patterns that this establishes. Are they just what you want? Perform an algorithm walk-through to verify that all of the appropriate conditions occur in the right places.

9. Trace the execution of the loop by hand with a code walk-through. Simulate the first few passes and the last few passes very carefully to see how the loop really behaves.

10. Use a *debugger* if your system provides one. A debugger is a program that runs your program in "slow motion," allowing you to execute one instruction at a time and to examine the contents of variables as they change. If you haven't already done so, check to see if a debugger is available on your system.

11. If all else fails, use *debug output statements*—output statements inserted into a program to help debug it. They output a message to a separate file that indicates the flow of execution in the program or reports the values of variables at certain points in the program.

 For example, if you want to know the value of variable `beta` at a certain point in a program, you could insert this statement:

```
logFile.println("beta = " + beta);
```

 If this output statement is in a loop, you will get as many values of `beta` on the file associated with `logFile` as there are iterations of the body of the loop.

 After you have debugged your program, you can remove the debug output statements or just precede them with `//` so that they'll be treated as comments.

(This practice is referred to as commenting out a piece of code.) You can remove the double slashes if you need to use the statements again.

12. An ounce of prevention is worth a pound of debugging. Use the checklist questions and design your loop correctly at the outset. It may seem like extra work, but it pays off in the long run.

Summary of Classes

Package Name

Class Name	Comments
`java.lang`	Automatically imported to every Java program
`String`	
Value-Returning Instance Methods:	
`valueOf(`*any numeric type*`)`	Class method that returns the string representation of its argument
`java.io`	
`BufferedReader throws IOException`	
Constructor: `BufferedReader(FileReader)`	
Value-Returning Instance Methods:	
`read()`	Returns `int`
`readLine`	Returns `String`
Void Instance Methods:	
`close()`	
`skip(long)`	
`FileReader`	Some methods can throw `IOException`
Constructor: `FileReader(String)`	
Value-Returning Instance Method:	
`read()`	Returns `int`
Void Instance Methods:	
`close()`	
`skip(long)`	
`FileWriter`	Some methods can throw `IOException`

(continued)

Package Name

Class Name	Comments

Constructor: `FileWriter(String)`

Void Instance Methods:

```
close()
flush()
write(char)
```

PrintWriter

Constructor: `PrintWriter(FileWriter)`

Void Instance Methods:

```
close()
flush()
print(char)
print(double)
print(float)
print(int)
print(long)
print(String)
println(char)
println(double)
println(float)
println(int)
println(long)
println(String)
write(char)
```

Summary

Programs operate on data. If data and programs are kept separate, the data is available to use with other programs, and the same program can be run with different sets of data. Noninteractive input/output allows data to be prepared before a program is run and allows the program to run again with the same data in the event that a problem crops up during processing.

Data files are often used for noninteractive processing and to permit the output from one program to be used as input to another program. In Java we use four types of file classes: `FileReader`, `FileWriter`, `BufferedReader`, and `PrintWriter`.

FileReader and FileWriter work with individual characters using the read and write methods, respectively. BufferedReader adds to FileReader a readLine method that inputs an entire line as a string. PrintWriter adds the print and println methods to FileWriter that enable the output of all the standard Java data types and classes.

To use files, you must do five things: (1) import the package java.io.*, (2) declare the file variables along with your other variable declarations, (3) instantiate each file object, (4) use methods associated with each file object to read or write it, and (5) call the close method associated with each file object when you are done with it. When using files, we must forward exceptions to the JVM by adding a throws IOException clause to the heading of main and any other method that uses the file operations.

The *while* statement is a looping construct that allows the program to repeat a statement as long as the value of an expression is true. When the value of the expression becomes false, the statement is skipped, and execution continues with the first statement following the loop.

With the *while* statement you can construct several types of loops that you use again and again. These types of loops fall into two categories: count-controlled loops and event-controlled loops.

In a count-controlled loop, the loop body is repeated a specified number of times. You initialize a counter variable right before the *while* statement. This variable is the loop control variable. The control variable is tested against the limit in the *while* expression. The last statement in the loop body increments the control variable.

Event-controlled loops continue executing until something inside the body signals that the looping process should stop. Event-controlled loops include those that test for a sentinel value in the data, end-of-file, or a change in a flag variable.

Sentinel-controlled loops are input loops that use a special data value as a signal to stop reading. EOF-controlled loops are loops that continue to input (and process) data values until there is no more data. To implement them with a *while* statement, you must test the value returned by the input method. The read method returns −1 when it reaches EOF and readLine returns null. Sentinel controlled loops usually require a priming read just before entry into the loop and an updating read at the end of the loop; however, Java's assignment expression can be used as a shortcut to combine these two input operations into one within the loop test. The assignment expression shortcut should be used only in simple cases where the intent is clear to a human reader. Otherwise, it is preferable to write a sentinel-controlled loop in the usual manner.

A flag is a variable that is set in one part of the program and tested in another. In a flag-controlled loop, you must set the flag before the loop begins, test it in the *while* expression, and change it somewhere in the body of the loop.

Counting is a looping operation that keeps track of how many times a loop is repeated or how many times some event occurs. This count can be used in computations or to control the loop. A counter is a variable that is used for counting. It may be the loop control variable in a count-controlled loop, an iteration counter in a counting loop, or an event counter that counts the number of times a particular condition occurs in a loop.

Summing is a looping operation that keeps a running total of certain values. It is like counting in that the variable that holds the sum is initialized outside the loop. The summing operation, however, adds up unknown values; the counting operation adds a constant (1) to the counter each time.

When you design a loop, there are seven points to consider: how the termination condition is initialized, tested, and updated; how the process in the loop is initialized, performed, and updated; and the state of the program upon loop exit. By answering the checklist questions, you can bring each of these points into focus.

To design a nested loop structure, begin with the outermost loop. When you get to where the inner loop must appear, make it a separate module and come back to its design later.

Quick Check

1. If a program is going to input 1,000 integer numbers, is interactive input appropriate? (p. 387)
2. What does a constructor for an input file do? (pp. 388–389)
3. What does the following series of statements write on the file `fileOut`? (pp. 390–391)

```
fileOut.write('W');
fileOut.write(88);
fileOut.write("  What letter comes next?");
```

4. What is the statement that reads in a string and stores the integer equivalent into `number`? (p. 398)
5. Write the first line of a *while* statement that loops until the value of the Boolean variable `done` becomes `true`. (p. 403)
6. What are the four parts of a count-controlled loop? (pp. 406–407)
7. Should you use a priming read with an EOF-controlled loop? (pp. 410–412)
8. How is a sentinel used to control a loop? (pp. 407–408)
9. What is the difference between a counting operation in a loop and a summing operation in a loop? (pp. 412–414)
10. What is the difference between a loop control variable and an event counter? (pp. 412–415)
11. What kind of loop would you use in a program that reads the closing price of a stock for each day of the week? (pp. 415–417)
12. How would you extend the loop in Question 11 to make it read prices for 52 weeks? (pp. 415–418)

Answers

1. No. File input is more appropriate for programs that input large amounts of data. 2. The constructor associates the name of the disk file with the file variable used in the program, and places the file pointer at the first piece of data in the file. 3. WX What letter comes next? 4. number = Integer.valueOf(infile.readln()).intValue();

5. `while ( !done )`   6. The process being repeated, plus initializing, testing, and incrementing the loop control variable.   7. Yes.   8. A sentinel is a value that is used to signal the end of data. The loop expression compares each data value to the sentinel and the loop continues until they are equal.   9. A counting operation increments by a fixed value with each iteration of the loop; a summing operation adds unknown values to the total.   10. A loop-control variable controls the loop; an event counter simply counts certain events during execution of the loop.   11. Because there are five days in a business week, you would use a count-controlled loop that runs from 1 to 5.   12. Nest the original loop inside a count-controlled loop that runs from 1 to 52.

Exam Preparation Exercises

1. What are the five steps in using file input?
2. What is the meaning of the parameter for the constructor for file classes `FileReader` and `FileWriter`?
3. Where should the file declarations and the calls to the appropriate constructors be placed in a program? Why?
4. What does the following statement do?

```
fileOut.flush();
```

5. What does the `read` method for class `FileReader` return?
6. a. What value does the `read` method return?
   b. What value does the `readLine` method return?
   c. Distinguish between a `null` string and an empty string.
7. Explain the difference between a loop and a branch.
8. What does the following loop print out? (`number` is of type `int`.)

```
number = 1;
while (number < 11)
{
   number++;
   out.println(number);
}
```

9. By rearranging the order of the statements (don't change the way they are written), make the loop in Exercise 8 print the numbers from 1 through 10.
10. When the following code is executed, how many iterations of the loop are performed?

```
number = 2;
done = false;
while ( !done )
{
   number = number * 2;
   if (number > 64)
      done = true;
}
```

11. What is the output of this nested-loop structure?

```
i = 4;
while (i >= 1)
{
    j = 2;
    while (j >= 1)
    {
        out.print (j + " ");
        j--;
    }
    out.println(i);
    i--;
}
```

12. The following code segment is supposed to write out the even numbers between 1 and 15. (n is an int variable.) The code has two flaws in it.

```
n = 2;
while (n != 15)
{
    n = n + 2;
    out.print(n + " ");
}
```

   a. What is the output of the code as written?
   b. Correct the code so that it works as intended.

13. The following code segment is supposed to copy one line from file infile to file outfile.

```
inChar = (char)infile.read();
while (inChar != '\n')
{
    inChar = (char)infile.read();
    outfile.write(inChar);
}
```

   a. What is the output if the input line consists of the characters ABCDE?
   b. Rewrite the code so that it works properly.

14. Does the following program segment need any priming reads? If not, explain why. If so, add the input statement(s) in the proper place. (letter is of type char.)

```
while (datum != -1)
{
    letter = (char) datum;
    while (letter != '\n')
```

```
{
    outFile.print(letter);
    inFile.read(datum);
    letter = (char)datum;
}
outFile.println;
outFile.println("Another line read...");
datum = inFile.read();
}
```

15. What sentinel value would you choose for a program that reads telephone numbers as integers?

16. Consider the following code segment:

```
sum = 0;
i = 1;
limit = 8;
finished = false;
while (i <= limit && !finished)
{
    number = Integer.valueOf(dataFile.readLine()).intValue();
    if (number > 0)
        sum = sum + number;
    else if (number == 0)
        finished = true;
    i++;
}
out.add(new Label("End of test. " + sum + ' ' + number));
```

and these data values (written one per line):

```
5   6   -3   7   -4   0   5   8   9
```

a. What are the contents of sum and number after exit from the loop?
b. Does the data fully test the program? Explain your answer.

17. What is the output of the following program segment? (All variables are of type int.)

```
i = 1;
while (i <= 5)
{
    sum = 0;
    j = 1;
    while (j <= i)
    {
        sum = sum + j;
        j++;
    }
```

```
        System.out.print(sum + " ");
        i++;
    }
```

18. The physical order of a program is the order in which the statements are _____ (written, executed).

19. The logical order of a program is the order in which the statements are _____ (written, executed).

20. a. What are the two major types of loops?
    b. Distinguish between a count-controlled loop and an event-controlled loop.
    c. What happens if you forget to increment the loop control variable in a count-controlled loop?
    d. What happens if you forget to change the event within the body of an event controlled-loop?
    e. Name three kinds of event-controlled loops.

21. Distinguish between an iteration counter and an event counter.

22. a. What is an assignment expression?
    b. Write the assignment expression that can be used to control a reading loop with method `read`.
    c. Write the assignment expression that can be used to control a reading loop with method `readLine`.

Programming Warm-Up Exercises

1. Write the statements that associate an object of class `FileReader` with file `infile.dat`.

2. Write the statements that associate an object of class `BufferedReader` with file `infile.dat`.

3. Write the statements that associate an object of `PrintWriter` with file `outfile.dat`.

4. What does the following series of statements write on the file `fileOut`?

```
fileOut.write('W');
fileOut.write('\n');
fileOut.write(88);
fileOut.write('\n');
fileOut.write("  What letter comes next?");
```

5. What is printed by the following series of statements?

```
fileOutPr.println('W');
fileOutPr.print(88);
fileOutPr.print("  What letter comes next?");
```

6. Write a code fragment that reads two characters from `fileIn` and stores them in two `char` variables, `first` and `second`. (`fileIn`, of class `FileReader` and has been declared and given a value.)
7. Write a code fragment that reads a line from `fileInBuf` and prints it on `fileOut` with blank lines before and after it.
8. Write the statements that close `fileOut` and associate it with file `dataOut.dat`.
9. Write a program segment that sets a Boolean variable `dangerous` to `true` and stops reading data if `pressure` (a `float` variable being read in) exceeds 510.0. Use `dangerous` as a flag to control the loop.
10. Here is a simple count-controlled loop:

```
count = 1;
while (count < 20)
   count++;
```

a. List three ways of changing the loop so that it executes 20 times instead of 19.
b. Which of those changes makes the value of `count` range from 1 through 21?
11. Write a program segment that counts the number of times the integer 28 occurs in a file of 100 integers.
12. Write a nested loop code segment that produces this output:

```
1
1 2
1 2 3
1 2 3 4
```

13. Write a program segment that reads a file of student scores for a class (any size) and finds the class average.
14. Write a program segment that reads in integers and then counts and prints out the number of positive integers and the number of negative integers. If a value is zero, it should not be counted. The process should continue until end-of-file occurs.
15. Write a program segment that adds up the even integers from 16 through 26, inclusive.
16. Write a statement(s) that increments `count` by 1 and sets it back to 0 when it reaches 13.
17. Write a program segment that prints out the sequence of all the hour and minute combinations in a day, starting with 1:00 A.M. and ending with 12:59 A.M.
18. Rewrite the code segment for Exercise 17 so that it prints the times in 10-minute intervals.
19. Write a loop to count the number of not-equal operators (!=) in a file that contains a Java program. Your algorithm should count the number of times an exclamation mark (!) followed by an equal sign (=) appears in the input. Read

the input file one character at a time, keeping track of the two most recent characters, the current value, and the previous value. In each iteration of the loop, a new current value is read and the old current value becomes the previous value. When EOF is reached, the loop is finished.

Programming Problems

1. Design and write a Java application that inputs an integer and a character from the screen. The output should be a diamond on the screen composed of the character and extending the width specified by the integer. For example, if the integer is 11 and the character is an asterisk (*), the diamond would look like this:

```
          *
        * * *
      * * * * *
    * * * * * * *
  * * * * * * * * *
* * * * * * * * * * *
  * * * * * * * * *
    * * * * * * *
      * * * * *
        * * *
          *
```

   If the input integer is an even number, it should be increased to the next odd number. Use meaningful variable names, proper indentation, appropriate comments, and good prompting messages. Use a `Frame` object for input and a `PrintWriter` object for output.

2. Write a design and a Java application that inputs an integer larger than 1 and calculates the sum of the squares from 1 to that integer. For example, if the integer equals 4, the sum of the squares is 30 (1 + 4 + 9 + 16). The output should be the value of the integer and the sum, properly labeled on the screen. The program should repeat this process for several input values. Use buttons and screen input and output.

3. You are putting together some music tapes for a party. You've arranged a list of songs in the order in which you want to play them. However, you would like to minimize the empty tape left at the end of each side of a cassette (the cassette plays for 45 minutes on a side). So you want to figure out the total time for a group of songs and see how well they fit. Write a design and a Java application to help you do this. The data is on file `songs.dat`. The time is entered as seconds. For example, if a song takes 7 minutes and 42 seconds to play, the data entered for that song would be

   462

   After all the data has been read, the program should print a message indicating the time remaining on the tape.

The output should be in the form of a table with columns and headings written on a file. For example,

Song Number	Song Time Minutes	Seconds	Total Time Minutes	Seconds
1	5	10	5	10
2	7	42	12	52
5	4	19	17	11
3	4	33	21	44
4	10	27	32	11
6	8	55	41	6

There are 3 minutes and 54 seconds of tape left on the 45-minute tape.

Note that the output converts the input from seconds to minutes and seconds.

4. Design and write an application that prints out the approximate number of words in a file of text. For our purposes, this is the same as the number of gaps following words. A *gap* is defined as one or more spaces in a row, so a sequence of spaces counts as just one gap. The newline character also counts as a gap. Anything other than a space or newline is considered to be part of a word. For example, there are 13 words in this sentence, according to our definition. The program should echo-print the data.

Solve this problem with two different programs:

a. Use a String object into which you input each line as a string. This approach is quite straightforward.

b. Assume the String class does not exist, and input the data one character at a time. This approach is more complicated. (*Hint:* Count a space as a gap only if the previous character read is something other than a space.)

Use meaningful variable names, proper indentation, and appropriate comments. Thoroughly test the programs with your own data sets.

Case Study Follow-Up Exercises

1. Change the Incomes program in the following ways.

a. The program prints an error message when a negative income value is input and then goes on processing any remaining data. Do not include the erroneous data in any of the calculations. Thoroughly test the modified program with your own data sets.

b. The program does not crash when there are no males in the input file or no females (or the file is empty). Instead, it prints an appropriate error message. Test the revised program with your own data sets.

c. The program rejects data sets that are coded with a letter other than 'F' or 'M' and prints an error message before continuing to process the remaining data. The program also prints a message indicating the number of erroneous data sets encountered in the file.

2. Develop a thorough set of test data for the Incomes program as modified in Exercise 1.

3. Rather than put the responsibility for reading in the application, redesign this problem to extend BufferedReader with two new methods, readGender and readSalary. Code and test your redesign.

4. Use the String methods valueOf, indexOf, and substring to print only two decimal places for all floating-point values. To accomplish this conversion, you must do the following tasks:

- Convert the floating point value to a string using the valueOf method.
- Find the location of the decimal point using the indexOf method.
- Create a new string that is a substring of the original with only two characters following the decimal point using the substring method.

Additional Control Structures and Exceptions

Goals

- To be able to write a *switch* statement for a multi-way branching problem.

- To be able to write a *do* statement and contrast it with a *while* statement.

- To be able to write a *for* statement as an alternative to a *while* statement.

- To be able to choose the most appropriate looping statement for a given problem.

- To be aware of Java's additional operators and their place in the precedence hierarchy with respect to each other.

- To be able to use the Java exception-handling mechanism using *try* and *catch*.

- To be able to define an exception class and throw an exception.

In Chapters 6 and 9, we introduced Java statements for the selection and loop control structures. In some cases, we introduced more than one way of implementing these structures. For example, selection may be implemented by an *if* structure. The *if*-(then) is sufficient to implement any selection structure, but Java provides the *if-else* for convenience because the two-way branch is frequently used in programming.

This chapter introduces four new statements that are also nonessential to, but nonetheless convenient for, programming. One, the *switch* statement, makes it easier to write selection structures that have many branches. Two new looping statements, *for* and *do*, make it easier to program certain types of loops.

This chapter also covers the try-catch statement used for exception-handling in Java. Rather than continuing to forward exceptions, we show how to handle one. We also show you how to generate exceptions of your own.

Finally, we examine the remaining operators in Java and their place in the precedence hierarchy.

10.1 Additional Control Structures

The switch Statement

Switch expression The expression whose value determines which *switch* label is selected. It must be an integer type other than `long`.

The *switch* statement is a selection control structure for multiway branches. A *switch* is similar to nested *if* statements. The value of a switch expression—an integer expression—determines which of the branches is executed. Look at the following example *switch* statement:

```
switch (digit)              // The switch expression is (digit)
{
   case 1 : Statement1;     // Statement1 is executed if digit is 1
            break;          // Go to Statement5
   case 2 :
   case 3 : Statement2;     // Statement 2 is executed if digit is 2 or 3
            break;          // Go to Statement5
   case 4 : Statement3;     // Statement3 is executed if digit is 4
            break;          // Go to Statement5
   default: Statement4;     // Else execute Statement4 and go to Statement5
}
Statement5;                 // Always executed
```

In this example, `digit` is the *switch* expression. The statement means "If `digit` is 1, execute Statement1 and break out of the switch statement and continue with Statement5. If `digit` is 2 or 3, execute Statement2 and continue with Statement5. If `digit` is 4, execute Statement3 and continue with Statement5. If `digit` is none of the values previously mentioned, execute Statement4 and continue with Statement5." Figure 10.1 shows the flow of control through this statement.

The *break* statement allows control to immediately jump to the statement following the *switch* statement. We see shortly what happens if we omit the *break* statements.

Let's look at the syntax template for the *switch* statement; then we look at what actually happens when it is executed.

The syntax template for the *switch* statement is

SwitchStatement

```
switch  (IntegralExpression )
{
    SwitchLabel . . . Statement   . . .
       .
       .
       .
}
```

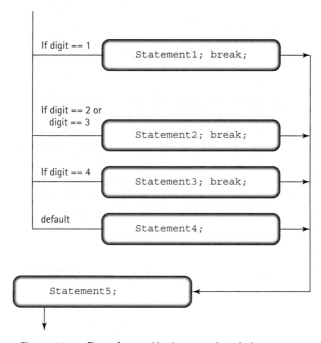

Figure 10.1   *Flow of control in the example switch statement*

IntegralExpression is an expression of one of the types `char`, `byte`, `short`, or `int`. The *switchLabel* in front of a statement is either a *case label* or a *default label:*

SwitchLabel

```
case ConstantExpression :

default :
```

In a case label, ConstantExpression is an expression of type `char`, `byte`, `short`, or `int`, whose operands must be literal or named constants. The following are examples of constant expressions (where `CLASS_SIZE` is a named constant of type `int`):

```
3
CLASS_SIZE
'A'
```

The data type of ConstantExpression is converted, if necessary, to match the type of the *switch* expression.

In our opening example that tests the value of `digit`, the following are the case labels:

```
case 1 :
case 2 :
case 3 :
case 4 :
```

As that example shows, multiple case labels may precede a single branch.

The value resulting from each ConstantExpression within a *switch* statement must be unique. If a value appears more than once among the case labels, a syntax error results. The compiler simply can't determine which of the identical cases to branch to. Also, there can be only one `default` label in a *switch* statement.

Be careful: `case 1` does not mean the first case. We've listed the values in order because that makes the statement easier to read. But Java allows us to place them in any order. The following *switch* statement behaves in exactly the same way as our earlier example.

```
switch (digit)              // The switch expression is (digit)
{
   case 3 :
   case 2 : Statement2;     // Statement2 is executed if digit is 2 or 3
            break;          // Go to Statement5
   case 4 : Statement3;     // Statement3 is executed if digit is 4
            break;          // Go to Statement5
```

```
  case 1 : Statement1;      // Statement1 is executed if digit is 1
           break;           // Go to Statement5
  default  : Statement4;    // Else execute Statement4 and go to Statement5
}
Statement5;                 // Always executed
```

The flow of control through a *switch* statement goes like this. First, the *switch* expression is evaluated. Then each expression beside the reserved word `case` is tested to see if it matches the *switch* expression. If the values match, control branches to the statement associated with that case label (the statement on the other side of the colon). From there, control proceeds sequentially until either a *break* statement or the end of the *switch* statement is encountered. If the value of the *switch* expression doesn't match any case value, then one of two things happens. If there is a `default` label, control branches to the associated statement. If there is no `default` label, the statements in the *switch* are skipped and control simply proceeds to the statement following the entire *switch* statement.

The following *switch* statement prints an appropriate comment based on a student's grade (`grade` is of type `char`). The *switch* expression can be `char` since Java considers `char` to be an integral type because it can be converted to type `int`.

```
switch (grade)
{
  case 'A' :
  case 'B' : outFile.print("Good Work");
             break;
  case 'C' : outFile.print("Average Work");
             break;
  case 'D' :
  case 'F' : outFile.print("Poor Work");
             numberInTrouble++;
             break;              // Unnecessary, but a good habit
}
```

Notice that the final *break* statement is unnecessary. But programmers often include it anyway. One reason is that it's easier to insert another case label at the end if a *break* statement is already present.

If `grade` does not contain one of the specified characters, none of the statements within the *switch* is executed. It would be wise to add a `default` label to account for an invalid grade:

```
switch (grade)
{
  case 'A' :
  case 'B' : outFile.print("Good Work");
             break;
```

```
      case 'C' : outFile.print("Average Work");
               break;
      case 'D' :
      case 'F' : outFile.print("Poor Work");
               numberInTrouble++;
               break;
      default  : outFile.print(grade + " is not a valid letter grade.");
               break;
}
```

A *switch* statement with a *break* statement after each case alternative behaves exactly like an *if-else-if* control structure. For example, our *switch* statement is equivalent to the following code:

```
if (grade == 'A' || grade == 'B')
  outFile.print("Good Work");
else if (grade == 'C')
  outFile.print("Average Work");
else if (grade == 'D' || grade == 'F')
{
  outFile.print("Poor Work");
  numberInTrouble++;
}
else
  outFile.print(grade + " is not a valid letter grade.");
```

Is either of these two versions better than the other? There is no absolute answer to this question. For this particular example, our opinion is that the *switch* statement is easier to understand because of its table-like form. When you are implementing a multiway branching structure, our advice is to use the one that you feel is easiest to read. Keep in mind that Java provides the *switch* statement as a matter of convenience. Don't feel obligated to use a *switch* statement for every multiway branch.

Finally, we said we would look at what happens if we omit the *break* statements inside a *switch* statement. Let's rewrite the preceding code statement as if we forgot to include the *break* statements, and we can see how it behaves:

```
switch (grade)    // Wrong version
{
  case 'A' :
  case 'B' : outFile.print("Good Work");
  case 'C' : outFile.print("Average Work");
  case 'D' :
  case 'F' : outFile.print("Poor Work");
               numberInTrouble++;
  default  : outFile.print(grade + " is not a valid letter grade.");
}
```

If `grade` happens to be `'H'`, control branches to the statement at the `default` label and the output to the file is

```
H is not a valid letter grade.
```

Unfortunately, this case alternative is the only one that works correctly. If `grade` is `'A'`, all of the branches are executed and the resulting output is this:

```
Good WorkAverage WorkPoor WorkA is not a valid letter grade.
```

Remember that after a branch is taken to a specific case label, control proceeds sequentially until either a *break* statement or the end of the *switch* statement is encountered. Forgetting a *break* statement in a case alternative is a very common source of errors in Java programs.

May We Introduce...
Admiral Grace Murray Hopper

From 1943 until her death on New Year's Day in 1992, Admiral Grace Murray Hopper was intimately involved with computing. In 1991, she was awarded the National Medal of Technology "for her pioneering accomplishments in the development of computer programming languages that simplified computer technology and opened the door to a significantly larger universe of users."

Admiral Hopper was born Grace Brewster Murray in New York City on December 9, 1906. She attended Vassar and received a Ph.D. in mathematics from Yale. For the next 10 years, she taught mathematics at Vassar.

In 1943, Admiral Hopper joined the U.S. Navy and was assigned to the Bureau of Ordnance Computation Project at Harvard University as a programmer on the Mark I. After the war, she remained at Harvard as a faculty member and continued work on the Navy's Mark II and Mark III computers. In 1949, she joined Eckert-Mauchly Computer Corporation and worked on the UNIVAC I. It was there that she made a legendary contribution to computing: She discovered the first computer "bug"—a moth caught in the hardware.

Admiral Hopper had a working compiler in 1952, a time when the conventional wisdom was that computers could do only arithmetic. Although not on the committee that designed the computer language COBOL, she was active in its design, implementation, and use. COBOL (which stands for Common Business-Oriented Language) was developed in the early 1960s and is still widely used in business data processing.

Admiral Hopper retired from the Navy in 1966, only to be recalled within a year to full-time active duty. Her mission was to oversee the Navy's efforts to maintain uniformity in programming languages. It has been said that just as Admiral Hyman Rickover was the

continued ▼

Admiral Grace Murray Hopper

father of the nuclear navy, Rear Admiral Hopper was the mother of computerized data automation in the Navy. She served with the Naval Data Automation Command until she retired again in 1986 with the rank of rear admiral. At the time of her death, she was a senior consultant at Digital Equipment Corporation.

During her lifetime, Admiral Hopper received honorary degrees from more than 40 colleges and universities. She was honored by her peers on several occasions, including the first Computer Sciences Man of the Year award given by the Data Processing Management Association, and the Contributions to Computer Science Education Award given by the Special Interest Group for Computer Science Education, which is part of the ACM (Association for Computing Machinery).

Admiral Hopper loved young people and enjoyed giving talks on college and university campuses. She often handed out colored wires, which she called nanoseconds because they were cut to a length of about one foot—the distance that light travels in a nanosecond (billionth of a second). Her advice to the young was, "You manage things, you lead people. We went overboard on management and forgot about leadership."

When asked which of her many accomplishments she was most proud of, she answered, "All the young people I have trained over the years."

The do Statement

The *do* statement is a looping control structure in which the loop condition is tested at the end (bottom) of the loop. This format guarantees that the loop body executes at least once. The syntax template for the *do* is this:

DoStatement

```
do
    Statement
while ( Expression ) ;
```

As usual in Java, Statement is either a single statement or a block. Also, note that the *do* ends with a semicolon.

The *do* statement

```
do
{
   Statement1;
   Statement2;
        .
        .
        .
   StatementN;
} while (Expression);
```

means "Execute the statements between `do` and `while` as long as Expression still has the value `true` at the end of the loop." This means that you execute the statements before you test the expression. Because there is the word `while` at the end of the block, this statement is sometimes called the *do-while* statement.

Let's compare a *while* loop and a *do* loop that do the same task: They find the first period in a file of data. Assume that there is at least one period in the file.

while Solution
```
inputChar  = (char)dataFile.read();
while (inputChar != '.')
   inputChar  = (char)dataFile.read();
```

do Solution
```
do
   inputChar  = (char)dataFile.read();
while (inputChar != '.');
```

The *while* solution requires a priming read so that `inputChar` has a value before the loop is entered. This isn't required for the *do* solution because the input statement within the loop is executed before the loop condition is evaluated.

We can also use the *do* to implement a count-controlled loop if we know in advance that the loop body should always execute at least once. Below are two versions of a loop to sum the integers from 1 through n.

while Solution
```
sum = 0;
counter = 1;
while (counter <= n)
{
   sum = sum + counter;
   counter++;
}
```

```
do Solution
sum = 0;
counter = 1;
do
{
    sum = sum + counter;
    counter++;
} while (counter <= n);
```

If n is a positive number, both of these versions are equivalent. But if n is 0 or negative, the two loops give different results. In the *while* version, the final value of sum is 0 because the loop body is never entered. In the *do* version, the final value of sum is 1 because the body executes once and *then* the loop test is made.

Because the *while* statement tests the condition before executing the body of the loop, it is called a *pretest loop*. The *do* statement does the opposite and thus is known as a *posttest loop*. Figure 10.2 compares the flow of control in the *while* and *do* loops.

When we finish introducing new looping constructs, we offer some guidelines for determining when to use each type of loop.

The for Statement

The *for* statement is designed to simplify the writing of count-controlled loops. The following statement prints out the integers from 1 through n:

```
for (count = 1; count <= n; count++)
    outFile.println("" + count);
```

This *for* statement means "Initialize the loop control variable count to 1. While count is less than or equal to n, execute the output statement and increment count by 1. Stop the loop after count has been incremented to n + 1."

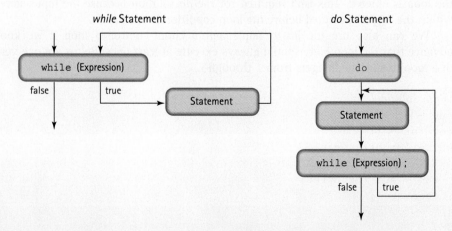

Figure 10.2 *Flow of control: while and do*

The syntax template for a *for* statement is

ForStatement

```
for ( Init ; Expression ; Update )
        Statement
```

Expression is the condition that ends the loop and must be of type `boolean`. *Init* can be any of the following: nothing, a local variable declaration, or an expression. Init can also be a series of local variable declarations and expressions separated by commas. *Update* can be omitted, it can be an expression, or it can be a series of expressions separated by commas.

Most often, a *for* statement is written such that Init initializes a loop-control variable and Update increments or decrements the loop-control variable. Here are two loops that execute the same number of times (50):

```
for (loopCount = 1; loopCount <= 50; loopCount++)
   .
   .
   .


for (loopCount = 50; loopCount >= 1; loopCount--)
   .
   .
   .
```

Just like *while* loops, *do* and *for* loops may be nested. For example, the nested *for* structure

```
for (lastNum = 1; lastNum <= 7; lastNum++)
{
   for (numToPrint = 1; numToPrint <= lastNum; numToPrint++)
     outFile.print("" + numToPrint);
   outFile.println();
}
```

prints the following triangle of numbers.

```
1
12
123
1234
12345
123456
1234567
```

Although *for* statements are used primarily for count-controlled loops, Java allows you to write any *while* loop by using a *for* statement. To use *for* loops intelligently, you should know the following facts.

1. In the syntax template, Init and Update are optional. If Update is omitted, the termination condition is not automatically updated.

2. According to the syntax template, Expression—the termination condition—is optional. Thus, the following is a valid *for* statement:

```
for ( ; ; )
  outFile.println("Hi");
```

If you omit the termination condition, the expression `true` is assumed, causing an infinite loop.

3. Init can be a declaration with initialization:

```
for (int i = 1; i <= 20; i++)
  outFile.println("Hi");
```

Here, the variable `i` has local scope, even though there are no braces creating a block. The scope of `i` extends only to the end of the *for* statement. Like any local variable, `i` is inaccessible outside its scope (that is, outside the *for* statement). Because `i` is local to the *for* statement, it's possible to write code like this:

```
for (int i = 1; i <= 20; i++)
  outFile.println("Hi");
for (int i = 1; i <= 100; i++)
  outFile.println("Ed");
```

This code does not generate a compile-time error (such as "MULTIPLY DEFINED IDENTIFIER"). We have declared two distinct variables named `i`, each of which is local to its own *for* statement.

The syntax for Init and Update allows them to have multiple parts, separated by commas. All of the parts are executed as if they are a block of statements. For example, it is sometimes useful to have a second variable in a loop that is a multiple of the iteration counter. The following loop has two variables, one that counts by one and is used as the loop control variable and another that counts by five.

```
for (int count = 1, int byFives = 5; count <= n; count++,
    byFives = count*5)
  outFile.println("Count = " + count + " * 5 = " + byFives);
```

The output of this loop, if n is 7, is:

```
Count = 1 * 5 = 5
Count = 2 * 5 = 10
Count = 3 * 5 = 15
```

```
Count = 4 * 5 = 20
Count = 5 * 5 = 25
Count = 6 * 5 = 30
Count = 7 * 5 = 35
```

Guidelines for Choosing a Looping Statement

Here are some guidelines to help you decide when to use each of the three looping statements (*while*, *do*, and *for*).

1. If the loop is a simple count-controlled loop, the *for* statement is a natural. Concentrating the three loop-control actions—initialize, test, and increment/decrement—into one location (the heading of the *for* statement) reduces the chances of forgetting to include one of them.

2. If the loop is an event-controlled loop whose body should execute at least once, a *do* statement is appropriate.

3. If the loop is an event-controlled loop and nothing is known about the first execution, use a *while* statement.

4. When in doubt, use a *while* statement.

10.2 Exception-Handling Mechanism

In the last chapter, we defined an exception as an unusual situation that is detected while a program is running. An exception halts the normal execution of a method. There are three parts to an exception-handling mechanism: defining the exception, raising or generating the exception, and handling the exception. We look first at handling exceptions and then at defining and raising them.

The try-catch-finally Statement

As part of introducing files in Chapter 9, it was necessary to forward an `IOException` to the JVM. We noted that the alternative to forwarding is to catch an exception. Because catching an exception involves a branch in control flow, it's natural to discuss it here.

When an error occurs in a method call, it isn't always possible for the method itself to take care of it. For example, suppose we ask the user for a file name in a dialog, get the name from a field, and then we attempt to open the file (prepare it for reading by calling the `FileReader` constructor). The constructor discovers that the file doesn't exist and is thus unable to open it. Perhaps the file has been deleted, or maybe the user just mistyped the name. The constructor has no way of knowing that the proper response to the error is to ask the user to reenter the name. Because the constructor can't appropriately deal with this error, it doesn't even try. It passes the problem on to the method that called it, such as `main`.

Exception handler A section of a program that is executed when an exception occurs. In Java, an exception handler appears within a *catch* clause of a *try-catch-finally* control structure.

When a call returns with an exception, normal execution ends and the JVM looks to see if there is code to take care of the problem. That code is called an exception handler and is part of a *try-catch-finally* statement.

The syntax diagram for a *try-catch-finally* statement is:

TryCatchFinally

```
try
    Block
catch (ExceptionType ObjectName)
    Block
    .
    .
    .
finally
    Block
```

As the diagram shows, the statement has three main parts. The first part is the keyword `try` and a block (a { } pair enclosing any number of statements). The second part is an optional series of *catch* clauses, each consisting of the keyword *catch*, a single parameter declaration enclosed in parentheses, and a block. The last part is also optional and consists of the keyword *finally* and a block.

When a statement or series of statements in a program might result in an exception, we enclose them in the block following `try`. For each type of exception that can be produced by the statements, we write a *catch* clause. Here's an example:

```
try
{
    . . .         // Statements  that try to open a file
}
catch (IOException except)
{
    . . .         // Statements that execute if the file can't be opened
}
finally
{
    . . .         // Statements that are always executed
}
```

The *try* statement is meant to sound something like the coach telling the gymnast, "Go ahead and try this move that you're unsure of, and I'll catch you if you fall." We are telling the computer to try executing some operations that might fail, and then we're providing code to catch the potential exceptions. The *finally* clause provides an opportunity to clean up, regardless of what happens in the `try` and `catch` blocks. We focus on the execution of a *try* statement without a *finally* clause (a *try-catch* statement) and briefly describe what happens when we add the *finally* clause.

Execution of try-catch   If none of the statements in the `try` block throws an exception, then control transfers to the statement following the entire *try-catch* statement. That is, we try some statements, and if everything goes according to plan, we just continue on with the succeeding statements.

When an exception occurs, control is immediately transferred to the block associated with the appropriate `catch`. It is important to realize that control jumps directly from whatever statement caused the exception to the `catch` block. If there are statements in the `try` block following the one that caused the exception, they are skipped. If the `catch` block completes without causing any new exceptions, then control transfers to the next statement outside of the *try-catch* structure.

How does the computer know which `catch` is appropriate? It looks at the class of the parameter declared in each one and selects the first one with a class that matches the thrown exception. Given how Java uses objects for just about everything, it should come as no surprise that an exception is an object and has a class. We've already seen one such class, `IOException`; another is `ArithmeticException`, which is thrown when we try to execute an invalid arithmetic operation (such as integer division by zero). Let's look at an example of a *try-catch* statement to illustrate this process.

```
try
{
  // Some statements
}
catch (IOException except)
{
  // Statements to handle IO errors
}
catch(ArithmeticException except)
{
  // Statements to handle division by zero
}
```

The computer begins by executing the statements within the `try` block. If one of them causes an `IOException`, then control jumps to the first `catch` block. If instead a statement causes an `ArithmeticException`, then control jumps to the second `catch` block.

What if a statement throws an exception that isn't among the *catch* clauses? In that case, the `try` statement fails to catch the error, and its enclosing method throws the exception to its caller. If the caller doesn't have a handler for the error, it throws the exception to its caller, and so on until the exception is either caught or ends up at the JVM, which halts the program and displays an error message.

The object that is passed to the `catch` block through its parameter has a value-returning method associated with it called `getMessage`. The `getMessage` method returns a string containing a message. For example, it might contain the name of the file that could not be opened. Thus, you could write the following statement in a `catch` block to display a message.

```
catch (IOException except)
{
  out.add(new Label("I/O Exception encountered for " +
    except.getMessage()));
}
```

Let's look at an actual example. Suppose we have prompted the user to enter a file name into a field, and upon clicking a button an event handler is called to open that file as a `PrintWriter`. We could use the following code in the button event handler to try to open the file. If the file can't be opened, we display an error message, and clear the input field so that the user can try again.

```
filename = fileField.getText();
try
{
  outFile = new PrintWriter(new FileWriter(filename));
}
catch (IOException except)
{
  errorLabel.setText("Unable to open file " + filename);
  fileField.setText("");
}
```

Execution of try-catch-finally   When a *finally* clause is present in a `try` statement, the block following `finally` is always executed no matter what happens in the `try` and `catch` blocks. Thus, even when a `catch` causes a new exception, the `finally` block is executed. The `finally` block gives us an opportunity to clean up after a failed `catch`. In writing the algorithm for the `finally` block, however, it is important to realize that it is always executed, even if the `try` succeeds.

In this text we use only *try-catch* statements, and we keep our exception handlers simple so that they won't produce additional exceptions. The `finally` clause is really only needed when a `catch` contains statements that might generate a new exception and we need to undo some of its processing before the exception is thrown.

Generating an Exception with throw

Standard library classes are not the only classes that can generate exceptions. Here we introduce the *throw* statement, which is the statement that we use when raising or generating an exception.

All exceptions are thrown by a *throw* statement. The syntax of the throw statement is quite simple.

ThrowStatement

```
throw ObjectExpression ;
```

The ObjectExpression must be either a variable or a value of a class that implements the `Throwable` interface. That is, it must be an object of class `Throwable` or a subclass of `Throwable` such as `Exception`. When an exception is thrown, the JVM goes looking for a *catch* statement that can handle that specific type of exception.

The *throw* statement may be written within a *try* statement that is intended to catch it. In that case, control is transferred to the *catch* clause with the corresponding type.

More often, the *throw* occurs inside a method that is called from within a *try* statement, as shown in Figure 10.3. The JVM first looks for a *catch* within the method. When it fails to find one, it causes the method to return. The JVM then looks around the point where the method was called, and finds an appropriate *catch* clause. The *catch* is executed and control proceeds to the statement following the *try-catch*.

If the JVM can't find a matching *catch*, it causes the method containing the call to also return. The series of returns can lead all the way back to `main`. If `main` fails to catch the exception, then the JVM handles it by stopping the program and displaying an error message.

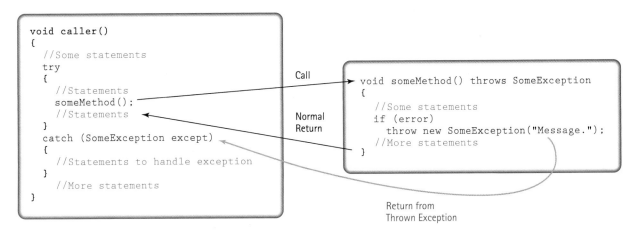

Figure 10.3   *Throwing an Exception to be Caught in a Calling Method*

As we've seen previously, we must handle each class of exception either by catching it or explicitly forwarding it with a *throws* clause in the method heading. Thus, an exception can cause a chain of returns that reaches the JVM only when our code is written to allow it. We can't generate an exception that is accidentally uncaught.

We can throw any of the standard exceptions that Java provides. For example,

```
throw new FileNotFoundException(filename);
```

It's actually quite rare to throw one of the predefined exceptions. One situation where we might do so is when we've caught such an exception in a *catch* clause but there is some aspect of handling it that must be passed to a higher level method.

Instead of throwing a predefined exception, we typically want to define and throw a new exception type that is unique to a class. A user of the class must then handle that type of exception. For example, in our Address class from Chapter 8, we could have validated the zip code. Basic zip codes are five digits or less. If a zip code is greater than 99,999, we can throw a ZipCodeInvalidException in the constructor for an Address object as follows.

```
public Address(String  name, String city, String state, int zipCode)
      throws ZipCodeInvalidException
{
  if (zipCode <= 99999)
    // If valid, store value
    this.zipCode = zipCode;
  else
    // If invalid, throw exception
    throw new ZipCodeInvalidException("" + zipCode);
  .
  .
  .
}
```

We would call this method within a *try-catch* statement.

```
try
{
  myAddress = new Address(myName, Austin, Texas, 7874);
}
catch (ZipCodeInvalidException  zipCode)
{
  // Exception handler
  // Print bad zip code
  System.out.println(zipCode.getMessage()+ " is invalid");
}
```

Whatever method is trying to create an `Address` object with an invalid zip code is then responsible for handling the error. But, of course, we also need to define the class called `ZipCodeInvalidException`.

Exception Classes

Notice that *throw* must have an exception object to throw. Exception objects are very simple to create. Their class name conveys the basic information that tells the JVM what sort of exception is being thrown. All we typically need to add is an error message or some other piece of information that helps the *catch* clause handle the error.

The predefined type `Exception` implements the `Throwable` interface and provides a field for an error message. Thus, all we have to do is extend it with our own class name and supply a pair of constructors that call `super`. Here is how we define `ZipCodeInvalid-Exception`.

```
package address;
public class ZipCodeInvalidException extends Exception
{
   public ZipCodeInvalidException()
   {
     super();
   }
   public ZipCodeInvalidException(String message)
   {
     super(message);
   }
}
```

Look at the *try-catch* in the previous section.

```
try
{
   myAddress = new Address(myName, Austin, Texas, 7874);
}
catch (ZipCodeInvalidException  zipCode)
{
   // Exception handler
   // Print bad area code
   System.out.println(zipCode.getMessge() + " is invalid");
}
```

In the *catch* clause we use `getMessage` to retrieve the same string that was used to instantiate the object of class `ZipCodeInvalidException`.

Whenever you design a class you should consider whether there are error conditions that cannot be handled strictly within the class. Exceptions are, as their name implies, meant to be used for exceptional situations. We recommend using an exception only when there is no simple way to handle an error.

10.3 Additional Java Operators

Java has a rich, sometimes bewildering, variety of operators that allow you to manipulate values of the primitive data types. Operators you have learned about so far include the assignment operator (=), the arithmetic operators (+, -, *, /, %), the increment and decrement operators (++, --), the relational operators (==, !=, <, <=, >, >=), the string concatenation operator (+), and the conditional (short-circuit evaluation) logical operators (!, &&, ||). In certain cases, a pair of parentheses is also considered to be an operator—namely, the type-cast operator

```
someFloat = (float)someInt;
```

Java also has many specialized operators that are seldom found in other programming languages. Here is a table of these additional operators. As you inspect the table, don't panic—a quick scan will do.

Operator	Remarks
Combined-assignment operators	
+=	Add and assign
-=	Subtract and assign
*=	Multiply and assign
/=	Divide and assign
%=	Remainder and assign
Increment and decrement operators	
++	Pre-increment	Example: `++someVar`
++	Post-increment	Example: `someVar++`
--	Pre-decrement	Example: `--someVar`
--	Post-decrement	Example: `someVar--`
Bitwise operators	**Integer operands only**
<<	Left shift
>>	Right shift with sign extension
>>>	Right shift with zero extension
&	Bitwise AND
|	Bitwise OR
^	Bitwise EXCLUSIVE OR
~	Complement (invert all bits)

(continued)

Operator	Remarks
Boolean full-evaluation operators	`boolean` **operands only**
`&` boolean AND	
`|` boolean OR	
`^` boolean EXCLUSIVE OR	
More combined-assignment operators	Integer operands only
`<<=` Shift left and assign	
`>>=` Shift right with sign extension and assign	
`>>>=` Shift right with zero extension and assign	
`&=` Bitwise AND and assign	
`|=` Bitwise OR and assign	
`^=` Bitwise EXCLUSIVE OR and assign	
Other operators	
`instanceof` Type comparison	object `instanceof` ClassName
`? :` Conditional operator	Form: Expr1 `?` Expr2 `:` Expr3

The operators in this table, along with those you already know, comprise all of the Java operators.

Assignment Operators and Assignment Expressions

Java has several assignment operators. The equal sign (=) is the basic assignment operator. When combined with its two operands, it forms an assignment expression (*not* an assignment statement). Every assignment expression has a *value* and a *side effect*, namely, that the value is stored into the object denoted by the left-hand side. For example, the expression

> **Assignment expression**   A Java expression with (1) a value and (2) the side effect of storing the expression value into a memory location
>
> **Expression statement**   A statement formed by appending a semicolon to an assignment expression, an increment expression, or a decrement expression

```
delta = 2 * 12
```

has the value 24 and the side effect of storing this value into `delta`.

In Java, an expression consisting of a variable and an increment or decrement expression also becomes an expression statement when it is terminated by a semicolon. All three of the following are valid Java statements:

```
alpha++;
beta--;
--gamma;
```

Each of these statements either increments or decrements the given variable.

Because an assignment is an expression, not a statement, you can use it anywhere an expression is allowed. Here is a statement that stores the value 20 into `firstInt`, the value 30 into `secondInt`, and the value 35 into `thirdInt`:

```
thirdInt = (secondInt = (firstInt = 20) + 10) + 5;
```

Although some Java programmers use this style of coding, we do not recommend it. It is hard to read and error-prone.

In Chapter 6, we cautioned against the mistake of using the = operator in place of the == operator:

```
if (alpha = 12)   // Wrong
  .
  .
  .
```

The condition in the *if* statement is an assignment expression, not a relational expression. The value of the expression is 12, which is not a `boolean` value, so a compiler error results.

In addition to the = operator, Java has several combined assignment operators (+=, *=, and the others listed in our table of operators). These operators have the following semantics:

Statement	Equivalent Statement
`i += 5;`	`i = i + 5;`
`pivotPoint *= n + 3;`	`pivotPoint = pivotPoint * (n + 3);`

The combined assignment operators are sometimes convenient for writing a line of code more compactly, but you can do just fine without them. We do not use them in this text.

Increment and Decrement Operators

The increment and decrement operators (++ and --) operate only on variables, not on constants or arbitrary expressions. Suppose a variable `someInt` contains the value 3. The expression ++someInt denotes pre-incrementation. The side effect of incrementing `someInt` occurs first, so the resulting value of the expression is 4. In contrast, the expression someInt++ denotes post-incrementation. The value of the expression is 3, and *then* the side effect of incrementing `someInt` takes place. The following code illustrates the difference between pre- and post-incrementation:

```
int1 = 14;
int2 = ++int1;
```

```
// At this point, int1 == 15  and  int2 == 15
int1 = 14;
int2 = int1++;
// At this point int1 == 15  and  int2 == 14
```

Some people make a game of seeing how much they can do in the fewest key-strokes possible by using side effects in the middle of larger expressions. But professional software development requires writing code that other programmers can read and understand. Use of side effects reduces readability. By far the most common use of ++ and -- is to do the incrementation or decrementation as a separate expression statement:

```
count++;
```

Here, the value of the expression is unused, but we get the desired side effect of incrementing count.

Bitwise Operators

The bitwise operators listed in the operator table (<<, >>, >>>, &, |, and so forth) are used for manipulating individual bits within a memory cell. This book does not explore the use of these operators; the topic of bit-level operations is most often covered in a course on computer organization and assembly-language programming. However, we should draw your attention to the fact that three of the bitwise operators, &, |, and ^, have a second meaning in Java. They can also be used with boolean operands to perform logical AND, OR, and EXCLUSIVE OR operations without short-circuit evaluation.

Recall from Chapter 6 that when the first operand of && is false, the second operand need not be evaluated because the result must be false. When used in combination with boolean operands, the & operator causes the second operand to be evaluated regardless of the value of the first operand. Similar rules apply to the | and ^ operators.

Here is an example that illustrates the difference between these logical operators:

```
// This works OK when i is 0 because m/i isn't evaluated
if (i != 0 && m/i >= 4)
  k = 20;
```

Now consider what happens if we use & in place of &&:

```
// This fails when i is 0 because of division by zero
if (i != 0 & m/i >= 4)
  k = 20;
```

There are rare cases where full evaluation is useful, but we recommend that you always use the relational operators && and || in your logical expressions.

The ?: Operator

The last operator in our operator table is the ?: operator, sometimes called the conditional operator. It is a ternary (three-operand) operator with the following syntax:

ConditionalOperator

Expression1 ? Expression2 : Expression3

Here's how it works. First, the computer evaluates Expression1. If the value is true, then the value of the entire expression is Expression2; otherwise, the value of the entire expression is Expression3.

A classic example of its use is to set a variable max equal to the larger of two variables a and b. Using an *if* statement, we would do it this way:

```
if (a > b)
   max = a;
else
   max = b;
```

With the ?: operator, we can use the following assignment statement:

```
max = (a > b) ? a : b;
```

The ?: operator is certainly not an intuitively obvious bit of Java syntax; it's one of the unusual features Java inherited from C. We do not recommend its use, but you should be aware of it in case you encounter it in reading code written by someone else.

Operator Precedence

Following is a summary of operator precedence for the Java operators we have encountered so far, excluding the bitwise operators. (Appendix B contains the complete list.) In Table 10.1, the operators are grouped by precedence level, and a horizontal line separates each precedence level from the next-lower level.

The column labeled Associativity describes grouping order. Within a precedence level, most operators group from left to right. For example,

```
a - b + c
```

Table 10.1 Precedence (highest to lowest)

Operator	Associativity	Remarks
++ --	Right to left	++ and -- as postfix operators
++ --	Right to left	++ and -- as prefix operators
Unary + Unary -	Right to left	
!	Right to left	
(cast)	Right to left	
* / %	Left to right	
+ -	Left to right	
+	Left to right	String concatenation
< <= > >=	Left to right	
instanceof	Left to right	
== !=	Left to right	
&	Left to right	boolean operands
^	Left to right	boolean operands
|	Left to right	boolean operands
&&	Left to right	
||	Left to right	
? :	Right to left	
= += -= *= /= %=	Right to left	

means

```
(a - b) + c
```

and not

```
a - (b + c)
```

Certain operators, though, group from right to left—specifically, the unary operators, the assignment operators, and the ? : operator. Look at the unary - operator, for example. The expression

```
sum = - -1
```

means

```
sum = -(-1)
```

instead of the meaningless

```
sum = (- -)1
```

This associativity makes sense because the unary – operation is naturally a right-to-left operation.

A word of caution: Although operator precedence and associativity dictate the *grouping* of operators with their operands, the precedence rules do not define the *order* in which subexpressions are evaluated. Java further requires that the left-hand operand of a two-operand operator be evaluated first. For example, if i currently contains 5, the statement

```
j = ++i + i;
```

stores 12 into j. Let's see why. There are three operators in the expression statement above: =, ++, and +. The ++ operator has the highest precedence, so it operates just on i, not the expression i + i. The addition operator has higher precedence than the assignment operator, giving implicit parentheses as follows:

```
j = (++i + i);
```

So far, so good. But now we ask this question: In the addition operation, is the left operand or the right operand evaluated first? As we just saw, the Java language tells us that the left-hand operand is evaluated first. Therefore, the result is 6 + 6, or 12. If Java had instead specified that the right operand comes first, the expression would have yielded 6 + 5, or 11.

In most expressions, Java's left-hand rule doesn't have any effect. But when side-effect operators like increment and assignment are involved, you need to remember that the left operand is evaluated first. To make the code clear and unambiguous, it's best to write the preceding example with two separate statements:

```
i++;
j = i + i;
```

The moral here is that it's best to avoid unnecessary side effects altogether.

Problem-Solving Case Study

Monthly Rainfall Averages

Statement of the Problem Meteorologists have recorded monthly rainfall amounts at several sites throughout a region of the country. You have been asked to write an application that reads one year's rainfall amounts from sites within the region from a file and prints out the average of the 12 values for each of the sites on a separate file. The first line of a data set is the name of the site, and the 12 values for the site follow on the next line with exactly one blank in between each value. The data file is named "rainData.dat".

Brainstorming This problem sounds familiar. We wrote an application in Chapter 5 that took rainfall amounts from observers and calculated the running average. In that problem we used a window for input and output; this problem asks for file input and output. Calculating an average should be the same, but where the calculation takes place is different. In the previous problem the calculation took place in the handler for the button event. There are no buttons in this problem.

There are other nouns in the problem, but they describe the context like region, country, and sites, so they are not objects in the solution. So, what are the objects? The application and the file objects.

Filtering This looks like a very sparse set of classes for a problem that includes calculating a series of averages. But this problem is one that has a process repeated over different data, but does not have any objects but numeric values and files. What about error conditions? Well we can't determine what they might be at this stage other than to say that the data might have been entered incorrectly on the file. Let's add an exception class to our list of classes. Before we look at the responsibilities of each class, let's name them. Let's call the application class `RainFall` and the exception class `DataSetExcetion`.

Scenarios The processing takes place within the application class `RainFall`: processing a data set, writing the average, and repeating the process until there are no more data sites. What happens if an input error occurs while reading the data file? What happens if a data value contains a non-numeric character? What happens if there is a negative rainfall amount?

These are all error conditions we must handle. For the moment, let's just say that `Rainfall` has the responsibility to throw exceptions if need be.

CRC Cards On the CRC card, we summarize `RainFall`'s responsibility as Process data.

Class Name: Rainfall	Superclass: Object	Subclasses:
Responsibilities	**Collaborations**	
Prepare the file for input	FileReader, BufferedReader	
Prepare the file for output	FileWriter, PrintWriter	
Process data	BufferedReader	
Throw exceptions if necessary	DataSetException	

Class Name: DataSetException	Superclass: Exception	Subclasses:
Responsibilities	**Collaborations**	
Create itself		
Pass message to super	Super	

Responsibility Algorithms Preparing the file for input and output has become so routine, that we do not need to write the algorithms for these. The third responsibility, Processing data, is the heart of the problem. At the topmost level of the design, we need a loop to process the data from all the sites. Each iteration must process one site's data, then check for a new site name. The program does not know in advance how many recording sites there are, so the loop cannot be a count-controlled loop. Although we can make any of *for*, *while*, or *do* work correctly, we use a *do* under the assumption that the file definitely contains at least one site's data. Therefore, we can set up the loop so that it processes the data from a recording site and then, at the *bottom* of the loop, decides whether to iterate again.

....

Process Data   Level 1

```
Prepare input file, rainData.dat
Prepare output file, outFile.dat
Read data set name
do
     Process one site
     Read data set name
while (more data)
Close files
```

Processing one site requires another loop to input 12 monthly rainfall amounts and form their sum. Using the summing technique we are familiar with by now, we initialize the sum to 0 before starting the loop, and each loop iteration reads another number and adds it to the accumulating sum. A *for* loop is appropriate for this task, because we know that exactly 12 iterations must occur. How are we going to handle the error conditions brought up in the scenarios? We had better put the *for* loop in a *try-catch* statement. Once we have the value we should throw an exception if it is negative.

....

Process One Site   Level 2

```
Set sum to 0.0
try to
     Get a line of values
     for months going from 1 to 12
          Get rainfall amount
          if amount is negative
               throw DataSetException("negative value found")
          else
               Set sum to sum + amount
     Write "Average for " + data set name + " is " + sum/12
catch and handle exceptions
```

Because all of the input values are on one line with a blank in between, we have to extract the characters that make up one value so we can convert it. We can use the `String` methods `indexOf` and `substring` to extract a string that represents exactly one floating-point value.

....

Get Rainfall Amount   Level 3

```
Set index to line.indexOf(' ')
Set currentValue to line.substring(0, index)
Set line to substring(index+1, line.length())
Set amount to Double.valueOf(currentValue).doubleValue
```

Before we go on, we had better hand-simulate this algorithm. Let's apply it to the following input string.

```
"23.5 5.6 5.44"
```

index	currentValue	line	amount
4	"23.5"	"5.6 5.44"	23.5
3	"5.6"	"5.44"	5.6
error	"5.44"		

There is an error in the logic. Unless there is a blank after the last value rather than an end of line, the `indexOf` method returns a −1, indicating that there isn't another blank. We then use the `index` in the next statement, producing an error in method `substring`. We need to check to be sure that a blank is found. If not, the remaining string is the last value in the line.

Get Rainfall Amount (revised)   Level 3

```
Set index to line.indexOf(' ')
if index > 0
    Set currentValue to line.substring(0, index)
    Set line to substring(index+1, line.length())
else
    Set currentValue to line
Set amount to Double.valueOf(currentValue).doubleValue
```

We now need to decide what other errors might occur, how to catch them, and how to handle them. The file can throw an `IOException` exception, the conversion operation can throw a `NumberFormatException`, and our own code can throw a `DataSetException`. Let's catch the `IOException`, print out the site name, and end the program. For the `NumberFormatException`, let's print out the site name with an error message, and continue processing with the next site. We can do the same for `DataSetException`.

Catch and Handle Exceptions

```
catch IOException
    Write "I/O Exception with site " + data set name
    exit program
catch NumberFormatException
    Write "NumberFormatException with site " + data set name
catch DataSetException
    Write except.getMessage()  + data set name
```

The only abstract step left is to determine when the outer loop finishes. If we read in a new site name and there is no more data, line will be `null`.

More Data

line != null

Assumptions   The file contains data for at least one site.

```java
package rainfall;
// Define an Exception class for signaling data set errors
class DataSetException extends Exception
{
  public DataSetException()
  {
    super();
  }
  public DataSetException(String message)
  {
    super(message);
  }
}
package rainfall;
import java.io.*;
public class Rainfall
//**********************************************************************
// RainFall application
// This program inputs 12 monthly rainfall amounts from a
//  recording site and computes the average monthly rainfall.
// This process is repeated for as many recording sites as
//  the user wishes.
//**********************************************************************
{
  static void processOneSite(BufferedReader inFile,
    PrintWriter outFile, String dataSetName)
  {
    int count;              // Loop control variable
    double amount;          // Rainfall amount for one month
    double sum = 0.0;       // Sum of amounts for the year
    String dataLine;        // String to input amount from inFile
    String currentValue;    // Floating point string
    int index;              // Position of blank

    try
    {
      // Next line could produce an IOException
      dataLine = inFile.readLine();
```

```
            for (count = 1; count <= 12; count++)   // For 12 months
            {
              index = dataLine.indexOf(' ');         // Find position of blank
              if (index > 0)
              { // Blank found
                currentValue = dataLine.substring(0, index);  // Extract a number
                // Remove current value from string
                dataLine =
                  dataLine.substring(Math.min(index+1, dataLine.length()),
                    dataLine.length());
              }
              else  // Remaining string is current value
                currentValue = dataLine;
              // Next line could produce NumberFormatException
              // Convert to double
              amount = Double.valueOf(currentValue).doubleValue();
              if (amount < 0.0)
                throw new DataSetException("Negative value in site ");
              else
                sum = sum + amount;
            }
            outFile.println("Average for " + dataSetName + " is " + sum/12.0);
          }
          catch (IOException except)
          {
            outFile.println("IOException  with site " + dataSetName);
            System.exit(0);
          }
          catch (NumberFormatException except)
          {
            outFile.println("NumberFormatException in site " + dataSetName);
          }
          catch (DataSetException except)
          {
            outFile.println(except.getMessage() + dataSetName);
          }
        }
        public static void main(String[] args)
          throws FileNotFoundException,IOException
        {
          String  dataSetName;                    // Name of reporting station
          BufferedReader inFile;                  // Data file
          PrintWriter outFile;                    // Output file
          inFile = new BufferedReader(new FileReader("rainData.dat"));
          outFile = new PrintWriter(new FileWriter("outfile.dat"));
          dataSetName = inFile.readLine();        // Get name of reporting station
```

```
    do
    {
      processOneSite(inFile, outFile, dataSetName);
      dataSetName = inFile.readLine();      // Get name of reporting station
    } while (dataSetName != null);
    inFile.close();
    outFile.close();
    System.exit(0);
  }
}
```

Testing   We should test two separate aspects of the Rainfall program. First, we should verify that the program works correctly given valid input data. Supplying arbitrary rainfall amounts of 0 or greater, we must confirm that the program correctly adds up the values and divides by 12 to produce the average. Also, we should make sure that the program behaves correctly when it reaches the end of the file.

The second aspect to test is the data-validation code that we included in the program. We should include negative numbers in the file to ensure that such data sets are not processed. Similarly, we need to include some values that are improperly formed floating values. Here's a sample input file that accomplishes the necessary testing:

```
Moose Lake
0.0 3.6 1.2 0.5 4.3 0.6 2.2 1.9 6.5 4.0 8.3 1.4
East Duckville
7.4 8.2 6.5 1.9 9.7 6.4 5.5 8.1 4.7 3.9 12.8 10.6
Dry Gulch
0.0 0.0 0.0 0.1 0.2 0.1 0.2 0.0 0.0 0.4 0.0 0.1
Bad Data City
-0.4 10.4 1000.9 21.1 0.0 0.0 0.0 0.0 0.0 0.0 0.0 0.0
Wrong Number Town
0.0 0.0 0.0 xyz.8 abc def ghi jkl mno pqr stu vwx
```

And here is the output from running the program on the data file:

```
Average for Moose Lake is 2.8749999999999996
Average for East Duckville is 7.141666666666667
Average for Dry Gulch is 0.09166666666666667
Negative value in site Bad Data City
NumberFormatException in site Wrong Number Town
```

Testing and Debugging

The same testing techniques we used with *while* loops apply to *do* and *for* loops. There are, however, a few additional considerations with these loops.

The body of a *do* loop always executes at least once. Thus, you should try data sets that show the result of executing a *do* loop the minimal number of times.

With a data-dependent *for* loop, it is important to test for proper results when the loop executes zero times. This occurs when the starting value is greater than the ending value (or less than the ending value if the loop control variable is being decremented).

When a program contains a *switch* statement, you should test it with enough different data sets to ensure that each branch is selected and executed correctly. You should also test the program with a switch expression whose value is not in any of the case labels.

A program that handles exceptions must be tested to ensure that the exceptions are generated appropriately and then properly handled. Test cases must be included to cause exceptions to occur and to specify the expected results from handling them.

Testing and Debugging Hints

1. In a *switch* statement, make sure there is a *break* statement at the end of each case alternative. Otherwise, control "falls through" to the code in the next case alternative.

2. Case labels in a *switch* statement are made up of values, not variables. They may, however, include named constants and expressions involving only constants.

3. A *switch* expression must be one of the types `char`, `byte`, `short`, or `int`. It cannot be of type `long` or a floating-point or string expression.

4. The case constants of a *switch* statement cannot be of type `long`, or be floating-point or string constants.

5. If there is a possibility that the value of the *switch* expression might not match one of the case constants, you should provide a `default` alternative.

6. Double-check long *switch* statements to make sure that you haven't omitted any branches.

7. The *do* loop is a posttest loop. If there is a possibility that the loop body should be skipped entirely, use a *while* statement or a *for* statement.

8. The *for* statement heading (the first line) always has three pieces within the parentheses. Typically, the first piece initializes a loop-control variable, the second piece tests the variable, and the third piece increments or decrements the variable. The three pieces must be separated by semicolons. Any of the pieces can be omitted, but the semicolons still must be present.

9. Make sure that all exceptions are either caught or forwarded as appropriate.

Summary of Classes

We have not introduced any new classes in the Java library in this chapter, nor have we designed any classes that should go into a library to use later.

Summary

The *switch* statement is a multiway selection statement. It allows the program to choose among a set of branches. A *switch* containing *break* statements can always be simulated by an *if-else-if* structure. If a *switch* can be used, however, it often makes the code easier to read and understand. A *switch* statement cannot be used with floating-point or string values in the case labels.

The *do* is a general-purpose looping statement. It is like the *while* loop except that its test occurs at the end of the loop, guaranteeing at least one execution of the loop body. As with a *while* loop, a *do* continues as long as the loop condition is `true`. A *do* is convenient for loops that test input values and repeat if the input is not correct.

The *for* statement is also a looping statement and is commonly used to implement count-controlled loops. The initialization, testing, and incrementation (or decrementation) of the loop-control variable are centralized in one location, the first line of the *for* statement.

An exception occurs when an error condition is encountered in a method and the method cannot directly resolve the problem. The method is said to throw an exception, which we can catch using a *try-catch* statement. Catching an exception and handling it properly enables the program to continue executing, rather than allowing the error to be passed to the JVM, which halts the program with an error message. Typical exceptions include `IOException`, `NumberFormatException`, and `ArithmeticException`.

The *throw* statement gives us the ability to throw exceptions when we detect them. When we create new classes derived from `Exception`, we can *throw* exceptions that are specific to our classes and methods. Those exceptions can then be caught and handled in ways that are more appropriate than would be possible if we were restricted to using the exception types in the Java library.

The *for, do, switch*, and *throw* statements are the ice cream and cake of Java. We can live without them if we absolutely must, but they are very nice to have.

Similarly, the additional operators that Java supplies, such as `+=`, `%=`, and `?:`, are sometimes convenient shortcuts. But we can program effectively without them. Often, the use of the less common operators results in code that is harder to understand and so we recommend that you avoid them. Even so, you must be aware of their meaning so that you can interpret them when you encounter code written by a programmer who values compact syntax over clarity.

Quick Check

1. Given a switch expression that is the `int` variable `nameVal`, write a *switch* statement that writes the following to `PrintWriter` file `outData`: your first name if `nameVal` = 1, your middle name if `nameVal` = 2, and your last name if `nameVal` = 3. (pp. 452–455)
2. How would you change the answer to Question 1 so that it writes an error message if the value is not 1, 2, or 3? (pp. 452–455)
3. What is the primary difference between a *while* loop and a *do* loop? (pp. 459–460)

4. A certain problem requires a count-controlled loop that starts at 10 and counts down to 1. Write the heading (the first line) of a *for* statement that controls this loop. (pp. 460–461)

5. What Java looping statement would you choose for a loop that is both count-controlled and event-controlled and whose body might not execute even once? (p. 463)

6. What is the difference between an expression and an expression statement in Java? (pp. 471–472)

7. Write a statement that converts a string to an integer and writes out the string if a `NumberFormatError` occurs. (p. 463)

8. What is the super class of most exceptions?

Answers

```
1. switch (nameVal)
   {
      case 1 : outData.println("Mary");
               break;
      case 2 : outData.println("Lynn");
               break;
      case 3 : outData.println("Smith");
               break;    // Not required
   }
2. switch (nameVal)
   {
      case 1   : outData.println("Mary");
                 break;
      case 2   : outData.println("Lynn");
                 break;
      case 3   : outData.println("Smith");
                 break;
      default  : outData.println("Invalid name value.");
                 break;    // Not required
   }
```

3. The body of a *do* always executes at least once; the body of a *while* may not execute at all.

4. `for (count = 10; count >= 1; count--)`

5. A *while* (or perhaps a *for*) statement

6. An expression becomes an expression statement when it is terminated by a semicolon.

7.
```
try
{
   intValue = Integer.valueOf("123").intValue();
}
catch(NumberFormatException except)
{
   System.out.println(except.getMessage);
}
```
8. `Exception`

Exam Preparation Exercises

1. Define the following terms:

   switch expression
   pretest loop
   posttest loop

2. (True or False?) A switch expression may be an expression that results in a value of type `int`, `float`, `boolean`, or `char`.

3. (True or False?) The values in case labels may appear in any order, but duplicate case labels are not allowed within a given *switch* statement.

4. (True or False?) All possible values for the switch expression must be included among the case labels for a given *switch* statement.

5. Rewrite the following code fragment using a *switch* statement.
```
if (n == 3)
   alpha++;
else if (n == 7)
   beta++;
else if (n == 10)
   gamma++;
```

6. What is written by the following code fragment if n equals 3? (Be careful here.)
```
switch (n + 1)
{
   case 2   : outData.println("Bill");
   case 4   : outData.println("Mary");
   case 7   : outData.println("Joe");
   case 9   : outData.println("Anne");
   default  : outData.println("Whoops!");
}
```

7. (True or False?) If a *while* loop whose condition is `delta <= alpha` is converted into a *do* loop, the loop condition of the *do* loop is `delta > alpha`.

8. (True or False?) A *do* statement always ends in a semicolon.

9. What is written by the following program fragment? (All variables are of type `int`.)

```
n = 0;
i = 1;
do
{
    outData.print(i);
    i++;
} while (i <= n);
```

10. What is written by the following program fragment? (All variables are of type `int`.)

```
n = 0;
for (i = 1; i <= n; i++)
    outData.print(i);
```

11. What is written by the following program fragment? (All variables are of type `int`.)

```
for (i = 4; i >= 1; i--)
{
    for (j = i; j >= 1; j--)
        outData.print (j + " ");
    outData.println(i);
}
```

12. What is written by the following program fragment? (All variables are of type `int`.)

```
for (row = 1; row <= 10; row++)
{
    for (col = 1; col <= 10 - row; col++)
        outData.print("*");
    for (col = 1; col <= 2*row - 1; col++)
        outData.print(" ");
    for (col = 1; col <= 10 - row; col++)
        outData.print("*");
    outData.println();
}
```

13. (True or False?) A *break* statement located inside a *switch* statement that is within a *while* loop causes control to exit the loop immediately.

14. Classify each of the following as either an expression or an expression statement.
    a. `sum = 0`
    b. `sqrt(x)`
    c. `y = 17;`
    d. `count++`

15. Rewrite each statement as described.
    a. Using the += operator, rewrite the statement

    ```
    sumOfSquares = sumOfSquares + x * x;
    ```

b. Using the decrement operator, rewrite the statement

```
count = count - 1;
```

c. Using a single assignment statement that uses the ?: operator, rewrite the following code segment.

```
if (n > 8)
    k = 32;
else
    k = 15 * n;
```

16. What is the control structure to use if you think an operation might throw an exception?
17. What is the statement that raises an exception?
18. What part of the *try-catch* must have a parameter of an exception object?
19. (True or False?) Our code can catch exceptions that it throws, but not exceptions that the system throws.
20. Mark the following statements True or False. If a statement is false, explain why.
    a. There can only be one *catch* clause for each try.
    b. The exception handler is within the *catch* clause.
    c. The *finally* clause is optional.
    d. The *finally* clause is rarely used.

Programming Warm-Up Exercises

1. Write a *switch* statement that does the following:

   If the value of grade is

   'A', add 4 to sum
   'B', add 3 to sum
   'C', add 2 to sum
   'D', add 1 to sum
   'F', print "Student is on probation" on PrintWriter file outData

2. Modify the code for Exercise 1 so that an error message is printed if grade does not equal one of the five possible grades.
3. Write a program segment that reads and sums integer values from a file until it has summed 10 data values or until a negative value is read, whichever comes first. Use a *do* loop for your solution.
4. Rewrite the following code segment using a *do* loop instead of a *while* loop.

```
response = inData.read();
while (response >= 0 && response <= 127)
{
    response = inData.read();
}
```

5. Rewrite the following code segment using a *while* loop.

```
inInt = inData.read();
if (inInt >= 0)
  do
  {
    outData.write(inInt);
    inInt = inData.read();
  } while (inInt >= 0);
```

6. Rewrite the following code segment using a *for* loop.

```
sum = 0;
count = 1;
while (count <= 1000)
{
  sum = sum + count;
  count++;
}
```

7. Rewrite the following *for* loop as a *while* loop.

```
for (m = 93; m >= 5; m--)
  outData.println( m + " " + m * m);
```

8. Rewrite the following *for* loop using a *do* loop.

```
for (k = 9; k <= 21; k++)
  outData.println( k + " " + 3 * k);
```

9. Write a value-returning method that accepts two `int` parameters, `base` and `exponent`, and returns the value of `base` raised to the `exponent` power. Use a *for* loop in your solution.

10. a. Declare an exception of class `MyException`.
    b. Write class `MyException`.
    c. Write the statement that throws an exception of class `MyException`.

11. Write a *try-catch* statement that attempts to open file `"data.in"` for reading and writes an error message if an exception is thrown.

Programming Problems

1. Develop a Java application that inputs a two-letter abbreviation for one of the 50 states from a field and displays the full name of the state in a label. If the abbreviation isn't valid, the program should display an error message and ask for an abbreviation again. The names of the 50 states and their abbreviations are given in the following table. Use two buttons: one to enter an abbreviation and one to quit.

State	Abbreviation	State	Abbreviation
Alabama	AL	Montana	MT
Alaska	AK	Nebraska	NE
Arizona	AZ	Nevada	NV
Arkansas	AR	New Hampshire	NH
California	CA	New Jersey	NJ
Colorado	CO	New Mexico	NM
Connecticut	CT	New York	NY
Delaware	DE	North Carolina	NC
Florida	FL	North Dakota	ND
Georgia	GA	Ohio	OH
Hawaii	HI	Oklahoma	OK
Idaho	ID	Oregon	OR
Illinois	IL	Pennsylvania	PA
Indiana	IN	Rhode Island	RI
Iowa	IA	South Carolina	SC
Kansas	KS	South Dakota	SD
Kentucky	KY	Tennessee	TN
Louisiana	LA	Texas	TX
Maine	ME	Utah	UT
Maryland	MD	Vermont	VT
Massachusetts	MA	Virginia	VA
Michigan	MI	Washington	WA
Minnesota	MN	West Virginia	WV
Mississippi	MS	Wisconsin	WI
Missouri	MO	Wyoming	WY

(*Hint:* Use nested *switch* statements, where the outer statement uses the first letter of the abbreviation as its switch expression.)

2. Design and write a Java application that reads a date in numeric form from a set of three fields and displays it in English within a label. Use appropriate buttons. For example:

Given the date:

```
10  27  1942
```

The program displays:

```
October twenty-seventh, nineteen hundred forty-two.
```

Here is another example:

Given the date:

```
12   10   2010
```

The program displays:

```
December tenth, two thousand ten.
```

The program should display an error message for any invalid date, such as `2  29 1883` (1883 wasn't a leap year).

3. Write a Java application that reads full names from an input file and writes the initials for the names to an output file named `initials`. For example, the input

```
John James Henry
```

should produce the output

```
JJH
```

The names are stored in the input file first name first, then middle name, then last name, separated by an arbitrary number of blanks. There is only one name per line. The first name or the middle name could be just an initial.

4. Write a Java application that converts letters of the alphabet into their corresponding digits on the telephone. The program should let the user enter letters repeatedly until a 'Q' or a 'Z' is entered. (Q and Z are the two letters that are not on the telephone.) An error message should be printed for any nonalphabetic character that is entered.

The letters and digits on the telephone have the following correspondence.

```
ABC  = 2    DEF  = 3    GHI = 4
JKL  = 5    MNO  = 6    PRS = 7
TUV  = 8    WXY  = 9
```

Here is an example:

When the user enters `P` the program displays:

```
The letter P corresponds to 7 on the telephone.
```

When the user enters `A` the program displays:

```
The letter A corresponds to 2 on the telephone.
```

When the user enters `D` the program displays:

```
The letter D corresponds to 3 on the telephone.
```

When the user enters `2` the program displays:

```
Invalid letter. Enter Q or Z to quit.
```

When the user enters `Z` the program quits.

5. Rewrite the `Rainfall` program so that it asks the user for the input file name using a `Frame`, and catches the `FileNotFoundException` if the name is invalid. In the case of an invalid file name, the user should be asked to re-enter the file name until a valid name is entered or they close the `Frame` (signaling that they want to stop the program).

Case Study Follow-Up Exercises

1. Rewrite the `processOneSite` method in the `Rainfall` application, replacing the *for* loop with a *do* loop.
2. Rewrite the `processOneSite` method in the `Rainfall` program, replacing the *for* loop with a *while* loop.
3. Change the *do* loop in `main` in the `Rainfall` program to be a *while* loop.
4. Could module Get RainFall Amount be made a method? Explain.

One-Dimensional Arrays

In Chapter 4, we showed a diagram of Java data types (repeated below as Figure 11.1). Java data types are broken into primitive and reference types. Recall that Java stores primitive types directly into the named location, but reference types are stored into the place whose address is stored in the named location. We have covered classes and primitive types in previous chapters. We extend the discussion of the Java data types in this chapter by examining the array. However, before we do, we step back and look at data types from a general perspective rather than from a Java perspective.

11.1 Atomic Data Types

Recall that a data type is a set of data values, along with a set of operations on those values. The definitions of integer and real numbers come from mathematics. Integer numbers are the set of whole numbers from negative to positive infinity, and the operations defined for them are the arithmetic operations, specified by +, -, / (integer division), *, and modulus, assignment, and the relational operations.

Real numbers are the set of all numbers from negative to positive infinity, and the operations are the same as those for the integers except that integer division and modulus are excluded. Because computers are finite, programming languages put limits on the range of integers and the range and precision of real numbers. Java provides four different types of integer numbers that differ only in the range of values that they can represent in memory: `byte`, `short`, `int`, and `long`. Java has two real types (called floating-point) that differ only in the range and precision that they can represent: `float` and `double`.

Alphanumeric characters, another simple type, are the symbols that we use in written language. These symbols vary from one natural language to another. The same is true of characters used to represent textual data in a computer. For many years, there were two main character sets: ASCII and EBCDIC. In these character sets, each character occupies one byte in memory, giving 256 possible characters. Some of the characters are nonprintable control characters used by the computer's hardware. Unicode, a character set that uses two bytes to represent each character, was developed to include characters for writing text in many natural languages. Unicode, which Java uses, contains ASCII as a subset.

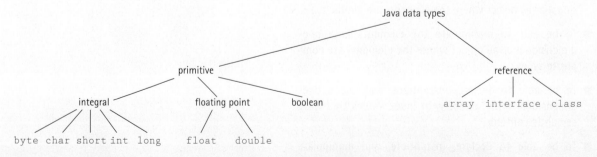

Figure 11.1   *Java data types*

The operations defined on alphanumeric characters are the relational operations and assignment. The ordering used by the relational operators is the collating sequence of the character set. Although the collating sequence is different for different character sets, the letters and digits are ordered as we would expect; that is, 'A'<'B'<'C' ... and '1'<'2'<'3'....

Characters are treated differently in different programming languages. In Pascal, the data type for a character is distinct. Arithmetic operations, applied to character data, cause a compile-time error. In C++, there is no real distinction between characters and numbers. Arithmetic operations may be applied to character data and often are. The only difference is that, when character data is printed, the character itself is printed rather than the numeric representation of the character. In Java, arithmetic operations applied to character data cause the compiler to insert a cast operation that converts the character to a numerical value.

Boolean values are another simple data type comprised of the two literals True and False. The operations allowed on these values are the logical operators AND, OR, NOT, the relational operations, and assignment operations. Although many languages consider Boolean values to be ordered, Java does not, so only equal and not equal can be applied to Boolean values in Java. Java calls the Boolean type `boolean` and the literals `true` and `false`.

Integers, reals, characters, and Booleans have two properties in common. Each is made up of indivisible, or atomic, elements, and each is ordered. Data types with these properties are called scalar data types. (Java's type `boolean` is not scalar because they aren't ordered.)

Scalar data type A data type in which the values are ordered and each value is atomic (indivisible)

When we say that a value is *atomic*, we mean that it has no component parts that can be accessed independently. For example, a single character is atomic, but the string "Good Morning" is not because it is composed of 12 characters. When we say that the values are ordered, we mean that exactly one of the relations less than, greater than, or equal is true for any pair of values. Some examples of ordered relationships are

```
1 < 2      'C' > 'A'      3.562 < 106.22
```

Integers, characters, and Booleans have an additional property: Each value (except the first) has a unique predecessor and each value (except the last) has a unique successor. A type with this property is called an ordinal data type.

Ordinal data type A data type in which each value (except the first) has a unique predecessor and each value (except the last) has a unique successor

Real numbers are not ordinal because a real value has no unique predecessor or successor. If one more digit of precision is added, the predecessor and successor change; that is, 0.52 and 0.520 are the same, but the predecessor of 0.52 is 0.51, and the predecessor of 0.520 is 0.519. Because Java's type `boolean` is not ordered, it is not ordinal.

Although the ordinals are a subset of the scalars, they are quite different. Mathematicians make this same distinction; they talk about continuous values versus discrete values. There are many real-life analogies that demonstrate this distinction as well: the continuous spectrum of colors in a real rainbow versus the discrete colors in a child's crayon drawing of a rainbow or the continuous tone of a violin sliding up the scale versus the discrete tones of a piano.

Java classifies the scalar types that it represents as "primitive." "Simple" is another name for scalar types.

11.2 Composite Data Types

There are times when it is necessary to show a relationship among variables or to store and reference collections of variables as a group. For this reason we need a way to associate an identifier with a collection of values. A data type made up of a collection of values is called a composite data type.

> **Composite data type** A data type that allows a collection of values to be associated with an identifier of that type.
>
> **Unstructured data type** A collection of components that are not organized with respect to one another
>
> **Structured data type** An organized collection of components; the organization determines the method used to access individual components.

Composite data types come in two forms: unstructured and structured. An unstructured data type is one in which no relationship exists among the values in the data type other than that they are members of the same collection. A structured data type, on the other hand, is an organized collection of components, one in which a relationship exists among the items in the collection. We use this relationship to access individual items within the collection as well as manipulate the collection as a whole.

A value in a simple type is a single data item; it cannot be broken down into component parts. For example, in Java each `int` value is a single integer number and cannot be further decomposed. In contrast, a composite data type is one in which each value is a collection of component items. The entire collection is given a single name, yet each component can still be accessed individually.

The class is an example of a composite data type. A class has a name and is composed of named data fields and methods. An instance of a class, including the data fields and methods, can be passed as a parameter. The data fields and methods can be accessed individually by name. A class is unstructured because the meaning is not dependent on the ordering of the data fields or the methods within the source code. That is, the order in which the members of the class are listed can be changed without changing the function of the class.

In Java, all composite types are either classes, interfaces, or arrays. Rather than talking about the type of a composite object, we talk about its class. An example of a composite object in Java is an instance of the `String` class, used for creating and manipulating strings. When you declare a variable `myString` to be of class `String`, `myString` does not represent just one atomic data value; it represents an entire collection of characters and the methods that manipulate the characters. But each of the components in the string can be accessed individually by using an expression such as `myString.charAt(3)`, which accesses the `char` value at position 3. Therefore, the characters within the string are organized according to their relative positions.

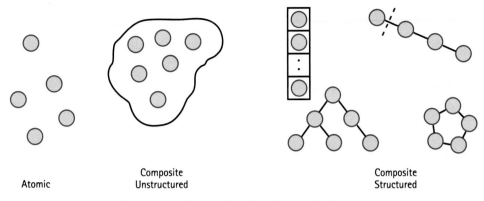

Atomic   Composite Unstructured   Composite Structured

Figure 11.2 *Atomic (simple) and composite data types*

Simple data types are the building blocks for composite types. A composite type gathers together a set of component values and usually imposes a specific arrangement on them (see Figure 11.2). If the composite type is a built-in type, the accessing mechanism is provided in the syntax of the language. If the composite type is a user-defined type, the accessing mechanism is built into the methods provided with the class.

In Chapters 1 through 10, we have discussed control structures and the `class`, an unstructured composite type. In the next three chapters we focus on structured composite data types. Of course, we do not abandon the class, but we focus on having a structured composite type as a field in a class.

11.3 One-Dimensional Arrays

How we organize our data plays an important role in the design process. If the internal data representation for a class is a composite type, that is, if it contains more than a single atomic field, we call the internal representation a data structure. The choice of data structure directly affects the design because it determines the algorithms used to process the data. The class gives us the ability to refer to an entire group of components by one name. This simplifies the design of many programs.

> **Data structure** The implementation of a composite data field in a class

Many problems, however, have so many components that it is difficult to process them if each one must have a unique field name. For example, if we use individually named values to read and print a file in reverse order, all the values must be read and saved before the last one can be printed. If there are 1,000 values, we must define 1,000 individual variables to hold the values and input and output each value separately–an incredibly tedious task! An array–the last of Java's built-in reference types–is the data type that allows us to program operations of this kind with ease.

Let's look at how we would have to solve this problem with simple variables.

```
// Read 1,000 numbers and print them in reverse order.
import java.io.*
public class ReadWrite
{
  private static BufferedReader inFile;
  private static PrintWriter outFile;
  public static void main(String[] args) throws IOException
  {
    inFile = new BufferedReader(new FileReader("infile.dat"));
    outFile = new PrintWriter(new FileWriter("outfile.dat"));

    // Declare 1,000 integer values.
    int value0;
    int value1;
    int value2;
    .
    .
    .
    int value999;

    // Read 1,000 integer values
    value0 = Integer.valueOf(inFile.readLine()).intValue();
    value1 = Integer.valueOf(inFile.readLine()).intValue();
    value2 = Integer.valueOf(inFile.readLine()).intValue();
    .
    .
    .
    value999 = Integer.valueOf(inFile.readLine()).integerValue();

    // Write out 1,000 values.
    outFile.println(value999);
    outFile.println(value998);
    outFile.println(value997);
    .
    .
    .
    outFile.println(value0);
    inFile.close();
    outFile.close();
    System.exit(0);
  }
}
```

This program is over 3,000 lines long, and we have to use 1,000 separate variables. Note that all the variables have the same name except for an appended number that distinguishes them. Wouldn't it be convenient if we could put the number into a counter variable and use *for* loops to go from 0 through 999, and then from 999 back down to 0? For example, if the counter variable were number, we could replace the 2,000 original input/output statements with the following four lines of code (we enclose number in brackets to set it apart from value):

```
for (number = 0; number < 1000; number++)
  value[number] = Integer.valueOf(inFile.readLine()).integerValue();
for (number = 999; number >= 0; number--)
  outFile.println(value[number]);
```

This code fragment is correct in Java *if* we declare value to be a *one-dimensional array,* which is a collection of variables—all of the same type—where the first part of each variable name is the same, and the last part is an *index value* enclosed in square brackets. In our example, the value stored in number is called the *index.*

The declaration of a one-dimensional array is similar to the declaration of a simple variable (a variable of a simple data type), with one exception. You must indicate that it is an array by putting square brackets next to the type.

```
int[] value;
```

Because an array is a reference type, it must be instantiated, at which time you specify how large the array is to be.

```
value = new int[1000];
```

value is an array with 1000 components, all of type int. The first component has index value 0, the second component has index value 1, and the last component has index value 999.

Here is the program to print out numbers in reverse order using an array. This is certainly much shorter than our first version of the program.

```
// Read 1,000 numbers and print them in reverse order.
import java.io.*
public class ReadWrite
{
  private static BufferedReader inFile;
  private static PrintWriter outFile;
  public static void main(String[] args) throws IOException
  { // Open files
    inFile = new BufferedReader(new FileReader("infile.dat");
    outFile = new PrintWriter(new FileWriter("outfile.dat");
    // Declare and instantiate an array variable.
    int[] value = new int[1000];
    // Read 1000 values
    for (int number = 0; number < 1000; number++)
      value[number] =
        Integer.valueOf(inFile.readLine()).intValue();
    // Print 1000 values in reverse order
    for (int number = 999; number >= 0; number--)
      outFile.println(value[number]);
```

```
    // Close files and exit
    inFile.close();
    outFile.close();
    System.exit(0);
  }
}
```

In general terminology, an array differs from a class in three fundamental ways:

1. An array is a *homogeneous* data structure (all components in the structure are of the same data type), whereas classes are heterogeneous types (their components may be of different types).

2. A component of an array is accessed by its *position* in the structure, whereas a component of a class is accessed by an identifier (the field name).

3. Because array components are accessed by position, an array is a structured data type.

Let's now define Java arrays formally and look at the rules for accessing individual components.

> **One-dimensional array** A structured collection of components, all of the same type, that is given a single name. Each component (array element) is accessed by an index that indicates the component's position within the collection.

Declaring an Array

A one-dimensional array is a structured collection of components (often called array elements) that can be accessed individually by specifying the position of a component with a single index value.

Here is a syntax template describing the simplest form of a one-dimensional array declaration:

ArrayDeclaration

> DataType [ ] ArrayName ;

In the syntax template, `DataType` describes what is stored in each component of the array. The brackets following `DataType` indicate that this is an array of `DataType` elements. Array components may be of almost any type, but for now we limit our discussion to atomic components. We know from Figure 11.1 that the array is a reference type. `ArrayName` is a location in memory that holds the address of an array when the `ArrayName` is instantiated. For example,

```
int[] numbers;
```

declares an array of integers. We tell the compiler how many components the array contains when we instantiate it.

Creating an Array

You create an array just like you create any object; you use `new`. Here is the syntax template for instantiating an array. Notice that arrays don't need to be initialized, so we don't pass a list of arguments. Instead, we put the number of slots to be in the array in brackets beside the type of the array.

ArrayCreation

```
new TypeName [IntExpression]
```

`IntExpression` is an integer expression that specifies the number of components in the array. This expression must have a value greater than or equal to 0. If the value is n, the range of index values is 0 through $n - 1$, not 1 through n. For example, the declarations

```
float[] angle;              // Declares the array variable
angle = new float[4];       // Instantiates the array object
int[] testScore;            // Declares the array variable
testScore = new int[10];    // Instantiates the array object
```

instantiate the arrays shown in Figure 11.3. The `angle` array has four components, each capable of holding one `float` value. The `testScore` array has a total of 10 components, all of type `int`.

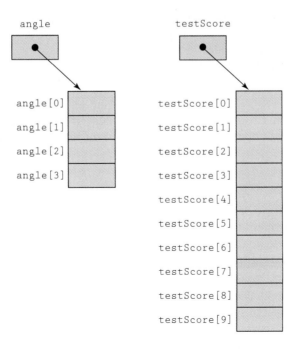

Figure 11.3   *angle and* testScore *arrays*

An array can be declared and instantiated in separate statements or the declaration and creation can be combined into one step as shown here.

```
// Declared and instantiated in one statement
float[] angle = new float[4];
// Declared and instantiated in one statement
int[] testScore = new int[10];
```

Because arrays are reference types in Java, they are instantiated at run time, not at compile time. Therefore, the IntExpression used to instantiate an array object does not have to be a constant. It can be a value that you have read into the program. For example, if you have read the value of dataSize from a file, the following declaration is legal:

```
int[] data = new int[dataSize];
```

Once instantiated, data always has dataSize components. For example, if dataSize is 10 when the array object data is instantiated but is later changed to 15, data still has 10 components.

Java provides an alternate syntax for declaring an array object; the brackets that signal an array can be placed after the array name as shown below:

```
char letters[];
char upperCase[];
char lowerCase[];
```

We do not recommend using this syntactic form, however. It is more consistent–and safer–to place the brackets with the type of the components. We say it is safer because, as you may recall from Chapter 2, Java also lets us declare multiple identifiers with a statement such as this:

```
char letters[], upperCase[], lowerCase;
```

Look closely at this example: letters and upperCase are composite variables of type char[], but lowerCase is a simple variable of type char. If you use the syntax that we introduced first, you cannot forget to put the brackets on one of the array identifiers:

```
char[] letters, upperCase, lowerCase;
```

Declaring and Creating an Array with an Initializer List

Java provides an alternative way to instantiate an array. You learned previously that Java allows you to initialize a variable in its declaration:

```
int delta = 25;
```

The value 25 is called an *initializer*. You also can initialize an array in its declaration, using a special syntax for the initializer. You specify a list of initial values for the array elements, separate them with commas, and enclose the list within braces:

```
int[] age = {23, 10, 16, 37, 12};
```

In this declaration, `age[0]` is initialized to 23, `age[1]` is initialized to 10, and so on. Notice two interesting things about this syntax. First, the `new` operator is not used; second, the number of components is not specified. When the compiler sees an initializer list, it determines the size by the number of items in the list, instantiates an array of that size, and stores the values into their proper places. Of course, the types of the values in the initializer list must match the type of the array.

What are the values in an array instantiated by using `new`? If the array components are primitive types, they are set to their default value. If the array components are reference types, the components are set to `null`.

There are only two ways that an object can be created without using `new`: by using an array initializer list and by creating a `String` literal.

Accessing Individual Components

Recall that to access an individual field of a class, we use dot notation—the name of the class object, followed by a period, followed by the field name. In contrast, to access an individual array component, we write the array name, followed by an expression enclosed in square brackets. The expression specifies which component to access. The syntax template for accessing an array component is

ArrayComponentAccess

```
ArrayName [IndexExpression]
```

The IndexExpression may be as simple as a constant or a variable name or as complex as a combination of variables, operators, and method calls. Whatever the form of the expression, it must result in an integer value. Index expressions can be of type `byte`, `char`, `short`, or `int`.[1] Using an index expression of type `long` causes a compile-time error. The simplest form of index expression is a constant. Using our `angle` array, the sequence of assignment statements

```
angle[0] = 4.93;
angle[1] = -15.2;
angle[2] = 0.5;
angle[3] = 1.67;
```

fills the array components one at a time (see Figure 11.4).

---

[1] Java inherits the notion that type `char` is a numeric type from C. The Java language specifications say that arrays must be indexed by `int` values but that values of type `short`, `byte`, or `char` may also be used because they are subjected to unary numeric promotion and become `int` values. However, for clarity we type cast `char` values to `int` when using them as an index.

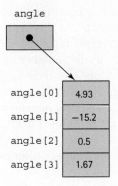

Figure 11.4 *angle array with values*

Each array component—angle[2], for instance—can be treated exactly the same as any simple variable of type float. For example, we can do the following to the individual component angle[2]:

```
// Assign it a value
angle[2] = 9.6;

// Read a value into it
angle[2] = Double.valueOf(inFile.readLine()).doubleValue();

// Write its contents
oufFile.println(angle[2]);

// Pass it as an argument
y = Math.sqrt(angle[2]);

// Use it in an expression
x = 6.8 * angle[2] + 7.5;
```

Let's look at a more complicated index expression. Suppose we declare a 1,000-element array of int values with the statement

```
int[] value = new int[1000];
```

and execute the following statement:

```
value[counter] = 5;
```

In this statement, 5 is stored into an array component. If counter is 0, 5 is stored into the first component of the array. If counter is 1, 5 is stored into the second place in the array, and so forth. If instead we execute this statement:

```
if (value[number+1] % 10 != 0)
```

then the expression number+1 selects an array component. The specific array component accessed is divided by 10 and checked to see if the remainder is nonzero. If number+1 is 0, we are testing the value in the first component; if number+1 is 1, we are testing the second place; and so on. Figure 11.5 shows the index expression as a constant, a variable, and a more complex expression.

Out-of-Bounds Array Indexes

Given the declaration

```
float[] alpha = new float[100];
```

the valid range of index values is 0 through 99. Starting at 0 seems awkward, because we are used to numbering things beginning with 1. However, you should not be surprised; the positions in a string begin with 0. What happens if we try to execute the statement

```
alpha[i] = 62.4;
```

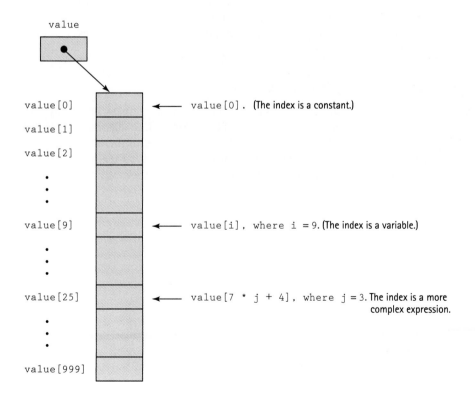

Figure 11.5 *An index as a constant, a variable, and an arbitrary expression*

when i is less than 0 or when i is greater than 99? The result is that a memory location outside the array would be accessed, which causes an error. This error is called an *out-of-bounds* error. Some languages, C++ for instance, do not check for this error, but Java does. If your program attempts to use an index that is not within the bounds of the array, an `ArrayIndexOutOfBoundsException` is thrown. Rather than try to catch this error, you should write your code to prevent it.

In Java, each array that is instantiated has a `public` instance variable, called `length`, associated with it that contains the number of components in the array. `length` can be used when processing the components in the array to keep from having an out-of-bounds error. Here's how. Array-processing algorithms often use *for* loops to step through the array elements one at a time. Here is a loop to zero out our 100-element `alpha` array:

> **Out-of-bounds error** An error caused by an index value that is either less than 0 or greater than the array size minus 1.

```
for (int i = 0; i < alpha.length; i++)
   alpha[i] = 0.0;
```

Use this pattern—initialize your counter to zero, use a less-than test against the size of the array object—and you can ensure that your counter is within the bounds of the array. If your program does crash with an `ArrayIndexOutOfBoundsException`, immediately check to be sure your relational operator is the less than operator, not the less than or equal operator.

Aggregate Array Operations

We can assign one array to another and we can compare two arrays for equality—but we might not get the answer we expect. Arrays, like classes, are reference types. This means that the value stored in the location assigned to the object name is not the object itself but the address of where the object is stored. Let's see what happens when we test two arrays for equality and assign one array to another.

```
int[] numbers = {2, 4, 6};
int[] values;
values[0] = 2;
values[1] = 4;
values[2] = 6;

if (numbers == values)
   . . .
numbers = values;
if (numbers == values)
   . . .
```

The first *if* expression is false because `numbers` and `values` occupy different places in memory. (See Figure 11.6a.) The next statement takes the contents of `values` (the

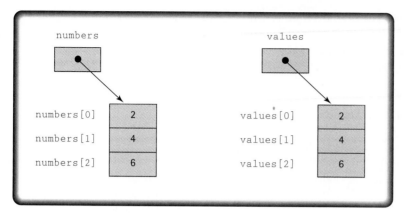

a. Result is `false`; these are two different arrays.

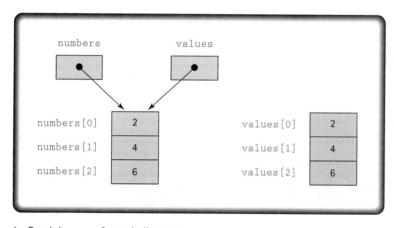

b. Result is `true` after a shallow copy.

Figure 11.6   *Comparison of array variables*

address of where the array is stored) and stores it into `numbers`. Now the *if* expression is true. `numbers` contains the address in memory of where the array referenced by `values` is stored. (See Figure 11.6b.)

You should not be surprised at this example. Assignment for reference types is a shallow assignment; an equality test for reference types is a shallow test. If you want to have a deep test, you must write a method to do the comparison, element by element:

```
int[] numbers = {2, 4, 6, 9};
int[] sameNumbers = new int[numbers.length];
// Deep copy of numbers to someNumbers
for (int index = 0; index < numbers.length; index++)
  sameNumbers[index] = numbers[index];
```

```
boolean compareArrays(int[] one, int[] two)
{
  if (one.length != two.length)
    return false;

  // Compare array objects component by component
  boolean result = true;
  int index = 0;
  while (index < one.length && result)
  {
    if (one[index] == two[index])
      index++;
    else
      result = false;
  }
  return result;
}
```

Now examine these comparisons:

```
if (numbers == sameNumbers)
  ...
if (compareArrays(numbers, sameNumbers))
  ...
```

The first expression is false. The array objects sameNumbers and numbers contain the same values, but the equality test is for addresses not values. The second expression is true because compareArrays is a method that performs a deep comparison.

11.4 Examples of Declaring and Processing Arrays

We now look in detail at some specific examples of declaring and accessing arrays. These examples demonstrate different applications of arrays in programs.

Occupancy Rates

Here are some declarations that a program might use to analyze occupancy rates in an apartment building:

```
final int BUILDING_SIZE = 350; // Number of apartments

int[] occupants = new int[BUILDING_SIZE];
// occupants[i] is the number of occupants in apartment i
int totalOccupants;              // Total number of occupants
```

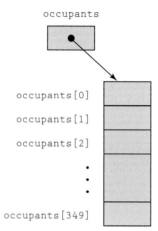

Figure 11.7   *occupants array*

occupants is a 350-element array of integers (see Figure 11.7): occupants[0] = 3 if the first apartment has three occupants; occupants[1] = 5 if the second apartment has five occupants; and so on. If values have been stored into the array object, then the following code totals the number of occupants in the building.

```
totalOccupants = 0;
for (int counter = 0; counter < occupants.length; counter++)
   totalOccupants = totalOccupants + occupants[counter];
```

The first time through the loop, counter is 0. We add the contents of totalOccupants (that is, 0) and the contents of occupants[0], storing the result into totalOccupants. Next, counter becomes 1 and the loop test occurs. The second loop iteration adds the contents of totalOccupants and the contents of occupants[1], storing the result into totalOccupants. Now counter becomes 2 and the loop test is made. Eventually, the loop adds the contents of occupants[349] and the sum and increments counter to 350. At this point, the loop condition is false, and control exits the loop.

Note how we used the named constant BUILDING_SIZE in the array declaration and occupants.length in the *for* loop. When a constant is used in this manner, changes are easy to make. If the number of apartments changes from 350 to 400, we just need to change the declaration of BUILDING_SIZE. We could also have written

```
for (int counter = 0; counter < BUILDING_SIZE; counter++)
```

but we prefer to use the length field because it is specifically associated with the array. In the future, the program might be changed to use a different constant to set the size of occupants. Then BUILDING_SIZE would no longer be the correct value to terminate the loop, but occupants.length is still correct.

Sales Figures

Now let's look at an example where the values stored in the array are sales figures and the indexes are the product numbers. (The products are gourmet hamburgers.) The product numbers range from 1 through 5. We can make the array object contain six components and just ignore the 0th position, or we can set up five components and make sure that we add (or subtract) 1 from the product number to get the proper slot. Let's use the latter strategy.

```
// Declare and instantiate an array with 5 real components.
double[] gourmetBurgers = new double[5];
```

The data for this example are (hamburger number, day's sales) pairs. The data file contains a week's worth of such pairs. The first value is an integer between 1 and 5 that represents one of the gourmet hamburgers. The next value is the sales amount for that hamburger for the day. Each value is on a line by itself. The following code segment reads in a hamburger number, sales figure pair.

```
inFile = new BufferedReader(new FileReader("infile.dat"));
outFile = new PrintWriter(new FileWriter("outfile.dat"));
int burgerNumber;
double salesAmount;
  . . .
burgerNumber = Integer.valueOf(inFile.readLine()).intValue();
salesAmount = Double.valueOf(inFile.readLine()).doubleValue();
```

To add the sales amount to the value in the appropriate slot in the array, we use `burgerNumber-1` as the index into the array `gourmetBurgers`.

```
gourmetBurgers[burgerNumber - 1] =
      salesAmount + gourmetBurgers[burgerNumber - 1];
```

If we put our input and processing within a loop, we can process the week's worth of sales figures. We can then write the totals out to a file with the following loop.

```
for (burgerNumber = 0; burgerNumber < gourmetBurgers.length; burgerNumber++)
{
  outFile.print("Gourmet Burger # " + (burgerNumber + 1));
  outFile.println(": " + gourmetBurgers[burgerNumber]);
}
```

Figure 11.8 shows the contents of array object `gourmetBurgers` after the data shown has been processed. Note that the data is shown all on one line with commas between pairs to save space.

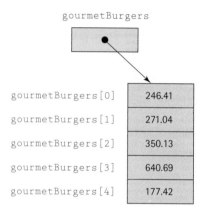

gourmetBurgers

gourmetBurgers[0]	246.41
gourmetBurgers[1]	271.04
gourmetBurgers[2]	350.13
gourmetBurgers[3]	640.69
gourmetBurgers[4]	177.42

Data
1 50.25, 2 44.75, 4 100.33, 3 85.12, 5 20.76
3 75.20, 1 50.20, 4 95.12, 5 77.44, 2 44.75
5 12.23, 4 125.12, 3 55.23 2 70.12, 1 44.75
1 55.66, 2 66.67, 3 77.78, 4 200.12, 5 44.75
2 44.75, 3 56.80, 4 120.00, 5 11.12, 1 45.55

Figure 11.8   *gourmetBurgers array*

This example, where the index into the array is one less than the number assigned to a type of hamburger, is a type of problem where the index has semantic content. That is, the index has meaning within the problem itself.

Letter Counts

As a final example in this section, let's use an array to count the number of times each letter in the English alphabet is used in text, either uppercase or lowercase. We declare an array of 26 integers, one for each letter.

```
int[] letterCount = new int[26];
```

letterCount[0] is the counter for the number of times we see an 'a', letterCount[1] is the counter for the number of times we see a 'b', and letterCount[25] is the number of times we see a 'z'. How do we convert a letter to its position in the array? Well, we read a character and see if it is a letter. If so, we convert it to uppercase. The uppercase letter minus 'A' gives us the letter's place in the array. The following code fragment accomplishes this conversion:

```
letter = dataFile.read();
if (((char)letter >= 'A' && (char)letter <= 'Z' ||
    ((char)letter >= 'a' && (char)letter <= 'z'))
```

The following statements convert the letter to an index and increment the counter for the character.

```
index = (int)Character.toUpperCase((char)letter) - (int) 'A';
letterCount[index] = letterCount[index] +1;
```

The following loop ties these pieces together.

```
letter = dataFile.read();          // Priming read
while (letter != -1)
{
  if (((char)letter >= 'A' && (char)letter <= 'Z') ||
      ((char)letter >= 'a' && (char)letter <= 'z'))
  {
    // Convert letter to an index
    index = (int)Character.toUpperCase((char)letter) - (int) 'A';
    // Increment counter
    letterCount[index] = letterCount[index] + 1;
  }
  letter = dataFile.read();     // Get a character
}
```

Now all we need is a loop that prints out the values:

```
for (index = 0; index < letterCount.length; index++)
  outFile.println("The number of all " + (char) (index + (int)'A')
    + letterCount[index]);
```

11.5 Arrays of Objects

Although arrays with atomic components are very common, many applications require a collection of composite objects. For example, a business needs a list of parts records, and a teacher needs a list of students in a class. Arrays are ideal for these applications. We simply define an array whose components are class objects.

Arrays of Strings

Let's define an array of strings, each of which is a grocery item. Declaring and creating the array of objects is exactly like declaring and creating an array where the components are atomic types.

```
String[] groceryItems = new String[10];  // Array of strings
```

groceryItems is an array of 10 strings. How many characters are there in each string? We don't know yet. The array of strings has been instantiated, but the string objects themselves have not. Another way of saying this is that groceryItems is an array of *references* to string objects, which are set to null when the array is instantiated. The string objects must be instantiated separately. The following code segment reads and stores 10 strings into groceryItems.

```
inFile = new BufferedReader(new FileReader("infile.dat"));
outFile = new PrintWriter(new FileWriter("outfile.dat"));
...
int index;      // index into groceryItems
String[] groceryItems = new String[10];

// Read and store strings from file inFile
for (index = 0; index < groceryItems.length; index++)
{
  groceryItems[index] = inFile.readLine();
}
```

The `readLine` method is a value returning method, which instantiates the string, stores values into it, and returns it. That is, the reference to the string is returned and stored into `groceryItems`. Figure 11.9 shows what the array looks like with values in it.

An array name with no brackets is the array object. An array name with brackets is a component. The component can be manipulated just like any other variable of that type.

Expression	Class/Type
groceryItems	An array
groceryItems[0]	A string
groceryItems[0].charAt(0)	A character

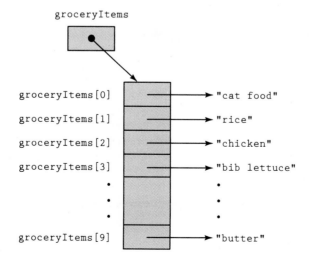

Figure 11.9 *groceryItems array*

How would you read in grocery items if you didn't know how many you had? You know that there are no more than 10, but you don't know exactly how many. You would have to use a *while* loop that reads in a grocery item and stores it in the first place. If there were another item, it would be stored in the second place, and so on. This means that you must keep a counter of how many items you read in. Here is a code fragment that would read and store grocery items until 10 had been read or the file is empty.

```
// Read and store strings from file inFile.
int index = 0;
String anItem = inFile.readLine();
while (index < groceryItems.length  && anItem != null)
{
   groceryItems[index] =  anItem;
   index++;
   anItem = inFile.readLine();
}
System.out.println(index + " grocery items were read and stored.");
```

Look carefully at Figures 11.9 and 11.10. In Figure 11.9, every slot in the array is filled with grocery items. In Figure 11.10, index items have been read in and stored. If index is equal to 10, then the two figures are the same. To process the items in Figure 11.10, you use a loop that goes from 0 through index-1.

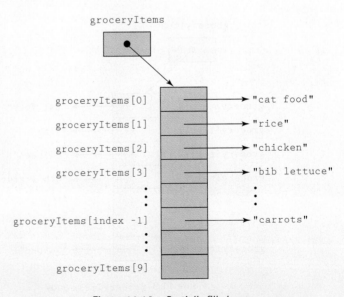

Figure 11.10 *Partially filled array*

You first saw a reference to an array of strings in Chapter 1. In class `Payroll` the following statement appears:

```
public static void main(String[] args) throws IOException
```

The parameter for method `main` is an array of strings, called `args` by convention. There are ways of running Java programs that allow you to pass string arguments to method `main`. We do not use this feature in our programs, but we still have to list the parameter on the heading.

Throughout this chapter we have drawn array variables with an arrow to the object structure to which they refer. An array type is a reference type. When we declare an array variable with the name `groceryItems`, one location in memory is assigned to that name. When the array is instantiated, the address of the place in memory where the actual structure begins is stored into location `groceryItems`. This address is called the base address of the array.

> **Base address** The memory address of the first element of an array

If the component type is an atomic type, the values are actually stored in the memory locations beginning at the base address. If the component type is a reference type, a reference to the first component is stored in the base address. We have used the arrow in our drawings as a visual reminder that the contents of a reference variable is the address of where the object can be found.

Clearly, strings and arrays are related. You can visualize a string as an array of characters. You can visualize an array as a string of values. Because of this similarity, the `String` class has methods that transform a string into an array of `char` and an array of `char` (`char[]`) into a string. Method `toCharArray` in class `String` converts a string value into a `char[]`. Method `valueOf` takes a `char[]` and converts it into a string.

Arrays of User-Defined Objects

In the last example, the components of the array were strings. Now let's look at an array of user-defined objects. In Chapter 7, we used the `Date` class as an example. The following code declares and instantiates an array of elements of class `Date`.

```
Date[] bigEvents = new Date[10];
```

and the following shows the types involved and how to access the various components.

Expression	Class/Type
bigEvents	An array
bigEvents[0]	A `Date` object
bigEvents[0].month	A string
bigEvents[0].day	An integer
bigEvents[0].year	An integer
bigEvents[0].month.charAt(1)	A character

11.6 Arrays and Methods

The only observer method provided for arrays is component access, which has its own special syntax: the array object's name, followed by an index enclosed in brackets. The index specifies which of the components to access.

However, when we use an array as a field in a class, we may need to pass an array object as a parameter to a method or pass a component of an array object to a method. Recall from Chapter 7 that all parameters in Java are passed by value. That is, a copy of each parameter is sent to the method. Because an array, like a class, is a reference type, what is passed to the method is the address of where the object is stored.

Suppose we define a `public` class method (say, in class `Accounting`) that takes an array as an argument and returns the sum of the components in the array:

```
public static double sumSales(double[] data)
{
  double sum = 0.0;
  for (int index = 0; index < data.length; index++)
    sum = sum + data[index];
  return sum;
}
```

The following statement uses method `sumSales` to sum the week's gourmet hamburger sales.

```
outFile.print("This week's sales of gourmet hamburgers: ");
outFile.println(Accounting.sumSales(gourmetBurgers));
```

What is passed as a parameter to `sumSales`? It is the base address of `gourmetBurgers` (the arrow in Figure 11.8).

There are two cases to consider when passing array components as arguments to a method: the component is a primitive type, or the component is a reference type. If the component is a primitive type, the method cannot change the value of its parameter. If the component is a reference type, the method can change the value of its parameter *but it should not.* Changing the value of a parameter is poor style.

11.7 Special Kinds of Array Processing

Two types of problems occur frequently that use arrays as part of the internal data structure for a class. One problem uses only part of the defined array in which to store data and the other problem is one in which the index values have specific meaning within the problem.

Partial (or Sub) Array Processing

The size of an array is the declared number of array components—the number of slots set aside for the array object in memory. Java has an instance field `length` associated with each array object that contains this value. In many problems, however, we do not know how many data values we actually have, so we declare the array to be as big as it would ever need to be. This means that we may not fill all of the array components with values. In order to avoid processing slots into which we have not stored valid data, we must keep track of how many components are actually filled.

As values are put into the array, we keep a count of how many components are filled. We then use this count to process only components that have values stored in them. Any remaining places are not processed. For example, if there are 250 students in a class, a program to analyze test grades would set aside 250 locations for the grades. However, some students may be absent on the day of the test. So the number of test grades must be counted, and that number, rather than 250, is used to control the processing of the array. This number becomes part of the internal representation of the class being defined. Figure 11.10 visualizes this type of processing.

Chapter 12 examines subarray processing in detail.

Indexes with Semantic Content

In some problems, an array index has meaning beyond simple position; that is, the index has semantic content. An example is the `gourmetBurgers` array we showed earlier. This array was indexed by the number of the type of hamburger minus 1. That is, the sales for the hamburger that the company called #1 occupied the 0th position in the array; hamburger #2 occupied the 1st position in the array; etc.

Problem-Solving Case Study

Comparison of Two Lists

Statement of the Problem You are writing an application that does not tolerate erroneous input data. Therefore, the data values are prepared by entering them twice into one file. The file contains two lists of positive integer numbers, separated by a negative number. These two lists of numbers should be identical; if they are not, then a data-entry error has occurred. For example, if the input file contains the sequence of numbers 17, 14, 8, −5, 17, 14, 8, then the two lists of three numbers are identical. However, the sequence 17, 14, 8, −5, 17, 12, 8 shows a data-entry error.

You decide to write a separate application to compare the lists and print out any pairs of numbers that are not the same. The exact number of integers in each list is unknown, but each list has no more than 500.

Brainstorming In all previous problems involving files, we just read and/or wrote them, value by value. Here we have to compare the first value on the file with the first value following a negative number; the second value with the second value following a negative number; and so on. The comparison cannot begin until the values have been read in. We need two container objects: one to hold the first list and one to hold the second list.

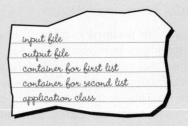

input file
output file
container for first list
container for second list
application class

Filtering Do we really need two container objects? If we were checking the lists by hand, we would write the numbers from the first list on a pad of paper, one per line. The line number would correspond to the number's position in the list; that is, the first number would be on the first line, the second number on the second line, and so on. The first number in the second list would then be compared to the number on the first line, the second number to the number on the second line, and so forth. We wouldn't write the second sequence on a sheet of paper in order to compare the values. So we need only one container object.

input file
output file
container for first list
application class

Scenarios Let's call our container class `FirstList`. What are its responsibilities? It must create itself by defining a constructor. What does the constructor do? It must set the number of values read so far to zero. Class `FirstList` is responsible for reading values from the file and storing them into the list. And finally, it is responsible for determining if the rest of the file matches the items on the list.

The application class must prepare the files for input and output, send a message to `FirstList` to read in values, and send a message to `FirstList` to compare itself with the rest of the file.

Who is responsible for letting the user know the results of the comparison? Since `FirstList` is responsible for making the comparison, let's assign the responsibility of informing the user of the result to `FirstList`.

Class Name: FirstList	Superclass: Object	Subclasses:
Responsibilities	**Collaborations**	
Create itself, Constructor		
Input first list, Transformer	FileReader, BufferedReader	
Compare first list with rest of file, Observer	BufferedReader	

Class Name: *DataValidation*	Superclass: *Object*	Subclasses:
Responsibilities	**Collaborations**	
Prepare the file for input	*FileReader, BufferedReader*	
Prepare the file for output	*FileWriter, PrintWriter*	
Tell FirstList to input first list	*FirstList*	
Tell FirstList to compare first list with rest of file	*FirstList*	
Close the files	*PrintWriter, BufferedReader*	

Data Representation   The by-hand algorithm tells us exactly what the container list must look like: an array, where each component represents a line on the paper. The only difference is that humans normally count from 1 and Java counts from zero. We also need a place to record how many values have been read in.

Responsibility Algorithms for `FirstList`   This class is both reading and writing to files. Which files? Let's let the driver pass the files as parameters to the constructor. Now we are ready to design the algorithms for our class methods.

....

public FirstList(in, out)

Set numItems to 0
Set dataFile to in
Set dataFile to out

....

public readFirstList()

Get first value from dataFile
while value greater than 0
    Set firstList[numItems] = value
    Increment numItems
    Get next value from dataFile

public compareListWithFile()

Set valuesTheSame to true
for counter going from 0 through numItems–1
 Get next value from dataFile
 if values are not the same
  Set valuesTheSame to false
  Print both values
if valuestheSame
 Print "The two lists are identical."

Values are not the same   Level 2

value != firstList[counter]

Print both values   Level 2

Print "Values at position " + (counter + 1) + ": " + firstList[counter]
 + " != " + value

Responsibility Algorithm for DataValidation

---

public static void main(String[] args)

Prepare dataFile for reading
Prepare outFile for output
Declare and instantiate checker of type FirstList(dataFile, outFile)
checker.readFirstList()
checker.compareListWithFile()
Close files

```java
package validation;
import java.io.*;
public class FirstList
{
  // Constructor
  public FirstList(BufferedReader in, PrintWriter out)
  {
    numItems = 0;
    firstList = new int[500]; // Default value for number of items
    dataFile = in;
    outFile = out;
  }
  // Transformer
  public void readFirstList() throws IOException
  // Reads in firstList[0]..firstList[numItems-1]
  {
    int value;
    value = Integer.valueOf(dataFile.readLine()).intValue();
    while (value > 0)
    {
      firstList[numItems] = value;
      numItems++;
      value = Integer.valueOf(dataFile.readLine()).intValue();
    }
  }
  // Observer
  public  void compareListWithFile() throws IOException
  // Compares the two lists and prints the results
  //  on outFile
  {
    int value;
    boolean valuesTheSame = true;
    for (int counter = 0; counter < numItems; counter++)
    {
      value = Integer.valueOf(dataFile.readLine()).intValue();
      if (value != firstList[counter])
      {
        outFile.println("Values at position " + (counter + 1) + ": "
          + firstList[counter] + " != " + value);
        valuesTheSame = false;
      }
    }
```

```
        if (valuesTheSame)
          outFile.println("The two lists are identical");
    }
    // Instance variables
    private int[] firstList;
    private int numItems;
    private BufferedReader dataFile;
    private PrintWriter outFile;
}
import validation.*;
import java.io.*;                              // File types
public class DataValidation
// Application DataValidation compares two positive integer data sets on
//  file dataFile, separated by a  negative number.
//  If the data sets are not identical, the pairs that do not match
//  are printed.
{
  private static PrintWriter outFile;          // Output data file
  private static BufferedReader dataFile;      // Input data file

  public static void main(String[] args) throws IOException
  {
    dataFile = new BufferedReader(
        new FileReader("datafile.dat"));      // Prepare input file
    outFile = new PrintWriter(
        new FileWriter("outfile.dat"));       // Prepare output file

    // Declare an object of type FirstList
    FirstList checker = new FirstList(dataFile, outFile);

    checker.readFirstList();
    checker.compareListWithFile();
    dataFile.close();
    outFile.close();
  }
}
```

Testing   The program is run with two sets of data, one in which the two lists are identical and one in which there are errors. The data and the results from each are shown on the next page.

Data Set 1	Data Set 2
21	21
32	32
76	76
22	22
21	21
-4	-4
21	21
32	32
76	176
22	12
21	21

Output

The two lists are identical.

Output

Position 2:   76 != 176

Problem-Solving Case Study

Grading True/False Tests

Statement of the Problem   Your History teacher gives True/False exams. Knowing that you are studying Computer Science, she asks you to write a program that grades True/False questions. The key to the exam is on the first line of data, followed by a line with the student's name and a line with the student's answers. She gives you the following example of the file to use as a guideline.

```
TFTFTFTFTTTFFFT
Joe Jones
TFTFTFTFTTTFFTT
Janet Jerome
TFTFTFTFTTTFFFF
Jeff Jubilee
TFTFTFTFTTTFFFT
...
```

As output, she wants the student's name followed by the number answered correctly written on a file, one student per line.

Brainstorming   How would you grade these exams by hand? If the student's answers were written as a sequence of Ts and Fs, you would probably take a sheet of paper, write down the Ts and Fs from the key, fold the paper so that the Ts and Fs were on the top, and line up the paper under a student's answer. You could then compare them one at a time marking through the student's answer that did not agree with the key. So, what are the objects in the problem?

We are working with an exam key and a student's answer, where the student's answer has two parts: the name and a series of Ts and Fs. We need a container to hold the key, and a container to hold a student's answer. We also need file objects.

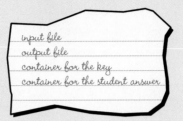

input file
output file
container for the key
container for the student answer

Filtering   Let's look at the key object first. An exam is made up of questions, the answers to which are either T or F. Therefore, the key is an ordered collection of Ts and Fs that represents the correct answers to the questions. Let's call this class `TheKey`. The student answer contains the student's name and a sequence of Ts and Fs. Yes, this set of objects looks complete. Oh, we forgot the class that contains `main`, the application class.

input file
output file
container for the key
container for the student answer
application class

Scenarios   What are the responsibilities of `TheKey` class? That is, what operations must the class perform on the Ts and Fs? The class must create itself, initialize the Ts and Fs to the correct pattern, and grade a student's answer.

The second object is a student's answer. This object contains a student's name and an ordered collection of Ts and Fs representing the student's answers to the exam questions. Let's call this class `AStudentAnswer`. What are the responsibilities of this class? It must create itself, input a name and a sequence of Ts and Fs, pass the Ts and Fs to the key to be graded, and print out the student name and the number of correct answers.

At this stage you should step back and see if there is anything missing from the design. You notice that the sample data your teacher gives you has 15 questions. The test you took last week had 20 questions. This means that the number of questions varies, so the number of questions on the exam must be input to the constructor for class `TheKey` to determine the number of Ts and Fs. Class `AStudentAnswer` also needs to know the number of questions.

CRC Cards

Class Name: TheKey	Superclass: Object	Subclasses:
Responsibilities		**Collaborations**
Create itself (number of items), Constructor		
Read the key, Transformer		BufferedReader
Grade a student's answer (student's Ts/Fs), Observer, V–R		BufferedReader
return int (number correct)		IOException

Class Name: AStudentAnswer	Superclass: Object	Subclasses:
Responsibilities		**Collaborations**
Create itself (number of items), constructor		
Read student's name (infile, outfile), constructor		BufferedReader, PrintWriter
Read student's answer (infile)		BufferedReader
Write student's name		PrintWriter
Write number correct (student's Ts/Fs), observer		TheKey, PrintWriter

Class Name: GradeExams	Superclass: Object	Subclasses:
Responsibilities		**Collaborations**
Prepare the file for input		FileReader, BufferedReader
Prepare the file for output		FileWriter, PrintWriter
Declare and instantiate variables		
Tell TheKey to get the key		TheKey
Process a student answer		AStudentAnswer

Data Representation The key and the answer are an ordered collection of Ts and Fs. The array is the obvious choice for holding the Ts and Fs. The index of an individual answer is the question number minus 1. Now we are ready to design the algorithms for the three classes.

Responsibility Algorithms for `TheKey`   In our by-hand algorithm, we wrote the key so that we could hold it next to the student answers and compare them, position by position. The operational verb in the discussion is "compare." To grade a student's answer, the operation must compare its ordered collections of Ts and Fs with the ordered collection of Ts and Fs representing a student's answer. The return value is the number of places where the values match.

public TheKey(int number)   Level 1

Create key as an array of number characters

public void readKey(BufferedReader inFile)

for counter going from 0 through key.length − 1
    Get next answer
    Set key[counter] to next answer

public int numberCorrect(char[] answer)

Set noCorrect to 0
for counter going from 0 through key.length − 1
    if (key[counter] == answer[counter])
        Increment noCorrect
return noCorrect

Responsibility Algorithms for `AStudentAnswer`

public AStudentAnswer(int number)

Create answer as an array of number characters

public void readStudentName(BufferedReader inFile)

Read a student name from inFile

public void readStudentAnswer(BufferedReader inFile)

for counter going from 0 through answer.length − 1
    Get next answer
    Set answer[counter] to next answer

public void writeStudentName(PrintWriter outFile)

> Write name

public void writeNumberCorrect(PrintWriter outFile, TheKey key)

> Set score to key.numberCorrect(answer)
> Print " number correct " + score

As is usually true in an object-oriented design, the work is done in the classes. The final algorithm that pulls the pieces together is in the `main` method of a driver.

public static void main(String[] args)

> Import TheKey class
> Import AStudentAnswer class
> Declare key of class TheKey
> Declare studentExam of class AStudentAnswer
> Prepare file inFile for input
> Prepare file outFile for output
> key.readKey(inFile)
> **while** more students
>   studentExam.readStudentName(inFile)
>   studentExam.readStudentAnswer(inFile)
>   studentExam.writeStudentName(outFile)
>   studentExam.writeNumberCorrect(outFile, key)
> Close files

"Declare...". We have forgotten something. How do we know how many questions there are on this exam? The user could enter it from the keyboard as an event or the user could enter the number of questions on the file on the line immediately before the key. Because this program does not need the user to be present to enter any other data, putting the number of questions on the data file is the better choice.

How should the loop be implemented? In the past the looping structure has been within the method that does the reading. Here the reading is done within a method invoked within the loop. When reading the student name, `readStudentName` can determine that there is no more data, but the algorithm did not do so. What is more, how does that information get back into `main` to control the loop? We need to add one more observer, `moreData`, to class `AStudentAnswer`, which checks to see if there was another student's name on the file.

public boolean moreData()

> **return** name != null

```
public static void main(String[] args)                          Revised

    Import TheKey class
    Import AStudentAnswer class
    Prepare file for input
    Prepare file for output
    Get noQuestions
    Declare key(noQuestions) of class TheKey
    Declare studentExam(noQuestions) of class AStudentAnswer
    key.readKey(inFile)
    studentExam.readStudentName(inFile)

    while studentExam.moreData()
        studentExam.readStudentAnswer(inFile)
        studentExam.writeStudentName(outFile)
        studentExam.writeNumberCorrect(outFile, key)
        studentExam.readStudentName(inFile)
    Close files
```

Now we are ready to code our solution. Let's implement the classes first and put them into a package called grader.

```java
package grader;                          // Package declaration
import java.io.*;                        // Access files
public class TheKey
{ // Private data fields
  private char[] key;

  // Methods
  public TheKey(int number)
  { // Constructor
    key = new char[number];              // Instantiate array object
  }

  public void readKey(BufferedReader inFile) throws IOException
  { // Transformer:  Input Ts and Fs
    int datum;
    for (int counter = 0; counter < key.length; counter++)
    {
      datum = inFile.read();
      key[counter] = (char) datum;
    }
    inFile.readLine();                   // Read past end of line
  }

  public int numberCorrect(char[] answer) throws IOException
  { // Observer: Returns the number of correct answers
```

```
    int noCorrect = 0;
    for (int counter = 0; counter < key.length; counter++)
      if (key[counter] == answer[counter])
        noCorrect++;
    return noCorrect;
  }
} // End of class TheKey

package grader;                      // Package declaration
import java.io.*;                    // Import files

public class AStudentAnswer
{ // Private data fields
  private char[] answer;
  private String name;
  // Methods
  public AStudentAnswer(int number)
  { // Constructor
    answer = new char[number];
  }

  public void readStudentName(BufferedReader inFile)
    throws IOException
  { // Transformer: Read in a student's name
    name = inFile.readLine();
  }

  public void writeStudentName(PrintWriter outFile)
  {
    // Observer: Output a name
    outFile.print(name);
  }
  public void readStudentAnswer(BufferedReader inFile)
    throws IOException
  { // Transformer: Read in a student's answers
    int datum;
    for (int counter = 0; counter < answer.length; counter++)
    {
      datum = inFile.read();
      answer[counter] = (char)datum;
    }
    inFile.readLine();               // Read past end of line
  }

  public boolean moreData()
  { // Observer: Returns true if there is more data
    return (name != null);
  }
```

```java
      public void writeNumberCorrect(PrintWriter outFile, TheKey key)
        throws IOException
      { // Observer: Write out the student name and score
        int score;
        score = key.numberCorrect(answer);
        outFile.println(" number correct " + score);
      }
} // End of class AStudentAnswer

// Driver for classes in package grader
import grader.*;
import java.io.*;
public class GradeExams
// Student true/false exams are graded
{
  // Variable declarations
  private static PrintWriter outFile;
  private static BufferedReader inFile;
  private static TheKey key;
  private static AStudentAnswer studentExam;

  public static void main(String[] args) throws IOException
  {
    int noQuestions;                    // Number of questions
    // Prepare files for input and output
    inFile = new BufferedReader(
            new FileReader("datafile.dat"));
    outFile = new PrintWriter(
            new FileWriter("outfile.dat"));

    // Set up key and student answer arrays
    noQuestions = Integer.valueOf(inFile.readLine()).intValue();
    key = new TheKey(noQuestions);
    studentExam = new AStudentAnswer(noQuestions);
    key.readKey(inFile);
    // Priming read
    studentExam.readStudentName(inFile);
    while (studentExam.moreData())
    { // Process exams until end of file
      studentExam.readStudentAnswer(inFile);
      studentExam.writeStudentName(outFile);
      studentExam.writeNumberCorrect(outFile, key);
      studentExam.readStudentName(inFile);
    }
    inFile.close();
    outFile.close();
  }  // End main
} // End of class GradeExams
```

Testing   This program has two classes and a driver. We have been using the word *driver* to refer to a simple program class that is used to test a method. Here we are using it in its other context: the main class in an object-oriented design. The driver in this Case Study is class `GradeExams`, the class that contains the `main` method. Actually, these two definitions are not dissimilar. In both cases, the driver starts the process. In a regular application, the driver implements the top-level algorithm, which might start any process. In a test driver, the process is always the same because its role is strictly to test one or more methods.

Does this mean that we need to design a test driver for this application and import class `GradeExams`? No, quite the contrary. We can let class `GradeExams` test itself by carefully choosing data sets. That is, we can use a black-box testing strategy.

What are the inputs to the program? There are three: an integer that specifies the number of questions, a sequence of Ts and Fs that represent the key and a student's answers, and a string that represents a student's name. For the moment, let's assume that the data is correct on the file, and concentrate on the main processing: the comparison of the key and a student exam. The following cases come immediately to mind.

1. The key and the student response match completely (all are correct).
2. The key and the student response do not match at all (all are wrong).
3. The key and the student response partially match (some are correct).

Depending on the number of questions, there could be thousands of cases in the third category. How many do we have to try to convince ourselves that the program is correct? The end cases here would be that they agree in the first and last positions, they do not agree in the first and last position, they agree somewhere in the middle, and they disagree somewhere in the middle.

As the algorithm is not dependent on the number of questions, let's use 5 for our test cases.

Test #	Reason for Test	Input	Expected Output
		5 TTTTT	
1	All correct (Also tests same in first and last position)	Jones TTTTT	Jones number correct 5
2	All wrong (Also tests different in first and last position)	Janes FFFFF	Janes number correct 0
3	Partially correct	Julian TFTFT	Julian number correct 3
4	Test ending condition	EOF on data file	Program ends

Provided our input is correct, if the implemented test plan produces the results expected, we should be fairly confident that the program is correct. *Provided our input is correct?* We have built in no error checking into these classes. This is a serious flaw in our design. The Case Study Follow-Up Exercises ask you to make these classes more robust by adding error checking.

Testing and Debugging

The most common error in processing arrays is an out-of-bounds array index. That is, the program attempts to access a component using an index that is either less than 0 or greater than the array size minus 1. For example, given the declarations

```
char[] line = new char[100];
int   counter;
```

the following *for* statement would print the 100 elements of the line array and then try to print a 101st value.

```
for (counter = 0; counter <= line.length; counter++)
  outfile.print(line[counter]);
```

This error is easy to detect, because your program will halt with an `ArrayIndexOutOf-BoundsException`. The loop test should be `counter < line.length`. But you won't always use a simple *for* statement when accessing arrays. Suppose we read data into the line array in another part of the program. Let's use a *while* statement that reads to the newline character:

```
counter = 0;
infile.read(ch);
while ((char) ch != '\n')
{
  line[counter] = (char) ch;
  counter++;
  infile.read(ch);
}
```

This code seems reasonable enough, but what if the input line has more than 100 characters? After the hundredth character is read and stored into the array, the loop executes one more time and the `ArrayIndexOutOfBoundsException` is thrown, causing the program to crash.

The moral is: When processing arrays, give special attention to the design of loop termination conditions. Always ask yourself if the loop could possibly keep running after the last array component has been processed.

Whenever an array index goes out of bounds, the first suspicion should be a loop that fails to terminate properly. The second thing to check is any array access involving an index that is based on an input value or a calculation. When an array index is input as data, a data validation check is an absolute necessity.

As we have demonstrated in many examples in the last several chapters, it is possible to combine data structures in various ways: classes whose components are objects, classes whose components are arrays, arrays whose components are objects, arrays whose components are strings, and so forth. When arrays of objects are used, there can be confusion about precisely where to place the operators for array element selection ([]) and class field selection (.).

To summarize the correct placement of these operators, let's use a StudentRec class, where the data fields are defined as:

```
private static class StudentRec
{
    private static String   stuName;      // Student's name
    private static float     gpa;          // Student's grade point average
    private static int[]     examScores;   // There are four exams
    private static char      courseGrade;  // A, B, C, D, or F
    ...
};
```

If we declare a variable of class StudentRec and an array of class StudentRec components

```
StudentRec student;
StudentRec[] members = new StudentRec[100];
```

the following chart shows how to access the fields of student. Recall that the dot operator is a binary (two-operand) operator; its left operand denotes a class variable or class name, and its right operand is a field. The [] operator is a unary (one-operand) operator; it comes immediately after an expression denoting an array:

Expression	Class/Type	Meaning
student	A StudentRec object	A single student
student.stuName	A string	A name
student.gpa	A real number	A gpa
student.examScores	An array of integers	
student.examScores[0]	An integer	The first exam score
student.examScores[4]	Crash!! Index out of range	
student.courseGrade	A character	
members[0].student	A StudentRec object	The first student
members[0].stuName	A string	The name of the first student
members[0].gpa	A real number	The gpa of the first student
members[0].examScores	An array of integers	The exam scores for the first student
members[0].examScores[1]	An integer	The second score for the first student

Testing and Debugging Hints

1. When an individual component of a one-dimensional array is accessed, the index must be within the range 0 through the array size minus 1. Attempting to use an index value outside this range causes your program to crash.

2. The individual components of an array are themselves variables of the component type. When values are stored into an array, they should either be of the component type or be explicitly converted to the component type; otherwise, implicit type conversion occurs.

3. As with all Java's composite data types, declaring an array variable and instantiating the variable are separate steps. The size of a one-dimensional array is omitted in its declaration but *must* be specified when the array object is being instantiated.

4. When an array is a parameter, the reference to the array object is passed to the method. The reference cannot be changed by the method, but the elements in the array can be changed.

5. An individual array component can be passed as an argument. If the component is a reference type, it can be changed within the method if it is a mutable object. If the component is an atomic type, it cannot be changed within the method.

6. Although reference types passed as a parameter can be changed if the type is mutable, it is bad style to do so.

7. Subarray processing is used to process array components when the actual number of data items is not known until the program is executing. The `length` field of the array object contains the number of slots in the array; the number of data values stored into the array may differ.

8. When methods perform subarray processing on a one-dimensional array, the array name and the number of data items actually stored in the array should be encapsulated together into a class.

9. When a one-dimensional array is instantiated, the constructor for the component class is called.

10. A one-dimensional array is an object, so a reference to it may be set to `null`.

11. When processing the components in a one-dimensional array, use a loop that begins at zero and stops when the counter is equal to the `length` field associated with the array object.

Summary of Classes

We have not introduced any new classes in the Java library in this chapter, nor have we designed any classes that should go into a library to use later.

    d. A list of addresses

    e. A list of hourly temperatures

    f. A list of passengers on an airliner, including names, addresses, fare class, and seat assignment

    g. A departmental telephone directory with last name and extension number

15. What happens in Java if you try to access an element that is outside the dimensions of the array?

16. What are the array components initialized to when the array is instantiated using `new`?

17. What are the array components initialized to when the array is instantiated using an initializer list?

Programming Warm-Up Exercises

Use the following declarations in Exercises 1–7. You may declare any other variables that you need.

```
final int NUM_STUDENTS = 100;  // Number of students
boolean[] failing = new boolean[NUM_STUDENTS];
boolean[] passing = new boolean[NUM_STUDENTS];
int  grade;
int[] score = new int[NUM_STUDENTS];
```

1. Write a Java instance method that initializes all components of `failing` to `false`.

2. Write a Java instance method that takes `score` as a parameter. Set the components of `failing` to `true` wherever the corresponding value in `score` is less than 60.

3. Write a Java instance method that has `score` as a parameter. Set the components of `passing` to `true` wherever the corresponding value in `score` is greater than or equal to 60.

4. Write a Java value-returning instance method `passTally` that reports how many components in `passing` are `true`.

5. Write a Java value-returning class method `error` that takes `passing` and `failing` as parameters. `error` returns `true` if any corresponding components in `passing` and `failing` are the same.

6. Write a Java value-returning instance method that takes `grade` as a parameter. The method reports how many values in `score` are greater than or equal to `grade`.

7. Write a Java instance method that takes `score` as a parameter and reverses the order of the components in `score`; that is, `score[0]` goes into `score[score.length-1]`, `score[1]` goes into `score[score.length-2]`, and so on.

8. Write a program segment to read in a set of part numbers and associated unit costs. Use an array of classes with two members, `number` and `cost`, to represent each pair of input values. Assume the end-of-file condition terminates the input.

Programming Problems

1. The local baseball team is computerizing its records. There are 20 players on the team, identified by the numbers 1 through 20. Their batting records are coded in a file as follows. Each line contains four numbers: the player's identification number and the number of hits, walks, and outs he or she made in a particular game. Here is a sample:

   3   2   1   1

   The example above indicates that during a game, player number 3 was at bat four times and made 2 hits, 1 walk, and 1 out. For each player there are several lines in the file. Each player's batting average is computed by adding the player's total number of hits and dividing by the total number of times at bat. A walk does not count as either a hit or a time at bat when the batting average is being calculated.

   Design and implement an application that prints a table showing each player's identification number, batting average, and number of walks. (Be careful: The players' identification numbers are 1 through 20, but Java array indexes start at 0.)

2. Design, implement, and test a class that calculates the mean and standard deviation of integers stored in a file. The output should be of type `float` and should be properly labeled and formatted to two decimal places. The formula for calculating the mean of a series of integers is to add all the numbers, then divide by the number of integers. Expressed in mathematical terms, the mean $\overline{X}$ of N numbers $X_1, X_2, \dots X_N$ is

$$\overline{X} = \frac{\sum_{i=1}^{N} X_i}{N}$$

   To calculate the standard deviation of a series of integers, subtract the mean from each integer (you may get a negative number) and square the result, add all these squared differences, divide by the number of integers minus 1, then take the square root of the result. Expressed in mathematical terms, the standard deviation S is

$$S = \frac{\sum_{i=1}^{N} \left(\overline{X}_i - X\right)^2}{N-1}$$

   The methods of the class that access the input data should take a file as a parameter.

3. One of the local banks is gearing up for a big advertising campaign and would like to see how long its customers are waiting for service at drive-up windows. Several employees have been asked to keep accurate records for the

12-hour drive-up service. The collected information, which is read from a file, consists of the time the customer arrived in hours, minutes, and seconds; the time the customer actually was served; and the ID number of the teller. Design and implement a class with the following responsibilities:

a. Reads in the wait data.
b. Computes the wait time in seconds.
c. Calculates the mean, standard deviation (defined in Programming Problem 2), and range.
d. Prints a single-page summary showing the values calculated in part c.

Input

The first data line contains a title.

The remaining lines each contain a teller ID, an arrival time, and a service time.

The times are broken up into integer hours, minutes, and seconds according to a 24-hour clock.

Processing

Calculate the mean and the standard deviation.

Locate the shortest wait time and the longest wait time for any number of records up to 100.

Output

The input data (echo print).

The title.

The following values, all properly labeled: number of records, mean, standard deviation, and range (minimum and maximum).

4. Your history professor has so many students in her class that she has trouble determining how well the class does on exams. She has discovered that you are a computer whiz and has asked you to write a program to perform some simple statistical analyses on exam scores. Your program must work for any class size up to 100. Write and test a computer program that does the following:

a. Reads the test grades from file inData.
b. Calculates the class mean, standard deviation (defined in Programming Problem 2), and percentage of the test scores falling in the ranges <10, 10–19, 20–29, 30–39, ... , 80–89, and ≥90.
c. Prints a summary showing the mean and the standard deviation, as well as a histogram showing the percentage distribution of test scores.

Input

The first data line contains the number of exams to be analyzed and a title for the report.

The remaining lines have 10 test scores on each line until the last line, and from one to 10 scores on the last. The scores are all integers.

Output

The input data as they are read.

A report consisting of the title that was read from the data, the number of scores, the mean, the standard deviation (all clearly labeled), and the histogram.

5. Write an application that reads an apartment number and the number of occupants in the apartment. The apartment number is to be used as an index into an array of apartments. The components in the array represent the number of people who live in the apartment. Use the data structure described in the chapter. Use window input and print the number of people in the building when the user presses the Quit button.

Case Study Follow-Up Exercises

1. The `ValidateData` application compares two lists of integers. Exactly what changes would be necessary for the program to compare two lists of `float` values?
2. Modify the `ValidateData` application so that it works even if the lists do not have the same number of elements. Print an appropriate error message and stop the comparison if the two lists do not have the same number of elements.
3. The exam grading application contains no error checking.
   a. What happens if a letter other than a T or F is entered in the key?
   b. What happens if a letter other than a T or F is entered for a student?
   c. It is easy to put in a check to be sure that the input values are a T or F, but what should the program do if an error occurs?
4. Redesign and rewrite the exam grading application to incorporate error checking based on the answers in Exercise 3.
5. When the authors ran the test plan originally, the names didn't print and a format exception occurred. In the original version of the application the following statement was not included after reading in a series of Ts and Fs:

```
inFile.readLine();
```

When this statement was added in two places, the application worked correctly. Explain.

Array-Based Lists

Goals

- To be able to distinguish between an array and a list.
- To be able to insert an item into a list.
- To be able to delete an item from a list.
- To be able to search for an item in a list.
- To be able to sort the items in a list into ascending or descending order.
- To be able to build a list in sorted order.
- To be able to search for an item in a sorted list using a linear search.
- To be able to search for an item using a binary search.
- To be able to use the Java `Comparable` interface.

Chapter 11 introduced the array, a structured data type that holds a collection of components of the same type or class given a single name. In general, a one-dimensional array is a structure used to hold a list of items. We all know intuitively what a "list" is; in our everyday lives we use lists all the time—grocery lists, lists of things to do, lists of addresses, lists of party guests. In computer programs, lists are very useful and common ways to organize the data. In this chapter, we examine algorithms that build and manipulate lists implemented using a one-dimensional array to hold the items.

12.1 Lists

From a logical point of view, a list is a homogeneous collection of elements, with a linear relationship between elements. Linear means that, at the logical level, each element in the list except the first one has a unique predecessor, and each element except the last one has a unique successor.[1] The number of items in the list, which we call the length of the list, is a property of a list. That is, every list has a length.

Linear relationship Each element except the first has a unique predecessor, and each element except the last has a unique successor

Length The number of items in a list; the length can vary over time

Unsorted list A list in which data items are placed in no particular order with respect to their content; the only relationship between data elements is the list predecessor and successor relationships.

Sorted list A list with predecessor and successor relationships determined by the content of the keys of the items in the list; there is a semantic relationship among the keys of the items in the list.

Key A member of a class whose value is used to determine the logical and/or physical order of the items in a list

Lists can be unsorted—their elements may be placed into the list in no particular order—or they can be sorted in a variety of ways. For instance, a list of numbers can be sorted by value, a list of strings can be sorted alphabetically, and a list of addresses could be sorted by zip code. When the elements in a sorted list are of composite types, their logical (and often physical) order is determined by one of the members of the structure, the key member. For example, a list of students on a class roll can be sorted alphabetically by name or numerically by student identification number. In the first case, the name is the key; in the second case, the identification number is the key. (See Figure 12.1.)

If a list cannot contain items with duplicate keys, it is said to have *unique keys*. (See Figure 12.2.) This chapter deals with both unsorted lists and lists of elements with unique keys, sorted from smallest to largest key value. The items on the list can be of any type, atomic or composite. In the following discussion, "item," "element," and "component" are synonyms; they are what is stored in the list.

[1]At the implementation level, there is also a relationship between the elements, but the physical relationship may not be the same as the logical one.

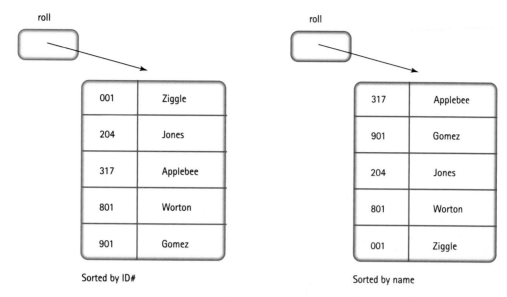

Figure 12.1 *List sorted by two different keys*

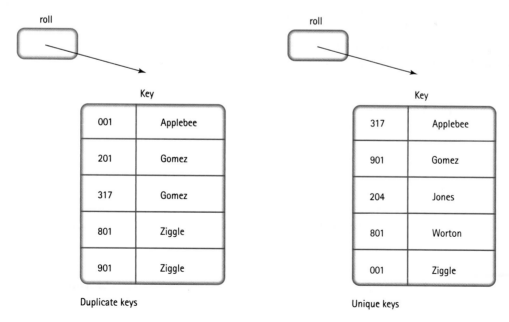

Figure 12.2 *(a)List with duplicate keys and (b) List with unique keys*

12.2 List Class

In this section, we design and implement a general-purpose class that represents a list of items. Let's think in terms of a to-do list. But before we begin to brainstorm, we must ask an important question: For whom are we designing the class? We may be designing it for ourselves to keep in our library of classes. We may be designing it for others to use in a team project. When we design a class, the software that uses it is called the client of the class. In our discussion, we use the terms client and user interchangeably, thinking of the client as referring to the people writing the software that uses the class, rather than the software itself.

> **Client** Software that declares and manipulates objects of a particular class

Brainstorming the List Class

Because we are designing a general-purpose class, our brainstorming must be more speculative. We don't have a specific problem to solve; we have to think in terms of what we do with our to-do lists and what other things we might like to do if we could. Hopefully, we start with an empty list each morning and add things to it. As we accomplish a task on the list, we cross it off. We check to see if an item is on the list. We check to see if there is any way that we can add one more item to the list. We check to see if the list is empty (we wish!). We go through the list one item at a time. Let's translate these observations into responsibilities for the list with their responsibility type.

CRC Card

Class Name: List		Superclass: Object	Subclasses:
Responsibilities		**Collaborations**	
Create itself (max Items)		None	
Is list full? Observer		None	
return boolean			
Is list empty? Observer		None	
return boolean			
Know length, Observer		None	
return int			
Is an item in the list? Observer		None	
return boolean			
Insert into list (item), Transformer		None	
Delete from list (item), Transformer		None	
Know each item, Iterator		None	

Although we have designed our CRC card for a to-do list, the responsibilities are valid for any kind of list. For example, if we are creating a list of people to invite to a wedding, all of these operations are valid. We add names to the list, check whether a name is on the list, count the names on the list, check to see if the list is full (i.e., the length is equal to the number of invitations bought), delete names, and review the names one at a time.

To make the rest of the discussion more concrete, let's assume that the items on the list are strings. We then show how the items can be made even more general.

Refining the Responsibilities

Let's go back through the responsibilities, refining them and converting them into method headings. Because we are designing a general-purpose class, we do not have any specific scenarios that we can use. Instead, we consider a variety of simplified scenarios that are examples of how we believe the class might be employed. Because the class is intended for widespread use, we should pay special attention to the documentation right from the design stage.

The observers, testing for full and empty, returning the number of items, and checking to see if an item is in the list, need no further discussion. Here are their method headings.

```
public boolean isFull();
// Returns true if no room to add a component; false otherwise

public boolean isEmpty();
// Returns true if no components in the list; false otherwise

public int length();
// Returns the number of components in the list

public boolean isThere(String item);
// Returns true if item is in the list; false otherwise
```

In designing the transformers, we have to make some decisions. For example, do we allow duplicates in our list? This has implications for deleting items as well as inserting items. If we allow duplicates, what do we mean by removing an item? Do we delete just one or all of them? Because the focus of this chapter is on algorithms, we just make a decision and design our algorithms to fit. We examine the effect of other choices in the exercises. Let's allow only one copy of an item in the list. This decision means that delete just removes one copy. However, do we assume that the item to be removed is in the list? Is it an error if it is not? Or does the delete operation mean "delete, if there?" Let's use the last meaning.

We now incorporate these decisions into the documentation for the method headings.

```
public void insert(String item);
// Adds item to the list
// Assumption: item is not already in the list
```

```
public void delete(String item);
// item is removed from the list if it is in the list
```

The iterator allows the user to see each item in the list one at a time. Let's call the method that implements the Know each item responsibility getNextItem. The list must keep track of the next item to return when the iterator is called. The list does this with a state variable that records the position of the next item to be returned. The constructor initializes this position to 0, and it is incremented in getNextItem. The client can use the length of the list to control a loop asking to see each item in turn. As a precaution, the current position should be reset after the last item has been accessed. In an application problem, we might need a transformer iterator that goes through the list applying an operation to each item; however, for our general discussion we provide only an observer iterator.

What happens if a user inserts or deletes an item in the middle of an iteration? Nothing good you can be sure! Adding and deleting items changes the length of the list, making the termination condition of our iteration-counting loop invalid. Depending on whether an addition or deletion occurs before or after the iteration point, our iteration loop could end up skipping or repeating items.

We have several choices of how to handle this possibly dangerous situation. The list can throw an exception, the list can reset the current position when inserting or deleting, or the list can disallow transformer operations while an iteration is taking place. We choose the latter here by way of an assumption in the documentation. In case the user wants to restart an iteration, let's provide a resetList method that reinitializes the current position.

```
public void resetList();
// The current position is reset
```

```
public String getNextItem();
// Assumption:  No transformers have been called since the iteration began
```

Before we go to the implementation phase, let's look at how we might use getNextItem. Suppose the client program wants to print out the items in the list. The client program cannot directly access the list items, but it can use getNextItem to iterate through the list. The following code fragment prints the string values in list.

```
String next;
for (int index = 1; index <= list.length(); index++)
{
  next = list.getNextItem();  // Get an item
  System.out.println(next + " is still in the list");
}
```

Now is also the time to look back over the list and see if we need to add any responsibilities. For example, do we need to provide an equals test? If we want to perform a deep comparison of two lists, we must provide equals; however, comparing lists is not a particularly useful operation, and we provide the client the tools to write a comparison operation if necessary. In fact, here is the client code to compare two lists. The algorithm determines if the lengths are the same and, if so, iterates through the lists checking to see if corresponding items are the same.

isDuplicate

```
if lengths are not the same
    return false
else
    Set counter to 1
    Set same to true
    Set limit to length of first list
    while they are still the same AND counter is less than or equal to limit
        Set next1 to next item in the first list
        Set next2 to next item in the second list
        Set same to result of seeing if next1.compareTo(next2) is 0
        Increment counter
return same
```

We can implement this algorithm without having to know anything about the list. We just use the instance methods supplied in the interface.

```java
public boolean isDuplicate(List list1, List list2)
// Returns true if the lists are identical
{
  if (list1.length() != list2.length())  // Number of items is not the same
    return false
  else
  {
    String next1;                        // An item from list1
    String next2;                        // An item from list2
    int counter = 1;                     // Loop control variable
    boolean same = true;                 // True if lists are equal so far
    int limit = list1.length();          // Number of items in each list
    list1.resetList();                   // Set up for iteration
    list2.resetList() ;
    while (same && counter <= limit)
    {
      next1 = list1.getNextItem();       // Get an item from list1
      next2 = list2.getNextItem();       // Get an item from list2
      same = next1.compareTo(next2) == 0;
      counter++;
    }
```

```
    }
  return same;
}
```

Internal Data Representation

How are we going to represent the items in the list? An array of strings is the obvious answer. What other data fields do we need? We have to keep track of the number of items in our list, and we need a state variable that tells us where we are in the list during an iteration.

```
public class List
{
  // Data fields
  protected String[] listItems;      // Array to hold list items
  protected int numItems;            // Number of items in the list
  protected int currentPos;          // State variable for iteration
  ...
}
```

We introduced the concept of subarray processing in the last chapter and pointed out that every Java array object has a `final` field called `length` that contains the number of components defined for the array object. The literature for lists uses the identifier "length" to refer to the number of items that have been put into the list. Faced with this ambiguity in terminology, we still talk about the length of the list, but we refer to the field that contains the number of items in the list as `numItems`.

It is very important to understand the distinction between the array object that contains the list items and the list itself. The array object is `listItems[0]..listItems[listItems.length-1]`; the items in the list are `listItems[0]..listItems[numItems-1]`. This distinction is illustrated in Figure 12.3. Six items have been stored into the list, which is instantiated with the following statement:

```
List myList = new List(10);
```

Responsibility Algorithms for Class List

As Figure 12.3 shows, the list exists in the array elements `listItems[0]` through `listItems[numItems−1]`. To create an empty list, it is sufficient to set the `numItems` field to 0. We do not need to store any special values into the data array to make the list empty, because only those values in `listItems[0]` through `listItems[numItems−1]` are processed by the list algorithms. We explain why `currentPos` is set to 0 when we look more closely at the iterator.

```
public List(int maxItems)
// Instantiates an empty list object with room for maxItems items
{
  numItems = 0;
```

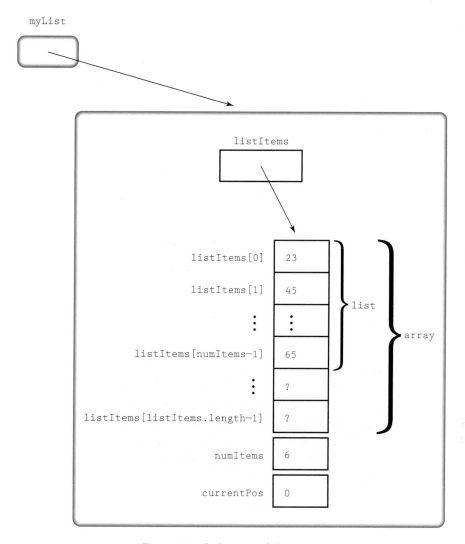

Figure 12.3 *An instance of class* `List`

```
    listItems = new String[maxItems];
    currentPos = 0;
}
```

Should the class provide a default constructor? Let's do so as a precaution.

```
public List()
// Instantiates an empty list object with room for 100 items
{
    numItems = 0;
```

```
        listItems = new String[100];
        currentPos = 0;
    }
```

The observers isFull, isEmpty, and length are very straightforward. Each is only one line long, as is so often the case in methods within the object-oriented paradigm.

```
public boolean isFull()
// Returns true if no room to add a component; false otherwise
{
    return (listItems.length == numItems);
}

public boolean isEmpty()
// Returns true if no components in the list; false otherwise
{
    return (numItems == 0);
}

public int length()
// Returns the number of components in the list
{
    return numItems;
}
```

We have one more observer to implement: isThere. Because isThere is an instance method, it has direct access to the items in the list. We just loop through the items in the list looking for the one specified on the parameter list. The loop ends when we find the matching item or have looked at all the items in the list. Our loop expression has two conditions: (1) the index is within the list and (2) the corresponding list item is not equal to the one for which we are searching. After the loop is exited, we return the assertion that the index is still within the list. If this assertion is true, then the search item was found.

---

isThere

Set index to 0
while more to examine and item not found
    Increment index
return (index is within the list)

This algorithm can be coded directly into Java, using the `compareTo` method of `String`.

```java
public boolean isThere(String item)
// Returns true if item is in the list.
{
  int index = 0;
  while (index < numItems && listItems[index].compareTo(item) != 0)
    index++;
  return (index < numItems);
}
```

This algorithm is called a *sequential* or *linear search* because we start at the beginning of the list and look at each item in sequence. We stop the search as soon as we find the item we are looking for (or when we reach the end of the list, concluding that the desired item is not present in the list).

We can use this algorithm in any program requiring a list search. In the form shown, it searches a list of `String` components, but the algorithm works for any class that has a `compareTo` method.

Let's look again at the heading for the operation that puts an item into the list.

```java
public void insert(String item);
// Adds item to the list
// Assumption:  item is not already in the list
```

Is there anything in the documentation that says where each new item should go? No, this is an unsorted list. Where we put each new item is up to the implementer. In this case, let's put each new item in the easiest place to reach: the next free slot in the array. Therefore, we can store a new item into `listItems[numItems]`—and then increment `numItems`.

This algorithm brings up a question: Do we need to check that there is room in the list for the new item? We have two choices. The `insert` method can test `numItems` against `listItems.length` and throw an exception if there isn't room, or we can let the client code make the test before calling `insert`. Our documentation is incomplete because it does not specify what occurs in this situation. Let's make the client code responsible for checking the `isFull` operation before an insertion. If the client fails to do so, the operation fails and the list is unchanged.

This algorithm is so simple, we just go directly to code.

```java
public void insert(String item)
// If the list is not full, puts item in the last position in the list;
//   otherwise list is unchanged.
{
  if (!this.isFull())
```

```
    {
      listItems[numItems] = item;
      numItems++;
    }
  }
```

Deleting a component from a list consists of two parts: finding the item and removing it from the list. We can use the same algorithm we used for isThere to look for the item. We know from the documentation that the item may or may not be in the list. If we find it, how do we remove it? We shift each item that comes after the one being deleted up one array slot.

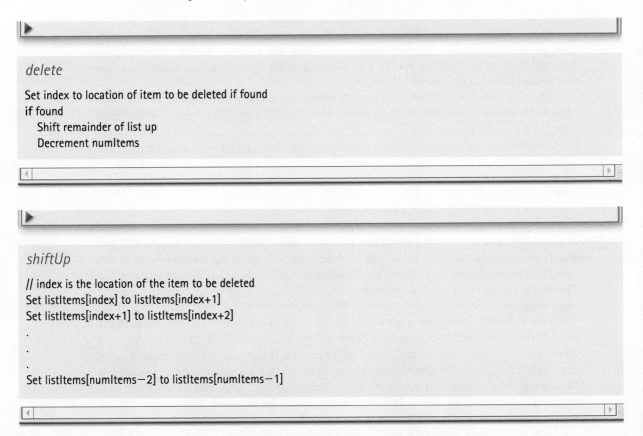

delete

Set index to location of item to be deleted if found
if found
   Shift remainder of list up
   Decrement numItems

shiftUp

// index is the location of the item to be deleted
Set listItems[index] to listItems[index+1]
Set listItems[index+1] to listItems[index+2]
.
.
.
Set listItems[numItems−2] to listItems[numItems−1]

We can implement this algorithm using a *for* loop.

```
public void delete(String item)
// Removes item from the list if it is there
{
```

```
  int index = 0;
  boolean found = false;
  while (index < numItems && !found)
  {
    if (listItems[index].compareTo(item) == 0)
      found = true;
    else
      index++;
  }
  if (found)
  { // Shift remainder of list up to delete item
    for (int count = index; count < numItems-1; count++)
      listItems[count] = listItems[count+1];
    numItems--;
  }
}
```

The resetList method is analogous to the open operation for a file in which the file pointer is positioned at the beginning of the file, so that the first input operation accesses the first component of the file. Each successive call to an input operation gets the next item in the file. Therefore, resetList must initialize currentPos to the first item in the list. Where is the first item in an array-based list? In the 0th position. The getNextItem operation is analogous to an input operation; it accesses the current item and then increments currentPos. When currentPos reaches numItems, we reset it to 0.

```
public void resetList()
// The iteration is initialized by setting currentPos to 0
{
  currentPos = 0;
}


public String getNextItem()
// Returns the item at the currentPos position; increments currentPos;
//  resets current position to first item after the last item is returned
// Assumption:  No transformers have been invoked since last call
{
  String next = listItems[currentPos];
  if (currentPos == numItems-1)
    currentPos = 0;
  else
    currentPos++;
  return next;
}
```

Both of the methods change `currentPos`. Shouldn't we consider them transformers? We could certainly argue that they are, but their *intention* is to set up an iteration through the items in the list, returning one item at a time to the client.

Test Plan

The documentation for the methods in class `List` helps us identify the tests necessary for a black-box testing strategy. The code of the methods determines a clear-box testing strategy. To test the `List` class implementation, we use a combination of black-box and clear-box strategies. We first test the constructor by testing to see if the list is empty (a call to `length` returns 0).

The methods `length`, `insert`, and `delete` must be tested together. That is, we insert several items and delete several items. How do we know that the `insert` and `delete` work correctly? We must write an auxiliary method `printList` that iterates through the list using `length` and `getNextItem` to print out the values. We call `printList` to check the status of the list after a series of insertions and deletions. To test the `isFull` operation, we must test it when the list is full and when it is not. We must also call `insert` when the list if full to see that the list is returned unchanged.

Are there any special cases that we need to test for `delete` and `isThere`? We look at the end cases. What are the end cases in a list? The item is in the first position in the list, the item is in the last position in the list, and the item is the only one in the list. So we must be sure that our `delete` can correctly delete items in these positions. We must check that `isThere` can find items in these same positions and correctly determine that values are not in the list.

These observations are summarized in the following test plan. The tests are shown in the order in which they should be performed.

Operation to be Tested Description of Action	Input Values	Expected Output	Observed Output
Constructor (4) print `length`		0	
`insert`			
`insert` four items and print	mary, john, ann, betty	mary, john, ann, betty	
`insert` item and print		mary, john, ann, betty	
`isThere`			
`isThere` susy and print whether found		item is not found	
`isThere` mary and print whether found		item is found	
`isThere` ann and print whether found		item is found	
`isThere` betty and print whether found		item is found	

Operation to be Tested Description of Action	Input Values	Expected Output	Observed Output
isFull			
invoke (list is full)		list is full	
delete ann and invoke		list is not full	
delete			
print		mary, john, betty	
delete betty and print		mary, john	
delete mary and print		john	
delete john and print		(empty)	
isEmpty		yes	

But what about testing resetList, and getNextItem? They do not appear explicitly in the test plan, but they are tested each time the auxiliary method printList is called to print the contents of the list. We do however have to add one additional test involving the iterator. We must print out length plus 1 items to test whether the current position is reset after the last item is returned.

To implement this test plan, we must construct a test driver that carries out the tasks outlined in the first column of the plan. We can make the test plan a document separate from the driver, with the last column filled in and initialed by a person running the program and observing the screen output. Or we can incorporate the test plan into the driver as comments and have the output go to a file. The key to properly testing any software is in the plan: It must be carefully thought out and it must be written.

12.3 Sorting the List Items

getNextItem presents the items to the user in the order in which they were inserted. Depending on what we are using the list for, there might be times when we want to rearrange the list components into a certain order before an iteration. For example, if we are using the list for wedding invitations, we might want to see the names in alphabetic order. Arranging list items into order is a very common operation and is known in software terminology as sorting.

> **Sorting** Arranging the components of a list into order (for instance, words into alphabetical order or numbers into ascending or descending order)

If you were given a sheet of paper with a column of 20 names on it and asked to write the numbers in ascending order, you would probably do the following:

1. Make a pass through the list, looking for the lowest name (the one that comes first alphabetically).
2. Write it on the paper in a second column.

3. Cross the number off the original list.

4. Repeat the process, always looking for the lowest name remaining in the original list.

5. Stop when all the names have been crossed off.

We could implement this algorithm as a client code, using `getNextItem` to go through the list searching for the lowest. When we find it, we could insert it into another list and delete it from the original. However, we would need two lists—one for the original list and a second for the sorted list. In addition the client would have destroyed the original list. If the list is large, we might not have enough memory for two copies even if one is empty. A better solution is to derive a class from `List` that adds a method that sorts the values in the list. Because the data fields in `List` are protected, we can inherit them and access them directly. By accessing the values directly, we can keep from having to have two lists.

Class Name: *ListWithSort*	Superclass: *List*	Subclasses:
Responsibilities	**Collaborations**	
Create itself (maxItems), Constructor	super	
Sort the items in the list, Transformer	string	

Responsibility Algorithms for Class `ListWithSort`

The constructor takes the maximum number of items and calls the `List`'s constructor. None of the other methods need to be overridden.

Going back to our by-hand algorithm, we can search `listItems` for the smallest value, but how do we "cross off" a list component? We could simulate crossing off a value by replacing it with `null`. We thus set the value of the crossed-off item to something that doesn't interfere with the processing of the rest of the components. However, a slight variation of our hand-done algorithm allows us to sort the components *in place*. We do not have to use a second list; we can put a value into its proper place in the list by having it swap places with the component currently in that list position.

We can state the algorithm as follows. We search for the smallest value in the array and exchange it with the component in the first position in the array. We search for the next-smallest value in the array and exchange it with the component in the second position in the array. This process continues until all the components are in their proper places.

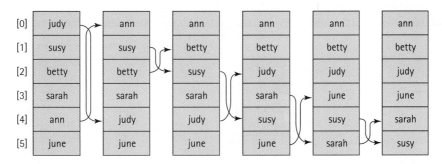

Figure 12.4 *Straight selection sort*

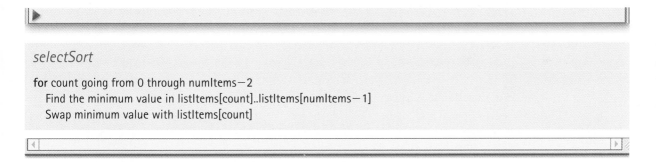

selectSort

for count going from 0 through numItems−2
  Find the minimum value in listItems[count]..listItems[numItems−1]
  Swap minimum value with listItems[count]

Figure 12.4 illustrates how this algorithm works.

Observe that we perform `numItems-1` passes through the list because `count` runs from 0 through `numItems-2`. The loop does not need to be executed when `count` equals `numItems-1` because the last value, `listItems[numItems-1]`, is in its proper place after the preceding components have been sorted.

This sort, known as the *straight selection sort*, belongs to a class of sorts called selection sorts. There are many types of sorting algorithms. Selection sorts are characterized by finding the smallest (or largest) value left in the unsorted portion at each iteration and swapping it with the value indexed by the iteration counter. Swapping the contents of two variables requires a temporary variable so that no values are lost (see Figure 12.5).

Class `ListWithSort`

We are now ready to code our derived class. We need to include in the documentation that the alphabetic order may be lost with future insertions.

```
public class ListWithSort extends List
{
  // The items in the list are rearranged into ascending order
  //  This order is not preserved in future insertions
```

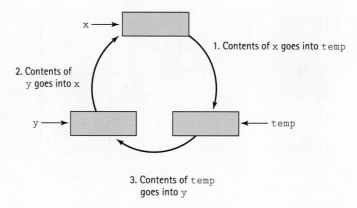

Figure 12.5 *Swapping the contents of two variables, x and y*

```
public ListWithSort(int maxItems)
{ // Constructor
  super(maxItems);
}

ListWithSort()
{ // Default constructor
  super();
}

public void selectSort()
// Arranges list items in ascending order;
//   selection sort algorithm is used.
{
  String temp;            // Temporary variable
  int passCount;          // Loop control variable for outer loop
  int searchIndex;        // Loop control variable for inner loop
  int minIndex;           // Index of minimum so far
  for (passCount = 0; passCount < numItems - 1; passCount++)
  {
    minIndex = passCount;
    // Find the index of the smallest component
    //   in listItems[passCount]..listItems[numItems-1]
    for (searchIndex = passCount + 1; searchIndex < numItems;
         searchIndex++)
      if (listItems[searchIndex].compareTo(listItems[minIndex]) <0)
```

```
        minIndex = searchIndex;
      // Swap listItems[minIndx] and listItems[passCount]
      temp = listItems[minIndex];
      listItems[minIndex] = listItems[passCount];
      listItems[passCount] = temp;
    }
  }
} // End of class ListWithSort
```

Note that with each pass through the outer loop in `selectSort`, we are looking for the minimum value in the rest of the array (`listItems[passCount]` through `list-Items[numItems-1]`). Therefore, `minIndex` is initialized to `passCount` and the inner loop runs from `searchIndex` equal to `passCount+1` through `numItems-1`. Upon exit from the inner loop, `minIndex` contains the position of the smallest value. (Note that the *if* statement is the only statement in the loop.)

This method may swap a component with itself, which occurs if no value in the remaining list is smaller than `listItems[passCount]`. We could avoid this unnecessary swap by checking to see if `minIndex` is equal to `passCount`. Because this comparison is made in each iteration of the outer loop, it is more efficient not to check for this possibility and just to swap something with itself occasionally.

This algorithm sorts the components into ascending order. To sort them into descending order, we must scan for the maximum value instead of the minimum value. Simply changing the test in the inner loop from less than to greater than accomplishes this. Of course, `minIndex` would no longer be an appropriate identifier and should be changed to `maxIndex`.

12.4 Sorted List

It is important to note that `ListWithSort` does not provide the user with a sorted list class. The `insert` and `delete` algorithms do not preserve ordering by value. The `insert` operation places a new item at the end of the list, regardless of its value. After `selectSort` has been executed, the list items remain in sorted order only until the next insertion or deletion takes place. Of course, the client could sort the list after every insertion, but this is inefficient. Let's now look at a sorted list design in which all the list operations cooperate to preserve the sorted order of the list components.

Brainstorming Sorted List

There is nothing about order in the design for class `List`. If we want the list items kept in sorted order, we need to specify this. Let's go back to the CRC card design for class `List` and indicate that we want the list to be sorted.

Class Name: *List*	Superclass: *Object*	Subclasses:
Responsibilities		**Collaborations**
Create itself (maxItems)		None
Is list full? Observer		None
return boolean		
Is list empty? Observer		None
return boolean		
Know length, Observer		None
return int		
Is an item in the list? Observer		None
return boolean		
Insert into list (item) keeping the list sorted, Transformer		String
Delete from list (item) keeping the list sorted, Transformer		String
Look at each item in sorted order, Iterator		String

The first thing to notice is that the observers do not change. They are the same whether the list is sorted by value or not. The transformers insert and delete and the iterator now have additional constraints. Rather than designing an entirely new class, we can derive SortedList from class List, overriding those methods whose implementations need changing.

Class Name: *SortedList*	Superclass: *List*	Subclasses:
Responsibilities		**Collaborations**
Create itself (maxItems)		None
Insert into list (item) keeping the list sorted, Transformer		String
Delete from list (item) keeping the list sorted, Transformer		String
Look at each item in sorted order, Iterator		String

Responsibility Algorithms for Class `SortedList`

Let's look first at `insert`. Figure 12.6 illustrates how it should work.

The first item inserted into the list can go into the first position. If there is only one item, the list is sorted. If a second item being inserted is less than the first item, the first item must be moved into the second position and the new item put into the first position. If the second item is larger, it goes into the second position. If we add a third item that is smaller than the first item, the other two are shifted down one and the third item goes into the first position. If the third item is greater than the first item but less than the second, the second is shifted down and the third item goes into the second position. If the third item is greater than the second item, it goes into the third position.

To generalize, we start at the beginning of the list and scan until we find an item greater than the one we are inserting. We shift that item and the rest of the items in the list down one position to make room for the new item. The new item goes in the list at that point.

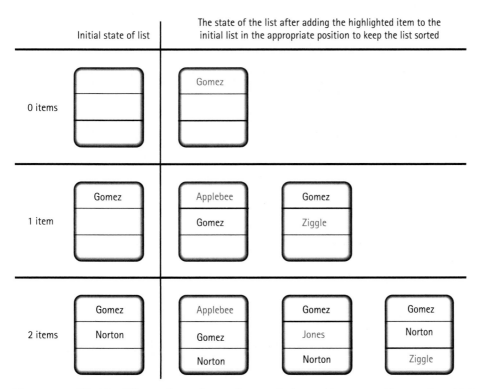

Figure 12.6 *All of the different places where an item can be inserted into a sorted list, starting with 0, 1, or 2 items already in the list.*

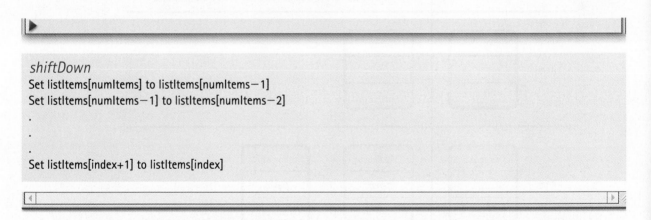

insert

if (list is not full)
    while place not found AND more places to look
        if item > current item in the list
            Increment current position
        else
            Place found
    Shift remainder of the list down
    Insert item
    Increment numItems

Assuming that `index` is the place where `item` is to be inserted, the algorithm for shifting the remainder down is as follows.

shiftDown
Set listItems[numItems] to listItems[numItems−1]
Set listItems[numItems−1] to listItems[numItems−2]
.
.
.
Set listItems[index+1] to listItems[index]

This algorithm is illustrated in Figure 12.7. Like the shiftUp algorithm, shiftDown can be implemented using a *for* loop.

This algorithm is based on how we would accomplish the task by hand. Often, such an adaptation is the best way to solve a problem. However, in this case, further thought reveals a slightly better way. Notice that we search from the front of the list (people always do), and we shift down from the end of the list upward. We can combine the searching and shifting by beginning at the *end* of the list.

If `item` is the new item to be inserted, compare `item` to the value in `listItems[numItems-1]`. If `item` is *less*, put `listItems[numItems-1]` into

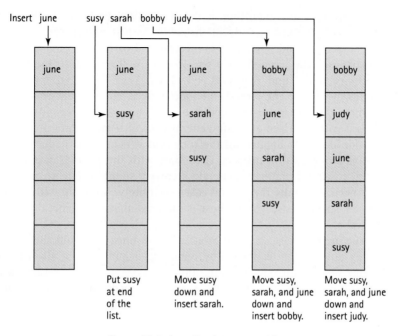

Insert june   susy sarah bobby judy

june	**june**	**june**	**bobby**
	susy	sarah	june
		susy	sarah
			susy

bobby
judy
june
sarah
susy

Put susy at end of the list.

Move susy down and insert sarah.

Move susy, sarah, and june down and insert bobby.

Move susy, sarah, and june down and insert judy.

Figure 12.7 *Inserting into a sorted list*

`listItems[numItems]` and compare `item` to the value in `listItems[numItems-2]`. This process continues until you find the place where `item` is greater than (or equal to if duplicates are allowed) the list item. Store `item` directly after it. Here is the algorithm:

insert (revised)

```
if (list is not full)
   Set index to numItems – 1
   while index >= 0 && (item .compareTo( listItems[index]) < 0)
      Set listItems[index+1] to listItems[index]
      Decrement index
   Set listItems[index+1] to item
   Increment numItems
```

Notice that this algorithm works even if the list is empty. When the list is empty, numItems is 0 and the body of the *while* loop is not entered. So item is stored into listItems[0], and numItems is incremented to 1. Does the algorithm work if item is the smallest? The largest? Let's see. If item is the smallest, the loop body is executed numItems times, and index is −1. Thus, item is stored into position 0, where it belongs. If item is the largest, the loop body is not entered. The value of index is still numItems − 1, so item is stored into listItems[numItems], where it belongs.

Are you surprised that the general case also takes care of the special cases? This situation does not happen all the time, but it occurs sufficiently often that we find it is good programming practice is to start with the general case. If we begin with the special cases, we may still generate a correct solution, but we may not realize that we don't need to handle the special cases separately. So begin with the general case, then treat as special cases only those situations that the general case does not handle correctly.

The methods delete and getNextItem must maintain the sorted order—but they already do! An item is deleted by removing it and shifting all of the items larger than the one deleted up one position, and getNextItem only returns a copy of an item, it does not change an item. Only insert needs to be overridden in derived class SortedList.

```java
public class SortedList extends List
{
  public SortedList()
  {
    super();
  }
  public SortedList(int maxItems)
  {
    super(maxItems);
  }


  public void insert(String item)
  // If the list is not full, puts item in its proper place in the
  //  list; otherwise list is unchanged
  // Assumption:  item is not already in the list
  {
    if (!this.isFull())
    {
      int index = numItems - 1;              // Loop control variable
      while (index >= 0 && (item.compareTo(listItems[index]) < 0))
      {
        listItems[index+1] = listItems[index]; // Find insertion point
        index--;
```

```
        }
      listItems[index+1] = item;        // Insert item
      numItems++;                        // Increment number of items
    }
  }
}
```

Test Plan

The same test plan can be used for the sorted list that we used for the unsorted version. The only difference is that in the expected output column, the list items should appear in sorted order.

12.5 The List Class Hierarchy and Abstract Classes

We have created a hierarchy with class `List` at the top and two derived classes. We can visualize the hierarchy as follows:

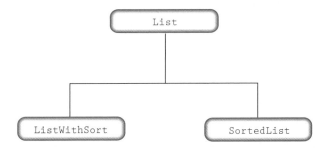

`ListWithSort` is a `List`. `SortedList` is a `List`. `ListWithSort` is not a `SortedList`, and `SortedList` is not a `ListWithSort`.

We could have organized the hierarchy using an abstract class. Recall from Chapter 8 that an abstract class is a class that is headed by the word `abstract` and leaves one or more methods incomplete. An abstract class cannot be instantiated. Another class must extend the abstract class and implement all of the abstract methods. We could have implemented the observers and iterator in the abstract class and left the implementation of the transformers to the derived class. Then the unsorted list and the sorted version could both inherit from the abstract class. The class and method headings would be as follows: (method implementations are indicated by "{...}"; the abstract methods are indicated by method signatures that end with ";").

```
public abstract class List
{
  public List() {...}
  public List(int maxItems) {...}
  public boolean isFull() {...}
  public boolean isEmpty() {...}
```

```
  public int length() {...}
  public boolean isThere(String item) {...}
  public void resetList() {...}
  public String getNextItem() {...}
  public abstract void delete(String item);
  public abstract void insert(String item);
}

public class UnsortedList extends List
{
  public UnsortedList() {...}
  public UnsortedList(int maxItems) {...}
  public void delete(String item) {...}
  public void insert(String item) {...}
}

public class SortedList extends List
{
  public SortedList() {...}
  public SortedList(int maxItems) {...}
  public void delete(String item) {...}
  public void insert(String item) {...}
}

public class ListWithSort extends UnsortedList
{
  public ListWithSort() {...}
  public ListWithSort(int maxItems) {...}
  public void selectSort() {...}
}
```

Under these conditions, the class hierarchy looks like this:

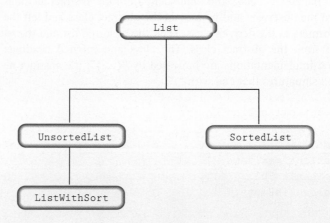

12.6   Searching

In our `SortedList` class we overrode the `insert` method, the only method that had to be rewritten to keep the list in sorted form. However, if the list is in sorted form, we can perform a more efficient search. In this section, we look at two searching algorithms that depend on the list items being in sorted order.

Sequential Search

The `isThere` algorithm assumes that the list to be searched is unsorted. A drawback to searching an unsorted list is that we must scan the entire list to discover that the search item is not there. Think what it would be like if your city telephone book contained people's names in random rather than alphabetical order. To look up Marcus Anthony's phone number, you would have to start with the first name in the phone book and scan sequentially, page after page, until you found it. In the worst case, you might have to examine tens of thousands of names only to find out that Marcus's name is not in the book.

Of course, telephone books *are* alphabetized, and the alphabetical ordering makes searching easier. If Marcus Anthony's name is not in the book, you discover this fact quickly by starting with the A's and stopping the search as soon as you have passed the place where his name should be. Although the sequential search algorithm in `isThere` works in a sorted list, we can make the algorithm more efficient by taking advantage of the fact that the items are sorted.

How does searching in a sorted list differ from searching in an unordered list? When we search for an item in an unsorted list, we won't discover that the item is missing until we reach the end of the list. If the list is already sorted, we know that an item is missing when we pass the place where it should be in the list. For example, if a list contains the values

and we are looking for judy, we need only compare judy with becca, bobby, and june to know that judy is not in the list.

If the search item is greater than the current list component, we move on to the next component. If the item is equal to the current component, we have found what we are looking for. If the item is less than the current component, then we know that it is not in the list. In either of the last two cases, we stop looking. In our original algorithm, the loop conditions were that the index was within the list and the corresponding list item was not the one searched for. In this algorithm, the second condition must be that the item being searched for is less than the corresponding list item. However, determining whether the item is found is a little more complex. We must first assert that the index is within the list and, if that is true, assert that the search item is equal to the corresponding list item.

---

isThere (in a sorted list)

Set index to 0
while index is within the list AND item is greater than listItems[index]
    Increment index
return (index is within the list AND item is equal to listItems[index])

Why can't we just test to see if `item` is equal to `listItems[index]` at the end of the loop? This works on all cases but one. What happens if `item` is larger than the last element in the list? We would exit the loop with `index` equal to `numItems`. Trying to access `listItems[index]` would then cause the program to crash with an index out of range error. Therefore, we must check on the value of `index` first.

```
public boolean isThere(String item)
// Returns true if item is in the list; false otherwise
// Assumption:  List items are in ascending order
{
   int index = 0;
   while (index < numItems && item.compareTo( listItems[index]) > 0)
     index++;
   return (index < numItems && item.compareTo(listItems[index])== 0);
}
```

On average, searching a sorted list in this way takes the same number of iterations to find an item as searching an unsorted list. The advantage of this new algorithm is that we find out sooner if an item is missing. Thus, it is slightly more efficient. There is another search algorithm that works only on a sorted list, but it is more complex: a binary search. However, the complexity is worth it.

Binary Search

The *binary search* algorithm on a sorted list is considerably faster both for finding an item and for discovering that an item is missing. A binary search is based on the principle of successive approximation. The algorithm divides the list in half (divides by 2—that's why it's called a *binary* search) and decides which half to look in next. Division of the selected portion of the list is repeated until the item is found or it is determined that the item is not in the list.

This method is analogous to the way in which we look up a name in a phone book (or word in a dictionary). We open the phone book in the middle and compare the name with one on the page that we turned to. If the name we're looking for comes before this name, we continue our search in the left-hand section of the phone book. Otherwise, we continue in the right-hand section of the phone book. We repeat this process until we find the name. If it is not there, we realize that either we have misspelled the name or our phone book isn't complete. See Figure 12.8.

We start with the whole list (indexes 0 through `numItems-1`) and compare our search value to the middle list item. If the search item is less than the middle list item, we continue the search in the first half of the list. If the search item is greater than the middle list item, we continue the search in the second half of the list. Otherwise, we have found a match. We keep comparing and redefining the part of the list in which to

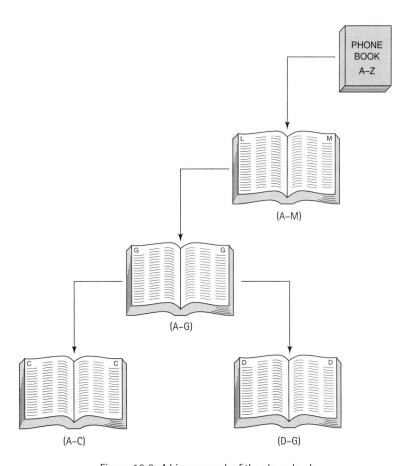

Figure 12.8 *A binary search of the phone book*

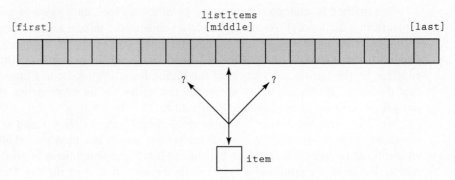

Figure 12.9 *Binary search*

look (the search area) until we find the item or the search area is empty. Let's write the algorithm bounding the search area by the indexes `first` and `last`. See Figure 12.9.

Binary Search

Set first to 0
Set last to numItems − 1
Set found to false
while search area is not empty and !found
    Set middle to (first + last) divided by 2
    if (item is equal to listItems[middle])
      Set found to true
    else if (item is less than listItems[middle])
      Set last to middle−1   // Look in first half
    else
      Set first to middle + 1 // Look in last half

This algorithm should make sense. With each comparison, at best, we find the item for which we are searching; at worst, we eliminate half of the remaining list from consideration. Before we code this algorithm, we need to determine when the search area is empty. If the search area is between `listItems[first]` and `listItems[last]`, then this area is empty if `last` is less than `first`.

Let's do a walk-through of the binary search algorithm. The item being searched for is `"bat"`. Figure 12.10a shows the values of `first`, `last`, and `middle` during the first iteration. In this iteration, `"bat"` is compared with `"dog"`, the value in `listItems[middle]`.

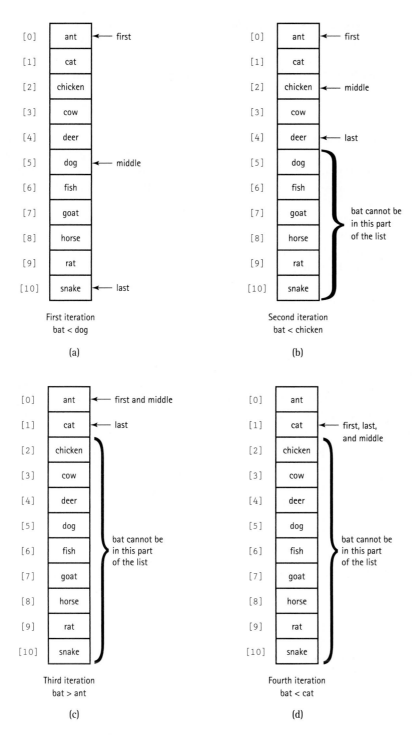

Figure 12.10 *Walk-through of binary search algorithm*

Because "bat" is less than (comes before) "dog", last becomes middle-1 and first stays the same. Figure 12.10b shows the situation during the second iteration. This time, "bat" is compared with "chicken", the value in listItems[middle]. Because "bat" is less than (comes before) "chicken", last becomes middle-1 and first again stays the same.

In the third iteration (Figure 12.10c), middle and first are both 0. The item "bat" is compared with "ant", the item in listItems[middle]. Because "bat" is greater than (comes after) "ant", first becomes middle+1. In the fourth iteration (Figure 12.10d), first, last, and middle are all the same. Again, "bat" is compared with the item in listItems[middle]. Because "bat" is less than "cat", last becomes middle-1. Now that last is less than first, the process stops; found is false.

The binary search is the most complex algorithm that we have examined so far. The following table shows first, last, middle, and listItems[middle] for searches of the items "fish", "snake", and "zebra", using the same data as in the previous example. Examine the results in this table carefully.

Iteration	first	last	middle	listItems[middle]	Terminating Condition
item: fish					
First	0	10	5	dog	
Second	6	10	8	horse	
Third	6	7	6	fish	found is true
item: snake					
First	0	10	5	dog	
Second	6	10	8	horse	
Third	9	10	9	rat	
Fourth	10	10	10	snake	found is true
item: zebra					
First	0	10	5	dog	
Second	6	10	8	horse	
Third	9	10	9	rat	
Fourth	10	10	10	snake	
Fifth	11	10			last < first

Notice in the table that whether we searched for "fish", "snake", or "zebra", the loop never executed more than four times. It never executes more than four times in a list of 11 components because the list is being cut in half each time through the loop. The table below compares a sequential search and a binary search in terms of the average number of iterations needed to find an item.

| | Average Number of Iterations | |
Length	Sequential Search	Binary Search
10	5.5	2.9
100	50.5	5.8
1,000	500.5	9.0
10,000	5000.5	12.0

If the binary search is so much faster, why not use it all the time? It certainly is faster in terms of the number of times through the loop, but more computations are performed within the binary search loop than in the other search algorithms. So if the number of components in the list is small (say, less than 20), the sequential search algorithms are faster because they perform less work at each iteration. As the number of components in the list increases, the binary search algorithm becomes relatively more efficient.

Here is the code for isThere that uses the binary search algorithm.

```
public boolean isThere(String item)
// Returns true if item is in the list; false otherwise
//   Binary search algorithm is used
// Assumption:  List items are in ascending order
{
  int first = 0;            // Lowest position in search area
  int last = numItems-1;    // Highest position in search area
  int middle;               // Middle position in search area
  boolean found = false;
  while (last >= first && !found)
  {
    middle = (first + last)/2;
    if (item.compareTo(listItems[middle])==0)
      found = true;
    else if (item.compareTo(listItems[middle])< 0)
      // Item not in listItems[middle]..listItems[last]
      last = middle - 1;
    else
      // Item not in listItems[first]..listItems[middle]
      first = middle + 1;
  }
  return found;
}
```

Theoretical Foundations
Complexity of Searching and Sorting

We introduced Big-O notation in Chapter 9 as a way of comparing the work done by different algorithms. Let's apply it to the algorithms that we've developed in this chapter and see how they compare with each other. In each algorithm, we start with a list containing some number of items, N.

In the worst case, the `isThere` sequential-search method scans all N components to locate an item. Thus, it requires N steps to execute. On average, `isThere` takes roughly $N/2$ steps to find an item; however, recall that in Big-O notation, we ignore constant factors (as well as lower-order terms). Thus, method `isThere` is an order N—that is, an $O(N)$—algorithm.

What about the algorithm we presented for a sequential search in a sorted list? The number of iterations is decreased for the case in which the item is missing from the list. However, all we have done is take a case that would require N steps and reduce its time, on average, to $N/2$ steps. Therefore, this algorithm is also $O(N)$.

Now consider `isThere` when the binary search algorithm is being used. In the worst case, it eliminates half of the remaining list components on each iteration. Thus, the worst-case number of iterations is equal to the number of times N must be divided by 2 to eliminate all but one value. This number is computed by taking the logarithm, base 2, of N (written $\log_2 N$). Here are some examples of $\log_2 N$ for different values of N:

N	$\text{Log}_2 N$
2	1
4	2
8	3
16	4
32	5
1,024	10
32,768	15
1,048,576	20
33,554,432	25
1,073,741,824	30

As you can see, for a list of over 1 billion values, the binary search algorithm takes only 30 iterations. It is definitely the best choice for searching large lists. Algorithms such as the binary search algorithm are said to be of *logarithmic order*.

Now let's turn to sorting. Method `selectSort` contains nested *for* loops. The total number of iterations is the product of the iterations performed by the two loops. The outer loop executes $N - 1$ times. The inner loop also starts out executing $N - 1$ times, but steadily decreases until it performs just one iteration: The inner loop executes $N/2$ iterations. The

continued ▼

> ### 🔲 Complexity of Searching and Sorting
>
> total number of iterations is thus
>
> $$\frac{(N-1) \times N}{2}$$
>
> Ignoring the constant factor and lower-order term, this is N^2 iterations, and `selectSort` is an O(N^2) algorithm. By contrast, `isThere`, when coded using the binary search algorithm, takes only 30 iterations to search a sorted array of 1 billion values. Putting the array into order takes `selectSort` approximately 1 billion times 1 billion iterations!
>
> The `insert` algorithm for a sorted list forms the basis for an insertion sort in which values are inserted into a sorted list as they are input. On average, `insert` must shift down half of the values ($N/2$) in the list; thus, it is an O(N) algorithm. If `insert` is called for each input value, we are executing an O(N) algorithm N times; therefore, an insertion sort is an O(N^2) algorithm.
>
> Is every sorting algorithm O(N^2)? Most of the simpler ones are, but O($N \times \log_2 N$) sorting algorithms exist. Algorithms that are O($N \times \log_2 N$) are much closer in performance to O(N) algorithms than are O(N^2) algorithms. For example, if N is 1 million, then an O(N^2) algorithm takes a million times a million (1 trillion) iterations, but an O($N \times \log_2 N$) algorithm takes only 20 million iterations—that is, it is 20 times slower than the O(N) algorithm but 50,000 times faster than the O(N^2) algorithm.

12.7 Generic Lists

Generic lists are lists where the operations are defined, but the objects on the list are not. Although we called the components of our lists "items," they are `Strings`. Is it possible to construct a truly general-purpose list where the items can be anything? For example, could we have a list of `Name` objects as defined in Chapter 7 or `Address` objects as defined in Chapter 8? Yes, we can. All we have to do is declare the objects on the list to be `Comparable`. What is `Comparable`? It's an `interface`. Now, let's see how we can use it to make our lists generic.

Comparable Interface

In Chapter 5, we defined the Java construct `interface` as a model for a class that specifies the constants (final fields) and instance methods that must be present in a class that implements the `interface`. The `Comparable interface` is part of the standard Java class library. Any class that implements this interface must implement method `compareTo`. This method compares two objects and returns an integer that determines the relative ordering of the two objects (the instance to which it is applied and the method's parameter). Consider

```
intValue = item.compareTo(listItems[index]);
```

`intValue` is negative if `item` comes before `listItems[index]`, is 0 if they are equal, and is positive if `item` comes after `listItems[index]`. We have used this method for comparing strings in the classes designed in this chapter because `String` implements interface `Comparable`.

To make our `List` class as generic as possible, we replace `String` with `Comparable` throughout the class. This means that any object of a class that implements the `Comparable` interface can be passed as a parameter to `insert`, `delete`, or `isThere`. This change also means that the array must hold `Comparable` objects and `getNextItem` must return a `Comparable` object. Here is the complete abstract class `List`.

```java
public abstract class List
{
   protected Comparable[] listItems;      // Array to hold list items
   protected int numItems;                // Number of items in the list
   protected int currentPos;              // State variable for iteration

   public List(int maxItems)
   // Instantiates an empty list object with room for maxItems items
   {
      numItems = 0;
      listItems = new Comparable[maxItems];
      currentPos = 0;
   }

   public List()
   // Instantiates an empty list object with room for 100 items
   {
      numItems = 0;
      listItems = new Comparable[100];
      currentPos = 0;
   }

   public boolean isFull()
   // Returns true if there is not room for another component;
   //   false otherwise
   {
      return (listItems.length == numItems);
   }
```

```java
public boolean isEmpty()
// Returns true if there are no components in the list;
//  false otherwise
{
  return (numItems == 0);
}


public int length()
// Returns the number of components in the list.
{
  return numItems;
}


public abstract boolean isThere(Comparable item);
// Returns true if item is in the list; false otherwise

// Transformers
public abstract void insert(Comparable item);
// If list is not full, inserts item into the list;
//  otherwise list is unchanged.
// Assumption:  item is not already in the list

public abstract void delete(Comparable item);
// Removes item from the list if it is there

// Iterator Pair
public void resetList()           // Prepare for iteration
{
  currentPos  = 0;
}
public Comparable getNextItem()
// Returns the item at the currentPos position;
//  resets current position to first item after the last item is returned
// Assumption:  No transformers have been invoked since last call
{
  Comparable next = listItems[currentPos];
  if (currentPos == numItems-1)
    currentPos = 0;
  else
    curentPos++;
  return next;
}
}
```

Notice that we have made the `isThere` method abstract. This way the derived class can determine which searching algorithm to use.

Polymorphism

We have discussed polymorphism several times as it is one of the major features of object-oriented programming. In a hierarchy of classes, polymorphism enables us to override a method name with a different implementation in a derived class. Thus there can be multiple forms of a given method within the hierarchy (literally, polymorphism means *having multiple forms*).

The Java compiler decides which form of a polymorphic instance method to use by looking at the class of its associated instance. For example, if `compareTo` is associated with a `String` variable, then the version of `compareTo` defined in class `String` is called.

Thus far, this is all straightforward. But consider the case where `compareTo` is applied to an object that has been passed as a parameter declared to be `Comparable`. The abstract `insert` method that we defined in the last section is precisely the example we have in mind.

```
public abstract void insert(Comparable item);
```

An instance of any class that implements `Comparable` can be passed as an argument to this parameter. The class of the argument object determines which form of `compareTo` is actually called within `insert`. At compile time, however, there is no way for the Java compiler to determine the class of the argument object. Instead, it must insert Bytecode that identifies the argument's class at run time and then calls the appropriate method. Programming language designers call this dynamic binding. When the compiler can identify the appropriate form of the method to use, it is called a static binding.

Dynamic binding Determining at run time which form of a polymorphic method to call

Static binding Determining at compile time which form of a polymorphic method to call

The practical implication of dynamic binding is that it allows us to define a generic `List` class that works with items that are of any class that implements `Comparable`. Whenever a method in the `List` class needs to compare two items, the appropriate form of `compareTo` is called, even when the class of the items isn't known until run time.

The other practical implication of dynamic binding is that it is slower than static binding. With static binding, the JVM transfers control directly to the appropriate method. But in dynamic binding, the JVM must first identify the class of the object and then look up the address of the associated method before transferring control to it.

Problem-Solving Case Study

Exam Attendance

Problem   You are the grader for a U.S. government class of 200 students. The instructor has asked you to prepare two lists: an alphabetical list of the students taking an exam and an alphabetical list of the students who have missed it. The catch is that she wants the lists before the exam is over. You decide to write an application for your notebook computer that takes each student's name as the student enters the exam room and prints the lists of absentees and attendees for your instructor.

Brainstorming   The words *student*, *name*, and *list* are sprinkled throughout the problem statement. The fundamental objects, then, are lists of students, each represented by his or her name. We need a window object to hold the student names as they enter the exam. We also need an object that represents the person checking in the students. This object is the driver class for the application.

a student name
a list of names
application
window object

Filtering   None of these classes overlap, so there is no consolidation that we can do. We may be missing a class, but we can't tell yet.

Scenarios   Let's look at a by-hand algorithm to get a better picture of the processing. You could stand at the door, ask the students their names as they enter, and check off the names from a master list. After all of the students have entered, you make a list of those that were not checked off and a list of those that were. Of course! You must have a master list of all the students in the class.

How do you simulate "ask the students their names"? You type each name on the keyboard of your laptop. How do you simulate "check off"? Your program reads the name and deletes it from the master list. If you then insert the name into a list of those present, you have both lists ready for printing as soon as the last student signs in.

You check with your instructor, and she says that the master class list is available on file "students.dat". You must add an input file object for reading the master list of students and a list to store them in. What about an output file? Yes, you need that too. You can write the two lists to a file and take it down the hall to be printed while the students are taking the exam. What about the student names? You have class `Name` that you can use from Chapter 7.

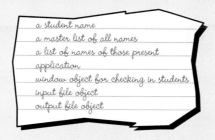

a student name
a master list of all names
a list of names of those present
application
window object for checking in students
input file object
output file object

CRC Cards This application makes use of two lists: the master list and the list of the attendees. We do not make a CRC card for this class because we can use one of the list classes developed in this chapter. Here is the CRC Card for the application class. Let's call it class `ExamAttendance`.

Class Name: ExamAttendance	Superclass: Object	Subclasses:
Responsibilities	**Collaborations**	
Prepare window object	Frame, Button, Label, Textfield	
Create master list of students	Name, BufferedReader, List	
Get a student name from the window	Name, Button	
Delete name from master list	List, Name	
Insert name into present list	List, Name	
Print list of those present	List, Name, PrintWriter	
Print list of those absent	List, Name, PrintWriter	

Internal Data Representation Your application must prepare the initial list of students from the class-roster file, which is ordered by social security number. If you use an unsorted list for the list of all students, the list must be sorted before printing (class `ListWithSort`). You decide to use class `SortedList` instead. So the internal representation is two sorted lists of `Name` objects. The interface for class `Name` is repeated here.

```java
package name;

public class Name implements Comparable
// This class defines a name consisting of three parts
{
  // Constructors
  public Name(String firstName, String middleName,
            String lastName)
  // Initializes a Name object with first, middle, and
  //  last name

  public String knowFirstName()
  public String knowMiddleName()
  public String knowLastName()
```

```
// Additional observers
public String firstLastMid()
public String lastFirstMid()
public boolean equals(Name otherName)
public int compareTo(Name otherName)
}
```

Responsibility Algorithms Preparing the window object involves setting up the `Frame` for the students to enter their names. The names are to be stored in a `Name` object, which requires a first name, a middle name, and a last name. This means that the `Frame` must have three `Labels` and three `TextFields`. There must be a button to signal the name is ready for input and a button to signal that the last student has entered the exam.

....

Prepare Window Objects

Create three labels
Create three text fields
Create "Enter" button
Create "Quit" button

Because creating `Frame` objects is second nature to you now, you can code this module directly.

Creating the master list of students requires preparing the file for input, reading the names, storing them into a `Name` object, and inserting the object into the list. Reading the names requires that you know how the data is written on file "students.dat". The file format is first name, middle name or initial, last name, and social security number. There is exactly one space between each part of the name. If there is an initial rather than a middle name, it is not followed by a period. We should extend `BufferedReader` to input this information and return a `Name` object. We design this class later.

....

Create MasterList

Prepare file
while more data
    Set name to dataFile.getName()
    Insert name into masterList

The next three responsibilities, getting a student name, deleting the name from the master list, and inserting the name in the present list, take place in the event handler for the "Enter" button.

Get a Student name

```
Set firstName to firstField.getText()
Set middleName to middleField.getText()
Set lastName to lastField.getText()
Set name to new Name(firstName, middleName, lastName)
```

Delete Name from Master List

```
masterList.delete(name)
```

Insert Name into Present List

```
presentList.insert(name)
```

The last two responsibilities, printing the list of those present and printing the list of those absent, take place within the event handler for the "Quit" button. Because the algorithm for printing a list is identical in both cases, you write it as a helper method that takes the file name and the list. The event handler can also close the window.

Print List(outFile, list)

```
list.resetList()
for index going from 1 to list.length()
    Set name to list.getNextItem()
    outFile.println(name.firstLastMid())
```

Now you need to design the class that does the file input. It is derived from `Buffered-Reader`. It must create itself, input a string, and break the string into the first name, middle name, and last name. It should also have a Boolean method that tells when the file is empty. Here is its CRC card for class `ExamDataReader`.

Class Name: ExamDataReader	Superclass: BufferedReader		Subclasses:
Responsibilities		**Collaborations**	
Create itself, Constructor		None	
Get name, Observer return name		BufferedReader	
More data? Observer return boolean		BufferedReader	

Because the fields of the name are delimited by blanks, you can use the `ReadLine` method in `BufferedReader` to input the entire line. In order to separate out the first, middle, and last names of a student, you can use the methods provided in the `String` class. The `indexOf` method finds the spaces. The first name begins at the 0th position and ends at the position before the space. The original line is replaced by the line with the first name removed. This process is repeated to get the middle name and the last name. The social security number can just be ignored. This problem doesn't need it.

We must be sure to read the first line of data in the constructor and read at the end of `get-Name`. The More data responsibility can then check to see if the last line read was `null`.

Get Name

> Set index to dataLine.indexOf(' ')
> Set firstName to dataLine.substring(0, index)
> Set dataLine to dataLine.substring(index+1, dataLine.length())
> Set index to dataLine.indexOf(' ')
> Set middleName to dataLine.substring(0, index)
> Set dataLine to dataLine.substring(index+1, dataLine.length())
> Set index to dataLine.indexOf(' ')
> Set lastName to dataLine.substring(0, index)
> Set name to new Name(firstName, middleName, lastName)
> Set dataLine to this.readLine()
>
> **return** name

```java
package exam;
import name.*;
import java.io.*;

public class ExamDataReader extends BufferedReader
{
  public static String dataLine;
  public ExamDataReader(BufferedReader inFile) throws IOException
  {
    super(inFile);
    dataLine = inFile.readLine();
  }
  public Name getName() throws IOException
  {
    String firstName;
    String middleName;
    String lastName;
    Name name;
    int index;
```

```
                // Extract first name
                index = dataLine.indexOf(' ');
                firstName = dataLine.substring(0, index);
                dataLine = dataLine.substring(index+1, dataLine.length());
                // Extract middle name
                index = dataLine.indexOf(' ');
                middleName = dataLine.substring(0, index);
                dataLine = dataLine.substring(index+1, dataLine.length());
                // Extract last name
                index = dataLine.indexOf(' ');
                lastName = dataLine.substring(0, index);
                name = new Name(firstName, middleName, lastName);
                dataLine = this.readLine();  // Get next data line

                return name;
        }
        public boolean moreData()
        {
                return dataLine != null;

        }
} // End of class ExamDataReader

import name.*;                        // Access Name class
import list.*;                        // Access List and SortedList

import exam.*;                        // Access ExamDataReader class
import java.awt.*;                    // Access Java events and files
import java.awt.event.*;
import java.io.*;

public class ExamAttendance
{
        // Define a button listener
        private static class ActionHandler implements ActionListener
        {
                public void actionPerformed(ActionEvent event)
                // Listener for the Enter and Quit buttons events
                {
                        // Declare string variables
                        String firstName;
                        String middleName;
```

```
    String lastName;
    Name name;

    if (event.getActionCommand().equals("Enter"))
    { // Handles Enter event
      firstName = firstText.getText();
      middleName = middleText.getText();
      lastName = lastText.getText();
      name = new Name(firstName, middleName, lastName);
      masterList.delete(name);
      presentList.insert(name);

      firstText.setText("");                         // Clear text fields
      middleText.setText("");
      lastText.setText("");
    }
    else
    { // Handles Quit event
      outFile.println("Students that took the exam:");
      printList(outfile, presentList);
      outfile.println("Students that missed the exam:");
      printList(outFile, masterList);
      outFile.close();
      inputFrame.dispose();                          // Close window
      System.exit(0);                                // Quit the program
    }
  }
  private void printList(PrintWriter outFile, SortedList list)
  { // Helper method to print a list
    Name name;
    list.resetList();
    int limit = list.length();
    for (int index = 1; index <= limit; index++)
    {
      name = list.getNextItem();
      outFile.println(name.firstLastMid());
    }
  }
} // End of class ActionHandler

// Class variables for class ExamAttendance
private static Frame inputFrame;
private static TextField firstText;                  // First name field
private static TextField middleText;                 // Middle name field
```

```
                  private static TextField lastText;          // Last name field
                  private static Name name;                   // A name
                  private static SortedList masterList;       // List of students
                  private static SortedList presentList;      // List of those present
                  private static ExamDataReader dataFile ;     // Master file of students
                  private static PrintWriter outFile;         // File for printing

                  public static void main(String[] args) throws IOException
                  { // Declare local variables
                    Label firstLabel;                         // Labels for input fields
                    Label middleLabel;
                    Label lastLabel;

                    Button enter;                                    // Enter button
                    Button quit;                                     // Quit button
                    ActionHandler action;                            // Declare listener

                    // Initialize/instantiate variables
                    inputFrame = new Frame();
                    firstLabel = new Label("First Name");
                    firstText = new TextField("", 15);
                    middleLabel = new Label("Middle Name");
                    middleText = new TextField("", 15);
                    lastLabel = new Label("Last Name");
                    lastText = new TextField("", 15);

                    // Instantiate/register buttons and button listener
                    enter = new Button("Enter");
                    quit = new Button("Quit");
                    action = new ActionHandler();
                    enter.addActionListener(action);
                    quit.addActionListener(action);

                    // Instantiate files and lists
                    outFile = new PrintWriter(new FileWriter("exam.out"));
                    dataFile = new ExamDataReader(new BufferedReader
                                          (new FileReader("students.dat")));
                    masterList = new SortedList(200);
                    presentList = new SortedList(200);

                    // Get the master list of students
                    while (dataFile.moreData())
                    {
                      name = dataFile.getName();
```

```
        masterList.insert(name);
    }

    // Add components to frame
    inputFrame.setLayout(new GridLayout(4,2));
    inputFrame.add(firstLabel);
    inputFrame.add(firstText);
    inputFrame.add(middleLabel);
    inputFrame.add(middleText);
    inputFrame.add(lastLabel);
    inputFrame.add(lastText);
    inputFrame.add(enter);
    inputFrame.add(quit);
    inputFrame.pack();                              // Pack the frame
    inputFrame.show();                              // Show the frame
  }
}
```

Here is a screen shot of the user interface.

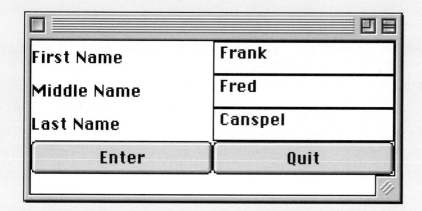

Testing This application is made up of five user-defined classes: Name, List, SortedList, ExamDataReader, and ExamAttendance. Fortunately, three of the five classes have already been tested. This is one of the main advantages of object-oriented programming: Classes can be created, tested, encapsulated into a package, and stored in your library.

    We leave the test plan for ExamDataReader and ExamAttendance as a Case Study Follow-Up Exercise.

Testing and Debugging

We have written a test plan for the unsorted list and the sorted list. However, we have not tested the sort method that was used in class ListWithSort. Method selectSort takes an array of items and rearranges the items so that they are in ascending order. If we write a black-box test plan, what are the end cases that we should test in addition to the general case? These cases fall into two categories based on length of the list of items and on the order of the items in the original list:

- The list is empty.
- The list contains one item.
- The list contains more than one item.
- The list contains the maximum number of items.
- The list is already sorted in ascending order.
- The list is sorted in descending order.

We leave it as an exercise to convert this list into a complete test plan.

Testing and Debugging Hints

1. Review the Testing and Debugging Hints from Chapter 11.

2. Be sure that any argument to a list method with a Comparable parameter belongs to a class that has implemented the Comparable interface.

3. Be careful: Primitive types cannot be passed to a method whose parameter implements the Comparable interface.

4. General-purpose methods should be tested outside the context of a particular program, using a test driver.

5. Choose test data carefully so that you test all end conditions and some in the middle. End conditions are those that reach the limits of the structure used to store them. For example, in a list, there should be test data in which the number of components is 0, 1, and array size, as well as somewhere in between.

Summary of Classes

Package Name Class Name	Comments

java.lang
  Comparable (an interface)

Observers:

compareTo(Object obj)	Returns −1 if object to which applied comes before obj; 0 if equal; +1 otherwise

(continued)

Package Name

Class Name	Comments
List	Abstract Class
Constructors:	
List()	Default with room for 100 items
List(int maxItems)	Sets up room for maxItems items
Observers:	
isEmpty()	Returns true if the list is empty
isFull()	Returns true if the list is full
abstract isThere(Comparable item)	Returns true if item is in list
Transformers:	
abstract insert(Comparable item)	Inserts item in the list
abstract delete(Comparable item)	Deletes item if it is there
Iterator:	
resetList()	Resets for another iteration
getNextItem()	Returns the next item in the list
UnsortedList **and** SortedList	
Observer:	
isThere(Comparable item)	Returns true if item is in list
Transformers:	
insert(Comparable item)	Inserts item in the list
delete(Comparable item)	Deletes item if it is there
ListWithSort **derived from** UnsortedList	
selectSort()	Sorts the values in the list

Summary

This chapter has provided practice in working with lists where the items are stored in a one-dimensional array. We have examined algorithms that insert, delete, and search data stored in an array-based unsorted list, and we have written methods to implement these algorithms. We have also examined an algorithm that takes the array in which the list items are stored and sorts them into ascending order.

We have examined several search algorithms: sequential search in an unsorted list, sequential search in a sorted list, and binary search. The sequential search in an unsorted list compares each item in the list to the one being searched for. All items must be examined before it can be determined that the search item is not in the list. The sequential search in a sorted list can determine that the search item is not in the list when the place where the item belongs has been passed. The binary search looks for the

search item in the middle of the list. If it is not there, then the search continues in the half where the item should be. This process continues to cut the search area in half until either the item is found or the search area is empty.

We have examined the insertion algorithm that keeps the items in the list sorted by value. We generalized the list in an abstract class `List`, leaving the `insert`, `delete`, and `isThere` methods abstract. We demonstrated the `Comparable interface` as a way to make the list items generic.

Quick Check

1. What is the difference between a list and an array? (pp. 552–553)
2. If the list is unsorted, does it matter where a new item is inserted? (p. 555)
3. The following code fragment implements the "Delete, if it's there" meaning for the Delete operation in an unsorted list. Change it so that the other meaning is implemented; that is, there is an assumption that the item *is* in the list. (pp. 555–556)

```
while (index < numItems && !found)
{
  if (listItems[index].compareTo(item) == 0)
    found = true;
  else
    index++;
}
if (found)
{
  for (int count = index; count < numItems-1; count++)
    listItems[count] = listItems[count+1];
  numItems--;
}
```

4. In a sequential search of an unsorted array of 1,000 values, what is the average number of loop iterations required to find a value? What is the maximum number of iterations? (pp. 578–579)
5. The following program fragment sorts list items into ascending order. Change it to sort into descending order. (pp. 560–562)

```
for (passCount = 0; passCount < numItems - 1; passCount++)
{
  minIndex = passCount;
  for (searchIndex = passCount + 1; searchIndex < numItems;
                    searchIndex++)
    if (listItems[searchIndex].compareTo(
        listItems[minIndex]) < 0)
```

```
        minIndex = searchIndex;
    temp = listItems[minIndex];                    // Swap
    listItems[minIndex] = listItems[passCount];
    listItems[passCount] = temp;
}
```

6. Describe how the `insert` operation can be used to build a sorted list from unsorted input data. (pp. 578–579)
7. Describe the basic principle behind the binary search algorithm. (pp. 572–575)

Answers

1. A list is a variable-sized structured data type; an array is a built-in type often used to implement a list.
2. No.
3.
```
index = 0;
while (listItems[index].compareTo(item) != 0)
  index++;
for (int count = index; count < numItems-1; count++)
  listItems[count] = listItems[count+1];
numItems-=;
```
4. The average number is 500 iterations. The maximum is 1000 iterations.   5. The only required change is to replace the less than with greater than in the inner loop. As a matter of style, the name `minIndex` should be changed to `maxIndex`.   6. The list initially has a length of 0. Each time a value is read, insert adds the value to the list in its correct position. When all the data values have been read, they are in the array in sorted order.   7. The binary search takes advantage of sorted list values, looking at a component in the middle of the list and deciding whether the search value precedes or follows the midpoint. The search is then repeated on the appropriate half, quarter, eighth, and so on, of the list until the value is located.

Exam Preparation Exercises

1. The following values are stored in an array in ascending order.

```
28   45   97   103   107   162   196   202   257
```

Applying the unsorted linear search algorithm to this array, search for the following values and indicate how many comparisons are required to either find the number or find that it is not in the list.

a. 28
b. 32
c. 196
d. 194

2. Repeat Exercise 1, applying the algorithm for a sequential search in a sorted list.
3. The following values are stored in an array in ascending order.

```
29   57   63   72   79   83   96   104   114   136
```

Apply the binary search algorithm looking for 114 in this list and trace the values of `first`, `last`, and `middle`. Indicate any undefined values with a *U*.

4. (True or False?) A binary search is always better to use than a sequential search.

5. If `resetList` initializes `currentPos` to -1 rather than 0, what corresponding change would have to be made in `getNextItem`?

6. We have said that arrays are homogeneous structures, yet Java implements them with an associated integer. Explain.

7. Why does the outer loop of the sorting method run from 0 through `numItems-2` rather than `numItems-1`?

8. A method that returns the number of days in a month is an example of (a) a constructor, (b) an observer, (c) an iterator, or (d) a transformer.

9. A method that adds a constant to the salary of everyone in a list is an example of (a) a constructor, (b) an observer, (c) an iterator, or (d) a transformer.

10. A method that stores values into a list is an example of (a) a constructor, (b) an observer, (c) an iterator, or (d) a transformer.

11. What Java construct is implemented using the keyword `implements`?

12. What kind of class cannot be instantiated?

13. What is the `interface` that contains method `compareTo`? What does `compareTo` return?

14. Class `List` assumes that there are no duplicate items in the list.
    a. Which method algorithms would have to be changed to allow duplicates?
    b. Would there still be options for the `delete` operation? Explain.

Programming Warm-Up Exercises

1. Complete the implementation of `UnsortedList` as a derived class from abstract class `List`.

2. Complete the implementation of `ListWithSort` as a class derived from `UnsortedList`.

3. Derive a subclass of `UnsortedList` that has the following additional methods:
    a. A value-returning instance method named `occurrences` that receives a single parameter, `item`, and returns the number of times `item` occurs in the list
    b. A Boolean instance method named `greaterFound` that receives a single parameter, `item`, and searches the list for a value greater than `item`. If such a value is found, the method returns `true`; otherwise, it returns `false`.
    c. An instance method named `component` that returns a component of the list given a position number (`pos`). The position number must be within the range 0 through `numItems-1`.
    d. A copy constructor for the `List` class that takes a parameter that specifies how much to expand the array holding the items. Implement the copy constructor by creating a larger array and copying all of the items in the list into the new array.

4. Complete the implementation of `SortedList` as a derived class from abstract class `List`.

5. Derive a subclass of `SortedList` that has the additional methods outlined in Exercise 3.

6. Write a Java Boolean method named `exclusive` that has three parameters: `item`, `list1`, and `list2` (both of class `List` as defined in this chapter). The method returns `true` if `item` is present in either `list1` or `list2` but not both.

7. The `insert` method in class `SortedList` inserts items into the list in ascending order. Derive a new class from `List` that sorts the items in descending order.
8. Exam Preparation Exercise 14 asked you to examine the implication of a list with duplicates.
    a. Design an abstract class `ListWithDuplicates` that allows duplicate keys.
    b. How does your design differ from `List`?
    c. Implement your design where the items are unsorted and `delete` deletes all of the duplicate items.
    d. Implement your design where the items are sorted and `delete` deletes all of the duplicate items.
    e. Did you use a binary search in part (d)? If not, why not?
9. Rewrite method `insert` in class `SortedList` so that it implements the first insertion algorithm discussed for sorted lists. That is, the place where the item should be inserted is found by searching from the beginning of the list. When the place is found, all the items from the insertion point to the end of the list are shifted down one position.

Programming Problems

1. A company wants to know the percentages of total sales and total expenses attributable to each salesperson. Each person has a pair of data lines in the input file. The first line contains his or her name, last name first. The second line contains his or her sales (`int`) and expenses (`float`). Write an application that produces a report with a header line containing the total sales and total expenses. Following this header should be a table with each salesperson's name, percentage of total sales, and percentage of total expenses, sorted by salesperson's name. Use one of the list classes developed in this chapter.
2. Only authorized shareholders are allowed to attend a stockholders' meeting. Write an application to read a person's name from the keyboard, check it against a list of shareholders, and print a message on the screen saying whether or not the person may attend the meeting. The list of shareholders is in a file `owners.dat` in the following format: first name, blank, last name. Use the end-of-file condition to stop reading the file. The maximum number of shareholders is 1,000.

    Design a user interface similar to the one in the Case Study. If the name does not appear on the list, the program should repeat the instructions on how to enter the name and then tell the user to try again. A message saying that the person may not enter should be printed only after he or she has been given a second chance to enter the name.
3. Enhance the program in Problem 2 as follows:
    a. Print a report file showing the number of stockholders at the time of the meeting, how many were present at the meeting, and how many people who tried to enter were denied permission to attend.
    b. Follow this summary report with a list of the names of the stockholders, with either *Present* or *Absent* after each name.

4. An advertising company wants to send a letter to all its clients announcing a new fee schedule. The clients' names are on several different lists in the company. The various lists are merged to form one file, "clients," but obviously, the company does not want to send a letter twice to anyone.

   Write an application that removes any names appearing on the list more than once. On each data line there is a four-digit code number, followed by a blank and then the client's name. For example, Amalgamated Steel is listed as

```
0231 Amalgamated Steel
```

Your program is to output each client's code and name, but no duplicates should be printed. Use one of the list classes developed in this chapter.

Case Study Follow-Up Exercises

1. Write a test plan for application `ExamAttendance`.
2. If the event handler does not delete the name from the class list when a student arrives, what other algorithm could be used to determine the names of those students that did not attend the exam?
3. Redesign the solution to this problem to use `ListWithSort`.
4. Implement the design in Question 3.

Multidimensional Arrays and Numeric Computation

- To be able to declare a two-dimensional array.

- To be able to perform fundamental operations on a two-dimensional array:

  - Access a component of the array.

  - Initialize the array.

  - Print the values in the array.

  - Process the array by rows.

  - Process the array by columns.

- To be able to declare a two-dimensional array as a parameter.

- To be able to view a two-dimensional array as an array of arrays.

- To be able to declare and process a multidimensional array.

- To be able to describe how floating-point numbers are represented in the computer.

- To be able to avoid errors caused by the limited numeric precision of the computer.

The structures that we choose to hold a collection of data objects play an important role in the design process. In the last two chapters, we have discussed the one-dimensional array and its use in problems where the logical representation of the data is a list of objects. The choice of data structure directly affects the design because it determines the algorithms used to process the data objects. For example, if the data items are stored in sorted order within the array, we can apply a binary search algorithm rather than a linear search.

In many problems, however, the relationships between data items are more complex than can be represented in a simple list. Examples of complex relationships can be found in simulations of board games such as chess, Tic-Tac-Toe, or Scrabble, in computer graphics, where points on the screen are arranged as a two-dimensional object, or in matrix operations in mathematics. In this chapter we examine the two-dimensional array, which is useful when we need to organize data in two dimensions. We usually call these dimensions rows and columns.

Then we extend the definition of an array to allow arrays with any number of dimensions, called multidimensional arrays. Each dimension represents a different feature of the data objects in the structure. For example, we might use a three-dimensional array to store objects representing sales figures by (1) store number, (2) month, and (3) item number.

Finally, we take a closer look at the limitations of the computer in doing calculations, how these limitations can cause numerical errors, and how to avoid such errors. This discussion relates directly to our Case Study, where we examine arrays as implementation structures for the mathematical object matrix.

13.1 Two-Dimensional Arrays

A one-dimensional array is used to represent items in a list or a sequence of values. A two-dimensional array is used to represent items in a table with rows and columns, provided each item in the table is of the same type or class. A component in a two-dimensional array is accessed by specifying the row and column indexes of the item in the array. This is a familiar task. For example, if you want to find a street on a map, you look up the street name on the back of the map to find the coordinates of the street, usually a number and a letter. The number specifies a row, and the letter specifies a column. You find the street where the row and column meet.

> **Two-dimensional array**   A collection of components, all of the same type or class, structured in two dimensions. Each component is accessed by a pair of indexes that represent the component's position in each dimension.

Figure 13.1 shows a two-dimensional array with 100 rows and 9 columns. The rows are accessed by an integer ranging from 0 through 99; the columns are accessed by an integer ranging from 0 through 8. Each component is accessed by a row–column pair—for example, [0][5].

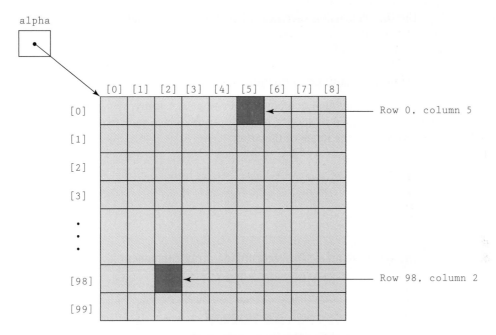

Figure 13.1 *alpha array*

Array Declaration and Instantiation

A two-dimensional array variable is declared in exactly the same way as a one-dimensional array variable, except that there are two pairs of brackets. A two-dimensional array object is instantiated in exactly the same way, except that sizes must be specified for two dimensions. Below is the syntax template for declaring an array with two dimensions, along with an example.

ArrayDeclaration

```
TypeName [] [] ArrayName;
```

The first two lines of the following code fragment would create the array shown in Figure 13.1, where the data in the table are floating-point numbers.

```
double[][] alpha;
alpha = new double[100][9];
String[][] beta;
beta = new String[10][10];
```

The first dimension specifies the number of rows, and the second dimension specifies the number of columns. Once the two-dimensional array has been created, `alpha.length` and `beta.length` give the number of rows in each array.

Accessing Individual Components

To access an individual component of the `alpha` array, two expressions (one for each dimension) are used to specify its position. We place each expression in its own pair of brackets next to the name of the array:

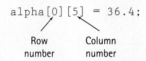

```
alpha[0][5] = 36.4;
```
    Row   Column
  number   number

The syntax template for accessing an array component is

ArrayComponentAccess

> ArrayName [IndexExpression] [IndexExpression] . . .

As with one-dimensional arrays, each index expression must result in an integer value between 0 and the number of slots in that dimension minus 1.

Let's look now at some examples. Here is the declaration of a two-dimensional array with 364 integer components (52 × 7 = 364):

```
int[][] hiTemp;
hiTemp = new int[52][7];
```

`hiTemp` is an array with 52 rows (indexed from 0 to 51) and 7 (indexed from 0 to 6) columns. Each place in the array (each component) can contain any `int` value. Our intention is that the array contains high temperatures for each day in a year. Each row represents one of the 52 weeks in a year, and each column represents one of the 7 days in a week. (To keep the example simple, we ignore the fact that there are 365—and sometimes 366—days in a year.) The expression `hiTemp[2][6]` refers to the `int` value in the third row and the seventh column. Semantically, `hiTemp[2][6]` is the temperature for the seventh day of the third week. The code fragment shown in Figure 13.2 would print the temperature values for the third week.

To obtain the number of columns in a row of an array we access the length field for the specific row. For example, the statement

```
midYear = hiTemp[26].length;
```

stores the length of row 26 of array `hiTemp`, which is 7, into the `int` variable `midYear`.

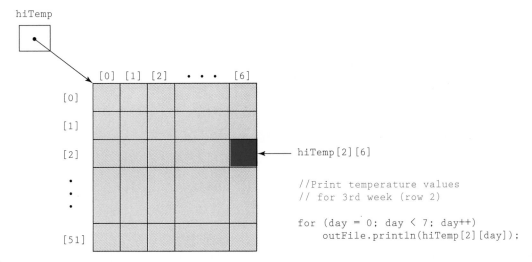

```
                                                        hiTemp[2][6]

                                                    //Print temperature values
                                                    // for 3rd week (row 2)

                                                    for (day = 0; day < 7; day++)
                                                        outFile.println(hiTemp[2][day]);
```

Figure 13.2 *hiTemp* array

Using Initializer Lists

Just as a one-dimensional array can be created with a list of values, a two-dimensional array can be created with a list of a list of values. For example, the following statement instantiates a two-dimensional array of hits. This array represents the hits for a five-day period for your four favorite baseball players.

```
int[][] hits = {{2, 1, 0, 3, 2}
                {1, 1, 2, 3, 4}
                {1, 0, 0, 0, 0}
                {0, 1, 2, 1, 1}};
```

As in the case of one-dimensional array, you do not use new with an initializer list. Now what would happen if one of your favorite players went into a slump, and the manager gave him a rest for a few days? How could you represent that in your array? Let's say that the third player sat out three games. Here is how you would represent it.

```
int[][] hits = {{2, 1, 0, 3, 2}
                {1, 1, 2, 3, 4}
                {1, 0}
                {0, 1, 2, 1, 1}};
```

The third row in the table would have only two columns, not five like the others. This array now is an example of a *ragged array*, one in which the lengths of the rows are not

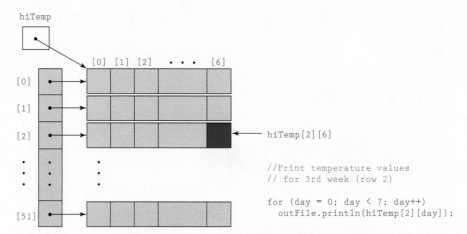

Figure 13.3 *Java implementation of* `hiTemp` *array*

the same. In fact, we could instantiate the same ragged array as follows:

```
int[][] hits;
hits = new int[4][];
hits[0] = new int[5];
hits[1] = new int[5];
hits[2] = new int[2];
hits[3] = new int[5];
```

If we then access the length of the second and third rows with the following code,

```
one = hits[1].length;
two = hits[2].length;
```

we would find that variable `one` has been assigned 5 and variable `two` contains 2.

The moral here is that in Java each row of a two-dimensional array is itself a one-dimensional array. Many programming languages directly support two-dimensional arrays; Java doesn't. In Java, a two-dimensional array is an array of references to array objects. Because of the way that Java handles two-dimensional arrays, the drawings in Figures 13.1 and 13.2 are not quite accurate. Figure 13.3 shows how Java actually implements the array `hiTemp`.

From the Java programmer's perspective, however, the two views are synonymous in the majority of applications. We typically instantiate arrays with the same number of columns in every row and rarely create a ragged array. So we continue to use the stylized version.

13.2 Processing Two-Dimensional Arrays

Processing data in a two-dimensional array generally means accessing the array in one of four patterns: randomly, along rows, along columns, or throughout the entire array. Each of these may also involve subarray processing.

The simplest way to access a component is to look directly in a given location. For example, a user enters map coordinates that we use as indexes into an array of street names to access the desired name at those coordinates. This process is referred to as *random access* because the user may enter any set of coordinates at random.

There are many cases in which we might wish to perform an operation on all the elements of a particular row or column in an array. Consider the `hiTemp` array defined previously, in which the rows represent weeks of the year and the columns represent days of the week. If we wanted the average high temperature for a given week, we would sum the values in that row and divide by 7. If we wanted the average for a given day of the week, we would sum the values in that column and divide by 52. The former case shows access by row; the latter case shows access by column.

Now suppose that we wish to determine the average for the year. We must access every element in the array, sum them, and divide by 364. In this case, the order of access—by row or by column—is not important. (The same is true if we initialize every element of an array to a constant.) This is access throughout the array.

There are times when we must access every array element in a particular order, either by rows or by columns. For example, if we wanted the average for every week, we would run through the entire array, taking each row in turn. However, if we wanted the average for each day of the week, we would run through the array a column at a time.

Let's take a closer look at these patterns of access by considering three common examples of array processing.

1. Sum the rows.
2. Sum the columns.
3. Initialize the array to some special value.

In the following discussion, we use the generic identifiers `row` and `col`, rather than problem-dependent identifiers, and we look at each algorithm in terms of generalized two-dimensional array processing. The array that we use is declared and instantiated by the following statement:

```
int[][] data = new int[50][30];  // A two-dimensional array
```

In what follows, we assume that `data` contains valid information.

Sum the Rows

Suppose we want to sum row number 3 (the fourth row) in the array and print the result. We can do this easily with a *for* loop:

```
int total = 0;
for (int col = 0; col < data[3].length; col++)
  total = total + data[3][col];
outFile.println("Row sum: " + total);
```

This *for* loop runs through each column of data while keeping the row index fixed at 3. Every value in row 3 is added to total.

Now suppose we want to sum and print two rows—row 2 and row 3. We can use a nested loop and make the row index a variable:

```
for (int row = 2; row <= 3; row++)
{
  total = 0;
  for (int col = 0; col < data[row].length; col++)
    total = total + data[row][col];
  outFile.println("Row sum: " + total);
}
```

The outer loop controls the rows, and the inner loop controls the columns. For each value of row, every column is processed; then the outer loop moves to the next row. In the first iteration of the outer loop, row is held at 2 and col goes from 0 through data[2].length. Therefore, the array is accessed in the following order:

```
data[2][0]    [2][1]    [2][2]    [2][3]    ...    [2][29]
```

In the second iteration of the outer loop, row is incremented to 3, and the array is accessed as follows:

```
data[3][0]    [3][1]    [3][2]    [3][3]    ...    [3][29]
```

We can generalize this row processing to run through every row of the array by having the outer loop run from 0 to data.length. However, if we want to access only part of the array (subarray processing), given variables declared as

```
int rowsFilled;    // Data is in 0..rowsFilled-1
int colsFilled;    // Data is in 0..colsFilled-1
```

then we write the code fragment as follows:

```
for (int row = 0; row < rowsFilled; row++)
{
  // Array is not ragged
  total = 0;
  for (int col = 0; col < colsFilled; col++)
    total = total + data[row][col];
  outFile.println("Row sum: " + total);
}
```

This is an example of subarray processing by row. Figure 13.4 illustrates subarray processing by row.

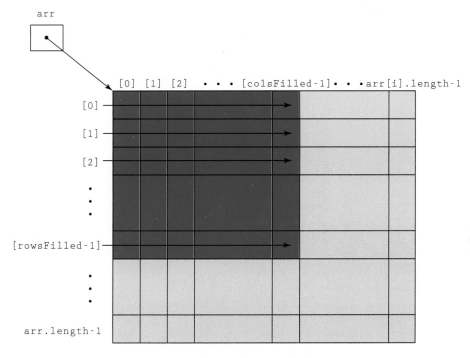

arr

[0] [1] [2] • • • [colsFilled-1]• • •arr[i].length-1

[0]

[1]

[2]

•
•
•

[rowsFilled-1]

•
•
•

arr.length-1

Figure 13.4 *Partial array processing by row*

Sum the Columns

Suppose we want to sum and print each column. The code to perform this task follows.
Again, we have generalized the code to sum only the portion of the array that contains
valid data.

```
for (int col = 0; col < colsFilled; col++)
{
  // Array is not ragged
  total = 0;
  for (int row = 0; row < rowsFilled; row++)
    total = total + data[row][col];
  outFile.println("Column sum: " + total);
}
```

In this case, the outer loop controls the column, and the inner loop controls the row. All
the components in the first column are accessed and summed before the outer loop
index changes and the components in the second column are accessed. Figure 13.5
illustrates subarray processing by column.

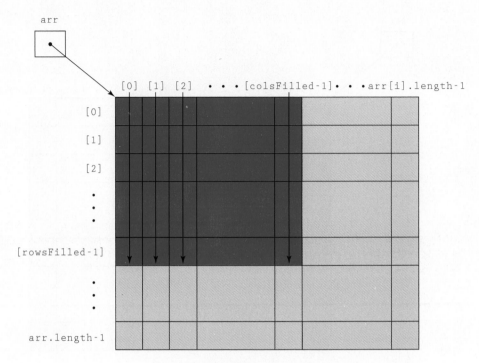

Figure 13.5 *Partial array processing by column*

Initialize the Array

Instantiating an array with initializer lists is impractical if the array is large. For a 100-row by 100-column array, you don't want to list 10,000 values. If the values are all different, you should store them into a file and input them into the array at run time. If the values are all the same, the usual approach is to use nested *for* loops and an assignment statement. Here is a general-purpose code segment that sets every item in the array to −1:

```
for (int row = 0; row < data.length; row++)
  for (int col = 0; col < data[row].length; col++)
    data[row][col] = -1;
```

In this case, we initialized the array a row at a time, but we could just as easily have run through each column instead. The order doesn't matter as long as we access every element.

Almost all processing of data stored in a two-dimensional array involves either processing by row or processing by column. The looping patterns for row processing and column processing are so useful that we summarize them on the following page. To make them more general, we use minRow for the first row number and minCol for the first column number. Remember that row processing has the row index in the outer loop, and column processing has the column index in the outer loop.

Row Processing

```
for (int row = minRow; row < rowsFilled; row++)
  for (int col = minCol; col < colsFilled; col++)
    // Whatever processing is required
```

Column Processing

```
for (int col = minCol; col < colsFilled; col++)
  for (int row = minRow; row < rowsFilled; row++)
    // Whatever processing is required
```

Two-Dimensional Arrays and Methods

Two-dimensional arrays can be parameters to methods, and they can be the return value type for a method. The syntax and semantics are identical to those for one-dimensional arrays, except there is an additional pair of brackets. Let's enclose the array initialization code fragment within a method.

```
public static void initialize(int[][] data)
// Set every cell in data to 0
{
  for (int row = 0; row < data.length; row++)
    for (int col = 0; col < data[row].length; col++)
      data[row][col] = 0;
}
```

Because Java has a field associated with each array that contains the number of slots defined for the array, we do not have to pass this information as a parameter as we do in many other languages. This is a consequence of the object orientation of the language. The array is an object and the information about the object is encapsulated with it.

As an example of a value returning method, let's design one that returns a copy of the array passed as a parameter. All the information we need to instantiate the new array is present in the one passed as a parameter. We just instantiate it and copy in the values.

```
public static int[][] copy(int[][] data)
// Returns a deep copy of data
{
  int[][] copyData = new int[data.length] [data[0].length];
  for (int row = 0; row < data.length; row++)
    for (int col = 0; col < data[row].length; col++)
      copyData[row][col] = data[row][col];
  return copyData;
}
```

13.3 Multidimensional Arrays

Java does not place a limit on the number of dimensions that an array can have. We can generalize our definition of an array to cover all cases.

> **Array** A collection of components, all of the same type or class, ordered on *N* dimensions (*N* >= 1). Each component is accessed by *N* indexes, each of which represents the component's position within that dimension.

You might have guessed that you can have as many dimensions as you want. How many should you have in a particular case? Use as many as there are features that describe the components in the array.

Take, for example, a chain of department stores. Monthly sales figures must be kept for each item by store. There are three important pieces of information about each item: the month in which it was sold, the store from which it was purchased, and the item number. We can define an array type to summarize this data as follows:

```
int[][][] sales;              // Declare array of sales figures
// First dimension represents number of stores;
//   second dimension represents months;
//   third dimension represents items
sales = new int[100][12][10];    // Instantiate array
```

A graphic representation of the sales array is shown in Figure 13.6.

The number of components in `sales` is 12,000 (10 × 12 × 100). If sales figures are available only for January through June, then half the array is empty. If we want to process the data in the array, we must use subarray processing. The following program fragment sums and prints the total number of each item sold this year to date by all stores.

```
int currentMonth = 6;     // Range: 1..12

for (int item = 0; item < sales[0][0].length; item++)
{
  numberSold = 0;
  for (int store = 0; store < sales.length; store++)
    for (int month = 0; month < currentMonth; month++)
      numberSold = numberSold + sales[store][month][item];
  outFile.println("Item # " + item + " Sales to date = "
                  + numberSold);
}
```

Because `item` controls the outer *for* loop, we are summing each item's sales by `month` and `store`. If we want to find the total sales for each `store`, we use `store` to control the outer *for* loop, summing its sales by `month` and `item` with the inner loops.

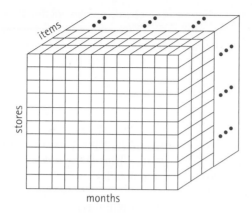

Figure 13.6 `sales` *array*

```
int currentMonth = 6;

for (int store = 0; store < sales.length; store++)
{
  numberSold = 0;
  for (item = 0; item < sales[0][0].length; item++)
    for (int month = 0; month < currentMonth; month++)
      numberSold = numberSold + sales[store][month][item];
  outFile.println("Store # "  + store + " Sales to date = "
                  + numberSold);
}
```

It takes two loops to access each component in a two-dimensional array; it takes three loops to access each component in a three-dimensional array. The task to be accomplished determines which index controls the outer loop, the middle loop, and the inner loop. If we want to calculate monthly sales by store, then `month` controls the outer loop and `store` controls the middle loop. If we want to calculate monthly sales by item, then `month` controls the outer loop and `item` controls the middle loop.

Multidimensional arrays can be passed as parameters and can be the return type of a method. Just be sure that you have as many brackets as you have dimensions following the type name.

Vector Class

We cannot leave the discussion of arrays without mentioning a class that is available in the `java.util` package: the `Vector` class. The functionality of the `Vector` class is similar to that of the array. In fact, the array is the underlying implementation structure used in the class. In contrast to an array, however, a vector can grow and shrink; its size is not fixed for its lifetime. The class provides methods to manipulate items at specified index positions. In many ways, the vector is like the general purpose list classes that we designed in the last chapter. We explore the `Vector` class in more detail in the exercises.

13.4 Floating-Point Numbers

We have used floating-point numbers off and on since we introduced them in Chapter 2, but we have not examined them in depth. Floating-point numbers have special properties when used on the computer. Thus far, we've almost ignored these properties, but now it's time to consider them in detail.

Representation of Floating-Point Numbers

As we know, Java represents numbers in the binary number system and its different numeric types use different numbers of bits. But let's assume, to simplify the following discussion, that we have a computer in which each memory location is the same size and is divided into a sign plus five decimal digits. When a variable or constant is defined, the location assigned to it consists of five digits and a sign. When an integral variable or constant is defined, the interpretation of the number stored in that place is straightforward. When a floating-point variable or constant is defined, the number stored there has both a whole number part and a fractional part, so it must be coded to represent both parts.

Let's see what such coded numbers might look like. The range of whole numbers we can represent with five digits is −99,999 through +99,999:

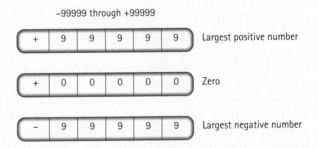

−99999 through +99999

| + | 9 | 9 | 9 | 9 | 9 | Largest positive number
| + | 0 | 0 | 0 | 0 | 0 | Zero
| − | 9 | 9 | 9 | 9 | 9 | Largest negative number

> **Precision** The maximum number of significant digits

Our precision (the number of digits we can represent) is five digits, and each number within that range can be represented exactly.

What happens if we allow one of those digits (the leftmost one, for example) to represent an exponent?

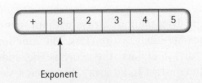

| + | 8 | 2 | 3 | 4 | 5 |

↑
Exponent

Then +82345 represents the number $+2345 \times 10^8$. The range of numbers we now can represent is much greater:

$$-9999 \times 10^9 \text{ through } 9999 \times 10^9$$

or

$$-9,999,000,000,000 \text{ through } +9,999,000,000,000$$

However, our precision is now only four digits; that is, only four-digit numbers can be represented exactly in our system. What happens to numbers with more digits? The four leftmost digits are represented correctly, and the rightmost digits, or least significant digits, are lost (assumed to be 0). Figure 13.7 shows what happens. Note that 1,000,000 can be represented exactly but −4,932,416 cannot, because our coding scheme limits us to four significant digits.

> **Significant digits**   Those digits from the first nonzero digit on the left to the last nonzero digit on the right (plus any 0 digits that are exact)

To extend our coding scheme to represent floating-point numbers, we must be able to represent negative exponents. Examples are

$$7394 \times 10^{-2} = 73.94$$

and

$$22 \times 10^{-4} = .0022$$

NUMBER	POWER OF TEN NOTATION	CODED REPRESENTATION	VALUE
+99,999	$+9999 \times 10^1$	Sign + / Exp 1 / 9 9 9 9	+99,990
−999,999	-9999×10^2	Sign − / Exp 2 / 9 9 9 9	−999,900
+1,000,000	-1000×10^3	Sign + / Exp 3 / 1 0 0 0	+1,000,000
−4,932,416	-4932×10^3	Sign − / Exp 3 / 4 9 3 2	−4,932,000

Figure 13.7 *Coding using positive exponents*

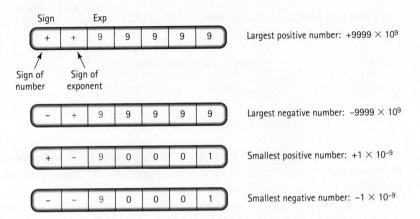

Figure 13.8 *Coding using positive and negative exponents*

Because our scheme does not include a sign for the exponent, let's change it slightly. The existing sign becomes the sign of the exponent, and we add a sign to the far left to represent the sign of the number itself (see Figure 13.8).

All the numbers between -9999×10^9 and 9999×10^9 can now be represented accurately to four digits. Adding negative exponents to our scheme allows us to represent fractional numbers as small as 1×10^{-9}.

Figure 13.9 shows how we would encode some floating-point numbers. Note that our precision is still only four digits. The numbers 0.1032, -5.406, and 1,000,000 can be represented exactly. The number 476.0321, however, with seven significant digits, is represented as 476.0; the 321 cannot be represented. (We should point out that some computers, including all JVMs, perform *rounding* rather than simple truncation when discarding excess digits. Using our assumption of four significant digits, rounding

NUMBER	POWER OF TEN NOTATION	CODED REPRESENTATION	VALUE
0.1032	$+1032 \times 10^{-4}$	+ − 4 1 0 3 2	0.1032
−5.4060	-5406×10^{-3}	− − 3 5 4 0 6	−5.406
−0.003	-3000×10^{-6}	− − 6 3 0 0 0	−0.0030
476.0321	$+4760 \times 10^{-1}$	+ − 1 4 7 6 0	476.0

Figure 13.9 *Coding of some floating-point numbers*

would store 476.0321 as 476.0 but would store 476.0823 as 476.1. We continue our discussion assuming simple truncation rather than rounding.)

Arithmetic with Floating-Point Numbers

When we use integer arithmetic, our results are exact. Floating-point arithmetic, however, is seldom exact. To understand why, let's add three floating-point numbers x, y, and z using our coding scheme.

First, we add x to y and then we add z to the result. Next, we perform the operations in a different order, adding y to z and then adding x to that result. The associative law of arithmetic says that the two answers should be the same—but are they? Let's use the following values for x, y, and z:

$$x = -1324 \times 10^3 \qquad y = 1325 \times 10^3 \qquad z = 5424 \times 10^0$$

Here is the result of adding z to the sum of x and y:

$$
\begin{array}{lll}
(x) & -1324 \times 10^3 & \\
(y) & \underline{1325 \times 10^3} & \\
& 1 \times 10^3 & = 1000 \times 10^0 \\
\\
(x + y) & 1000 \times 10^0 & \\
(z) & \underline{5424 \times 10^0} & \\
& 6424 \times 10^0 & \leftarrow (x + y) + z
\end{array}
$$

Now here is the result of adding x to the sum of y and z:

$$
\begin{array}{lll}
(y) & 1325000 \times 10^0 & \\
(z) & \underline{5424 \times 10^0} & \\
& 1330424 \times 10^0 & = 1330 \times 10^3 \text{ (truncated to four digits)} \\
\\
(y + z) & 1330 \times 10^3 & \\
(x) & \underline{-1324 \times 10^3} & \\
& 6 \times 10^3 & = 6000 \times 10^0 \leftarrow x + (y + z)
\end{array}
$$

These two answers are the same in the thousands place but are different thereafter. The error behind this discrepancy is called representational error.

Because of representational errors, it is unwise to use a floating-point variable as a loop-control variable. Because precision may be lost in calculations involving floating-point numbers, it is difficult to predict when (or even *if*) a loop-control variable of type `float`

Representational error   Arithmetic error that occurs when the precision of the true result of an arithmetic operation is greater than the precision of the machine

(or `double`) equals the termination value. A count-controlled loop with a floating-point control variable can behave unpredictably.

Also because of representational errors, you should never compare floating-point numbers for exact equality. Rarely are two floating-point numbers exactly equal, and thus you should compare them only for near equality. If the difference between the two numbers is less than some acceptable small value, you can consider them equal for the purposes of the given problem.

Implementation of Floating-Point Numbers in the Computer

All computers limit the precision of floating-point numbers, although modern machines use binary rather than decimal arithmetic. In our representation, we used only five digits to simplify the examples, and some computers really are limited to only four or five digits of precision. Some systems provide six significant digits, 15 significant digits, and 19 significant digits, respectively, for three sizes of floating-point types. We have shown only a single-digit exponent, but most systems allow two digits for the smaller floating-point type and up to four-digit exponents for a longer type.

Some languages leave the range and precision of floating-point types to each individual compiler, but Java states the range and precision in the language specification in the following formula:

$$s \times m \times 2^e$$

where s is $+1$ or -1, m is a positive integer less than 2^{24}, and e is between -149 and 104, inclusive, for values of type `float`. For values of type `double`, m is less than 253 and e is between -1075 and 970. No, we don't expect you to calculate this. Each Java numeric type provides constants `MAX_VALUE` and `MIN_VALUE`. One of the exercises asks you to print out these values for each type.

When you declare a floating-point variable, part of the memory location contains the exponent, and the number itself (called the mantissa) is assumed to be in the balance of the location. The system is called floating-point representation because the number of significant digits is fixed, and the decimal point conceptually is allowed to float (move to different positions as necessary). In our coding scheme, every number is stored as four digits, with the leftmost digit being nonzero and the exponent adjusted accordingly. Numbers in this form are said to be *normalized*. The number 1,000,000 is stored as

+	+	3	1	0	0	0

and 0.1032 is stored as

+	–	4	1	0	3	2

Normalization provides the maximum precision possible.

In Java, values of type `float` use 32 bits with an approximate range of $\pm 1.4E-45$ to $\pm 3.4E+38$ with seven significant digits. Values of type `double` use 64 bits with an approximate range of $\pm 4.9E-324$ to $1.7E+308$ with 15 significant digits.

Model Numbers   Any real number that can be represented exactly as a floating-point number in the computer is called a *model number*. A real number whose value cannot be represented exactly is approximated by the model number closest to it. In our system with four digits of precision, 0.3021 is a model number. The values 0.3021409, 0.3021222, and 0.30209999999 are examples of real numbers that are represented in the computer by the same model number. The following table shows all of the model numbers for an even simpler floating-point system that has one digit in the mantissa and an exponent that can be -1, 0, or 1.

0.1×10^{-1}	$0.1 \times 10^{+0}$	$0.1 \times 10^{+1}$
0.2×10^{-1}	$0.2 \times 10^{+0}$	$0.2 \times 10^{+1}$
0.3×10^{-1}	$0.3 \times 10^{+0}$	$0.3 \times 10^{+1}$
0.4×10^{-1}	$0.4 \times 10^{+0}$	$0.4 \times 10^{+1}$
0.5×10^{-1}	$0.5 \times 10^{+0}$	$0.5 \times 10^{+1}$
0.6×10^{-1}	$0.6 \times 10^{+0}$	$0.6 \times 10^{+1}$
0.7×10^{-1}	$0.7 \times 10^{+0}$	$0.7 \times 10^{+1}$
0.8×10^{-1}	$0.8 \times 10^{+0}$	$0.8 \times 10^{+1}$
0.9×10^{-1}	$0.9 \times 10^{+0}$	$0.9 \times 10^{+1}$

The difference between a real number and the model number that represents it is a form of representational error called *rounding error*. We can measure rounding error in two ways. The *absolute error* is the difference between the real number and the model number. For example, the absolute error in representing 0.3021409 by the model number 0.3021 is 0.0000409. The *relative error* is the absolute error divided by the real number and is sometimes stated as a percentage. For example, 0.0000409 divided by 0.3021409 is 0.000135, or 0.0135%.

The maximum absolute error depends on the *model interval*—the difference between two adjacent model numbers. In our example, the interval between 0.3021 and 0.3022 is 0.0001. The maximum absolute error in this system, for this interval, is less than 0.0001. Adding digits of precision makes the model interval (and thus the maximum absolute error) smaller.

The model interval is not a fixed number; it varies with the exponent. To see why the interval varies, consider that the interval between 3021.0 and 3022.0 is 1.0, which is 10^4 times larger than the interval between 0.3021 and 0.3022. This makes sense, because 3021.0 is simply 0.3021 times 10^4. Thus, a change in the exponent of the model numbers adjacent to the interval has an equivalent effect on the size of the interval. In practical terms, this means that we give up significant digits in the fractional part in order to represent numbers with large integer parts. Figure 13.10 illustrates this by graphing all of the model numbers listed in the preceding table.

Figure 13.10 *A graphical representation of model numbers*

We also can use relative and absolute error to measure the rounding error resulting from calculations. For example, suppose we multiply 1.0005 by 1,000. The correct result is 1000.5, but because of rounding error, our four-digit computer produces 1000.0 as its result. The absolute error of the computed result is 0.5, and the relative error is 0.05%. Now suppose we multiply 100,050.0 by 1,000. The correct result is 100,050,000, but the computer produces 100,000,000 as its result. If we look at the relative error, it is still a modest 0.05%, but the absolute error has grown to 50,000. Notice that this example is another case of changing the size of the model interval.

Whether it is more important to consider the absolute error or the relative error depends on the situation. It is unacceptable for an audit of a company to discover a $50,000 accounting error; the fact that the relative error is only 0.05% is not important. On the other hand, a 0.05% relative error is acceptable in representing prehistoric dates because the error in measurement techniques increases with age. That is, if we are talking about a date roughly 10,000 years ago, an absolute error of 5 years is acceptable; if the date is 100,000,000 years ago, then an absolute error of 50,000 years is equally acceptable.

Comparing Floating-Point Numbers We have cautioned against comparing floating-point numbers for exact equality. Our exploration of representational errors in this chapter reveals why calculations may not produce the expected results even though it appears that they should. In Chapter 10, we wrote an expression that compares two floating-point variables r and s for near equality using the floating-point absolute value method abs:

```
Math.abs(r - s) < 0.00001
```

From our discussion of model numbers, you now can recognize that the constant 0.00001 in this expression represents a maximum absolute error. We can generalize this expression as

```
Math.abs(r - s) < ERROR_TERM
```

where ERROR_TERM is a value that must be determined for each programming problem.

What if we want to compare floating-point numbers with a relative error measure? We must multiply the error term by the value in the problem that the error is relative to. For example, if we want to test whether r and s are "equal" within 0.05% of s, we write the following expression:

```
Math.abs(r - s) < 0.0005 * s
```

Keep in mind that the choice of the acceptable error and whether it should be absolute or relative depends on the problem being solved. The error terms we have shown in our example expressions are completely arbitrary and may not be appropriate for most problems. In solving a problem that involves the comparison of floating-point numbers, you typically want an error term that is as small as possible. Sometimes the choice is specified in the problem description or is reasonably obvious. Some cases require careful analysis of both the mathematics of the problem and the representational limits of the particular computer. Such analyses are the domain of a branch of mathematics called *numerical analysis* and are beyond the scope of this text.

Underflow and Overflow In addition to representational errors, there are two other problems to watch out for in floating-point arithmetic: *underflow* and *overflow*.

Underflow is the condition that arises when the value of a calculation is too small to be represented. Going back to our decimal representation, let's look at a calculation involving small numbers:

$$
\begin{array}{r}
4210 \times 10^{-8} \\
\times\ 2000 \times 10^{-8} \\
\hline
8420000 \times 10^{-16} = 8420 \times 10^{-13}
\end{array}
$$

This value cannot be represented in our scheme because the exponent -13 is too small. Our minimum is -9. One way to resolve the problem is to set the result of the calculation to 0.0. Obviously, any answer depending on this calculation will not be exact.

Overflow is a more serious problem because there is no logical recourse when it occurs. For example, the result of the calculation

$$
\begin{array}{r}
9999 \times 10^{9} \\
\times\ 1000 \times 10^{9} \\
\hline
9999000 \times 10^{18} = 9999 \times 10^{21}
\end{array}
$$

cannot be stored, so what should we do? To be consistent with our response to underflow, we could set the result to 9999×10^{9} (the maximum representable value in this case). Yet this seems intuitively wrong. The alternative is to stop with an error message.

In Java, if an overflow occurs, the result is set to signed infinity. If an underflow occurs, the result is set to a signed zero. No exception is thrown in either case.

Although we are discussing problems with floating-point numbers, integer numbers also can overflow both negatively and positively. All implementations of Java ignore integer overflow and underflow. To see how your system handles the situation, try adding 1 to a `byte` variable that has been set to 127 and adding -1 to a `byte` variable that has been set to -127.

Sometimes you can avoid overflow by arranging computations carefully. Suppose you want to know how many different five-card poker hands can be dealt from a deck of cards. What we are looking for is the number of *combinations* of 52 cards taken 5 at a time. The standard mathematical formula for the number of combinations of *n* things taken *r* at a time is

$$\frac{n!}{r!(n-r)!}$$

We could write a method `factorial` and write this formula in an assignment statement:

```
hands = factorial(52) / (factorial(5) * factorial(47));
```

The only problem is that 52! is a very large number (approximately 8.0658×10^{67}). And 47! is also large (approximately 2.5862×10^{59}). Both of these numbers are well beyond the capacity of the JVM to represent exactly (52! requires 68 digits of precision). Even though these numbers can be represented as floating-point numbers, most of the precision is still lost. By rearranging the calculations, however, we can achieve an exact result with any integral type with nine or more digits of precision (with `int` in Java). How? Consider that most of the multiplications in computing 52! are canceled when the product is divided by 47!

$$\frac{52!}{5! \times 47!} = \frac{52 \times 51 \times 50 \times 49 \times 47 \times 46 \times 45 \times 44 \times \ldots}{(5 \times 4 \times 3 \times 2 \times 1)(47 \times 46 \times 45 \times 44 \times \ldots)}$$

So, we really only have to compute

```
hands = 52 * 51 * 50 * 49 * 48 / Factorial(5);
```

which means the numerator is 311,875,200 and the denominator is 120. If we have nine or more digits of precision, we get an exact answer: 2,598,960 poker hands.

Cancellation Error Another type of error that can happen with floating-point numbers is called *cancellation error*, a form of representational error that occurs when numbers of widely differing magnitudes are added or subtracted. Let's look at an example:

$$(1 + 0.00001234 - 1) = 0.00001234$$

The laws of arithmetic say this equation should be true. But is it true if the computer does the arithmetic?

$$
\begin{array}{r}
100000000 \times 10^{-8} \\
+ \qquad 1234 \times 10^{-8} \\
\hline
100001234 \times 10^{-8}
\end{array}
$$

To four digits, the sum is 1000×10^{-3}. Now the computer subtracts 1:

$$
\begin{array}{r}
1000 \times 10^{-3} \\
-1000 \times 10^{-3} \\
\hline
0
\end{array}
$$

The result is 0, not .00001234.

Sometimes you can avoid adding two floating-point numbers that are drastically different in size by carefully arranging the calculations. Suppose a problem requires many small floating-point numbers to be added to a large floating-point number. The result is more accurate if the program first sums the smaller numbers to obtain a larger number and then adds the sum to the large number.

 ## Background Information
Practical Implications of Limited Precision

A discussion of representational, overflow, underflow, and cancellation errors may seem purely academic. In fact, these errors have serious practical implications in many problems. We close this section with three examples illustrating how limited precision can have costly or even disastrous effects.

During the Mercury space program, several of the spacecraft splashed down a considerable distance from their computed landing points. This delayed the recovery of the spacecraft and the astronaut, putting both in some danger. Eventually, the problem was traced to an imprecise representation of Earth's rotation period in the program that calculated the landing point.

As part of the construction of a hydroelectric dam, a long set of high-tension cables had to be constructed to link the dam to the nearest power-distribution point. The cables were to be several miles long, and each one was to be a continuous unit. (Because of the high power output from the dam, shorter cables couldn't be spliced together.) The cables were constructed at great expense and strung between the two

continued ▼

Practical Implications of Limited Precision

points. It turned out that they were too short, however, so another set had to be manufactured. The problem was traced to errors of precision in calculating the length of the catenary curve (the curve that a cable forms when hanging between two points).

An audit of a bank turned up a mysterious account with a large amount of money in it. The account was traced to an unscrupulous programmer who had used limited precision to his advantage. The bank computed interest on its accounts to a precision of a tenth of a cent. The hundredths of cents were not added to the customers' accounts, so the programmer had the extra tenths for all the accounts summed and deposited into an account in his name. Because the bank had thousands of accounts, these tiny amounts added up to a large amount of money. And because the rest of the bank's programs did not use as much precision in their calculations, the scheme went undetected for many months.

The moral of this discussion is twofold: (1) The results of floating-point calculations are often imprecise, and these errors can have serious consequences; and (2) if you are working with extremely large numbers or extremely small numbers, you need more information than this book provides and should consult a numerical analysis text.

 ## Software Engineering Tip
Choosing a Numeric Data Type

A first encounter with all the numeric data types of Java may leave you feeling overwhelmed. To help in choosing an alternative, you may even feel tempted to toss a coin. You should resist this temptation because each data type exists for a reason. Here are some guidelines:

1. In general, `int` is preferable. As a rule, you should use floating-point types only when absolutely necessary—that is, when you definitely need fractional values. Not only is floating-point arithmetic subject to representational errors, it also is significantly slower than integer arithmetic on most computers.
2. For ordinary integer data, use `int` instead of `byte` or `short`. It's easy to make overflow errors with these smaller data types.
3. Use `long` only if the range of `int` values is too restrictive. Compared to `int`, the `long` type requires twice the memory space.
4. `double` is the default floating type in Java and should be used unless you are certain that a problem can be solved with the lower precision of the `float` type.

By following these guidelines, you'll find that the simple types you use most often are `int` and `double`, along with `char` for character data and `boolean` for Boolean data. Only rarely do you need the longer or shorter variations of these fundamental types.

Problem-Solving Case Study

MatrixManipulation

Problem   Many mathematical problems, such as rotations in graphics, require the addition, subtraction, and multiplication of two matrices. Design and implement a general-purpose `Matrix` class that provides the operations addition, subtraction, and multiplication for real matrices.

Brainstorming   You reach for your algebra book to refresh your memory on what matrices are and how matrix addition, subtraction, and multiplication are defined. You find that a matrix is just like an array data type—well, not exactly. A matrix is a mathematical object; an array is a structured data type. A more accurate statement is that an array is a perfect structure to implement a matrix.

   Before we start to design the user interface for the `Matrix` class, we review what the operations on matrices mean. To add two matrices, you add the values in the corresponding positions: result[i][j] = A[i][j] + B[i][j]. To subtract one matrix from another, you subtract the values in the corresponding positions: result[i][j] = A[i][j] − B[i][j]. A + B and A − B are only defined on matrices with the same dimensions.

$$A = \begin{bmatrix} 5 & 0 & 1 & 4 \\ 2 & 1 & 3 & 2 \\ 1 & 1 & 0 & 0 \\ 1 & 2 & 3 & 4 \\ 2 & 3 & 1 & 0 \end{bmatrix} \qquad B = \begin{bmatrix} 1 & 1 & 1 & 2 \\ 2 & 1 & 0 & 3 \\ 1 & 2 & 4 & 1 \\ 0 & 0 & 4 & 5 \\ 0 & 0 & 1 & 1 \end{bmatrix}$$

$$A + B = \begin{bmatrix} 6 & 1 & 2 & 6 \\ 4 & 2 & 3 & 5 \\ 2 & 3 & 4 & 1 \\ 1 & 2 & 7 & 9 \\ 2 & 3 & 2 & 1 \end{bmatrix} \qquad A - B = \begin{bmatrix} 4 & -1 & 0 & 2 \\ 0 & 0 & 3 & -1 \\ 0 & -1 & -4 & -1 \\ 1 & 2 & -1 & -1 \\ 2 & 3 & 0 & -1 \end{bmatrix}$$

   Matrix multiplication is slightly more complex. If matrix E is the result of multiplying matrix C and matrix D, then

$$E[i][j] = C[i][1]*D[1][j] + C[i][2]*D[2][j] + \cdots + C[i][n]*D[n][j].$$

Why didn't we use the same matrices, A and B, for multiplication that we used for addition and subtraction? Well, matrices A and B cannot be multiplied. Look carefully at the formula: The first row of C is being multiplied item by item by the first column of D and the values summed. Therefore, the number of columns in C must be equal to the number of rows in D in the preceeding formula. Here is an example.

$$C = \begin{bmatrix} 1 & 2 & 3 & 4 \\ 0 & 2 & 1 & 3 \\ 1 & 1 & 0 & 0 \end{bmatrix} \qquad D = \begin{bmatrix} 1 & 1 \\ 0 & 1 \\ 1 & 3 \\ 4 & 2 \end{bmatrix}$$

$$C*D = \begin{bmatrix} 20 & 20 \\ 13 & 11 \\ 1 & 2 \end{bmatrix}$$

The sum of multiplying a row by a column is called the *dot product*. Another way of stating multiplications is that for any position i, j in E

$$E[i][j] = \text{dot product of row i and column j}$$

Now that we understand the semantics of the operations, we are ready to determine the responsibilities.

Scenario   If we were the users of the class, what facilities would we need? First, of course, we would need to create the matrix itself by telling it how many rows and columns there should be. Next, we would need a way to put values into the slots of the matrix. We would probably want to print out the matrix after it is constructed to be sure the values were correct. At that point, we would be ready to apply one of the binary operations, say, addition. We send the message to one matrix to add itself to the matrix in the message parameter and return the result to us. We follow the same process for subtraction and multiplication.

Are there any states of the matrix object we might want to know about? Well, it might be useful to view the value at a particular matrix position, so let's add that to the list of responsibilities. We also might want to access the number of rows and columns in a matrix.

What about error conditions? Matrix addition and subtraction require that the matrices have the same dimensions, and matrix multiplication requires that the number of columns in the first matrix must be equal to the number of rows in the second matrix. It makes sense for the matrix that is being told to perform an operation to check to be sure the operation is legal before complying with the request. If the operation is not legal, the matrix can throw an exception.

CRC Card   We can summarize our observations in a CRC card.

Class Name: *Matrix*		Superclass: *Object*	Subclasses:
Responsibilities		**Collaborations**	
Create itself (rows, columns), Constructor		None	
Know value at (row, col) return double			
Know number of rows, Observer return int		None	
Know number of columns, Observer return int		None	
Set a value at [row, col] (row, col, value), Transformer		None	
Print matrix, Observer		PrintWriter	
Add self to (two), Transformer, Constructor return Matrix		None	
Subtract (two) from self, Transformer, Constructor return Matrix		None	
Multiply self times (two), Transformer, Constructor return Matrix		None	

Internal Data Representation   We said earlier that an array is the ideal implementation structure for a matrix. In many languages, we would have to include the number of rows and number of columns as data fields in the `Matrix` class, but Java provides them for us as instance fields in the array object. Let's represent the numeric values in the matrices as `double`; this allows us to handle the largest range of values.

```
public class Matrix
{
  // Private data field
  private  double[][] matrix;
  ...
}
```

Responsibility Algorithms   To create itself, we need a constructor that takes the number of rows and the number of columns as parameters and creates the array.

```
public Matrix(int rows, int columns)
// Create empty matrix
{
  matrix = new double[rows][columns];
}
```

The next method simply asks the object to return a copy of an item at a particular slot in the array.

```
public double knowValueAt(int row, int col)
// Returns the value at matrix[row][col]
{
  return matrix[row][col];
}
```

The next two observer methods return the number of rows and the number of columns. Because Java implements a two-dimensional array as an array of references to arrays and each one-dimensional array object has an instance field that contains the number of slots in the array, we have direct access to this information. The `length` field of the two-dimensional array gives the number of rows; the `length` of each row gives the number of columns in that row. We do not need to worry about ragged arrays because of the way that we have implemented the constructor.

```
public int knowRows()
// Returns the number of rows in matrix
{
  return matrix.length;
}
```

```
public int knowColumns()
// Returns the number of columns in matrix
{
  return matrix[0].length;
}
```

The main transformer method takes a value and a row and column number. The value is stored in the matrix at the `[row][col]` position.

```
public void setValue(double dataItem, int row, int col)
// Sets matrix[row][col] to dataItem
{
  matrix[row][col] = dataItem;
}
```

The remaining observer is `printMatrix`. The matrix is to be printed by row. We have a pattern that we can follow exactly for our general discussion about arrays. Because we don't know how many columns the matrix has, we should print a blank line between rows.

```
public void printMatrix(PrintWriter outFile)
// Matrix is written on outFile by row
{
  for (int row = 0; row < matrix.length; row++)
  {
    for (int col = 0; col < matrix[0].length; col++)
      outFile.print(matrix[row][col] + "   ");
    outFile.println();
  }
}
```

The last three methods are what this problem is all about: adding, subtracting, and multiplying matrices. One matrix is the one to which the method is applied and the other matrix is a parameter.

add (two)

```
if the addition is not legal
    throw MatException
else
    Create result matrix with the same dimensions as this
    for row going from 0 through matrix.length−1
        for col going from 0 through matrix[0].length−1
            Set result[row][col] to matrix[row][col] + two.matrix[row][col]
return result
```

Each of these steps is concrete. Determining if the addition is legal is a matter of checking the dimensions of `this` against the dimensions of the parameter. The string that goes with the exception can simply state that the addition is not legal.

```
public Matrix add(Matrix two) throws MatException
  // Returns the sum of this and two
  {
    if (matrix.length != two.matrix.length ||
        matrix[0].length != two.matrix[0].length)
      throw new MatException(new String("Illegal matrix addition."));
    else
    {
      Matrix result = new Matrix(matrix.length, matrix[0].length);
      for (int row = 0; row < matrix.length; row++)
```

```
                for (int col = 0; col < matrix[0].length; col++)
                    result.matrix[row][col] = matrix[row][col] +
                        two.matrix[row][col];
            return result;
        }
    }
```

sub (two)

> **if** the subtraction is not legal
>   **throw** MatException
> **else**
>   Create result matrix with the same dimensions as this
> **for** row going from 0 through matrix.length−1
>   **for** col going from 0 through matrix[0].length−1
>   Set result[row][col] to matrix[row][col] − two.matrix[row][col]
> **return** result

```
public Matrix sub(Matrix two) throws MatException
    // Returns two subtracted from this
    {
        if (matrix.length != two.matrix.length ||
            matrix[0].length != two.matrix[0].length)
            throw new MatException(new String("Illegal matrix subtraction."));
        else
        {
            Matrix result = new Matrix(matrix.length, matrix[0].length);
            for (int row = 0; row < matrix.length; row++)
                for (int col = 0; col < matrix[0].length; col++)
                    result.matrix[row][col] = matrix[row][col] -
                        two.matrix[row][col];
            return result;
        }
    }
```

multiply (two)

> **if** multiplication is not legal
>> **throw** MatException
> **else**
>> Create result matrix with number of rows in this and number of columns in two
>> **for** row going from 0 through matrix.length − 1
>>> **for** col going from 0 through two.matrix[0].length − 1
>>>> Set result[row][col] to dot product of row of matrix
>>>> and column of two.matrix

dotProduct(row, col, two)

> Set total to 0
> **for** index going from 0 through number of columns of matrix
>> Set total to matrix[row][index] * two.matrix[index][col]+ total

Let's make `dotProduct` a helper function.

```
public Matrix multiply(Matrix two)   throws MatException
  // Returns this times two
  {
    if (matrix[0].length != two.matrix.length)
      throw new MatException(new String("Illegal matrix multiplication."));
    else
    {
      Matrix  result = new Matrix(matrix.length, two.matrix[0].length);
      for (int row = 0; row < matrix.length; row++)
        for (int col = 0; col < two.matrix[0].length; col++)
          result.matrix[row][col] = dotProduct(row, col, two);
      return result;
    }
  }

private double dotProduct(int row, int col, Matrix two)
// Returns the dot product of row of this and column of two
{
  double total = 0;
  for (int index = 0; index < two.matrix.length; index++)
    total = total + matrix[row][index]*two.matrix[index][col];
  return total;
}
```

Before we collect these methods into a complete class, have we forgotten anything? The class creates itself, has three observer methods that return its state variables, has a transformer that sets a value in a specified row and column—what happens if the specified row and column are not within the bounds of the matrix? The class should check for this error and throw an exception. The same is true for the operation that returns a value at a specified position. What about the binary matrix operations? We know that these numeric operations can cause underflow and overflow. If there is underflow, the values are automatically set to zero, but if there is overflow, the values are set to a signed infinity. If overflow occurs, the operation should throw an exception. The Double class has a boolean class method isInfinite that we can use to determine if there has been overflow. In the following class, overflow is checked, but the other error conditions are left to a Case Study Follow-Up Exercise.

```java
package matrix;
public class MatException extends Exception
{
  public MatException()
  {
    super();
  }

  public MatException(String message)
  {
    super(message);
  }
} // End of class MatException

package matrix;
import java.io.*;

public class Matrix
{
  // Private data field
  private  double[][] matrix;

  public Matrix(int rows, int columns)
  // Create empty matrix
  {
    matrix = new double[rows][columns];
  }

  public double knowValueAt(int row, int col)
  // Returns the value at matrix[row][col]
  {
    return matrix[row][col];
  }
```

```java
public int knowRows()
// Returns the number of rows in matrix
{
  return matrix.length;
}


public int knowColumns()
// Returns the number of columns in matrix
{
  return matrix[0].length;
}


public void setValue(double dataItem, int row, int col)
// Sets matrix[row][col] to dataItem
{
  matrix[row][col] = dataItem;
}


public void printMatrix(PrintWriter outFile)
// Matrix is written on outFile by row
{
  for (int row = 0; row < matrix.length; row++)
  {
    for (int col = 0; col < matrix[0].length; col++)
      outFile.print(matrix[row][col] + "   ");
    outFile.println();
  }
}


public Matrix add(Matrix two)   throws MatException
// Returns the sum of this and two
// Throws MatException if the matrices cannot be added or overflow occurs
{
  if (matrix.length != two.matrix.length ||
      matrix[0].length != two.matrix[0].length)
    throw new MatException(new String("Illegal matrix addition."));
  else
  {
    Matrix result = new Matrix(matrix.length, matrix[0].length);
    for (int row = 0; row < matrix.length; row++)
      for (int col = 0; col < matrix[0].length; col++)
      {
        result.matrix[row][col] = matrix[row][col] + two.matrix[row,col];
```

```
            if (Double.isInfinite(result.matrix[row][col]))
                throw new MatException(new String("Addition overflow"));
        }
      return result;
  }
}


public Matrix sub(Matrix two) throws MatException
// Returns two subtracted from this
// Throws MatException if the matrices cannot be subtracted
//    or overflow occurs

{
  if (matrix.length != two.matrix.length ||
      matrix[0].length != two.matrix[0].length)
    throw new MatException(new String("Illegal matrix subtraction."));
  else
  {
    Matrix result = new Matrix(matrix.length, matrix[0].length);
    for (int row = 0; row < matrix.length; row++)
      for (int col = 0; col < matrix[0].length; col++)
      {
        result.matrix[row][col] = matrix[row][col] -
            two.matrix[row, col];
        if (Double.isInfinite(result.matrix[row][col]))
            throw new MatException(new String("Subtraction overflow"));
      }
    return result;
  }
}


public Matrix multiply(Matrix two)  throws MatException
// Returns this times two
// Throws MatException if the matrices cannot be multiplied
//    or overflow occurs

{
  if (matrix[0].length != two.matrix.length)
    throw new MatException(new String("Illegal matrix multiplication."));
  else
  {
    Matrix  result = new Matrix(matrix[0].length, two.matrix.length);
    for (int row = 0; row < matrix.length; row++)
```

```
        for (int col = 0; col < two.matrix[0].length; col++)
        {
            result.matrix[row][col] = dotProduct(row, col, two);
            if (Double.isInfinite(result.matrix[row][col]))
                throw new MatException(new String("Multiplication overflow"));
        }
        return result;
    }
}


private double dotProduct(int row, int col, Matrix two)
// Returns the dot product of row of this and column of two
{
    double total = 0;
    for (int index = 0; index < two.matrix.length; index++)
        total = total + matrix[row][index]*two.matrix[index, col];
    return total;
}
} // End of class Matrix
```

Testing Because the branching statements check for errors and throw exceptions only if they occur, a clear or white-box testing strategy is appropriate. The end cases for addition and subtraction would be for dimensions of one by one and something larger. For multiplication, the outer dimensions should be one and the inner dimensions something else, the inner dimensions should be one and the outer dimensions something else. Then the error conditions must all be checked. A complete test plan is left as a Case Study Follow-up Exercise.

Testing and Debugging

Errors with multidimensional arrays usually fall into two major categories: index expressions that are out of order and index range errors. We have been very careful to use an array object's own length value in loop expressions to minimize range errors. However, inadvertent switching of indexes can cause index range errors. Take a look at the code for dotProduct. What happens if the indexes are reversed in the following statement?

```
total = total + matrix[row][index]*two.matrix[index][col];
```

That is, what happens if the statement is coded as follows?

```
total = total + matrix[index][row]*two.matrix[col][index];
```

If the first matrix is a 3 × 5 and the second is a 5 × 2, `index` goes from 0 through 4 while `row` and `col` remain at 0. `matrix[0][0]` and `two.matrix[0][0]` are accessed; then `matrix[1][0]` and `two.matrix[0][1]` are accessed; then `matrix[2][0]` and `two.matrix[0][2]` are accessed. This last access causes an `IndexOutOfBoundsException` to be thrown: `two.matrix[0][2]` doesn't exist.

How can you avoid such errors? There is no simple answer. You just have to be careful and thoroughly test your code.

Testing and Debugging Hints

1. With multidimensional arrays, use the proper number of indexes when referencing an array component and make sure the indexes are in the correct order.

2. In loops that process multidimensional arrays, double check the upper and lower bounds on each index variable to be sure they are correct for that dimension of the array.

3. When declaring a multidimensional array as a parameter, be sure that you have the proper number of brackets beside the type on the parameter list.

4. When passing an array object as an argument, be sure that is has the same number of dimensions as the parameter of the method to which it is being passed.

5. Be aware of representational, cancellation, overflow, and underflow errors. If possible, try to arrange calculations in your program to keep floating-point numbers from becoming too large or too small.

6. If your program increases the value of a positive integer and the result suddenly becomes a negative number, you should suspect integer overflow.

7. Avoid mixing data types in expressions, assignment operations, argument passing, and the return of a method value. If you must mix types, explicit type casts can prevent unwelcome surprises caused by implicit type coercion.

Summary of Classes

Package Name	Comments
Class Name	

`matrix`
  `Matrix`

Constructor: `Matrix(int, int)`	Number of rows, number of columns
`Matrix add(Matrix)`	Returns result of matrix addition
`Matrix sub(Matrix)`	Returns result of matrix subtraction
`Matrix multiply(Matrix)`	Returns result of matrix multiplication

(continued)

Package Name		Comments
Class Name		
Transformer: `setValue(double, int, int)`		Sets `[row][col]` to double value
Observers:	`double knowValueAt(int, int)`	Returns value at `[row][col]`
	`int knowRows()`	Returns the number of rows
	`int knowColumns()`	Returns number of columns
	`printMatrix(PrintWriter)`	Prints matrix by row on file

Summary

Two-dimensional arrays are useful for processing information that is represented naturally in tabular form. Processing data in two-dimensional arrays usually takes one of two forms: processing by row or processing by column. Java implements a two-dimensional array as an array of references to one-dimensional arrays. Associated with each two-dimensional array is a final instance variable `length` that contains the number of rows. Associated with each row of the table is a final instance variable `length` that contains the number of items in the row (the column length). The number of items in a row is usually the same for each row, but does not need to be. If the rows are uneven, the array is called a ragged array.

A multidimensional array is a collection of like components that are ordered on more than two dimensions. Each component is accessed by a set of indexes, one for each dimension, which represents the component's position on the various dimensions. Each index may be thought of as describing a feature of a given array component.

The floating-point types built into the Java language are `float` and `double`. Floating-point numbers are represented in the computer with a fraction and an exponent. This representation permits numbers that are much larger or much smaller than those that can be represented with the integral types. Floating-point representation also allows us to perform calculations on numbers with fractional parts.

However, there are drawbacks to using floating-point numbers in arithmetic calculations. Representational errors, for example, can affect the accuracy of a program's computations. When using floating-point numbers, keep in mind that if two numbers are vastly different from each other in size, adding or subtracting them can produce the wrong answer. Remember, also, that the computer has a limited range of numbers that it can represent. If a program tries to compute a value that is too large or too small, the result is unusual or unexpected values.

Quick Check

1. Declare a two-dimensional array named `plan` and create an array object with 30 rows and 10 columns. The component type of the array is `float`. (pp. 600–602)
2. Given the array created in Question 1, answer the following questions.
   a. Assign the value 27.3 to the component in row 13, column 7 of the array `plan` from Question 1. (pp. 602–604)
   b. Nested *for* loops can be used to sum the values in each row of array `plan`. What range of values would the outer *for* loop count through to do this? (pp. 605–607)
   c. Nested *for* loops can be used to sum the values in each column of array `plan`. What range of values would the outer *for* loop count through to do this? (p. 607)
   d. Write a program fragment that initializes array `plan` to all ones. (p. 608)
   e. Write a program fragment that prints the contents of array `plan`, one row per line of output. (pp. 606–609)
3. Suppose array `plan` is passed as an argument to a method in which the corresponding parameter is named `someArray`. What would the declaration of `someArray` look like in the parameter list? (p. 609)
4. Given the declarations

   ```
   final  int SIZE = 10;
   char[][][][] quick = new[SIZE][SIZE][SIZE][SIZE-1];
   ```

   a. How many components does array `quick` contain? (p. 610)
   b. Write a program fragment that fills array `quick` with blanks. (pp. 610–611)
5. Why is it inappropriate to use a variable of a floating-point type as a loop-control variable? (p. 618)
6. If a computer has four digits of precision, what would be the result of the following addition operation? (pp. 620–621)

   $$400400.000 + 199.9$$

Answers

1. ```
   float[][] plan;
   plan = new float[30][10];
   ```
2. a. ```
      plan[13][7] = 27.3;
      ```
   b. ```
      for (row = 0; row < 30; row++)
      ```
   c. ```
      for (col = 0; col < 10; col++)
      ```
   d. ```
      for (row = 0; row < 30; row++)
          for (col = 0; col < 10; col++)
              plan[row][col] = 0.0;
      ```
   e. ```
      for (row = 0; row < 30; row++)
      {
          for (col = 0; col < 10; col++)
            outFile.print(plan[row][col]);
          outFile.println();
      }
      ```

3. `float[][] someArray`
4. a. Nine thousand ($10 \times 10 \times 10 \times 9$)

   b.
```
for (dim1 = 0; dim1 < SIZE; dim1++)
    for (dim2 = 0; dim2 < SIZE; dim2++)
        for (dim3 = 0; dim3 < SIZE; dim3++)
            for (dim4 = 0; dim4 < SIZE - 1; dim4++)
                    quick[dim1][dim2][dim3][dim4] = ' ';
```

5. Because representational errors can cause the loop-termination condition to be evaluated with unpredictable results.   6. 400500.000 (Actually, 4.005E+5)

Exam Preparation Exercises

1. Given the declarations

```
final int NUM_SCHOOLS = 10;
final int NUM_SPORTS = 3;
int[][]  kidsInSports = new int[NUM_SCHOOLS][NUM_SPORTS];
double[][] costOfSports = new double[NUM_SPORTS][NUM_SCHOOLS];
```

   answer the following questions:
   a. What is the number of rows in `kidsInSports`?
   b. What is the number of columns in `kidsInSports`?
   c. What is the number of rows in `costOfSports`?
   d. What is the number of columns in `costOfSports`?
   e. How many components does `kidsInSports` have?
   f. How many components does `costOfSports` have?
   g. What kind of processing (row or column) would be needed to total the amount of money spent on each sport?
   h. What kind of processing (row or column) would be needed to total the number of children participating in sports at a particular school?

2. Given the following code segments, draw the arrays and their contents after the code is executed. Indicate any undefined values with the letter *U*.
   a.
```
int[][] exampleA;
exampleA =  new int[4][3];
int i, j;
for (i = 0; i < 4; i++)
  for (j = 0; j < 3; j++)
     exampleA[i][j] = i * j;
```
   b.
```
int[][] exampleB;
exampleB = new int[4][3];
int i, j;
for (i = 0; i < 3; i++)
  for (j = 0; j < 3; j++)
     exampleB[i][j] = (i + j) % 3;
```

c.
```
int[][] exampleC;
exampleC = new int[8][2];
int i, j;
exampleC[7][0] = 4;
exampleC[7][1] = 5;
for (i = 0; i < 7; i++)
{
   exampleC[i][0] = 2;
   exampleC[i][1] = 3;
}
```

3. a. Define an `int` variable `teamType` and an `int` variable `resultType`.

   b. Define a two-dimensional array variable `outcome`.

   c. This array is to be used to keep track of the wins and losses for the baseball season. `teamType` represents the classes, freshman (0), sophomore (1), junior (2), and senior (3). `resultType` represents whether they won (0), tied (1), or lost (2). Instantiate the array object referenced by `outcome`.

   d. Write a code fragment that increases the number of freshman wins by 1.

   e. Write a code fragment that determines which class won the most games.

   f. Write a code fragment that determines the total number of wins for all classes.

4. (True or False?) The number of rows in the array must be specified on the parameter list of a method that takes the array as a parameter.

5. Declare and instantiate the two-dimensional arrays described below.

   a. An array with five rows and six columns which contains Boolean values.

   b. An array, indexed from 0 through 39 and 0 through 199, which contains `double` values.

   c. An array, indexed from 0 through 3 and 0 through 2, which contains `char` values.

6. A logging operation keeps records of 37 loggers' monthly production for purposes of analysis, using the following array structure:

```
final int NUM_LOGGERS = 37;
int logsCut[NUM_LOGGERS][12];  // Logs cut per logger per month
int monthlyHigh;
int[][] logsCut;  // Logs cut per logger per month
logsCut = new int[NUM_LOGGERS][12];
int yearlyTotal;
int high;
int month;
int bestMonth;
int logger;
int bestLogger;
```

   a. (True or False?) The following statement assigns the January log total for logger number 7 to `monthlyTotal`.

   ```
   monthlyTotal = logsCut[7][0];
   ```

b. (True or False?) The following statements compute the yearly total for logger number 11.

```
yearlyTotal = 0;
for (month = 0; month < NUM_LOGGERS; month++)
   yearlyTotal = yearlyTotal + logsCut[month][10];
```

c. (True or False?) The following statements find the best logger (most logs cut) in March.

```
monthlyHigh = 0;
for (logger = 0; logger < NUM_LOGGERS; logger++)
   if (logsCut[logger][2] > monthlyHigh)
   {
      bestLogger = logger;
      monthlyHigh = logsCut[logger][2];
   }
```

d. (True or False?) The following statements find the logger with the highest monthly production and the logger's best month.

```
high = -1;
for (month = 0; month < 12; month++)
   for (logger = 0; logger < NUM_LOGGERS; logger++)
      if (logsCut[logger][month] > high)
      {
         high = logsCut[logger][month];
         bestLogger = logger;
         bestMonth = month;
      }
```

7. Declare and instantiate the `double` array variables described below.
   a. A three-dimensional array in which the first dimension is indexed from 0 through 9, the second dimension is indexed from 0 through 6 representing the days of the week, and the third dimension is indexed from 0 through 20.
   b. A four-dimensional array in which the first two dimensions are indexed from 0 through 49, and the third and fourth have 20 and 30 slots, respectively.
8. If a system supports 10 digits of precision for floating-point numbers, what are the results of the following computations?
   a. 1.4E+12 + 100.0
   b. 4.2E–8 + 100.0
   c. 3.2E–5 + 3.2E+5
9. Define the following terms:

   significant digits
   exponent
   representational error
   overflow
   underflow

Programming Warm-Up Exercises

1. Using the declarations in Exam Preparation Exercise 1, write code fragments to do the following tasks.
   a. Determine which school spent the most money on football.
   b. Determine which sport the last school spent the most money on.
   c. Determine which school had the most students playing basketball.
   d. Determine in which sport the third school had the most students participating.
   e. Determine the total amount spent by all the schools on volleyball.
   f. Determine the total number of students who played any sport. (Assume that each student played only one sport.)
   g. Determine which school had the most students participating in sports.
   h. Determine which was the most popular sport in terms of money spent.
   i. Determine which was the most popular sport in terms of student participation.

2. Examine the following class declaration.

```
public class TwoDimensions
{
  // Private data
  private int[][] data;
  private int rowsUsed;       // Number of rows that contain data
  private int columnsUsed;    // Number of columns that contain data
  // Methods
  public TwoDimensions(int maxRows, int maxColumns)
  // Constructor: Creates a maxRows  x maxColumns array
  public void inputData(BufferedReader inFile)
  // Reads data into the array
  // Data is on the file as follows:
  // First line: number of rows (rowsUsed)
  // Second line: number of columns (columnsUsed)
  // The data is stored one value per line in row order.  That is,
  //  the first columnsUsed values go into row 0; the next
  //  columnsUsed values go into row 1; etc.
  public void print(PrintWriter outFile)
  // Prints the values in the array on outFile, one row per line
  public int maxInRow(int row)
  // Returns the maximum value in the specified row
  public int maxInCol(int column)
  // Returns the maximum value in the specified column
  public int maxInArray()
  // Returns the maximum value in the entire array
  public int sum()
  // Returns the sum of the values in the array
  public int sumInRow(int row)
```

```
// Returns the sum of the values in the specified row
public int sumInCol(int column)
// Returns the sum of the values in the specified column
public boolean allPlus()
// Returns true if all the values are positive; false otherwise
```

    a. Write the code for method `TwoDimensions`.
    b. Write the code for method `inputData`.
    c. Write the code for method `print`.
    d. Write the code for method `maxInRow`.
    e. Write the code for method `maxInCol`.
    f. Write the code for method `maxInArray`.
    g. Write the code for method `sum`.
    h. Write the code for method `sumInRow`.
    i. Write the code for method `sumInCol`.
    j. Write the code for method `allPlus`.

3. Write a code segment that finds the largest value in a two-dimensional `double` array of 50 rows and 50 columns.

4. Given the following declarations

```
final int NUM_DEPTS = 100;
final int NUM_STORES = 10;
final int NUM_MONTHS = 12;
```

    a. Declare an array variable `sales` that is indexed by number of departments, number of stores, and number of months and contains `double` values.
    b. Instantiate the array object referenced by `sales`.
    c. What values do the variables in `sales` have after it is created?
    d. Write a code segment to calculate the sum of the sales for January.
    e. Write a code segment to calculate the sum of the sales for store 2.
    f. Write a code segment to calculate the sum of the sales for department 33.

5. In a program you are writing, a `double` variable `beta` potentially contains a very large number. Before multiplying `beta` by 100.0, you want the program to test whether it is safe to do so. Write an *if* statement that tests for a possible overflow *before* multiplying by 100.0. Specifically, if the multiplication would lead to overflow, print a message and don't perform the multiplication; otherwise, go ahead with the multiplication.

6. Write an application to print out MAX_VALUE and MIN_VALUE for types `float` and `double`.

7. The `Vector` class in `java.util` provides a functionality very similar to that of an array. In fact, the underlying data structure is an array. The advantage of a `Vector` is that it can grow and shrink; the disadvantage is that this capability is time consuming. To grow beyond the initial size requires the system to create a larger array and move the objects into it. Listed below are some of the useful methods in the `Vector` class and the corresponding array operations.

Method	Array equivalent/Explanation
`Vector myVector;`	`Object[] myVector;`
`myVector = new Vector(10);`	`myVector = new Object[10];`
`myVector.setElementAt(item, 9);`	`myVector[9] = item;`
`item = myVector.elementAt(5);`	`item = myVector[5];`
`myVector.addElement(item);`	`myVector[numItems] = item;`
	`numItems++;`
`int myVector.size();`	Returns the number of items in `myVector`
`int capacity()`	`myVector.length`

    a. Run an experiment to determine how many slots are added to a `Vector` object when you add one more item than you originally stated should be in the vector.

    b. Make a chart like the one shown above showing five other useful methods in the class.

Programming Problems

1. Write an application that plays Tic-Tac-Toe. Represent the board as a 3 × 3 `char` array. The array is initialized to blanks and each player is asked in turn to input a position. The first player's position is marked on the board with an 0, and the second player's position is marked with an X. Continue the process until a player wins or the game is a draw. To win, a player must have three marks in a row, in a column, or on a diagonal. A draw occurs when the board is full and no one has won.

   Each player's position should be input as indexes into the Tic-Tac-Toe board—that is, a row number and a column number. Make the program user-friendly.

   After each game, print out a diagram of the board showing the ending positions. Keep a count of the number of games each player has won and the number of draws. Before the beginning of each game, ask each player if he or she wishes to continue. If either player wishes to quit, print out the statistics and stop. Use buttons as appropriate.

2. Photos taken in space by the Galileo spacecraft are sent back to earth as a stream of numbers. Each number represents a level of brightness. A large number represents a high brightness level, and a small number represents a low level. Your job is to take a matrix (a two-dimensional array) of the numbers and print it as a picture.

   One approach to generating a picture is to print a dark character (such as a $) when the brightness level is low, and to print a light character (such as a blank or a period) when the level is high. Unfortunately, errors in transmission sometimes occur. Thus, your program should first attempt to find and correct these errors. Assume a value is in error if it differs by more than 1 from each of its four neighboring values. Correct the erroneous value by giving it the average of its neighboring values, rounded to the nearest integer.

Example:

```
      5              The 2 would be regarded as an error and would be given
4     2     5        a corrected value of 5.
      5
```

Note that values on the corners or boundaries of the matrix have to be processed differently than the values on the interior. Your application should print an image of the uncorrected picture and then an image of the corrected picture.

3. The following diagram represents an island surrounded by water (shaded area).

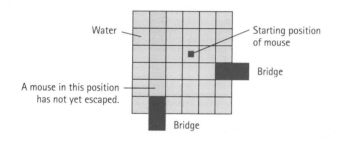

Two bridges lead off of the island. A mouse is placed on the black square. Write a program to make the mouse take a walk across the island. The mouse is allowed to travel one square at a time, either horizontally or vertically. A random number from 1 through 4 should be used to decide which direction the mouse is to take. The mouse drowns when he hits the water; he escapes when he enters a bridge. You may generate a random number up to 100 times. If the mouse does not find his way by the hundredth try, he will die of starvation. Restart the mouse in a reinitialized array and go back and repeat the whole process. Count the number of times he escapes, drowns, and starves.

Input

First input line—the size of the array, including border of water and bridges (not larger than 20 × 20).

Next N input lines—the rows of the two-dimensional array, where the positions containing negative numbers represent the water, the positions in the edge containing a 0 represent the bridges, the position containing a 1 represents the starting position of the mouse, and all other positions contain 0s.

Output

A line stating whether the mouse escaped, drowned, or starved
A line showing the mouse's starting position and the position of the two bridges
A map showing the frequency of the mouse's visits to each position

You should print the items above (double spaced between trips) for each trip by the mouse.

4. In competitive diving, each diver makes three dives of varying degrees of difficulty. Nine judges score each dive from 0 through 10 in steps of 0.5. The total score is obtained by discarding the lowest and highest of the judges' scores, adding the remaining scores, and then multiplying the scores by the degree of difficulty. The divers take turns, and when the competition is finished, they are ranked according to score. Write a program to calculate the outcome of a competition, using the following input and output specifications.

Input

Number of divers

Diver's name (10 characters), difficulty (`double`), and judges' ratings (nine `double`s)

There is a line of data for each diver for each dive. All the data for Dive 1 are grouped together, then all for Dive 2, then all for Dive 3.

Output

The input data, echo printed in tabular form with appropriate headings—for example,

Name	Difficulty	Judge's number (1–9)

A table that contains the following information:

Name	Dive 1	Dive 2	Dive 3	Total

where Name is the diver's name; Dive 1, Dive 2, and Dive 3 are the total points received for a single dive, as described above; and Total is the overall total.

5. You are to test what happens when overflow occurs. Write a simple application that does the following tasks:

Calculates the factorial of an integer number.
Embeds the factorial in a loop that goes from 1 to 100.
Prints out the result of each factorial within the loop.

Run your application with the factorial calculated using each of the integer types. Record the results of each run.

Redo the experiment taking the factorial of a real number. Record the results of each run.

Write a report describing what you have learned about overflow and Java.

6. Implement the Exam Attendance problem from Chapter 12 using the `Vector` class.

Case Study Follow-Up Exercises

1. There are no checks for row and column parameters being in bounds in the Matrix Manipulation Case Study. List the methods in which this error might occur.

2. Implement checks for this error and recode the solution.

3. Design a test plan for class `Matrix` as modified in Case Study Follow-Up Exercise 2.

4. The `java.math` package contains the `BigInteger` and `BigDecimal` classes that allow you to work with arbitrary-size and arbitrary-precision integers and floating-point values. How would you have to change class `Matrix` to define the operations using `BigInteger` rather than `double`?

Recursion

■ To be able to identify the base case(s) and the general case in a recursive definition.

■ To be able to identify the size of the problem that must decrease.

■ To be able to write a recursive algorithm for a problem involving only simple variables.

■ To be able to write a recursive algorithm for a problem involving structured variables.

In Java, any method can call another method. A method can even call itself! When a method calls itself, it is making a recursive call. The word *recursive* means "having the characteristic of coming up again, or repeating." In this case, a method call is being repeated by the method itself. Recursion is a powerful technique that can be used in place of iteration (looping).

> **Recursive call** A method call in which the method being called is the same as the one making the call

Recursive solutions can be less efficient than iterative solutions to the same problem. However, some problems lend themselves to simple, elegant, recursive solutions and are exceedingly cumbersome to solve iteratively. Some programming languages, such as early versions of FORTRAN, BASIC, and COBOL, do not allow recursion. Other languages are especially oriented to recursive algorithms—LISP is one of these. Java lets us take our choice: We can implement both iterative and recursive algorithms.

Our examples are broken into two groups: problems that use only simple variables and problems that use structured variables. If you are studying recursion before reading Chapter 11 on structured data types, then cover only the first set of examples and leave the rest until you have completed the chapters on structured data types.

Rather than one large Case Study at the end of the chapter, there are several small problems solved using recursion throughout the chapter.

14.1 What Is Recursion?

You may have seen a set of gaily painted Russian dolls that fit inside one another. Inside the first doll is a smaller doll, inside of which is an even smaller doll, inside of which is yet a smaller doll, and so on. A recursive algorithm is like such a set of Russian dolls. It reproduces itself with smaller and smaller examples of itself until a solution is found—that is, until there are no more dolls. The recursive algorithm is implemented by using a method that makes recursive calls to itself.

Power Function Definition

Let's examine a method that calculates the result of raising an integer to a positive power. If x is an integer and n is a positive integer,

$$x^n = \underbrace{x * x * x * x * \cdots * x}_{n \text{ times}}$$

We could also write this formula as

$$x^n = x * \underbrace{(x * x * x * \cdots * x)}_{(n-1) \text{ times}}$$

or even as

$$x^n = x * x * \underbrace{(x * x * \cdots * x)}_{(n-2) \text{ times}}$$

In fact, we can write the formula most concisely as

$$x^n = x * x^{n-1}$$

This definition of x^n is a classic recursive definition—that is, a definition given in terms of a smaller version of itself.

x^n is defined in terms of multiplying x times x^{n-1}. How is x^{n-1} defined? Why, as x times x^{n-2}, of course! And x^{n-2} is x times x^{n-3}, x^{n-3} is x times x^{n-4}, and so on. In this example, "in terms of smaller versions of itself" means that the exponent is decremented each time.

When does the process stop? It ends when we have reached a case for which we know the answer without resorting to a recursive definition. In this example, it is the case where n equals 1: x^1 is x. The case (or cases) for which an answer is explicitly known is called the base case. The case for which the solution is expressed in terms of a smaller version of itself is called the recursive or general case. A recursive algorithm is an algorithm that expresses the solution in terms of a call to itself, a recursive call. A recursive algorithm must terminate; that is, it must have a base case.

> **Recursive definition** A definition in which something is defined in terms of smaller versions of itself
>
> **Base case** The case for which the solution can be stated nonrecursively
>
> **General case** The case for which the solution is expressed in terms of a smaller version of itself; also known as the *recursive case*
>
> **Recursive algorithm** A solution that is expressed in terms of (a) smaller instances of itself and (b) a base case

Power Function Implementation

The code uses an *if* statement to determine which case is being executed. Here is a method that implements the power function with the general case and the base case marked in the comments.

```
public static int power(int x, int n)
// Returns x raised to the power n
// Assumption:  x is a valid integer and n is greater than 0
// Note: Large exponents may result in integer overflow
```

```
{
  if (n == 1)
    return x;                     // Base case
  else
    return x * power(x, n - 1); // Recursive call
}
```

Each recursive call to power can be thought of as creating a completely new copy of the method, each with its own copies of the parameters x and n. The value of x remains the same for each version of power, but the value of n decreases by 1 for each call until it becomes 1.

Let's trace the execution of this recursive method with the following initial call.

```
xToN = power(2, 3);
```

We use a new format to trace recursive routines: We number the calls and then discuss what is happening in paragraph form. This trace is also summarized in Figure 14.1, where each box represents a call to the power method. The values for the parameters for that call are shown in each box. Look at the figure as you are working through the trace in paragraph form.

Call 1: power is called with the number equal to 2 and the exponent equal to 3. Within power, the parameters x and n are initialized to 2 and 3, respectively. Because n is not equal to 1, power is called recursively with x and n - 1 as arguments. Execution of Call 1 pauses until an answer is sent back from this recursive call.

Call 2: x is equal to 2 and n is equal to 2. Because n is not equal to 1, the method power is called again, this time with x and n - 1 as arguments. Execution of Call 2 pauses until an answer is sent back from this recursive call.

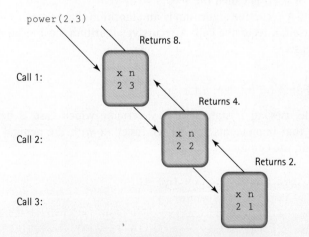

Figure 14.1 *Execution of power (2, 3)*

Call 3: x is equal to 2 and n is equal to 1. Because n equals 1, the value of x is to be returned. This call to the method has finished executing, and the method return value (which is 2) is passed back to the place in the statement from which the call was made in Call 2.

Call 2: This call to the method can now complete the statement that contained the recursive call because the recursive call has returned. Call 3's return value (which is 2) is multiplied by x. This call to the method has finished executing, and the method return value (which is 4) is passed back to the place in the statement from which the call was made in Call 1.

Call 1: This call to the method can now complete the statement that contained the recursive call because the recursive call has returned. Call 2's return value (which is 4) is multiplied by x. This call to the method has finished executing, and the method return value (which is 8) is passed back to the place in the statement from which the call was made. Because the first call (the nonrecursive call) has now completed, this is the final value of the method power.

What happens if there is no base case? We have infinite recursion, the recursive equivalent of an infinite loop. For example, if the condition

> **Infinite recursion**   The situation in which a method calls itself over and over endlessly

```
if (n == 1)
```

were omitted, power would be called over and over again. Infinite recursion also occurs if power is called with n less than or equal to 0.

In actuality, recursive calls can't go on forever. Here's the reason. When a method is called, either recursively or nonrecursively, the computer system creates temporary storage for the parameters and the method's local variables. This temporary storage is a region of memory called the *run-time stack*. When the method returns, its parameters and local variables are released from the run-time stack. With infinite recursion, the recursive method calls never return. Each time the method calls itself, a little more of the run-time stack is used to store the new copies of the variables. Eventually, all the memory space on the stack is used. At that point, the program crashes with an error message such as "RUN-TIME STACK OVERFLOW" (or the computer may simply hang).

14.2 More Examples with Simple Variables

For some people thinking recursively is intuitive; for others it is a mysterious process verging on the supernatural. The objective of the rest of the chapter is to de-mystify the recursive process by working through a collection of examples.

Calculating the Factorial Function

Let's look at another example: calculating a factorial. The factorial of a number n (written $n!$) is n multiplied by $n - 1$, $n - 2$, $n - 3$, and so on. Another way of expressing factorial is

$$n! = n * (n - 1)!$$

This expression looks like a recursive definition. $(n - 1)!$ is a smaller instance of $n!$—that is, it takes one less multiplication to calculate $(n - 1)!$ than it does to calculate $n!$ If we can find a base case, we can write a recursive algorithm. Fortunately, we don't have to look too far: $0!$ is defined in mathematics to be 1.

factorial

```
if number is 0
    return 1
else
    return number * factorial(number − 1)
```

This algorithm can be coded directly in the following method.

```
public static int factorial (int number)
// Returns the factorial of number
// Assumption: number is greater than or equal to 0
// Note: Large values of number may cause integer overflow
{
    if (number == 0)
        return 1;                              // Base case
    else
        return number * factorial(number - 1); // General case
}
```

Let's trace this method with an original number of 4.

Call 1: number is 4. Because number is not 0, the else branch is taken. The return statement cannot be completed until the recursive call to factorial with number - 1 as the argument has been completed.

Call 2: number is 3. Because number is not 0, the else branch is taken. The return statement cannot be completed until the recursive call to factorial with number - 1 as the argument has been completed.

Call 3: number is 2. Because number is not 0, the else branch is taken. The return statement cannot be completed until the recursive call to factorial with number - 1 as the argument has been completed.

Call 4: number is 1. Because number is not 0, the else branch is taken. The return statement cannot be completed until the recursive call to factorial with number - 1 as the argument has been completed.

Call 5: number is 0. Because number equals 0, this call to the method returns, sending back 1 as the result.

Call 4: The return statement in this copy can now be completed. The value to be returned is number (which is 1) times 1. This call to the method returns, sending back 1 as the result.

Call 3: The `return` statement in this copy can now be completed. The value to be returned is `number` (which is 2) times 1. This call to the method returns, sending back 2 as the result.

Call 2: The `return` statement in this copy can now be completed. The value to be returned is `number` (which is 3) times 2. This call to the method returns, sending back 6 as the result.

Call 1: The `return` statement in this copy can now be completed. The value to be returned is `number` (which is 4) times 6. This call to the method returns, sending back 24 as the result. Because this is the last of the calls to `factorial`, the recursive process is over. The value 24 is returned as the final value of the call to `factorial` with an argument of 4. Figure 14.2 summarizes the execution of the `factorial` method with an argument of 4.

Let's organize what we have done in these two solutions into an outline for writing recursive algorithms.

1. Understand the problem. (We threw this in for good measure; it is always the first step.)

2. Determine the base case(s). A base case is one to which you know the answer. It does not involve any further recursion.

3. Determine the recursive case(s). A recursive case is one in which you can express the solution in terms of a smaller version of itself.

We have used the factorial and the power algorithms to demonstrate recursion because they are easy to visualize. In practice, one would never want to calculate either of these methods using the recursive solution. In both cases, the iterative solutions are simpler and much more efficient because starting a new iteration of a loop is a faster

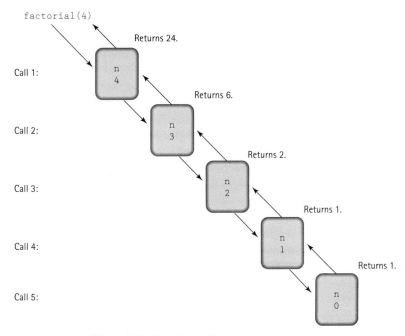

Figure 14.2 *Execution of* `factorial(4)`

operation than calling a method. Let's compare the code for the iterative and recursive versions of the factorial problem.

Iterative Solution

```
public static int factorial(int number)
{
  int factor;
  int count;

  factor = 1;
  for (count = 2; count <= number; count++)
    factor = factor * count;
  return factor;
}
```

Recursive Solution

```
public static int factorial(int number )
{
  if (number == 0)
    return 1;
  else
    return number * factorial(number - 1);
}
```

The iterative version has two local variables, whereas the recursive version has none. There are usually fewer local variables in a recursive routine than in an iterative routine. Also, the iterative version always has a loop, whereas the recursive version always has a selection statement—either an *if* or a *switch*. A branching structure is the main control structure in a recursive routine. A looping structure is the main control structure in an iterative routine.

Converting Decimal Integers to Binary

You enter integer data in decimal form, and the computer converts these decimal numbers to binary for use within a program. Do you know how decimal integers are converted to binary? The algorithm for this conversion is as follows:

1. Take the decimal number and divide it by 2.
2. Make the remainder the rightmost digit in the answer.
3. Replace the original dividend with the quotient.
4. Repeat, placing each new remainder to the left of the previous one.
5. Stop when the quotient is 0.

This is clearly an algorithm for a calculator and paper and pencil. Expressions such as "to the left of" certainly cannot be implemented in Java as yet. Let's do an example—convert 42 from base 10 to base 2—to get a feel for the algorithm before we try to write a computer solution. Remember, the quotient in one step becomes the dividend in the next.

Step 1

21 ← Quotient
2)42
4
2
2
0 ← Remainder

Step 2

10 ← Quotient
2)21
2
1
0
1 ← Remainder

Step 3

5 ← Quotient
2)10
10
0 ← Remainder

Step 4

2 ← Quotient
2)5
4
1 ← Remainder

Step 5

1 ← Quotient
2)2
2
0 ← Remainder

Step 6

0 ← Quotient
2)1
0
1 ← Remainder

The answer is the sequence of remainders from last to first. Therefore, the decimal number 42 is 101010 in binary.

It looks as though the problem can be implemented with a straightforward iterative algorithm. Each remainder is obtained from the remainder operation (% in Java), and each quotient is the result of the / operation.

convert

```
while number > 0
    Set remainder to number % 2
    Print remainder
    Set number to number / 2
```

Let's do a walk-through to test this algorithm.

Number	Remainder
42	0
21	1
10	0
5	1
2	0
1	1

Answer:	0	1	0	1	0	1
(remainder from step	1	2	3	4	5	6)

The answer is backwards! An iterative solution (using only simple variables) doesn't work. We need to print the last remainder first. The first remainder should be printed only after the rest of the remainders have been calculated and printed.

In our example, we should print 42 % 2 after (42 / 2) % 2 has been printed. But this, in turn, means that we should print (42 / 2) % 2 after ((42 / 2) / 2) % 2 has been printed. Now this begins to look like a recursive definition. We can summarize by saying that, for any given number, we should print number % 2 after (number / 2) % 2 has been printed. What is the base case? We know the answer when number is zero: We have finished and there is nothing left to do. What is the recursive case? Convert number divided by 2. When this conversion is complete, print the remainder of number divided by 2 (number % 2). This becomes the following algorithm:

▶

convert (Recursive)

if number > 0
  convert(number /2)
  Print number % 2

If number is 0, we have called convert as many times as we need to and can begin printing the answer. The base case is simply when we do nothing. The recursive solution to this problem is encoded in the convert method.

```
public static void convert(int number)
// Converts number to binary and prints it.
// Assumption:  number >= 0.
{
  if (number > 0)
  {
    convert(number / 2);    // Recursive call
    outFile.print(number % 2);
  }
    // Empty else-clause is the base case
}
```

Let's do a code walk-through of convert(10). We pick up our original example at Step 3, where the dividend is 10.

Call 1: convert is called with an argument of 10. Because number is not equal to 0, the *then-clause* is executed. Execution pauses until the recursive call to convert with an argument of (number / 2) has completed.

Call 2: number is 5. Because number is not equal to 0, execution of this call pauses until the recursive call with an argument of (number / 2) has completed.

Call 3: number is 2. Because number is not equal to 0, execution of this call pauses until the recursive call with an argument of (number / 2) has completed.

Call 4: number is 1. Because number is not equal to 0, execution of this call pauses until the recursive call with an argument of (number / 2) has completed.

Call 5: number is 0. Execution of this call to convert is complete. Control returns to the preceding call.

Call 4: Execution of this call resumes with the statement following the recursive call to convert. The value of number % 2 (which is 1) is printed. Execution of this call is complete.

Call 3: Execution of this call resumes with the statement following the recursive call to convert. The value of number % 2 (which is 0) is printed. Execution of this call is complete.

Call 2: Execution of this call resumes with the statement following the recursive call to convert. The value of number % 2 (which is 1) is printed. Execution of this call is complete.

Call 1: Execution of this call resumes with the statement following the recursive call to convert. The value of number % 2 (which is 0) is printed. Execution of this call is complete. Because this is the nonrecursive call, execution resumes with the statement immediately following the original call.

Figure 14.3 shows the execution of the convert method with the values of the parameters.

In the next section, we examine a more complicated problem—one in which the recursive solution is not immediately apparent.

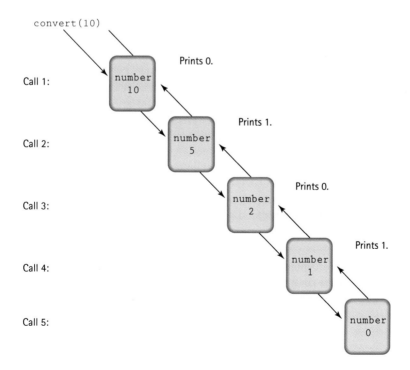

Figure 14.3 *Execution of* convert (10)

Towers of Hanoi

One of your first toys may have been a disk with three pegs with colored circles of different diameters. If so, you probably spent countless hours moving the circles from one peg to another. If we put some constraints on how the circles or discs can be moved, we have an adult game called the Towers of Hanoi. When the game begins, all the circles are on the first peg in order by size, with the smallest on the top. The object of the game is to move the circles, one at a time, to the third peg. The catch is that a circle cannot be placed on top of one that is smaller in diameter. The middle peg can be used as an auxiliary peg, but it must be empty at the beginning and at the end of the game.

To get a feel for how this might be done, let's look at some sketches of what the configuration must be at certain points if a solution is possible. We use four circles or discs. The beginning configuration is:

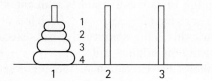

To move the largest circle (circle 4) to peg 3, we must move the three smaller circles to peg 2. Then circle 4 can be moved into its final place:

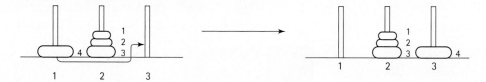

Let's assume we can do this. Now, to move the next largest circle (circle 3) into place, we must move the two circles on top of it onto an auxiliary peg (peg 1 in this case):

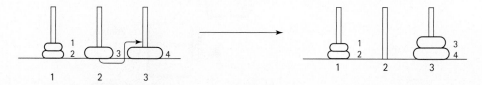

To get circle 2 into place, we must move circle 1 to another peg, freeing circle 2 to be moved to its place on peg 3:

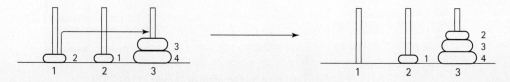

The last circle (circle 1) can now be moved into its final place, and we are finished:

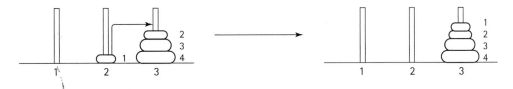

Get n Circles Moved from Peg 1 to Peg 3

Get n−1 circles moved from peg 1 to peg 2
Move nth circle from peg 1 to peg 3
Get n−1 circles moved from peg 2 to pet 3

This algorithm certainly sounds simple; surely there must be more. But this really is all there is to it.

Let's write a recursive method that implements this algorithm. We can't actually move discs, of course, but we can print out a message to do so. Notice that the beginning peg, the ending peg, and the auxiliary peg keep changing during the algorithm. To make the algorithm easier to follow, we call the pegs beginPeg, endPeg, and auxPeg. These three pegs, along with the number of circles on the beginning peg, are the parameters of the method.

We have the recursive or general case, but what about a base case? How do we know when to stop the recursive process? The clue is in the expression "Get n circles moved." If we don't have any circles to move, we don't have anything to do. We are finished with that stage. Therefore, when the number of circles equals 0, we do nothing (that is, we simply return).

```
public static void doTowers(
    int circleCount,     // Number of circles to move
    int beginPeg,        // Peg containing circles to move
    int auxPeg,          // Peg holding circles temporarily
    int endPeg       )   // Peg receiving circles being moved
// Moves are written on file outFile
{
  if (circleCount > 0)
  {
    // Move n - 1 circles from beginning peg to auxiliary peg
    doTowers(circleCount - 1, beginPeg, endPeg, auxPeg);
    outFile.println("Move circle from peg " + beginPeg
            + " to peg " + endPeg);
```

```
      // Move n - 1 circles from auxiliary peg to ending peg
      doTowers(circleCount - 1, auxPeg, beginPeg, endPeg);
  }
}
```

It's hard to believe that such a simple algorithm actually works, but we'll prove it to you. We enclose the method within a driver class that invokes the doTowers method. Output statements have been added so you can see the values of the arguments with each recursive call. Because there are two recursive calls within the method, we have indicated which recursive statement issued the call.

```
// Driver class for doTowers method
// Reads the number of circles from a file and calls doTowers
import java.io.*;                    // File types

public class Towers
{
  private static PrintWriter outFile;    // Output data file
  private static BufferedReader inFile;  // Input data file

  public static void main(String[] args) throws IOException
  {
    // Prepare files
    inFile = new BufferedReader(
            new FileReader("datafile.dat"));
    outFile = new PrintWriter(
            new FileWriter("outfile.dat"));
    int circleCount;    // Number of circles on starting peg
    circleCount = Integer.valueOf(inFile.readLine()).intValue();

    outFile.println("Input number of circles: " + circleCount);
    outFile.println("OUTPUT WITH " + circleCount + " CIRCLES");
    outFile.println("From original: ");
    doTowers(circleCount, 1, 2, 3);
  }

  public static void doTowers(
          int circleCount,    // Number of circles to move
          int beginPeg,       // Peg containing circles to move
          int auxPeg,         // Peg holding circles temporarily
          int endPeg     )    // Peg receiving circles being moved
// Moves are written on file outFile
//  This recursive method moves circleCount circles from beginPeg
//  to endPeg.  All but one of the circles are moved from beginPeg
//  to auxPeg, then the last circle is moved from beginPeg to
//  endPeg, and then the circles are moved from auxPeg to endPeg.
```

```
//  The subgoals of moving circles to and from auxPeg are what
//  involve recursion
{
  outFile.println("#circles: " + circleCount + " Begin: " +
    beginPeg + " Auxil: " + auxPeg + " End: " + endPeg);
  if (circleCount > 0)
  {
    // Move n - 1 circles from beginning peg to auxiliary peg
    outFile.print("From # first:    ");
    doTowers(circleCount - 1, beginPeg, endPeg, auxPeg);
    outFile.println("Move circle " + circleCount + "from "
            + beginPeg + "to " + endPeg);

    // Move n - 1 circles from auxiliary peg to ending peg
    outFile.println("From second:    ");
    doTowers(circleCount - 1, auxPeg, beginPeg, endPeg);
  }
 }
}
```

The output from a run with three circles follows. "Original" means that the parameters listed beside it are from the nonrecursive call, which is the first call to doTowers. "From first" means that the parameters listed are for a call issued from the first recursive statement. "From second" means that the parameters listed are for a call issued from the second recursive statement. Notice that a call cannot be issued from the second recursive statement until the preceding call from the first recursive statement has completed execution.

```
OUTPUT WITH 3 CIRCLES
From original: #circles: 3 Begin: 1 Auxil: 2 End: 3
From  first:   #circles: 2 Begin: 1 Auxil: 3 End: 2
From  first:   #circles: 1 Begin: 1 Auxil: 2 End: 3
From  first:   #circles: 0 Begin: 1 Auxil: 3 End: 2
Move circle 1 from 1 to 3
From second:   #circles: 0 Begin: 2 Auxil: 1 End: 3
Move circle 2 from 1 to 2
From second:   #circles: 1 Begin: 3 Auxil: 1 End: 2
From  first:   #circles: 0 Begin: 3 Auxil: 2 End: 1
Move circle 1 from 3 to 2
From second:   #circles: 0 Begin: 1 Auxil: 3 End: 2
Move circle 3 from 1 to 3
From second:   #circles: 2 Begin: 2 Auxil: 1 End: 3
From  first:   #circles: 1 Begin: 2 Auxil: 3 End: 1
From  first:   #circles: 0 Begin: 2 Auxil: 1 End: 3
Move circle 1 from 2 to 1
From second:   #circles: 0 Begin: 3 Auxil: 2 End: 1
```

```
Move circle 2 from 2 to 3
From second:    #circles: 1 Begin: 1 Auxil: 2 End: 3
From  first:    #circles: 0 Begin: 1 Auxil: 3 End: 2
Move circle 1 from 1 to 3
From second:    #circles: 0 Begin: 2 Auxil: 1 End: 3
```

14.3 Recursive Algorithms with Structured Variables

In our definition of a recursive algorithm, we said there were two cases: the recursive or general case, and the base case for which an answer can be expressed nonrecursively. In the general case for all our algorithms so far, an argument was expressed in terms of a smaller value each time. When structured variables are used, the recursive case is often in terms of a smaller structure rather than a smaller value; the base case occurs when there are no values left to process in the structure.

Printing the Values in an Array

Let's write a recursive algorithm for printing the contents of a one-dimensional array of n elements to show what we mean. What is the base case? It occurs when there are no elements left to print. What is the general case? It is to print the item in the first position in the array and print the rest of the items.

Print Array

if more elements
    Print the item in the first position
    Print the rest of the array

The recursive case is to print the values in an array that is one element "smaller"; that is, the size of the array decreases by 1 with each recursive call. The base case is when the size of the array becomes 0—that is, when there are no more elements to print.

Our arguments must include the index of the first element (the one to be printed). How do we know when there are no more elements to print (that is, when the size of the array to be printed is 0)? We know we have printed the last element in the array when the index of the next element to be printed is beyond the index of the last element in the array. Therefore, the index of the last array element must be passed as an argument. We call the indexes `first` and `last`. When `first` is greater than `last`, we are finished. The name of the array is `data`.

```
public static void printArray(int[] data,    // Array to be printed
                              int first,     // Index of first element
                              int last  )    // Index of last element
// Prints an array
{
  if (first <= last)
  {                                          // Recursive case
    outFile.println(data[first]+ " ");
    printArray(data, first + 1, last);
  }
  // Empty else-clause is the base case
}
```

Here is a code walk-through of the method call

```
print(data, 0, 4);
```

using the pictured array.

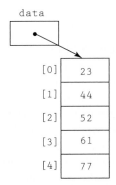

data

[0]	23
[1]	44
[2]	52
[3]	61
[4]	77

Call 1: first is 0 and last is 4. Because first is less than last, the value in data[first] (which is 23) is printed. Execution of this call pauses while the array from first + 1 through last is printed.

Call 2: first is 1 and last is 4. Because first is less than last, the value in data[first] (which is 44) is printed. Execution of this call pauses while the array from first + 1 through last is printed.

Call 3: first is 2 and last is 4. Because first is less than last, the value in data[first] (which is 52) is printed. Execution of this call pauses while the array from first + 1 through last is printed.

Call 4: first is 3 and last is 4. Because first is less than last, the value in data[first] (which is 61) is printed. Execution of this call pauses while the array from first + 1 through last is printed.

Call 5: first is 4 and last is 4. Because first is equal to last, the value in data[first] (which is 77) is printed. Execution of this call pauses while the array from first + 1 through last is printed.

Call 6: `first` is 5 and `last` is 4. Because `first` is greater than `last`, the execution of this call is complete. Control returns to the preceding call.

Call 5: Execution of this call is complete. Control returns to the preceding call.

Calls 4, 3, 2, and 1: Each execution is completed in turn, and control returns to the preceding call.

Notice that once the deepest call (the call with the highest number) was reached, each of the calls before it returned without doing anything. When no statements are executed after the return from the recursive call to the method, the recursion is known as tail recursion. Tail recursion often indicates that the problem could be solved more easily using iteration. We used the array example because it made the recursive process easy to visualize; in practice, an array should be printed iteratively.

Tail recursion A recursive algorithm in which no statements are executed after the return from the recursive call

Figure 14.4 shows the execution of the `print` method with the values of the parameters for each call. Notice that the array gets smaller with each recursive call (`data[first]` through `data[last]`). If we want to print the array elements in reverse order recursively, all we have to do is interchange the two statements within the *if* statement.

Binary Search

Do you remember the binary search in Chapter 12? Here is the description of the algorithm. "The algorithm divides the list in half (divides by 2—that's why it's called a *binary* search) and decides which half to look in next. Division of the selected portion of the list is repeated until the item is found or it is determined that the item is not in the list." There is something inherently recursive about this description.

Though the method that we wrote in Chapter 12 was iterative, this really is a *recursive algorithm*. The solution is expressed in smaller versions of the original problem: If the answer isn't found in the middle position, perform a binary search (a recursive call) to search the appropriate half of the list (a smaller problem). In the iterative version we kept track of the bounds of the current search area with two local variables, `first` and `last`. In the recursive version we call the method with these two values as parameters. The recursive binary search method must be called from the `isThere` method of the `SortedList` class rather than being written as part of it.

```
private boolean binIsThere(int first, int last, int item)
// Returns true if item is in the list
{
  if (first > last)       // Base case 1
    return false;
  else
  {
    int midPoint;
    midPoint = (first + last) / 2;
```

print(data, 0, 4)

data, which is the array, is not shown in the boxes.

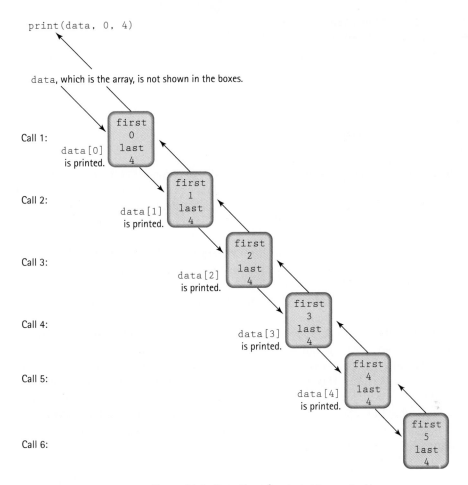

Figure 14.4 *Execution of* print *(data, 0, 4)*

```
if (item < listItems[midPoint])
   return binIsThere(first, midPoint-1, item);
else if (item == listItems[midPoint])
    return true;    // Base case 2
else
    return binIsThere(midPoint+1, last, item);
}
}
```

```
public boolean isThere(int item)
// Returns true if item is in the list.
{
  return binIsThere(0, numItems-1, item);
}
```

14.4 Recursion or Iteration?

Recursion and iteration are alternative ways of expressing repetition in a program. When iterative control structures are used, processes are made to repeat by embedding code in a looping structure such as a *while*, *for*, or *do*. In recursion, a process is made to repeat by having a method call itself. A selection statement is used to control the repeated calls.

Which is better to use—recursion or iteration? There is no simple answer to this question. The choice usually depends on two issues: efficiency and the nature of the problem being solved.

Historically, the quest for efficiency, in terms of both execution speed and memory usage, has favored iteration over recursion. Each time a recursive call is made, the system must allocate stack space for all parameters and local variables. The overhead involved in any method call is time-consuming. On early, slow computers with limited memory capacity, recursive algorithms were visibly—sometimes painfully—slower than the iterative versions. However, studies have shown that on modern, fast computers, the overhead of recursion is often so small that the increase in computation time is almost unnoticeable to the user. Except in cases where efficiency is absolutely critical, then, the choice between recursion and iteration more often depends on the second issue—the nature of the problem being solved.

Consider the factorial and power algorithms we discussed earlier in the chapter. In both cases, iterative solutions were obvious and easy to devise. We imposed recursive solutions on these problems only to demonstrate how recursion works. As a rule of thumb, if an iterative solution is more obvious or easier to understand, use it; it is probably more efficient. However, there are problems for which the recursive solution is more obvious or easier to devise, such as the Towers of Hanoi problem. (It turns out that the Towers of Hanoi problem is surprisingly difficult to solve using iteration.) Computer science students should be aware of the power of recursion. If the definition of a problem is inherently recursive, then a recursive solution should certainly be considered.

Testing and Debugging

Recursion is a powerful technique when used correctly. Improperly used, recursion can cause errors that are difficult to diagnose. The best way to debug a recursive algorithm is to construct it correctly in the first place. To be realistic, however, we give a few hints about where to look if an error occurs.

Testing and Debugging Hints

1. Be sure there is a base case. If there is no base case, the algorithm continues to issue recursive calls until all memory has been used. Each time the method is called, either recursively or nonrecursively, stack space is allocated for the parameters and automatic local variables. If there is no base case to end the recursive calls, the run-time stack eventually overflows. An error message such as "STACK OVERFLOW" indicates that the base case is missing.

2. Be sure you have not used a *while* structure. The basic structure in a recursive algorithm is the *if* statement. There must be at least two cases: the recursive case and the base case. If the base case does nothing, the *else* clause is omitted. The selection structure, however, must be there. If a *while* statement is used in a recursive algorithm, the *while* statement usually should not contain a recursive call.

3. Use your system's debugger program (or use debug output statements) to trace a series of recursive calls. Inspecting the values of parameters and local variables often helps to locate errors in a recursive algorithm.

Summary

A recursive algorithm is expressed in terms of a smaller instance of itself. It must include a recursive case, for which the algorithm is expressed in terms of itself, and a base case, for which the algorithm is expressed in nonrecursive terms.

In many recursive problems, the smaller instance refers to a numeric argument that is being reduced with each call. In other problems, the smaller instance refers to the size of the data structure being manipulated. The base case is the one in which the size of the problem (value or structure) reaches a point for which an explicit answer is known.

In the conversion of decimal integers to binary, the size of the problem is the number to be converted. When this number is 0, the conversion is finished. In the Towers of Hanoi game, the size of the problem was the number of discs to be moved. When there was only one left on the beginning peg, it could be moved to its final destination.

In the example for printing an array using recursion, the size of the problem was the size of the array being printed. When the array size became 1, the solution was known. In the binary search algorithm, the size of the problem was the size of the search area. There are two base cases in this algorithm: when the search item is found or when the search area becomes empty and you know that the search value is not there.

Quick Check

1. What distinguishes the base case from the recursive case in a recursive algorithm? (p. 649)
2. What is the size of the problem in the recursive power algorithm? (pp. 649–650, 667)
3. What is the base case in the Towers of Hanoi algorithm? (pp. 658–661)
4. In working with simple variables, the recursive case is often stated in terms of a smaller value. What is typical of the recursive case in working with structured variables? (p. 662)
5. In the binary search algorithm, what is the base case? (pp. 664–665)

Answers
1. The base case is the simplest case, the case for which the solution can be stated nonrecursively.
2. The size of the problem is the power to which the number is taken. It is decreased by one in each call.   3. When there are no more circles left to move.   4. It is often stated in terms of a smaller structure.   5. When the search area is empty.

Exam Preparation Exercises

1. Recursion is an example of
   a. selection
   b. a data structure
   c. repetition
   d. data-flow programming
2. (True or False?) A void method can be recursive, but a value-returning method cannot.
3. (True or False?) When a method is called recursively, the arguments and local variables of the calling version are saved until its execution is resumed.
4. Given the recursive formula $F(N) = -F(N - 2)$, with base case $F(0) = 1$, what are the values of $F(4)$, $F(6)$, and $F(5)$? (If any of the values are undefined, say so.)
5. What algorithm error(s) leads to infinite recursion?
6. What control structure appears most commonly in a recursive method?
7. If you develop a recursive algorithm that employs tail recursion, what should you consider?
8. A recursive algorithm depends on making something smaller. When the algorithm works on a data structure, what might become smaller?
   a. Distance from a position in the structure
   b. The data structure
   c. The number of variables in the recursive method
9. What is the name of the memory area used by the computer system to store a method's parameters and local variables?
10. Given the following input data (where \n denotes the newline character):

    ABCDE\n

    what is the output of the following method?

    ```
    public static void rev()
    {
      char ch;

      ch = (char)inFile.read();
      if (ch != '\n')
      {
        rev();
        outFile.print(ch);
      }
    }
    ```

11. Repeat Exercise 10, replacing the `rev` method with the following version:

```
public static void rev()
{
  char ch;

  ch = (char)inFile.read();
  if (ch != '\n')
  {
    outFile.print(ch);
    rev();
  }
}
```

12. Given the following input:

```
15
23
21
19
```

what is the output of the following method?

```
public static void printNums()
{
  int n;
  String line;
  line = inFile.readLine();
  if (line != null)                 // If not EOF...
  {
    n = Integer.valueOf(line).intValue();
    outFile.print(n + " ");
    printNums();
    outFile.print(n + " ");
  }
}
```

Programming Warm-Up Exercises

1. Write a Java value-returning method that implements the recursive formula $f(n) = f(n-1) + f(n-2)$ with base cases $f(0) = 1$ and $f(1) = 1$.
2. Add whatever is necessary to fix the following method so that `func(3)` equals 10.

```
public static int func(int n )
{
  return func(n - 1) + 3;
}
```

3. Rewrite the following `doubleSpace` method without using recursion.

```
public static void doubleSpace()
{
    char ch;
    int data;
    data = inFile.read();
    if (data != -1)              // If not EOF...
    {
        ch = (char) data;
        outFile.print(ch);
        if (ch == '\n')
            outFile.println();
        doubleSpace();
    }
}
```

4. Rewrite the following `printSquares` method using recursion.

```
public static void printSquares()
{
    int count;
    for (count = 1; count <= 10; count++)
        outFile.println(count + " " + count * count);
}
```

5. Modify the `factorial` method of this chapter to print its parameter and returned value indented two spaces for each level of call to the method. The call `factorial(3)` should produce the following output on `System.out`:

```
3
  2
    1
      0
      1
    1
  2
6
```

6. Write a recursive value-returning method that sums the integers from 1 through n.

7. Rewrite the following method so that it is recursive.

```
public static void printSqRoots(int n )
{
    int i;

    for (i = n; i > 0; i--)
        outFile.println(i + " " + Math.sqrt((double)i));
}
```

8. The `printArray` method of this chapter prints the contents of an array from first element to last. Write a recursive method that prints from last element to first.

9. Write an `isThere` method that takes an array as a parameter and performs a recursive linear search.

10. Rewrite the `power` method using another base case.

11. Rewrite the `power` method using the following formula.

if n == 0, return 1
if n = 1, return x
if n is even, return power (x*x, n/2)
else return x*power(x, n–1)

Programming Problems

1. Use recursion to solve the following problem.

A *palindrome* is a string of characters that reads the same forward and backward. Write a program that reads in strings of characters and determines if each string is a palindrome. Each string is on a separate input line. Print each string on an output file, followed by "Is a palindrome" if the string is a palindrome or "Is not a palindrome" if the string is not a palindrome. For example, given the input string

`Able was I, ere I saw Elba.`

the program would print "Is a palindrome." In determining whether a string is a palindrome, consider uppercase and lowercase letters to be the same and ignore punctuation characters.

2. Write a program to place eight queens on a chessboard in such a way that no queen is attacking any other queen. This is a classic problem that lends itself to a recursive solution. The chessboard should be represented as an 8 × 8 Boolean array. If a square is occupied by a queen, the value is `true`; otherwise, the value is `false`. The status of the chessboard when all eight queens have been placed is the solution.

3. A maze is to be represented by a 10 × 10 array of three characters: P (for path), H (for hedge), and E (for Exit). There is one exit from the maze. Write a program to determine if it is possible to exit the maze from a given starting point. You may move vertically or horizontally in any direction that contains P; you may not move to a square that contains H. If you move into a square that contains E, you have exited.

The input data consists of two parts: the maze and a series of starting points. The maze is entered as 10 lines of 10 characters (P, H, and E). Each succeeding line contains a pair of integers that represents a starting point (that is, row and column numbers). Continue processing entry points until end-of-file occurs.

Appendix A

Java Reserved Words

abstract	do	if	package	synchronized
boolean	double	implements	private	this
break	else	import	protected	throw
byte	extends	instanceof	public	throws
case	false	int	return	transient
catch	final	interface	short	true
char	finally	long	static	try
class	float	native	strictfp	void
const	for	new	super	volatile
continue	goto	null	switch	while
default				

Appendix B

Operator Precedence

In the following table, the operators are grouped by precedence level (highest to lowest), and a horizontal line separates each precedence level from the next-lower level.

Precedence (highest to lowest)

Operator	Assoc.*	Operand Type(s)	Operation Performed
.	LR	object, member	object member access
[]	LR	array, int	array element access
(args)	LR	method, arglist	method invocation
++, --	LR	variable	post-increment, decrement
++, --	RL	variable	pre-increment, decrement
+, -	RL	number	unary plus, unary minus
~	RL	integer	bitwise complement
!	RL	boolean	boolean NOT
new	RL	class, arglist	object creation
(type)	RL	type, any	cast (type conversion)
*, /, %	LR	number, number	multiplication, division, remainder
+, -	LR	number, number	addition, subtraction
+	LR	string, any	string concatenation
<<	LR	integer, integer	left shift
>>	LR	integer, integer	right shift with sign extension
>>>	LR	integer, integer	right shift with zero extension
<, <=	LR	number, number	less than, less than or equal
>, >=	LR	number, number	greater than, greater than or equal
instanceof	LR	reference, type	type comparison
==	LR	primitive, primitive	equal (have identical values)
!=	LR	primitive, primitive	not equal (have different values)
==	LR	reference, reference	equal (refer to the same object)
!=	LR	reference, reference	not equal (refer to different objects)
&	LR	integer, integer	bitwise AND
&	LR	boolean, boolean	boolean AND
^	LR	integer, integer	bitwise XOR
^	LR	boolean, boolean	boolean XOR

Precedence (highest to lowest)

Operator	Assoc.*	Operand Types(s)	Operation Performed
|	LR	integer, integer	bitwise OR
|	LR	boolean, boolean	boolean OR
&&	LR	boolean, boolean	conditional AND (short circuit evaluation)
||	LR	boolean, boolean	conditional OR (short circuit evaluation)
? :	RL	boolean, any, any	conditional (ternary) operator
=	RL	variable, any	assignment
*=, /=, %=, +=, -=, <<=, >>=, >>>=, &=, ^=, |=	RL	variable, any	assignment with operation

*LR means left to right associativity; RL means right to left associativity.

Appendix C

Primitive Data Types

Type	Value Stored	Default Value	Size	Range of Values
char	Unicode character	Character code 0	16 bits	0 to 65535
byte	Integer value	0	8 bits	−128 to 127
short	Integer value	0	16 bits	−32768 to 32767
int	Integer value	0	32 bits	−2147483648 to 2147483647
long	Integer value	0	64 bits	−9223372036854775808 to 9223372036854775807
float	Real value	0.0	32 bits	±1.4E-45 to ±3.4028235E+38
double	Real value	0.0	64 bits	±4.9E-324 to ±1.7976931348623157E+308
boolean	true or false	false	1 bit	NA

Appendix D

ASCII Subset of Unicode

The following chart shows the ordering of characters in the ASCII (American Standard Code for Information Interchange) subset of Unicode. The internal representation for each character is shown in decimal. For example, the letter *A* is represented internally as the integer 65. The space (blank) character is denoted by a "□".

Left Digit(s) \ Right Digit	0	1	2	3	4	5	6	7	8	9
0	NUL	SOH	STX	ETX	EOT	ENQ	ACK	BEL	BS	HT
1	LF	VT	FF	CR	SO	SI	DLE	DC1	DC2	DC3
2	DC4	NAK	SYN	ETB	CAN	EM	SUB	ESC	FS	GS
3	RS	US	□	!	"	#	$	%	&	'
4	(	)	*	+	,	−	.	/	0	1
5	2	3	4	5	6	7	8	9	:	;
6	<	=	>	?	@	A	B	C	D	E
7	F	G	H	I	J	K	L	M	N	O
8	P	Q	R	S	T	U	V	W	X	Y
9	Z	[	\	]	^	_	`		a	b	c
10	d	e	f	g	h	i	j	k	l	m
11	n	o	p	q	r	s	t	u	v	w
12	x	y	z	{			}	~	DEL		

ASCII is the heading over columns 0–9.

Codes 00–31 and 127 are the following nonprintable control characters:

NUL	Null character	VT	Vertical tab	SYN	Synchronous idle
SOH	Start of header	FF	Form feed	ETB	End of transmitted block
STX	Start of text	CR	Carriage return	CAN	Cancel
ETX	End of text	SO	Shift out	EM	End of medium
EOT	End of transmission	SI	Shift in	SUB	Substitute
ENQ	Enquiry	DLE	Data link escape	ESC	Escape
ACK	Acknowledge	DC1	Device control one	FS	File separator
BEL	Bell character (beep)	DC2	Device control two	GS	Group separator
BS	Back space	DC3	Device control three	RS	Record separator
HT	Horizontal tab	DC4	Device control four	US	Unit separator
LF	Line feed	NAK	Negative acknowledge	DEL	Delete

Left Digit(s) \ Right Digit	EBCDIC 0	1	2	3	4	5	6	7	8	9
6					□					
7					¢	.	<	(	+	|
8	&									
9	!	$	*	)	;	¬	–	/		
10							^	,	%	_
11	>	?								
12		`	:	#	@	´	=	"		a
13	b	c	d	e	f	g	h	i		
14						j	k	l	m	n
15	o	p	q	r						
16		~	s	t	u	v	w	x	y	z
17								\	{	}
18	[	]								
19				A	B	C	D	E	F	G
20	H	I								J
21	K	L	M	N	O	P	Q	R		
22							S	T	U	V
23	W	X	Y	Z						
24	0	1	2	3	4	5	6	7	8	9

In the EBCDIC table, nonprintable control characters—codes 00–63, 250–255, and those for which empty spaces appear in the chart—are not shown.

Appendix E

Decimal Format Type

To give more precise control over the formatting of numbers, Java provides a class called `DecimalFormat` that is part of a package called `java.text`. The `DecimalFormat` class allows us to create patterns that can be used to format numbers for output. These patterns are in the form of strings, made up of characters that represent the parts of a formatted number. For example, the pattern

`"###,###"`

indicates that a number should be formatted with up to six decimal digits, and when there are more than three digits in the number, a comma should be used to separate the thousands from the rest of the number.

There are four steps we must follow to use `DecimalFormat` patterns to format numbers:

- `import java.text.*;`
- Declare an object of type `DecimalFormat` for each number format we wish to use.
- Give the object a value of type `DecimalFormat` that contains the pattern.
- Format the number using the format method associated with each of the `DecimalFormat` variables.

Let's examine each of these steps in turn. You are familiar with writing `import` declarations, so all you need to do for the first step is remember to put the declaration at the start of your program. Declaring objects of type `DecimalFormat` is done in the same way as declaring objects of type `String` or `Frame`. For example:

```
DecimalFormat dollar;      // Format for dollar amounts
DecimalFormat percent;     // Format for percentages
DecimalFormat accounting;  // Format for negative values in ()
```

The third step involves using new and the DecimalFormat constructor to create a value that we can assign to the object. The call to the constructor contains the string representing the pattern. Here are statements that assign patterns to each of the variables declared previously. Don't be concerned yet with trying to interpret the specific patterns shown; we explain them below.

```
dollar = new DecimalFormat("$###,##0.00");
percent = new DecimalFormat("##0.00%");
accounting = new DecimalFormat("$###,##0.00;($###,##0.00)");
```

The last step is to format the number using a method called format, which is a value returning method associated with each of the DecimalFormat objects. The format method takes as its parameter a numerical value and returns a value of type String that contains the formatted number. For example, if we write

```
out.add(new Label(dollar.format(2893.67));
```

then a label is added to the frame called out, which contains a string of the form

```
$2,893.67
```

Now that we have seen the process for using patterns to format numeric values, let's look at how to write the patterns themselves. The following table shows the characters that can appear in a pattern string and their meanings.

Character	Meaning
0	Display one digit here. If no digit is present in this place, display a zero.
#	Display one digit here. If no digit is present in this place, display nothing here (not even a blank).
,	If there are digits on both sides of this place, insert a comma to separate them. The comma is only meaningful in the integer part of the pattern (the part to the left of the decimal point).
.	Put the decimal point here. If the pattern doesn't have any digits (0 or #) to the right of the period, and the number doesn't have a fractional part, don't insert the decimal point.
%	When used anywhere to the right of the rightmost digit in the pattern, this indicates that the number is a percentage. Multiply it by 100 before displaying it, and put the % sign here.
;	The pattern to the left of ; is for positive numbers. The pattern to the right is for negative numbers.
'	The character following is one of the special pattern characters, but should be printed literally (For example, use '# to show a # in the formatted number.)
other	Anything else is inserted exactly as it appears.

Now we can interpret the patterns we assigned to the `DecimalFormat` variables. The pattern we gave to `dollar` is `"$###,##0.00"`, which means the number should have a decimal point with at least two fractional digits and one digit in the integer part. When the integer part has more than three digits, use a comma as a separator. The number should start with a dollar sign to the left of the first digit.

We use the pattern `"##0.00%"` to tell `format` that the number is a percentage that should first be multiplied by 100. After that, it is formatted with at least two fractional digits and one digit in the integer part. The percent sign is to be placed to the right of the last digit.

The third pattern, `"$###,##0.00;($###,##0.00)"`, is the most complex of the three, but is really just a minor variation on the `dollar` format. The semicolon indicates that the pattern on the left, which is the same as the pattern we gave to `dollar`, is to be used when the number is positive. The pattern on the right (the same pattern but in parentheses) is to be used when the number is negative.

Here is a code segment that shows the definition and use of these patterns. Note that we are also using `Label.RIGHT` to align the numbers to the right within their labels.

```
dollar = new DecimalFormat("$###,##0.00");
percent = new DecimalFormat("##0.00%");
accounting = new DecimalFormat("$###,##0.00;($###,##0.00)");

out.add(new Label(dollar.format(2893.67), Label.RIGHT));
out.add(new Label(dollar.format(-2893.67), Label.RIGHT));
out.add(new Label(dollar.format(4312893.6), Label.RIGHT));
out.add(new Label(dollar.format(0), Label.RIGHT));
out.add(new Label(percent.format(0.23679), Label.RIGHT));
out.add(new Label(percent.format(1), Label.RIGHT));
out.add(new Label(accounting.format(2893.67), Label.RIGHT));
out.add(new Label(accounting.format(-2893.67), Label.RIGHT));
```

Let's take a closer look at each of the labels in this frame. The first label demonstrates what happens when a positive floating-point value is formatted with the dollar format. Only as many digits are used as are necessary, and the dollar sign is immediately adjacent to the leftmost digit. The second label shows the result of formatting a negative number. The format is the same as in the first case, but a minus sign precedes the dollar sign.

The third label is an example of formatting a number with more digits than the pattern specifies. Notice that the pattern is expanded to fit. The separation between the decimal point (or the rightmost digit, in the case of an integer) and the comma closest to it are used as a guide to the placement of additional commas. In this case, the comma is three places to the left of the decimal point, so additional commas are inserted every three places. We can't split up the fractional part of a number with a separator character such as comma or period. If you try to use a comma in the fractional part, it simply ends up being pushed to the right end of the number. It is also interesting to compare the value in the code segment with the value displayed—this is a perfect example of what we said earlier about the kind of minor inaccuracies you often encounter with floating-point numbers!

The fourth label demonstrates that an integer value can be formatted to look like a floating-point value. It also shows that placing a zero in the pattern forces a zero to appear in the resulting string when there is no corresponding digit in the number.

The fifth label shows the use of the `percent` format. Notice that the value is multiplied by 100 before it is formatted. This example also shows that when there are more digits of precision in the fractional part than in the pattern, it is not expanded to show the additional fractional digits. The sixth label shows the application of the `percent` format to an integer.

The last two labels in the frame demonstrate the use of the pattern we assigned to `accounting`. When the number is positive, it is formatted normally, and when it is negative, it is enclosed in parentheses. Using two different patterns separated by a semicolon suppresses the automatic insertion of the minus sign and allows us to use other characters to indicate that the number is negative. As a safeguard, however, if we mistakenly use the same pattern on both sides of the semicolon, `format` ignores the semicolon and reverts to using the minus sign.

`DecimalFormat` gives us a powerful mechanism to format numbers in the patterns we typically use in our programs. However, it has some limitations. For example, when printing a dollar amount on a check, it is typical to fill the extra space around the number with asterisks or dashes to prevent tampering. `DecimalFormat` doesn't enable us to do this directly. However, because the `format` method returns its value as a string, we can store a formatted number into a `String` variable and then use string operations to further refine its formatting.

Suppose we write the assignments

```
dollar = new DecimalFormat("###,##0.00");
value = 8239.41;
```

then the expression

```
dollar.format(value)
```

has the value `"8,239.41"`. Further suppose that we want to display this in a fixed space of thirteen character positions, where the first character is the dollar sign and the spaces between the dollar sign and the first digit are filled with stars: `"$****8,239.41"`. If the number has more digits, fewer stars are needed, and if it has fewer digits then more stars must be concatenated. The number of stars to add is

```
12 - dollar.format(value).length
```

because the dollar sign takes up one of the thirteen character positions. The maximum value of this expression is 8, because the format requires at least three decimal digits and a decimal point. Thus, if we use a string constant called `stars` that contains eight stars, we can write

```
stars.substring(0, 12 - dollar.format(value).length)
```

to get a string with the proper number of stars. All we have left to do is to concatenate the pieces to form the desired string.

```
"$" + stars.substring(0, 12 - dollar.format(value).length) +
    dollar.format(value)
```

Look closely at this expression to be certain that you understand how it works. Many programming problems require that output values be precisely formatted. In such cases, you may need to use complex combinations of the string operations that Java provides. Breaking an output format into its component pieces and deciding how to format each piece before concatenating them together is a common strategy for dealing with this complexity.

Appendix F

Program Style, Formatting, and Documentation

Useful programs have very long lifetimes, during which they must be modified and updated. Good style and documentation are essential if another programmer is to understand and work with your program.

General Guidelines

Style is of benefit only for a human reader of your programs—differences in style make no difference to the computer. Good style includes the use of meaningful identifiers, comments, and indentation of control structures, all of which help others to understand and work with your program. Perhaps the most important aspect of program style is consistency. If the style within a program is not consistent, it then becomes misleading and confusing.

Comments

Comments are extra information included to make a program easier to understand. You should include a comment anywhere the code is difficult to understand. However, don't overcomment. Too many comments in a program can obscure the code and be a source of distraction.

In our style, there are four basic types of comments: headers, declarations, in-line, and sidebar.

Header comments appear at the top of a class, method, or package and should include your name, the date that the code was written, and its purpose. It is also useful to include sections describing the input, output, and assumptions that form the basis for the design of the code. The header comments serve as the reader's introduction to your program. Here is an example:

```
// This method computes the sidereal time for a given date and solar
//  time
//
// Written by: Your Name
//
// Date completed: 4/8/02
//
// Input: java.util.calendar object for the date and solar time
//
```

```
// Output: a java.util.calendar object containing the corresponding
//   sidereal time
//
// Assumptions: Solar time is specified for a longitude of 0 degrees
```

Declaration comments accompany the field declarations in a class. Anywhere that an identifier is declared, if is helpful to include a comment that explains its purpose. For example:

```
//Class constants
static final String FIRST  = "Herman";    // Person's first name
static final String LAST   = "Herrmann";  // Person's last name
static final char   MIDDLE = 'G';         // Person's middle initial
// Instance variables
Frame outputDisplay;                      // Declare frame object
String firstLast;                         // Name in first-last format
String lastFirst;                         // Name in last-first format
int studentCount;                         // Number of students
int sumOfScores;                          // Sum of their scores
long sumOfSquares;                        // Sum of squared scores
double average;                           // Average of the scores
float deviation;                          // Standard deviation of scores
char grade;                               // Student's letter grade
String stuName;                           // Student's name
```

Notice that aligning the comments gives the code a neater appearance and is less distracting.

In-line comments are used to break long sections of code into shorter, more comprehensible fragments. It is generally a good idea to surround in-line comments with blank lines to make them stand out. In this text we save space by printing the in-line comments in color rather than using blank lines. Some editors also color comments automatically, which makes it easier to spot them on the screen. However, blank lines are still helpful because code is often printed on paper in black and white. Here is an example:

```
//Instantiate labels and input field

resultLabel = new Label("Result:");
register = new Label("0.0", Label.RIGHT);
entryLabel = new Label("Enter #:");
inputField = new TextField("", 10);


//Instantiate button objects

add = new Button("+");
subtract = new Button("-");
clear = new Button("Clear");
```

```
//Name the buttons

add.setActionCommand("add");
subtract.setActionCommand("subtract");
clear.setActionCommand("clear");

//Register the button listeners

add.addActionListener(operation);
subtract.addActionListener(operation);
clear.addActionListener(clearOperation);
```

Even if comments aren't needed, blank lines can be inserted wherever there is a logical break in the code that you would like to emphasize.

Sidebar comments appear to the right of executable statements and are used to shed light on the purpose of the statement. Sidebar comments are often just pseudocode statements from your responsibility algorithms. If a complicated Java statement requires some explanations, the pseudocode statement should be written to its right. For example:

```
while ((line = dataFile.readLine()) != null ) // Get a line if not EOF
```

Because the page of a textbook has a fixed width, it is sometimes difficult to fit a sidebar comment next to a long line of code. In those cases, we place the sidebar comment before the statement to which it refers. Most computer screens can now display more characters on a line than fit across a page, so this situation is less common in practice. However, if lines of code become too long, they are hard to read. It is then better to place the sidebar comment before the line of code.

In addition to the four main types of comments that we have discussed, there are some miscellaneous comments that we should mention. Although we do not do this in the text, to conserve space, we recommend that classes and methods be separated in a compilation unit file by a row of asterisks.

```
//************************************************************************
```

Programmers also sometimes place a comment after the right brace of a block to indicate which control structure the block belongs to. This is especially helpful in a package file where there may be multiple classes. Indicating where a class or long method ends helps readers keep track of where they are looking in scanning the code.

```
    return noCorrect;
  }
} // End of class TheKey
```

Identifiers

The most important consideration in choosing a name for a field or method is that the name convey as much information as possible about what the field is or what the method does. The name should also be readable in the context in which it is used. For example, the following names convey the same information, but one is more readable than the other:

```
datOfInvc     invoiceDate
```

Although an identifier may be a series of words, very long identifiers can become quite tedious and can make the program harder to read. The best approach to designing an identifier is to try writing out different names until you reach an acceptable compromise—and then write an especially informative declaration comment next to the declaration.

Formatting Lines and Expressions

Java allows you to break a long statement in the middle and continue onto the next line. The split can occur at any point where it would be possible to insert spaces without affecting the behavior of the code. When a line is so long that it must be split, it's important to choose a breaking point that is logical and reasonable. Compare the readability of the following code fragments:

```
outFile.println(" for a radius of " + radius + "the diameter of the cir"
                + "cle is " + diameter);
outFile.println(" for a radius of " + radius +
                " the diameter of the circle is " + diameter);
```

When writing expressions, keep in mind that spaces improve readability. Usually you should include one space on either side of the == operator as well as most other operators. Occasionally, spaces are left out to emphasize the order in which operations are performed. Here are some examples:

```
if (x+y > y+z)
   maximum = x + y;
else
   maximum = y + z;
hypotenuse = Math.sqrt(a*a + b*b);
```

Indentation

The purpose of indenting statements in a program is to provide visual cues to the reader and to make the program easier to debug. When a program is properly indented, the way the statements are grouped is immediately obvious. Compare the following two program fragments:

```
while (count <= 10)
{
num = Integer.valueOf(in.readLine()).intValue();
if (num == 0)
{
count++;
num = 1;
}
out.println(num);
out.println(count);
}

while (count <= 10)
{
   num = Integer.valueOf(in.readLine()).intValue();
   if (num == 0)
   {
     count++;
     num = 1;
   }
   out.println(num);
   out.println(count);
}
```

As a basic rule in this text, each nested or lower level item is indented by two spaces. Exceptions to this rule are parameter declarations and statements that are split across two or more lines. Indenting by two spaces is a matter of personal preference. Some people prefer to indent by more spaces.

In this text, we prefer to place the braces on separate lines so that it is easy to scan down the left edge of a block of code and find them. Placing them on separate lines also reminds us to consider whether the beginning or the end of a block would benefit from an in-line comment and automatically gives us a place to write one. This is just one style of placement, and you will encounter other styles as you encounter code written by other programmers.

As we noted at the beginning of this appendix, the most important aspect of code formatting is consistency. You may frequently find it necessary to adopt the style of another programmer in order to update their code in a consistent manner. Even when you believe your own favorite style to be superior, resist the temptation to mix your style with a different, existing style. The mixture is likely to be more confusing than either style alone.

Appendix G

Applets

In this text we write all of our programs as Java applications. That is, we write a class that contains a method called `main` to act as the driver for whatever set of scenarios our objects support. Java provides a second type of program called an applet. As its name implies, it is intended to be a small application.

Applets are used as elements of web pages. Most web browsers include a special JVM that can execute the bytecode contained in an applet. When the browser encounters a link to an applet bytecode file, it copies the file into memory and calls its JVM to execute the bytecode.

The ability for a browser to execute applets means that we can create web pages that are as sophisticated as almost any program we can write in Java. We say almost because applets are subject to certain limitations that Java applications are not. For example, you would not want your browser to run an applet that destroys the files on your computer. Thus, applets are prohibited from accessing files.[1] Likewise, an applet cannot send messages to other computers from your computer (except the one from which it was loaded). These security restrictions are included in Java to prevent the creation of harmful applets by malicious programmers.

From an educational viewpoint, we thus present only applications in this text because they enable us to use all of Java's features. They also do not require the use of a browser or a separate program (called an applet viewer) to run compiled code.

Creating an applet instead of an application is reasonably straightforward. Like an application, an applet resides in a class and has specially named methods that are called by the JVM. Whereas an application is a class derived from `Object`, however, an applet is written in a class derived from a class called `Applet`. Thus the beginning of any applet must contain statements similar to these:

```
import java.applet.Applet;

public class SomeName extends Applet
{
```

The `Applet` class provides several methods that we can override with our derived class. One of these is called `init`.

---

[1] Later versions of Java ease this restriction to allow special cases of file access when a user permits it.

Because of the way that applets are executed, they should not have constructors. Instead, the operations that we would normally place into a constructor (such as initializing fields or setting up the user interface) should be written in the applet's `init` method. When a browser first downloads an applet, its JVM executes this method. The `init` method is equivalent to `main` in an application. It contains the main block of code that begins the work of the applet.

The applet class contains additional methods called `start`, `stop`, and `destroy` that are used with more sophisticated applets that employ features of Java that we do not cover in this text. For example, if an applet is showing a graphics animation, we may want it to `stop` when the user moves to a different web page and resume (`start`) when the user returns to the page with the applet.

The `Applet` class is derived from `Container`, as is `Frame`. Thus, they share much in common. However, in our applications, we had to instantiate a `Frame` into which we added our user interface components. Because an applet is itself a container, we simply call methods such as `add` and `setLayout` directly. All of the components we have introduced in the text can be used with applets. Thus, to demonstrate how an applet is written, we present the code for the `Calculator` application of Chapter 6, rewritten into the form of an applet. In rewriting the code we have condensed the event handlers into a single `ActionListener` to illustrate that an applet can directly implement a listener. We have also added exception handling (see Chapter 10) to check for an improperly formatted input value.

```java
import java.applet.Applet;                     // Applet class
import java.awt.event.*;                        // Event handling classes
import java.awt.*;                              // User interface classes


public class Calculator extends Applet implements ActionListener
{
    // Define action listener for numeric buttons
    public  void actionPerformed(ActionEvent event)
    // Handles events from the buttons in calcFrame
    {
        double secondOperand;                    // Holds input value
        String whichButton;                      // Holds the button's name
        // Get the operand, checking for numeric format error
        try
        {
            secondOperand = Double.valueOf(inputField.getText()).doubleValue();
        }
        catch (NumberFormatException except)
        {
            secondOperand = 0.0;                 // If error, set to zero
        }
```

```
        whichButton = event.getActionCommand();              // Get the button's name

        if (whichButton.equals("add"))                        // When the name is "add"
          result = result + secondOperand;                    //   add the operand
        else  if (whichButton.equals("subtract"))             // When "subtract"
          result = result - secondOperand;                    //   subtract the operand
        else                                                  // Otherwise
          result = 0.0;                                       // Clear result to zero

        register.setText("" + result);                        // Display result
        inputField.setText("");                               // Clear input
      }

      private static TextField inputField;                    // Data field
      private static Label register;                          // Result shown on screen
      private static double result;                           // Keeps current value

      public void init()
      {
        Label resultLabel;                                    // Indicates output area
        Label entryLabel;                                     // Label for input field
        Button add;                                           // Add button
        Button subtract;                                      // Subtract button
        Button clear;                                         // Clear button
        result = 0.0;                                         // Initialize result

        // Instantiate labels and initialize input field
        resultLabel = new Label("Result:");
        register = new Label("0.0", Label.RIGHT);
        entryLabel = new Label("Enter #:");
        inputField = new TextField("", 10);

        // Instantiate button objects
        add = new Button("+");
        subtract = new Button("-");
        clear = new Button("Clear");

        // Name the button events
        add.setActionCommand("add");
        subtract.setActionCommand("subtract");
        clear.setActionCommand("clear");

        // Register the button listeners
        add.addActionListener(this);
        subtract.addActionListener(this);
```

```
    clear.addActionListener(this);

    // Add interface elements to applet
    setLayout(new GridLayout(4,2));            // Set the layout manager
    add(resultLabel);
    add(register);
    add(entryLabel);
    add(inputField);
    add(add);
    add(subtract);
    add(clear);
  }
}
```

Appendix H

Converting from AWT to Swing

With the release of Java 1.2[1], Sun introduced a new package for writing graphical user interfaces. Called Swing, this package replaces the functionality of AWT, which we have used throughout this book. Although Swing offers many new features, most of them are not essential for learning to program. The new features permit the creation of more sophisticated user interfaces than our programs require. At the time of this writing, Swing is still not fully supported under all operating systems. However, if you would like to explore its use, this Appendix presents the essential differences between Swing and AWT and the changes that you must make to your programs to substitute Swing for AWT. The process is relatively easy because Swing implements nearly all of the same basic classes that are in AWT.

As you might expect, the first change is to import the Swing packages. The import statements you need are:

```
import javax.swing.*;
import.javax.swing.event.*;
```

If you're converting an AWT program, you may still need to import `java.awt.*` and `java.awt.event.*`. For example, Swing provides a new set of layout managers, and Swing is also compatible with our old layout manager friends `flowLayout` and `grid-Layout`, which are part of AWT. So if you want to make use of the AWT layout managers, you must still import the AWT package.

Next, you must change all of the AWT class names to the corresponding Swing classes. To do so, just add the letter J to the front of the AWT class name:

```
Frame     → JFrame
Button    → JButton
Label     → JLabel
TextField → JTextField
```

The next step is somewhat more complicated. With a `Frame` object, we add components such as Buttons directly to the `Frame`. But with a `JFrame` there is another layer that we must go through. A `JFrame` object consists of multiple parts that affect its appearance

---

[1]Java 1.2 is sometimes also confusingly referred to as Java 2 because at the same time, Sun released version two of their Java software development tools. The version of the language at that time was 1.2, so technically, Java 1.2 was part of the Java Software Development Kit version 2, which many people shorten to just Java 2.

on the screen (we could select a different style of window to display, for example). The part to which we add our components is called the content pane (as in a pane of glass in a window). Once we instantiate a `JFrame`, we must ask it to return a reference to its content pane. The content pane is an object of class `Container`, which is the superclass for `Frame`, `JFrame`, and all other user interface classes that can contain components. So we may write:

```
private static JFrame calcFrame;
private static Container calcPane;

calcFrame = new JFrame();
calcPane = calcFrame.getContentPane();
```

Then we can add components to the content pane. For example:

```
calcPane.setLayout(new GridLayout(4,2));
calcPane.add(new JLabel("Result:"));
```

Two methods from AWT that are not implemented by Swing are `Pack` and `Show`. Instead, we set the size of a `JFrame` and then set its visibility to true. The size is specified in terms of the number of horizontal and vertical pixels on the screen. Here is an example that sets the `calcFrame` to 300 pixels wide by 200 pixels high and then shows it on the screen.

```
calcFrame.setSize(300, 200);
calcFrame.setVisible(true);
```

You may need to experiment with different sizes to get a window that is just right for your needs.

With AWT we needed to use a `WindowAdapter` to define an event handler method for closing a window. In all of our programs, we merely disposed of the frame and exited the program. In Swing, we no longer need to do this. A single method tells the `JFrame` what to do when its window is closed, as long the action is one of a small set of common choices. The `JFrame` class provides the following class constants that name these choices:

```
JFrame.DISPOSE_ON_CLOSE
JFrame.DO_NOTHING_ON_CLOSE
JFrame.HIDE_ON_CLOSE
```

These are passed to an instance method called `setDefaultCloseOperation`. Here is an example:

```
calcFrame.setDefaultCloseOperation(JFrame.DO_NOTHING_ON_CLOSE);
```

The example tells `calcFrame` not to click on the window's close button, which is the usual behavior of a `Frame` if we fail to specify an event handler.

There is one additional choice, which does not have a named constant. If we pass the integer 3 to `setDefaultCloseOperation`, then the program disposes of the window and exits (just what we've always done). Here's how that call would look:

```
calcFrame.setDefaultCloseOperation(3); //Exit program on closing window
```

So that you can see how all of this works in the context of a real program, we present below the code for program Calculator in Chapter 6. Compare this to the code on pages 267–269 to see the differences. We've marked the lines that have changed significantly by starting their comments with a + sign. (Some of the changes are simply a result of introducing a new variable name, because of the need to provide a container for the content pane. We haven't marked these changes.)

```java
import javax.swing.*;                            //+User interface classes
import javax.swing.event.*;                      //+Event handling classes
import java.awt.*;                               //Older interface classes
import java.awt.event.*;                         //Older event classes

public class SwingCalculator
{
 //Define action listener for numeric buttons
 private static  class NumericHandler implements ActionListener
  {
    public void actionPerformed(ActionEvent event)
    //Handles events from the buttons in calcPane
    {
      double secondOperand;                      //Holds input value
      String whichButton;                        //Holds the button's name
      //Get the operand
      secondOperand =
        Double.valueOf(inputField.getText()).doubleValue();
      whichButton = event.getActionCommand(); //Get the button's name

      if (whichButton.equals("add"))             //When the name is "add"
        result = result + secondOperand;         //  add the operand
      else                                       //Otherwise
            result = result - secondOperand;     //  subtract the operand

        register.setText("" + result);           //Display result
        inputField.setText("");                  //Clear input
      }
    }
```

```
private static class ClearHandler implements ActionListener
  {
    public void actionPerformed(ActionEvent event)
    //Handles events from the Clear button in calcPane
    {
      result = 0.0;                            //Set result back to zero
      register.setText("0.0");                 //Reset result in register
      inputField.setText("");                  //Clear input
    }
  }

  private static JTextField inputField;        //+Data field
  private static JLabel register;              //+Result shown on screen
  private static JFrame calcFrame;             //+Declare a frame
  private static Container calcPane;           //+Container to hold
                                               //  content pane of frame
  private static double result;                //Keeps current value

  public static void main(String[] args)
  {
    NumericHandler operation;                  //Declare numeric listener
    ClearHandler clearOperation;               //Declare clear listener
    JLabel resultLabel;                        //+Indicates output area
    JLabel entryLabel;                         //+Label for input field
    JButton add;                               //+Add button
    JButton subtract;                          //+Subtract button
    JButton clear;                             //+Clear button

    operation = new NumericHandler();          //Instantiate operation
    clearOperation = new ClearHandler();       //Instantiate clear
    result = 0.0;                              //Initialize result

    //Instantiate labels and initialize input field
    resultLabel = new JLabel("Result:");            //+
    register = new JLabel("0.0", JLabel.RIGHT);     //+
    entryLabel = new JLabel("Enter #:");            //+
    inputField = new JTextField("", 10);            //+

    //Instantiate button objects
    add = new JButton("+");                         //+
    subtract = new JButton("-");                    //+
    clear = new JButton("Clear");                   //+
```

```
    //Name the button events
    add.setActionCommand("add");
    subtract.setActionCommand("subtract");
    clear.setActionCommand("clear");

    //Register the button listeners
    add.addActionListener(operation);
    subtract.addActionListener(operation);
    clear.addActionListener(clearOperation);

    //Add interface elements to calcFrame
    calcFrame = new JFrame();                    //+Give the frame a value
    calcPane = calcFrame.getContentPane();       //+Get the content pane
    calcPane.setLayout(new GridLayout(4,2));     //Set the layout manager
    calcPane.add(resultLabel);
    calcPane.add(register);
    calcPane.add(entryLabel);
    calcPane.add(inputField);
    calcPane.add(add);
    calcPane.add(subtract);
    calcPane.add(clear);
    calcFrame.setSize(300, 200);                 //+Specify size of frame
    calcFrame.setVisible(true);                  //+Show the frame
    calcFrame.setDefaultCloseOperation(3);       //+Set close op to exit
  }
}
```

And here is the Swing JFrame that is displayed when the program runs:

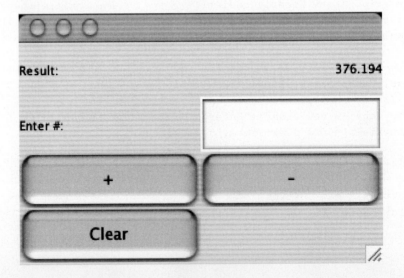

abstract   a modifier of a class or field that indicates that it is incomplete and must be fully defined in a derived class

abstract data type (ADT)   a class of data objects with a defined set of properties and a set of operations that process the data objects while maintaining the properties

abstract step   an algorithmic step for which some implementation details remain unspecified

abstraction   a model of a complex system that includes only the details essential to the perspective of the viewer of the system; the separation of the logical properties of data or actions from their implementation details; the separation of the logical properties of an object from its implementation

abstraction (in OOD)   the essential characteristics of an object from the viewpoint of the user

aggregate operation   an operation on a data structure as a whole, as opposed to an operation on an individual component of the data structure

algorithm   a logical sequence of discrete steps that describes a complete solution to a given problem computable in a finite amount of time; instructions for solving a problem or subproblem in a finite amount of time using a finite amount of data; a verbal or written description of a logical sequence of actions

allocate   to assign memory space at run time for use by an object

ALU   see *arithmetic/logic unit*

anonymous class   a class that does not have an identifier (a name) associated with it

argument   a variable, constant, or expression listed in the call to a method

arithmetic/logic unit (ALU)   the component of the central processing unit that performs arithmetic and logical operations

array a collection of components, all of the same type, ordered on n dimensions ($n >= 1$); each component is accessed by n indices, each of which represents the component's position within that dimension

assembler a program that translates an assembly language program into machine code

assembly language a low-level programming language in which a mnemonic represents each of the machine language instructions for a particular computer

assertion a logical proposition that is either true or false

assignment expression a Java expression with (1) a value and (2) the side effect of storing the expression value into a memory location

assignment statement a statement that stores the value of an expression into a variable

asynchronous not occurring at the same moment in time as some specific operation of the computer; in other words, not synchronized with the program's actions

atomic data type a data type that allows only a single value to be associated with an identifier of that type

auxiliary storage device a device that stores data in encoded form outside the computer's memory

binary operator an operator that has two operands

base address the memory address of the first element of an array

base case the case for which the solution can be stated nonrecursively

base class the class being inherited from

big-O notation a notation that expresses computing time (complexity) as the term in a function that increases most rapidly relative to the size of a problem

binary expressed in terms of combinations of the numbers 1 and 0 only

binary search a search algorithm for sorted lists that involves dividing the list in half and determining, by value comparison, whether the item would be in the upper or lower half; the process is performed repeatedly until either the item is found or it is determined that the item is not on the list

bit short for binary digit; a single 1 or 0

block a group of zero or more statements enclosed in braces

body the statement(s) to be repeated within the loop; the executable statement(s) within a function

boolean a data type consisting of only two values: true and false

boolean expression an assertion that is evaluated as either true or false, the only values of the boolean data type

boolean operators operators applied to values of the type boolean; in Java these are the special symbols &&, ||, and !

booting the system the process of starting up a computer by loading the operating system into its main memory

branch a code segment that is not always executed; for example, a switch statement has as many branches as there are case labels

branching control structure see *selection control structure*

brainstorming (in OOD) the beginning phase of an object-oriented design in which possible classes of objects in the problem are identified

button a component of a frame that fires an event (called a *button event*) when the user clicks on it with the mouse

byte eight bits

Bytecode a standard machine language into which Java source code is compiled

CRC Cards index cards on which a class name is written along with its super and subclasses and a listing of the class's responsibilities and collaborators; *C*lass, *R*esponsibility, *C*ollaboration

call the point at which the computer begins following the instructions in a subprogram is referred to as the subprogram call

cancellation error a form of representational error that occurs when numbers of widely differing magnitudes are added or subtracted

catch the processing of a thrown exception by a section of code called an exception handler

central processing unit (CPU) the part of the computer that executes the instructions (program) stored in memory; consists of the arithmetic/logic unit and the control unit

char data type whose values consist of one alphanumeric character (letter, digit, or special symbol)

character set a standard set of alphanumeric characters with a given collating sequence and binary representation

class (general sense) a description of the behavior of a group of objects with similar properties and behaviors

class (Java construct) a pattern for an object

class data data that is associated with a class and accessible by all objects of that class

class method a method that is associated with a class but not with a specific object; it is called by writing the name of the class followed by a period and then the name of the method and its parameter list

client software that declares and manipulates objects of a particular class

code data type specifications and instructions for a computer that are written in a programming language

code walk-through a verification process for a program in which each statement is examined to check that it faithfully implements the corresponding algorithmic step

coding translating an algorithm into a programming language; the process of assigning bit patterns to pieces of information

collating sequence the ordering of the elements of a set or series, such as the characters (values) in a character set

compiler a program that translates a high-level language (such as C++, Pascal, or Java) into machine code

compiler listing a copy of a program into which have been inserted messages from the compiler (indicating errors in the program that prevent its translation into machine language if appropriate)

complexity a measure of the effort expended by the computer in performing a computation, relative to the size of the computation

composite data type a data type that allows a collection of values to be associated with an object of that type

composition (containment) a mechanism by which an internal data member of one class is defined to be an object of another class type

computer (electronic) a programmable device that can store, retrieve, and process data

computer program data type specifications and instructions for carrying out operations that are used by a computer to solve a problem

computer programming the process of specifying the data types and the operations for a computer to apply to data in order to solve a problem

concrete step a step for which the implementation details are fully specified

conditional test the point at which the boolean expression is evaluated and the decision is made to either begin a new iteration or skip to the first statement following the loop

constant an item in a program whose value is fixed at compile time and cannot be changed during execution

constant time an algorithm whose big-O work expression is a constant

constructor an operation that creates a new instance of a class; a method that has the same name as the class type containing it, which is called whenever an object of that type is instantiated

container class a class into which you can add other elements

control abstraction the separation of the logical properties of a control structure from its implementation

control structure a statement used to alter the normally sequential flow of control

control unit the component of the central processing unit that controls the action of other components so that instructions (the program) are executed in sequence

conversion function a function that converts a value of one type to another type so that it can be assigned to a variable of the second type; also called transfer function or type cast

copy constructor an operation that creates a new instance of a class by copying an existing instance, possibly altering some or all of its state in the process

count-controlled loop a loop that executes a predetermined number of times

counter a variable whose value is incremented to keep track of the number of times a process or event occurs

CPU see *central processing unit*

crash the cessation of a computer's operations as a result of the failure of one of its components; cessation of program execution due to an error

data information that has been put into a form a computer can use

data abstraction the separation of a data type's logical properties from its implementation

data encapsulation the separation of the representation of data from the applications that use the data at a logical level; a programming language feature that enforces information hiding

data representation the concrete form of data used to represent the abstract values of an abstract data type

data structure a collection of data elements whose organization is characterized by accessing operations that are used to store and retrieve the individual data elements; the implementation of the composite data members in an abstract data type; the implementation of a composite data field in an abstract data type

data type the general form of a class of data items; a formal description of the set of values (called the domain) and the basic set of operations that can be applied to it

data validation a test added to a program or a function that checks for errors in the data

debugging the process by which errors are removed from a program so that it does exactly what it is supposed to do

deallocate to return the storage space for an object to the pool of free memory so that it can be reallocated to new objects

decision see *selection control structure*

declaration a statement that associates an identifier with a field, a method, a class, or a package so that the programmer can refer to that item by name

deep copy an operation that not only copies one class object to another but also makes copies of any pointed-to data

demotion (narrowing) the conversion of a value from a "higher" type to a "lower" type according to a programming language's precedence of data types; demotion may cause loss of information

derived class a class that is created as an extension of another class in the hierarchy

desk checking tracing an execution of a design or program on paper

development environment a single package containing all of the software required for developing a program

dialog a style of user interface in which the user enters data and then performs a separate action (such as clicking a button) when the entered values are ready to be processed by the program

direct execution the process by which a computer performs the actions specified in a machine language program

documentation the written text and comments that make a program easier for others to understand, use, and modify

down a descriptive term applied to a computer when it is not in a usable condition

driver a simple dummy main program that is used to call a method being tested; a main method in an object-oriented program

dynamic allocation allocation of memory space for a variable at run time (as opposed to static allocation at compile time)

dynamic binding determining at run time which form of a polymorphic method to call; the run-time determination of which implementation of an operation is appropriate

dynamic memory management the allocation and deallocation of storage space as needed while an application is executing

echo printing   printing the data values input to a program to verify that they are correct

editor   an interactive program used to create and modify source programs or data

encapsulation (in OOD)   the bundling of data and actions in such a way that the logical properties of the data and actions are separated from the implementation details; the practice of hiding a module implementation in a separate block with a formally specified interface; designing a class so that its implementation is protected from the actions of external code except through the formal interface

evaluate   to compute a new value by performing a specified set of operations on given values

event   an action, such as a mouse click, that takes place asynchronously with respect to the execution of the program

event counter   a variable that is incremented each time a particular event occurs within a loop control structure

event handler   a method that is part of an event listener and is invoked when the listener receives a corresponding event

event handling   the process of responding to events that can occur at any time during execution of the program

event listener   an object that is waiting for one or more events to occur

event loop   The repetative calling of an event handler to respond to a series of events until some condition causes the application to exit the cycle

event-controlled loop   a loop control structure that terminates when something happens inside the loop body to signal that the loop should be exited

exception   an unusual situation that is detected while a program is running; throwing an exception halts the normal execution of the method

exception handler   a section of a program that is executed when an exception occurs; in Java, an exception handler appears within a catch clause of a *try-catch-finally* control structure

executing   the action of a computer performing as instructed by a given program

execution trace   going through the program with actual values and recording the state of the variables

expression   an arrangement of identifiers, literals, and operators that can be evaluated to compute a value of a given type

expression statement   a statement formed by appending a semicolon to an expression

external file   a file that is used to communicate with people or programs and is stored externally to the program

external representation   the printable (character) form of a data value

fetch-execute cycle   the sequence of steps performed by the central processing unit for each machine language instruction

field   a component of a frame in which the user can type a value; the user must first place the cursor in the field by clicking inside the field; a named place in memory that holds a data value or a reference to an object

file   a named area in secondary storage that is used to hold a collection of data; the collection of data itself

filtering (in OOD)   the phase in an object-oriented design in which the proposed classes of objects from the brainstorming phase are refined and overlooked ones are added.

finite state machine   an idealized model of a simple computer consisting of a set of states, the rules that specify when states are changed, and a set of actions that are performed when changing states

firing an event   an event source generates an event

flag   a Boolean variable that is set in one part of the program and tested in another to control the logical flow of a program

flat implementation   the hierarchical structure of a solution written as one long sequence of steps; also called inline implementation

floating point number   the value stored in a type `float` or `double` variable, so called because part of the memory location holds the exponent and the balance of the location the mantissa, with the decimal point floating as necessary among the significant digits

flow of control   the order of execution of the statements in a program

formatting   the planned positioning of statements or declarations and blanks on a line of a program; the arranging of program output so that it is neatly spaced and aligned

forward   when a method calls another method that throws an exception, it may pass the exception to its own caller rather than catch the exception

free pool (heap)   an area of memory, managed by the JVM, which is used to provide storage space for objects

functional decomposition   a technique for developing software in which the problem is divided into more easily handled subproblems, the solutions of which create a solution to the overall problem

garbage   the set of currently unreachable objects

garbage collection   the process of finding all unreachable objects and destroying them by deallocating their storage space

general (recursive) case   the case for which the solution is expressed in terms of a smaller version of itself

hardware   the physical components of a computer

heuristics   assorted problem-solving strategies

hide   to provide a field in a derived class that has the same name as a field in its superclass; to provide a class method that has the same form of heading as a class method in its superclass; the field or class method is said to hide the corresponding component of the superclass

hierarchy (in OOD)   structuring of abstractions in which a descendant object inherits the characteristics of its ancestors

high-level programming language   any programming language in which a single statement translates into one or more machine language instructions

homogeneous   a descriptive term applied to structures in which all components are of the same data type (such as an array)

identifier   a name associated with a package, class, method, or field and used to refer to them

immutable an object whose state cannot be changed once it is created

implementation phase the second set of steps in programming a computer: translating (coding) the algorithm into a programming language; testing the resulting program by running it on a computer, checking for accuracy, and making any necessary corrections; using the program

implementing coding and testing an algorithm

implementing a test plan running the program with the test cases listed in the test plan

implicit matching see *positional matching*

in place describes a kind of sorting algorithm in which the components in an array are sorted without the use of a second array

index a value that selects a component of an array

infinite loop a loop whose termination condition is never reached and which therefore is never exited without intervention from outside of the program

infinite recursion the situation in which a subprogram calls itself over and over continuously

information any knowledge that can be communicated

information hiding the practice of hiding the details of a class with the goal of controlling access to them; the programming technique of hiding the details of data or actions from other parts of the program

inheritance a design technique used with a hierarchy of classes by which each descendant class acquires the properties (data and operations) of its ancestor class; a mechanism that enables us to define a new class by adapting the definition of an existing class; a mechanism by which one class acquires the properties – the data fields and methods – of another class

inline implementation see *flat implementation*

input the process of placing values from an outside data set into variables in a program; the data may come from either an input device (keyboard) or an auxiliary storage device (disk or tape)

input prompts messages printed by an interactive program, explaining what data is to be entered

input transformation an operation that takes input values and converts them to the abstract data type representation

input/output (i/o) devices the parts of a computer that accept data to be processed (input) and present the results of that processing (output)

inspection a verification method in which one member of a team reads the program or design line by line and the others point out errors

instance data data that is associated with a specific object

instance method a method that is associated with an object of a given type; it is called by writing the name of the object followed by a period and then the name of the method and its parameter list

instantiate to create an object based on the description supplied by a class

instantiation creating an object, an instance of a class

integer number a positive or negative whole number made up of a sign and digits (when the sign is omitted, a positive sign is assumed)

interactive system a system that allows direct communication between the user and the computer

interface a connecting link (such as a keyboard) at a shared boundary that allows independent systems (such as the user and the computer) to meet and act on or communicate with each other; the formal definition of the behavior of a subprogram and the mechanism for communicating with it; a Java construct that specifies method headings and constants to be included in any class that implements it

interpretation the translation, while a program is running, of non-machine-language instructions (such as Bytecode) into executable operations

interpreter a program that inputs a program in a high-level language and directs the computer to perform the actions specified in each statement; unlike a compiler, an interpreter does not produce a machine language version of the entire program

invoke to call on a subprogram, causing the subprogram to execute before control is returned to the statement following the call

iteration an individual pass through, or repetition of, the body of a loop

iteration counter a counter variable that is incremented with each iteration of a loop

iterator an operation that allows us to process–one at a time–all the components in an object

key a member of a class whose value is used to determine the logical and/or physical order of the items in a list

layout manager a method in the `Frame` class that automatically manages the placement of display elements within this particular style of window on the screen

length the number of items in a list; the length can vary over time

lifetime for a variable, constant, or object, the portion of an application's execution time during which it is assigned storage space in the computer's memory

linear relationship each element except the first has a unique predecessor, and each element except the last has a unique successor

linear time for an algorithm, when the big-O work expression can be expressed in terms of a constant times n, where n is the number of values in a data set

listing a copy of a source program, output by a compiler, containing messages to the programmer

literal value any constant value written in a program

local variable a variable declared within a block; it is not accessible outside of that block

local data data that is associated with a specific call to a method

logarithmic order for an algorithm, when the big-O work expression can be expressed in terms of the logarithm of n, where n is the number of values in a data set

logical order the order in which the programmer wants the statements in the program to be executed, which may differ from the physical order in which they appear

loop a method of structuring statements so that they are repeated while certain conditions are met

loop control variable (lcv) a variable whose value is used to determine whether the loop executes another iteration or exits

loop entry the point at which the flow of control first passes to a statement inside a loop

loop exit that point when the repetition of the loop body ends and control passes to the first statement following the loop

loop test the point at which the loop expression is evaluated and the decision is made either to begin a new iteration or skip to the statement immediately following the loop

machine language the language, made up of binary-coded instructions, that is used directly by the computer

mainframe a large computing system designed for high-volume processing or for use by many people at once

maintenance the modification of a program, after it has been completed, in order to meet changing requirements or to take care of any errors that show up

maintenance phase period during which maintenance occurs

mantissa with respect to floating point representation of real numbers, the digits representing a number itself and not its exponent

member a field or method declaration within a class

memory unit internal data storage in a computer

metalanguage a language that is used to write the syntax rules for another language

method a subprogram that defines one aspect of the behavior of a class; a subprogram in Java

microcomputer see *personal computer*

mixed type expression an expression that contains operands of different data types; also called a mixed mode expression

modifiability the property of an encapsulated class definition that allows the implementation to be changed without having an effect on code that uses it (except in terms of speed or memory space)

modular programming see *top-down design*

modularity (in OOD) meaningful packaging of objects

module a self-contained collection of steps that solves a problem or subproblem; can contain both concrete and abstract steps

mutable an object whose state can be changed after it is created

name precedence the priority treatment accorded a local identifier in a block over a global identifier with the same spelling in any references that the block makes to that identifier

named constant a location in memory, referenced by an identifier, where a data value that cannot be changed is stored

narrowing conversion a type conversion that may result in a loss of some information, as in converting a value of type `double` to type `float`

nested control structure a program structure consisting of one control statement (selection, iteration, or subprogram) embedded within another control statement

nested if an *if* statement that is nested within another *if* statement

nested loop a loop that is within another loop

new an operator that takes a class name and returns an object of the class type

object a collection of data values and associated operations

object (general sense) an entity or thing that is relevant in the context of a problem

object (Java) an instance of a class

object code a machine language version of a source code

object-oriented design a technique for developing software in which the solution is expressed in terms of objects—self-contained entities composed of data and operations on that data that interact by sending messages to one another

object program the machine-language version of a source program

object-based programming language a programming language that supports abstraction and encapsulation, but not inheritance

observer an operation that allows us to observe the state of an instance of an abstract data type without changing it

one-dimensional array a structured collection of components of the same type given a single name; each component is accessed by an index that indicates its position within the collection

operating system a set of programs that manages all of the computer's resources

ordinal data type a data type in which each value (except the first) has a unique predecessor and each value (except the last) has a unique successor

out-of-bounds array index an index value that is either less than 0 or greater than the array size minus 1

output transformation an operation that takes an instance of an abstract data type and converts it to a representation that can be output

overflow the condition that arises when the value of a calculation is too large to be represented

overloading the repeated use of a method name with a different signature

override to provide an instance method in a derived class that has the same form of heading as an instance method in its superclass; the method in the derived class redefines (overrides) the method in its superclass; we cannot override class methods

package a named collection of program building blocks or components in Java that can be imported by a class

parameter a variable declared in a method heading

parameter passing the transfer of data between the arguments and parameters in a method call

pass by address a parameter-passing mechanism in which the memory address of the argument is passed to the parameter; also called pass by reference (not used in Java)

pass by reference see *pass by address*

pass by value a parameter-passing mechanism in which a copy of an argument's value is passed to the parameter (used in Java)

password a unique series of letters assigned to a user (and known only by that user) by which that user identifies himself or herself to a computer during the logging-on procedure; a password system protects information stored in a computer from being tampered with or destroyed

path a combination of branches that might be traversed when a program or function is executed

path testing a testing technique whereby the tester tries to execute all possible paths in a program or function

pc see *personal computer*

peripheral device an input, output, or auxiliary storage device attached to a computer

personal computer (pc) a small computer system (usually intended to fit on a desktop) that is designed to be used primarily by a single person

polymorphic an operation that has multiple meanings depending on the class of object to which it is bound

polymorphism the ability to determine which of several operations with the same name is appropriate; a combination of static and dynamic binding

positional matching a method of matching arguments and parameters by their relative positions in the two lists; also called *relative* or *implicit* matching

postfix operator an operator that follows its operand(s)

precision a maximum number of significant digits

prefix operator an operator that precedes its operand(s)

priming read an initial reading of a set of data values before entry into an event-controlled loop in order to establish values for the variables

problem-solving phase the first set of steps in programming a computer: analyzing the problem; developing an algorithm; testing the algorithm for accuracy

procedural abstraction the separation of the logical properties of an action from its implementation

programming planning, scheduling, or performing a task or an event; see also *computer programming*

programming language a set of rules, symbols, and special words used to construct a program

pseudocode a mixture of English statements and Java-like control structures that can easily be translated into a programming language

public interface the members of a class that can be accessed outside of the class, together with the modes of access that are specified by other modifiers

range of values the interval within which values must fall, specified in terms of the largest and smallest allowable values

real number a number that has a whole and a fractional part and no imaginary part

recursion the situation in which a subprogram calls itself

recursive call a subprogram call in which the subprogram being called is the same as the one making the call

recursive case see *general case*

recursive definition a definition in which something is defined in terms of a smaller version of itself

registering the listener adding the listener to an event source object's list of interested listeners

relational operators operators that state that a relationship exists between two values; in Java, symbols that cause the computer to perform operations to verify whether or not the indicated relationship exists

representational error arithmetic error caused when the precision of the true result of arithmetic operations is greater than the precision of the machine

reserved word a word that has special meaning in a programming language; it cannot be used as an identifier

responsibility algorithms   the algorithms for the class methods in an object-oriented design; the phase in the design process where the algorithms are developed

return   the point at which the flow of control comes back from executing a method

reuse   the ability to import a class into any program without additional modification to either the class or the program; the ability to extend the definition of a class

right-justified   placed as far to the right as possible within a fixed number of character positions

robust   a descriptive term for a program that can recover from erroneous inputs and keep running

scalar data type   a data type in which the values are ordered and each value is atomic (indivisible)

scenarios (in OOD)   the phase in an object-oriented design in which responsibilities are assigned to the classes

scope of access (scope)   the region of program code where it is legal to reference (use) an identifier

scope rules   the rules that determine where in a program an identifier may be referenced, given the point where the identifier is declared and its specific access modifiers

secondary storage device   see *auxiliary storage device*

selection control structure   a form of program structure allowing the computer to select one among possible actions to perform based on given circumstances; also called a *branching control structure*

self-documenting code   a program containing meaningful identifiers as well as judiciously used clarifying comments

semantics   the set of rules that gives the meaning of instruction written in a programming language

sentinel   a special data value used in certain event-controlled loops as a signal that the loop should be exited

sequence   a structure in which statements are executed one after another

shallow copy   an operation that copies one class object to another without copying any pointed-to data

short-circuit (conditional) evaluation   evaluation of a logical expression in left-to-right order with evaluation stopping as soon as the final boolean value can be determined

side effect   any effect of one function on another that is not part of the explicitly defined interface between them

signature   the distinguishing features of a method heading the combination of the method name with the number and type(s) of its parameters in their given order

significant digits   those digits from the first nonzero digit on the left to the last nonzero digit on the right (plus any 0 digits that are exact)

simulation   a problem solution that has been arrived at through the application of an algorithm designed to model the behavior of physical systems, materials, or processes

size (of an array)   the physical space reserved for an array

software computer programs; the set of all programs available on a computer

software engineering the application of traditional engineering methodologies and techniques to the development of software

software life cycle the phases in the life of a large software project including requirements analysis, specification, design, implementation, testing, and maintenance

software piracy the unauthorized copying of software for either personal use or use by others

sorted list a list with predecessor and successor relationships determined by the content of the keys of the items in the list; there is a semantic relationship among the keys of the items in the list

sorting arranging the components of a list into order (for instance, words into alphabetical order or numbers into ascending or descending order)

source program a program written in a high-level programming language

stable sort a sorting algorithm that preserves the order of duplicates

standardized made uniform; most high-level languages are standardized, as official descriptions of them exist

state the current values contained within an object

static binding determining at compile time which form of a polymorphic method to call

string (general sense) a sequence of characters, such as a word, name, or sentence, enclosed in double quotes

string (Java construct) an object, an instance of the `String` class

structured data type an organized collection of components; the organization determines the method used to access individual components

stub a dummy method that assists in testing part of a program; it has the same function that would actually be called by the part of the program being tested, but is usually much simpler

style the individual manner in which computer programmers translate algorithms into a programming language

subprogram see *method*

supercomputer the most powerful class of computers

switch expression the expression whose value determines which *switch* label is selected; it must be an integer type other than long

syntax the formal rules governing how valid instructions are written in a programming language

system software a set of programs—including the compiler, the operating system, and the editor—that improves the efficiency and convenience of the computer's processing

tail recursion a recursive algorithm in which no statements are executed after the return from the recursive call

team programming the use of two or more programmers to design a program that would take one programmer too long to complete

termination condition the condition that causes a loop to be exited

test driver see *driver*

test plan a document that specifies how a program is to be tested

test plan implementation using the test cases specified in a test plan to verify that a program outputs the predicted results

testing checking a program's output by comparing it to hand-calculated results; running a program with data sets designed to discover any errors

text file a file in which each component is a character; each numeric digit is represented by its code in the collating sequence

throw the act of signaling that an exception has occurred; throwing an exception is said to abnormally terminate execution of a method

transformer an operation that builds a new value of an ADT, given one or more previous values of the type

traverse a list to access the components of a list one at a time from the beginning of the list to the end

two-dimensional array a collection of components, all of the same type, structured in two dimensions; each component is accessed by a pair of indices that represent the component's position within each dimension

type casting (type conversion) the explicit conversion of a value from one data type to another

type coercion an automatic conversion of a value of one type to a value of another type, called type conversion in Java

unary operator an operator that has just one operand

underflow the condition that arises when the value of a calculation is too small to be represented

unreachable a condition of an object wherein there is no way to refer to it

unstructured data type a collection consisting of components that are not organized with respect to one another

user name the name by which a computer recognizes the user, and which must be entered to log on to a machine

value-returning method a method that returns a single value to its caller and is invoked from within an expression

variable a location in memory, referenced by an identifier, that contains a data value that can be changed

virtual machine a program that makes one computer act like another

virus a computer program that replicates itself, often with the goal of spreading to other computers without authorization, possibly with the intent of doing harm

visible accessible; a term used in describing a scope of access

void method a method that is called as a separate statement; the method does not return a value

walk-through a verification method in which a *team* performs a manual simulation of the program or design

widening conversion a type conversion that does not result in a loss of information

word a group of 16, 32, or 64 bits; a group of bits processed by the arithmetic-logic unit in a single instruction

work a measure of the effort expended by the computer in performing a computation

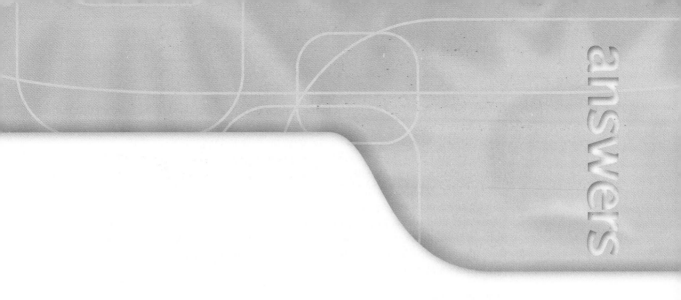
Chapter 1   Exam Preparation Exercises

1. The steps keep repeating forever, because there is no way for the algorithm to stop. (Also, it is a poor algorithm because the last action is lathering—you wouldn't want to leave the lather in your hair.) Corrected algorithm:

   1. Wet hair
   2. Lather
   3. Rinse
   4. Repeat steps 2 and 3 once

3. In the following recipe for chocolate pound cake, the statements that are branches, loops, or subalgorithm references are marked.

   Preheat the oven to 350 degrees
   Line the bottom of a 9-inch tube pan with wax paper
   Sift 2 ¾ c flour, ¾ t cream of tartar, ½ t baking soda, 1 ½ t salt, and 1 ¾ c sugar into a large bowl
   Add 1 c shortening to the bowl
   If [BRANCH] using butter, margarine, or lard, then
       add ⅔ c milk to the bowl,
   else
       (for other shortenings) add 1 c minus 2 T of milk to the bowl
   Add 1 t vanilla to the mixture in the bowl
   If [BRANCH] mixing with a spoon, then
       see [SUBALGORITHM REFERENCE] the instructions in the introduction to the chapter on cakes,
   else
       (for electric mixers) beat the contents of the bowl for 2 minutes at medium speed, scraping the
           bowl and beaters as needed
   Add 3 eggs plus 1 extra egg yolk to the bowl
   Melt 3 squares of unsweetened chocolate and add to the mixture in the bowl
   Beat the mixture for 1 minute at medium speed
   Pour the batter into the tube pan

Put the pan into the oven and bake for 1 hour and 10 minutes
Perform [SUBALGORITHM REFERENCE] the test for doneness described in the introduction to the chapter on cakes
Repeat [LOOP] the test once each minute until the cake is done
Remove the pan from the oven and allow the cake to cool for 2 hours
Follow [SUBALGORITHM REFERENCE] the instructions for removing the cake from the pan, given in the introduction to the chapter on cakes
Sprinkle powdered sugar over the cracks on top of the cake just before serving

5. Hardware: disk drive, memory, arithmetic/logic unit, and central processing unit
   Software: compiler, editor, operating system, object program, and Java Virtual Machine
7. One approach to finding a job, using the divide-and-conquer strategy, is reflected in the following algorithm.

Main Algorithm

Find information on available jobs
Apply for jobs

Find information on available jobs

Check newspaper
Call employment service

Apply for jobs

Write resume
Submit resume to potential employers
Arrange interviews
Attend interviews
Make follow-up calls after promising interviews

Each of these steps can be further subdivided.

Chapter 1 Programming Warm-Up Exercises

2. Algorithm for making a peanut butter and jelly sandwich

Open refrigerator door by pulling on door handle.
Remove bread bag, jelly jar, and peanut butter jar from refrigerator.
Place bread bag, jelly jar, and peanut butter jar on counter.
Close refrigerator door.
Open bread bag by removing twist-tie.
Remove 2 bread slices from bread bag.
Place 2 bread slices on counter.
Close bread bag using twist-tie.
Open jelly jar by unscrewing lid.
Place jelly jar lid on counter.
Open drawer under counter.
Remove knife from drawer.

Close drawer.
Use knife blade to scoop desired amount of jelly out of jar.
Spread jelly on face-up side of one slice of bread.
Close jelly jar by screwing on lid.
Open peanut butter jar by unscrewing lid.
Place peanut butter jar lid on counter.
Use knife blade to scoop out desired amount of peanut butter.
Spread peanut butter on face-up side of other slice of bread.
Close peanut butter jar by screwing on lid.
Place face-up sides of bread slices together so that their edges align.
Open refrigerator door by pulling on door handle.
Place bread bag, jelly jar, and peanut butter jar in refrigerator.
Close refrigerator door.

Chapter 1   Case Study Follow-Up Exercises

1. A divide-and-conquer diagram for a Company Payroll.

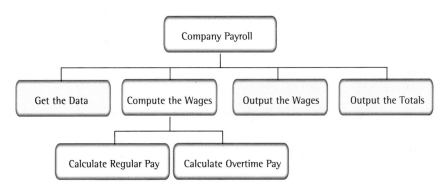

3. The starting point is the set of data values; the end is the payroll for the week.

Chapter 2   Exam Preparation Exercises

1. **Valid:** `data, y, PAY_DAY, num5`
   Invalid: `item#1, 3Set, bin-2, Sq Ft`
3. program (15), algorithm (14), compiler (3), identifier (1), compilation phase (12), execution phase (10), variable (11), constant (2), memory (13), syntax (6), semantics (8), block (7)
5. False; reserved words cannot be used as variable names.
7. a. `s1 = blues2 = bird`
   b. `Result:bluebird`
   c. `Result:   bluebird`
   d. `Result:   blue bird`
8. A rollingstonegathersnomoss

9. Only one character can be stored into a variable of type char.

11. False; a variable of type `String` can not be assigned to a variable of type `char`.

13. The identifier `computer` is used to name something, such as an application or a variable. `"computer"` is the character string made up of the characters: `'c'`, `'o'`, `'m'`, `'p'`, `'u'`, `'t'`, `'e'`, and `'r'`.

Chapter 2   Programming Warm-Up Exercises

```
2. System.out.println("The moon "));
   System.out.println("is ");
   System.out.println("blue."));
4. System.out.println("Make: " + make);
   System.out.println("Model: " + model);
   System.out.println("Color: " + color);
   System.out.println("Plate type: " + plateType);
   System.out.println("Classification: " + classification);
6. a. System.out.println("Four score ");
      System.out.println("and seven years ago ");
   b. System.out.println("Four score ");
      System.out.println("and seven ");
      System.out.println("years ago");
   c. System.out.println("Four score ");
      System.out.println("and ");
      System.out.println("seven ");
      System.out.println("years ago ");
   d. System.out.println("Four ");
      System.out.println("score ");
      System.out.println("and ");
      System.out.println("seven ");
      System.out.println("years ");
      System.out.println("ago ");
```

Chapter 2   Case Study Follow-Up Exercises

2. The string stored in constant `MONTH_NUMBER`, the symbol `"/"`, the string stored in constant `DAY`, the symbol `"/"`, and the string stored in constant `YEAR` are all concatenated together and stored into the `String` variable `third`.

Chapter 3   Exam Preparation Exercises

1. Add a label to the frame; show the frame; pack the frame.

3. `Frame out = new Frame;`

5. class methods, instance methods, helper methods

7. `print`, `println`

9. A parameter list contains information that a method needs to do its job.

11. The `add` method adds an object to a frame.

13. Constructors must be spelled exactly like the name of the class, and class names begin with uppercase letters.

15. a. The `setLayout` method tells the `Frame` object how to arrange the items in the frame.
    b. `FlowLayout` and `GridLayout`. `FlowLayout` leaves the placement of items up to the class. `GridLayout` allows the user to determine the number of columns and rows in the window.

16. The second parameter is a constant that determines the placement of the first parameter within the label. The constants are `Label.LEFT`, `Label.CENTER`, and `Label.RIGHT`.

18. An event handler is the code within an event listener that takes care of the event.

20. An event source is an object that can fire an event.

21. Registering an event listener means adding a listener object to the event source's list of listeners. In the `Frame` class, the method to register a listener is `addWindowListener`. When the event is fired, control passes to the appropriate method within the listener object.

25. `1425B Elm St. Amaryllis , Iowa`

26. This program may be corrected in several ways. Here is one correct version.

```java
// This program is full of errors
import java.awt.*;
public class LotsOfErrors

{
    private static final String FIRST = "Martin";
    private static final String MID = "Luther";
    private static final String LAST = "King";
    private static Frame outputDisplay;

    public static void main (string[] args)
    {
        outputDisplay = new Frame();
        outputDisplay.setLayout(new FlowLayout());
        String name;
        char initial;

        name = FIRST + ' ' + MID + ' ' + LAST;
        outputDisplay.add(new Label("Name = " + name + " Jr."));
        outputDisplay.pack();
        outputDisplay.show();
    }
}
```

Chapter 3   Programming Warm-Up Exercises

1. `display.add(new Label("Nell Dale"));`
2. `display.add(new Label("The moon "));`
   `display.add(new Label("is "));`
   `display.add(new Label("blue."));`

4. ```
auto.add(new Label("Make: " + make));
auto.add(new Label("Model: " + model));
auto.add(new Label("Color: " + color));
auto.add(new Label("Plate type: " + plateType));
auto.add(new Label("Classification: " + classification));
```
6. ```
private static Frame address;
address = new Frame();
address.setLayout(new FlowLayout());
```
8. `Hello world. Hello world. Hello world. is written in the window.`
10. `outDisplay.setLayout(new GridLayout(0,3));`
11. `outDisplay.add(new Label("Hello world.", Label.CENTERED));`

Chapter 3   Case Study Follow-Up Exercises

2. The string stored in constant MONTH_NUMBER, the symbol "/", the string stored in constant DAY, the symbol "/", and the string stored in constant YEAR are all concatenated together and stored into the String variable third.
3. The changed statements are as follows:

```
third = MONTH_NUMBER + "-" + DAY + "-" + YEAR;  // Create mm/dd/yyyy format
fourth = DAY + "-" + MONTH_NUMBER + "-" + YEAR; // Create dd/mm/yyyy format
```

Chapter 4   Exam Preparation Exercises

2. a. 27   b. 13   c. 5   d. 0   e. 3   f. 8   g. 3
3. All expressions are legal. The real values are shown with decimal points.
   a. 13.333   b. 2   c. 5   d. 13.750   e. −4   f. 1   g. 0.33
4. a. 3   b. 4   c. 37   d. 22   e. 23   f. 5

7. $$\frac{-b \pm \sqrt{b^2 - 4ac}}{2a}$$

8. a. 0.235294   b. 2.25   c. 44.20   d. 5   e. 0   f. 21   g. 8   h. 5   i. 1   j. 3
10. a. 9.1   b. 7.0   c. 24   d. 16.0   e. 5.0   f. 3.0
12. False; incorrect formatting does not cause an error when running the program, but it may cause the person reading the program to make an error.

Chapter 4   Programming Warm-Up Exercises

1. The following statement is the only one that must be changed: LBS must be set to 15 instead of 10.

   ```
   final int LBS = 15;
   ```

2. ```
int sum;
sum = n*(n+1)/2;
```
```

3.

a. x / y - 3
b. (x + y) * (x - y)
c. 1.0 / (x + y)
d. 1.0 / x + y
e. (float) i / (float) j
f. i / j
g. (((x + y) / 3) -((x - y) / 5)) / (4 * x)

6. This is a laboratory exercise for the student and requires no answer here.

9. (sentence.indexOf("res")) The first occurrence of the string "res" occurs at position 12.

10.
```
saveSentence = substring(0, sentence.length());  // save original
position = sentence.indexOf("res");
out.add(new Label("first occurrence is at position " + position));
sentence = substring(position + 2, sentence.length());
position = sentence.indexOf("res");
out.add(new Label("second occurrence is at position " + position));
sentence = substring(position + 2, sentence.length());
position = sentence.indexOf("res");
out.add(new Label("third occurrence is at position" + position));
sentence = substring(position + 2, sentence.length());
```

Chapter 4   Case Study Follow-Up Exercises

1. The advantage of using named constants over literal values is that if we decide to change the values, we only need to change the program in one place, where the constants are declared, thus reducing the effort and the chance of error.

3. The round-off factor should be a constant because it does not change throughout the entire program.

Chapter 5   Exam Preparation Exercises

1. A label, a button, and a field

3. The text to be displayed in the label

5. The frame never appears on the screen.

7. Declare the button variable and assign it a value with new.

8. Declare a variable of the listener class, instantiate the listener class, register it with the event.

10. A model for an object type that specifies the fields and methods that must be present in any class that implements the type.

12. Any class that implements ActionListener must be declared and contained within an application class and must contain a method called actionPerformed rather than a method main. An application class uses the modifier public; the ActionListener class uses the modifiers private static and must have the clause implements Action-Listener following the name of the class.

14. Declare a variable of the event listener class, give the object a value with new, and call the addActionListener method associated with the button, passing it an object of the listener type.

16. The person interacting with the application. If the person is not familiar with computers, the prompts must be more detailed. If the person is familiar with computers, less information is necessary.

17. We must enter a number as a string and convert it to the appropriate numeric type, using methods from Java's library.

19. An instance method is a method associated with an object of a class and is always applied to an object. A class method is a method associated with a class and is always applied to a class.

21. Functional design

23. A concrete step is one in which all the implementation details are fully specified. An abstract step is one in which some details are not fully specified.

25. Refining the responsibility algorithms.

Chapter 5 Programming Warm-Up Exercises

2. a. `Button stop;`
   b. `stop = new button("Stop");`
   c. `stop.setActionCommand("stop");`
   d. `ButtonListener action;`
      `action = new ButtonListener();`
      `// ButtonListener implements ActionListener`
   e. `stop.addActionListener(action);`
   f. `dataFrame.add(stop);`

4. a. The type of this expression is `Integer` (not `int`).
   b. In part (a), `valueOf` is a class method; it is applied to class `Integer`.
   c. The method `intValue` applied to an object of class `Integer` converts the object to an instance of type `int`.

7. a. Brainstorming The objects in the problem are all numeric values, which are built into the language. If the input and output are from the screen, you need a frame object. If the input and output are from different sources, you need a screen object and a file object. You also need an application class.

   Filtering You decide to make the input screen-oriented and use `System.out` for the output. The final objects are a window object, an application class, and `System.out`.

   Scenarios The processing is in the button handler. Two values are input, two formulas are calculated, and two answers are written to the screen.

CRC cards

Class Name: *Quadratic*	Superclass:	Subclassess:
Responsibilities	**Collaborations**	
Prepare the window for input	*TextField, Label, String, Buttons*	
Handle input events (using buttons)	*Buttons, Button handler class*	
Handle window closing	*Frame*	

Class Name: *ButtonHandler*	Superclass:	Subclassess:
Responsibilities	**Collaborations**	
Get the three input values	*TextField, Label, String, Buttons*	
Calculate the formula		
Display the output	*System.out*	

Prepare Window

Declare, instantiate, and add label for first value
Declare, instantiate, and add label for second value
Declare, instantiate, and add label for third value
Declare, instantiate, and add text field for first value
Declare, instantiate, and add text field for second value
Declare, instantiate, and add text field for third value
Declare, instantiate, and add enter button
Declare, instantiate, and register ButtonHandler as the button listener

Handle inputs are taken care of in the ButtonHandler class

Handle Window Closing

Dispose of the frame
Exit the program

Get Three Values

Get first value from text field
Get second value from text field
Get third value from text field

Calculate Formula

Set root1 to ((−second + Math.sqrt(second*second − 4*first*third)) /(first+first)
Set root2 to ((−second − Math.sqrt(second*second − 4*first*third)) /(first+first)

Display Output

System.out.println("root1 is " + root1)
System.out.println("root2 is " + root2)

b. For the functional decomposition version, screen input and file output is used.

Main Module

Prepare window
Open file
Get three input values
Calculate two Real solutions
Write solutions to output file

Prepare window

Prepare labels
Prepare text fields

Open file

Open file OutQuad for output

Get three input values

Get first value from text field
Get second value from text field
Get third value from text field

Calculate two Real solutions

First solution S1 = (−B + Math.sqrt(Sqr(B) − 4*A*C))/(2*A)
Second solution S2 = (−B − Math.sqrt(Sqr(B) − 4*A*C))/(2*A)

Write solutions to file

Write S1 to file OutQuad
Write S2 to file OutQuad

c. The object-oriented design determined the objects and their responsibilities. The functional design created a hierarchy of tasks that the main module must accomplish. Each task was further refined. The tasks in the functional design were distributed in the object-oriented design between the application, the frame object, and the button handler.

Chapter 5 Case Study Follow-Up Exercises

1. No, the application doesn't crash. If the window is closed before any values have been entered, the window disappears and the program halts normally. Of course, no output is generated.
3. A second button (call it Quit) could be added to the display. The user could press the Quit button to stop processing.

Chapter 6 Exam Preparation Exercises

3.

Expression	Meaning in English
one == two	The value stored in variable one is equal to the value stored in variable two.
one != two	The value stored in variable one is not equal to the value stored in variable two.
one > two	The value stored in variable one is greater than the value stored in variable two.
one < two	The value stored in variable one is less than the value stored in variable two.
one >= two	The value stored in variable one is greater than or equal the value stored in variable two.
one <= two	The value stored in variable one is less than or equal the value stored in variable two.

4. a. T   b. T   c. T   d. F
5. a. Ok as is; == has higher precedence than ||.
   b. Ok as is; relational operators have higher precedence than Boolean operators and && has higher precedence than ||.
   c. Ok as is; true or not true is always true.
   d. !(q && q)
7. a. xy
      xy
   b. The value of x is 3
   c. 3
      7
      6
      z (Despite the indention, the final output statement is not part of the *else* clause.)
9. a. 4   b. 2   c. 5   d. 3   e. 1
12. a. *if-else*. There are two alternative actions.
    b. *if*. There is one action to be taken or not taken.
    c. *if*. There is one action to be taken or not taken.
    d. *if-else*. There are two alternative actions.

14.
```
if (typeA || typeB)
{
    if (typeA && typeB)
        out.add(new Label("Type AB"));
}
else
        out.add(new Label("Type O"));
```

15.

Data Set	ch1, ch2, ch3	Expected Output
Set 1	A, A, A	All initials are the same.
Set 2	A, A, B	First two initials are the same.
Set 3	B, A, A	Last two initials are the same.
Set 4	A, B, A	First and last initials are the same.
Set 5	A, B, C	All initials are different.

18. a. The `String` class provides methods that can be used to compare two strings.

b.

Method Name	Parameter	Returns	English Description
`equals`	`String`	`boolean`	Returns true if two strings are equal; false otherwise.
`compareTo`	`String`	`int`	Returns 0: two strings are equal
			Returns <0: object comes before parameter
			Returns >0: object comes after parameter
`toUpperCase`	`none`	`String`	Returns object string in all uppercase letters.
`toLowerCase`	`none`	`String`	Returns object string in all lowercase letters.

20. One string is displayed with the button in the window; one string names the button within the system.

Chapter 6   Programming Warm-Up Exercises

1.
```
boolean eligible;
eligible = true;
```

2.
```
available = (numberOrdered <= (numberOnHand - numberReserved));
```
An *if* statement could have been used, but it isn't necessary.

6.
```
if (year % 4 == 0)
   out.add(new Label(year + " is a leap year."));
else
{
  year = year + 4 - year % 4;
  out.add(new Label(year + " is the next leap year."));
}
```

8. The wrong operator is used in the *if* condition: = is used in place of ==.

10.
```
if (x1 == x2)
   out.add(new Label("Slope undefined."));
else
{
  m = (y1 - y2) / (x1 - x2);
  out.add(new Label("the slope is " + m));
}
```

13. a.
```
private static Button1Handler action1;
private static Button2handler action2;
private static Button enter;
private static Button quit;
```
b.
```
enter = new Button("Enter");
quit = new Button("Quit");
action1 = new Button1Handler;
action2 = new Button2Handler;
```
c.
```
enter.setActionCommand("enter");
quit.setActionCommand("quit");
```
d.
```
outDisplay.add(enter);
outdisplay.add(quit);
```
e.
```
enter.addActionListener(action1);
quit.addActionListener(action2);
```
f.
```
private static class Button1Handler implements ActionListener
{
   public void actionPerformed(ActionEvent event)
   {
     String name;
     name = event.getActionCommand();
     if (name.equal("enter"))
       out.add(new Label("Enter was pressed."));
     else
       out.add(newLabel("An unexpected event occurred."));
   }
}
```

```
private static class Button2Handler implements ActionListener
{
  public void actionPerformed(ActionEvent event)
  {
    String name;
    name = event.getActionCommand();
    if (name.equal("quit"))
        out.add(new Label("Quit was pressed."));
    else
        out.add(newLabel("An unexpected event occurred.")):
  }
}
```

Chapter 6   Case Study Follow–Up Exercises

```
2. private static class ClearHandler implements ActionListener
   {
     public void actionPerformed(ActionEvent event)
     {
       result = 0.0;
       register.setText("0.0");
       inputField.setText("");
     }
   }
```

Class `ClearHandler` is the listener for the Clear button. When the Clear button is pressed, `result` is set to 0.0, `register` is set to 0.0, and the `inputField` is set to blank.

```
Button clear;
```
Declares a button variable named `clear`.

```
clear = new Button("Clear");
```
Instantiates the button.

```
clear.setActionCommand("clear");
```
Names the button event.

```
clear.addActionListener(clearOperation);
```
Registers the button listener.

```
calcFrame.add(clear);
```
Adds the button event to the frame.

4.

Data Set	Command	Operand	Observed Output
Set 1	add	12.5	12.5
Set 2	subtract	12.5	0.0
Set 3	add	5.5	5.5
Set 4	multiply	10.0	55.0
Set 5	divide	5.0	11.0
Set 6	clear		
	add	−12.5	−12.5
Set 7	subtract	−12.5	0.0
Set 8	add	−1.0	−1.0
Set 9	multiply	5.0	−5.0
Set 10	divide	2.0	−2.5
Set 11	divide	0.0	exception thrown

Chapter 7   Exam Preparation Exercises

2. Encapsulation is the basis of abstraction, and abstraction is how we handle complexity in programming.
3. Modifiability and reuse
5. A class can be imported into a program without having to change either the class or the program.
7. Sequence, selection, loop, method call, and asynchronous event
8. Constructors have the same name as the class and do not have a return type or void.
10. a. Data abstraction is the separation of the logical properties of data from their implementation.
    b. Control abstraction is the separation of the logical properties of operations from their implementation.
    c. An object is a collection of values and a set of operations. Data abstraction refers to an object's data representation, and control abstraction refers to an object's operations (methods).
12. A class method has the `static` modifier. It is applied with the name of the class, dot, and the method name. An instance method does not have the `static` modifier. It is applied with the name of an instance, dot, and the method name.
15. a. A reference to the object   b. Yes   c. No, the reference is not changed, but the object to which it refers can be changed.
17. At the logical level, a constructor creates a new instance of a class. In Java, the operator `new` creates the new instance and the constructor performs initializations. For example,

```
String myName = new String("Nell");
```

creates a new `String` that contains the string "`Nell`".

18. a. A transformer changes the state of an object. For example, `changeColor` and `decrementTimeRemaining` in class `TrafficLight` are transformers.

b. An observer allows us to observe the state of an object without changing it. For example, `knowCurrentColor` and `knowTimeRemaining` are observers.

19. a. An iterator allows the user to process the components in an object one at a time.

b. An observer iterator views the components one at a time; a transformer iterator changes each component as it processes it.

20.

Types of Data	Lifetime of Data	From where Data is Accessible
Instance Data	Lifetime of the instance object in which it is defined.	Instance data is accessible to methods applied to the object.
Class Data	Lifetime of class data is the entire execution of the program in which the class is defined.	Class data is accessible to all objects of that type.
Local Data	Lifetime of local data is the execution of the method in which it is defined.	Local data is accessible from within the block in which it is defined.

21. Class data has the modifier `static` preceding field.

26. An immutable object is an object that cannot be changed after it is created. A mutable object is one in which the values may be changed. If an object has transformer operations, it is mutable. If an object does not have transformer operations, it is immutable.

28. a. You cannot. You must create a new object that has the same values as the previous one except for the one you want to change.

b. Write a copy constructor. A copy constructor creates a new instance of the class by copying the existing instance, possibly altering some or all of its state in the process.

Chapter 7   Programming Warm-Up Exercises

2. ```
public AddressLabel(AddressLabel oldLabel, String newAddress)
   // Creates an AddressLabel object with the same name, and
   //   state as oldLabel, but with the address set to newAddress.
```

4. ```
public AddressLabel(String  name, String address, String city,
        String state, long zipCode, String country)
   // Creates an AddressLabel object with its name, address, state,
   //   zipCode  and country set to the values in the corresponding
   //   parameters.
```

6. ```
package somePackage;
public class AddressLabel {...}
class PrintLabel {...}
```

8. Different Java systems do it different ways. Check the documentation of the system you are using.

10. `public int myExample()`

11. `return 1066;`

13. ```
private float returnFloat(TextField data)
{
    return Float.valueOf(data.getText()).floatValue();
}
```

Chapter 7   Case Study Follow-Up Exercises

2.

Class	Method	Test #	Reason for Test	Input Values	Expected Output
Name	Name	4	Iterator	"John", "Kirk", "Herrel"	
Name	knowNext	4	Iterator		"John"
Name	knowNext	5	Iterator		"Kirk"
Name	knowNext	6	Iterator		"Herrel"
Name	knowNext	7	Iterator		"John"

Chapter 8   Exam Preparation Exercises

1. a. Internal scope and external scope
   b. No. Internal scope does not depend on the access modifiers.
   c. Internal scope refers to the scope within a class. Any identifier in a class can be used anywhere within the class.
   d. You can't use a class variable to initialize another before it has been defined. A local identifier overrides a class member with the same name.
   e. Name precedence is a scope rule that specifies that a local identifier hides the class identifier with the same name.
   f. Yes
2. Derived classes, members of the same package, and code external to the package
4. a. Protected members
   b. They are automatically part of the interface.
7. `Object`
9. Data fields and methods that are `public` or `protected`.
10. `super`
12. The derived method overrides the method in its superclass.
14. Overriding refers to instance methods; hiding refers to data fields and class method.

16.

Situation	Hiding	Overriding	Overloading
A class method has the same name and signature of a superclass method.	X		
An instance method has the same name and signature of a superclass instance method.		X	
A class has two methods with the same name but different signatures.			X
A field in a derived class has the same name as a field in its superclass.	X		
An instance method has the same name but a different signature of a superclass instance method.			X
A method declares a field with the same name as a field in the class.	X		
A method has a formal parameter with the same name as a field in the class.	X		

17. Constructors and any component declared with the private or package (default) modifiers.

Chapter 8   Programming Warm-Up Exercises

1. ```
public MyClass()
public MyClass(String name)
public MyClass(int name)
```

5. a. `public void someMethod()`
   b. `int someMethod()`
   c. `private int someMethod()`

6. ```
public static class someClass
{
   public static int var;              // Class member
   public static final int const;      // Class member const
   public static void someMethod(int param)
   {
     int var;                          // Local variable
     var = param * const;
     final int const = 10;
     {
       var = 5;                        // Local variable
       label1.setText(" " + this.var); // Class member
     }
   }
}
```

Chapter 8   Case Study Follow-Up Exercises

1. You would need three new methods: `getfloat`, `setfloat`, and `getSelectedfloat`.

3.

Class Name: *FloatField*	Superclass: *NumericField*	Subclassess:
Responsibilities	**Collaborations**	
Create itself, default	*TextField*	
Create itself (int columns)	*TextField*	
Create itself (float value, int columns)	*TextField*	
Get float, Observer return float	*TextField*	
Set float (float value), Transformer	*TextField*	
Get selected float, Observer return float	*TextField*	

Chapter 9   Exam Preparation Exercises

2. The parameter is a string that names the file on the disk. It binds the external name for the file with the internal name in the application.
4. Write the material in the buffer immediately.
6. a. `read` returns a character converted to its `int` value.
   b. `readLine` returns a string.
   c. An empty string is a string with no characters. A null string is a unique value in Java that does not correspond to any valid data value.
8. The loop prints the integers 2 through 11, one number per line.
10. Six iterations are performed.
13. a. The output is BCDE, followed by an echo of the newline character. The A that is input by the priming read is discarded.
    b.
```
inChar = (char)infile.read();
while (inChar != ' \n' )
{
   outfile.write(inChar);
   inChar = (char)infile.read();
}
```

15. Many different values can be used as a sentinel if telephone numbers are read as long integers. In the United States, a standard telephone number is a positive seven-digit number (ignoring area code) and cannot start with 0, 1, 411, or 911. Therefore, any negative value, a value greater than 9999999, or a value less than 2000000 would be good sentinels.
17. The output is 1 3 6 10 15.
18. Written

20. a. Count-controlled and event-controlled
    b. A count-controlled loop executes a predetermined number of times. An event-controlled loop executes as long as an event is true and exits the loop when the event becomes false.
    c. The loop runs forever (or until the program is manually terminated by the operating system).
    d. The loop runs forever (or until the program is manually terminated by the operating system).
    e. Sentinel-controlled, end-of-file-controlled, and flag-controlled
21. An iteration counter keeps track of the number of times a loop is executed; an event counter keeps track of the number of times an event occurs.

Chapter 9   Programming Warm-Up Exercises

1. `infile = new FileReader("infile.dat");`

3. `outfile = new PrintWriter(new FileWriter("outfile.dat"));`

5. W
   88   What letter comes next?

6.
```
private static char first;
private static char first;
private static char second;
private static int digit;
digit = fileIn.read();
first = (char)digit;
digit = fileIn.read();
second = (char)digit;
```

8.
```
fileOut.close();
fileOut = new FileWriter("dataOut.dat");
```

11.
```
count28 = 0;
loopCount = 1;
while (loopCount <= 100)
{
  number = Integer.valueOf(inFile.readLine()).intValue();
  if (number == 28)
    count28++;
  loopCount++;
}
```

13.
```
count = 0
sum = 0;
scoreLine = scoreFile.readLine();
while (scoreLine != null)
{
  score = Integer.valueOf(scoreLine).intValue();
  sum = sum + score;
```

```
      count++;
      scoreLine = scoreFile.readLine();
    }
    if (count > 0)
      average = (float)sum / (float)count;
```

15.
```
    sum = 0;
    evenInt = 16;
    while (evenInt <= 26)
    {
      sum = sum + evenInt;
      evenInt = evenInt + 2;
    }
```

17.
```
    hour = 1;
    minute = 0;
    am = true;
    done = false;
    while (!done)
    {
      timeOut.print(hour + ":");
      if (minute < 10)
        timeOut.print('0');
      timeOut.print(minute);
      if (am)
        timeOut.println(" A.M.");
      else
        timeOut.println(" P.M.");
      minute++;
      if (minute > 59)
      {
        minute = 0;
        hour++
        if (hour == 13)
          hour = 1;
        else if (hour == 12)
          am = !am;
      }
      done = (hour == 1 && minute == 0 && am);
    }
```

Chapter 9 Case Study Follow-Up Exercises

2. To test the modified program Incomes, we use four test files. The first file tests the case where there are no females in the data set; the second file tests the case where there are no males in the data set; the third file tests the case where there are no errors in the file; and the fourth file tests for the handling of the various data errors that may occur.

Test File 1: This data set does not contain any females.

```
M  10000.00
M  20000.00
```

Expected output:

```
For 0 Females, the average income is 0.0
For 2 Males, the average income is 15000.00
There were 0 bad data sets in the file.
```

Test File 2: This data set does not contain any males.

```
F  30000.00
F  40000.00
F  50000.00
```

Expected output:

```
For 3 females, the average income is 40000.00
For 0 males, the average income is 0.0.
There were 0 bad data sets in the file.
```

Test File 3: This data set does not contain any errors

```
M  10000.00
F  30000.00
M  20000.00
F  50000.00
```

Expected output:

```
For 2 females, the average income is 40000.00
For 2 Males, the average income is 15000.00
There were 0 bad data sets in the file.
```

Test File 4: This data set contains many data errors. Note that the program only prints that there were two errors in the data file, because the only type of error that is to be counted is an incorrect code. However, no entries with any type of error are used in the calculation of the averages.

```
M  10000.00
m  20000.00
F  20000.00
c  20000.00
M -20000.00
```

Expected output:

```
Letter other than F or M in file.
Negative value in file.
For 1 females, the average income is 20000.00
For 1 Males, the average income is 10000.00
There were 2 bad data sets in the file.
```

4. Write a helper function that takes the original value and converts it to a string.

```
private String format(double value)
{
  String stringForm;
  int index;
  stringForm = new String(String.valueOf(value));
  index =  stringForm.indexOf(".");
  return stringForm.substring(0, index+3);
}
```

Chapter 10 Exam Preparation Exercises

1. A switch expression is the expression in a switch statement whose value determines which case label is selected.

   A pretest loop is a loop in which the test occurs before the body of the loop. If the loop expression is false, the loop body is not executed.

   A posttest loop is a loop in which the test occurs after the loop body. Therefore, a posttest loop always executes at least once.
3. True
4. False
6. MaryJoeAnneWhoops!
8. True
9. 1
11. 4 3 2 1 4
    3 2 1 3
    2 1 2
    1 1

12. ```
    * * * * * * * *  * * * * * * * *
    * * * * * * * *  * * * * * * * *
    * * * * * * *    * * * * * * *
    * * * * * *      * * * * * *
    * * * * *        * * * * *
    * * * *          * * * *
    * * *            * * *
    * *              * *
    *                *
    ```
14. a. expression
    b. expression
    c. expression statement
    d. expression
16. Use a *try-catch* statement.
20. a. False. There can be many *catch* clauses as long as they each have a different parameter object.
    ```

b. True
c. True
d. True

Chapter 10 Programming Warm-Up Exercises

2.
```java
switch (grade)
{
    case 'A' : sum = sum + 4;
               break;
    case 'B' : sum = sum + 3;
               break;
    case 'C' : sum = sum + 2;
               break;
    case 'D' : sum++;
               break;
    case 'F' : System.out.println("Student is on probation");
               break;
    default  : System.out.println("Invalid letter grade");
               break;    // Not required
}
```

4.
```java
response = inData.read();
if(response >= 0 && response <= 127)
  do
  {
    response = inData.read();
  } while (response >= 0 && response <= 127);
```

6.
```java
sum = 0;
count = 1;
for (count = 1; count <= 1000; count++)
  sum = sum + count;
```

8. Rewrite the following *for* loop using a *do* loop.

```java
k = 9;
do
{
  outData.println(k + " " + 3 * k);
  k++;
} while (k <= 21);
```

10. a. MyException. anException;

b. `public class MyException extends Exception`

```
{
    public MyException()
    {
        super();
    }
    public MyException(String message)
    {
        super(message);
    }
}
```

c. `throw new MyException("Error somewhere.");`

Chapter 10   Case Study Follow-Up Exercises

4. Module Get Rainfall Amount has two outputs: the rainfall amount and the changing line. The only way we could make it a method would be to bind the two values into a class and make the class the return value of the method.

Chapter 11   Exam Preparation Exercises

2. False

4. a. `static final int CLASS_SIZE = 30;`
   b. `float[] quizAverage;`
   c. `quizAvg = new float[CLASS_SIZE];`

6. a. Because the array is of type `int`, the values are automatically set to 0 by the constructor.
   b.
   ```
   for (int index = 0; index < count.length; count++)
       count[index] =
               Integer.valueOf(inFile.readLine()).intValue();
   ```
   c.
   ```
   int sum = 0;
   for (int index = 0; index < count.length; count++)
       sum = sum + count[index];
   ```

7.
```
 1   3 -2
17   6 11
 4   2  2
19  14  5
11  15 -4

52  40 12
```

8. The exception was thrown because the last array access is out of bounds. The loop should go from 0 through 3. If the ending condition is written `arr.length` rather than an integer literal, the problem would not have happened. Of course, if the initial value isn't changed to 0, only part of the data would be printed.

12. A class is a heterogeneous, unstructured type in which the components are accessed by name; an array is a homogeneous, structured type in which the components are accessed by position.

14. For each of the following descriptions of data, determine which general type of data structure (array of primitive types, class, array of classes) is appropriate.
    a. class containing classes
    b. class
    c. class
    d. array of classes
    e. array of primitive types
    f. array of classes containing classes
    g. array of classes

15. An `ArrayOutOfBounds` exception is thrown.

17. The values in the initializer list

Chapter 11   Programming Warm-Up Exercises

1.
```java
public void setToFalse()
{
   for (int index = 0; index <= failing.length; index++)
     failing[index] = false;
}
```

3.
```java
public void setPassing(int[] score)
{
   for (int index = 0; index <= passing.length; index++)
     if (score[index] >= 60)
       passing[index] = true;
}
```

5.
```java
public static boolean error(boolean[] passing, boolean[] failing)
{
   for (int index = 0; index <= failing.length; index++)
     if (passing[index] == failing[index])
        return true;
   return false;
}
```

7.
```
public void reverse(int[] score)
{
   int tempScore;
   int halfLength = score.length/2;
   for (int index = 0; index < halfLength; index++)
   {
     tempScore = score[index];
     score[index] = score[score.length - (index + 1)];
     score[score.length - (index + 1)] = tempScore;
   }
}
```

Chapter 11   Case Study Follow-Up Exercises

1. The following changes would be necessary:

   firstList must be made a double array
   value must be declared double (two places)
   the input line must be converted to double rather than int (two places)

3. a. If a letter other than a T or F is entered in the key, each student answer is checked against that erroneous letter.
   b. If a letter other than a T or F is entered for a student, that answer is incorrect unless, by some chance, the same erroneous letter was entered in the same spot for the key.
   c. If an error occurs in the key, the application should be aborted. If an error occurs in a student's answer, the processing of that student should be halted and the application should continue with the next student.

5. Because we are reading one character at a time from the file using read, we must explicitly read past the end of line.

Chapter 12   Exam Preparation Exercises

3.

item	first	last	middle	result
114	0	9	4	
	5	9	7	
	8	9	8	found is true

4. False

6. At the logical level, an array is a homogeneous data type. Java implements an array with an extra integer variable that contains the number of cells in the array.

7. In this sorting algorithm, if the items in 0 through `numItems-2` are sorted, then the remaining item must be the largest one and is therefore in its proper place.
10. Transformer
13. The `Comparable` interface has only one method, named `compareTo`. `compareTo` returns a value less than 0 if the object comes before the parameter, 0 if the object and the parameter are equal, and a value greater than 0 if the parameter comes first.

Chapter 12   Programming Warm-Up Exercises

```
2. public class ListWithSort extends UnsortedList
   {
     // The items in the list are rearranged into ascending order.
     //  This order is not preserved in future insertions

     public ListWithSort()
     {
       super();
     }

     public ListWithSort(int maxItems)
     { // Constructor
       super(maxItems);
     }

     public void selectSort()
     // Arranges list items in ascending order;
     //  selection sort algorithm is used.
     {
       Comparable temp;        // Temporary variable
       int passCount;          // Loop control variable for outer loop
       int searchIndex;        // Loop control variable for inner loop
       int minIndex;           // Index of minimum so far

       for (passCount = 0; passCount < numItems - 1; passCount++)
       {
         minIndex = passCount;
         // Find the index of the smallest component
         //  in listItems[passCount]..listItems[numItems-1]
         for (searchIndex = passCount + 1; searchIndex < numItems;
               searchIndex++)
           if (listItems[searchIndex].compareTo( listItems[minIndex]) <0)
             minIndex = searchIndex;
```

```
            // Swap listItems[minIndx] and listItems[passCount]
            temp = listItems[minIndex];
            listItems[minIndex] = listItems[passCount];
            listItems[passCount] = temp;
        }
    }
}
```

5. The code does not have to be changed because the list is sorted. All you have to do is change the extends clause from `UnsortedList` to `SortedList` and change the names of the constructors.

6.
```
public boolean exclusive(int item, List list1, List list2)
{
    if (list1.isThere(item))
    {
        if (list2.isThere(item))
            return false;
        else
            return true;
    }
    return list2.isThere(item);
}
```

7. All you have to do is change the direction of the relational operator in the comparison in the implementation and change the names of the constructors and the class.

9.
```
public void insert(String item)
// If the list is not full, puts item in its proper position in the
//   list; otherwise list is unchanged.
{
    boolean placeFound = false;
    int index = 0;
    while (!placeFound && index < numItems)
        if (item.compareTo(listItems[index]) > 0)
            index++;
        else
            placeFound = true;
    for (int count = numItems; count > index; count--)
        listItems[count] = listItems[count - 1];
    listItems[index] = item;
    numItems++;
}
```

Chapter 12 Case Study Follow-Up Exercises

2. If the event handler does not delete the name from the list when a student arrives, two other algorithms could be used:

- As the list of those present is being printed, each name could be removed from the master list, or
- You could iterate through the master list and print those names that are not in the list of those present.

3. The unsorted list could be used rather than the sorted list. The master list and the list of those present could be sorted before they are written to the file to be printed.

Chapter 13 Exam Preparation Exercises

1. a. 10   b. 3   c. 3   d. 10   e. 30   f. 30   g. row   h. row
6. a. True   b. False   c. True   d. True
10. A
    B
    413 is the value of n
    21.8 is the value of y

Chapter 13 Programming Warm-Up Exercises

2. a.
```
public TwoDimensions(int maxRows, int maxColumns)
// Creates a maxRows  x maxColumns array
{
   data = new int[maxRows][maxColumns];
}
```
b.
```
public void inputData(BufferedReader inFile)
// Reads data into the array.
// Data is on the file as follows:
//  First line: number of rows (rowsUsed)
//  Second line: number of columns (columnsUsed)
// The data is stored one value per line in row order.  That is,
//  the first columnsUsed values go into row 0; the next
//  columnsUsed values go into row 1; etc.
{
  rowsUsed = Integer.valueOf(inFile.readLine()).intValue();
  columnsUsed = Integer.valueOf(inFile.readLine()).intValue();
  for (int row = 0; row < rowsUsed; row++)
    for (int column = 0; column < columnsUsed; column++)
      data[row][column] =
         Integer.valueOf(inFile.readLine()).intValue();
}
```

c.
```
public void print(PrintWriter outFile)
// Prints the values in the array on outFile, one row per line
{
  for (int row = 0; row < rowsUsed; row++)
  {
    for (int column = 0 ; column < columnsUsed; column++)
      outFile.print(data[row][col]+ " ");
    outfile.println();
  }
}
```

d.
```
public int maxInRow(int row)
// Returns the maximum value in the specified row
{
  int maxSoFar = 0;
  for (int column = 1; column < columnsUsed; column++)
    if (data[row][column] > data[row][maxSoFar])
      maxSoFar = column;
  return data[row][maxSoFar];
}
```

e.
```
public int maxInCol(int column)
// Returns the maximum value in the specified column
{
  int maxSoFar = 0;
  for (int row = 1; row < rowsUsed; row++)
    if (data[row][column] > data[maxSoFar][column])
      maxSoFar = row;
  return data[maxSoFar][column];
}
```

f.
```
public int maxInArray()
// Returns the maximum value in the entire array
{
  int maxValue = data[0][0];
  for (int row = 0; row < rowsUsed; row++)
    for (int column  = 0; column < columnsUsed; column++)
      if (data[row][column] > maxValue)
        maxValue = data[row][column];
  return maxValue;
}
```

g.
```
public int sum()
// Returns the sum of the values in the array
{
   int sum = 0;
   for (int row = 0; row < rowsUsed; row++)
     for (int column == 0; column < columnsUsed; column++)
       sum = sum + data[row][column];
   return sum;
}
```

h.
```
public int sumInRow(int row)
// Returns the sum of the values in the specified row
{
   int sum = data[row][0]
   for (int column = 1; column < columnsUsed; column++)
       sum = sum + data[row][column];
   return sum;
}
```

i.
```
public int sumInCol(int column)
// Returns the sum of the values in the specified column
{
   int sum = 0;
   for (int row = 0; row < rowsUsed; row++)
     sum = sum + data[row][column];
   return sum;
}
```

j.
```
public boolean allPlus()
// Returns true if all the values are positive; false otherwise
{
   for (int row = 0; row < rowsUsed; row++)
     for (int column == 0; column < columnsUsed; column++)
       if (data[row][column] <= 0)
         return false;
   return true;
}
```

5. Include the following statement before multiplying:

```
if (beta > Double.MAX_VALUE/100.0)
   System.out.println(" " + beta + " is too large to multiply" +
     " by 100.");
else
   someFloat = beta*100.0;
```

7. a. This question asks you to run an experiment. We do not give the answer away here.

b.
Method	Array Equivalent/Explanation
myVector.insertElementAt(Object obj, int index)	Insert object at the index position in the array
myVector.firstElement()	Return myVector[0]
myVector.removeElementAt(int index)	Delete the element at the index position and close up the array
myVector.lastElement()	Return myVector[numItems-1]
myVector.removeAllElements()	Remove all the elements, setting numItems to 0

Chapter 13   Case Study Follow-Up Exercises

1. This error might occur in knowValueAt and setValue.

Chapter 14   Exam Preparation Exercises

2. False
4. F(4) = 1, F(6) = −1, and F(5) is undefined
6. *if* or *switch* are the control structures used in recursion.
8. In a recursive algorithm on a data structure, either the distance from a position in the structure or the size of the data structure can get smaller.
12. 15 23 21 19 19 21 23 15

Chapter 14   Programming Warm-Up Exercises

1.
```
public static int f(int n)
{
  if (n == 0 || n == 1)
    return 1;
  else
    return f(n - 1) + f(n - 2);
}
```

3.
```
public static void doubleSpace()
{
  char ch;
  int data;
  data = inFile.read();
  while (data != -1)                    // While not EOF...
```

```
      {
        ch = (char) data;
        outFile.print(ch);
        if (ch == '\n')
          outFile.println();
        data = inFile.read();
      }
    }
```

```
5. public static int factorial(int n, int level)
   {
     int tempFactorial;
     int loopCount;
     for (loopCount = 1; loopCount <= level; loopCount++)
       System.out.print("  ");
     System.out.println(n);
     if (n == 0)
       tempFactorial = 1;
     else
       tempFactorial = n * factorial(n - 1, level + 1);
     for (loopCount = 1; loopCount <= level; loopCount++)
       System.out.print("  ");
     System.out.println(tempFactorial);
     return tempFactorial;
   }
```

```
7. public static void printSqRoots(int n )
   {
     if (n > 0)
     {
       outFile.println(n + " " + Math.sqrt((double)n));
       printSqRoots(n - 1);
     }
   }
```

```
9. public static boolean isThere(
     int[] data,    // Array to be searched
     int first,     // Index of first element
     int last,      // Index of last element
     int item )     // Item to be searched for
```

```
{
  if (first <= last)
  {                              // Recursive case
    if (data[first] == item)
      return true;
    else
      return isThere(data, first + 1, last, item);
  }
  return false;
}
```

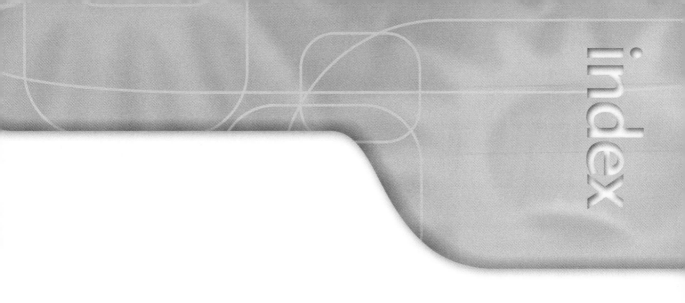